(ex•ploring) SERIES

1. To investigate in a systematic way: examine. 2. To search into or range over for the purpose of discovery.

(ex•ploring) • SERIES

1. To investigate in a systematic way: examine. 2. To search into or range over for the purpose of discovery.

Microsoft® Office

Access 2007

COMPREHENSIVE

Robert T. Grauer

Maurie Wigman Lockley | Keith Mulbery

Upper Saddle River
New Jersey 07458

Library of Congress Cataloging-in-Publication Data
Grauer, Robert T., 1945-
Microsoft Office Access 2007 comprehensive / Robert T. Grauer, Maurie Wigman Lockley, Keith Mulbery.
p. cm.
ISBN-13: 978-0-13-156788-7
ISBN-10: 0-13-156788-8
1. Microsoft Access. 2. Database management. I. Lockley, Maurie Wigman. II. Mulbery, Keith. III. Title.
QA76.9.D3G7195952 2007
005.75'85—dc22

2007025033

Vice President and Publisher: Natalie E. Anderson
Associate VP/ Executive Acquisitions Editor, Print: Stephanie Wall
Executive Acquisitions Editor, Media: Richard Keaveny
Sr. Acquisitions Editor: Melissa Sabella
Product Development Manager: Eileen Bien Calabro
Sr. Editorial Project Manager/Development: Eileen Clark
Editorial Project Manager/Assistant Editor: Jenelle J. Woodrup
Market Development Editor: Claire Hunter
Editorial Assistant: Rebecca Knauer
Executive Producer: Lisa Strite
Content Development Manager: Cathi Profitko
Project Manager, Media: Ashley Lulling
Director of Marketing: Margaret Waples
Sr. Marketing Manager: Scott Davidson
Sr. Sales Associate: Rebecca Scott
Sr. Managing Editor: Cynthia Zonneveld
Associate Managing Editor: Camille Trentacoste
Production Project Manager: Lynne Breitfeller
Sr. Operations Supervisor: Nick Sklitsis
Design Director: Maria Lange
Art Director/Interior and Cover Design: Blair Brown
Cover Illustration/Photo: Courtesy of Getty Images/Laurent Hamels
Composition: GGS Book Services
Project Management: GGS Book Services
Project Manager: Kevin Bradley
Production Editors: Blair Woodcock and Andrea Shearer
Cover Printer: Phoenix Color
Printer/Binder: Banta/Menasha

10 9 8 7 6 5 4 3 2
ISBN-978-0-13-156788-7
ISBN-10: 0-13-156788-8

Dedications

To Marion—my wife, my lover, and my best friend.

Robert Grauer

I would like to express appreciation for my family's patience and support as I have worked on this project. Elizabeth, Aaron, and James were extraordinarily understanding and cooperative about letting me work. I need to acknowledge Dan Bullard for his continuing source of motivation and inspiration. Most of all, I need to thank my best friend and husband, Jim, for always believing in me.

Maurie Wigman Lockley

I would like to dedicate this book to my family and close friends who provided a strong community of emotional support and patience as I completed my doctorate program and worked on this edition of the Exploring series.

Keith Mulbery

About the Authors

Dr. Robert T. Grauer

Dr. Robert T. Grauer is an Associate Professor in the Department of Computer Information Systems at the University of Miami, where he has been honored with the Outstanding Teacher Award in the School of Business. He is the vision behind the Exploring Series, which is about to sell its 3 millionth copy.

Dr. Grauer has written more than 50 books on programming and information systems. His work has been translated into three foreign languages and is used in all aspects of higher education at both national and international levels.

Dr. Grauer also has been a consultant to several major corporations including IBM and American Express. He received his Ph.D. in operations research in 1972 from the Polytechnic Institute of Brooklyn.

Maurie Wigman Lockley

Maurie Wigman Lockley teaches desktop applications and management information systems classes at the University of North Carolina Greensboro. She has been an instructor there since 1990.

She lives in a tiny piedmont North Carolina town with her husband, daughter, and two preschool-aged grandsons. She spends her free time playing with the boys, reading, camping, playing computer games, and singing. She serves on several not-for-profit boards and is active at her church.

Dr. Keith Mulbery

Dr. Keith Mulbery is an Associate Professor in the Information Systems and Technology Department at Utah Valley State College, where he teaches computer applications, programming, and MIS classes. He has written more than 15 software textbooks and business communication test banks. In January 2001, he received the Utah Valley State College Board of Trustees Award of Excellence for authoring *MOUS Essentials Word 2000*. In addition to his series editor and authoring experience, he also served as a developmental editor on two word processing textbooks. In 2007, he received the UVSC School of Technology and Computing Scholar Award.

He received his B.S. and M.Ed. (majoring in Business Education) from Southwestern Oklahoma State University and earned his Ph.D. in Education with an emphasis in Business Information Systems at Utah State University in 2006. His dissertation topic was computer-assisted instruction using TAIT to supplement traditional instruction in basic computer proficiency courses.

Contributing Authors

John Blackwood

John Blackwood is a computer information systems instructor at the Umpqua Community College in Roseburg, Oregon. He previously taught at the Louisiana Technical College - Hammond Area Campus where he earned an Outstanding Teacher award. He holds an M.S in Computer Systems from City University (Bellevue, WA), B.A. from Indiana University, A.E in Software Engineering Technology from the Oregon Institute of Technology, and an A.A.S. in Accounting from the College of Lake County (Grayslake, IL). He holds the MCSE: Security (Server 2003), CCNA/CCAI, and A+ industry certifications. He has several years of experience in software development and call center management. He is the author of his own book about his family's experience in Hurricane Katrina.

Philip Koneman, Ph.D.
Dr. Koneman manages the global certification program at Autodesk, Inc., a company that creates design, visualization, and collaboration software for the manufacturing, architecture, building, civil engineering, and media and entertainment industries. Prior to joining Autodesk, Dr. Koneman managed the IT certification programs at PeopleSoft and J.D. Edwards.

Dr. Koneman has a wide professional portfolio that includes 10 years as a faculty member at Colorado Christian University. He has written computer textbooks for Addison Wesley and Prentice Hall. As the former President of Instructional Design Consultants, Inc. he managed the design and development of CD-ROM instructional materials for medical technology education.

Dr. Koneman received his Ph.D. from the University of Colorado at Denver, School of Education, Division of Instructional Technology. His research interests include computer-based learning, educational testing and measurement, and the ethical implications of technology in a post-modern society. Dr. Koneman is an avid bicyclist and mountaineer, and enjoys many outdoor pursuits in his native Colorado Rocky Mountains.

Linda Ericksen, Office Fundamentals Chapter
Linda Ericksen is Associate Professor of Software Engineering at the University of Advancing Technology in Tempe, Arizona. She is the author of over 20 college-level computer textbooks on topics ranging from the Internet through many software applications, writing for major publishers such as Que, Addison-Wesley, and Course Technology. She was also the author of her own popular series for Prentice Hall, the Quick Simple Series, which featured Microsoft Office 2000.

Brief Contents

Contents

CHAPTER ONE | Office Fundamentals: Using Word, Excel, Access, and PowerPoint 1

Microsoft Office Access 2007

CHAPTER ONE | Introduction to Access: Finding Your Way through a Database 69

CHAPTER TWO | Relational Databases and Multi-Table Queries: Designing Databases and Using Related Data 129

CHAPTER THREE | Customize, Analyze, and Summarize Query Data: Creating and Using Queries to Make Decisions 201

CHAPTER FOUR | Create, Edit, and Perform Calculations in Reports: Creating Professional and Useful Reports 253

CHAPTER EIGHT | Get Connected: Exchanging Data Between Access and Other Applications 511

CHAPTER NINE | Bulletproofing the Database: Protecting Data and Analyzing Database Performance 577

CHAPTER TEN | Macros and Visual Basic for Applications: Customizing a Database 639

Acknowledgments

The success of the Exploring series is attributed to contributions from numerous individuals. First and foremost, our heartfelt appreciation to Melissa Sabella, senior acquisitions editor, for providing new leadership and direction to capitalize on the strength and tradition of the Exploring series while implementing innovative ideas into the Exploring Office 2007 edition. Scott Davidson, senior marketing manager, was an invaluable addition to the team who believes in the mission of this series passionately and did an amazing job communicating its message.

During the first few months of the project, Eileen Clark, senior editorial project manager, kept the team focused on the vision, pedagogy, and voice that has been the driving force behind the success of the Exploring series. Claire Hunter, market development editor, facilitated communication between the editorial team and the reviewers to ensure that this edition meets the changing needs of computer professors and students at the collegiate level. Keith Mulbery gave up many nights and weekends (including Thanksgiving) to jump in and help out with anything that was asked of him, including assisting with topical organization, reviewing and revising content, capturing screenshots, and ensuring chapter manuscripts adhered to series guidelines.

Jenelle Woodrup, editorial project manager/assistant editor, masterfully managed the flow of manuscript files among the authors, editorial team, and production to ensure timely publication of series. Laura Town, developmental editor, provided an objective perspective in reviewing the content and organization of selected chapters. Eileen Calabro, product development manager, facilitated communication among the editorial team, authors, and production during a transitional stage. The team at GGS worked through software delays, style changes and anything else we threw at them to bring the whole thing together. Art director Blair Brown's conversations with students and professors across the country yielded a design that addressed the realities of today's students with function and style.

A special thanks to the following for the use of their work in the PowerPoint section of the text: Cameron Martin, Ph.D., Assistant to the President, Utah Valley State College, for the use of the Institutional Policies and Procedures Approval Process flowchart; Nick Finner, Paralegal Studies, Utah Valley State College, for the use of his research relating to the elderly population residing in the prisons of Utah; Ryan Phillips, Xeric Landscape and Design (XericUtah.com), for sharing Xeric's concepts for creating beautiful, drought-tolerant landscapes and for the photographs illustrating these concepts; Jo Porter, Photographer, Mapleton, Utah, for allowing the use of her beautiful engagement and wedding photographs; and David and Ali Valeti for the photographs of their baby and their family.

The following organizations and individuals generously provided data and structure from their organizational databases: Replacements, Ltd., Shweta Ponnappa, JC Raulston Arboretum at North Carolina State University, and Valerie Tyson. We deeply appreciate the ability to give students a feel for "real" data.

The new members of the Exploring author team would like to especially thank Bob Grauer for his vision in developing Exploring and his leadership in creating this highly successful series.

Maryann Barber would like to thank Bob Grauer for a wonderful collaboration and providing the opportunities through which so much of her life has changed.

The Exploring team would like to especially thank the following instructors who drew on their experience in the classroom and their software expertise to give us daily advice on how to improve this book. Their impact can be seen on every page:

Barbara Stover, Marion Technical College

Bob McCloud, Sacred Heart University

Cassie Georgetti, Florida Technical College

Dana Johnson, North Dakota State University

Jackie Lamoureux, Central New Mexico Community College

Jim Pepe, Bentley College

Judy Brown, The University of Memphis

Lancie Anthony Affonso, College of Charleston

Mimi Duncan, University of Missouri – St. Louis

Minnie Proctor, Indian River Community College

Richard Albright, Goldey-Beacom College

We also want to acknowledge all the reviewers of the Exploring 2007 series. Their valuable comments and constructive criticism greatly improved this edition:

Aaron Schorr
Fashion Institute of Technology

Alicia Stonesifer
La Salle University

Allen Alexander, Delaware
Tech & Community College

Amy Williams, Abraham
Baldwin Agriculture College

Annie Brown
Hawaii Community College

Barbara Cierny
Harper College

Barbara Hearn
Community College of Philadelphia

Barbara Meguro
University of Hawaii at Hilo

Bette Pitts
South Plains College

Beverly Fite
Amarillo College

Bill Wagner
Villanova

Brandi N. Guidry
University of Louisiana at Lafayette

Brian Powell
West Virginia University – Morgantown
Campus

Carl Farrell
Hawaii Pacific University

Carl Penzuil
Ithaca College

Carole Bagley;
University of St. Thomas

Catherine Hain
Central New Mexico CC

Charles Edwards
University of Texas of the Permian Basin

Christine L. Moore
College of Charleston

David Barnes
Penn State Altoona

David Childress;
Ashland Community College

David Law, Alfred
State College

Dennis Chalupa
Houston Baptist

Diane Stark
Phoenix College

Dianna Patterson
Texarkana College

Dianne Ross
University of Louisiana at Lafayette

Dr. Behrooz Saghafi
Chicago State University

Dr. Gladys Swindler
Fort Hays State University

Dr. Joe Teng
Barry University

Dr. Karen Nantz
Eastern Illinois University

Duane D. Lintner
Amarillo College

Elizabeth Edmiston
North Carolina Central University

Erhan Uskup
Houston Community College

Fred Hills, McClellan
Community College

Gary R. Armstrong
Shippensburg University of Pennsylvania

Glenna Vanderhoof
Missouri State

Gregg Asher
Minnesota State University, Mankato

Hong K. Sung
University of Central Oklahoma

Hyekyung Clark
Central New Mexico CC

J Patrick Fenton
West Valley College

Jana Carver
Amarillo College

Jane Cheng
Bloomfield College

Janos T. Fustos
Metropolitan State College of Denver

Jeffrey A Hassett
University of Utah

Jennifer Pickle
Amarillo College

Jerry Kolata
New England Institute of Technology

Jesse Day
South Plains College

John Arehart
Longwood University

John Lee Reardon
University of Hawaii, Manoa

Joshua Mindel
San Francisco State University

Karen Wisniewski
County College of Morris

Karl Smart
Central Michigan University

Kathryn L. Hatch
University of Arizona

Krista Terry
Radford University

Laura McManamon
University of Dayton

Laura Reid
University of Western Ontario

Linda Johnsonius
Murray State University

Lori Kelley
Madison Area Technical College

Lucy Parker,
California State University, Northridge

Lynda Henrie
LDS Business College

Malia Young
Utah State University

Margie Martyn
Baldwin Wallace

Marianne Trudgeon
Fanshawe College

Marilyn Hibbert
Salt Lake Community College

Marjean Lake
LDS Business College

Mark Olaveson
Brigham Young University

Nancy Sardone
Seton Hall University

Patricia Joseph
Slippery Rock University.

Patrick Hogan
Cape Fear Community College

Paula F. Bell
Lock Haven University of Pennsylvania

Paulette Comet
Community College of Baltimore County, Catonsville

Pratap Kotala
North Dakota State University

Richard Blamer
John Carroll University

Richard Herschel
St. Joseph's University

Richard Hewer
Ferris State University

Robert Gordon
Hofstra University

Robert Marmelstein
East Stroudsburg University

Robert Stumbur
Northern Alberta Institute of Technology

Roberta I. Hollen
University of Central Oklahoma

Roland Moreira
South Plains College

Ron Murch
University of Calgary

Rory J. de Simone
University of Florida

Ruth Neal
Navarro College

Sandra M. Brown
Finger Lakes Community College

Sharon Mulroney
Mount Royal College

Stephen E. Lunce
Midwestern State University

Steve Schwarz
Raritan Valley Community College

Steven Choy
University of Calgary

Susan Byrne
St. Clair College

Thomas Setaro
Brookdale Community College

Todd McLeod
Fresno City College

Vickie Pickett
Midland College

Vipul Gupta
St Joseph's University

Vivek Shah
Texas State University - San Marcos

Wei-Lun Chuang
Utah State University

William Dorin
Indiana University Northwest

Finally, we wish to acknowledge reviewers of previous editions of the Exploring series—we wouldn't have made it to the 7th edition without you:

Alan Moltz
Naugatuck Valley Technical Community College

Alok Charturvedi
Purdue University

Antonio Vargas
El Paso Community College

Barbara Sherman
Buffalo State College

Bill Daley
University of Oregon

Bill Morse
DeVry Institute of Technology

Bonnie Homan
San Francisco State University

Carl M. Briggs
Indiana University School of Business

Carlotta Eaton
Radford University

Carolyn DiLeo
Westchester Community College

Cody Copeland
Johnson County Community College

Connie Wells
Georgia State University

Daniela Marghitu
Auburn University

David B. Meinert
Southwest Missouri State University

David Douglas
University of Arkansas

David Langley
University of Oregon

David Rinehard
Lansing Community College

David Weiner
University of San Francisco

Dean Combellick
Scottsdale Community College

Delores Pusins
Hillsborough Community College

Don Belle
Central Piedmont Community College

Douglas Cross
Clackamas Community College

Ernie Ivey
Polk Community College

Gale E. Rand
College Misericordia

Helen Stoloff
Hudson Valley Community College

Herach Safarian
College of the Canyons

Jack Zeller
Kirkwood Community College

James Franck
College of St. Scholastica

James Gips
Boston College

Jane King
Everett Community College

Janis Cox
Tri-County Technical College

Jerry Chin
Southwest Missouri State University

Jill Chapnick
Florida International University

Jim Pruitt
Central Washington University

John Lesson
University of Central Florida

John Shepherd
Duquesne University

Judith M. Fitspatrick
Gulf Coast Community College

Judith Rice
Santa Fe Community College

Judy Dolan
Palomar College

Karen Tracey
Central Connecticut State University

Kevin Pauli
University of Nebraska

Kim Montney
Kellogg Community College

Kimberly Chambers
Scottsdale Community College

Larry S. Corman
Fort Lewis College

Lynn Band
Middlesex Community College

Margaret Thomas
Ohio University

Marguerite Nedreberg
Youngstown State University

Marilyn Salas
Scottsdale Community College

Martin Crossland
Southwest Missouri State University

Mary McKenry Percival
University of Miami

Michael Hassett
Fort Hayes State University

Michael Stewardson
San Jacinto College – North

Midge Gerber
Southwestern Oklahoma State University

Mike Hearn
Community College of Philadelphia

Mike Kelly
Community College of Rhode Island

Mike Thomas
Indiana University School of Business

Paul E. Daurelle
Western Piedmont Community College

Ranette Halverson
Midwestern State University

Raymond Frost
Central Connecticut State University

Robert Spear, Prince
George's Community College

Rose M. Laird
Northern Virginia Community College

Sally Visci
Lorain County Community College

Shawna DePlonty
Sault College of Applied Arts and Technology

Stuart P. Brian
Holy Family College

Susan Fry
Boise State Universtiy

Suzanne Tomlinson
Iowa State University

Vernon Griffin
Austin Community College

Wallace John Whistance-Smith
Ryerson Polytechnic University

Walter Johnson
Community College of Philadelphia

Wanda D. Heller
Seminole Community College

We very much appreciate the following individuals for painstakingly checking every step and every explanation for technical accuracy, while dealing with an entirely new software application:

Barbara Waxer
Bill Daley
Beverly Fite
Dawn Wood
Denise Askew
Elizabeth Lockley
James Reidel
Janet Pickard
Janice Snyder
Jeremy Harris
John Griffin
Joyce Neilsen
LeeAnn Bates
Mara Zebest
Mary E. Pascarella
Michael Meyers
Sue McCrory

Preface

The Exploring Series

Exploring has been Prentice Hall's most successful Office Application series of the past 15 years. For Office 2007 Exploring has undergone the most extensive changes in its history, so that it can truly move today's student "beyond the point and click."

The goal of Exploring has always been to teach more than just the steps to accomplish a task – the series provides the theoretical foundation necessary for a student to understand when and why to apply a skill. This way, students achieve a broader understanding of Office.

Today's students are changing and Exploring has evolved with them. Prentice Hall traveled to college campuses across the country and spoke directly to students to determine how they study and prepare for class. We also spoke with hundreds of professors about the best ways to administer materials to such a diverse body of students.

Here is what we learned

Students go to college now with a different set of skills than they did 5 years ago. The new edition of Exploring moves students beyond the basics of the software at a faster pace, without sacrificing coverage of the fundamental skills that everybody needs to know. This ensures that students will be engaged from Chapter 1 to the end of the book.

Students have diverse career goals. With this in mind, we broadened the examples in the text (and the accompanying Instructor Resources) to include the health sciences, hospitality, urban planning, business and more. Exploring will be relevant to every student in the course.

Students read, prepare and study differently than they used to. Rather than reading a book cover to cover students want to easily identify what they need to know, and then learn it efficiently. We have added key features that will bring students into the content and make the text easy to use such as objective mapping, pull quotes, and key terms in the margins.

Moving students beyond the point and click

All of these additions mean students will be more engaged, achieve a higher level of understanding, and successfully complete this course. In addition to the experience and expertise of the series creator and author Robert T. Grauer we have assembled a tremendously talented team of supporting authors to assist with this critical revision. Each of them is equally dedicated to the Exploring mission of **moving students beyond the point and click.**

Key Features of the Office 2007 revision include

- **New** **Office Fundamentals Chapter** efficiently covers skills common among all applications like save, print, and bold to avoid repetition in each Office application's first chapter, along with coverage of problem solving skills to prepare students to apply what they learn in any situation.

- **New** **Moving Beyond the Basics** introduces advanced skills earlier because students are learning basic skills faster.

- **White Pages/Yellow Pages clearly** distinguish the theory (white pages) from the skills covered in the Hands-On exercises (yellow pages) so students always know what they are supposed to be doing.

- **New** **Objective Mapping** enables students to skip the skills and concepts they know, and quickly find those they don't, by scanning the chapter opener page for the page numbers of the material they need.

- **New** **Pull Quotes e**ntice students into the theory by highlighting the most interesting points.

- **New** **Conceptual Animations** connect the theory with the skills, by illustrating tough to understand concepts with interactive multimedia.

- **New** **More End of Chapter Exercises** offer instructors more options for assessment. Each chapter has approximately 12–15 exercises ranging from Multiple Choice questions to open-ended projects.

- **New** **More Levels of End of Chapter Exercises,** including new Mid-Level Exercises tell students what to do, but not how to do it, and Capstone Exercises cover all of the skills within each chapter.

- **New** **Mini Cases with Rubrics** are open ended exercises that guide both instructors and students to a solution with a specific rubric for each mini case.

Instructor and Student Resources

Instructor Chapter Reference Cards

A four page color card for every chapter that includes a:

- *Concept Summary* that outlines the KEY objectives to cover in class with tips on where students get stuck as well as how to get them un-stuck. It helps bridge the gap between the instructor and student when discussing more difficult topics.
- *Case Study Lecture Demonstration Document* which provides instructors with a lecture sample based on the chapter opening case that will guide students to critically use the skills covered in the chapter, with examples of other ways the skills can be applied.

The Enhanced Instructor's Resource Center on CD-ROM includes:

- **Additional Capstone Production Tests** allow instructors to assess all the skills in a chapter with a single project.
- **Mini Case Rubrics** in Microsoft® Word format enable instructors to customize the assignment for their class.
- **PowerPoint® Presentations** for each chapter with notes included for online students.
- **Lesson Plans** that provide a detailed blueprint for an instructor to achieve chapter learning objectives and outcomes.
- **Student Data Files**
- **Annotated Solution Files**
- **Complete Test Bank**
- **Test Gen Software with QuizMaster**

TestGen is a test generator program that lets you view and easily edit testbank questions, transfer them to tests, and print in a variety of formats suitable to your teaching situation. The program also offers many options for organizing and displaying testbanks and tests. A random number test generator enables you to create multiple versions of an exam.
QuizMaster, also included in this package, allows students to take tests created with TestGen on a local area network. The QuizMaster Utility built into TestGen lets instructors view student records and print a variety of reports. Building tests is easy with Test-Gen, and exams can be easily uploaded into WebCT, BlackBoard, and CourseCompass.

Prentice Hall's Companion Web Site

www.prenhall.com/exploring offers expanded IT resources and downloadable supplements. This site also includes an online study guide for student self-study.

Online Course Cartridges

Flexible, robust and customizable content is available for all major online course platforms that include everything instructors need in one place.
www.prenhall.com/webct
www.prenhall.com/blackboard
www.coursecompass.com

my**it**lab for Microsoft Office 2007, is a solution designed by professors that allows you to easily deliver Office courses with defensible assessment and outcomes-based training.

The new *Exploring Office 2007* System will seamlessly integrate online assessment and training with the new my**it**lab for Microsoft Office 2007!

Integrated Assessment and Training

To fully integrate the new my**it**lab into the *Exploring Office 2007* System we built my**it**lab assessment and training directly from the *Exploring* instructional content. No longer is the technology just mapped to your textbook.

This 1:1 content relationship between the *Exploring* text and my**it**lab means that your online assessment and training will work with your textbook to move your students beyond the point and click.

Advanced Reporting

With my**it**lab you will get advanced reporting capabilities including a detailed student click stream. This ability to see exactly what actions your students took on a test, click-by-click, provides you with true defensible grading.

In addition, myitlab for Office 2007 will feature. . .

Project-based assessment: Test students on Exploring projects, or break down assignments into individual Office application skills.

Outcomes-based training: Students train on what they don't know without having to relearn skills they already know.

Optimal performance and uptime: Provided by a word-class hosting environment.

Dedicated student and instructor support: Professional tech support is available by phone and email when you need it.

No installation required! my**it**lab runs entirely from the Web.

And much more!

www.prenhall.com/myitlab

Visual Walk-Through

Office Fundamentals Chapter

efficiently covers skills common among all applications like save, print, and bold to avoid repetition in each 1st application chapter.

chapter 1 | Office Fundamentals

Using Word, Excel, Access, and PowerPoint

Objectives

After you read this chapter you will be able to:

1. Identify common interface components **(page 4)**.
2. Use Office 2007 Help **(page 10)**.
3. Open a file **(page 18)**.
4. Save a file **(page 21)**.
5. Print a document **(page 24)**.
6. Select text to edit **(page 31)**.
7. Insert text and change to the Overtype mode **(page 32)**.
8. Move and copy text **(page 34)**.
9. Find, replace, and go to text **(page 36)**.
10. Use the Undo and Redo commands **(page 39)**.
11. Use language tools **(page 39)**.
12. Apply font attributes **(page 43)**.
13. Copy formats with the Format Painter **(page 47)**.

Hands-On Exercises

Exercises	Skills Covered
1. IDENTIFYING PROGRAM INTERFACE COMPONENTS AND USING HELP (page 12)	• Use PowerPoint's Office Button, Get Help in a Dialog Box, and Use the Zoom Slider • Use Excel's Ribbon, Get Help from an Enhanced ScreenTip, and Use the Zoom Dialog Box • Search Help in Access • Use Word's Status Bar • Search Help and Print a Help Topic
2. PERFORMING UNIVERSAL TASKS (page 28) **Open:** chap1_ho2_sample.docx **Save as:** chap1_ho2_solution.docx	• Open a File and Save it with a Different Name • Use Print Preview and Select Options • Print a Document
3. PERFORMING BASIC TASKS (page 48) **Open:** chap1_ho3_internet_docx **Save as:** chap_ho3_internet_solution.docx	• Cut, Copy, Paste, and Undo • Find and Replace Text • Check Spelling • Choose Synonyms and Use Thesaurus • Use the Research Tool • Apply Font Attributes • Use Format Painter

Microsoft Office 2007 Software Office Fundamentals 1

chapter 3 | **Access**

Customize, Analyze, and Summarize Query Data

Creating and Using Queries to Make Decisions

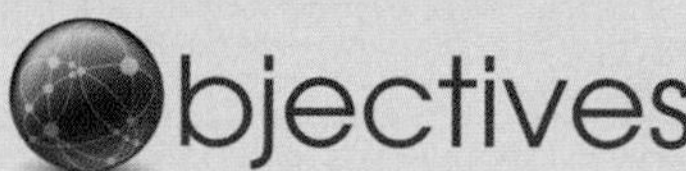

After you read this chapter you will be able to:

1. Understand the order of precedence **(page 679)**.
2. Create a calculated field in a query **(page 679)**.
3. Create expressions with the Expression Builder **(page 679)**.
4. Create and edit Access functions **(page 690)**.
5. Perform date arithmetic **(page 694)**.
6. Create and work with data aggregates **(page 704)**.

Hands-On Exercises

Exercises	Skills Covered
1. CALCULATED QUERY FIELDS (PAGE 683) **Open:** chap3_ho1-3_realestate.accdb **Save:** chap3_ho1-3_realestate_solution.accdb **Back up as:** chap3_ho1_realestate_solution.accdb	• Copy a Database and Start the Query • Select the Fields, Save, and Open the Query • Create a Calculated Field and Run the Query • Verify the Calculated Results • Recover from a Common Error
2. EXPRESSION BUILDER, FUNCTIONS, AND DATE ARITHMETIC (page 695) **Open:** chap3_ho1-3_realestate.accdb (from Exercise 1) **Save:** chap3_ho1-3_realestate_solution.accdb (additional modifications) **Back up as:** chap3_ho2_realestate_solution.accdb	• Create a Select Query • Use the Expression Builder • Create Calculations Using Input Stored in a Different Query or Table • Edit Expressions Using the Expression Builder • Use Functions • Work with Date Arithmetic
3. DATA AGGREGATES (page 707) **Open:** chap3_ho1-3_realestate.accdb (from Exercise 2) **Save:** chap3_ho1-3_realestate_solution.accdb (additional modifications)	• Add a Total Row • Create a Totals Query Based on a Select Query • Add Fields to the Design Grid • Add Grouping Options and Specify Summary Statistics

Access 2007 677

Objective Mapping

allows students to skip the skills and concepts they know and quickly find those they don't by scanning the chapter opening page for the page numbers of the material they need.

Case Study

begins each chapter to provide an effective overview of what students can accomplish by completing the chapter.

CASE STUDY

West Transylvania College Athletic Department

The athletic department of West Transylvania College has reached a fork in the road. A significant alumni contingent insists that the college upgrade its athletic program from NCAA Division II to Division I. This process will involve adding sports, funding athletic scholarships, expanding staff, and coordinating a variety of fundraising activities.

Tom Hunt, the athletic director, wants to determine if the funding support is available both inside and outside the college to accomplish this goal. You are helping Tom prepare the five-year projected budget based on current budget figures. The plan is to increase revenues at a rate of 10% per year for five years while handling an estimated 8% increase in expenses over the same five-year period. Tom feels that a 10% increase in revenue versus an 8% increase in expenses should make the upgrade viable. Tom wants to examine how increased alumni giving, increases in college fees, and grant monies will increase the revenue flow. The Transylvania College's Athletic Committee and its Alumni Association Board of Directors want Tom to present an analysis of funding and expenses to determine if the move to NCAA Division I is feasible. As Tom's student assistant this year, it is your responsibility to help him with special projects. Tom prepared the basic projected budget spreadsheet and has asked you to finish it for him.

Case Study

Your Assignment

- Read the chapter carefully and pay close attention to mathematical operations, formulas, and functions.
- Open *chap2_case_athletics*, which contains the partially completed, projected budget spreadsheet.
- Study the structure of the worksheet to determine what type of formulas you need to complete the financial calculations. Identify how you would perform calculations if you were using a calculator and make a list of formulas using regular language to determine if the financial goals will be met. As you read the chapter, identify formulas and functions that will help you complete the financial analysis. You will insert formulas in the revenue and expenditures sections for column C. Use appropriate cell references in formulas. Do not enter constant values within a formula; instead enter the 10% and 8% increases in an input area. Use appropriate functions for column totals in both the revenue and expenditures sections. Insert formulas for the Net Operating Margin and Net Margin rows. Copy the formulas.
- Review the spreadsheet and identify weaknesses in the formatting. Use your knowledge of good formatting design to improve the appearance of the spreadsheet so that it will be attractive to the Athletic Committee and the alumni board. You will format cells as currency with 0 decimals and widen columns as needed. Merge and center the title and use an attractive fill color. Emphasize the totals and margin rows with borders. Enter your name and current date. Create a custom footer that includes a page number and your instructor's name. Print the worksheet as displayed and again with cell formulas displayed. Save the workbook as **chap2_case_athletics_solution**.

380 CHAPTER 2 | Formulas and Functions

Key Terms

are called out in the margins of the chapter so students can more effectively study definitions.

Pull Quotes

entice students into the theory by highlighting the most interesting points.

Tables

A *table* is a series of rows and columns that organize data.

A *cell* is the intersection of a row and column in a table.

A ***table*** is a series of rows and columns that organize data effectively. The rows and columns in a table intersect to form ***cells***. The table feature is one of the most powerful in Word and is an easy way to organize a series of data in a columnar list format such as employee names, inventory lists, and e-mail addresses. The Vacation Planner in Figure 3.1, for example, is actually a 4x9 table (4 columns and 9 rows). The completed table looks impressive, but it is very easy to create once you understand how a table works. In addition to the organizational benefits, tables make an excellent alignment tool. For example, you can create tables to organize data such as employee lists with phone numbers and e-mail addresses. The Exploring series uses tables to provide descriptions for various software commands. Although you can align text with tabs, you have more format control when you create a table. (See the Practice Exercises at the end of the chapter for other examples.)

> The table feature is one of the most powerful in Word and is the basis for an almost limitless variety of documents. It is very easy to create once you understand how a table works.

Vacation Planner			
Item	Number of Days	Amount per Day (est)	Total Amount
Airline Ticket			449.00
Amusement Park Tickets	4	50.00	200.00
Hotel	5	120.00	600.00
Meals	6	50.00	300.00
Rental Car	5	30.00	150.00
Souvenirs	5	20.00	100.00
TOTAL EXPECTED EXPENSES			$1799.00

Figure 3.1 The Vacation Planner

In this section, you insert a table in a document. After inserting the table, you can insert or delete columns and rows if you need to change the structure. Furthermore, you learn how to merge and split cells within the table. Finally, you change the row height and column width to accommodate data in the table.

Inserting a Table

You can create a table from the Insert tab. Click Table in the Tables group on the Insert tab to see a gallery of cells from which you select the number of columns and rows you require in the table, or you can choose the Insert Table command below the gallery to display the Insert Table dialog box and enter the table composition you prefer. When you select the table dimension from the gallery or from the Insert Table dialog box, Word creates a table structure with the number of columns and rows you specify. After you define a table, you can enter text, numbers, or graphics in individual cells. Text

Tables | Word 2007 197

White Pages/ Yellow Pages

clearly distinguishes the theory (white pages) from the skills covered in the Hands-On exercises (yellow pages) so students always know what they are supposed to be doing.

Keyword for search

Collections to be searched

Type of clips to be included in results

Search results

Link to Microsoft Clip Organizer

Link to more clips online

CIS 101 Review Session
Test #2

Monday
7pm
Glass 102

Figure 3.18 The Clip Art Task Pane

You can access the Microsoft Clip Organizer (to view the various collections) by clicking Organize clips at the bottom of the Clip Art task pane. You also can access the Clip Organizer when you are not using Word; click the Start button on the taskbar, click All Programs, Micros
Clip Organizer. Once in the Organiz
ous collections, reorganize the exis
add new clips (with their associated
the bottom of the task pane in Figur
and tips for finding more relevant c

Insert a Picture

In addition to the collection of clip
you also can insert your own pictur
ital camera attached to your comput
Word. After you save the picture to
on the Insert tab to locate and insert
opens so that you can navigate to t
insert the picture, there are many c
mands are discussed in the next sec

Formatting a Grap

Remember that graphical elements should enhance a document, not overpower it.

When you inse
fined size. For
very large and
resized. Most ti
within the d

Step 2
Move and Resize the Clip Art Object

Refer to Figure 3.24 as you complete Step 2.

a. Click once on the clip art object to select it. Click **Text Wrapping** in the Arrange group on the Picture Tools Format tab to display the text wrapping options, and then select **Square**, as shown in Figure 3.24.

You must change the layout in order to move and size the object.

b. Click **Position** in the Arrange group, and then click **More Layout Options.** Click the **Picture Position tab** in the Advanced Layout dialog box, if necessary, then click **Alignment** in the *Horizontal* section. Click the **Alignment drop-down arrow** and select **Right**. Deselect the **Allow overlap check box** in the *Options* section. Click **OK**.

c. Click **Crop** in the Size group, then hold your mouse over the sizing handles and notice how the pointer changes to angular shapes. Click the **bottom center handle** and drag it up. Drag the side handles inward to remove excess space surrounding the graphical object.

d. Click the Shape **Height box** in the Size group and type **2.77**.

Notice the width is changed automatically to retain the proportion.

e. Save the document.

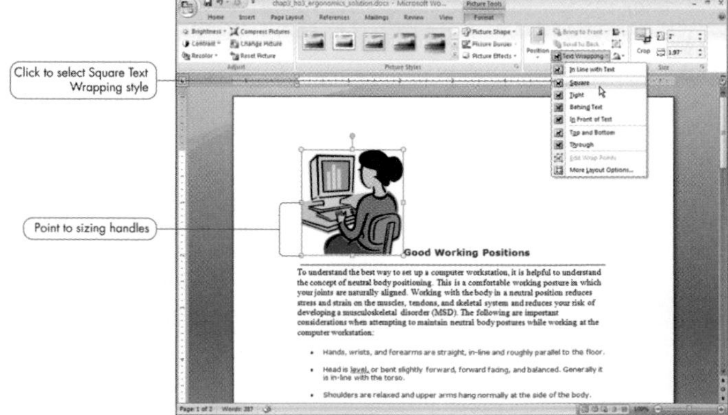

Figure 3.24 Formatting Clip Art

Step 3
Create a WordArt Object

Refer to Figure 3.25 as you complete Step 3.

a. Press **Ctrl+End** to move to the end of the document. Click the **Insert tab**, and then click **WordArt** in the Text group to display the WordArt gallery.

b. Click **WordArt Style 28** on the bottom row of the gallery.

The Edit WordArt Text dialog box displays, as shown in Figure 3.25.

Summary

1. **Create a presentation using a template.** Using a template saves you a great deal of time and enables you to create a more professional presentation. Templates incorporate a theme, a layout, and content that can be modified. You can use templates that are installed when Microsoft Office is installed, or you can download templates from Microsoft Office Online. Microsoft is constantly adding templates to the online site for your use.
2. **Modify a template.** In addition to changing the content of a template, you can modify the structure and design. The structure is modified by changing the layout of a slide. To change the layout, drag placeholders to new locations or resize placeholders. You can even add placeholders so that elements such as logos can be included.
3. **Create a presentation in Outline view.** When you use a storyboard to determine your content, you create a basic outline. Then you can enter your presentation in Outline view, which enables you to concentrate on the content of the presentation. Using Outline view keeps you from getting buried in design issues at the cost of your content. It also saves you time because you can enter the information without having to move from placeholder to placeholder.
4. **Modify an outline structure.** Because the Outline view gives you a global view of the presentation, it helps you see the underlying structure of the presentation. You are able to see where content needs to be strengthened, or where the flow of information needs to be revised. If you find a slide with content that would be presented better in another location in the slide show, you can use the Collapse and Expand features to easily move it. By collapsing the slide content, you can drag it to a new location and then expand it. To move individual bullet points, cut and paste the bullet point or drag-and-drop it.
5. **Print an outline.** When you present, using the outline version of your slide show as a reference is a boon. No matter how well you know your information, it is easy to forget to present some information when facing an audience. While you would print speaker's notes if you have many details, you can print the outline as a quick reference. The outline can be printed in either the collapsed or the expanded form, giving you far fewer pages to shuffle in front of an audience than printing speaker's notes would.
6. **Import an outline.** You do not need to re-enter information from an outline created in Microsoft Word or another word processor. You can use the Open feature to import any outline that has been saved in a format that PowerPoint can read. In addition to a Word outline, you can use the common generic formats Rich Text Format and Plain Text Format.
7. **Add existing content to a presentation.** After you spend time creating the slides in a slide show, you may find that slides in the slide show would be appropriate in another show at a later date. Any slide you create can be reused in another presentation, thereby saving you considerable time and effort. You simply open the Reuse Slides pane, locate the slide show with the slide you need, and then click on the thumbnail of the slide to insert a copy of it in the new slide show.
8. **Examine slide show design principles.** With a basic understanding of slide show design principles you can create presentations that reflect your personality in a professional way. The goal of applying these principles is to create a slide show that focuses the audience on the message of the slide without being distracted by clutter or unreadable text.
9. **Apply and modify a design theme.** PowerPoint provides you with themes to help you create a clean, professional look for your presentation. Once a theme is applied you can modify the theme by changing the color scheme, the font scheme, the effects scheme, or the background style.
10. **Insert a header or footer.** Identifying information can be included in a header or footer. You may, for example, wish to include the group to whom you are presenting, or the location of the presentation, or a copyright notation for original work. You can apply footers to slides, handouts, and Notes pages. Headers may be applied to handouts and Notes pages.

908 CHAPTER 2 | Introduction to PowerPoint

Summary

links directly back to the objectives so students can more effectively study and locate the concepts that they need to focus on.

More End-of-Chapter Exercises with New Levels of Assessment

offer instructors more options for assessment. Each chapter has approximately 12-15 projects per chapter ranging from multiple choice to open-ended projects.

Practice Exercises

reinforce skills learned in the chapter with specific directions on what to do and how to do it.

New Mid-Level Exercises

assess the skills learned in the chapter by directing the students on what to do but not how to do it.

New Capstone Exercises

cover all of the skills with in each chapter without telling students how to perform the skills.

Mini Cases with Rubrics

are open ended exercises that guide both instructors and students to a solution with a specific rubric for each Mini Case.

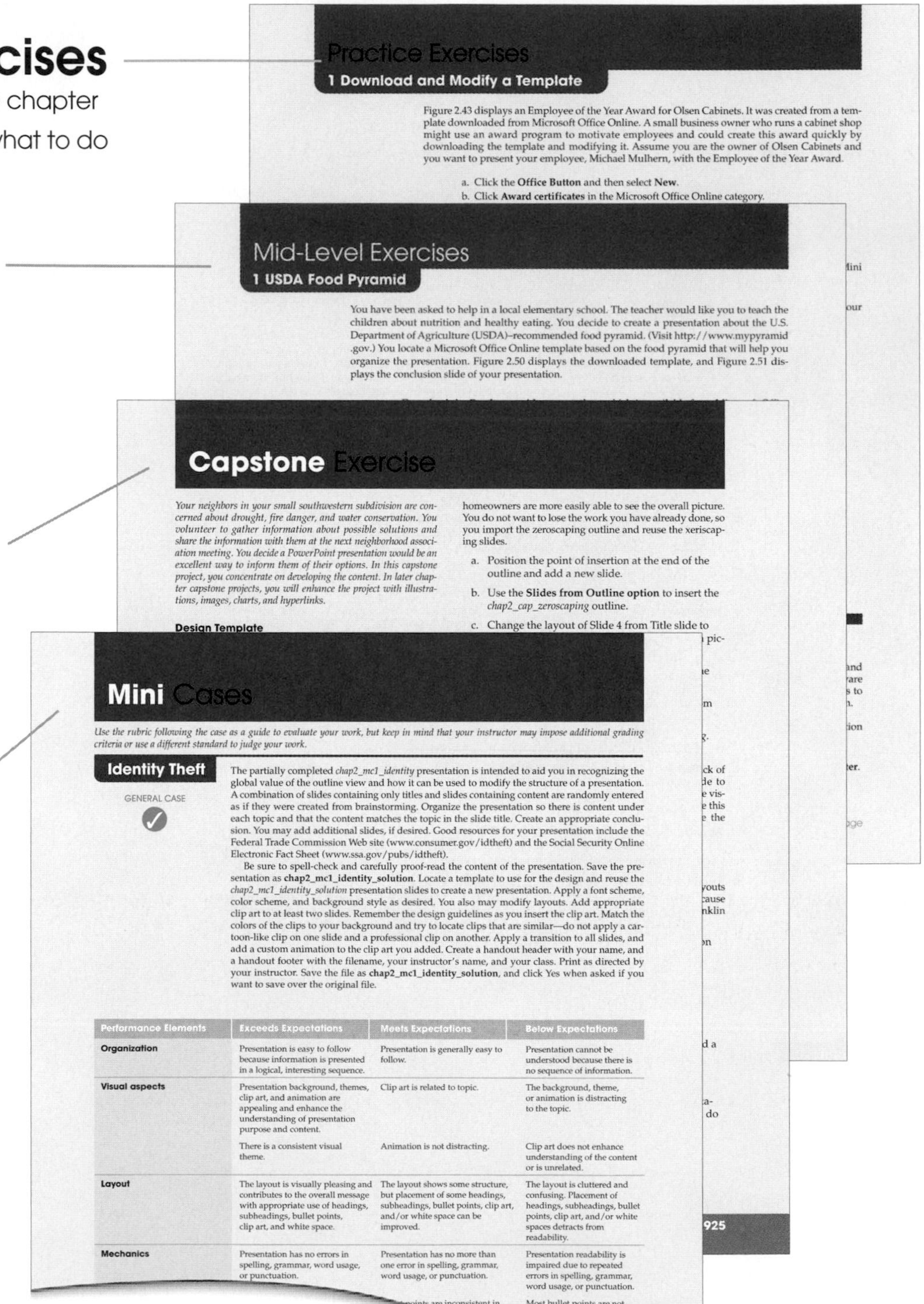

Practice Exercises

1 Download and Modify a Template

Figure 2.43 displays an Employee of the Year Award for Olsen Cabinets. It was created from a template downloaded from Microsoft Office Online. A small business owner who runs a cabinet shop might use an award program to motivate employees and could create this award quickly by downloading the template and modifying it. Assume you are the owner of Olsen Cabinets and you want to present your employee, Michael Mulhern, with the Employee of the Year Award.

a. Click the **Office Button** and then select **New**.
b. Click **Award certificates** in the Microsoft Office Online category.

Mid-Level Exercises

1 USDA Food Pyramid

You have been asked to help in a local elementary school. The teacher would like you to teach the children about nutrition and healthy eating. You decide to create a presentation about the U.S. Department of Agriculture (USDA)–recommended food pyramid. (Visit http://www.mypyramid.gov.) You locate a Microsoft Office Online template based on the food pyramid that will help you organize the presentation. Figure 2.50 displays the downloaded template, and Figure 2.51 displays the conclusion slide of your presentation.

Capstone Exercise

Your neighbors in your small southwestern subdivision are concerned about drought, fire danger, and water conservation. You volunteer to gather information about possible solutions and share the information with them at the next neighborhood association meeting. You decide a PowerPoint presentation would be an excellent way to inform them of their options. In this capstone project, you concentrate on developing the content. In later chapter capstone projects, you will enhance the project with illustrations, images, charts, and hyperlinks.

Design Template

homeowners are more easily able to see the overall picture. You do not want to lose the work you have already done, so you import the zeroscaping outline and reuse the xeriscaping slides.

a. Position the point of insertion at the end of the outline and add a new slide.
b. Use the **Slides from Outline option** to insert the *chap2_cap_zeroscaping* outline.
c. Change the layout of Slide 4 from Title slide to

Mini Cases

Use the rubric following the case as a guide to evaluate your work, but keep in mind that your instructor may impose additional grading criteria or use a different standard to judge your work.

Identity Theft

GENERAL CASE

The partially completed *chap2_mc1_identity* presentation is intended to aid you in recognizing the global value of the outline view and how it can be used to modify the structure of a presentation. A combination of slides containing only titles and slides containing content are randomly entered as if they were created from brainstorming. Organize the presentation so there is content under each topic and that the content matches the topic in the slide title. Create an appropriate conclusion. You may add additional slides, if desired. Good resources for your presentation include the Federal Trade Commission Web site (www.consumer.gov/idtheft) and the Social Security Online Electronic Fact Sheet (www.ssa.gov/pubs/idtheft).

Be sure to spell-check and carefully proof-read the content of the presentation. Save the presentation as **chap2_mc1_identity_solution**. Locate a template to use for the design and reuse the *chap2_mc1_identity_solution* presentation slides to create a new presentation. Apply a font scheme, color scheme, and background style as desired. You also may modify layouts. Add appropriate clip art to at least two slides. Remember the design guidelines as you insert the clip art. Match the colors of the clips to your background and try to locate clips that are similar—do not apply a cartoon-like clip on one slide and a professional clip on another. Apply a transition to all slides, and add a custom animation to the clip art you added. Create a handout header with your name, and a handout footer with the filename, your instructor's name, and your class. Print as directed by your instructor. Save the file as **chap2_mc1_identity_solution**, and click Yes when asked if you want to save over the original file.

Performance Elements	Exceeds Expectations	Meets Expectations	Below Expectations
Organization	Presentation is easy to follow because information is presented in a logical, interesting sequence.	Presentation is generally easy to follow.	Presentation cannot be understood because there is no sequence of information.
Visual aspects	Presentation background, themes, clip art, and animation are appealing and enhance the understanding of presentation purpose and content.	Clip art is related to topic.	The background, theme, or animation is distracting to the topic.
	There is a consistent visual theme.	Animation is not distracting.	Clip art does not enhance understanding of the content or is unrelated.
Layout	The layout is visually pleasing and contributes to the overall message with appropriate use of headings, subheadings, bullet points, clip art, and white space.	The layout shows some structure, but placement of some headings, subheadings, bullet points, clip art, and/or white space can be improved.	The layout is cluttered and confusing. Placement of headings, subheadings, bullet points, clip art, and/or white spaces detracts from readability.
Mechanics	Presentation has no errors in spelling, grammar, word usage, or punctuation.	Presentation has no more than one error in spelling, grammar, word usage, or punctuation.	Presentation readability is impaired due to repeated errors in spelling, grammar, word usage, or punctuation.
		...points are inconsistent in	Most bullet points are not parallel.

Using Word, Excel, Access, and PowerPoint

Objectives

After you read this chapter, you will be able to:

1. Identify common interface components (page 4).
2. Use Office 2007 Help (page 10).
3. Open a file (page 18).
4. Save a file (page 21).
5. Print a document (page 24).
6. Select text to edit (page 31).
7. Insert text and change to the Overtype mode (page 32).
8. Move and copy text (page 34).
9. Find, replace, and go to text (page 36).
10. Use the Undo and Redo commands (page 39).
11. Use language tools (page 39).
12. Apply font attributes (page 43).
13. Copy formats with the Format Painter (page 47).

Hands-On Exercises

Exercises	Skills Covered
1. IDENTIFYING PROGRAM INTERFACE COMPONENTS AND USING HELP (page 12)	• Use PowerPoint's Office Button, Get Help in a Dialog Box, and Use the Zoom Slider • Use Excel's Ribbon, Get Help from an Enhanced ScreenTip, and Use the Zoom Dialog Box • Search Help in Access • Use Word's Status Bar • Search Help and Print a Help Topic
2. PERFORMING UNIVERSAL TASKS (page 28) **Open:** chap1_ho2_sample.docx **Save as:** chap1_ho2_solution.docx	• Open a File and Save It with a Different Name • Use Print Preview and Select Options • Print a Document
3. PERFORMING BASIC TASKS (page 48) **Open:** chap1_ho3_internet_docx **Save as:** chap_ho3_internet_solution.docx	• Cut, Copy, Paste, and Undo • Find and Replace Text • Check Spelling • Choose Synonyms and Use Thesaurus • Use the Research Tool • Apply Font Attributes • Use Format Painter

CASE STUDY

Color Theory Design

Natalie Trevino's first job after finishing her interior design degree is with Color Theory Design of San Diego. Her new supervisor has asked her to review a letter written to an important client and to make any changes or corrections she thinks will improve it. Even though Natalie has used word processing software in the past, she is unfamiliar with Microsoft Office 2007. She needs to get up to speed with Word 2007 so that she can open the letter, edit the content, format the appearance, re-save the file, and print the client letter. Natalie wants to successfully complete this important first task, plus she wants to become familiar with all of Office 2007 because she realizes that her new employer, CTD, makes extensive use of all the Office products.

Case Study

In addition, Natalie needs to improve the appearance of an Excel workbook by applying font attributes, correcting spelling errors, changing the zoom magnification, and printing the worksheet. Finally, Natalie needs to modify a short PowerPoint presentation that features supplemental design information for CTD's important client.

Your Assignment

- Read the chapter and open the existing client letter, *chap1_case_design*.
- Edit the letter by inserting and overtyping text and moving existing text to improve the letter's readability.
- Find and replace text that you want to update.
- Check the spelling and improve the vocabulary by using the thesaurus.
- Modify the letter's appearance by applying font attributes.
- Save the file as **chap1_case_design_solution**, print preview, and print a copy of the letter.
- Open the *chap1_case_bid* workbook in Excel, apply bold and blue font color to the column headings, spell-check the worksheet, change the zoom to 125%, print preview, and print the workbook. Save the workbook as **chap1_case_bid_solution**.
- Open the *chap1_case_design* presentation in PowerPoint, spell-check the presentation, format text, and save it as **chap1_case_design_solution**.

Microsoft Office 2007 Software

> Which software application should you choose? You have to start with an analysis of the output required.

Microsoft Office 2007 is composed of several software applications, of which the primary components are Word, Excel, PowerPoint, and Access. These programs are powerful tools that can be used to increase productivity in creating, editing, saving, and printing files. Each program is a specialized and sophisticated program, so it is necessary to use the correct one to successfully complete a task, much like using the correct tool in the physical world. For example, you use a hammer, not a screwdriver, to pound a nail into the wall. Using the correct tool gets the job done correctly and efficiently the first time; using the wrong tool may require redoing the task, thus wasting time. Likewise, you should use the most appropriate software application to create and work with computer data.

Choosing the appropriate application to use in a situation seems easy to the beginner. If you need to create a letter, you type the letter in Word. However, as situations increase in complexity, so does the need to think through using each application. For example, you can create an address book of names and addresses in Word to create form letters; you can create an address list in Excel and then use spreadsheet commands to manipulate the data; further, you can store addresses in an Access database table and then use database capabilities to manipulate the data. Which software application should you choose? You have to start with an analysis of the output required. If you only want a form letter as the final product, then you might use Word; however, if you want to spot customer trends with the data and provide detailed reports, you would use Access. Table 1.1 describes the main characteristics of the four primary programs in Microsoft Office 2007 to help you decide which program to use for particular tasks.

Word processing software is used primarily with text to create, edit, and format documents.

Spreadsheet software is used primarily with numbers to create worksheets.

Presentation graphics software is used primarily to create electronic slide shows.

Relational database software is used to store data and convert it into information.

Table 1.1 Office Products

Office 2007 Product	Application Characteristics
Word 2007	Word processing software is used with text to create, edit, and format documents such as letters, memos, reports, brochures, resumes, and flyers.
Excel 2007	Spreadsheet software is used to store quantitative data and to perform accurate and rapid calculations with results ranging from simple budgets to financial analyses and statistical analyses.
PowerPoint 2007	Presentation graphics software is used to create slide shows for presentation by a speaker, to be published as part of a Web site, or to run as a stand-alone application on a computer kiosk.
Access 2007	Relational database software is used to store data and convert it into information. Database software is used primarily for decision-making by businesses that compile data from multiple records stored in tables to produce informative reports.

In this section, you explore the common interface among the programs. You learn the names of the interface elements. In addition, you learn how to use Help to get assistance in using the software.

Identifying Common Interface Components

A ***user interface*** is the meeting point between computer software and the person using it.

A ***user interface*** is the meeting point between computer software and the person using it and provides the means for a person to communicate with a software program. Word, Excel, PowerPoint, and Access share the overall Microsoft Office 2007 interface. This interface is made up of three main sections of the screen display shown in Figure 1.1.

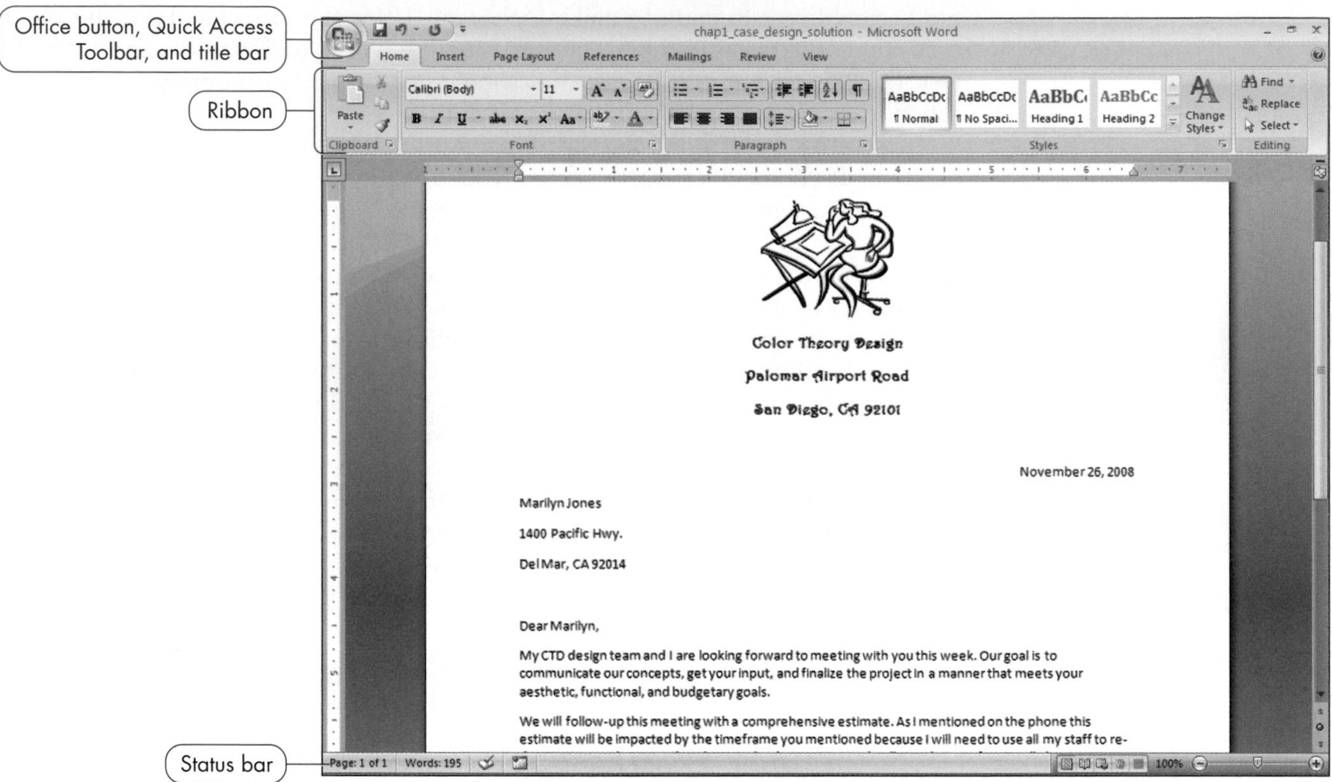

Figure 1.1 Office 2007 Interface

Use the Office Button and Quick Access Toolbar

The first section of the Office 2007 interface contains three distinct items: the Microsoft Office Button (referred to as Office Button in the Exploring series), Quick Access Toolbar, and the title bar. These three items are located at the top of the interface for quick access and reference. The following paragraphs explain each item.

Click the ***Office Button*** to display the Office menu.

The ***Office menu*** contains commands that work with an entire file or with the program.

The ***Office Button*** is an icon that, when clicked, displays the ***Office menu***, a list of commands that you can perform on the entire file or for the specific Office program. For example, when you want to perform a task that involves the entire document, such as saving, printing, or sharing a file with others, you use the commands on the Office menu. You also use the Office menu commands to work with the entire program, such as customizing program settings or exiting from the program. Some commands on the Office menu perform a default action when you click them, such as Save—the file open in the active window is saved. However, other commands open a submenu when you point to or click the command. Figure 1.2 displays the Office menu in Access 2007.

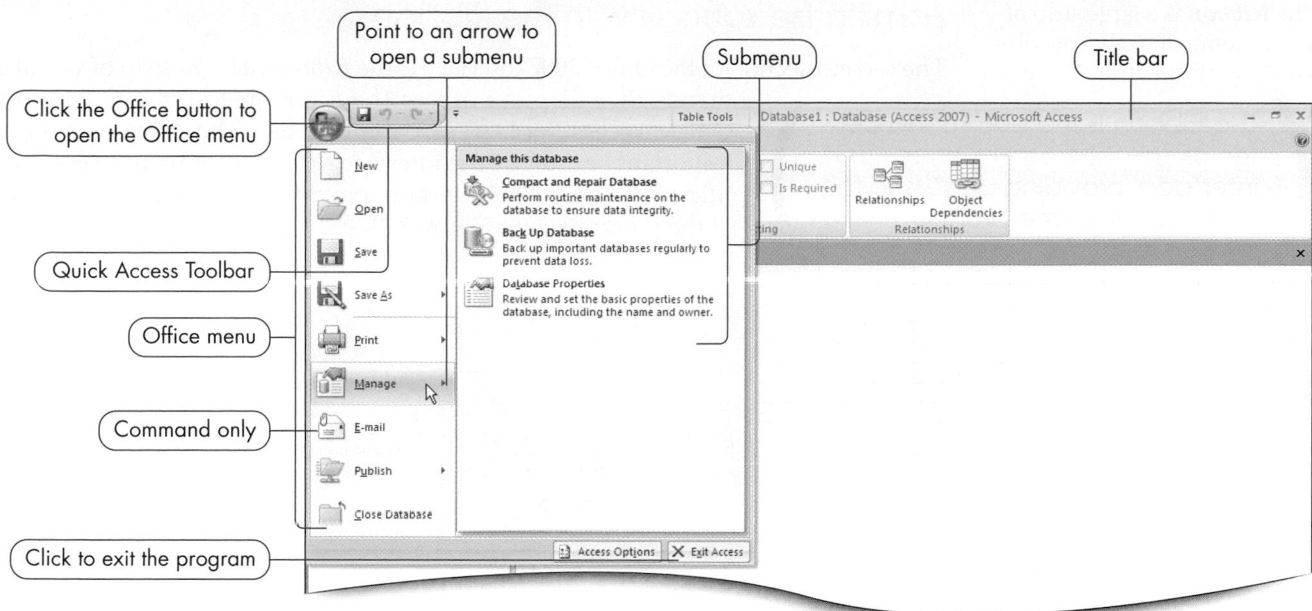

Figure 1.2 Access Office Menu

TIP Displaying the Office Menu from the Keyboard

If you prefer to use a keyboard shortcut to display the Office menu instead of clicking the Office Button, press Alt+F.

The ***Quick Access Toolbar*** contains buttons for frequently used commands.

The second item at the top of the window is the ***Quick Access Toolbar***, which contains buttons for frequently used commands, such as saving a file or undoing an action. This toolbar keeps buttons for common tasks on the screen at all times, enabling you to be more productive in using these frequently used commands.

TIP Customizing the Quick Access Toolbar

As you become more familiar with Microsoft Office 2007, you might find that you need quick access to additional commands, such as Print Preview or Spelling & Grammar. You can easily customize the Quick Access Toolbar by clicking the Customize Quick Access Toolbar drop-down arrow on the right end of the toolbar and adding command buttons from the list that displays. You also can customize the toolbar by changing where it displays. If you want it closer to the document window, you can move the toolbar below the Ribbon.

A ***title bar*** displays the program name and file name at the top of a window.

The third item at the top of the screen is the ***title bar***, which displays the name of the open program and the file name at the top of a window. For example, in Figure 1.1, *chap1_case_design_solution* is the name of a document, and *Microsoft Word* is the name of the program. In Figure 1.2, *Database1* is the name of the file, and *Microsoft Access* is the name of the program.

The ***Ribbon*** is a large strip of visual commands that enables you to perform tasks.

Familiarize Yourself with the Ribbon

The second section of the Office 2007 interface is the ***Ribbon***, a large strip of visual commands that displays across the screen below the Office Button, Quick Access Toolbar, and the title bar. The Ribbon is the most important section of the interface: It is the command center of the Microsoft Office 2007 interface, providing access to the functionality of the programs (see Figure 1.3).

The Ribbon is the command center of the Microsoft Office 2007 interface, providing access to the functionality of the programs.

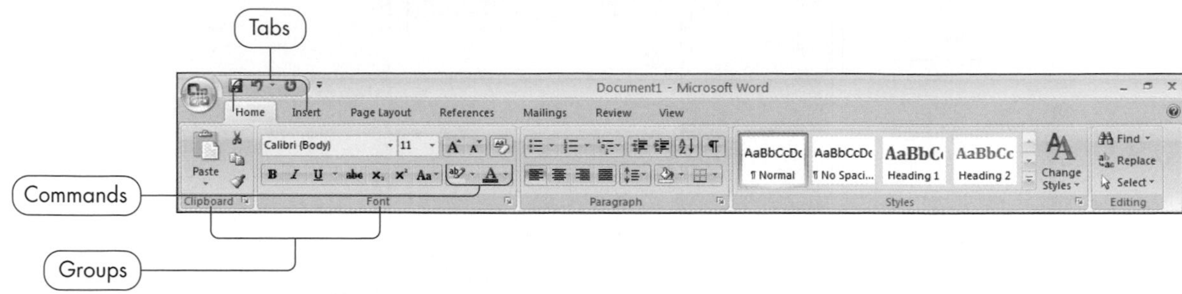

Figure 1.3 The Ribbon

The Ribbon has three main components: tabs, groups, and commands. The following list describes each component.

Tabs, which look like folder tabs, divide the Ribbon into task-oriented categories.

- ***Tabs***, which look like folder tabs, divide the Ribbon into task-oriented sections. For example, the Ribbon in Word contains these tabs: Home, Insert, Page Layout, Reference, Mailings, Review, and View. When you click the Home tab, you see a set of core commands for that program. When you click the Insert tab, you see a set of commands that enable you to insert objects, such as tables, clip art, headers, page numbers, etc.

Groups organize similar commands together within each tab.

- ***Groups*** organize related commands together on each tab. For example, the Home tab in Word contains these groups: Clipboard, Font, Paragraph, Styles, and Editing. These groups help organize related commands together so that you can find them easily. For example, the Font group contains font-related commands, such as Font, Font Size, Bold, Italic, Underline, Highlighter, and Font Color.

A ***command*** is a visual icon in each group that you click to perform a task.

- ***Commands*** are specific tasks performed. Commands appear as visual icons or buttons within the groups on the Ribbon. The icons are designed to provide a visual clue of the purpose of the command. For example, the Bold command looks like a bolded B in the Font group on the Home tab. You simply click the desired command to perform the respective task.

The Ribbon has the same basic design—tabs, groups, and commands—across all Microsoft Office 2007 applications. When you first start using an Office 2007 application, you use the Home tab most often. The groups of commands on the Home tab are designed to get you started using the software. For example, the Home tab contains commands to help you create, edit, and format a document in Word, a worksheet in Excel, and a presentation in PowerPoint. In Access, the Home tab contains groups of commands to insert, delete, and edit records in a database table. While three of the four applications contain an Insert tab, the specific groups and commands differ by application. Regardless of the application, however, the Insert tab contains commands to *insert something*, whether it is a page number in Word, a column chart in Excel, or a shape in PowerPoint. One of the best ways to develop an understanding of the Ribbon is to study its structure in each application. As you explore each program, you will notice the similarities in how commands are grouped on tabs, and you will notice the differences specific to each application.

TIP Hiding the Ribbon

If you are creating a large document or worksheet, you might find that the Ribbon takes up too much of the screen display. Microsoft enables you to temporarily hide a large portion of the Ribbon. Double-click the active tab, such as Home, to hide all the groups and commands, greatly reducing the size of the Ribbon. When you want to display the entire Ribbon, double-click the active tab. You also can press **Ctrl+F1** to minimize and maximize the Ribbon.

The Ribbon provides an extensive sets of commands that you use when creating and editing documents, worksheets, slides, tables, or other items. Figure 1.4 points out other important components of the Ribbon.

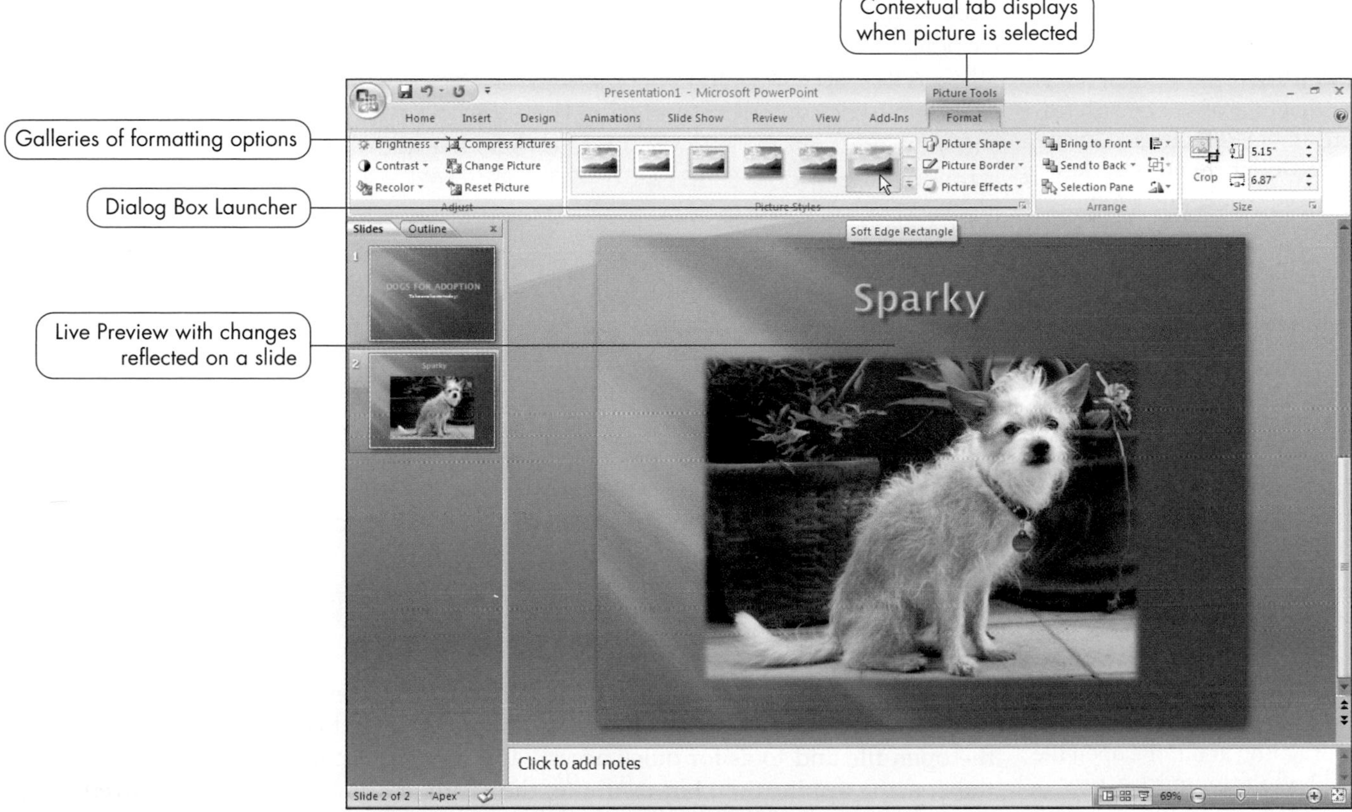

Figure 1.4 PowerPoint with Ribbon

A ***dialog box*** is a window that provides options related to a group of commands.

A ***Dialog Box Launcher*** is a small icon that, when clicked, opens a related dialog box.

A ***gallery*** is a set of options that appears as thumbnail graphics.

Live Preview provides a preview of the results for gallery options.

Figure 1.4 shows examples of four other components of the Ribbon. These components include a Dialog Box Launcher, a gallery, Live Preview, and a contextual tab. The following list describes each component:

- A ***Dialog Box Launcher*** is a small icon located on the right side of some group names that you click to open a related ***dialog box,*** which is a window that provides options related to a group of commands.
- A ***gallery*** is a set of options that appear as thumbnail graphics that visually represent the option results. For example, if you create a chart in Excel, a gallery of chart formatting options provides numerous choices for formatting the chart.
- ***Live Preview*** works with the galleries, providing a preview of the results of formatting in the document. As you move your mouse pointer over the gallery

thumbnails, you see how each formatting option affects the selected item in your document, worksheet, or presentation. This feature increases productivity because you see the results immediately. If you do not like the results, keep moving the mouse pointer over other gallery options until you find a result you like.

A ***contextual tab*** is a tab that provides specialized commands that display only when the object they affect is selected.

- A ***contextual tab*** provides specialized commands that display only when the object they affect is selected. For example, if you insert a picture on a slide, PowerPoint displays a contextual tab on the Ribbon with commands specifically related to the selected image. When you click outside the picture to deselect it, the contextual tab disappears.

A ***Key Tip*** is the letter or number that displays over each feature on the Ribbon and Quick Access Toolbar and is the keyboard equivalent that you press.

TIP Using Keyboard Shortcuts

Many people who have used previous Office products like to use the keyboard to initiate commands. Microsoft Office 2007 makes it possible for you to continue to use keyboard shortcuts for commands on the Ribbon. Simply press Alt on the keyboard to display the Ribbon and Quick Access Toolbar with shortcuts called Key Tips. A Key Tip is the letter or number that displays over each feature on the Ribbon or Quick Access Toolbar and is the keyboard equivalent that you press. Notice the Key Tips that display in Figure 1.5 as a result of pressing Alt on the keyboard. Other keyboard shortcuts, such as Ctrl+C to copy text, remain the same from previous versions of Microsoft Office.

Press the letter on the keyboard to initiate a command

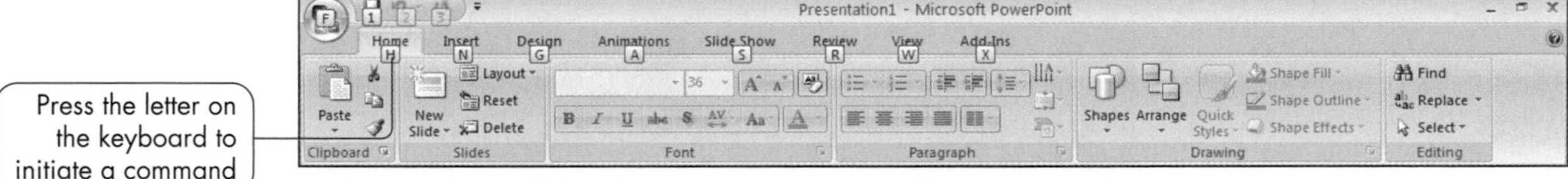

Figure 1.5 Key Tips Displayed for Ribbon and Quick Access Toolbar

Use the Status Bar

The ***status bar*** displays below the document and provides information about the open file and buttons for quick access.

The third major section of the Office 2007 user interface is the status bar. The ***status bar*** displays at the bottom of the program window and contains information about the open file and tools for quick access. The status bar contains details for the file in the specific application. For example, the Word status bar shows the current page, total number of pages, total words in the document, and proofreading status. The PowerPoint status bar shows the slide number, total slides in the presentation, and the applied theme. The Excel status bar provides general instructions and displays the average, count, and sum of values for selected cells. In each program, the status bar also includes View commands from the View tab for quick access. You can use the View commands to change the way the document, worksheet, or presentation displays onscreen. Table 1.2 describes the main characteristics of each Word 2007 view.

Table 1.2 Word Document Views

View Option	Characteristics
Print Layout	Displays the document as it will appear when printed.
Full Screen Reading	Displays the document on the entire screen to make reading long documents easier. To remove Full Screen Reading, press the Esc key on the keyboard.
Web Page	Displays the document as it would look as a Web page.
Outline	Displays the document as an outline.
Draft	Displays the document for quick editing without additional elements such as headers or footers.

The ***Zoom slider*** enables you to increase or decrease the magnification of the file onscreen.

The ***Zoom slider***, located on the right edge of the status bar, enables you to drag the slide control to change the magnification of the current document, worksheet, or presentation. You can change the display to zoom in on the file to get a close up view, or you can zoom out to get an overview of the file. To use the Zoom slider, click and drag the slider control to the right to increase the zoom or to the left to decrease the zoom. If you want to set a specific zoom, such as 78%, you can type the precise value in the Zoom dialog box when you click Zoom on the View tab. Figure 1.6 shows the Zoom dialog box and the elements on Word's status bar. The Zoom dialog box in Excel and PowerPoint looks similar to the Word Zoom dialog box, but it contains fewer options in the other programs.

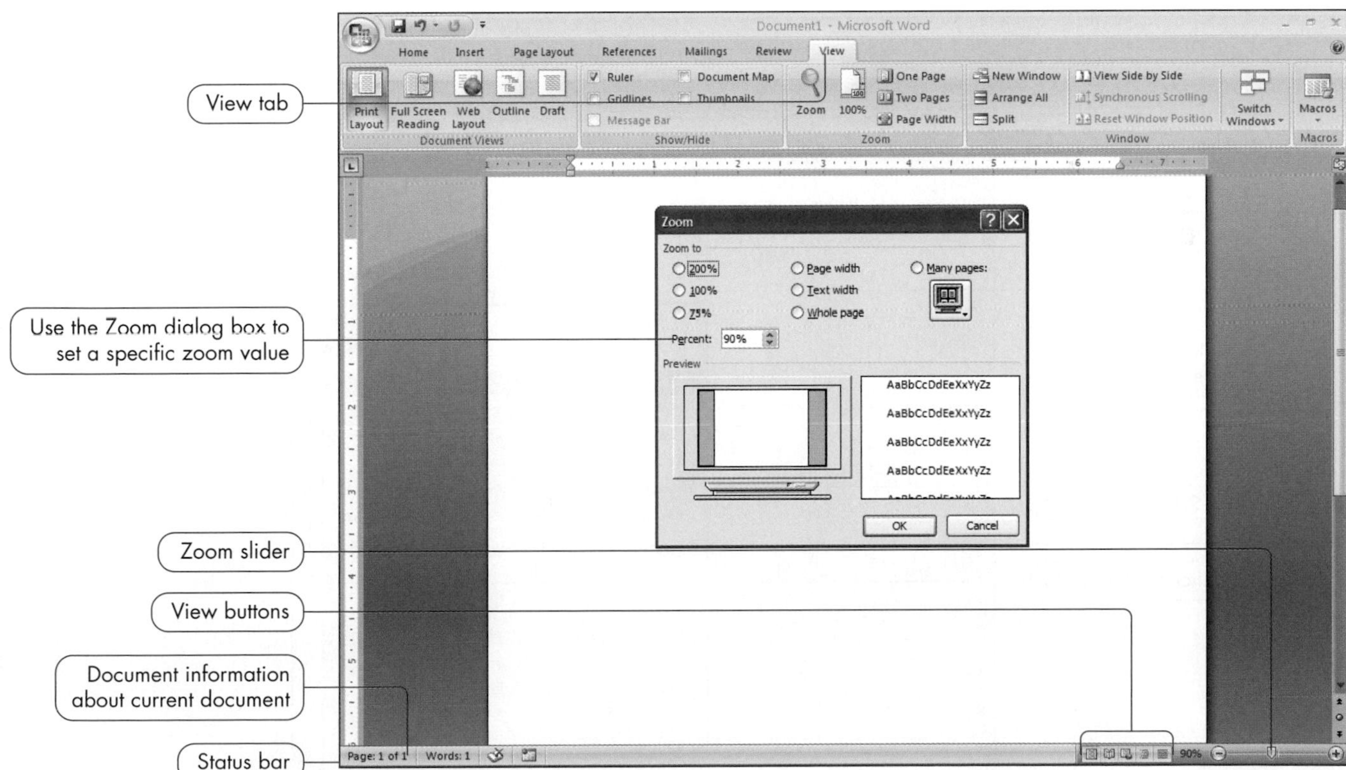

Figure 1.6 View Tab, Zoom Dialog Box, and the Status Bar in Word

Using Office 2007 Help

> Help is always available when you use any Office 2007 program.

Have you ever started a project such as assembling an entertainment center and had to abandon it because you had no way to get help when you got stuck? Microsoft Office includes features that keep this type of scenario from happening when you use Word, Excel, Access, or PowerPoint. In fact, several methods are available to locate help when you need assistance performing tasks. Help is always available when you use any Office 2007 program. Help files reside on your computer when you install Microsoft Office, and Microsoft provides additional help files on its Web site. If you link to Microsoft Office Online, you not only have access to help files for all applications, you also have access to up-to-date products, files, and graphics to help you complete projects.

Use Office 2007 Help

To access Help, press F1 on the keyboard or click the Help button on the right edge of the Ribbon shown in Figure 1.7. If you know the topic you want help with, such as printing, you can type the key term in the Search box to display help files on that topic. Help also displays general topics in the lower part of the Help window that are links to further information. To display a table of contents for the Help files, click the Show Table of Contents button, and after locating the desired help topic, you can print the information for future reference by clicking the Print button. Figure 1.7 shows these elements in Excel Help.

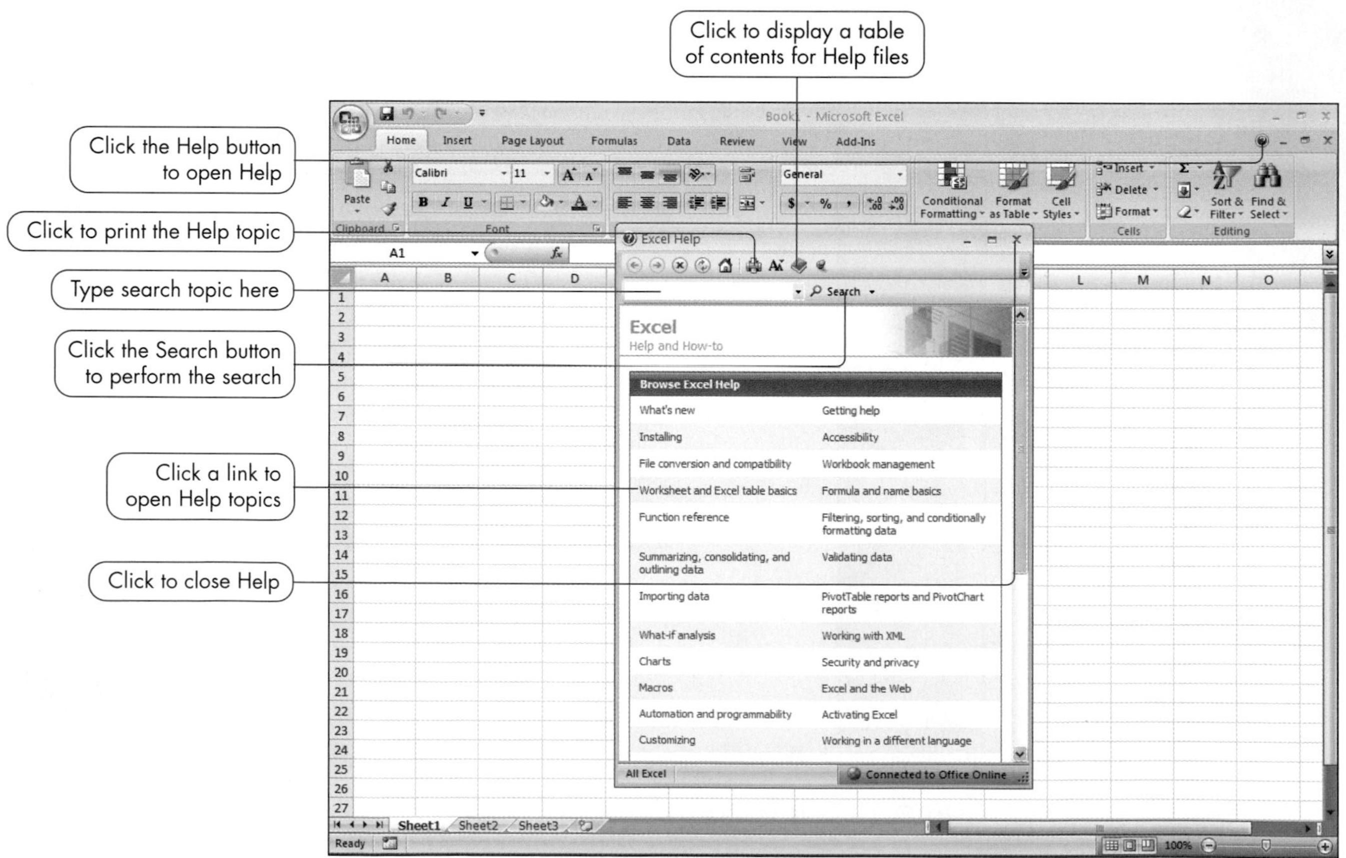

Figure 1.7 Excel Help

Use Enhanced ScreenTips

An ***Enhanced ScreenTip*** displays the name and brief description of a command when you rest the pointer on a command.

Another method for getting help is to use the Office 2007 Enhanced ScreenTips. An *Enhanced ScreenTip* displays when you rest the mouse pointer on a command. Notice in Figure 1.8 that the Enhanced ScreenTip provides the command name, a brief description of the command, and a link for additional help. To get help on the specific command, keep the pointer resting on the command and press F1 if the Enhanced ScreenTip displays a Help icon. The advantage of this method is that you do not have to find the correct information yourself because the Enhanced ScreenTip help is context sensitive.

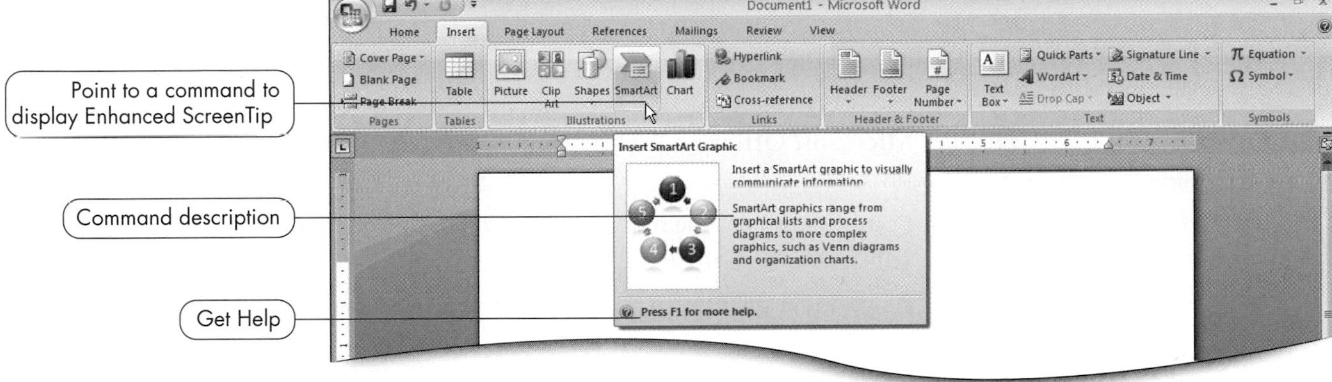

Figure 1.8 Enhanced ScreenTip

Get Help with Dialog Boxes

As you work within a dialog box, you might need help with some of the numerous options contained in that dialog box, but you do not want to close the dialog box to get assistance. For example, if you open the Insert Picture dialog box and want help with inserting files, click the Help button located on the title bar of the dialog box to display help for the dialog box. Figure 1.9 shows the Insert Picture dialog box with Help displayed.

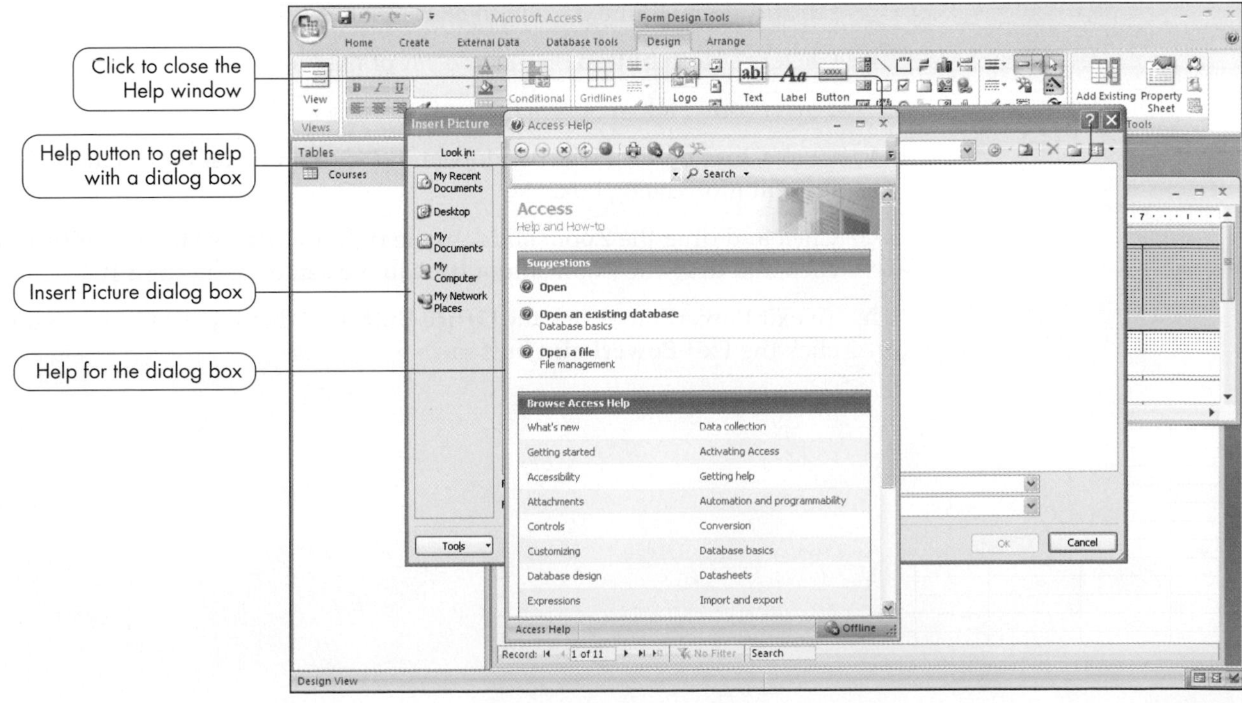

Figure 1.9 Help with Dialog Boxes

Hands-On Exercises

1 | Identifying Program Interface Components and Using Help

Skills covered: 1. Use PowerPoint's Office Button, Get Help in a Dialog Box, and Use the Zoom Slider **2.** Use Excel's Ribbon, Get Help from an Enhanced ScreenTip, and Use the Zoom Dialog Box **3.** Search Help in Access **4.** Use Word's Status Bar **5.** Search Help and Print a Help Topic

Step 1
Use PowerPoint's Office Button, Get Help in a Dialog Box, and Use the Zoom Slider

Refer to Figure 1.10 as you complete Step 1.

a. Click **Start** to display the Start menu. Click (or point to) **All Programs**, click **Microsoft Office**, then click **Microsoft Office PowerPoint 2007** to start the program.

b. Point to and rest the mouse on the Office Button, and then do the same to the Quick Access Toolbar.

   As you rest the mouse pointer on each object, you see an Enhanced ScreenTip for that object.

   TROUBLESHOOTING: If you do not see the Enhanced ScreenTip, keep the mouse pointer on the object a little longer.

c. Click the **Office Button** and slowly move your mouse down the list of menu options, pointing to the arrow after any command name that has one.

   The Office menu displays, and as you move the mouse down the list, submenus display for menu options that have an arrow.

d. Select **New**.

   The New Presentation dialog box displays. Depending on how Microsoft Office 2007 was installed, your screen may vary. If Microsoft Office 2007 was fully installed, you should see a thumbnail to create a Blank Presentation, and you may see additional thumbnails in the *Recently Used Templates* section of the dialog box.

e. Click the **Help button** on the title bar of the New Presentation dialog box.

   PowerPoint Help displays the topic *Create a new file from a template.*

f. Click **Close** on the Help Window and click the **Cancel** button in the New Presentation dialog box.

g. Click and drag the **Zoom slider** to the right to increase the magnification. Then click and drag the **Zoom slider** back to the center point for a 100% zoom.

h. To exit PowerPoint, click the **Office Button** to display the Office menu, and then click the **Exit PowerPoint button**.

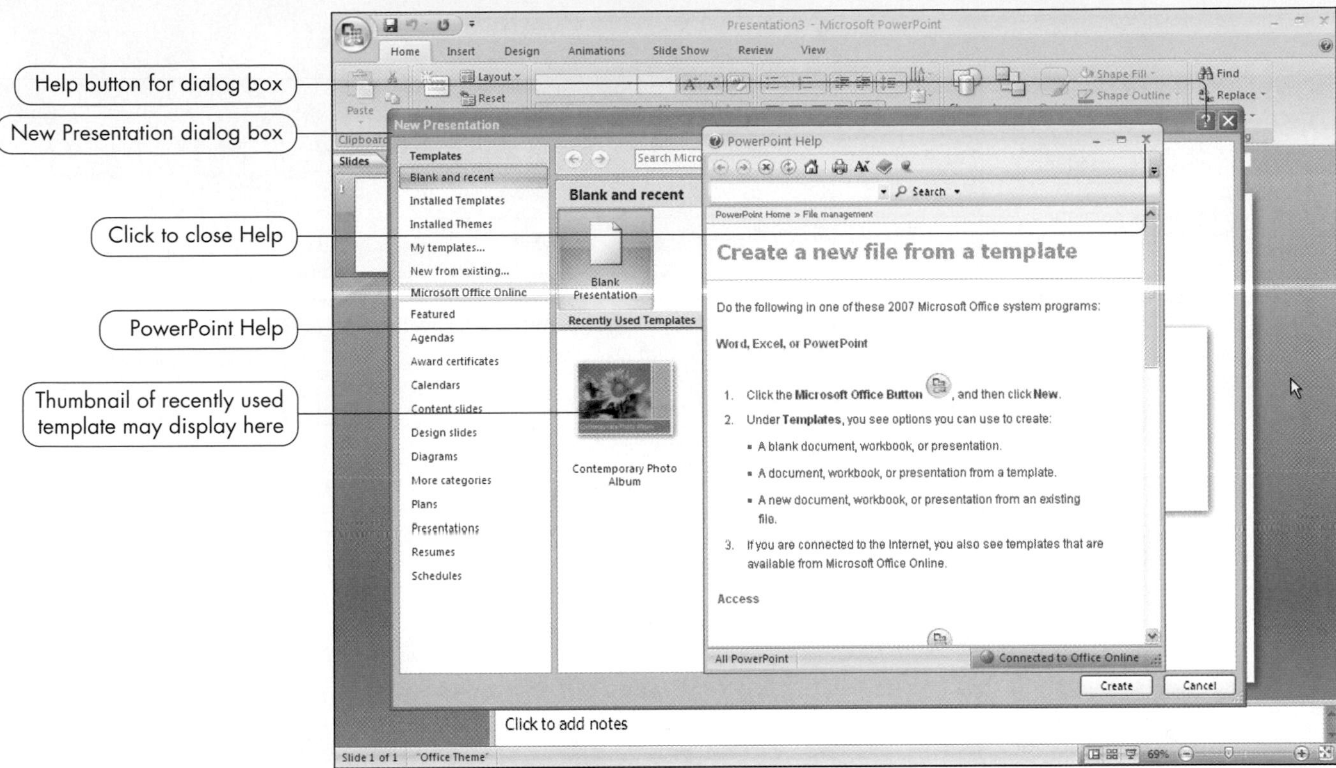

Figure 1.10 PowerPoint Help for New Presentations Dialog Box

Step 2
Use Excel's Ribbon, Get Help from an Enhanced ScreenTip, and Use the Zoom Dialog Box

Refer to Figure 1.11 as you complete Step 2.

a. Click **Start** to display the Start menu. Click (or point to) **All Programs**, click **Microsoft Office**, then click **Microsoft Office Excel 2007** to open the program.

b. Click the **Insert tab** on the Ribbon.

The Insert tab contains groups of commands for inserting objects, such as tables, illustrations, charts, links, and text.

c. Rest the mouse on **Hyperlink** in the Links group on the Insert tab.

The Enhanced ScreenTip for Hyperlinks displays. Notice the Enhanced ScreenTip contains a Help icon.

d. Press **F1** on the keyboard.

Excel Help displays the *Create or remove a hyperlink* Help topic.

TROUBLESHOOTING: If you are not connected to the Internet, you might not see the context-sensitive help.

e. Click the **Close button** on the Help window.

f. Click the **View tab** on the Ribbon and click **Zoom** in the Zoom group.

The Zoom dialog box appears so that you can change the zoom percentage.

g. Click the **200%** option and click **OK**.

The worksheet is now magnified to 200% of its regular size.

h. Click **Zoom** in the Zoom group on the View tab, click the **100%** option, and click **OK**.

The worksheet is now restored to 100%.

i. To exit Excel, click the **Office Button** to display the Office menu, and then click the **Exit Excel button**.

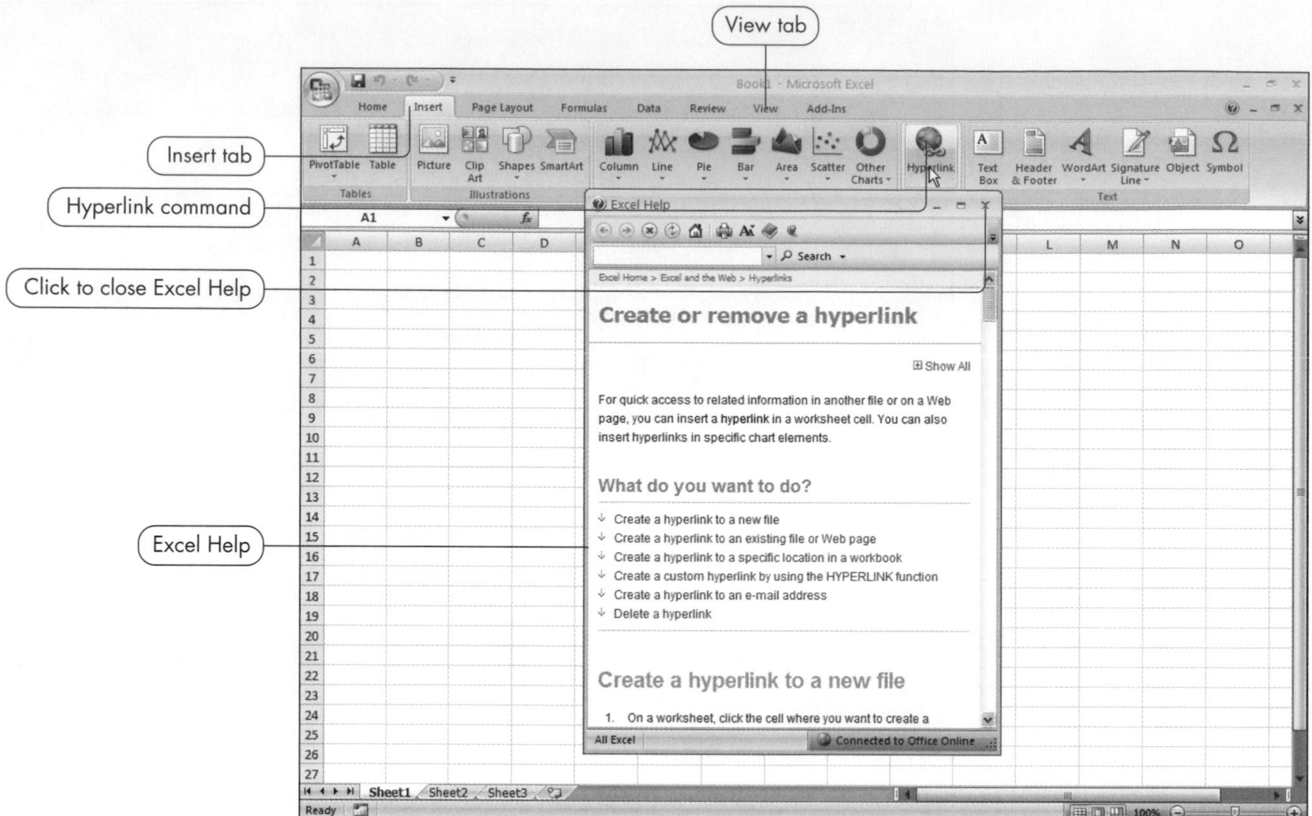

Figure 1.11 Excel Ribbon with Help

Step 3
Search Help in Access

Refer to Figure 1.12 as you complete Step 3.

a. Click **Start** to display the Start menu. Click (or point to) **All Programs**, click **Microsoft Office**, then click **Microsoft Office Access 2007** to start the program.

   Access opens and displays the Getting Started with Microsoft Access screen.

   TROUBLESHOOTING: If you are not familiar with Access, just use the opening screen that displays and continue with the exercise.

b. Press **F1** on the keyboard.

   Access Help displays.

c. Type **table** in the Search box in the Access Help window.

d. Click the **Search** button.

   Access displays help topics.

e. Click the topic **Create a table in a database**.

   The help topic displays.

f. Click the **Close** button on the Access Help window.

   Access Help closes.

g. To exit Access, click the **Office Button** to display the Office menu, and then click the **Exit Access button**.

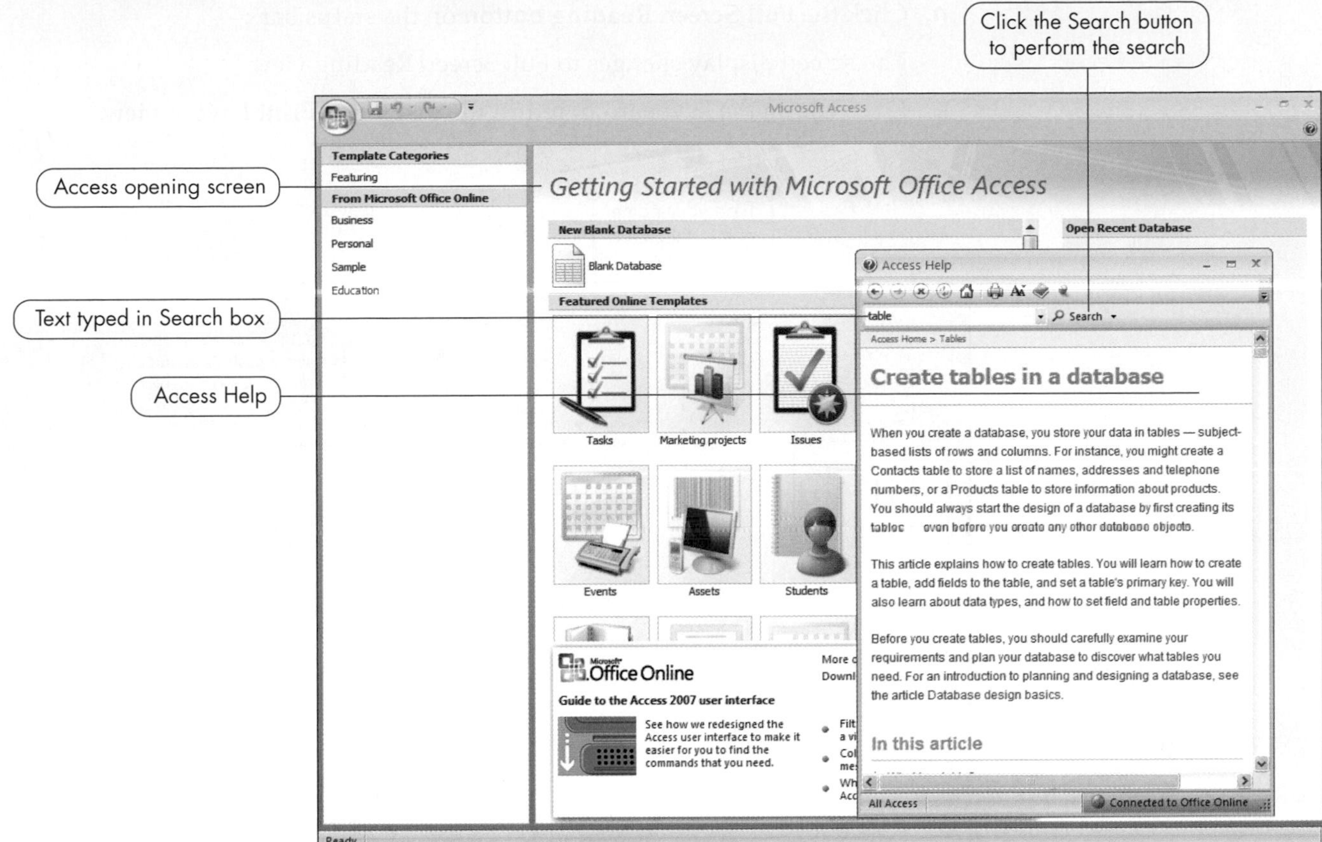

Figure 1.12 Access Help

Step 4
Use Word's Status Bar

Refer to Figure 1.13 as you complete Step 4.

a. Click **Start** to display the Start menu. Click (or point to) **All Programs**, click **Microsoft Office**, then click **Microsoft Office Word 2007** to start the program.

Word opens with a blank document ready for you to start typing.

b. Type your first name.

Your first name displays in the document window.

c. Point your mouse to the **Zoom slider** on the status bar.

d. Click and drag the **Zoom slider** to the right to increase the magnification.

The document with your first name increases in size onscreen.

e. Click and drag the slider control to the left to decrease the magnification.

The document with your first name decreases in size.

f. Click and drag the **Zoom slider** back to the center.

The document returns to 100% magnification.

g. Slowly point the mouse to the buttons on the status bar.

A ScreenTip displays the names of the buttons.

h. Click the **Full Screen Reading button** on the status bar.

The screen display changes to Full Screen Reading view.

i. Press **Esc** on the keyboard to return the display to Print Layout view.

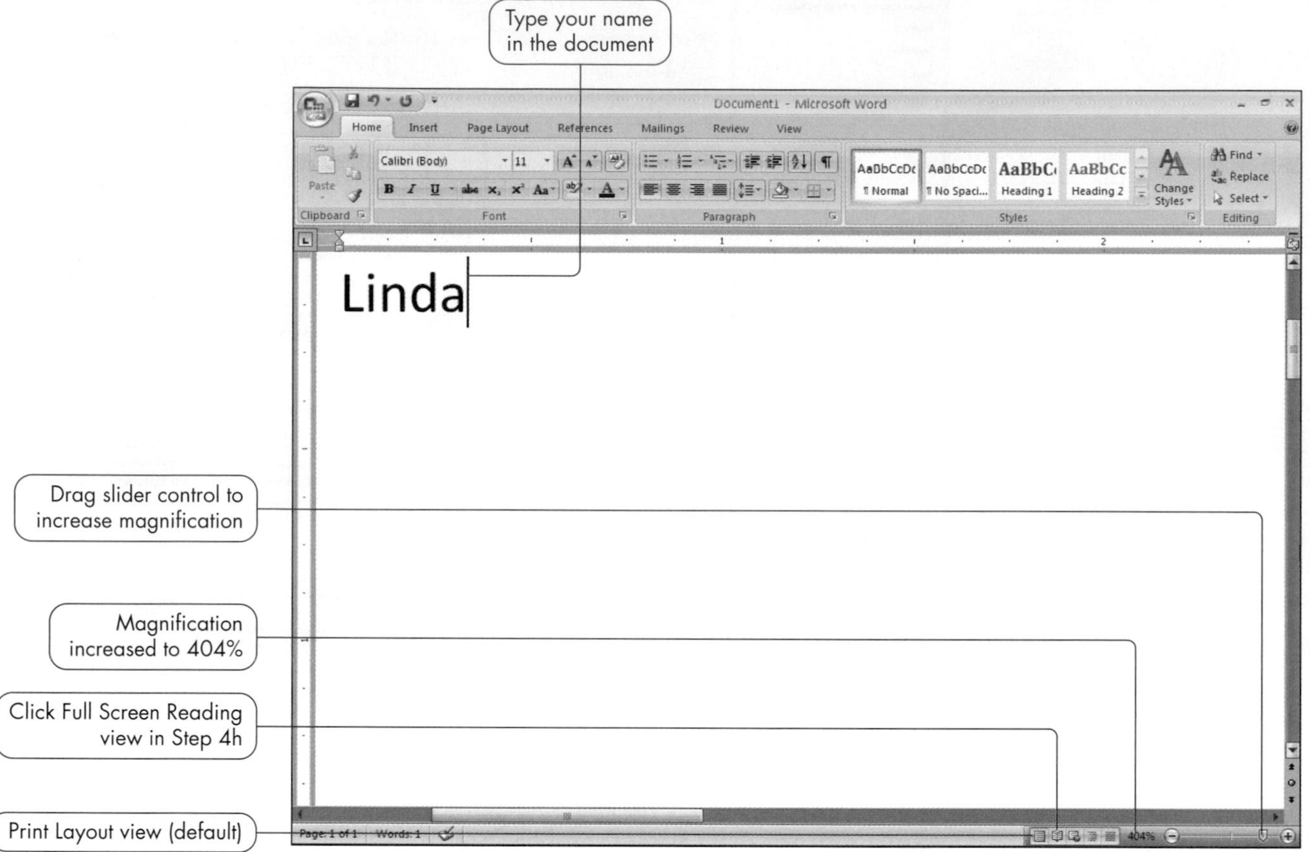

Figure 1.13 The Word Status Bar

Step 5
Search Help and Print a Help Topic

Refer to Figure 1.14 as you complete Step 5.

a. With Word open on the screen, press **F1** on the keyboard.

Word Help displays.

b. Type **zoom** in the Search box in the Word Help window.

c. Click the **Search** button.

Word Help displays related topics.

d. Click the topic **Zoom in or out of a document, presentation, or worksheet**.

The help topic displays.

TROUBLESHOOTING: If you do not have a printer that is ready to print, skip Step 5e and continue with the exercise.

e. Turn on the attached printer, be sure it has paper, and then click the Word Help **Print** button.

The Help topic prints on the attached printer.

f. Click the **Show Table of Contents** button on the Word Help toolbar.

The Table of Contents pane displays on the left side of the Word Help dialog box so that you can click popular Help topics, such as *What's new*. You can click a closed book icon to see specific topics to click for additional information, and you can click an open book icon to close the main Help topic.

g. Click the **Close** button on Word Help.

Word Help closes.

h. To exit Word, click the **Office Button** to display the Office menu, and then click the **Exit Word button**.

A warning appears stating that you have not saved changes to your document.

i. Click **No** in the Word warning box.

You exit Word without saving the document.

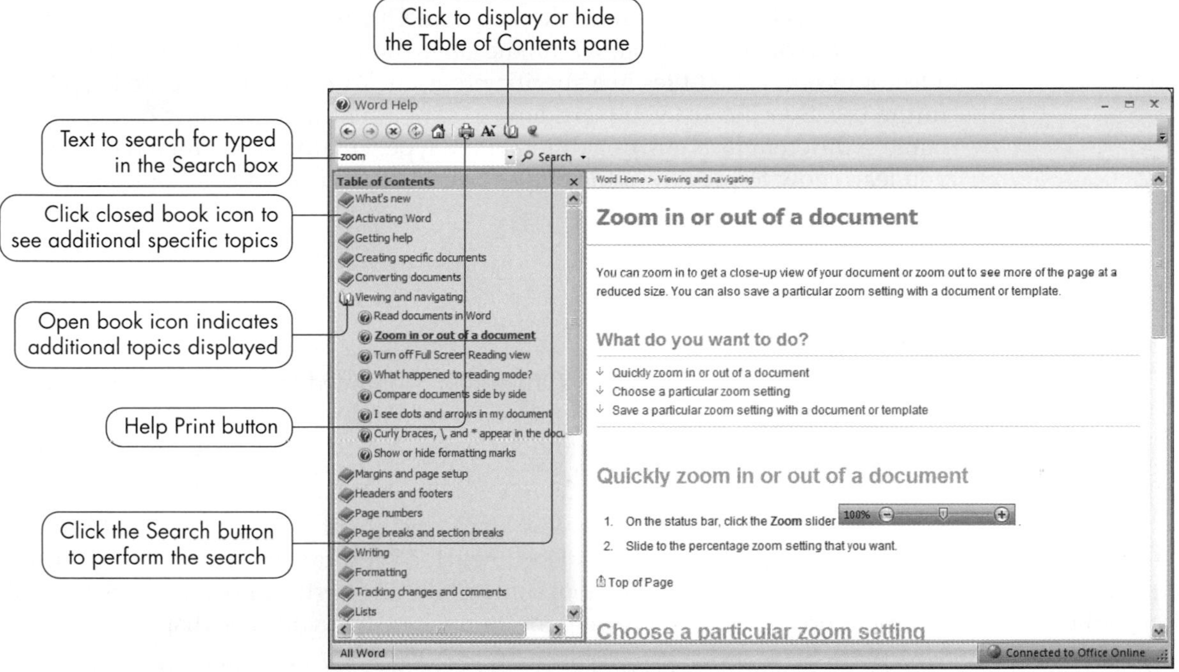

Figure 1.14 Word Help

Universal Tasks

Today, storing large amounts of information on a computer is taken for granted, but in reality, computers would not have become very important if you could not save and re-use the files you create.

One of the most useful and important aspects of using computers is the ability to save and re-use information. For example, you can store letters, reports, budgets, presentations, and databases as files to reopen and use at some time in the future. Today, storing large amounts of information on a computer is taken for granted, but in reality, computers would not have become very important if you could not save and re-use the files you create.

Three fundamental tasks are so important for productivity that they are considered universal to most every computer program, including Office 2007:

- opening files that have been saved
- saving files you create
- printing files

In this section, you open a file within an Office 2007 program. Specifically, you learn how to open a file from within the Open dialog box and how to open a file from a list of recently used files in a specific program. You also save files to keep them for future use. Specifically, you learn how to save a file with the same name, a different name, a different location, or a different file type. Finally, you print a file. Specifically, you learn how to preview a file before printing it and select print options within the Print dialog box.

Opening a File

When you start any program in Office 2007, you need to start creating a new file or open an existing one. You use the Open command to retrieve a file saved on a storage device and place it in the random access memory (RAM) of your computer so you can work on it. For example:

The ***insertion point*** is the blinking vertical line in the document, cell, slide show, or database table designating the current location where text you type displays.

- When you start Word 2007, a new blank document named Document1 opens. You can either start typing in Document1, or you can open an existing document. The ***insertion point***, which looks like a blinking vertical line, displays in the document designating the current location where text you type displays.
- When you start PowerPoint 2007, a new blank presentation named Presentation1 opens. You can either start creating a new slide for the blank presentation, or you can open an existing presentation.
- When you start Excel 2007, a new blank workbook named Book1 opens. You can either start inputting labels and values into Book1, or you can open an existing workbook.
- When you start Access 2007—unlike Word, PowerPoint, and Excel—a new blank database is not created automatically for you. In order to get started using Access, you must create and name a database first or open an existing database.

Open a File Using the Open Dialog Box

Opening a file in any of the Office 2007 applications is an easy process: Use the Open command from the Office menu and specify the file to open. However, locating the file to open can be difficult at times because you might not know where the file you want to use is located. You can open files stored on your computer or on a remote computer that you have access to. Further, files are saved in folders, and you might need to look for files located within folders or subfolders. The Open dialog box, shown in Figure 1.15, contains many features designed for file management; however, two features are designed specifically to help you locate files.

- **Look in**—provides a hierarchical view of the structure of folders and subfolders on your computer or on any computer network you are attached to. Move up or down in the structure to find a specific location or folder and then click the desired location to select it. The file list in the center of the dialog box displays the subfolders and files saved in the location you select. Table 1.3 lists and describes the toolbar buttons.
- **My Places bar**—provides a list of shortcut links to specific folders on your computer and locations on a computer network that you are attached to. Click a link to select it, and the file list changes to display subfolders and files in that location.

Table 1.3 Toolbar Buttons

Buttons	Characteristics
Previous Folder	Returns to the previous folder you viewed.
Up One Level	Moves up one level in the folder structure from the current folder.
Delete	Deletes the selected file or selected folder.
Create New Folder	Creates a new folder within the current folder.
Views	Changes the way the list of folders and files displays in the File list.

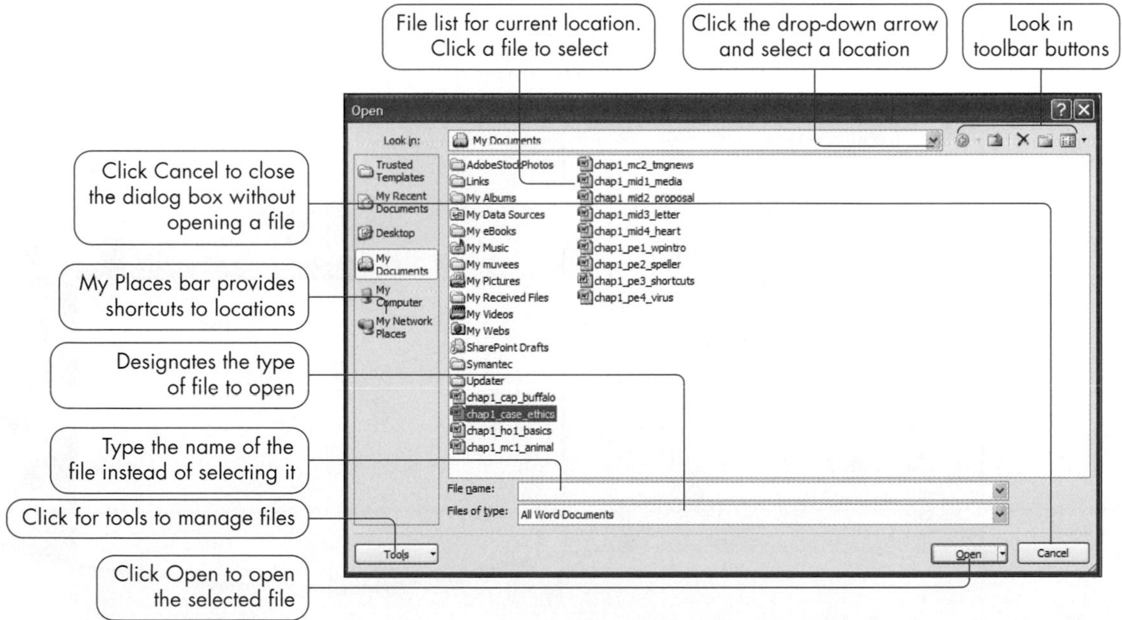

Figure 1.15 Open Dialog Box in Word

After you locate and select the file, click the Open button in the dialog box to display the file on the screen. However, if, for example, you work as part of a workgroup that shares files with each other, you might find the need to open files in a more specialized way. Microsoft Office programs provide several options for opening files when you click the drop-down arrow on the Open button. For example, if you want to keep the original file intact, you might open the file as a copy of the original. Table 1.4 describes the Open options.

Table 1.4 Open Options

Open Options	Characteristics
Open	Opens the selected file with the ability to read and write (edit).
Open Read-Only	Opens the selected file with the ability to read the contents but prevents you from changing or editing it.
Open as Copy	Opens the selected file as a copy of the original so that if you edit the file, the original remains unchanged.
Open in Browser	Opens the selected file in a Web browser.
Open with Transform	Opens a file and provides the ability to transform it into another type of document, such as an HTML document.
Open and Repair	Opens the selected file and attempts to repair any damage. If you have difficulty opening a file, try to open it by selecting Open and Repair.

Open Files Using the Recent Documents List

Office 2007 provides a quick method for accessing files you used recently. The Recent Documents list displays when the Office menu opens and provides a list of links to the last few files you used. The list changes as you work in the application to reflect only the most recent files. Figure 1.16 shows the Office menu with the Recent Documents list.

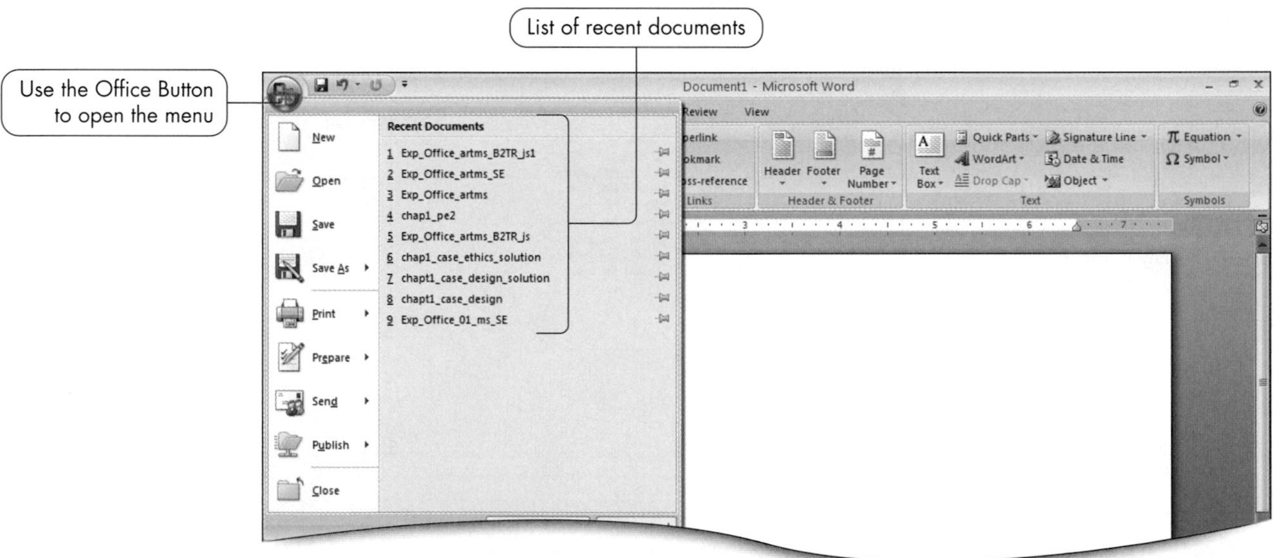

Figure 1.16 The Recent Documents List

TIP Keeping Files on the Recent Documents List

As you use the Office application and open several files, the list of Recent Documents changes; however, you can designate files to keep displayed on the Recent Documents list at all times. Notice the icon of the pushpin that displays immediately following each file name on the Recent Documents list. Just as you use pushpins to post an important notice in the real world, you use pushpins here to designate important files that you want easy access to. To pin a specific file to the Recent Documents list, click the icon of a gray pushpin. The shape of the pin changes as if pushed in, and the color of the pin changes to green designating that the file is pinned permanently on the list. However, if later you decide to remove the file from the list, you can unpin it by simply clicking the green pushpin, changing the icon back to gray, and the file will disappear from the list over time. Notice the Recent Documents list with both gray and green pushpins in Figure 1.17.

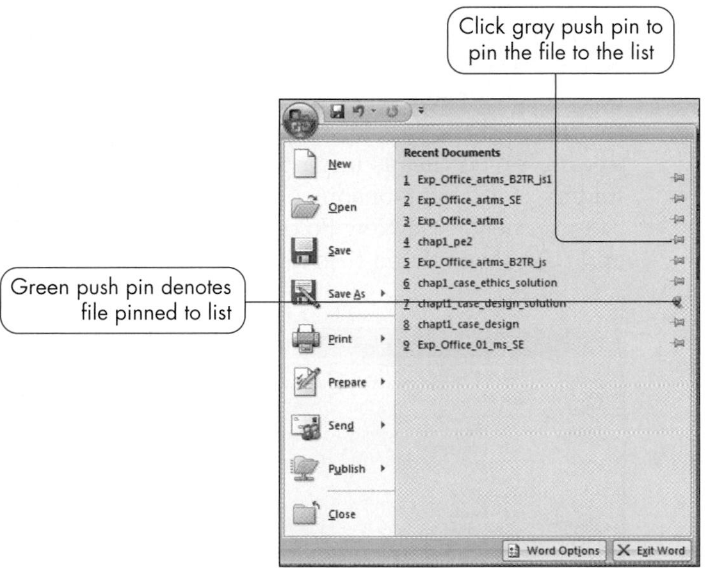

Figure 1.17 The Recent Documents List

Saving a File

As you work with any Office 2007 application and create files, you will need to save them for future use. While you are working on a file, it is stored in the temporary memory or RAM of your computer. When you save a file, the contents of the file stored in RAM are saved to the hard drive of your computer or to a storage device such as a flash drive. As you create, edit, and format a complex file such as a report, slide show, or budget, you should consider saving several versions of it as you work. For example, you might number versions or use the date in the file name to designate each version. Using this method enables you to revert to a previous version of the document if necessary. To save a file you create in Word, PowerPoint, or Excel, click the Office Button to display the Office menu. Office provides two commands that work similarly: Save and Save As. Table 1.5 describes the characteristics of these two commands.

> As you create, edit, and format a complex file such as a report, slide show, or budget, you should consider saving several versions of it as you work.

Table 1.5 Save Options

Command	Characteristics
Save	Saves the open document: • If this is the first time the document is being saved, Office 2007 opens the Save As dialog box so that you can name the file. • If this document was saved previously, the document is automatically saved using the original file name.
Save As	Opens the Save As dialog box: • If this is the first time the document is being saved, use the Save As dialog box to name the file. • If this document was saved previously, use this option to save the file with a new name, in a new location, or as a new file type preserving the original file with its original name.

When you select the Save As command, the Save As dialog box appears (see Figure 1.18). Notice that saving and opening files are related, that the Save As dialog box looks very similar to the Open dialog box that you saw in Figure 1.15. The dialog box requires you to specify the drive or folder in which to store the file, the name of the file, and the type of file you wish the file to be saved as. Additionally, because finding saved files is important, you should always group related files together in folders, so that you or someone else can find them in a location that makes sense. You can use the Create New Folder button in the dialog box to create and name a folder, and then save related files to it.

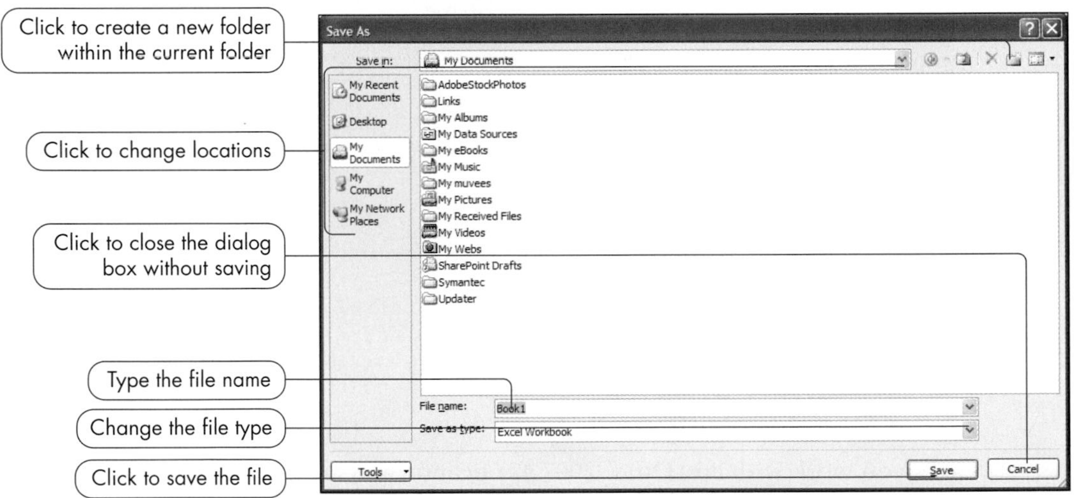

Figure 1.18 Save As Dialog Box in Excel

All subsequent executions of the Save command save the file under the assigned name, replacing the previously saved version with the new version. Pressing Ctrl+S is another way to activate the Save command. If you want to change the name of the file, use the Save As command. Word, PowerPoint, and Excel use the same basic process for saving files, which include the following options:

- naming and saving a previously unsaved file
- saving an updated file with the same name and replacing the original file with the updated one
- saving an updated file with a different name or in a different location to keep the original intact
- saving the file in a different file format

TIP Saving from the Office Menu

You should select the Save As command on the Office menu rather than pointing to the arrow that follows the command. When you point to the arrow, menu options display for saving the file in an alternative format. Always check the Save as type box in the dialog box to be sure that the correct file type is specified.

A ***macro*** is a small program that automates tasks in a file.

A ***virus checker*** is software that scans files for a hidden program that can damage your computer.

A ***template*** is a file that contains formatting and design elements.

Office 2007 saves files in a different format from previous versions of the software. Office now makes use of XML formats for files created in Word, PowerPoint, and Excel. For example, in previous versions of Word, all documents were saved with the three-letter extension .doc. Now Word saves default documents with the four-letter extension .docx. The new XML format makes use of file compression to save storage space for the user. The files are compressed automatically when saved and uncompressed when opened. Another important feature is that the XML format makes using the files you create in Office 2007 easier to open in other software. This increased portability of files is a major benefit in any workplace that might have numerous applications to deal with. The new file format also differentiates between files that contain ***macros***, which are small programs that automate tasks in a file, and those that do not. This specification of files that contain macros enables a virus checker to rigorously check for damaging programs hidden in files. A ***virus checker*** is software that scans files for a hidden program that can damage your computer. Table 1.6 lists the file formats with the four-letter extension for Word, PowerPoint, and Excel, and a five-letter extension for Access.

Table 1.6 Word, PowerPoint, Excel, and Access File Extensions

File Format	Characteristics
Word	.docx—default document format .docm—a document that contains macros .dotx—a template without macros (a template is a file that contains formatting and design elements) .dotm—a template with macros
PowerPoint	.pptx—default presentation format .pptm—a presentation that contains macros .potx—a template .potm—a template with macros .ppam—an add-in that contains macros .ppsx—a slide show .ppsm—a slide show with macros .sldx—a slide saved independently of a presentation .sldm—a slide saved independently of a presentation that contains a macro .thmx—a theme used to format a slide
Excel	.xlsx—default workbook .xlsm—a workbook with macros .xltx—a template .xltm—a template with a macro .xlsb—non-XML binary workbook—for previous versions of the software .xlam—an add-in that contains macros
Access	.accdb—default database

Access 2007 saves data differently from Word, PowerPoint, and Excel. When you start Access, which is a relational database, you must create a database and define at least one table for your data. Then as you work, your data is stored automatically. This powerful software enables multiple users access to up-to-date data. The concepts of saving, opening, and printing remain the same, but the process of how data is saved is unique to this powerful environment.

A ***shortcut menu*** displays when you right-click the mouse on an object and provides a list of commands pertaining to the object you clicked.

TIP Changing the Display of the My Places Bar

Sometimes finding saved files can be a time-consuming chore. To help you quickly locate files, Office 2007 provides options for changing the display of the My Places bar. In Word, PowerPoint, Excel, and Access, you can create shortcuts to folders where you store commonly used files and add them to the My Places bar. From the Open or Save As dialog box, select the location in the Look in list you want to add to the bar. With the desired location selected, point to an empty space below the existing shortcuts on the My Places bar. Right-click the mouse to display a shortcut menu, which displays when you right-click the mouse on an object and provides a list of commands pertaining to the object you clicked. From the shortcut menu, choose Add (folder name)—the folder name is the name of the location you selected in the Look in box. The new shortcut is added to the bottom of the My Places bar. Notice the shortcut menu in Figure 1.19, which also provides options to change the order of added shortcuts or remove an unwanted shortcut. However, you can only remove the shortcuts that you add to the bar; the default shortcuts cannot be removed.

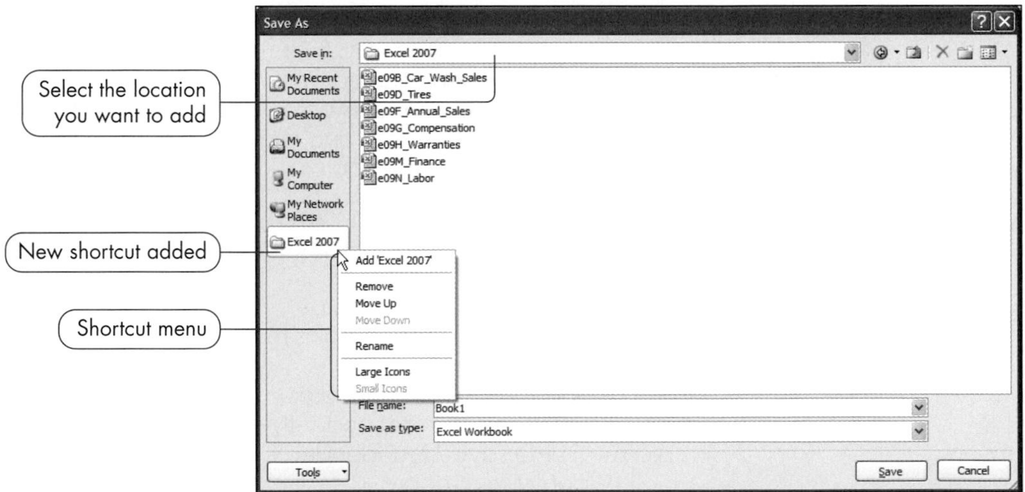

Figure 1.19 Save As Dialog Box with New Shortcut Added to My Places Bar

Printing a Document

As you work with Office 2007 applications, you will need to print hard copies of documents, such as letters to mail, presentation notes to distribute to accompany a slide show, budget spreadsheets to distribute at a staff meeting, or database summary reports to submit. Office provides flexibility so that you can preview the document before you send it to the printer; you also can select from numerous print options, such as changing the number of copies printed; or you can simply and quickly print the current document on the default printer.

Preview Before You Print

It is highly recommended that you preview your document before you print because Print Preview displays all the document elements, such as graphics and formatting, as they will appear when printed on paper. Previewing the document first enables you to make any changes that you need to make without wasting paper. Previewing documents uses the same method in all Office 2007 applications, that is, point to the arrow next to the Print command on the Office menu and select Print Preview to display the current document, worksheet, presentation, or database table in the Print Preview window. Figure 1.20 shows the Print Preview window in Word 2007.

It is highly recommended that you preview your document before you print because Print Preview displays all the document elements, such as graphics and formatting, as they will appear when printed on paper.

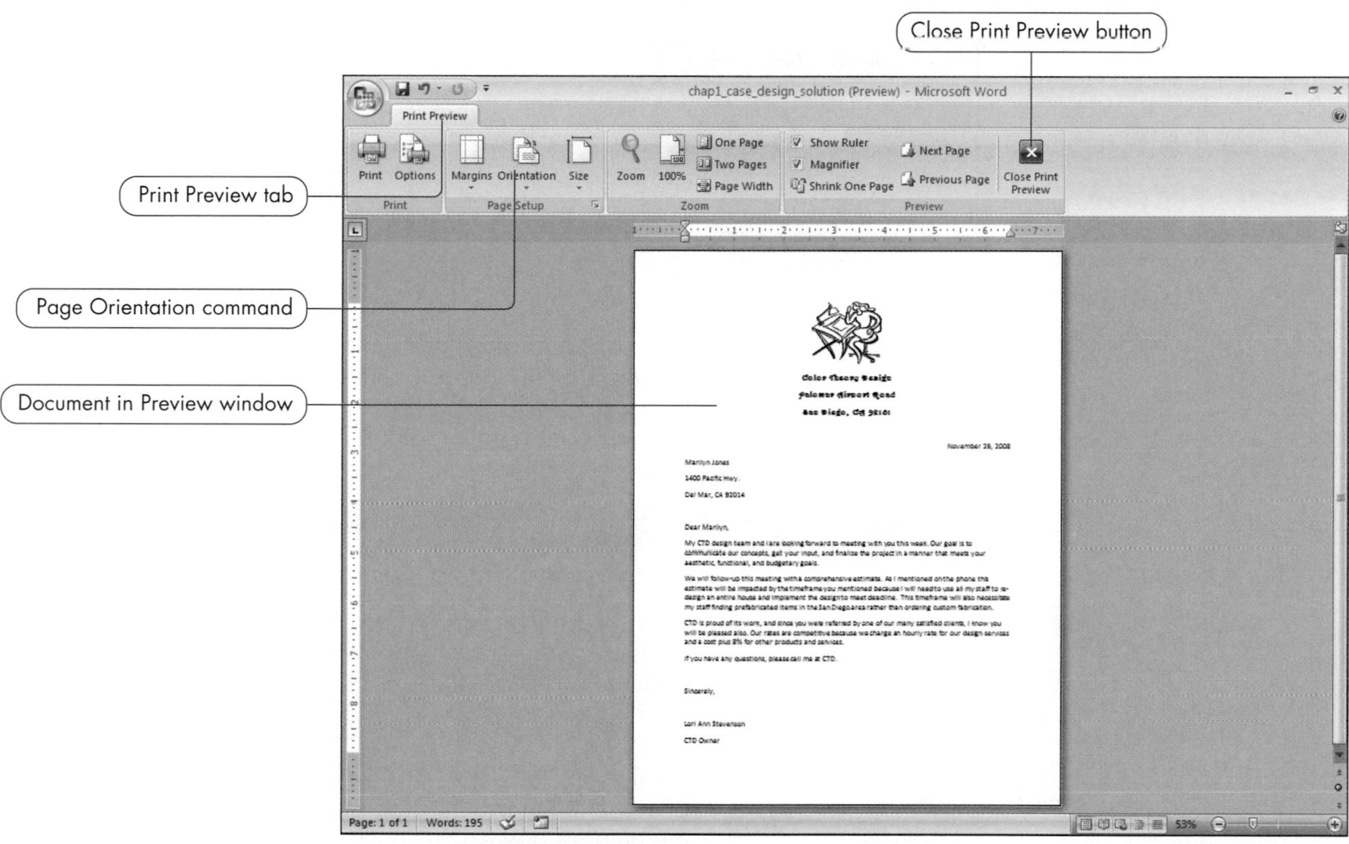

Figure 1.20 Print Preview Window

As you preview the document, you can get a closer look at the results by changing the zoom. Notice that the mouse pointer displays in the Preview window as a magnifying glass with a plus sign, so that you can simply click in the document to increase the zoom. Once clicked, the plus sign changes to a minus sign, enabling you to click in the document again to decrease the zoom. You also can use the Zoom group on the Print Preview tab or the Zoom slider on the status bar to change the view of the document.

Portrait orientation is longer than it is wide—like the portrait of a person.

Landscape orientation is wider than it is long, resembling a landscape scene.

Other options on the Print Preview tab change depending on the application that you are using. For example, you might want to change the orientation to switch from portrait to landscape. Refer to Figure 1.20. ***Portrait orientation*** is longer than it is wide, like the portrait of a person; whereas, ***landscape orientation*** is wider than it is long, resembling a landscape scene. You also can change the size of the paper or other options from the Print Preview tab.

If you need to edit the document before printing, close the Print Preview window and return to the document. However, if you are satisfied with the document and want to print, click Print in the Print group on the Print Preview tab. The Print dialog box displays. Figure 1.21 shows Word's Print dialog box.

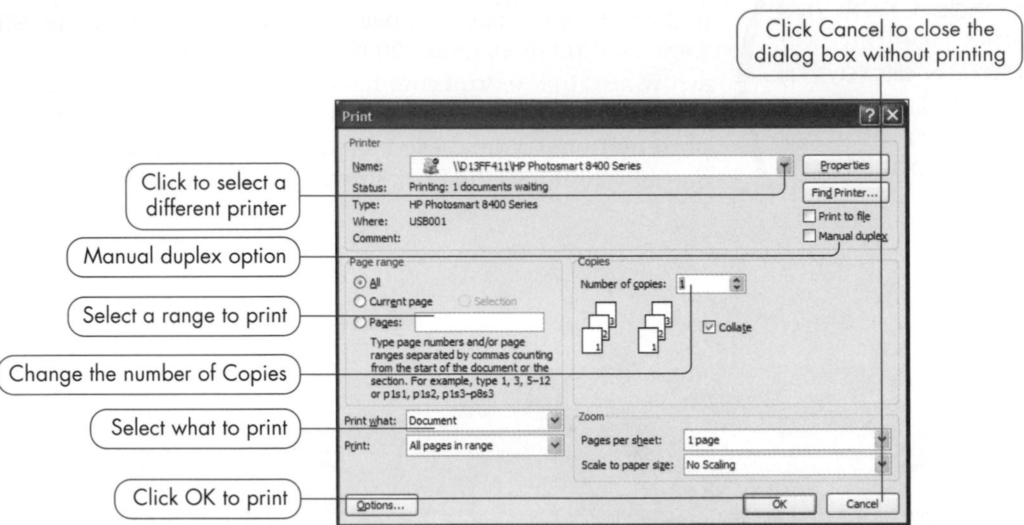

Figure 1.21 Print Dialog Box

The Print dialog box provides numerous options for selecting the correct printer, selecting what to print, and selecting how to print. Table 1.7 describes several important and often-used features of the Print dialog box.

Table 1.7 Print Dialog Box

Print Option	Characteristics
All	Select to print all the pages in the file.
Current page/slide	Select to print only the page or slide with the insertion point. This is a handy feature when you notice an error in a file, and you only want to reprint the corrected page.
Pages	Select to print only specific pages in a document. You must specify page numbers in the text box.
Number of Copies	Change the number of copies printed from the default 1 to the number desired.
Collate	Click if you are printing multiple copies of a multi-page file, and you want to print an entire first copy before printing an entire second copy, and so forth.
Print what	Select from options on what to print, varying with each application.
Selection	Select to print only selected text or objects in an Excel worksheet.
Active sheet(s)	Select to print only the active worksheet(s) in Excel.
Entire workbook	Select to print all worksheets in the Excel workbook.

As you work with other Office 2007 applications, you will notice that the main print options remain unchanged; however, the details vary based on the specific task of the application. For example, the *Print what* option in PowerPoint includes options such as printing the slide, printing handouts, printing notes, or printing an outline of the presentation.

A ***duplex printer*** prints on both sides of the page.

A ***manual duplex*** operation allows you to print on both sides of the paper by printing first on one side and then on the other.

TIP Printing on Both Sides of the Paper

Duplex printers print on both sides of the page. However, if you do not have a duplex printer, you can still print on two sides of the paper by performing a manual duplex operation, which prints on both sides of the paper by printing first on one side, and then on the other. To perform a manual duplex print job in Word 2007, select the Manual duplex option in the Print dialog box. Refer to Figure 1.21. With this option selected, Word prints all pages that display on one side of the paper first, then prompts you to turn the pages over and place them back in the printer tray. The print job continues by printing all the pages that appear on the other side of the paper.

Print Without Previewing the File

If you want to print a file without previewing the results, select Print from the Office menu, and the Print dialog box displays. You can still make changes in the Print dialog box, or just immediately send the print job to the printer. However, if you just want to print quickly, Office 2007 provides a quick print option that enables you to send the current file to the default printer without opening the Print dialog box. This is a handy feature to use if you have only one printer attached and you want to print the current file without changing any print options. You have two ways to quick print:

- Select Quick Print from the Office menu.
- Customize the Quick Access toolbar to add the Print icon. Click the icon to print the current file without opening the Print dialog box.

Hands-On Exercises

2 | Performing Universal Tasks

Skills covered: 1. Open a File and Save It with a Different Name **2.** Use Print Preview and Select Options **3.** Print a Document

Step 1
Open a File and Save It with a Different Name

Refer to Figure 1.22 as you complete Step 1.

a. Start Word, click the **Office Button** to display the Office menu, and then select **Open**.

The Open dialog box displays.

b. If necessary, click the **File Type List** button to locate the files for this textbook to find *chap1_ho2_sample*.

TROUBLESHOOTING: If you have trouble finding the files that accompany this text, you may want to ask your instructor where they are located.

c. Select the file and click **Open**.

The document displays on the screen.

d. Click the **Office Button**, and then select **Save As** on the Office menu.

The Save As dialog box displays.

e. In the *File name* box, type **chap1_ho2_solution**.

f. Check the location listed in the **Save in** box. If you need to change locations to save your files, use the **Save in drop-down arrow** to select the correct location.

g. Make sure that the *Save as type* option is Word Document.

TROUBLESHOOTING: Be sure that you click the **Save As** command rather than pointing to the arrow after the command, and be sure that Word Document is specified in the Save as type box.

h. Click the **Save** button in the dialog box to save the file under the new name.

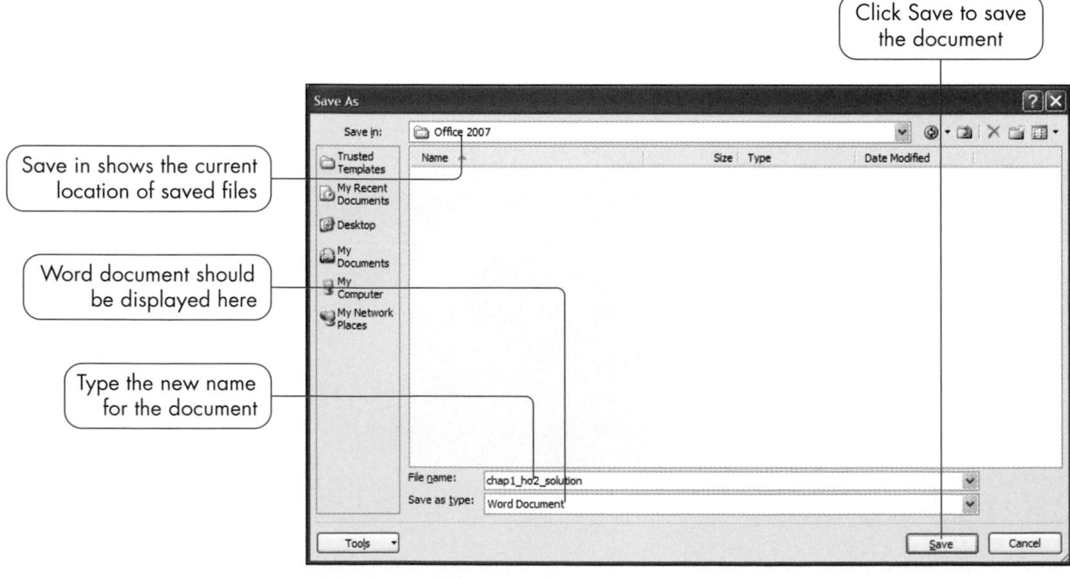

Figure 1.22 Save As Dialog Box

Step 2
Use Print Preview and Select Options

Refer to Figure 1.23 as you complete Step 2.

a. With the document displayed on the screen, click the **Office Button** and point to the arrow following **Print** on the Office menu.

The Print submenu displays.

b. Select **Print Preview**.

The document displays in the Print Preview window.

c. Point the magnifying glass mouse pointer in the document and click the mouse once.

TROUBLESHOOTING: If you do not see the magnifying glass pointer, point the mouse in the document and keep it still for a moment.

The document magnification increases.

d. Point the magnifying glass mouse pointer in the document and click the mouse again.

The document magnification decreases.

e. Click **Orientation** in the Page Setup group on the Print Preview tab.

The orientation options display.

f. Click **Landscape**.

The document orientation changes to landscape.

g. Click **Orientation** a second time, and then choose **Portrait**.

The document returns to portrait orientation.

h. Click the **Close Print Preview** button on the Print Preview tab.

i. The Print Preview window closes.

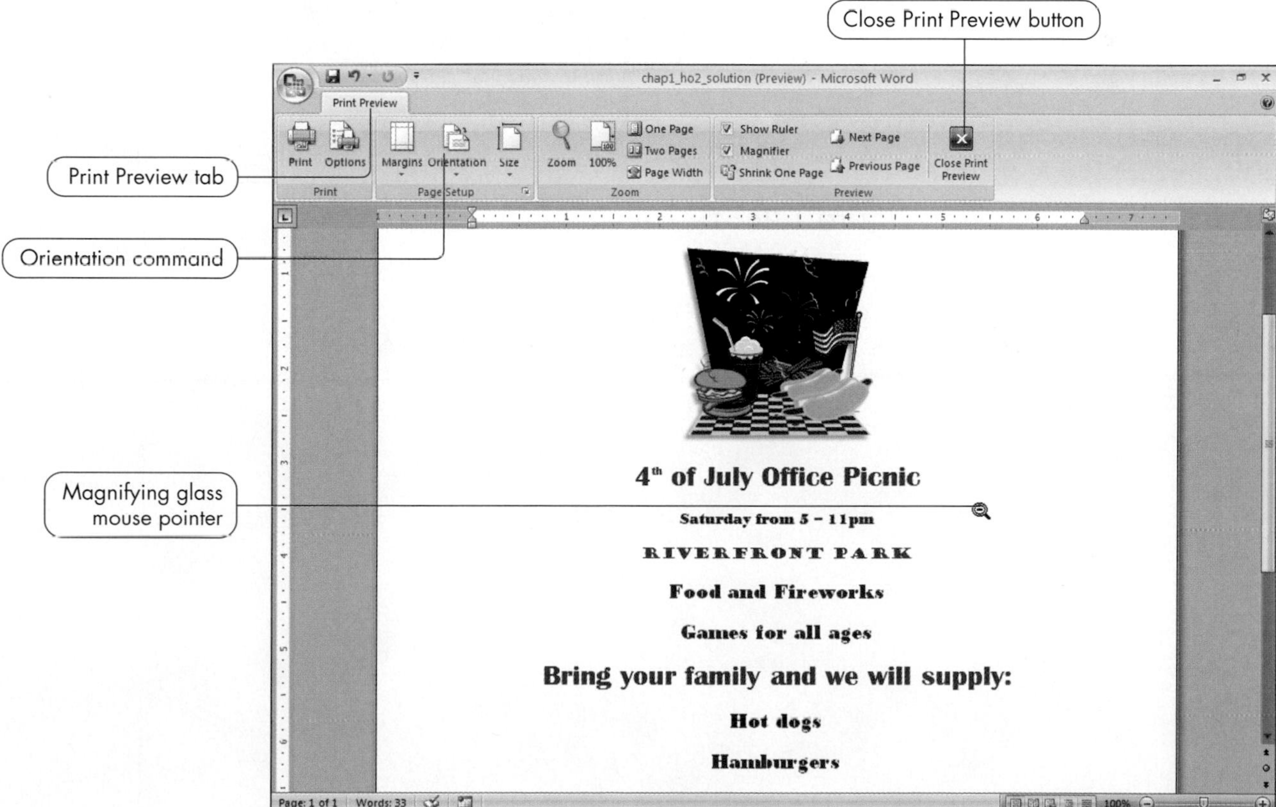

Figure 1.23 Print Preview

Step 3
Print a Document

Refer to Figure 1.24 as you complete Step 3.

a. Click the **Office Button**, and then point to the arrow next to **Print** on the Office menu.

   The print options display.

b. Select **Print**.

   The Print dialog box displays.

   TROUBLESHOOTING: Be sure that your printer is turned on and has paper loaded.

c. If necessary, select the correct printer in the **Name box** by clicking the drop-down arrow and selecting from the resulting list.

d. Click **OK**.

   The Word document prints on the selected printer.

e. To exit Word, click the **Office Button**, and then click the **Exit Word button**.

f. If prompted to save the file, choose **No**.

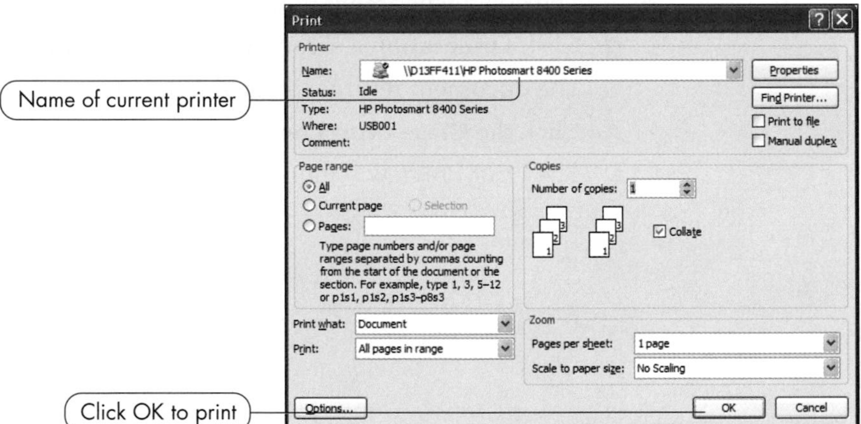

Figure 1.24 The Print Dialog Box

Basic Tasks

Many of the operations you perform in one Office program are the same or similar in all Office applications. These tasks are referred to as basic tasks and include such operations as inserting and typing over, copying and moving items, finding and replacing text, undoing and redoing commands, checking spelling and grammar, using the thesaurus, and using formatting tools. Once you learn the underlying concepts of these operations, you can apply them in different applications.

Most basic tasks in Word fall into two categories:

- editing a document
- formatting a document

Most successful writers use many word processing features to revise and edit documents, and most would agree that the revision process takes more time than the initial writing process. Errors such as spelling and grammar need to be eliminated to produce error-free writing. However, to turn a rough draft into a finished document, such as a report for a class or for a business, requires writers to revise and edit several times by adding text, removing text, replacing text, and moving text around to make the meaning clearer. Writers also improve their writing using tools to conduct research to make the information accurate and to find the most appropriate word using the thesaurus. Modern word processing applications such as Word 2007 provide these tools and more to aid the writer.

> Most successful writers use many word processing features to revise and edit documents, and most would agree that the revision process takes more time than the initial writing process.

The second category of basic tasks is formatting text in a document. Formatting text includes changing the type, the size, and appearance of text. You might want to apply formatting to simply improve the look of a document, or you might want to emphasize particular aspects of your message. Remember that a poorly formatted document or workbook probably will not be read. So whether you are creating your résumé or the income statement for a corporation's annual report, how the output looks is important. Office 2007 provides many tools for formatting documents, but in this section, you will start by learning to apply font attributes and copy those to other locations in the document.

In this section, you learn to perform basic tasks in Office 2007, using Word 2007 as the model. As you progress in learning other Office programs such as PowerPoint, Excel, and Access, you will apply the same principles in other applications.

Selecting Text to Edit

Most editing processes involve identifying the text that the writer wants to work with. For example, to specify which text to edit, you must select it. The most common method used to select text is to use the mouse. Point to one end of the text you want to select (either the beginning or end) and click-and-drag over the text. The selected text displays highlighted with a light blue background so that it stands out from other text and is ready for you to work with. The ***Mini toolbar*** displays when you select text in Word, Excel, and PowerPoint. It displays above the selected text as semitransparent and remains semitransparent until you point to it. Often-used commands from the Clipboard, Font, and Paragraph groups on the Home tab are repeated on the Mini toolbar for quick access. Figure 1.25 shows selected text with the Mini toolbar fully displayed in the document.

The ***Mini toolbar*** displays above the selected text as semitransparent and repeats often-used commands.

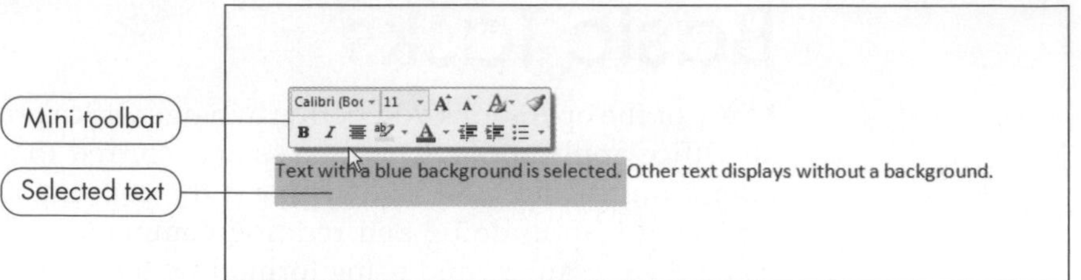

Figure 1.25 Selected Text

Sometimes you want to select only one word or character, and trying to drag over it to select it can be frustrating. Table 1.8 describes other methods used to select text.

Table 1.8 Easy Text Selection in Word

Outcome Desired	Method
Select a word	Double-click the word.
One line of text	Point the mouse to the left of the line, and when the mouse pointer changes to a right-pointing arrow, click the mouse.
A sentence	Hold down Ctrl and click in the sentence to select.
A paragraph	Triple-click the mouse in the paragraph.
One character to the left of the insertion point	Hold down Shift and press the left arrow key.
One character to the right of the insertion point	Hold down Shift and press the right arrow key.

TIP Selecting Large Amounts of Text

As you edit documents, you might need to select a large portion of a document. However, as you click-and-drag over the text, you might have trouble stopping the selection at the desired location because the document scrolls by too quickly. This is actually a handy feature in Word 2007 that scrolls through the document when you drag the mouse pointer at the edge of the document window.

To select a large portion of a document, click the insertion point at the beginning of the desired selection. Then move the display to the end of the selection using the scroll bar at the right edge of the window. Scrolling leaves the insertion point where you placed it. When you reach the end of the text you want to select, hold down Shift and click the mouse. The entire body of text is selected.

Inserting Text and Changing to the Overtype Mode

Insert is adding text in a document.

As you create and edit documents using Word, you will need to ***insert*** text, which is adding text in a document. To insert or add text, point and click the mouse in the location where the text should display. With the insertion point in the location to insert the text, simply start typing. Any existing text moves to the right, making room for the new inserted text. At times, you might need to add a large amount of text in a document, and you might want to replace or type over existing text instead of inserting text. This task can be accomplished two ways:

Overtype mode replaces the existing text with text you type character by character.

- Select the text to replace and start typing. The new text replaces the selected text.
- Switch to ***Overtype mode***, which replaces the existing text with text you type character by character. To change to Overtype mode, select the Word Options button on the Office menu. Select the option Use Overtype Mode in the Editing Options section of the Advanced tab. Later, if you want to return to Insert mode, repeat these steps to deselect the overtype mode option. Figure 1.26 shows the Word Options dialog box.

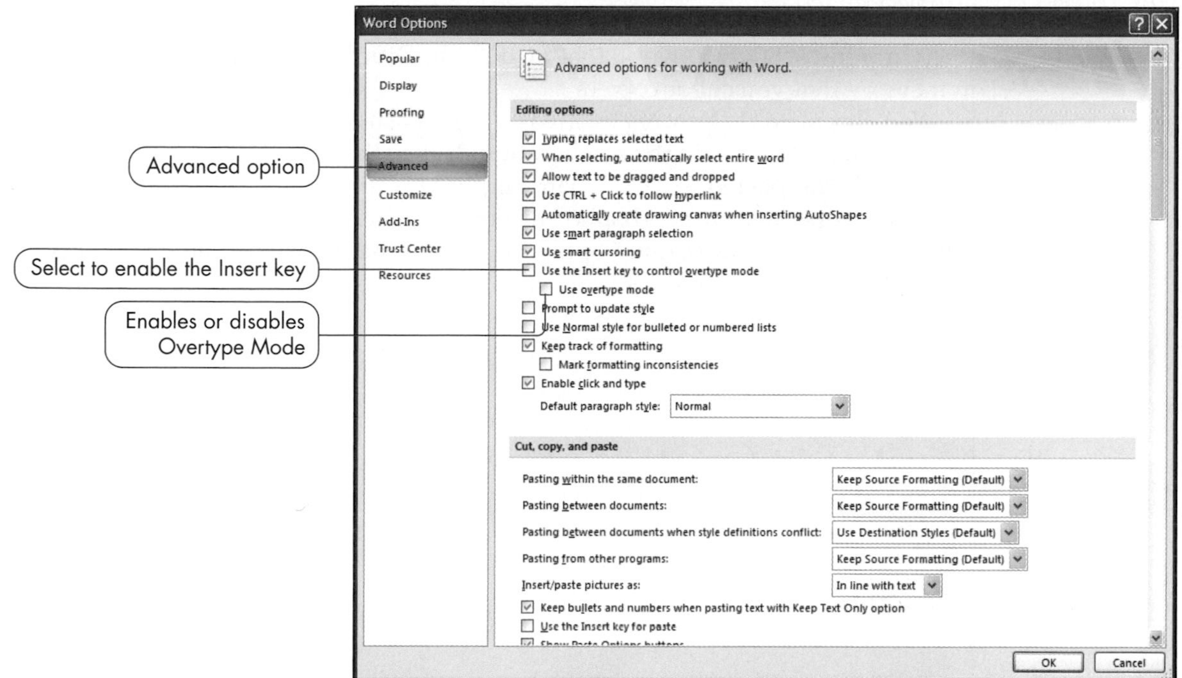

Figure 1.26 The Word Options Dialog Box

TIP Using the Insert Key on the Keyboard

If you find that you need to switch between Insert and Overtype mode often, you can enable Insert on the keyboard by clicking the Word Options button on the Office menu. Select the option Use the Insert Key to Control Overtype Mode in the Editing Options section on the Advanced tab. Refer to Figure 1.26. You can now use Insert on the keyboard to switch between the two modes, and this option stays in effect until you go back to the Word Options dialog box and deselect it.

Moving and Copying Text

As you revise a document, you might find that you need to move text from one location to another to improve the readability of the content. To move text, you must cut the selected text from its original location and then place it in the new location by pasting it there. To duplicate text, you must copy the selected text in its original location and then paste the duplicate in the desired location. To decide whether you should use the Cut or Copy command in the Clipboard group on the Home tab to perform the task, you must notice the difference in the results of each command:

Cut removes the original text or object from its current location.

Copy makes a duplicate copy of the text or object, leaving the original intact.

- ***Cut*** removes the selected original text or object from its current location.
- ***Copy*** makes a duplicate copy of the text or object, leaving the original text or object intact.

Keep in mind while you work, that by default, Office 2007 retains only the last item in memory that you cut or copied.

Paste places the cut or copied text or object in the new location.

You complete the process by invoking the Paste command. ***Paste*** places the cut or copied text or object in the new location. Notice the Paste Options button displays along with the pasted text. You can simply ignore the Paste Options button, and it will disappear from the display, or you can click the drop-down arrow on the button and select a formatting option to change the display of the text you pasted. Figure 1.27 shows the options available.

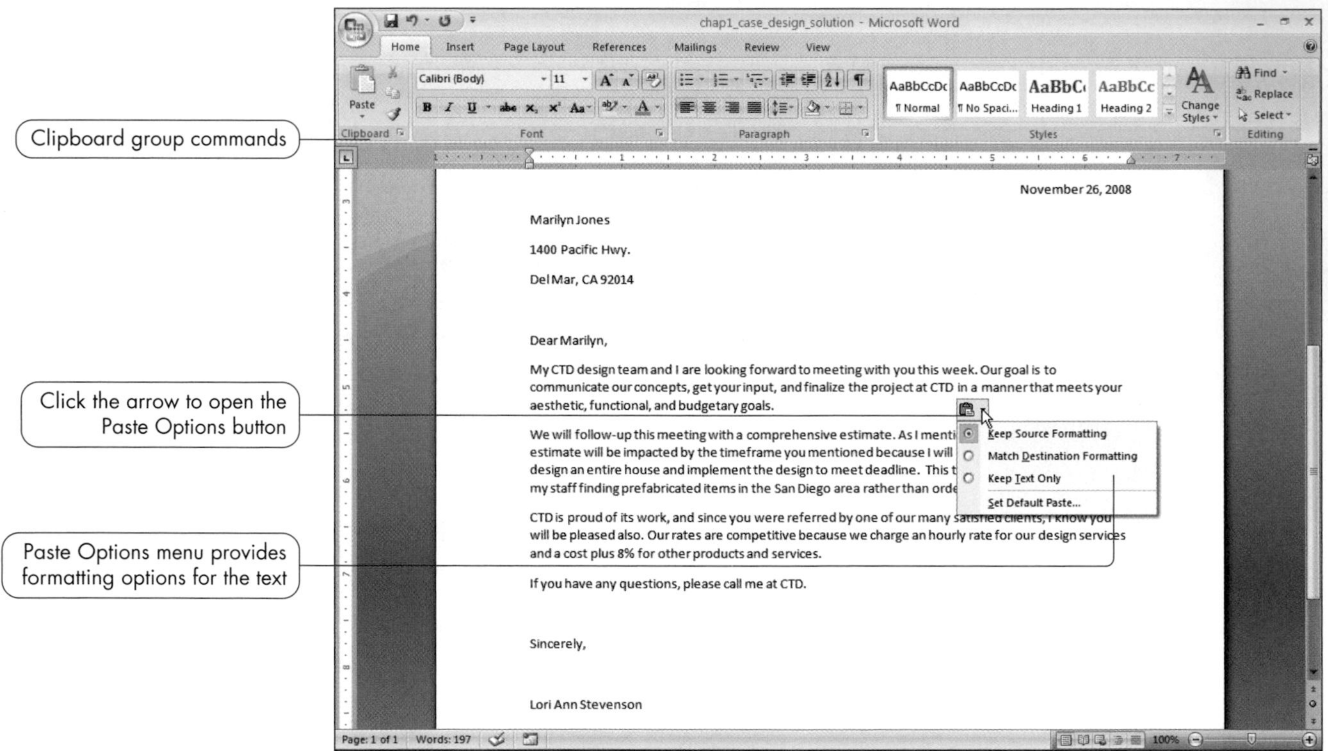

Figure 1.27 Text Pasted in the Document

TIP Moving and Copying Using Shortcuts

You can use alternative methods instead of using the commands located on the Home tab to cut, copy, and paste text. Office 2007 provides the following shortcuts:

- After selecting text, point back to the selected text and right-click the mouse. The shortcut menu displays, allowing you to choose Cut or Copy. Move the insertion point to the desired location, right-click the mouse again, and choose Paste from the shortcut menu.
- After selecting text, use the keyboard shortcut combinations Ctrl+C to copy or Ctrl+X to cut text. Move the insertion point to the new location and press Ctrl+V to paste. These keyboard shortcuts work in most Windows applications, so they can be very useful.
- After selecting text, you can move it a short distance in the document by dragging to the new location. Point to the selected text, hold down the left mouse button, and then drag to the desired location. While you are dragging the mouse, the pointer changes to a left-pointing arrow with a box attached to it. Release the mouse button when you have placed the insertion point in the desired location, and the text displays in the new location.

Use the Office Clipboard

The ***Clipboard*** is a memory location that holds up to 24 items for you to paste into the current document, another file, or another application.

Office 2007 provides an option that enables you to cut or copy multiple items to the ***Clipboard***, which is a memory location that holds up to 24 items for you to paste into the current file, another file, or another application. The Clipboard stays active only while you are using one of the Office 2007 applications. When you exit from all Office 2007 applications, all items on the Clipboard are deleted. To accumulate items on the Clipboard, you must first display it by clicking the Dialog Box Launcher in the Clipboard group on the Home tab. When the Clipboard pane is open on the screen, its memory location is active, and the Clipboard accumulates all items you cut or copy up to the maximum 24. To paste an item from the Clipboard, point to it, click the resulting drop-down arrow, and choose Paste. To change how the Clipboard functions, use the Options button shown in Figure 1.28. One of the most important options allows the Clipboard to accumulate items even when it is not open on the screen. To activate the Clipboard so that it works in the background, click the Options button in the Clipboard, and then select Collect without Showing Office Clipboard.

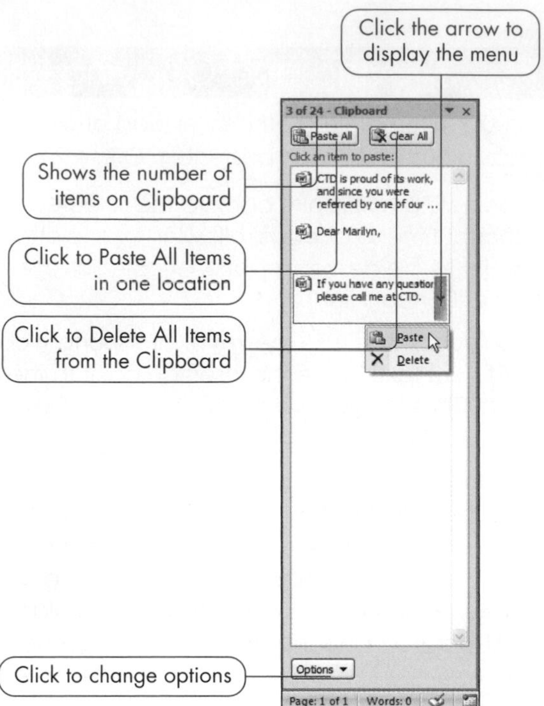

Figure 1.28 Clipboard

Finding, Replacing, and Going to Text

You can waste a great deal of time slowly scrolling through a document trying to locate text or other items. Office 2007 provides features that speed up editing by automatically finding text and objects in a document, thus making you more productive. Office 2007 provides the following three related operations that all use the Find and Replace dialog box:

Find locates a word or group of words in a document.

Replace not only finds text, it replaces a word or group of words with other text.

Go To moves the insertion point to a specific location in the document.

- The ***Find*** command enables you to locate a word or group of words in a document quickly.
- The ***Replace*** command not only finds text quickly, it replaces a word or group of words with other text.
- The ***Go To*** command moves the insertion point to a specific location in the document.

Find Text

To locate text in an Office file, choose the Find command in the Editing group on the Home tab and type the text you want to locate in the resulting dialog box, as shown in Figure 1.29. After you type the text to locate, you can find the next instance after the insertion point and work through the file until you find the instance of the text you were looking for. Alternatively, you can find all instances of the text in the file at one time. If you decide to find every instance at once, the Office application temporarily highlights each one, and the text stays highlighted until you perform another operation in the file.

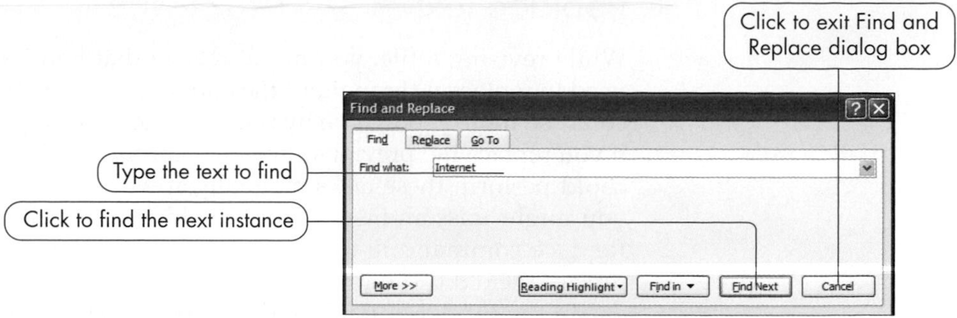

Figure 1.29 Find Tab of the Find and Replace Dialog Box

TIP Finding and Highlighting Text in Word

Sometimes, temporarily highlighting all instances of text is not sufficient to help you edit the text you find. If you want Word to find all instances of specific text in a document and keep the highlighting from disappearing until you want it to, you can use the Reading Highlight option in the Find dialog box. One nice feature of this option is that even though the text remains highlighted on the screen, the document prints normally without highlighting. Figure 1.30 shows the Find and Replace dialog box with the Reading Highlight options that you use to highlight or remove the highlight from a document.

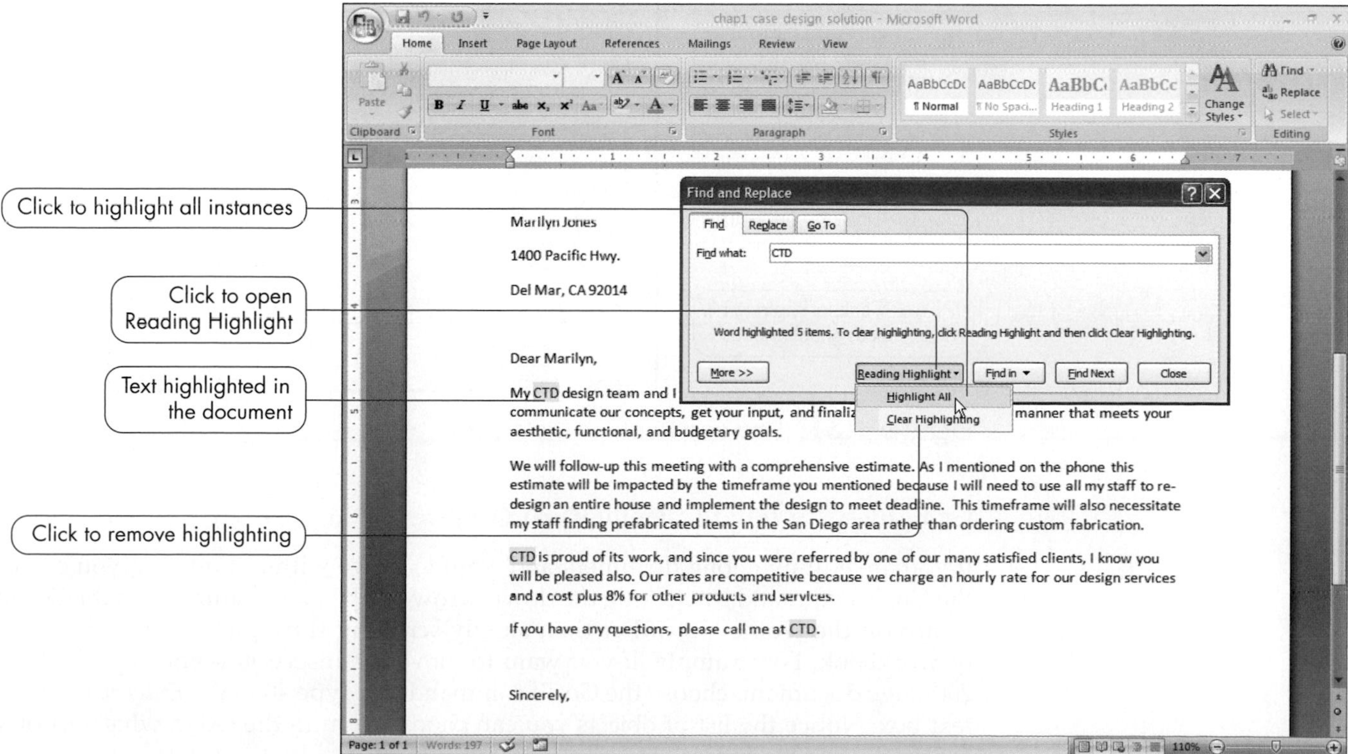

Figure 1.30 Find and Replace Dialog Box with Highlighting Options

Replace Text

While revising a file, you might realize that you have used an incorrect term and need to replace it throughout the entire file. Alternatively, you might realize that you could be more productive by re-using a letter or report that you polished and saved if you replace the previous client's or corporation's name with a new one. While you could perform these tasks manually, it would not be worth the time involved, and you might miss an instance of the old text, which could prove embarrassing. The Replace command in the Editing group on the Home tab can quickly and easily replace the old text with the new text throughout an entire file.

In the Find and Replace dialog box, first type the text to find, using the same process you used with the Find command. Second, type the text to replace the existing text with. Third, specify how you want Word to perform the operation. You can either replace each instance of the text individually, which can be time-consuming but allows you to decide whether to replace each instance one at a time, or you can replace every instance of the text in the document all at once. Word (but not the other Office applications) also provides options in the dialog box that help you replace only the correct text in the document. Click the More button to display these options. The most important one is the Find whole words only option. This option forces the application to find only complete words, not text that is part of other words. For instance, if you are searching for the word *off* to replace with other text, you would not want Word to replace the *off* in *office* with other text. Figure 1.31 shows these options along with the options for replacing text.

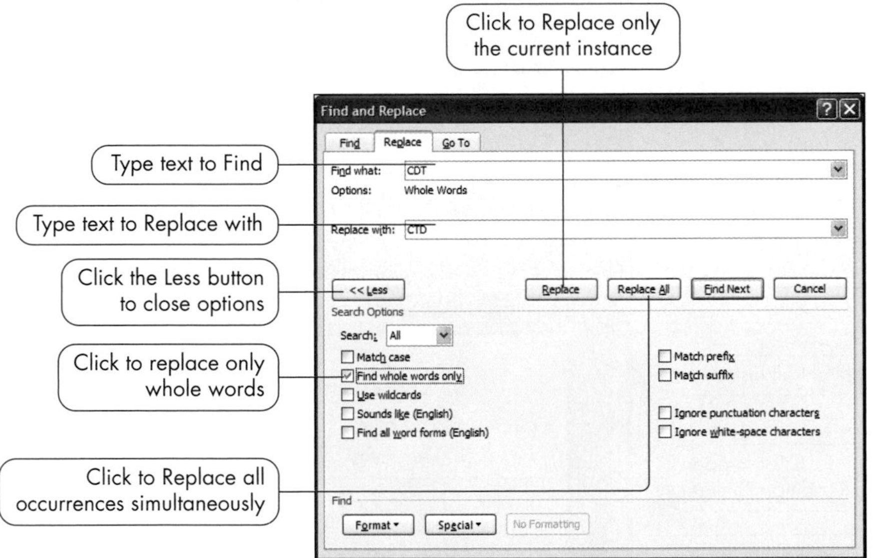

Figure 1.31 Find and Replace Dialog Box

Go Directly to a Location in a File

If you are editing a long document and want to move within it quickly, you can use the Go To command by clicking the down arrow on the Find command in the Editing group on the Home tab rather than slowly scrolling through an entire document or workbook. For example, if you want to move the insertion point to page 40 in a 200-page document, choose the Go To command and type 40 in the *Enter page number* text box. Notice the list of objects you can choose from in the Go to what section of the dialog box in Figure 1.32.

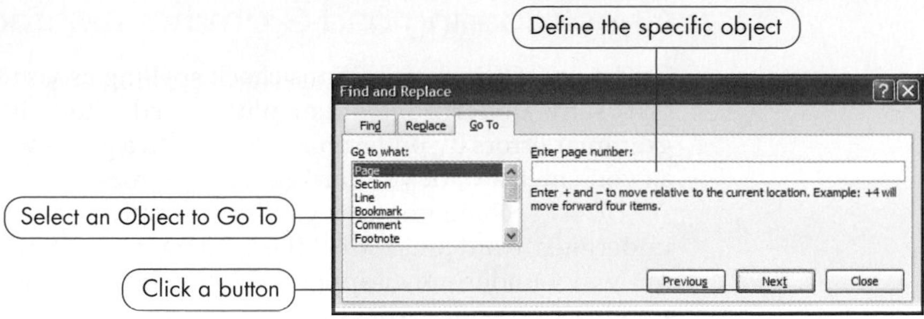

Figure 1.32 Go To Tab of the Find and Replace Dialog Box

Using the Undo and Redo Commands

The ***Undo*** command cancels your last one or more operations.

The ***Redo*** command reinstates or reverses an action performed by the Undo command.

As you create and edit files, you may perform an operation by mistake or simply change your mind about an edit you make. Office applications provide the ***Undo*** command, which can cancel your previous operation or even your last few operations. After using Undo to reverse an action or operation, you might decide that you want to use the ***Redo*** command to reinstate or reverse the action taken by the Undo command.

To undo the last action you performed, click Undo on the Quick Access Toolbar. For example, if you deleted text by mistake, immediately click Undo to restore it. If, however, you deleted some text and then performed several other operations, you can find the correct action to undo, with the understanding that all actions after that one will also be undone. To review a list of the last few actions you performed, click the Undo drop-down arrow and select the desired one from the list—Undo highlights all actions in the list down to that item and will undo all of the highlighted actions. Figure 1.33 shows a list of recent actions in PowerPoint. To reinstate or reverse an action as a result of using the Undo command, click Redo on the Quick Access Toolbar.

The ***Repeat*** command repeats only the last action you performed.

The ***Repeat*** command provides limited use because it repeats only the last action you performed. To repeat the last action, click Repeat on the Quick Access Toolbar. If the Office application is able to repeat your last action, the results will display in the document. Note that the Repeat command is replaced with the Redo command after you use the Undo command. For example, Figure 1.33 shows the Redo command after the Undo command has been used, and Figure 1.34 shows the Repeat command when Undo has not been used.

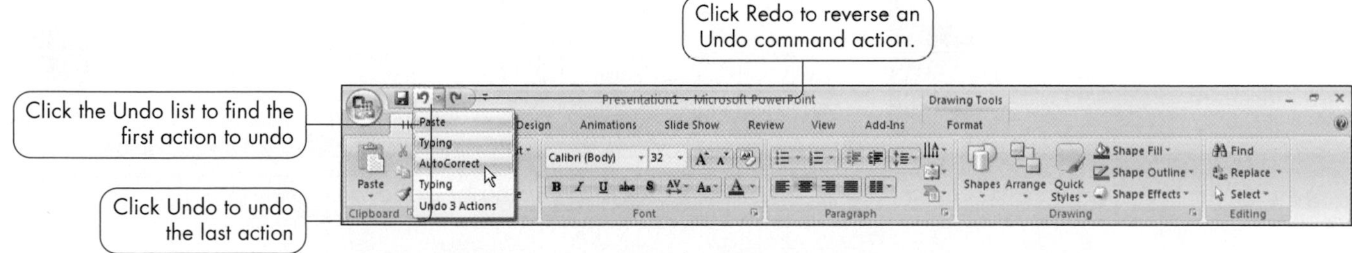

Figure 1.33 Undo and Redo Buttons

Using Language Tools

Documents, spreadsheets, and presentations represent the author, so remember that errors in writing can keep people from getting a desired job, or once on the job, can keep them from getting a desired promotion. To avoid holding yourself back, you should polish your final documents before submitting them electronically or as a hard copy. Office 2007 provides built-in proofing tools to help you fix spelling and grammar errors and help you locate the correct word or information.

Check Spelling and Grammar Automatically

By default, Office applications check spelling as you type and flag potential spelling errors by underlining them with a red wavy line. Word also flags potential grammar errors by underlining them with a green wavy line. You can fix these errors as you enter text, or you can ignore the errors and fix them all at once.

To fix spelling errors as you type, simply move the insertion point to a red wavy underlined word and correct the spelling yourself. If you spell the word correctly, the red wavy underline disappears. However, if you need help figuring out the correct spelling for the flagged word, then point to the error and right-click the mouse. The shortcut menu displays with possible corrections for the error. If you find the correction on the shortcut menu, click it to replace the word in the document. To fix grammar errors, follow the same process, but when the shortcut menu displays, you can choose to view more information to see rules that apply to the potential error. Notice the errors flagged in Figure 1.34. Note that the Mini toolbar also displays automatically.

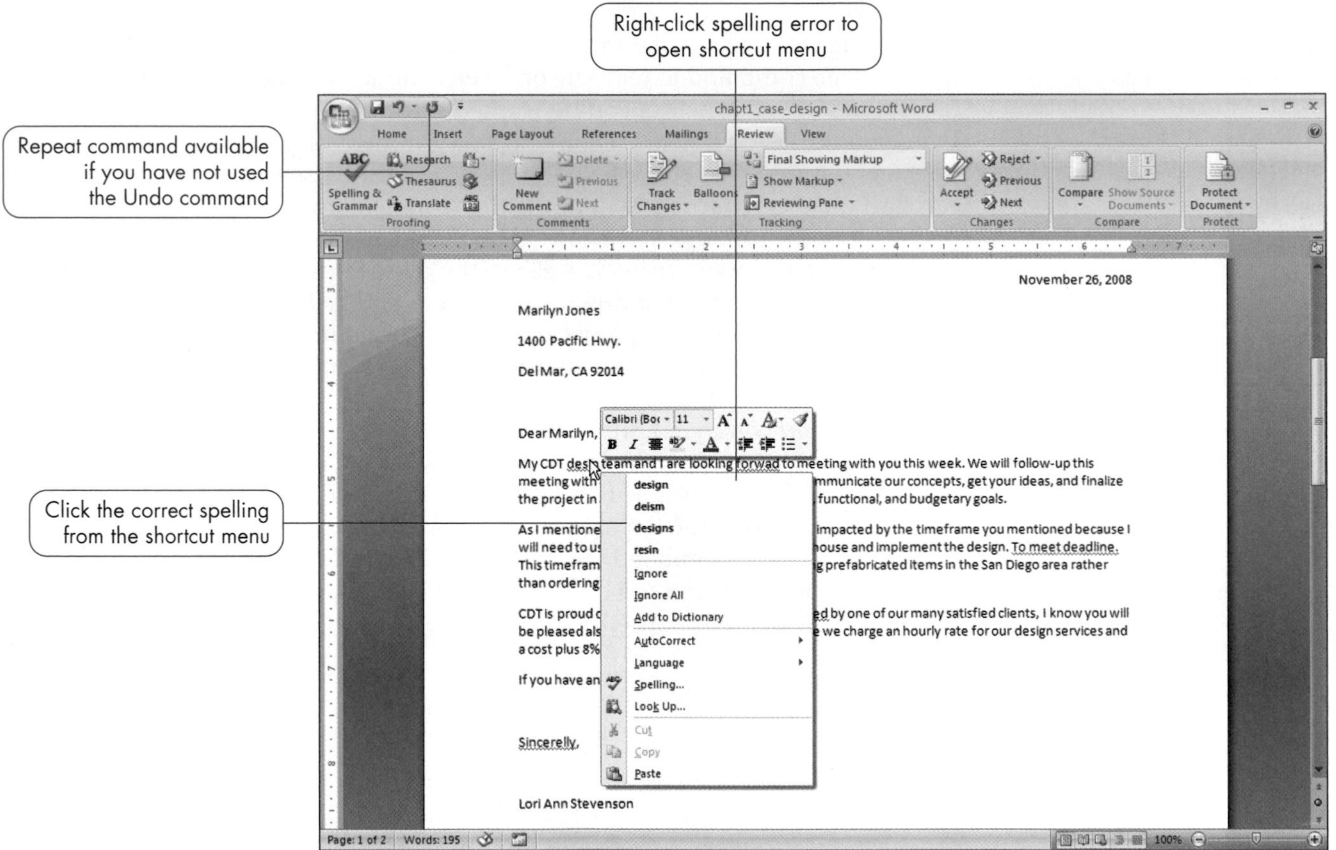

Figure 1.34 Automatic Spell and Grammar Check

Check Spelling and Grammar at Once

Some people prefer to wait until they complete typing the entire document and then check spelling and grammar at once. To check for errors, click Spelling & Grammar in Word (Spelling in Excel or PowerPoint) in the Proofing group on the Review tab. As the checking proceeds through the file and detects any spelling or grammar errors, it displays the Spelling dialog box if you are using Excel or PowerPoint, or the Spelling and Grammar dialog box in Word. You can either correct or ignore the changes that the Spelling checker proposes to your document. For example, Figure 1.35 shows the Spelling and Grammar dialog box with a misspelled word in the top section and Word's suggestions in the bottom section. Select the correction from the list and change the current instance, or you can change all instances of the error throughout the document. However, sometimes the flagged word might be a specialized term or a person's name, so if the flagged word is not a spelling error, you can ignore it once in the current document or throughout the entire document; further, you could add the word to the spell-check list so that it never flags that spelling again.

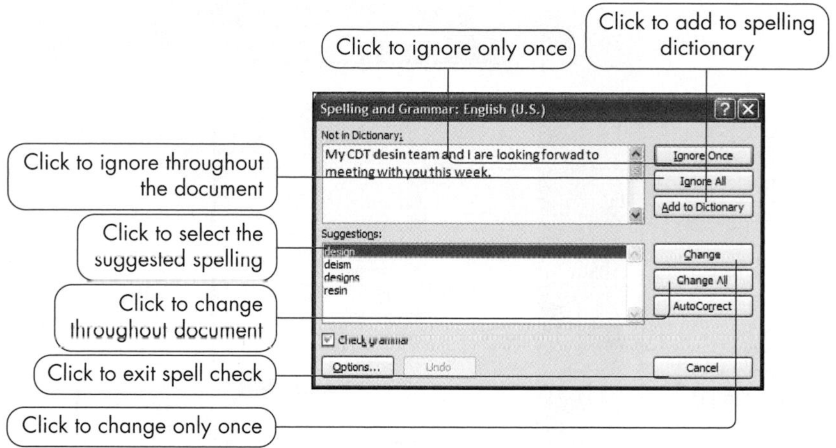

Figure 1.35 Spelling and Grammar Dialog Box

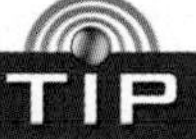

TIP Proofreading Your Document

The spelling and grammar checks available in Word provide great help improving your documents. However, you should not forget that you still have to proofread your document to ensure that the writing is clear, appropriate for the intended audience, and makes sense.

Use the Thesaurus

As you edit a document, spreadsheet, or presentation, you might want to improve your writing by finding a better or different word for a particular situation. For example, say you are stuck and cannot think of a better word for *big*, and you would like to find an alternative word that means the same. Word, Excel, and PowerPoint provide a built-in thesaurus, which is an electronic version of a book of synonyms. Synonyms are different words with the same or similar meaning, and antonyms are words with the opposite meaning.

The easiest method for accessing the Thesaurus is to point to the word in the file that you want to find an alternative for and right-click the mouse. When the shortcut menu displays, point to Synonyms, and the program displays a list of alternatives. Notice the shortcut menu and list of synonyms in Figure 1.36. To select one of the alternative words on the list, click it, and the word you select replaces the original word. If you do not see an alternative on the list that you want to use and you want to investigate further, click Thesaurus on the shortcut menu to open the full Thesaurus.

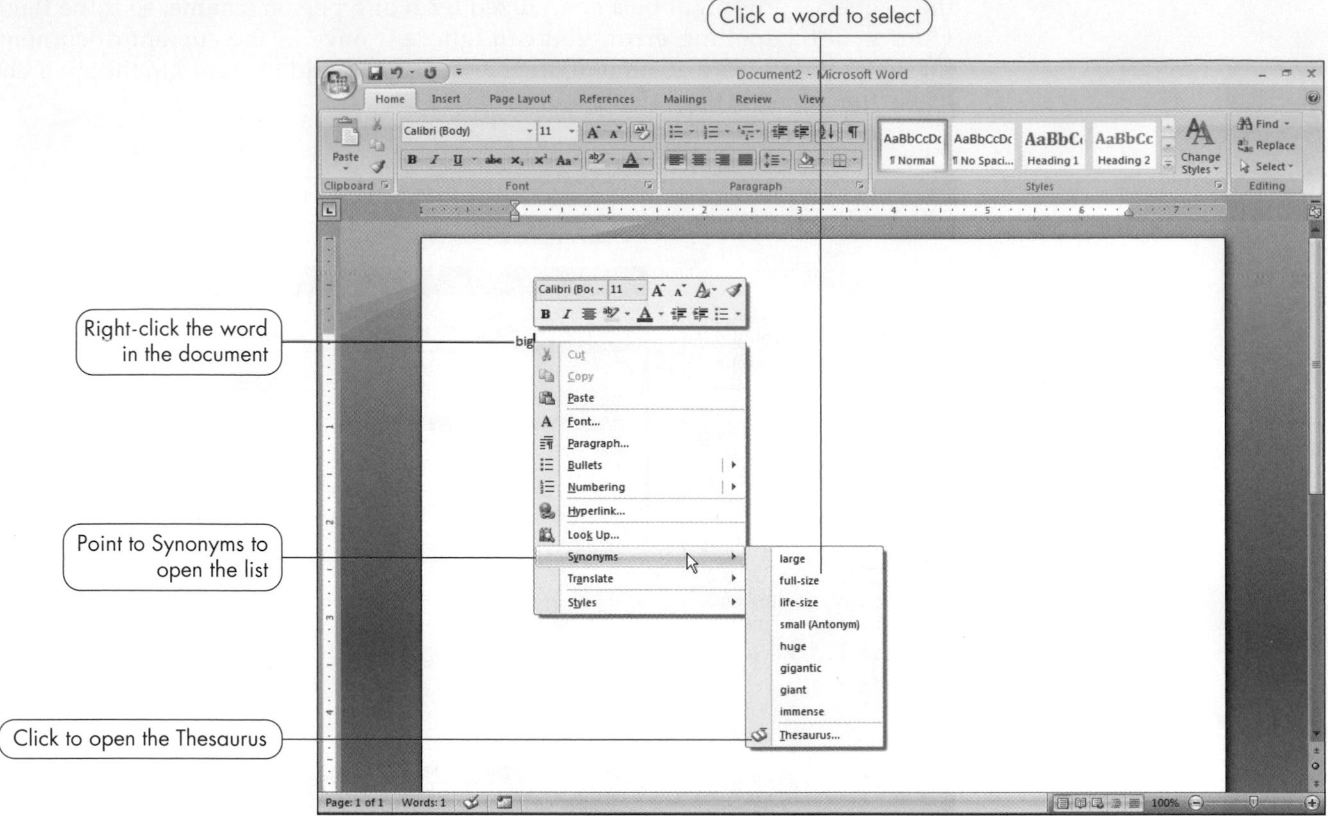

Figure 1.36 Shortcut Menu with Synonyms

An alternative method for opening the full Thesaurus is to place the insertion point in the word you want to look up, and then click the Thesaurus command in the Proofing group on the Review tab. The Thesaurus opens with alternatives for the selected word. You can use one of the words presented in the pane, or you can look up additional words. If you do not find the word you want, use the Search option to find more alternatives. Figure 1.37 shows the Thesaurus.

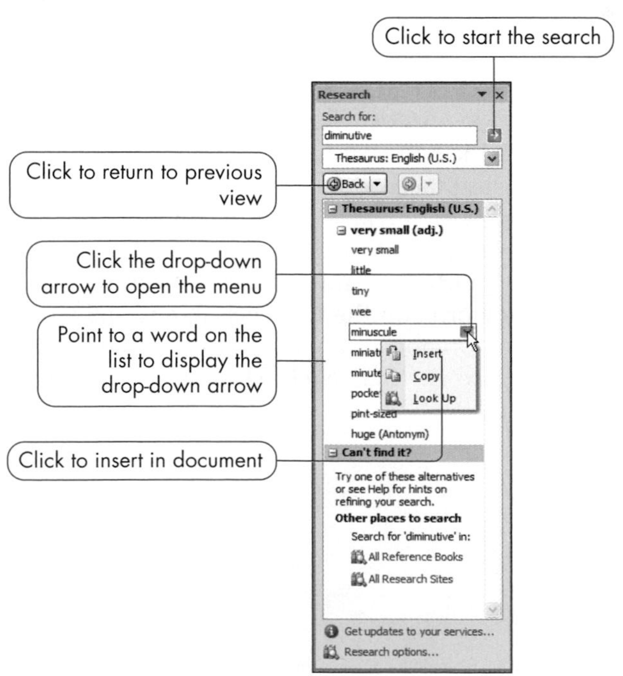

Figure 1.37 The Thesaurus

Conduct Research

As you work in Word, Excel, or PowerPoint, you might need to find the definition of a word or look up an item in the encyclopedia to include accurate information. Office 2007 provides quick access to research tools. To access research tools, click the Research button in the Proofing group on the Review tab. Notice in Figure 1.38 that you can specify what you want to research and specify where to Search. Using this feature, you can choose from reference books, research sites, and business and financial sites.

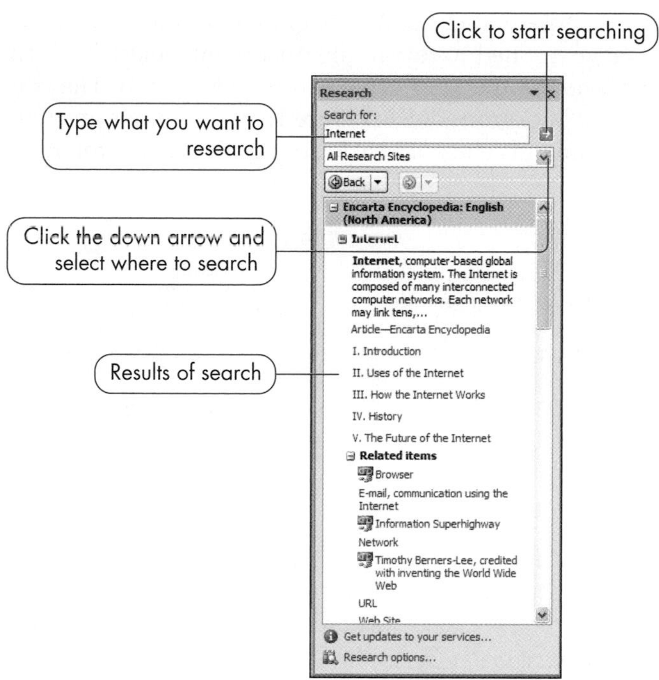

Figure 1.38 Research Task Pane

TIP Avoiding Plagiarism

If you use the research feature in Office to find information in an encyclopedia or in other locations to help you create your document, then you need to credit the source of that information. Avoid the problem of plagiarism, which is borrowing other people's words or ideas, by citing all sources that you use. You might want to check with your instructor for the exact format for citing sources.

Applying Font Attributes

> Taking the time to format text helps the reader find important information in the document by making it stand out and helps the reader understand the message by emphasizing key items.

After you have edited a document, you might want to improve its visual appeal by formatting the text. ***Formatting text*** changes an individual letter, a word, or a body of selected text. Taking the time to format text helps the reader find important information in the document by making it stand out and helps the reader understand the message by emphasizing key items. You can format the text in the document by changing the following font attributes:

Formatting text changes an individual letter, a word, or a body of selected text.

- font face or size
- font attributes such as bold, underline, or italic
- font color

The Font group on the Home tab—available in Word, Excel, PowerPoint, and Access—provides many formatting options, and Office provides two methods for applying these font attributes:

- Choose the font attributes first, and then type the text. The text displays in the document with the formatting.
- Type the text, select the text to format, and choose the font attributes. The selected text displays with the formatting.

You can apply more than one attribute to text, so you can select one or more attributes either all at once or at any time. Also, it is easy to see which attributes you have applied to text in the document. Select the formatted text and look at the commands in the Font group on the Home tab. The commands in effect display with a gold background. See Figure 1.39. To remove an effect from text, select it and click the command. The gold background disappears for attributes that are no longer in effect.

Gold background denotes attributes used to format text

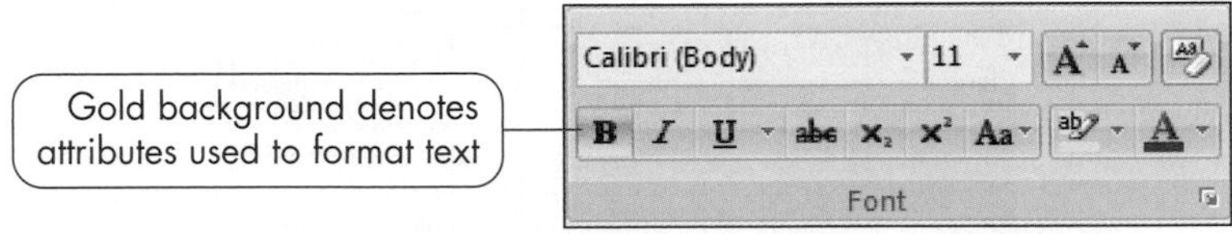

Figure 1.39 Font Group of the Home tab

Change the Font

A ***font*** is a named set of characters with the same design.

A ***font*** is a named set of characters with the same design, and Office 2007 provides many built-in fonts for you to choose from. Remember that more is not always better when applied to fonts, so limit the number of font changes in your document. Additionally, the choice of a font should depend on the intent of the document and should never overpower the message. For example, using a fancy or highly stylized font that may be difficult to read for a client letter might seem odd to the person receiving it and overpower the intended message.

> Remember that more is not always better when applied to fonts, so limit the number of font changes in your document.

One powerful feature of Office 2007 that can help you decide how a font will look in your document is Live Preview. First, select the existing text, and then click the drop-down arrow on the Font list in the Font group on the Home tab. As you point to a font name in the list, Live Preview changes the selected text in the document to that font. Figure 1.40 shows the selected text displaying in a different font as a result of Live Preview.

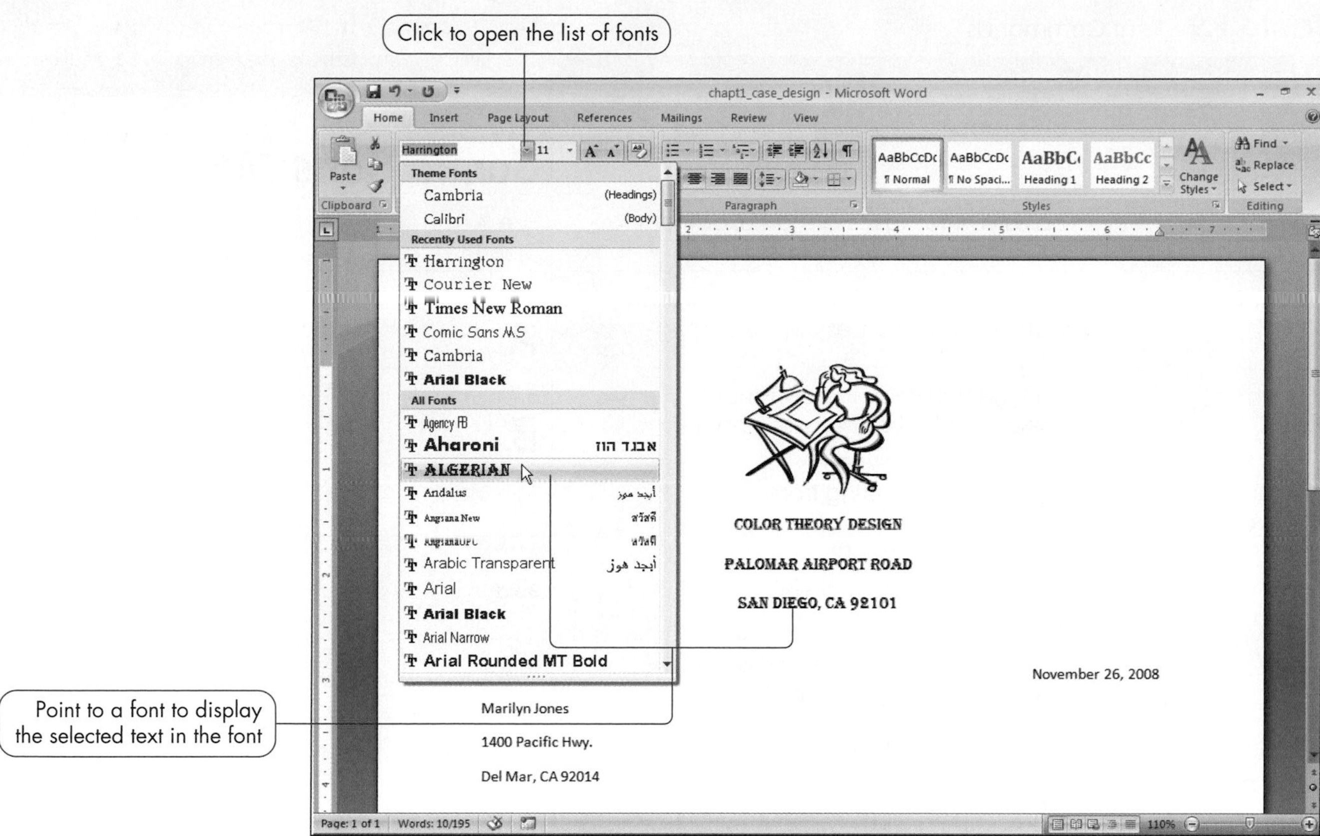

Figure 1.40 Font List

Change the Font Size, Color, and Attributes

Besides changing the font, you also can change the size, color, and other attributes of text in a document. Because these formatting operations are used so frequently, Office places many of these commands in several places for easy access:

- in the Font group on the Home tab
- on the Mini toolbar
- in the Font dialog box

Table 1.9 describes the commands that display in the Font group of the Home tab and in the Font dialog box.

Table 1.9 Font Commands

Command	Description	Example
Font	Enables you to designate the font.	Arial Comic Sans MS
Font Size	Enables you to designate an exact font size.	Size 8 Size 18
Grow Font	Each time you click the command, the selected text increases one size.	A A
Shrink Font	Each time you click the command, the selected text decreases one size.	B B
Clear Formatting	Removes all formatting from the selected text.	Formatted Cleared
Bold	Makes the text darker than the surrounding text.	**Bold**
Italic	Places the selected text in italic, that is, slants the letters to the right.	Italic
Underline	Places a line under the text. Click the drop-down arrow to change the underline style.	Underline
Strikethrough	Draws a line through the middle of the text.	~~Strikethrough~~
Subscript	Places selected text below the baseline.	$\text{Sub}_{\text{script}}$
Superscript	Places selected text above the line of letters.	$\text{Super}^{\text{script}}$
Change Case	Changes the case of the selected text. Click the drop-down arrow to select the desired case.	lowercase UPPERCASE
Text Highlight Color	Makes selected text look like it was highlighted with a marker pen. Click the drop-down arrow to change color and other options.	Highlighted
Font Color	Changes the color of selected text. Click the drop-down arrow to change colors.	Font Color

If you have several formatting changes to make, click the Dialog Box Launcher in the Font group on the Home tab to display the Font dialog box. The Font dialog box is handy because all the formatting features display in one location, and it provides additional options such as changing the underline color. Figure 1.41 shows the Font dialog box in Word.

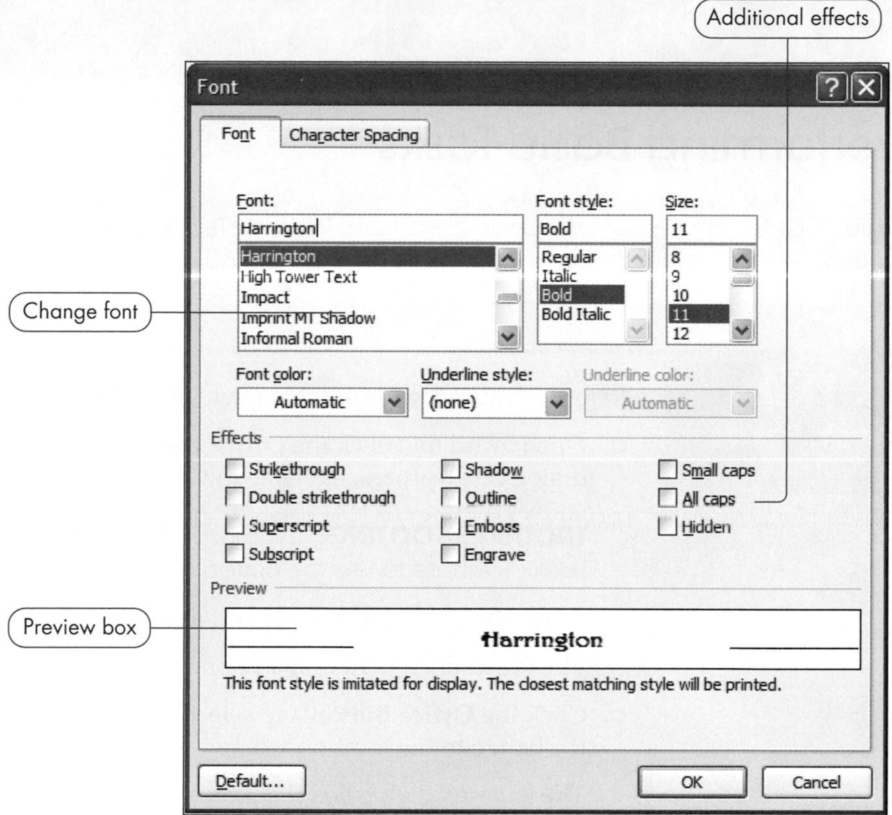

Figure 1.41 Font Dialog Box

Copying Formats with the Format Painter

The ***Format Painter*** copies the formatting of text from one location to another.

After formatting text in one part of a document, you might want to apply that same formatting to other text in a different location in the document. You could try to remember all the formatting options you selected, but that process would be time-consuming and could produce inconsistent results. Office 2007 provides a shortcut method called the ***Format Painter***, which copies the formatting of text from one location to another.

Select the formatted text you want to copy and click the Format Painter in the Clipboard group on the Home tab to copy the format. Single-click the command to turn it on to copy formatting to one location—the option turns off automatically after one copy—or double-click the command to turn it on for unlimited format copying—you must press Esc on the keyboard to turn it off.

Hands-On Exercises

3 | Performing Basic Tasks

Skills covered: 1. Cut, Copy, Paste, and Undo **2.** Find and Replace Text **3.** Check Spelling **4.** Choose Synonyms and Use Thesaurus **5.** Use the Research Tool **6.** Apply Font Attributes **7.** Use Format Painter

Step 1 Cut, Copy, Paste, and Undo

Refer to Figure 1.42 as you complete Steps 1 and 2.

a. Open Word and click the **Office Button**, click **Open**, and then using the Open dialog box features, navigate to your classroom file location.

   TROUBLESHOOTING: If you have trouble finding the file, remember to use the Look in feature to find the correct location.

b. Select the file *chap1_ho3_internet* and click the **Open** button.

   The Word document displays on the screen.

c. Click the **Office Button** and select **Save As**. If necessary, use the **Look in** feature to change to the location where you save files.

   The Save As dialog box displays.

d. Type the new file name, **chap1_ho3_internet_solution**, be sure that *Word Document* displays in the *Save as type* box, and click **Save**.

   The file is saved with the new name.

e. Click to place the insertion point at the beginning of the second sentence in the first paragraph. Type **These developments brought together**, and then press **Spacebar**.

   The text moves to the right, making room for the new inserted text.

f. Press and hold down **Ctrl** as you click this sentence below the heading The World Wide Web: *The Netscape browser led in user share until Microsoft Internet Explorer took the lead in 1999.*

g. Click **Cut** in the Clipboard group on the Home tab.

   The text disappears from the document.

h. Move the insertion point to the end of the last paragraph and click **Paste** in the Clipboard group on the Home tab.

   The text displays in the new location.

i. Reselect the sentence you just moved and click **Copy** in the Clipboard group on the Home tab.

j. Move the insertion point to the end of the first paragraph beginning *The idea* and click the right mouse button.

   The shortcut menu displays.

k. Select **Paste** from the shortcut menu.

   The text remains in the original position and is copied to the second location.

l. Click **Undo** on the Quick Access Toolbar to undo the last paste.

Step 2
Find and Replace Text

Refer to Figure 1.42 to complete Step 2.

a. Press **Ctrl + Home** to move the insertion point to the beginning of the document. Click **Replace** in the Editing group on the Home tab.

   The Find and Replace dialog box displays.

b. Type **Internet** in the *Find what* box and type **World Wide Web** in the *Replace with* box.

c. Click the **Replace All** button. Click **OK** to close the information box that informs you that Word has made seven replacements. Click **Close** to close the Find and Replace dialog box.

   All instances of Internet have been replaced with World Wide Web in the document.

d. Click **Undo** on the Quick Access Toolbar.

   All instances of *World Wide Web* have changed back to *Internet* in the document.

e. Click **Replace** in the Editing group on the Home tab.

   The Find and Replace dialog box displays with the text you typed still in the boxes.

f. Click the **Find Next** button.

   The first instance of the text *Internet* is highlighted.

g. Click the **Replace** button.

   The first instance of Internet is replaced with World Wide Web, and the next instance of Internet is highlighted.

h. Click the **Find Next** button.

   The highlight moves to the next instance of Internet without changing the previous one.

i. Click the **Close** button to close the Find and Replace dialog box.

   The Find and Replace dialog box closes.

The World Wide Web

By Linda Ericksen

The idea of a complex computer network that would allow communicatin among users of various computers developed over time. These developments brought together the network of networks known as the Internet, which included both technological developments and the merging together of existing network infrastructure and telecommunication systems. This network provides users with email, chat, file transfer, Web pages and other files.

History of Internet

In 1957, the Soviet Union lanched the first satellite, Sputnik I, triggering President Dwight Eisenhower to create the ARPA agency to regain the technological lead in the arms race. Practical implementations of a large computer network began during the late 1960's and 1970's. By the 1980's, technologies we now recognise as the basis of the modern Internet began to spread over the globe.

In 1990, ARPANET was replaced by NSFNET which connected universities in North America, and later research facilities in Europe were added. Use of the Internet exploded after 1990, causing the US Government to transfer management to independent orginizations.

The World Wide Web

The World Wide Web was developed in the 1980's in Europe and then rapidly spread around the world. The World Wide Web is a set of linked documents on computers connected by the Internet. These documents make use of hyperliks to link documents together. To use hyperlinks, browser software was developed.

Browsers

The first widely used web browser was Mosaic, and the programming team went on to develop the first commercial web browser called Netscape Navigator. The Netscape browser led in user share until Microsoft Internet Explorer took the lead in 1999.

Figure 1.42 Edited Document (Shown in Full Screen Reading View)

Step 3
Check Spelling

Refer to Figure 1.43 as you complete Steps 3–5.

a. Right-click the first word in the document that displays with the red wavy underline: *communicatin*.

   TROUBLESHOOTING: If the first word highlighted is the author's last name, ignore it for now. The name is spelled correctly, but if it is not listed in the spell check, then Word flags it.

   The shortcut menu displays with correct alternatives.

b. Click **communication** to replace the misspelled word in the document.

   The incorrect spelling is replaced, and the red wavy underline disappears.

c. Click the **Review tab**, and then click **Spelling & Grammar** in the Proofing group.

   The Spelling and Grammar dialog box opens with the first detected error displayed.

d. Move through the document selecting the correct word from the suggestions provided and choosing to **Change** the errors.

e. Click **OK** to close the Spelling and Grammar checker when the process is complete.

Step 4
Choose Synonyms and Use Thesaurus

a. Place the insertion point in the word **complex** in the first sentence and right-click the mouse.

   The shortcut menu displays.

b. Point to **Synonyms** on the shortcut menu.

   The list of alternative words displays.

c. Click the alternative word **multifaceted**.

   The new word replaces the word *complex* in the document.

d. Click in the word you just replaced, *multifaceted*, and click the **Thesaurus** button on the Review tab.

   The Thesaurus displays with alternatives for **multifaceted**.

e. Scroll down the list and point to the word *comprehensive*.

   A box displays around the word with a drop-down arrow on the right.

f. Click the drop-down arrow to display the menu and click **Insert**.

   The word *comprehensive* replaces the word in the document.

Step 5
Use the Research Tool

Refer to Figure 1.43 to complete Step 5.

a. Place the insertion point in the Search for text box and type **browser**.

b. Click the drop-down arrow on the **Reference** list, which currently displays the Thesaurus.

   The list of reference sites displays.

c. Click **Encarta Encyclopedia: English (North American)** option.

   A definition of the browser displays in the results box.

d. Click the **Close** button on the Research title bar.

   The Research pane closes.

The World Wide Web

By Linda Ericksen

The idea of a comprehensive computer network that would allow communication among users of various computers developed over time. These developments brought together the network of networks known as the Internet, which included both technological developments and the merging together of existing network infrastructure and telecommunication systems. This network provides users with email, chat, file transfer, Web pages and other files.

History of Internet

In 1957, the Soviet Union launched the first satellite, Sputnik I, triggering President Dwight Eisenhower to create the ARPA agency to regain the technological lead in the arms race. Practical implementations of a large computer network began during the late 1960's and 1970's. By the 1980's, technologies we now recognize as the basis of the modern Internet began to spread over the globe.

In 1990, ARPANET was replaced by NSFNET which connected universities in North America, and later research facilities in Europe were added. Use of the Internet exploded after 1990, causing the US Government to transfer management to independent organizations.

The World Wide Web

The World Wide Web was developed in the 1980's in Europe and then rapidly spread around the world. The World Wide Web is a set of linked documents on computers connected by the Internet. These documents make use of hyperlinks to link documents together. To use hyperlinks, browser software was developed.

Browsers

The first widely used web browser was Mosaic, and the programming team went on to develop the first commercial web browser called Netscape Navigator. The Netscape browser led in user share until Microsoft Internet Explorer took the lead in 1999.

Figure 1.43 Language Tools Improved the Document

Step 6
Apply Font Attributes

Refer to Figure 1.44 as you complete Steps 6 and 7.

a. Select the title of the document.

The Mini toolbar displays.

b. Click **Bold** on the Mini toolbar, and then click outside the title.

TROUBLESHOOTING: If the Mini toolbar is hard to read, remember to point to it to make it display fully.

The text changes to boldface.

c. Select the title again and click the drop-down arrow on the **Font** command in the Font group on the Home tab.

The list of fonts displays.

d. Point to font names on the list.

Live Preview changes the font of the selected sentence to display the fonts you point to.

e. Scroll down, and then select the **Lucinda Bright** font by clicking on the name.

The title changes to the new font.

f. With the title still selected, click the drop-down arrow on the **Font Size** command and select **16**.

The title changes to font size 16.

g. Select the byline that contains the author's name and click the **Underline** command, the **Italic** command, and the **Shrink Font** command once. All are located in the Font group on the Home tab.

The author's byline displays underlined, in italic, and one font size smaller.

h. Select the first heading *History of Internet* and click the **Font Color** down arrow command in the Font group on the Home tab. When the colors display, under Standard Colors, choose **Purple**, and then click outside the selected text.

The heading displays in purple.

i. Select the heading you just formatted as purple text and click **Bold**.

Step 7
Use Format Painter

Refer to Figure 1.44 to complete Step 7.

a. Click the **Format Painter** command in the Clipboard group on the Home tab.

   The pointer changes to a small paintbrush.

b. Select the second unformatted heading and repeat the process to format the third unformatted heading.

   The Format Painter formats that heading as purple and bold and automatically turns off.

c. Press **Ctrl** while you click the last sentence in the document and click the **Dialog Box Launcher** in the Font group.

d. Select **Bold** in the Font style box and **Double strikethrough** in the *Effects* section of the dialog box, then click **OK**.

e. Click outside the selected sentence to remove the selection and view the effects, and then click back in the formatted text.

   The sentence displays bold with two lines through the text. The Bold command in the Font group on the Home tab displays with a gold background.

f. Select the same sentence again, click **Bold** in the Font group on the Home tab, and then click outside the sentence.

   The Bold format has been removed from the text.

g. Click **Save** on the Quick Access Toolbar.

   The document is saved under the same name.

h. To exit Word, click the **Office Button**, and then click the **Exit Word** button.

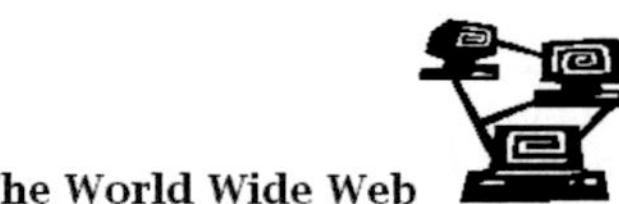

The World Wide Web

By Linda Ericksen

The idea of a big computer network that would allow communication among users of various computers developed over time. These developments brought together the network of networks known as the Internet, which included both technological developments and the merging together of existing network infrastructure and telecommunication systems. This network provides users with email, chat, file transfer, Web pages and other files.

History of Internet

In 1957, the Soviet Union launched the first satellite, Sputnik I, triggering President Dwight Eisenhower to create the ARPA agency to regain the technological lead in the arms race. Practical implementations of a large computer network began during the late 1960's and 1970's. By the 1980's, technologies we now recognize as the basis of the modern Internet began to spread over the globe.

In 1990, ARPANET was replaced by NSFNET which connected universities in North America, and later research facilities in Europe were added. Use of the Internet exploded after 1990, causing the US Government to transfer management to independent organizations.

The World Wide Web

The World Wide Web was developed in the 1980's in Europe and then rapidly spread around the world. The World Wide Web is a set of linked documents on computers connected by the Internet. These documents make use of hyperlinks to link documents together. To use hyperlinks, browser software was developed.

Browsers

The first widely used web browser was Mosaic, and the programming team went on to develop the first commercial web browser called Netscape Navigator. ~~The Netscape browser led in user share until Microsoft Internet Explorer took the lead in 1999.~~

Figure 1.44 Formatted Document

Summary

1. **Identify common interface components.** You learned to identify and use the common elements of the Office 2007 interface and apply them in Word, PowerPoint, Excel, and Access. The top of the application window contains the Office Button that, when clicked, displays the Office menu. The Quick Access Toolbar provides commonly used commands, such as Save and Undo. The primary command center is the Ribbon, which contains tabs to organize major tasks. Each tab contains groups of related commands. The bottom of the window contains a status bar that gives general information, view options, and the Zoom slider.
2. **Use Office 2007 Help.** When you need help to continue working with Office 2007, you can use the Help feature from your computer or get help at Microsoft Office Online. You can position the mouse pointer on a command to see an Enhanced ScreenTip. You can click some Enhanced ScreenTips to display help. You can often get context-sensitive help by clicking Help within dialog boxes.
3. **Open a file.** To retrieve a file you have previously saved, you use the Open command. When you open a file, it is copied into RAM so that you can view and work on it.
4. **Save a file.** As you create and edit documents, you should save your work for future use. Use the Save or Save As command to save a file for the first time, giving it a name and location. To continue saving changes to the same file name, use Save. To assign a new name, location, or file type, use Save As.
5. **Print a document.** Producing a perfect hard copy of the document is an important task, and you can make it easier by previewing, selecting options, and printing. You can select the printer, how many copies to print, and the pages you want to print. In addition, each program has specific print options.
6. **Select text to edit.** In order to edit text, you have to identify the body of text you want to work with by selecting it first. You can select text by using the mouse.
7. **Insert text and change to the Overtype mode.** To edit text in the document, you need to be able to insert text and to replace text by typing over it. The Insert mode inserts text without deleting existing text. The Overtype mode types over existing text as you type.
8. **Move and copy text.** You can move text from one location to another to achieve a better flow in a document, worksheet, or presentation. You can use the Copy command to duplicate data in one location and use the Paste command to place the duplicate in another location.
9. **Find, replace, and go to text.** Another editing feature that can save you time is to find text by searching for it or going directly to a specific element in the document. You can also replace text that needs updating.
10. **Use the Undo and Redo commands.** If you make a mistake and want to undo it, you can easily remedy it by using the Undo feature. Likewise, to save time, you can repeat the last action with the Redo command.
11. **Use language tools.** Office 2007 provides tools to help you create and edit error-free documents. You can use the spelling check and grammar check, the built-in thesaurus, and even conduct research all from your Word document. You can check spelling and conduct research in Excel and PowerPoint as well.
12. **Apply font attributes.** Applying font formats can help make the message clearer. For example, you can select a different font to achieve a different look. In addition, you can adjust the font size and change the font color of text. Other font attributes include bold, underline, and italic.
13. **Copy formats with the Format Painter.** You might want to copy the format of text to another location or to several locations in the document. You can easily accomplish that with the Format Painter.

Key Terms

Multiple Choice

1. Software that is used primarily with text to create, edit, and format documents is known as:
   (a) Electronic spreadsheet software
   (b) Word processing software
   (c) Presentation graphics software
   (d) Relational database software

2. Which Office feature displays when you rest the mouse pointer on a command?
   (a) The Ribbon
   (b) The status bar
   (c) An Enhanced ScreenTip
   (d) A dialog box

3. What is the name of the blinking vertical line in a document that designates the current location in the document?
   (a) A command
   (b) Overtype mode
   (c) Insert mode
   (d) Insertion point

4. If you wanted to locate every instance of text in a document and have it temporarily highlighted, which command would you use?
   (a) Find
   (b) Replace
   (c) Go To
   (d) Spell Check

5. The meeting point between computer software and the person using it is known as:
   (a) A file
   (b) Software
   (c) A template
   (d) An interface

6. Which of the following is true about the Office Ribbon?
   (a) The Ribbon displays at the bottom of the screen.
   (b) The Ribbon is only available in the Word 2007 application.
   (c) The Ribbon is the main component of the Office 2007 interface.
   (d) The Ribbon cannot be used for selecting commands.

7. Which element of the Ribbon looks like folder tabs and provides commands that are task oriented?
   (a) Groups
   (b) Tabs
   (c) Status bar
   (d) Galleries

8. Which Office 2007 element provides commands that work with an entire document or file and displays by default in the title bar?
   (a) Galleries
   (b) Ribbon
   (c) Office Button
   (d) Groups

9. If you needed the entire screen to read a document, which document view would you use?
   (a) Outline view
   (b) Draft view
   (c) Print Layout
   (d) Full Screen Reading

10. The default four-letter extension for Word documents that do not contain macros is:
    (a) .docx
    (b) .pptx
    (c) .xlsx
    (d) .dotm

11. Before you can cut or copy text, you must first do which one of the following?
    (a) Preview the document.
    (b) Save the document.
    (c) Select the text.
    (d) Undo the previous command.

12. What is the name of the memory location that holds up to twenty-four items for you to paste into the current document, another document, or another application?
    (a) My Places bar
    (b) My Documents
    (c) Ribbon
    (d) Clipboard

Multiple Choice Continued...

13. Word flags misspelled words by marking them with which one of the following?
    (a) A green wavy underline
    (b) Boldfacing them
    (c) A red wavy underline
    (d) A double-underline in black

14. Which of the following displays when you select text in a document?
    (a) The Mini toolbar
    (b) The Quick Access Toolbar
    (c) A shortcut menu
    (d) The Ribbon

15. Formatting text allows you to change which of the following text attributes?
    (a) The font
    (b) The font size
    (c) The font type
    (d) All of the above

Practice Exercises

1 Using Help and Print Preview in Access 2007

a. Open Access. Click the **Office Button**, and then select **Open**. Use the Look in feature to find the *chap1_pe1* database, and then click **Open**.
b. At the right side of the Ribbon, click the **Help** button. In the Help window, type **table** in the **Type words to search for** box. Click the **Search** button.
c. Click the topic *Create a Table*. Browse the content of the Help window, and then click the **Close** button in the Help window.
d. Double-click the **Courses table** in the left pane. The table opens in Datasheet view.
e. Click the **Office Button**, point to the arrow after the **Print** command, and select **Print Preview** to open the Print Preview window with the Courses table displayed.
f. Point the mouse pointer on the table and click to magnify the display. Compare your screen to Figure 1.45.
g. Click the **Close Print Preview** button on the Print Preview tab.
h. Click the **Office Button**, and then click the **Exit Access button**.

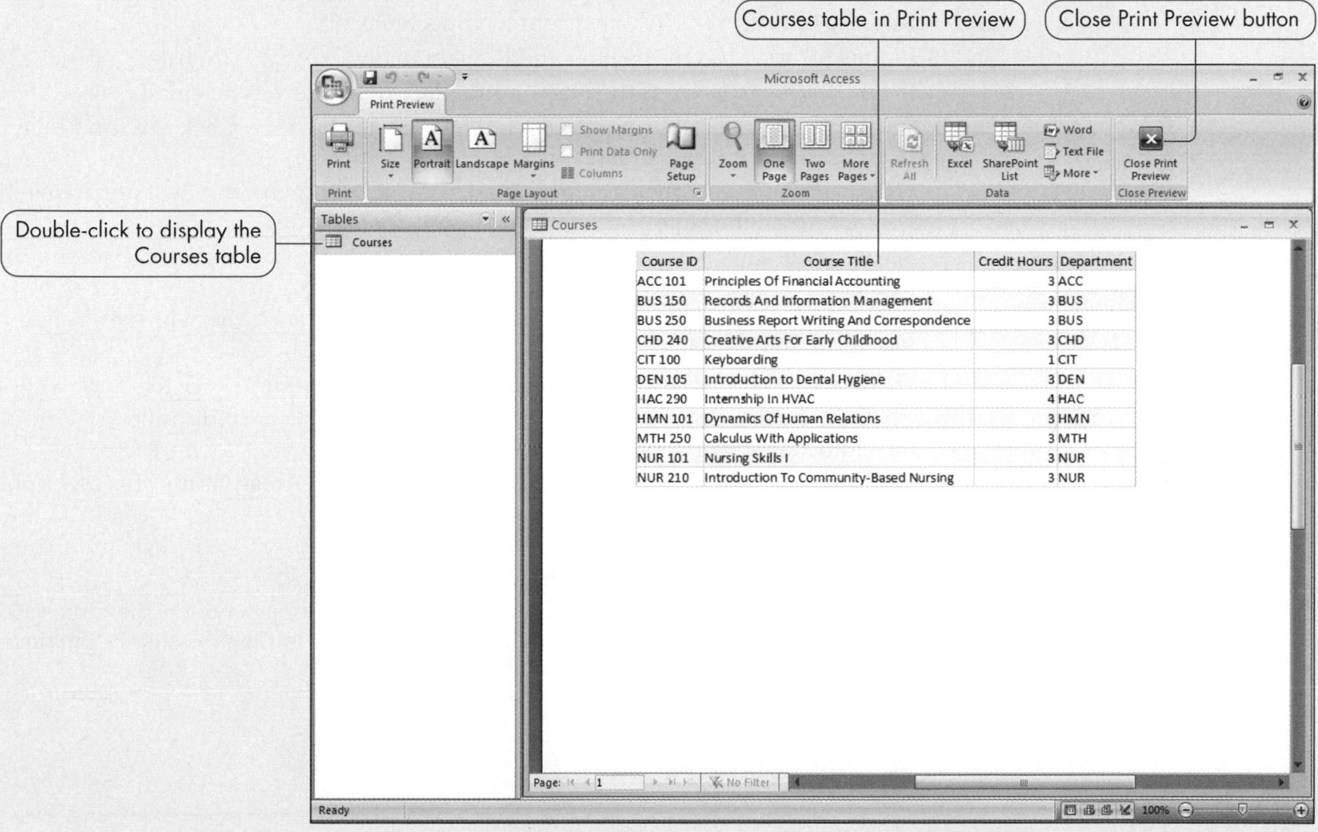

Course ID	Course Title	Credit Hours	Department
ACC 101	Principles Of Financial Accounting	3	ACC
BUS 150	Records And Information Management	3	BUS
BUS 250	Business Report Writing And Correspondence	3	BUS
CHD 240	Creative Arts For Early Childhood	3	CHD
CIT 100	Keyboarding	1	CIT
DEN 105	Introduction to Dental Hygiene	3	DEN
HAC 290	Internship In HVAC	4	HAC
HMN 101	Dynamics Of Human Relations	3	HMN
MTH 250	Calculus With Applications	3	MTH
NUR 101	Nursing Skills I	3	NUR
NUR 210	Introduction To Community-Based Nursing	3	NUR

Figure 1.45 Access Print Preview

...continued on Next Page

2 Avoiding Fraud Report

As part of your Introduction to Computers course, you have prepared an oral report on phishing. You want to provide class members with a handout that summarizes the main points of your report. This handout is in the rough stages, so you need to edit it, and you also realize that you can format some of the text to emphasize the main points.

a. Start Word. Click the **Office Button**, and then select **Open**. Use the *Look in* feature to find the *chap1_pe2* document, and then click **Open**.
b. Click the **Office Button**, and then select **Save As**. In the *File name* box, type the document name, **chap1_pe2_solution**, be sure that Word document displays in the *Save as type* box, and use the *Look in* option to move to the location where you save your class files. Click **Save**.
c. In the document, click after the word Name and type **your name**.
d. Select your name, and then click **Bold** and **Italic** on the Mini toolbar—remember to point to the Mini toolbar to make it display fully. Your name displays in bold and italic.
e. Move the insertion point immediately before the title of the document and click the **Replace** button in the Editing group on the Home tab.
f. In the *Find what* box of the Find and Replace dialog box, type **internet**.
g. In the *Replace with* box of the Find and Replace dialog box, type **email**.
h. Click the **Replace All** button to have Word replace the text. Click **OK**, and then click **Close** to close the dialog boxes.
i. To format the title of the document, first select it, and then click the **Font arrow** in the Font group on the Home tab to display the available fonts.
j. Scroll down and choose the **Impact** font if you have it; otherwise, use one that is available.
k. Place the insertion point in the word *Phishng*. Right-click the word, and then click **Phishing** from the shortcut menu.
l. To emphasize important text in the list, double-click the first **NOT** to select it.
m. Click the **Font Color** arrow and select Red, and then click **Bold** in the Font group on the Home tab to apply bold to the text.
n. With the first instance of NOT selected, double-click **Format Painter** in the Clipboard group on the Home tab.
o. Double-click the second and then the third instance of **NOT** in the list, and then press **Esc** on the keyboard to turn off the Format Painter.
p. Compare your document to Figure 1.46. Save by clicking **Save** on the Quick Access Toolbar. Close the document and exit Word or proceed to the next step to preview and print the document.

...continued on Next Page

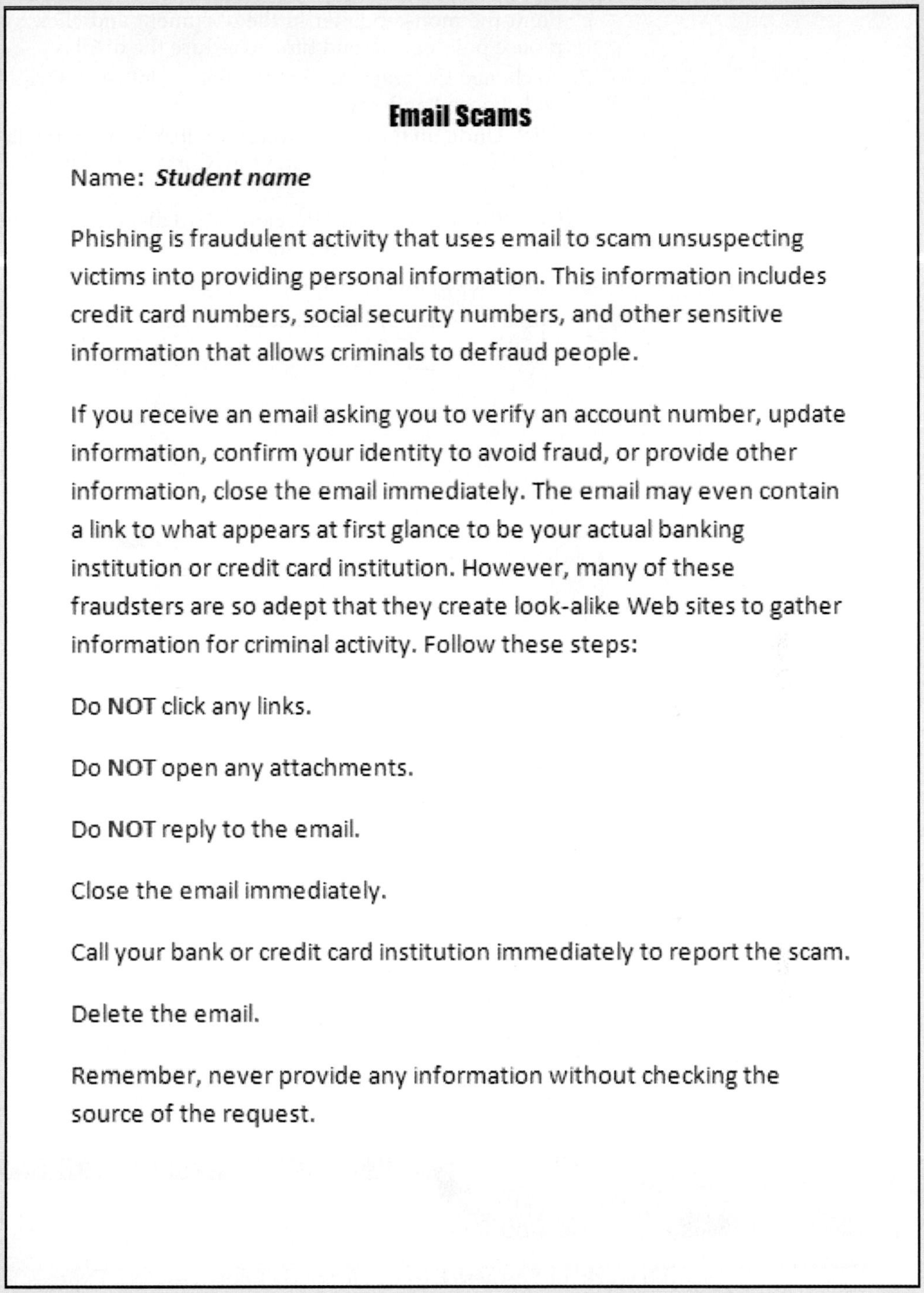

Email Scams

Name: ***Student name***

Phishing is fraudulent activity that uses email to scam unsuspecting victims into providing personal information. This information includes credit card numbers, social security numbers, and other sensitive information that allows criminals to defraud people.

If you receive an email asking you to verify an account number, update information, confirm your identity to avoid fraud, or provide other information, close the email immediately. The email may even contain a link to what appears at first glance to be your actual banking institution or credit card institution. However, many of these fraudsters are so adept that they create look-alike Web sites to gather information for criminal activity. Follow these steps:

Do **NOT** click any links.

Do **NOT** open any attachments.

Do **NOT** reply to the email.

Close the email immediately.

Call your bank or credit card institution immediately to report the scam.

Delete the email.

Remember, never provide any information without checking the source of the request.

Figure 1.46 Phishing Document

3 Previewing and Printing a Document

You created a handout to accompany your oral presentation in the previous exercise. Now you want to print it out so that you can distribute it.

a. If necessary, open the *chap1_pe2_solution* document that you saved in the previous exercise.
b. Click the **Office Button**, point to the arrow after the Print command, and select **Print Preview** to open the Print Preview window with the document displayed.

...continued on Next Page

c. Point the mouse pointer in the document and click to magnify the display. Click the mouse pointer a second time to reduce the display.

d. To change the orientation of the document, click **Orientation** in the Page Setup group and choose **Landscape**.

e. Click **Undo** on the Quick Access Toolbar to undo the last command, which returns the document to portrait orientation. Compare your results to the zoomed document in Figure 1.47.

f. Click **Print** on the Print Preview tab to display the Print dialog box.

g. Click **OK** to print the document.

h. Close the document without saving it.

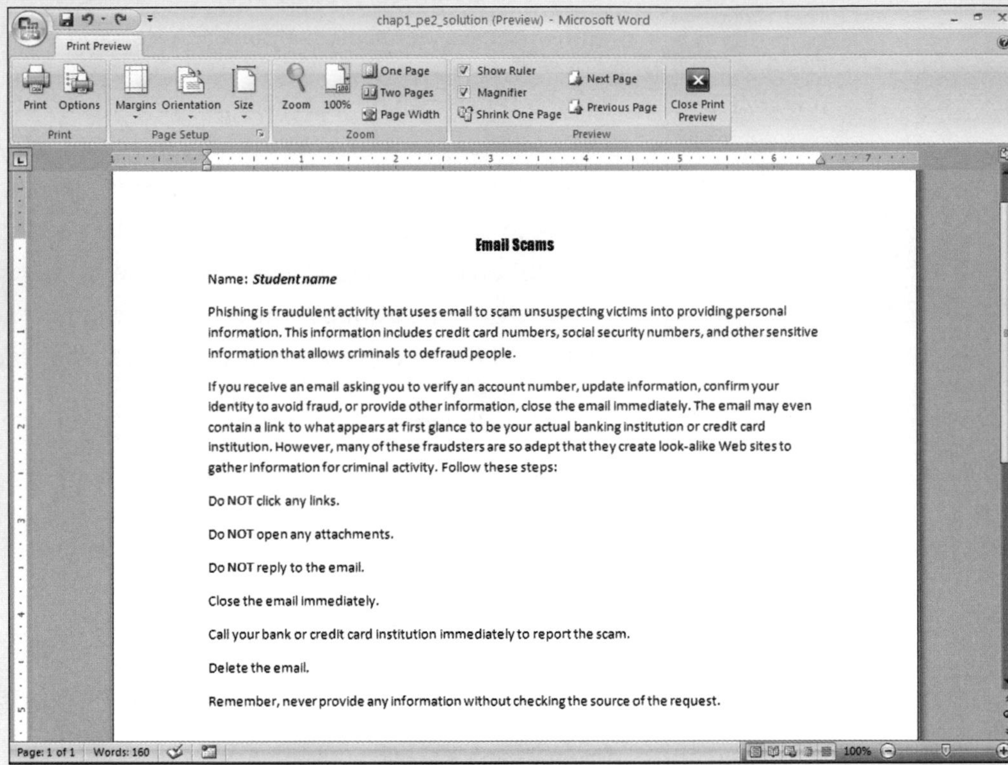

Figure 1.47 Document in Print Preview Window

4 Editing a Promotion Flyer

You work for Business Express, formerly known as Print Express, a regional company specializing in business centers that design and produce documents for local businesses and individuals. Business Express has just undergone a major transition along with a name change. Your job is to edit and refine an existing flyer to inform customers of the new changes. Proceed as follows:

a. Open Word. Click the **Office Button**, and then select **Open**. Use the *Look in* feature to find the *chap1_pe4* document.

b. Click the **Office Button** again and select **Save As**. Type the document name, **chap1_pe4_solution**, be sure that Word document displays in the *Save as type* box, and use the *Look in* option to move to the location where you save your class files.

c. Place the insertion point at the beginning of the document, and then click **Spelling & Grammar** in the Proofing group on the Review tab to open the Spelling and Grammar dialog box.

d. Click the **Change** button three times to correct the spelling errors. Click **OK** to close the completion box.

...continued on Next Page

e. Place the insertion point at the end of the first sentence of the document—just before the period. To insert the following text, press **Spacebar** and type **that offers complete business solutions**.
f. Place the insertion point in *good* in the first sentence of the third paragraph and right-click the mouse.
g. Point to **Synonyms**, and then click **first-rate** to replace the word in the document.
h. Place the insertion point in *bigger* in the last sentence of the third paragraph and click **Thesaurus** in the Proofing group on the Review tab. Point to **superior** and click the drop-down arrow that displays. Click **Insert** from the menu to replace the word in the document, and then click the **Close** button on the Thesaurus.
i. Select the last full paragraph of the document and click **Cut** in the Clipboard group on the Home tab to remove the paragraph from the document.
j. Place the insertion point at the beginning of the new last paragraph and click **Paste** in the Clipboard group on the Home tab to display the text.
k. Click **Undo** on the Quick Access Toolbar twice to undo the paste operation and to undo the cut operation—placing the text back in its original location.
l. Place the insertion point after the colon at the bottom of the document and type **your name**.
m. Compare your results to Figure 1.48, and then save and close the document.

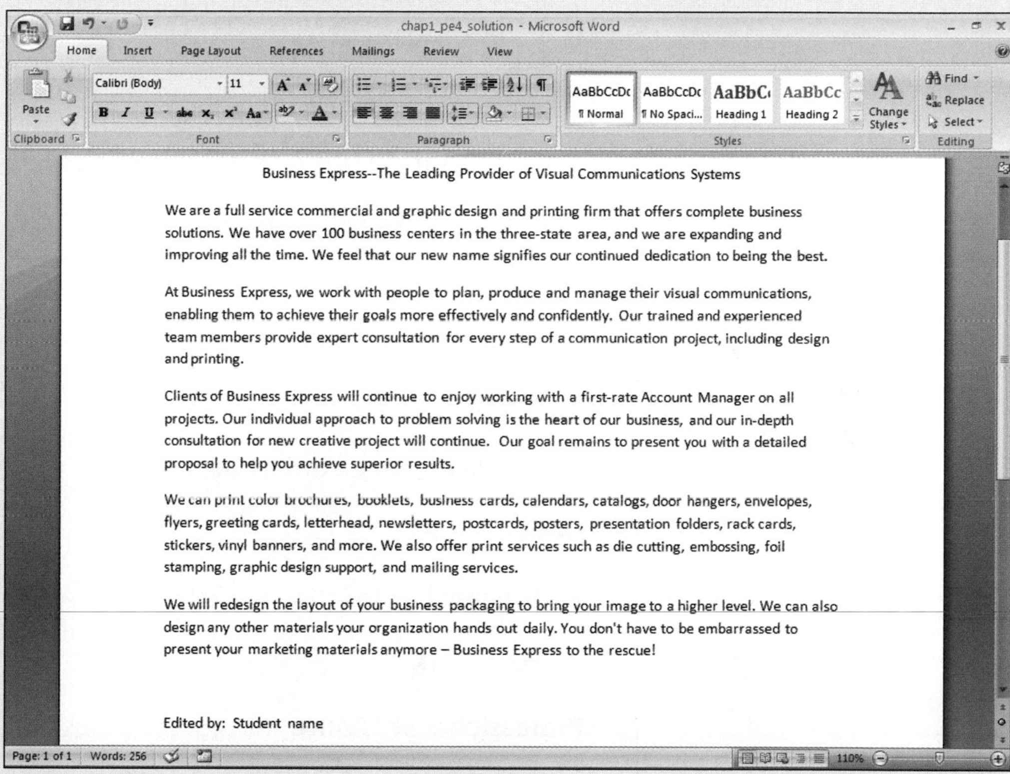

chap1_pe4_solution - Microsoft Word
Home
Insert
Page Layout
References
Mailings
Review
View
Paste
Calibri (Body)
11
AaBbCcDc
¶ Normal
AaBbCcDc
¶ No Spaci...
AaBbCc
Heading 1
AaBbCc
Heading 2
Change Styles
Find
Replace
Select
Clipboard
Font
Paragraph
Styles
Editing
Business Express--The Leading Provider of Visual Communications Systems
We are a full service commercial and graphic design and printing firm that offers complete business solutions. We have over 100 business centers in the three-state area, and we are expanding and improving all the time. We feel that our new name signifies our continued dedication to being the best.
At Business Express, we work with people to plan, produce and manage their visual communications, enabling them to achieve their goals more effectively and confidently. Our trained and experienced team members provide expert consultation for every step of a communication project, including design and printing.
Clients of Business Express will continue to enjoy working with a first-rate Account Manager on all projects. Our individual approach to problem solving is the heart of our business, and our in-depth consultation for new creative project will continue. Our goal remains to present you with a detailed proposal to help you achieve superior results.
We can print color brochures, booklets, business cards, calendars, catalogs, door hangers, envelopes, flyers, greeting cards, letterhead, newsletters, postcards, posters, presentation folders, rack cards, stickers, vinyl banners, and more. We also offer print services such as die cutting, embossing, foil stamping, graphic design support, and mailing services.
We will redesign the layout of your business packaging to bring your image to a higher level. We can also design any other materials your organization hands out daily. You don't have to be embarrassed to present your marketing materials anymore – Business Express to the rescue!
Edited by: Student name
Page: 1 of 1
Words: 256
110%

Figure 1.48 Business Flyer

Mid-Level Exercises

1 Updating a Training Document

Your position as trainer for a large building supply company involves training all new employees. It is your job to familiarize new employees with the services provided by Castle Home Building Supply. You distribute a list at the training session and you realize that it needs updating before the next session, so you decide to edit and format it.

a. Start Word. Open the *chap1_mid1* file and save it as **chap1_mid1_solution**.
b. Change the title font to Arial Rounded MT Bold size 16 and change the font color to dark brown.
c. Make the subtitle Arial Unicode MS and italic.
d. Cut the item *Help with permits* and make it the second item on the list.
e. In the first list item, insert **and** after the word *fair*.
f. Change the word *help* in the last list item to **Assistance**.
g. Select the list of items excluding the heading, Services Provided.
h. Bold the list and change the font size to 16.
i. Save the document and compare it to Figure 1.49.

Castle Home Building Supply

Where the Customer Comes First

Services Provided:

Fair and accurate estimates

Help with permits

Free delivery on all orders over $100

Design help

Professional Installation available

Custom work

Professional assistance

New building and renovations

Assistance with inspections

Figure 1.49 Training Document

...continued on Next Page

2 Formatting a Menu

The owner of the Bayside Restaurant wants your help formatting his menu so that it is more pleasing to customers; follow the steps below:

a. Open the *chap1_mid2* document and save it as **chap1_mid2_solution**.

b. Format the menu title as Broadway size 16.

c. Format the three headings: Appetizers, Soups and Salads, and Lunch or Dinner Anytime! as Bodoni MT Black, size 12, and change the font color to Dark Red. Remember to format the first one and use the Format Painter for the second two headings.

d. Format all the dish names, such as Nachos, using the Outline Font Effects.

e. Bold all the prices in the document.

f. Preview the document, compare to Figure 1.50, and then print it.

g. Save and close the document.

Bayside Menu - Great Food & Prices!

APPETIZERS

NACHOS: tri-color tortilla chips, melted cheddar cheese topped with tomato, onion and jalapeno **$ 9.00**

CHICKEN WINGS: baked, served with celery sticks and blue cheese dip **$ 9.00**

MOZZARELLA STICKS: baked, then served with a hearty marinara sauce **$ 9.00**

CRAB & ARTICHOKE DIP: a creamy blend of artichoke hearts, lump meat crab meat and cheese, served with toasted bread **$ 12.00**

STEAMED SHRIMP: half-pound of extra large shrimp, served with cocktail sauce **$14.00**

SOUPS and SALADS

CHILE: beef and bean chili with tortilla chips on the side **$ 7.00**

HOUSE SALAD: mixed greens and garden vegetables **$ 5.00**

LUNCH or DINNER ANYTIME!

CRAB CAKE SANDWICH: jumbo crab meat on a toasted roll served with chips and dip **$ 15.00**

CLASSIC CLUB: turkey, ham, cheddar and provolone cheese, bacon, lettuce, tomato and mayo on toasted bread, served with chips and dip **$ 10.00**

DOUBLE BURGER: half-pound Black Angus beef burger, cooked the way you order it, topped with American cheese, bacon, onion, lettuce and tomato on a toasted roll with French fries **$ 11.00**

BBQ PULLED PORK SANDWICH: pulled pork with BBQ sauce served on a toasted roll with chips **$ 10.00**

SWISS CHICKEN: breast topped with Swiss cheese, bacon and tomato with ranch dressing, served on a toasted roll and French fries **$ 10.00**

TURKEY WRAP: sliced turkey breast, lettuce, tomato and mayo, rolled on a flour tortilla, served with chips and dip **$ 10.00**

RUEBEN: corned beef, sauerkraut, Swiss cheese and Russian dressing on toasted rye, served with French fries **$ 10.00**

CHICKEN TENDERS: breaded and baked just right, served with BBQ sauce, honey mustard and French Fries **$ 10.00**

ITALIAN PIZZA: mozzarella, pepperoni, and marinara **$ 8.00**

Figure 1.50 The Formatted Menu

...continued on Next Page

3 Enhance the Insurance Letter

Your job duties at Health First Insurance, Inc., involve maintaining the correspondence. You need to update the welcome letter you send to clients to reflect the company's new name, new address, and other important elements, and then address it to a new client. Proceed as follows.

a. Open the *chap1_mid3* document and save it as **chap1_mid3_solution**.
b. Run the Spelling check to eliminate the errors.
c. Use Replace to change **University Insurance, Inc**. to **Health First Insurance, Inc**. throughout the letter.
d. Change the Address from **123 Main St**. to **1717 N. Zapata Way**.
e. Change the inside address that now has **Client name, Client Address, Client City, State and Zip Code** to **your name and complete address**. Also change the salutation to your name.
f. Move the first paragraph so that it becomes the last paragraph in the body of the letter.
g. Preview the letter to be sure that it fits on one page, compare it with Figure 1.51, and then print it.
h. Save and close the document.

Health First Insurance, Inc.

1717 N. Zapata Way

Laredo, TX 78043

Student name

Student Address

Student City, State, and Zip Code

Dear Student name:

Welcome to the Health First Insurance, Inc. We have received and accepted your application and premium for health insurance. Please detach and the ID cards attached to this letter and keep with you at all times for identification, reference and access to emergency phone assistance and Pre Notification numbers in the event of a claim.

Enclosed you will find a Certificate of Coverage detailing the benefits, limits, exclusions and provisions of the Health First Insurance, Inc. Medical Plan. Please review the Certificate of Coverage thoroughly and contact us if you have any questions regarding the terms and provisions.

In order for you and your dependents to receive adequate medical treatment and for your assistance, the Health First Insurance, Inc. Medical Plan requires any insured (or someone on their behalf) to Pre-notify Health First Insurance, Inc., for any hospital admission prior to admittance (or within 36 hours after an emergency admission). Additionally, the Health First Insurance, Inc. Medical Plan requires all insured to utilize the provider network.

We appreciate your confidence in our organization and look forward to serving your insurance needs.

Sincerely,

Maria Fernandez

Agent

Health First Insurance, Inc.

Figure 1.51 The Updated Letter

Capstone Exercise

In this project, you work with a business plan for Far East Trading Company that will be submitted to funding sources in order to secure loans. The document requires editing to polish the final product and formatting to enhance readability and emphasize important information.

Editing the Document

This document is ready for editing, so proceed as follows:

a. Open the *chap1_cap* document. Save the document as **chap1_cap_solution**.

b. Run the Spelling and Grammar check to eliminate all spelling and grammar errors in the document.

c. Use the Thesaurus to find a synonym for the word **unique** in the second paragraph of the document.

d. Use the Go To command to move to page 3 and change the $175,000 to $250,000.

e. Move the entire second section of the document (notice the numbers preceding it) now located at the end of the document to its correct location after the first section.

f. Insert the street **1879 Columbia Ave.** before Portland in the first paragraph.

g. Copy the inserted street address to section 2.3 and place it in front of Portland there also.

h. Replace the initials **FET** with **FETC** for every instance in the document.

i. Type over 1998 in the third paragraph so that it says 2008.

Formatting the Document

Next, you will apply formatting techniques to the document. These format options will further increase the readability and attractiveness of your document.

a. Select the two-line title and change the font to Engravers MT, size 14, and change the color to Dark Red.

b. Select the first heading in the document: 1.0 Executive Summary, then change the font to Gautami, bold, and change the color to Dark Blue.

c. Use the Format Painter to make all the main numbered headings the same formatting, that is 2.0, 3.0, 4.0, and 5.0.

d. The first three numbered sections have subsections such as 1.1, 1.2. Select the heading 1.1 and format it for bold, italic, and change the color to a lighter blue—Aqua, Accents, Darker 25%.

e. Use the Format Painter to make all the numbered subsections the same formatting.

Printing the Document

To finish the job, you need to print the business plan.

a. Preview the document to check your results.

b. Print the document.

c. Save your changes and close the document.

Mini Cases

Use the rubric following the case as a guide to evaluate our work, but keep in mind that your instructor may impose additional grading criteria or use a different standard to judge your work.

A Thank-You Letter

GENERAL CASE

As the new volunteer coordinator for Special Olympics in your area, you need to send out information for prospective volunteers, and the letter you were given needs editing and formatting. Open the *chap1_mc1* document and make necessary changes to improve the appearance. You should use Replace to change the text (insert your state name), use the current date and your name and address information, format to make the letter more appealing, and eliminate all errors. Your finished document should be saved as **chap1_mc1_solution**.

Performance Elements	Exceeds Expectations	Meets Expectations	Below Expectations
Corrected all errors	Document contains no errors.	Document contains minimal errors.	Document contains several errors.
Use of character formatting features such as font, font size, font color, or other attributes	Used character formatting options throughout entire document.	Used character formatting options in most sections of document.	Used character formatting options on a small portion of document.
Inserted text where instructed	The letter is complete with all required information inserted.	The letter is mostly complete.	Letter is incomplete. .

The Information Request Letter

RESEARCH CASE

Search the Internet for opportunities to teach abroad or for internships available in your major. Have fun finding a dream opportunity. Use the address information you find on the Web site that interests you, and compose a letter asking for additional information. For example, you might want to teach English in China, so search for that information. Your finished document should be saved as **chap1_mc2_solution**.

Performance Elements	Exceeds Expectations	Meets Expectations	Below Expectations
Use of character formatting	Three or more character formats applied to text.	One or two character formats applied to text.	Does not apply character formats to text.
Language tools	No spelling or grammar errors.	One spelling or grammar error.	More than one spelling or grammar error.
Presentation	Information is easy to read and understand.	Information is somewhat unclear.	Letter is unclear.

Movie Memorabilia

DISASTER RECOVERY

Use the following rubrics to guide your evaluation of your work, but keep in mind that your instructor may impose additional grading criteria.

Open the *chap1_mc3* document that can be found in the Exploring folder. The advertising document is over-formatted, and it contains several errors and problems. For example, the text has been formatted in many fonts that are difficult to read. The light color of the text also has made the document difficult to read. You should improve the formatting so that it is consistent, helps the audience read the document, and is pleasing to look at. Your finished document should be saved as **chap1_mc3_solution**.

Performance Elements	Exceeds Expectations	Meets Expectations	Below Expectations
Type of font chosen to format document	Number and style of fonts appropriate for short document.	Number or style of fonts appropriate for short document.	Overused number of fonts or chose inappropriate font.
Color of font chosen to format document	Appropriate font colors for document.	Most font colors appropriate.	Overuse of font colors.
Overall document appeal	Document looks appealing.	Document mostly looks appealing.	Did not improve document much.

chapter 1 | **Access**

Introduction to Access

Finding Your Way Through a Database

After you read this chapter, you will be able to:

1. Explore, describe, and navigate among the objects in an Access database **(page 71)**.
2. Understand the difference between working in storage and memory **(page 78)**.
3. Practice good file management **(page 79)**.
4. Back up, compact, and repair Access files **(page 80)**.
5. Create filters **(page 89)**.
6. Sort table data on one or more fields **(page 92)**.
7. Know when to use Access or Excel to manage data **(page 94)**.
8. Use the Relationship window **(page 102)**.
9. Understand relational power **(page 103)**.

Hands-On Exercises

Exercises	Skills Covered
1. INTRODUCTION TO DATABASES (page 81) **Open:** chap1_ho1-3_traders.accdb **Copy, rename, and back up as:** chap1_ho1-3_traders_solution.accdb and chap1_ho1_traders_solution.accdb	• Create a Production Folder and Copy an Access File • Open an Access File • Edit a Record • Navigate an Access Form and Add Records • Recognize the Table and Form Connectivity and Delete a Record • Back Up and Compact the Database
2. DATA MANIPULATION: FILTERS AND SORTS (page 96) **Open:** chap1_ho1-3_traders_soution.accdb (from Exercise 1) **Copy, rename, and back up as:** chap1_ho1-3_traders_solution.accdb (additional modifications), chap1_ho2_traders_solution.docx, and chap1_ho2_traders_solution.accdb	• Use Filter by Selection with an Equal Setting • Use Filter by Selection with a Contains Setting • Use Filter by Form with an Inequity Setting • Sort a Table
3. INTRODUCTION TO RELATIONSHIPS (page 105) **Open:** chap1_ho1-3_traders_solution.accdb (from Exercise 2) **Copy, rename, and back up as:** chap1_ho1-3_traders_solution.accdb (additional modifications)	• Examine the Relationships Window • Discover That Changes in Table Data Affect Queries • Use Filter by Form with an Inequity Setting and Reapply a Saved Filter • Filter a Report • Remove an Advanced Filter

CASE STUDY

Medical Research—The Lifelong Learning Physicians Association

Case Study

Today is the first day of your information technology internship appointment with the *Lifelong Learning Physicians Association*. This medical association selected you for the internship because your résumé indicates that you are proficient with Access. Bonnie Clinton, M.D., founded the organization with the purpose of keeping doctors informed about current research and to help physicians identify qualified study participants. Dr. Clinton worries that physicians do not inform their patients about study participation opportunities. She expressed further concerns that the physicians in one field, e.g., cardiology, are unfamiliar with research studies conducted in other fields, such as obstetrics.

Because the association is new, you have very little data to manage. However, the system was designed to accommodate additional data. You will need to talk to Dr. Clinton on a regular basis to determine the association's changing information needs. You may need to guide her in this process. Your responsibilities as the association's IT intern include many items.

Your Assignment

- Read the chapter, paying special attention to learning the vocabulary of database software.
- Copy the *chap1_case_physicians.accdb* file to your production folder, rename it **chap1_case_physicians_solution.accdb**, and enable the content.
- Open the Relationships window and examine the relationships among the tables and the fields contained within each of the tables to become acquainted with this database.
- Open the Volunteers table. Add yourself as a study participant by replacing the last record with your own information. You should invent data about your height, weight, blood pressure, and your cholesterol. Examine the values in the other records and enter a realistic value. Do not change the stored birthday.
- Identify all of the volunteers who might be college freshmen (18- and 19-year-olds). After you identify them, print the table listing their names and addresses. Use a filter by form with an appropriately set date criterion to identify the correctly aged participants.
- Identify all of the physicians participating in a study involving cholesterol management.
- Open the *Studies and Volunteers Report*. Print it.
- Compact and repair the database file.
- Create a backup of the database. Name the backup **chap1_case_physicians_backup.accdb**.

Data and Files Everywhere!

You probably use databases often. Each time you download an MP3 file, you enter a database via the Internet. There, you find searchable data identifying files by artist's name, music style, most frequently requested files, first lines, publication companies, and song titles. If you know the name of the song but not the recording artist or record label, you generally can find it. The software supporting the Web site helps you locate the information you need. The server for the Web site provides access to a major database that contains a lot of data about available MP3 files.

(Each time you download an MP3 file, you enter a database via the internet.)

You are exposed to other databases on a regular basis. For example, your university uses a database to support the registration process. When you registered for this course, you entered a database. It probably told you how many seats remained but not the names of the other students. In addition, Web-based job and dating boards are based on database software. Organizations rely on data to conduct daily operations, regardless of whether the organization exists as a profit or not-for-profit environment. The organization maintains data about employees, volunteers, customers, activities, and facilities. Every keystroke and mouse click creates data about the organization that needs to be stored, organized, and analyzed. Microsoft Access provides the organizational decision-maker a valuable tool facilitating data retrieval and use.

In this section, you explore Access database objects and work with table views. You also learn the difference between working in storage and memory to understand how changes to database objects are saved. Finally, you practice good file management techniques by backing up, compacting, and repairing databases.

Exploring, Describing, and Navigating Among the Objects in an Access Database

A ***field*** is a basic entity or data element, such as the name of a book or the telephone number of a publisher.

A ***record*** is a complete set of all of the data (fields) about one person, place, event, or idea.

A ***table*** is a collection of records. Every record in a table contains the same fields in the same order.

A ***database*** consists of one or more tables and the supporting objects used to get data into and out of the tables.

To understand database management effectively and to use Access productively, you should first learn the vocabulary. A ***field*** is a basic entity, data element, or category, such as book titles or telephone numbers. The field does not necessarily need to contain a value. For example, a field might store fax numbers for a firm's customers. However, some of the customers may not have a fax machine so the Fax field is blank for that record. A ***record*** is a complete set of all of the data (fields) about one person, place, event, or idea. For example, your name, homework, and test scores constitute your record in your instructor's grade book. A ***table***, the foundation of every database, is a collection of related records that contain fields to organize data. If you have used Excel, you will see the similarities between a spreadsheet and an Access table. Each column represents a field, and each row represents a record. Every record in a table contains the same fields in the same order. An instructor's grade book for one class is a table containing records of all students in one structure. A ***database*** consists of one or more tables and the supporting objects used to get data into and out of the tables.

Prior to the advent of database management software, organizations managed their data manually. They placed papers in file folders and organized the folders in multiple drawer filing cabinets. You can think of the filing cabinet in the manual system as a database. Each drawer full of folders in the filing cabinet corresponds to a table within the database. Figure 1.1 shows a college's database system from before the information age. File drawers (tables) contain student data. Each folder (record) contains facts (fields) about that student. The cabinet also contains drawers (tables) full of data about the faculty and the courses offered. Together, the tables combine to form a database system.

TIP Data Versus Information

Data and information are not synonymous, although, the terms often are used interchangeably. Data is the raw material and consists of the table (or tables) that comprise a database. Information is the finished product. Data is converted to information by selecting (filtering) records, by sequencing (sorting) the selected records, or by summarizing data from multiple records. Decisions in an organization are based on information compiled from multiple records, as opposed to raw data.

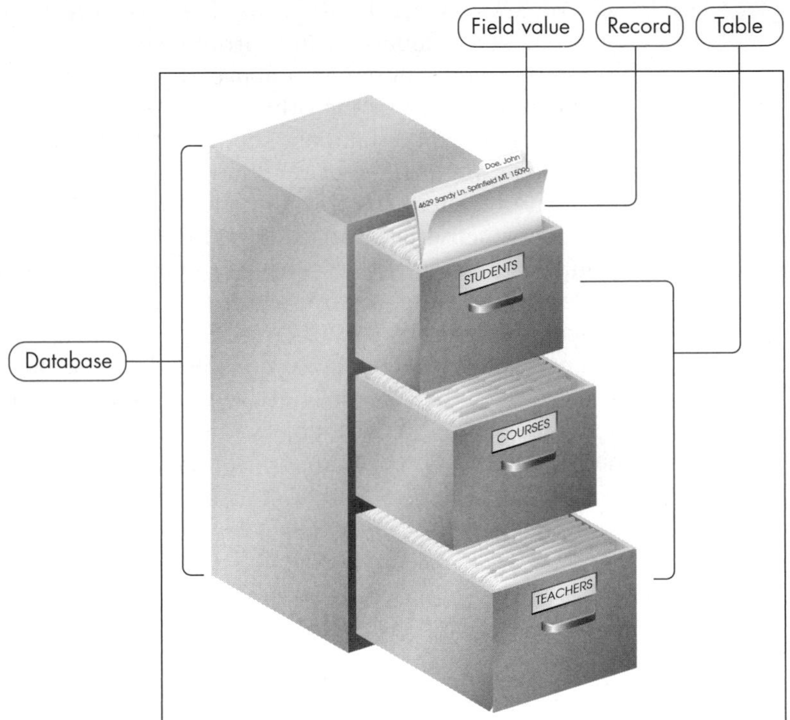

Figure 1.1 Primitive Database

Identify Access Interface Elements

Figure 1.2 shows how Microsoft Access appears onscreen. It contains two open windows—an application window for Microsoft Access and a document (database) window for the open database. Each window has its own title bar and icons. The title bar in the application window contains the name of the application (Microsoft Access) and the Minimize and Maximize (or Restore) icons. The title bar in the document (database) window contains the name of the object that is currently open (Employees table). Should more than one object be open at a time, the top of the document window will display tabs for each open object. The Access application window is maximized; therefore, Restore is visible.

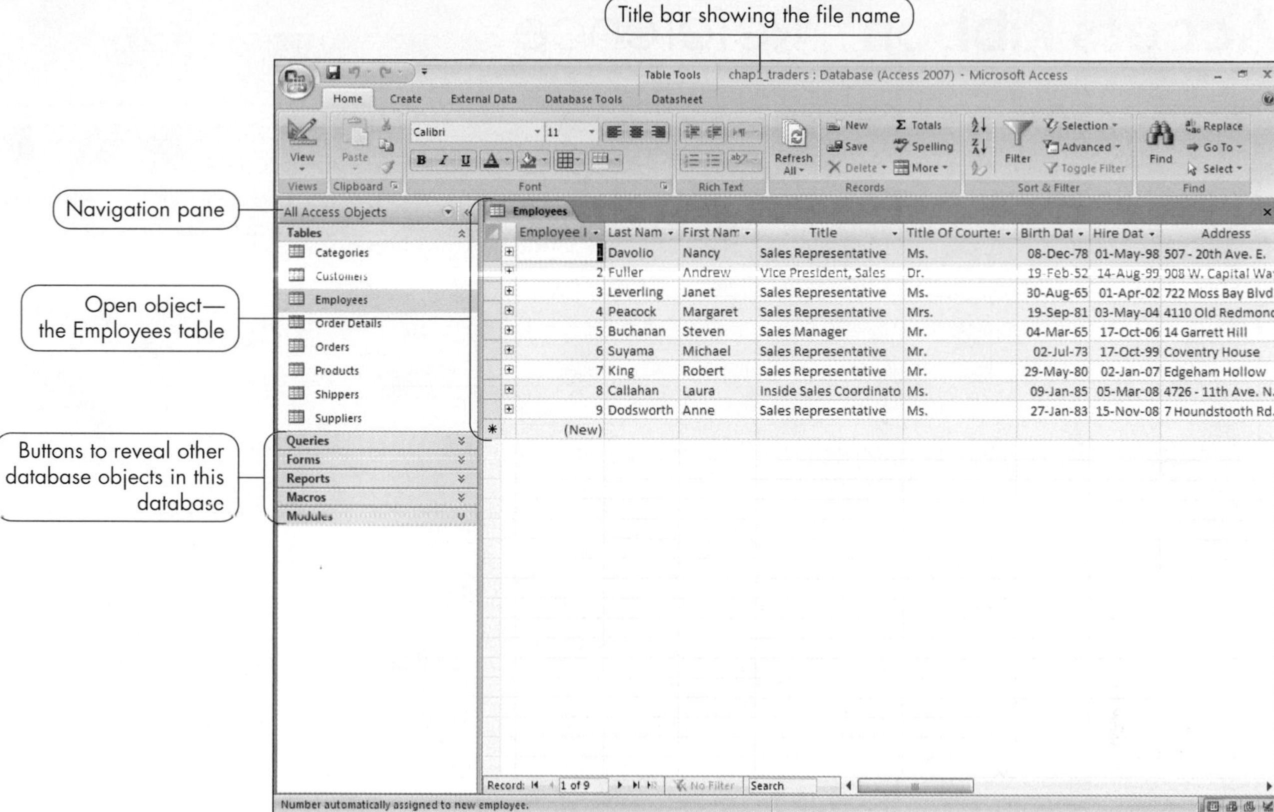

Figure 1.2 An Access Database

Let us look at an example of a database for an international food distribution company—The Northwind Traders. This firm sells specialty food items to restaurants and food shops around the world. It also purchases the products it sells from diversely located firms. The Northwind Traders Company database contains eight tables: Categories, Customers, Employees, Order Details, Orders, Products, Shippers, and Suppliers. Each table, in turn, consists of multiple records, corresponding to the folders in the file cabinet. The Employees table, for example, contains a record for every employee. Each record in the Employees table contains 17 fields—where data about the employee's education, address, photograph, position, and so on are stored. Occasionally, a field does not contain a value for a particular record. One of the employees, Margaret Peacock, did not provide a picture. The value of that field is missing. Access provides a placeholder to store the data when it is available. The Suppliers table has a record for each vendor from whom the firm purchases products, just as the Orders table has a record for each order. The real power of Access is derived from a database with multiple tables and the relationships that connect the tables.

An Access ***object*** contains the basic elements of the database.

The database window displays the various objects in an Access database. An Access ***object*** stores the basic elements of the database. Access uses six types of objects—tables, queries, forms, reports, macros, and modules. Every database must contain at least one table, and it may contain any, all, or none of the other objects. Each object type is accessed through the appropriate tab within the database window. Because of the interrelationships among objects, you may either view all of the objects of a type in a single place or view all of the related objects in a way that demonstrates their inner-connectivity. You select an object for viewing using the Navigation pane. The Navigation pane on the left side groups related objects.

The Reference page describes the tabs and groups on the Ribbon in Access 2007. You do not need to memorize most of these tabs and groups now. You will learn where things are located as you explore using the features.

Access Ribbon | Reference

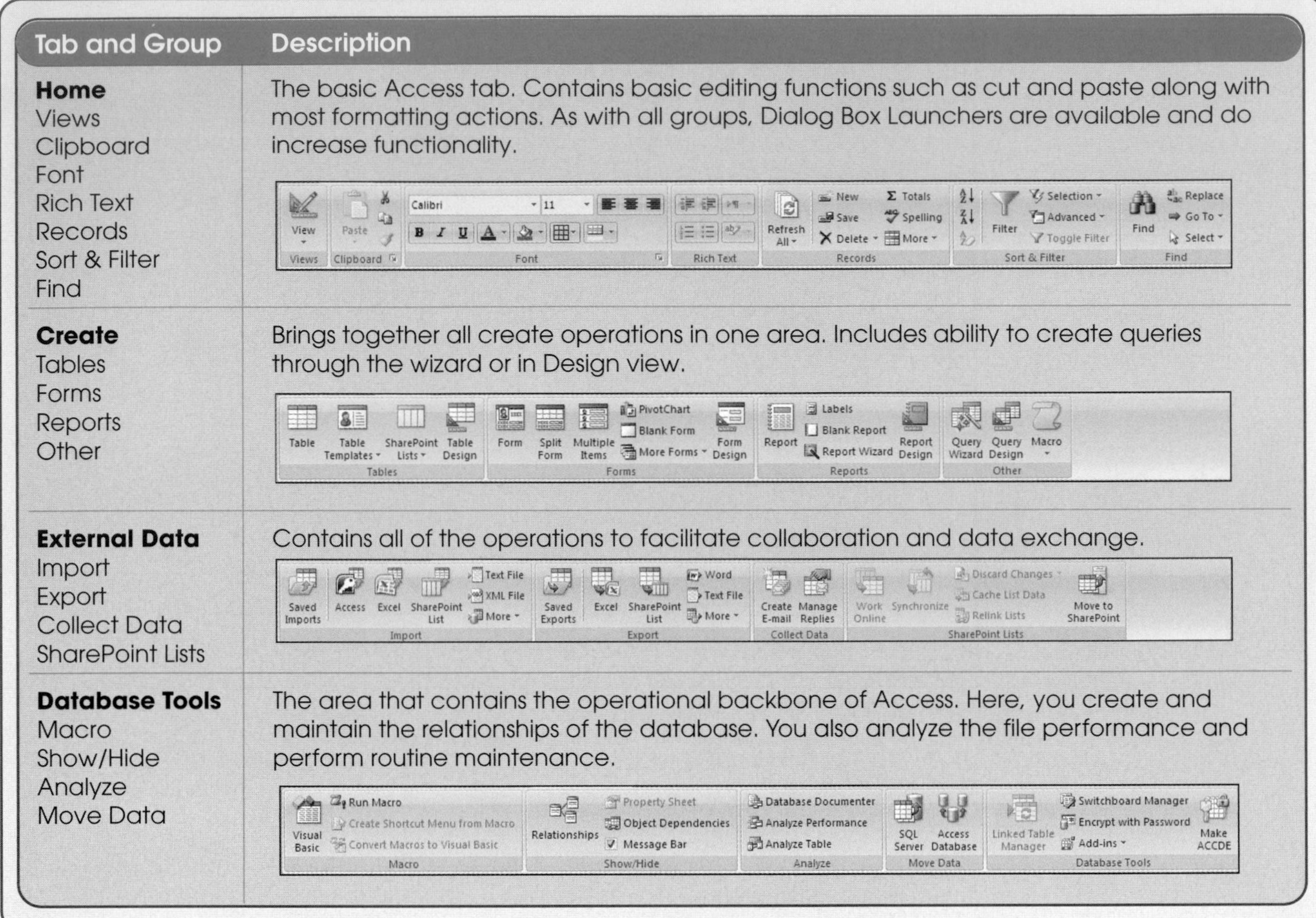

Tab and Group	Description
Home Views Clipboard Font Rich Text Records Sort & Filter Find	The basic Access tab. Contains basic editing functions such as cut and paste along with most formatting actions. As with all groups, Dialog Box Launchers are available and do increase functionality.
Create Tables Forms Reports Other	Brings together all create operations in one area. Includes ability to create queries through the wizard or in Design view.
External Data Import Export Collect Data SharePoint Lists	Contains all of the operations to facilitate collaboration and data exchange.
Database Tools Macro Show/Hide Analyze Move Data	The area that contains the operational backbone of Access. Here, you create and maintain the relationships of the database. You also analyze the file performance and perform routine maintenance.

Work with Table Views

The ***Datasheet view*** is a grid where you add, edit, and delete the records of a table.

The ***Design view*** is a different grid where you create and modify the properties of the table.

Access provides different ways in which to view a table and most other objects. The ***Datasheet view*** is a grid containing columns (fields) and rows (records). You can view, add, edit, and delete records of a table in the Datasheet view. You can use the ***Design view*** to create and modify the table by specifying the fields it will contain and their associated properties. The field type (for example, text or numeric data) and the field length are examples of field properties. If you need the values stored in a particular field to display as currency, you would modify the property of that field to ensure all values display appropriately.

Figure 1.3 shows the Datasheet view for the Customers table. The first row in the table displays the field names. Each additional row contains a record (the data for a specific customer). Each column represents a field (one fact about a customer). Every record in the table contains the same fields in the same order.

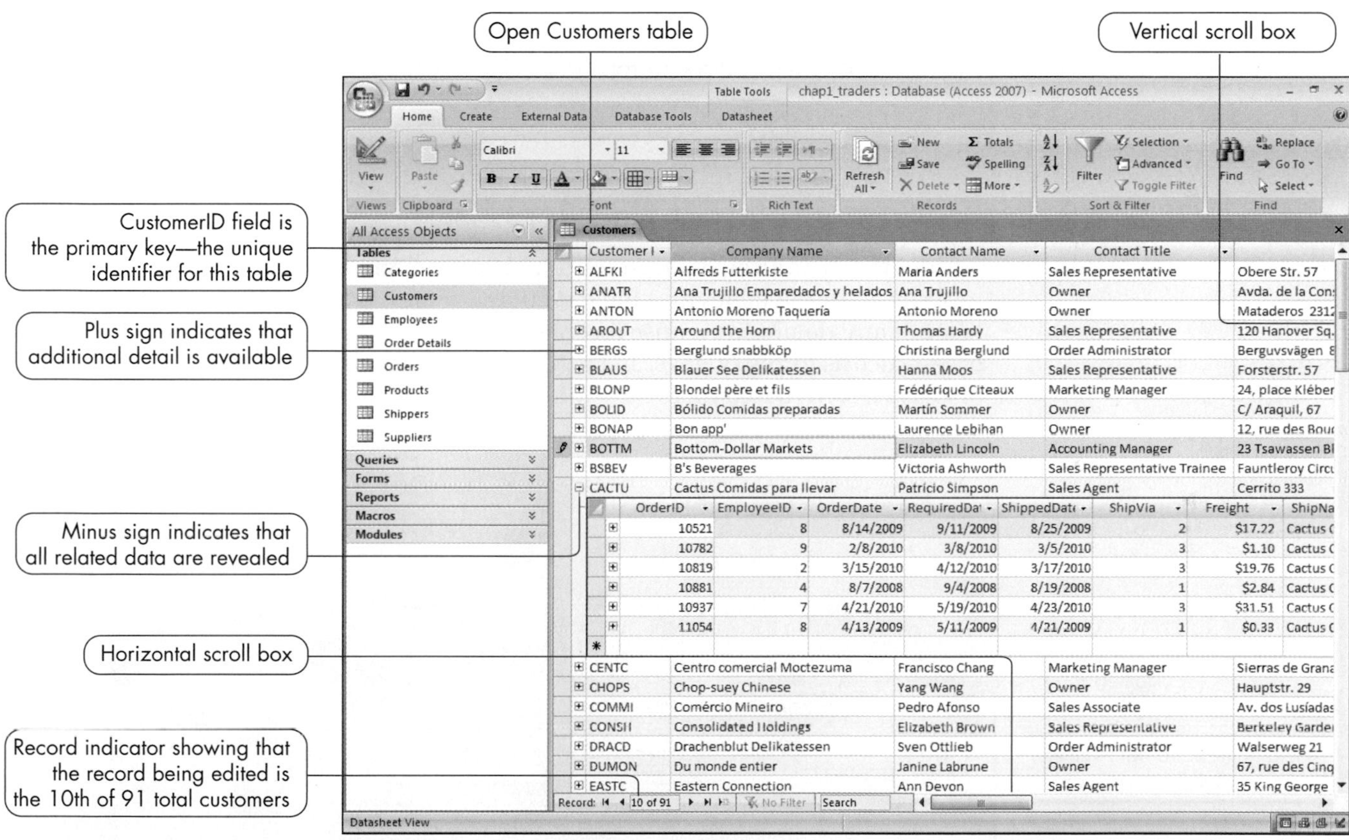

Figure 1.3 The Customers Table and Related Order Information

The ***primary key*** is the field that makes each record in a table unique.

The ***primary key*** is the field (or combination of fields) that makes each record in a table unique. The CustomerID is the primary key in the Customers table; it ensures that every record in a table is different from every other record, and it prevents the occurrence of duplicate records. Primary key fields may be numbers, letters, or a combination of both. In this case the primary key is text (letters).

The Navigation bar at the bottom of Figure 1.3 shows a table with 91 records and record number 10 as the current record. You can work on only one record at a time. The vertical scroll bar at the right of the window shows that more records exist in the table than you can see at one time. The horizontal scroll bar at the bottom of the window indicates that you cannot see an entire record.

The pencil icon at the left of the record indicates that the data in the current record are being edited and that the changes have not yet been saved. The pencil icon disappears after you complete the data entry and move to another record, because Access saves data automatically as soon as you move from one record to the next.

Figure 1.4 displays the navigation buttons that you use to move within most Access objects. You may navigate using commands to go to the last and first records, advance and go back one record, and add a new record.

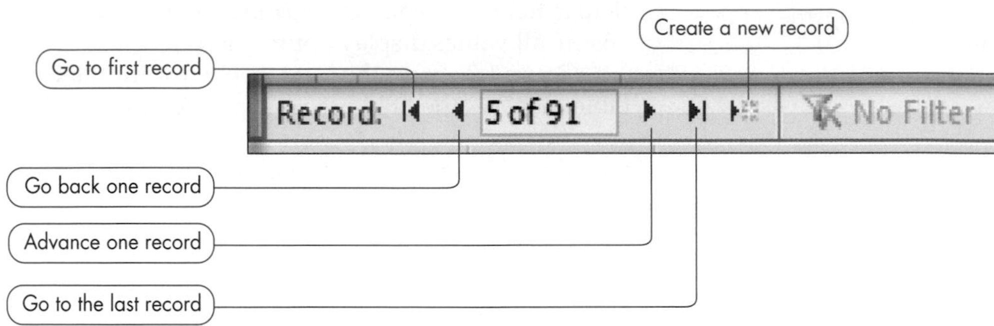

Figure 1.4 Navigation Buttons

Use Forms, Queries, and Reports

As previously indicated, an Access database is made up of different types of objects together with the tables and the data they contain. A table (or set of tables) is at the heart of any database because it contains the actual data. The other objects in a database—such as forms, queries, and reports—are based on an underlying table. Figure 1.5 displays a form based on the Customers table shown earlier.

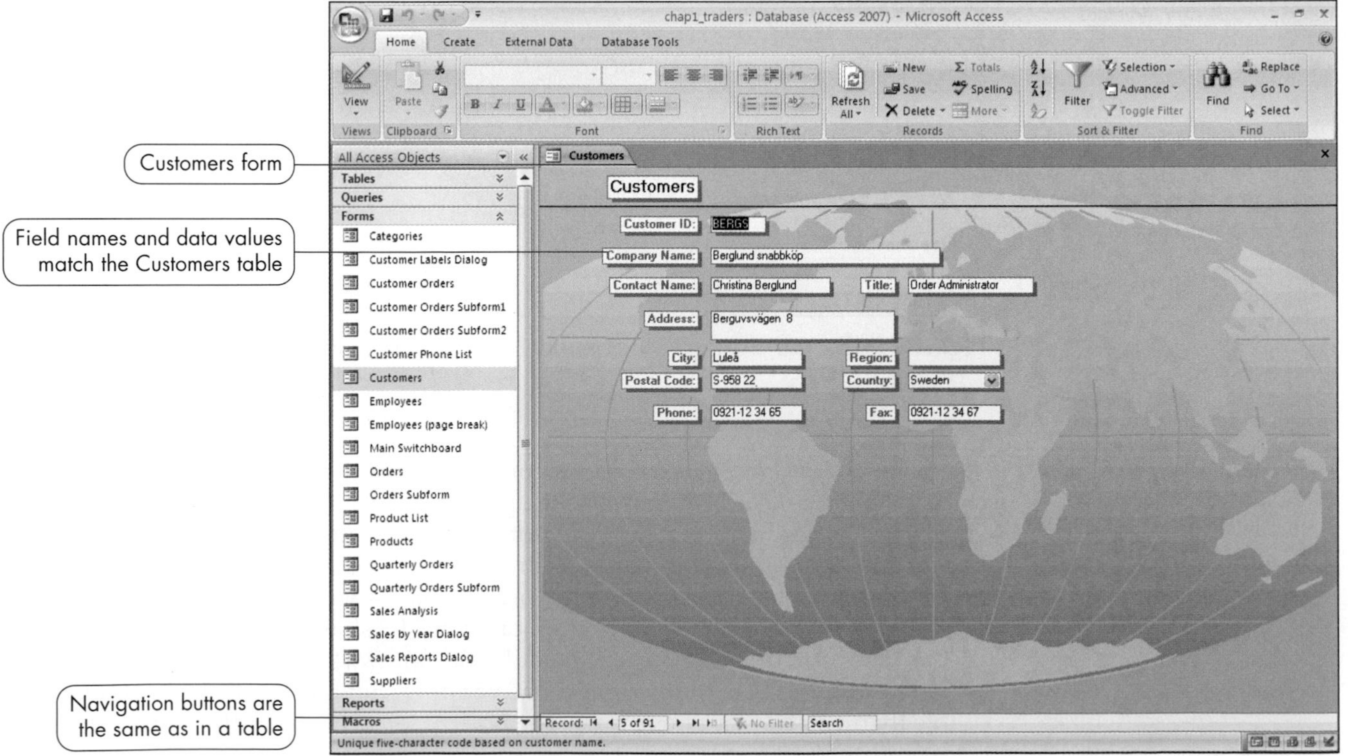

Figure 1.5 Customers Form

A ***form*** is an interface that enables you to enter or modify record data.

A ***form*** is an interface that enables you to enter or modify record data. Commands may appear in the form to add a new record, print a record, or close the form. The form provides access to all of the data maintenance operations that are available through a table. The status bar and navigation buttons at the bottom of the form are similar to those that appear at the bottom of a table. You use the form in Datasheet view, but create and edit the form structure in Design view.

A ***query*** provides information that answers a question.

A ***criterion*** (***criteria***, pl) is a rule or norm that is the basis for making judgments.

Figure 1.6 displays a query that lists the products that the firm purchases from a particular supplier. A ***query*** provides information that answers a question based on the data within an underlying table or tables. The Suppliers table, for example, contains records for many vendors, but the query in Figure 1.6 shows only the products that were supplied by a specific supplier. If you want to know the details about a specific supplier, you establish a criterion to specify which supplier you need to know about. A ***criterion*** (***criteria***, pl) is a rule or norm that is the basis for making judgments. If you need the names of all the suppliers in New York, you set a criterion to identify the New York suppliers. The results would yield only those suppliers from New York. Query results are similar in appearance to the underlying table, except that the query contains selected records and/or selected fields for those records. The query also may list the records in a different sequence from that of the table. (You also can use a query to add new records and modify existing records.) If you have a query open and notice an error in an address field, you can edit the record, and the edited value would immediately and permanently transfer to the table storing that record. Queries may be opened in Datasheet view or Design view. You use the Datasheet view to examine the query output and use the Design view to specify which fields and records to include in the query.

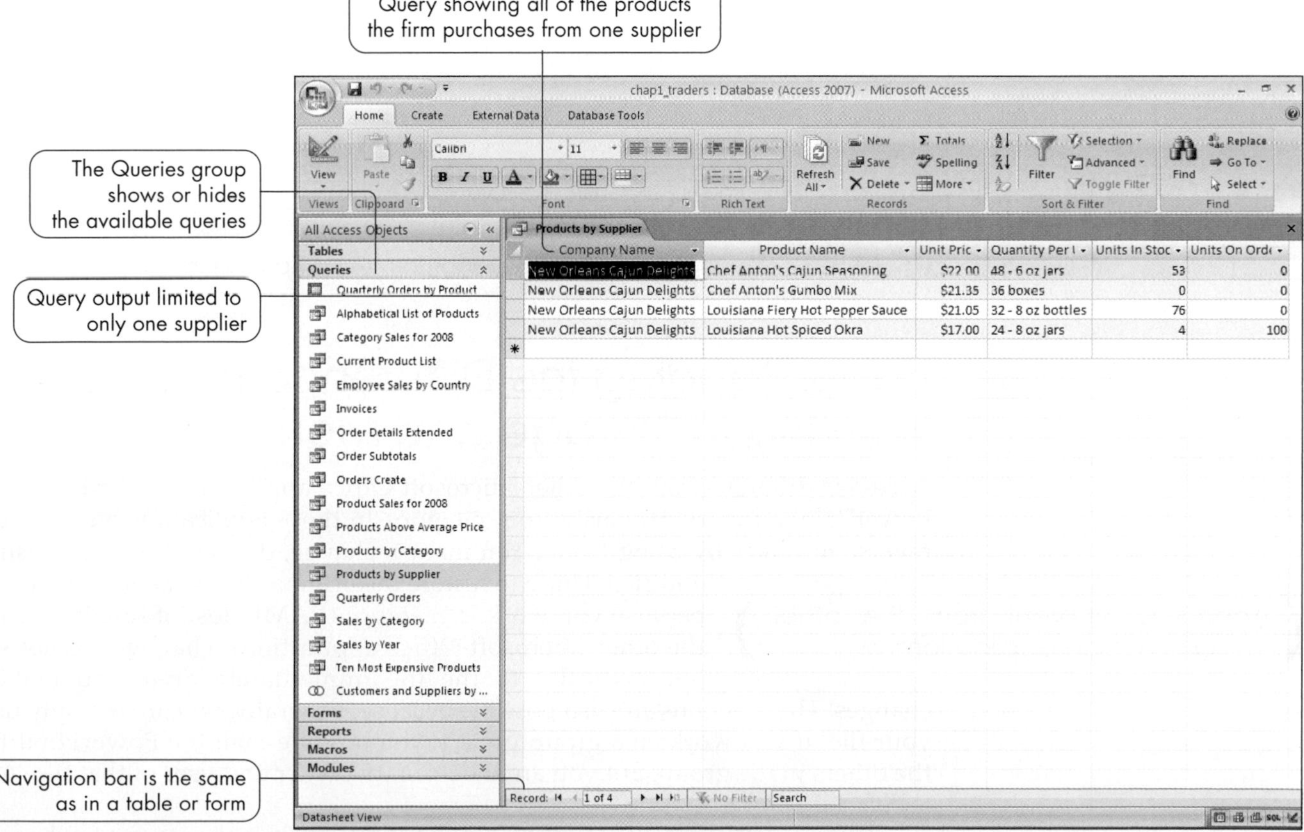

Figure 1.6 Results of a Query Shown in Datasheet View

A ***report*** presents database information professionally.

Figure 1.7 displays a report that contains the same information as the query in Figure 1.6. A ***report*** contains professionally formatted information from underlying tables or queries. Because the report information contains a more enhanced format than a query or table, you place database output in a report to print. Access provides different views for designing, modifying, and running reports. Most Access users use only the Print Preview, Print Layout, and Report views of a report.

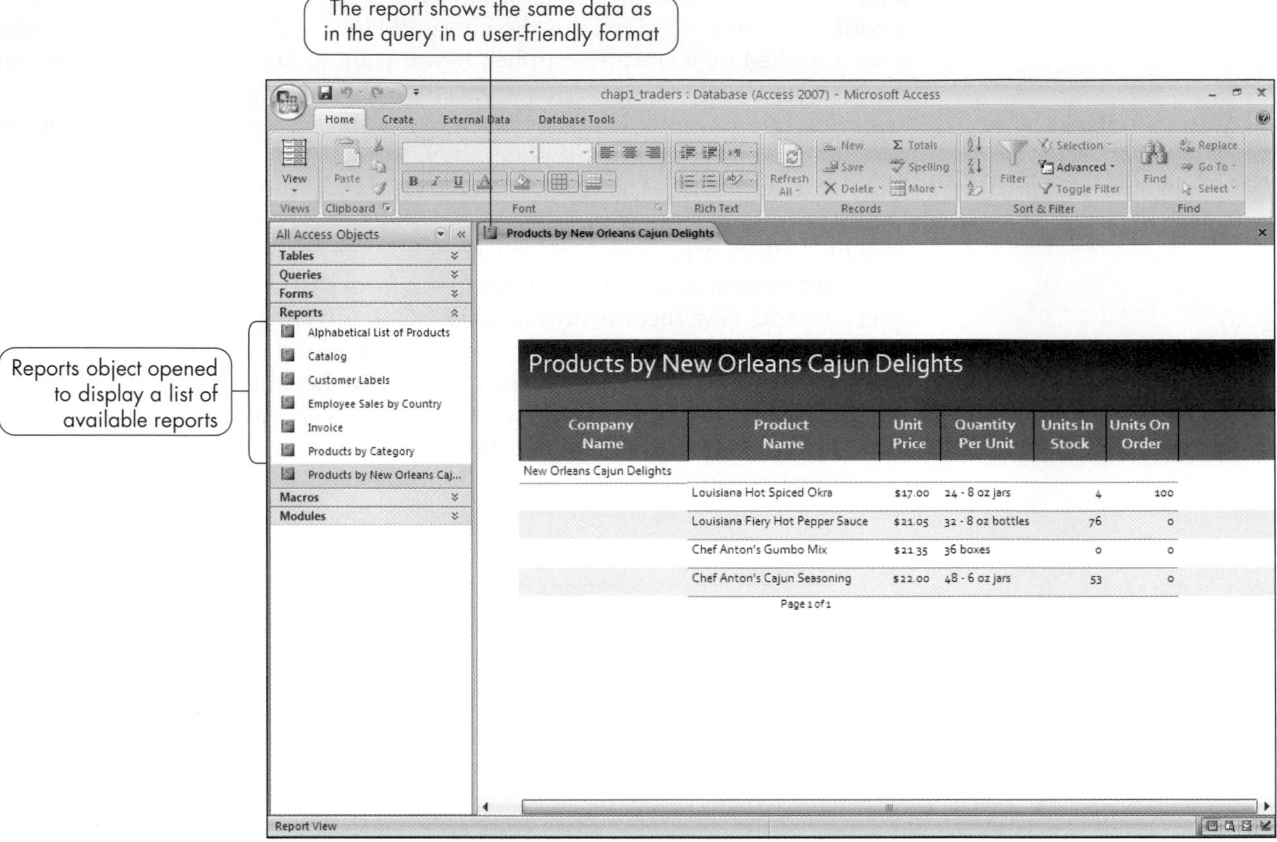

Figure 1.7 Report Displaying the Query Information from Figure 1.6

Understanding the Difference Between Working in Storage and Memory

Access is different from the other Microsoft Office applications. Word, Excel, and PowerPoint all work primarily from memory. In those applications you can easily reverse mistakes by using Undo. You make a change, discover that you dislike it, and click Undo to restore the original. These actions are possible because you work in memory (RAM) most of the time while in the other Microsoft Office applications; changes are not saved automatically to the file immediately after you make the changes. These actions are also possible because, generally, you are the only user of your file. If you work on a group project, you might e-mail the PowerPoint file to the others in the group, but you are the primary owner and user of that file. Access is *different*.

(Access is different from the other Microsoft Office applications.)

Access works primarily from storage. When you make a change to a field's content in an Access table (for example, changing a customer's area code), Access saves your changes as soon as you move the insertion point to a different record; you do not need to click Save. You can click Undo to reverse several editing changes (such as changing an area code and a contact name) for a single record **immediately** after making the changes to that record. However, unlike other Office programs that let you continue

Undoing actions, you cannot use Undo to reverse edits to more than the last record you edited or to restore a field if you delete it.

Multiple users can work on the database simultaneously. As long as no two users attempt to interact with the same record at the same time, the system updates as it goes. This also means that any reports extracting the information from the database contain the most up-to-date data. The only time you need to click Save is when you are creating or changing a structural element, such as a table, query, form, or report.

TIP Save Edits While Keeping a Record Active

When you want to save changes to a record you are editing while staying on the same record, press Shift+Enter. The pencil icon, indicating an editing mode, disappears, indicating that the change is saved.

Be careful to avoid accidentally typing something in a record and pressing Enter. Doing so saves the change, and you can retrieve the original data if you are lucky enough to remember to click Undo immediately before making or editing other records. Because Access is a relational database, several other related objects (queries, reports, or forms) could also be permanently changed. In Access, one file holds everything. All of the objects—tables, forms, queries, and reports—are saved both individually and as part of the Access collection.

TIP Data Validation

No system, no matter how sophisticated, can produce valid output from invalid input. Thus, good systems are built to anticipate errors in data entry and to reject those errors prior to saving a record. Access will automatically prevent you from adding records with a duplicate primary key or entering invalid data into a numeric or date field. The database developer has the choice whether to require other types of validation, such as requiring the author's name.

Practicing Good File Management

You must exercise methodical and deliberate file management techniques to avoid damaging data. Every time you need to open a file, this book will direct you to copy the file to your production folder and rename the copied file. Name the production folder with **Your Name Access Production**. You would not copy a real database and work in the copy often. However, as you learn, you will probably make mistakes. Following the practice of working in a copied file will facilitate mistake recovery during the learning process.

Further, it matters to which type of media you save your files. Access does not work from some media. Access runs best from a hard or network drive because those drives have sufficient access speed to support the software. Access speed measures the time it takes for the storage device to make the file content available for use. If you work from your own computer, create the production folder in the My Documents folder on the hard drive. Most schools lock their hard drives so that students cannot permanently save files there. If your school provides you with storage space on the school's network, store your production folder there. The advantage to using the network is that the network administration staff backs up files regularly. If you have no storage on the school network, your next best storage option is a thumb drive, also known as USB jump drive, flash drive, Pen drive, or stick drive.

TIP Do Not Use This Media

Because storage space is limited, you should not use floppy disks or Zip disks. Furthermore, you should not use CDs or DVDs because Access must constantly save changes to the file, a process that does not work with storage media that have slow access speed or limited write privileges. ***Access speed*** measures the time it takes for the storage device to locate the file, open it, and transfer it to memory so that the file content is available for use. However, you may back up your work or archive it to these storage devices.

Access speed measures the time it takes for the storage device to make the file content available for use.

All of the objects in an Access database are stored in a single file. You can open a database from within Windows Explorer by double-clicking the file name. You also can open the database from within Access through the Recent Documents list or by clicking the Microsoft Office Button (noted as Office Button only in this textbook) and selecting Open from the Office menu. The individual objects within a database are opened from the database window.

Backing Up, Compacting, and Repairing Access Files

Data is the lifeblood of any organization. Imagine what would happen to a firm that loses the records of the orders placed but not shipped or the charity that loses the list of donor contribution records or the hospital that loses the digital records of patient X-rays. What would happen to the employee who "accidentally" deleted mission-critical data? What would happen to the other employees who did not lose the mission-critical data? Fortunately, Access recognizes how critical backup procedures are to organizations and makes backing up the database files easy.

Back Up a Database

You back up an Access file (and all of the objects it contains) with just a few mouse clicks. To back up files, click the Office Button and select Manage from the Office menu. When you select Back Up Database, the Save As dialog box opens. You may use controls in the Save As dialog box to specify storage location and file name. Access provides a default file name that is the original file name followed by the date. In most organizations, this step is useful because the Information Technology department backs up every database each day.

Compact and Repair a Database

All databases have a tendency to expand with use. This expansion will occur without new information being added. Simply using the database, creating queries and running them, or applying and removing filters may cause the file to store inefficiently. Because the files tend to be rather large to start with, any growth creates problems. Access provides another utility, Compact and Repair, under the Manage submenu in the Office menu that addresses this issue. The Compact and Repair utility acts much like a disk defragmenter utility. It finds related file sectors and reassembles them in one location if they become scattered from database use. You should compact and repair your database each day when you close the file. This step often will decrease file size by 50% or more. Access closes any open objects during the compact and repair procedure, so it is a good idea to close any objects in the database prior to compacting so that you will control if any design changes will be saved or not.

In the next hands-on exercise, you will work with a database from an international gourmet food distributor, the Northwind Traders. This firm purchases food items from suppliers and sells them to restaurants and specialty food shops. It depends on the data stored in the Access database to make daily decisions.

Hands-On Exercises

1 | Introduction to Databases

Skills covered: 1. Create a Production Folder and Copy an Access File **2.** Open an Access File **3.** Edit a Record **4.** Navigate an Access Form and Add Records **5.** Recognize the Table and Form Connectivity and Delete a Record **6.** Back Up and Compact the Database

Step 1 Create a Production Folder and Copy an Access File

Refer to Figure 1.8 as you complete Step 1.

a. Right-click **My Computer** on the desktop and select **Explore** from the shortcut menu.

   This step opens the Explore utility in a two-pane view that facilitates transferring materials between folders.

b. Determine where your production folder will reside and double-click that location. For example, double-click the **My Documents** folder if that is where your files will reside.

   For the remainder of this book, it is assumed that your production folder resides in the My Document folder on the hard drive. Your folder may actually exist on another drive. What is important is that you (1) create and use the folder and (2) remember where it is.

c. Right-click anywhere on a blank spot in the right pane of the Exploring window. Select **New**, and then select **Folder** from the shortcut menu.

   A new folder is created with the default name, New Folder, selected and ready to be renamed.

d. Type **Your Name Access Production** and press **Enter**.

e. Open the folder that contains the student data files that accompany this textbook.

f. Find the file named *chap1_ho1-3_traders.accdb*, right-click the file, and select **Copy** from the shortcut menu.

g. Go to the newly created production folder named with your name. Right-click a blank area in the right side of the Exploring window and select **Paste**.

   You have created a copy of the original *chap1_ho1-3_traders.accdb* file. You will work with the copy. In the event that you make mistakes, the original remains intact in the student data folder. You can recopy it and rework the exercise if necessary.

h. Rename the newly copied file **your_name_chap1_ho1-3_traders_solution.accdb**.

   You need to remember to rename all of the solution files with your name. If your instructor requests that you submit your work for evaluation using a shared folder on the campus network, each file must have a unique name. You risk overwriting another student's work (or having someone overwrite your work) if you do not name your files with your name and the file designation.

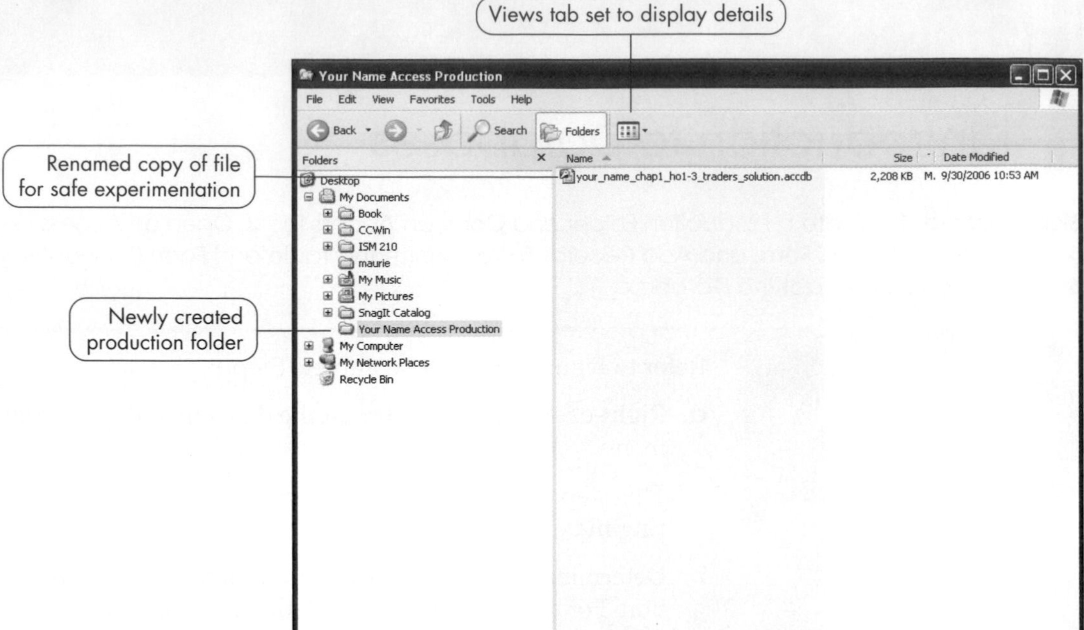

Figure 1.8 Production Folder Created Showing Copied and Renamed File

Step 2
Open an Access File

Refer to Figure 1.9 as you complete Step 2.

a. Double-click the *your_name_chap1_ho1-3_traders_solution* file to open it.

This step launches Access and opens the Explore file. From now on, this book will refer to the files without the *your_name* prefix.

b. Click **Options** on the Security Warning toolbar. See Figure 1.9.

Each time you open an Access file for the remainder of the class, you will need to enable the content. Several viruses and worms may be transmitted via Access files. You may be reasonably confident of the trustworthiness of the files in this book. However, if an Access file arrives as an attachment from an unsolicited e-mail message, you should not open it. Microsoft warns all users of Access files that a potential threat exists every time the file is opened.

c. Click **Enable this content**, and then click **OK**.

The Microsoft Office Security Options dialog box closes and the Security Warning toolbar disappears.

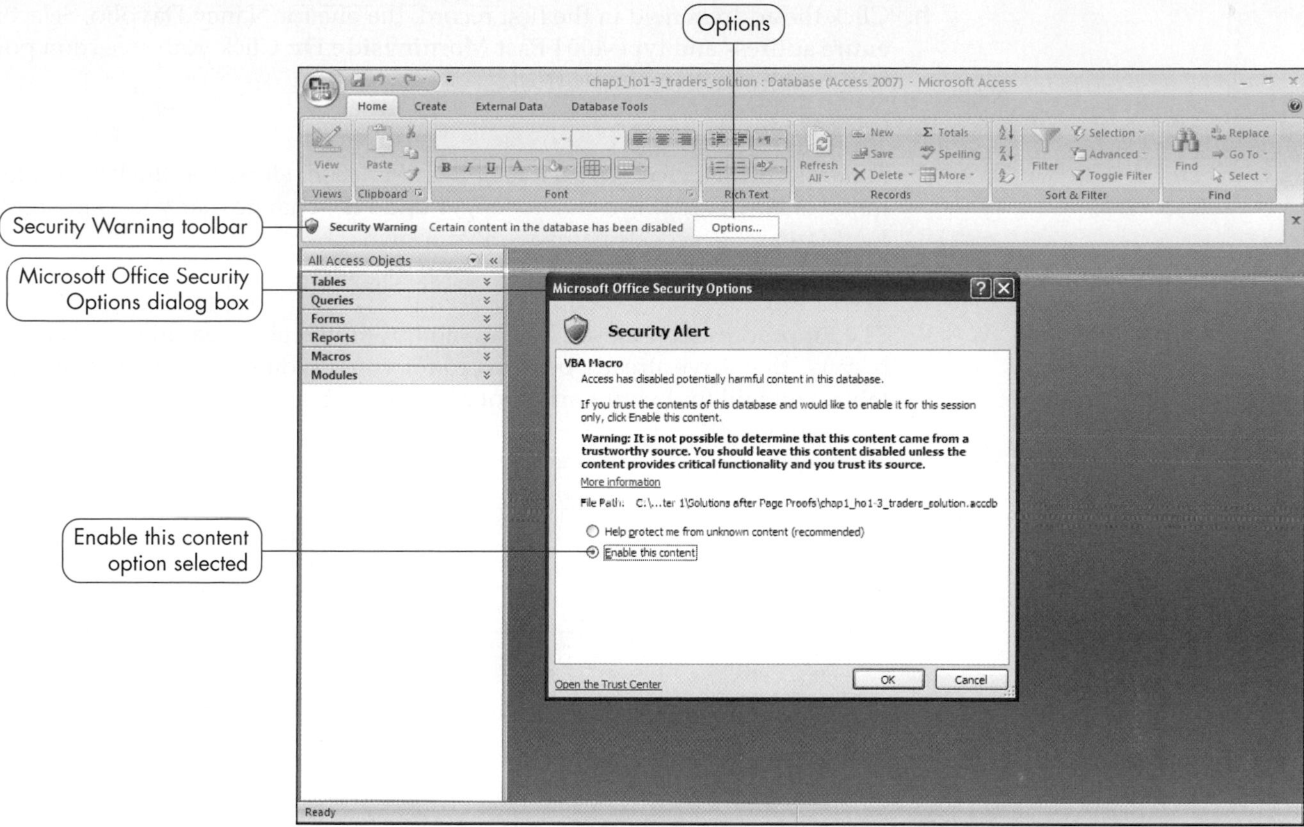

Figure 1.9 Microsoft Office Security Options Dialog Box

Step 3
Edit a Record

Refer to Figure 1.10 as you complete Step 3.

a. Click **Tables** in the Navigation pane to expand the list of available tables.

The list of tables contained in the database file opens.

b. Double-click the **Employees table** to open it. See Figure 1.10.

c. Click the insertion point in the fourth row. Double-click *Peacock* in the LastName field. The entire name highlights. Type **your last name** to replace *Peacock*.

d. Press **Tab** to move to the next field in the fourth row. Replace *Margaret* with **your first name**.

You have made changes to two fields in the same record (row); the pencil displays in the row selector box.

e. Click **Undo** on the Quick Access Toolbar.

Your first name reverts back to Margaret because you have not yet left the record.

f. Type your name again to replace *Margaret* with **your first name**. Press **Enter**.

You should now be in the Title field and your title, *Sales Representative*, is selected. The pencil icon still displays in the row selector.

g. Click anywhere in the third row where Janet Leverling's data are stored.

The pencil icon disappears; your changes to the table have been saved.

h. Click the address field in the first record, the one for Nancy Davolio. Select the entire address and type **4004 East Morningside Dr**. Click your insertion point into Andrew Fuller's name field.

i. Click **Undo**.

Nancy's address changes back to *507 - 20th Ave. E.* However, the Undo command is now faded. You can no longer undo the change that you made replacing Margaret Peacock's name with your own.

j. Click **Close** to close the Employees table. See Figure 1.10.

The Employees table closes. You are not prompted about saving your changes, because they have already been saved for you. If you reopen the Employees table, you will find your name, not Margaret's, because Access works in storage, not memory.

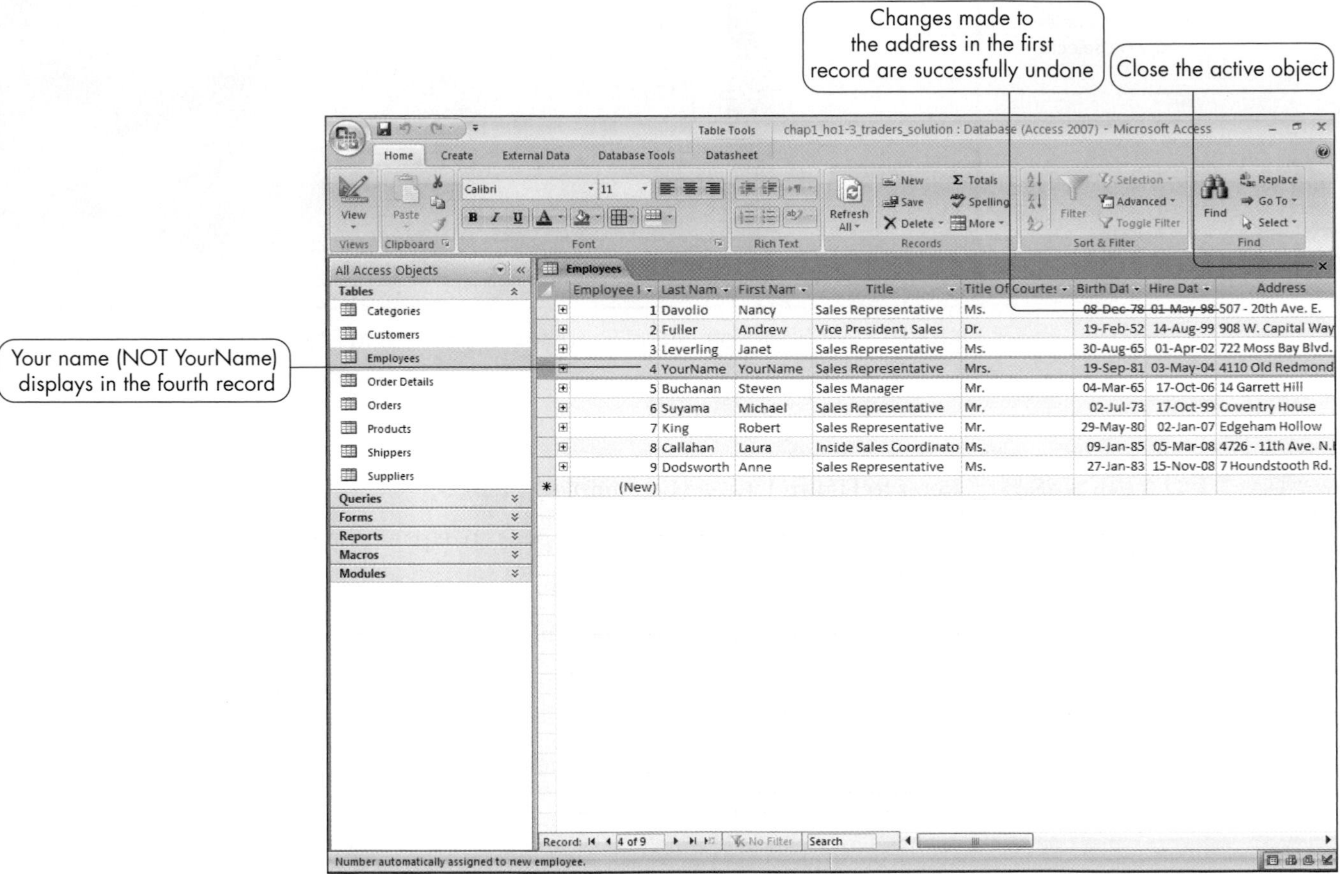

Figure 1.10 The Edited Employees Table

Step 4
Navigate an Access Form and Add Records

Refer to Figure 1.11 as you complete Step 4.

a. Click **Tables** in the Navigation pane to close it.

The list of available tables collapses.

b. Click **Forms** in the Navigation pane to expand it.

c. Double-click the **Products form** to open it.

d. Refer to Figure 1.4 and practice with the navigation buttons above the status bar to move from one record to the next. Click **Next record**, and then click **Last record**.

e. Click **Find** in the Find group on the Home tab.

The Find command is an ideal way to search for specific records within a table, form, or query. You can search a single field or the entire record, match all or part of the selected field(s), move forward or back in a table, or specify a case-sensitive search. The Replace command can be used to substitute one value for another. Be careful, however, about using the Replace All option for global replacement because unintended replacements are far too common.

f. Type **ikura** in the *Find What* section of the Find and Replace dialog box. Check to make sure that the *Look In* option is set to **Product Name** and the *Match* option is set to **Whole Field**. The *Search* option should be set to **All**. Click **Find Next**.

You should see the information about *ikura*, a seafood supplied by Tokyo Traders.

g. Type **Grandma** in the *Find What* box, click the **Match drop-down arrow**, and select **Any Part of Field**. Click **Find Next**.

You should see information about Grandma's Boysenberry Spread. Setting the match option to any part of the field will return a match even if it is contained in the middle of a word.

h. Close the Find and Replace dialog box.

i. Click **New (blank) record** located on the Navigation bar.

j. Enter the following information for a new product. Press **Tab** to navigate the form.

Field Name	**Value to Type**
Product Name	Your Name Pecan Pie
Supplier	Grandma Kelly's Homestead (Note, display the drop-down list to enter this information quickly)
Category	Confections (Use the drop-down box here, too)
Quantity Per Unit	1
Unit Price	25.00
Units in Stock	18
Units on Order	50
Reorder Level	20

As soon as you begin typing in the product name box, Access assigns a Product ID, in this case 78, to the record. The Product ID is used as the primary key in the Products table.

k. Close the Products form.

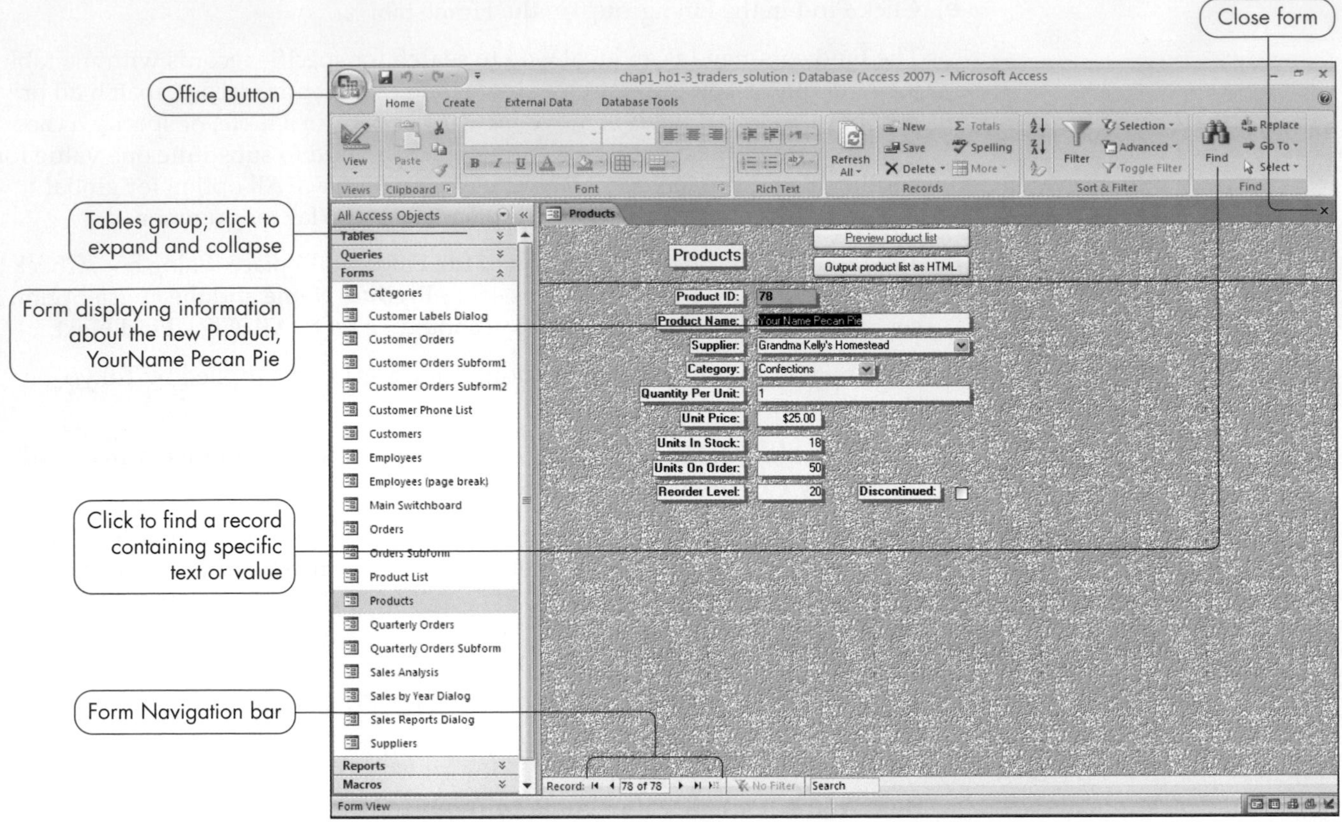

Figure 1.11 The Newly Created Record in the Products Form

Step 5
Recognize the Table and Form Connectivity and Delete a Record

Refer to Figure 1.12 as you complete Step 5.

a. Click **Forms** in the Navigation pane to close it.

   The list of available forms collapses.

b. Click **Tables** in the Navigation pane to expand it.

   The list of available tables expands. You need to assure yourself that the change you made to the Products form will transfer to the Products table.

c. Double-click the **Products table** to open it.

d. Click **Last record** on the Navigation bar.

   The Products form was designed to make data entry easier. It is linked to the Products table. Your newly created record about the Pecan Pie product name is stored in the Products table even though you created it in the form.

e. Navigate to the fifth record in the table, *Chef Anton's Gumbo Mix*.

f. Use the horizontal scroll bar to scroll right until you see the *Discontinued* field.

   The check mark in the Discontinued check box tells you that this product has been discontinued.

g. Click the row selector box at the left of the window (see Figure 1.12).

   The row highlights with a gold-colored border.

h. Press **Delete**.

An error message appears. It tells you that you cannot delete this record because the table, Order Details, has related records. Even though the product is now discontinued and none of it is in stock, it cannot be deleted from the table because related records are connected to it. A customer in the past ordered this product. If you first deleted all of the orders in the Order Details table that referenced this product, you would be permitted to delete the product from the Products table.

i. Read the error message. Click **OK**.

j. Navigate to the last record. Click the *row selector* to highlight the entire row.

k. Press **Delete**. STOP. Read the error message.

A warning box appears. It tells you that this action cannot be undone. This product can be deleted because it was just created. No customers have ever ordered it so no related records are in the system.

l. Click **No**. You do not want to delete this record.

TROUBLESHOOTING: If you clicked Yes and deleted the record, return to Step 4j. Reenter the information for this record. You will need it later in the lesson.

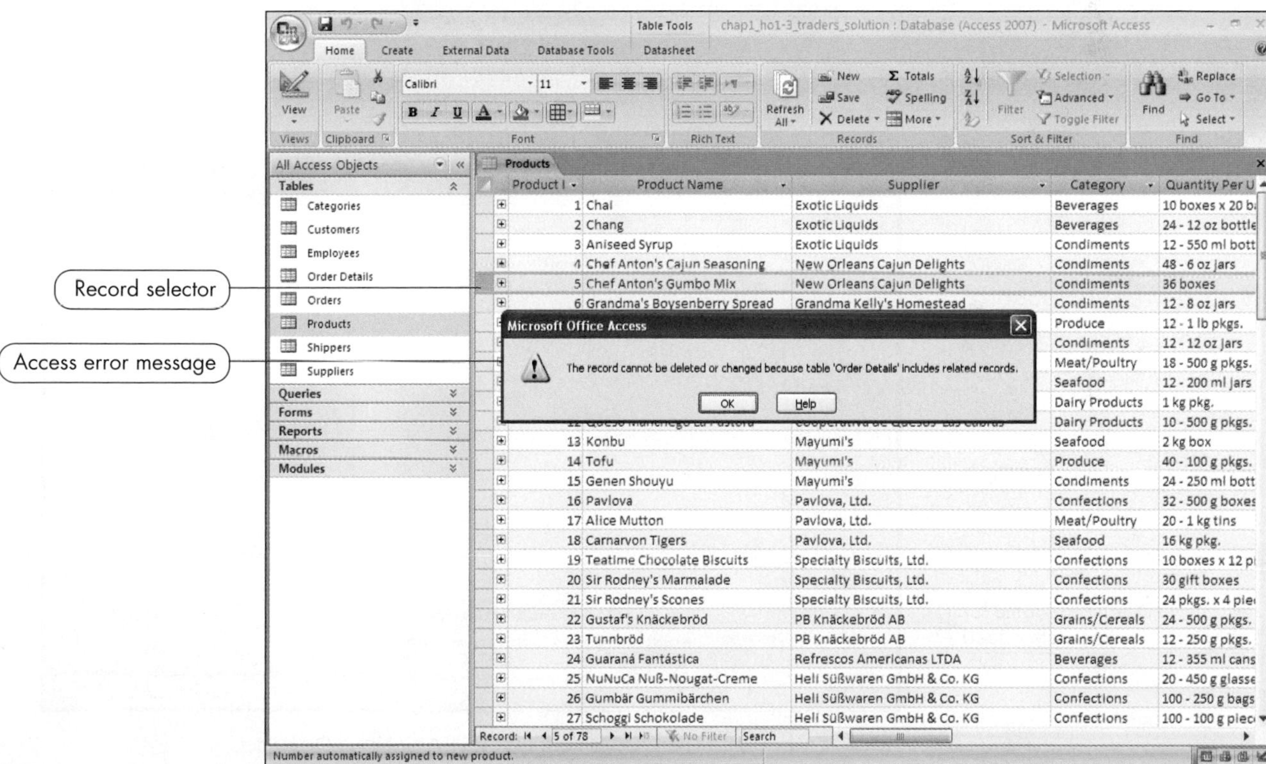

Figure 1.12 How Databases Work to Protect Data

Step 6
Back Up and Compact the Database

Refer to Figure 1.13 as you complete Step 6.

a. Click the **Office Button** and select **Manage**.

   The Manage menu gives you access to three critically important tools.

b. Select **Compact and Repair Database**.

   Databases tend to get larger and larger as you use them. This feature acts as a defragmenter and eliminates wasted space. As it runs, it closes any open objects in the database.

c. Click the **Office Button**, select **Manage**, and then select **Back Up Database**.

   The Save As dialog box opens. The backup utility assigns a default name by adding a date to your file name.

d. Type **chap1_ho1_traders_solution** and click **Save**.

   You just created a backup of the database after completing the first hands-on exercise. The original database *chap1_ho1-3_traders_solution* remains onscreen. If you ruin the original database as you complete the second hands-on exercise, you can use the backup file you just created.

e. Close the file and exit Access if you do not want to continue with the next exercise at this time.

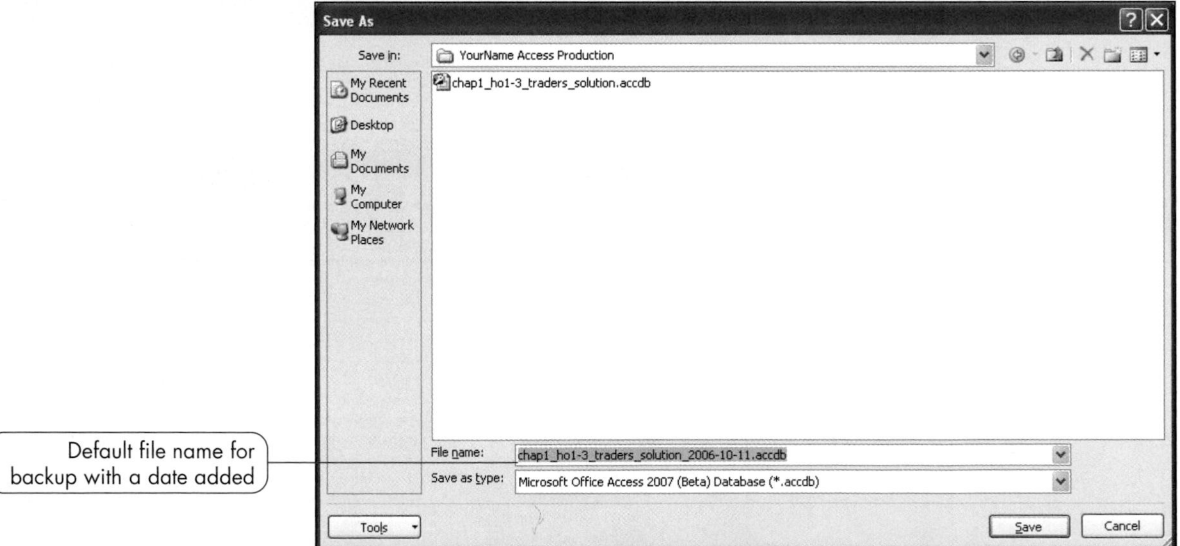

Figure 1.13 Save As Dialog Box to Back Up a Database

Filters, Sorts, and Access Versus Excel

Microsoft Office provides you with many tools that you may use to identify and extract only the records needed at the moment. For example, you might need to know which suppliers are located in New Orleans or which customers have not ordered any products in the last 60 days. You might use that information to identify possible disruptions to product deliveries or customers who may need a telephone call to see if all is well. Both Access and Excel contain powerful tools that enable you to sift through data and extract the information you need and arrange it in a way that makes sense to you. An important part of becoming a proficient computer user is recognizing when to use which tool to accomplish a task.

In this section, you learn how to create filters to examine records and organize these records by sorting table data. You also will examine the logic of Access and Excel in more detail. You will investigate when to use which application to complete a given task.

Creating Filters

A ***filter*** lets you find a subset of data meeting your specifications.

In the first hands-on exercise, you used data from an existing table to obtain information from the database. You created new records and saw that the changes made in a form update data in the associated table data. You found the pecan pie, but you also saw lots of other products. When all of the information needed is contained in a single table, form, report, or query, you can open the object in the Datasheet view, and then apply a filter to display only the records of interest to you. A ***filter*** displays a subset of records; from the object according to specified criteria. You use filters to examine data. Applying a filter does not delete any records; it simply hides extraneous records from your view.

Figure 1.14 displays a Customers table with 91 records. The records in the table are displayed in sequence according to the CustomerID, which is also the primary key (the field or combination of fields that uniquely identifies a record). The status bar indicates that the active record is the sixth in the table. Let's explore how you would retrieve a partial list of those records, such as records of customers in Germany only.

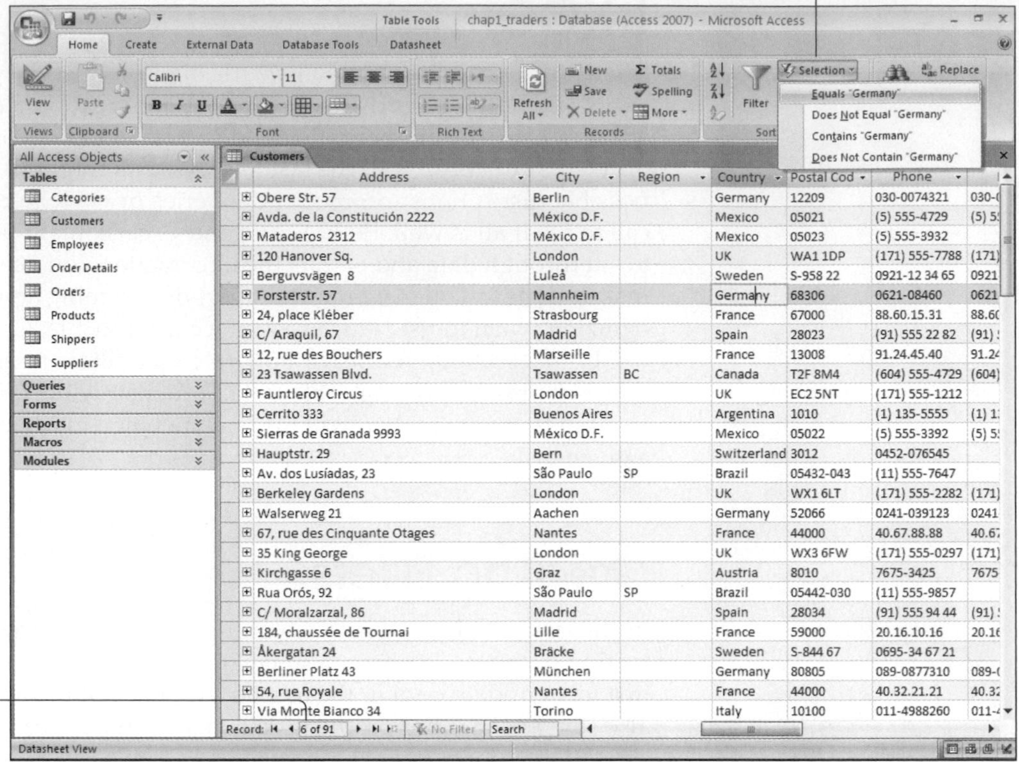

Figure 1.14 Unfiltered Table with Appropriate Sort Options Selected

Figure 1.15 displays a filtered view of the same table in which we see only the customers in Germany. The Navigation bar shows that this is a filtered list and that the filter found 11 records satisfying the criteria. (The Customers table still contains the original 91 records, but only 11 records are visible with the filter applied.)

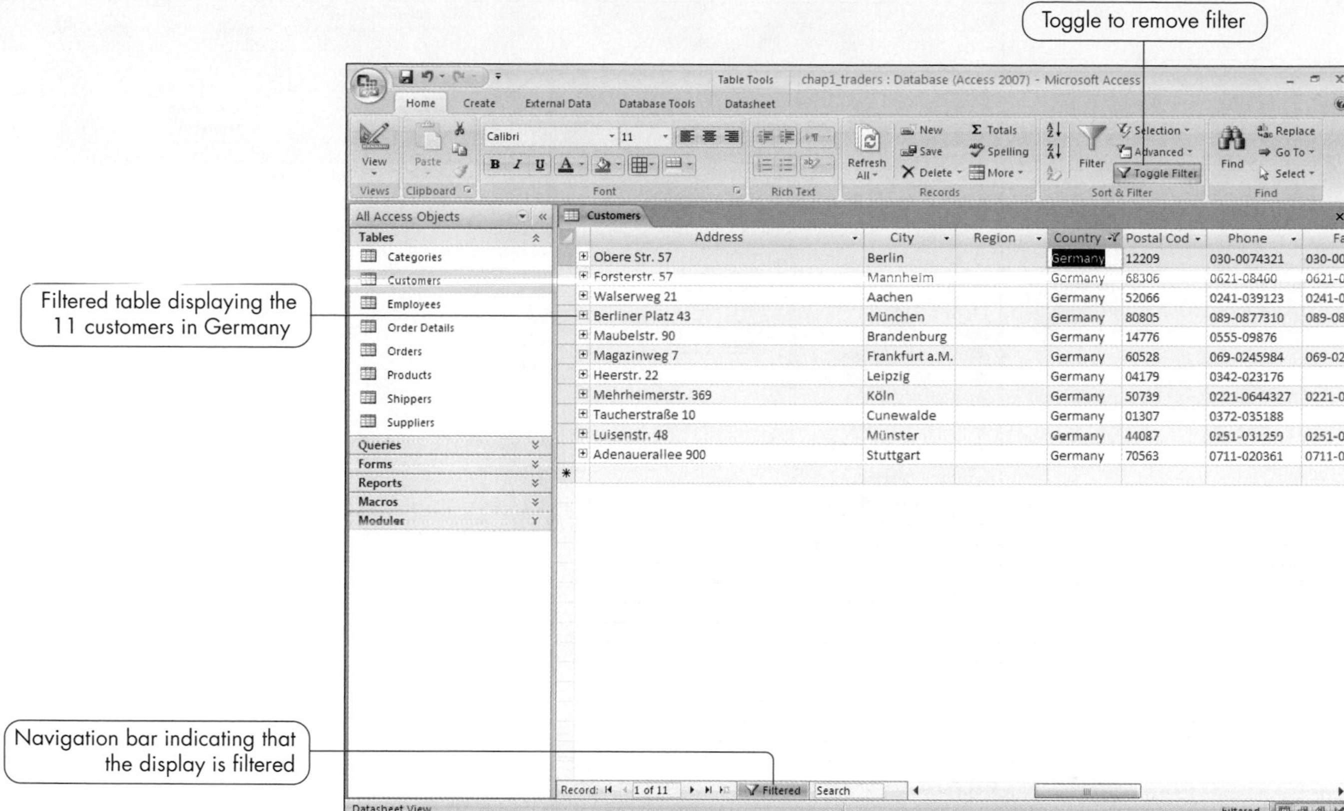

Figure 1.15 Filtered Table with Appropriate Sort Options Selected

TIP Use Quick Keyboard Shortcuts

Look for underlined letters in Access menus. They indicate the letters to use for the keyboard shortcuts. For example, when you click in a field and click the Selection down arrow in the Sort & Filter group, you can click the Equals "London" menu selection or simply type the letter e because the letter E in Equals is underlined, indicating a shortcut key.

Filter by Selection selects only the records that match the pre-selected criteria.

Filter by Form permits selecting criteria from a drop-down list or applying multiple criteria.

An ***inequity*** examines a mathematical relationship such as equals, not equals, greater than, less than, greater than or equal to, or less than or equal to.

The easiest way to implement a filter is to click in any cell that contains the value of the desired criterion (such as any cell that contains *Account Rep* in the Title field), then click Filter by Selection in the Sort & Filter group. ***Filter by Selection*** selects only the records that match the pre-selected criteria.

Figure 1.16 illustrates an alternate and more powerful way to apply a filter. ***Filter by Form*** permits selecting the criteria from a drop-down list and/or applying multiple criteria simultaneously. However, the real advantage of the Filter by Form command extends beyond these conveniences to two additional capabilities. First, you can specify relationships within a criterion; for example, you can use an inequity setting to select products with an inventory level greater than (or less than) 30. An ***inequity*** examines a mathematical relationship such as equals, not equals, greater than, less than, greater than or equal to, or less than or equal to. Filter by Selection, on the other hand, requires you to specify criteria equal to an existing value. Figure 1.16 shows the filtered query setup to select Beverages with more than 30 units in stock.

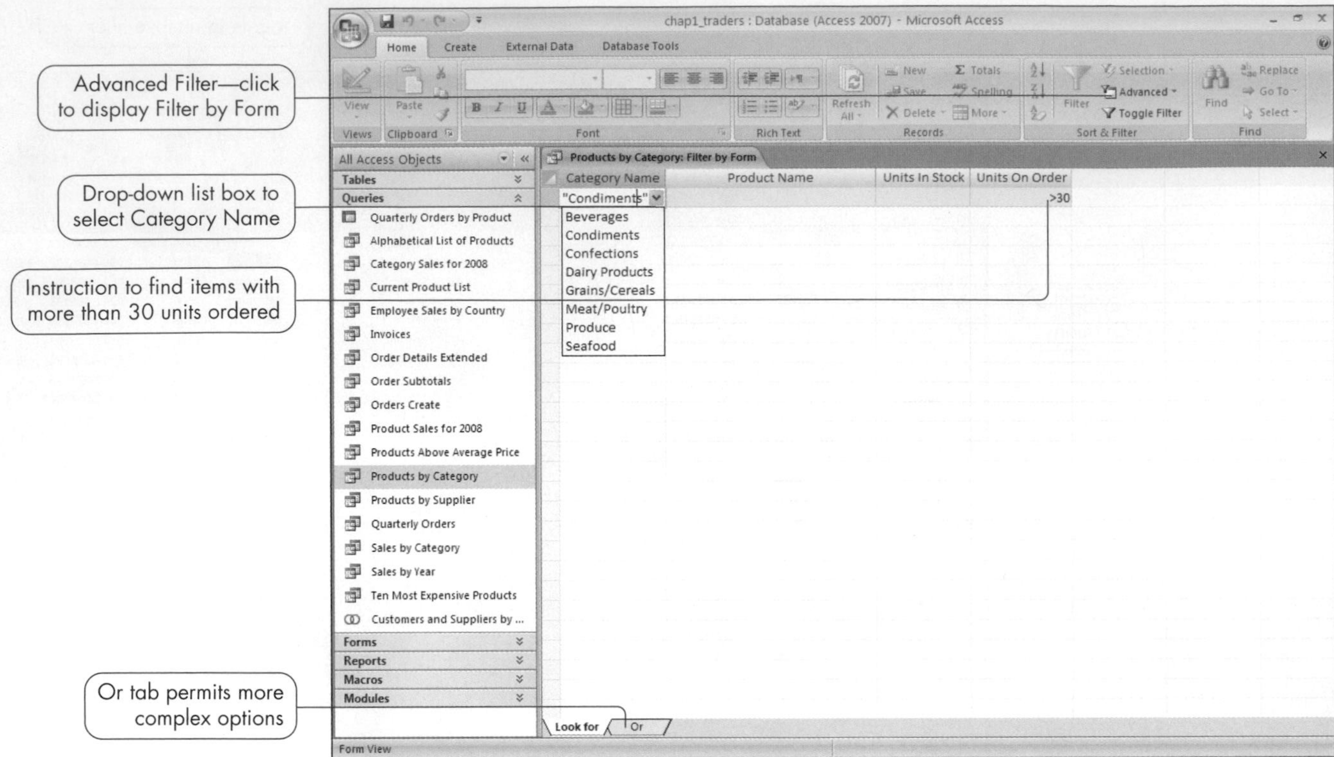

Figure 1.16 Filter by Form Design Grid

A second advantage of the Filter by Form command is that you can specify alternative criteria (such as customers in Germany or orders for over 30 units) by clicking the Or tab. (The latter capability is not implemented in Figure 1.16.) However, the availability of the various filter and sort commands enables you to obtain information from a database quickly and easily without creating a query or report.

Sorting Table Data on One or More Fields

A ***sort*** lists those records in a specific sequence, such as alphabetically by last name.

Sort Ascending provides an alphabetical list of text data or a small to large list of numeric data.

Sort Descending displays records with the highest value listed first.

You also can change the order of the information by sorting by one or more fields. A ***sort*** lists those records in a specific sequence, such as alphabetically by last name or by EmployeeID. To sort the table, click in the field on which you want to sequence the records (the LastName field in this example), then click Sort Ascending in the Sort & Filter group on the Home tab. ***Sort Ascending*** provides an alphabetical list of text data or a small to large list of numeric data. ***Sort Descending*** is appropriate for numeric fields such as salary, if you want to display the records with the highest value listed first. Figure 1.17 shows the Customers table sorted in alphabetical order by country. You may apply both filters and sorts to table or query information to select and order the data in the way that you need to make decisions.

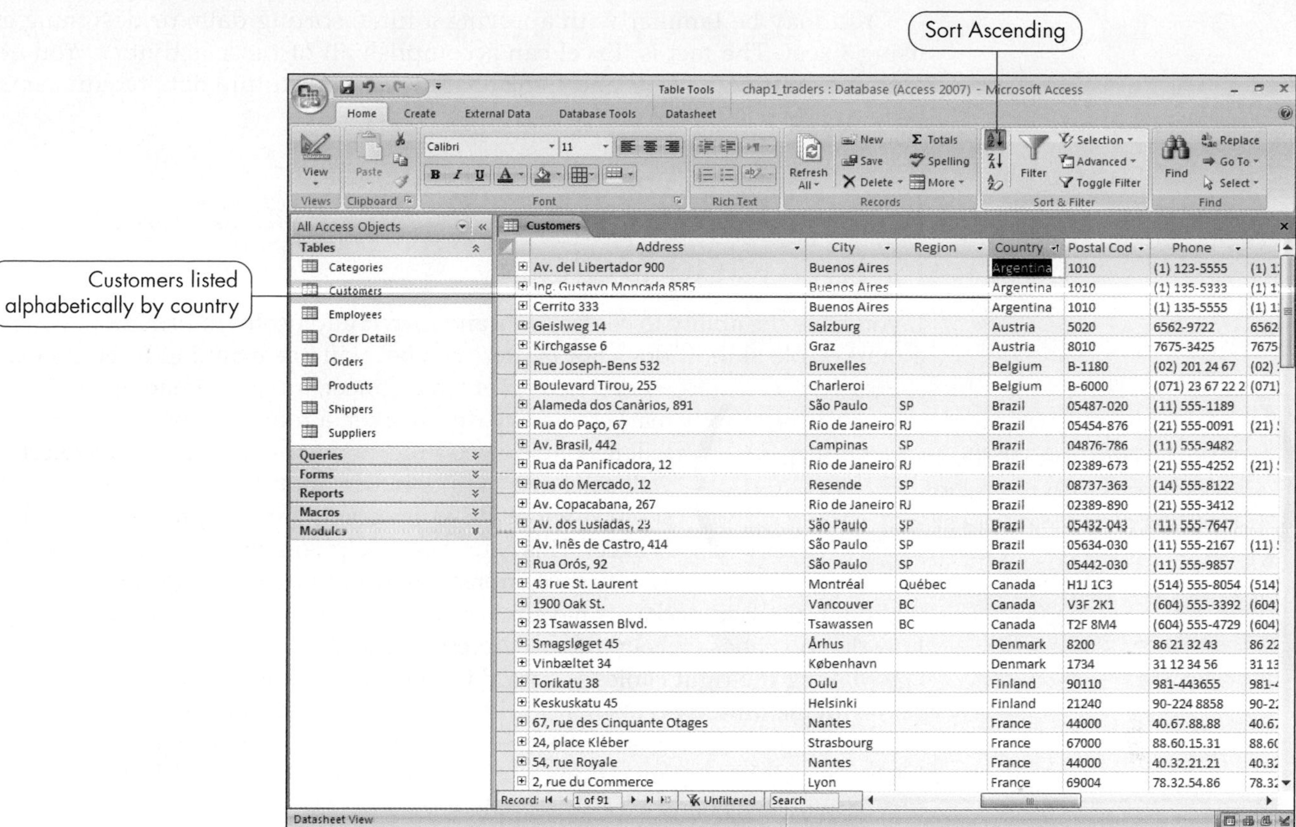

Figure 1.17 Customers Table Sorted by Country

The operations can be done in any order; that is, you can filter a table to show only selected records, then you can sort the filtered table to display the records in a different order. Conversely, you can sort a table, and then apply a filter. It does not matter which operation is performed first, and indeed, you can go back and forth between the two. You can also filter the table further, by applying a second (or third) criterion; for example, click in a cell containing *USA* and apply a Filter by Selection. Then click in a record for Oregon (OR) and apply a Filter by Selection a second time to display the customers from Oregon. You also can click Toggle Filter at any time to display all of the records in the table. Filters are a temporary method for examining subsets of data. If you close the filtered table or query and reopen it, all of the records display.

TIP The Sort or Filter—Which Is First?

It doesn't matter whether you sort a table, and then apply a filter or filter first, and then sort. The operations are cumulative. Thus, after you sort a table, any subsequent display of filtered records for that table will be in the specified sequence. Alternatively, you can apply a filter, and then sort the filtered table by clicking in the desired field and clicking the appropriate sort command. Remember, too, that all filter commands are cumulative and hence, you must remove the filter to see the original table.

You may be familiar with applying a filter, sorting data, or designing a form using Excel. The fact is, Excel can accomplish all of these activities. You need to examine your data needs and think about what your future data requirements may be to decide whether to use Access or Excel.

Knowing When to Use Access or Excel to Manage Data

If you have the ability to control data and turn it into useful information, you possess a marketable skill. It does not matter whether you are planning to become a social worker, a teacher, an engineer, an entrepreneur, a radiologist, a marketer, a day care worker, a musician, or an accountant. You will need to collect, store, maintain, manage, and protect data as well as convert it into information used to make strategic decisions. A widely used program that you probably already know is Excel. This course will help you become familiar with Access. You can accomplish many of the same things in either software. Although the two packages have much in common, they each have advantages. So, how do you choose whether to use Access or Excel?

If you have the ability to control data and turn it into useful information, you possess a marketable skill.

Making the right choice is critical if you want to find and update your information with maximum performance and accuracy. Ideally, your data needs and the type and amount of data used will determine how to pick the program that will work best. Sometimes organizations use Access when they probably would be better served with Excel and vice versa. The answer to the question of which to use may depend on who you ask. An accountant probably will use Excel. The information technology professional probably will use a more sophisticated database software like Oracle, but not Access. The middle manager in the marketing or manufacturing department will probably use Access. The question remains.

Select the Software to Use

A contacts list is an example of flat data. Each column of data (names, addresses, and phone numbers) is logically related to the others. If you can store your data logically in a single table or worksheet, then do. Update your data in the same type of file. Data contained in a single page or sheet (not multiple) are called ***flat or non-relational data***. You would never store your friend's last name on a different sheet from the sheet containing the friend's cell phone number.

Data contained in a single page or sheet (not multiple) are called ***flat or non-relational data***.

Suppose you had a spreadsheet of club members' names and contact information. Your club decides to sell cookies as a fundraiser. You might create a new worksheet listing how many boxes of which type of cookie each member picked up to sell. Your third worksheet might show how much money each member has turned in from the cookie sales. These data are different. They are not flat. Can you imagine needing to know someone's phone number or how many cookie boxes he or she promised to sell while looking at the worksheet of data about how much money has been turned in? These data are multi-dimensional and need to be stored in more than one worksheet or table. This describes relational data. Each table holds a particular type of data (number of boxes collected, contact information, funds turned in). Relational data are best stored in Access. In this example, you would create a database with three tables. You need to adhere to the following rules about assigning data to the appropriate table.

Assign table data so that each table:

- Represents only a single subject
- Has a field(s) that uniquely identifies each record
- Does not contain duplicate fields
- Has no repetition of the same type of value
- Has no fields belonging in other tables

As the quantity and complexity of data increase, the need to organize it efficiently also increases. Access affords better data organization than Excel. Access accomplishes the organization through a system of linkages among the tables. Each record (row) should be designated with a primary key—a unique identifier that sets it apart from all of the other records in the table. The primary key might be an account number, a student identification number, or an employee access code. All data in Excel have a unique identifier—the cell address. In life, you have a Social Security Number. It is the best unique identifier you have. Ever notice how, when at the doctor's office or applying for college admission, you are asked for your Social Security Number as well as your name? Your record in its database system probably uses your Social Security Number as a unique identifier.

You still need to answer the question of when to use Access and when to use Excel.

Use Access

You should use Access to manage data when you:

- Require a relational database (multiple tables or multi-dimensional tables) to store your data or anticipate adding more tables in the future.

  For example, you may set your club membership contact list in either software, but if you believe that you also will need to keep track of the cookie sales and fund collection, use Access.
- Have a large amount of data.
- Rely on external databases to derive and analyze the data you need.

  If you frequently need to have Excel exchange data to or from Access, use Access. Even though the programs are compatible, it makes sense to work in Access to minimize compatibility issues.
- Need to maintain constant connectivity to a large external database, such as one built with Microsoft SQL Server or your organization's Enterprise Resource Planning system.
- Need to regroup data from different tables in a single place through complex queries.

  You might need to create output showing how many boxes of cookies each club member picked up and how much money they turned in along with the club member's name and phone number.
- Have many people working in the database and need strong options to update the data.

  For example, five different clerks at an auto parts store might wait on five different customers. Each clerk connects to the inventory table to find out if the needed part is in stock and where in the warehouse it is located. When the customer says, "Yes, I want that," the inventory list is instantly updated and that product is no longer available to be purchased by the other four customers.

Use Excel

You should use Excel to manage data when you:

- Require a flat or non-relational view of your data (you do not need a relational database with multiple tables).

  This idea is especially true if that data is mostly numeric—for example, if you need to maintain an expense statement.
- Want to run primarily calculations and statistical comparisons on your data.
- Know your dataset is manageable in size (no more than 15,000 rows).

In the next exercise, you will create and apply filters, perform sorts, and develop skills to customize the data presentation to answer your questions.

Hands-On Exercises

2 | Data Manipulation: Filters and Sorts

Skills covered: 1. Use Filter by Selection with an Equal Setting **2.** Use Filter by Selection with a Contains Setting **3.** Use Filter by Form with an Inequity Setting **4.** Sort a Table

Step 1
Use Filter by Selection with an Equal Setting

Refer to Figure 1.18 as you complete Step 1.

a. Open the *chap1_ho1-3_traders_solution* file if necessary, and click **Options** on the Security Warning toolbar, click the **Enable this content option** in the Microsoft Office Security Options dialog box, and click **OK**.

   TROUBLESHOOTING: If you create unrecoverable errors while completing this hands-on exercise, you can delete the *chap1_ho1-3_traders_solution* file, copy the *chap1_ho1_traders_solution* backup database you created at the end of the first hands-on exercise, and open the copy of the backup database to start the second hands-on exercise again.

b. Open the **Customers table**; navigate to record 4 and replace *Thomas Hardy's* name with **your name** in the **Contact Name field**.

c. Scroll right until the **City field** is visible. Look through the record values of the field until you locate a customer in **London**, for example, the fourth record. Click in the field box to select it.

   The word *"London"* will have a gold colored border around it to let you know that it is active.

d. Click **Selection** in the Sort & Filter group on the Home tab.

e. Choose **Equals "London"** from the menu.

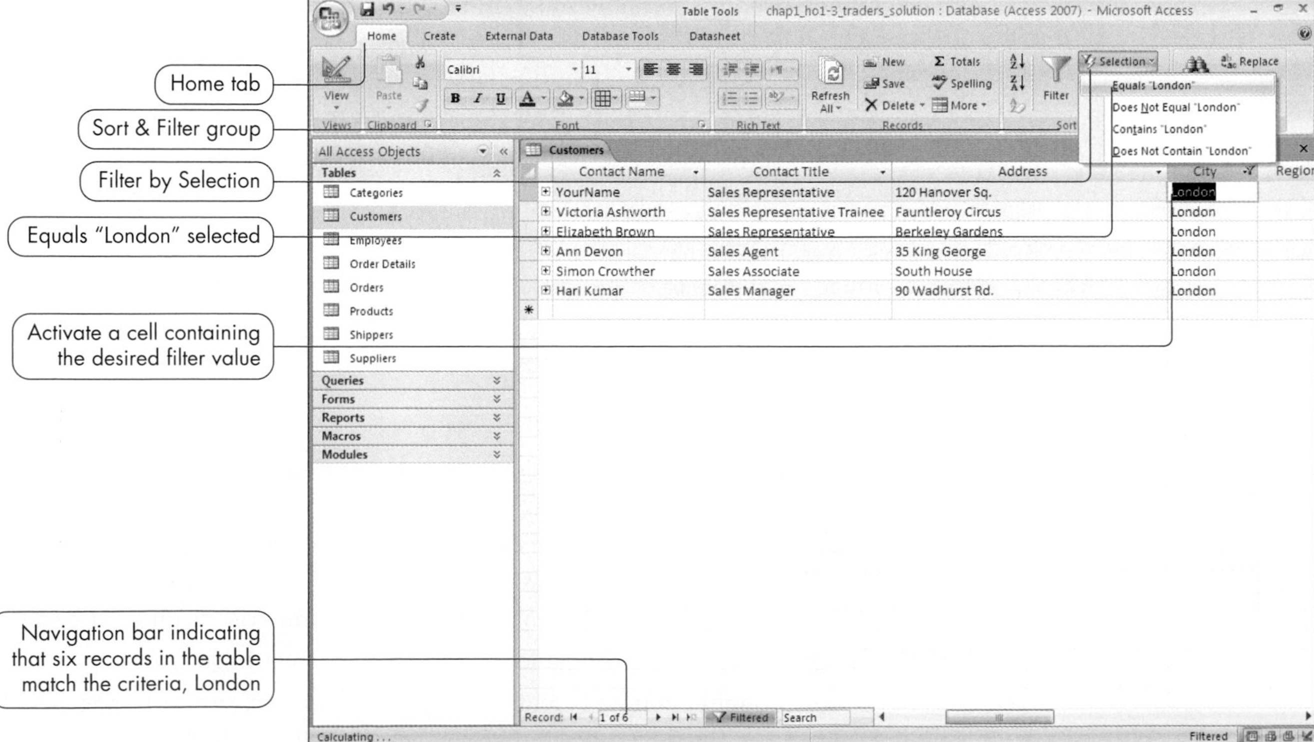

Figure 1.18 Customers Table Filtered to Display London Records Only

Step 2

Use Filter by Selection with a Contains Setting

Refer to Figure 1.19 as you complete Step 2.

a. Find a record with the value **Sales Representative** in the **Contact Title field**. Click your insertion point to activate that field. The first record has a value of *Sales Representative* for the Contact Title field.

   Sales Representative will have a gold colored border around it to let you know that it is activated.

b. Click **Selection** on the Sort & Filter group located on the Home tab.

c. Click **Contains "Sales Representative"**.

   You have applied a second layer of filtering to the customers in London. The second layer further restricts the display to only those customers who have the words Sales Representative contained in their title.

d. Scroll left until you see your name. Compare your results to those shown in Figure 1.19.

e. Click the **Office Button**, position the mouse pointer over **Print**, and then select **Quick Print**.

f. Click **Toggle Filter** in the Sort & Filter group to remove the filters.

g. Close the Customers table. Click **No** if a dialog box asks if you want to save the design changes to the Customers table.

TIP Removing Versus Deleting a Filter

Removing a filter displays all of the records that are in a table, but it does not delete the filter because the filter is stored permanently with the table. To delete the filter entirely is more complicated than simply removing it. Click Advanced on the Sort & Filter group and select the Clear All Filters option from the drop-down list box. Deleting unnecessary filters may reduce the load on the CPU and will allow the database manager to optimize the database performance.

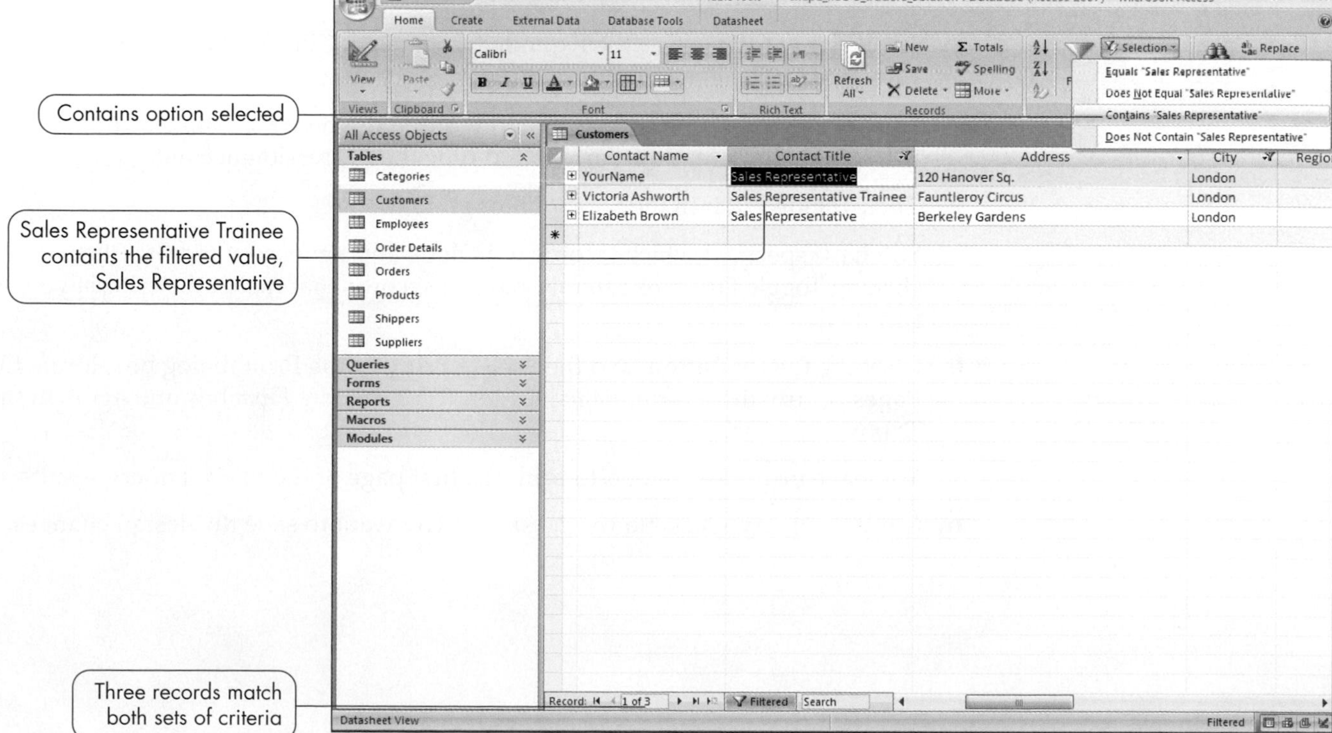

Contains option selected
Sales Representative Trainee contains the filtered value, Sales Representative
Three records match both sets of criteria

Figure 1.19 Customers Table Filtered to Display London and Sales Representative Job Titles

Step 3
Use Filter by Form with an Inequity Setting

Refer to Figure 1.20 as you complete Step 3.

a. Click **Tables** in the Navigation pane to collapse the listed tables.

b. Click **Queries** in the Navigation pane to expand the lists of available queries.

c. Locate and double-click the **Order Details Extended** query to open it.

   This query contains information about orders. It has fields containing information about the salesperson, the Order ID, the product name, the unit price, quantity ordered, the discount given, and an extended price. The extended price is a term used to total order information.

d. Click **Advanced** in the Sort & Filter group on the Home tab.

   The process to apply a filter by form is identical in a table or a query.

e. Select **Filter By Form** from the list.

   All of the records seem to vanish and you see only a list of field names.

f. Click in the **first row** under the **First Name** field.

   A down arrow appears at the right of the box.

g. Click the **First Name down arrow**. A list of all available first names appears.

   Your name should be on the list. It may be in a different location than that shown in Figure 1.20 because the list is in alphabetical order.

   TROUBLESHOOTING: If you do not see your name and you do see Margaret on the list, you probably skipped Steps 3c and 3d in Hands-On Exercise 1. Close the query without saving changes, turn back to the first hands-on exercise, and rework it, making sure not to omit any steps. Then you can return to this spot and work the remainder of this hands-on exercise.

h. Select **your first name** from the list.

i. Click in the *first row* under the *Last Name field* to turn on the drop-down arrow. Locate and select **your last name** by clicking it.

j. Scroll right until you see the Extended Price field. Click in the *first row* under the Extended Price field and type **<50**.

   This will select all of the items that you ordered where the total was under $50. You ignore the drop-down arrow and type the expression needed.

k. Click **Toggle Filter** in the Sort & Filter group.

   You have specified which records to include and have executed the filtering by clicking Toggle Filter. You should have 31 records that match the criteria you specified.

l. Click the **Office Button**, and then select **Print**. In the Print dialog box, locate the **Pages** control in the *Print Range* section. Type **1** in the *From* box and again in the *To* box. Click **OK**.

   You have instructed Access to print the first page of the filtered query results.

m. Close the query. Click **No** when asked if you want to save the design changes.

TIP Deleting Filter by Form Criterion

The Filter by Form command has all of the capabilities of the Filter by Selection command and provides two additional capabilities. First, you can use relational operators such as >, >=, <, or <= as opposed to searching for an exact value. Second, you can search for records that meet one of several conditions (the equivalent of an "Or" operation). Enter the first criterion as you normally would, then click the Or tab at the bottom of the window to display a second form in which you enter the alternate criteria. (To delete an alternate criterion, click the associated tab, and then click Delete on the toolbar.)

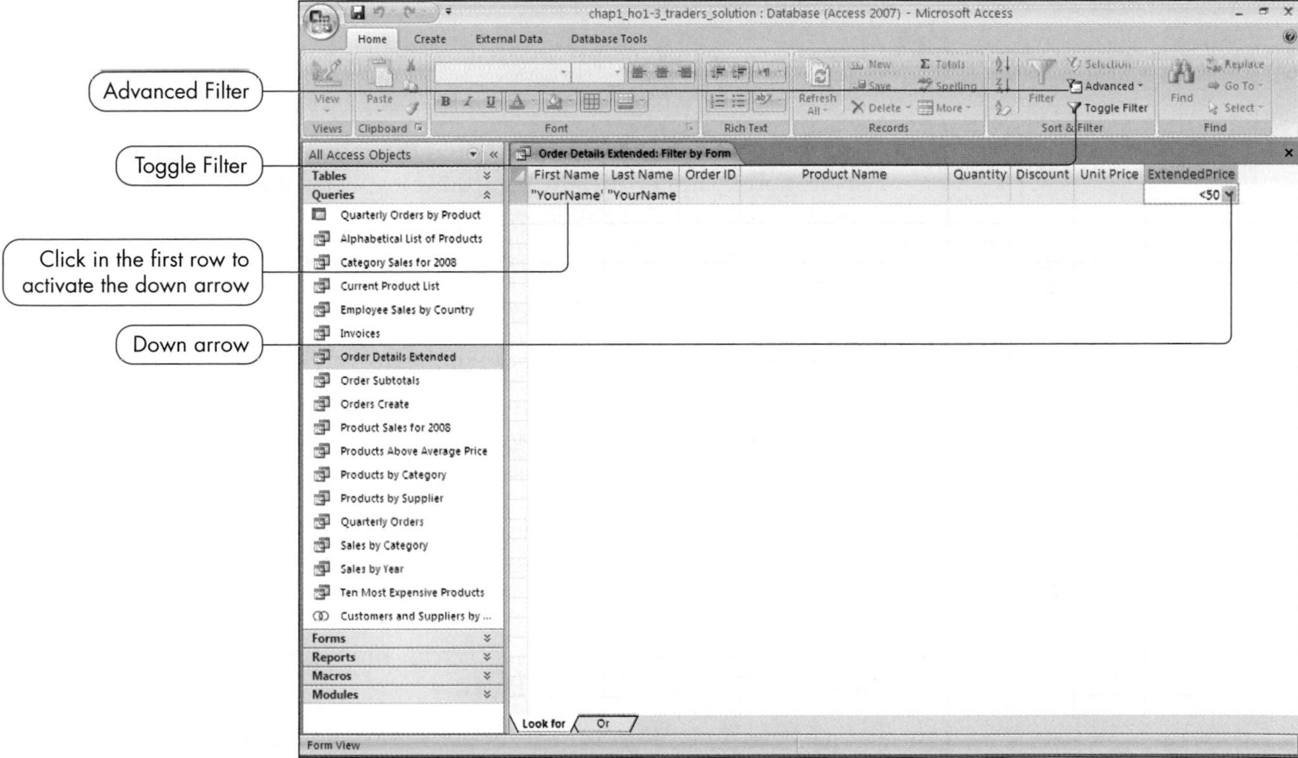

Figure 1.20 Filter by Selection Criteria Settings

Step 4
Sort a Table

Refer to Figure 1.21 as you complete Step 4.

a. Click **Queries** in the Navigation pane to collapse the listed queries.

b. Click **Tables** in the Navigation pane to expand the lists of available tables.

c. Locate and double-click the **Customers table** to open it.

This table contains information about customers. It is sorted in ascending order by the Customer ID field. Because this field contains text, the table is sorted in alphabetical order.

d. Click any value in the **Customer ID field**. Click **Sort Descending** in the Sort & Filter group on the Home tab.

Sorting in descending order on a character field produces a reverse alphabetical order.

e. Scroll right until you can see both the **Country** and **City fields**.

You will sort the customers by country and then by city within the countries. You can sort on more than one field as long as you sort on the primary field (in this case the country) last.

f. Click the field name for **Country**.

The entire column selects.

g. Click the **Country field name box** and hold the left mouse down.

A thick dark blue line displays on the left edge of the Country field column.

h. Check to make sure that you see the thick blue line. When you do, drag the country field to the **left**. When the thick black line moves to between the *Address and City* fields, release the mouse and the Country field position moves to the left of the City field.

i. Click any city name in the **City field** and click **Sort Ascending**.

j. Click any country name in the **Country field** and click **Sort Ascending**.

The countries are sorted in alphabetical order. The cities within each country also are sorted alphabetically. For example, the customer in Graz, Austria, is listed before the one in Saltzburg.

k. Scroll down until you see the *UK* customers listed.

l. Scroll to the left until the *Contact Name* is the first field in the left of the screen.

m. Press **PrntScrn** located somewhere in the upper right of your keyboard.

You have captured a picture of your screen. If nothing seemed to happen, it is because the picture was saved to the Clipboard. You must retrieve the picture from the Clipboard in order to see it.

TROUBLESHOOTING: Some notebook computers have Print Screen as a function. If the words Print Screen on the key are a different color, you must press **Fn+Print Screen**.

n. Launch Word, open a *new blank document*, and type **your name and section number** on the first line. Press **Enter**.

o. Press **Ctrl+V** to paste your picture of the screenshot into the Word document. Save the document as **chap1_ho2_traders_solution.docx**. Print the Word document. Close Word.

p. Close the **Customers table**. Do not save the changes.

q. Click the **Office Button**, select **Manage**, and then select **Compact and Repair Database**.

r. Click the **Office Button** again, select **Manage**, and then select **Back Up Database**. Type **chap1_ho2_traders_solution** as the file name and click **Save**.

You just created a backup of the database after completing the second hands-on exercise. The original database *chap1_ho1-3_traders_solution* remains onscreen. If you ruin the original database as you complete the third hands-on exercise, you can use the backup file you just created.

s. Close the file and exit Access if you do not want to continue with the next exercise at this time.

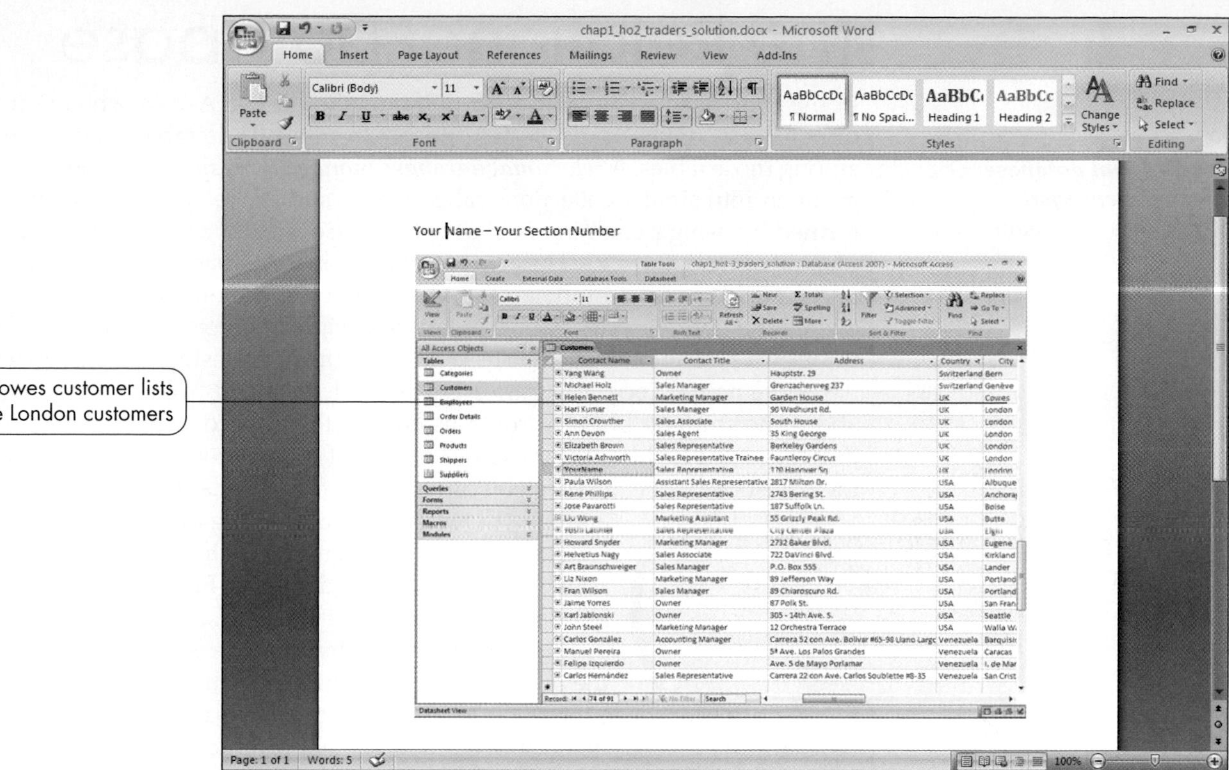

The Cowes customer lists before the London customers

Figure 1.21 The Customers Table Sorted by Country and Then by City in Word

The Relational Database

A ***relational database management system*** is one in which data are grouped into similar collections, called tables, and the relationships between tables are formed by using a common field.

In the previous section, you read that you should use Access when you have multidimensional data. Access derives power from multiple tables and the relationships among those tables. A ***relational database management system*** is one in which data are grouped into similar collections called tables, and the relationships between tables are formed by using a common field or fields. The design of a relational database system is illustrated in Figure 1.22. The power of a relational database lies in the software's ability to organize data and combine items in different ways to obtain a complete picture of the events the data describe. Good database design connects the data in different tables through a system of linkages. These links are the relationships that give relational databases the name. Look at Figure 1.1. The student record (folder) contains information about the student, but also contains cross-references to data stored in other cabinet drawers, such as the advisor's name or a list of courses completed. If you need to know the advisor's phone number, you can open the faculty drawer, find the advisor's record, and then locate the field containing the phone number. The cross-reference from the student file to the faculty file illustrates how a relationship works in a database. Figure 1.22 displays the cross-references between the tables as a series of lines connecting the common fields. When the database is set up properly, the users of the data can be confident that if they search a specific customer identification number, they will be given accurate information about that customer's order history and payment balances, and his/her product or shipping preferences.

(The power of a relational database lies in the software's ability to organize data and combine items in different ways to obtain a complete picture of the events the data describe.)

In this section, you will explore the relationships among tables, learn about the power of relational integrity, and discover how the software protects the organization's data.

Using the Relationship Window

A ***foreign key*** is a field in one table that also is stored in a different table as a primary key.

The relationship (the lines between the tables in Figure 1.22) is like a piece of electronic string that travels throughout the database, searching every record of every table until it finds the data satisfying the user's request. Once identified, the fields and records of interest will be tied to the end of the string, pulled through the computer and reassembled in a way that makes the data easy to understand. The first end of the string was created when the primary key was established in the Customers table. The primary key is a unique identifier for each table record. The other end of the string will be tied to a field in a different table. If you examine Figure 1.22, you will see that the CustomerID is a foreign field in the Orders table. A ***foreign key*** is a field in one table that also is stored in a different table as a primary key. Each value of the CustomerID can occur only once in the Customers table because it is a primary key. However, the CustomerID may appear multiple times in the Orders table because one customer may make many different purchases. The CustomerID field is a foreign key in the Orders table but the primary key in the Customers table.

Examine Referential Integrity

Referential integrity is the set of rules that ensure that data stored in related tables remain consistent as the data are updated.

The relationships connecting the tables will be created using an Access feature that uses referential integrity. Integrity means truthful or reliable. When ***referential integrity*** is enforced, the user can trust the "threads" running through the database and "tying" related items together. The sales manager can use the database to find the names and phone numbers of all the customers who have ordered Teatime Chocolate Biscuits (a specific product). Because referential integrity has been enforced, it will not matter that the order information is in a different table from the customer data. The invisible threads will keep the information accurately connected. The threads also provide a method of ensuring data accuracy. You cannot enter a record in the Orders table that references a ProductID or a CustomerID that does not exist elsewhere in the system. Nor can you easily delete a record in one table if it has related records in related tables.

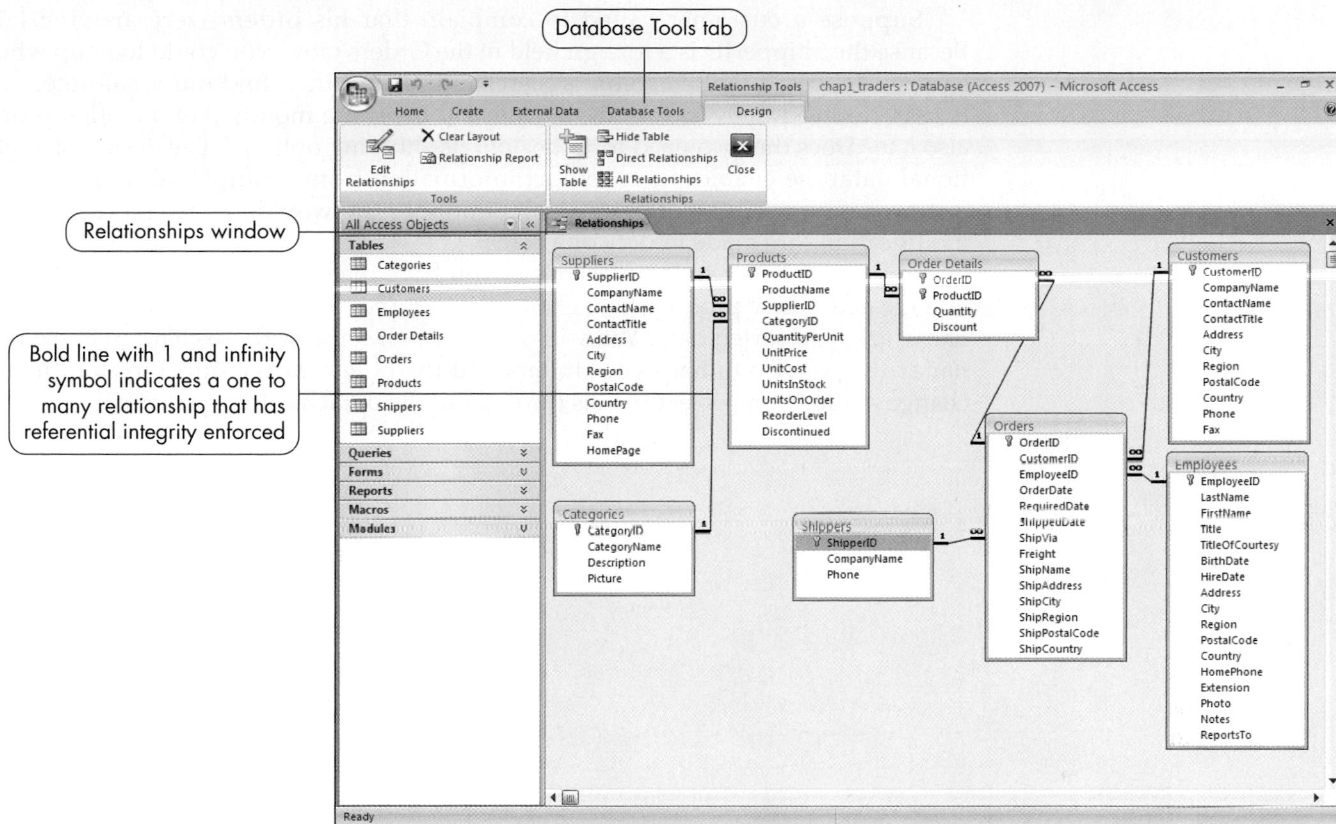

Figure 1.22 The Relationships Window Displaying Table Connections

If this were a real organization's data system, the files would be much, much larger and the data more sophisticated. When learning database skills, you should start with smaller, more manageable files. The same design principles apply regardless of the database size. A small file gives you the ability to check the tables and see if your results are correct. Even though the data amounts are small, you need to develop the work practices needed to manage large amounts of data. With only a handful of records, you can easily count the number of employees at the Washington state office. In addition to learning how to accomplish a task, you also should begin to learn to anticipate the computer's response to an instruction. As you work, ask yourself what the anticipated results should be and then verify. When you become skilled at anticipating output correctly, you are surprised less often.

As you work, ask yourself what the anticipated results should be and then verify. When you become skilled at anticipating output correctly, you are surprised less often.

Understanding Relational Power

In the previous section, you read that you should use Access when you have multidimensional data. Access derives power from multiple tables and the relationships between those tables. This type of database is known as a relational database and is illustrated in Figure 1.22. This figure describes the database structure. Examine some of the connections. The EmployeeID is a foreign field in the Orders table. For example, you can produce a document displaying the history of each order a customer had placed and the employee's name (from the Employees table) that entered the order. The Orders table references the Order Details table where the OrderID is a foreign field. The ProductID relates to the Products table (where it is the primary key). The CategoryID is the primary key in the Categories table, but shows up as a foreign field in the Products table. The table connections, even when more than one table is involved, provide the decision-maker power. This feature gives the manager the ability to find out sales by category. How many different beverages were shipped last week? What was the total revenue generated from seafood orders last year?

Suppose a customer called to complain that his orders were arriving late. Because the ShipperID is a foreign field in the Orders table, you could look up which shipper delivered that customer's merchandise, and then find out what other customers received deliveries from that shipper the same month. Are the other orders also late? Does the firm need to reconsider its shipping options? The design of a relational database enables us to extract information from multiple tables in a single query or report. Equally important, it simplifies the way data are changed in that modifications are made in only one place.

In the previous hands-on exercises, you have made modifications to table data. You created a new product, you changed an employee and customer name to your name, and you sorted data. You will trace through some of those changes in the next hands-on exercise to help you understand the power of relationships and how a change made to one object travels throughout the database file structure.

3 | Introduction to Relationships

Skills covered: 1. Examine the Relationships Window **2.** Discover That Changes in Table Data Affect Queries **3.** Use Filter by Form with an Inequity Setting and Reapply a Saved Filter **4.** Filter a Report **5.** Remove an Advanced Filter

Step 1 Examine the Relationships Window

Refer to Figure 1.23 as you complete Step 1.

a. Open the *chap1_ho1-3_traders_solution* file if necessary, click **Options** on the *security warning* toolbar, click the **Enable this content option** in the Microsoft Office Security Options dialog box, and click **OK**.

TROUBLESHOOTING: If you create unrecoverable errors while completing this hands-on exercise, you can delete the *chap1_ho1-3_traders_solution* file, copy the *chap1_ho2_traders_solution* database you created at the end of the second hands-on exercise, and open the copy of the backup database to start the third hands-on exercise again.

b. Click the **Database Tools tab** and click **Relationships** in the Show/Hide group.

Examine the relationships that connect the various tables. For example, the Products table is connected to the Suppliers, Categories, and Order Details tables.

c. Click **Show Table** in the Relationships group on the Relationship Tools Design tab.

The Show Table dialog box opens. It tells you that there are eight available tables in the database. If you look in the Relationship window, you will see that all eight tables are in the relationship diagram.

d. Click the **Queries tab** in the Show Table dialog box.

You could add all of the queries to the Relationships window. Things might become cluttered, but you could tell at a glance where the queries get their information.

e. Close the Show Table dialog box.

f. Click the **down arrow** in the All Access Objects bar of the Navigation pane.

g. Click **Tables and Related Views**.

You can now see not only the tables, but also the queries, forms, and reports that connect to the table data. If a query is sourced on more than one table, it will appear multiple times in the Navigation pane. This view provides an alternate method of viewing the relationships connecting the tables.

h. Close the Relationships window.

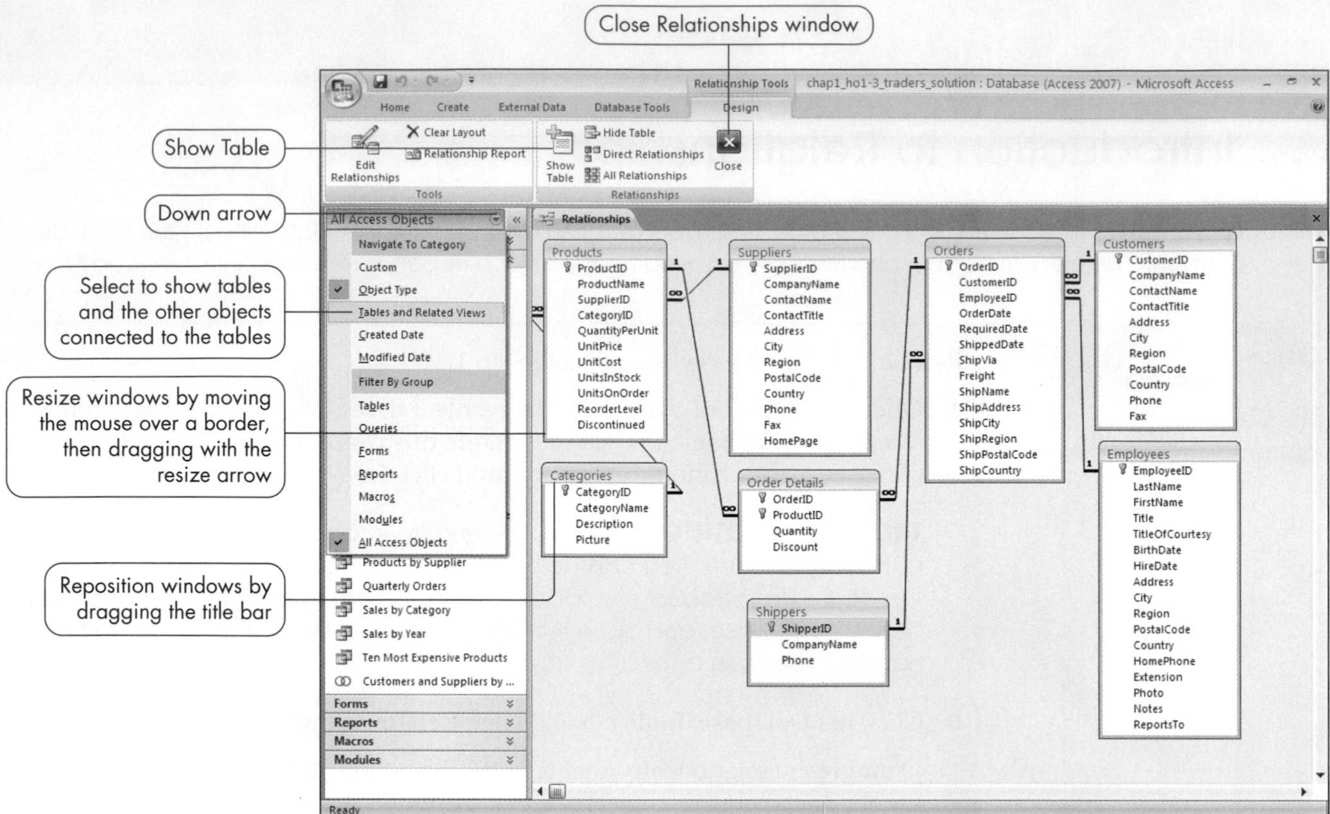
Close Relationships window
Show Table
Down arrow
Select to show tables and the other objects connected to the tables
Resize windows by moving the mouse over a border, then dragging with the resize arrow
Reposition windows by dragging the title bar

Figure 1.23 The Relationships Window Displaying the Northwind Table Relationships

Step 2

Discover That Changes in Table Data Affect Queries

Refer to Figure 1.24 as you complete Step 2.

a. Scroll in the Navigation pane until you see the *Products table and Related Objects*. Locate and double-click the **Order Details Extended query**.

b. Examine the icons on the left edge of the Navigation pane. Figure 1.24 identifies the object type for each of the objects.

c. Find an occurrence of *your last name* anywhere in the query (record 7 should show your name) and click your last name to make it active.

The query contains your name because in Hands-On Exercise 1 you replaced Margaret Peacock's name in the Employees table with your name. The Employees table is related to the Orders table, the Orders table to the Order Details table, and the Order Details table to the Products table. Therefore, any change you make to the Employees table is carried throughout the database via the relationships.

d. Click **Selection** in the Sort & Filter group. Select **Equals "YourName"** from the selection menu.

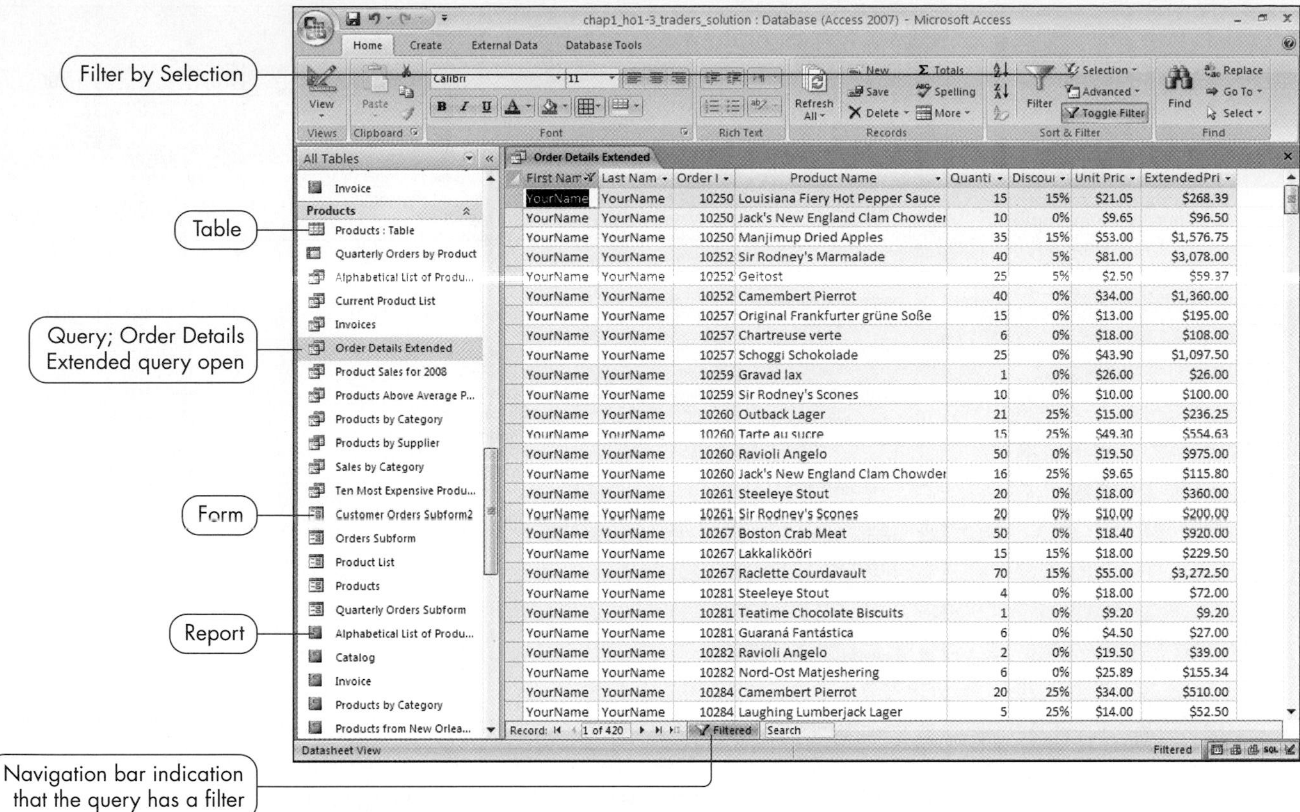

Figure 1.24 Filtered Query Results

Step 3
Use Filter by Form with an Inequity Setting and Reapply a Saved Filter

Refer to Figure 1.25 as you complete Step 3.

a. Click **Advanced Filter Options** in the Sort & Filter group.

b. Select **Filter By Form** from the drop-down list.

Because you already applied a filter to these data, the Filter By Form design sheet opens with one criterion already filled in. Your name displays in the selection box under the Last Name field.

c. Scroll right (or press **Tab**) until the Extended Price field is visible. Click the insertion point in the **first row** under the Extended Price field.

d. Type **>2000**.

The Extended Price field shows the purchased amount for each item ordered. If an item sold for $15 and a customer ordered 10, the Extended Price would display $150.

e. Click **Toggle Filter** in the Sort & Filter group. Examine the filtered results.

Your inequity instruction, >2000, identified the items ordered where the extended price exceeded $2,000.

f. Press **Ctrl+S** to save the query. Close the query by clicking the X in the object window.

g. Open the **Order Details Extended query**.

The filter disengages when you close and reopen the object. However, your filtering directions have been stored with the query design. You may reapply the filter at any time by clicking the Toggle Filter command.

h. Click **Toggle Filter** in the Sort & Filter group.

i. Compare your work to Figure 1.25. If it is correct, close the query.

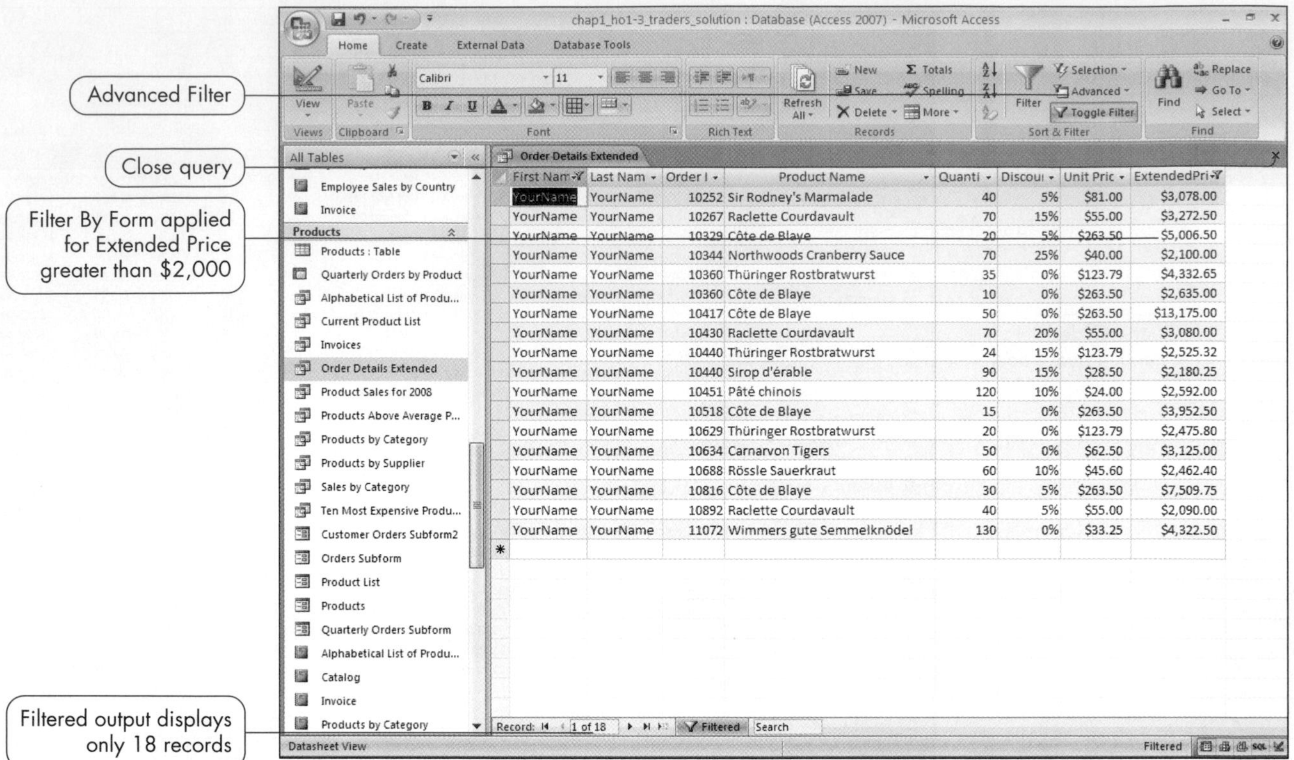
Advanced Filter
Close query
Filter By Form applied for Extended Price greater than $2,000
Filtered output displays only 18 records

Figure 1.25 Filtered Query Results After Limiting Output to Extended Prices over $2,000

Step 4
Filter a Report

Refer to Figure 1.26 as you complete Step 4.

a. Open the **Products by Category report** located in the Navigation pane under the Products group. You may need to scroll down to locate it.

   The report should open in Print Preview with a gray stripe highlighting the report title. The Print Preview displays the report exactly as it will print. This report was formatted to display in three columns.

   TROUBLESHOOTING: If you do not see the gray stripe and three columns, you probably opened the wrong object. The database also contains a Product by Category query. It is the source for the Products by Category report. Make sure you open the report (shown with the green report icon) and not the query. Close the query and open the report.

b. Examine the Confections category products. You should see **Your Name Pecan Pie**.

   You created this product by entering data in a form in Hands-On Exercise 1. You later discovered that changes made to a form affect the related table. Now you see that other related objects also change when the source data changes.

c. Right-click the **gold report tab** within Products by Category. Select **Report View** from the shortcut menu.

   The Report view displays the information a little differently. It no longer shows three columns. If you clicked the Print command while in Report view, the columns would print even though you do not see them. The Report view permits limited data interaction (for example, filtering).

d. Scroll down in the report until you see the title *Category: Confections*. **Right-click** the word **Confections** in the title. Select **Equals "Confections"** from the shortcut menu.

Right-clicking a selected data value in an Access table, query, form, or report activates a shortcut to a Filter by Selection menu. Alternatively, you can click the selected value, in this case, Confections, and then click the Filter by Selection command in the Sort & Filter group.

e. Right-click the **gold report tab** within Products by Category. Select **Print Preview** from the shortcut menu.

You need to print this report. Always view your reports in Print Preview prior to printing.

f. Click the **Office Button**, position the mouse pointer over **Print**, and then select **Quick Print** to produce a printed copy of the filtered report. Click **OK**.

The Quick Print command sends your work to the default printer as soon as you click it. You can use this safely when you have already viewed your work in Print Preview.

g. Save and close the report.

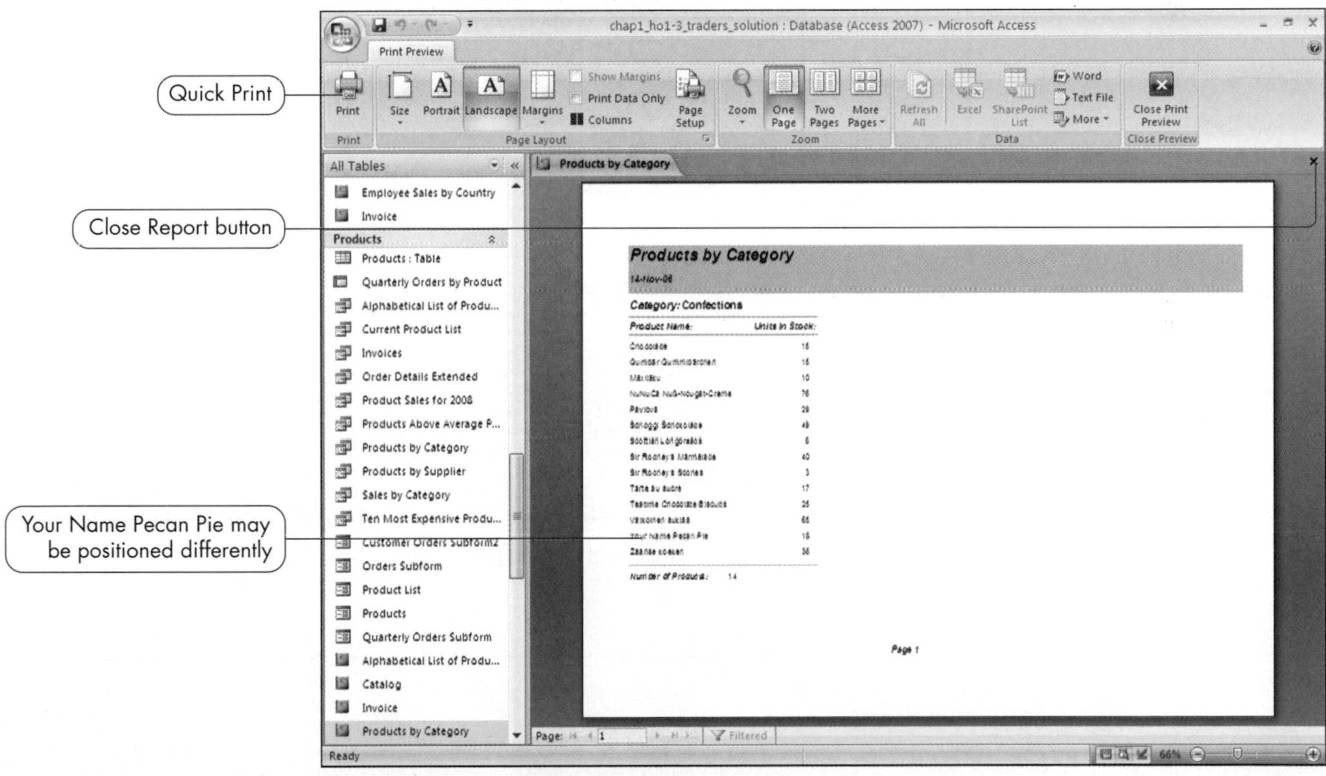

Figure 1.26 Filtered Report Results

Step 5 Remove an Advanced Filter

Refer to Figure 1.27 as you complete Step 5.

a. Open the **Order Details Extended query**.

All 2,155 records should display in the query. You have unfiltered the data. However, the filter still exists.

b. Click **Toggle Filter** in the Sort & Filter group.

   You will see the same 18 filtered records that you printed in Step 3.

c. Click **Advanced** in the Sort & Filter group and click **Clear All Filters**.

d. Close the query. A dialog box opens asking if you want to save changes. Click **Yes**.

e. Open the **Order Details Extended query**.

f. Click **Advanced Filter Options** in the Sort & Filter group.

g. Check to ensure the *Clear All Filters* option is dim. Save and close the query.

h. Click the **Office Button**, select **Manage**, and select **Compact and Repair Database**. Close the file and exit Access.

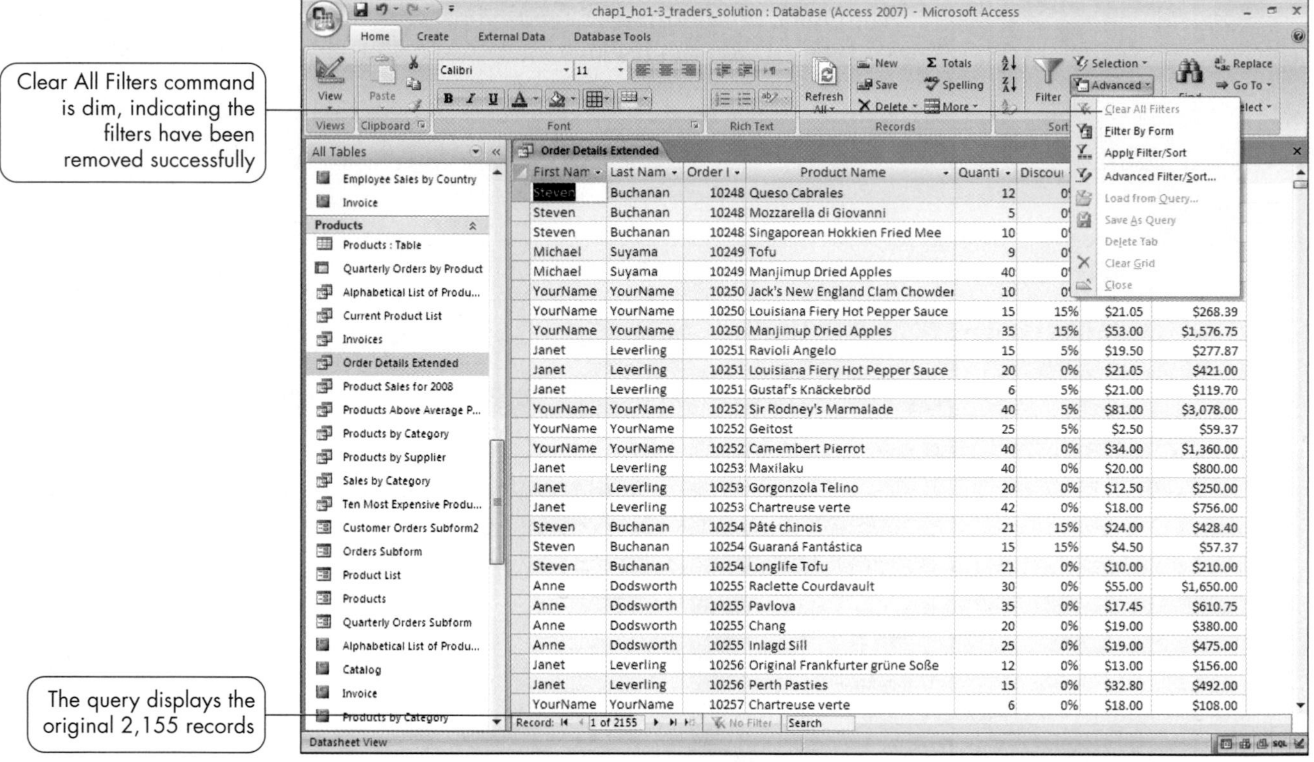
Clear All Filters command is dim, indicating the filters have been removed successfully
The query displays the original 2,155 records
chap1_ho1-3_traders_solution : Database (Access 2007) - Microsoft Access

Figure 1.27 Query Results with Filters Removed

Summary

1. **Explore, describe, and navigate among objects in an Access database.** An Access database has six types of objects: tables, forms, queries, reports, macros, and modules. The database window displays these objects and enables you to open an existing object or create new objects. You may arrange these objects by type or by relationship views. The relationship view provides a listing of each table and all other objects in the database that use that table as a source. Thus, one query or report may appear several times, listed once under each table from which it derives information. Each table in the database is composed of records, and each record is in turn composed of fields. Every record in a given table has the same fields in the same order. The primary key is the field (or combination of fields) that makes every record in a table unique.
2. **Understand the difference between working in storage and memory.** Access automatically saves any changes in the current record as soon as you move to the next record or when you close the table. The Undo Current Record command cancels (undoes) the changes to the previously saved record.
3. **Practice good file management.** Because organizations depend on the data stored in databases, database users need to be intentional about exercising good file management practices. You need to be intentional about where you save your files. As you learn new Access skills, you need to make a copy of the database file and practice on the copy. This practice provides a recovery point should you make data-damaging errors.
4. **Back up, compact, and repair your database.** Because using a database tends to increase the size of the file, you should always close any database objects and compact the database prior to closing the file. This step may reduce the storage requirement by half. Adequate backup is essential when working with an Access database (or any other Office application). A duplicate copy of the database should be created at the end of every session and stored off-site (away from the computer).
5. **Create filters.** A filter is a set of criteria that is applied to a table to display a subset of the records in that table. Microsoft Access lets you Filter by Selection or Filter by Form. The application of a filter does not remove the records from the table, but simply suppresses them from view.
6. **Sort table data on one or more fields.** The records in a table can be displayed in ascending or descending order by clicking the appropriate command on the Home tab.
7. **Know when to use Access or Excel to manage data.** Excel data typically is flat. All of the needed information easily presents in a one-dimensional spreadsheet. Use Excel when the data are primarily numeric. Access handles multi-dimensional data more effectively. Use Access when you need to exchange data with other databases, for large amounts of data, or if your data needs are likely to expand.
8. **Use the Relationships window.** The Relationships window provides a summarizing overview of the database design. Use it to discover which fields are stored in what table. It displays the system of linkages among the table data. The Relationships window provides an excellent tool for you to become acquainted with a new database quickly.
9. **Understand relational power.** A relational database contains multiple tables and enables you to extract information from those tables in a single query. The related tables must be consistent with one another, a concept known as referential integrity. Thus, Access automatically implements additional data validation to ensure the integrity of a database. No system, no matter how sophisticated, can produce valid output from invalid input. Changes made in one object travel through the database and affect other, related objects. The relationships are based on linking primary and foreign key fields between tables.

Key Terms

Access speed 80
Criterion (criteria, pl) 77
Database 71
Datasheet view 75
Design view 75
Field 71
Filter 89
Filter by Form 91
Filter by Selection 91
Flat or non-relational data 94
Foreign key 102
Form 77
Inequity 91
Object .73
Primary key 75
Query 77
Record .71
Referential integrity 102
Relational database management system 102
Report .78
Sort 92
Sort Ascending 92
Sort Descending 92
Table 71

Multiple Choice

1. Which sequence represents the hierarchy of terms, from smallest to largest?
   (a) Database, table, record, field
   (b) Field, record, table, database
   (c) Record, field, table, database
   (d) Field, record, database, table

2. Which of the following is not true regarding movement within a record (assuming you are not in the first or last field of that record)?
   (a) Press Tab or the right arrow key to move to the next field.
   (b) Press Spacebar to move to the next field to the right.
   (c) Press Shift+Tab or the left arrow key to return to the previous field.
   (d) Press the Enter key and move to the next record.

3. You are performing routine maintenance on a table within an Access database. When should you execute the Save command?
   (a) Immediately after you add, edit, or delete a record
   (b) Periodically during a session—for example, after every fifth change
   (c) Once at the end of a session
   (d) None of the above since Access automatically saves the changes as they are made

4. Which of the following objects are not contained within an Access database?
   (a) Tables and forms
   (b) Queries and reports
   (c) Macros and modules
   (d) Web sites and worksheets

5. You have opened an Access file. The left pane displays a table with forms, queries, and reports listed under the table. Then another table and its objects display. You notice some of the object names are repeated under different tables. Why?
   (a) The database has been set to Object Type View. The object names repeat because a query or report is frequently based on multiple tables.
   (b) The database has been set to Tables and Related View. The object names repeat because a query or report is frequently based on multiple tables.
   (c) The database has been set to Most Recently Used View. The object names repeat because an object has been used frequently.
   (d) The database objects have been alphabetized.

6. Which of the following is not true of an Access database?
   (a) Every record in a table has the same fields as every other record. The fields are in the same order in each record.
   (b) Every table contains the same number of records as every other table.
   (c) Every record in a table has the same fields as every other record. The fields may be ordered differently depending on the record.
   (d) All records contain the same data as all other records.

7. Which of the following is true regarding the record selector symbol?
   (a) A pencil indicates that the current record already has been saved.
   (b) An empty square indicates that the current record has not changed.
   (c) An asterisk indicates the first record in the table.
   (d) A gold border surrounds the active record.

8. You have finished an Access assignment and wish to turn it in to your instructor for evaluation. As you prepare to transfer the file, you discover that it has grown in size. It is now more than double the original size. You should:
   (a) Zip the database file prior to transmitting it to the instructor.
   (b) Turn it in; the size does not matter.
   (c) Compact and repair the database file prior to transmitting it to the instructor.
   (d) Delete extra tables or reports or fields to make the file smaller.

9. Which of the following will be accepted as valid during data entry?
   (a) Adding a record with a duplicate primary key
   (b) Entering text into a numeric field
   (c) Entering numbers into a text field
   (d) Omitting an entry in a required field

10. In a Replace command, the values for the Find and Replace commands must be:
    (a) The same length
    (b) The same case
    (c) Any part of a word
    (d) Either the same or a different length and case

...continued on Next Page

Multiple Choice Continued...

11. Which of the following capabilities is available through Filter by Selection?
    (a) The imposition of a relational condition
    (b) The imposition of an alternate (OR) condition
    (c) The imposition of an Equal condition
    (d) The imposition of a delete condition

12. You open an Access form and use it to update an address for customer Lee Fong. You exited the record and closed the form. Later you open a report that generates mailing labels. What will the address label for Lee Fong show?
    (a) The new address
    (b) The old address
    (c) The new address if you remembered to save the changes made to the form
    (d) The old address until you remember to update it in the report

13. You have created a Filter by Form in an Order Total field. You set the criterion to >25. Which of the following accurately reflects the instruction given to Access?
    (a) All orders with an Order Total of at least 25
    (b) All orders with an Order Total of less than 25
    (c) All orders with an Order Total over 25
    (d) All orders with an Order Total of 25 or less

14. You have used Find and Replace to find all occurrences of the word "his" with "his/her." You typed only his in the Find box and only his/her in the Replace box. What will the result be?
    (a) History will become His/Herstory
    (b) This will become This/Her
    (c) His will become His/Her
    (d) All of the above
    (e) None of the above

15. You are looking at an Employees table in Datasheet view. You want the names sorted alphabetically by last name and then by first name, e.g., Smith, Andrea is listed before Smith, William. To accomplish this, you must:
    (a) First sort ascending on first name, and then on last name
    (b) First sort descending on first name, and then on last name
    (c) First sort ascending on last name, and then on first name
    (d) First sort descending on last name, and then on first name

Practice Exercises

1 Comfort Insurance

The Comfort Insurance Agency is a midsized company with offices located across the country. You are the human resource director for the company. Your office is located in the home office in Miami. Each employee receives an annual performance review. The review determines employee eligibility for salary increases and the performance bonus. The employee data are stored in an Access database. This database is used by the Human Resource department to monitor and maintain employee records. Your task is to identify the employees who have a performance rating of excellent and a salary under $40,000 per year (if any). Once you identify the appropriate records, you need to sort them alphabetically by the employee's last name. Verify your work by examining Figure 1.28.

a. Copy the partially completed file in *chap1_pe1_insurance.accdb* from the Exploring Access folder to your production folder. Rename it **chap1_pe1_insurance_solution**. Double-click the file name to open it. Enable the security content by clicking the **Options** command in the Security Warning bar. Select **Enable this content**, and then click **OK**.
b. Click the **Database Tools tab** and click **Relationships** in the Show/Hide group. Examine the table structure, relationships, and fields. Once you are familiar with the database, close the Relationships window.
c. Double-click the **Raises and Bonuses query** in the Navigation pane to open it. Find *Debbie Johnson*'s name in the seventh record. Double-click *Debbie* and type your **first name**. Double-click *Johnson* and type your **last name**. Click a different record to save your change.
d. Examine the number of records in the query and remember it for future reference.
e. Find a record that has a value of *Excellent* in the *Performance field*. The record for Johnny Park (sixth record) is one. Click your insertion point in that field on the word **Excellent**.
f. Activate the **Filter by Selection** in the Sort & Filter group. Select **Equals "Excellent"** from the menu. Examine the number of records in the query and remember it for future reference.
g. Click **Advanced Filter** in the Sort & Filter group and select **Filter By Form**.
h. Position the insertion point in the first row in the *Salary field*. Type **<40000**. (Make sure you apply this number to the Salary field and not the NewSalary field.)
i. Click **Toggle Filter** in the Sort & Filter group. Examine the number of records in the query and remember it for future reference. As you add additional criteria, the number of filtered results should decrease.
j. Click **Sort Ascending** in the Sort & Filter group on the Home tab to sort the filtered output by the employee's last name alphabetically.
k. Compare your results with Figure 1.28. Your name will be sorted into the list so your results may not match exactly. The number of records should exactly match.
l. Click the **Office Button** and position the mouse pointer over **Print**. Select **Quick Print** and click **OK**. Save the query.
m. Click the **Office Button**, select **Manage**, and select **Compact and Repair Database**. Close the file.

...continued on Next Page

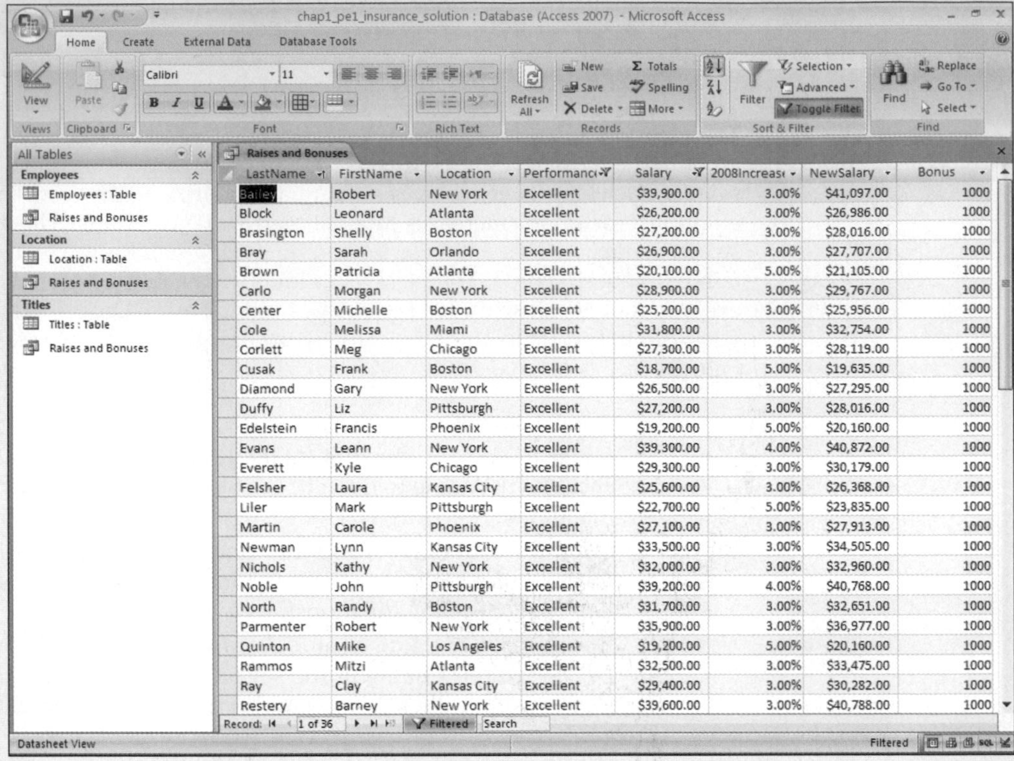

Figure 1.28 Sorted and Filtered Query Results

2 Member Rewards

The Prestige Hotel chain caters to upscale business travelers and provides state of the art conference, meeting, and reception facilities. It prides itself on its international, four-star cuisines. Last year, it began a member rewards club to help the marketing department track the purchasing patterns of its most loyal customers. All of the hotel transactions are stored in the database. Your task is to update a customer record and identify the customers who had weddings in St. Paul. Verify your work by examining Figure 1.29.

a. Copy the partially completed file in *chap1_pe2_memrewards.accdb* from the Exploring Access folder to your production folder. Rename it **chap1_pe2_memrewards_solution**. Double-click the file name to open it. Enable the security content by clicking the **Options** command in the Security Warning bar. Select **Enable this content** and then click **OK**.

b. Open the **Members Form form** and click **New (blank) record** in the Navigation bar. (It has a yellow asterisk.)

c. Enter the information below in the form. Press **Tab** to move from field to field.

Field Name	Value
MemNumber	1718
LastName	Your Last Name
FirstName	Your First Name
JoinDate	7/30/2008
Address	124 West Elm Apt 12
City	Your hometown
State	Your state (2 character code)
Zip	00001

...continued on Next Page

Phone	9995551234
Email	Your e-mail
OrderID	9325
ServiceDate	8/1/2008
ServiceID	3
NoInParty	2
Location	20

d. Click **Close form** in the database window (X) to close the form.
e. Double-click the **Members table** in the Navigation pane. Find Boyd Pegel in the first and last name field and replace his name with **your name**. Close the table.
f. Double-click the **Member Service by City query** in the Navigation pane. Find a record that displays **St Paul** as the value in the *City field*. Click **St Paul** to select that data entry.
g. Select **Selection** in the Sort & Filter group on the Home tab. Click **Equals "St Paul"**.
h. Find a record that displays **Wedding** as the value in the *ServiceName* field. Click **Wedding** to select that data entry.
i. Select **Selection** in the Sort & Filter group on the Home tab. Click **Equals "Wedding"**.
j. Click any value in the **FirstName** field. Click **Sort Ascending** in the Sort & Filter group on the Home tab. Click any value in the **LastName** field. Click **Sort Ascending** in the Sort & Filter group on the Home tab.
k. Click the **Office Button**, select **Print**, and click **OK** to print the sorted and filtered query.
l. Save and close the query.
m. Click the **Office Button**, select **Manage**, and then select **Compact and Repair Database**. Close the file.

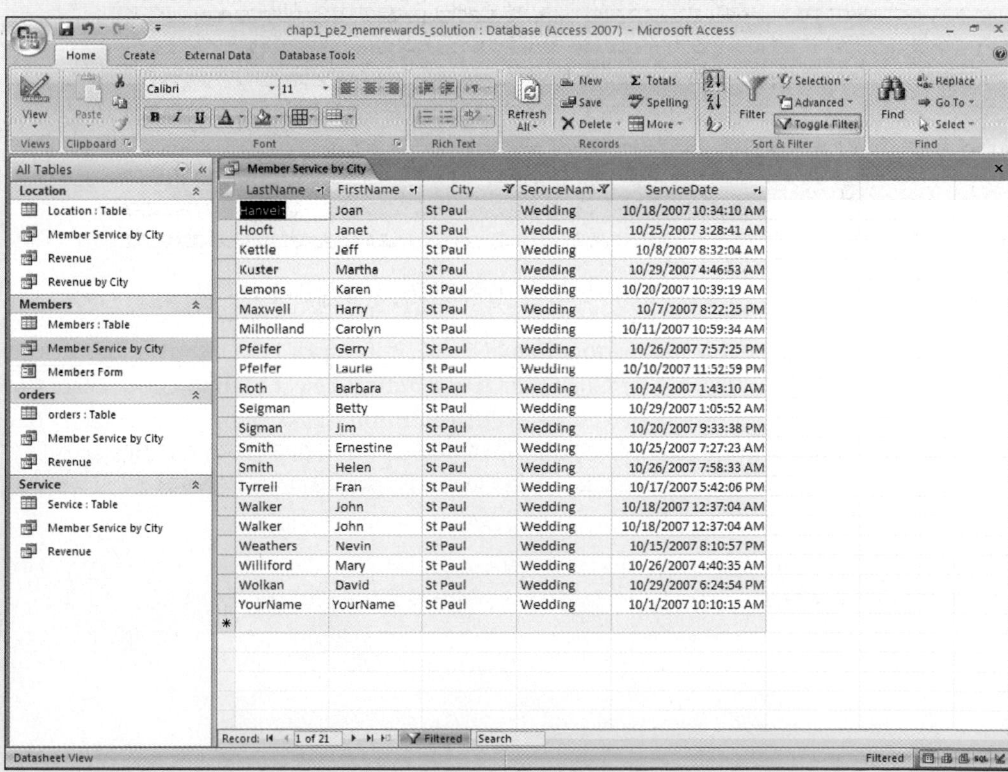

Figure 1.29 Sorted and Filtered Query Results

3 Vancouver Preschool

The Vancouver Preschool is a dynamic and exciting educational environment for young children. It launches each school year with a fundraiser that helps provide classroom supplies. Patrons are asked to donate goods and services, which are auctioned at a welcome-back-to-school dinner for students, parents, grandparents, and friends. All of the data about the donations are contained in an Access file. Your task is to make some modifications to the data and print a form and a report. Verify your work by comparing it to Figure 1.30. The report in the figure is displayed at a higher zoom percentage so that you can read the report easily. Your report may appear as a full page.

a. Copy the partially completed file *chap1_pe3_preschool.accdb* from the Exploring Access folder to your production folder. Rename it **chap1_pe3_preschool_solution.accdb**. Double-click the file name to open it. Click **Options** on the Security Warning bar, click **Enable this content**, and then click **OK**.

b. Open the **Donors form**. Navigate to a **new blank record** by clicking the navigation button with the yellow asterisk on it.

c. Enter the information below in the form.

Field Name	Value
DonorID	(New)
FirstName	Your First Name
LastName	Your Last Name
Address	124 West Elm Apt 12
City	Your hometown
State	Your state
Zip	00001
Phone	9995551234
Notes	Your e-mail
Item Donated	Car wash and hand wax
Number Attending	2
Item Value	100
Category	Service

d. Click **Print Record**. Close the form.

e. Open the **Items for Auction** report. Check to ensure that the *car wash and hand wax* donation is listed. If it is, print the report. Close Print preview.

f. Click the **Office Button**, select **Manage**, and select **Compact and Repair Database**.

g. Click the **Office Button**, select **Manage**, and select **Back Up Database**. Use the default backup file name.

h. Close the file.

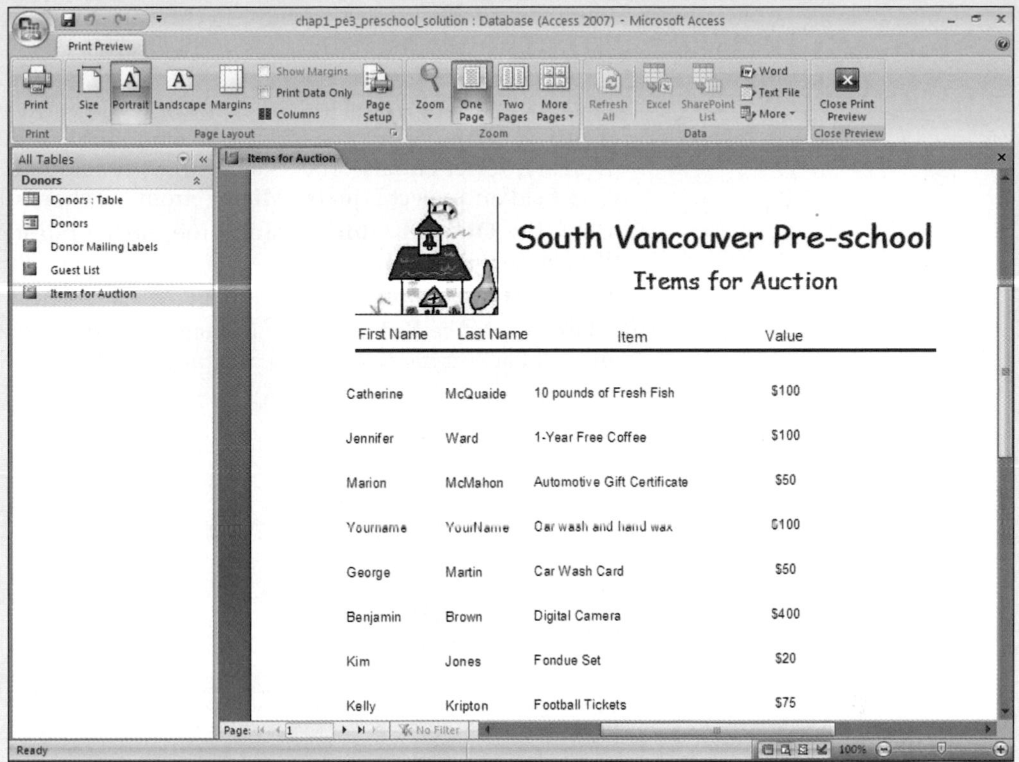

Figure 1.30 Report

4 Custom Coffee

The Custom Coffee Company is a small service organization that provides coffee, tea, and snacks to offices. Custom Coffee also provides and maintains the equipment for brewing the beverages. Although the firm is small, its excellent reputation for providing outstanding customer service has helped it grow. Part of the customer service is determined through a database the firm owner set up to organize and keep track of customer purchases. Verify your work by comparing it to Figure 1.31. The report in the figure is displayed at a higher zoom percentage so that you can read the report easily. Your report may appear as a full page.

a. Copy the partially completed file *chap1_pe4_coffee.accdb* from the Exploring Access folder to your production folder. Rename it **chap1_pe4_coffee_solution.accdb**. Double-click the file name to open the file. Click **Options** in the Security Warning bar, click **Enable this content**, and then click **OK**.

b. Click the **Navigation pane down arrow** to change the object view from Tables and Related Views to **Object Type**.

c. Examine the other objects, reports, forms, and queries in the database. Click the **Navigation pane down arrow** and restore the **Tables and Related Views** method of looking at the objects.

d. Double-click the **Sales Reps table** to open it. Replace *YourName* with **your name** in both the Last Name and First Name fields. Close the table by clicking Close in the database window.

e. Double-click the **Customers Form** to open it. Navigate to a **new blank record** by clicking the navigation button with the yellow asterisk on it. Use **your name** for the *Customer* and *Contact* fields. Invent an address, phone, and e-mail. Type **Miami** for the city and **FL** for the state fields. The *Service Start Date* is **01/17/2005**. The *Credit Rating* is **A**. Type a **2** for the *Sales Rep ID*. It will convert to *S002* automatically.

f. Close the Customers Form.

g. Double-click the **Orders form** to open it. Navigate to a new blank record by clicking the bottom navigation button with the yellow asterisk on it.

h. Type **16** as the *Customer ID*. The database will convert it to *C0016*. In the *Payment Type*, type **Cash** or select **Cash** using the drop-down arrow.

...continued on Next Page

i. Type **4** in the *Product ID box* and **2** in *Quantity*. In the next row, type **6** and **1** for *Product ID* and *Quantity*. The Product IDs will convert to P0004 and P0006. Close the form, saving changes if requested.

j. Open the **Order Details Report**. Scroll down to verify that your name appears both as a customer and as a sales rep (LastName). Right-click **your name** in the LastName field and select **Equals "Your Name"** from the shortcut menu. Right click **Miami** in the City field and select **Equals "Miami"** from the shortcut menu.

k. Click the **Office Button**, position the mouse pointer over **Print**, and select **Print Preview**. Click **Print**.

l. Click the **Office Button**, select **Manage**, and then select **Compact and Repair Database**.

m. Click the **Office Button**, select **Manage**, and then select **Back Up Database**. Use the default backup file name. Close the file.

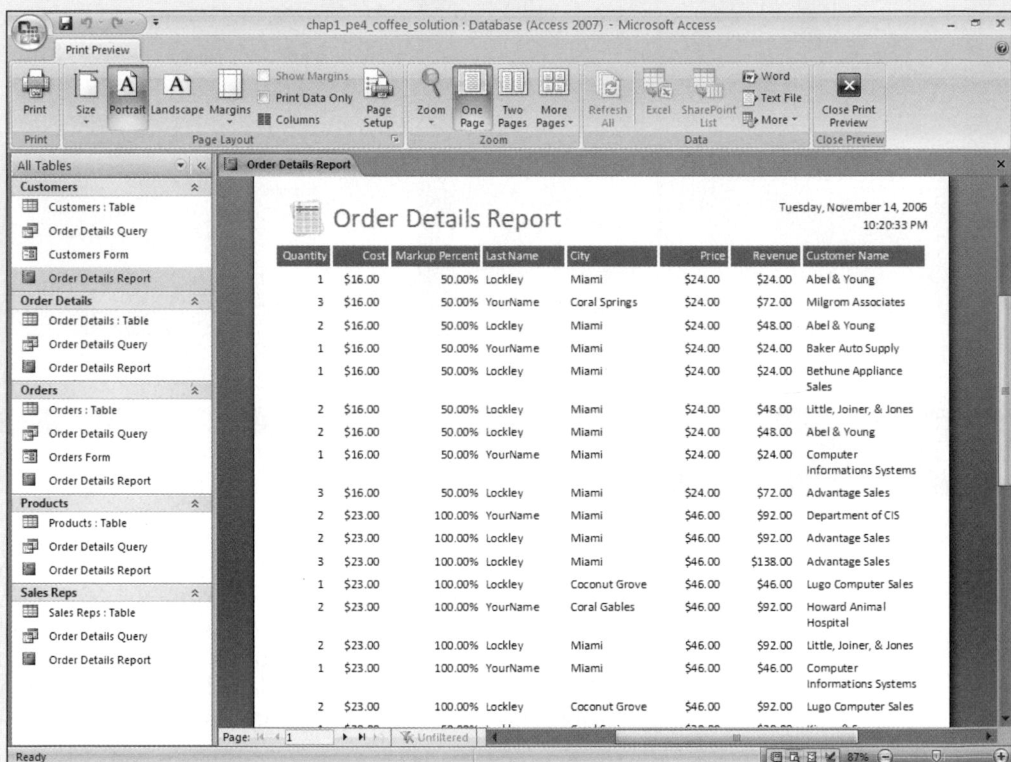

Figure 1.31 Report Showing Changes Made Using Forms

Mid-Level Exercises

1 Object Navigation, Data Entry, and Printing Database Objects

Your little sister lives to play soccer. She told her coach that you have become a computer expert. Coach (who is also the league director) called you to ask for help with the Access database file containing all of the league information. You agreed, and he promptly delivered a disc containing a copy of the league's database. The file contains information on the players, the coaches, and the teams. Players are classified by skill and experience level, with the best players described as "A." The Coaches table classifies coaching status as level 1 (head coaches) or 2 (assistant coaches). Coach asks that you add new players to the database and then identify all of the players not yet assigned to teams. He also needs you to identify the teams without coaches, the unassigned coaches, and asks that you assign each team a head and an assistant coach. Finally, Coach convinces you to volunteer as a coach in the league. Verify your work by looking at Figure 1.32.

a. Locate the file named *chap1_mid1_soccer.accdb*, copy it to your working folder, and rename it **chap1_mid1_soccer_solution.accdb**. Open the file and enable the content.

b. Open the Relationships window and examine the tables, the relationships, and the fields located in each table. Close the Relationships window.

c. Examine all of the objects in the database and think about the work Coach asked you to do. Identify which objects will assist you in accomplishing the assigned tasks.

d. Open the **Players form** and create a new record. Use your name, but you may invent the data about your address and phone. You are classified as an "A" player. Print the form containing your record. Close the form.

e. Open the **Coaches table**. Replace record 13 with **your instructor's name**. Add **yourself** as a new record. You are a *coach status* **1**.

f. Identify the players not assigned to teams. Assign each player to a team while balancing skill levels. (You would not want one team in the league to have all of the "A" skill level players because they would always win.)

g. Identify the teams without coaches and the coaches not assigned to teams. Assign a head coach and an assistant coach to each team. You may need to assign a person with head coaching qualifications to an assistant position. If you do, change his or her *status* to **2**.

h. After you assign all of the players and coaches to teams, open and print the **Master Coaching List report**.

i. After you assign all of the players and coaches to teams, open and print the **Team Rosters report**. Close the database.

...continued on Next Page

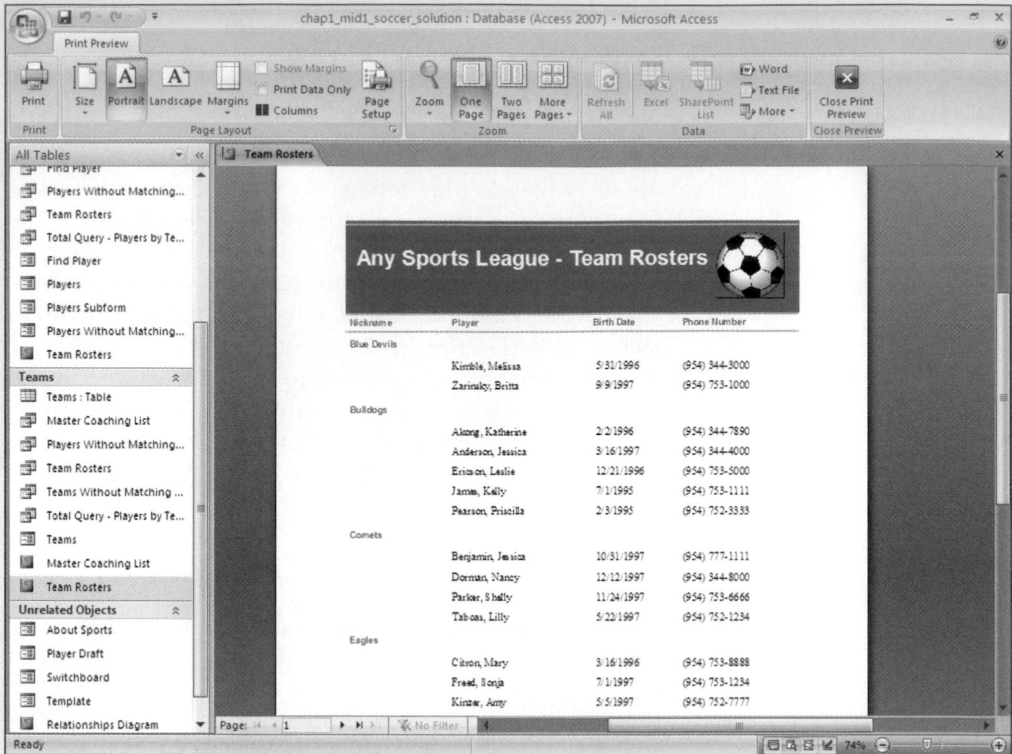

Figure 1.32 Team Roster Report

2 Sorting and Filtering Table Data Using Advanced Filters

You are the senior partner in a large, independent real estate firm that specializes in home sales. Although you still represent buyers and sellers in real estate transactions, you find that most of your time is spent supervising the agents who work for your firm. This fact distresses you because you like helping people buy and sell homes. There is a database containing all of the information on the properties your firm has listed. You believe that by using the data in the database more effectively, you can spend less time supervising the other agents and spend more time doing the part of your job that you like doing the best. Your task is to determine how many three-bedroom, two-bathroom, and garage properties your firm has listed for sale with a listing price under $400,000. Finally, you need to sort the data by list price in descending order. Refer to Figure 1.33 to verify that your results match the results shown.

a. Locate the file named *chap1_mid2_realestate.accdb;* copy it to your working folder and rename it **chap1_mid2_realestate_solution.accdb**. Open the file and enable the content. Open the *Agents* table. Find and replace *YourName* with **your name** in the first and last name fields. Close table after making the changes.

b. Create a filter by form on the data stored in the *Under 400K query*. Set the criteria to identify **three or more bedrooms**, **two or more bathrooms**, and **garage**: (i.e., not a carport) properties you have listed for sale with a listing price **under $400,000**.

c. Sort the filtered results in **descending** order by the **ListPrice** field.

d. After you are sure that your results are correct, save the query.

e. Capture a screenshot of the sorted and filtered Under 400K query. With the sorted and filtered table open on your computer, press **PrintScrn**. Open Word; launch a new blank document, type **your name and section number**, and press **Enter**. Press **Ctrl+V** or

...continued on Next Page

click Paste. Print the word document. Save it as **chap1_mid2_realestate_solution.docx**. Close the Word document.

f. Compact, repair, and back up the database. Name the backup **chap1_mid2_realestate_backup.accdb**. Close the database.

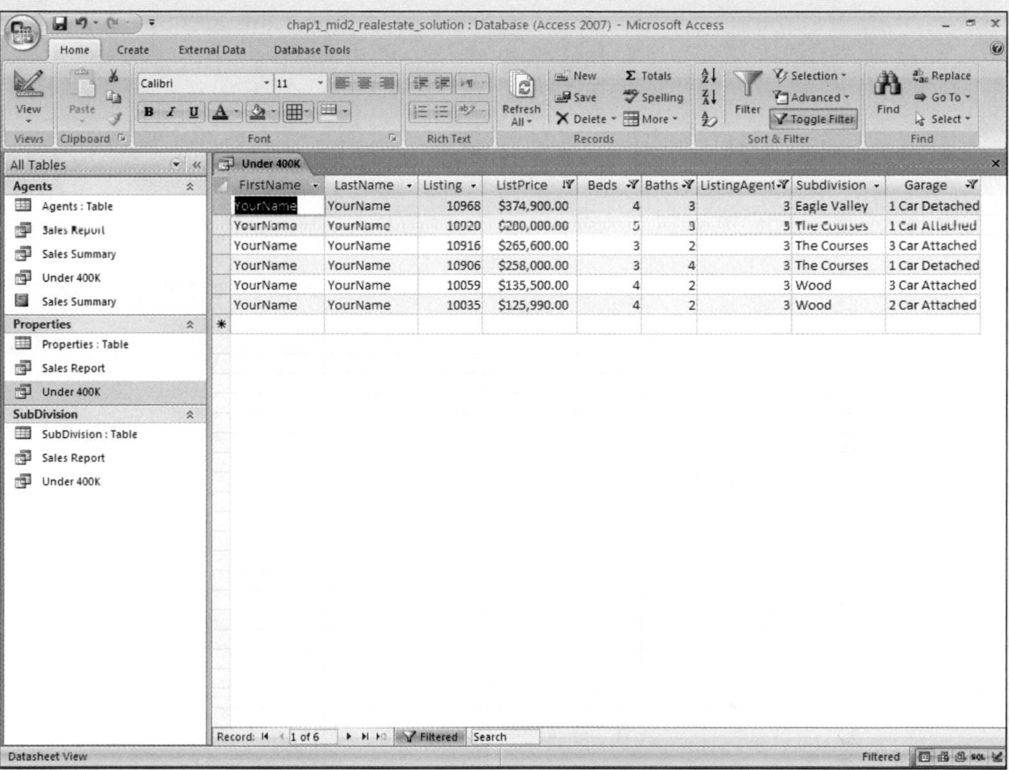

Figure 1.33 Sorted, Filtered Table

3 Sorting and Filtering Table Data Using Advanced Filters, Printing a Report

You work for the Office of Residence Life at your university as a work/study employee. The dean of student affairs, Martha Sink, Ph.D., placed you in this position because your transcript noted that you were enrolled in a computing class covering Microsoft Access. Dr. Sink has a special project for you. Each year, the Association of Higher Education hosts a national conference to share new ideas and best practices. Next year, the conference will be held on your campus, and the Office of Residence life has the responsibility of planning and organizing the events, speakers, and physical meeting spaces. To facilitate the work, the IT department has created a database containing information on the rooms, speakers, and sessions. Dr. Sink needs your assistance with extracting information from the database. Examine Figure 1.34 to verify your work.

a. Locate the file named *chap1_mid3_natconf.accdb*; copy it to your working folder and rename it **chap1_mid3_natconf_solution.accdb**. Open the file and enable the content. Open the **Speakers table**. Find and replace *YourName* with **your name**. Close the Speakers table.

...continued on Next Page

b. Open the **Speaker - Session Query** and apply a filter to identify the sessions where you or Holly Davis are the speakers. Use Filter by Form and engage the Or tab.

c. Sort the filtered results in descending order by the RoomID field.

d. Capture a screenshot of the sorted and filtered Speaker Session query. With the sorted and filtered query open on your computer press **PrintScrn**. Open Word, launch a new blank document, type **your name and section number**, and press **Enter**. Press **Ctrl+V** or click **Paste**. Print the Word document. Save it as **chap1_mid3_natconf_solution.docx**. Close the query but do not save it.

e. Open the **Master List – Sessions and Speakers report** in Report View. Apply a filter that limits the report to sessions where you are the speaker. Print the report. Close the report.

f. Compact, repair, and back up the database. Name the backup **chap1_mid3_natconf_backup.accdb**. Close the database.

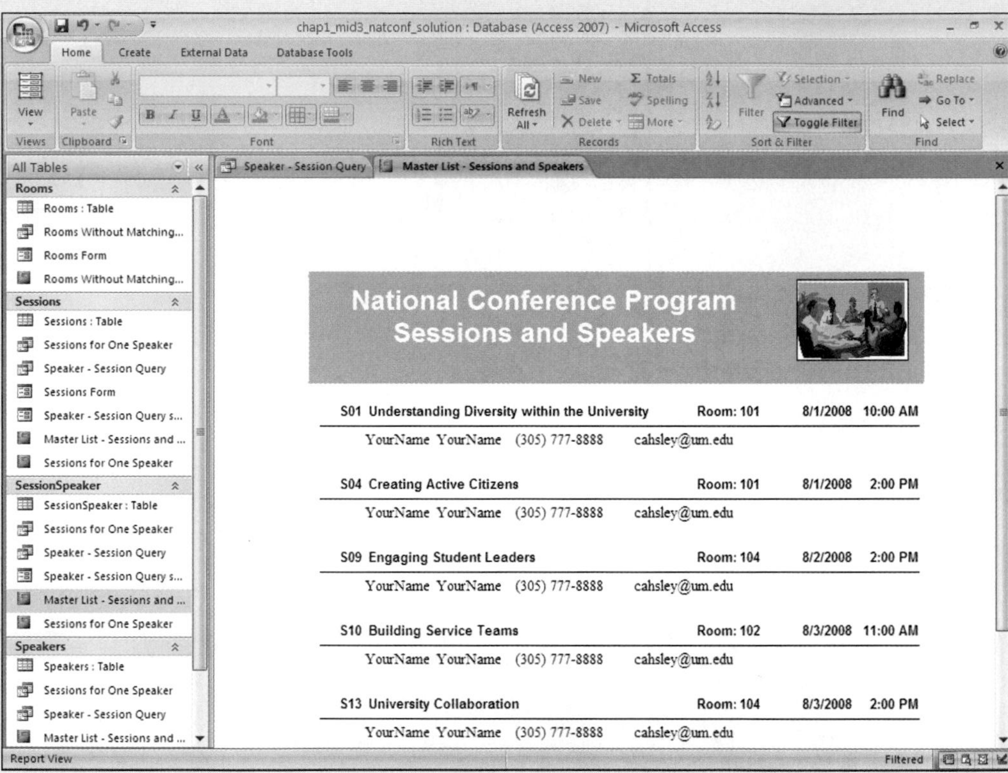

Figure 1.34 Master Sessions and Speakers Report

Capstone Exercise

Your boss expressed a concern about the accuracy of the inventory reports in the bookstore. He needs you to open the inventory database, make modifications to some records, and determine if the changes you make carry through to the other objects in the database. You will make changes to a form and then visit those changes in a table, a query, and a report. When you have verified that the changes update automatically, you will compact and repair the database and make a backup of it.

Database File Setup

You need to copy an original database file, rename the copied file, and then open the copied database to complete this capstone exercise. After you open the copied database, you will replace an existing employee's name with your name.

a. Locate the file named *chap1_cap_bookstore.accdb* and copy it to your working folder.

b. Rename the copied file as **chap1_cap_bookstore_solution.accdb**.

c. Open the *chap1_cap_bookstore_solution.accdb* file and enable the content.

d. Open the **Author Form** form.

e. Navigate to record 7 and replace *YourName* with **your name**.

f. Add a new *Title*, **Computer Wisdom II**. The *ISBN* is **0-684-80416-5**, the *PubID* is **SS**, the *PublDate* is **2007**, the *Price* is **$28.00** (just type 28, no $, period, or zeros), and *StockAmt* is **27** *units*.

g. Navigate to record 6 (or any other record). Close the form.

h. Open the **Author Form** again and navigate to record 7. The changes are there because Access works from storage, not memory. Close the form.

Sort a Query and Apply a Filter by Selection

You need to reorder a detail query so that the results are sorted alphabetically by the publisher name.

a. Open the **Publishers, Books, and Authors Query**.

b. Click in any record in the PubName field and sort the field in alphabetical order.

c. Check to make sure that two books list you as the author.

d. Click *your name* in the Author field and filter the records to show your books.

e. Close the query without saving the changes.

View a Report

You need to examine the Publishers, Books, and Authors report to determine if the changes you made to the Author form carried through to the report.

a. Open the **Publishers, Books, and Authors Report**.

b. Check to make sure that the report shows two books listing you as the author.

c. Print the report.

d. Close the report.

Filter a Table

You need to examine the Books table to determine if the changes you made to the Author form carried through to the related table. You also will filter the table to display books published after 2004 with fewer than 30 copies in inventory.

a. Open the **Books** table.

b. Click **Advanced** in the Sort & Filter group, and then select **Filter by Form** from the drop-down list.

c. Create the criteria that will identify all records published after 2004 with fewer than 30 items in stock.

d. Apply the filter.

e. Print the filtered table.

f. Close the table. Do not save the design changes.

Compact, Repair, and Back Up a Database

Now that you are satisfied that any changes made to a form, table, or query carry through the database, you are ready to compact, repair, and back up your file.

a. Select the option to compact and repair your database.

b. Select the option to create a backup copy of your database, accept the default file name, and save it.

c. Close the file.

Mini Cases

Use the rubric following the case as a guide to evaluate your work, but keep in mind that your instructor may impose additional grading criteria or use a different standard to judge your work.

Applying Filters, Printing, and File Management

GENERAL CASE

The *chap1_mc1_safebank.accdb* file contains data from a small bank. Copy the *chap1_mc1_safebank.accdb* file to your working storage folder, name it **chap1_mc1_safebank_solution.accdb**, and open the copied file. Use the skills from this chapter to perform several tasks. Open the Customer table, replace YourName with your name, and sort the data in alphabetical order by LastName. Print the Customer table. Open the Branch table and make yourself the manager of the Campus branch. Close both tables. Open the Branch Customers query and filter it to show only the accounts at the Campus branch with balances over $1,500.00. Print the filtered query results. Close the query but do not save it. Compact, repair, and backup your work.

Performance Elements	Exceeds Expectations	Meets Expectations	Below Expectations
Sort and print table data	Printout displays data sorted in requested order.	The table was successfully printed, but the order is incorrect.	Output missing or corrupted.
Apply filters and print query data	Appropriate filters successfully created and printed.	One of the requested filters but not both work correctly. Output created.	Output missing or corrupted.
Data entry	Data were entered correctly.	Some but not all of the requested data were entered correctly, or other data were overwritten.	Output missing or corrupted.
File management	Database was correctly compacted, repaired, and backed up.	The database was successfully compacted but not backed up or vice versa.	Files not submitted.

Combining Name Fields

RESEARCH CASE

This chapter introduced you to the power of using Access filters and setting criteria, but you have much more to explore. Copy the file named *chap1_mc2_traders.accdb* to your production folder and rename it **chap1_mc2_traders_solution.accdb**. Open the file and enable the content. Open the Employees table and replace YourName with your first and last names. Open the Revenue report and switch to the appropriate view. Use the tools that you have learned in this chapter to filter the report. You wish to limit the output to only your sales of Seafood. You may need to use Access Help to get the filters to work. Once the report is filtered, print it. Write your instructor a letter explaining how you accomplished this step. Use a letter template in Word, your most professional writing style, and clear directions that someone could follow in order to accomplish this task. Attach the printout of the name list to the letter. Turn the printouts in to the instructor if instructed to do so. Back up, compact, and repair your database.

Performance Elements	Exceeds Expectations	Meets Expectations	Below Expectations
Use online help	Appropriate articles located, and letter indicates comprehension.	Appropriate articles located, but letter did not demonstrate comprehension.	Articles not found.
Report filtered to display only your sales of seafood	Printed list attached to letter in requested format.	Printed list is attached, but the filter failed to screen one or more salespeople or categories.	List missing or incomprehensible.
Summarize and communicate	Letter clearly written and could be used as directions.	Letter text indicates some understanding but also weaknesses.	Letter missing or incomprehensible.
File management	Database was correctly compacted, repaired, and backed up.	Database was successfully compacted but not backed up or vice versa.	Files not submitted.
Esthetics	Letter template correctly employed.	Template employed but signed in the wrong place or improperly used.	Letter missing or incomprehensible.

Coffee Revenue Queries

DISASTER RECOVERY

A co-worker called you into his office and explained that he was having difficulty with Access 2007 and asked you to look at his work. Copy the *chap1_mc3_coffee.accdb* file to your working storage folder, rename it **chap1_mc3_coffee_solution.accdb**, and open the file. Your co-worker explains that the report is incorrect. It shows that Lockley is the sales representative for "Coulter Office Supplies" and the "Little, Joiner, and Jones" customers, when in fact, you are those customers' sales representative. Make sure your name replaces YourName in the Sales Reps table. Find the source of the error and correct it. Run and print the report and turn the printout and file in to your instructor if instructed to do so. Compact, repair, and backup your database.

Performance Elements	Exceeds Expectations	Meets Expectations	Below Expectations
Error identification	Correct identification and correction of all errors.	Correct identification of all errors and correction of some errors.	Errors neither located nor corrected.
Reporting	Report opened, run, and printed successfully.	Printout submitted, but with errors.	No printout submitted for evaluation.
File management	Database was correctly compacted, repaired, and backed up.	Database was successfully compacted but not backed up or vice versa.	Files not submitted.

chapter 2 | **Access**

Relational Databases and Multi-Table Queries

Designing Databases and Using Related Data

After you read this chapter, you will be able to:

1. Design data **(page 131)**.
2. Create tables **(page 136)**.
3. Understand table relationships **(page 149)**.
4. Share data with Excel **(page 150)**.
5. Establish table relationships **(page 154)**.
6. Create a query **(page 166)**.
7. Specify criteria for different data types **(page 169)**.
8. Copy and run a query **(page 173)**.
9. Use the Query Wizard **(page 173)**.
10. Understand large database differences **(page 177)**.

Hands-On Exercises

Exercises	Skills Covered
1. TABLE DESIGN, PROPERTIES, VIEWS, AND WIZARDS (page 142) **Open:** a new blank database **Save as:** chap2_ho1-3_safebank_solution.accdb **Back up as:** chap2_ho1_safebank_solution.accdb	• Create a New Database • Create a Table by Entering Data • Change the Primary Key, Modify Field Properties, and Delete a Field • Modify Table Fields in Design View • Create a New Field in Design View • Switch Between the Table Design and the Table Datasheet Views
2. IMPORTS AND RELATIONSHIPS (page 159) **Open:** chap2_ho1-3_safebank_solution.accdb (from Exercise 1) and chap2_ho2_safebank.xlsx **Save as:** chap2_ho1-3_safebank_solution.accdb (additional modifications) **Back up as:** chap2_ho2_safebank_solution. accdb	• Import Excel Data into an Access Table • Import Additional Excel Data • Modify an Imported Table's Design • Add Data to an Imported Table • Establish Table Relationships • Understand How Referential Integrity Protects Data
3. MULTIPLE-TABLE QUERY (page 178) **Open:** chap2_ho1-3_safebank_solution.accdb (from Exercise 2) **Save as:** chap2_ho1-3_safebank_solution.accdb (additional modifications)	• Create a Query Using a Wizard • Specify Simple Query Criteria • Change Query Data • Add a Table to a Query Using Design View and Sort a Query

CASE STUDY

National Conference

You received a work-study assignment to the Office of Student Life at your school. This morning, the dean of Student Affairs, Jackie Cole, invited you to come to her office. Dr. Cole returned from the National Conference of Student Service Providers yesterday. Thousands of educators participate in this conference annually. She volunteered your school to host the event next year. She explained that this is a wonderful opportunity to showcase your school to the rest of the education world, but that the conference details need to be planned carefully so that the scheduled events execute flawlessly. Then Dr. Cole explained that she selected you as the work-study student because of your Access skills. She explained that no one else in the office knew anything about Access. She noted that a project of this magnitude required a database to efficiently manage the data. Then she said, "We are depending on you to create and manage the database and make our school look good."

Dr. Cole asked the IT department to help you design the database. The IT staff has created a small database with a table for the speakers and a table that joins the speakers and sessions together. An Excel spreadsheet contains information about the sessions. You will need to import the Excel data into the Access file, connect it with the rest of the database, and update the data.

Case Study

The IT staff did not think about the conference participants when they designed the database. You need to design a table that will hold the information about the conference participants. Think carefully about what information might be needed about each registrant. Then think about how to connect the registration information to the rest of the database. You need to establish the primary and foreign keys for the Registrant table as you plan the other fields in that table.

Your Assignment

- Copy the file named *chap2_case_natconf.accdb* to your production folder. Name the copy **chap2_case_natconf_solution.accdb**.
- Open each table and familiarize yourself with the data.
- Open the Relationships window and acquaint yourself with the tables, fields, and relationships among the tables in the database.
- Import the data contained in the Excel file, *chap2_case_sessions.xlsx*. As you create the import, think about which field will be the primary key and establish appropriate properties.
- Establish a relationship between the Sessions table and the other tables in the database. Remember that a relationship may only be formed on data of like type and size.
- Replace the first record in the Speakers table with information about you.
- Create a new record in the Speakers table. Add yourself as a speaker. Your area of expertise is Student Life.
- Create a new Session. Title it **Undergraduate Challenges**. Examine the session times and rooms and schedule this session so that it does not conflict with the other sessions.
- Create a query that will show the speaker's name, the session title, and the room number. Add parameters to limit the output to sessions conducted by **Davis**, **Kline**, and **you**. Print the query results.
- Create a table for conference participant's registrations. Carefully anticipate which fields need to be included. Participants must pay a $500 registration fee.
- Create a new record in the registration table. Add yourself as a participant.
- Capture a screenshot of the Relationships window. Paste the screenshot into a Word file. Save the file as **chap2_case_natconf_solution.docx**.
- Compact and repair your file. Back up the database as **chap2_case_natconf_solution_backup.accdb**.

Table Design, Properties, Views, and Wizards

Good database design provides the architectural framework supporting the work the database accomplishes. If the framework is flawed, the resulting work will always have flaws, too. You may remember the period leading to New Year's Eve in 1999, Y2K. Many people stocked up on groceries, withdrew cash from their checking accounts, and filled their gas tanks because they believed that the computer-operated grocery checkouts, automatic banking machines, and gasoline pumps would not function properly (if at all) on New Year's Day, 2000. These frightened people had legitimate reasons due to poor database design. Electronic data storage was (and remains) relatively expensive. Principles of good design dictate saving storage space when possible. As a space-saving measure, most dates in most computers prior to the mid-1990s stored the year as a two-digit number. For example, 1993 was stored as 93. The Information Systems and Computer Science professionals responsible for managing the databases in the world failed to anticipate the consequences of flawed database design.

Computers perform relatively simple arithmetic computations to measure time lapses. When subtracting 1993 from 1995, the computer knows that two years have passed. The results do not change when the dates are stored as 93 and 95. However, what would happen when the computer subtracted 99 from 01? You know that a two-year period has passed. But, the computer would believe that a *negative* 98 years had passed! Before New Year's Day, 2000, IS professionals worked extra hours correcting the design flaws in the way their systems handled and processed dates. On January 1, 2000, computerized grocery stores, ATMs, and gas pumps virtually all worked. The overtime hours combined with the new hardware and software required cost an estimated $21 billion globally to fix.

This chapter introduces the Safebank database case study to present the basic principles of table and query design. You use tables and forms to input data, and you create queries and reports to extract information from the database in a useful and organized way. The value of that information depends entirely on the quality of the underlying data, which must be both complete and accurate.

In this section, you learn about the importance of proper design and essential guidelines that are used throughout the book. After developing the design, you implement that design in Access. You create a table, and then refine its design by changing the properties of various fields. You will gain an understanding of the importance of data validation during data entry.

Designing Data

As a consumer of financial services, you know that your bank or credit union maintains data about you. Your bank has your name, address, phone number, and Social Security number. It knows if you have a credit card and what your balances are. Additionally, your bank keeps information about its branches. Think about the information your bank generates and then make a list of the data needed to produce that information. The key to the design process is to visualize the output required to determine the input needed to produce that output. Think of the specific fields you need and characterize each field according to the type of data it contains (such as text, numbers, or dates) as well as its size (length). Figure 2.1 shows one sample list of fields. Your list may vary. The order of the fields within the table and the specific field names are not significant. What is important is that the tables contain all necessary fields so that the system can perform as intended.

Customer's Last Name–Text
Customer's First Name–Text
Customer's Identification Number–Either text or number
Address–Text
City–Text
State–Text
Postal Code–Number
Phone–Text
Branch Identification–Either text or number
Branch Manager's Name–Text
Branch Manager's Start Date–Number date formatted
Branch Location–Text
Account Number–Either text or number
Balance–Number formatted as currency

Figure 2.1 Data Needed for a Bank Database

Figure 2.1 reflects the results of a careful design process based on seven essential guidelines:

1. Include the necessary data.
2. Design for the next 100 years.
3. Design in compliance with Sarbanes Oxley.
4. Design in compliance with PNPI Regulations.
5. Store data in its smallest parts.
6. Avoid calculated fields in table data.
7. Design to accommodate date arithmetic.

The following paragraphs discuss these guidelines. As you proceed through the text, you will begin developing the experience necessary to design your own systems. Design is an important skill. You also must understand how to design a database and its tables to use Access effectively.

Include the Necessary Data

> . . . ask yourself what information will be expected from the system, and then determine the data required to produce that information.

The best way to determine what data are necessary is to create a rough draft of the reports you will need, and then design tables that contain the fields necessary to create those reports. In other words, ask yourself what information will be expected from the system, and then determine the data required to produce that information. Consider, for example, the type of information that can and cannot be produced from the table in Figure 2.1:

- You can determine which branch a customer uses. You cannot, however, tell the customer with multiple accounts at different locations what the total balance of all accounts might be.

- You can calculate a total of all account balances by adding individual account balances together. You could also calculate the sum of all deposits at a branch. You cannot tell when a deposit was made because this small exercise does not store that data.
- You can determine who manages a particular branch and which accounts are located there. You cannot determine how long the customer has banked with the branch because the date that he or she opened the account is not in the table.

Whether these omissions are important depends on the objectives of the system. Of course, the data stored in a real bank's database is far more complex and much larger than the data you will use. This case has been simplified.

Design for the Next 100 Years

A fundamental law of information technology states that systems evolve continually and that information requirements change. Try to anticipate the future needs of the system, and then build in the flexibility to satisfy those demands. Include the necessary data at the outset, and be sure that the field sizes are large enough to accommodate future expansion. The ***field size property*** defines how many characters to reserve for a specific field.

The ***field size property*** defines how much space to reserve for each field.

When you include all possible elements of data that anyone might ever need, you drive up the cost of the database. Each element costs employee time to enter and maintain the data and consumes storage space. Computers have a finite amount of space. Good database design must balance the current and future needs of the system against the cost of recording and storing unnecessary data elements. Even with using data warehouses, the amount of data that we can store is limited.

Good database design must balance the current and future needs of the system against the cost of recording and storing unnecessary data elements.

Suppose you are designing a database for your college. You would need to include students' on-campus and permanent addresses. It might be useful for someone to know other places a student might have lived or even visited during their lives. A worker in the Student Life office could help an international student connect with someone who used to live in or at least visited the international student's homeland. A student who had moved often or traveled extensively might need an extra page on his or her application form. Completing the application might take so long that the student might apply to a different college. A worker in the admissions office would need extra time to enter all the places of residence and travel into the database. The school's database file would grow and require additional storage space on the university computer system. The benefits provided to the international student from connecting him to someone who had been in his country may not justify the cost of entering, maintaining, and storing the additional data.

The data will prove useful only if they are accurate. You need to anticipate possible errors a data entry operator might commit. Access provides tools to protect data from user error. A ***validation rule*** restricts data entry in a field to ensure the correct type of data is entered or that the data does not violate other enforced properties, such as exceed a size limitation. The validation rule checks the authenticity of the data entered when the user exits the field. If the data entry violates the validation rule, an error message appears and prevents the invalid data from being stored in the field.

A ***validation rule*** checks the authenticity of the data entered in a field.

Design in Compliance with Sarbanes Oxley

Following the financial and accounting scandals involving Enron and World Com in 2002, the U.S. Congress passed the ***Sarbanes Oxley Act (SOX)***. Its intent is to protect the general public and companies' shareholders against fraudulent practices and accounting errors. The Securities and Exchange Commission (SEC) enforces the act. Although primarily focused on the accounting practices followed by publicly traded companies, SOX permeates corporate Information Technology policies and practices. The act requires that all business records, including electronic messages, be saved for a period of five years and be made available to the SEC on request. Penalties for

Sarbanes Oxley Act (SOX) protects the general public and companies' shareholders against fraudulent practices and accounting errors.

non-compliance include fines, imprisonment, or both. The IT department faces the challenge of archiving all the required information in a cost-effective and efficient way.

Design in Compliance with PNPI Regulations

PNPI—Federal laws governing the safeguarding of personal, non-public information such as Social Security Numbers (SSNs), credit card or bank account numbers, medical or educational records, or other sensitive data.

Federal laws and regulations govern the safeguarding of personal, non-public information (***PNPI***), such as Social Security Numbers (SSNs), credit or bank account numbers, medical or educational records, or other sensitive, confidential or protected data (i.e., grades used in context with personally identifiable information such as name, address, or other easily traceable identifiers). Organizations must store your personal information in computer systems. For example, without your Social Security Number, the financial aid office cannot release scholarship money to pay your tuition. Your employer cannot cut a paycheck without knowing your Social Security Number. Your doctor cannot tell the student health service at your school whether you have been immunized against the measles without your written permission. The data must be stored with protected and restricted access. Congress has passed several laws to protect you from identity theft or other misuse of your private, personal information. The most important of these laws include the following:

- Family Educational Rights and Privacy Act (FERPA) [educational records]
- Gramm-Leach-Bliley Act (GLBA) [financial institution and customer data]
- Health Insurance Portability and Accountability Act (HIPAA) [health information]

Store Data in Their Smallest Parts

The design in Figure 2.1 divides a customer's name into two fields (first and last name) to reference each field individually. You might think it easier to use a single field consisting of both the first and last name, but that approach is inadequate. Consider this list in which the customer's name is stored as a single field:

- Allison Foster
- Brit Reback
- Carrie Graber
- Danielle Ferrarro
- Evelyn Adams
- Frances Coulter

The first problem in this approach is lack of flexibility: You could not easily create a salutation of the form *Dear Allison* or *Dear Ms. Foster* because the first and last names are not accessible individually. In actuality you could write a procedure to divide the name field in two, but that is beyond the capability of the Access novice.

A second difficulty is that the list of customers cannot be put into alphabetical order by last name very easily because the last name begins in the middle of the field. The names are already alphabetized by first name because sorting always begins with the left position in a field. Thus the "A" in Allison comes before the "B" in Brit, and so on. The proper way to sort the data is on the last name, which can be done more efficiently if the last name is stored as a separate field.

Think of how an address might be used. The city, state, and postal code should always be stored as separate fields. Any type of mass mailing requires you to sort on postal codes to take advantage of bulk mail. Other applications may require you to select records from a particular state or postal code, which can be done more efficiently if you store the data as separate fields. Often, database users enter the postal code, and the database automatically retrieves the city and state information. You may need to direct a mailing to only a neighborhood or to a single street. The guideline is simple: Store data in their smallest parts.

Avoid Calculated Fields in Table Data

A ***calculated field*** is a field that derives its value from a formula that references one or more existing fields.

A *calculated field* produces a value from an expression—a formula or function that references an existing field or combination of fields. Although the information derived from calculations can be incredibly valuable to the decision maker, it is useful only at the moment the calculation is made. It makes no sense to store outdated data when recalculating; it will provide the decision maker with fresh, accurate information. Calculated fields should not be stored in a table because they are subject to change and waste space.

The total account balance for a customer with multiple accounts is an example of a calculated field because it is computed by adding the balances in all of the customer's accounts together. It is unnecessary to store the calculated sum of account balances in the Account table, because the table contains the fields on which the sum is based. In other words, Access is able to calculate the sum from these fields whenever it is needed, which is much more efficient than doing it manually.

Design to Accommodate Date Arithmetic

A ***constant*** is an unchanging value, like a birth date.

Date arithmetic is the process of subtracting one date from another.

A ***date/time field*** is a field that facilitates calculations for dates and times.

A person's age and date of birth provide equivalent information, as one is calculated from the other. It might seem easier, therefore, to store the age rather than the birth date to avoid the calculation. That would be a mistake because age changes continually and needs to be updated continually, but the date of birth remains *constant*—an unchanging value. Similar reasoning applies to an employee's length of service versus date of hire. Like Excel, Access stores all dates as a serial integer. You can use *date arithmetic* to subtract one date from another to find out the number of days, months, or years that have lapsed between them. Access provides a special data definition for *date/time fields* to facilitate calculations.

Design Multiple Tables

After listing all of the data items that you want to include in the database, you need to group them into similar items. Group the customer information into one table, the branch information into another, and the account information into a third table. A well-designed database provides a means of recombining the data when needed. When the design is sound, the **referential integrity** rules ensure that consistent data is stored in a related table. For example, the Customers and Account tables are linked by relationship. Referential integrity ensures that only valid customer IDs that exist in the Customers table are used in the Account table; it prevents you from entering an invalid customer ID in the Account table.

Data redundancy occurs when unnecessary duplicate information exists in a database.

Avoid *data redundancy*, which is the unnecessary inclusion of duplicate data among tables. You should never store duplicate information in multiple tables in a database. The information about a customer's address should only exist in a single table, the Customers table. It would be poor database design to also include the customer's address in the Account table. When duplicate information exists in a database, errors may result. Suppose the address data were stored in both the Customers and Account tables. You need to anticipate the consequences that may result when a customer moves. A likely outcome would be that the address would be updated in one but not both tables. The result would be unreliable data. Depending on which table served as the source for the output, either the new or the old address might be provided to the manager requesting the information. It is a much stronger design to have the address stored in only one table but tied to the rest of the database through the power of the relationships. See Figure 2.2.

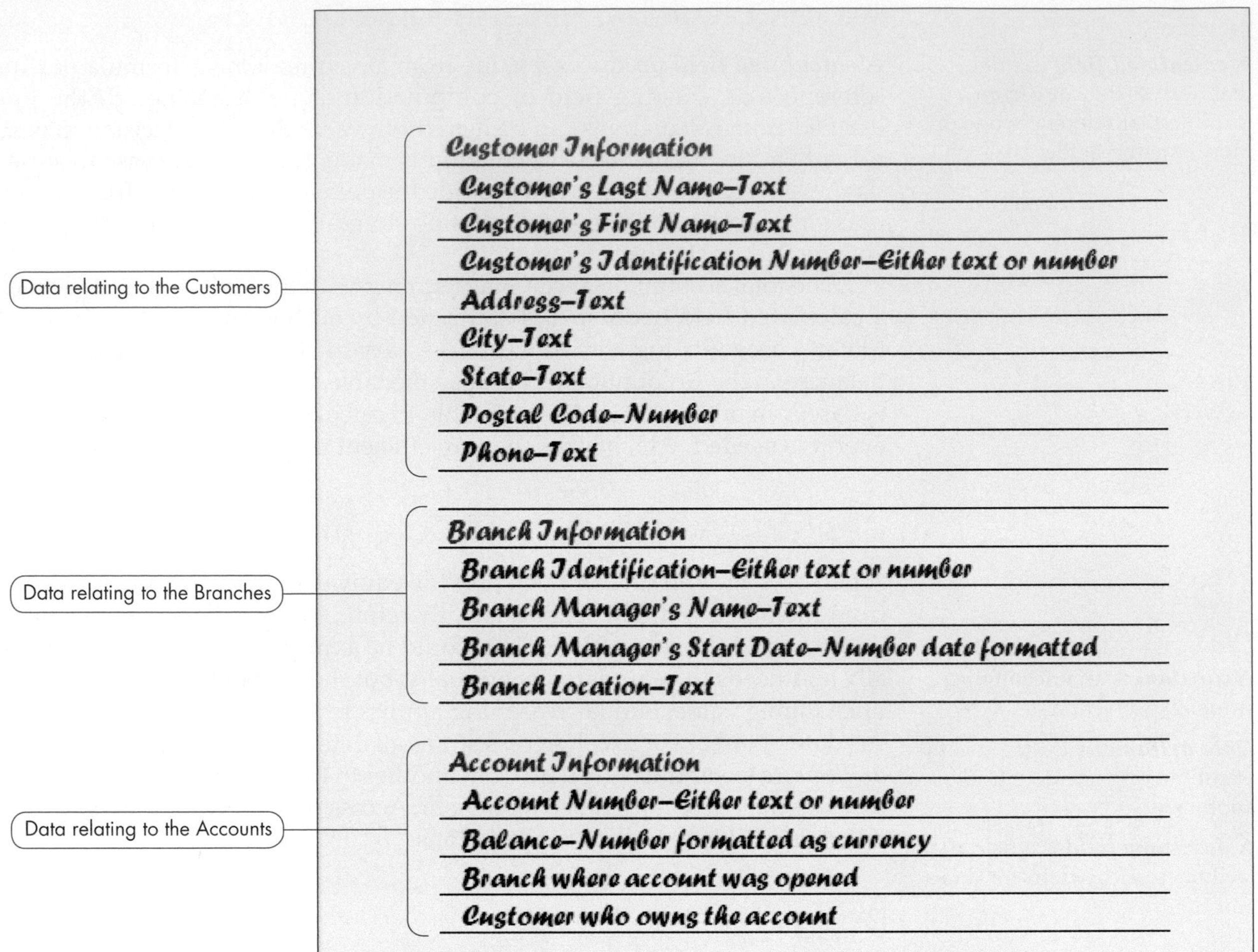

Figure 2.2 Bank's Database Data Grouped to Form a Table

Creating Tables

A table and all Access objects must be created within an Access file. To create a table, you must first create the file that will house it. Access works from storage, not memory. The other Microsoft Office programs work from memory: You create first and then save. With Access you must save a file first, and then create its contents. You will open a new blank database and save it to a specific storage location before you can begin creating your tables.

Access provides several ways to create a table. You can create a table by entering the table data into a field. You also can import table data from another database or application, for example, Excel. Regardless of how a table is created, you can modify it to include a new field or to delete an existing field.

CamelCase notation uses no spaces in multi-word field names, but uses uppercase letters to distinguish the first letter of each new word.

Every field has a field name to identify the data that is entered into the field. The field name should be descriptive of the data and can be up to 64 characters in length, including letters, numbers, and spaces. Actual databases employ ***CamelCase notation*** for fields, objects, and file names. Instead of spaces in multi-word field names, use uppercase letters to distinguish the first letter of each new word, for example, ProductCost or LastName. Access is used frequently as a user-friendly means to connect to large databases stored on mainframes. Using Access, the manager can enter the organization's databases without needing courses in specialized computer languages. The manager then can find the data needed to make a decision and convert it to information. Most large databases and most mainframe computer systems will not accept spaces in field names.

A ***data type*** determines the type of data that can be entered and the operations that can be performed on that data.

Every field also has a ***data type*** that determines the type of data that can be entered and the operations that can be performed on that data. Access recognizes nine data types.

Illustrations of Data Types and Uses | Reference

Data Type	Description	Example
Attachment	The **Attachment** data type is new to Office Access 2007 .accdb files. You can attach images, spreadsheet files, charts, and other types of supported files to the records in your database.	A photo of a product
Number	A **Number** field contains a value that can be used in a calculation, such as the number of credits a student has earned. The contents of a number field are restricted to numbers, a decimal point, and a plus or minus sign.	Height
Text	A **Text** field stores alphanumeric data, such as a student's name or address. It can contain alphabetic characters, numbers, and/or special characters (i.e., an apostrophe in O'Malley). Fields that contain only numbers but are not used in a calculation (i.e., Social Security Number, telephone number, or postal code) should be designated as text fields. A text field can hold up to 255 characters.	City
Memo	A **Memo** field can be up to 65,536 characters long. Memo fields are used to hold descriptive data (several sentences or paragraphs).	Library databases that store research papers
Date/Time	A **Date/Time** field holds formatted dates or times (i.e., mm/dd/yyyy) and allows the values to be used in date or time arithmetic.	March 31, 2008
Currency	A **Currency** field can be used in a calculation and is used for fields that contain monetary values.	Your checking account balance
Yes/No	A **Yes/No** field (also known as a Boolean or Logical field) assumes one of two values, such as Yes or No, True or False, or On or Off.	Dean's list
OLE	An **OLE** Object field contains an object created by another application. OLE objects include pictures, sounds, or graphics.	Excel workbook
AutoNumber	An **AutoNumber** field is a special data type that Access uses to assign the next consecutive number each time you add a record. The value of an AutoNumber field is unique for each record in the file, and thus, AutoNumber fields are frequently used as the primary key. The numbering may be sequential or random.	Customer account number
Hyperlink	A **Hyperlink** field stores a Web address (URL). All Office documents are Web-enabled so that you can click a hyperlink and display the associated Web page.	www.UNCG.edu

Establish a Primary Key

The **primary key** is a unique field (or combination of fields) that identifies each record in a table. Access does not require that each table have a primary key. Good database design strongly recommends the inclusion of a primary key in each table. You should select infrequently changing data for the primary key. For example, a complete address (street, city, state, and postal code) may be unique but would not make a good primary key because it is subject to change when someone moves.

You probably would not use a person's name as the primary key because many people have the same name. A Customer Identification Number, on the other hand, is unique and is a frequent choice for the primary key, as in the Customers table in this chapter. The primary key emerges naturally in many applications, such as a part number in an inventory system, or the ISBN in the Books table of a bookstore or library. At your school, you have a Student ID that uniquely identifies you. No other student has the same Student ID. When no primary key occurs naturally, you can create a new field with the ***AutoNumber field*** type, and Access will assign a unique identifying number to each new record. Figure 2.3 illustrates two types of table data. In the table shown at the top of the figure, the book's ISBN is the natural primary key because no two book titles have the same ISBN. It uniquely identifies the records in the table. The lower table depicts a table where no unique identifier emerged naturally from the data, so Access automatically numbered the records in order to distinguish them.

The ***AutoNumber field*** type assigns a unique identifying number to each record.

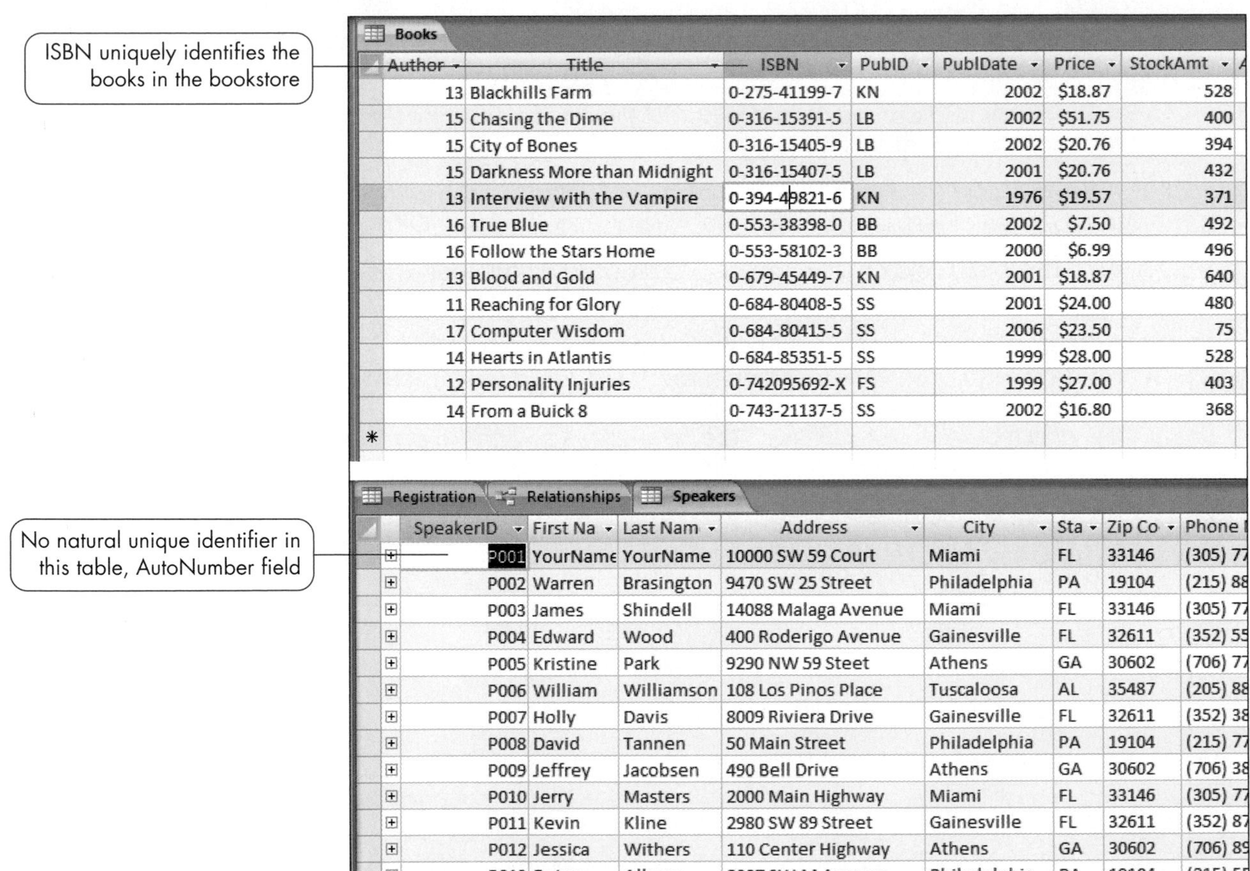

ISBN uniquely identifies the books in the bookstore
No natural unique identifier in this table, AutoNumber field
Books
Registration
Relationships
Speakers

Author	Title	ISBN	PubID	PublDate	Price	StockAmt
13	Blackhills Farm	0-275-41199-7	KN	2002	$18.87	528
15	Chasing the Dime	0-316-15391-5	LB	2002	$51.75	400
15	City of Bones	0-316-15405-9	LB	2002	$20.76	394
15	Darkness More than Midnight	0-316-15407-5	LB	2001	$20.76	432
13	Interview with the Vampire	0-394-49821-6	KN	1976	$19.57	371
16	True Blue	0-553-38398-0	BB	2002	$7.50	492
16	Follow the Stars Home	0-553-58102-3	BB	2000	$6.99	496
13	Blood and Gold	0-679-45449-7	KN	2001	$18.87	640
11	Reaching for Glory	0-684-80408-5	SS	2001	$24.00	480
17	Computer Wisdom	0-684-80415-5	SS	2006	$23.50	75
14	Hearts in Atlantis	0-684-85351-5	SS	1999	$28.00	528
12	Personality Injuries	0-742095692-X	FS	1999	$27.00	403
14	From a Buick 8	0-743-21137-5	SS	2002	$16.80	368

SpeakerID	First Na	Last Nam	Address	City	Sta	Zip Co	Phone
P001	YourName	YourName	10000 SW 59 Court	Miami	FL	33146	(305) 77
P002	Warren	Brasington	9470 SW 25 Street	Philadelphia	PA	19104	(215) 88
P003	James	Shindell	14088 Malaga Avenue	Miami	FL	33146	(305) 77
P004	Edward	Wood	400 Roderigo Avenue	Gainesville	FL	32611	(352) 55
P005	Kristine	Park	9290 NW 59 Steet	Athens	GA	30602	(706) 77
P006	William	Williamson	108 Los Pinos Place	Tuscaloosa	AL	35487	(205) 88
P007	Holly	Davis	8009 Riviera Drive	Gainesville	FL	32611	(352) 38
P008	David	Tannen	50 Main Street	Philadelphia	PA	19104	(215) 77
P009	Jeffrey	Jacobsen	490 Bell Drive	Athens	GA	30602	(706) 38
P010	Jerry	Masters	2000 Main Highway	Miami	FL	33146	(305) 77
P011	Kevin	Kline	2980 SW 89 Street	Gainesville	FL	32611	(352) 87
P012	Jessica	Withers	110 Center Highway	Athens	GA	30602	(706) 89

Figure 2.3 Tables Illustrating AutoNumbered and Naturally Emerging Primary Keys

Explore Foreign Key

A **foreign key** is a primary key from one table that is used in a different table as the basis for the relationship between the tables. The Customer ID may be the primary key in the Customers table. It serves to uniquely identify each customer. It often will appear as a foreign key in a related table. For example, the Order table may contain a field establishing which customer placed an individual order. Although a single Customer Identification Number can appear only one time in the Customers table, it may appear repeatedly in the Order table. A single customer may place multiple orders.

If you were the database administrator for the Youth Soccer League, you would assign a primary key to each player in the Players table and to each team in the Teams table. The Players table would have a field to show for which team the players play. The primary key in the Players table would uniquely identify the child with a PlayerID and also would show which team he or she played on using a TeamID (foreign key). Because each team has several players, you will find the TeamID repeated frequently in the Players table. Figure 2.4 depicts portions of the Players and Teams tables.

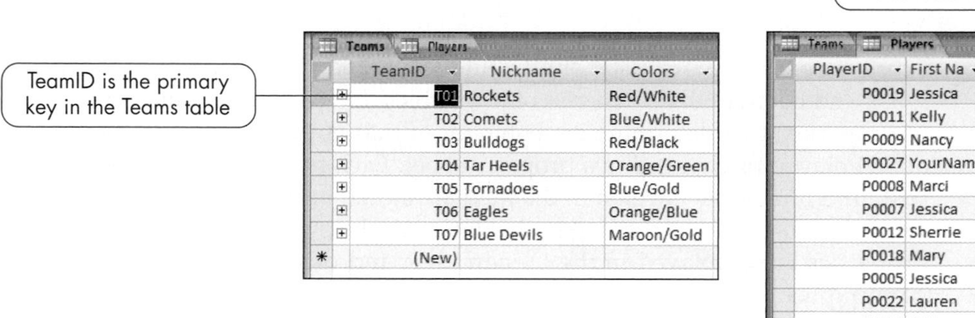

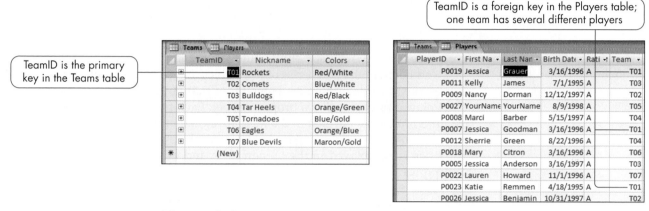

Figure 2.4 Tables Illustrating Primary and Foreign Keys

Use Table Views

The ***PivotTable view*** provides a convenient way to summarize and organize data about groups of records.

The ***PivotChart view*** displays a chart of the associated PivotTable View.

You may view your table in different ways. For example, you work in Datasheet view to add, edit, and delete records. The Datasheet view of an Access table resembles an Excel spreadsheet and displays data in rows (records) and columns (fields). In this chapter, you will use the Design view to create and modify a table's structure, properties, and appearance. The ***PivotTable view*** provides a convenient way to summarize and organize data about groups of records. The ***PivotChart view*** displays a chart of the associated PivotTable view. Figure 2.5 displays a table in Datasheet view that corresponds to the table you saw in Figure 2.1. The Datasheet view displays the record selector symbol for the current record. It displays an asterisk in the record selector column next to the blank record at the end of the table.

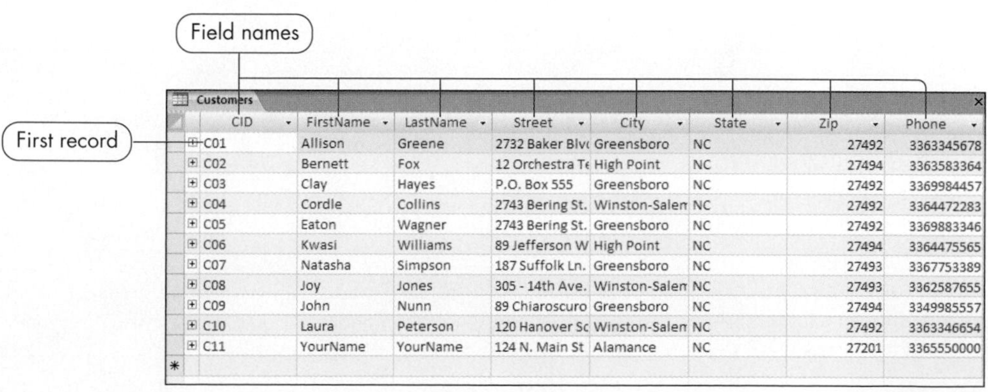

Figure 2.5 Customers Table in Datasheet View

TIP Toggle Between Datasheet and Design Views

To toggle from the Datasheet view to the Design view, click View in the Views group on the Home tab or right-click the table tab that appears above the datasheet and choose Design View from the menu. To toggle from the Design view to the Datasheet view, click View in the Views group on the Design tab or right-click the table tab that appears above the Design view grid and choose Datasheet View from the menu.

Work with Properties

A ***property*** is a characteristic or attribute of an object that determines how the object looks and behaves.

A ***property*** is a characteristic or attribute of an object that determines how the object looks and behaves. Every Access object (tables, forms, queries, and reports) has a set of properties that determine the behavior of that object. The properties for an object are displayed or changed in a property sheet. Each field has its own set of properties that determine how the data in the field are stored and displayed. The properties are set to default values according to the data type, but you can modify if necessary. The properties are displayed in the Design view and described briefly in the following paragraphs.

A ***caption property*** specifies a label other than the field name that appears at the top of a column in Datasheet view, forms, and reports.

Exclusively using CamelCase notation provides a consistent method to name your fields, but it may make the information difficult to read and understand. Therefore, you can use the ***caption property*** to create a more readable label that appears at the top of a column in Datasheet view and in forms and reports. For example, a field named ProductCostPerUnit can have the caption *Per Unit Product Cost*. The caption displays at the top of a table or query column in Datasheet view and when the field is used in a report or form. You use the formal field name, ProductCostPerUnit, in any expressions.

In the following hands-on exercise, you begin by creating a database and entering data into a table. Then you switch to the Design view to add additional fields and modify selected properties of various fields within the table.

Before launching Access, use Windows Explorer to verify that you have a folder named **Your Name Access Production** on your storage device. Remember that you cannot run Access from a floppy or a Zip disk or a CD, even a CD-RW. The access speed of most USB thumb drives is adequate. Access runs best from the My Documents folder or a network drive.

Access Table Property Types and Descriptions | Reference

Property Type	Description
Field Size	The **Field Size** property adjusts the size of a text field or limits the allowable value in a number field. Microsoft Access uses only the amount of space it needs even if the field size allows a greater number. However, Access often connects to other database programs that reserve space for the specified field length. Good practice limits the field size to reduce system storage requirements.
Format	The **Format** property changes the way a field is displayed or printed, but does not affect the stored value.
Input Mask	The **Input Mask** property facilitates data entry by displaying literal characters that are displayed but not stored, such as hyphens in a Social Security Number or slashes in a date. It also imposes data validation by ensuring that the data entered by the user fits within the mask (i.e., it prevents typing an additional digit in a phone number).
Caption	The **Caption** property specifies a label other than the field name for forms and reports. It also displays on the table's Datasheet view. It permits a more user-friendly way to View the data.
Default Value	The **Default Value** property automatically enters a designated (default) value for the field in each record that is added to the table. If 90 percent of your customers lived in North Carolina, you might consider setting the default value for the State field to NC in order to save data entry time.
Validation Rule	The **Validation Rule** property rejects any record in which the data entered does not conform to the specified rules for data entry.
Validation Text	The **Validation Text** property specifies the error message that is displayed when the validation rule is violated.
Required	The **Required** property rejects any record that does not have a value entered for this field.
Allow Zero Length	The **Allow Zero Length** property enables text or memo strings of zero length.
Indexed	The **Indexed** property increases the efficiency of a search on the designated field. (The primary key in a table is always indexed.)
Unicode Compression	The **Unicode Compression** property is set to "Yes" by default for Text, Memo, and Hyperlink fields to store the data more efficiently.
IME Mode IME Sentence Mode	The **IME Mode and IME Sentence Mode** properties refer to the Input Method Editor for East Asian languages.
Smart Tags	The properties permit advanced users to add action buttons to a field. If you were using a database offering products for sale, a Smart Tag button embedded in a product name might open an inventory file and tell the database user what products are in stock.

Hands-On Exercises

1 | Table Design, Properties, Views, and Wizards

Skills covered: 1. Create a New Database **2**. Create a Table by Entering Data **3**. Change the Primary Key, Modify Field Properties, and Delete a Field **4**. Modify Table Fields in Design View **5**. Create a New Field in Design View **6**. Switch Between the Table Design and the Table Datasheet Views

Step 1 Create a New Database

Refer to Figure 2.6 as you complete Step 1.

a. Start Microsoft Access.

   You should see the Welcome Window.

b. Click **Blank Database** in the New Blank Database section of the *Getting Started with Microsoft Office Access* window.

   The lower right corner of the window displays the Blank Database section with file management tools.

c. Click **Browse**—the little yellow folder.

d. Click the **Save in drop-down arrow** and select the appropriate drive. Double-click the **Your Name Access Production** folder. Click **OK**.

   You need to be intentional about where you save your database file. Otherwise, you may have difficulty finding it again.

e. Click in the **File name** box and select *Database1.accdb*. Type **chap2_ho1-3_safebank_solution.accdb** to name your database and click **OK**. Click the **Create command** in the Blank Database section of the *Getting Started with Microsoft Office Access* window.

   The Database window for the *chap2_ho1-3_safebank_solution.accdb* should appear.

   TROUBLESHOOTING: If you skipped the instructions in Step 1d, you may have problems finding your file. From the desktop, right-click Computer and select Explore from the shortcut menu. Click the Search tool. Select All Files or Folders. In the box, type **chap2_ho1-3_safebank_solution.accdb**. When the search results return, copy the file, and then paste it into the appropriate folder. Open and work the remainder of the hands-on exercises from the appropriate folder.

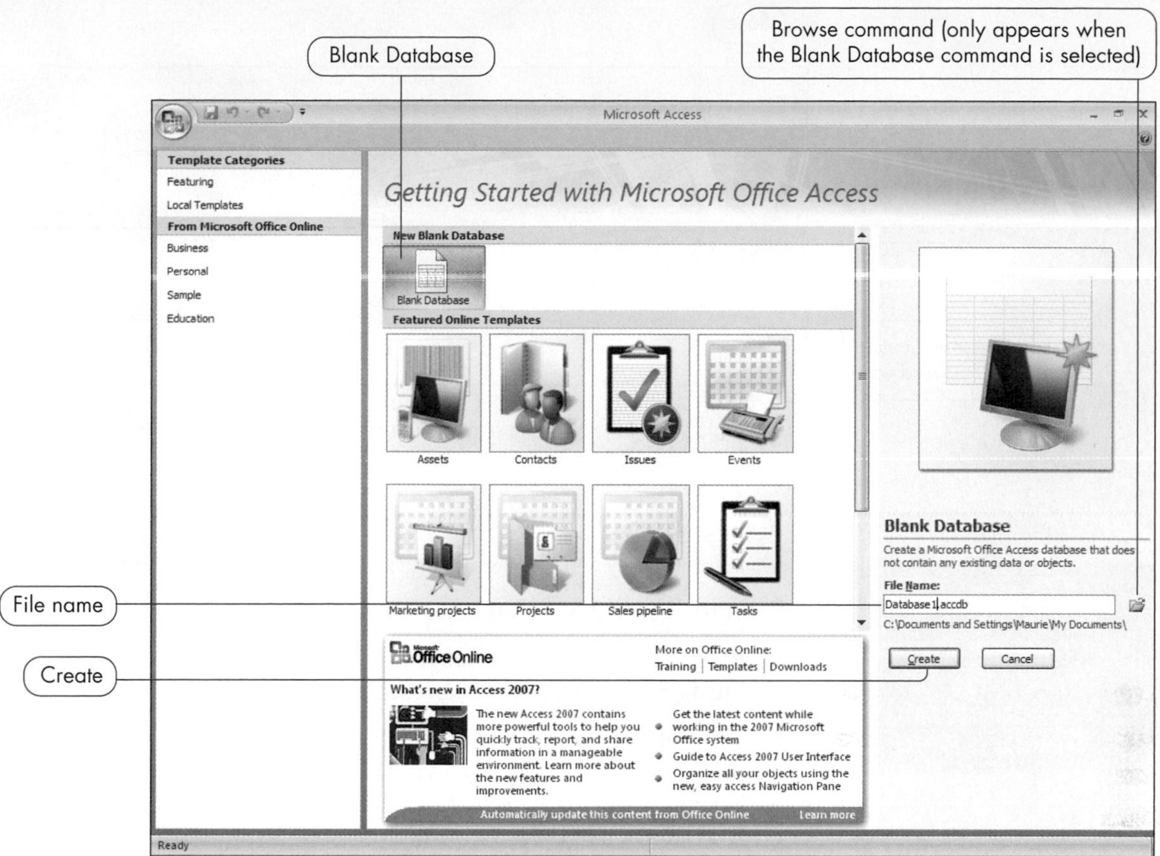

Figure 2.6 Welcome to Microsoft Office Access

Step 2
Create a Table by Entering Data

Refer to Figure 2.7 as you complete Step 2.

a. Type **B1** in the gold bordered cell and press **Enter**. The insertion point moves to the right. You also may navigate between the cells in the table by pressing **Tab** or the **arrow keys**.

b. Type **Lockley** in the first row of the third column. Press **Enter** and type **Uptown** in the next column.

c. Click in the cell below B1 and type **B2**, **Weeks**, and **Eastern**.

   If your ID numbers do not match those shown in Figure 2.7, do not be concerned. You will be deleting that field in a later step.

d. Enter the additional data for the new table, as shown in Figure 2.7. Replace YourName with your first and last names.

e. Click **Save** on the Quick Access Toolbar. Type **Branch** in the Save As dialog box and click **OK**.

   Entering data provides an easy way to create the table initially. You can now modify the table in Design view as described in the next several steps.

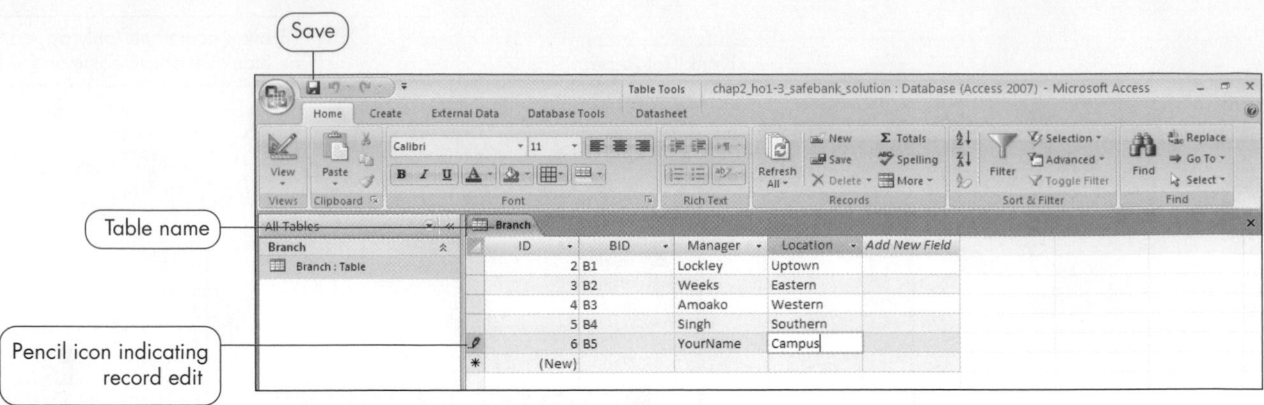

Figure 2.7 Table Data for the (Unnamed) Branch Table

Step 3
Change the Primary Key, Modify Field Properties, and Delete a Field

Refer to Figure 2.8 as you complete Step 3.

a. Right-click the **Branch table** under All Tables in the Navigation Pane and select **Design View** from the shortcut menu.

b. The fields are named ID, Field1, Field2, and Field3. These field names are not descriptive of the data, so you need to change Field1, Field2, and Field3 to BID, Manager, and Location, respectively. Click and Drag *Field1* to select it and type **BID**. Replace *Field2* with **Manager** and *Field3* with **Location**.

c. Click the **row selector** to the left of the *BID* field. The entire row selects, as shown in Figure 2.8.

d. Click **Primary Key** in the Tools group on the Design tab.

   You changed the primary key in this table from the automatically generated one that Access created for you to the one you intended, the BID. As soon as you identified BID as the primary key, the Indexed property updated to Yes (No Duplicates). The primary key must be a unique identifier for each record.

   TROUBLESHOOTING: A primary key must be a unique identifier for each record in the table. If you had trouble here, check to make sure the Indexed property is set to Indexed, Yes (No Duplicates). Return to Datasheet view and examine your data entry to ensure that you typed the correct values in the BID field.

e. Right-click the row selector to the left of the ID field. Select **Delete Rows** from the shortcut menu. Click **Yes** in the warning box instructing Access to permanently delete the selected field.

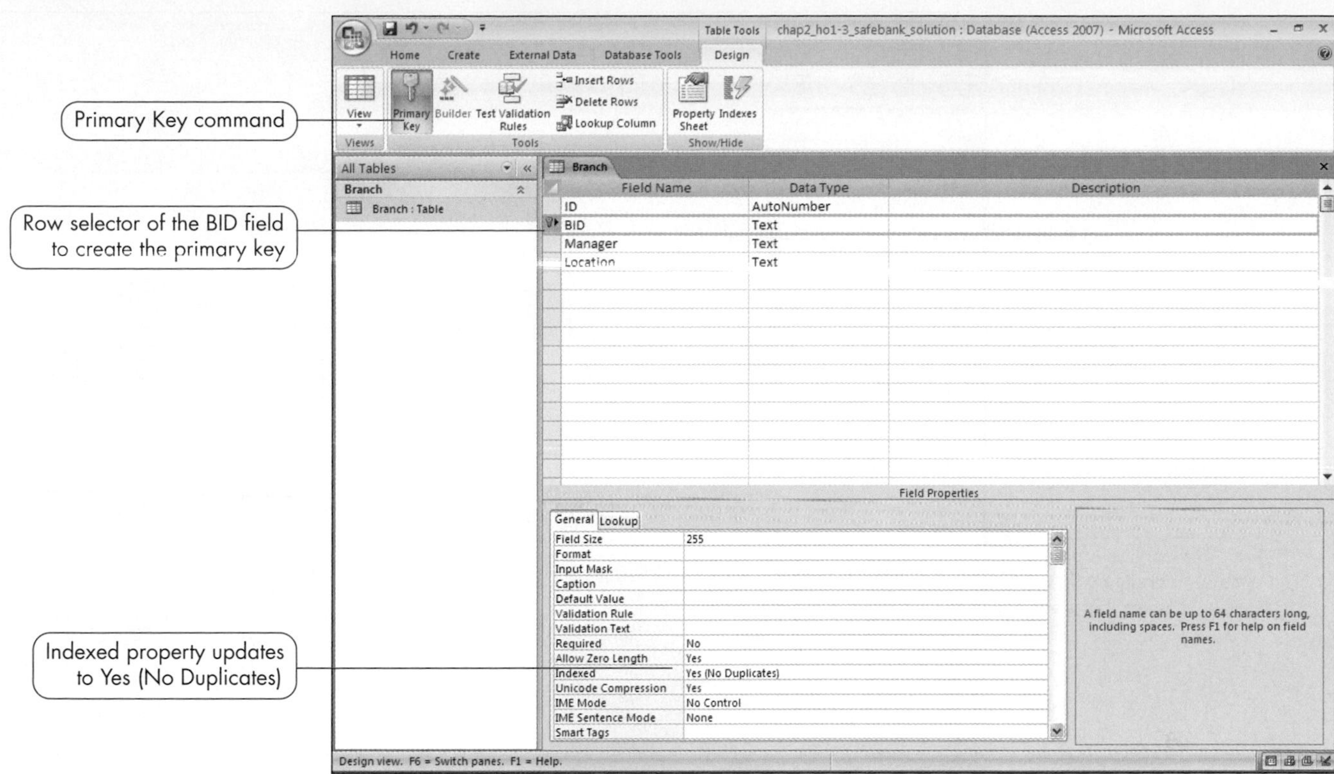

Figure 2.8 Branch Table in Design View

Step 4
Modify Table Fields in Design View

Refer to Figures 2.8 and 2.9 as you complete Step 4.

a. Modify some of the properties of the **BID** field.

1. Click in the **BID** field in the top section of the design window.
2. Click in the **Field Size** property box in the Field Properties section and type **10**.
3. Click in the **Caption** property box and type **Branch ID**.
4. Check the **Indexed** property box to make sure it is **Yes (No Duplicates)**.

If you need to change it, click in the Indexed property box. A drop-down arrow displays on the right side of the box. Scroll to select **Yes (No Duplicates)**, as shown in Figure 2.8.

For the next several tasks, you will toggle between the top of the design screen and the Field Property box on the bottom of the design screen.

b. Click the **Manager** field name at the top of the window. Look in the Field Properties section. In the **Field Size** property box, replace *255* with **30**. In the **Caption** property box, type **Manager's Name**.

A caption provides a more descriptive field name. It will head the column in Datasheet view and describe data in other database objects, such as reports, forms, and queries.

c. Click the **Location** field name at the top of the window. In the **Field Size** property box, change *255* to **30**. In the **Caption** property, type **Branch Location**.

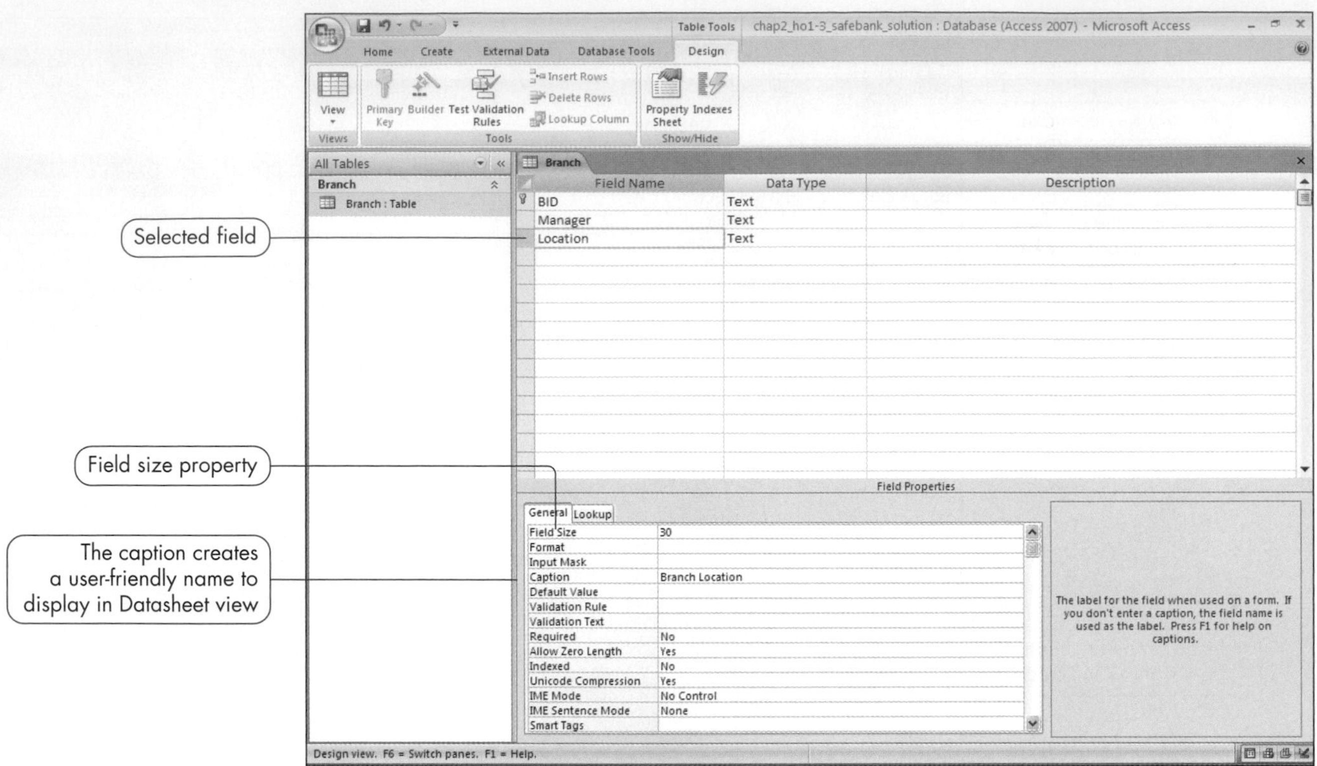

Selected field
Field size property
The caption creates a user-friendly name to display in Datasheet view

Figure 2.9 Change Field Properties to Increase Efficiency

Step 5
Create a New Field in Design View

Refer to Figure 2.10 as you complete Step 5.

a. Click the blank cell below the *Location* field name. Create a new field by typing the field name named **StartDate**.

b. Press **Tab** to move to the *Data Type* column. Click the **Data Type drop-down arrow** and select **Date/Time**.

c. Press **Tab** to move to the *Description* column and type **This date is the date the manager started working at this location.**

d. Click in the **Caption** property box and type **Manager's Start Date**.

e. Click the **Format property drop-down arrow** and select **Short Date** from the list of Date formats.

f. Click **Save** on the Quick Access Toolbar to save the Branch table within the *chap2_ho1-3_safebank_solution* database.

   A warning dialog box opens to indicate that the size of the BID, Manager, and Location field properties were shortened. It asks if you want to continue anyway. Always read the Access warnings! In this case, you are OK. You changed the size of the BID field from 255 to 10 in Step 4a. You did not need 255 characters to identify the BID. Your bank only has five locations. You changed the other two field sizes in Steps 4b and 4c.

g. Click **Yes** in the warning box.

   The table Design view is useful to modify the structure of fields or to add fields to an existing table. However, tables cannot be populated in the Design view. The Datasheet view must be used to add data to a table.

TIP Keyboard Shortcut for Data Types

You also can type the first letter of the field type such as D for Date/Time, T for Text, or N for number. Click into the data type column in the field's row and, using the keyboard, type the first letter of the field type.

Click in the Data Type column to reveal a hidden drop-down list of data types

Click to toggle between Design View and Datasheet View

Right-click to switch and select Datasheet View

Click in the first blank Field Name column to create a new field

Click to reveal a hidden drop-down list of data formats

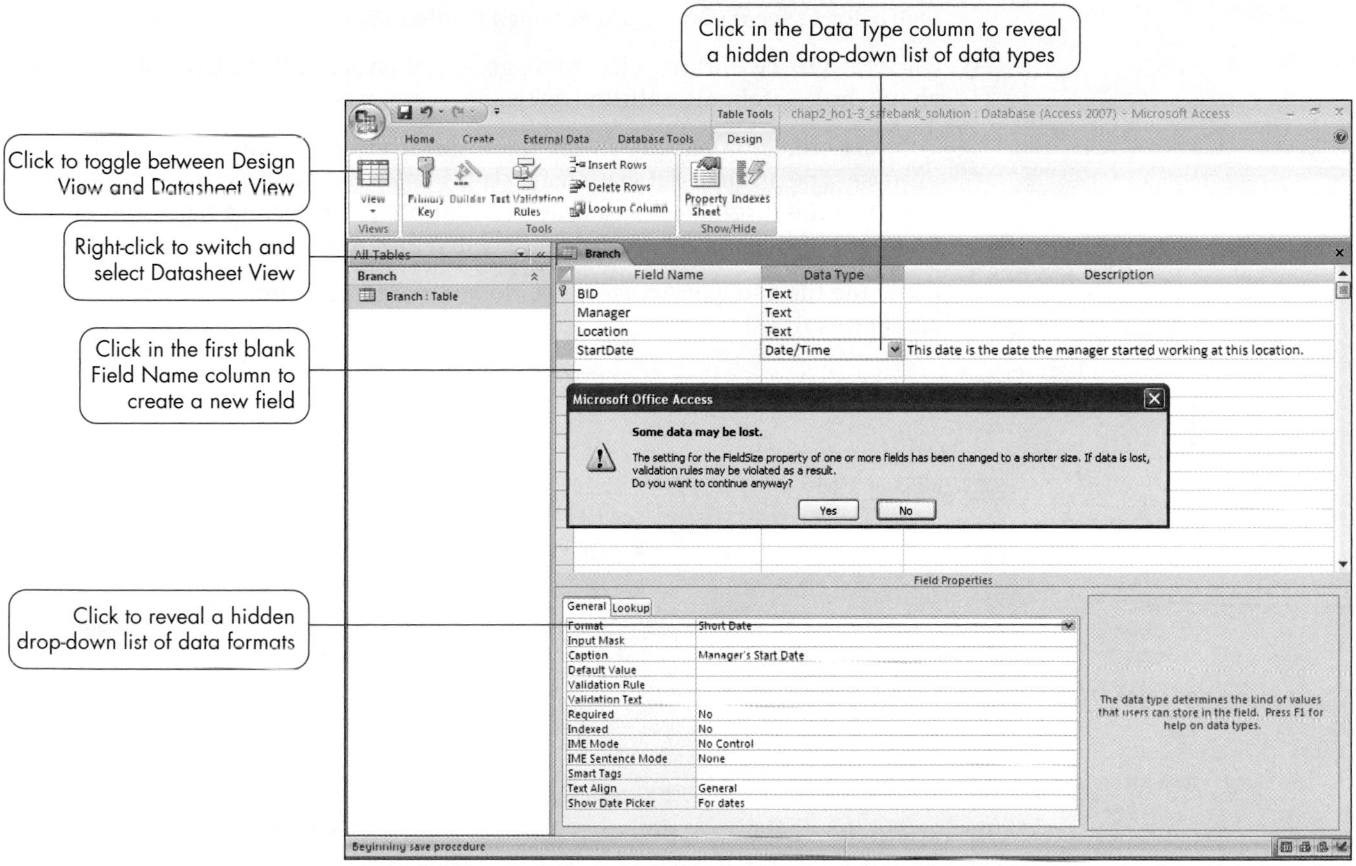

Figure 2.10 Change Field Properties to Increase Efficiency

Step 6
Switch Between the Table Design and the Table Datasheet Views

Refer to Figure 2.11 as you complete Step 6.

a. Right-click the gold tab shown in Figure 2.10 and select **Datasheet View** from the shortcut menu. (To return to the Design view, right-click the tab in Datasheet view and select Design View or click **View** in the Views group on the Design tab.)

b. Enter the dates each manager started work, as shown in Figure 2.11.

After entering the date for yourself, you remember that you started work on October 11. Therefore, you need to change the date from December 12 to October 11 using the calendar command.

c. Click the **calendar command** and click the **October 11** date on the calendar.

d. Click the table's **Close command**.

e. Double-click the **Branch table** in the Navigation Pane to open the table. Check the start dates.

You did not save any changes you made; you closed the table without saving changes. The dates are correct because Access works from storage, not memory.

f. Click the **Office Button**, position the mouse pointer over **Print**, and then select **Quick Print**.

Most users do not print Access table data. Tables store and organize data and rarely generate output. People do not spend time formatting table data. Check with your instructor to see if you should submit a printed Branch table for feedback.

g. Click the **Office Button**, select **Manage**, and then select **Back Up Database**. Type **chap2_ho1_safebank_solution** as the file name, and then click **Save**.

You just created a backup of the database after completing the first hands-on exercise. The original database *chap2_ho1-3_safebank_solution* remains onscreen. If you ruin the original database as you complete the second hands-on exercise, you can use the backup file you just created and rework the second exercise.

h. Close the file and exit Access if you do not want to continue with the next exercise at this time.

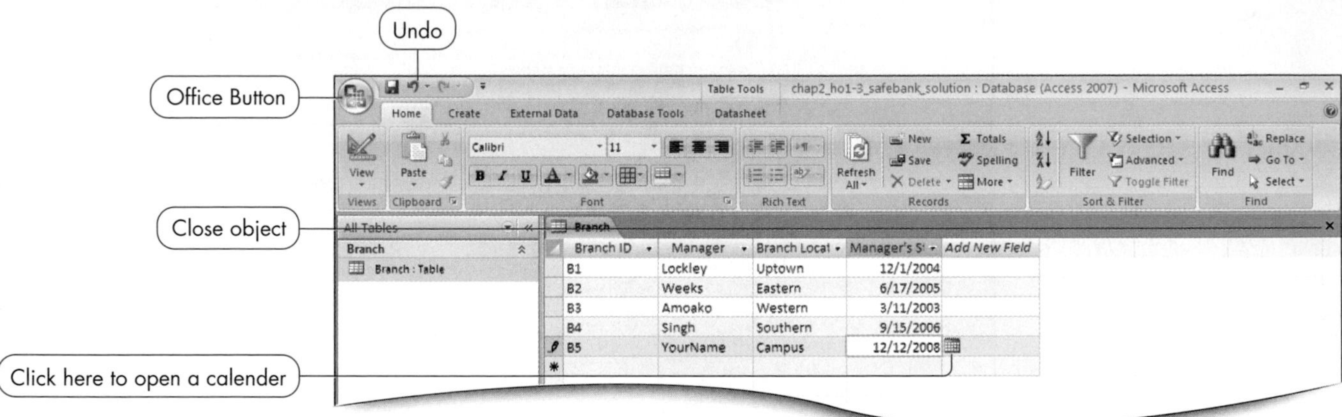

Figure 2.11 Calendar Facilitates Data Entry

Multiple Table Database

Earlier, you designed a database and combined similar data items into groupings called tables. You have completed the first table in the database, the Branch table. If you re-examine your design notes and Figure 2.2, recall that you planned for two additional tables in the Safebank database. The power of a relational database lies in its ability to organize and combine data in different ways to obtain a complete picture of the events the data describe. Good database design connects the data in different tables through links. These links are the relationships that give relational databases the name. In your Safebank database, one customer can have many accounts or can bank at any of the bank locations. That is, the customer's ID may be listed for many account numbers in the Accounts table, but the customer's ID is listed only one time in the Customers table. When the database is set up properly, database users can be confident that if they search for a specific customer identification number, they will be given accurate information about that customer's account balances, address, or branch preferences.

In this section, you learn about table relationships, referential integrity, indexing, and importing data from Excel.

Understanding Table Relationships

The relationship is like a piece of electronic string that travels throughout the database, searching every record of every table until it finds the events of interest. Once identified, the fields and records of interest will be tied to the end of the string, pulled through the computer, and reassembled in a way that makes the data easy to understand. The first end of the string was created when the primary key was established in the Branch table. The primary key is a unique identifier for each table record. The other end of the string ties to a field in a different table. You will include the Branch ID as a foreign field in the Accounts table. A foreign key is a field in one table that is also stored in a different table as a primary key. Each value of the Branch ID (BID) can occur only once in the Branch table because it is a primary key. However, the BID may appear multiple times in the account table because many different accounts are at the same branch.

Establish Referential Integrity

The relationships will be created using an Access feature that enforces referential integrity. Integrity means truthful or reliable. When referential integrity is enforced, the user can trust the threads running through the database and tying related items together. The Campus branch manager can use the database to find the names and phone numbers of all the customers with accounts at the Campus branch. Because referential integrity has been enforced, it will not matter that the branch information is in a different table from the customer data. The invisible threads keep the information accurately connected. Managers need organized and dependable data upon which they base decisions. The threads also provide a method of ensuring data accuracy. You cannot enter a record in the Account table that references a Branch ID or a Customer ID that does not exist in the system. Nor can you delete a record in one table if it has related records in other tables.

Ask yourself what the anticipated results should be, and then verify. When you become skilled at anticipating output correctly, you are surprised less often.

If this were a real bank's data system, the files would be much larger and the data more sophisticated. However, the same design principles apply regardless of the database size. A small file gives you the ability to check the tables and see if your results are correct. Even though the data amounts are small, you need to develop the work practices to manage large amounts of data. With only a handful of records, you can easily count the number of accounts at the Campus branch. In addition to learning HOW to accomplish a task, you should learn to anticipate the computer's response to an instruction. Ask yourself what the anticipated results should be, and then verify. When you become skilled at anticipating output correctly, you are surprised less often.

Identify Cascades

Cascades permit data changes to travel from one table to another.

Cascade delete searches the database and deletes all of the related records.

Cascade update connects any primary key changes to the tables in which it is a foreign key.

Cascades are an Access feature that helps update related data across tables. In databases, ***cascades*** permit data changes to travel from one table to another. The database designer may establish cascades to update or delete related records. The string tying related items together can also make global changes to the data. If one bank branch closed and the accounts were not transferred to a different branch, the ***cascade delete*** feature would search the database and delete all of the accounts and customers who banked solely at the closed branch. (This may not be an optimal business practice, but it explains how the cascade delete feature works.) If a customer with an account at one branch opens a new account at a different branch, the ***cascade update*** will travel through the databases and connect the new account to the customer's address in the Customers table and the new account balance in the Accounts table.

As a general rule, you do not want changes cascading through the database. An inattentive data entry clerk could, with the click of a mouse, delete hundreds of records in various tables throughout the database. However, you need the power of a cascade occasionally. Suppose your company and another firm merged. Your firm has always stored customer account numbers as a five-digit number. The other firm has always used a three-digit account number. In this case, you would turn the cascade update feature on, open the Customers table, and change all of the three digit numbers to five digit ones. The new account numbers would cascade through the database to any records in any table related to the Customers table—for example, the Payments or Orders tables.

Retrieve Data Rapidly by Indexing

The ***indexed property*** is a list that relates the field values to the records that contain the field value.

In Hands-On Exercise 1, you created the Branch table and established the BID as the primary key. Access changed the ***indexed property*** to Yes (No Duplicates). Access uses indexing exactly like you would read a book on U.S. history. If you need to know who succeeded Van Buren as president, you could start on page 1 and read the book in order page by page. Alternatively, you could go to the index and discover where the information about Van Buren may be found and open directly to that page. Using the index in a book makes finding (retrieving) information quicker. Indexing a database field has the same effect; it greatly reduces retrieval time. The actual index is a list that relates the field values to the records that contain the field value. Without an index, each row in the database would need to be scanned sequentially, an inefficient search method. The increased search time would adversely affect the performance of the database. All primary keys must be indexed. Additional table fields also may be indexed.

Sharing Data with Excel

Many Access and Excel tasks overlap. Although you are learning the highly valuable skill of using Access, more people know how to use Excel than Access. Therefore, a lot of data resides within Excel spreadsheets. Often, the data stored in those spreadsheets fits well into an Access database design. Therefore, you need to be able to integrate existing Excel spreadsheet data into the organization's database. Fortunately, Access provides you with wizards that facilitate data sharing with Excel. Access can both import data from Excel and export data to Excel easily.

Figures 2.12–2.18 show how to use the Get External Data – Excel Spreadsheet wizard. You launch the wizard by clicking the External Data tab. Table 2.1 lists and describes the four groups on the External Data tab.

Table 2.1 Access and Other Applications Share Data

Process	When Used
Get External Data	Used to bring data into an Access database. The data sources include Excel, other Access files, XML, SharePoint Lists, and Text files.
Export Data	Used to send a portion of a database to other applications. You might use this to create a Mail Merge letter and envelopes in Word. You could create an Excel file for a co-worker who does not know how to use (or does not have) Access, or could share your data over the Internet via a SharePoint List.
Collect and Update	You could create an e-mail mail merge to send e-mails to your clients, and then use Access to manage the clients' responses.
Offline SharePoint Lists	This process might be used when traveling, if an immediate Internet connection is not available.

Launch the wizard by clicking the Excel command in the Get External Data Group.

Figure 2.12 shows the External Data tab that contains the Import Excel command. After you specify the data storage location, you can use the imported data to create a new table in Access, to ***append*** new records to an existing Access table, or to create a link between the Excel file and the Access table. When linked, any changes made to the Excel file will be updated automatically in the database, too.

You ***append*** records to an existing table by adding new records to the end of the table.

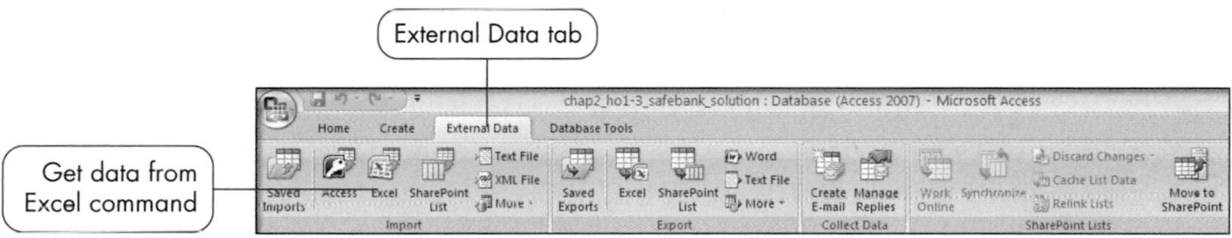

Figure 2.12 Select the Source and Destination for the Data

Figure 2.13 shows the Get External Data – Excel Spreadsheet dialog box. This feature controls where you find the data to import. It asks you to choose among three options governing what to do with the data in Access: place it in a new table, append the data to an existing table, or link the Access table to the Excel source.

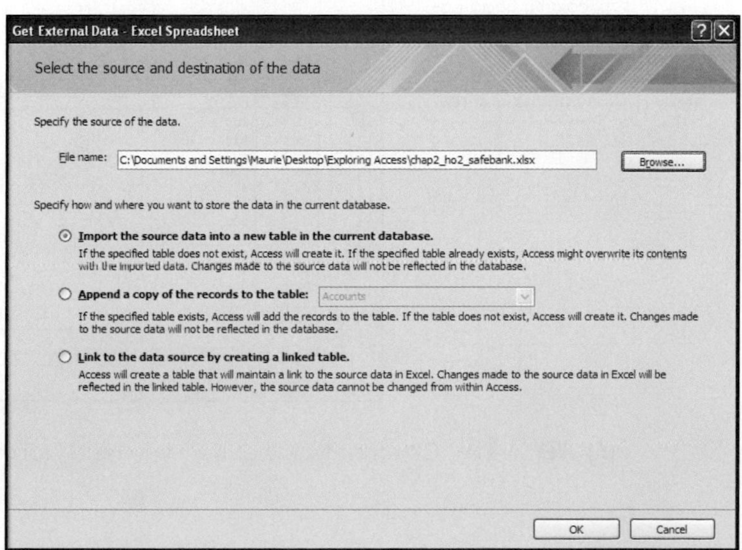

Figure 2.13 Select the Source and Destination of the Data

After you select the Excel workbook, you see the Import Spreadsheet Wizard dialog box, which displays a list of the worksheets in the specified workbook (see Figure 2.14). Use the options to specify a worksheet, in this case, the Customers worksheet. The bottom of the Import Spreadsheet Wizard dialog box displays a preview of the data stored in the specified worksheet.

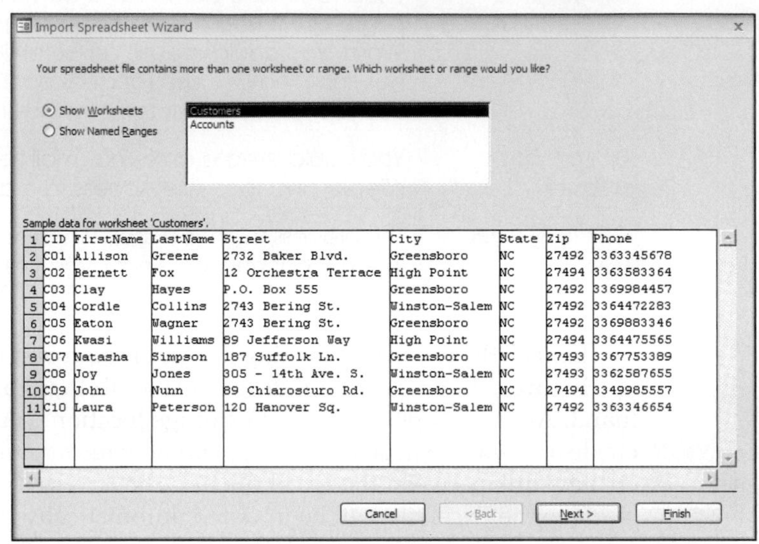

Figure 2.14 Show Available Worksheets and Preview Data

Although well-designed spreadsheets include descriptive labels, not all Excel users practice good spreadsheet design. The second window of the Import Spreadsheet Wizard dialog box contains a check box that gives you a chance to describe the data to Access (see Figure 2.15). When you find a label row in a spreadsheet, check the box. Access will use the Excel labels to generate the Access field names. When you find unlabeled data, do not check the box, and the data will import using Field1, Field2, and so on as field names.

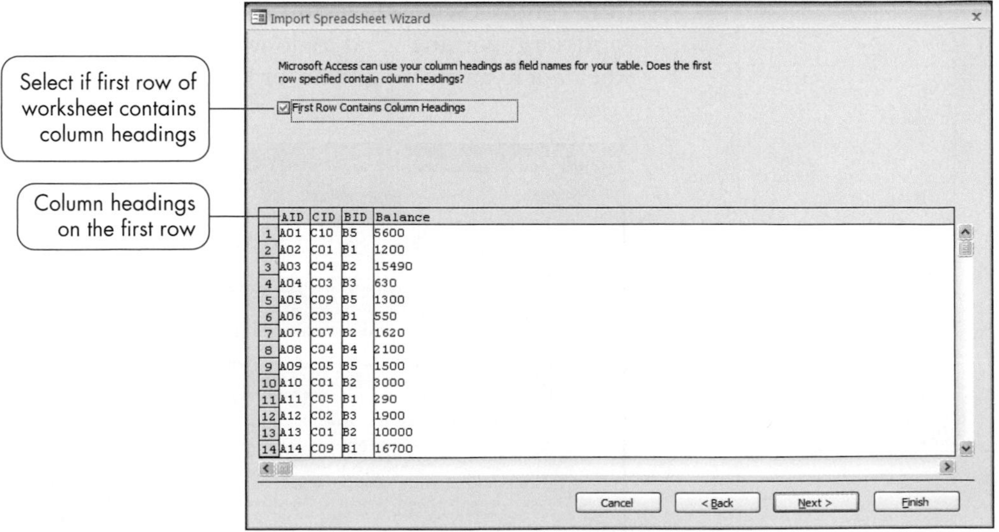

Figure 2.15 Column Headings Become Field Names

The third window of the Import Spreadsheet Wizard dialog box enables you to stipulate field properties (see Figure 2.16). The AID field is shown in the figure. Because it will become this table's primary key, you need to set the Index Property to Yes (No Duplicates). Use the Field Name box to select other fields (columns) in the worksheet and establish their properties. Not all Access table properties are supported by the wizard. You will need to open the table in Design view after importing it and make some additional property changes.

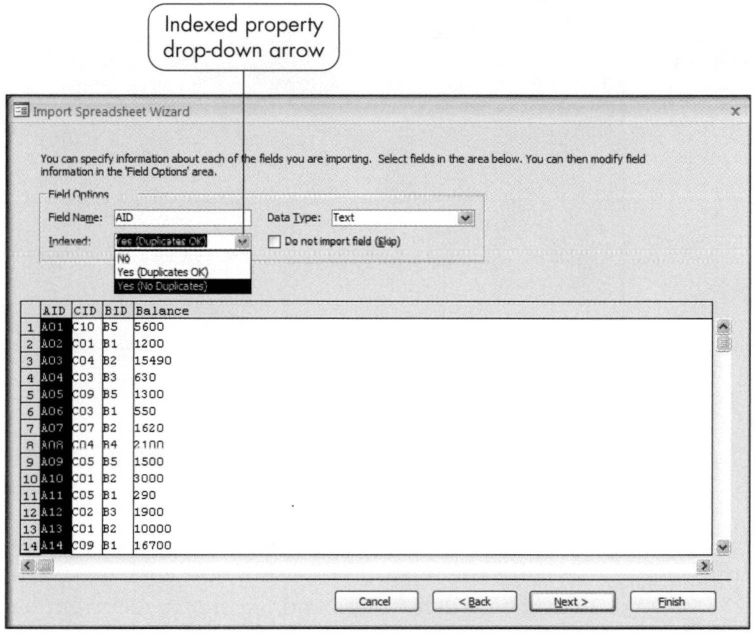

Figure 2.16 Field Options for Importing the Spreadsheet

The fourth window of the Import Spreadsheet Wizard dialog box enables you to establish the primary key before the import takes place (see Figure 2.17). If the option for *Let Access add primary key* is selected, Access will generate an AutoNumber field and designate it as the primary key. In the import described in the figure, the Excel data has a unique identifier that will become the table's primary key on import.

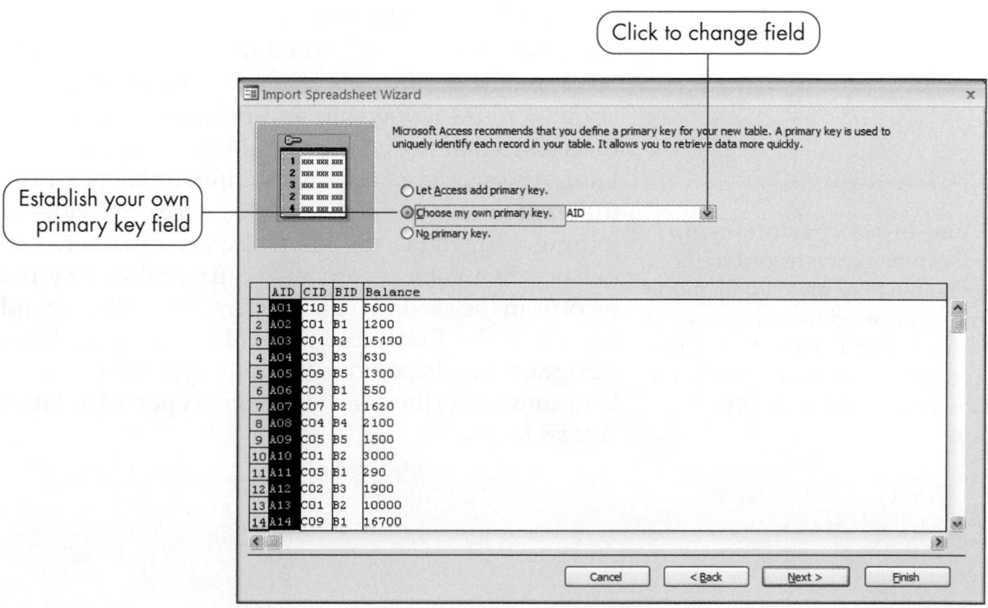

Figure 2.17 Primary Key Designation

Use the final window of the Import Spreadsheet Wizard dialog box prompts you to name the Access table. If the worksheet in the Excel workbook was named, Access uses the worksheet name as the table name (see Figure 2.18).

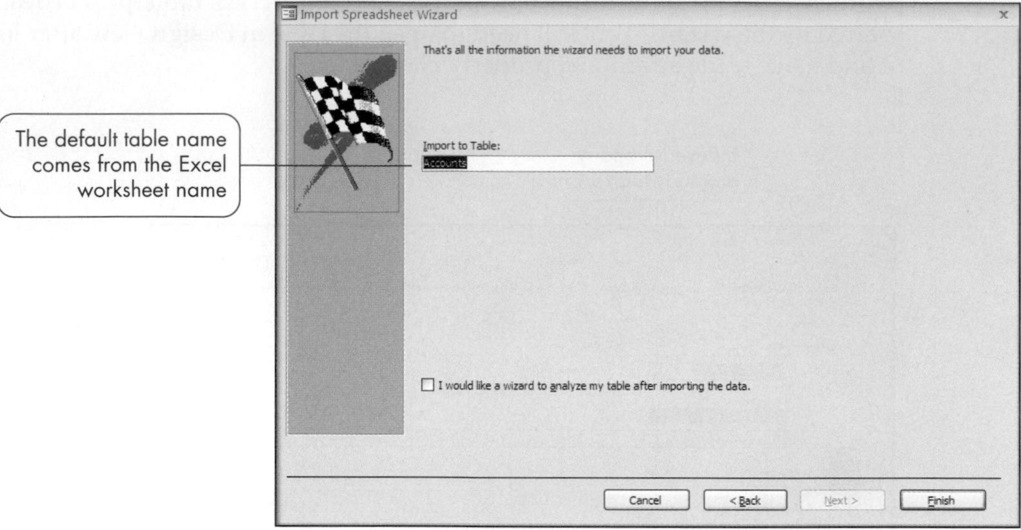

Figure 2.18 Table Name for Import Spreadsheet

Finally, the wizard will ask if you wish to save the import steps. Frequently data is shared between Access and Excel on a recurrent basis. At the close of a day or week or month, data from Excel are routinely imported and updated in Access. Saving the import steps expedites the data re-importation the next time it is needed. The imported data become a permanent part of the Access file. Access will open a final dialog box asking if you want to save the import specifications. In your hands-on exercise, the data import is a one-time only event so you do not need to save the import parameters.

Establishing Table Relationships

You should store like data items together using a logical file management structure. The customer data are stored in the Customers table. The Branch table stores data about the bank's branch, management, and location. The Accounts table stores data about account ownership and balances. You learned earlier that relationships form the strings that tie the related table data together. When you tie something, you use a knot. Any scout or sailor uses different knots for different purposes. Just as you use different knots for differing tasks, Access provides several differing relationships for joining your data. You have already discovered that a ***one-to-many relationship*** exists when each record in the first table may match one, more than one, or no records in the second table. Each record in the second table matches one and only one record in the first table to establish a powerful knot or relationship. In a well-designed database, you use this type of relationship most frequently. Table 2.2 lists and describes the different types of relationships you can form between Access tables.

A ***one-to-many relationship*** exists when each record in the first table may match one, more than one, or no records in the second table. Each record in the second table matches one and only one record in the first table.

Table 2.2 Relationship Types

Relationship Name	Definition
One-To-Many	This relationship is between a primary key in the first table and a foreign key in the second table. The first table must have only one occurrence of each value. That is: Each customer must have a unique identification number in the Customers table or each employee must have a unique employee identification number in the Employee table. The foreign key field in the second table may have recurrent values. For example, one customer may have many different account numbers, or one employee can provide service to many customers.
One-To-One	Two different tables use the same primary key. Exactly one record exists in the second table for each record in the first table. Sometimes security reasons require a table to be split into two related tables. For example, anyone in the company can look in the Employee table and find the employee's office number, department assignment, or telephone extension. However, only a few people need to have access to the employee's salary, Social Security Number, performance review, or marital status. Both tables use the same unique identifier to identify each employee.
Many-To-Many	This is an artificially constructed relationship giving many matching records in each direction between tables. It requires construction of a third table called a juncture table. For example, a database might have a table for employees and one for projects. Several employees might be assigned to one project, but one employee might also be assigned to many different projects. When Access connects to databases using Oracle or other software, you find this relationship type. When using Access as a stand-alone software, you would specify a Multivalue field and record multiple items as legitimate entries in a single field.

Establish a One-To-Many Relationship

When you click the Database Tools tab, you see the Show/Hide group (see Figure 2.19). The first command is the tool that opens the Relationship window. If this were a long established database, the Relationship window would be populated with the related tables in the database.

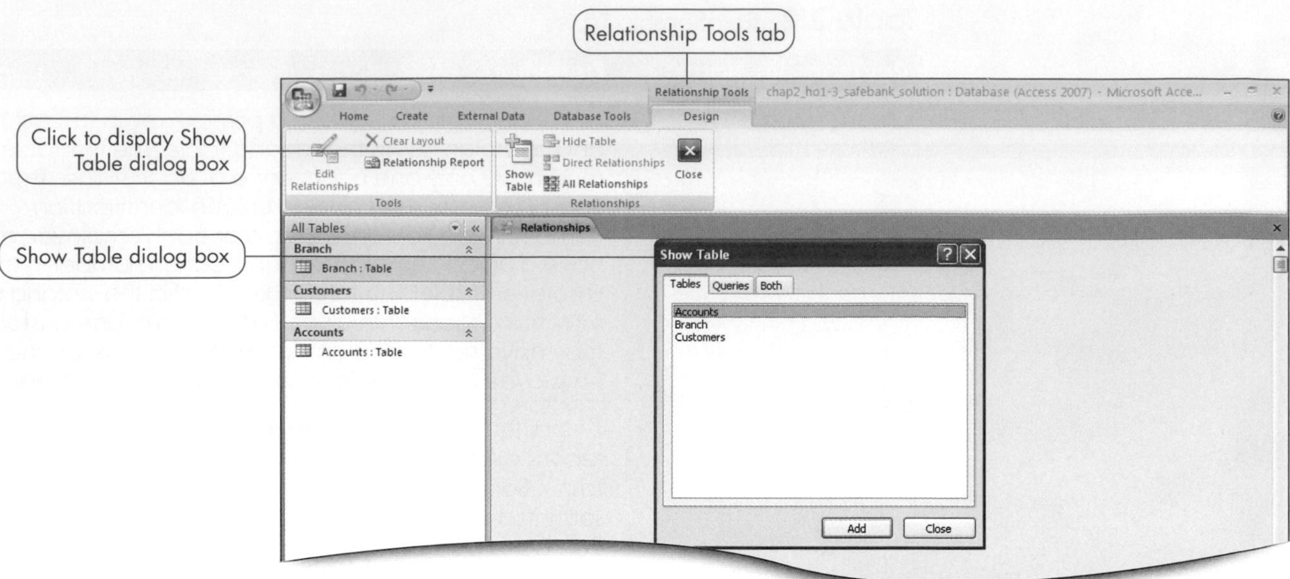

Figure 2.19 The Show/Hide Group and Show Table Dialog Box

Because the first time you will use the Relationship window you will be working in a newly created database, you must first use the Show Table dialog box to add the necessary tables to the Relationship window (see Figure 2.19). Select the tables you want to use in relation to other tables and add them to the Relationship window by clicking Add.

TIP Navigation Between the Relationship Window and a Table's Design

When you right-click the table title bar in the Relationship window, the shortcut menu offers you a chance to open the table in Design view. Because relationships may be established only between data with the same definition, you have a chance to check how the data in different tables have been defined.

When possible, expand the table windows to display the complete list of field names shown in the table (see Figure 2.20). You may rearrange the tables by clicking and dragging the table window title bar.

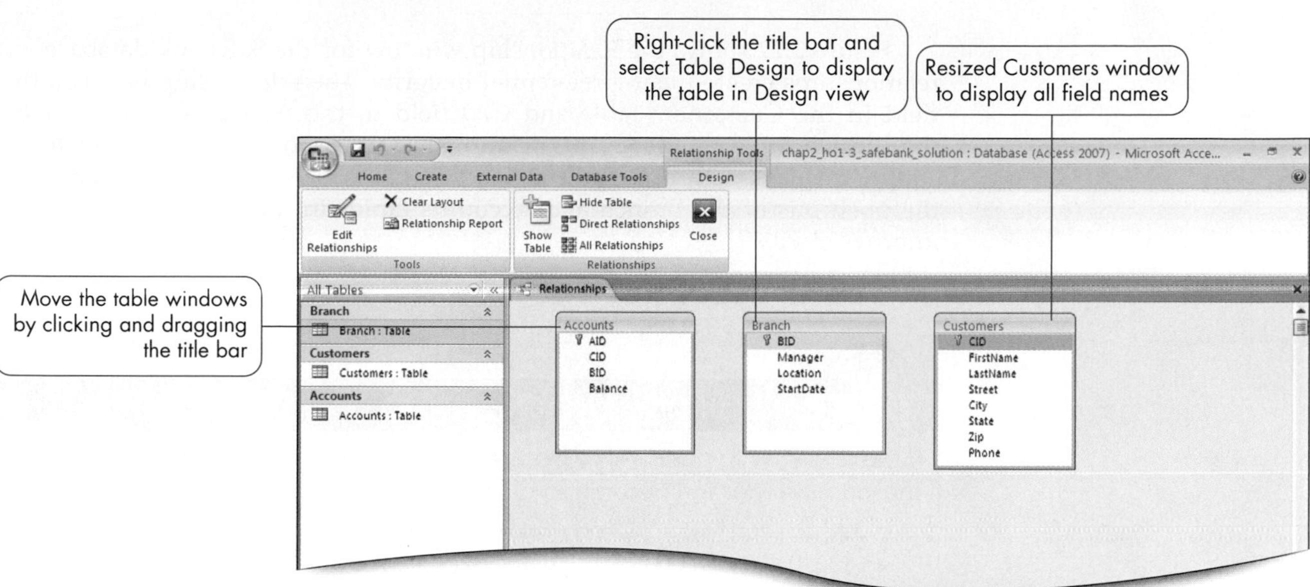

Figure 2.20 The Relationship Window with Resized Tables

Establish the relationships by clicking and dragging the field name from one table to the field name in the related table. When you release the mouse, the Edit Relationships dialog box opens (see Figure 2.21). Prior to establishing a relationship, Access runs through the table data to ensure that the rules you attempt to establish in the relationship can be met. For example, it checks to make sure that the branch identification number in the Accounts table (foreign key) exactly matches a Branch ID in the Branch table where it is the primary key. If all of the Branch IDs do not match exactly between the tables, Access cannot establish the relationship with referential integrity enforced. It will attempt to make a connection, but it will warn you that a problem exists with the data.

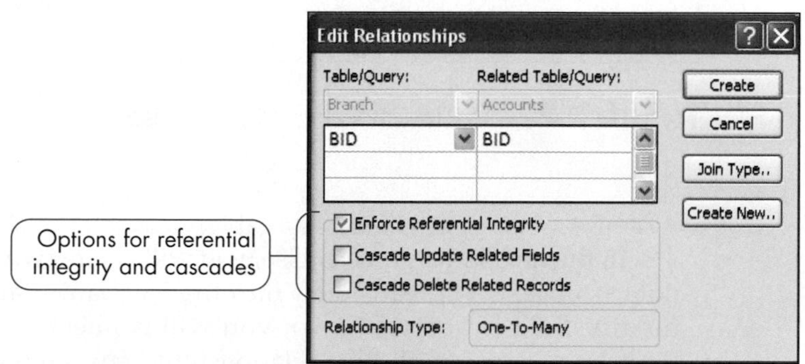

Figure 2.21 The Edit Relationships Dialog Box

Figure 2.22 shows the Relationship window for the Safebank database with all relationships created using referential integrity. The relationship between the CID field in the Customers table and CID field in the Accounts table runs behind the Branch table window. This relationship does not affect the Branch table; it simply displays with part of the connecting line obscured. You may want to switch the positions of the Branch and Accounts tables in the Relationship window to improve clarity.

TIP Editing a Relationship

If the relationship has already been established and you need to edit it, right-click the juncture line. You also right-click the juncture line to delete a relationship.

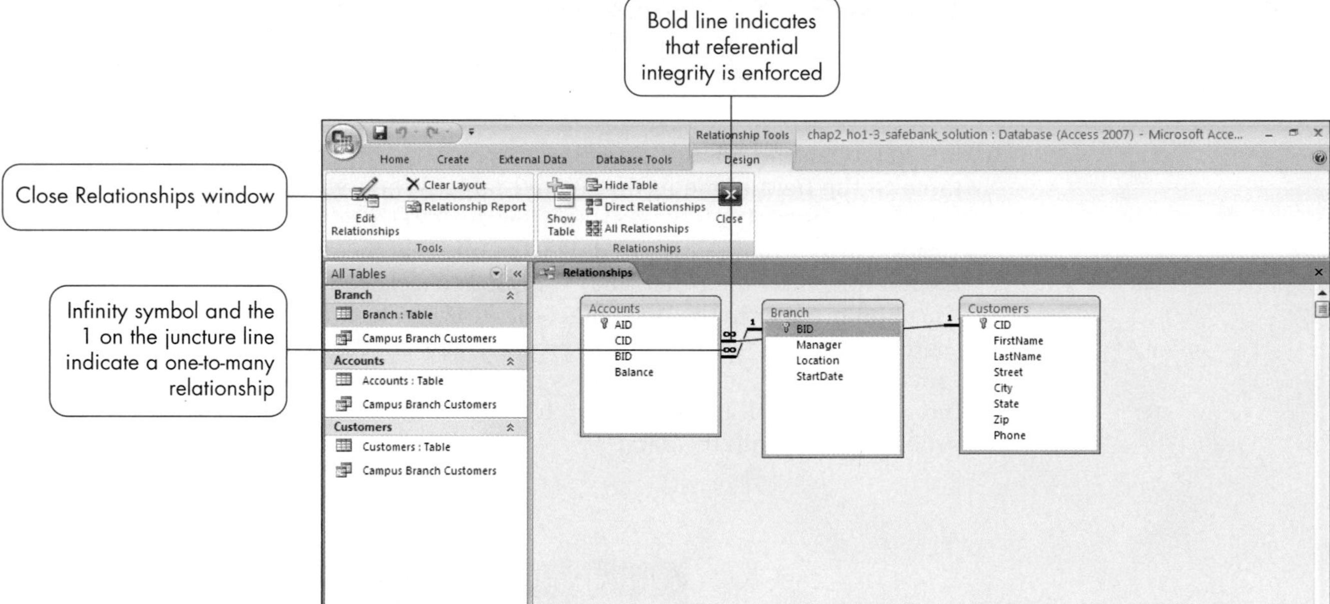

Figure 2.22 The Relationship Window Displaying One-to-Many Relationships

In the next hands-on exercise, you will create two additional tables by importing data from Excel spreadsheets into the Safebank database. You will establish and modify field properties. Then you will connect the newly imported data to the Branch table by establishing relationships between the tables.

Hands-On Exercises

2 | Imports and Relationships

Skills covered: 1. Import Excel Data into an Access Table **2.** Import Additional Excel Data **3.** Modify an Imported Table's Design **4.** Add Data to an Imported Table **5.** Establish Table Relationships **6.** Understand How Referential Integrity Protects Data

Step 1
Import Excel Data into an Access Table

Refer to Figure 2.23 and Figures 2.13 through 2.18 as you complete Step 1.

a. Open the *chap2_ho1-3_safebank_solution.accdb* file if necessary, then click **Options** on the Security Warning toolbar, click the **Enable this content option** in the Microsoft Office Security Options dialog box, and click **OK**.

   TROUBLESHOOTING: If you create unrecoverable errors while completing this hands-on exercise, you can delete the *chap2_ho1-3_safebank_solution* file, copy the *chap2_ho1_safebank_solution* database you created at the end of the first hands-on exercise, and open the copy of the backup database to start the second hands-on exercise again.

b. Click the **External Data tab** (see Figure 2.12). Click **Import Excel Spreadsheet** in the Import group to launch the Get External Data – Excel Spreadsheet wizard. Select the **Import the source data into a new table in the current database option**, if necessary, as shown in Figure 2.13.

c. Click **Browse** and go to your **Exploring Access Production folder**. Select the *chap2_ho2_ safebank.xlsx* workbook. Click **Open**.

   Click **OK** in the Get External Data-Excel Spreadsheet to open the **Import Spreadsheet Wizard**. The first window shows all of the worksheets in the workbook. This particular workbook contains only two worksheets: Accounts and Customers. The Customers worksheet is active, and a list of the data contained in the Customers worksheet displays in the Wizard.

d. Click on the **Accounts worksheet** and click **Next** (see Figure 2.14).

e. Click in the **First Row Contains Column Headings check box** to tell Access that column headings exist in the Excel file (see Figure 2.15).

   The field names, AID, CID, BID, and Balance will import from Excel along with the data stored in the rows in the worksheet.

f. Click **Next**.

   The AID (Account ID) will become the primary key in this table. It needs to be a unique identifier, so we must change the properties to disallow duplicates.

g. Click the **Indexed drop-down arrow** in the Field Options section and select **Indexed Yes (No Duplicates)**. Click **Next** (see Figure 2.16).

h. Click the **Choose my own primary key** option. Make sure that the **AID** field is selected. Click **Next** (see Figure 2.17).

   The final screen of the Import Spreadsheet Wizard asks you to name your table. The name of the Excel worksheet was Accounts and Access defaults to the worksheet name. It is an acceptable name (see Figure 2.18).

i. Click **Finish**.

A dialog box opens asking if you wish to save the parameters of this import to use again. If this were sales data that were collected in Excel and updated to the database on a weekly basis, saving the import would save time.

j. Click **Close**.

Saving these import parameters is not necessary. The new table displays in Datasheet view and resides in the Safebank database (see Figure 2.18).

k. Open the newly imported **Accounts table** in Datasheet view.

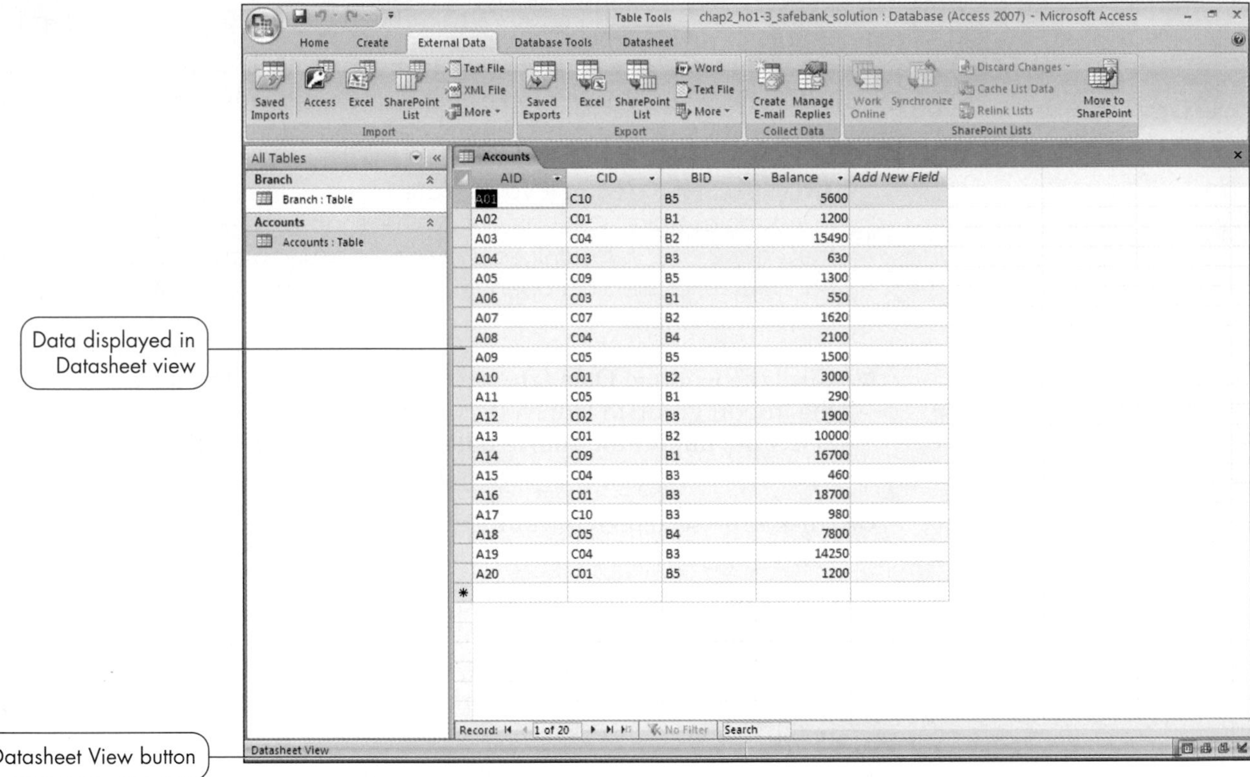

Figure 2.23 The Newly Imported Accounts Table

Step 2
Import Additional Excel Data

Refer to Figure 2.24 and Figures 2.13 through 2.18 as you complete Step 2.

a. Turn back to the beginning of Step 1 and repeat the instructions a through k, with the following changes.

b. Click on the **Customers worksheet** in Step 1d.

c. Change the index property of the **CID** field to **Yes (No Duplicates)** in Step 1g.

d. Identify the **CID** (Customer ID) as the primary key in Step 1h.

The default table name will be the Customers table. This is a good name so accept it.

e. Click **Finish** and click **Close**. The All Tables view will display three tables: Branch, Accounts, and Customers.

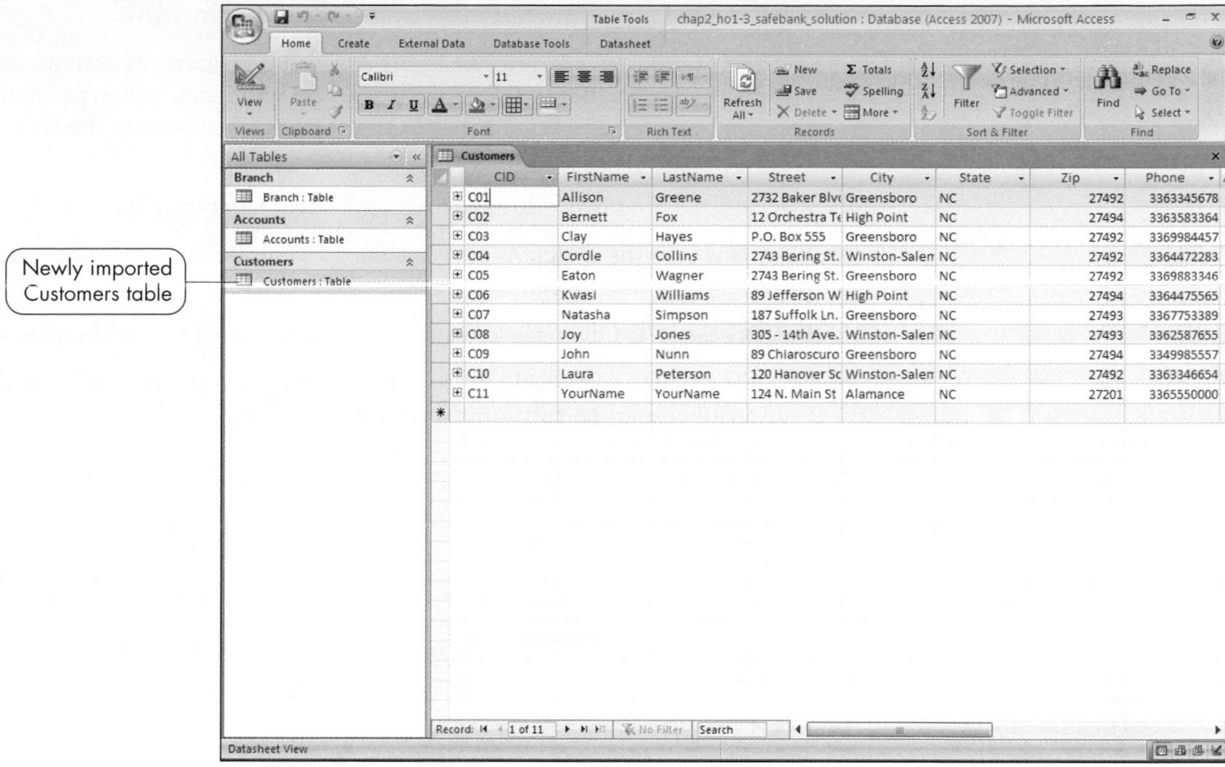

Figure 2.24 The Newly Imported Customers Table

Step 3
Modify an Imported Table's Design

Refer to Figure 2.25 as you complete Step 3.

a. Open the **Accounts table** in Design view and click the **AID** field if necessary.

b. Change the **AID** field size to **10**. Look at the bottom of the window in the Field Properties box.

   The field size was set at 255. Importing data from Excel saves typing but does not always create an efficiently designed database.

c. Type **Account ID** in the **Caption** property box for the AID field.

d. Click the **CID** field in the top of the Design view window to activate the *Properties* for the CID field.

e. Type **10** in the **Field Size** property box for the CID field using the Field Properties box in the bottom of the window.

f. Type **Customer ID** in the **Caption** property for the CID field.

g. Click the **BID** field in the top of the Design View window to activate the Properties for the BID field.

h. Type **10** in the **Field Size** property box for the BID field in the Field properties box at the bottom of the window.

i. Type **Branch ID** in the **Caption** property box for the BID field.

j. Click the **Balance** field in the top of the Design view window to activate the Properties for the Balance field.

k. Click in the **Format** property box to see a drop-down arrow.

Access often hides drop-down arrows until the property is activated. As you become more familiar with the software, you will learn which properties contain these hidden drop-down arrows. In the meanwhile, develop the habit of clicking around each new screen.

l. Click the **Format drop-down arrow** and select **Currency** from the list.

m. Click **Save** on the Quick Access Toolbar to save the design changes you made to the Accounts table. **Read the Warning Box!** Click **Yes**.

In this case, it is OK to click Yes because the size of three fields were shortened.

n. Open the **Customers table** in Design view. Change the **field size** of the **CID** field to **10** and add a **caption**, **Customer ID**.

o. Save the design changes to the Customers table.

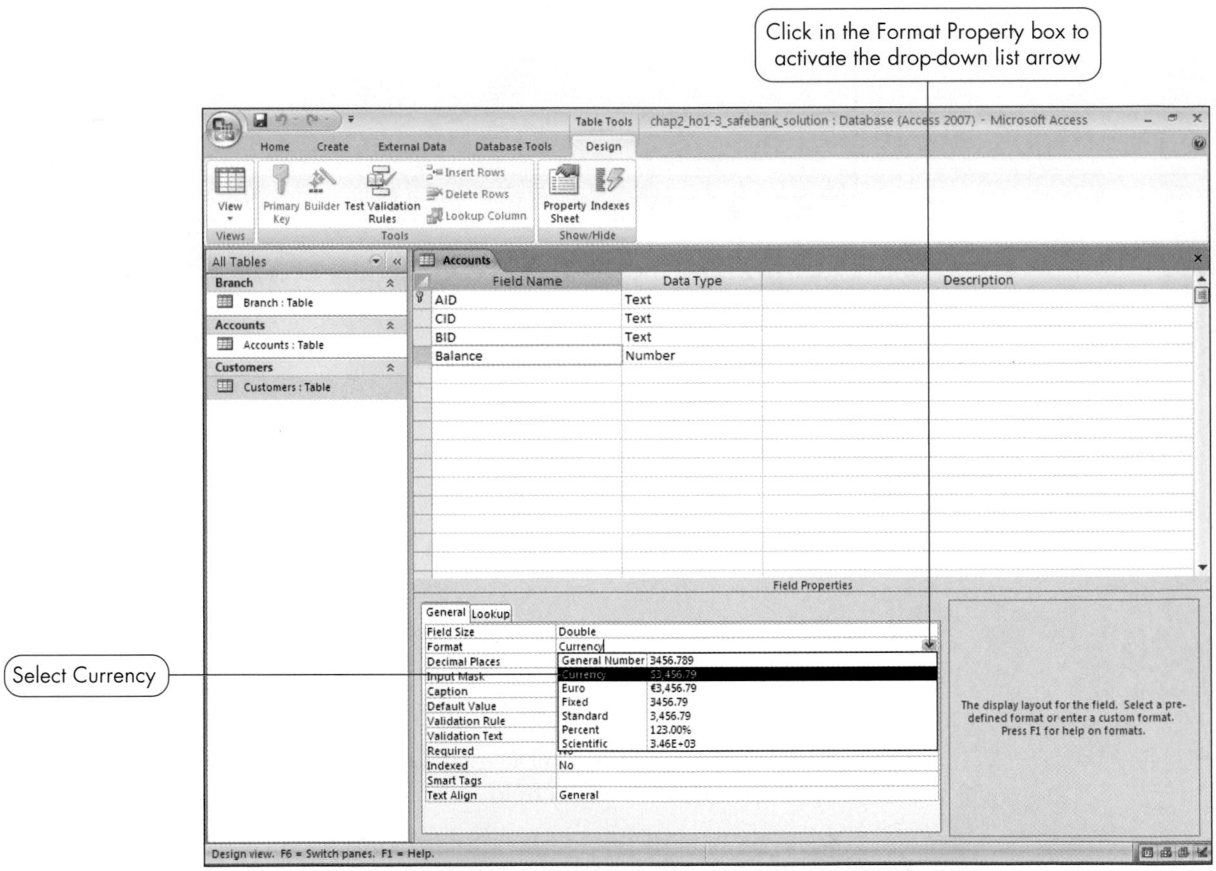

Figure 2.25 The Format Property of the Balance Field Set to Currency

Step 4
Add Data to an Imported Table

Refer to Figure 2.26 as you complete Step 4.

a. Open the **Customers table** in Datasheet view.

The asterisk in the row selector area is the indicator of a place to enter a new record.

b. Click the **Customer ID** field in the record after C10. Type **C11**. Fill in the rest of the data using your information as the customer. You may use a fictitious address and phone number.

c. Open **Accounts table** in Datasheet view. Create a new account ID A21. Enter **C11** as the Customer ID and **B5** as the Branch ID. Use your course number and section for the Balance field value.

If you were a student in section 04 of ISM 210, you would enter 21004 as the Balance.

d. Close all of the tables; keep the database open.

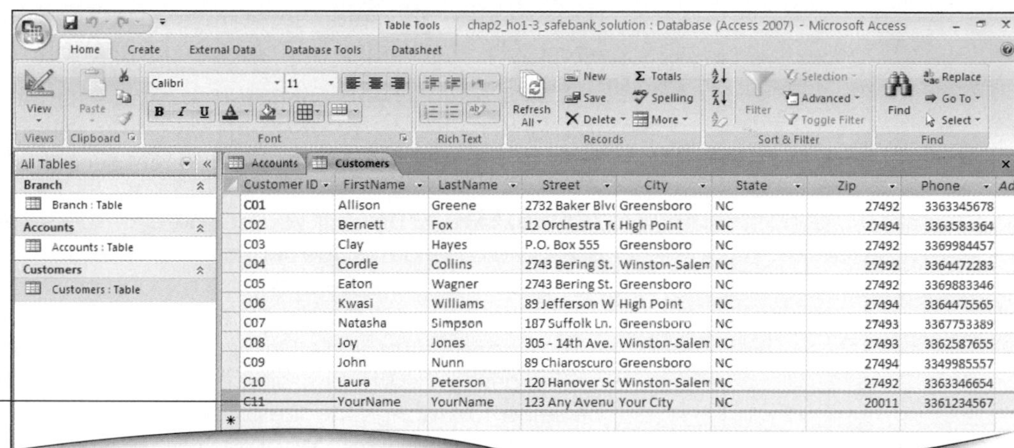

Figure 2.26 The Customers Table Displaying the New Account

Step 5
Establish Table Relationships

Refer to Figures 2.27 and 2.21 as you complete Step 5.

a. Click the **Database Tools tab**. Click **Relationships** in the Show/Hide group.

The Relationship window opens to the Show Table dialog box.

TROUBLESHOOTING: If the Show Table dialog box does not open, click Show Table in the Relationships group on the Design tab.

b. Double-click each of the three tables to add them to the Relationship window. (Alternatively, click a table, and then click **Add**.) Click **Close** in the Show Table dialog box.

The Accounts and Branch table boxes are large enough to display all of the field names. The Customers table has a scroll bar because it has too many fields to display in the small space.

TROUBLESHOOTING: If you duplicate a table, you may have gotten carried away clicking and adding. The duplicate table will display in the Relationship window with a number after its name, i.e. Branch1 or Customer2. Close the Show Table dialog box. Click the title bar of the duplicated table and press Delete. This procedure also works if you add the same table twice to a Query's design grid.

c. Run your mouse over the **blue line** at the bottom of the Customers table box until its shape changes to the **resize arrow**. With the double-headed arrow showing, click the left mouse button and drag down until all the field names display and the scroll bar disappears. Move or drag each table so all the relationship lines are visible.

d. Click the **BID** field in the **Branch table**. Drag to the **BID** field in the **Accounts table** and release the mouse. The Edit Relationships dialog box opens. Check the **Enforce Referential Integrity** box. Click **Create**.

   A thick black line displays joining the two tables. It has a 1 on the end near the Branch table signifying that it is connecting the primary key (unique identifier) to an infinity symbol on the end next to the Accounts table. You have established a one-to-many relationship between the Branch and Accounts tables.

e. Click the **CID** field in the **Customers table** to select it. Drag to the **CID** field in the **Accounts table** and release the mouse. The Edit Relationships dialog box opens. Check the **Enforce Referential Integrity** box. Click **Create**.

   You have established a one-to-many relationship between the Customers and Accounts tables. A customer will have only a single Customer ID number. The same customer may have many different accounts: Savings, Checking, CDs, etc.

   TROUBLESHOOTING: If you get an error message when you click Create, you possibly did not get all the field properties established correctly in Steps 3 and 4 of Hands-On Exercise 2. Relationships may be created only between like data types and sizes. Right-click the blue title bar of the Accounts window in the Relationship window and select Table Design from the shortcut menu. Click on the CID field and examine the size property. It should be set to 10. Click the BID field. It should be set to 10. Change the size property of one or both fields. Save your changes to the table design. Try to establish the relationship again. If it still does not work, check the size of the CID field in the Customers table. It should also be 10.

f. Click **Save** on the Quick Access Toolbar to save the changes to the Relationships. Close the Relationships window.

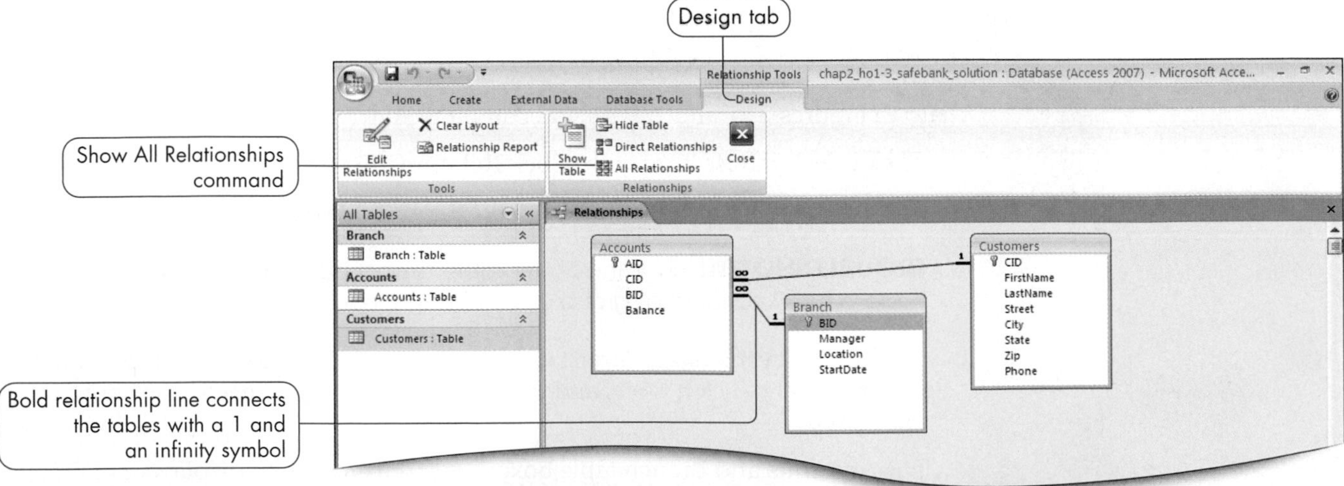

Figure 2.27 Properly Constructed Relationships Among the Tables

Step 6
Understand How Referential Integrity Protects Data

Refer to Figure 2.28 as you complete Step 6.

a. Open the **Accounts table** in Datasheet view. Add a new record: Account ID – A22; Customer ID – **C03** (Note, that is a zero, not a letter O); Branch ID – **B6**; Balance – **4000**. Press **Enter**.

   A warning box appears. This bank has five branches. A sixth branch does not exist. In this case, the warning message is telling exactly what is wrong. There is no related record for B6 in the Branch table. Access does not permit data entry of unconnected data. Referential integrity was enforced between the Branch ID in the Branch table and the Branch ID in the Accounts table. Access prevents the entry of an invalid Branch ID.

b. Click **OK**. Replace *B6* with **B5** and press **Enter** twice. As soon as you move to a different record, the pencil symbol disappears and your data are saved.

   You successfully identified a Branch ID that Access recognizes. Because referential integrity between the Accounts and Branch tables has been enforced, Access looks at each data entry item in a foreign key and matches it to a corresponding value in the table where it is the primary key. In Step 6a, you attempted to enter a nonexistent Branch ID and were not allowed to make that error. In Step 6b, you entered a valid Branch ID. Access examined the index for the Branch ID in the Branch table and found a corresponding value for B5.

c. Close the Accounts table. Reopen the **Accounts table** and you will find that the record you just entered for A22 has been saved.

d. Click the **Office Button**, select **Manage**, and then select **Back Up Database**. Type **chap2_ho2_safebank_solution** as the file name and click **Save**.

   You just created a backup of the database after completing the second hands-on exercise. The original database *chap2_ho1-3_safebank_solution* remains onscreen. If you ruin the original database as you complete the third hands-on exercise, you can use the backup file you just created and rework the third exercise.

e. Close the file and exit Access if you do not want to continue with the next exercise at this time.

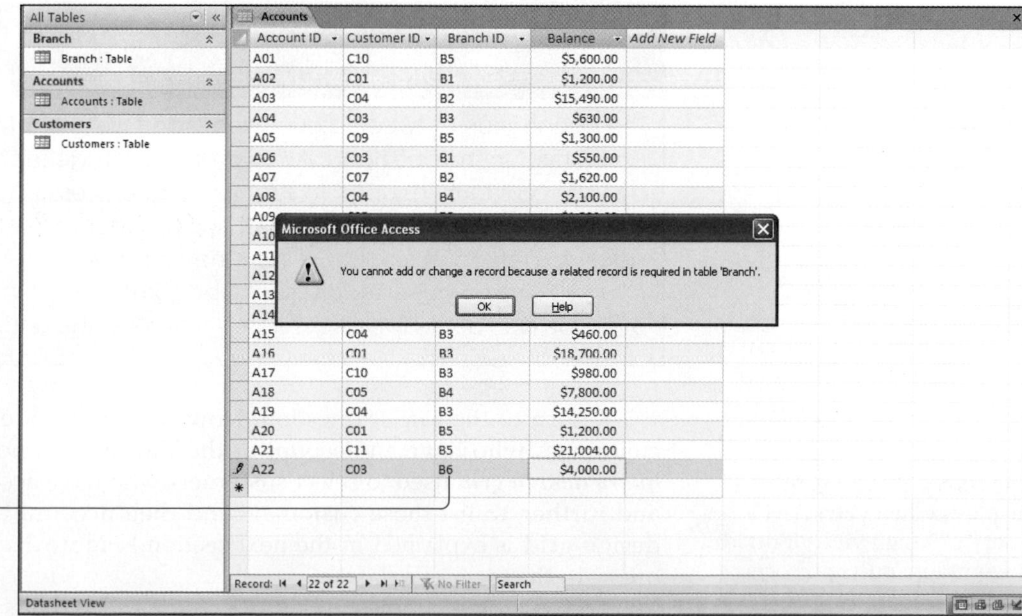

Figure 2.28 How Referential Integrity Works to Protect Data Accuracy

Queries

What if you wanted to see just the customers who bank at a specific branch or who have accounts with balances over $5,000? Perhaps you need to know the customers who have accounts at multiple branches. Maybe you will need a list of all the customers who bank with the branch managed by a specific manager. The manager's name is stored in the Branch table and the customer's name in the Customers table. In this small database, you could open both tables and mentally trace through the strings of the relationships and extract the information. But in a real world database with thousands of records, you would be unable to do this accurately. A query provides the ability to ask questions based on the data or a smaller grouping of data and to find the answers to those questions.

A ***query*** enables you to ask questions about the data stored in a database and returns the answers from the records in the order that matches your instructions.

A ***query*** permits you to see the data you want arranged in the sequence that you need. It enables you to select specific records from a table (or from several tables) and show some or all of the fields for the selected records. You can perform calculations to display data that are not explicitly stored in the underlying table(s), such as the amount of interest each bank account earned during the previous month.

In this section, you use the Query Wizard to create a query. You set specific conditions to display only records that meet the condition. Finally, you learn about large databases.

Creating a Query

The ***Query Wizard*** is an Access tool that facilitates new query development.

A ***dataset***, which contains the records that satisfy the criteria specified in the query, provides the answers to the user's questions.

Create a query either by using the ***Query Wizard*** or specifying the tables and fields directly in Design view. Like all of the Microsoft wizards, the Query Wizard is a method to automate your work. It facilitates new query development. The results of the query display in a ***dataset***, which contains the records that satisfy the criteria specified in the query.

A dataset looks and acts like a table, but it is not a table; it is a dynamic subset of a table that selects, sorts, and calculates records as specified in the query. A dataset is similar to a table in appearance and, like a table, it enables you to enter a new record or modify or delete an existing record. Any changes made in the dataset are reflected automatically in the underlying table.

TIP Changes Made to Query Results Overwrite Table Data

The connection between a query result and the underlying table data may create problems. On the one hand, it is to your advantage that you can correct an error in data if you should happen to spot it in a query result. You save time by not having to close the query, open the table, find the record in error, fix it, and run the query again to get robust results. On the other hand, you must be careful not to accidentally click into a query record and type something. If you press Enter or Tab, whatever you accidentally typed is stored forever in the underlying table.

The ***query design grid*** displays when you select a query's Design view; it divides the window into two parts.

Return to the earlier question. How would you identify the names of all of the customers who have an account at the Campus branch? Figure 2.29 contains the ***query design grid*** used to select customers who have accounts at the Campus Branch and further, to list those customers and their account balances alphabetically. (The design grid is explained in the next section.) Figure 2.30 displays the answer to the query in the form of a dataset.

The Customers table contains 21 records. The dataset in Figure 2.30 has only six records, corresponding to the customers who have Campus branch accounts. The records in the table are ordered by the Customer ID (the primary key), whereas the records in the dataset are in alphabetical order by last name. Changing the order of data displayed in a query has no effect on the underlying table data.

TIP Examine the Record Number

An experienced Access user always examines the number of records returned in a query's results. As you add additional criteria, the number of records returned should decrease.

Create a Select Query

A ***select query*** searches the underlying tables to retrieve the data that satisfy the query parameters.

The query in Figures 2.29 and 2.30 is an example of a select query, which is the most common type of query. A ***select query*** searches the underlying tables to retrieve the data that satisfy the query parameters. The data displayed in a dataset (see Figure 2.30), which can be modified to update the data in the underlying table(s). The specifications for selecting records and determining which fields will be displayed for the selected records, as well as the sequence of the selected records, are established within the design grid of Figure 2.29. The select query is one of many different query operations Access supports.

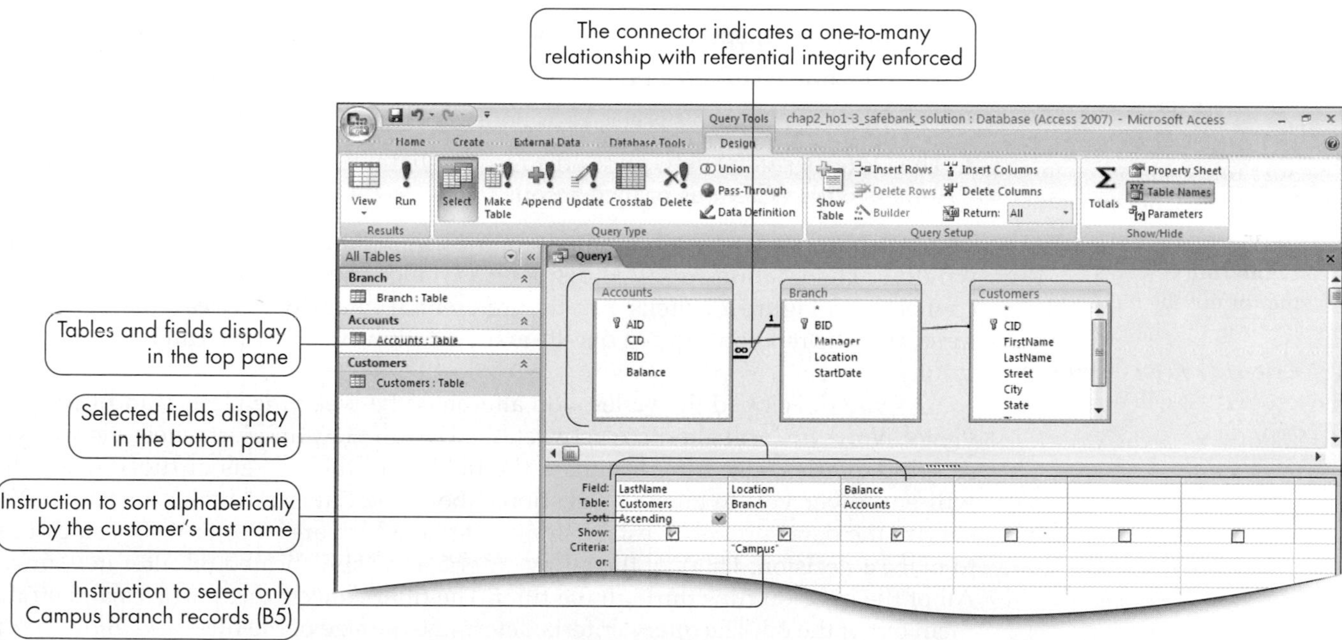

Figure 2.29 The Query Design View

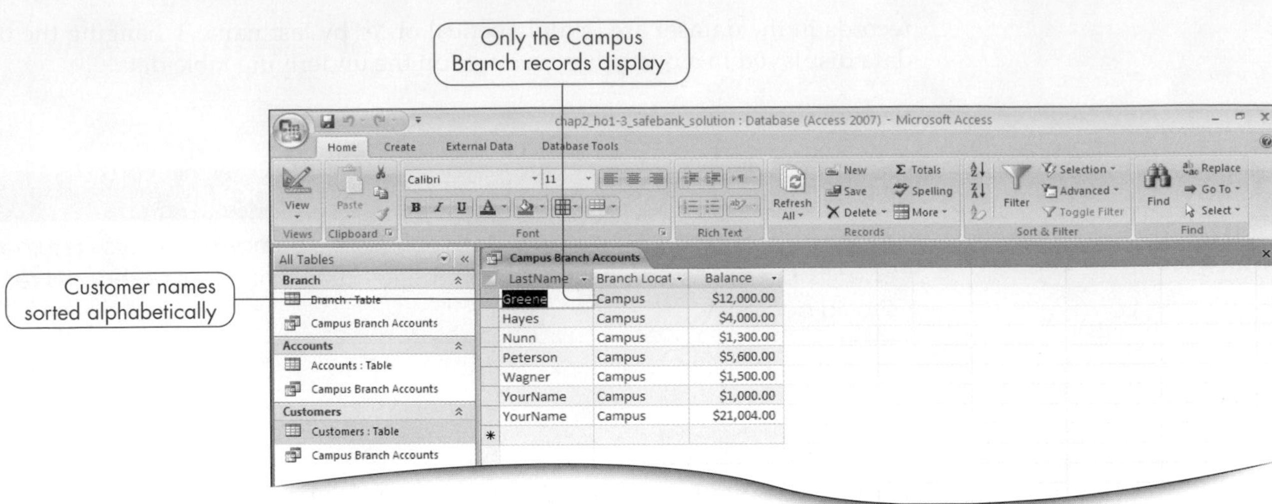

Figure 2.30 The Query Datasheet View

Use the Query Design Grid

The query design grid consists of two panes. The lower pane contains columns and rows. Each field in the query has its own column and contains multiple rows. The rows permit you to control query results.

The ***Table row*** displays the data source.

The ***Field row*** displays the field name.

The ***Sort row*** enables you to sort in ascending or descending sequence.

The ***Show row*** controls whether or not the field will be displayed in the dataset.

The ***Criteria row(s)*** determines the records that will be selected.

- The ***Table row*** displays the data source. The ***Field row*** displays the field name.
- The ***Sort row*** enables you to sort in ascending or descending sequence.
- The ***Show row*** controls whether or not the field will be displayed in the dataset.
- The ***Criteria row*(s)** determines the records that will be selected, such as customers with a Campus branch account.

The top pane contains table names in a design that resembles the relationship window. The relationship type displays as the connector between the tables. The connector in Figure 2.29 tells you that referential integrity between the tables is in force, that the relationship is a one-to-many relation, and that we can trust the query results.

As you developed the tables, you alternated between the Design and Datasheet views. Now, you will alternate between the Design view and Datasheet view as you develop queries. Use it to designate the fields and the subsets of those fields that will empower you to answer questions about the data and make decisions. You specify the data subsets by establishing criteria, which are rules or tests you can use to make a decision. Think of the query criteria as a sophisticated oil filter in your car. All of the car's oil runs through the filter. The filter collects dirt particles and strains them out of the oil. The query criteria determine the size of the filter and allow you to sift through the data to find the records of interest. The criteria operate much like a filter in a table. The difference between a filter and a query is that the query becomes a permanent part of the database. A filter gives you a temporary method to view the data.

Specifying Criteria for Different Data Types

A *currency* is the medium of exchange; in the United States, currency formatted values display with a dollar sign.

The field data type determines how the criteria are specified for that field. You need to enter criteria for a text field enclosed in quotation marks. To find only the records of customers with accounts at the Campus branch, you would enter "Campus" as the criteria under the Location field. You enter the criteria for number, ***currency*** (e.g., $3.00 in the United States), and counter fields as digits with or without a decimal point and/or a minus sign. (Commas and dollar signs are not allowed.) When the criterion is in a date field, you enclose the criterion in pound signs. You should enter date criteria in the mm/dd/yyyy format, such as #10/14/2008#. You enter criteria for a Yes/No field as Yes (or True) or No (or False).

Access accepts values for text and date fields in the design grid in multiple formats. You can enter the text with or without quotation marks, such as *Campus* or *"Campus."* You can enter a date with or without the pound signs, such as *1/1/2008* or *#1/1/2008#*. Access will enter the quotation marks or pound signs, respectively, for you when you move to the next cell in the design grid. Thus, text entries are always shown in quotation marks and dates in pound signs.

Use Wildcards

Select queries recognize the question mark and asterisk wildcards that enable you to search for a pattern within a text field. A question mark stands for a single character in the same position as the question mark; thus *H?ll* will return *Hall*, *Hill*, and *Hull*. An asterisk stands for any number of characters in the same position as the asterisk; for example, *S*nd* will return *Sand*, *Stand*, and *Strand*. If you search a two-letter state code field for *?C*, Access will return *NC*, *SC*, and *DC*. If you search the same field with either **C* or *C**, Access will return *CA*, *CO*, *CT*, *DC*, *NC*, and *SC*.

Use Operands in Queries

An ***operator*** is a mathematical symbol, such as +, -, *, and /.

An ***operand*** is the portion of the mathematical expression that is being operated on.

A numeric field may be limited through standard numeric operators; ***operators*** such as plus, minus, equals, greater than, less than, multiply (*), divide (/), and not equals (<>). An ***operand*** is a portion of the mathematical expression that is being operated on, such as the value stored in a field. In Access, you use the field name as an operand, such as Date() - 30. Both the Date() field and 30 are operands. Table 2.4 shows sample expressions and discusses their results.

Table 2.4 Criteria Operands

Expression	Result
>10	For a Price field, items with a price over $10.00
<10	For a Price field, items with a price under $10.00
>=10	For a Price field, items with a price of at least $10.00
<=10	For a Price field, items with a price of $10.00 or less
=10	For a Price field, items with a price of exactly $10.00
<> 10	For a Price field, items with a price not equal to $10.00
!=10	For a Price field, items with a price not equal to $10.00
#2/2/2008#	For a ShippedDate field, orders shipped on February 2, 2008
'2/2/2008'	For a ShippedDate field, orders shipped on February 2, 2008
Date()	For an OrderDate field, orders for today's date
Between 1/1/2007 and 3/31/2007	For a specified interval between a start and end date
Between Date( ) And DateAdd ("M", 3, Date( ))	For a RequiredDate field, orders required between today's date and three months from today's date
< Date( ) – 30	For an OrderDate field, orders more than 30 days old
Year([OrderDate]) = 2005	For an OrderDate field, orders with order dates in 2005
DatePart("q", [OrderDate]) = 4	For an OrderDate field, orders for the fourth calendar quarter
DateSerial(Year ([OrderDate]), Month ([OrderDate]) + 1, 1) – 1	For an OrderDate field, orders for the last day of each month
Year([OrderDate]) = Year(Now()) And Month([OrderDate]) = Month(Now())	For an OrderDate field, orders for the current year and month

Work with Null and Zero-Length Strings

A ***null*** value is the formal, computer term for a missing value.

Sometimes finding what is *not* known is an important part of making a decision. For example, which orders have been accepted but not shipped? Are we missing phone numbers or addresses for some of our customers? The computer term for a missing value is ***null***. Table 2.5 gives the following illustrations on how to use the Null criterion in a query.

Table 2.5 Establishing Null Criteria Expressions

Expression	Result
Is Null	For an Employee field in the Customers table when the customer has not been assigned a sales representative. (Some fields, such as primary key fields, can't contain Null.)
Is Not Null	For a ShipDate field, orders already shipped to customers.
" "	For an E-mail field for customers who don't have an email address. This is indicated by a zero-length string. This is different from a Null value. Use this only when you know a customer has no e-mail, not when he or she has e-mail but you do not know what it is. You enter a zero-length string by typing two double quotation marks with no space between them (" ").

Understand Query Sort Order

The ***query sort order*** determines the order of items in the query Datasheet View.

The ***query sort order*** determines the order of items in the query Datasheet view. You can change the sort order of a query by specifying the sort order in the design grid. The sorts work from left to right. The leftmost field with a sort order specified will be the primary sort field; the next sort specified field to the right will be the secondary sort field, and so forth. Change the order of the query fields in the design grid to change the sort order of the query result. Alter the field order within the design grid by clicking in the Table row (the second row) of the design grid and specifying the table and then in the Field row and selecting a different field name. The table must be specified first because each field row drop-down list shows only the names of the fields in the specified table. You also may insert additional columns in the design grid by selecting the column, right-clicking the selection, and choosing Insert column from the shortcut menu. The inserted column will insert to the right of the highlighted column.

TIP Reorder Query Fields

With a query open in Design view, move your mouse above a field name. The mouse pointer will change shape to a bold black arrow. When you see the bold black arrow, click the mouse. The field's column selects. Move your mouse slowly over the top of the selected area until the pointer shape changes to the move shape (a thick white arrow). When the white arrow shape shows, click and drag the field to a new position on the design grid. A thick black border moves with your mouse to tell you where the field will move. Release the mouse when the border moves to the desired position.

Establish And, Or, and Not Criteria

Until now, all of the questions that you have asked the database to answer through queries have been relatively simple. Access adapts to more complex query specifications. What if you need a list of all of the customers who bank at the Campus branch and do not have accounts at any other branches? Which customers bank only at the Campus or Uptown branches? Are there customers of the Campus branch with deposits over $5,000? These questions involve multiple field interaction. The

The ***And operator*** returns only records that meet all criteria.

The ***Or operator*** returns records meeting any of the specified criteria.

The ***Not operator*** returns the opposite of the specified criteria.

moment you specify criteria in multiple fields, Access combines the fields using the And or the Or operator. When the expressions are in the same row of the query design grid, Access uses the ***And operator***. This means that only the records that meet *all* criteria in all of the fields will be returned. If the criteria are positioned in different rows of the design grid, Access uses the ***Or operator*** and will return records meeting *any* of the specified criteria. The ***Not operator*** returns the *opposite* of the specification.

Figure 2.31 shows a query in Design view that specifies an And operator. It will return all of the Campus branch accounts with balances over $5,000. Both conditions must be met for the record to be included. Figure 2.32 shows a query in Design view that specifies an Or operator. It will return all of the Campus branch accounts with any balance plus all accounts at any branch with balances over $5,000. Either condition may be met for a record to be included. Figure 2.33 shows a query in Design view that specifies a Not operator. It will return all of the accounts at all of the branches excluding the Campus branch. You may combine And, Or, and Not operators to achieve the desired result. If you need a list of the accounts with balances over $5,000 at the Campus and Uptown branches, you set the criteria so that the >5000 expression is duplicated for each location specified (see Figure 2.34).

Field:	LastName	Location	Balance
Table:	Customer	Branch	Account
Sort:	Ascending		
Show:	☑	☑	☑
Criteria:		"Campus"	>5000
or:			

Figure 2.31 And Criterion—Only Records Satisfying Both Conditions Will Return

Field:	LastName	Location	Balance
Table:	Customer	Branch	Account
Sort:	Ascending		
Show:	☑	☑	☑
Criteria:		"Campus"	
or:			>5000

Figure 2.32 Or Criterion—Records Meeting Either Condition Will Return

Field:	LastName	Location	Balance
Table:	Customer	Branch	Account
Sort:	Ascending		
Show:	☑	☑	☑
Criteria:		Not "Campus"	
or:			>5000

Figure 2.33 Not Criterion—Any Record Except the Matching Will Return

Field:	LastName	Location	Balance
Table:	Customer	Branch	Account
Sort:	Ascending		
Show:	☑	☑	☑
Criteria:		"Campus"	>5000
or:		"Uptown"	>5000

Figure 2.34 And and Or Criteria—Records Meeting Both Conditions at Both Branches Return

Copying and Running a Query

After you create a query, you may want to duplicate it to use as the basis for creating similar queries. Duplicating a query saves time in selecting tables and fields for queries that need the same structure but different criteria. After you create and save one or more queries, you can execute them whenever you need them to produce up-to-date results.

Copy a Query

Sometimes, you have one-of-a-kind questions about your data. Then you create and run the query, find the answer and close it. If you create the query with the wizard, you save and name it in the last step. If you create the query in Design view, it is possible for you to exit the query without saving changes. Most queries answer recurrent questions. What were sales last week in Houston, in Dallas, in Chicago? In cases like this, you set up the query for the dates and places of interest one time, then copy it, rename the copy and establish the parameters for a different city or date.

Frequently, you will need to examine multiple subsets of the data. In Hands-On Exercise 3, you will create a query displaying the names and account balances of the customers who have accounts at the Campus branch. Should you need to know the same information about the customers who have Uptown accounts, you would select the query in the Navigation pane, and then copy and paste it to a blank space at the bottom pane. Right-click the copy and rename it Uptown. Open the newly created Uptown query in Design view and replace the Campus criterion with Uptown. When you run and save the query, the resulting dataset displays customers and account balances from the Uptown branch. Using this method takes you a few minutes to create branch specific queries for all five locations.

Run a Query

When you ***run a query***, Access processes the query instructions and displays records that meet the conditions.

After you create the query by specifying criteria and save it, you are ready to run it. You ***run a query*** by clicking the Run command (the red exclamation point) to direct Access to process the instructions specified by the query. In our databases, the queries run quickly. Even in the largest database you will use in the end of chapter exercises, no query will take more than a few seconds to run. As you learn how to work with these databases, keep in mind that real-world databases can be massive. Think through the query design carefully. Include all necessary fields and tables, but do not include fields or tables that are not necessary to answer the question. Unnecessary fields slow the query's run time.

Using the Query Wizard

You may create a query directly in Design view or by using the Query Wizard. Even if you initiate the query with a wizard, you will need to learn how to modify it in Design view. Often, it is much faster to copy an existing query and make slight modifications to its design than it would be to start at the beginning of the wizard. You also will need to know how to add additional tables and fields to an existing query in case you failed to think through the design thoroughly and you omitted a necessary field. To launch the Query Wizard, click the Create tab and click Query Wizard in the Other group (see Figure 2.35).

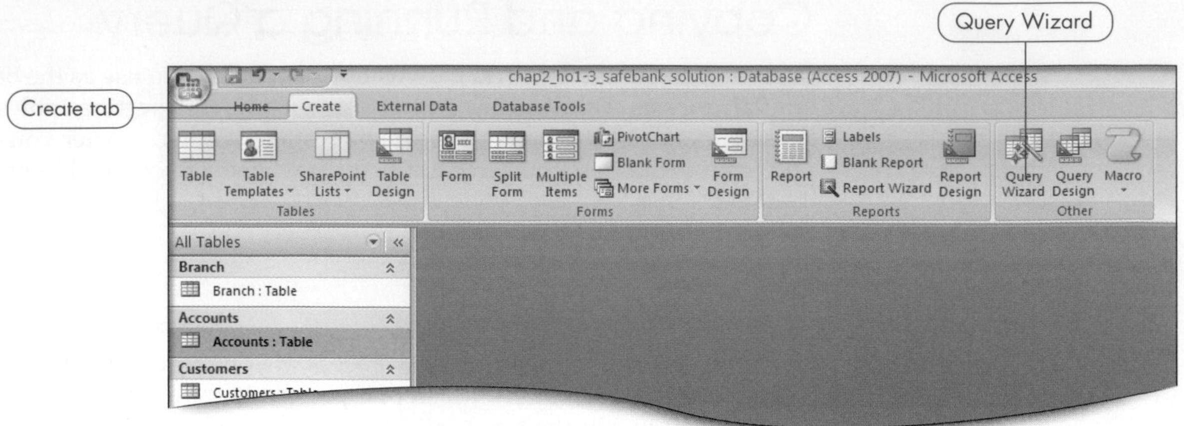

Figure 2.35 Launching the Query Wizard

Access produces many different kinds of queries. Here we will work with the most common query type, the Simple query. This is a powerful and sophisticated tool. Select the Simple Query Wizard in the first dialog box of the Query Wizard, as shown in Figure 2.36.

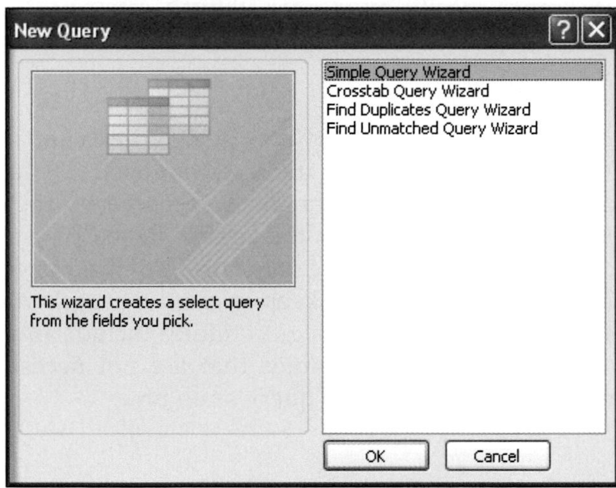

Figure 2.36 The Simple Query Wizard Step 1

In the second step of the Simple Query Wizard dialog box, you specify the tables and fields needed in your query. As soon as you click on the table in the Tables/Queries drop-down box, a list of that table's fields display in the Available fields box. See Figures 2.37 and 2.38.

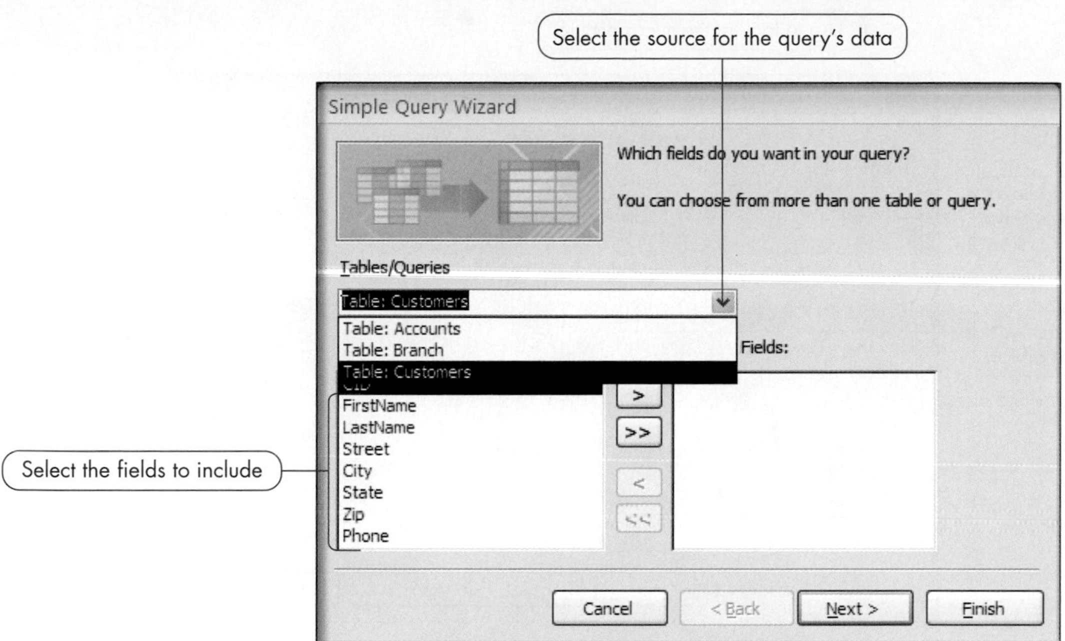

Figure 2.37 Specify Which Tables or Queries to Use as Input

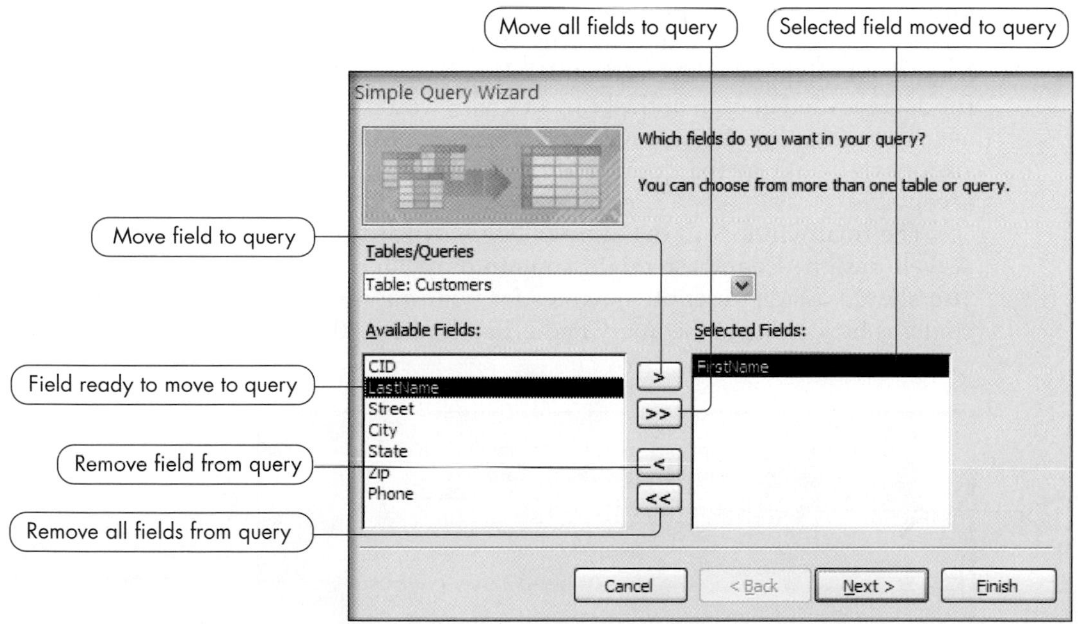

Figure 2.38 Specify the Fields for the Query

Select the necessary fields by clicking them to highlight, and then using the navigation arrows described in Figure 2.39.

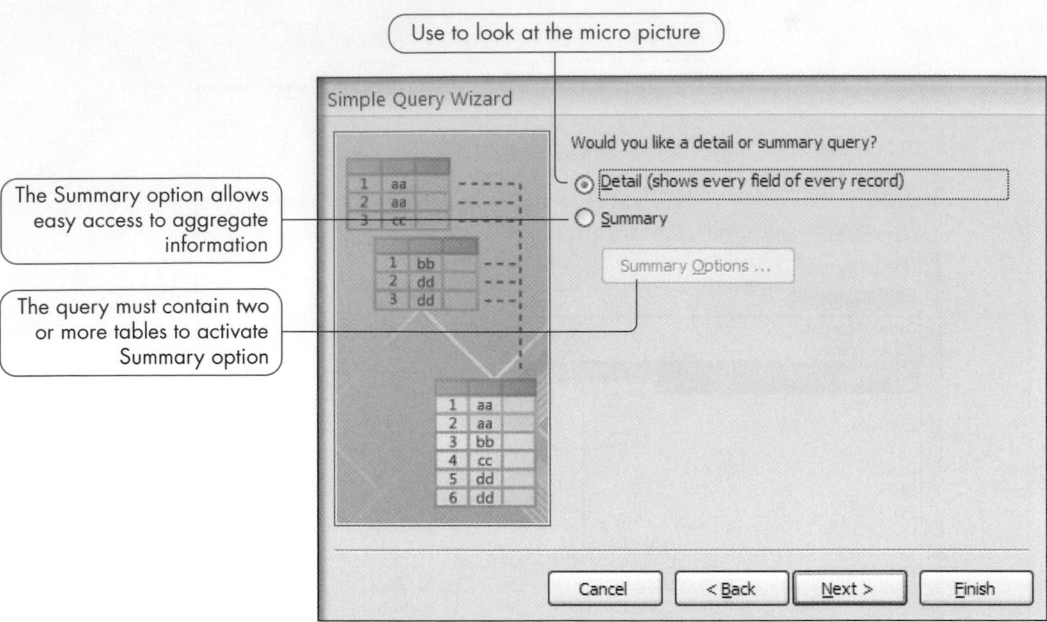

Figure 2.39 Select to Display Detail or to Summarize the Data

Aggregate means the collection of individual items into a total.

In the Simple Query Wizard, you choose between a detailed or a summary query. The detail query provides every record of every field. The summary enables you to aggregate data and View only summary statistics. ***Aggregate*** means the collection of individual items into a total. If you were only interested in the total of the funds deposited at each of the branches, you would set the query to a summary and ask Access to sum the balances of all accounts in that branch. Some Access users summarize data in the queries and others do so in reports. Either approach is acceptable.

The final window in the Simple Query Wizard directs you to name the query. A well-designed database might contain only 5 tables and 500 queries. Therefore, you should assign descriptive names for your queries so that you know what each contains by looking at the query name. See Figure 2.40.

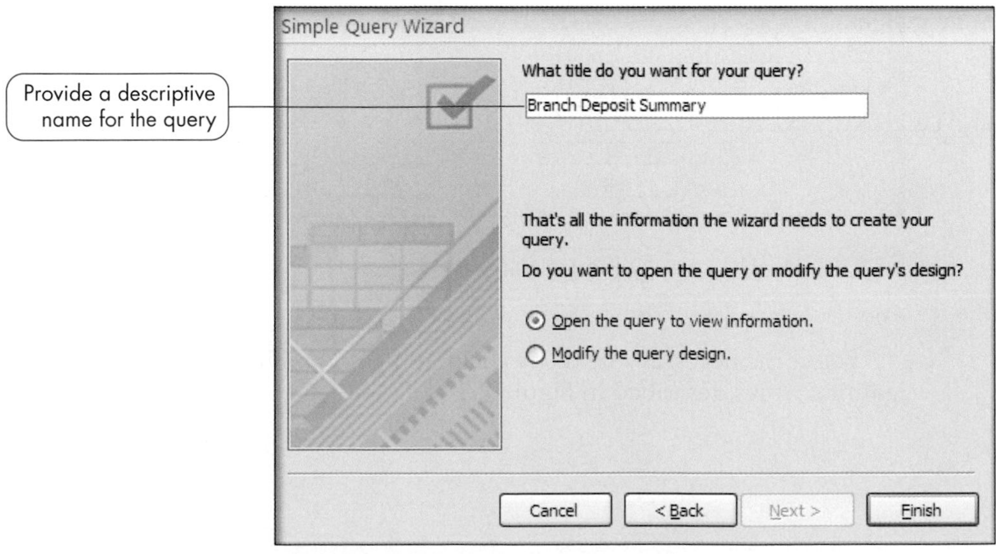

Figure 2.40 Name the Query Descriptively

Understanding Large Database Differences

Suppose you work for a large university. You need to identify all of the students at your university who are business majors, their advisor's names, and their specific majors. The Student table contains student names, identification numbers, majors, faculty advisor's identification number, class standing, addresses, and so on. The Faculty table contains faculty names, departmental affiliation, identification number, and rank. Your query needs to include fields for the student's name, major, and the advisor's name. You would not need the student's address or the faculty member's ID because those fields are unnecessary to answer the question. You need to establish criteria to select business majors: Accounting, Finance, Information Systems, Management, Marketing, and Economics.

Even if your computer is state-of-the-art, fast, powerful, and loaded with memory, this query might take up to 15 minutes to run. If you include unnecessary fields or tables, the run time increases. At the author's university, each additional table roughly doubles the query run time. As an Access beginner, your queries might contain too much or too little information. You will make frequent modifications to the query design as you learn. As you apply your database skills to work with large databases, you will learn to carefully design queries prior to running them to minimize the time to run the queries.

In addition to the earlier mentioned size difference between real world databases and those you will use in the class, real world databases involve multiple users. Typically, the organization stores the database file on the network. Multiple people may simultaneously log into the database. Each user makes changes to tables or forms. At your school, thousands of users can extract data from the university's database. Prior to meeting your advisor, you check your transcript online. You enter a database to find out how many hours you have completed and whether or not you have met the prerequisites. You have permission to view your transcript but you do not have the necessary permission to change what is recorded there. Several hundred other users have more extensive privileges in your school's database. Your Access professor can enter and probably change your grade in this class. If the securities are appropriately set on the database, your Access professor is not able to change the grade that you earned in other courses.

Most large organizations employ database administrators and managers that ensure data security, efficacy, and integrity. These professionals are well paid to make sure that no one inside or outside the firm has access to classified data or can corrupt the data resident in the system. Additionally, SOX rules mandate backup and security measures.

These positions involve a great deal of responsibility. How does someone charged with this vital role do it? One common method involves splitting the database into front and back ends. Typically, the ***front end*** of a database contains the objects, like queries, reports, and forms, needed to interact with data, but not the tables where the record values reside. The tables are safely stored in the ***back end*** system where users cannot inadvertently destroy or corrupt data. Most often, the front and back ends of the database are stored on different systems placed in different locations to provide an extra security measure. Users within the organization are divided into groups by their data needs. Then the groups are assigned rights and privileges. For example, a professor has privileges to record grades for students registered in his or her classes but not for other professors' classes. The financial aid officer may look at student grades and financial records, but may not alter either. The dean may look at student grades, but probably not their financial records. The student health center physician may view a student's immunization records and update it when necessary, but cannot see the student's grades.

The ***front end*** of a database contains the objects, like queries, reports, and forms, needed to interact with data, but not the tables where the record values reside.

The ***back end*** of the system protects and stores data so that users cannot inadvertently destroy or corrupt the organization's vital data.

The next hands-on exercise introduces queries as a more useful way to examine data. You use the Query Wizard to create a basic query, and then modify that query by adding an additional field and an additional table, and performing simple query criteria specifications.

Hands-On Exercises

3 | Multiple-Table Query

Skills covered: 1. Create a Query Using a Wizard **2.** Specify Simple Query Criteria **3.** Change Query Data **4.** Add a Table to a Query Using Design View and Sort a Query

Step 1
Create a Query Using a Wizard

Refer to Figure 2.41 as you complete Step 1.

a. Open the *chap2_ho1-3_safebank_solution.accdb* database from Hands-On Exercise 2 (if necessary), click **Options** on the Security Warning toolbar, click the **Enable this content option** in the Microsoft Office Security Options dialog box, and click **OK**.

   TROUBLESHOOTING: If you create unrecoverable errors while completing this hands-on exercise, you can delete the *chap2_ho1-3_safebank_solution* file, copy the *chap2_ho2_safebank_solution* database you created at the end of the second hands-on exercise, and open the copy of the backup database to start the third hands-on exercise again.

b. Click the **Create tab** and click **Query Wizard** in the Other group to launch the wizard.

   The New Query Dialog box opens.

c. Simple Query Wizard is selected by default. Click **OK**.

d. Click the **Tables/Queries drop-down arrow** and select **Table: Customers**.

   This step asks you to specify the tables and fields needed in the query. A list of the fields in the Customers table displays in the Available Fields box.

e. Double-click the **FirstName** field.

   The FirstName field moves from the Available Fields box to the Selected Fields box. You can also double-click a field in the Selected Fields box to move it back to the Available box.

f. Click the **LastName** field and click the **Move Field to Query command** (see Figure 2.38).

g. Click the **Tables/Queries drop-down arrow** and select **Table**: **Accounts**.

h. From the list of fields in the Accounts table, select **BID** and **Balance** and move them one at a time to the Fields in Query box. Click **Next**.

   Your query should have four fields: First and Last names, BID, and Balance.

i. Select **Detail**, if necessary, to choose between a Detail and Summary Query. Click **Next**.

j. Name your query **Campus Branch Customers**. Click **Finish**.

   This name describes the data that will eventually populate the query. The default name, Customers Query, comes from the first table selected when you started the query wizard.

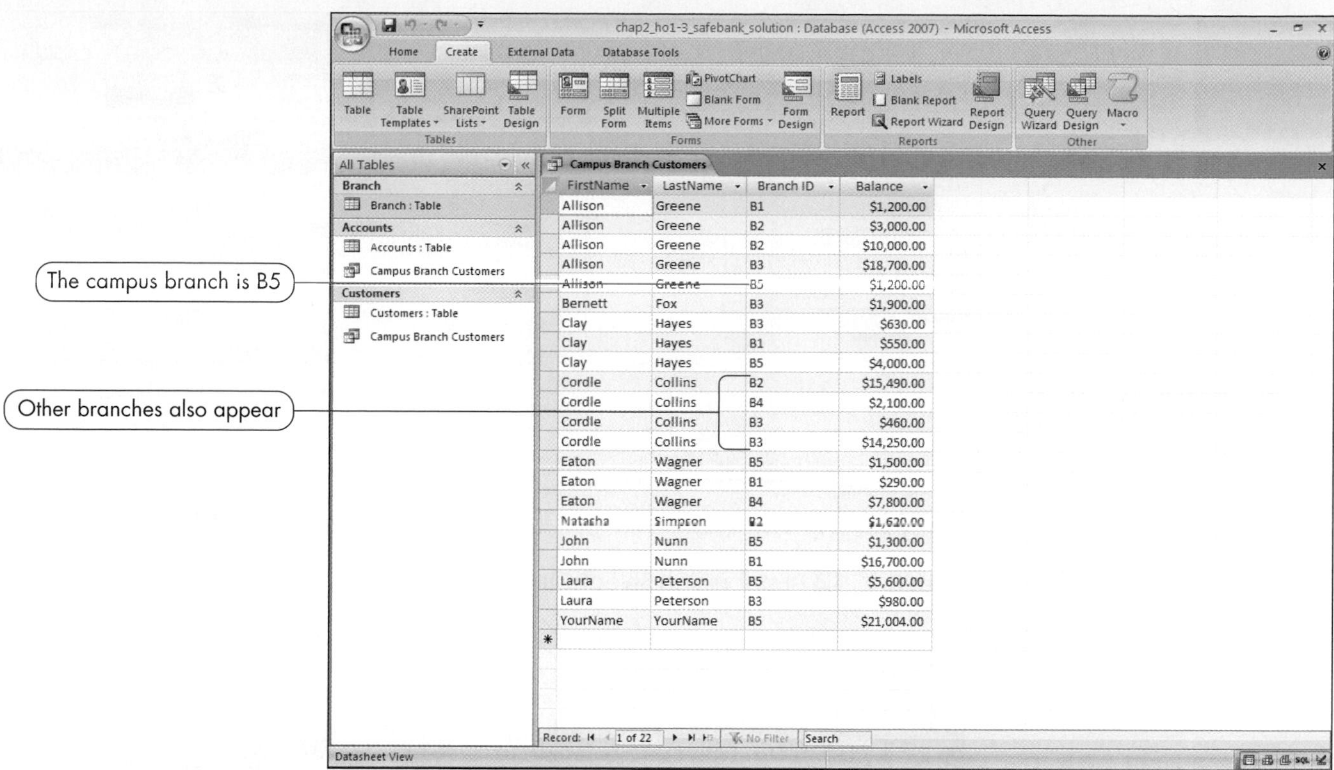
The campus branch is B5
Other branches also appear

Figure 2.41 Criteria Have Not Been Applied

Step 2
Specify Simple Query Criteria

Refer to Figure 2.42 as you complete Step 2.

a. Right-click the **Campus Branch Customers tab** and select **Design View** from the shortcut menu.

   You have created the Campus Branch Customers query to view only those customers who have accounts at the Campus branch. However, other branch's accounts also display. You need to limit the query results to only the records of interest.

b. Click in the fifth row (the **criteria row**) under the **BID** field and type **b5**.

   Access is not case sensitive but is frequently used to connect to larger databases for which case matters.

c. Click in the **Sort row** (third row) under the **LastName field** to activate the drop-down arrow. (This is another of the hidden arrows that only provides selections when the cell is active.) Select **Ascending** from the drop-down list.

d. Click **Run** in the Results group on the Design tab.

   You should have six records in the dataset.

e. Save your query.

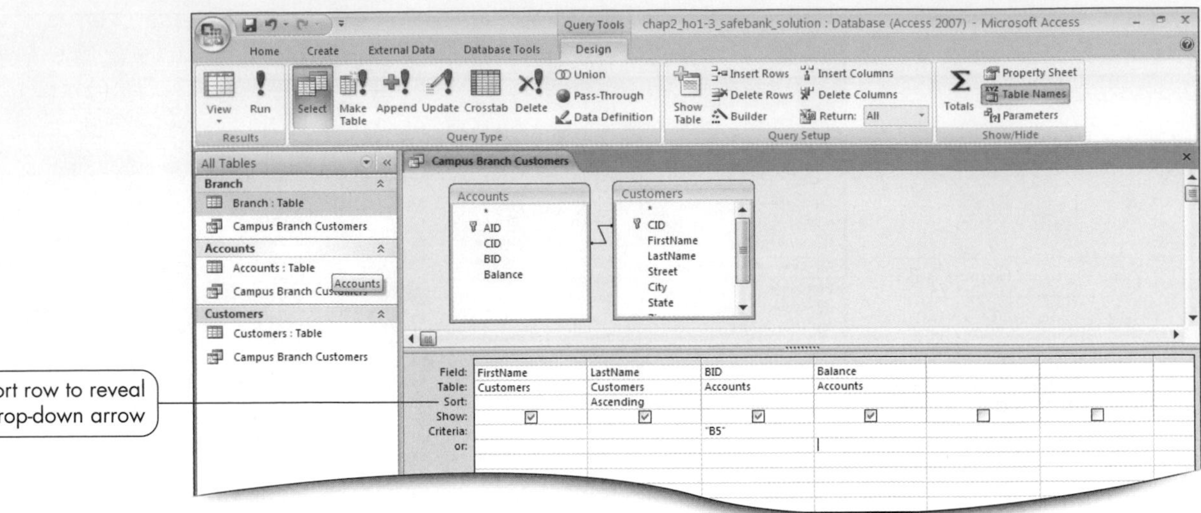

Figure 2.42 Establishing Select Criteria and Sort Order

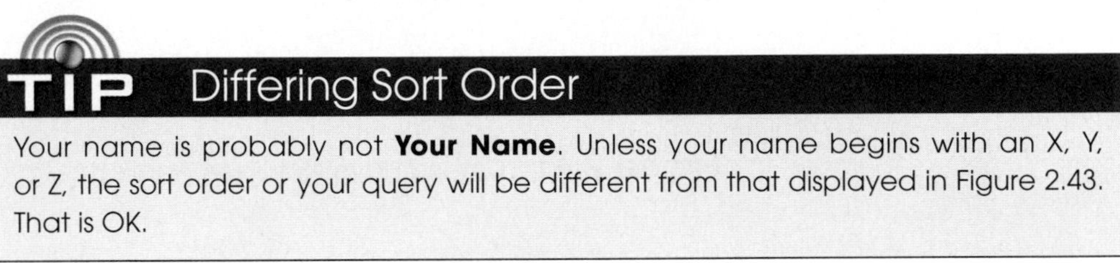

TIP Differing Sort Order

Your name is probably not **Your Name**. Unless your name begins with an X, Y, or Z, the sort order or your query will be different from that displayed in Figure 2.43. That is OK.

Step 3 Change Query Data

Refer to Figure 2.43 as you complete Step 3.

a. Click on the **Balance** field in the record for *Allison Greene's* account. Change **$1200** to **$12,000**. Press **Enter**. Close the query. Do ***not*** save your changes.

b. Open the **Accounts table.**

Only one account shows a $12,000 balance. The Customer ID is C01.

c. Open the **Customers table**. Find the name of the customer whose Customer ID is **C01**. Close the **Customers table**.

Allison Green's CID number is C01. The change you made in the query datasheet has permanently changed the data stored in the underlying table.

TROUBLESHOOTING: Changes in query data change table data! As soon as you pressed Enter in Step 3a, the balance for Allison's account saved. (Remember Access works in storage, not memory.) A wise Access user is extremely careful about the position of the cursor and about typing stray characters while a table or query is open. As soon as you move to a different record, any edits are saved automatically, whether you intend the save or not!

d. Add a new record to the **Accounts table**. The Accounts table should be open. If not, open it now.

e. Type **A23**, **C11**, **B5**, and **1000**. Press **Enter**.

f. Open the **Campus Branch Customers query**. Right click to open the shortcut menu and choose **Design View**. Click **Run** on the Design tab.

You (as a bank customer) now show two accounts, one with a balance that matches your course and section number and one with a balance of $1,000.

Because you closed and reopened the query, it re-ran prior to opening. Access reruns queries to ensure that the data the query returns is the most recent in the database.

g. Close the **Accounts table.**

You successfully created a multi-table query. It does almost everything that you intended. Because this bank is so small, everybody who works there (and probably most of the customers) knows that the Campus branch is B5. But what if this were the database for a real bank? How many thousands of branches does it have? (Remember you are designing your database for 100 years.) You decide that you want to display the branch name, not the ID number. The branch name is a field in the Branch table. The Campus Branch Customers query was based on the Accounts and Customers tables. In order to display the branch name, you need to connect the Branch table to the query.

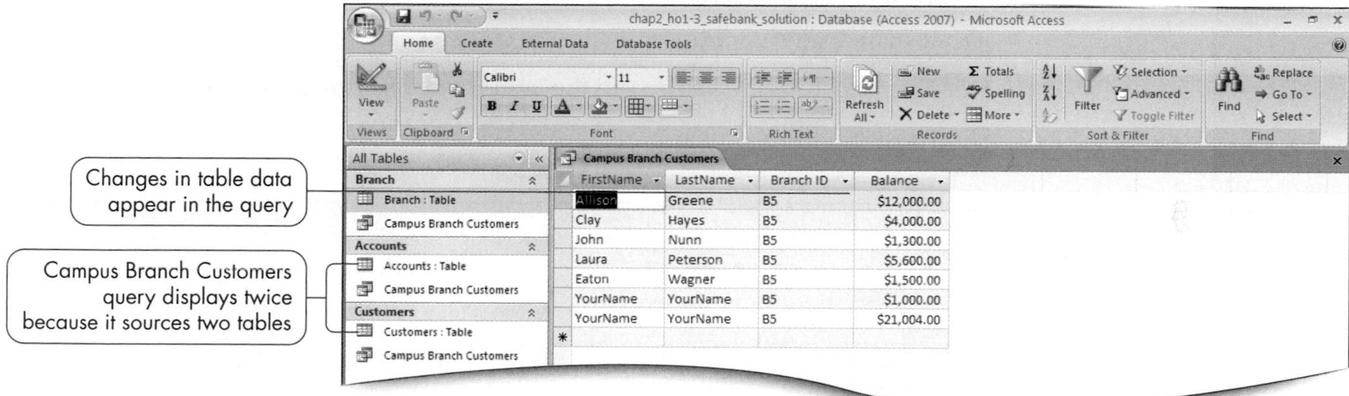

Figure 2.43 Campus Branch Customers Query Following Data Modifications

Step 4
Add a Table to a Query Using Design View and Sort a Query

Refer to Figure 2.44 as you complete Step 4.

a. Open the *Campus Branch Customers Query* if necessary. Right-click the query tab and select **Design View** from the shortcut menu.

b. Click the **Branch: table** under the **All Tables list** on the left-most window pane.

It will turn gold to indicate that it is selected.

c. Click and drag the selected **Branch table** to the **top pane** of the Query design grid.

Your mouse pointer shape will change to a Table as you drag.

d. Drop the **Branch table** next to the **Accounts table.**

The one-to-many relationship lines automatically connect the Branch table to the Accounts table. The query inherits the relationship specifications from the database design.

e. Click the **Location** field name in the Branch table and **drag** it down to the **first empty column**. It should be to the right of the Balance column.

f. Click the **Show row check box** under the **BID** field to hide this field.

The BID field is no longer needed because we have a more descriptive and easily understood name.

g. Remove the **b5** criterion under the Branch ID by highlighting, and then deleting it.

h. Type **Campus** as a criterion in the **Location** field.

The syntax actually requires that you enter text criteria within quotation marks, such as "Campus". Access will enter these quotes for you if you forget. If you use Access to get into large databases, you may need to remember the quotation marks while setting parameters for character fields.

i. Click the word *Location*. As soon as you leave the criteria row, Access adds the missing quotes for you.

j. Click in the **Sort row** of the **Balance** field to activate the drop-down list. Select **Descending**.

The query will still be sorted alphabetically by the customer's last name because that is the left-most sort field in the design grid. You have added an additional, or secondary, sort. Customers with multiple accounts will have their accounts sorted from the largest to smallest balances.

k. Run and save your query.

Your accounts are listed with the largest balance first in the dataset.

l. Close the file and exit Access.

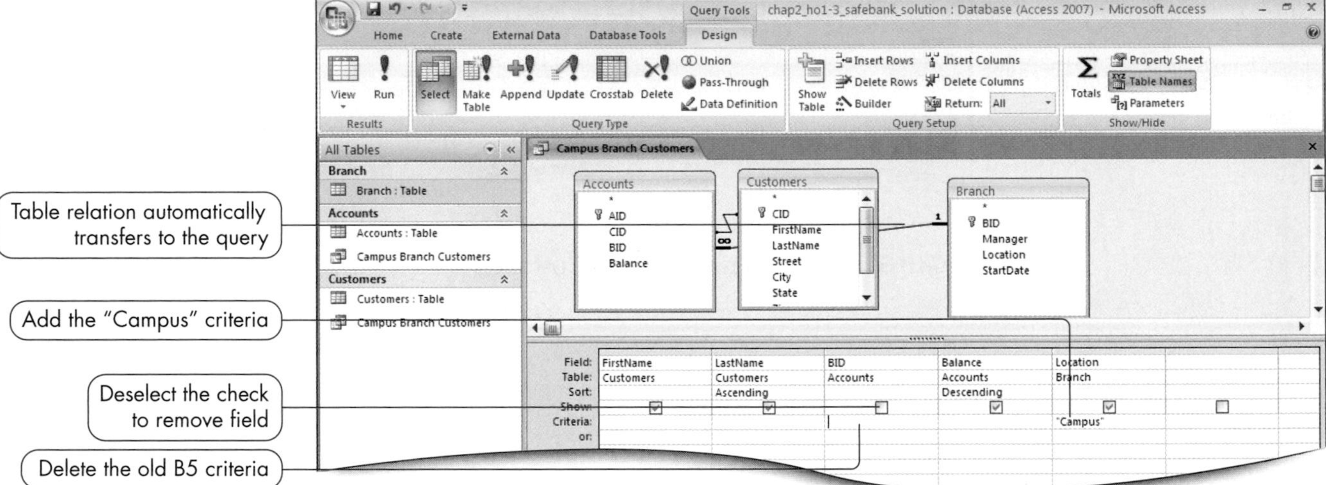

Figure 2.44 Drag and Drop the Branch Table to Add to the Query Design Grid

Summary

1. **Design data.** The architectural infrastructure that supports the database needs to be driven by the output the database will need to generate. You learned that good database design requires that you anticipate how the data will be used, both now and for a long time to come. Creating a database adds costs to the firm, and the designer must balance the costs of including data against the costs of needing it at some point in the future and not having it available. The Sarbanes Oxley Act governs how, where, and when publicly traded firms must store data. You learned that good design principles avoid making calculations in table data, that data should be stored in their smallest parts, and that like data should be grouped together to form tables.

2. **Create tables.** Access employs several ways to create a table. You can create a table yourself by entering the table data into a field. You also can import table data from another database or application, for example, Excel. You learned that each field needs a unique and descriptive name and were introduced to the CamelCase notation naming convention. Access accommodates many different types of data including: text, number, Date/Time, Yes/No, Memo, and others.

3. **Understand table relationships.** Data stored in different tables may be linked using the powerful tool of referential integrity enforcement. Typically, the primary key from one table (unique identifier) resides as a foreign key in another table. This becomes the means of creating the link.

4. **Share data with Excel.** Access facilitates data exchanges with Excel through imports and exports. You used the Import Wizard to import an Excel worksheet into an Access database table. The settings of the Import Wizard may be saved and reused when the import is recurrent.

5. **Establish table relationships.** You created links between tables in the database and attempted to enter an invalid branch number in a related table. You discovered that the enforcement of referential integrity prevented you from creating an account in a non-existent branch. Cascades give the database manager a powerful tool that facilitates updating or deleting multiple records in different tables simultaneously.

6. **Create a query.** You manipulated the data to display only those records of interest by creating a select query. Later, you learned to add additional fields or tables to an existing query.

7. **Specify criteria for different data types.** Establishing criteria empowers you to see only the records that meet the criteria. Different data types require different criteria specifications. Date fields are enclosed in pound signs (#) and text fields with quote marks (""). Additionally, you learned that there are powerful operators, And, Or, and Not, that return the results needed to answer complex questions. You established a sort order for arranging the query results. The Primary sort field needs to be in the left-most position in the query design grid. You may specify additional sort fields; their priority is determined by their left-to-right positions in the grid.

8. **Copy and run a query.** After specifying tables, fields, and conditions for one query, you can copy the query and modify only the criteria in the duplicate query. Copying queries saves time so that you do not have to select tables and fields again for queries that need the same structure but different criteria. After saving queries, you can run them whenever you need to display up-to-date results based on the query conditions.

9. **Use the Query Wizard.** An alternative to creating a select query is to use the Query Wizard. The wizard enables you to select tables and fields from lists. The last step of the wizard prompts you to save the query.

10. **Understand large database differences.** Large database queries may take a long time to run. Therefore, you should think carefully about what fields and tables to include in the query prior to executing it. You learned that database administrators often split the database into front and back ends. Different users of a large database have different levels of access and privilege in order to protect the data validity.

Key Terms

Aggregate 176
And operator 172
Append 151
AutoNumber field 138
Back end 177
Calculated field 135
CamelCase notation 136
Caption property 140
Cascade delete 150
Cascade update 150
Cascades 150
Constant 135
Criteria row(s) 168
Currency 169
Data redundancy 135
Data type 136
Dataset 166
Date arithmetic 135
Date/time field 135
Field row 168
Field size property 133
Front end 177
Indexed property 150
Not operator 172
Null 170
One-to-many relationship 154
Operand 169
Operator 169
Or operator 172
PivotChart view 139
PivotTable view 139
PNPI 134
Property 140
Query 166
Query design grid 166
Query sort order 171
Query Wizard 166
Run a query 173
Sarbanes Oxley Act (SOX) 133
Select query 167
Show row 168
Sort row 168
Table row 168
Validation rule 133

Multiple Choice

1. When entering, deleting or editing table data:
   (a) The table must be in Design view.
   (b) The table must be in Datasheet view.
   (c) The table may be in either Datasheet or Design view.
   (d) Data may be entered only in a form.

2. Which of the following is implemented automatically by Access?
   (a) Rejecting misspelled field entries in a record
   (b) Rejecting redundant field specifications among tables
   (c) Rejecting a record of a foreign key without a matching value in a related table
   (d) Rejecting a record in a primary key without a matching value in a related table

3. Social Security Number, phone number, and postal code should be designated as:
   (a) Number fields
   (b) Text fields
   (c) Yes/No fields
   (d) Any of the above, depending on the application

4. Which of the following is true of the primary key?
   (a) Its values must be unique.
   (b) It must be defined as a text field.
   (c) It must be the first field in a table.
   (d) It can never be changed.

5. Social Security Number should not be used as a primary key because:
   (a) The Social Security Number is numeric, and primary key fields should be text.
   (b) The Social Security Number is not unique.
   (c) The Social Security Number is too long.
   (d) Using the Social Security Number may expose employees or customers to identity theft.

6. An illustration of a one-to-many relationship would be:
   (a) A unique city name relates to a single postal code.
   (b) A customer ID may be related to multiple account numbers.
   (c) A branch location may contain many branch identification numbers.
   (d) A balance field may contain many values.

7. Which of the following was not a suggested guideline for designing a table?
   (a) Include all necessary data
   (b) Store data in its smallest parts
   (c) Avoid calculated fields
   (d) Designate at least two primary keys

8. A query's specifications providing instructions about which fields to include must be entered:
   (a) On the Show row of the query design grid
   (b) On the Sort row of the query design grid
   (c) On the Criteria row of the query design grid
   (d) On the Table Row of the query design grid

9. Which view is used to modify field properties in a table?
   (a) Datasheet view
   (b) Design view
   (c) PivotTable view
   (d) PivotChart view

10. Which of the following is true?
    (a) Additional tables may be added to a query only by restarting the Query Wizard.
    (b) Additional tables or fields may be added to a query by clicking and dragging in the query design grid.
    (c) Access does not permit the addition of additional tables or fields to an existing query.
    (d) Additional tables may be added by copying and pasting the fields from the table to the query.

11. In which view will you see the record selector symbols of a pencil and a triangle?
    (a) Only the Datasheet view of a table
    (b) Only the Datasheet view of a query
    (c) Neither the Datasheet view of a table or query
    (d) Both the Datasheet view of a table nor query

12. You attempt to make a data edit in the Datasheet view of a query by changing an account balance, and then pressing Enter.
    (a) The change also must be made to the underlying table for it to be a permanent part of the database.
    (b) The change must be saved for it to be a permanent part of the database.
    (c) An error message will display because queries are used only to view data, not edit.
    (d) The change is saved, and the underlying table immediately reflects the change.

...continued on Next Page

Multiple Choice Continued...

13. Data in a Name field is stored as Janice Zook, Zachariah Allen, Tom Jones, and Nancy Allen. If the field was sorted in ascending order, which name would be last?
    (a) Janice Zook
    (b) Zachariah Allen
    (c) Tom Jones
    (d) Nancy Allen

14. Which data type appears as a check box in a table?
    (a) Text field
    (b) Number field
    (c) Yes/No field
    (d) Name field

15. Which properties would you use to provide the database user with "user-friendly" column headings in the Datasheet View of a table?
    (a) Field Size and Format
    (b) Input Mask, Validation Rule, and Default Value
    (c) Caption
    (d) Required

16. Which of the following is true with respect to an individual's hire date and years of service, both of which appear on a query that is based on an employee table?
    (a) Hire date should be a calculated field; years of service should be a stored field.
    (b) Hire date should be a stored field; years of service should be a calculated field.
    (c) Both should be stored fields.
    (d) Both should be calculated fields.

17. What is the best way to store an individual's name in a table?
    (a) As a single field consisting of the last name, first name, and middle initial, in that order.
    (b) As a single field consisting of the first name, last name, and middle initial, in that order.
    (c) As three separate fields for first name, last name, and middle initial.
    (d) All of the above are equally suitable.

18. Which of the following would not be a good primary key?
    (a) Student Number
    (b) Social Security Number
    (c) An e-mail address
    (d) A branch identification number

19. A difference between student database files and "real world" files is not:
    (a) Split between front and back end storage.
    (b) Many users add, delete, and change records in "real world" files.
    (c) Student files tend to be much smaller than "real world" files.
    (d) Students work in live databases but "real world" files have multiple copies of the database on all user's desktops.

20. Your query has a date field. If you wanted the records for the month of March 2007 returned, how would you set the criteria?
    (a) <3/31/2007
    (b) between 3/1/2007 and 3/31/2007
    (c) >3/31/2007
    (d) = March 2007

Practice Exercises

1 Martha's Vineyard Bookstore—Creation

One of your aunt's friends, Jennifer Frew, owns and operates a tiny bookstore during the tourist season on Martha's Vineyard. Jennifer asked you to help her after your aunt bragged that you are becoming quite the computer whiz because of this class. You believe that you can help Jennifer by creating a small database. She has stored information about the publication companies and the books that she sells in Excel spreadsheets. You, in consultation with Jennifer, determine that a third table—an author table— also is required. Your task is to design and populate the three tables, establish appropriate linkages between them, and enforce referential integrity. This project follows the same set of skills as used in Hands-On Exercises 1 and 2 in this chapter. If you have problems, reread the detailed directions presented in the chapter. Refer to Figure 2.45 as you complete your work.

a. Start Access and click **Blank Database** in the New Blank Database section of the *Getting Started with Microsoft Office Access* window. Click **Browse**, navigate to the Your Name Access Production folder, type **chap2_pe1_bookstore_solution.accdb**, and click **OK**. Then click **Create** in the Blank Database section of the *Getting Started with Microsoft Office Access* window.

b. Create a new table by entering data into what will become the Author table. Enter the following data.

Field1	Field2	Field3
11	Benchloss	Michael R.
12	Turow	Scott
13	Rice	Anne
14	King	Stephen
15	Connelly	Michael
16	Rice	Luanne

c. Click **Save** on the Quick Access Toolbar. Type **Author** in the Save As dialog box and click **OK**.

d. Right-click the **Author table** under All Tables in the Navigation Pane and select **Design View**. Access will automatically create a primary key; however, it is not the correct field for the primary key.

e. Click the row selector for the second row (Field1) and click **Primary Key** in the Tools group on the Design tab.

f. Check the properties of **Field1** to ensure that the *Indexed* property has been set to **Yes (No Duplicates)**, which is appropriate for a primary key. Select *Field1* and type **AuthorID** to rename the field, type **Author ID** as the caption, and select **Long Integer** as the field size.

g. Rename *Field2* as **LastName**, type **Author's Last Name** as the caption, and type **20** as the field size. Rename *Field3* as **FirstName**, type **Author's First Name** as the caption, and type **15** as the field size.

h. Click the **ID field row selector** to select the row and press **Delete**. Click **Yes**.

i. Click **Save** on the Quick Access toolbar to save the design changes. It is safe to ignore the lost data warning because you did shorten the field sizes.

j. Click the **External Data tab** and click **Import Excel Spreadsheet** in the Import group to launch the Get External Data Wizard – Get External Spreadsheet Wizard. Select the **Import the source data into a new table in the current database option**, click **Browse**, and go to your Exploring Access folder. Select the *chap2_pe1_bookstore.xlsx* workbook, click **Open**, and click **OK**. This workbook contains two worksheets.

k. Select the **Publishers worksheet**. Use the **PubID** field as the primary key. Set the *Indexed Field Options* property box to **Yes (No Duplicates)**. In the next wizard screen, select the **PubID** as your primary key. Name the table **Publishers**. Do not save the import steps.

...continued on Next Page

l. Repeat the Import Wizard to import the **Books worksheet** from the same file into the Access database as a table named **Books**. Set the *Indexed Field Options* property box for the ISBN to **Yes (No Duplicates)**. Set the **ISBN** as the primary field. Do not save the import steps.

m. Open the **Books table** in Design view. Make sure the **PubID** field is selected, click in the *Field Size* property box, and type **2**. Change the **ISBN** *Field size* property to **15**. Change the **Price** field *Format* property to **Currency**. Change the **AuthorCode** field *Field Size* property to **Long Integer** to create the relationship later. Click **Save** on the Quick Access toolbar to save the design changes to the **Books table**.

n. Open the **Publishers table** in Design view. Make sure the **PubID** field is selected, click in the *Field Size* property box and type **2**, and click in the *Caption* property box and type **Publisher's ID**. For each of the following fields, click in the *Field Size* property box and type **50: PubName, PubAddress**, and **PubCity** fields. Set the *Field Size* property for **PubState** field to **2**. Change the *Pub Address* field name to **PubAddress** and change the *Pub ZIP* field name to **PubZIP** (without the spaces to be consistent with the other field names). Click **Save** on the Quick Access Toolbar to save the design changes to the **Publishers table**. Close all open tables.

o. Click the **Database Tools tab** and click **Relationships** in the Show/Hide group. Double-click each table name to add it to the Relationship window. Click and drag the **AuthorID** field from the **Author table** to the **AuthorCode** field in the **Books table**. Click the **Enforce Referential Integrity check box** in the Edit Relationships dialog box. Then click **Create** to create a one-to-many relationship between the Author and Books tables.

p. Click and drag the **PubID** field from the **Publishers table** to the **PubID** field in the **Books table**. Click the three check boxes in the Edit Relationships dialog box and click **Create** to establish a one-to-many relationship between the Publishers and Books tables.

q. Click **Save** on the Quick Access Toolbar to save the changes to the Relationship window. Press **PrintScreen** to capture a screenshot. Nothing seems to happen because the screenshot is saved to the Clipboard. Launch Microsoft Word. Type **your name and section number** and press **Enter**. Paste the screenshot into the Word file, save the file as **chap2_pe1_bookstore_solution.docx**, and print it. Close Word. The Access file should still be open.

r. Close the Relationship window. Click the **Office Button**, select **Manage**, and then select **Back Up Database**. Name the backup **chap2_pe1_bookstore_solution_backup.accdb**. Close the database.

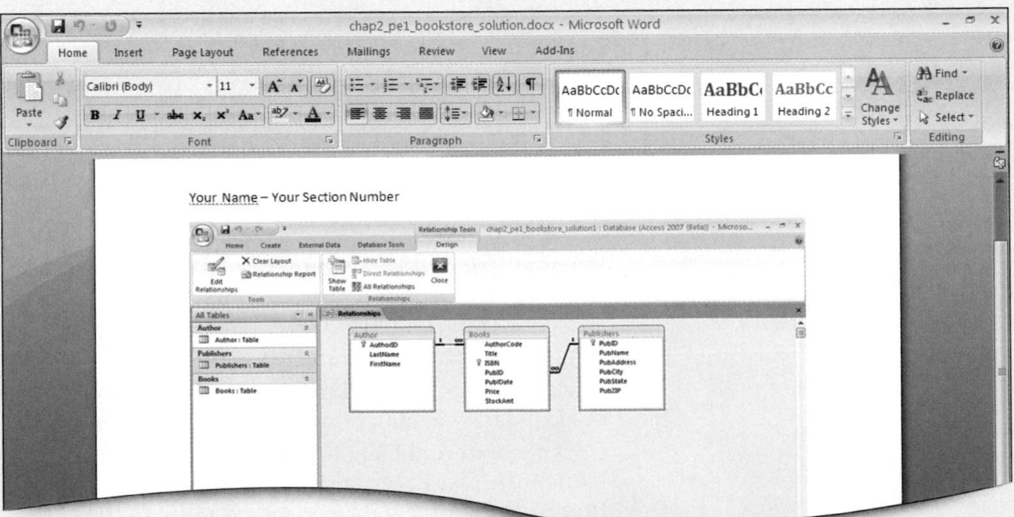

Figure 2.45 Word Screen Showing Capture of the Access Relationship Window

...continued on Next Page

2 Martha's Vineyard Bookstore—Querying

Your mother's friend is thrilled with the work that you have completed on the bookstore's database. She has received additional stock and asks you to update the file with the new information. Once updated she wants you to provide a printout of all of the books in stock that were published by Simon & Shuster. **You must complete Exercise 1 before you can start this one.** This project follows the same set of skills as used in Hands-On Exercise 3 in this chapter. If you have problems, reread the detailed directions presented in the chapter. Refer to Figure 2.46 as you complete your work.

a. Use Windows to copy the *chap2_pe1_bookstore_solution.accdb* database. Rename the copied database as **chap2_pe2_bookstore_solution.accdb**. Open the *chap2_pe2_bookstore_solution* file. Click **Options** in the Security Warning bar, click **Enable this content** in the Microsoft Office Security Options dialog box, and click **OK.**
b. Double-click the **Author table** in the All Tables pane to open the table in Datasheet view. Locate the new record indicator (the one with the * in the row selector) and click the first field. Enter data for the new record using **17** as Author ID and **your name** as the first and last names. Press **Enter**.
c. Open the **Books table** and click the **New (blank) record command**. Type **17** in the AuthorCode field, **Computer Wisdom** in the Title field, **0-684-80415-5** in the ISBN field, **KN** in the PubID field, **2006** in the PubDate field, **23.50** in the Price field, and **75** in the StockAmt field. Press **Enter**.
d. Click the **Create tab** and click **Query Wizard** in the Other group. Choose the **Simple Query Wizard**. From the **Author table**, select the Author's **LastName** and **FirstName** fields. From the **Books table**, select **Title**. Select the **PubName** field from the **Publishers table**. Name the query **Your Name Publishers, Books, and Authors**.
e. Open the query in Design view. Click in the criteria row of the PubName field. Type Knopf to create a criterion to limit the output to only books published by **Knopf**. Click **Run** in the Results group on the Design tab.
f. Return to Design view. Click the Sort row in the **LastName** field and select **Ascending**.
g. Move your mouse over the top of the **Title** field until the mouse pointer shape changes to a bold down arrow, and then click. With the Title column selected, click and drag it to the left of the **LastName** field. Click the Sort row in the **Title** field and select **Ascending**. You will see sort commands on both the Title and LastName fields.
h. Click **Run** in the Results group on the Design tab. Save the query. Click the **Office Button**, position the mouse pointer over **Print**, and select **Quick Print**.
i. Click the **Office Button**, select **Manage**, and then select **Compact and Repair Database**. Close the database.

...continued on Next Page

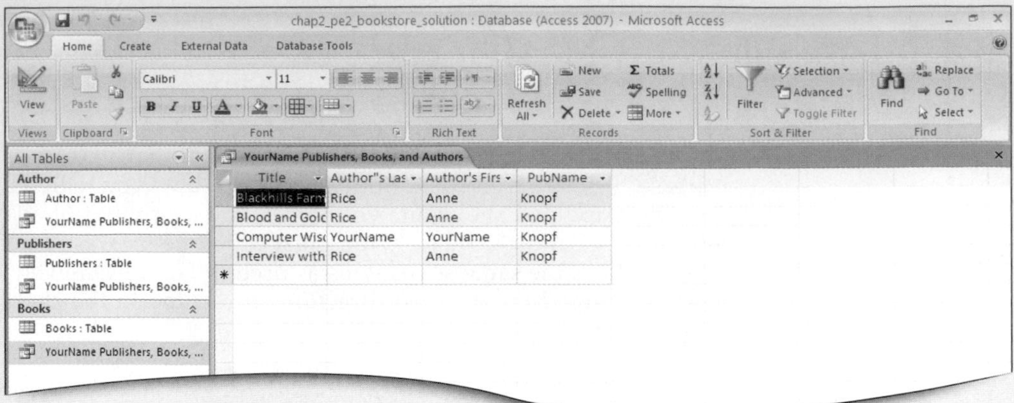

Figure 2.46 Sorted Query Results

3 Combs Insurance

The Comb's Insurance Company offers a full range of insurance services in four locations: Miami, Boston, Chicago, and Atlanta. Until now, they have stored all of the firm's Human Resource data in Excel spreadsheets. These files contain information on employee performance, salary, and education. Some of the files contain information on each of the company's job classifications, including education requirements and the salary range for that position. The firm is converting from Excel to Access to store this important data. There already is a database file containing two of the tables. You need to import the data for the third table from Excel. Once imported, you will need to modify field properties and connect the new table to the rest of the database. The Human Resources vice president is concerned that the Atlanta office ignores the salary guidelines published by the home office. He asks that you create a query to investigate the salary practices of the Atlanta office. This project follows the same set of skills as used in Hands-On Exercises 2 and 3 in this chapter. If you have problems, reread the detailed directions presented in the chapter. Refer to Figure 2.47 as you complete your work.

a. Copy the *chap2_pe3_insurance.accdb* file and rename it **chap2_pe3_insurance_solution**. Open the *chap2_pe3_insurance_solution* database, click **Options in the Security Warning and Enable the Content**, then open and examine the data stored in the **Location** and **Titles** tables. Become familiar with the field names and the type of information stored in each table. Pay particular attention to the number of different Position titles.

b. Click the **External Data tab** and click **Import Excel Spreadsheet** in the Import group to import the *chap2_pe3_employees.xlsx* file. Select the **Employees worksheet** and click the **First Row Contains Column Headings check box**. Set the *Indexed Field Options box* for the **EmployeeID** field to **Yes (No Duplicates)**. In the next wizard screen, select the **EmployeeID** as your primary key. Name the table **Employees**.

c. Open the **Employees table** in Design view. In the top of the design window, position the insertion point on the **Location ID** field. Locate the *Field Size property* in the lower portion of the table Design view window and change the Field Size for the *Location ID* to **3**. Click in the *Caption* property box and type **Location ID**. In the top of the Design view

...continued on Next Page

window, position the insertion point on the **TitleID** field. Click in the *Field Size* property box in the lower portion of the table Design view window and type **3**. Click in the *Caption* property box and type **Title ID**. Save the design changes.

d. Switch the **Employees table** to the Datasheet view and examine the data. Click any record in the Title ID field and click **Descending** in the Sort & Filter group on the Home tab. How many different position titles are in the table? Does this match the number in the Titles table?

e. Locate the new record row, the one with the * in the row selector box. Click the first field. Add yourself as a new record. Your EmployeeID is **27201**. You are a **Trainee** (T03) in the **Atlanta** (L01) office earning **$27,350** and your performance rating is **Good**. Press **Enter**.

f. Open the **Titles table** in Datasheet view and add the missing title. The *TitleID* is **T04**; the *Title* is **Senior Account Rep**. The rest of the record is **A marketing position requiring a technical background and at least three years of experience.** It requires a **Four year degree**. The minimum salary is **$45,000**. The maximum is **$75,000**. Do not type the dollar sign or comma as you enter the salary data. Close all open tables. Answer Yes if prompted to save.

g. Click **Relationships** in the Show/Hide group on the Database Tools tab. Add the three tables to the Relationship window by double-clicking them one at a time (You may have to click the Show Table button to bring up the Show Table dialog box.) Close the Add Table dialog box.

h. Click the **LocationID** in the Location table and drag it to the **LocationID** in the Employees table. Drop it. In the Relationship dialog box, click the **Enforce referential integrity check box**. Click **Create**. Click the **TitleID** in the **Titles** table and drag it to the **TitleID** in the **Employees** table and drop it. In the Relationship dialog box, click the **Enforce Referential Integrity check box**. Click **Create**. Save the changes to the relationships and close the Relationship window.

i. Click **Query Wizard** in the Other group on the Create tab. In the first screen of the Query Wizard, select **Simple Query Wizard**. Select **Table: Location** in the Tables/Queries list. Double-click **Location** to move it to the *Selected Fields* list. Select the **Employees table** in the Tables/Queries list. Double-click **LastName**, **FirstName**, and **Salary**. Select the **Titles** table in the Tables/Queries list. Double-click **MinimumSalary** and **MaximumSalary**. Click **Next**. Select the **Detail (shows every field of every record)** option and click **Next**. Type **Your Name Atlanta** as the query title and click **Finish**.

j. Open the **Your Name Atlanta query** in Design view. Click in the criteria row in the Location field. Type **Atlanta**. Click **Run** in the Results group on the Design tab. Check to ensure that the results display only Atlanta employees. Save and close the query.

k. Right-click the **Your Name Atlanta query** in the Navigation pane and select **Copy**. Right-click a white space in the All Objects pane and select **Paste**. In the Paste As window, type **Your Name Boston** for the query name. Click OK.

l. Open the **Your Name Boston query** in Design view. Click in the criteria row in the Location field. Type **Boston**. Click **Run** in the Results group on the Design Tab. Check to ensure that the results display only Boston employees. Save and close the query.

m. Open the **Your Name Atlanta** query and the **Your Name Boston** query. *Your screen should appear similar to Figure 2.47*. Print both queries.

n. Click the **Office Button**, select **Manage**, and then select **Compact and Repair Database**.

...continued on Next Page

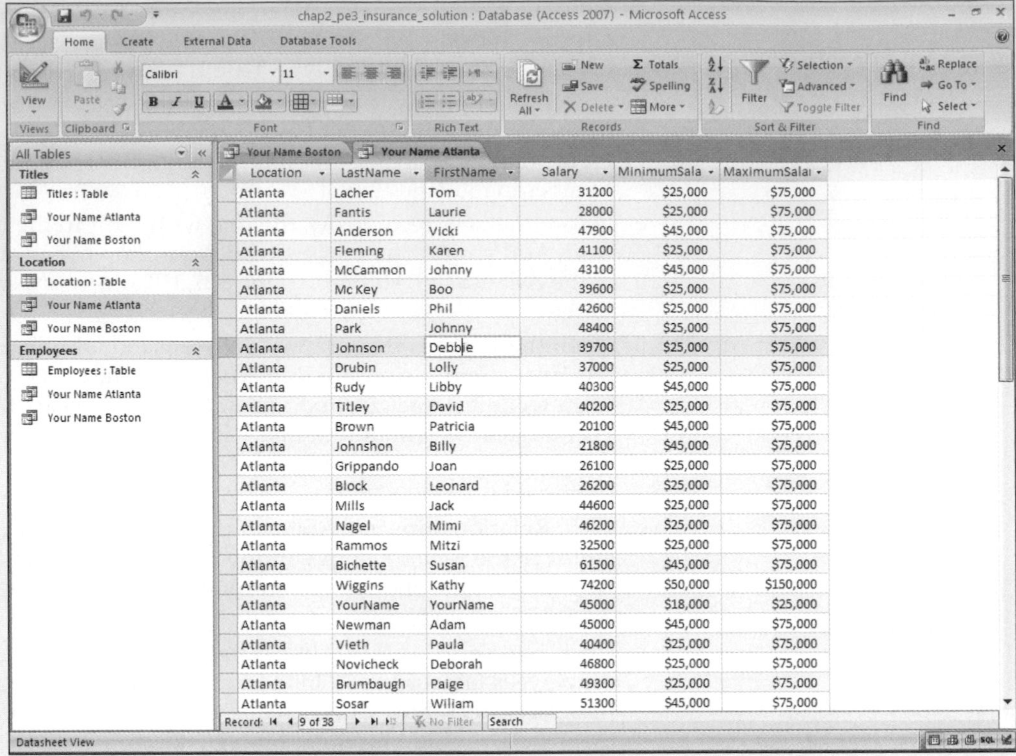

Figure 2.47 Atlanta Query Results

4 Coffee Service Company

The Coffee Service Company provides high-quality coffee, tea, snacks, and paper products to its customers. Most of the customers are offices in the area: IT firms, insurance offices, financial services. Coffee Service employees go to the customer location and restock the coffee, tea, and snacks supplied daily. A few accounts elect to pick up the merchandise at the Coffee Service Office. You have been asked to help convert the Excel files to an Access database. Once the database is set up, you need to use queries to help the owner do some market analysis. This project follows the same set of skills as used in Hands-On Exercises 2 and 3 in this chapter. The instructions are less detailed to give you a chance to practice your skills. If you have problems, reread the detailed directions presented in the chapter. Refer to Figure 2.48 as you complete your work.

a. Copy the *chap2_pe4_coffee.accdb* file. Rename the copy **chap2_pe4_coffee_solution.accdb**. Open the copied file, then open, enable the content, and examine the data stored in the tables. Become familiar with the field names and the type of information stored in each table.

b. Click the **External Data tab** and click **Import Excel Spreadsheet** in the Import group. Select the **Import the source data into a new table in the current database** option. Click **Browse**, select the *chap2_pe4_products.xlsx* workbook, click **Open**, then click **OK**. Select the **Products worksheet** and click **Next**. Click the **First Row Contains Column Headings check box**, and then click **Next**. Click the **Indexed property drop-down arrow** and select to **Yes** (No Duplicates**)**. Make sure the ProductID field is active. Click **Next**. Click the **Choose my own primary** key **option** and select the **ProductID**. Click **Next**, type **Products** as the table name, and then click **Finish**.

c. Open the **Products table** in Design view. In the top of the design grid, click the **ProductID** field to select it. In the bottom portion of the window, change the *Field size* property to **Long Integer**. Click in the *Caption* property box and type **Product ID**. Save the changes to the Products table. Close the Products table.

...continued on Next Page

d. Click the **Database Tools tab**, and then click **Relationships** in the Show/Hide group. Click **Show Table** to open the Show Table dialog box. Double-click the **Products table** to add it to the Relationships window, if it is not already shown. Close the Show Table dialog box.

e. Click the **ProductID** in the **Products table** and drag and drop it on the **ProductID** in the **Order Details table**. The Edit Relationships dialog box opens. Click the **Enforce Referential Integrity check box**. Click **Create**. Save the changes to the Relationship window and close it.

f. Open the **Sales Reps table** and replace YourName in the *FirstName* and *LastName* fields with **YourName**.

g. Launch the **Query Wizard** in the Other group on the Create tab. Create a **Simple Select Query**. Select the **Sales Reps table** in the Tables/Queries list. Double-click the **LastName** and **FirstName** fields to move them to the Selected Fields list. Select the **Order Details table** in the Tables/Queries list. Double-click the **Quantity** field to move it to the query. Select the **Customers table** and double-click the **CustomerName** field. Select the **Products table** in the Tables/Queries list. Double-click the **ProductName**, **RefrigerationNeeded**, and **YearIntroduced** fields to move them to the query. This is a detail query. Name the query **Product Introduction**.

h. Open the **Product Information query** in Design view. Click in the sort row in the **YearIntroduced** field and select **Ascending**. Click the sort row of the **ProductName** field and select **Ascending**.

i. Click the criteria row in the LastName field and type **Your Last Name**. Click the criteria row in the FirstName field and type **YourName**. Click the criteria row in the YearIntroduced field and type **2004**. Click into the or row (the next row down) and type **2005**. Reenter your first and last name in the or criteria row for the FirstName and LastName fields. This establishes criteria so that only sales by you on products introduced in 2004 and 2005 display.

j. Click the **Design tab** and click **Run** in the Results group. Save the design changes to the query and close it. Right-click the query name in the Navigation pane and select **Rename**. Rename the query **2004–5 Product Introduction by YourName**. Print the query results.

k. Click the **Office Button**, select **Manage**, and then select **Compact and Repair Database**.

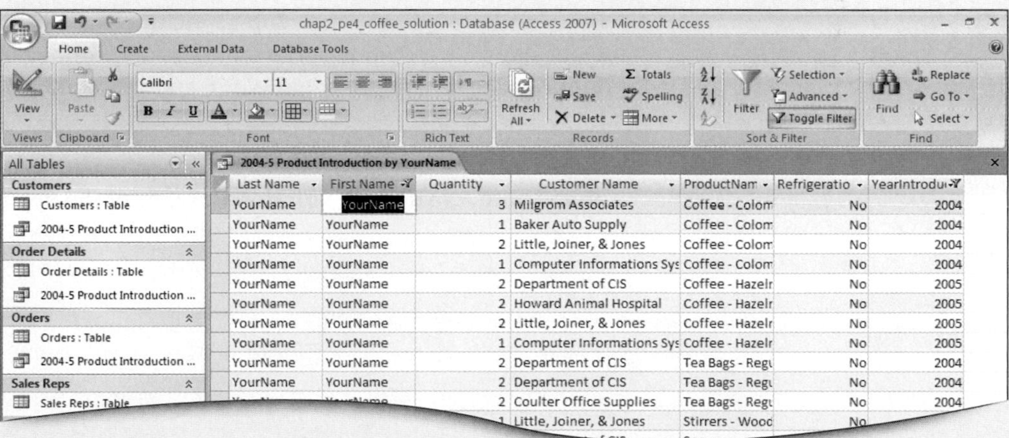

Figure 2.48 Sorted Product Introduction Query Results

Mid-Level Exercises

1 Creating a Query and Working with Criteria

You are an intern in a large, independent real estate firm that specializes in home sales. A database contains all of the information on the properties marketed by your firm. Most real estate transactions involve two agents—one representing the seller (the listing agent) and the other the buyer (the selling agent). The firm owner has asked that you examine the records of recent listings (real estate is listed when the home owner signs a contract with an agent that offers the property for sale) and sort them by subdivision (neighborhood) and the listing agent's name. The results need to include only the sold properties and be sorted by subdivision and the listing agent's last name. Refer to Figure 2.49 as you complete your work.

a. Locate the file named *chap2_mid1_realestate.accdb*, copy it to your working folder, and rename it **chap2_mid1_realestate_solution.accdb**. Open the file and enable the content. Open the **Agents table**. Find and replace *Kia Hart*'s name with your name. Close the **Agents** table.

b. Create a detail query. You need the following fields: **LastName**, **FirstName**, **DateListed**, **DateSold**, **ListPrice**, **SellingAgent**, and **Subdivision**. Name the query **YourName Sold Property by Subdivision and Agent**. Run the query and examine the number of records.

c. In Design view, enter the criteria that will remove all of the properties from the Water Valley Subdivision. Run the query and examine the number of records. It should be a smaller number than in Step b.

d. Rearrange the fields in the query so that the Subdivision field is in the leftmost column and the LastName field is the second from the left. Add the appropriate sort commands to the design grid to sort first by subdivision, and then by LastName.

e. Add a criterion that will limit the results to the properties sold after October 31, 2008.

f. Capture a screenshot of the Sales Summary query results. Have it open on your computer and press **PrnScrn**. to copy a picture of what is on the monitor to the clipboard. Open Word, type your name and section number in a new blank document, press **Enter**, paste the screenshot in Word, and press **Enter** again.

g. Return to Design view and capture a screenshot of the query in Design view. Paste this screenshot below the first in the Word document. Save the Word document as **chap2_mid1_realestate_solution.docx**. Print the document.

...continued on Next Page

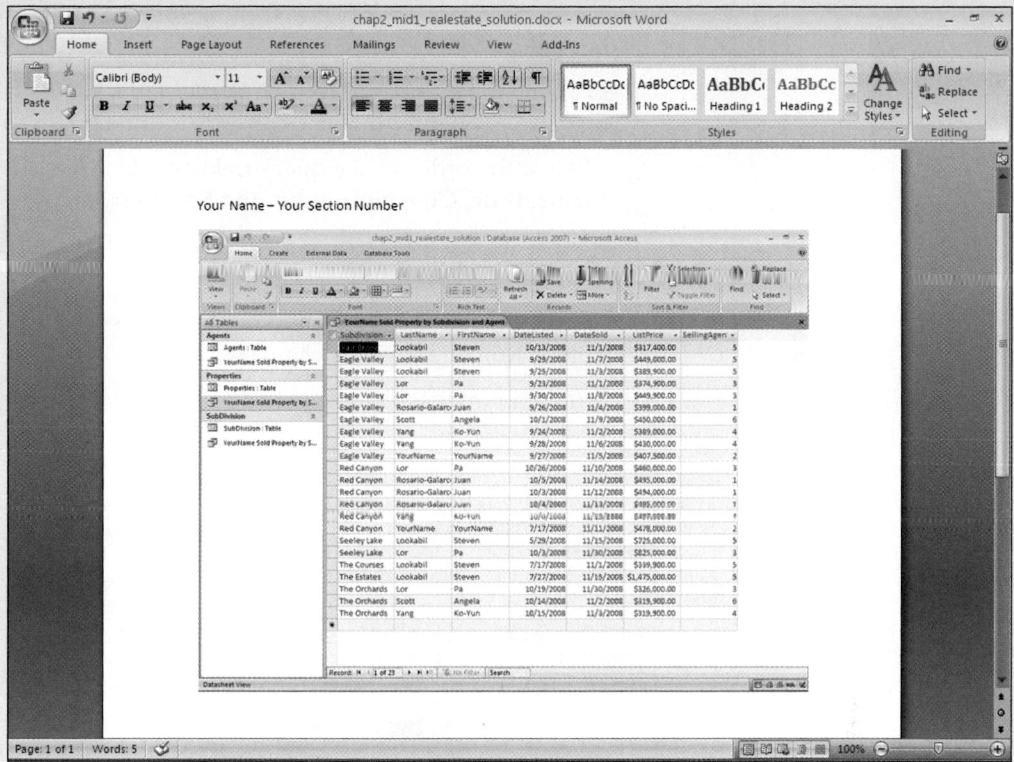

Figure 2.49 Sorted Product Introduction Query Results

2 Importing Excel Data, Creating, and Sorting a Query

The Prestige Hotel chain caters to upscale business travelers and provides state-of-the-art conference, meeting, and reception facilities. It prides itself on its international, four-star cuisines. Last year, it began a member rewards club to help the marketing department track the purchasing patterns of their most loyal customers. All of the hotel transactions are stored in the database. Your task is to help the manager of the Boston hotel identify the customers who used suites last year and who had more than two persons in their party. Refer to Figure 2.50 as you complete your work.

a. Copy the *chap2_mid2_memrewards.accdb* database and name the copy **chap2_mid2_memrewards_solution.accdb.** Open and tour the newly copied file. Gain an understanding of the relationships and the data contained in the different tables. Specifically look for the tables and fields containing the information you need: dates of stays in Boston suites, the member's name, and the number in the party.

b. Import the Excel file *chap2_mid2_location.xlsx* into your database as a new table. Name the table as **Location**. Use the LocationID field as the primary key. Set the field size to Double.

c. Establish a relationship between the LocationID field in the **Location table** and the Location field in the **Orders table**. Enforce referential integrity.

d. Open the **Members table** and find Fred White's name. Replace Fred's name with your own first and last name. Now find *Karen Korte*'s name and replace it with your name.

e. Create a query that contains the fields you identified in Step a. Set a condition to limit the output to Boston, service from August–December 2007, and private parties greater than 2. Run the query and **sort** the results in descending order by the Service Date.

...continued on Next Page

Name the query **Your Name Boston Suites**. See Figure 2.50 if you need help figuring out which fields to select.

f. Examine the number of records in the status bar at the bottom of the query. It should display 23. If your number of records is different, examine the criteria.

g. Change the order of the query fields so that they display as **FirstName**, **LastName**, **ServiceDate**, **City**, **NoInParty**, and **ServiceName**.

h. Save and close the query. Copy it and in the Paste As dialog box, name the new query **YourName Miami Suites**.

i. Open the Miami Suites query in Design view and replace the Boston criterion with Miami. Run and save the changes.

j. Print your queries if directed to do so by your instructor. Compact, repair, and back up your file.

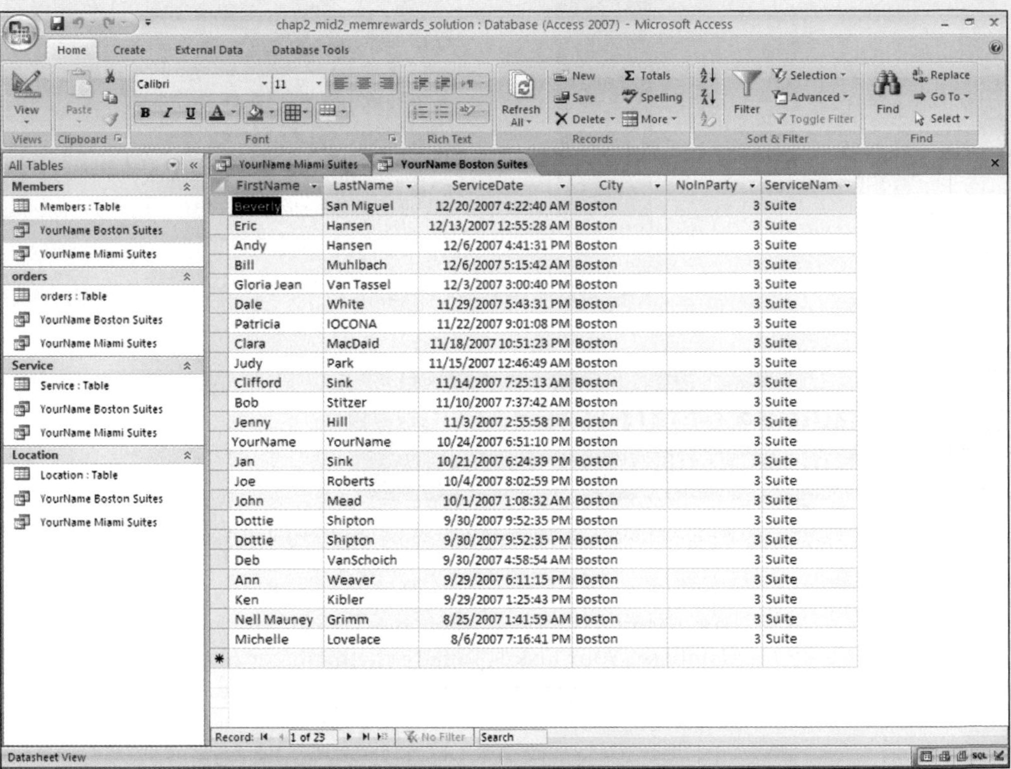

FirstName	LastName	ServiceDate	City	NoInParty	ServiceNam
Beverly	San Miguel	12/20/2007 4:22:40 AM	Boston	3	Suite
Eric	Hansen	12/13/2007 12:55:28 AM	Boston	3	Suite
Andy	Hansen	12/6/2007 4:41:31 PM	Boston	3	Suite
Bill	Muhlbach	12/6/2007 5:15:42 AM	Boston	3	Suite
Gloria Jean	Van Tassel	12/3/2007 3:00:40 PM	Boston	3	Suite
Dale	White	11/29/2007 5:43:31 PM	Boston	3	Suite
Patricia	IOCONA	11/22/2007 9:01:08 PM	Boston	3	Suite
Clara	MacDaid	11/18/2007 10:51:23 PM	Boston	3	Suite
Judy	Park	11/15/2007 12:46:49 AM	Boston	3	Suite
Clifford	Sink	11/14/2007 7:25:13 AM	Boston	3	Suite
Bob	Stitzer	11/10/2007 7:37:42 AM	Boston	3	Suite
Jenny	Hill	11/3/2007 2:55:58 PM	Boston	3	Suite
YourName	YourName	10/24/2007 6:51:10 PM	Boston	3	Suite
Jan	Sink	10/21/2007 6:24:39 PM	Boston	3	Suite
Joe	Roberts	10/4/2007 8:02:59 PM	Boston	3	Suite
John	Mead	10/1/2007 1:08:32 AM	Boston	3	Suite
Dottie	Shipton	9/30/2007 9:52:35 PM	Boston	3	Suite
Dottie	Shipton	9/30/2007 9:52:35 PM	Boston	3	Suite
Deb	VanSchoich	9/30/2007 4:58:54 AM	Boston	3	Suite
Ann	Weaver	9/29/2007 6:11:15 PM	Boston	3	Suite
Ken	Kibler	9/29/2007 1:25:43 PM	Boston	3	Suite
Nell Mauney	Grimm	8/25/2007 1:41:59 AM	Boston	3	Suite
Michelle	Lovelace	8/6/2007 7:16:41 PM	Boston	3	Suite

Figure 2.50 Boston Query Results

3 Creating and Using Queries

Northwind Traders is a small, international, specialty food company. It sells products in eight different divisions: Beverages, Confections (candy), Condiments, Dairy Products, Grains and Cereals, Meat and Poultry, Produce, and Seafood. Although most of its customers are restaurants and gourmet food shops, it has a few retail customers, too. It purchases the merchandise from a variety of suppliers. All of the order information is stored in the company's database. The marketing department uses this database to monitor and maintain sales records. You are the marketing

...continued on Next Page

manager. Your task is to identify which customers purchase Chai (tea) and Chang (Chinese Beer) in 2007. It would be valuable for you to discover the order quantities and the countries where the orders ship. After you complete the query, you will copy it and add the salesperson's name field to the copy. Refer to Figure 2.51 as you complete your work.

a. Copy the *chap2_mid3_traders.accdb* file and rename the copy **chap2_mid3_traders_solution.accdb**. Open the newly copied file and enable the content. Tour the database Relationship window to gain an understanding of the relationships and the data contained in the different tables. As you tour, specifically look for the tables and fields containing the information you need, that is, orders shipped in **2007** for the **beverages Chai** and **Chang**, the quantities purchased, the date the order shipped, and the countries the purchases were shipped to. You are interested in all of the countries *excluding* the United States.
b. After you identify the necessary fields, create a query that includes the fields of interest. Name this query **YourName Shipping for Chai and Chang**.
c. Set the query criteria to select the records of interest—2007 orders of Chai and Chang shipped to all of the world except for the United States.
d. Sort the query results by the Company name (alphabetically), and then by the quantity ordered. (If the same company is listed twice, the largest quantity should be listed first.)
e. Print the query results. Save and close the query.
f. Copy the query and name the copy **YourName Chai and Chang Sales by Employee**.
g. Open the **Employees table** and replace *Andrew* Fuller's name with your own name.
h. Add the employee's First and Last Name fields to the newly copied query.
i. Rearrange the fields so that the employee last name field is the first in the design grid and the Employee's FirstName is the second. Sort the results by the Employee's LastName.
j. Run, save, and print the query. Compact, repair, and back up your file.

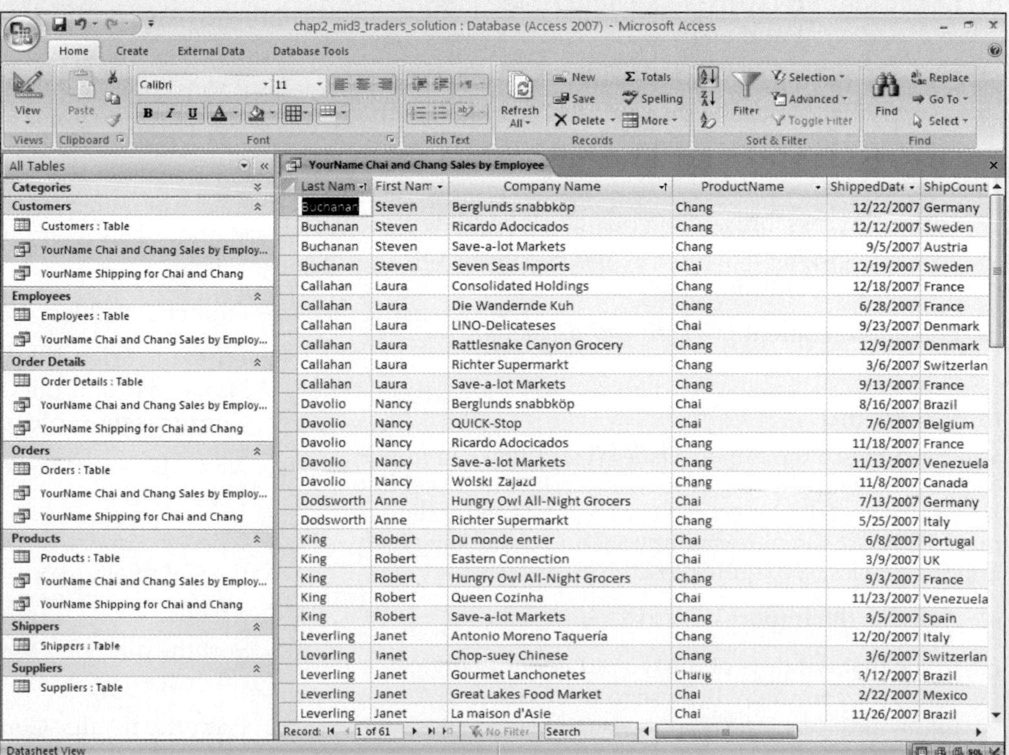

Last Nam	First Nam	Company Name	ProductName	ShippedDate	ShipCount
Buchanan	Steven	Berglunds snabbköp	Chang	12/22/2007	Germany
Buchanan	Steven	Ricardo Adocicados	Chang	12/12/2007	Sweden
Buchanan	Steven	Save-a-lot Markets	Chang	9/5/2007	Austria
Buchanan	Steven	Seven Seas Imports	Chai	12/19/2007	Sweden
Callahan	Laura	Consolidated Holdings	Chang	12/18/2007	France
Callahan	Laura	Die Wandernde Kuh	Chang	6/28/2007	France
Callahan	Laura	LINO-Delicateses	Chai	9/23/2007	Denmark
Callahan	Laura	Rattlesnake Canyon Grocery	Chang	12/9/2007	Denmark
Callahan	Laura	Richter Supermarkt	Chang	3/6/2007	Switzerlan
Callahan	Laura	Save-a-lot Markets	Chang	9/13/2007	France
Davolio	Nancy	Berglunds snabbköp	Chai	8/16/2007	Brazil
Davolio	Nancy	QUICK-Stop	Chai	7/6/2007	Belgium
Davolio	Nancy	Ricardo Adocicados	Chang	11/18/2007	France
Davolio	Nancy	Save-a-lot Markets	Chang	11/13/2007	Venezuela
Davolio	Nancy	Wolski Zajazd	Chang	11/8/2007	Canada
Dodsworth	Anne	Hungry Owl All-Night Grocers	Chai	7/13/2007	Germany
Dodsworth	Anne	Richter Supermarkt	Chang	5/25/2007	Italy
King	Robert	Du monde entier	Chai	6/8/2007	Portugal
King	Robert	Eastern Connection	Chai	3/9/2007	UK
King	Robert	Hungry Owl All-Night Grocers	Chang	9/3/2007	France
King	Robert	Queen Cozinha	Chai	11/23/2007	Venezuela
King	Robert	Save-a-lot Markets	Chang	3/5/2007	Spain
Leverling	Janet	Antonio Moreno Taquería	Chang	12/20/2007	Italy
Leverling	Janet	Chop-suey Chinese	Chang	3/6/2007	Switzerlan
Leverling	Janet	Gourmet Lanchonetes	Chang	3/12/2007	Brazil
Leverling	Janet	Great Lakes Food Market	Chai	2/22/2007	Mexico
Leverling	Janet	La maison d'Asie	Chai	11/26/2007	Brazil

Record: 1 of 61

Figure 2.51 2007 Chai and Chang Sales by Employee

Capstone Exercise

The JC Raulston Arboretum at NC State University staff have been carefully saving their data in Excel for years. One particular workbook contains a worksheet that lists the names of all the Arboretum's "friends." This not-for-profit organization solicits contributions in the form of cash gifts, volunteer service, and "in-kind" gifts. An in-kind gift is a gift of a plant to the arboretum. Each year, one of the major fundraising events is the Gala. This is a formal event held on a delightful spring afternoon with cocktails, gourmet hors d'oeuvres, live music, and a silent auction featuring a plethora of unique plants and an eclectic array of many other distinctive items. As friends contribute service or funds to the Arboretum, another reward they receive are connoisseur plants. Connoisseur plants are rare new plants or hard-to-find old favorites, and they are part of the annual appeal and membership drive to benefit the Arboretum's many fine programs and its day-to-day operational expenses. These wonderful plants are sent to those who join the Friends of JC Raulston Arboretum at the Sponsor, Patron, Benefactor, or Philanthropist levels. The organization has grown. The files are too large to handle easily in Excel. Your task will be to begin the conversion of the files from Excel to Access.

Database File Setup

You need to open an Excel workbook that contains data on four named worksheets. Examine the data in the worksheets, paying attention to which fields will become the primary keys in each table and where those fields will appear as foreign keys in other tables in order to form the relationships.

a. Locate the Excel workbook named *chap2_cap_friends.xlsx* and open it.

b. Locate the Excel workbook named *chap2_cap_connplants.xlsx* and open it.

c. Examine the data, identify what will become the primary field in each table, and look for that field to reappear in other tables so that you can form relationships.

d. Launch Access, browse to your working folder, and create a new, blank database named **chap2_cap_arboretum_solution.accdb**.

e. Enable the content in *chap2_cap_arboretum_solution.accdb*.

Import Wizard

You need to use the Import Data Wizard twice to import each of the worksheets in the workbook from Excel into Access. You need to select the worksheets, specify the primary keys, set the indexing option, and name the newly imported tables (see Figures 2.12 through 2.18).

a. Activate the Import Wizard.

b. In the first window of the wizard, identify the source of your data. Browse to the Exploring Access folder and select the *chap2_cap_friends.xlsx* file.

c. The FriendID field will become the primary key. Set its indexing option to **Yes (No Duplicates)**.

d. When prompted, select the **FriendID** as the primary key.

e. Name the table **Friends**.

f. Import the *chap2_cap_connoisseur.xlsx* file, set the ID field as the primary key, and name the table as **Connoisseur**.

g. In Datasheet view, examine the newly imported tables.

Create Relationships

You need to create the relationship between the tables. Identify the primary fields in each table and, using the Relationships window, connect them with their foreign key counterparts in other tables. Enforce referential integrity.

a. Close any open tables, and then display the Relationships window.

b. Add the two tables to the Relationship window with the Show Table dialog box. Then, close the Show Tables dialog box.

c. Drag the FriendID from the **Friends table** to the FriendNumber field in the **Connoisseur table**. Enforce Referential Integrity.

d. Print the Relationships window.

e. Close the Relationship window and save your changes.

Create, Add Criteria to, and Sort a Query

You need to create a query that identifies the people who have received at least one connoisseur plant and who are not attending the Gala. Use the Query Wizard to identify the tables, Friends and Connoisseur, and fields necessary. Establish criteria that will limit the results to only records where one or more plant has been sent and there is no Gala reservation. This query will need to be sorted by the last name field.

a. Launch the Query Wizard.

b. From the **Friends table** select the NameFirst, NameLast, and the Gala fields. From the **Connoisseur table**, select the SendPlant field.

c. Name the query as **YourName Gala No, Conn Plant Yes**.

d. Open the query in Design view and set criteria in the Gala field to **No** and in the SendPlants field to **>0**.

e. Sort the query by the NameLast field in alphabetical order.

f. Print the results. Compact, repair, and back up the file.

Mini Cases

Use the rubric following the case as a guide to evaluate your work, but keep in mind that your instructor may impose additional grading criteria or use a different standard to judge your work.

Employee Performance Review

GENERAL CASE

The *chap2_mc1_insurance.accdb* file contains data from a large insurance agency. Copy the *chap2_mc1_insurance.accdb* file, name it **chap2_mc1_insurance_solution.accdb**, and open the copied file. Use the skills from this chapter to perform several tasks. The firm's employee policy states that an employee needs to maintain a performance rating of good or excellent to maintain employment. If an employee receives an average or poor performance rating, she receives a letter reminding her of this policy and advising her to improve or suffer the consequences. You are the manager of the Atlanta office. You need to identify the employees who need a letter of reprimand. Once the query has been completed, it will be used to generate a form letter to be sent to the employees. You need to include fields for the letter that contain the employees' first and last names, their position titles, and their salary. You do not need to write the letter, only assemble the data for the letter to be written. The results need to be alphabetized by the employee's names. As you work, consider the order that the fields will need to be used in the letter and order the query fields accordingly.

Performance Elements	Exceeds Expectations	Meets Expectations	Below Expectations
Create query	All necessary and no unneeded fields included.	All necessary fields included but also unnecessary fields.	Not all necessary fields were included in the query.
Establish criteria	The query results correctly identified and selected records.	The query results correctly identified and selected records.	Incorrect criteria specifications.
Sorting	Query fields were logically ordered and appropriately sorted.	Query fields were appropriately sorted but not logically ordered.	Both the order and the sort were incorrect.
Query name	The query name described the content.	The query name partially described the content.	The query employed the default name.

Database Administrator Position

RESEARCH CASE

This chapter introduced you to the idea that employees who administer and manage databases receive high pay, but you have much more to explore. Use the Internet to search for information about database management. One useful site is published by the federal government's Bureau of Labor Statistics. It compiles an Occupational Outlook Handbook describing various positions, the type of working environment, the education necessity, salary information, and the projected growth. The Web site is **http://www.bls.gov/oco**. Your challenge is to investigate the position of Database Administrator. Use the BLS Web site and at least one other source. Write your instructor a memo describing this position. Use a memo template in Word, your most professional writing style, and specify the data sources.

Performance Elements	Exceeds Expectations	Meets Expectations	Below Expectations
Use online resources	Appropriate articles located and memo indicates comprehension.	Appropriate articles located but memo did not demonstrate comprehension.	Articles not found.
Extract useful information from the resources	Most major components of the position described accurately.	Many elements of the position described.	Many elements of the position missing or the description incomprehensible.
Summarize and communicate	Memo clearly written and free of misspellings.	Memo text indicates some understanding but also weaknesses.	Memo missing or incomprehensible.
Esthetics	Memo template correctly employed.	Template employed but signed in the wrong place or improperly used.	Memo missing or incomprehensible.

May and Beverage Queries

DISASTER RECOVERY

A co-worker called you into his office and explained that he was having difficulty with Access 2007 and asked you to look at his work. Copy the *chap2_mc3_traders.accdb* file to your working storage folder, name it **chap2_mc3_traders_solution.accdb**, and open the file. It contains two queries, May 2007 Orders of Beverages and Confections and 2007 Beverage Sales by Ship Country. The May 2007 Orders of Beverages and Confections query is supposed to only have information from May. You find other dates included in the results. Your challenge is to find and correct the error(s). The 2007 Beverage Sales by Ship Country returns no results. It needs to be ordered by country. It needs to be repaired and resorted. Print the Datasheet View of both queries.

Performance Elements	Exceeds Expectations	Meets Expectations	Below Expectations
Error identification	Correct identification and correction of all errors.	Correct identification of all errors and correction of some errors.	Errors neither located nor corrected.
May query	Correct criteria and sorted logically.	Correct criteria but inadequately sorted.	Incorrect criteria.
Beverage query	Correct criteria and sorted logically.	Correct criteria but inadequately sorted.	Incorrect criteria.

chapter 3 | Access

Customize, Analyze, and Summarize Query Data

Creating and Using Queries to Make Decisions

After you read this chapter, you will be able to:

1. Understand the order of precedence **(page 203)**.
2. Create a calculated field in a query **(page 203)**.
3. Create expressions with the Expression Builder **(page 213)**.
4. Create and edit Access functions **(page 214)**.
5. Perform date arithmetic **(page 218)**.
6. Create and work with data aggregates **(page 228)**.

Hands-On Exercises

Exercises	Skills Covered
1. CALCULATED QUERY FIELDS (page 207) **Open:** chap3_ho1-3_realestate.accdb **Save as:** chap3_ho1-3_realestate_solution.accdb **Back up as:** chap3_ho1_realestate_solution.accdb	• Copy a Database and Start the Query • Select the Fields, Save, and Open the Query • Create a Calculated Field and Run the Query • Verify the Calculated Results • Recover from a Common Error
2. EXPRESSION BUILDER, FUNCTIONS, AND DATE ARITHMETIC (page 219) **Open:** chap3_ho1-3_realestate.accdb (from Exercise 1) **Save as:** chap3_ho1-3_realestate_solution.accdb (additional modifications) **Back up as:** chap3_ho2_realestate_solution.accdb	• Create a Select Query • Use the Expression Builder • Create Calculations Using Input Stored in a Different Query or Table • Edit Expressions Using the Expression Builder • Use Functions • Work with Date Arithmetic
3. DATA AGGREGATES (page 231) **Open:** chap3_ho1-3_realestate.accdb (from Exercise 2) **Save as:** chap3_ho1-3_realestate_solution.accdb (additional modifications)	• Add a Total Row • Create a Totals Query Based on a Select Query • Add Fields to the Design Grid • Add Grouping Options and Specify Summary Statistics

CASE STUDY

Replacements, Ltd.

(Replacements, Ltd exists. The data in the case file are actual data. The customer and employee information have been changed to ensure privacy. However, the inventory and sales records reflect actual transactions.)

Today is the first day in your new position as associate marketing manager at Replacements, Ltd. In preparation for your first day on the job you have spent hours browsing the Replacements Web site, www.replacements.com. There you learned that Replacements, Ltd. (located in Greensboro, N.C.) has the world's largest selection of old and new dinnerware, including china, stoneware, crystal, glassware, silver, stainless, and collectibles. Its 300,000-square-foot facilities (the size of five football fields!) house an incredible inventory of 10 million pieces in 200,000 patterns, some more than 100 years old. While interviewing for the position, you toured the show room and warehouses. You learned that Replacements provides its customers with pieces that exactly match their existing patterns of china, silver, crystal, etc. People who break a cup or accidentally drop a spoon in the disposal purchase replacement treasures.

Case Study

You have been given responsibility for managing several different patterns of merchandise. You need to maintain adequate inventory levels. On the one hand you need to have merchandise available so that when a customer wishes to purchase a fork in a specific pattern, the customer service representatives can find it and box it for shipment. To accomplish this task, you need to closely monitor past sales in the various patterns in order to understand purchasing habits and product demand. On the other hand, the firm cannot afford to stock inventory of patterns no one wishes to purchase. You exchange information with the customer service representatives and monitor their performance. If you discover that one of the patterns you manage has excess inventory, you will need to direct the buyers to stop purchasing additional pieces in that pattern and encourage the customer service representatives to suggest the pattern to customers. You will determine if and when a pattern should be discounted or if an incentive program or contest should be implemented to reward the sales associates for successfully selling the overstocked merchandise.

Your Assignment

- Copy the *chap3_case_replacement.accdb* file to your production folder. Name the copy **chap3_case_replacement_solution.accdb**.
- Open the Relationships window and acquaint yourself with the tables, fields, and relationships among the tables in the database.
- You need to convert the data into useful information. To accomplish this task, you will need to create a query that identifies the revenue generated from sales in each of the patterns you manage.
- You also must determine which patterns customers purchase most often.
- Replacements encourages the customer service representatives by paying them bonuses based on the orders that they fill. You will calculate each customer service representative's total sales and calculate their bonuses. The bonus will be calculated based on ½% of the representative's total sales.
- Finally, you need to compare the inventory levels of each pattern piece with its sales volume. Careful monitoring of stock levels will prevent excessive inventory. For each item calculate the percent of the inventory level that was sold in the past month. For example, if there were 100 cups in a specific pattern in inventory at the beginning of the month and 18 of them were sold during the month, the sales-inventory ratio would be 18%. Set criteria so that the zero OnHandQuantity items are excluded from the calculation.

Data Summary and Analysis

Practicing good database design discourages storing calculations as table data. Although storing calculated results in a table is not a good idea, Access *can* perform arithmetic calculations using formulae and functions much like Excel. However, the calculated results do not belong in tables. Instead, calculations needed to summarize and analyze data are found in three places: queries, forms, and reports. Professionals who use Access to develop applications within organizations have very different opinions about the most appropriate placement of calculations in Access. One group assembles and manipulates data inside a query. After you establish the calculations and criteria, the data are sent to an Access report to be cosmetically enhanced. (This is the practice that you will employ throughout the exercises in this book.) The other group does all of the calculations inside of forms and reports. This group uses fewer queries but creates far more sophisticated reports and forms.

In this section, you learn about the order of precedence and create a calculated field in a query.

Understanding the Order of Precedence

The ***order of precedence*** establishes the sequence by which values are calculated.

The *order of precedence* establishes the sequence by which values are calculated in an expression. Evaluate parenthetically expressed values, then exponents, multiplication and division, and, finally, addition and subtraction. Access calculates exactly what you tell it to calculate—even if your formulae are incorrect! Table 3.1 shows some examples of arithmetic order. You must have a solid understanding of these rules in order to "teach" the computer to generate the required output. Access, like Excel, uses the following symbols:

- Addition +
- Subtraction –
- Multiplication *
- Division /
- Exponentiation ^

Creating a Calculated Field in a Query

You instruct Access to perform calculations in the Design view of the query. (Query Design is displayed in the Other section of the Create tab.) Create the calculated values in the first row of a blank column. You may scroll, if necessary, to find a blank column in the design grid or insert a blank column where you want

Table 3.1 Examples of Order of Precedence

Expression	Order to Perform Calculations	Output
= 2 + 3 * 3	Multiply first, and then add.	11
= (2 + 3) * 3	Add the values inside the parenthesis first, and then multiply.	15
= 2 + 2 ^ 3	Simplify the exponent first. 2^3 = 2*2*2 or 8. Then add.	10
= (2 + 2) ^3	Add the parenthetical values first (2 + 2 = 4), and then raise the result to the 3rd power. 4^3 = 4*4*4.	64
= 10/2 + 3	Divide first, and then add.	8
= 10/(2+3)	Add first to simplify the parenthetical expression, and then divide.	2
= 10 * 2 – 3 * 2	Multiply first, and then subtract.	14

the calculated value to appear. A formula used to calculate new fields from the values in existing fields is also known as an *expression*. An expression consists of a number of different items to produce the answers needed. The items used in an expression may include the following:

An ***expression*** is a formula used to calculate new fields from the values in existing fields.

- Identifiers (the names of fields, controls or properties)
- Operators (arithmetic instructions about what to do with the identifiers like + or –)
- Functions (as in Excel, Access has built-in functions to perform routine calculations, like SUM or Average)
- ***Constants*** and values (numbers that may be used as a part of a calculation but are unlikely to change)

A ***constant*** refers to a value that does not change.

You may use the expression to perform calculations, retrieve a value from a field, set query criteria, verify data created, calculate fields or controls, and set grouping levels in reports. Access not only organizes and protects a firm's valuable data but also enables you to summarize, understand, and make decisions based on the data. Your value to an organization dramatically increases when you master the skills that surround expression building in Access.

Build Expressions with Correct Syntax

Syntax is the set of rules by which the words and symbols of an expression are correctly combined.

Enter the expression in the first row of the column. Using simple ***syntax*** rules you instruct the software to calculate the necessary values. You can create expressions to perform calculations using either field values or constants. You must correctly spell the field names for Access to find the appropriate values. You should assign descriptive names to the calculated fields. Access ignores spaces in calculations. The general syntax follows:

CalculatedFieldName: [InputField1] operator [InputField2]

Although this is the most appropriate format, Access enters the brackets for you if it recognizes the field name. Remember that an **operator** is a symbol, such as *, that performs some operation, such as multiplication. An **operand** is the value that is being manipulated or operated on. In calculated fields in Access, the operand is either a literal value or a field name. Figure 3.1 shows a calculated field named Interest. The calculated field first calculates the monthly interest rate by dividing the 3.5% (0.035) annual rate by 12. The monthly interest rate is then multiplied by the value in the Balance field to determine the amount of interest owed. The query contains a second calculated field named NewBalance. Its value is the product of the value in the Interest field and the result of the Balance calculated field.

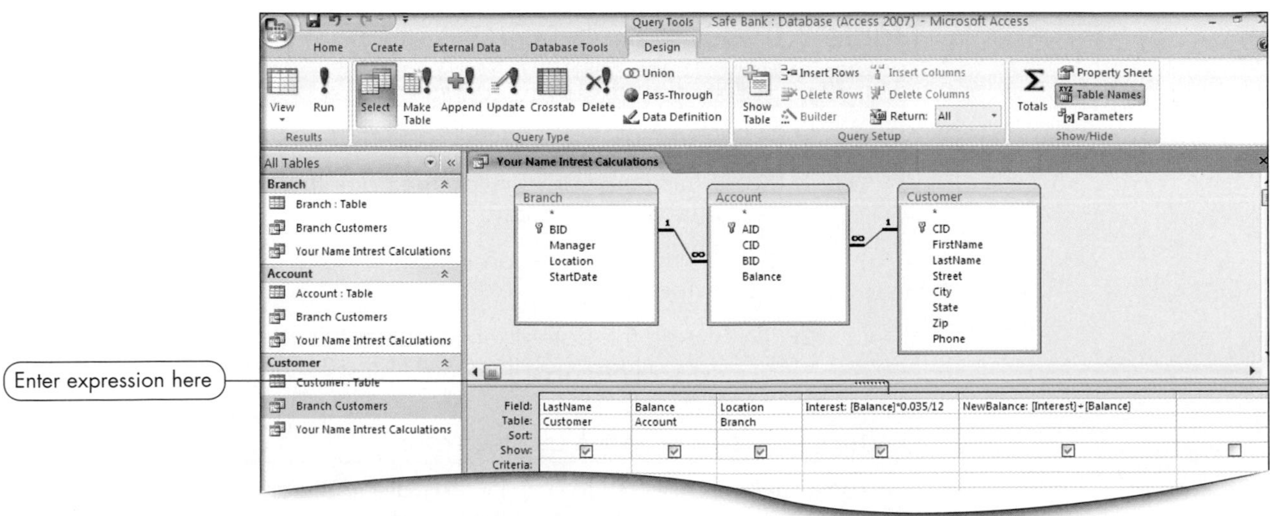

Figure 3.1 The Correct Location for a Calculated Query Expression

To help reinforce how calculated fields work, suppose you need to calculate the revenue from a purchase order. Revenue is the name of the calculated field. The following expression generates the calculated field by multiplying the unit price by the quantity ordered:

Revenue: Price*Quantity

Access enters the brackets for you and converts the expression to the following:

Revenue: [Price]*[Quantity]

For a final example of calculated fields, suppose you need to calculate a 10% price increase on all products you sell. NewPrice is the name of the calculated field. The following expression multiplies the old price by 110%:

NewPrice: Price*1.1

Access enters the brackets for you and converts the expression to the following:

NewPrice: [Price]*1.1

When you run the query, the calculated results display in the query's Datasheet view. Using the above example, Access goes to the table(s) where the prices and order quantities are stored, extracts the current data, loads it into the query, and uses the data to perform the calculation. When you direct Access to collect fields that are stored in related tables, Access uses the "strings" that form the relationship to collect the appropriate records and deliver them to the query. For example, suppose you create a query that retrieves customers' names from the customer table and the dates that the orders were placed from the Order table. The Customers table might contain 50,000 customer records. The query will return only those customers who ordered something because the relationship integrity will limit the output to only the records of interest. After the data are assembled, you can manipulate the data in each record by entering expressions. After you run the query, you need to examine the calculated results to verify that the output is what you need. Access has the ability to process a lot of numbers very quickly. Unfortunately, Access can also return incorrectly calculated results equally quickly if the formula you create is incorrect. Remember and avoid GIGO—Garbage In; Garbage Out!

(GIGO—Garbage In; Garbage Out!)

Verify Calculated Results

After your query runs, look at the values of the input field and then look at the calculated results returned. Ask yourself, "Does this answer make sense?" Use a pocket calculator or the Windows calculator to perform the same calculation using the same inputs and compare the answers. Alternatively, you can use Excel to check your calculated results. Copy and paste a few records into Excel. Repeat all of the calculations and compare the answers. The Access calculated field, the calculator, and the Excel calculations should return identical results.

After verifying the calculated results, you should save the query to run the next time you need to perform the same calculations.

Save a Query Containing Calculated Fields

Saving a query does *not* save the data. It saves only your instructions about what data to select and what to do with it once it is selected. Think of a query as a set of instructions directing Access to deliver data and the form the data are to assume at delivery. Writing a query is like placing an order with a restaurant server. You may order a medium rare steak, a baked potato, and tossed salad with blue cheese dressing. Your server writes the order and any special instructions and delivers it to the kitchen. In the kitchen the cook fills the order based on your instructions. Then the server delivers the ordered food to you. The data in a database is like the raw food in the kitchen. It is stored in the freezer or refrigerator or the cupboard (the tables). Data from the query (server's order) are assembled and "cooked." The big difference is that in the restaurant, once your steak is delivered to you, it is no longer available to other diners to order. The data in a database are *never* consumed. Data can be ordered simultaneously by multiple queries in a multiple user database environment. The data physically reside in the tables and never move from their storage location. Running the query collects the field values in the records of interest. The query contains only the instructions governing how Access selects and interacts with the data. If you type over a data item in a query table view, the new value automatically replaces the old one in the table.

After you run, verify, and save the query, you can use the newly created calculated fields in subsequent calculations. You may use a calculated field as input for other calculated fields. However, you must first save the query so that the calculation's results will be available.

In the first hands-on exercise, you will create calculated expressions, practice verification techniques, and generate and recover from a common error.

Hands-On Exercises

1 | Calculated Query Fields

Skills covered: 1. Copy a Database and Start the Query **2.** Select the Fields, Save, and Open the Query **3.** Create a Calculated Field and Run the Query **4.** Verify the Calculated Results **5.** Recover from a Common Error

Step 1
Copy a Database and Start the Query

Refer to Figure 3.2 as you complete Step 1.

a. Use Windows Explorer to locate the file named *chap3_ho1-3_realestate.accdb*. Copy the file to your production folder and rename the copied file as **chap3_ho1-3_realestate_solution.accdb**.

b. Open the *chap3_ho1-3_realestate_solution.accdb* file.

c. Click **Options** on the Security Warning toolbar, and then click **Enable this content** in the Microsoft Office Security Options dialog box and click **OK**.

d. Click the **Create tab**, and then click **Query Wizard** in the Other group.

e. Select **Simple Query Wizard** in the New Query dialog box. Click **OK**.

The Simple Query Wizard dialog box displays so that you can specify the table(s) and fields to include in the query design.

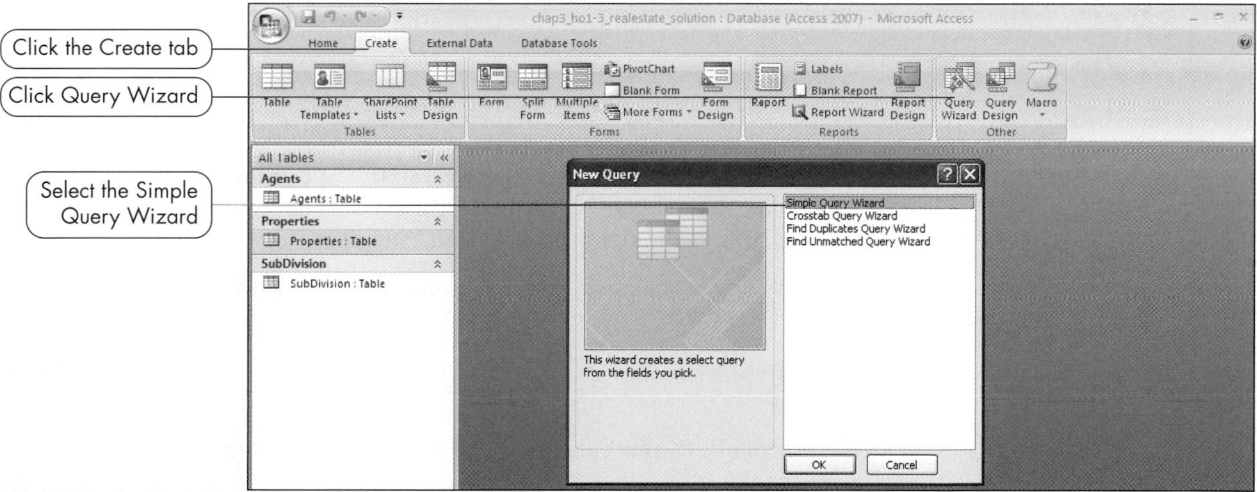

Figure 3.2 New Query Dialog Box

Step 2
Select the Fields, Save, and Open the Query

Refer to Figure 3.3 as you complete Step 2.

a. Click the **Tables/Queries drop-down arrow** and select **Table: Agents**. Double-click the **FirstName** and **LastName** fields in the **Available Fields list** to select them.

b. Click the **Tables/Queries drop-down arrow** and select **Table: Properties**. Double-click the following fields to select them: **DateListed, DateSold, ListPrice, SalePrice, SqFeet**, and **Sold**.

c. Compare your selected fields to those shown in Figure 3.3, and then click **Next**.

d. Verify that the **Detail (shows every field of every record) option** is selected in the *Would you like a detail or summary query?* screen in the Simple Query Wizard dialog box. Click **Next**.

e. Type **YourName Sale Price per SqFt** for the query title. Click **Finish**.

The results of the query appear in the Datasheet view.

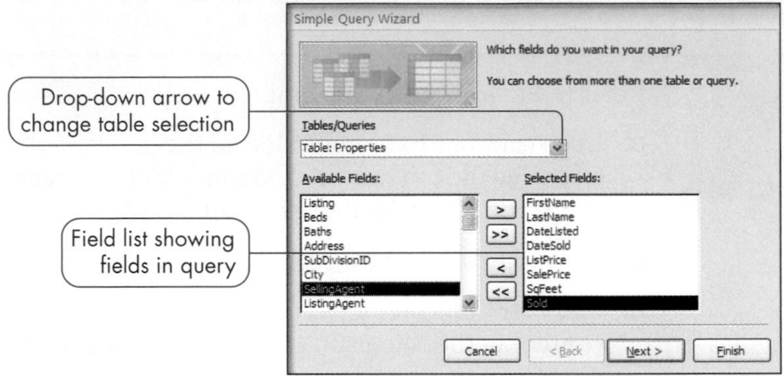

Figure 3.3 Select Fields for the Query

Step 3
Create a Calculated Field and Run the Query

Refer to Figure 3.4 as you complete Step 3.

a. Click the **Home tab** and click **View** in the View group to toggle to the Design view.

TROUBLESHOOTING: If you click View and Access does not toggle to the Design view, click the View arrow and select Design View.

This query was based on two tables, so the upper half of the Design view displays the two tables, Agents and Properties. The lower portion of the Design view displays the fields currently in the query.

b. Use the horizontal scroll bar to scroll the design grid to the right until you see a blank column.

c. Click in the first row of the first blank column to position your insertion point there.

d. Type **PricePerSqFt: SalePrice/SqFeet** and press **Enter**.

This expression creates a new calculated field named PricePerSqFt by dividing the values in the SalePrice field by the values in the SqFeet field. In this calculated field, the operator is the division symbol (/) and the operands are the SalePrice and SqFeet fields. Look at Figure 3.4 if you need help with the syntax for the expression.

TIP Increasing Width of Columns

To increase the column width so that you can see the entire calculated field expression, double-click the vertical line in the gray area above the field names between the calculated field column and the blank column.

e. Right-click the field text box in the design grid that contains the PricePerSqFt calculated field. Select **Properties** from the shortcut menu. Click the **Format drop-down arrow** in the Property Sheet window and select **Currency**. Click the X to close the Property Sheet window.

f. Click the **Design tab**, if needed, and then click **Run** in the Results group.

When you run the query, Access performs all of the calculations and opens in the table view to display the results.

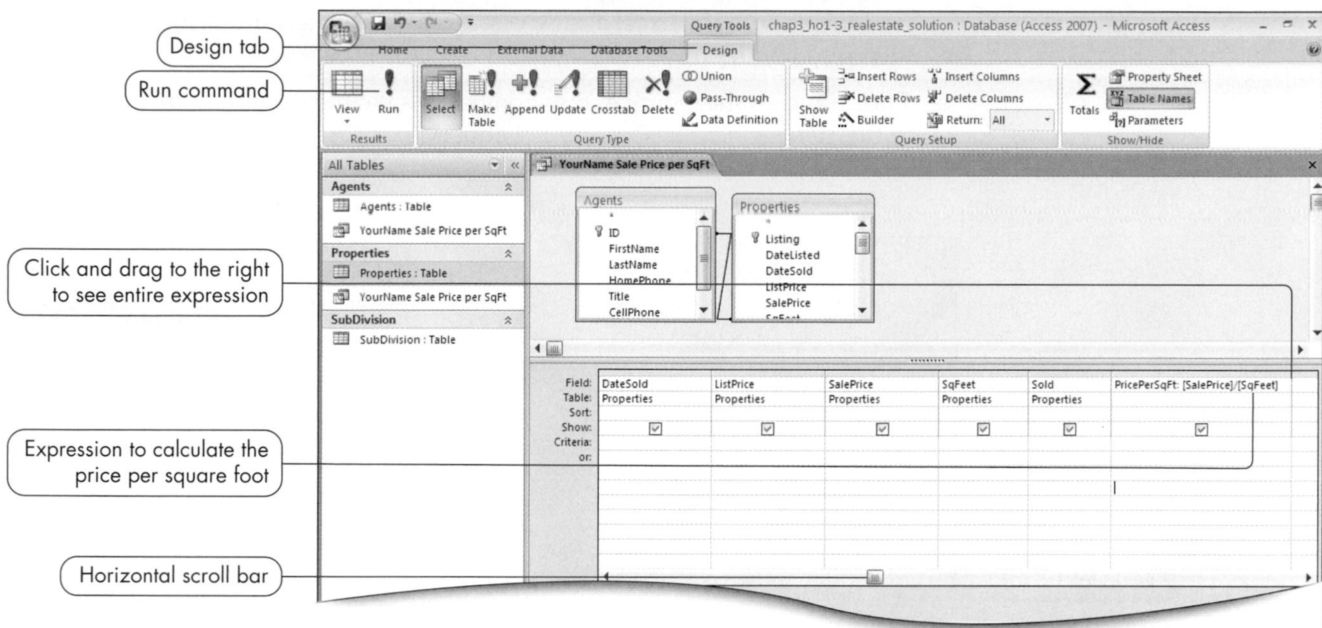

Figure 3.4 Expression Syntax

Step 4 Verify the Calculated Results

Refer to Figure 3.5 as you complete Step 4.

a. Examine the results of the calculation. Ask yourself if the numbers make sense to you.

TROUBLESHOOTING: Are you having a problem? You may wish to read Step 5 now. Often, a typo entered in a calculated field will result in a parameter box opening. Step 5 discusses how to recover from this error.

Look at the fourth record. The sale price is $155,000, and the number of square feet is 1,552. You can probably verify these results by dividing the values in your head. The result is about $100. The PricePerSqFt field in Figure 3.5 displays $99.87.

b. Use the row selectors to select the first four records by clicking and dragging. After you select the four records, right-click them and select **Copy** from the shortcut menu.

c. Launch Excel, activate **cell A1** of a blank workbook and paste the Access records into Excel.

The field names appear in the first row, and the four records appear in the next four rows. The fields are located in Columns A–I. The calculated field results are pasted in Column I as values rather than as a formula.

TROUBLESHOOTING: If you see pound signs (#####) instead of numbers in an Excel column, that means the column is too narrow to display the values. Position the mouse pointer on the vertical line between the column letters, such as between D and E, and double-click the vertical line to increase the width of column D.

d. In **cell J2**, type **=F2/G2** and press **Enter**.

The formula divides the sale price by the square feet. Compare the results in the I and J columns. The numbers should be the same. If the numbers are the same, close Excel without saving the workbook and return to Access. If the values differ, look at both the Excel and Access formulae. Determine which is correct and then find and fix the error in the incorrect formula.

e. Click **Save** on the Quick Access Toolbar to save the design modifications made to the *Your_Name Sale Price per SqFt* query.

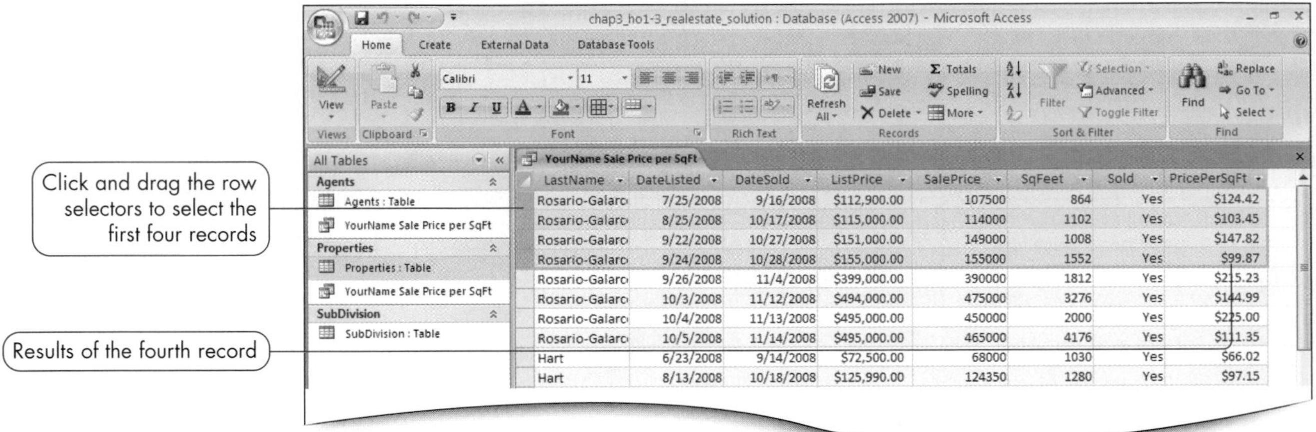

Click and drag the row selectors to select the first four records
Results of the fourth record

Figure 3.5 Examine Calculated Results

Step 5
Recover from a Common Error

Refer to Figure 3.6 as you complete Step 5.

a. In the *YourName Sale Price per SqFt query*, click **View** in the Views group to switch to Design view. Scroll to the first empty column and click in the first row to position the insertion point.

Because Access users occasionally make a typing error when creating an expression, it is useful to learn how to recover from this type of error. You will intentionally misspell a field name used in a calculation by typing the field name SalePrice as SaleSPrice and SqFeet as SqRFeet.

b. Type **WrongPricePerSqFt: SaleSPrice/SqRFeet.**

Be sure that you added the extra *S* and *R* to the field names. You are making intentional errors to learn how Access will respond.

c. Click **Run** in the Results group.

You should see the Enter Parameter Value dialog box. Examine the dialog box. What is it asking you to do? The dialog box indicates that Access could not find a value for SaleSPrice in the first record. This error occurs because the table does not contain a SaleSPrice field. Because Access is asking you to supply a value, you will type in a value.

TROUBLESHOOTING: You should carefully read the contents of a warning box or a parameter box when one appears. Access tries to tell you what is wrong. As your experience builds, the messages will become clearer to you.

d. Type **100000** in the parameter box. Before you click OK, try to anticipate what the software will do next. You intentionally misspelled *two* field names. Press **Enter** or click **OK**.

   Another Enter Parameter Value dialog box displays, asking that you supply a value for SqRFeet. This error occurs because the table does not contain a SqRFeet field.

e. Type **1000** and press **Enter**.

   The query has the necessary information to run and returns the results in Datasheet view.

f. Scroll right and examine the results of the calculation for WrongPricePerSqFt.

   All of the records show 100. This result occurs because you entered the values 100000 and 1000, respectively, in the Enter Parameter Value dialog boxes, which used those literal values in the expression. The result of 100 appears for all records.

g. Return to Design view and correct the errors in the WrongPricePerSqFt field by changing the formula to **WrongPricePerSqFt: SalePrice/SqFeet**.

h. Right-click the field text box in the design grid that contains the WrongPricePerSqFt calculated field. Select **Properties** from the shortcut menu. Click the **Format drop-down arrow** in the Property Sheet window and select **Currency**. Click the X to close the Property Sheet window.

i. Run and save the query again.

   The calculated values in the last two columns should be the same.

j. Close the query.

k. Click the **Office Button**, select **Manage**, and then select **Back Up Database**. Enter the file name **chap3_ho1_realestate_solution** (note *ho1* instead of *ho1-3*) and click **Save**.

   You just created a backup of the database after completing the first hands-on exercise. The original database *chap3_ho1-3_realestate_solution* remains onscreen. If you ruin the original database as you complete the second hands-on exercise, you can use the backup file you just created.

l. Close the file and exit Access if you do not want to continue with the next exercise at this time.

TIP Learning Software

Following step-by-step instructions is a way to begin learning application software. If you want to become proficient in software, you must learn how to recover from errors. As you work through the rest of the Hands-On Exercises in this book, follow the instructions as presented and save your work. Then go back a few steps and make an intentional error just to see how Access responds. Read the error messages (if any) and learn from your mistakes in a safe environment.

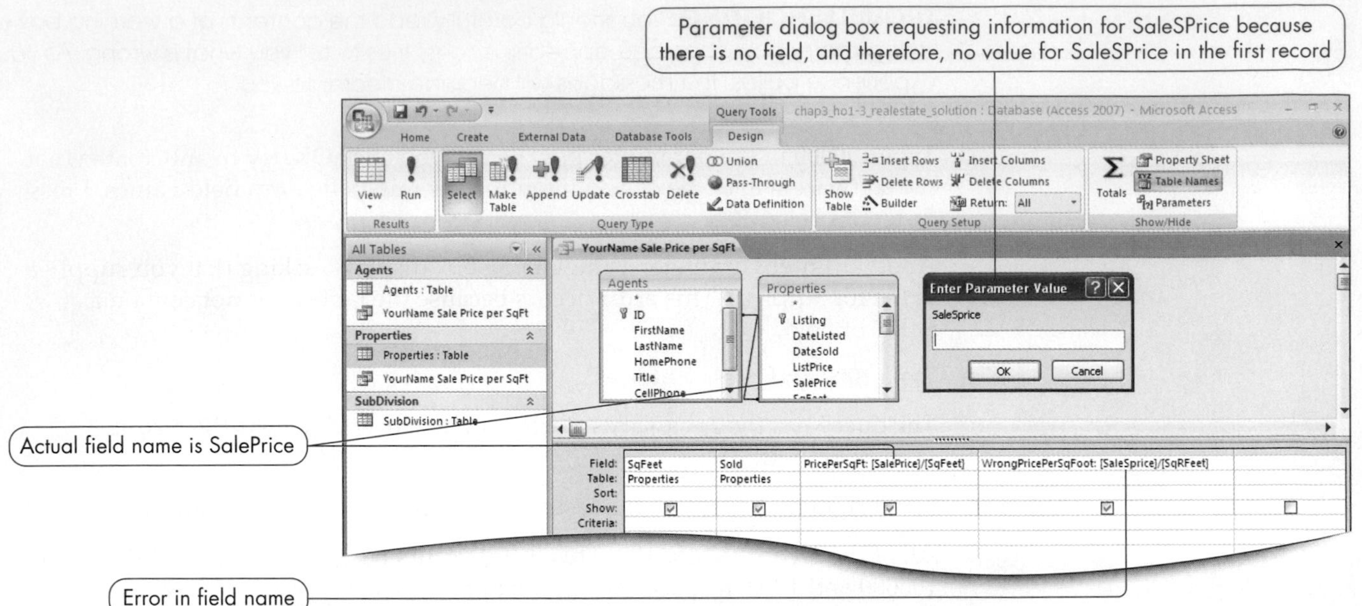
Parameter dialog box requesting information for SaleSPrice because there is no field, and therefore, no value for SaleSPrice in the first record
Actual field name is SalePrice
Error in field name

Figure 3.6 Error Recovery

Expression Builder

Before people used electronic database programs, decision makers were hampered because they could not find valid, timely, and accurate data to base decisions on. In today's world, data remains a problem for decision makers; however, the nature of the problem has changed. The data are current, accurate, and authentic. But because so much data are available, managers can become overwhelmed. In the last hands-on exercise, you calculated a price per square foot for real estate listings. That simple calculation can assist a decision maker to ascribe value to a property. It is a useful way to examine a complex transaction in a simplified fashion. Access enables you to calculate the value, but typing (and spelling correctly) all of those field names in the calculation is a lot of work. Fortunately, you can use the ***Expression Builder*** as an alternative, easier method to perform calculations. When you create an expression in the field text box, you must scroll to see the entire expression. The Expression Builder's size permits you to see even long, complex formulae and functions in their entirety.

The ***Expression Builder*** is a tool to help you create a formula that performs calculations easily.

In this section, you learn how to create expressions with the Expression Builder. You then learn how to create and edit functions. Finally, you perform date arithmetic.

Creating Expressions with the Expression Builder

You can use the Expression Builder in a query design grid to assist you in properly crafting the appropriate syntax. It is a blend of a calculator and a spreadsheet. You also can use the Expression Builder in other Access objects where calculations are needed. These objects include the control properties in forms and reports and table field properties. The Expression Builder requires some practice for you to learn how to use it effectively. Once you master the Expression Builder, you may use it to create a formula from scratch, or you can use it to select some pre-built expressions or functions. Additionally, the Expression Builder enables you to include useful items such as page numbers and the current date or time.

(The Expression Builder . . . is a blend of a calculator and a spreadsheet.)

Access automatically assigns placeholder names to all expressions created with the Expression Builder as Expr1, Expr2, Expr3. You need to develop the habit of running the query, verifying the calculation results and then returning to the design grid and replacing Exp1 with a descriptive field name. Good work habits will save you hours and hours when you return to your calculations in six weeks or six months.

After you save the query, the newly calculated field and descriptively named field are available to use in subsequent calculations.

Launch the Expression Builder

Open the query in Design view and display the Design tab. The Builder command is found in the Query Setup group. Figure 3.7 shows the components of the Expression Builder. The middle column contains a list of fields available in the current query. Occasionally, you may need to use a field as a calculation input that is not contained in the current query. Everything in the database is available to you through the builder. If you click the plus sign to the right of the Tables or Queries folder in the left column, the folder will open and reveal the other tables and fields in the database. This is a wonderful feature for someone who forgot to include a needed field in a query.

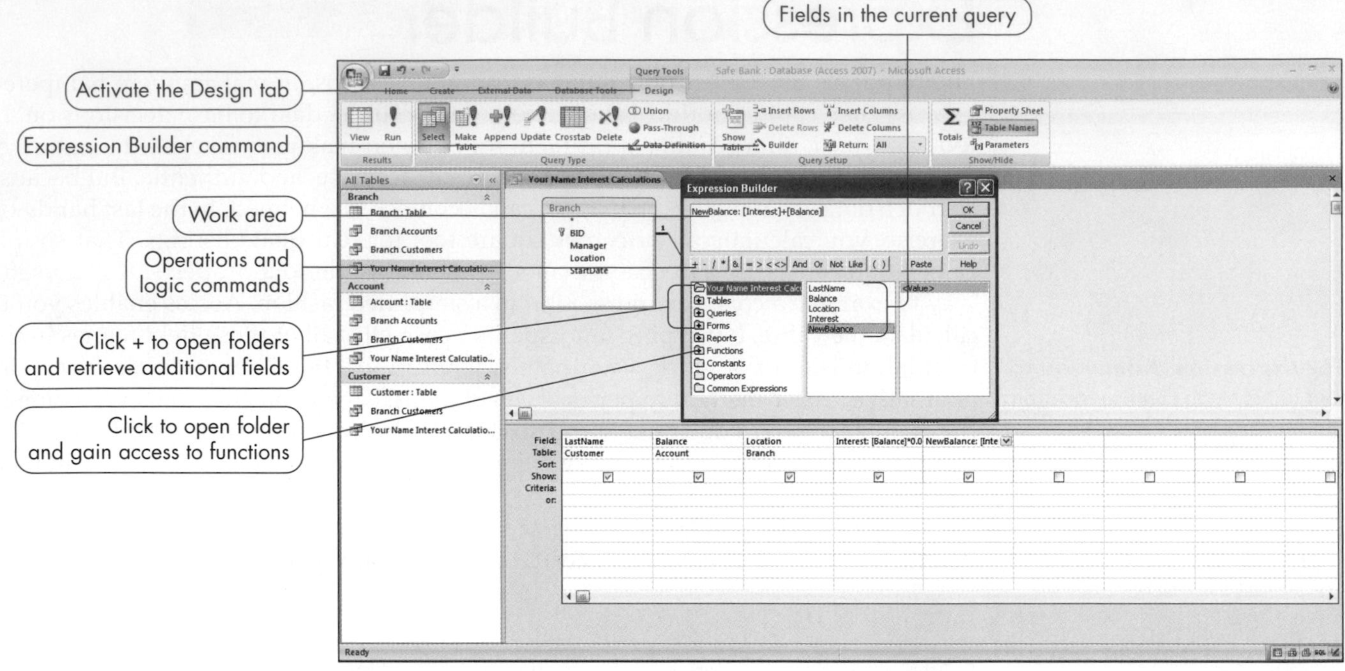

Figure 3.7 Expression Builder

The work area is the large rectangle at the top of the dialog box. Just as in Excel, an Access expression created using the Expression Builder begins with an equal sign. You may either type it or click the equal sign in the logic and operands area under the work area. When you need a field entered, find the field (look first in the middle column) and double-click it to add it to the expression. The field is added with the syntactically appropriate brackets inserted. Type or click operands (+, –, *, /) as needed and add additional fields to complete the expression. When you finish the expression, click OK.

Creating and Editing Access Functions

An ***Access function*** performs an operation using input supplied as arguments and returns a value.

An ***argument*** is a necessary input component required to produce the output for a function.

An *Access function* calculates commonly used expressions using "canned" instructions and input values to return a calculated value. You must know the function's name and provide it arguments in order to use it. Access functions work much like Excel functions. You identify the function by its name (e.g., Average, Sum, PMT) and enter the required *arguments*—what input values should be averaged, added, or calculated as a payment. They are grouped into categories of similar functions: Math, Financial, Date/Time, General, etc.

Calculate Payments with the PMT Function

The ***PMT function*** calculates a periodic loan payment given a constant interest rate, term, and original value.

Figure 3.8 shows the ***PMT function***, which calculates a periodic loan payment given a constant interest rate, specific term of the loan, and the original value of the loan. To use this function, you need to fill in values from data stored in fields from underlying tables or supply constants in the formula.

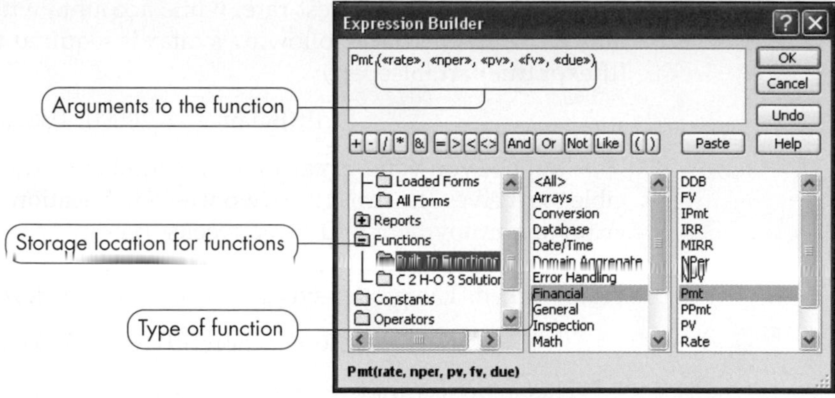

Figure 3.8 Access Function Shown in Expression Builder

The following syntax is required for the PMT function. Table 3.2 lists and describes the arguments for the PMT function.

Pmt(*rate, nper, pv, fv, type*)

Pmt(.065/12, 4*12, 12500,0,0)

Table 3.2

Part	Description
( )	Everything inside the parentheses is an argument to the function. The arguments are separated by commas. This function requires three arguments.
rate	Required. Expression or value specifying interest rate per period. (The period is the term of the loan payment, such as monthly or quarterly. For example, a car loan at an annual percentage rate (APR) of 6.5% with monthly payments gives the rate per period (month) of 0.065/12, or 0.005417).
nper	Required. Expression or Integer value specifying total number of payment periods in the annuity. For example, monthly payments on a four-year car loan gives a total of 4 * 12 (or 48) payment periods.
pv	Required. Expression or value specifying present value (or how much you borrow) that a series of payments to be paid in the future is worth now. For example, the loan amount is the present value to the lender of the monthly car payments.
fv	Optional. Value specifying future value or cash balance you want after you've made the final payment. For example, most loans have a future value of $0 because that's what is owed after the final payment. However, if you want to save $50,000 over 18 years for your child's education, then $50,000 is the future value.
type	Optional. Value (0 or 1) identifying when payments are due. Use 0 if payments are due at the end of the payment period (the norm), or 1 if payments are due at the beginning of the period.

Execute Actions with the IIf Function

The ***IIf function*** evaluates a condition and executes one action when the condition is true and an alternate action when the condition is false.

Another useful function is the ***IIf function,*** which evaluates a condition and executes one action when the expression is true and an alternate action when the condition is false. The condition must evaluate as true or false only. For example, if balance >=10,000 or if City = "Chicago" illustrate appropriate conditions. Access evaluates the expression, determines whether it is true or false, and performs alternative actions based on the determination. For example, accounts with balances over

$10,000 earn a 3.5% interest rate, while accounts with balances below $10,000 earn only 2.75% interest. The following syntax is required for the IIf function: IIf(expr,truepart,falsepart)

IIf(Balance >= 10000, .035, .0275)

Suppose you want to calculate the number of vacation weeks an employee is eligible to receive. The firm gives two weeks of vacation to employees with five or fewer years of employment and three weeks to employees who have worked more than five years for the firm. Your query has a field showing the number of years worked, YearsWorked. The proper syntax to calculate vacation weeks is the following:

WksVacation:IIf([YearsWorked]>5, 3,2)

This expression evaluates each record and determines if the number of years worked is more than five. When the number of years is greater than 5 (true), the expression returns the number 3 in the WksVacation field, indicating that the employee receives three weeks of vacation. If the years worked are not greater than 5 (false), the expression returns 2 in the WksVacation field, indicating that the employee receives two weeks of vacation. It is important that you write the expression so that it returns only a value of True or False for every record because Access cannot deal with ambiguities. The IIf function always evaluates both the true and false parts although the function returns only one part. When the expression, the truepart, or the falsepart references a character string (words instead of numbers), you must type the string inside of quotation marks, such as

IIf([City]="Tulsa","Oklahoma","Other State")

TIP Structure IIf Logic Carefully

Even experienced Access users get surprised sometimes when using IIf functions because the false part is evaluated even when the expression is true. Occasionally, this false part evaluation will result in a *divide by zero* error. You can prevent this error by rewriting the expression and reversing the operator. For example, change > to <=. You also must reverse the truepart and falsepart actions.

When you complete the expression, click OK. The Expression Builder dialog box closes, but nothing seems to happen. You have written the instruction in a form the computer understands, but you have not yet given the command to the computer to execute your instructions. The next step is to force an execution of your command by clicking Run. Your newly calculated result displays in the Datasheet view of the table. The column heading shows the default name, Expr1. Examine and verify the results of the calculation. When you are satisfied that the results are correct, return to Design view. In the design grid, double-click <Expr1> to select it, type over <Expr1> with a descriptive field name, run, and save the query.

TIP Calculated Field Availability

A calculated query field will not be available to use in subsequent calculations until after you save the query. When you need to make multiple-step calculations, you must author the steps one at a time, then run, verify, and save after each step.

Using the Expression Builder Steps | Reference

1. Open the query in Design view.
2. Position the insertion point in a blank column.
3. Select the Design tab.
4. Click the Builder icon to launch the Expression Builder.
5. When entering a formula, type (or click) an equal sign, =.
6. Double-click field names to add to the expression.
7. Type or click the icons for operators.
8. Double-click the Functions folder and select the type of function needed, then from the right column, select the individual function.
9. Click OK to exit the Builder box.
10. Run the query.
11. Examine and verify the output.
12. Return to the Design view.
13. Highlight <Expr1> in the design grid and rename the field with a descriptive field name.
14. Run the query and save it.

Because dates are stored as sequential numbers, you can calculate an age . . . or . . . how many days past due an invoice is.

Performing Date Arithmetic

Access, like Excel, stores all dates as serial numbers. You may format the stored dates with a format that makes sense to you. In Europe, the date *November 20, 2008*, might be formatted as *20-11-2008* or *20.11.2008*. In the United States, the same date might be formatted as *11/20/2008*, and in South Asia, the date might be formatted as *20/11/2008*. ***Date formatting*** affects the date's display without changing the serial value. All dates and times in Access are stored as the number of days that have elapsed since December 31, 1899. For example, January 1, 1900, is stored as 1, indicating one day after December 31, 1899. If the time were 9:00 PM on November 20, 2008, no matter how the date or time is formatted, Access stores it as 39772.857. The 39772 represents the number of days elapsed since December 31, 1899, and the .857 reflects the fraction of the 24-hour day that has passed at 9:00 PM. This storage method may seem complicated, but it affords an Access user power and flexibility when working with date values. For example, because dates are stored as sequential numbers, you can calculate the total numbers of hours worked in a week if you record the starting and ending times for each day. Using ***date arithmetic***, you can create expressions to calculate an age in years from a birth date or tell a business owner how many days past due an invoice is.

Date formatting affects the date's display without changing the serial value.

Using ***date arithmetic*** you can create expressions to calculate lapsed time.

Identify Partial Dates with the DatePart Function

You can look at entire dates or simply a portion of the date that is of interest. If your company increases the number of weeks of annual vacation from two weeks to three weeks after an employee has worked for five or more years, then the only part of the date of interest is the time lapsed in years. Access has a function, the ***DatePart function***, to facilitate this. Table 3.3 shows the DatePart function parameters.

The ***DatePart function*** enables users to identify a specific part of a date, such as only the year.

DatePart("yyyy",[Employees]![HireDate])

Do not let the syntax intimidate you. After you practice using the DatePart function, the syntax will get much easier to understand.

Useful date functions are:

- **Date**—Inserts the current date into an expression.
- **DatePart**—Examines a date and returns only the portion of interest.
- **DateDiff**—Measures the amount of time elapsed between two dates. This is most often today's date as determined by the date function and a date stored in a field. For example, you might calculate the number of days a payment is past due by comparing today's date with the payment DueDate.

Table 3.3 Using the DatePart Function

Function Portion	Explanation
DatePart	An Access function that examines a date and focuses on a portion of interest.
"yyyy"	The first argument, the interval, describes the portion of the date of interest. We specified the years. It could also be "dd" or "mmm".
(Employees)!(HireDate)	The second argument, the date, tells Access where to find the information. In this case, it is stored in the Employee Table in a field named HireDate.

Hands-On Exercises

2 | Expression Builder, Functions, and Date Arithmetic

Skills covered: 1. Create a Select Query **2.** Use the Expression Builder **3.** Create Calculations Using Input Stored in a Different Query or Table **4.** Edit Expressions Using the Expression Builder **5.** Use Functions **6.** Work with Date Arithmetic

Step 1
Create a Select Query

Refer to Figure 3.9 as you complete Step 1.

a. Open the *chap3_ho1-3_realestate_solution* file if necessary, click **Options** on the Security Warning toolbar and click the **Enable this content option** in the Microsoft Office Security Options dialog box, and click **OK**.

   TROUBLESHOOTING: If you create unrecoverable errors while completing this hands-on exercise, you can delete the *chap3_ho1-3_realestate_solution* file, copy the *chap3_ho1_realestate_solution* backup database you created at the end of the first hands-on exercise, and open the copy of the backup database to start the second hands-on exercise again.

b. Open the **Agents table** and replace **Angela Scott's** name with your name. Close the Agents table.

c. Click the **Create tab** and click **Query Wizard** in the Other group. Select **Simple Query Wizard** and click **OK**.

d. Select the fields (in this order) from the Agents table: **LastName** and **FirstName**. From the Properties table, select **DateListed**, **DateSold**, **ListPrice**, **SalePrice**, and **SqFeet**. From the SubDivision table, select the **Subdivision** field. Click **Next**.

   You have selected fields from three related tables. Because relationships exist among the tables, you can trust that the agent's name that returns when the query runs will be the agent associated with the property.

e. Check to make sure that the option for **Detail** query is selected and click **Next**.

f. Name this query **YourName Commissions** and click **Finish**.

   The query should run and open in Datasheet view. An experienced Access user always checks the number of records when a query finishes running and opens. This query should have 54 records. See Figure 3.9.

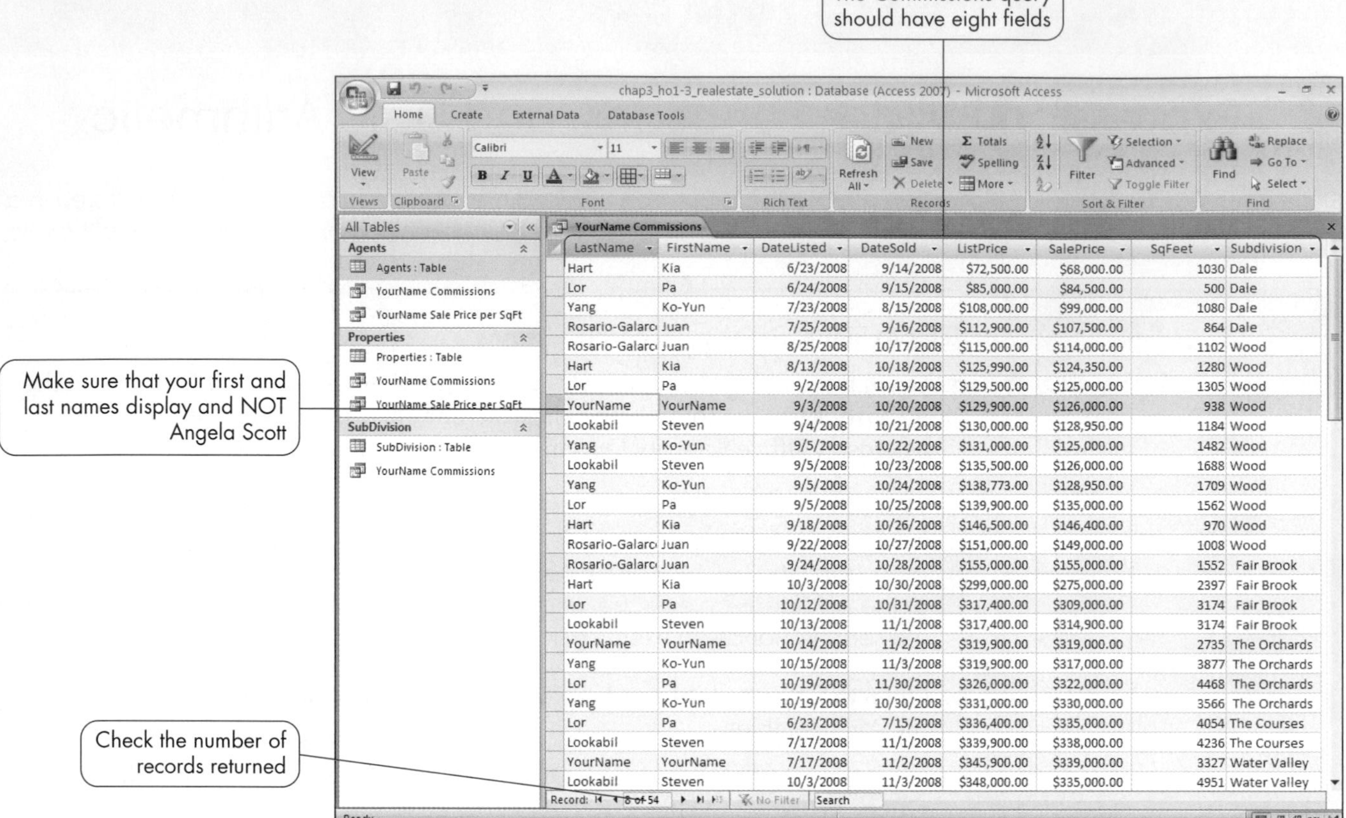

Figure 3.9 Datasheet View of the YourName Commissions Query

Step 2
Use the Expression Builder

Refer to Figure 3.10 as you complete Step 2.

a. Click the **Home tab** and switch to Design view by clicking the **View** button. Scroll to the right to locate the first empty column in the design grid and position your insertion point in the first row.

b. Verify that the Design tab is selected and click **Builder** in the Query Setup group.

   The Expression Builder dialog box opens. You may click the title bar and reposition it to a more convenient location if necessary.

c. Repeat the PricePerSqFt calculation from Hands-On Exercise 1 by using the Expression Builder. Click or type =.

d. Locate the list of fields in the Commissions query in the middle column and double-click the **SalePrice** field.

   The work area of the Expression Builder dialog box should now display **= [SalePrice]**. The Expression Builder adds the **brackets** and always spells the field names correctly.

e. Click or type the divide operator (the forward slash, /), and then double-click the **SqFeet** field name in the middle column.

   Now, the work area of the expression builder will display **= [SalePrice] / [SqFeet]**.

f. Click **OK**. Run the query. Scroll right in the Datasheet view to find the newly calculated field, which is named Expr1.

g. Verify the results of the calculation, adjusting column width if necessary.

The fifth record has values that can be rounded more easily in your head—$114,000 and 1102 Sq. Ft. That should return a result slightly higher than $100. The actual result is 103.448275862069. Once you are satisfied with the accuracy of the calculation, continue with the next step.

h. Activate the **Home tab** (if necessary) and change the view to Design view by clicking the **View** button.

TIP Switching Between Design and Datasheet Views

An easy way to alternate views for an Access object is to right-click the object window's title bar and select the appropriate view from the shortcut menu. You can also click the views buttons in the bottom-right corner of the Access window. In this case, the object title bar says YourName Commissions. See Figure 3.10 for instructions on where to right-click.

i. Double-click **Expr1** in the field row of the right column. Type **PricePerSqFt**.

j. Right-click the field text box in the design grid that contains the PricePerSqFt calculated field. Select **Properties** from the shortcut menu. Click the **Format drop-down arrow** in the Property Sheet window and select **Currency**. Click the X to close the Property Sheet window.

k. Run the query. Click **Save** (or press **Ctrl + S**) and return to Design view.

l. Click the insertion point in the Field row of the first empty column and activate the Expression Builder. Look in the middle column that shows the list of available fields in this query. The last listed field should be the newly saved PricePerSqFt.

TROUBLESHOOTING: Sometimes, you need to edit an expression created using the Expression Builder. When you open the Expression Builder to make the edits, you will find that Access adds <Expr1> to any unsaved expressions. Locate and double-click the <Expr1> to select it and delete it prior to making the necessary edits to the expression.

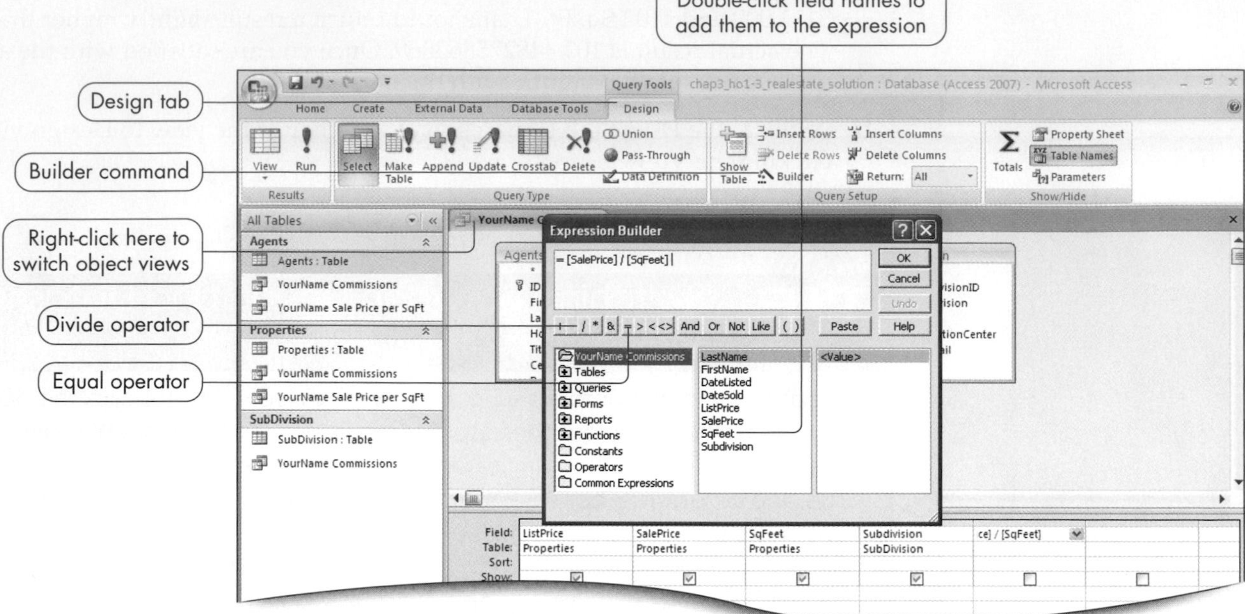

Figure 3.10 Working with the Expression Builder

Step 3
Create Calculations Using Input Stored in a Different Query or Table

Refer to Figure 3.11 as you complete Step 3.

a. Open **Expression Builder** dialog box, type = (equal sign) in the work area of the Expression Builder. Double-click **SalePrice** in the middle column to add it to the expression. Type or click / (divide symbol). Your formula in the work area should be **= [SalePrice]/**.

In addition to calculating the price per square foot, you decide that it would be helpful if you knew the price of the sold properties per bedroom, but you did not include a field for the number of bedrooms in the query. You have two options. One, you can cancel the expression, add the missing field to the query, and then restart the expression. Two, you also can use a field in a calculation that is not resident in the query. You need only tell Access where the field is stored.

b. Double-click the **Tables folder** in the left column of the Expression Builder.

The Tables folder expands to reveal the table objects in the database. Because you have not yet selected a table, the middle and right columns of the Expression Builder dialog box are empty.

c. Click the **Properties table**.

The middle column is populated with the names of the fields available from the Properties table. You will use this data to calculate the per bedroom sale price of the homes in the database.

d. Double-click the **Beds field**. Your expression will look like this:

= [SalePrice] / [Properties]![Beds]

This expression gives Access the instruction to go to the Properties table, locate the values of the number of bedrooms for each of the records in the Commissions query, and use that value to calculate a price per bedroom value. The appropriate number of bedrooms will be returned in each calculation because relationships exist between the tables. The query will inherit the referential integrity of the source tables.

e. Click **OK**. Click **Run**. Verify the calculated results.

f. Return to Design view. Double-click **Expr1** in the design grid to select it and type **PricePerBR**.

You have renamed Expr1, but the name change does not become permanent until you save the query design.

g. Right-click the PricePerBR calculated field. Select **Properties** from the shortcut menu. Click the **Format drop-down arrow** in the Property Sheet window and select **Currency**. Click the X to close the Property Sheet window.

h. Save the query.

i. Position the insertion point anywhere in the Field row in the PricePerBR column.

j. Click **Builder** in the Query Setup group on the Design tab.

The Expression Builder dialog box displays the renamed calculated field, PricePerBR, and a colon at the beginning of the expression without the equal sign (see Figure 3.11).

k. Click **OK** to close the Expression Builder dialog box.

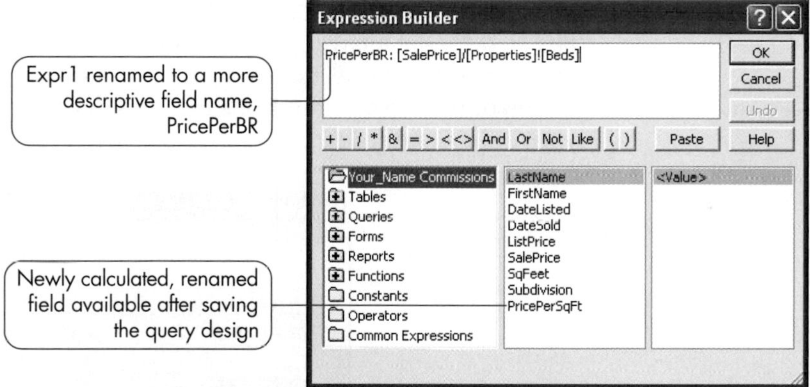

Figure 3.11 A Completed Expression

Step 4
Edit Expressions Using the Expression Builder

Refer to Figure 3.12 as you complete Step 4.

a. Click and drag to select the entire **PricePerBR** expression in the design grid. Right-click the selected expression and select **Copy**.

Be careful that you select and copy the entire expression. You need the new field name, all of the input fields, and the operands.

TROUBLESHOOTING: You cannot click into the next field in the design grid while the Expression Builder dialog box is open. Generally, any open dialog box in a Microsoft product is assigned top priority, and you must first deal with the dialog box before you can do anything anywhere else in the file. Close the Expression Builder dialog box if it is open.

b. Right-click in the field box of the first blank column and select **Paste**.

Your next task is to edit the copied formula so that it reflects the price per bathroom.

c. Position the insertion point anywhere in the copied formula and click **Builder**.

d. Move the I-beam pointer over any portion of the word *Beds* in the formula. Double-click.

   The entire portion of the formula, [Properties]![Beds], should highlight.

e. Double-click the **Tables folder** in the left column, and then click the **Properties table** to open the folder and table, respectively.

   Make sure that the middle column displays the field names of the available fields in the Properties table.

f. Double click the **Baths field**.

   The edited expression now displays **PricePerBR: [SalePrice] / [Properties]! [Baths].**

g. Drag to select the word **BR** in the *PricePerBR*. Replace BR with **Bath**.

   The edited expression is **PricePerBath: [SalePrice] / [Properties]! [Baths]**.

h. Click **OK**. Click **Run**. Click **Save**, and then return to Design view.

i. Right-click the PricePerBath calculated field. Select **Properties** from the shortcut menu. Click the **Format drop-down arrow** in the Property Sheet window and select **Currency**. Click the X to close the Property Sheet window.

j. Run the query. Examine the calculated results in the Datasheet view.

   Do your results make sense? Which field has larger numbers in it, the price per bedroom or the price per bathroom? Do most houses have more bedrooms or bathrooms? Which number would you expect to be larger? Remember, you are dividing in these calculations. As the number on the bottom of a fraction gets larger, does the answer get larger or smaller? You do not need to write the answers to these questions on paper. You do need to develop a critical eye and force yourself to ask questions like these every time you calculate a value.

k. Click **Save**.

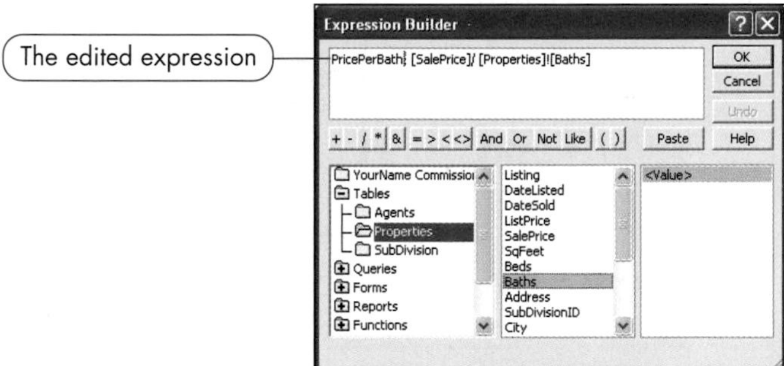

Figure 3.12 The Correctly Edited Formula

Step 5
Use Functions

Refer to Figures 3.13 and 3.14 as you complete Step 5.

a. Position the insertion point in the field row of the first blank column of the query in Design view.

   You are going to use a financial function to calculate an estimated house payment for each of the sold properties. You make the following assumptions: 90% of the sale price financed, a 30-year period, monthly payments, and a fixed 6.5% annual interest rate. The first task is to calculate the amount financed. Assume a 10% down payment means that there will be 90% of the purchase price remaining to finance.

b. Right-click in the field box of the first blank column and select **Build** from the shortcut menu to display the Expression Builder dialog box. Type the formula **= [SalePrice]** * **.9** and click **OK**.

   You will need to use this calculated value in subsequent calculations.

c. Run and save the query, return to Design view, double-click **Expr1**, and type **AmountFinanced**. Save the query.

d. Position the insertion point in the field row of the next available column. Launch the Builder.

e. Double-click the **Functions folder** in the left column. Click **Built-In Functions folder**.

f. Look in the middle column. Click the **Financial** function category.

g. Look in the right column. Double-click the **Pmt function**.

The builder work area displays
Pmt(<<rate>>,<<nper>>,<<pv>>,<<fv>>,<<due>>)

We are assuming monthly payments at a 6½% interest rate over 30 years with no balloon payment at the end of the 30-year period and that the finance charges are calculated at the end of each period.

h. Double-click each formula argument to select it. Substitute the appropriate information:

Argument	Replacement Value
<<rate>>	0.065/12
<<nper>>	30*12
<<pv>>	(AmountFinanced)—Click the YourName Commissions folder to display a list of field names available to use in the query.
<<fv>>	0
<<due>>	0

TROUBLESHOOTING: If you do not see the AmountFinanced field in the list of available field names, you probably forgot to save the query after running it. Press Esc to close the Expression Builder dialog box. Click Save or press Ctrl+S to save the query design changes and re-work steps d through h.

i. Examine Figure 3.13 to make sure that you have entered the correct arguments. Click **OK**. Run the query.

The payments are all negative numbers. That is normal. You will edit the formula to return positive values.

j. Click **OK**. Return to Design view. Click in the Payment calculated field and open the Expression Builder. Position the insertion point to the left of the left bracket, [, and type a hyphen, –. Double-click **Expr1** and type **Payment**. The expression will now be:

Payment: Pmt(0.065/12, 30*12, –[AmountFinanced], 0,0). Click **OK**.

k. Right-click the Payment calculated field. Select **Properties** from the shortcut menu. Click the **Format drop-down arrow** in the Property Sheet window and select **Currency**. Click the **X** to close the Property Sheet window.

l. Run and save the query.

The calculated field values now appear as positive, rather than negative, values.

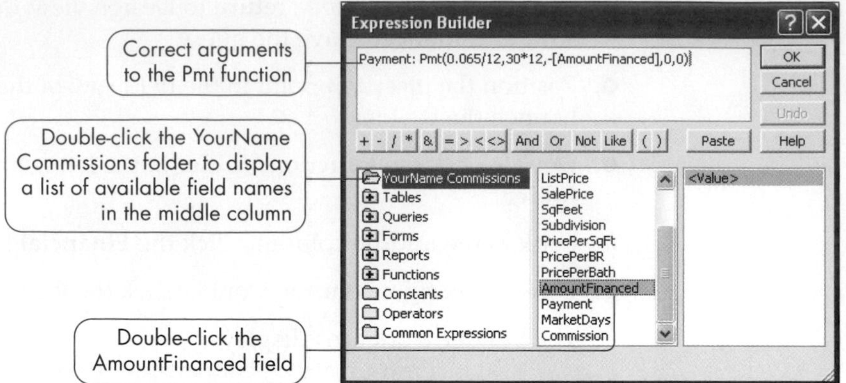

Figure 3.13 The Payment Function Arguments

Step 6 Work with Date Arithmetic

Refer to Figure 3.14 as you complete Step 6.

a. Position the insertion point in the field row of the first blank column of the query in Design view. Launch the Expression Builder.

You are going to calculate the number of days that each property was on the market prior to its sale.

b. Enter the formula = **[DateSold] – [DateListed]**. Run the query. Return to Design view and replace Expr1 with **MarketDays**. Save the query. Open the Property Sheet window and *format* the field as **Fixed** and set the *Decimal Places* to **0**.

Because Access stores all dates as serial numbers, the query returns the number of days on the market. The first property was placed on the market on June 23, and it sold on September 14. Look at your query result. This property was for sale all of July, all of August, and for parts of June and September. This is about three months. Does the query result reflect about three months?

c. Create a new field. Use the Expression Builder to multiply the SalePrice field by the commission rate of 7%. The formula in the Expression Builder is = **[SalePrice] * .07**. Run the query and replace Expr1 with **Commission**. Save the query.

The Commission calculated field calculates the total commission. The agent earns 7% of the sale price. The first agent's commission is $4,760.00.

d. Right-click the Commission calculated field. Select **Properties** from the shortcut menu. Click the **Format drop-down arrow** in the Property Sheet window and select **Currency**. Click the **X** to close the Property Sheet window.

The values in the Commission calculated field now appear in Currency format. The first agent's commission displays as $4,760.00.

e. Click the **Office Button**, select **Manage**, and then select **Back Up Database**. Enter the file name **chap3_ho2_realestate_solution** (note *ho2* instead of *ho1-3*) and click the **Save** button on the Quick Access Toolbar.

You just created a backup of the database after completing the second hands-on exercise. The original database *chap3_ho1-3_realestate_solution* remains onscreen. If you ruin the original database as you complete the third hands-on exercise, you can use the backup file you just created.

f. Close the file and exit Access if you do not want to continue with the next exercise at this time.

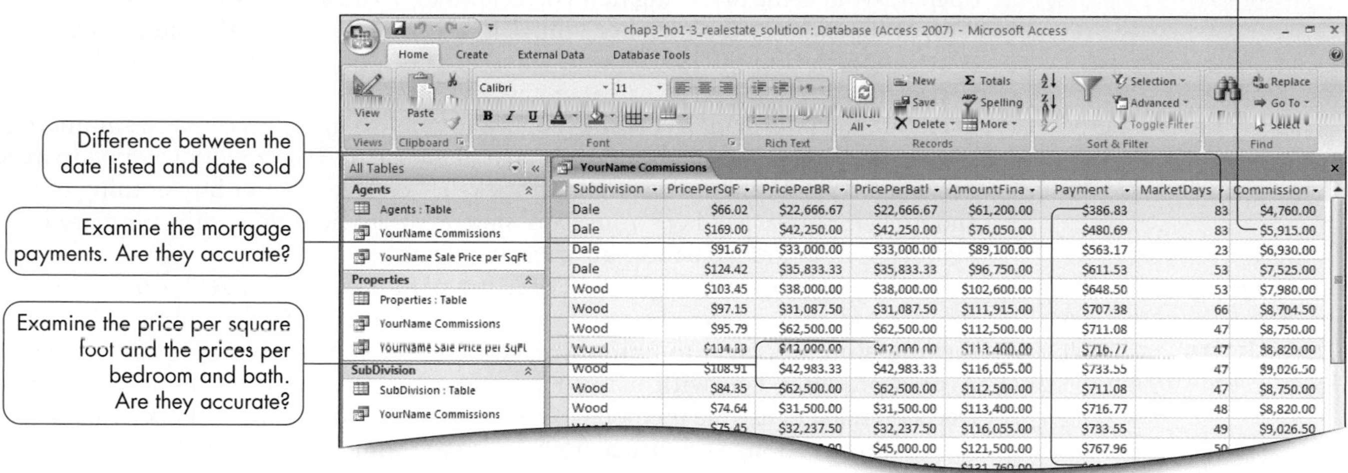

This property sold for $84,500. The commission rate is 7%. Does $5,915 reflect 7% of the sale price? Did you use a calculator or Excel to verify your calculation?
Difference between the date listed and date sold
Examine the mortgage payments. Are they accurate?
Examine the price per square foot and the prices per bedroom and bath. Are they accurate?
chap3_ho1-3_realestate_solution : Database (Access 2007) - Microsoft Access
YourName Commissions

Figure 3.14 Verify, Verify, Verify!

Data Aggregates

Assume that you have an old-fashioned bank that still sends paper statements at the end of the month through the mail. Your statement arrives at your mailbox, and you open it. What is the first thing that you examine? If you are like most people, you first look at the balance for each account. The checking account information lists each transaction during the last month, whether it is a deposit or withdrawal, and the transaction method—ATM or paper check. These records provide vitally important data. But, the information contained in the account balances gives you a summarized snapshot of your financial health. You may then use the balance information to make decisions. "Yes, I can buy those concert tickets!" or "No, I better buy nothing but gas and groceries until payday." Your bank statement provides you with summary information. Your account balances are data aggregates.

A ***data aggregate*** is a collection of many parts that come together from different sources and are considered a whole.

A ***data aggregate*** is a collection of many parts that come together from different sources and are considered a whole. Commonly employed aggregating calculations include sum, average, minimum, maximum, standard deviation, and variance. Access provides you with many methods of summarizing or aggregating data. Decision makers use the methods to help make sense of an array of choices.

In this section, you learn how to create and work with data aggregates. Specifically, you learn how to use the totals row and create a totals query.

Creating and Working with Data Aggregates

A ***total row*** displays as the last row in the Datasheet view of a table or query and provides a variety of summary statistics.

Aggregates may be used in a query, table, form, or report. Access provides two methods of adding aggregate functions to a query. A ***total row*** displays as the last row in the Datasheet view of a table or query and provides a variety of summary statistics. The first method enables you to add a total row from the Datasheet view. This method is quick and easy, works in the Datasheet view of a table, and has the additional advantage that it provides the total information without altering the object design. You will recall that some databases are split into front and back end portions. Different users have different levels of privileges when interacting with the database. Adding a total row to a query or table can be accomplished by the lowest-privilege-level employee because it does not alter the structure of the object. The second method enables you to alter the query design and create a totals query. This method has the advantage of permitting you to group your data into relevant subcategories. For example, you can subtotal all houses sold in a specific subdivision or by each salesperson. After the summary statistics are assembled, you can employ them to make decisions. Who is the leading salesperson? In which neighborhood do houses sell most often or least often? This method requires that the user have rights to alter the design of a query. In a large, split database, a front-end user may not be afforded the rights to create or alter a query design. The query design is generally restricted to back-end users—the IT professionals only.

Data aggregation gives the decision maker a powerful and important tool. The ability to summarize and consolidate mountains of data into a distilled and digestible format makes the Access software a popular choice for managerial users. You already have learned that data aggregates may be created in queries. Access also permits aggregation in reports. In the first section, you learned that some users calculate all of their expressions in queries, whereas others perform needed calculations in forms and reports. The positioning of data aggregates also may be accomplished in a variety of ways. Some users aggregate and calculate summary statistics in queries, others in reports. You will need to learn both methods of aggregation because the practices and procedures governing database use differ among firms. Some firms allow users relatively free access to both the front and rear ends of the database; other firms grant extremely limited front-end rights only.

Create a Total Row in a Query or Table

Figure 3.15 illustrates adding a total row to the Datasheet view. Access can total or average numeric fields only. Begin by positioning your insertion point in a numeric or currency field of any record. Then click Totals in the Records group on the Home tab. The word Total is added below the new record row of the query. The highlighted numeric field shows a box with an arrow in the Total row. You may choose from several different aggregate functions by clicking the arrow. This method works in the same way if you want to add a total row to a numeric field in a table.

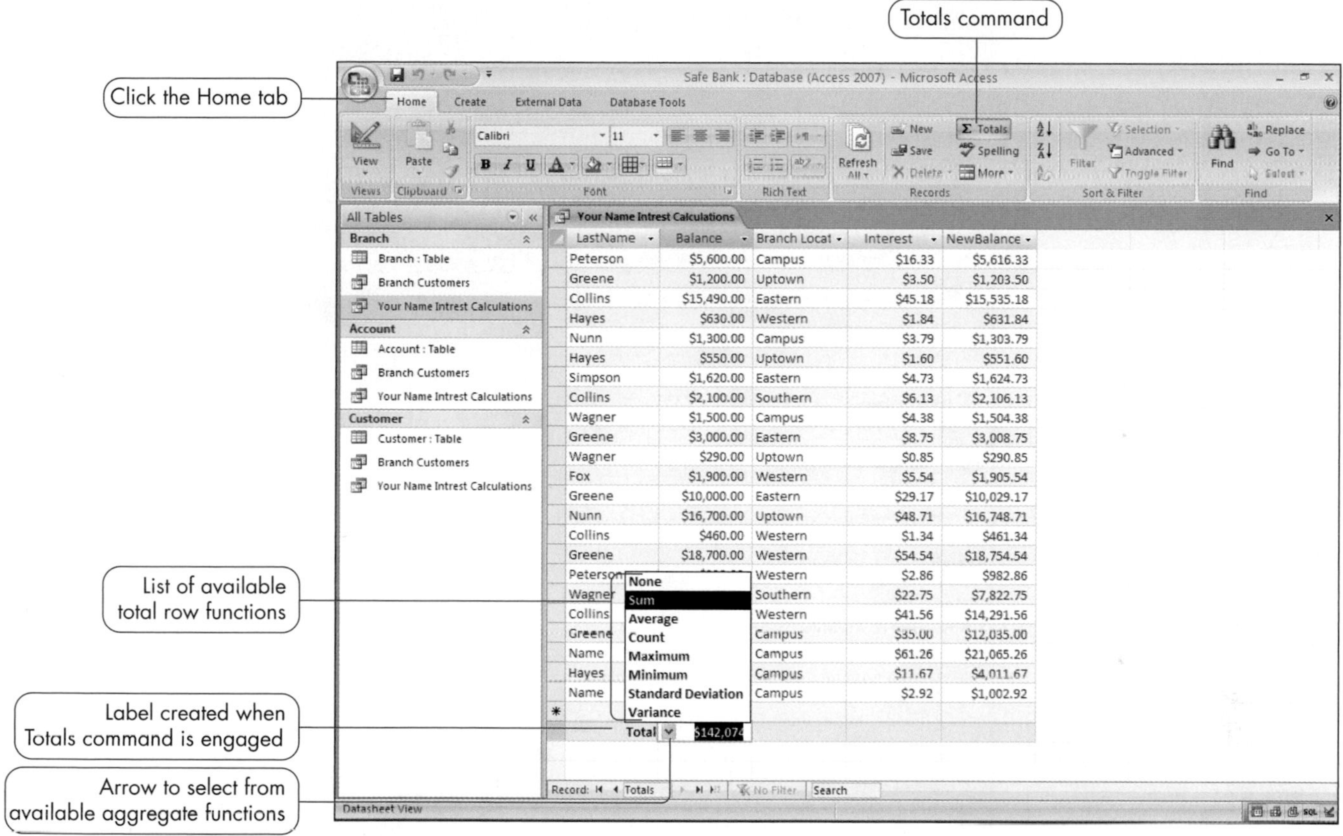

Figure 3.15 Adding a Total Row to a Query in Datasheet View

Group Totals in a Totals Query

The Total row, when added to a query, provides the decision maker with useful information. However, it does not provide any method of subtotaling the data. The total row is useful when a decision maker needs to know the totals or averages of all the data in a query or table. Sometimes knowing only the total is insufficient. The decision maker needs to know more detail. For example, knowing the total sales of houses during a period is good information. Knowing subtotals by salespeople would be more useful. Knowing subtotals by subdivision also would be useful information. Instead of using a total row, you can create a ***totals query*** to organize the results of a query into groups to perform aggregate calculations. It contains a minimum of two fields. The first field is the grouping field, such as the salesperson's last name. The second field is the numeric field that the decision maker wishes to summarize, such as the sale price of the homes. You may add other numeric fields to a totals query to provide additional information. The totals query in Access helps you provide a more detailed snapshot of the data.

A ***totals query*** organizes query results into groups by including a grouping field and a numeric field for aggregate calculations.

The SafeBank database that you created in Chapter 2 has five branch locations. If you need to know the total deposits by location, you would create a totals query. The two fields necessary would be the Location field in the Branch table and the Account

> . . . a totals query can only include the field or fields that you want to total and the grouping field.

Balance field in the Accounts table. After you create and run the query, you may add parameters to limit the totals query to a specific data subset. The process of adding criteria in a totals query is identical to any other query. Remember that a totals query can include only the field or fields that you want to total and the grouping field. No additional descriptive fields are allowed in the totals query. If you need to see the salesperson's last name, the sale price of the house, *and* the salesperson's first name, you would need to create two queries. The first query would be the totals query summarizing the sales data by last name. Then you would need to create a second query based on the totals query and add the additional descriptive field (the first name) to the new query. Figure 3.16 shows the setup for a totals query.

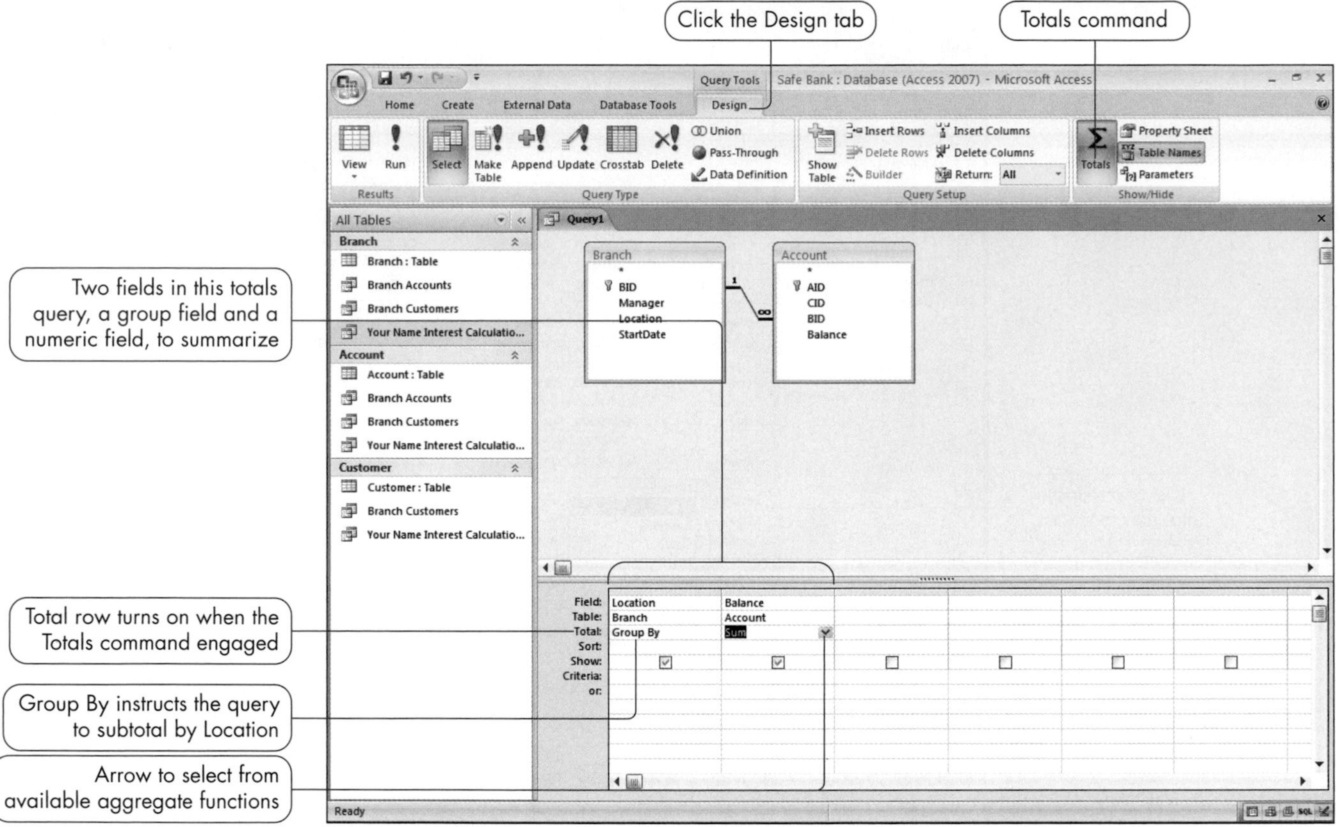

Figure 3.16 Constructing a Totals Query

Hands-On Exercises

3 | Data Aggregates

Skills covered: 1. Add a Total Row **2.** Create a Totals Query Based on a Select Query **3.** Add Fields to the Design Grid **4.** Add Grouping Options and Specify Summary Statistics

Step 1
Add a Total Row

Refer to Figure 3.17 as you complete Step 1.

a. Open the *chap3_ho1-3_realestate_solution* file if necessary, click **Options** on the Security Warning toolbar, click the **Enable this content option** in the Microsoft Office Security Options dialog box, and click **OK**.

   TROUBLESHOOTING: If you create unrecoverable errors while completing this hands-on exercise, you can delete the *chap3_ho1-3_realestate_solution* file, copy the *chap3_ho2_realestate_solution* backup database you created at the end of the second hands-on exercise, and open the copy of the backup database to start the third hands-on exercise again.

b. Open the **YourName Commissions query** in the Datasheet view.

c. Click the **Home tab** and click **Totals** in the Records group.

   Look at the last row of the query. The Totals command is a toggle: Click it once to display the Total row. Click it again to hide the Total row. You need the Total row turned on to work the next steps.

d. Click in the cell that intersects the **Total row** and the **SalePrice** column.

   This is another place in Access that when selected, a drop-down list becomes available. Nothing indicates that the drop-down menu exists until the cell or control is active. You need to remember that this is one of those places in order to aggregate the data.

e. Click the **drop-down arrow** and select **Sum** to calculate the total of all the properties sold. Widen the SalePrice field if you can't see the entire total value.

   The total value of the properties sold is $19,936,549.00.

f. Scroll right, locate the **Subdivision field**, and click in the Total row to activate the drop-down list.

   The choices from the total list are different. You may have the summary statistics set to None or Count. Subdivision is a character field. Access recognizes that it cannot add or average words and automatically limits your options to only tasks that Access is able to do with words.

g. Select **Count** from the drop-down list in the Total row for the Subdivision field.

h. Click in the **Total row** in the **PricePerSqFt** field. Click the **drop-down arrow** and select **Average**.

i. Click in any record of any field. Close the query.

   A dialog box opens that asks if you wish to save the changes to the ***layout*** of the YourName Commissions query. It does NOT ask if you wish to save the changes made to the design. Toggling a Total row on and off is a layout (cosmetic) change only and does not affect the architectural structure of the query or table design.

j. Click **Yes**. The query saves the layout changes and closes.

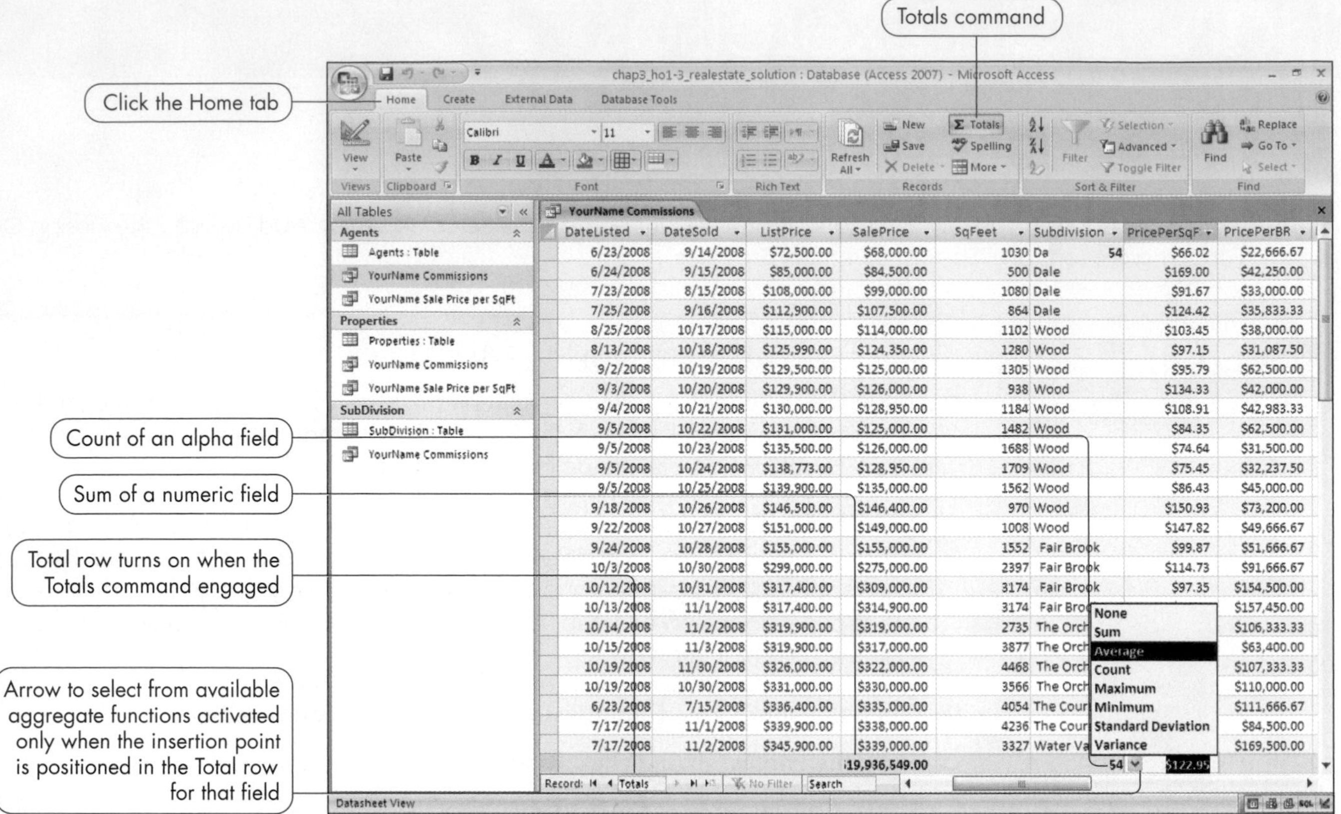

Figure 3.17 Add a Total Row to the Query Datasheet View

Step 2
Create a Totals Query Based on a Select Query

Refer to Figure 3.18 as you complete Step 2.

a. Click the **Create tab** and click **Query Design** in the Other group.

The Show Table dialog box opens. You could source this query on the tables. However, because you already have made many useful calculations in the Commissions query, it will save you time to source the Totals query on the Commissions query.

b. Click the **Queries tab** in the Show Table dialog box.

c. Select the **YourName Commissions query** and click **Add**.

d. Click **Close**.

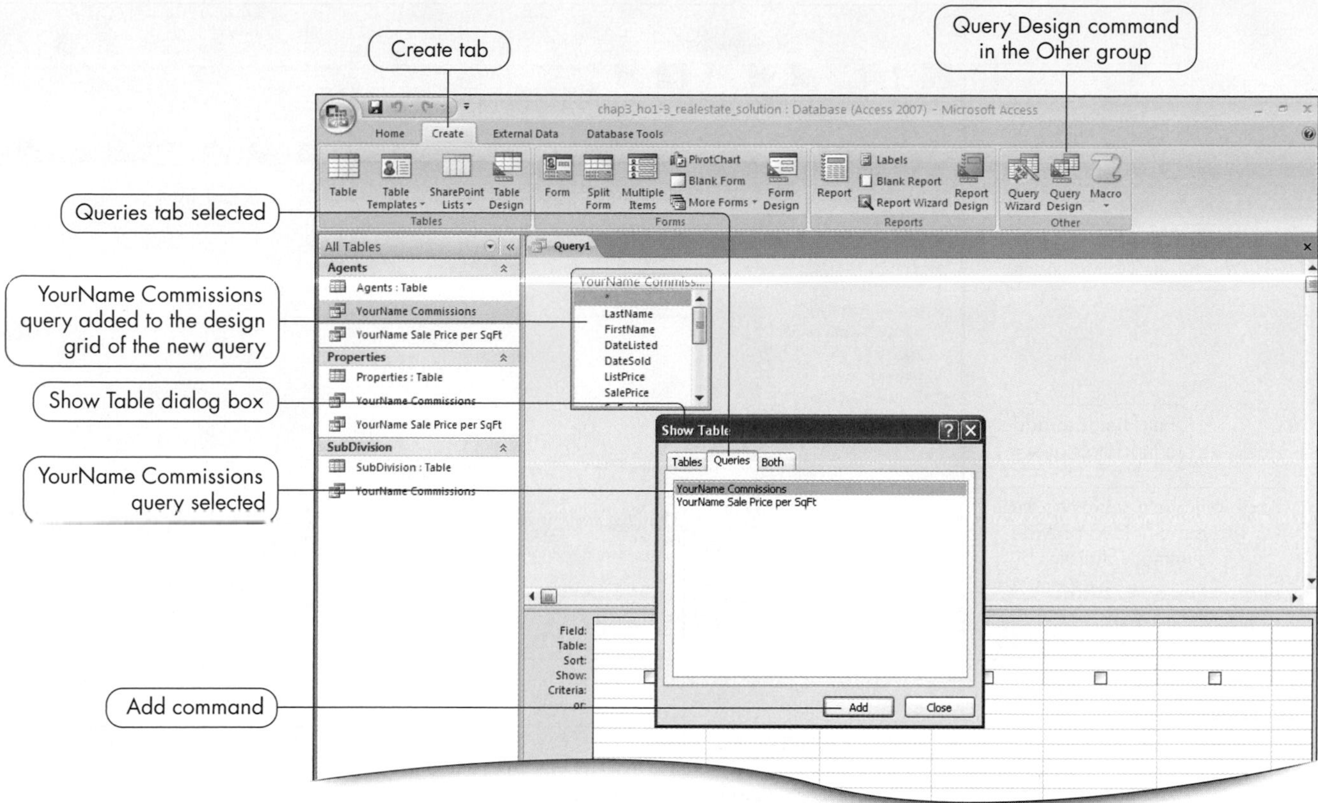

Figure 3.18 Create a Totals Query

Step 3
Add Fields to the Design Grid

Refer to Figure 3.19 as you complete Step 3.

a. Locate the **LastName** field in the YourName Commissions field list box.

You may add fields from the YourName Commissions query to the new query by clicking and dragging them to the design grid or by double-clicking.

b. Double-click the **LastName** field to add it to the grid.

You will create summary statistics based on each salesperson's activities. The LastName field is the grouping field in this totals query.

TROUBLESHOOTING: If you attempt to double-click a field name and the computer "beeps" at you, you probably forgot to close the Show Table dialog box.

c. Double-click the **SalePrice** field to add it to the grid.

d. Scroll down in the list of available fields box and double-click **MarketDays** to add it to the new query.

e. Add the **Commission** field to the new query.

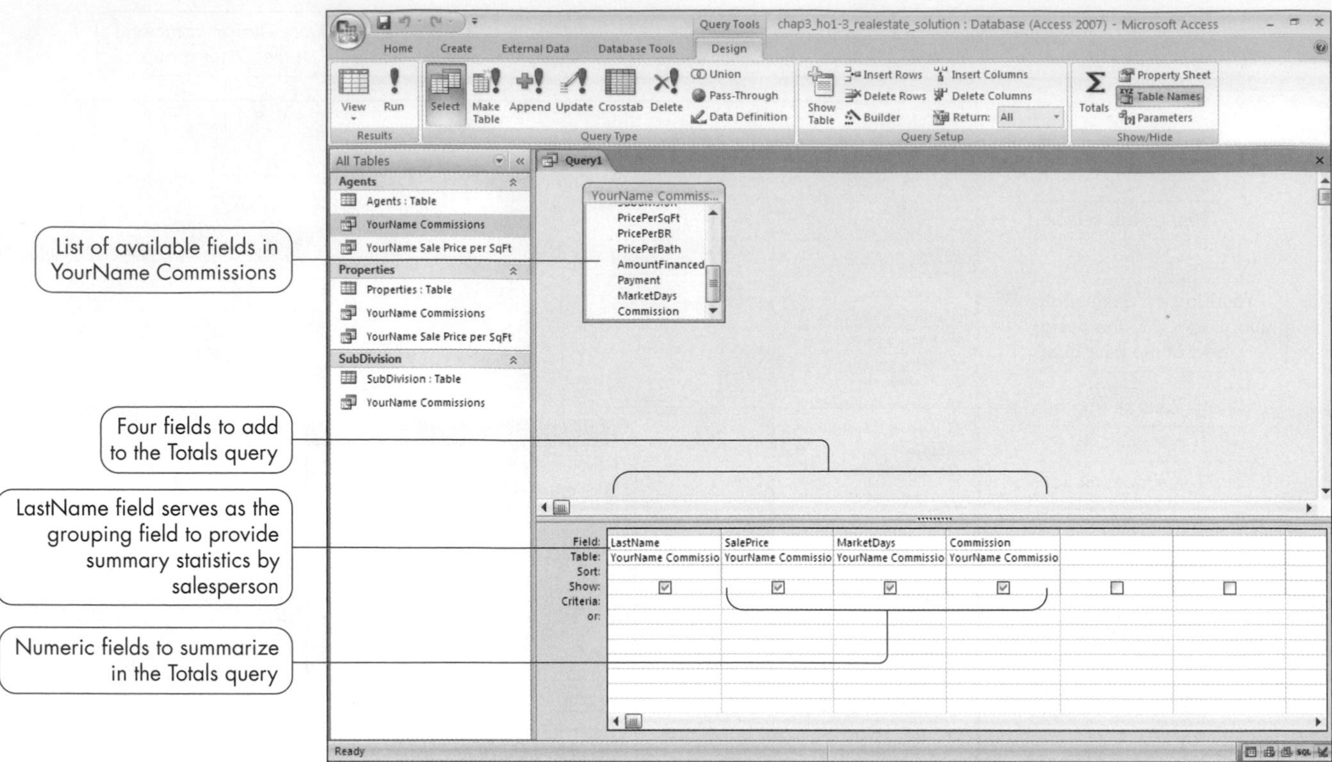

Figure 3.19 Setting Up the Totals Query

Step 4
Add Grouping Options and Specify Summary Statistics

Refer to Figures 3.20 and 3.21 as you complete Step 4.

a. Click **Totals** in the Show/Hide group on the Design tab.

   Look at the lower part of the design grid. The Totals command toggles a new row between the Table and Sort rows of the design grid. When the Totals command is activated, all fields are set to Group by. You only want one Group by field, the LastName field.

b. Click in the **Total row** for the **SalePrice** field. Click the **drop-down arrow** and select **Sum** from the list.

   Here is another of those hidden drop-down lists. As you gain experience, you will learn where to look for them. For now, simply memorize that one will show up in the Total row.

c. Click in the **Total row** of the **MarketDays** field. Click the **drop-down arrow** and select **Avg**.

d. Click the **Total row** in the **Commission** field and select **Sum**.

e. Run the query. Return to Design view and set the properties of the SalePrice and Commission fields as **Currency**. Set the Format property of the MarketDays field to **Fixed**. Set the Decimal Places property to **0**. Close the Property Sheet.

f. Verify results of the calculated summaries. Save the query as **YourName Commission Summary**.

g. Close the *chap3_ho1-3_realestate_solution* file.

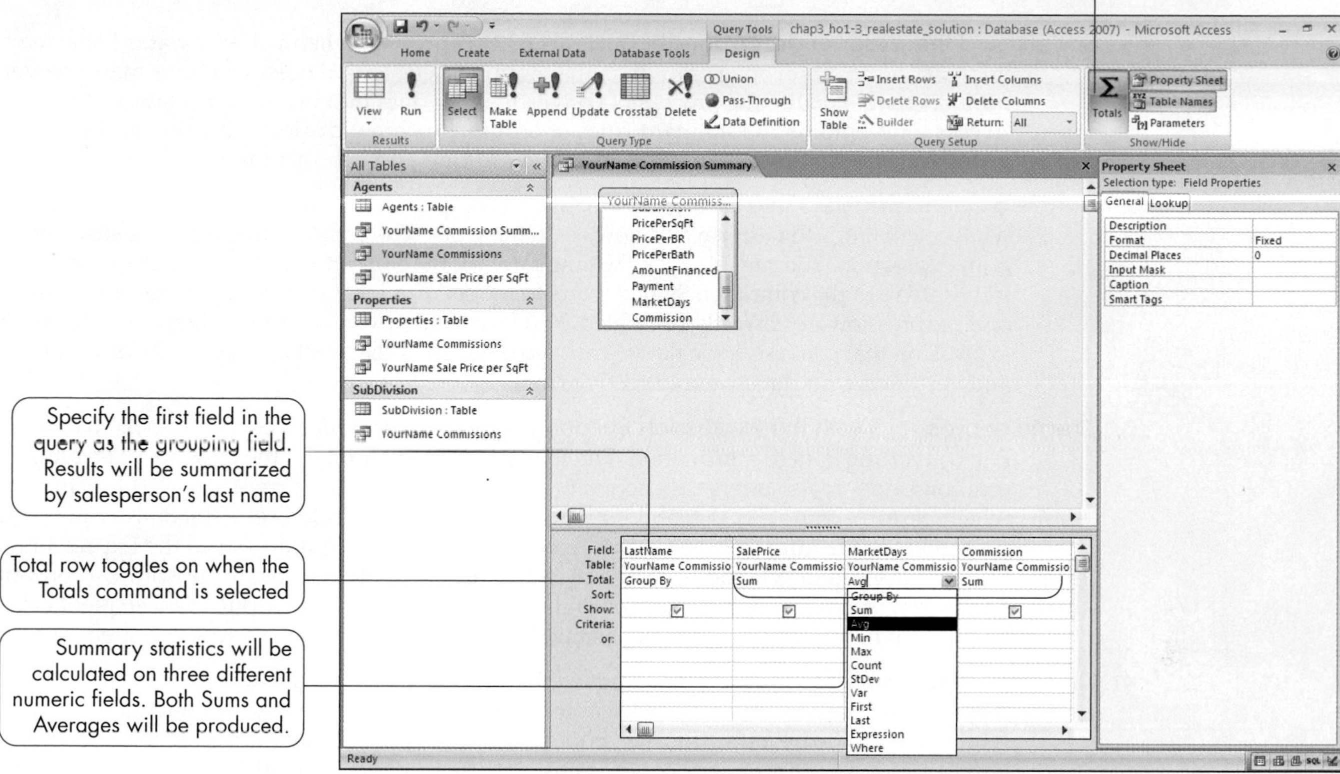
Totals command located in the Show/Hide group on the Design tab
Specify the first field in the query as the grouping field. Results will be summarized by salesperson's last name
Total row toggles on when the Totals command is selected
Summary statistics will be calculated on three different numeric fields. Both Sums and Averages will be produced.

Figure 3.20 Specify Grouping Field and Summary Statistics

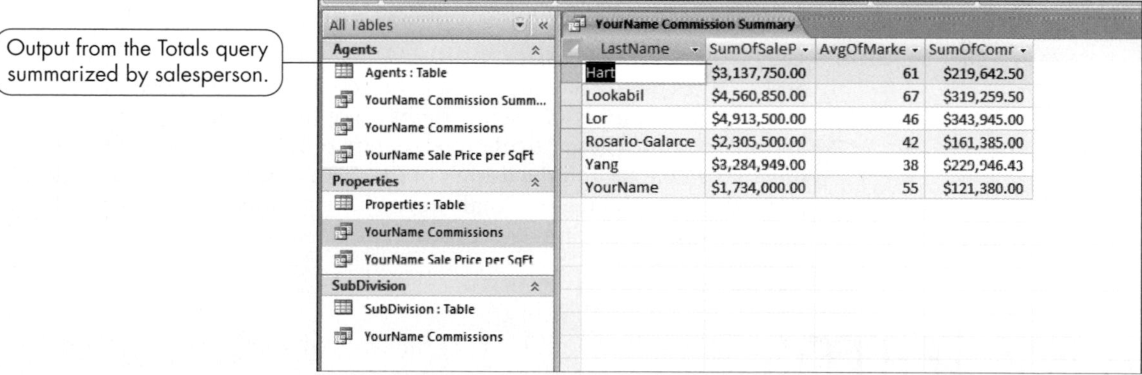
Output from the Totals query summarized by salesperson.

LastName	SumOfSaleP	AvgOfMarke	SumOfComr
Hart	$3,137,750.00	61	$219,642.50
Lookabil	$4,560,850.00	67	$319,259.50
Lor	$4,913,500.00	46	$343,945.00
Rosario-Galarce	$2,305,500.00	42	$161,385.00
Yang	$3,284,949.00	38	$229,946.43
YourName	$1,734,000.00	55	$121,380.00

Figure 3.21 Specify Grouping Field and Summary Statistics

Summary

1. **Understand the order of precedence.** Decision makers are overwhelmed with data. They need information that they may employ to make sound decisions. Access provides many powerful tools that expedite the process of converting raw data into useful information. The Access tools employ the standard rules of order in arithmetic calculations: parentheses, exponents, multiplication and division, and addition and subtraction.
2. **Create a calculated field in a query.** Access, like all computer software, must be instructed in what calculations to perform and how to do the work. The formal name for those instructions is an expression. You must "speak the language" of the software in order to accurately communicate with the computer. Syntax refers to the set of rules by which the words and symbols of an expression are correctly combined. You learned that you can write a syntactically correct expression that contains logic flaws. You also developed the practice of critically examining and verifying your data to avoid costly errors.
3. **Create expressions with the Expression Builder.** The chapter introduced powerful tools that facilitate converting data to information. The Expression Builder makes the logistics of formula creation easier. It also offers easy access to a number of pre-built formulae, called functions, which perform complex calculations relatively painlessly. Using Access functions requires the user to know the function's name and arguments. The arguments appear in the Expression Builder enclosed in symbols (<<XXX>>) as a visual cue that you need to substitute a constant or a field name. Access can use the output of earlier calculations as input to subsequent calculations, but the expression must be renamed and the query saved prior to subsequent use.
4. **Create and edit Access functions.** You learned that Access, like Excel, has a variety of functions that can perform complex tasks in an automated fashion. You employ the functions by identifying the function by name (IIf, Avg, Sum, Pmt), and then entering the arguments in the appropriate order. Arguments are the input data Access uses to create the output. They may be field names or values.
5. **Perform date arithmetic.** Dates in Access are stored as serial numbers based on the number of days that have elapsed from an arbitrarily chosen base date, December 31, 1899. Access provides several functions to facilitate date handling. Additionally, you can simply subtract one date from another or add a number to a date to create a different date.
6. **Create and work with data aggregates.** Data aggregates provide powerful means to summarize and analyze data. You may add a Total row to the Datasheet view of a table or query and select from a number of useful summary options including count, sum, average, minimum, and maximum. These calculations require only a few mouse clicks to create. Additionally, they have no effect on the design of the table or query. When a more robust summary is needed, you may create a Totals query. This permits you to establish grouping levels for the data to make summaries more meaningful.

Key Terms

Multiple Choice

1. Which statement most accurately describes the differences between a table field and a calculated field?
   (a) All data entries to a table field are permanently stored, but calculated field data do not exist in the database. They appear in the datasheet, form or report but are not a part of the dataset.
   (b) A calculated field is permanently stored in the dataset when the query, table, form, or report design is saved. Only the properties governing the data are saved when a table is saved.
   (c) Query data and Table data are dynamic, and no data are permanently stored.
   (d) None of the above.

2. Which of the following correctly identify the rules of order of arithmetic operations?
   (a) Exponentiation, Parenthesis, Addition, Subtraction, Multiplication, Division
   (b) Parenthesis, Exponentiation, Addition, Subtraction, Multiplication, Division
   (c) Parenthesis, Exponentiation, Multiplication, Division, Addition, Subtraction
   (d) Addition, Subtraction, Multiplication, Division, Exponentiation, Parenthesis

3. Which set of parentheses is unnecessary in the following expression?
   = (3 * 5) + (7 / 2) – (6^2) * (36 *2)
   (a) (3 * 5)
   (b) (7 / 2)
   (c) (6^2)
   (d) (36 *2)
   (e) All of the above

4. Which statement about saving a query is true?
   (a) Data are extracted from the source table and saved in query form.
   (b) Data are duplicated from the source table and saved in query form.
   (c) Data created using expressions are saved when the query is saved, but the source data stays in the original table.
   (d) No data are saved in a query.

5. The Expression Builder icon may be found in the:
   (a) Manage group on the Databases Tools tab
   (b) Query Setup group on the Design tab
   (c) Database Management group on the Design tab
   (d) Design group on the Query Setup tab

6. Your database contains a Price field stored in the Products table and a Quantity field stored in the Orders table. You have created a query but forgot to add the Price field in the design. Now, you need to use the price field to calculate the total for the order. The correct syntax is:
   (a) OrderTotal:(Quantity)*(Products)!(Price)
   (b) OrderTotal=(Quantity)*(Products)!(Price)
   (c) OrderTotal:[Quantity]*[Products]![Price]
   (d) OrderTotal=[Quantity]*[Products]![Price]

7. Which of the following is true about a select query?
   (a) It may reference fields from more than one table or query.
   (b) It may reference fields from a table, but not a query.
   (c) It may reference fields from either a table or a query but not both.
   (d) It may reference fields from a form.

8. You correctly calculated a value for the OrderAmount using an expression. Now, you need to use the newly calculated value in another expression calculating sales tax. The most efficient method is to:
   (a) Run and save the query to make OrderAmount available as input to subsequent expressions.
   (b) Create a new query based on the query containing the calculated Order amount, and then calculate the sales tax in the new query.
   (c) Close the Access file, saving the changes when asked; reopen the file and reopen the query; calculate the sales tax.
   (d) Create a backup of the database, open the backup and the query, then calculate the sales tax.

9. If state law requires that wait staff be over age 21 to serve alcohol and you have a database that stores each employee's birthdate in the Employee table, which of the following is the proper syntax to identify the employees' year of birth.
   (a) Age:DatePart("yyyy",[Employee]![BirthDate])
   (b) Age=DatePart("yyyy",[Employee]![BirthDate])
   (c) Age:DatePart("yyyy",[BirthDate]![Employee])
   (d) Age=DatePart("yyyy",[BirthDate]![Employee])

...continued on Next Page

Multiple Choice Continued...

10. You want to add a Totals row in a query Datasheet view. Where will you find the Totals command?
    (a) In the Data group on the Home tab
    (b) In the Home group on the Data tab
    (c) In the Records group on the Home tab
    (d) In the Home group on the Records tab

11. Which statement about a Totals query is true?
    (a) A Totals query may contain only one descriptive field but several aggregating fields.
    (b) A Totals query may contain several descriptive fields but only one aggregating field.
    (c) A Totals query has a limit of only two fields, one descriptive field, and one aggregating field.
    (d) A Totals query can aggregate data, but to find a grand total, you must create a new query based on the Totals query and turn on the Total row in the new query.

12. You built a query expression and clicked Run. A parameter dialog box pops up on your screen. Which of the following actions is the most appropriate if you expected results to display and do not want to enter an individual value?
    (a) Click OK to make the parameter box go away.
    (b) Read the field name specified in the parameter box and look for that spelling in the calculated expression.
    (c) Type numbers in the parameter box and click OK.
    (d) Close the query without saving changes. Re-open it and try running the query again.

13. A query contains fields for StudentName and Address. You have created and run a query and are in Datasheet view examining the output. You notice a spelling error on one of the student's names. You correct the error in the query Datasheet view.
    (a) The name is correctly spelled in this query but will be misspelled in the table and all other queries based on the table.
    (b) The name is correctly spelled in the table and in all queries based on the table.
    (c) The name is correctly spelled in this query and any other queries, but will remain misspelled in the table.
    (d) You cannot edit data in a query.

14. Which of the following is not available as an aggregate function within a query?
    (a) Sum
    (b) Min
    (c) Division
    (d) Avg

15. Which of the following is not true about the rows in the query design grid?
    (a) The Total row can contain different functions for different fields.
    (b) The Total row can source fields stored in different tables.
    (c) The Total row is located between the Table and Sort rows.
    (d) The Total row can be applied only to numeric fields.

Practice Exercises

1 Comfort Insurance—Salaries and Bonuses

The Comfort Insurance Agency is a midsized company with offices located across the country. Each employee receives a performance review annually. The review determines employee eligibility for salary increases and the annual performance bonus. The employee data are stored in an Access database, which is used by the human resource department to monitor and maintain employee records. Your task is to calculate the salary increase for each employee and his or her performance bonuses (if any). You are the human resource department manager. If you correctly calculate the employee salaries and bonuses, you will receive a bonus. Work carefully and check the accuracy of the calculations. This project follows the same set of skills as used in Hands-On Exercises 1 and 2 in this chapter. The instructions are less detailed to give you a chance to practice your skills. If you have problems, reread the detailed directions presented in the chapter. Compare your results to Figure 3.22.

a. Copy the partially completed file *chap3_pe1_insurance* to your production folder. Rename it **chap3_pe1_insurance_solution**, open the file, and enable security.

b. Click the **Database Tools tab**, and then click **Relationships** in the Show/Hide group. Examine the table structure, relationships, and fields. Once you are familiar with the database, close the Relationships window.

c. Click the **Create tab** and click **Query Wizard** in the Other group. Select **Simple Query Wizard** in the first screen of the dialog box. Click **OK**.

d. From the **Employees table** select the **LastName**, **FirstName**, **Performance**, and **Salary** fields to add fields to the query. From the **Titles table** select the **2008Increase** field. Click **Next**. This needs to be a detail query. Name the query **YourName Raises and Bonuses**. Click **Finish**.

e. Right-click the query window title bar or the Query tab and select **Design View** from the shortcut menu to switch to Design view.

f. Position the insertion point in the first blank column in the Field row. Type **NewSalary:[Salary]*[2008Increase]+[Salary]** to create an expression.

g. Click **Run** in the Results group on the Design tab to run the query. (If you receive the Enter Parameter Value dialog box, check your expression carefully for typos.) Look at the output in the Datasheet view. Verify that your answers are correct. If they are, use the Property Sheet window to format the **NewSalary** field as **Currency** and save the query.

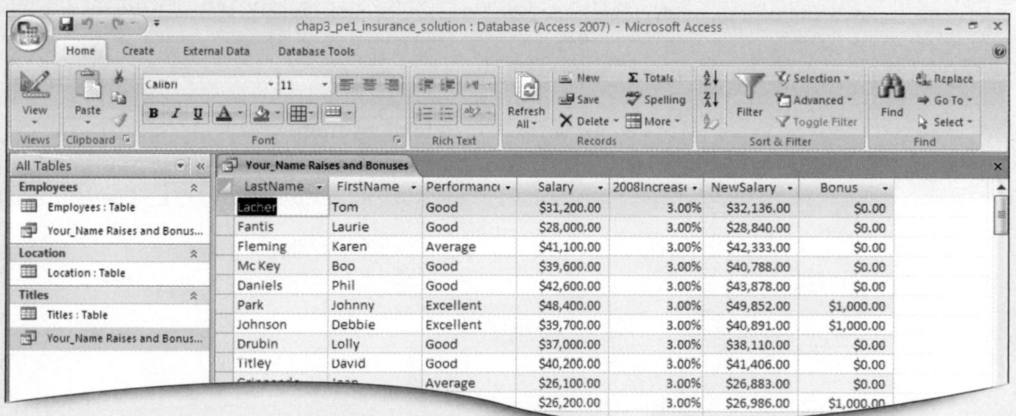

Figure 3.22 Raises and Bonuses

...continued on Next Page

h. Return to Design view. Position the insertion point in the first blank column in the Field row. Click **Builder** in the Query Setup group on the Design tab. In the **left column**, open the folder for **functions**. Open the **Built-In Functions** folder. Scroll the **right column** to locate the **IIf function**. Double-click to insert the function.

i. Double-click **<<expr>>** and replace it with **[Performance] = "Excellent"**; double-click **<<truepart>>** and replace it with **1000**; double-click **<<falsepart>>** and replace it with **0**. (That is zero, not the letter O.)

j. Run the query. Return to the Design view and double-click **Expr1** in the field row of the last column. Type **Bonus**. Format the field as Currency. Run and save the query. Close the database.

2 Comfort Insurance—Vacation

The Comfort Insurance Agency is a midsized company with offices located across the country. The human resource office is located in the home office in Miami. Each year, each employee receives a performance review. The review determines employee eligibility for salary increases and the annual performance bonus. The employee data are stored in an Access database. This database is used by the human resource department to monitor and maintain employee records. Your task is to calculate the salary increase for each employee, the number of years they have worked for the firm, and the number of vacation days they are eligible to receive. You are the human resource department manager. If you correctly calculate the employee salaries and vacations, you will receive a bonus. Work carefully and check the accuracy of the calculations. This project follows the same set of skills as used in Hands-On Exercises 1 and 2 in this chapter. The instructions are less detailed to give you a chance to practice your skills. If you have problems, feel free to reread the detailed directions presented in the chapter. Compare your results to Figure 3.23.

a. Copy the partially completed file *chap3_pe2_insurance.accdb* to your production folder. Rename it **chap3_pe2_insurance_solution.accdb**, open the copied file, and enable the security content.

b. Click the **Database Tools tab**, and then click **Relationships** in the Show/Hide group. Examine the table structure, relationships, and fields. Once you are familiar with the database, close the Relationships window.

c. Create a new query using the Query Wizard. Click the **Create tab** and click **Query Wizard** in the Other group. Select **Simple Query Wizard** in the first screen of the dialog box. Click **OK**.

d. Add fields to the query. From the **Employees table** select the **LastName**, **FirstName**, **HireDate**, and **Salary** fields. From the **Titles table**, select the **2008Increase** field. Click **Next**. This needs to be a detail query. Name the query **Your_Name Raises and Tenure**. Click **Finish**.

e. Switch to Design view by right-clicking the query window tab and selecting **Design View** from the shortcut menu.

f. Position the insertion point in the first blank column in the Field row. Create an expression by typing **2008Raise:[Salary]*[2008Increase]**. Format it as **Currency**.

...continued on Next Page

g. Click **Run** in the Results group on the Design tab. Look at the output in the Datasheet view. Verify that your answers are correct. If they are, save the query.

h. Return to Design view. Position the insertion point in the first blank column in the Field row. Click **Builder** in the Query Setup group on the Design tab. In the left column, open the folder for functions. Open the Built-In Functions folder. Scroll the right column to locate the **DatePart** function. Double-click to insert the function to the work area.

i. Double-click <<*interval*>> in the function in the work area of the Expression Builder dialog box. Type **"yyyy"**. Double-click <<*date*>> and replace it with **[HireDate]**. Delete the rest of the arguments and commas but do not delete the closing parenthesis. Your expression should look like this:

   DatePart ("yyyy", [HireDate])

j. Run and verify the output. Return to Design view and replace Expr1 in the field row of the last column with **YearHired**. Save the query.

k. Use the Expression Builder or type to create an expression that measures how long each employee has worked. Assume that this year is 2008. The finished expression will look like this:

   YearsWorked:2008 – [YearHired]

l. Run and save the query. Sort the output in descending order by the YearsWorked field. Save the query and close the database.

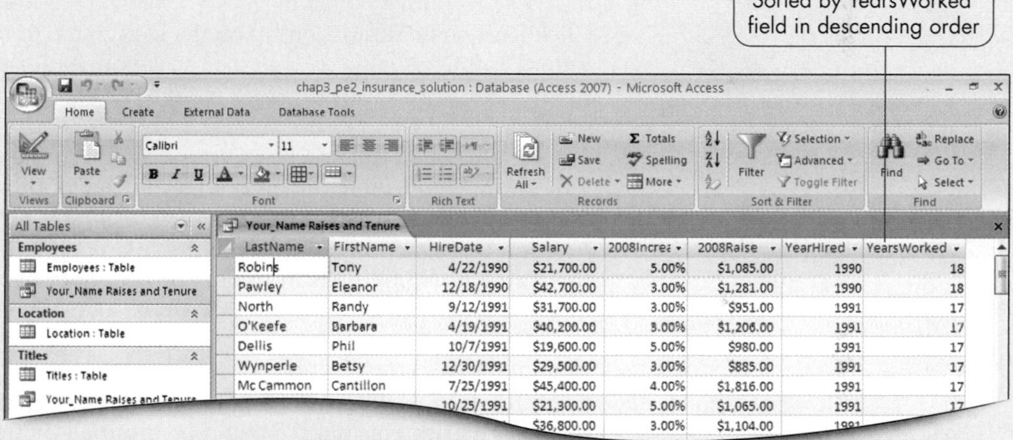

Figure 3.23 Raises and Tenure

3 Northwind Traders

Northwind Traders is a small, international, specialty food company. It sells products in eight different divisions: beverages, confections (candy), condiments, dairy products, grains and cereals, meat and poultry, produce, and seafood. The company offers discounts to some customers. Different customers receive differing discount amounts. The firm purchases merchandise from a variety of suppliers. All of the order and inventory information is stored in the company's database. This database is used by the marketing department to monitor and maintain sales records. You are the marketing manager. Your task is to determine the revenue from each order and to summarize the revenue figures by product category. This project follows the same set of skills as used in Hands-On Exercises 2 and 3 in this chapter. The instructions are less detailed to give you a chance to practice your skills. If you have problems, feel free to reread the detailed directions presented in the chapter. Compare your results to Figure 3.24.

...continued on Next Page

a. Copy the partially completed file *chap3_pe3_traders.accdb* to your production folder. Rename it **chap3_pe3_traders_solution.accdb**, open the file, and enable the content.
b. Click the **Database Tools tab**, and then click **Relationships** in the Show/Hide group. Examine the table structure, relationships, and fields. After you are familiar with the database, close the Relationships window.
c. Click the **Create tab** and click **Query Wizard** in the Other group. Select **Simple Query Wizard** in the first screen of the dialog box. Click **OK**.
d. From the **Order Details table**, select the **Quantity** and **Discount** fields to add the fields to the query. From the **Products table**, select the **UnitPrice** and **ProductCost** fields. From the **Categories table**, select the **CategoryName** Field. Click **Next**. This needs to be a detail query. Name the query **Your_Name Revenue**. Click **Finish**.

   The UnitPrice field contains data on what customers pay to purchase the products. The ProductCost field contains data on what the company pays suppliers to purchase the products.
e. Right-click the query window tab and select **Design View** from the shortcut menu to switch to Design view.
f. Position the insertion point in the first blank column in the Field row. Create an expression that calculates revenue. Some customers receive discounts on their orders so you need to calculate the discounted price in the expression that calculates revenue.

   Revenue:[UnitPrice] * (1 – [Discount]) * [Quantity]
g. Click **Run** in the Results group on the Design tab to run the query. (If you receive the Enter Parameter Value dialog box, check your expression carefully for typos.) Look at the output in the Datasheet view. Verify that your answers are correct. Save the query, then close.
h. Click the **Create tab** and click **Query Design** in the Other group. Click the **Queries Tab** in the Show Table dialog box. Double-click the **Your_Name Revenue** query to add it to the design grid. Click **Close** in the Show Table dialog box.
i. Position the insertion point in the first blank column in the Field row. Double-click the **CategoryName** field in the list of available fields in the Your_Name Revenue query. Click the insertion point in the next available column in the field row. Double-click **Revenue** to add it to the grid. Click the insertion point in the next available column in the field row. Double-click **Discount** to add it to the grid.
j. Click **Totals** in the Show/Hide group on the Design tab. The Total row will turn on in the design grid. This query should be grouped by the **CategoryName** field. Click in the Total row of the **Revenue** field to activate the drop down list and select **Sum**. Select **Avg** for the summary statistic in the **Discount** column.
k. Right-click the **Revenue** field name and select **Properties**. Click the box in the Property Sheet window to the right of **Format**. Select **Currency** from the drop down list to format the Revenue field as currency. With the Property Sheet Window still open, click the **Discount** field in the design grid. Click the box in the Property Sheet window to the right of **Format**. Select **Percent** from the drop-down list. Close the Property Sheet window by clicking the **X**.
l. Run the query. Verify the results. Name this query **Your_Name Revenue by Category**.
m. Close the database.

...continued on Next Page

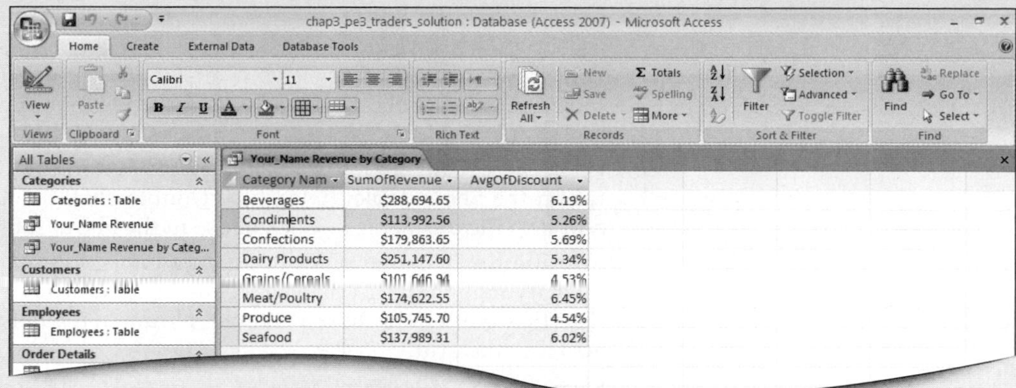

Figure 3.24 Revenue by Category

4 Member Rewards

The Prestige Hotel chain caters to upscale business travelers and provides state-of-the-art conference, meeting, and reception facilities. It prides itself on its international, four-star cuisines. Last year the chain began a member rewards club to help the marketing department track the purchasing patterns of its most loyal customers. All of the hotel transactions are stored in the database. Your task is to determine the revenue from each order and to summarize the revenue figures by location. This project follows the same set of skills as used in Hands-On Exercises 2 and 3 in this chapter. The instructions are less detailed to give you a chance to practice your skills. If you have problems, feel free to reread the detailed directions presented in the chapter. Compare your results to Figure 3.25.

a. Copy the partially completed file *chap3_pe4_memrewards.accdb* to your production folder. Rename it **chap3_pe4_memrewards_solution.accdb**, open the file, and enable the security content.
b. Click the **Database Tools tab**, and then click **Relationships** in the Show/Hide group. Examine the table structure, relationships, and fields. After you are familiar with the database, close the Relationships window.
c. Create a new query using the Query Wizard. Click the **Create tab** and click **Query Wizard** in the Other group. Select **Simple Query Wizard** in the first screen of the dialog box. Click **OK**.
d. Add fields to the query. From the **Location table**, select the **City**. From the **Orders table**, select the **NoInParty** Field. From the **Service table**, select the **PerPersonCharge** field. Click **Next.** This needs to be a detail query. Name the query **Your_Name Revenue**. Click **Finish**.
e. Right-click the query window tab and select **Design View** from the shortcut menu to Switch to Design view. Right-click **PerPersonCharge** and select **Properties** from the shortcut menu. Click the box to the right of **Format** in the Property Sheet. Select **Currency** from the drop-down. Click **X** to close the Property Sheet window.
f. Position the insertion point in the first blank column in the Field row. Create an expression that calculates revenue and format the field as **Currency**.

   Revenue:[NoInParty] * [PerPersonCharge]

...continued on Next Page

g. Click **Run** in the Results group on the Design tab. (If you receive the parameter dialog box, check your expression carefully for typos.) Look at the output in the Datasheet view. Verify that your answers are correct. If they are, return to Design view and format the **PerPersonCharge** and **Revenue** fields as **Currency** by setting the appropriate properties. Save and close the query.
h. Click the **Create tab** and click **Query Design** in the Other group. Click the **Queries tab** in the Show Table dialog box. Double-click the **Your_Name Revenue** query to add it to the design grid. Click **Close** in the Show Table dialog box.
i. Position the insertion point in the first blank column in the Field row. Double-click the **City** field in the list of available fields in the Your_Name Revenue query. Click the insertion point in the next available column in the field row. Double-click **Revenue** to add it to the grid.
j. Click **Totals** in the Show/Hide group on the Design tab. The Total row will turn on in the design grid. This query should be grouped by the **City** field. Click in the Total row of the **Revenue** field to activate the drop-down list and select **Sum**.
k. Right-click **Revenue** and select **Properties** from the shortcut menu. Click the box to the right of **Format** in the Property Sheet. From the drop down menu select **Currency**. Click **X** to close the Property Sheet window. Run the query.
l. Click the **Home tab** in Datasheet view. Click **Totals** in the Records group to turn on the Totals row. Click the **SumOfRevenue** column in the Total row. Click the drop-down arrow and select **Sum**.
m. Save this query as **Your_Name Revenue by City**.
n. Run and save the query. Close the database.

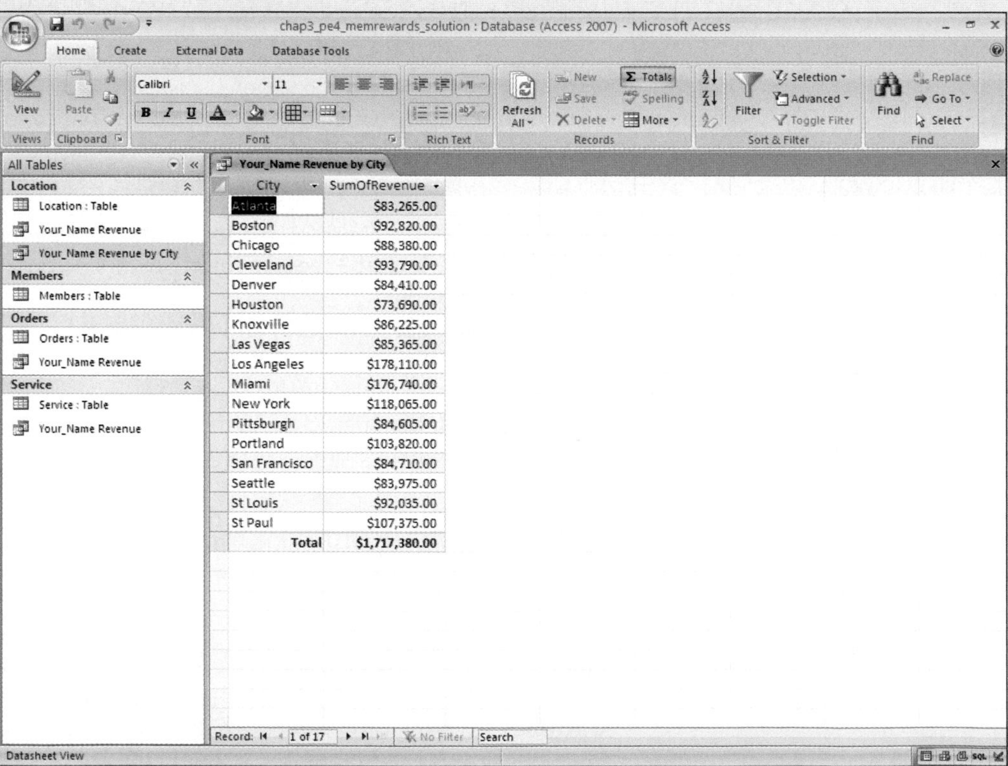

Figure 3.25 Revenue by City

Mid-Level Exercises

1 Calculating and Summarizing Specialty Food Data in a Query

Northwind Traders is a small, international, specialty food company. It sells products in eight different divisions: beverages, confections (candy), condiments, dairy products, grains and cereals, meat and poultry, produce, and seafood. Although most of its customers are restaurants and gourmet food shops, it has a few retail customers, too. The company offers discounts to some customers. Different customers receive differing discount amounts. The firm purchases merchandise from a variety of suppliers. All of the order information is stored in the company's database. This database is used by the finance department to monitor and maintain sales records. You are the finance manager. Your task is to determine the revenue and profit from each order and to summarize the revenue, profit, and discount figures by salesperson. *Revenue* is the money the firm takes in. *Profit* is the difference between revenue and costs. The salespeople may offer discounts to customers to reward loyal purchasing or to appease an angry customer when a shipment is late. Occasionally the sales people discount so deeply that the company loses money on an order, that is, the costs exceed the revenue. It is important that your calculations are correct. If the firm's profitability figures do not accurately reflect the firm's financial health, the employee's paychecks (including yours) might be returned as insufficient funds. Compare your results to Figure 3.26.

a. Locate the file named *chap3_mid1_traders.accdb*, copy it to your working folder, and rename it **chap3_mid1_traders_solution.accdb**. Open the file and enable the content. Open the **Employee table**. Find and replace **Margaret Peacock**'s name with **your name**. Close the table.

b. Create a detail query that you will use to calculate profits for each product ordered. You will need the **LastName** field from the **Employees table**. You will also need the fields for **Quantity**, **Discount**, **OrderDate**, **ShippedDate**, **UnitPrice**, and **ProductCost**. Save the query as **Your_Name Profit**.

c. In Design view, calculate **Revenue** and **Profit**. Because the discounts vary, some (not all) of the profit numbers will be negative. You must factor the discount into the price as you calculate revenue. If a product price (UnitPrice) is $100 and is sold with a 20% discount, the discounted price would be $80. Calculate **revenue** by multiplying the discounted price by the quantity sold. Calculate **total costs** by multiplying the product cost by quantity. Calculate **profit** by subtracting total cost from revenue. UnitPrice is the price for which the company sells merchandise. ProductCost is what the company pays to purchase the merchandise.

d. Save and close the query.

e. Create a **Totals query** based on **Your_Name Profit**. Group by **LastName** and summarize the fields for **Discount (average)**, **Revenue**, and **Profit (sums)**.

f. Format the **Discount** field as a percentage and the **SumOfRevenue** and **SumOfProfit** fields as currency.

g. Add a Total row to the Datasheet view. Average the discount field and sum the **SumOfRevenue** and **SumOfProfit** fields.

h. Save the totals query as **Your_Name Profit by Employee**.

i. Capture a screenshot of the Your_Name Profit by Employee query. Have it open on your computer and press **PrintScrn**. Open Word and press **Ctrl+V** or click **Paste** in the Clipboard group. Save the Word document as **chap3_mid1_solution**. Print the Word document. Close the Word document and close the database.

...continued on Next Page

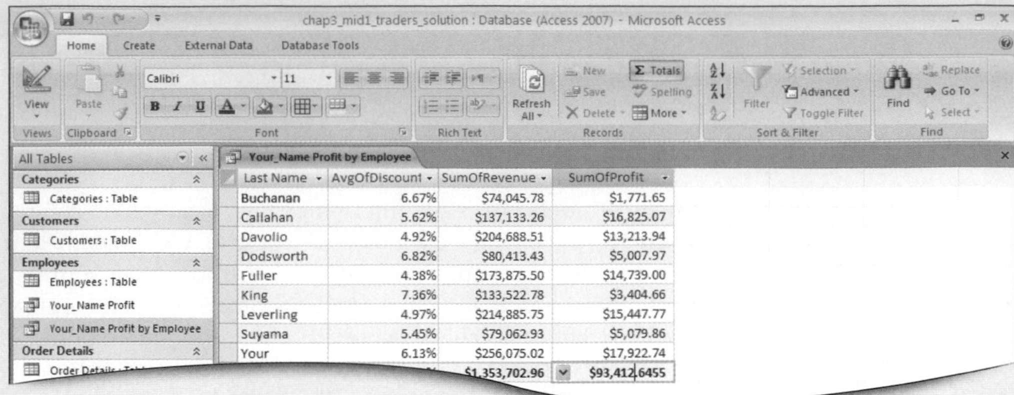

Last Name	AvgOfDiscount	SumOfRevenue	SumOfProfit
Buchanan	6.67%	$74,045.78	$1,771.65
Callahan	5.62%	$137,133.26	$16,825.07
Davolio	4.92%	$204,688.51	$13,213.94
Dodsworth	6.82%	$80,413.43	$5,007.97
Fuller	4.38%	$173,875.50	$14,739.00
King	7.36%	$133,522.78	$3,404.66
Leverling	4.97%	$214,885.75	$15,447.77
Suyama	5.45%	$79,062.93	$5,079.86
Your	6.13%	$256,075.02	$17,922.74
		$1,353,702.96	$93,412.6455

Figure 3.26 Profit by Employee

2 Calculating and Summarizing Bank Data in a Query

You are the manager of the loan department of the National Bank. Several customers have multiple loans with your institution. A single customer might have a mortgage loan, one or more car loans, and a home improvement loan. You need to monitor the total indebtedness of your customers to help them manage their debt load. Your task is to use the information stored in the database to calculate the loan payments for each loan and then to summarize the loans by customer. The PMT function requires five arguments. The first is the interest rate per period. The interest rates in the table are annual rates, so you will need to convert them to monthly rates in the function. The second argument is the number of periods (in years). Because the payments are monthly, you also need to convert the years for each loan to months in the function. The next argument is the PV, the present value of the loan—what the loan is worth today. It tells you how much each customer has borrowed. You generally supply zeros for the last two arguments, FV, and Type. FV shows the amount the borrower will owe after the last payment has been made—the future value of the monies borrowed. Generally this is zero. The type argument tells Access whether the payment is made at the beginning or the end of the period (month). Most loans accept payments and charge interest on the unpaid balance throughout the period. Use zero as the argument for this function. See Table 3.2 for more information about the arguments to the PMT function. Compare your results to Figure 3.27.

a. Locate the file named *chap3_mid2_nationalbank.accdb*, copy it to your working folder, and rename it **chap3_mid2_nationalbank_solution.accdb**. Open the file and enable the content. Open the **Customers table**. Find and replace **Michelle Zacco's** name with your name.

b. Create a detail query that you will use to calculate the payments for each loan. You will need the following fields: **LastName**, **Amount**, **InterestRate**, **Term**, and **Type**. Save the query as **Your_Name Payment**.

...continued on Next Page

c. In Design view, use the **Pmt** function to calculate the loan payment on each loan. Divide the annual interest rate by 12 and multiply the loan's term by 12 because every year has 12 months. Include a minus sign in front of the loan amount in the expression so the result returns a positive value. The last two arguments will be zero.

d. In the Datasheet view, add a Total row. Use it to calculate the **average** interest rate and the **sum** for the **payment**.

e. Create a Totals query based on Your_Name Loan Payment. **Group by LastName** and summarize the **sum** of the **Payment** field.

f. Format the **SumOfPayment** field as currency.

g. Add a total row to the Datasheet view that will sum the Payments. Save this query as **Your_Name Payment Summary**.

h. Capture a screenshot of the Payment Summary query. Have it open on your computer and press **PrintScrn**. Open Word and press **Ctrl+V** or click **Paste** in the Clipboard group. Save the Word document as **chap3_mid2_solution**. Print the Word document displaying the screenshot. Close the Word document and close the database.

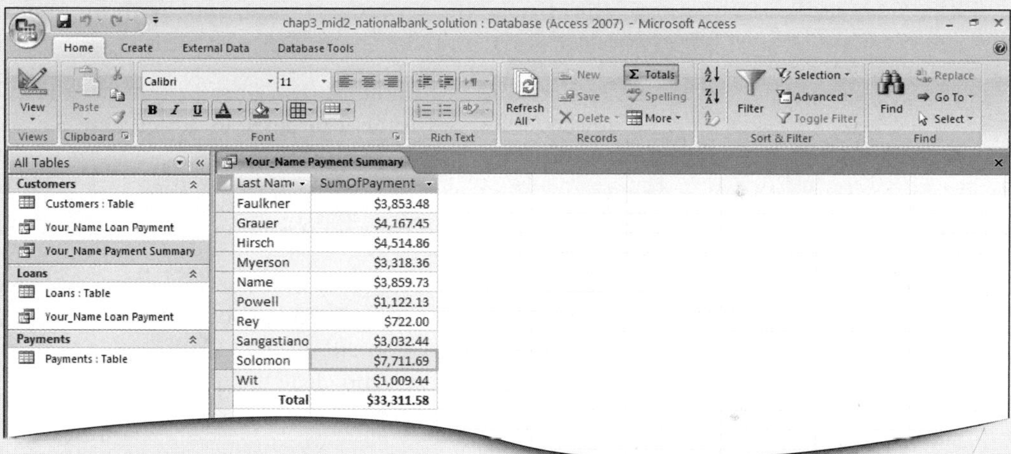

Figure 3.27 Payment Summary

3 Calculating and Summarizing Data in a Query, Working with Dates

You are the senior partner in a large, independent real estate firm that specializes in home sales. Although you still represent buyers and sellers in real estate transactions, you find that most of your time is spent supervising the agents who work for your firm. This fact distresses you because you like helping people buy and sell homes. Your firm has a database containing all of the information on the properties your firm has listed. You believe that by using the data in the database more effectively, you can spend less time supervising the other agents and spend more time doing the part of your job that you like doing the best. Your task is to determine the length of time each sold property was on the market prior to sale. Then calculate the commission from each property sale. Most real estate transactions involve two agents—one representing the seller (the listing agent) and the other the buyer (the selling agent). The two agents share the commission. Finally, you need to summarize the sales data by employee and calculate the average number of days each employee's sales were on the market prior to selling and the total commission earned by the employees. Compare your results to Figure 3.28.

a. Locate the file named *chap3_mid3_realestate.accdb*, copy it to your working folder, and rename it **chap3_mid3_realestate_solution.accdb**. Open the file and enable the content. Open the **Agents table**. Find and replace **Pa Lor**'s name with your name.

...continued on Next Page

b. Create a detail query that you will use to calculate the number of days each sold property has been on the market prior to sale. You will need the following fields: **LastName**, **DateListed**, **DateSold**, **SalePrice**, **SellingAgent**, **ListingAgent**, and **Subdivision**. Save the query as **Your_Name Sales Report**.

c. In Design view, build an expression, **DaysOnMarket**, to calculate the number of days each sold property has been on the market prior to sale. Subtract the **DateListed** field from the **DateSold** field. [Hint: The answers will *never* be negative numbers!]

d. Calculate the **Commission** for the selling and listing agents. Multiply the **SalePrice** by the Commission rate of **3.5%**. Name the newly created fields **SellComm** and **ListComm**. Both fields contain the same expression. They need to be named differently so that the proper agent—the listing agent or the selling agent—gets paid.

e. After you are sure that your calculations are correct, save the query. In Datasheet view, add a total row. Use it to calculate the average number of days on the market and the sums for the **SalePrice**, **SellComm**, and **ListComm** fields. Format the **SellComm**, **ListComm**, and **SalePrice** fields as **Currency**.

f. Create a Totals query based on **Your_Name Sales Report**. Group by **LastName** and summarize the **DaysOnMarket** field with an **average**. Summarize the **SalePrice**, **SellComm**, and **ListComm** fields as **sums**.

g. Add a Total row to the Datasheet view that will sum the price and commission fields and average the number of days on the market. Save this query as **Your_Name Sales Summary**.

h. Format the **AveOfDaysOnMkt** field so that it displays only two decimal places. Format the remaining numeric fields as Currency.

i. Capture a screenshot of the Sales Summary query. Have it open on your computer and press **PrintScrn**. Open Word and press **Ctrl+V** or click **Paste** in the Clipboard group. Save the Word document as **chap3_mid3_solution**. Print the Word document. Close the Word document and close the database.

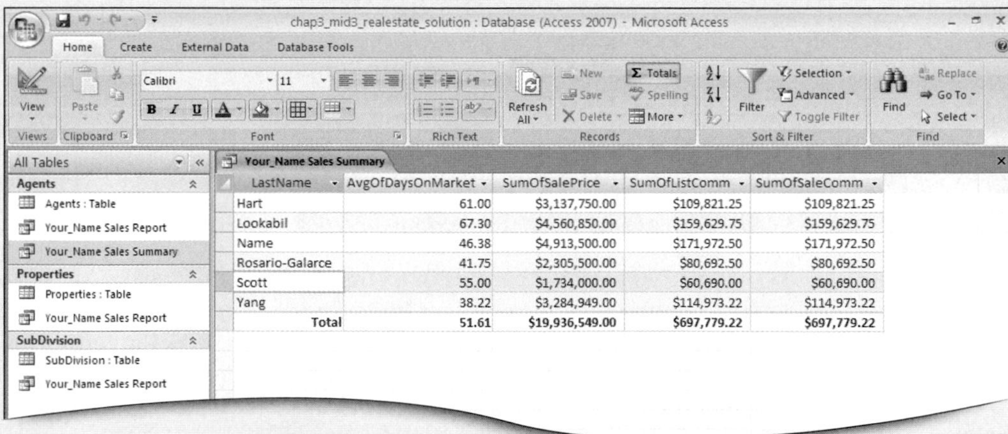

LastName	AvgOfDaysOnMarket	SumOfSalePrice	SumOfListComm	SumOfSaleComm
Hart	61.00	$3,137,750.00	$109,821.25	$109,821.25
Lookabil	67.30	$4,560,850.00	$159,629.75	$159,629.75
Name	46.38	$4,913,500.00	$171,972.50	$171,972.50
Rosario-Galarce	41.75	$2,305,500.00	$80,692.50	$80,692.50
Scott	55.00	$1,734,000.00	$60,690.00	$60,690.00
Yang	38.22	$3,284,949.00	$114,973.22	$114,973.22
Total	51.61	$19,936,549.00	$697,779.22	$697,779.22

Figure 3.28 Sales Summary

Capstone Exercise

Your boss expressed a concern about shipping delays. She believes that customers are not receiving the products they order in a timely fashion. Because your firm's reputation as a provider of high-quality customer service is at risk, she asks that you investigate the sales and shipping records for the last six months and report what you have discovered. In addition, the sales staff is permitted to discount the prices for some customers. Your boss is worried that the discounting erodes profits. She wants you to identify the sales staff who discount the most deeply.

Database File Setup

You need to copy an original database file, rename the copied file, and then open the copied database to complete this capstone exercise. After you open the copied database, you will replace an existing employee's name with your name.

a. Locate the file named *chap3_cap_traders.accdb* and copy it to your production folder.
b. Rename the copied file as **chap3_cap_traders_solution.accdb**.
c. Open the *chap3_cap_traders_solution.accdb* file and enable the content.
d. Open the **Employees table**.
e. Find and replace *Margaret Peacock's* name with your name.

Sales Report Query

You need to create a detail query to calculate the number of days between the date an order was placed and the date the order was shipped for each order. You also need the query to determine the amount of a discount, calculate the revenue, calculate the total cost, and calculate the profit. Furthermore, the query should calculate the employee's commission on the sale.

a. Set a criterion that limits the query to only the most recent six months' worth of shipped orders.
b. Sort the records in the datasheet view by order date to determine the most recent order, if you want.
c. Include the following fields: **LastName** (from the Employee Table), **OrderDate**, **ShippedDate**, **UnitPrice**, **ProductCost**, **Quantity**, and **Discount**.
d. Save the query as **Your_Name Sales Report**.
e. Build an expression, DaysToShip, to calculate the number of days taken to fill each order. Subtract the OrderDate field from the ShippedDate field. (Hint: The answers will never be negative numbers.)
f. Calculate the profit for each product ordered. Multiply the UnitPrice by the Discount to determine the amount of the discount. Then subtract the Discount amount from the UnitPrice and multiply the result by Quantity to calculate Revenue. Calculate TotalCost for each item ordered by multiplying ProductCost by Quantity. Subtract TotalCost from Revenue to calculate Profit.
g. Calculate the Commission for each profitable order. When the profit on the ordered item is positive, calculate Commission by multiplying profit by the commission rate of 3.5%. If the profit on the ordered item is negative (a loss), the salesperson receives no commission. Name the newly created field Commission.
h. Verify that the query calculations are correct and save the query.
i. In Datasheet view, add a total row to calculate the average number of DaysToShip and the sums for the Revenue, TotalCost, Profit, and Commission fields. Format the Revenue, TotalCost, Profit, and Commission fields as currency.

Totals Query

You need to create a totals query based on the Your_Name Sales Report query. You will group the totals query by last name to provide aggregate statistics that summarize each salesperson's performance and income. It also will provide the average number of days each salesperson's orders take to ship. Compare your results to Figure 3.28.

a. Create a **Totals** query based on Your_Name Sales Report. Group by **LastName** and summarize the **DaysToShip** field with an average. Summarize the **Revenue**, **TotalCost**, **Profit**, and **Commission** fields as sums. Format the Revenue, TotalCost, Profit, and Commission fields as currency.
b. Add a Total row to the Datasheet view that will sum the Revenue, TotalCost, Profit, and Commission fields and average the DaysToShip field.
c. Save this query as **Your_Name Shipping and Commission**.
d. Capture a screenshot of the Sales Summary query. Open the query on your computer and press **PrintScrn**. Open Microsoft Word and press **Ctrl+V** or click **Paste**. Save the Word document as **chap3_cap_solution**. Print the Word document.
e. Close the Word document and close the database.

...continued on Next Page

Mini Cases

Use the rubric following the case as a guide to evaluate your work, but keep in mind that your instructor may impose additional grading criteria or use a different standard to judge your work.

Vacation Time for Bank Employees

GENERAL CASE

The *chap3_mc1_safebank.accdb* file contains data from a small bank. Copy the *chap3_mc1_safebank.accdb* file to your working storage folder, name it **chap3_mc1_safebank_solution.accdb**, and open the copied file. Use the skills from this chapter to perform several tasks. The bank's employee policy states that an employee is eligible for three weeks of vacation after two years of employment. Before two full years, the employee may take two weeks of vacation. The Branch table stores the start date of each manager. You need to figure out how long each manager has worked for the bank. Once you have done that, you need to calculate the number of weeks of vacation the manager is eligible to enjoy. Set these calculations up so that when the query is opened in the future (for example, tomorrow, a month, or two years from now), the length of service and vacation values will update automatically. Summarize each customer's account balances. This summary should list the customer's name and a total of all account balances.

Performance Elements	Exceeds Expectations	Meets Expectations	Below Expectations
Create query	All necessary and no unneeded fields included.	All necessary fields included but also unnecessary fields.	Not all necessary fields were included in the query.
Compute length of service	Calculations and methods correct.	Calculations correct but method inefficient.	Calculations incorrect and methods inefficient.
Compute vacation entitlement	Calculations and methods correct, updates automatically.	Calculations and methods correct but fail to update.	Calculations incorrect, methods inefficient, no updates.
Summarize balances	Correct method, correct totals.	Correct totals but inefficient method.	Totals incorrect or missing.

Combining Name Fields

RESEARCH CASE

This chapter introduced you to the power of using Access Expressions, but you have much more to explore. Use Access help to search for Expressions. Open and read the articles titled *Create an expression* and *A guide to expression syntax*. Put your new knowledge to the test. Copy any of the database files that you used in this chapter and rename the copy with the prefix, **chap3_mc2**. For example, if you copy the safebank database, the file name should be **chap3_mc2_description_solution.accdb**. Open the file. Find a table that stores names in two fields: FirstName and LastName. Add your name to the table. Your challenge is to figure out a way of combining the last and first name fields into one field that prints the last name, a comma, a space, and then the first name. Once you successfully combine the fields somewhere, alphabetize the list. Print it. Write your instructor a memo explaining how you accomplished this. Use a memo template in Word, your most professional writing style, and clear directions that someone could follow in order to accomplish this task. Attach the printout of the name list to the memo. Save the Word document as **chap3_mc2_solution**.

Performance Elements	Exceeds Expectations	Meets Expectations	Below Expectations
Use online help	Appropriate articles located and memo indicates comprehension.	Appropriate articles located but memo did not demonstrate comprehension.	Articles not found.
Prepare list of names	Printed list attached to memo in requested format.	Printed list is attached but the formatting has minor flaws.	List missing or incomprehensible.
Summarize and communicate	Memo clearly written and could be used as directions.	Memo text indicates some understanding but also weaknesses.	Memo missing or incomprehensible.
Aesthetics	Memo template correctly employed.	Template employed but signed in the wrong place or improperly used.	Memo missing or incomprehensible.

...continued on Next Page

Coffee Revenue Queries

DISASTER RECOVERY

A co-worker called you into his office and explained that he was having difficulty with Access 2007 and asked you to look at his work. Copy the *chap3_mc3_coffee.accdb* file to your working storage folder, name it **chap3_mc3_coffee_solution.accdb**, and open the file. It contains two queries, Your_Name Revenue and Your_Name Revenue by City. The Revenue query is supposed to calculate product Price (based on a markup percentage on Cost) and Revenue (the product of Price and Quantity). Something is wrong with the Revenue query. Your challenge is to find and correct the error(s). Your co-worker also tried to use the Revenue query as input for a Totals by City query that should show revenue by city. Of course, since the Revenue query doesn't work correctly, nothing based upon it will work, either. After correcting the Revenue query, create the Totals by City query. Run the queries. Display all of the Balance values as currency. Save the queries with your name and descriptive titles. Print the Datasheet view of the Totals by City query and turn the printout and file in to your instructor if instructed to do so.

Performance Elements	Exceeds Expectations	Meets Expectations	Below Expectations
Error identification	Correct identification and correction of all errors.	Correct identification of all errors and correction of some errors.	Errors neither located nor corrected.
Summary query	Correct grouping options and summarization selected.	Correct grouping but some summaries incorrectly selected.	Incorrect group by option selection.
Naming	Descriptive query name selected and employed.	Query name is only partially descriptive.	Query missing or default names used.

chapter 4 | **Access**

Create, Edit, and Perform Calculations in Reports

Creating Professional and Useful Reports

After you read this chapter, you will be able to:

1. Plan a report **(page 255)**.
2. Use different report views **(page 257)**.
3. Create and edit a report **(page 261)**.
4. Identify report elements, sections, and controls **(page 271)**.
5. Add grouping levels in Layout view **(page 274)**.
6. Add fields to a report **(page 279)**.
7. Use the Report Wizard **(page 289)**.

Hands-On Exercises

Exercises	Skills Covered
1. INTRODUCTION TO ACCESS REPORTS (page 263) **Open:** chap4_ho1-3_coffee.accdb and chap4_ho1-3_coffee.gif **Save as:** chap4_ho1-3_coffee_solution.accdb **Back up as:** chap4_ho1_coffee_solution.accdb	• Create a Report Using the Report Tool • Create and Apply a Filter in a Report • Remove Fields from a Report and Adjust Column Widths • Reposition Report Objects and Insert Graphic Elements in a Report • Use AutoFormat and Format Report Elements
2. CREATE, SORT, EDIT, NEST, AND REMOVE GROUPS FROM REPORTS (page 281) **Open:** chap4_ho1-3_coffee_solution.accdb (from Exercise 1) **Save as:** chap4_ho1-3_coffee_solution.accdb (additional modifications) **Back up as:** chap4_ho2_coffee_solution.accdb	• Sort a Report • Create a Grouped Report and Sort It • Add Additional Grouping Levels and Calculate Summary Statistics • Remove Grouping Levels • Reorder Grouping Levels
3. REPORT WIZARD (page 294) **Open:** chap4_ho1-3_coffee_solution.accdb (from Exercise 2) **Save as:** chap4_ho1-3_coffee_solution.accdb (additional modifications)	• Assemble the Report Data • Create a Query-Based Report and Add Grouping • Create Summary Statistics • Select Layout and AutoFormatting • Modify the Report

CASE STUDY

Northwind Traders

Northwind Traders is a small, international, specialty food company. It sells products in eight different divisions: beverages, confections (candy), condiments, dairy products, grains and cereals, meat and poultry, produce, and seafood. Although most of its customers are restaurants and gourmet food shops, it has a few retail customers, too. All of the order information is stored in the company's database. This database is used by the finance department to monitor and maintain sales records. You are the finance manager. Your task is to determine the revenue from each order and to summarize the first-quarter revenue for each month and by each category. You need only report on gross revenue—the total amount the firm receives. This report does not need to calculate any costs or expenses. It is important that you report accurately. Figure 4.1 presents a rough layout of the report. You must identify the source data, prepare a report, and group it to match the layout.

Case Study

Your Assignment

- Copy the file named *chap4_case_traders.accdb*. Rename the copy **chap4_case_traders_solution.accdb**. Open the copied file and enable the content.
- Locate and rename the Your Name Revenue query with your first and last name. Use this query as the source for your report. It contains all the needed fields for the report plus several fields you do not need.
- Create a report based on the Your Name Revenue query. Use any report creation method you learned about in the chapter.
- Add appropriate grouping levels to produce the output shown in Figure 4.1. Name the report **Your Name First Quarter Sales by Month and Category**. You may select formatting as you want, but the grouping layout should match the design shown.
- Print the completed report.
- Compact and repair the file.
- Back up the database.

Appearances Matter

By now, you know how to plan a database, create a table, establish relationships among table data, and extract, manipulate, and summarize data using queries. You generated output by printing table or query datasheets. If you look back at your earlier work, you will see that the information exists, but it is bland. You probably have worked in other application software sufficiently to wonder if Access can enhance the print files. Access provides a powerful tool, giving you the ability to organize and present selected data clearly. Most of the printed output generated by Access users comes from reports.

Enhanced data improves the functionality of database information. Just as in the other Microsoft Office applications, you can change the size, style, and placement of printed matter. You may highlight portions of output to call attention to them. You may also add graphs, pictures, or charts to help the report reader more easily convert the database data into useful information. Designing and producing clear, functional, and organized reports facilitates decision-making. Report production begins with planning the report's design.

In this section, you plan reports. First, you create reports using the Report Tool, and then you edit the report by using the Layout view.

Planning a Report

A ***report*** is a printed document that displays information from a database.

A ***report*** is a printed document that displays information from a database in a manner that provides clear information to managers. You can design a report to create a catalog, a telephone directory, a financial statement, a graph showing sales by month, a shipping label, or a letter to customers reminding them about a past due payment. All documents you create using table data are Access reports. You should carefully consider what information you need and how you can optimally present it. Access provides powerful tools to help you accomplish this goal. However, if you do not take the time to plan the report in advance, the power of the tools may impede the report process. You should think through what elements you need and how they should be arranged on the printed page prior to launching the software. The time invested planning the report's appearance at the start of the process leads to fewer surprises with the end result. The report plan helps you take charge of the computer instead of the computer controlling you.

The report plan helps you take charge of the computer instead of the computer controlling you.

Draw a Paper Design

The most important tool you use to create an Access report may be a pencil. If you sketch your desired output before touching the mouse, you will be happier with the results. As you sketch, you must ask a number of questions.

- What is the purpose of the report?
- Who uses this report?
- What elements, including labels and calculations, need to be included? What formulae will produce accurate results?
- Will the results be sensitive or confidential? If so, does there need to be a warning printed on the report?
- How will the report be distributed? Will users pull the information directly from Access or will they receive it through e-mail, a fax, the Internet, Word, or Excel?

Sketch the report layout on paper. Identify the field names, their locations, their placement on the page, and other design elements as you sketch. Figure 4.1 provides a sample report layout.

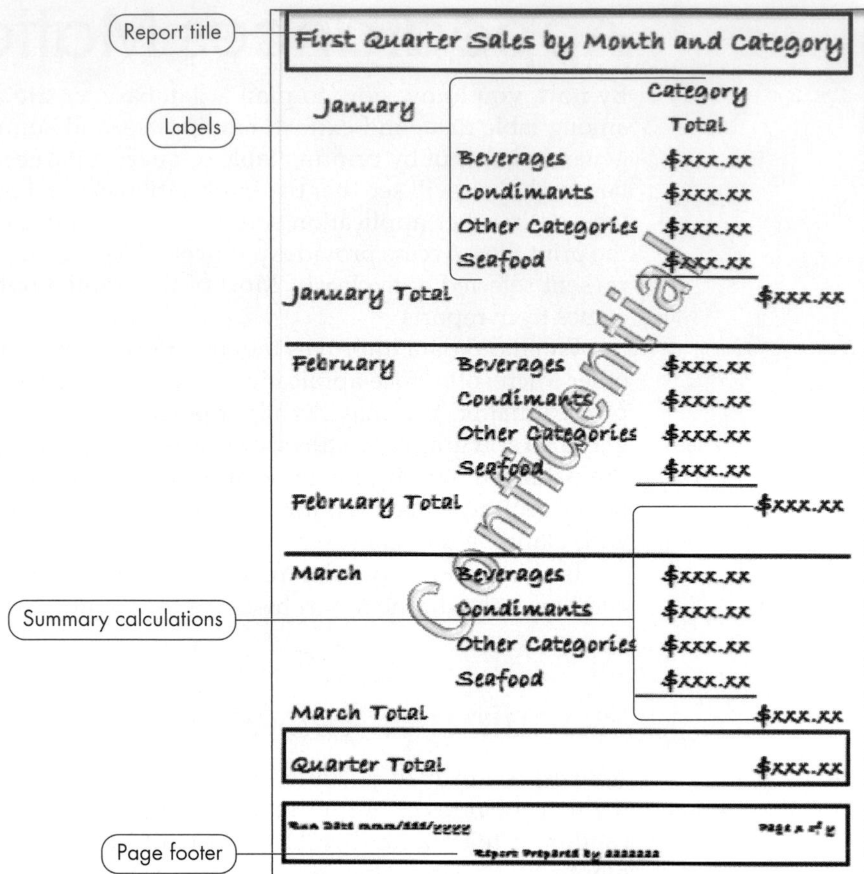

Figure 4.1 Report Plan

Identify Data Sources

In the next step of planning your report, you need to identify the data source(s) of each report element. You may use one or more tables, queries, or a combination of tables and queries as the report's source. Occasionally, a single table or query contains all of the records you need for the report. Typically, however, you need to specify several tables. When multiple tables are needed to create a report, you may assemble all necessary data in a single query, and then base the report on that query. Reports frequently contain graphics as well as data. As you identify the sources of report input, you also need to specify the graphic source. Frequently, a company logo on an invoice or a watermark, indicating that the material is confidential or proprietary, is printed on the report.

Select a Reporting Tool

Access gives you several tools to facilitate report creation. Which one you select depends on the data source and complexity of the report design. Table 4.1 summarizes the available tools and their usage.

Table 4.1 Report Tools, Location, and Usage

Report Tool	Location	Data Source	Output Complexity
Report Tool	Create Tab, Reports Group, Reports command	Single table or query	Limited. This creates a report showing all of the fields in the data source.
Report Wizard	Create Tab, Reports Group, Report Wizard command	Single or multiple tables or queries or a mixture of tables and queries	More sophisticated. Include (or exclude) fields. Add grouping and sorting instructions. Choose between detailed or summary data presentation.
Label Wizard	Create Tab, Reports Group, Labels command	Single or multiple tables or queries or a mixture of tables and queries	Limited. This feature only produces mailing labels (or name badges) but does so formatted to fit a variety of commercially available mailing labels. The output displays in multiple columns only in Print Preview. Filterable to exclude records.
Blank Report	Create Tab, Reports Group, Blank Report command	Single or multiple tables or queries or a mixture of tables and queries	Limited and extremely complex. Use to quickly assemble a few fields from multiple tables without stepping through the wizard. Alternatively, use to customize the most sophisticated reports with complex grouping levels and sorts.

Using Different Report Views

You have worked with Datasheet and Design views of tables and queries to perform different tasks. For example, you cannot perform data entry in an Access table in Design view, nor can you establish query criteria in Datasheet view. Similarly, Access 2007 provides different views of your report. You view and edit the report using different views depending on what you need to accomplish. Because Access reports may be more sophisticated than queries or tables, you have more views available. Each view accommodates different actions.

Use Print Preview

The ***Print Preview*** displays the report as it will be printed.

The ***Print Preview*** displays the report exactly as it will appear on the printed output. You may look at or print your reports in this view, but you cannot edit the report data. You may specify which pages to print in the Print dialog box. The default value will print all pages in the report. Figure 4.2 shows an Access report in Print Preview.

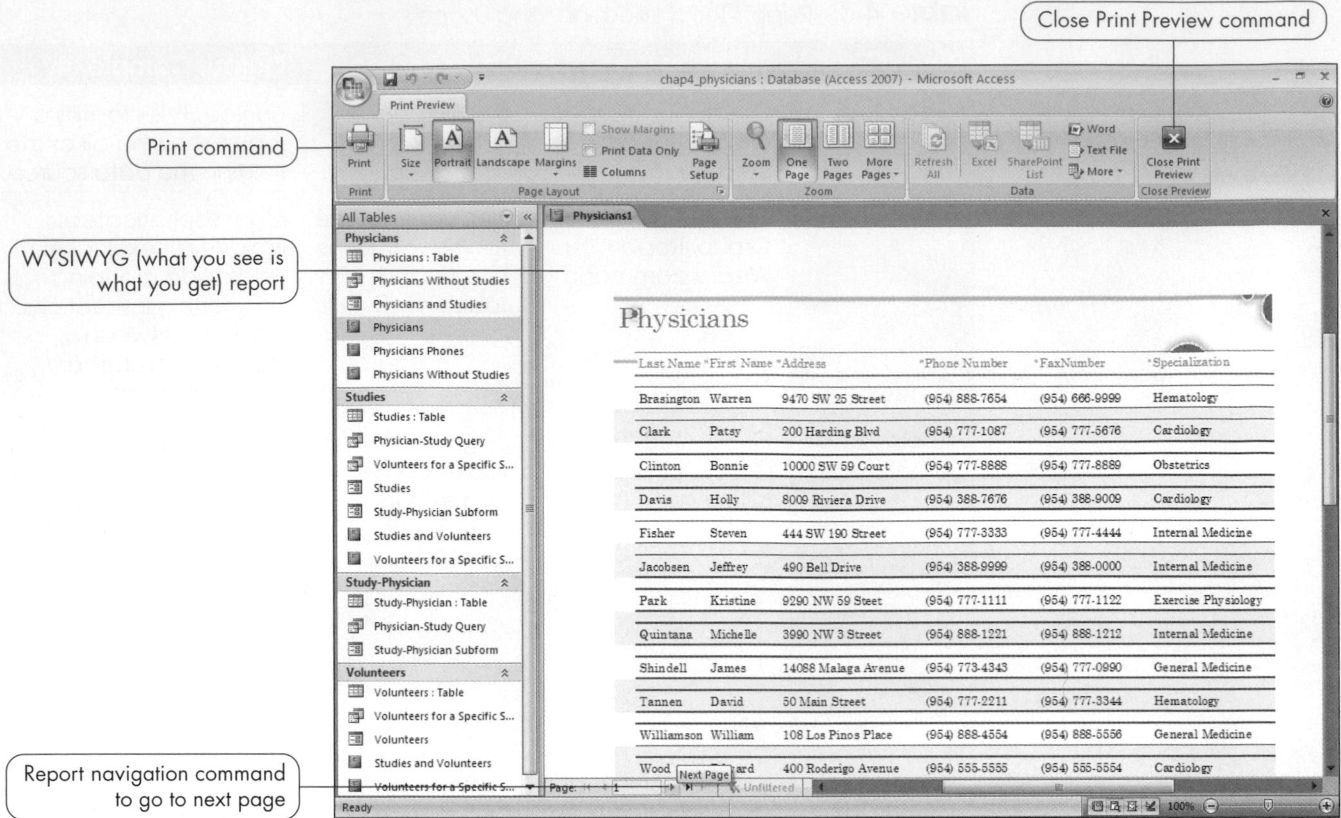

Figure 4.2 Print Preview of an Access Report

TIP Always Preview Access Reports Prior to Printing

Because databases contain a great deal of information, Access reports may become very long and may require many pages to print. Experienced Access users **always** preview their work and go to the last page of the report by using the navigation commands. Although some reports require hundreds of pages to print, many that have multiple pages may be reformatted to print on one or a few pages. The rule is preview before printing.

View and Interact with Data in Report View

Use the ***Report view*** to make temporary changes to data while viewing it as it will print.

The second way to view Access reports, the ***Report view***, provides you the ability to see what the printed report will look like and to make temporary changes to how the data are viewed. You can identify portions of the output by applying a filter. For example, if you need a list of physicians practicing Internal Medicine, you can right-click the record value and select the appropriate filtering option, *equals Internal Medicine*, from the shortcut menu. All of the other types of physicians are hidden temporarily (see Figure 4.3). If you print the filtered report, the printout will not show the hidden records. When you close and open a filtered report again, the filter disappears and all records appear in Report view. You may reapply the filter to reproduce the filtered results. The Report view permits you to copy selected formatted records to the Clipboard and paste them in other applications. Even when the security controls on the report have been tightly set by the database administrator, this view gives the report user a measure of customization and interactivity with the data.

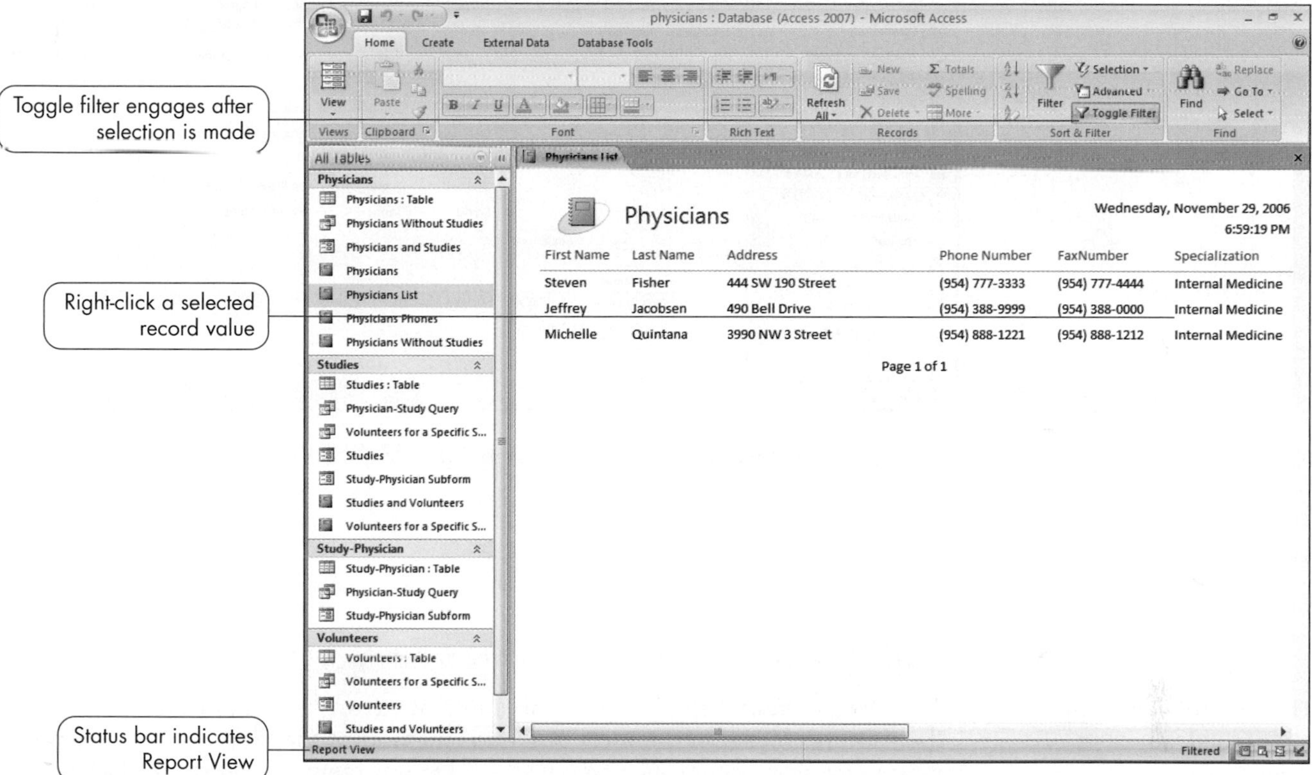

Figure 4.3 Filtered Report Output Shown in Report View

Modify Reports in Layout View

Use the ***Layout view*** to alter the report design while viewing the data.

The third (and perhaps the most useful) report view is the Layout view. Use the ***Layout view*** to alter the report design while viewing the data. You should use Layout view to add or delete fields to the report, modify field control properties, change the column widths or row height to ensure that the entire field displays without truncation, add grouping and sorting levels to a report, or to filter reported data to extract only specific records. Although the display appears as what you see is what you get (WYSIWYG), you will find sufficient variations between the Layout and Print Preview views that you will need to use Print Preview. You do most of the report's modification using Layout view. Figure 4.4 shows a report in Layout view.

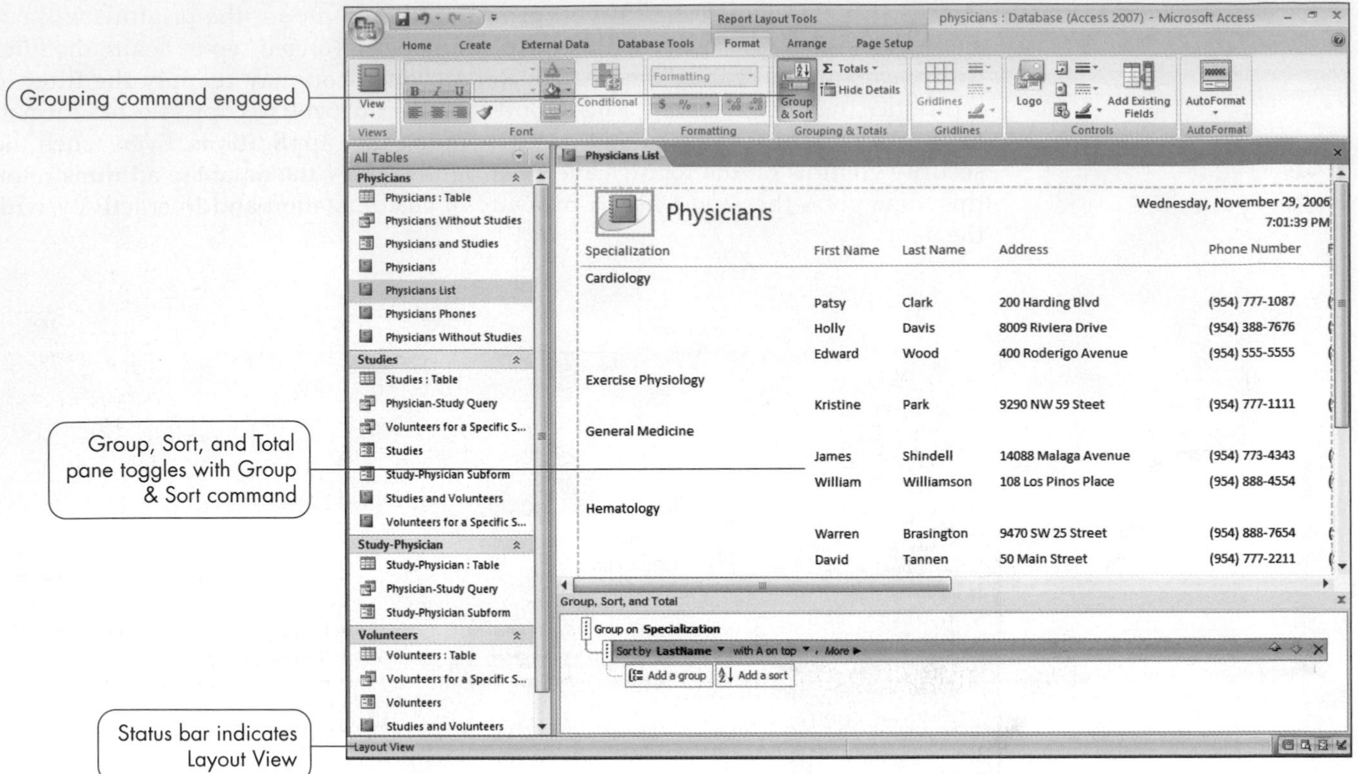
Grouping command engaged
Group, Sort, and Total pane toggles with Group & Sort command
Status bar indicates Layout View

Figure 4.4 Report in Layout View with Grouping and Sorting

Perfect a Report in Design View

The ***Design view*** displays the report's infrastructure but no data.

The ***Design view*** displays the report's infrastructure design, but it does not display data. It provides you the most powerful method of viewing an Access report. You may perform many of the same tasks in Design view as you can in Layout view—add and delete fields, add and remove sorting and grouping layers, rearrange data elements, adjust column widths, and customize report elements. You do not see any of the report's data while in this view. When the report is very lengthy, hiding the data as you alter the design may be an advantage because you save time by not scrolling. However, the Design view looks so different from the final output, it may be confusing. You need to experiment with using both the Layout and Design views and decide which view fits your style. Figure 4.5 displays the Physicians report in Design view. The next section provides explanations for all of the little boxes and stripes.

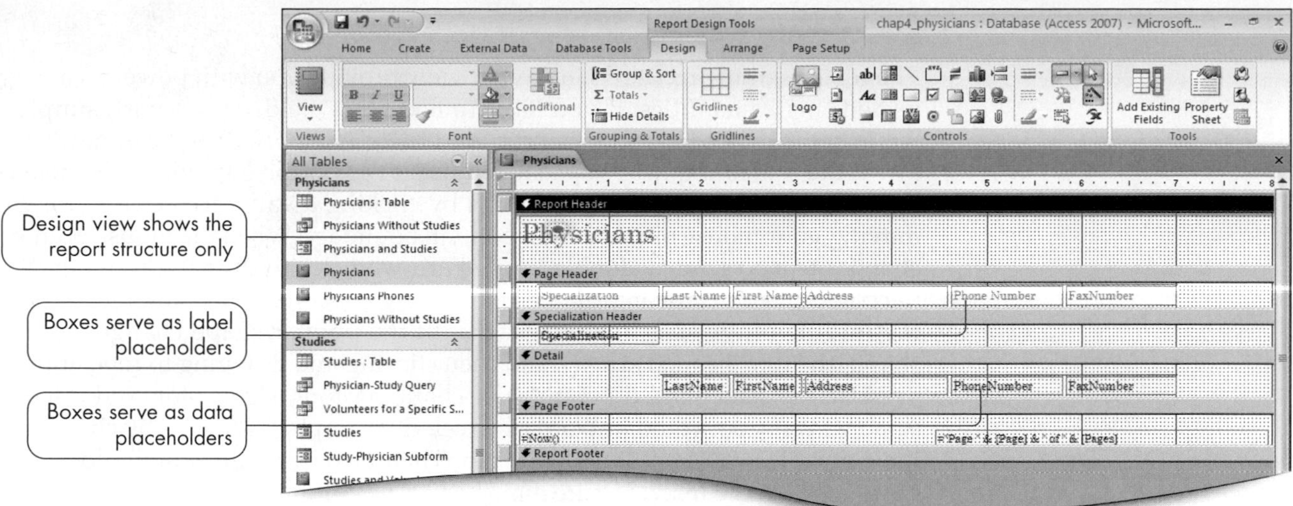

Design view shows the report structure only
Boxes serve as label placeholders
Boxes serve as data placeholders

Figure 4.5 Reports Shown in Design View Do Not Display Record Values

Create and Edit a Report

Access gives you several different methods to generate a report. You will first learn how to use the Report tool. Start by determining all of the fields needed for the report. To use the Report tool, you need to assemble all of the necessary data in one place. This tool is extremely easy to use and will adequately serve your needs much of the time. Occasionally, a table contains all of the fields for a report. More often, you will need to create or open a query containing the necessary fields. If an existing query has all of the fields needed for the report but also some unneeded fields, you will probably use the existing query. You can delete the extraneous fields.

Create a Report with the Report Tool

First, you need to determine the record source for the report. Open the record source in Datasheet view. Click the Create tab and click Report in the Reports group. Access creates the report and displays it in Layout view (see Figure 4.6). If you like the look of the report, you may print, save, and close it from the Layout view. When you reopen the saved report file, Access automatically returns to the record source and loads the most recent data into the report.

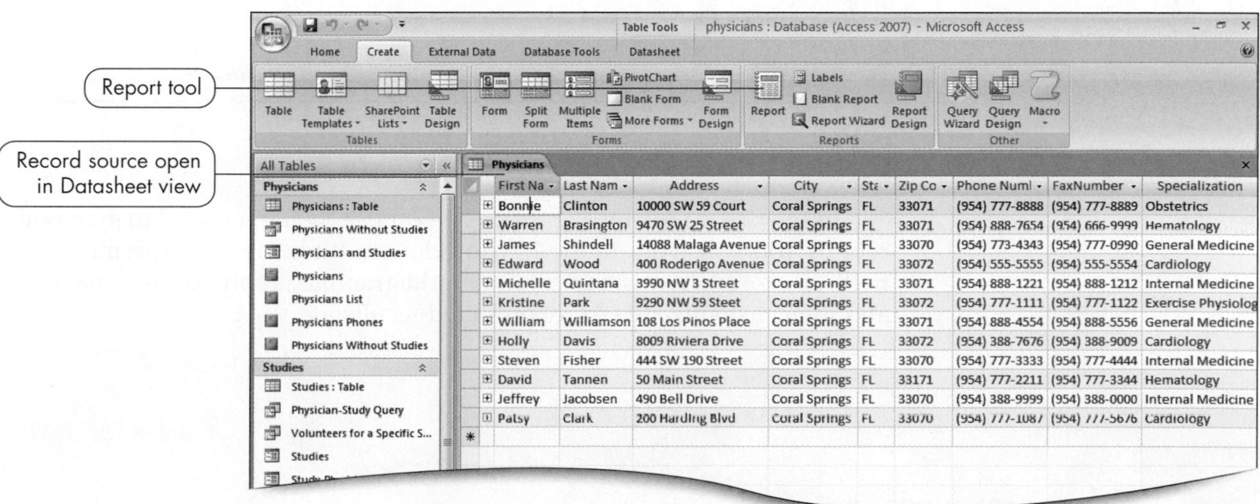

Report tool
Record source open in Datasheet view

Figure 4.6 Set Up for Using Report Tool

Edit a Report in Layout View

The report-editing functions in Layout view provide you with powerful and easy-to-use editing capabilities. If you have unnecessary fields in a report, simply click a value in the unneeded column and press Delete. Not only does the unneeded field go away, the remaining field's spacing adjusts to cover the gap where the deleted data had been. Change the column widths by clicking a value in the column, and then moving your mouse over the right column boundary. When the mouse pointer shape changes to a horizontal, double-headed arrow, click and drag the boundary to adjust the column width. You may move an object by selecting it, positioning your mouse in the middle of the selection, waiting until the pointer shape changes to the move shape (the four-headed arrow), and then clicking and dragging to reposition.

Use the select-and-do method of changing font, size, color, and effects in the same way as you would in Word or Excel. Add graphic elements by clicking Logo in the Controls group on the Format tab. Then browse to the storage location of the graphic file in the Insert Picture dialog box. The editing skills you already know from working in other software applications work is essentially the same way when you edit an Access report in the Layout view. Access provides many predefined formats that you may apply to the report. Figure 4.7 shows a report in Layout view.

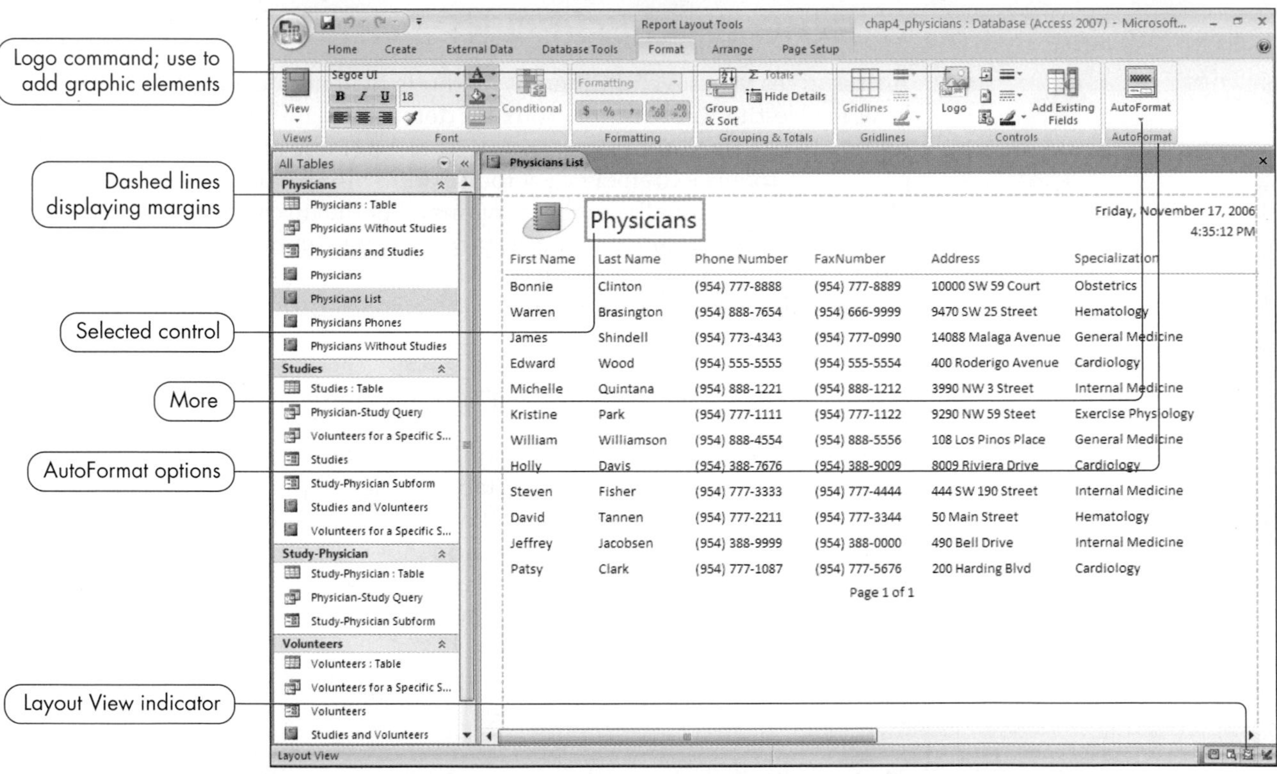

Figure 4.7 Report Layout View Elements

In the first hands-on exercise, you will use the Report tool to generate an Access report. You will work in the Layout view to filter the report, remove unnecessary fields, resize and reposition columns, add graphics, apply AutoFormats to the report, and then customize the AutoFormatted results.

Hands-On Exercises

1 | Introduction to Access Reports

Skills covered: 1. Create a Report Using the Report Tool **2.** Create and Apply a Filter in a Report **3.** Remove Fields from a Report and Adjust Column Widths **4.** Reposition Report Objects and Insert Graphic Elements in a Report **5.** Use AutoFormat and Format Report Elements

Step 1
Create a Report Using the Report Tool

Refer to Figure 4.8 as you complete Step 1.

a. Use Windows Explorer to locate the file named *chap4_ho1-3_coffee.accdb*. Copy the file and rename it as **chap4_ho1-3_coffee_solution.accdb**.

b. Open the *chap4_ho1-3_coffee_solution.accdb* file.

c. Click **Options** on the Security Warning toolbar, click **Enable this content** in the Microsoft Office Security Options dialog box, and then click **OK**.

d. Open the **Sales Reps table** and replace *Your Name* with your first and last names. Close the Sales Reps table.

e. Right-click the **Your Name Revenue** query in the *All Tables window* and select **Rename**. Replace *Your Name* with your first and last names.

f. Open the **Your Name Revenue query** in Datasheet view.

g. Click the **Create tab**, and then click **Report** in the Reports group.

Access creates the report and opens it in the Layout view. The report opens with the Format tab active because you almost always need to modify the format of a newly generated report.

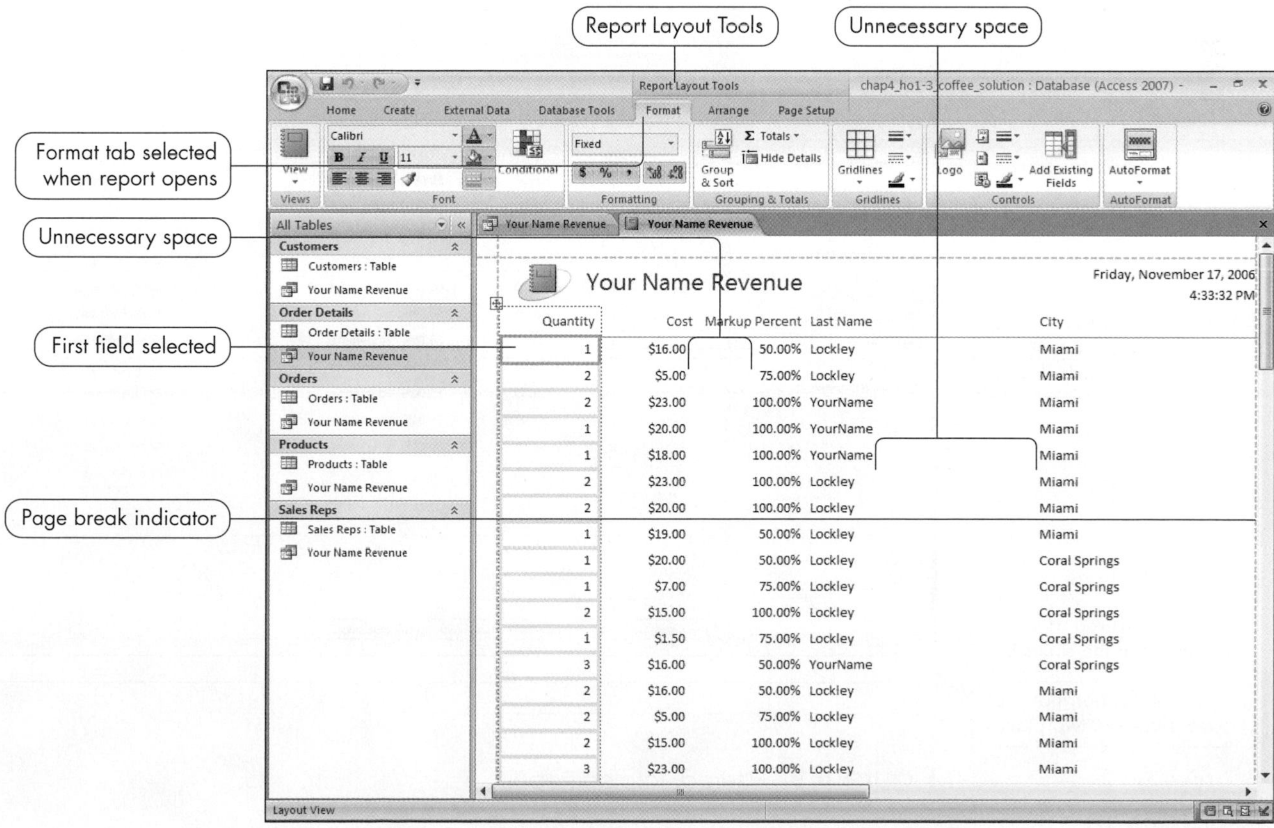

Figure 4.8 Newly Created Report Opens in Layout View

Step 2
Create and Apply a Filter in a Report

Refer to Figure 4.9 as you complete Step 2.

a. Right-click **Your Name** in the LastName field and select **Equals "Your Name"** from the shortcut menu.

   You have created and applied a filter that displays only your orders. The status bar in the lower-right corner of the window tells you that the report has a filter applied. Only your records should display.

b. Right-click the word *Miami* and select **Does Not Equal "Miami"** from the shortcut menu.

   Additional records are filtered out of the report, and a total for the Revenue field moves into view. Note that the total did not inherit the currency format from the source data. You may need to scroll right to see the total of the Revenue column.

c. Compare your selected fields to those shown in Figure 4.9 and then click **Save**.

   The Save As dialog box opens with the default name (inherited from the source query) highlighted.

d. Type **Your Name Sales Outside of Miami**. Click **OK**.

e. Close the report and close the query.

   You saved the report based on the query, so it no longer needs to be open. Although this is a small database, working with unnecessary objects open may slow your computer's response time. You should always close unnecessary objects.

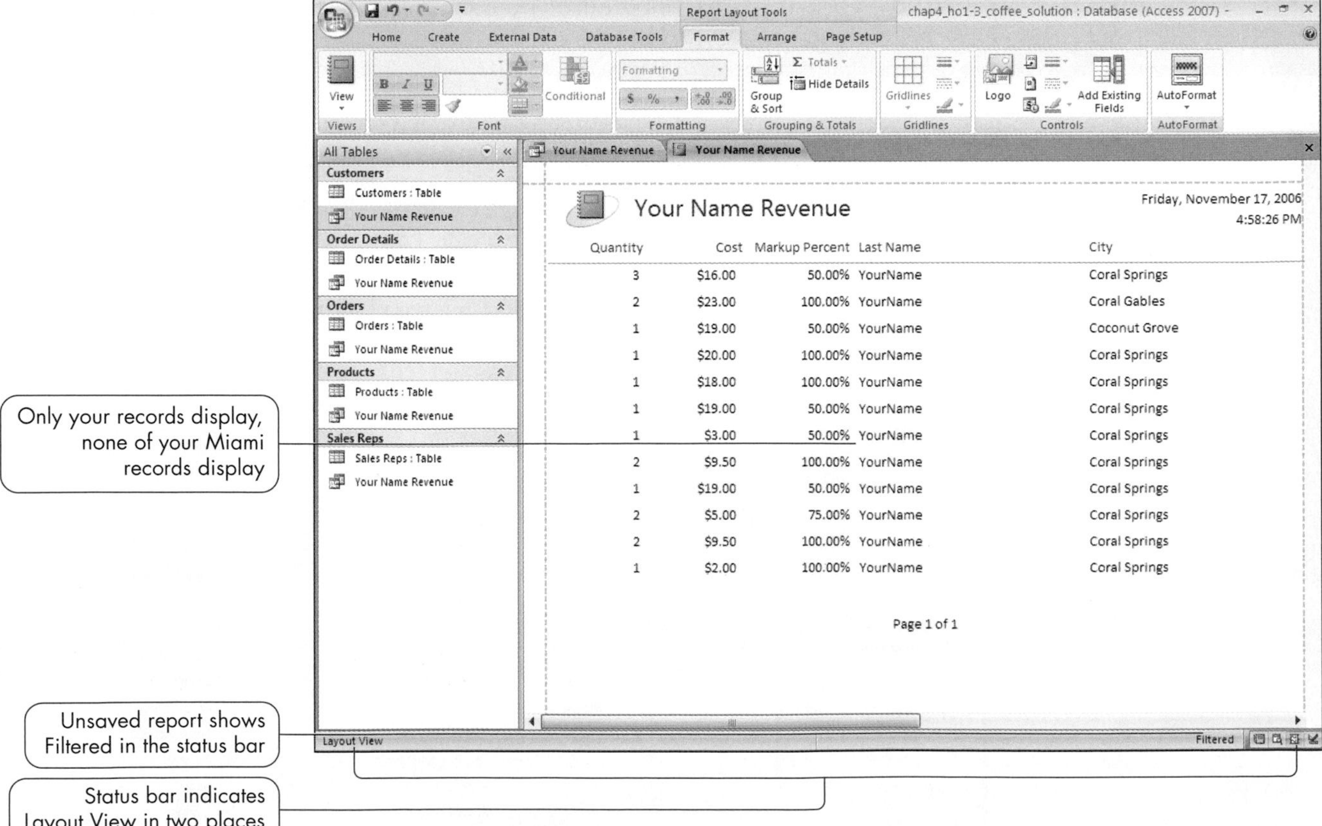

Figure 4.9 Filtered, Totaled Report

Step 3
Remove Fields from a Report and Adjust Column Widths

Refer to Figure 4.10 as you complete Step 3.

a. Open the **Your Name Sales Outside of Miami report**. Look at the left side of the status bar. It displays *Report View*. The status bar no longer indicates that the report is filtered.

   When you reopen an existing report, it opens in Report view. This view lets you look at the report and permits limited filtering capabilities. Because this view provides limited editing interaction, you need to change to Layout view.

b. Right-click the **Your Name Sales Outside of Miami tab** and select **Layout View** from the shortcut menu.

c. Click the label **Quantity**.

   A gold box surrounds the selected field name, and a dotted border surrounds the record values in the field.

   TROUBLESHOOTING: The gold box should only be around the word Quantity. If it surrounds the entire label row, you are still in Report view. Switch to Layout view and then click Quantity again.

d. Press **Delete**.

   The column disappears from the report. The remaining columns move left to fill the empty space.

e. Click **Your Name** in any record. Move your mouse to the right boundary of the gold border and, when the pointer shape changes to a double-headed arrow, click and drag the boundary to the left to decrease the column width.

f. Click a **city name** in any record. Move your mouse to the right boundary of the gold border and, when the pointer shape changes to a double-headed arrow, click and drag the boundary to the left to decrease the column width.

   The report should fit on a single page now. You notice that the column heading for the Markup Percent column is much wider than the values in the column.

g. Click the **Markup Percent** column label to activate the gold border. Single-click **Markup Percent** again to edit the label.

   You know you are in edit mode because the border color changes to black, and a flashing insertion point appears inside the border.

h. Position the insertion point to the left of the ***P*** in *Percent*. Press **Ctrl+Enter**. Click anywhere on the report to exit edit mode. Save the report.

   The Ctrl+Enter command forces a line break. The word *Percent* moves below the word *Markup*.

TIP Forced Line Break

A similar command, Alt+Enter, may be used in Excel to force a line break, when the width of the column name greatly exceeds the width of the data displayed in the column. Although word wrapping may achieve the same effect, you can more precisely control which word prints on what line by forcing the break yourself.

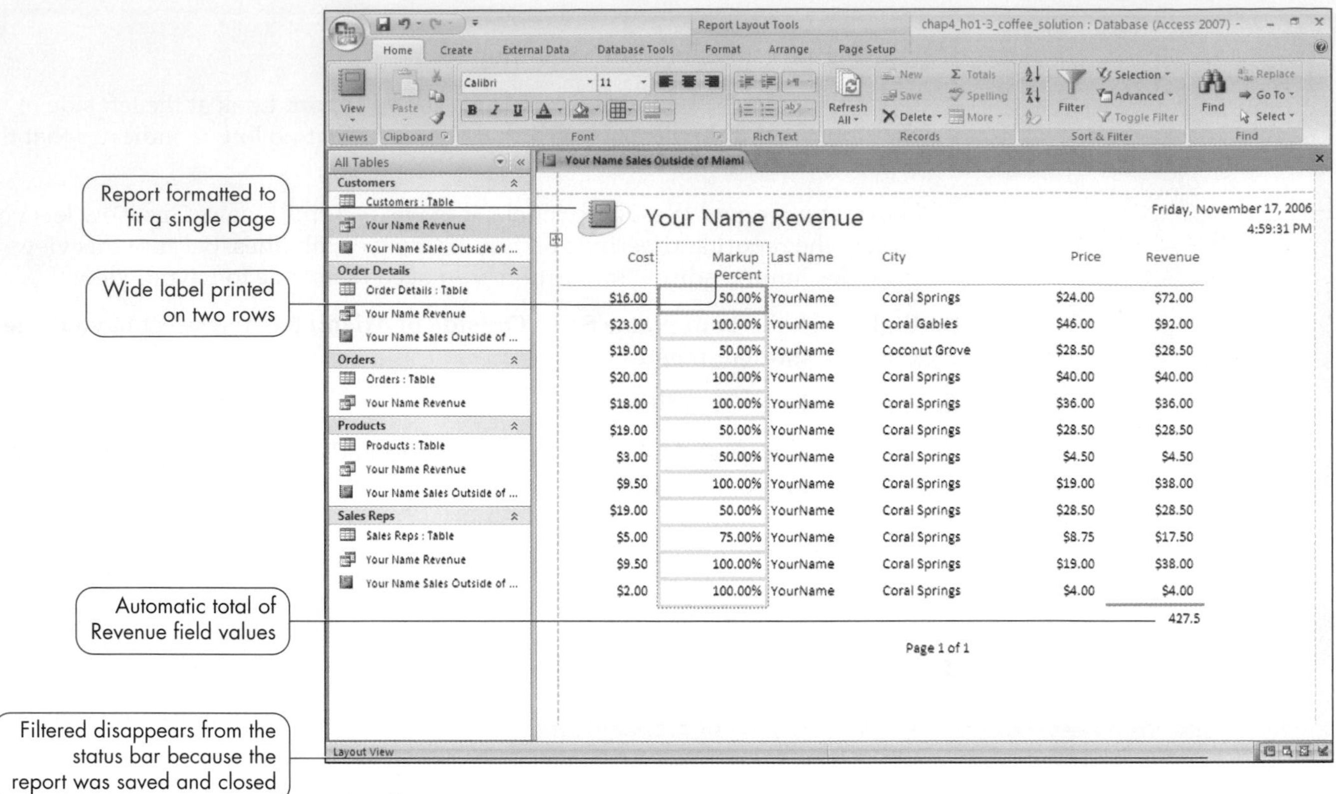

Figure 4.10 Resized Report

Step 4

Reposition Report Objects and Insert Graphic Elements in a Report

Refer to Figure 4.11 as you complete Step 4.

a. Click any record in the **City** column to select it. Move the mouse to the middle of the selected column. When the pointer shape changes to a *four-headed arrow*, click and drag to the left until the vertical gold line is on the left edge of the report. Release the mouse.

As you drag past other columns in the report, a gold line moves to tell you the column's current position. When you release the mouse, the City column moves to the first position.

TROUBLESHOOTING: When you begin to drag while located in a record, Access assumes that you want to change the height of the row until you move out of the column. While the mouse is inside the selected cell, a black boundary forms across the entire row. Keep dragging left. As soon as the mouse moves outside the original boundaries, the gold line will appear.

b. Click any record in the **Last Name** column to select it. Move the mouse to the middle of the selected column. When the pointer shape changes to a *four-headed arrow*, click and drag right. Continue the drag until the vertical gold line is on the right edge of the report. Release the mouse.

The Last Name column is the last column in the report.

c. Click the report title, *Your Name Revenue*, to select it, and then click it again to edit it. Type **Your Name Non–Miami Sales**.

d. Click the picture of the **report binder** to select it.

e. Click **Logo** in the Controls group on the Format tab.

The Insert Picture dialog box opens to the default folder, My Pictures, but the file you need is stored in the folder with the rest of the Access files.

f. Browse to your file storage folder; locate and open the file named *chap4_ho1-3_coffee.gif*. Click **OK**.

g. Move your mouse over the lower right corner of the picture until the pointer shape changes to a diagonal, double-headed arrow. Click and drag the lower-right picture corner until the picture's size roughly doubles.

The picture enlarges, but now it covers part of your name.

TIP Use the Properties Sheet to Exactly Size an Object

If you right-click the picture and select Properties from the shortcut menu, you may use measurements to exactly size the picture. You also may add special effects, like stretch or zoom.

h. Click the report's title, *Your Name Non–Miami Sales,* to select it. Position the mouse pointer in the middle of the box. When the pointer shape changes to the four-headed move arrow, click and drag the report title right and down (see Figure 4.11).

i. Click **Save** on the Quick Access Toolbar to save the design changes to the report.

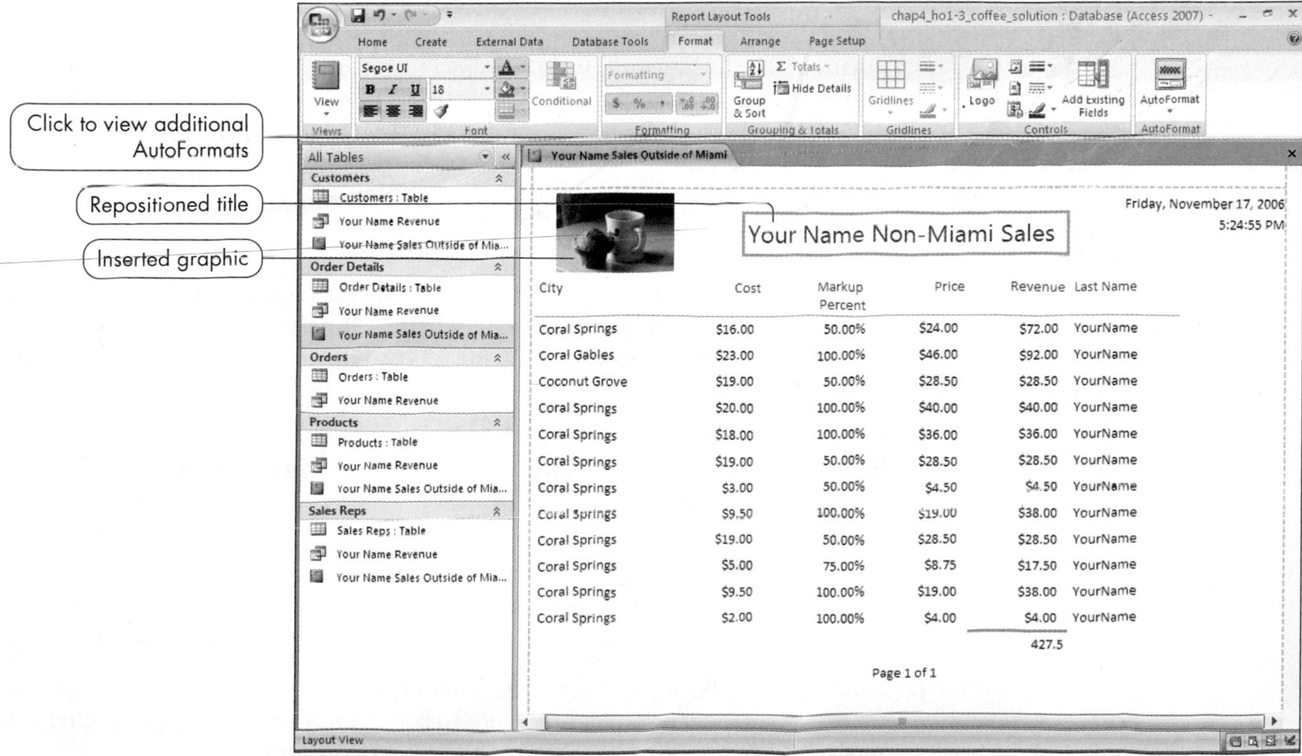

Figure 4.11 Graphic and Title Repositioned

Step 5

Use AutoFormat and Format Report Elements

Refer to Figure 4.12 as you complete Step 5.

a. Check to ensure the *Your Name Non–Miami Sales report* remains in Layout view. Right-click the **Revenue Total cell** (427.5) to select it and open the shortcut menu.

b. Select **Properties** from the shortcut menu.

   The Property Sheet opens in the task pane.

c. Click the **Format tab** (if necessary), and then click the **drop-down arrow** in the *Format Property box* and select **Currency**.

   You should see the value of the Revenue field total change to $427.50. Close the Property Sheet.

d. Click **More** in the AutoFormat group on the Format tab (see Figure 4.7).

   The AutoFormat list expands to display several formats. The last choice activates the AutoFormat Wizard.

e. Select the **Median AutoFormat** (2nd column, 3rd row) and click it.

   The AutoFormat applies to the entire report. It does not matter what portion of the report you selected when you applied the AutoFormat. Every element of the report gets a format change. This effect may create problems.

f. Examine the results. Identify problems.

   Although the Layout view gives you powerful editing capabilities, it does not perfectly duplicate the printed output. You need to use Print Preview to determine if the problem needs action.

g. Right-click the report tab and change to **Print Preview**. Examine the report's date and time. You should check the Report view, also. Right-click the report tab and change to **Report View**. Often, reports get copied and pasted or e-mailed directly from the Report view, so you need to make sure everything works there, too.

   Fortunately, the date and time display correctly in Print Preview. You decide that you do not like the font color looks in the Revenue total. You think it would look better if it matched the other numbers in size, font, and color.

h. Right-click the report tab and change to **Layout View**. Click any record in the **Revenue** field. Click **Format Painter** in the Font group on the Format tab. Move to the **Revenue total** value and click it.

   Clicking the format command instructs Access to save the source format. The mouse pointer has a paintbrush attached to it as you move to remind you that you will paint the stored format wherever you next click. When you reach the destination and click, the defined formats transfer.

i. Click to select the **brown** report header. Right-click the **brown area** at the top of the report and select **Properties** on the shortcut menu. Check to make sure the *Format tab* is open. Look in the *Back Color Property box*. The brown background color is color number **#775F55**.
   Select and **copy** the number or remember it.

   You need to match the heading color to replace the blue background of the column headings. By looking up the property, you may make an exact color match.

j. Click the blue background for the **Cost heading**. Find the Back color property on the Format sheet. Click and drag to select its contents and press **Ctrl + V** to paste the brown color number in the box. Press **Enter**.

   The color change does not take effect until you move to the next row. You like the new color but decide the type font will look better larger, centered, and boldfaced.

k. Click the **Font Size arrow** in the Font group and select **12**. Click **Bold**. Click the **Center text** command.

l. Scroll in the Property Sheet for the *Cost Heading* until you locate the Top Margin property. Type **0** and press **Enter**.

m. Duplicate the format changes to the cost heading to the other headings by double-clicking **Format Painter** located in the Font group. Click the headings for *Markup Percent*, *Last Name*, *City*, *Price*, and *Revenue*. Press **Esc**.

Double clicking the Format Painter permits painting a format to multiple areas without redefining the source after each painting. Pressing Esc or clicking the Format Painter again turns the Format Painter off.

n. Right-click the *Markup Percent* heading and change its Top Margin property in the Property Sheet to **0** (zero).

Because this heading is two lines, it needs to start higher up than the one line heading beside it.

o. Close the Property Sheet. Widen each column about a quarter inch so the entire page is filled (see Figure 4.12). Refer to Step 3e for instructions if necessary, except drag to widen rather than to narrow the column. Save your report.

TROUBLESHOOTING: Be sure to look at the report in Print Preview. Remember, the Layout view is not perfectly WYSIWYG. It is easy to make the right column a little too wide and push the report to an extra page. Check to make sure your report is still a single page. If it is not, make the columns a little narrower.

p. Click the **Office Button**, select **Manage**, and then select **Back Up Database**. Type **chap4_ho1_coffee_solution** (note *ho1* instead of *ho1-3*) and click **Save**.

You just created a backup of the database after completing the first hands-on exercise. The original database *chap4_ho1-3_coffee_solution* remains onscreen. If you ruin the original database as you complete the second hands-on exercise, you can use the backup file you just created.

q. Close the file and exit Access if you do not want to continue with the next exercise at this time.

TIP Learning Software

Following step-by-step instructions is a way to begin learning application software. If you want to become proficient in software, you must explore on your own. The properties sheet contains dozens of features that you did not cover in this lesson. You have finished Hands-On Exercise 1 and saved your file. You should experiment a little. Make a copy of the report and experiment on the copy. Activate the Property Sheet for a field and change properties to see the results.

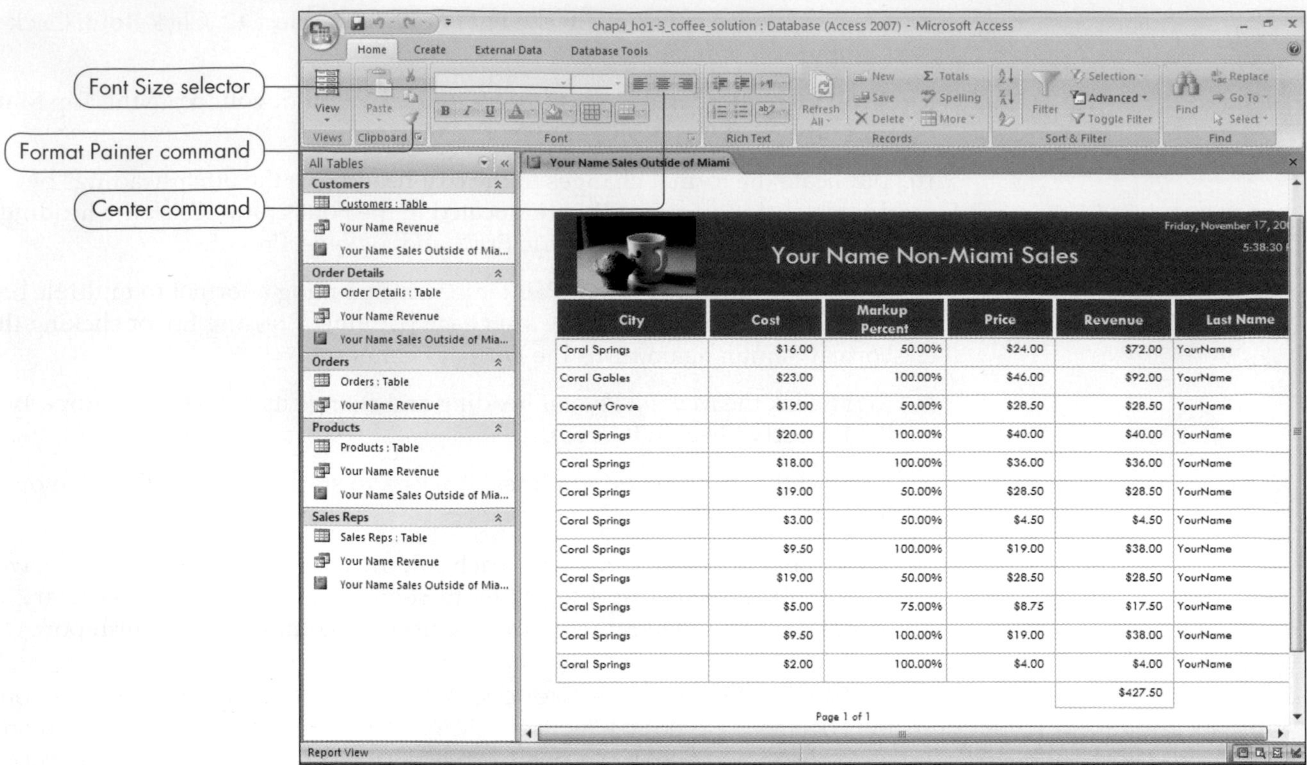

Figure 4.12 The Complete Single-Page Report

The Anatomy of a Report

You have produced reasonable, sophisticated output. Look at the report design depicted in Figure 4.13. It, too, contains summary statistics but on multiple levels. The desired layout contains indents to visually classify the differing elements. The finished report will likely require several pages. It would be much easier to read if the headings repeated at the start of each new page. Access can accomplish all of this, and more.

In this section, you will learn more about a report's sections and controls. You will also learn how to group an Access report into nested sections.

Identifying Report Elements, Sections, and Controls

Access divides all reports into sections, although you only see the sectional boundaries when you display the report in Design view. You need to become familiar with the sectional areas so that you can control report output completely. For example, if you place an instruction to add field values together in the detail section, the resulting calculation will duplicate each record's value for that field. The field in the detail section contains a single value from a single record.

Understand Sectional Divisions

The ***detail section*** repeats once for each record in the underlying record source.

The ***report header section*** prints once at the beginning of each report.

The ***report footer section*** prints once at the conclusion of each report.

The ***group header section(s)*** appear once at the start of each new grouping level in the report.

The ***group footer section(s)*** appear at the end of each grouping level.

The ***detail section*** repeats once for each record in the underlying record source. If you copied the calculation and placed it in a report header or footer, the result would display the sum of all that field's values for the entire report. The ***report header section*** prints once at the beginning of each report. The ***report footer section*** prints once at the conclusion of each report. Should you find all the stripes and little boxes confusing, you still must learn something about them to accurately produce the output you desire. You will begin by learning about the stripes—the sectional boundaries.

In Figure 4.13, each blue stripe marks the upper boundary of a report area. The top stripe denotes the upper boundary of the report header. The bottom stripe displays the top boundary of the report's footer. The gray, grid-patterned area beneath the stripes shows the space allotted to that element. Notice that the report has no space allocated to the report footer. You may change the space between areas by moving your mouse over the stripe's bottom. When the pointer shape changes to a double-headed arrow, click and drag to move the boundary. Use this method if you decide to add a footer to the report. A gray, grid-patterned work space appears as your mouse drags down. If you expand or contract the space allotment for a middle sectional boundary, the lower boundaries all move also. The ***group header section(s)*** appear once at the start of each new grouping level in the report. The ***group footer section(s)*** appear at the end of each grouping level.

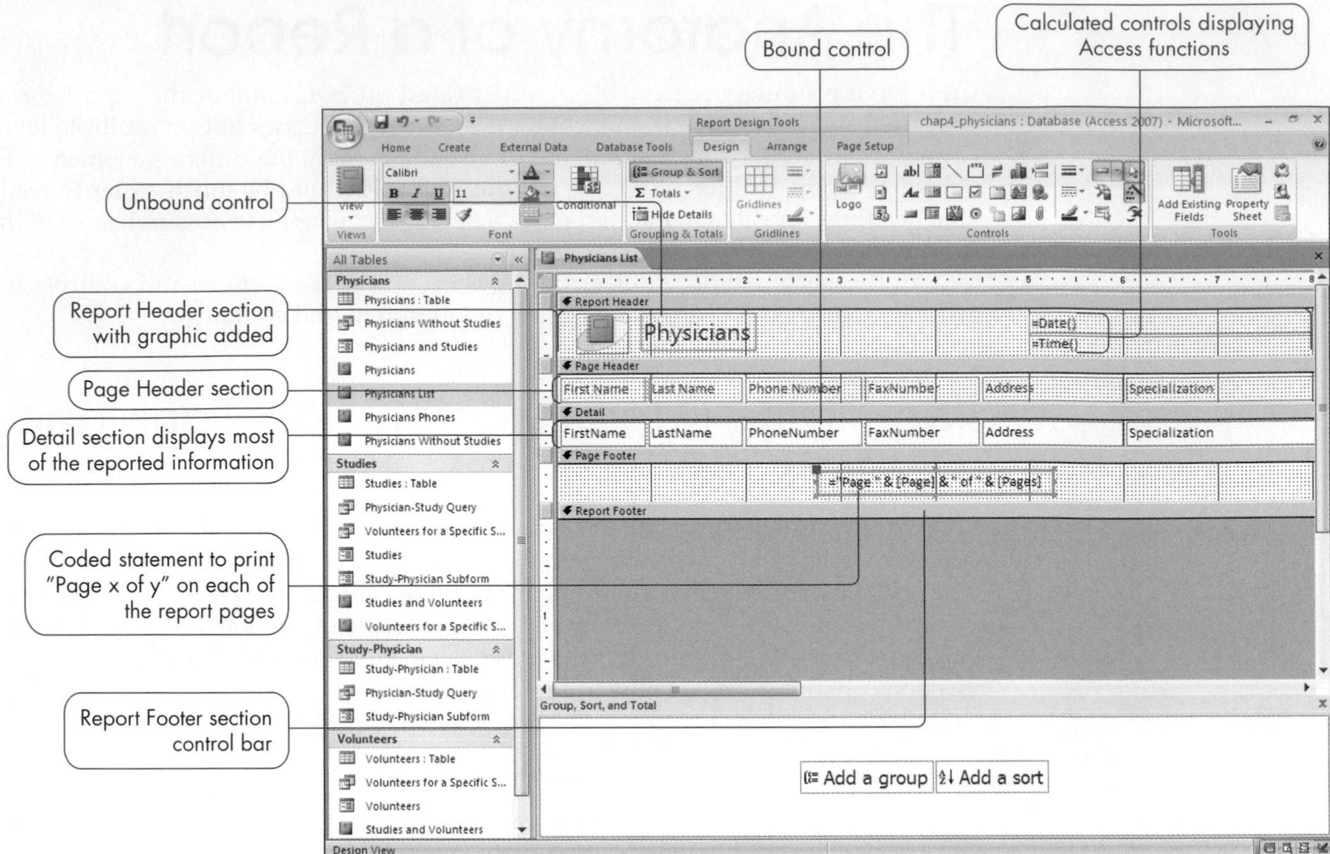

Figure 4.13 Reports Shown in Design View Do Not Display Record Values

If you decide that the allotted space for a particular section is not needed, you may reposition the top of the next sectional boundary so that the boundary stripes touch. The element will remain in the report's design but will consume no space on the printed output and will not show in any other report view. Use the page header section to repeat column headings on the top of each new page. You will place information like page numbers in the page footer. ***Page headers*** and ***page footers*** appear once for each page in the report at the top and bottom of the report's pages, respectively.

Page headers and ***page footers*** appear once for each page in the report at the top and bottom of the pages.

All reports contain several different sections; see the reference page for more information about their placement and usage.

Report Tools, Location, and Usage | Reference

Design Element	Location	Frequency	Usage	Required
Report Header	Top of the report	Once	Think of the report header as the title page. It includes information like the organization's name, the report's name, and the run date.	Yes
Page Header	Top of each page	One per page	Page headers generally contain the column headings. In a multi-page report, the labels repeat at the top of each page to provide clarity	Yes
Group Header	At the start of each new group	One at the start of each new group (up to 10)	This element begins and identifies each new group. It generally contains the group name, i.e., in a report grouped by state, the state name would be the header. Any aggregating functions in a group header will summarize the group records, e.g., a SUM function will add all of the record values within the group.	No
Detail	Middle	Once per record reported	This element is repeated once for each selected record in the data source. If there were 500 records in the data source for the report, the report would have 500 detail lines. In a grouped report, there may be multiple detail sections—one per group. Often, you omit the detail section entirely. You might show state total without population information showing the population per county. You might do this even when the state population was calculated by adding the county figures.	No
Group Footer	At the end of each group	Once at the end of each group (up to 10)	This element generally repeats the group name, e.g., in a report grouped by state, the state name would repeat in the footer along with a descriptor of aggregating information. An annual sales report might group by month, and one group's footer may display the Total Revenue in May. Any aggregating functions in a group's footer will summarize the group records, e.g., a SUM function will add all of the record values within the group.	No
Page Footer	Bottom of the page	Once per page in the report	Use this feature to print page numbers, page summary statistics, contact information, or report preparation/run date.	Yes, but it need not contain any data
Report Footer	End of the report	One per report	You would use this feature to print grand totals or other summary information for entire project. Often, the date, authorship, or contact information displays here.	Yes

TIP Report Footer Placement

In Design view, the report footer section displays below the page footer section. However, all other views and the printed output position the report footer above the page footer. Although this effect can be disconcerting the first time you notice it, it makes good sense. It ensures that the page numbers and other page footer items print in the same position on the last page of the report as on other report pages.

Work with Controls

The position and instructions about what to do with the data once retrieved from the table or query come through the use of controls (the little boxes in Design view). You use ***controls*** to position, display, format, and calculate the report data. Access reports use different types of controls for different purposes.

Use ***controls*** to position, display, format, and calculate the report data.

You use ***bound controls*** most frequently in preparing an Access report. These controls enable you to pull information from the underlying table or query data. Like the source data, the value of a bound control may be text, dates, numbers, pictures, graphs, or Yes/No values. The latter typically displays as a check box. The binding means that the control inherits most properties—size, formatting, and relationships—from the source table. For example, a text box may display a product's price in currency format. It is bound (tied) to the UnitPrice field in the Products table, which is also set to currency format. Most bound controls display with two small boxes in the report's Design view. The left box is the control's label, the right box or text box displays the record value. A bound control's label automatically comes from the field name or caption (if one exists).

Bound controls enable you to pull information from the underlying table or query data.

Unbound controls do not have any record source for their contents. The values contained there exist only in the report and nowhere else in the database. You use them to display information (the report's title), cosmetic elements (borders or lines to visually separate report sections), boxes, and pictures.

Unbound controls do not have any record source for their contents.

A ***calculated control*** uses an expression as opposed to a record value as its data source. The expression usually is bound to the record values of the fields referenced. A report expression, like a query expression, combines field names, operators, constants, and functions to instruct Access on how to perform a calculation. For example, you might use an expression to calculate a discounted price in a sales report. For example:

A ***calculated control*** uses an expression as opposed to a record value as its data source.

=[UnitPrice] * (1-[Discount] * [Quantity])

This expression would likely retrieve the UnitPrice data from the Products table, and the Discount and Quantity values from the Order Details table if you are using a retail store database that contains records for products, including unit price, selling price, and quantity.

Adding Grouping Levels in Layout View

Access provides you with several methods of creating data summaries.

- Create a Totals query by specifying a group by field and the field or fields to summarize.
- Create a grouped report using the Layout view's Sorting and Grouping tool.
- Create a grouped report using the Report Wizard and specifying the group layers within the Wizard.

Reports provide you with the same power as a Totals query and provide the added advantage of enhanced appearance. This section explores grouping and sorting in the Layout view method. The next section introduces you to the Report Wizard.

Engage the Group & Sort Tool

Open the report in Layout view. The report shown in Figure 4.14 contains over 2,000 records. Imagine that you must use this data to make decisions about your firm's operations. You would not easily identify trends and patterns by examining 50 or more printed pages. This data needs to be summarized. Begin summarizing by clicking Group & Sort in the Grouping & Totals group on the Format tab. The Group, Sort, and Total pane displays in the bottom of the report.

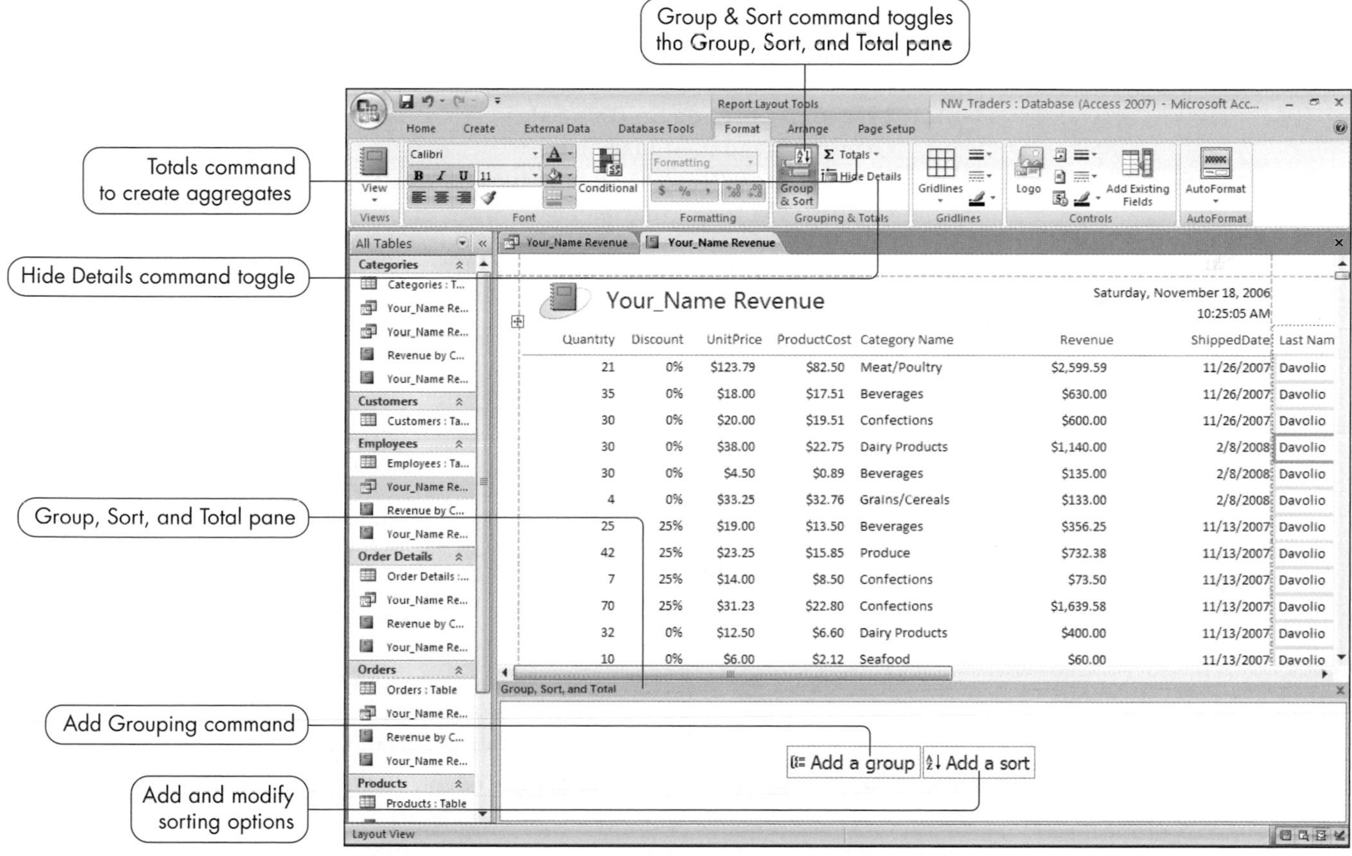

Figure 4.14 Display the Group, Sort, and Total Pane

Select the Primary Grouping Field

Nested groups provide a power-layering tool to organize information.

You may nest groups in different levels—up to 10. ***Nested groups*** provide a powerful layering tool to organize information. In this report, you need the sales figures summarized by the categories of products offered. Once created, each group contains introductory and summary information as well as the record values. Generally, the group header provides identification information, for example the name of the category. You use the group footer to present summary information for the group. Figure 4.15 depicts the Add a Group command engaged with the categories field selected as the primary grouping level.

After you establish the primary group, you may add additional levels. This feature works much like an outline. Suppose you needed a sales report grouped by salesperson, and then by quarter. Each successive grouping layer gets tucked between the header and footer of the previous layer.

Group 1 Header — Joe Adams' Sales

Group 2 Header—Quarter 1

Many Rows of Details for Quarter 1

Group 2 Footer—Quarter 1 Summary

Group 2 Header—Quarter 2

Many Rows of Details for Quarter 2

Group 2 Footer—Quarter 2 Summary

Group 2 Header—Quarter 3

Many Rows of Details for Quarter 3

Group 2 Footer—Quarter 3 Summary

Group 2 Header—Quarter 4

Many Rows of Details for Quarter 4

Group 2 Footer—Quarter 4 Summary

Group 1 Footer—Joe Adams' Sales Totals

Group 2 Header—Brenda Smith's Sales

Group 2 Header—Quarter 1

Many Rows of Details for Quarter 1

Group 2 Footer—Quarter 1 Summary

The pattern repeats.

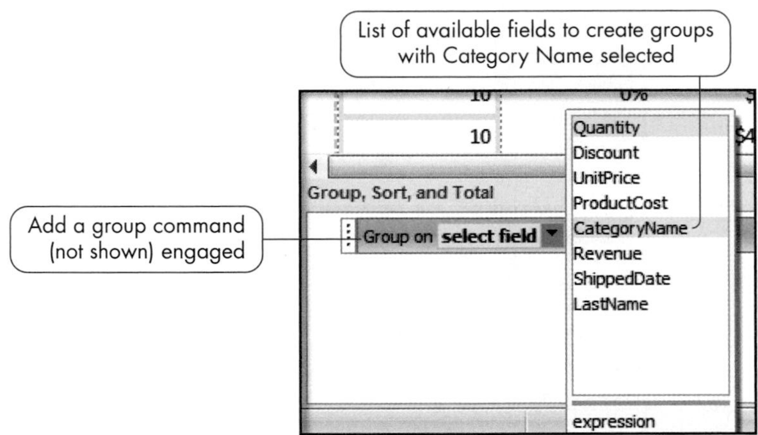

Figure 4.15 Select a Primary Grouping Level

Hide or Display Details

You must decide if the details—the values stored in each record that report used as a source—need to be displayed in the report. Many reports only display data summaries. How you decide to display details will depend on how the report will be used. Most Access report writers follow the general rule that the less detail and more summarizing information included, the more useful the report. Access makes it easy for you to add and remove detail levels. If you omit the detail and later discover that you need it, you can easily add it back. Engage the Hide Detail command to hide or display report details (see Figure 4.16).

(. . . the less detail and more summarizing information included, the more useful the report.)

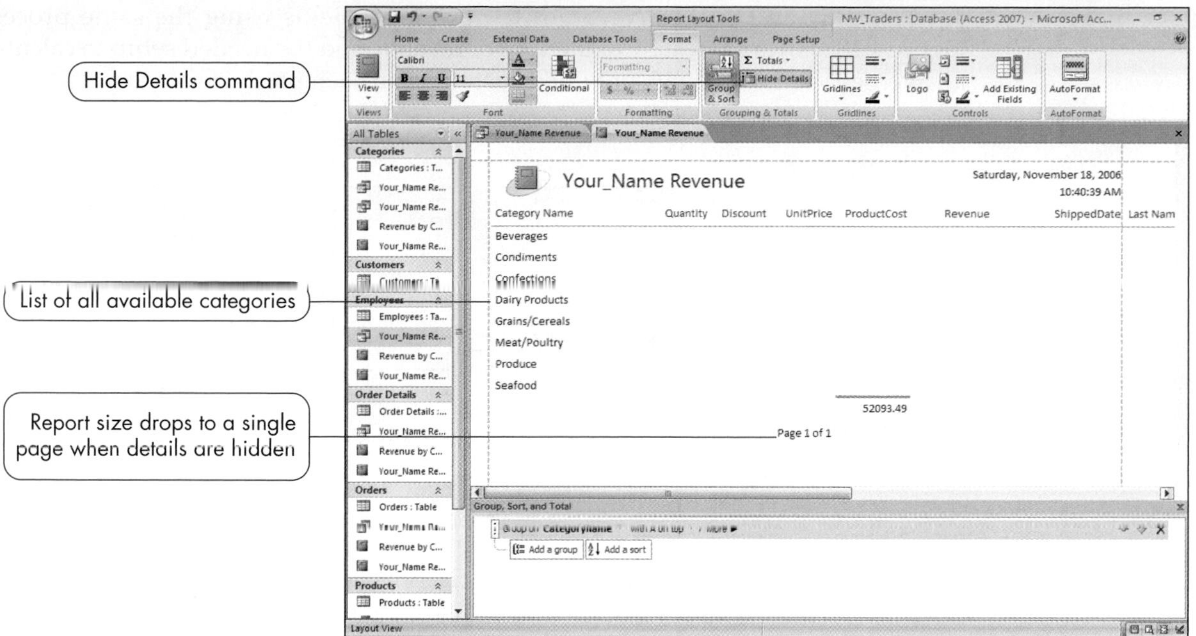

Figure 4.16 Summary Report with Details Hidden

Calculate Summary Statistics

The report in Figure 4.17 displays a list of the names of the categories of merchandise sold by the firm. The Totals command in the Grouping & Totals group helps you summarize data. First, select the control label for the data you want summarized. Then click Totals and select the necessary aggregating function from the drop-down list.

Decision-makers may wish to examine the same data using different aggregating functions to answer different questions. For example, a sum of all revenue generated by each product category will tell the manager important total sales information. Changing the report to display the maximum revenue will provide the decision-maker with information about which products generated the largest revenue. After you establish the grouping levels, Access makes it easy for you to examine the output in a variety of ways.

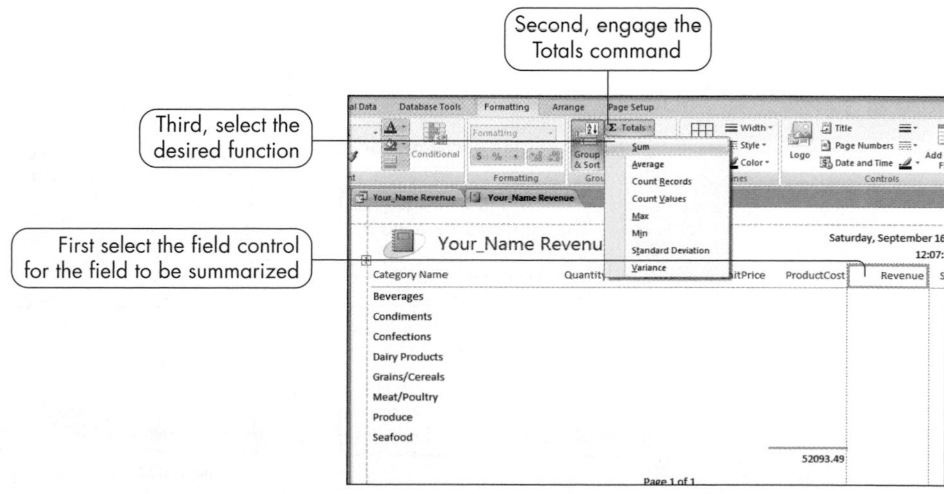

Figure 4.17 Creating a Sum of the Revenue Field

You may add summary values to additional fields using the same process. Figure 4.18 shows the results of the sum of revenue and the needed setup to calculate an average of the discounts provided customers in each product category.

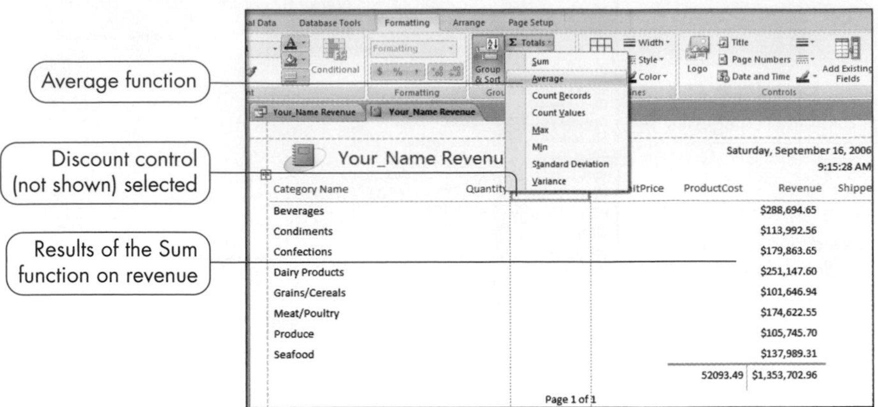

Figure 4.18 Creating an Average of the Discount Field

Add Additional Grouping Levels

You decide that having the report grouped by category is useful, but you also want to know who sells each category's products. You can add additional grouping levels to an existing report in Layout view by selecting the control that you need to group on and then clicking the Add a Group command in the Group, Sort, and Total pane. In the report displayed in Figure 4.19, you would first select the control for LastName field and then click the Add a group command. The figure displays the results of adding an additional grouping level to the report. The More command controlling the Category name group expands when selected, granting you access to additional features. The figure displays the settings necessary to display the totals (averages) for the categories below the salesperson totals.

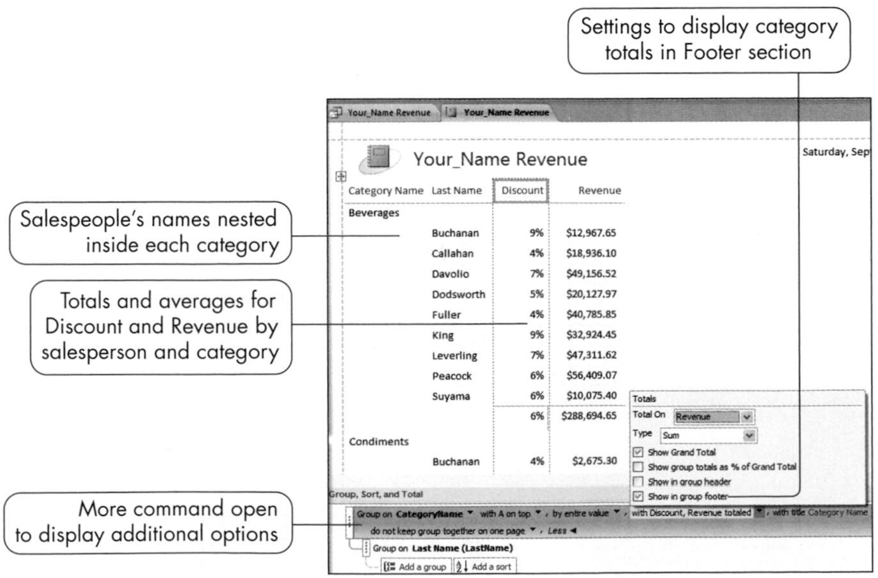

Figure 4.19 Nested Group Report with Totals Moved to Footer

Sort a Report

While working in the Layout view, you can interact with the sort order of the report's fields. Figure 4.20 shows a report with two sorting levels applied. The primary sort is the area of specialization. The secondary sort is by the physician's last name. This order groups the cardiologists together with Clark preceding Davis in the alphabetical listing.

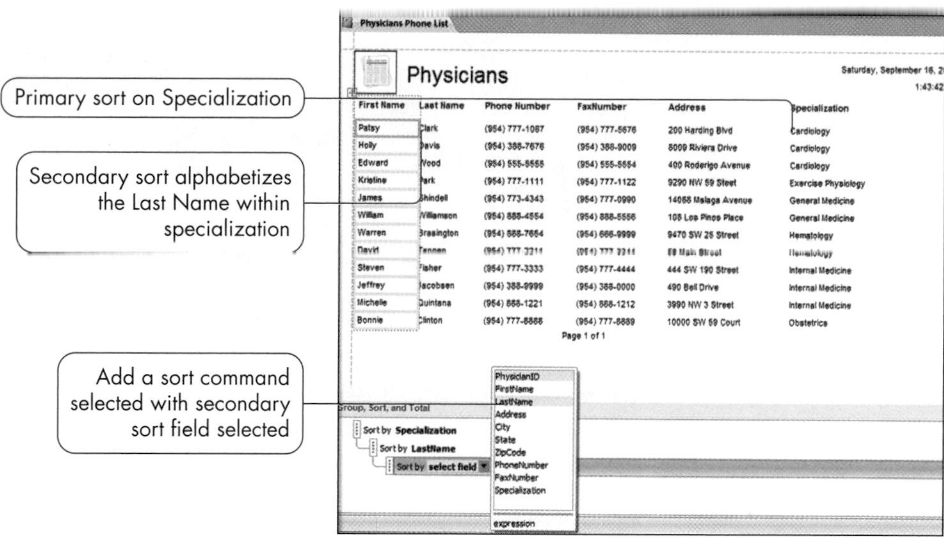

Figure 4.20 Sorted Report

Adding Fields to a Report

It is possible to omit a necessary field when designing a report. Even if a report has no errors, data needs change with time. You may need to add a new field to an existing report. Access provides an easy way to do that.

Open the report in Layout view. Activate the Format tab. Click Add Existing Fields in the Controls group. The Field List pane opens on the right side of the screen. The ***Field List pane*** displays a list of all of the tables and fields in the database. Once you locate the needed field in the Field List pane, drag and drop it on the report in the position that you want it to occupy. (Alternatively, you can double-click it.) Access creates the needed control to hold the new field, for example, a text box, and then binds the field to the newly created control (see Figure 4.21). Occasionally, you might

The ***Field List pane*** displays a list of all of the tables and fields in the database.

want a different control type than the one Access creates for you. You may edit the newly created control's properties to get exactly the control you want. But, you cannot use Layout view to do so. You cannot change the control type property in Layout view. This change must be accomplished in Design view. Of course, you may only specify a control that is appropriate to that data type. For example, a Yes/No field might display as a check box, but you would rather have the words, Yes or No, display.

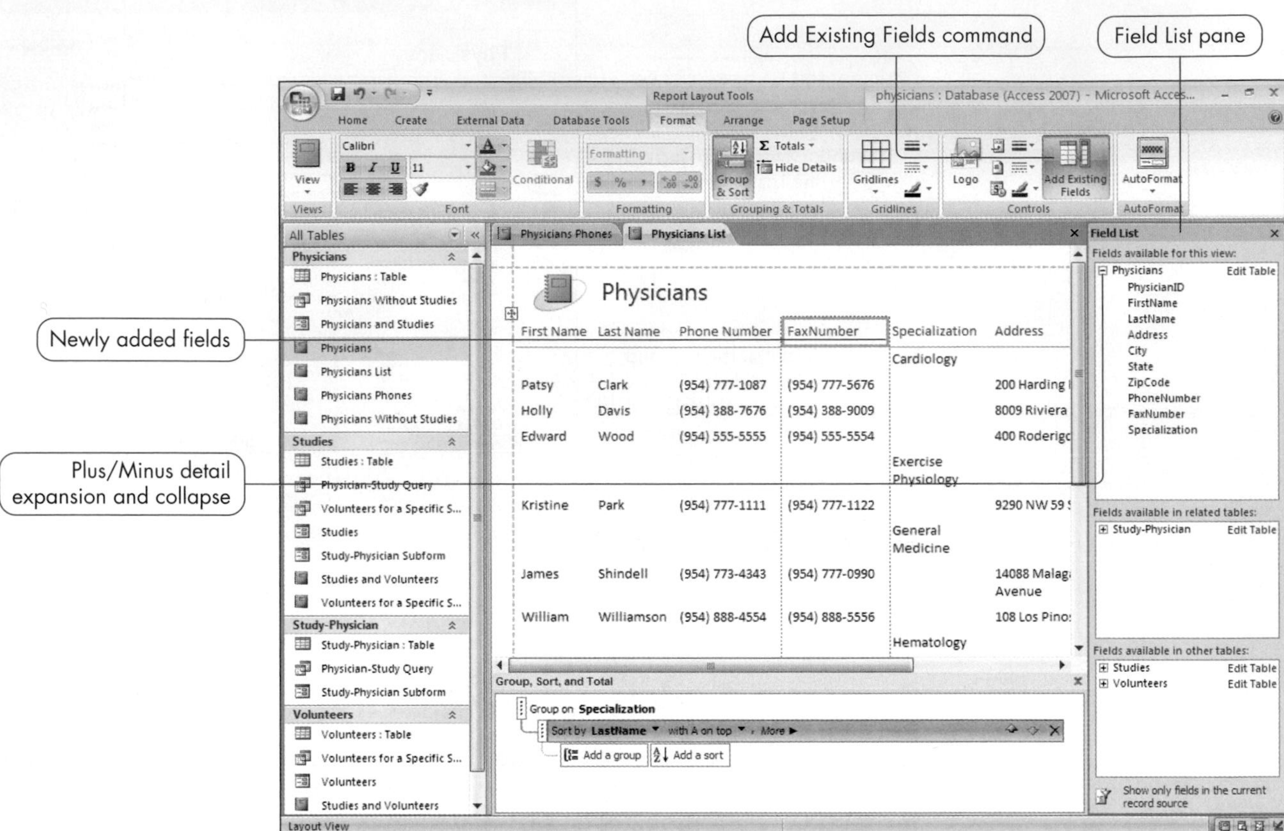

Figure 4.21 Sorted Report

In the next hands-on exercise, you will create a report, add sorting and grouping to refine the content, work with data aggregates, and add a new field to the report.

Hands-On Exercises

2 | Create, Sort, Edit, Nest, and Remove Groups from Reports

Skills covered: 1. Sort a Report **2.** Create a Grouped Report and Sort It. **3.** Add Additional Grouping Levels and Calculate Summary Statistics **4.** Remove Grouping Levels **5.** Reorder Grouping Levels

Step 1 Sort a Report

Refer to Figure 4.22 as you complete Step 1.

a. Open the *chap4_ho1-3_coffee_solution* file if necessary, click **Options** on the Security Warning toolbar, click the **Enable this content option** in the Microsoft Office Security Options dialog box, and click **OK**.

   TROUBLESHOOTING: If you create unrecoverable errors while completing this hands-on exercise, you can delete the chap4_ho1-3_coffee_solution file, copy the chap4_ho1_coffee_solution backup database you created at the end of the first hands-on exercise, and open the copy of the backup database to start the second hands-on exercise again.

b. Open the **Your Name Revenue query** in Datasheet view. Click the **Create tab** and click **Report**.

c. Click **Group & Sort** in the Grouping & Totals group to turn on the Group, Sort, and Total pane at the bottom of the screen.

   TROUBLESHOOTING: The Group & Sort command is a toggle. If you do not see the Group, Sort, and Total pane, click the Group & Sort command again. It may have been on, and you turned it off.

d. Click **Add a sort** in the Group, Sort, and Total pane.

   A list box opens displaying the names of all the reports fields.

e. Click **LastName** from the list and select it.

   Scroll through the list to see two names: Lockley and your name. If your name comes before Lockley alphabetically, your sales are reported first. If your name comes after Lockley alphabetically, Lockley's sales will be first. In the next step, you will sort the list so that your name is on the top—ascending or descending, depending on what letter your name begins with.

f. Find the **Sort with A on top drop-down arrow** in the Group, Sort, and Total pane. Click it to reveal two choices—with A on top and with Z on top. Click the choice that will position your name at the top of the list.

   If your name is not on top, sort again, and select the other option.

g. Click the **Office Button**, choose **Save As**, and type **Sales by Employee and City**. Click **OK**.

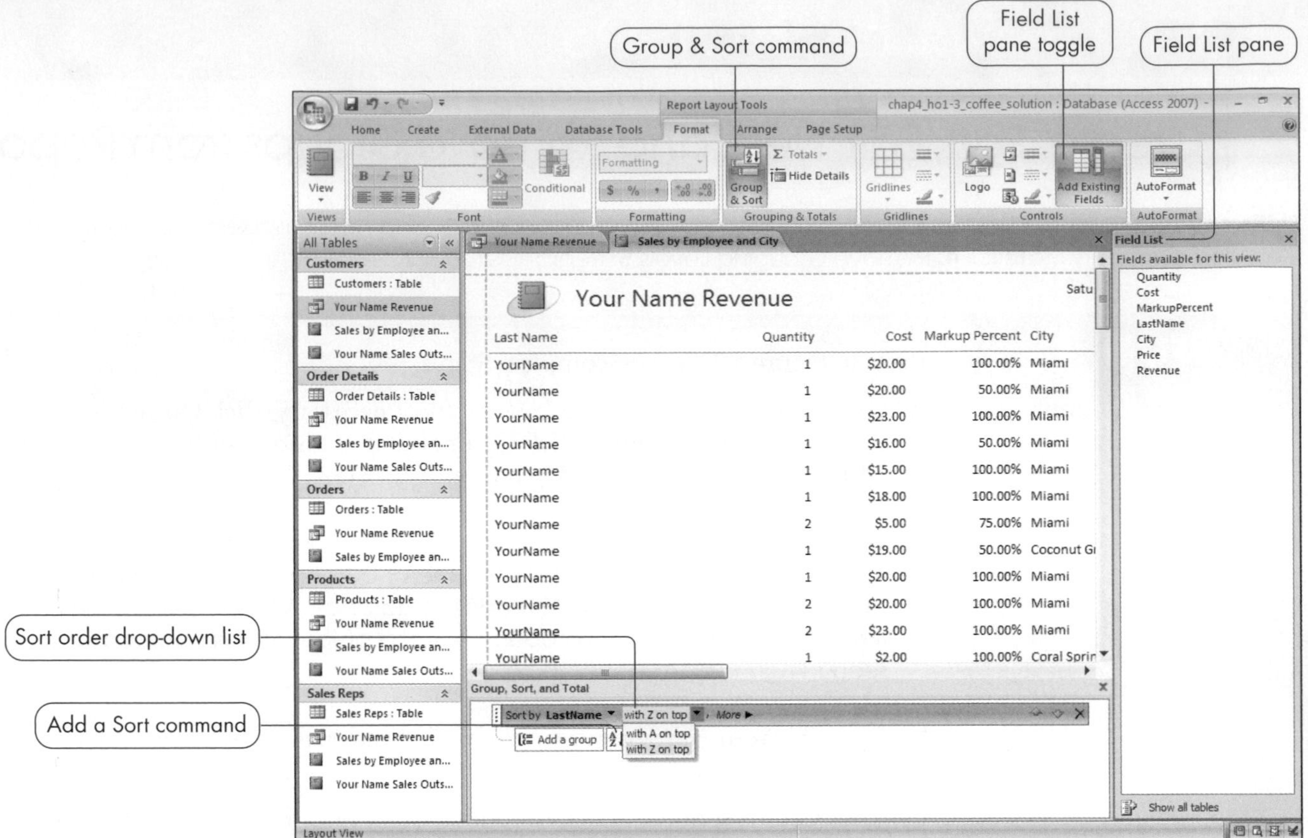

Figure 4.22 Correctly Sorted Report

Step 2
Create a Grouped Report and Sort It

Refer to Figure 4.23 as you complete Step 2.

a. Click **Add a group** in the Group, Sort, and Total pane.

A list box pops up asking you to select the field name that you want to group by.

b. Select the **LastName** field in the list box.

TROUBLESHOOTING: If your screen does not look like Figure 4.23, it may be because you selected a different group by value. Click close on the gold Group on LastName bar in the Group, Sort, and Total pane to remove the incorrect grouping. Then rework Steps 2a and 2b.

c. Scroll right until you can see the label control box for the **Revenue** field. (It is blue.) Click to select it.

d. Click the **Format tab** and click **Totals** in the Grouping & Totals group.

A drop-down list providing function options appears.

e. Click **Sum**.

f. Save the report.

A sum has been added to the Revenue field after each group. You probably cannot see it because it is scrolled off-screen. Use the scrollbar to see that your revenue is 1599.125.

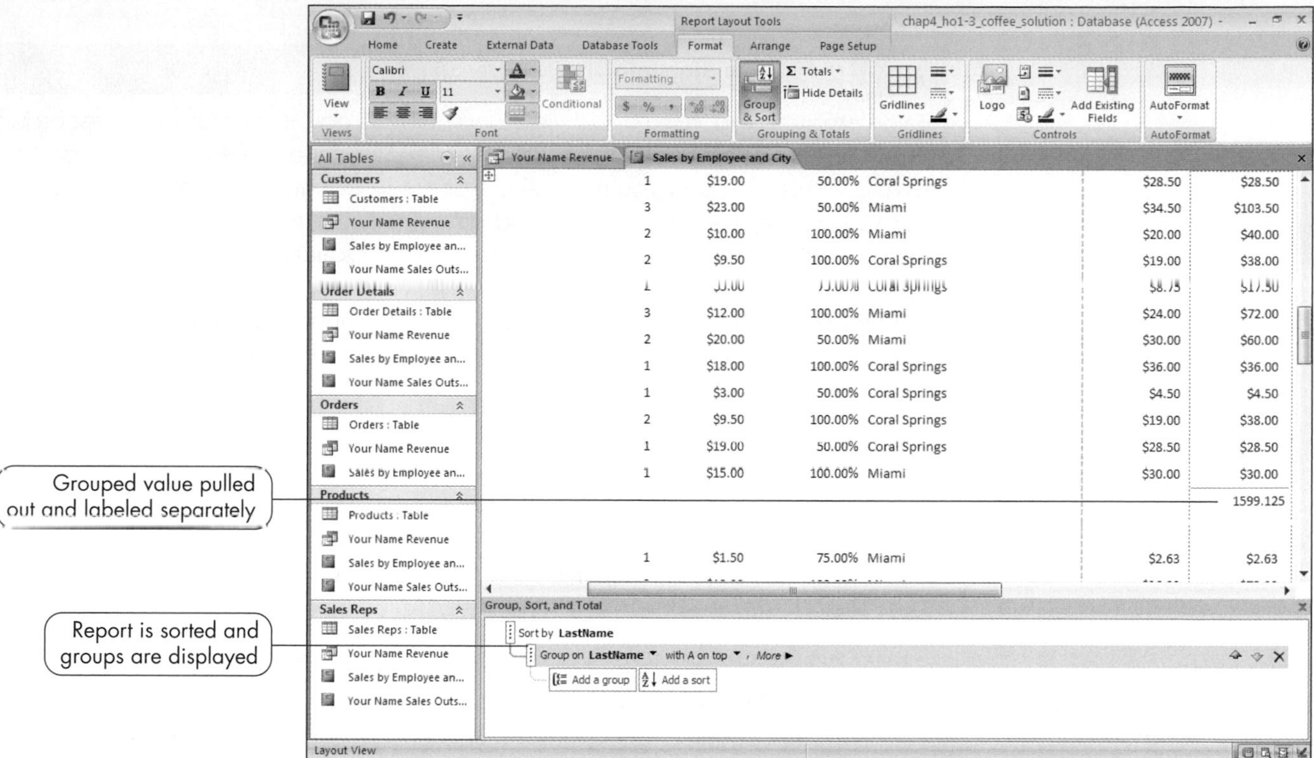

Figure 4.23 Correctly Sorted Report with Primary Group

Step 3 Add Additional Grouping Levels and Calculate Summary Statistics

Refer to Figure 4.24 as you complete Step 3.

a. Ensure that you are still in Layout view. Click **Add a group** in the Group, Sort, and Total pane.

b. Scroll left to locate and select the **City** field in the Field List box.

   The Primary grouping level is still the salesperson's last name. Now the customer's city is grouped together nested inside the LastName field. During this period, you sold one order to a customer in Coconut Grove, once to a customer in Coral Gables, 10 orders to customers in Coral Springs, and the rest of your orders came from Miami-based customers. You decide to create summary statistics by city and salesperson to analyze the sales information.

c. Click the **Cost** label to select it. Click **Totals** in the Grouping & Totals group. Select **Average** from the function list.

   Scroll down until you see the average cost for the orders to Coral Springs displayed. You will see the average cost of an order from a Coral Springs customer was only $12.10, while the average costs of orders to Coral Gables and Coconut Grove were much higher.

d. Scroll up and click the **City** label to select it. Click **Totals** in the Grouping & Totals group. Select **Count Records** from the function list.

   The City field is defined as a text field. Access presents different functions depending on whether the field contains text or numbers.

TIP Counting Records

If you create a report in Layout view and need to count the number of records, be sure to select a field that contains a non-null value for each record. If a report contained 20 records and you instructed Access to count a field that contained two null values, the resulting count would display 18. The missing values would not be included in the count. An easy way to fix this situation is to count only fields that have their Required property set to Yes. Alternatively, you can edit the field's control property. Select the text box containing the Count value, right-click, and select Properties. Click the Data tab. In the Control Source box, select and delete the expression and type =count(*).

e. Scroll to the last of the records from your customers (that is just above the name of the other salesperson, Lockley).

   You see the number of records of orders sold by you—39.

f. Press **Ctrl+Home** to return to the top of the report. Select the **Markup Percent** label. Click **Totals** in the Grouping & Totals group. Select **Average** from the function list.

g. Scroll to the right. Select the **Price** label. Click the **Totals** command in the Grouping & Totals group. Select **Average** from the function list. Format as currency.

   Like the Cost field, the Price field records a per-unit cost, so it does not make sense to sum it.

h. Scroll to the right. Select the **Revenue** label. Click **Totals** in the Grouping & Totals group. Select **Sum** from the function list. Check to make sure the value is formatted as currency.

   TROUBLESHOOTING: A group summary statistic should automatically inherit its formatting properties from the field's format. Occasionally, the group total or average calculates correctly, but it is incorrectly formatted. To correct the format, right-click the incorrectly formatted value in the Layout view of the report and select Properties from the shortcut menu. Set the Format property to the correct value, e.g., currency, and close the Property Sheet. This action forces a format correction.

i. Narrow the first two columns so that the report fits on one page horizontally. Refer to Hands-On Exercise 1, Step 3e, if you do not remember how to do this step.

j. Save the report.

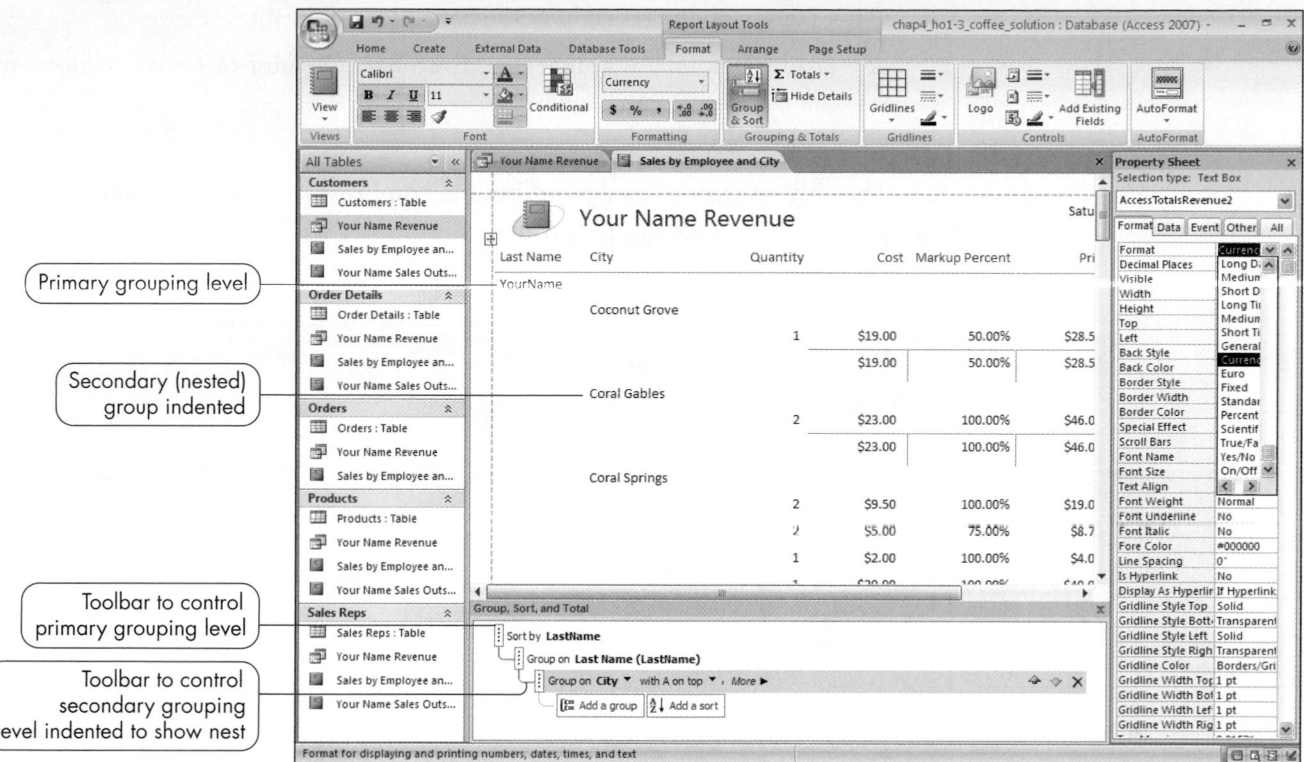

Figure 4.24 Report with Two Grouping Levels Added

Step 4 Remove Grouping Levels

Refer to Figure 4.25 as you complete Step 4.

a. Save and close the Sales by Employee and City report.

You need practice deleting grouping levels, but you need to preserve the work from Step 3. You will copy the report and delete the group levels in the copy.

b. Right-click the **Sales by Employee and City report** in the All Tables pane. Select **Copy** from the shortcut menu. Move your mouse to a white space in the All Tables pane, right-click, and select **Paste**.

c. Name the copy **Sales by Employee**. Click **OK**.

d. Move your mouse to a white space in the All Tables pane. (Do this a second time.) Right-click and select **Paste**.

e. Name the copy **Sales by City**.

TROUBLESHOOTING: If your monitor resolution is set low, you may have trouble finding white space in which to paste. This file was set to display tables and related objects in the All Tables pane. That view repeats multi-table query and report names. A view that uses less space is the Objects view. Click the All Tables pane title bar and select Object Type. That should free up some white space for you to paste the copied report. After your copied report is pasted and renamed, switch back to the Tables and related view.

f. Open the **Sales by Employee report** in Layout view.

g. Click **Group & Sort** in the Grouping & Totals group on the Format tab to display the Group, Sort, and Total pane (if necessary).

h. Click the **Group on City bar** to select it.

The entire bar turns gold when selected.

i. Click **Delete** on the far right of the bar (it looks like an X).

A warning box tells you that the group has a header or footer section and the controls there also will be deleted.

j. Click **Yes**.

The City grouping disappears, but the employee grouping remains.

k. Click **Save**. Close your report.

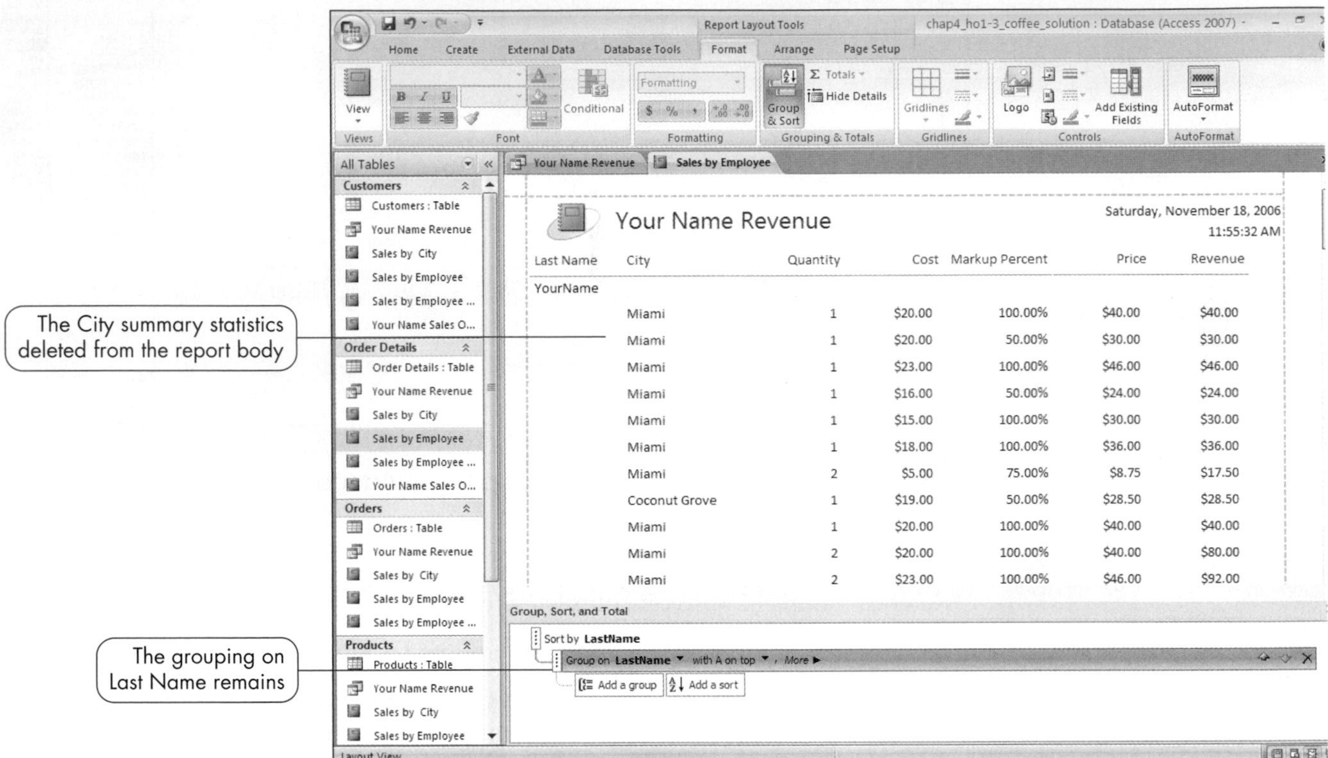

Figure 4.25 Sales by Employee

Step 5
Reorder Grouping Levels

Refer to Figure 4.26 as you complete Step 5.

a. Open the **Sales by City report** in Layout view.

You are going to change the order of the grouping fields so that the primary group will be the City and the secondary group the employee.

b. Click **Group & Sort** in the Grouping & Totals group on the Format tab to display the grouping pane (if necessary).

c. Click the **Group on LastName bar** in the Group, Sort, and Total pane to select it.

d. Click the **down arrow** in the right side of the Group on Last Name bar one time.

You might have expected that the report would now be grouped by city and then by your sales and Lockley's sales grouped within each city. Your sales are together in the top of the report, Lockley's in the bottom of the report. Examine the grouping window more carefully. There is a sort in effect. It receives the top priority. So the employee sales will not group in each city.

e. Click the **Sort by LastName bar** to select it.

f. Click **Delete** (X) on the right of the Sort by Last Name bar.

When you delete the sort, the grouping prioritization changes; now, the employees are sorted within the cities as expected.

g. Check to make sure the formats of the group totals and grand totals are appropriately formatted. If not, apply the Currency format.

h. Click the text box containing the report title, *Your Name Revenue*. Click it again to edit it. Change the report name to **Your Name City Revenue**. Save the report.

i. Click **Group & Sort** in the Grouping & Totals group on the Format tab.

j. Click the **Office Button**, select **Manage**, and then select **Back Up Database**. Enter the file name **chap4_ho2_coffee_solution** (*note ho2 instead of ho1-3*) and click **Save**.

You just created a backup of the database after completing the second hands-on exercise. The original database *chap4_ho1-3_coffee_solution* remains onscreen. If you ruin the original database as you complete the third hands-on exercise, you can use the backup file you just created.

k. Close the file and exit Access if you do not want to continue with the next exercise at this time.

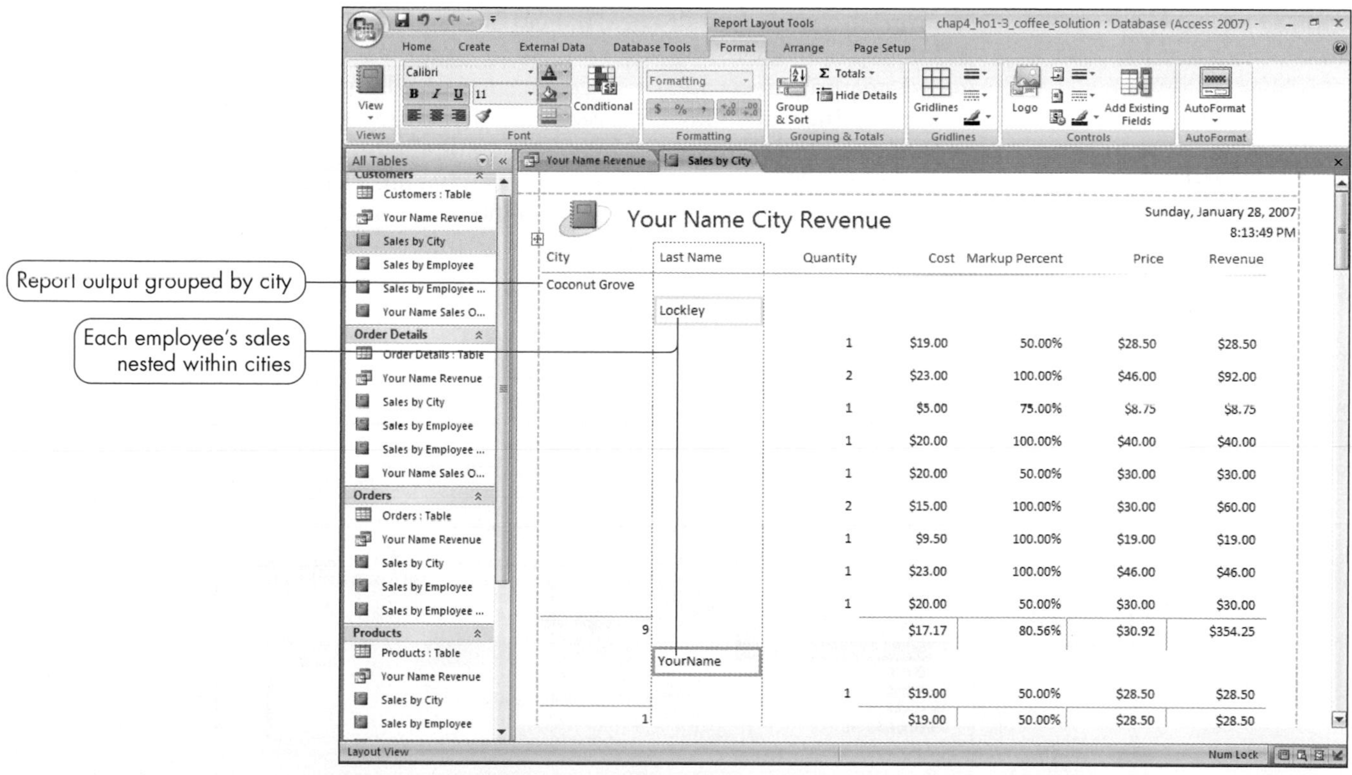

Figure 4.26 The City Report

The Report and Label Wizards

Earlier in this chapter, you created a polished, professional report with grouping levels, sorts, and summary statistics by using the Report tool. You edited the report through a GUI interface and immediately saw the effect on the output. You may recall that Access provides four ways of creating a report (see Table 4.1). In this section, you will create a report using the Report Wizard and edit it using both the Layout and Design views.

The ***Report Wizard*** asks you questions and then, depending on how you answer, generates the report.

The ***Report Wizard*** asks you questions and then, depending on how you answer, generates the report. Many of the wizard's dialog boxes contain commands that lead you to further levels of options. As you read this section and work through the hands-on exercise, you should explore the additional options and think about how and when you might use them. Access provides so many methods of report generation because Access users require so many differing types of reports. As you gain experience, you will learn which tool is most appropriate for your tasks.

If no query exists that assembles the necessary fields for a report, the Report Wizard is probably the best option. It enables you to pull fields from multiple sources relatively easily. Access reports generated by using the Report Wizard sometimes require extensive revision to make them intelligible. Occasionally, the necessary revision time greatly exceeds the time needed to assemble the needed fields in a query in order to use the Report tool. You will need to experiment with the differing methods of report generation to discover which works most effectively with your data and computing usage style.

Mailing labels are self-stick, die-cut labels that you print with names, addresses, and postal barcodes.

The ***Label Wizard*** asks you questions and then, depending on how you answer, generates the report formatted to print on mailing labels.

Mailing labels are self-stick, die-cut labels that you print with names, addresses, and postal barcodes. You purchase name-brand labels at an office supply store. In Access, mailing labels are considered a specialized report. You use the ***Label Wizard*** to help produce a mailing label report. In the wizard, you specify the label manufacturer and the label product number shown on the box of labels. For example, Avery 5660 contains 30 individual labels per sheet that are 1″ x 2⅝″. After selecting the label type, you place and format the fields in the label prototype (see Figure 4.27). The finished report is shown in Figure 4.28.

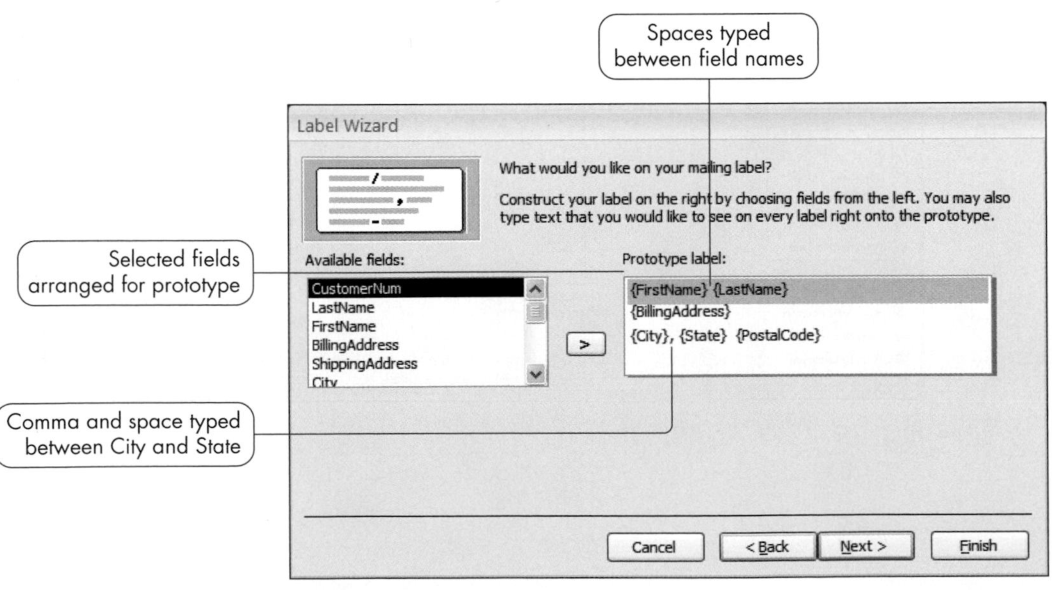

Figure 4.27 Label Prototype

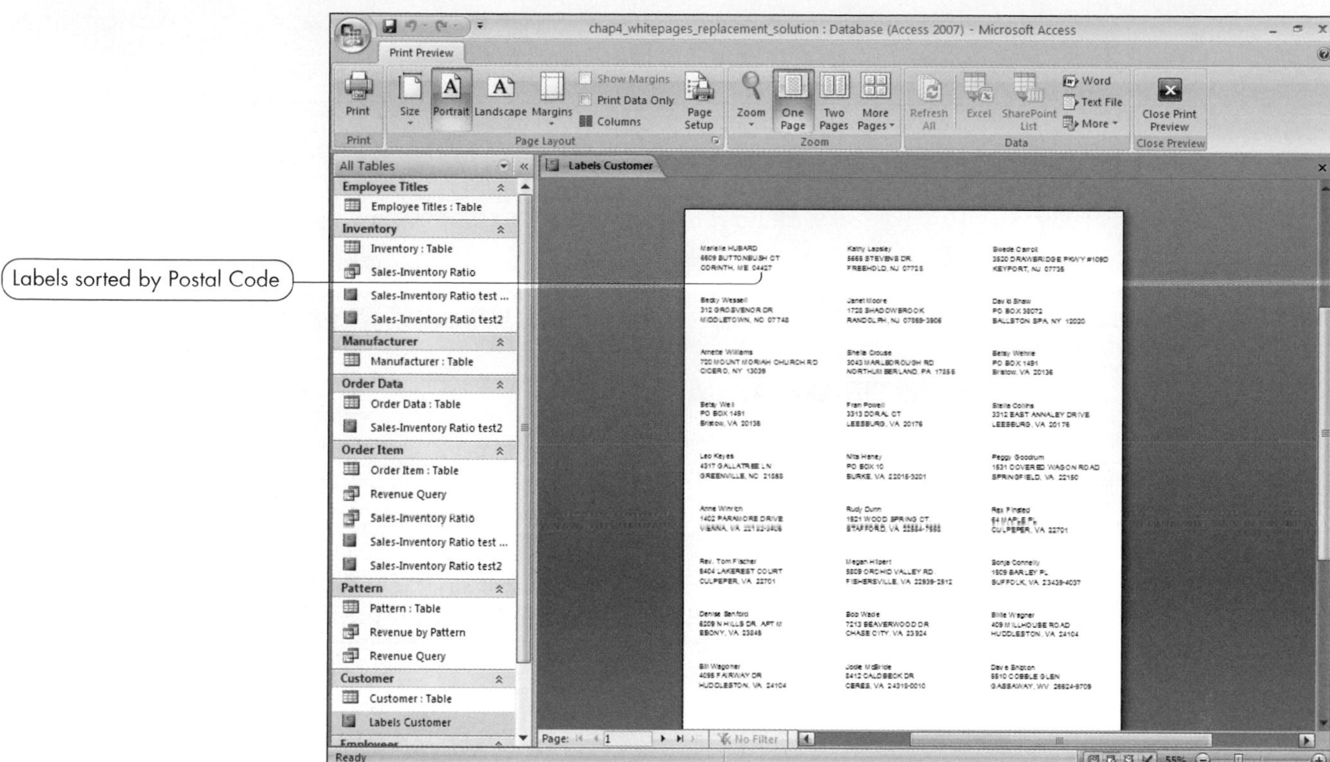

Figure 4.28 Completed Labels

Using the Report Wizard

Even when using a wizard to guide your report formation, you need to pre-plan the desired output. Suppose you needed a monthly sales report that grouped the products by category and provided summary statistics monitoring the average discounts offered to customers and the revenue generated from product sales. This report would require one grouping level and two summary calculations—one for total revenue and the other for average discount rate. Next, you need to identify the report's record source. For this illustration, you may assume that all necessary records exist in a query. In actual practice, you may need to first create the query assembling the needed records. Some Access users source reports directly from table data. After thinking through the design and record source, you launch the wizard.

> Even when using a wizard to guide your report formation, you need to pre-plan the desired output.

Start the Report Wizard

You do not need to have the report record source open to launch the Report Wizard like you do when using the Report tool. You may wish to close any open objects in your database before launching the wizard. Find the Report Wizard on the Create tab in the Reports group. The first dialog box asks you to specify the record source (see Figure 4.29).

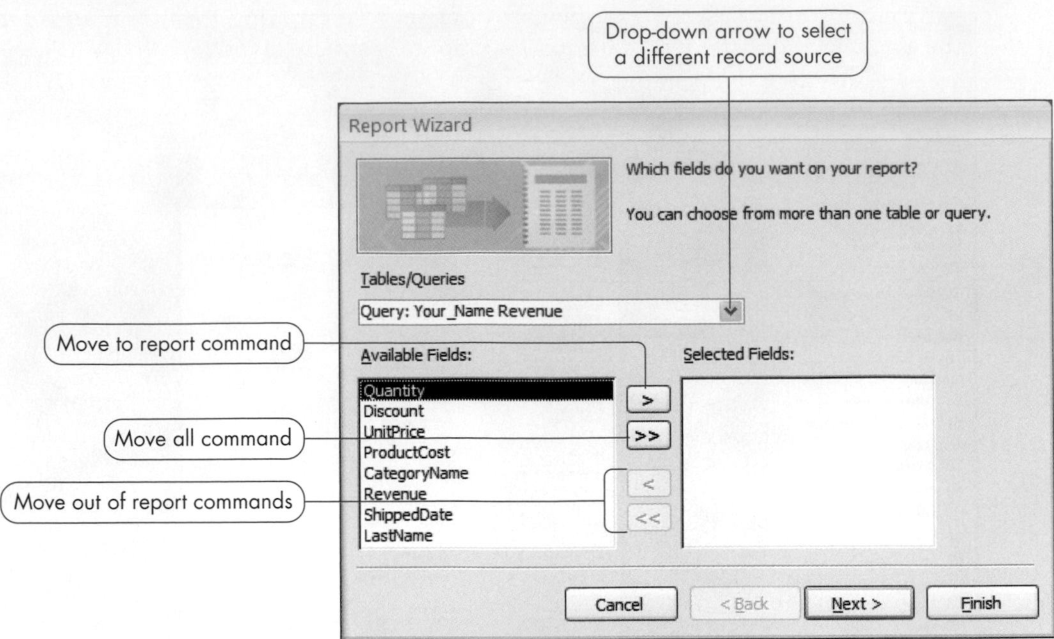

Figure 4.29 Select Records

Group Records

Grouping lets you organize and consolidate your data. You also can calculate aggregating information. In this report, you need the data grouped by the Category Name field, so in the wizard's box under "Do you want to add any grouping levels?" you would identify and double-click the Category Name field. If you needed additional grouping levels, you would double-click those field names also. The order in which you select the groups dictates the order of nesting in the report (see Figure 4.30). The Priority commands let you change your mind and restructure the nest levels. If you select a date/time field to group by, click Grouping Options to find an interval specification box. Use it to designate the grouping interval, such as week, month, or quarter.

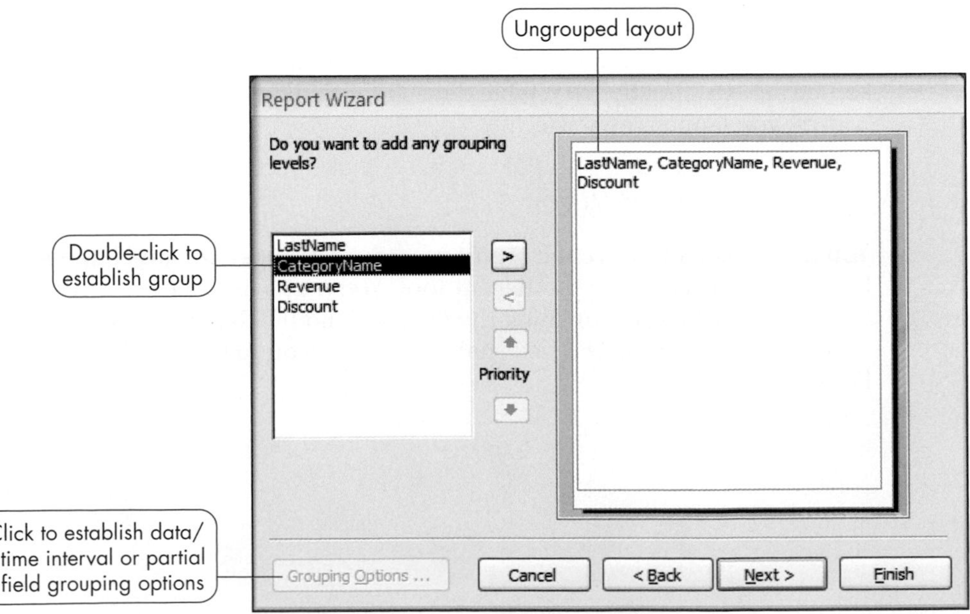

Figure 4.30 Specify Grouping Options

Figure 4.31 shows the grouping options set to group on Category Name. Once the group is established, the Grouping Options command activates. If the group field was a date/time field, you would establish the interval in the Grouping Intervals dialog box. Because this grouping field is a text field, the intervals displayed contain portions of the field name, i.e. the first two letters. You might use this feature if you were grouping an inventory list and the inventory IDs within a category started with the same letters. For example, FJW123, FJR123, FJB123 might be inventory numbers for the fine jewelry department for watches, rings, and bracelets. If you set the grouping interval option to the two initial letters, you would include the fine jewelry department's entire inventory.

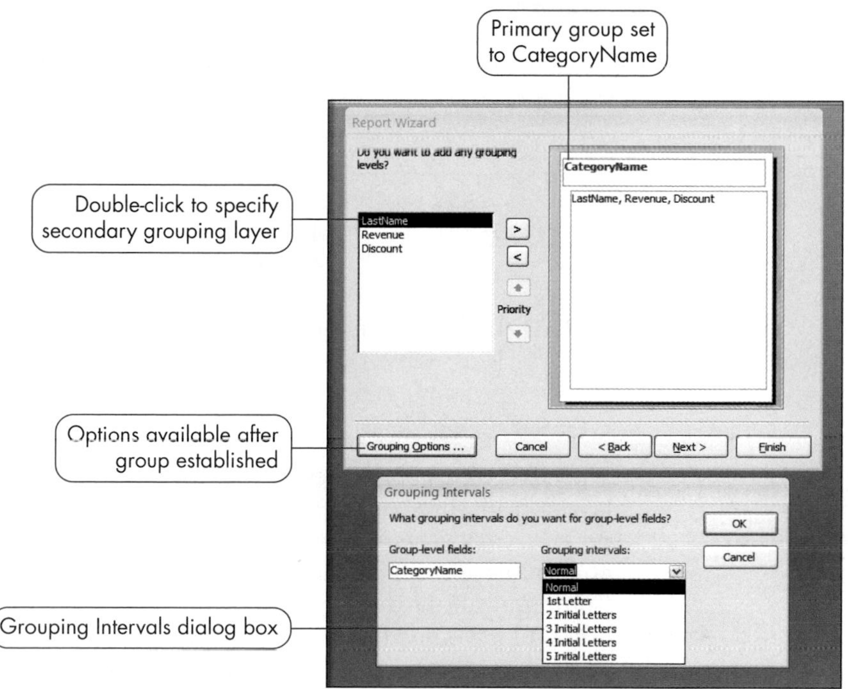

Figure 4.31 Grouping Options Set on Category

Add Sorts and Summary Instructions

The next dialog box asks "What sort order and summary information do you want for detail records?" Notice that the sorts apply only to a detail record. Some reports omit the detail, making the sort order moot. If this were a detail report, you might specify that the details be sorted first by category in ascending order, and then by revenue in descending order. Because you have decided to create a summary report, you need to click the Summary Options command. This step takes you to a screen where you may choose summary statistics (sum, average, minimum, and maximum), and whether or not you want the details presented (see Figure 4.32). Clicking either OK or Cancel returns you to the wizard.

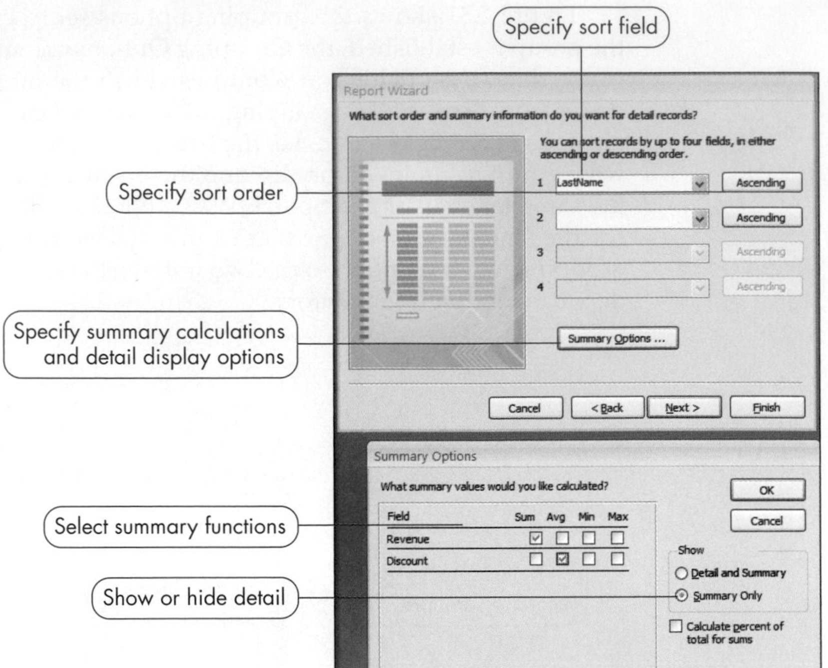

Figure 4.32 Specify Sort Options

Design the Report

The next two dialog boxes control the report's appearance. In the first, you select the layout from three options. Clicking an option will give you a general preview in the preview area. The final dialog box offers you options among the AutoFormats available (see Figure 4.33). In actual organizations, the Public Relations and Graphic Communications departments dictate the design of all printed output. The organization will have one template for all internal reports and one or two others for reports generated for external consumption (e.g., an invoice).

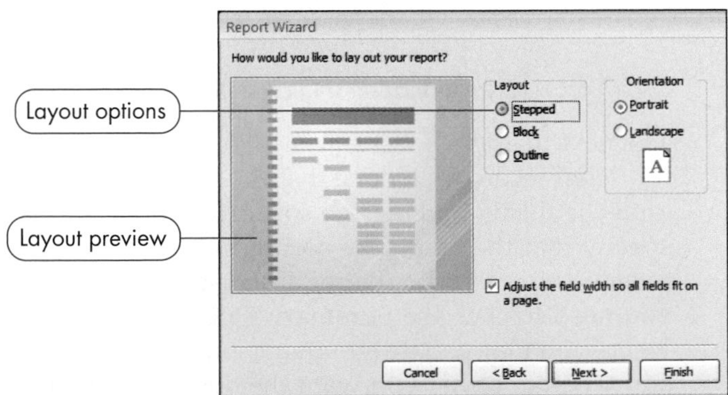

Figure 4.33 Specify Layout Options

A ***work-around*** acknowledges that a problem exists, and develops a sufficing solution.

Ironically, the design selection variety makes life more difficult for students than for real-world practitioners. On the job, you typically employ fewer than five templates. You use them all day, every day. You become intimately acquainted with all of their quirks. You develop functional work-arounds. A ***work-around*** acknowledges that a problem exists and develops a sufficing solution. In a course, you use a variety of differing templates and never fully understand any of them. Figure 4.34 shows AutoFormat choices.

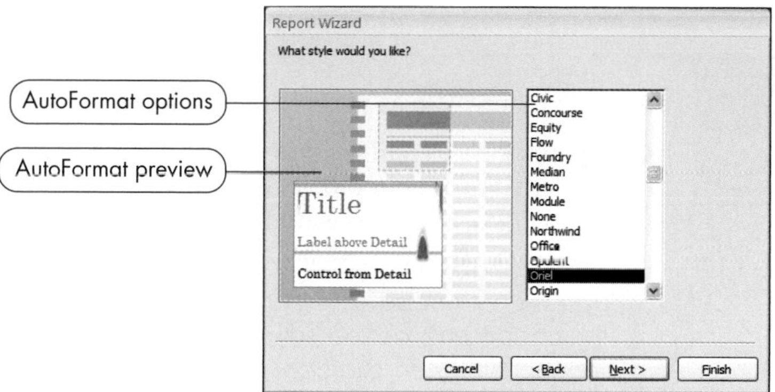

Figure 4.34 AutoFormat

Save and Name the Report

A well-designed database may contain only a few tables, but it may have many queries and reports. You should name all report objects descriptively to save you time and minimize frustration. Always name your report something that not only makes sense to you today, but also will communicate the report's contents to a co-worker or to you in six months (see Figure 4.35).

In the next hands-on exercise, you will create a report using the Report Wizard and edit it using the Layout view.

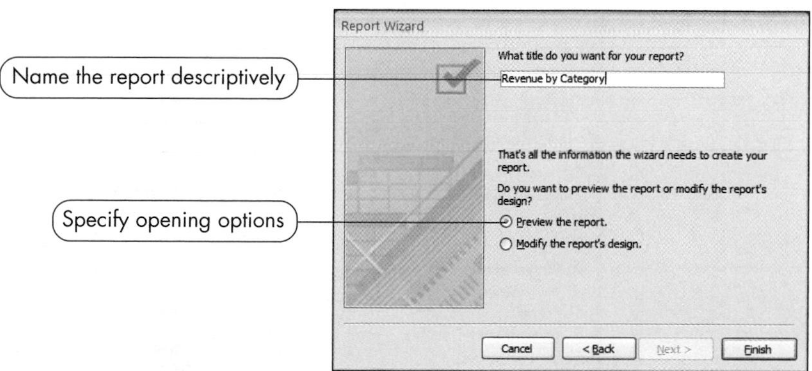

Figure 4.35 Use Descriptive Report Names

Hands-On Exercises

3 | Report Wizard

Skills covered: 1. Assemble the Report Data **2.** Create a Query-Based Report and Add Grouping **3.** Create Summary Statistics **4.** Select Layout and AutoFormatting **5.** Modify the Report

Step 1
Assemble the Report Data

Refer to Figure 4.36 as you complete Step 1.

a. Open the *chap4_ho1-3_coffee_solution* file if necessary, click **Options** on the Security Warning toolbar, click the **Enable this content option** in the Microsoft Office Security Options dialog box, and click **OK**.

TROUBLESHOOTING: If you create unrecoverable errors while completing this hands-on exercise, you can delete the chap4_ho1-3_coffee_solution file, copy the chap4_ho2_coffee_solution backup database you created at the end of the second hands-on exercise, and open the copy of the backup database to start the third hands-on exercise again.

b. Open the **Your Name Revenue query** in Design view.

c. Add the **OrderDate** field located in the *Orders* table to the design grid by double-clicking it.

d. Add the **ProductName** field located in the *Products* table to the design grid by double-clicking it.

e. Click **Run** in the Results group on the Design tab to run the query. Scroll right to ensure that the newly added fields exist.

f. Save the changes. Close the query. Check to make sure the query name is selected in the Navigation pane.

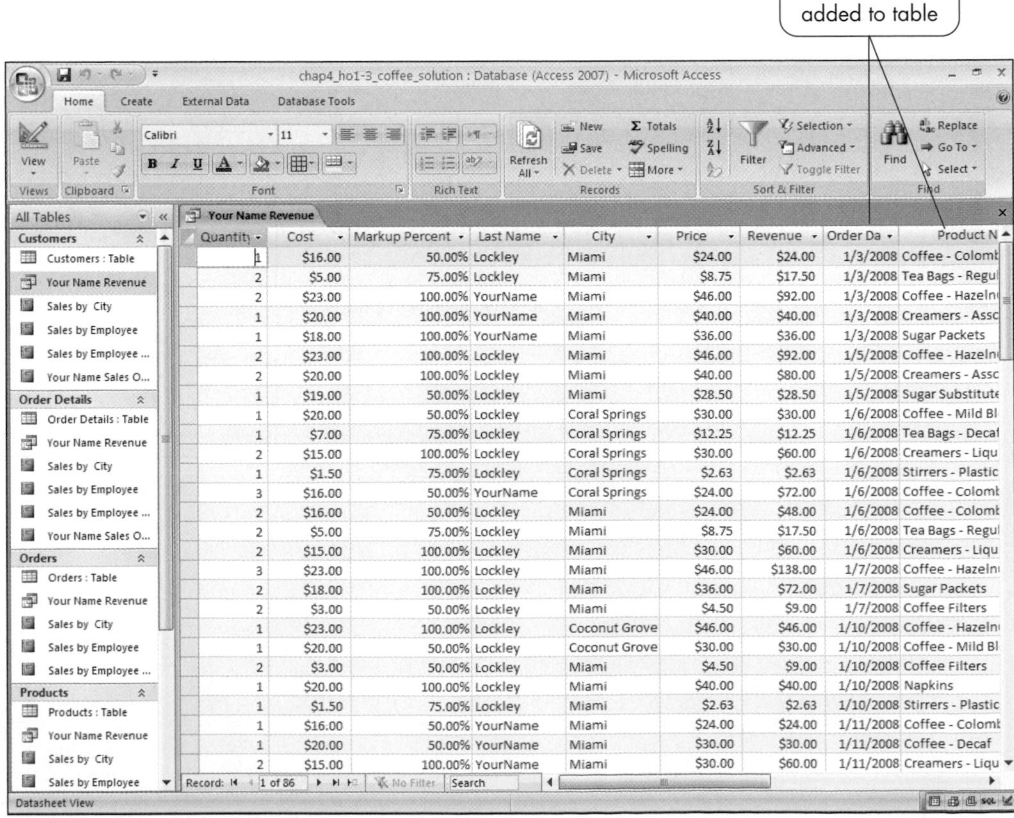

Figure 4.36 Assemble the Record Source

Step 2
Create a Query-Based Report and Add Grouping

Refer to Figure 4.37 as you complete Step 2.

a. Click the **Create tab** and click **Report Wizard** in the Reports group.

The wizard launches, and the Your Name Revenue query selects as the record source because it was highlighted when you started the wizard.

b. Click the **Move All command (>>)** to move all of the query fields to the Selected Fields box. Click **Next**.

c. Double-click **OrderDate** in the grouping level box.

The right box displays the default date grouping, OrderDate by Month. In this case, you want a monthly report so you do not need to change the grouping options command.

d. Double-click the **LastName** field in the left box to add it as a grouping level.

e. Compare your grouping levels to those shown in Figure 4.37. If they match, click **Next**.

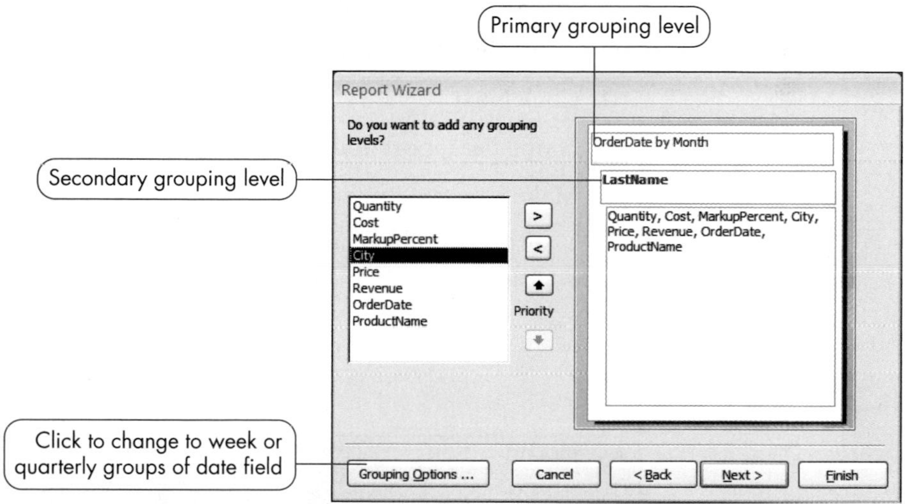

Figure 4.37 Create Groups

Step 3
Create Summary Statistics

Refer to Figure 4.38 as you complete Step 3.

a. Click the drop-down arrow beside the first sort box. Select **City** as the primary sort field.

b. Click **Summary Options**.

TROUBLESHOOTING: As long as the Report Wizard dialog box remains open, you can click Back and revisit your work.

c. Click the **Sum** check box for the **Revenue** field.

d. Click the **Calculate percent of total for sums** check box.

e. Compare your Summary Options to those shown in Figure 4.38. If they match, click **OK**, and then click **Next**.

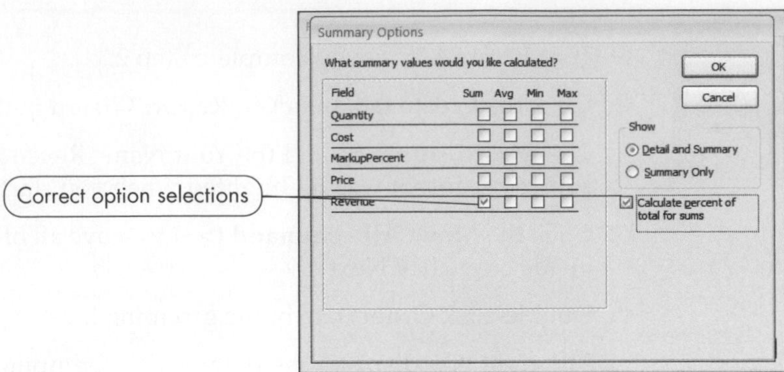

Figure 4.38 Summary Calculation Specifications

Step 4
Select Layout and AutoFormatting

Refer to Figure 4.39 as you complete Step 4.

a. Select a **Stepped** layout and a **Portrait** orientation.

b. Click **Next**.

Spend some time exploring in the Report AutoFormats of the wizard.

c. Select the **Module** style.

d. Click **Next**.

e. Name the report **Your Name Monthly Revenue by Salesperson**.

f. Make sure the **Preview the report** option is selected. Click **Finish**.

You successfully generated output, but it has flaws. Examine your work critically, and then compare the problems you spot to those highlighted in Figure 4.39.

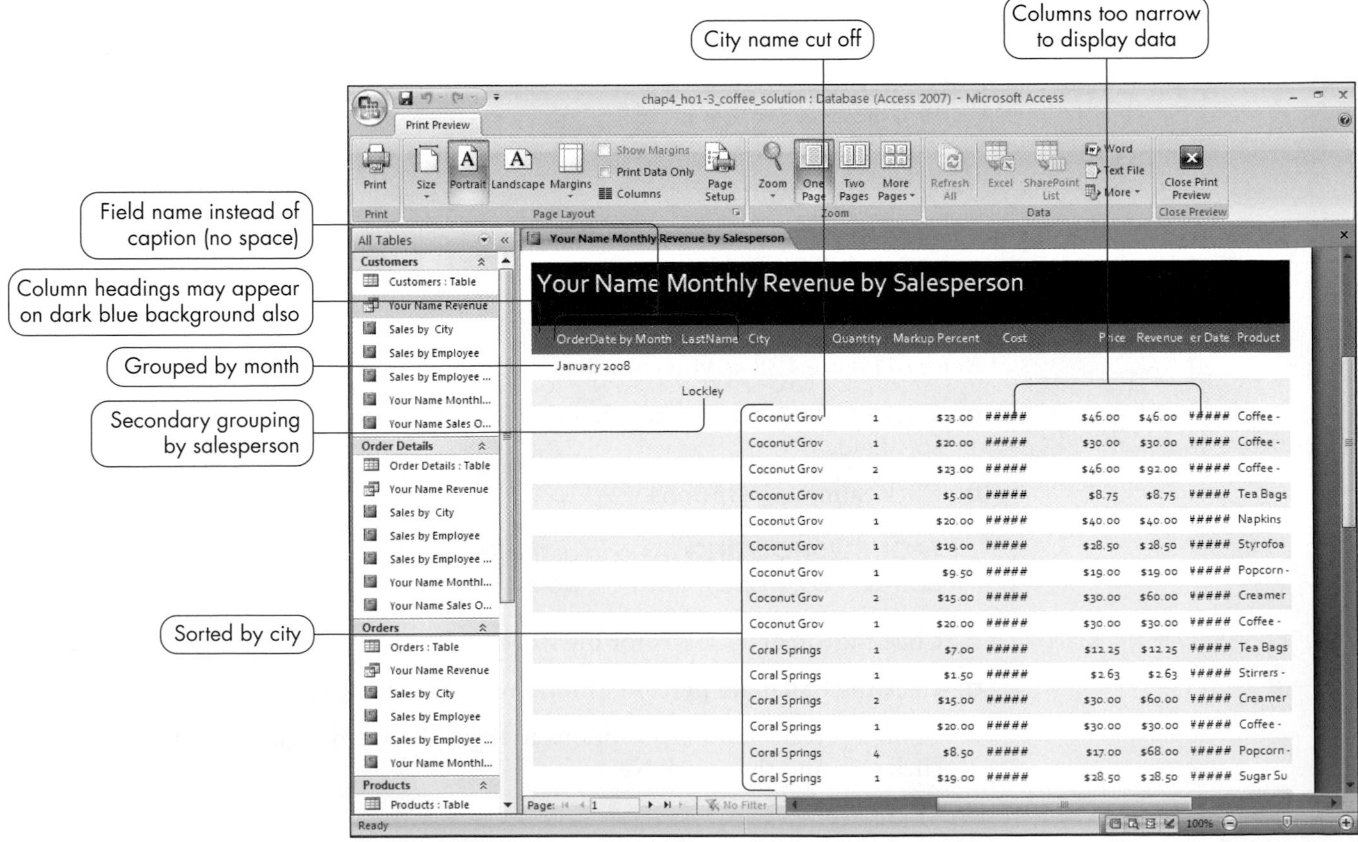

Figure 4.39 Create Groups

Step 5
Modify the Report

Refer to Figure 4.40 as you complete Step 4.

a. Right-click the report tab and select **Layout View**.

b. Select the text box for the OrderDate by Month control. Click it again to edit the text to **Order Month**. Press **Enter**.

   Ideally, you should save and close the report, open the Orders table, switch to Design view and add a caption for the OrderDate field. Save the design change to the table and close it. Run the query the report sources. Reopen the report. The caption will replace the field name in the text box in this and all other reports and forms that source on OrderDate. Because you also changed from OrderDate by Month to Order Month, it is excusable to make this a one-time change.

c. Ensure the **Order Month** control is still selected. Move your mouse over the right boundary and when the mouse pointer shape changes to the double-headed arrow, click and drag left about a quarter of an inch.

d. Select the text box for the **LastName** control. Click it again to edit the text. Type a **space** between Last and Name.

e. Select the **City** control text box and widen the column using the click and drag technique presented in Step 5c. Make sure the entire city name, Coconut Grove, displays.

   You determine that the report is too crowded and that several fields do not need to be displayed. You decide to delete the Quantity, Markup Percent, Cost, and Price fields.

f. Click the **Quantity** field control text box and press **Delete**.

g. Delete the **Markup Percent**, **Cost**, and **Price** fields.

h. Widen the **Product Name** and **Order Date** fields.

i. Click the **Format tab**, if necessary. Click **Hide Details** in the Grouping & Totals group.

   The details of the report hide. This result makes it easier for you to find and edit the summary statistics.

j. Find the words, *Summary for 'LastName' = Lockley (47 detail records)*. On the line below in blue, it says Sum. Look right. You should see a small text box with some numbers or pound signs in it. The control box is too small to display the value. Click the too-small control.

k. Mouse over the control's right boundary, get the double-headed resize arrows, and then click and drag to the **right** to widen the control.

   When the box is large enough, you will see that the value of Lockley's total revenue is 1836.5. It is not formatted as currency.

l. Enlarge the controls for **Sum and Grand Total**. Check to see that the text boxes are large enough to display the percent values, too. Enlarge those text boxes if necessary.

m. Click the **Sum** value for Lockley, 1836.5. **Right-click** and select **Properties** from the shortcut menu. Set the **Format** property to **Currency**. With the Properties Sheet still open, click the grand total and format it as **Currency**.

   All of the sums should display in Currency format. Because there are two grouping levels, the Report Wizard repeats the grand total twice. You want to keep the bottom one because it is in the report footer along with the words, *Grand Total*.

n. Find the repeated Grand Total value (the one labeled Sum). Select it and press **Delete**. Select and delete the word *Sum*.

o. Click **Hide Details** in the Grouping & Totals group on the Format tab to return the details to the report.

   You hid the details to format the totals. It moves them out of the way and makes it easier to format the total information.

p. Move the **Sum** and **Standard** control boxes left and position them under the Summary for 'LastName' = Your name. Align the total with the Revenue column. You also need to move the grand total controls.

q. Move the **percent** control boxes left under the Order Date column. Make the boxes wide enough to display the values. the control box containing **100%** and the **label**.

r. Locate the text box containing the **page number**. If necessary, move the right boundary left so that it no longer crosses the dotted line indicating the page break.

s. Right-click the report tab and select **Print Preview**.

t. Click **Two Pages** in the Zoom group. Use the navigation commands to preview the last page. Print the report. Save the report.

u. Click the **Office Button**, select **Manage**, and then select **Compact and Repair Database**.

v. Close the file and exit Access.

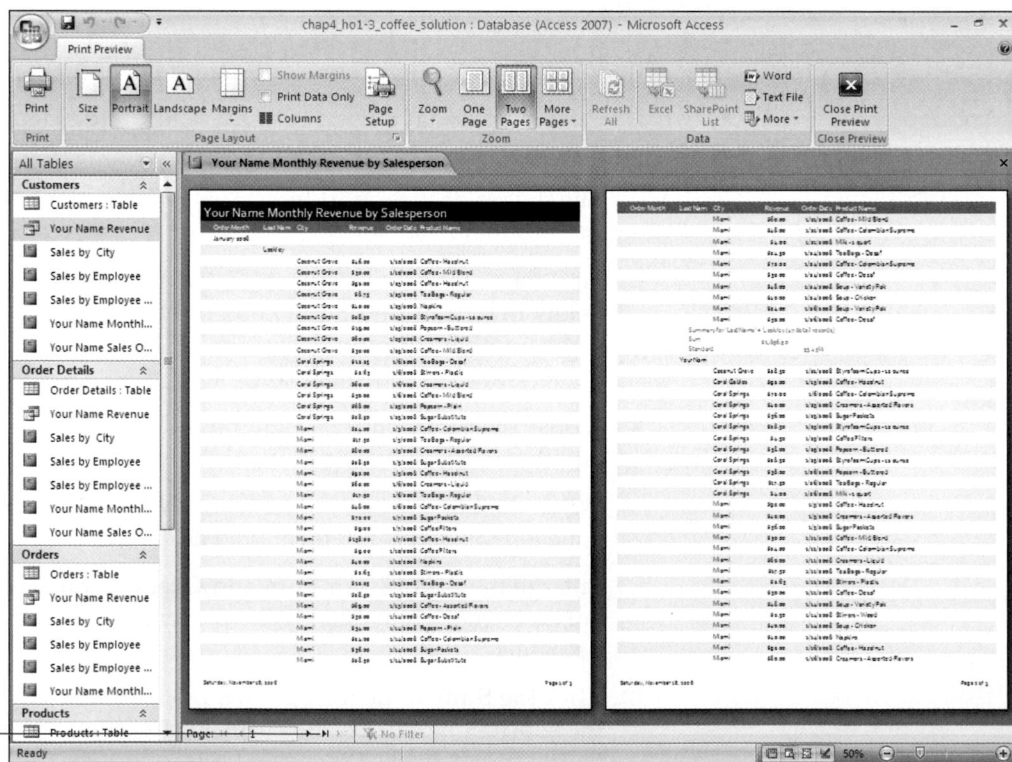

Figure 4.40 The Report in Print Preview

Summary

1. **Plan a report.** A report is a printed document that displays information from a database. Telephone directories, financial statements, shipping labels, and receipts are examples of reports. You should carefully consider what information you need and how you can optimally present it. A paper and pencil may be the best tools for planning. Develop a series of questions to ask to determine what the report should answer. Identify the data sources for the report. Select a reporting tool.

2. **Use different report views.** Access provides different views of your report depending on the operation you need to accomplish. Print Preview is an invaluable tool while designing reports. Use it liberally to preview your reports. Report view enables you to organize the data for the report by sorting and filtering it. Layout view enables you to alter the report design. This is the most powerful view and where you will spend most of your time. Design view displays the report's infrastructure design, but no data. This view has its advantages in large reports, but may be more difficult to use to make exact tweaks to the formatting.

3. **Create and edit a report.** To use the Report tool, you need to assemble all of the necessary data in one place. Occasionally, a table contains all of the necessary fields for a report. More often, you will need to create or open a query containing the necessary fields. If an existing query has all of the fields needed for the report but also some unneeded fields, you probably will use the existing query. You can delete the extraneous fields in Layout view. Access does a lot of the cosmetic work in your reports for you, by adjusting column widths as you add and remove columns. You can do the rest in Layout view.

4. **Identify report elements, sections, and controls.** Access divides all reports into sections, although you only see the sectional boundaries when you display the report in the Design view. Detail Section is the body of the report, containing each record. The Report Header (Footer) Section prints at the beginning (end) of each report. Group headers and footers appear at the tops and bottoms of each report group. Page headers and footers display at the top and bottom of each report page. You can edit these areas in the Design or Layout views. Controls display, position, format, and calculate the report data. You will use bound controls, those that are bound or tied to a source table or query, most frequently. Unbound controls have no record source in the underlying data. An example of an unbound control would be the report's title. A calculated control uses an expression as opposed to a record value as its data source. The expression usually is bound to record values of the fields referenced.

5. **Add grouping levels in Layout view.** Access provides several methods of grouping and summarizing data. You can create (1) a Totals query by specifying a group by field and the field or fields to summarize, (2) a grouped report using the Layout view's Sorting and Grouping tools, and (3) a grouped report using the Report Wizard and specifying the group layers within the wizard. Since most reports will have many thousands of records, you should sort them using the Group Sort tool. Nested groups make the report look similar to an outline. You also can hide and display details in reports and calculate summary statistics. You can add sub-groupings as needed.

6. **Add fields to a report.** Inevitably, after a report has been used, someone will say, "It would be nice to have this in the report, too." Use the Layout view to add additional fields to a report.

7. **Use the Report Wizard.** Access contains several wizards that will print common repeatedly used reports such as mailing labels. It is important that you organize your desired output for wizards just as you would if you designed the report from scratch. Unlike the Report tool, when using a Report Wizard, you should close any open objects in the data source. Like in the Report tool, you can customize the reports from the Report Wizard with groups, sorts, and summaries to tweak the overall design to best present your data. A well-designed database may only have a few tables, but dozens of queries and reports. Chances are good that they will be reused, so they should be saved and descriptively named.

Key Terms

Bound control 274
Calculated control 274
Controls 274
Design view 260
Detail section 271
Field List pane 279
Group footer section 271
Group header section 271
Label Wizard 288
Layout view 259
Mailing labels 288
Nested groups 275
Page footer 272
Page header 272
Print Preview 257
Report 255
Report footer section 271
Report header section 271
Report view 258
Report Wizard 288
Unbound controls 274
Work-around 293

Multiple Choice

1. Which statement most accurately describes the appropriate time to use a report in Access?
   (a) Entering data
   (b) Printing output for presentation
   (c) Querying data
   (d) Sorting records based on preset criteria

2. Which of the following is true?
   (I) You can edit the appearance of reports by changing fonts and styles.
   (II) You can add graphs, pictures, and charts to reports.
   (a) I but not II
   (b) II but not I
   (c) Neither I nor II
   (d) Both I and II

3. Which is an example of a report from a database?
   (a) A shipping label
   (b) A telephone directory
   (c) A sales receipt
   (d) All of the above

4. Which statement about saving a report is true?
   (a) Saved reports are static, and the data represented in a report will be the same every time you run a saved report.
   (b) Saving reports is generally not done in the real world because people rarely need the same information repeatedly.
   (c) You can edit a saved report to add additional fields at a later time.
   (d) Using a saved report can be costly and time-consuming.

5. The most important tool to create an Access report may be:
   (a) The Report Grid tool
   (b) A calculator
   (c) A pencil
   (d) The Report Creator tool

6. It is always best to ask _______ questions about what the report should look like and do.
   (a) the programmer
   (b) the end user
   (c) the customer
   (d) your manager

7. Which of the following are important things to know as you create an Access report?
   (a) Access cannot calculate data in a report.
   (b) Reports can be summarized, but the summaries have to be designed in the underlying query.
   (c) Reports cannot draw data from multiple tables.
   (d) What type of delivery mechanism will be used, fax, e-mail Word, Excel, PowerPoint, Internet, or printer, and what type and size of paper will be used for the report.

8. If you want to create mailing labels from your Customers table, the fastest and easiest tool would be Access':
   (a) Report Tool
   (b) Report Wizard
   (c) Label Wizard
   (d) Mailing Wizard

9. Which of the following is the most sophisticated and flexible tool for report generation?
   (a) Report Wizard
   (b) Report Tool
   (c) Free form report
   (d) WYSIWYG report

10. Use the ___________ to see what the printed report will look like before printing. This step helps with the overall layout and makes the report easy to read and understand.
    (a) Report Tool
    (b) Report Wizard
    (c) Group Wizard
    (d) Print Preview

11. You should modify column widths and row heights for a report in:
    (a) Layout view
    (b) Print Preview
    (c) Group view
    (d) Report view

12. Which of the following is true?
    (I) Access can create a report from multiple tables.
    (II) You will usually have to create a new query to create a report.
    (a) I but not II
    (b) II but not I
    (c) Both I and II
    (d) Neither I nor II

... continued on Next Page

Multiple Choice Continued...

13. What happens if you click a value in Layout view and press Delete?

(a) The entire column is deleted from the report, and column widths are adjusted to use the empty space.

(b) Nothing; you cannot change data in Layout view.

(c) The record is deleted from the report but remains in the database.

(d) An error message appears, saying that you should not attempt to manipulate records in a report.

14. Your pointer shape should be a ____________ to widen or narrow a column in Layout view.

(a) single arrow

(b) hand

(c) two-headed arrow

(d) dashed-tail arrow

15. Which of these is not a sectional division used in Access?

(a) Detail section

(b) Report header and footer sections

(c) Group header and footer sections

(d) Summary section

16. Bound controls are so called because they are bound or attached to:

(I) source data

(II) the report's margins

(a) I but not II

(b) II but not I

(c) Both I and II

(d) Neither I nor II

17. Which of the following is true?

(a) Unbound controls are used infrequently within reports.

(b) Unbound controls are used to display cosmetic elements in a report.

(c) Unbound controls must be saved separately because they are not part of a record.

(d) Unbound controls cannot be used with bound controls in the same report.

18. To organize your data in a highly usable and readable report, you may use:

(a) Nested tables

(b) Nested groups

(c) Nested queries

(d) Calculated fields

Practice Exercises

1 Comfort Insurance Raises and Bonuses Report

The Comfort Insurance Agency is a midsized company with offices located across the country. The Human Resource office is located in the home office in Miami. Each year, each employee receives a performance review. The review determines employee eligibility for salary increases and the annual performance bonus. The employee data are stored in an Access database, which is used by the Human Resource department to monitor and maintain employee records. Your task is to prepare a report showing the salary increase for each employee and his or her performance bonuses (if any). You are the Human Resource department manager. If you correctly report the employee salaries and bonuses, you will receive a bonus. Work carefully and check the accuracy of the calculations. This project follows the same set of skills as used in Hands-On Exercises 1 and 2 in this chapter. If you have problems, reread the detailed directions presented in the chapter. Compare your results to Figure 4.41.

a. Copy the partially completed file *chap4_pe1_insurance* to your production folder. Rename it **chap4_pe1_insurance_solution**, open the file, and enable the security content.
b. Click the **Database Tools tab** and click **Relationships** in the Show/Hide group. Examine the table structure, relationships, and fields. After you are familiar with the database, close the Relationships window.
c. Rename the query with **your name**. Open the **Your Name Raises and Bonus query**.
d. Click the **Create tab** and click **Report** in the Reports group.
e. Click **Group & Sort** in the Grouping & Totals group, if necessary. Click **Add a sort** in the Group, Sort, and Total pane and select **LastName**.
f. Click the **LastName** label. Click it again to edit it and add a **space** between *Last* and *Name*. Click outside the text box to turn off editing. Move the mouse to the **right** control boundary and when the pointer shape changes to the double-headed arrow, click and drag the boundary about a half-inch to the left to make the column narrower.
g. Repeat Step f to add a space to the *FirstName* control and decrease its width. Also reduce the width for the *Performance* column. The report should only be one page wide. Add spaces to the *2008Increase* and *NewSalary* controls.
h. Click the **Report Graphic** (the picture in the upper left) to select it. Click **Logo** in the Controls group on the Format tab. Browse to and locate the file named *chap4_pe1_confident.jpg*. Click **OK** in the Insert Picture dialog box.
i. Click the report title *Your Name Raises and Bonuses* to select it. Point the mouse at the middle of the control box and when the pointer shape changes to the four-headed move arrow, move the report title right.
j. Click the **Confidential graphic** and drag the **right** boundary right to enlarge the warning.
k. Right-click any number in the **New Salary** field and select **Properties** from the shortcut menu. Set the Format property in the Property Sheet to **Currency** and close the Property Sheet.
l. Right-click any number in the **Bonus** field and select **Properties**. Set the **Format property** to **Currency**. Close the Property Sheet.
m. Right-click the report tab and switch to **Print Preview**. If your report looks like the one in the figure, save the report as **Your Name Raises and Bonuses**.
n. Close the database.

...continued on Next Page

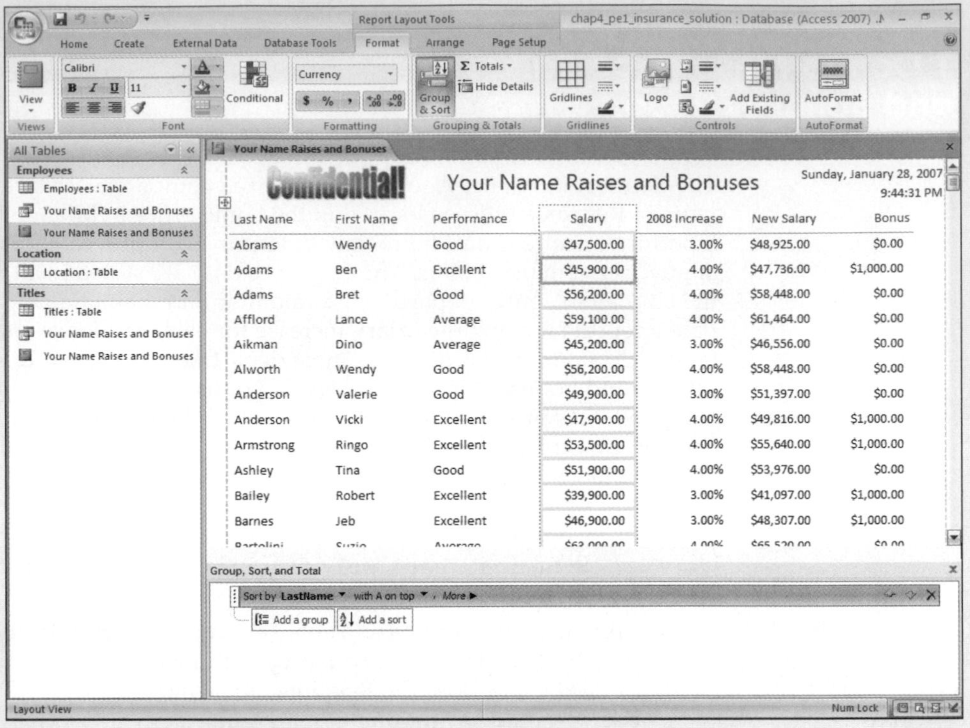

Figure 4.41 Raises and Bonuses Report

2 Comfort Insurance Raises by Location

The Comfort Insurance Agency is a midsized company with offices located across the country. The Human Resource office is located in the home office in Miami. Each year, each employee receives a performance review. The review determines employee eligibility for salary increases and the annual performance bonus. The employee data are stored in an Access database. This database is used by the Human Resource department to monitor and maintain employee records. Your task is to prepare a report showing employee raises and bonuses by city. You will need to total the payroll and bonus data for each city. You are the Human Resource department manager. If you correctly prepare the report, you will receive a bonus. This project follows the same set of skills as used in Hands-On Exercises 1 and 2 in this chapter. If you have problems, reread the detailed directions presented in the chapter. Compare your results to Figure 4.42.

a. Copy the partially completed file *chap4_pe2_insurance.accdb* to your production folder. Rename it **chap4_pe2_insurance_solution.accdb**, open the copied file, and enable the security content.
b. Click the **Database Tools tab** and click **Relationships** in the Show/Hide group. Examine the table structure, relationships, and fields. After you are familiar with the database, close the Relationships window.
c. Open the **Employees Query** in Datasheet view. Click the **Create tab** and click **Report** in the Reports group.
d. Click **Add Existing Fields** in the Controls group on the Format tab. The Field List pane opens on the right. In the bottom of the Field List pane is the *Fields available in related tables pane*. Click the **Show all tables** link. The Location table is listed with a plus sign next to it. Click the **plus sign** to reveal the hidden fields available in the Location table.
e. Double-click the **Location** field (not the LocationID field) to add it to the report. Because this field is in a table not in the original record source, Access asks if it is OK to create a new query that contains the Location field. Click **Yes**. The city names add to the report. The new field is selected. Close the Field List pane.
f. Click the **Location** text box at the top of the field. Move the mouse to the middle of the selected Location field and when the mouse pointer assumes the four-headed move shape, click and drag the field to the **leftmost** position in the report.

...continued on Next Page

g. Click the **LastName** text box at the top of the field to select it. Click it a second time to edit it. Type a **space** between Last and Name. Add spaces to **FirstName**, **HireDate**, **2008Increase**, **2008Raise**, **YearHired**, and **YearsWorked**.

h. Select the **Last Name** field. Move the mouse pointer over the right boundary and when the pointer shape changes to a double-headed arrow, click and drag **left** to narrow the column. Repeat this step for the **First Name** field.

i. Right-click any record in the **2008 Raise** field and select **Properties**. In the Properties Sheet, set the Format property to **Currency**. Close the Property Sheet.

j. Select the **Year Hired** field and delete it. Adjust any field column widths as necessary to make sure all the columns fit on one page.

k. Click **Group & Sort** in the Grouping & Totals group to turn on the Group, Sort, and Total pane (if necessary). Click **Add a group** in the Group, Sort, and Total pane. Click **Location** in the Group on Select field box.

l. Click the **More Options** command on the Group on Location bar. Click the drop-down arrow beside "with LastName totaled." Click the drop-down arrow in the Total On box and select **2008Raise**. Click the **Show Grand Total** and **Show in group footer** check boxes. Click anywhere outside the Total by box.

m. Click the report title and change it to **Your Name**.

n. Click the **Office Button**. Position the mouse pointer over **Print** and click **Print Preview**. Print the report.

o. Save the report as **Your Name Raises by Location**. Close the database.

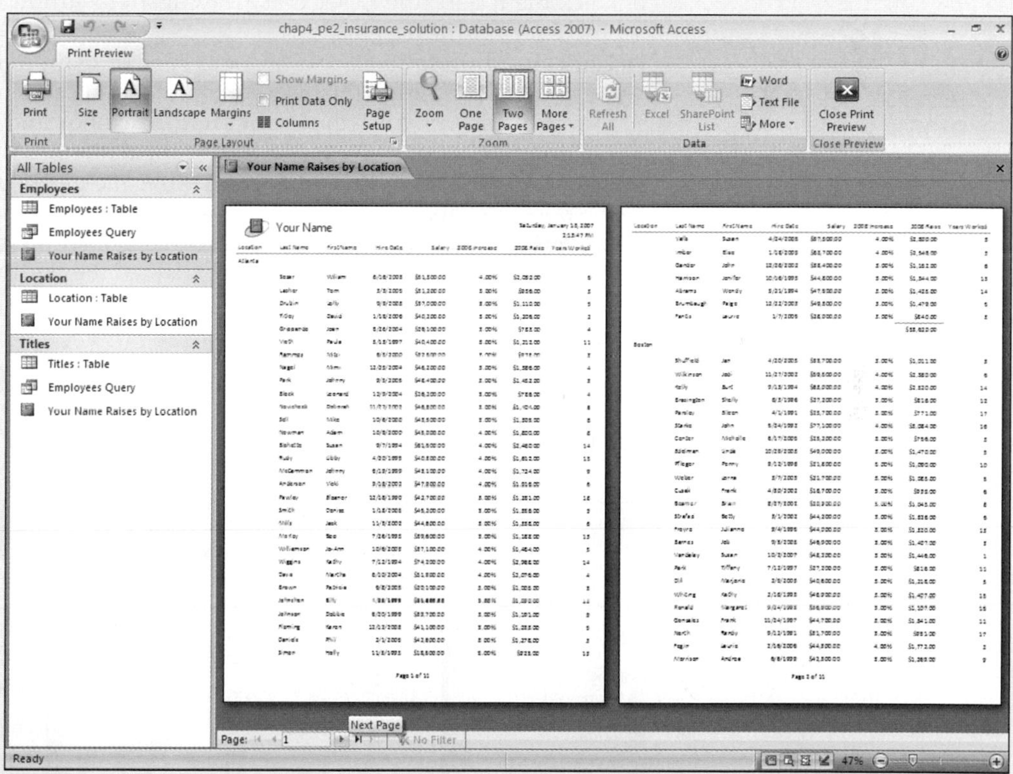

Figure 4.42 Raises by Location Shown in Print Preview

3 Northwind Traders

Northwind Traders is a small, international, specialty food company. It sells products in eight different divisions: beverages, confections (candy), condiments, dairy products, grains and cereals, meat and poultry, produce, and seafood. Although most of its customers are restaurants and gourmet food shops, it has a few retail customers, too. The firm purchases merchandise from a variety of suppliers. All of the order and inventory information is stored in the company's database. This database is used by the management to monitor and maintain records. You are the marketing manager. Your task is to prepare a report showing the profitability of the products in your inventory. You need to group the products by their categories. You also need to average the profit

...continued on Next Page

margin by category. (A profit margin is the profit divided by the price.) This project follows the same set of skills as used in Hands-On Exercises 1, 2, and 3. If you have problems, reread the detailed directions presented in the chapter. Compare your results to Figure 4.43.

a. Copy the partially completed file *chap4_pe3_traders.accdb* to your production folder. Rename it **chap4_pe3_traders_solution.accdb**, open the file, and enable the security content.
b. Click the **Database Tools tab** and click **Relationships** in the Show/Hide group. Examine the table structure, relationships, and fields. After you are familiar with the database, close the Relationships window.
c. Click the **Create tab** and click **Report Wizard** in the Reports group. Select the **Profit Margin query** in the first screen of the dialog box. Click the **Move all to Report command (>>)** to move all of the fields in the query to the report. Click **Next**.
d. Select **by Categories** to answer the "How do you want to view your data?" question. This step creates the necessary grouping level. Click **Next**. You already have established the grouping level so click **Next** only one time.
e. Click **Summary Options** and indicate that you would like the **Avg** for the *PerUnitProfit* field. Click **OK**, and then **Next**.
f. Ensure that **Stepped** layout and **Portrait** orientation are selected and click **Next**.
g. Select the **Aspect** style and click **Next**. Name the report **Your Name Profit Margin**. Set it to open to **Preview**. Click **Finish**.
h. Right-click the report tab and select Layout View.
i. Click the report title to select it. Click again to edit it. Change the title to **Your Name Category Profit Margins**.
j. Click the **UnitsInStock** text box and click it again to edit it. Insert a **space** between Units and In. Position the insertion point left of the **S** in Stock and type **Ctrl+Enter** to force a line break. Click the **Profit Margin** text box and click it again to edit it. Position the insertion point left of the **M** in Margin and type **Ctrl+Enter** to force a line break.
k. Click the text box for **Per Unit Profit**. Move the mouse over the **right boundary**. When the pointer shape changes to the double-headed arrow, click and drag the right boundary **left** to make the column narrower. Make the Product Name and Category columns wider to display the record contents. Adjust the widths of the remaining columns as necessary to fit all on one page.

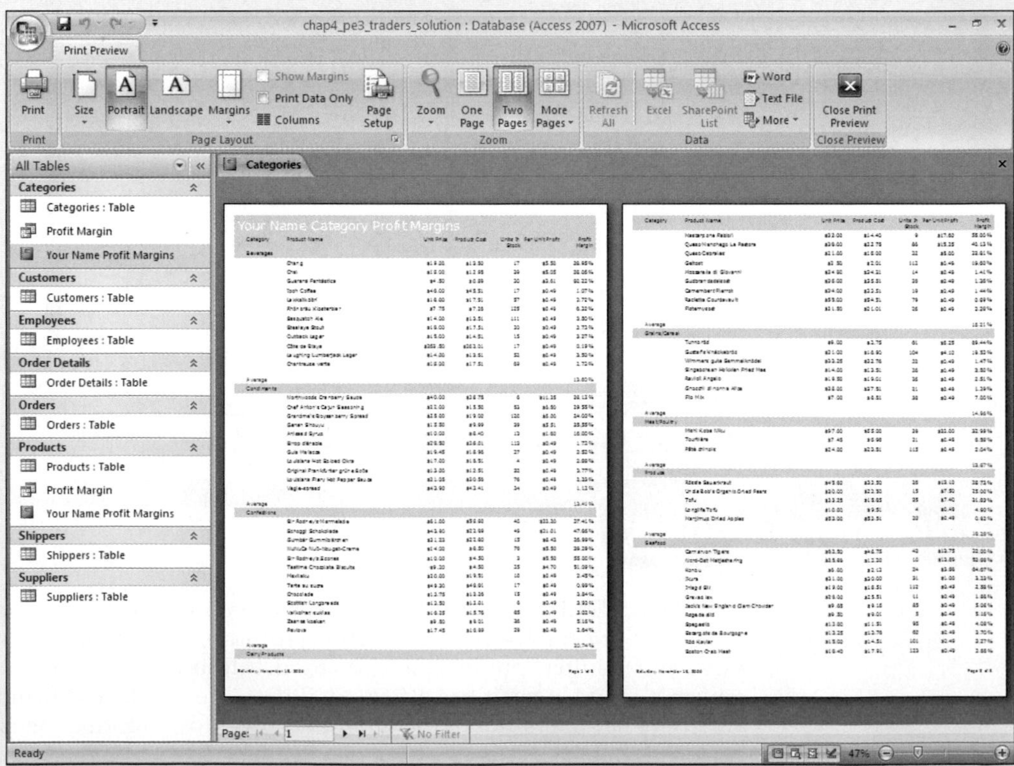

Figure 4.43 Profit Margin by Category

...continued on Next Page

l. Select the **Summary for Category Name . . .** and press **Delete**. Select **Avg** and replace it with **Average**.
m. Save the report. Print the report. Close the database.

4 Member Rewards

The Prestige Hotel chain caters to upscale business travelers and provides state-of-the-art conference, meeting, and reception facilities. It prides itself on its international, four-star cuisines. Last year, it began a member rewards club to help the marketing department track the purchasing patterns of its most loyal customers. All of the hotel transactions are stored in the database. Your task is to determine the revenue from each order and to summarize the revenue figures by location and service type. This project follows the same set of skills as used in Hands-On Exercises 2 and 3. If you have problems, reread the detailed directions presented in the chapter. Compare your results to Figure 4.44.

a. Copy the partially completed file *chap4_pe4_memrewards.accdb* to your production folder. Rename it **chap4_pe4_memrewards_solution.accdb**, open the file, and enable the security content.
b. Click the **Database Tools tab** and click **Relationships** in the Show/Hide group. Examine the table structure, relationships, and fields. After you are familiar with the database, close the Relationships window. Rename the **Your Name Revenue** query with **your name**.
c. Open the **Your Name Revenue** query in Datasheet view.
d. Click the **Create tab** and click **Report** in the Reports group.
e. Click **Group & Sort** in the Grouping & Totals group to turn on the Group, Sort, and Total pane (if necessary). Click **Add a group** in the Group, Sort, and Total pane. Click **City** in the Group on list box. Click **Add a group** and select **ServiceName** in the Group on list box.
f. Click **Hide Details** in the Grouping & Totals group.
g. Click **Group on ServiceName** in the Group, Sort, and Total pane to activate the group bar. Click the **More** command. Click the **with City totaled drop-down arrow**. In the **Total On** box, select **NoInParty**. In the **Type** box, select **Average**. Click the **Show in group header** check box.
h. Return to the Totals dialog box, click the drop-down arrow, and click **PerPersonCharge**. Set **Type** to **Average** and check **Show in group header**.
i. Return to the **Totals** dialog box, click the drop-down arrow, and click **Revenue**. Set **Type** to **Sum** and check **Show in group header**.
j. Click **Group on City** to activate the group bar. Click **More**. Locate and click the **with City totaled drop-down arrow**. In the **Total On** box, select **NoInParty**. In the **Type** box, select **Average.** Click the **Show in group footer check box.**
k. Return to the Totals dialog box, click the drop-down arrow, and click **PerPersonCharge**. Set **Type** to **Average** and check **Show in group footer.**
l. Return to the Totals dialog box, click the drop-down arrow, and click **Revenue**. Set **Type** to **Sum** and check **Show in group footer** and **Show Grand Total.**
m. Click the **ServiceName** text box and click it again to edit it. Insert a **space** between Service and Name. Click NoInParty to select and type **Number In Party**. Position the insertion point right of the **r** in Number and type **Ctrl+Enter** to force a line break. Click the **PerPerson Charge** text box and click it again to edit it. Add a space between Per and Person. Position the insertion point left of the **C** in Charge and type **Ctrl+Enter** to force a line break.

...continued on Next Page

n. Click the text box for **City**. Move the mouse over the **right boundary**. When the pointer shape changes to the double-headed arrow, click and drag the right boundary **left** to make the column narrower. Adjust the widths of the remaining columns as necessary to fit all on one page.

o. Right-click a value in the **Number in Party** field. Select **Properties** from the shortcut menu. Set the **Format** property to **Fixed**. Click the **Decimal Place** property and select **1**. Click a value in the Per Person Charge field. Set the **Format property** to **Currency**. Click a value in the Revenue field to set the **Format property** to **Currency**. Examine the formats of the city and grand totals and adjust their formats if necessary.

p. Right-click the report tab and select **Print Preview**. Save the report as **Your Name Revenue by City and Service**. Close the database.

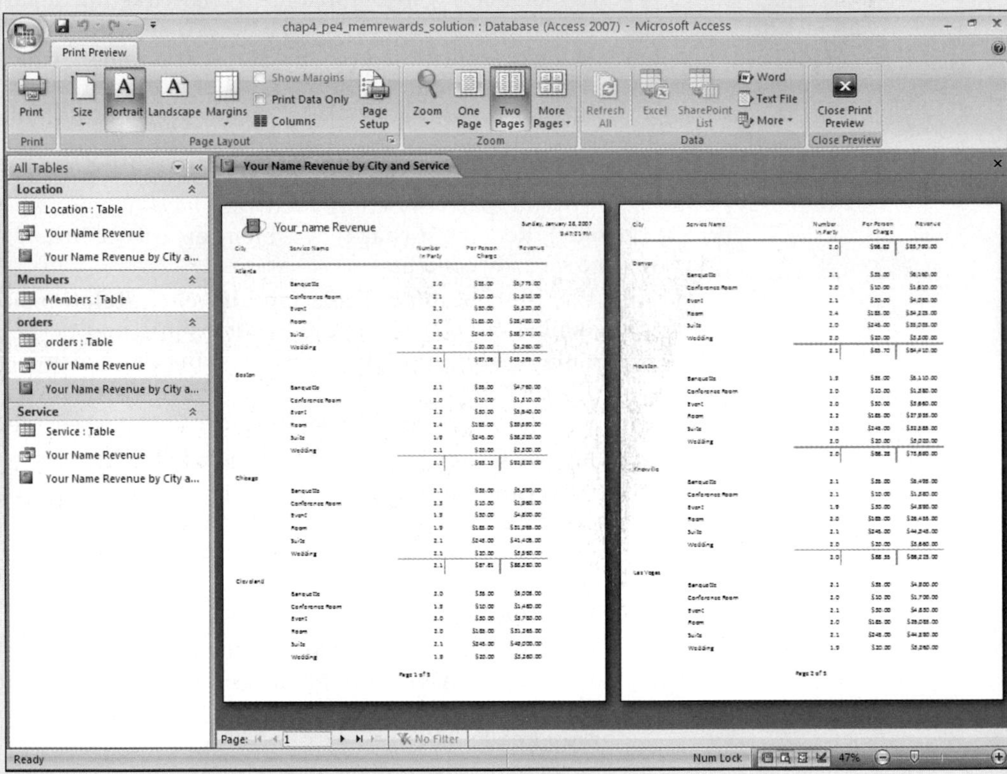

Figure 4.44 Revenue by City and Service

Mid-Level Exercises

1 Grouping and Totaling Dinnerware Revenue

(Replacements, Ltd is a real company located in Greensboro, North Carolina. The data in the case file are actual data. The customer and employee information have been changed to ensure privacy. However, the inventory and sales records reflect actual transactions.)

Today is the first day in your new position as associate marketing manager at Replacements, Ltd., which has the world's largest selection of old and new dinnerware, including china, stoneware, crystal, glassware, silver, stainless, and collectibles. In preparation for your first day on the job, you have spent hours browsing the Replacements Web site, www.replacements.com. You classify the merchandise by category number where 1 is dinnerware, 2 is crystal/glassware, and 3 is flatware (knives and forks). You are responsible for managing several different patterns of merchandise. To accomplish this task, you need to closely monitor past sales in the various patterns to understand purchasing habits and product demand. You exchange information with the customer service representatives and monitor their performance. You need to create a report that summarizes sales by pattern for the merchandise in Product Category 1, dinnerware. Compare your work to Figure 4.45.

a. Locate the file named *chap4_mid1_replacement.accdb*, copy it to your working folder, and rename it **chap4_mid1_replacement_solution.accdb**. Open the file and enable the content.

b. Open the **Revenue query**. It contains information about all three product classifications. Today, you are interested only in dinnerware. Create a report and set a filter to select only product category 1.

c. Group the report on the **LongPatName** field. Click the **More Options** command on the group bar in the Group, Sort, and Total pane. Locate the Totals drop-down arrow and select Revenue. Eventually you will hide the details, so set the total to display in the group header.

d. Hide the details. Remove all of the fields except for the LongPatName and Revenue from the report. Replace the label, *LongPatName*, with **Pattern Name**.

e. Save the report as **Your Name Revenue by Dinnerware Pattern**. Title the report appropriately.

f. Insert the *chap4_mid1_replacement.jpg* picture in the logo area. This image depicts the Spode pattern. It is copyrighted by Replacements, Ltd., and is used with permission.

g. Select the **Wide** margin choice. **Enlarge** the picture and **move the controls** in the Report Header and Footer sections to make the report a single page and attractive.

h. Capture a screenshot of the report. Have it open on your computer and press **PrintScrn**. Open Word, type **Your Name and Section Number** and press **Enter**. Press **Ctrl+V**. Save the Word document as **chap4_mid1_replacement_solution**. Print the Word document. Close the Word document and close the database.

...continued on Next Page

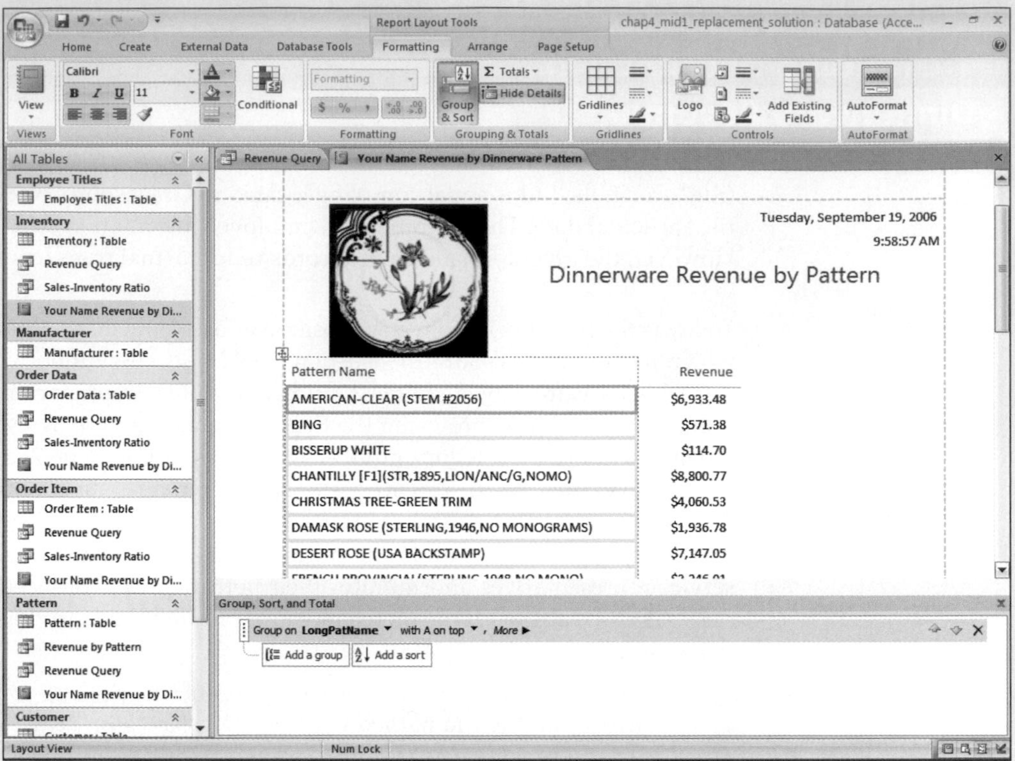

Figure 4.45 Dinnerware Revenue by Pattern

2 Calculating and Summarizing Bank Data in a Query

You are the manager of the loan department of the National Bank. Several customers have multiple loans with your institution. A single customer might have a mortgage loan, one or more car loans, and a home improvement loan. The loan department's database contains the records of all of the customer indebtedness. Your task is to use the information stored in the database to summarize the loan payments by month. Compare your results to Figure 4.46.

a. Locate the file named *chap4_mid2_nationalbank.accdb*, copy it to your working folder, and rename it **chap4_mid2_nationalbank_solution.accdb**. Open the file and enable the content. Open the **Customers table**. Find and replace **Michelle Zacco's** name with your name.

b. Open the **Payments Received** query. Use it to create a report.

c. In Report Layout view, use the Group, Sort, and Total pane to add a group. Group these data on the **Payment Date** field.

d. Click the **More** command on the Group on PaymentDate bar in the Group, Sort, and Total pane and set the grouping interval to **Month**.

e. Click the drop-down arrow beside with Amount Received totaled to launch the Totals box. Select **AmountReceived** as the value for Totals on. Show this total in the **group footer**. Also show a **grand total**.

f. Make the name fields narrower. Save the report as **Your Name Payments Received**.

...continued on Next Page

g. Add spaces as needed to the boxes controlling the report labels. Examine the report in Print Preview. Click and drag the Zoom slider to 75%.

h. Capture a screenshot of the Payment Summary query. Have it open on your computer and press **PrintScrn**. Open Word, then type **your name and section number**. Press **Enter**, and then press **Ctrl+V** or click **Paste** in the Clipboard group. Save the Word document as **chap4_mid2_nationalbank_solution.docx**. Print the Word document displaying the screenshot. Close the Word document and close the database.

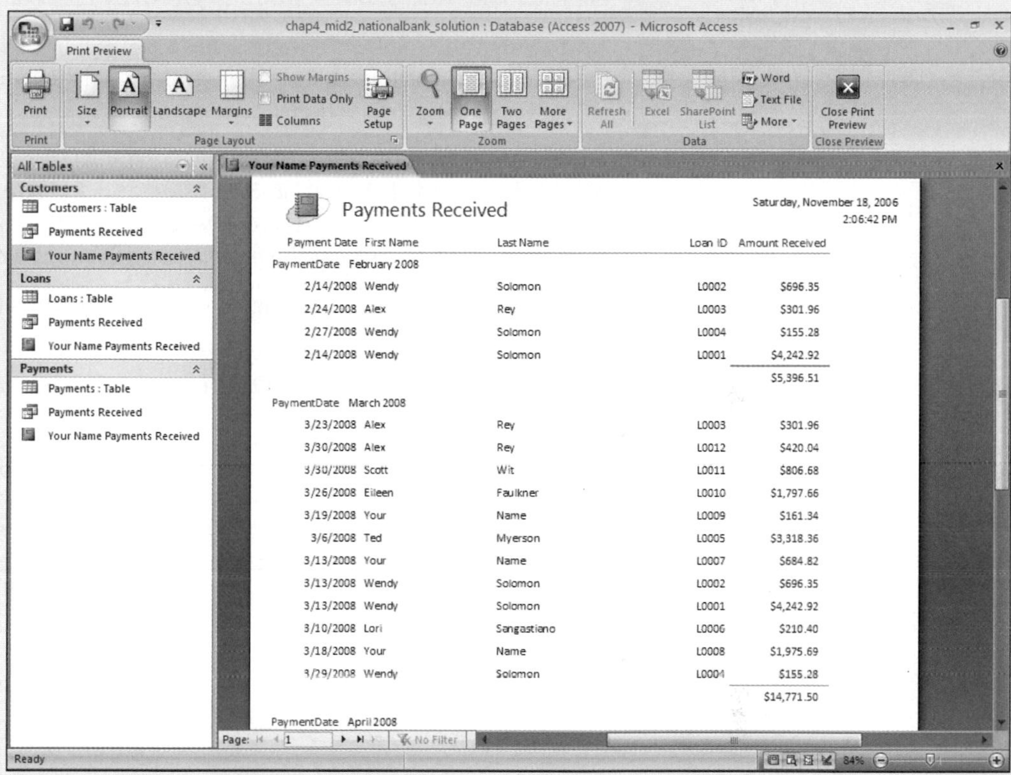

Figure 4.46 Payment Summary

3 Real Estate Report by Month and Salesperson

You are the senior partner in a large, independent real estate firm that specializes in home sales. Although you still represent buyers and sellers in real estate transactions, you find that most of your time is spent supervising the agents who work for your firm. This fact distresses you because you like helping people buy and sell homes. Your firm has a database containing all of the information on the properties your firm has for sale. You believe that by using the data in the database more effectively, you can spend less time supervising the other agents and spend more time doing the part of your job that you like doing the best. Your task is to prepare a sales report listing all recent transactions by month and salesperson. Finally, you need to summarize the sales and commission data by employee and calculate the average number of days each employee's sales were on the market prior to selling. Compare your results to Figure 4.47.

...continued on Next Page

a. Locate the file named *chap4_mid3_realestate.accdb*; copy and rename it **chap4_mid3_realestate_solution.accdb**. Open the file and enable the content. Open the **Agents** table. Find and replace **Pa Lor's** name with your name.

b. Rename the **Your Name Sales Report query** with **your name**. Open it. Create a report. Save the report as **Your Name Sales Report**. Open it in Layout view.

c. Add **spaces** as needed in the labels in the report header. Use **Ctrl + Enter** to force a line break between *On* and *Market* in *DaysOnMarket*. Make the **Subdivision** and **LastName** fields narrower so the report fits on a single page.

d. Activate the Group, Sort, and Total pane. Add a group to group the data monthly by the DateSold. Add another group to group by Last Name.

e. Add totals to the **SalePrice** and **SaleComm** fields that sum. Calculate the Average of the DaysOn Market field. Calculate grand totals for all three summary fields. Display all values in the group footers.

f. Use the Property Sheet to format the **DaysOnMarket** field as fixed with zero decimal places displayed. Format the **SalePrice** and **SaleComm** fields as Currency. Scroll through the complete report to ensure that all of the totals display fully and totals are formatted correctly. Adjust the text box widths if they do not.

g. Insert a picture of a house as the logo. Set the margins to wide.

h. Click the AutoFormat drop-down arrow and select the **AutoFormat Wizard** option. In the AutoFormat box select the Oriel format (3rd column, 4th row). View your report as two pages in Print Preview.

i. Capture a screenshot of the Sales Summary report. Have it open on your computer and press **PrintScrn**. Open Word and press **Ctrl+V** or click **Paste** in the Clipboard group. Save the Word document as **chap4_mid3_realestate_solution**. Print the screen. Close the Word document and close the database.

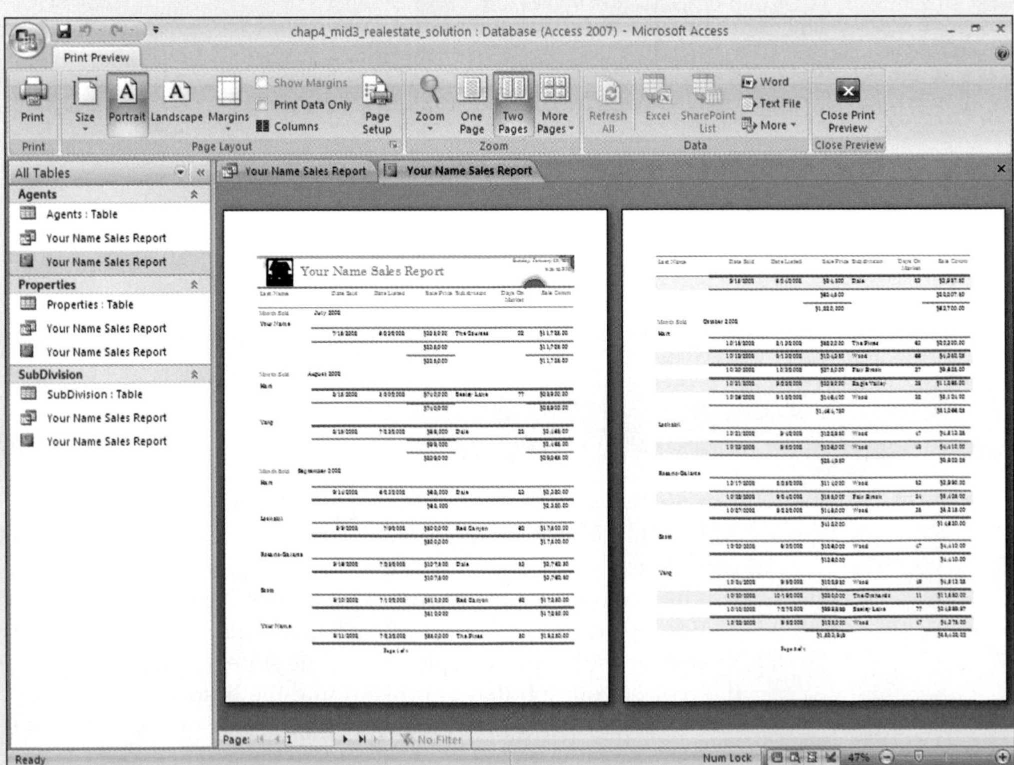

Figure 4.47 Sales Summary

Capstone Exercise

Your boss asked you to prepare a schedule for each speaker for the national conference being hosted next year on your campus. She wants to mail the schedules to the speakers so that they may provide feedback on the schedule prior to its publication. She believes that each speaker will find it easier to review his or her schedule if each speaker's schedule was printed in the same place. You assure her that you (and Access) can accomplish this task.

Database File Setup

You need to copy an original database file, rename the copied file, and then open the copied database to complete this capstone exercise. After you open the copied database, you will replace an existing employee's name with your name.

a. Locate the file named *chap4_cap_natconf.accdb* and copy it to a different folder.

b. Rename the copied file as **chap4_cap_natconf_ solution.accdb**.

c. Open the *chap4_cap_natconf_solution.accdb* file and enable the content.

d. Open the **Speakers table**.

e. Find and replace **Your Name** with your name.

Report Wizard

You need to create a report based on the Speakers and Sessions with Rooms query. You decide to use the Report Wizard to accomplish this task.

a. Activate the **Report Wizard**.

b. Select **Query: Speakers and Sessions with Rooms** as the data source for the report.

c. Move all fields to the report.

d. You want to view your data by speakers. Select **by speakers** if necessary.

e. You want the **LastName** and **FirstName** fields established as the primary grouping level. If they are not already moved into a box at the top of the report, double-click LastName and then FirstName to group by them.

f. Click the drop-down arrow for the first box and select **Date** as the primary sort field. Click **Next**.

g. Select the **Stepped** and **Portrait** options.

h. Choose the **Flow** style.

i. Name the report **Your Name Speaker Schedule**.

Report Edits

The report opens in the Print Preview. You need to examine the report and look for problems. Once they are identified, you will need to switch to Layout view and correct them.

a. Switch to the two page view.

b. Right-click the report tab and select **Layout View**.

c. Click the **Page Setup tab**. Click **Margins** in the Page Layout group. Select **Wide** from the drop-down menu.

d. Click the text box for **SessionTitle**. Insert a **space** between the words. Add a space to **RoomID**.

e. Move the **Date** field to the right of the Room ID column.

f. Resize the **FirstName** field by making it more narrow. Widen the **Session Title** field. Make the **RoomID** and **Date** fields more narrow.

g. Move the title right. Set the font size to **28 point**.

h. Click the **Logo command** in the Controls group. Insert a picture of a campus. Resize to about the same width as the Speakers title.

Additional Field

You realize the session times were not included in the query and you need them added to the report.

a. Click the Add Existing Fields Command in the Controls group.

b. Click **Show only fields in current record** and then **Show All Tables** in the bottom of the **Field List pane**. Find and **double-click** the **StartingTime** field in the Sessions table on the top of the Field List pane.

c. Click **Yes** in the warning box. Close the Field List pane. Add a **space** between Starting and Time. Adjust columns as needed to fit all columns on one page.

d. Scroll to the end of the page. Find and select the text box for the page number and move it left so the page number prints under the Starting Time field.

e. Change the view to Print Preview, two-page view.

f. Capture a screenshot of the Speaker Schedule report. Open the report on your computer and press **PrintScrn**. Open Microsoft Word and press **Ctrl+V** or click **Paste**. Save the Word document as **chap4_ cap_natconf_solution**. Print the screenshot file. Close the Word document and close the database.

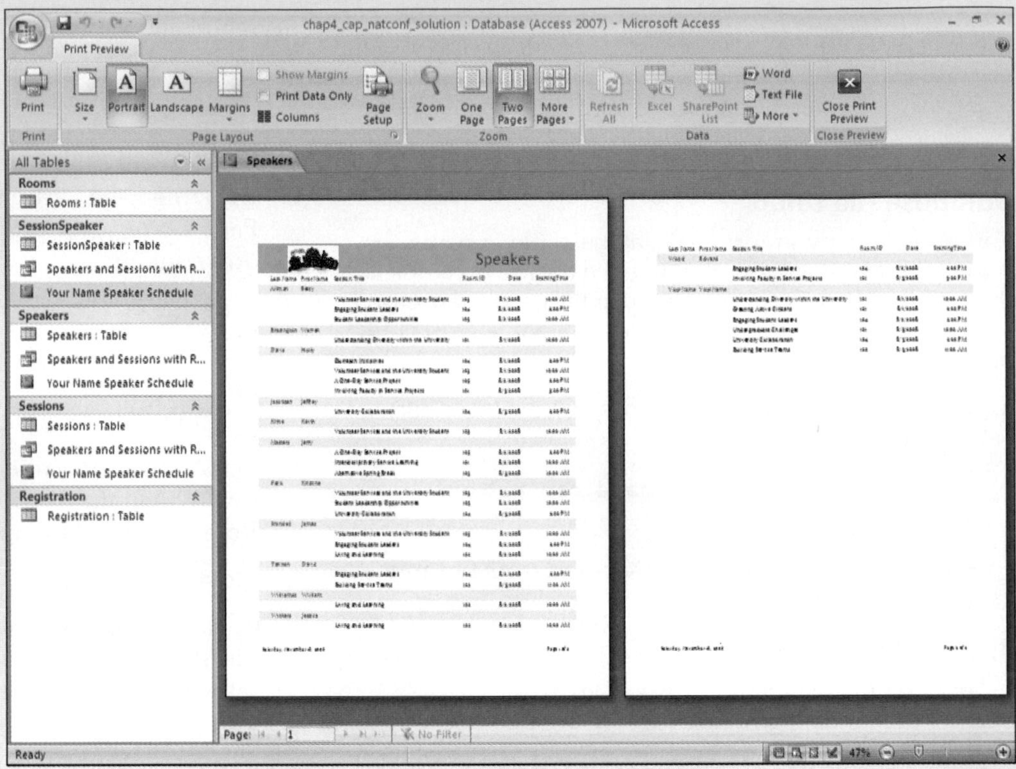

Figure 4.48 Speaker Schedule Report

Mini Cases

Use the rubric following the case as a guide to evaluate your work, but keep in mind that your instructor may impose additional grading criteria or use a different standard to judge your work.

Inventory Value

GENERAL CASE

The owner of a small bookstore called and asked for your help. Her insurance company requires that she provide the company with a report on the values of the inventory she stocks. Copy the *chap4_mc1_bookstore.accdb* file to your working storage folder, name it **chap4_mc1_bookstore_solution.accdb**, and open the copied file. Use the skills from this chapter to perform several tasks. Create a report that shows the publisher's name, the author's first and last names, the book title, the book price, the number in stock, and the value of the stock. The report needs to be grouped by publisher with appropriate summary statistics calculated. The books within each publisher's group should be listed in alphabetical order by the author's last name. The report needs to contain an appropriate graphic and a grand total. The file contains a query that you may use to create the report.

Performance Elements	Exceeds Expectations	Meets Expectations	Below Expectations
Create report	All necessary and no unneeded fields included.	All necessary fields included but also unnecessary fields.	Not all necessary fields were included.
Appropriate grouping and sorting	The grouping and sorting were correctly identified and executed.	Grouping correct but sorting incorrect or vice-versa.	Neither grouping nor sorting properly employed.
Summary statistics	Correct group aggregating information selected and appropriately displayed.	Correct group aggregating information selected, but the display had problems.	Group aggregating information not selected and/or inappropriately displayed.
Summarize balances	Correct method, correct totals.	Correct totals but inefficient method.	Totals incorrect or missing.

Producing Mailing Labels

RESEARCH CASE

This chapter introduced you to the power of using reports, but you have much more to explore. Use Access Help to search for mailing labels. Open and read the articles titled, *Use Access to Create and Print Labels* and *Learn Tips and Tricks for Creating Labels*. Put your new knowledge to the test. Copy the *chap4_mc2_arboretum.accdb* file and rename the copy as **chap4_mc2_arboretum_solution.accdb**. Open the file. It contains a query identifying volunteers who need to be invited to this year's gala. Your challenge is to figure out how to print the names and addresses as mailing labels. You have purchased Avery product number 5260 labels to print on. They are 1½″ x 2⅝″ with three columns of labels on each page. The mailing will be sent bulk rate, so the labels need to print sorted by postal code. After you successfully produce the report, print it on plain paper. Write your instructor a memo explaining how you accomplished this task. Use a memo template in Word, your most professional writing style, and clear directions that someone could follow in order to accomplish this task. Attach the printout of the labels to the memo. Save the Word document as **chap4_mc2_ arboretum_solution**.

Each label should be set up in this fashion:

Mr. (Dr., Ms., Mrs.,) John Doe, Jr.
Street Address
City, State Postal Code

Performance Elements	Exceeds Expectations	Meets Expectations	Below Expectations
Use online help	Appropriate articles located and memo indicates comprehension.	Appropriate articles located, but memo did not demonstrate comprehension.	Articles not found.
Prepare labels	Printed list attached to memo in requested format.	Printed list is attached, but the formatting has minor flaws.	List missing or incomprehensible.
Summarize and communicate	Memo clearly written and could be used as directions.	Memo text indicates some understanding but also weaknesses.	Memo missing or incomprehensible.
Aesthetics	Memo template correctly employed.	Template employed but signed in the wrong place or improperly used.	Memo missing or incomprehensible.

Real Estate Development Report

DISASTER CASE

A co-worker called you into her office, explained that she was having difficulty with Access 2007 and asked you to look at her work. Copy the *chap4_mc3_realestate.accdb* file to your working storage folder, name it **chap4_mc3_realestate_solution.accdb**, and open the file. It contains a query, Your Name Sales Report. It also contains a report based on the query. The report is supposed to show each agent's total sales with each development listed under the agent's name. There should be totals for the sales and commissions columns for each salesperson and each development. Your challenge is to find and correct the error(s) and then to produce an attractive, easy-to-read report.

Performance Elements	Exceeds Expectations	Meets Expectations	Below Expectations
Error identification	Correct identification and correction of all errors.	Correct identification of all errors and correction of some errors.	Errors neither located nor corrected.
Grouping order	Correct grouping options and summarization selected.	Correct grouping, but some summaries incorrectly selected.	Incorrect group by option selection.
Aesthetics	Report design aids reader.	Inconsistent formatting, but all necessary data displays.	Controls improperly sized. Information obscured.

chapter 5 | **Access**

PivotTables and PivotCharts

Data Mining

After you read this chapter, you will be able to:

1. Create a PivotTable view **(page 319)**.
2. Calculate aggregate statistics **(page 324)**.
3. Modify a PivotTable **(page 326)**.
4. Select an appropriate chart type **(page 336)**.
5. Identify chart elements **(page 337)**.
6. Edit a PivotChart **(page 339)**.
7. Create calculations in a PivotTable **(page 351)**.

Hands-On Exercises

Exercises	Skills Covered
1. CREATE AND USE A PIVOTTABLE (page 329) **Open:** chap5_ho1-3_insurance.accdb **Save as:** chap5_ho1-3_insurance_solution.accdb **Back up as:** chap5_ho1_insurance_solution.accdb	• Create a PivotTable from a Query • Add Fields Using the Design Grid • Remove Fields Using the Design Grid • Calculate Summary Statistics and Alter Formats and Captions • Add and Rearrange PivotTable Fields • Remove a Field and Modify Summary Calculations
2. PIVOTCHARTS AND MODIFICATIONS (page 345) **Open:** chap5_ho1-3_insurance_solution.accdb (from Exercise 1) **Save as:** chap5_ho1-3_insurance_solution.accdb (additional modifications) and chap5_ho2_insurance_solution.docx **Back up as:** chap5_ho2_insurance_solution.accdb	• Remove a PivotChart Field • Add a PivotChart Field • Change AutoCalc Calculation and Set PivotChart Properties and Captions • Edit Series Colors and Patterns
3. CALCULATING FIELD VALUES IN PIVOTTABLES (page 355) **Open:** chap5_ho1-3_insurance_solution.accdb (from Exercise 2) **Save as:** chap5_ho1-3_insurance_solution.accdb (additional modifications)	• Add a Field to a PivotTable • Identify and Add Fields Needed for Calculations • Create a PivotTable Calculation and Apply Formatting • Total a Calculated Field and Change Formatting • Set Captions

CASE STUDY

Encouraging Volunteerism

You find that your internship at the JC Ralston Arboretum in Raleigh, North Carolina, has a new challenge each day. Today you will work with a group of dedicated volunteers and board members who want to share their love of gardening. They are dedicated to the mission of enriching urban landscapes by promoting a greater diversity of creative, environmentally sound landscapes. The organization enjoys the labor of hundreds of volunteers who donate thousands of hours of service each year. The volunteers enjoy the companionship and the creativity of the arboretum. The group you have been assigned to assist believes that they can increase volunteer participation by tracking involvement by community. Volunteers come from Raleigh and nearby communities such as Cary, Wake Forest, and Chapel Hill. You need to help track which communities the volunteers come from and how many total hours of volunteer time may be attributed to each local community.

Case Study

Your supervisor tells you that the volunteer hours and city names are stored in the database. You suggest that a chart might be an easy way to communicate these data. The chart could have the city names along the bottom of the chart and different bar heights depicting the total number of volunteer hours for each city. Your supervisor thinks your chart idea is wonderful and asks that you show her your work.

Your Assignment

- Read the chapter, paying special attention to learning the vocabulary of PivotTables and PivotCharts.
- Copy the *chap5_case_arboretum.accdb* file to your production folder, rename it **chap5_case_arboretum_solution.accdb**, and enable the content.
- Open the Relationships window and examine the relationships among the tables and the fields contained within each of the tables to become acquainted with this database.
- Open the Vol + Gala Invite query and then switch to PivotTable view.
- Aggregate the volunteer hours (named Volwork) by summing across the cities.
- Create a PivotChart that displays the total volunteer hours by city.
- Print the table and chart.
- Compact and repair the database file.

Data Mining

At the grocery store's checkout, the cashier asks for your customer membership card and scans it. Many major grocery, bookstore, and electronics store chains employ some form of customer purchase tracking through memberships. You happily provide your membership card because it entitles you to discounts and special prices. You probably filled out a short form to enroll in the frequent buyer or important customer membership program. On the form, you answered questions about your age, education, income, race, and hobbies. The store provides you with a card containing a bar code (a unique identifier) that links your purchases to the promised discounts as well as to the demographic information stored about you from the questions you answered on the application form. ***Demographics*** are data describing population segments broken down by age, race, education, and so on by geographic regions.

Demographics are data describing population segments by age, race, education, and other variables.

The store analyzes the data describing you and your purchase habits and uses it to decide where to position merchandise in the store and what items to promote. For example, a major electronics retailer might use a frequent-buyer program to identify your purchase patterns and sends you an e-mail containing information on related products. If you purchase several movies of the same genre, you might receive an announcement of a new movie that has a similar theme. Most grocery chains sell the data about customer purchases to food manufacturing, health, and beauty aid companies; advertising firms; and marketing consulting firms. The data sold probably do not contain any of your personal information, such as your name or checking account number. The data are sold as aggregates. For example, the sold data might indicate the total number of 15-ounce boxes of Brand X cereal purchased by single, white females between the ages of 18 and 24 years who do not have a dog or a cat living with them.

Companies perform data mining to analyze consumer purchasing patterns and habits. ***Data mining*** is the process of analyzing large volumes of data and using advanced statistical techniques to identify patterns and relationships to assist managers in making informed decisions and help predict future customer behavior. Some data mining software is extraordinarily sophisticated and will, once a pattern has been identified, drill more deeply into the data to test further combinations of data without receiving additional instructions. Access provides two tools to help you perform limited data mining—PivotTables and PivotCharts.

Data mining is the process of analyzing large volumes of data to identify patterns and relationships.

PivotTables and PivotCharts enable the managerial decision maker to summarize and organize data with a variety of arrangements and multiple groupings. With the ability to collapse and expand groups and perform a range of calculations, PivotTables and PivotCharts empower the decision maker with the ability to discern patterns and trends in historical data in an attempt to predict and control the future.

In this section, you explore PivotTables and PivotCharts and work with query views. You also learn the specialized vocabulary that relates to PivotTables and PivotCharts. You will create a PivotTable based on a query and edit the result.

Creating a PivotTable View

The PivotTable views provide you with another method of summarizing and aggregating data. You have already worked with summary queries and grouped reports, which provide similar abilities. Sometimes managers need database reports on a regular basis. For example, a manager might need a weekly report summarizing payroll and overtime authorization by department. Often, the IT staff that manages the database generates that type of report and distributes it to the departmental managers who need the information. Routine and recurrent reports provide the decision maker with information to make routine and recurrent decisions. However, managerial information needs change when the decision is not routine. Opportunities arise and managers need the tools to adjust to changed circumstances. Even absent a surprise, decision makers sometimes have single-use data needs.

(Opportunities arise and managers need the tools to adjust to changed circumstances.)

PivotTables and PivotCharts provide powerful aggregation and summarization tools. You can construct a PivotTable very quickly. Because of that, decision makers employ them to answer single-use questions. It would be an expensive use of IT staff time to assemble a report for one person to view only once. Because the PivotTables and PivotCharts can be constructed easily, the person who needs the single-use information may organize it without involving the IT staff. After a PivotTable is constructed, you can alter it easily to examine additional aspects.

Create a Query PivotTable View

You may employ PivotTable and PivotChart views to forms, tables, and queries. However, a PivotTable works with only one table or query at a time. Because the power of PivotTables and PivotCharts lies in their ability to combine complex data in different ways to discover patterns, you will primarily use query data to construct PivotTables and PivotCharts. The elements of good database table design that group only similar items in a table make table and form data less suitable for PivotTable analysis. For example, the human resource (HR) manager may wish to examine the pay raise percentage throughout the organization to ensure that employees receive equitable raises. The HR manager may need to examine raises by office location (from the Location table), by job classification (the Position table), or by employee performance rating (the Employee table). Complex data analysis tools need complex data to realize their potential. Therefore, you will create PivotTables and PivotCharts based on queries.

The first step in analysis of data using PivotTables and PivotCharts requires that you assemble your source data in a single object. Often, the database will contain a query containing the necessary data. If no query exists that contains the appropriate data, you need to create it or modify an existing query. After you assemble the source data, open the query and switch to PivotTable view. Figure 5.1 illustrates the PivotTable design grid.

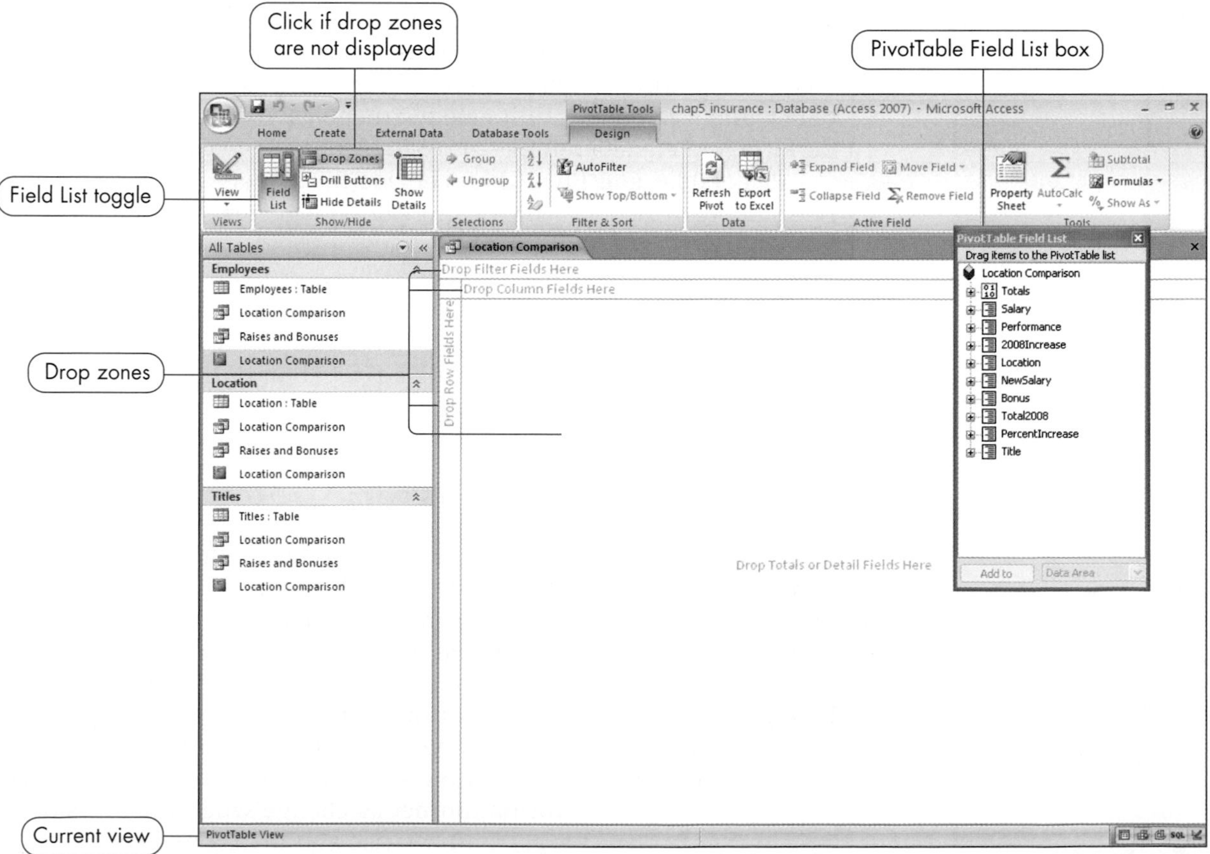

Figure 5.1 PivotTable Design Grid

Add Fields to the PivotTable View

A ***drop zone*** is an area in a PivotTable or PivotChart design grid where you drop fields to organize the data.

The ***row field*** is the field that you assign to group data horizontally into rows.

The PivotTable view appears blank when initiated because Access is waiting for your instructions on how to display the data. The light blue rectangles identify the drop zones. ***Drop zones*** are areas in the PivotTable or PivotChart design grid where you drop fields to organize the data. The primary drop zones are row field, column field, totals or detail field, and filter field. You use the row, column, and filter fields to define how to organize the data for analysis. The ***row field*** is the data source field that you use to group data horizontally into rows. Row fields are generally created by fields containing text, such as states or cities. In Figure 5.2, the Location field is selected. Notice the Drop Row Fields Here drop zone border is blue, indicating that the contents of the Location field are appropriate for a row field. After you click and drag the Location field to the Drop Row Fields Here drop zone, the PivotTable displays an alphabetical list of cities where the firm has offices.

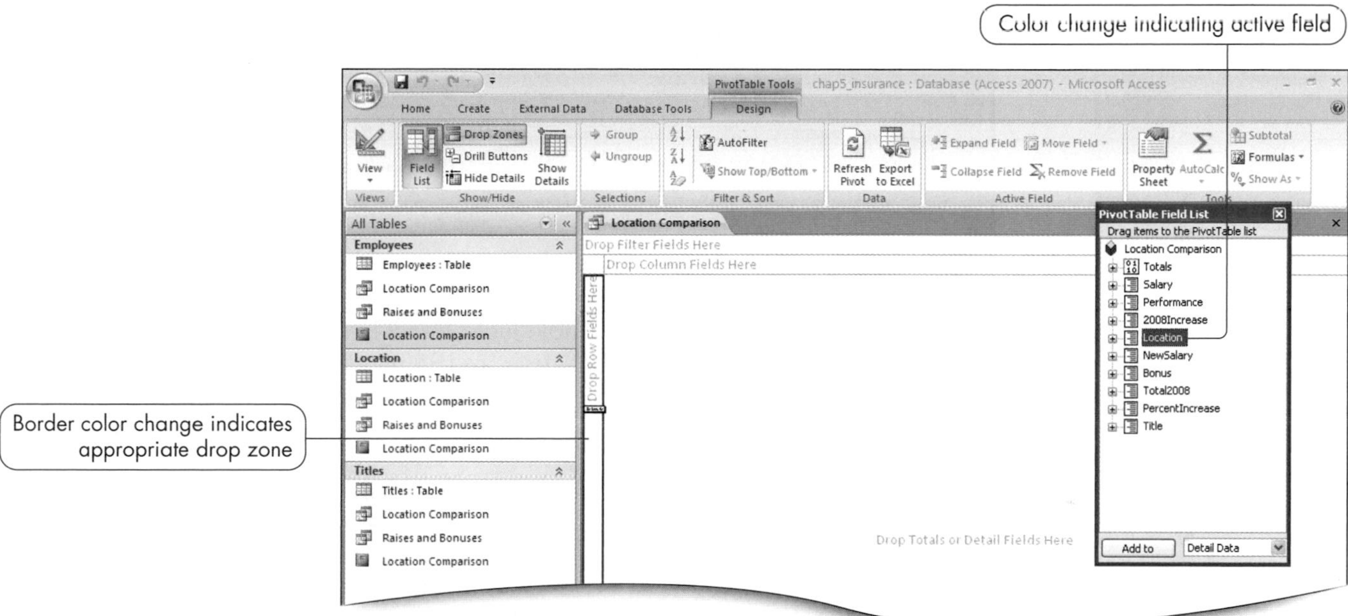

Figure 5.2 Field Selected for Row Field

The ***detail field*** contains individual values to be summarized.

The largest drop zone contains the ***detail field***, which is the location where you position the field or fields that contain data to be analyzed. Generally, the detail field is a field that contains individual numerical data, such as quantities, monetary values, or percentages. In Figure 5.3, the PercentIncrease field was added to the Drop Totals or Data Fields Here drop zone. This instructs Access to summarize the PercentIncrease field by city, the field used to organize data into rows. Dropping the PercentIncrease field in the detail field helps you analyze the data to see if pay raises across locations and positions are equitable. These data from the PercentIncrease field are averaged instead of totaled because the underlying values are percentages. For example, the average increase for Phoenix managers is 5.93%.

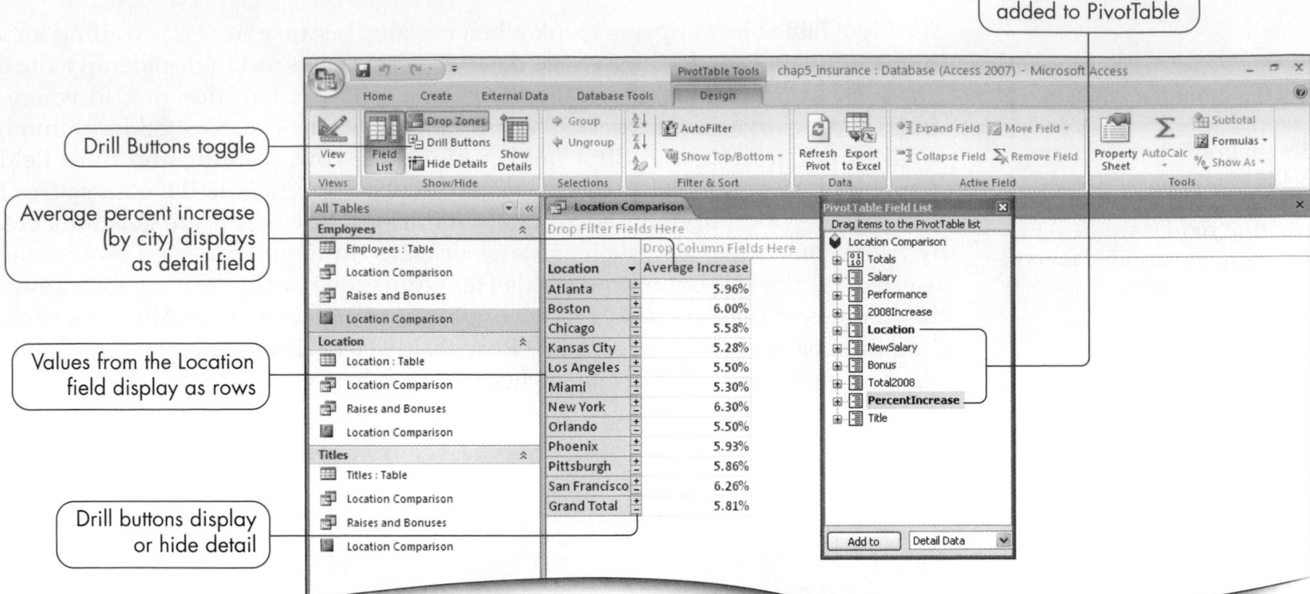

Figure 5.3 Average Increase (Detail Field) by City (Row Field)

A ***drill button*** is the plus (+) or minus (–) sign that enables you to show or collapse details.

You should notice a couple of things after adding fields to the drop zones. First, field names are bold in the PivotTable Field List window after you add them to the PivotTable. In Figure 5.3, the Location and PercentIncrease fields are bold after adding them to the drop zones. Second, you see ***drill buttons***, the little plus (+) and minus (–) signs to the right of individual groups, such as Location in the current PivotTable. Click the + drill button to display additional details for a particular group, or click the – drill button to collapse a group that is currently expanded. These buttons are useful as you experiment with the PivotTable to get the right amount of detail to analyze the data properly. If the drill buttons do not appear in the PivotTable, click Drill Buttons in the Show/Hide group on the Design tab.

The ***column field*** is the field that you assign to group data vertically into columns.

The ***column field*** is the data source field that you use to assign to group data vertically in columns in a PivotTable. Figure 5.4 shows the Title field dropped in the Drop Column Fields Here drop zone to display each job title as an analysis specification to determine percentage increase equity. Now, you can compare the average percent increase in each city by every position title: account rep, manager, senior rep, and trainee.

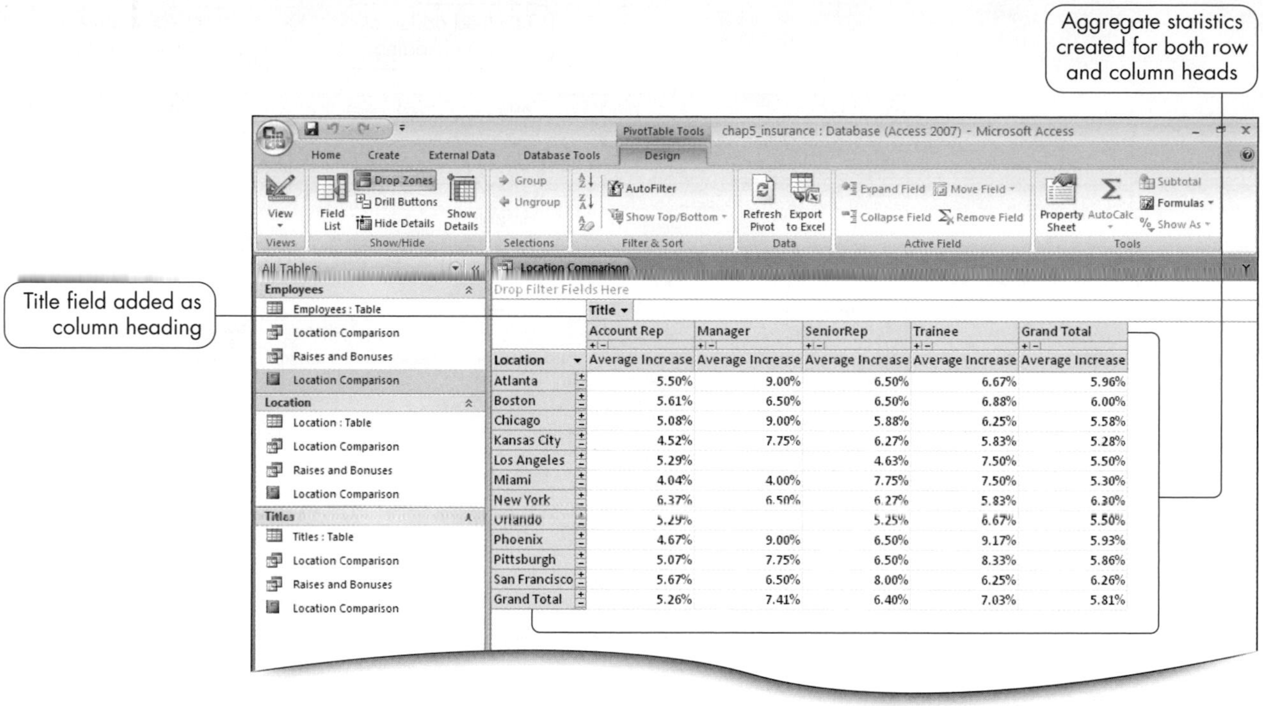

Aggregate statistics created for both row and column heads

Title field added as column heading

	Title				
	Account Rep	Manager	SeniorRep	Trainee	Grand Total
Location	Average Increase	Average Increase	Average Increase	Average Increase	Average Increase
Atlanta	5.50%	9.00%	6.50%	6.67%	5.96%
Boston	5.61%	6.50%	6.50%	6.88%	6.00%
Chicago	5.08%	9.00%	5.88%	6.25%	5.58%
Kansas City	4.52%	7.75%	6.27%	5.83%	5.28%
Los Angeles	5.29%		4.63%	7.50%	5.50%
Miami	4.04%	4.00%	7.75%	7.50%	5.30%
New York	6.37%	6.50%	6.27%	5.83%	6.30%
Orlando	5.29%		5.25%	6.67%	5.50%
Phoenix	4.67%	9.00%	6.50%	9.17%	5.93%
Pittsburgh	5.07%	7.75%	6.50%	8.33%	5.86%
San Francisco	5.67%	6.50%	8.00%	6.25%	6.26%
Grand Total	5.26%	7.41%	6.40%	7.03%	5.81%

Figure 5.4 Title Field Added to Column Field Drop Zone

TIP What Should Be in Rows or in Columns

You will need to experiment with each new PivotTable you construct to discover which layout best displays the data. An experienced user tends to put the field with the most possible choices in the row area and shorter ones in columns. Once you have thought through what questions to answer, you simply drag the appropriate field from the Field List pane to the appropriate drop zone. If you do not like the results, you can easily reverse the positions of the fields.

A ***filter field*** is the field that you use to filter data based on specified criteria.

A ***filter field*** is the data source field that you use to create specific criteria to filter data in a PivotTable. You use a filter to analyze data based on a particular condition; all other data are excluded from the analysis. For example, you can set a filter to display data for a particular state, department, job position, and so on. Figure 5.5 displays the Performance field added to the Drop Filter Fields Here drop zone. The filter is set to Good so that you can analyze data for all sales representatives who received a Good performance rating. The HR manager can then examine the results to determine if this year's salary increases are equitable for all of the employees with a good performance rating across locations and position titles. In this case, the raises are remarkably consistent. Good managers in Kansas City and New York received the same percentage increase in their salaries.

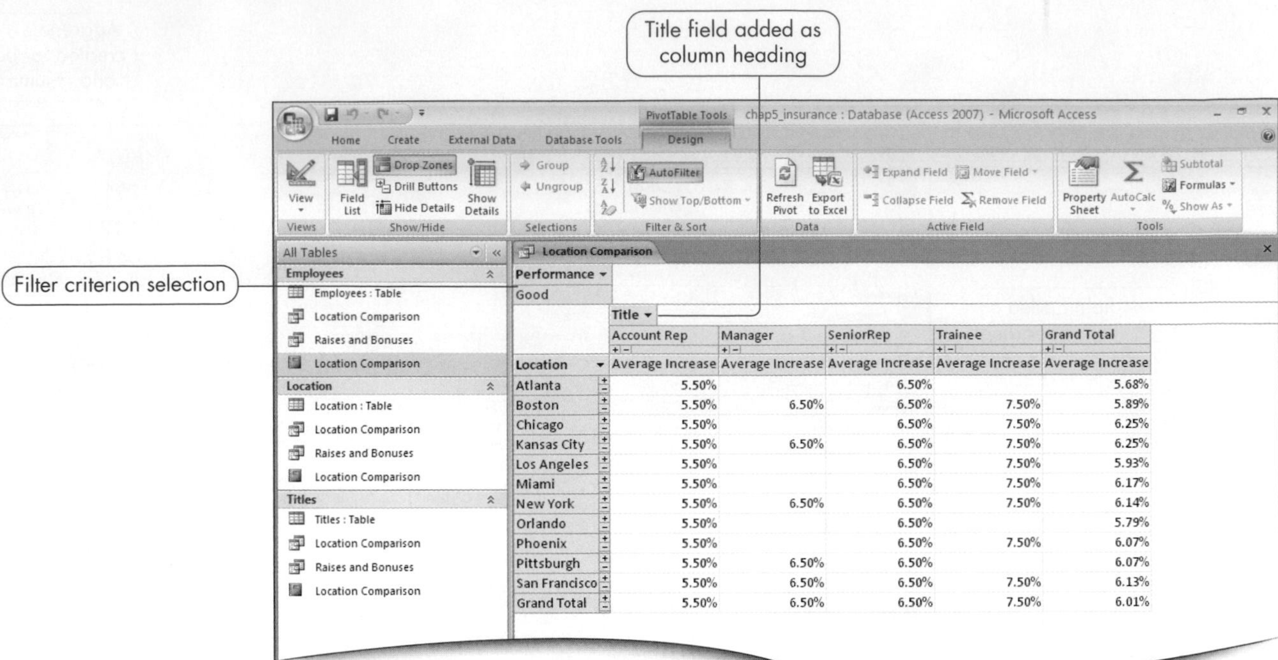

Location	Account Rep Average Increase	Manager Average Increase	SeniorRep Average Increase	Trainee Average Increase	Grand Total Average Increase
Atlanta	5.50%		6.50%		5.68%
Boston	5.50%	6.50%	6.50%	7.50%	5.89%
Chicago	5.50%		6.50%	7.50%	6.25%
Kansas City	5.50%	6.50%	6.50%	7.50%	6.25%
Los Angeles	5.50%		6.50%	7.50%	5.93%
Miami	5.50%		6.50%	7.50%	6.17%
New York	5.50%	6.50%	6.50%	7.50%	6.14%
Orlando	5.50%		6.50%		5.79%
Phoenix	5.50%		6.50%	7.50%	6.07%
Pittsburgh	5.50%	6.50%	6.50%		6.07%
San Francisco	5.50%	6.50%	6.50%	7.50%	6.13%
Grand Total	5.50%	6.50%	6.50%	7.50%	6.01%

Figure 5.5 Completed PivotTable with a Filtered Field Permits Easy Analysis

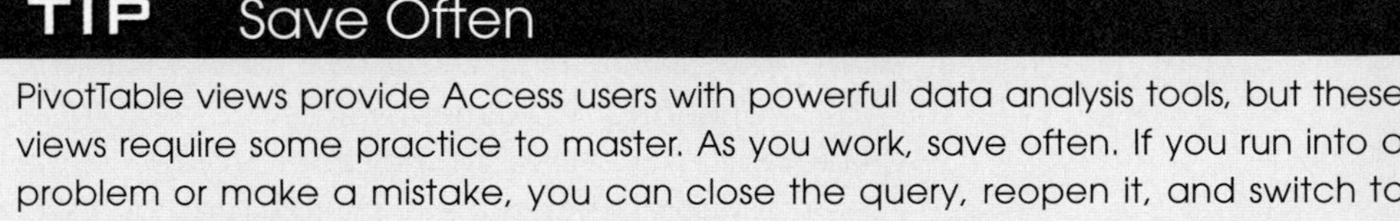

PivotTable views provide Access users with powerful data analysis tools, but these views require some practice to master. As you work, save often. If you run into a problem or make a mistake, you can close the query, reopen it, and switch to PivotTable view to try again.

Calculating Aggregate Statistics

A ***data aggregate*** is a collection of parts from different sources to form a whole.

After you assemble data in the PivotTable, you can use Access tools to help analyze and extract the information. The PivotTable view provides the same aggregating functions as found in reports and other query views. A ***data aggregate*** is a collection of many parts that come together from different sources and are considered a whole. Commonly employed aggregating calculations include sum, average, minimum, maximum, standard deviation, and variance. Table 5.1 describes the aggregating functional usage. Access provides you with many methods of summarizing or aggregating data. Decision makers use the methods to help make sense of an array of choices.

Table 5.1 Aggregate Functions

Aggregate Name	Definition	Example
Sum	Adds values together.	Total contributions for a political campaign by state.
Count	Counts the non-null items.	The number of students who earned an A in a computer class.
Min	Returns the smallest value.	The employee with the smallest percent increase.
Max	Returns the highest value.	The employee with the largest salary increase.
Average	Calculates the arithmetic mean—the mean obtained by adding several quantities together and dividing the sum by the number of quantities. It ignores null values.	The average cost of a three-bedroom house in Tulsa.
Standard Deviation	Measures how widely spread the values are from the average when the data describe a sample of the population instead of the entire population.	If the average percent increase were 3 and the standard deviation were 5, these pay increases differ more than if the average were 3 and the standard deviation were 2. The range is more varied in the sample distribution.
Standard Deviation Population	Measures how widely spread the values are from the average when the data describe an entire population.	If the average percent increase were 3 and the standard deviation were 5, these pay increases differ more than if the average were 3 and the standard deviation were 2. The range is more varied in a population distribution.
Variance Population	Measures the square of the population standard deviation.	Spread or dispersion of salaries for employees in similar positions in an organization.

When the field is a text or a yes/no value, you may count its values. You may also count numeric fields and also calculate the sum, count, minimum value, maximum value, average, standard deviation, variance, standard deviation population, and population variance from the data fields in the data area. You must activate a data point in the Drop Totals or Detail Fields zone (the large center box) prior to performing any aggregating calculations. For example, the Bonus field displayed in Figure 5.6 shows the detail for the Atlanta location. Before you use the AutoCalc tool, you must first activate any detail (here the fourth record in the AccountRep column) before you click AutoCalc. The AutoCalc feature generates a drop-down list for you to select the necessary function.

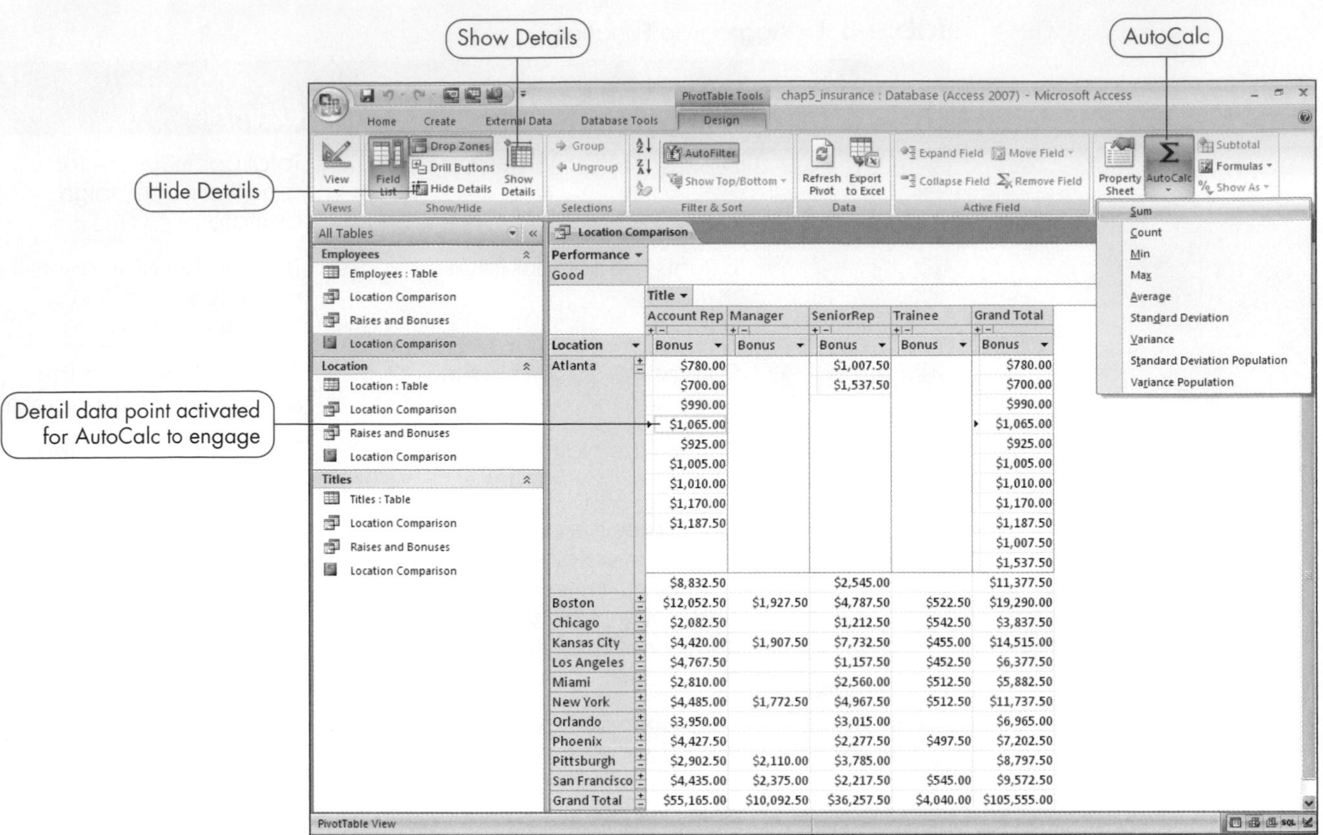

Figure 5.6 Calculating Summary Statistics

> **TIP** Turn the Field List Box Off or Move It
>
> Look through Figures 5.1 through 5.8. The Field List Box appears, moves around, and disappears. You can display, hide, or move the Field List Box as you work. The toggle controlling it is in the Show/Hide group on the Design tab.

Modifying a PivotTable

After you create a PivotTable, you may want to modify the structure or format of the PivotTable. For example, you may decide to reorganize the PivotTable by rearranging fields from rows to columns, select other fields for displaying details, or remove a filter and set a different filter. In addition, you might want to change the format of the PivotTable to be easier to read.

Add and Remove PivotTable Fields

Data mining uses statistical tools to analyze patterns and relationships in data. Once the original PivotTable has been constructed, the decision maker can use the existing form to examine other fields. For example, after the HR manager examines the percent increase across locations, position titles, and good performance rating to ensure equity, he or she may wish to examine the annual bonuses to validate them. You can add additional data items to the drop zone by clicking them in the Field List Box to select them and dragging them to the Drop Totals or Detail Fields drop zone. Figure 5.7 demonstrates the Bonus field added to the PivotTable view. It displays totals for the Bonus field and averages for the PercentIncrease field. The summary shows the information needed by the HR manager, but it is presented in a rather cluttered format.

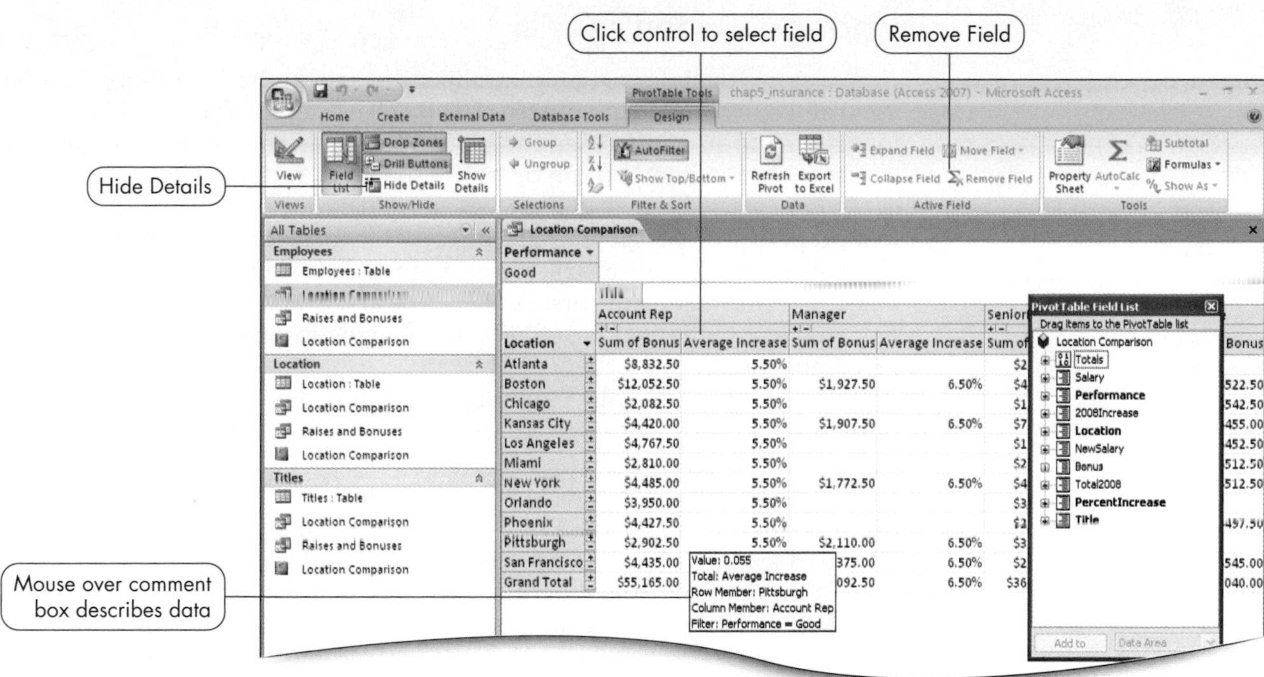

Figure 5.7 Bonus Field Added to an Existing Pivot

After establishing the PivotTable grid, you can easily add and remove data fields to analyze the data. Should you decide that displaying both the average percent increase and the bonus fields makes the information too cluttered to be useful, you can remove the PercentIncrease field data from the grid by clicking the field control button, and then clicking Remove Field in the Active Field group (shown in Figure 5.7). The resulting PivotTable demonstrates an important accounting concept, crossfooting. Accountants use ***crossfooting*** by summing the rows, summing the columns, and making sure the totals match. It provides an important check figure—a way to verify the accuracy of your data. See Figure 5.8.

Crossfooting sums the rows, sums the columns, and compares the totals.

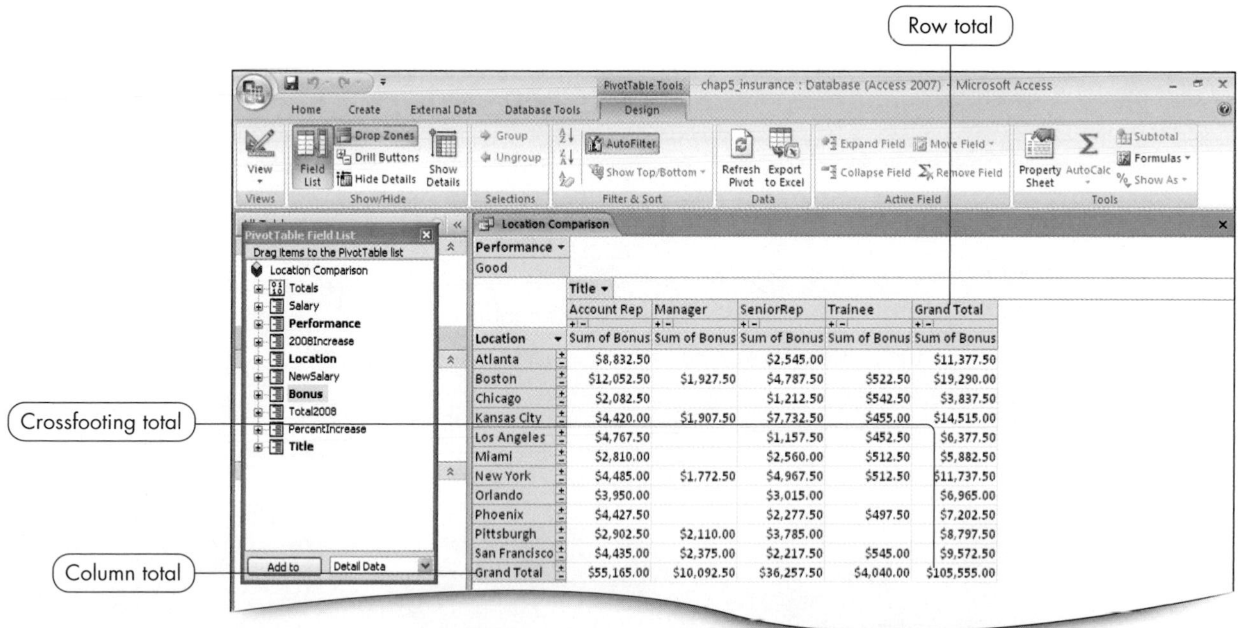

Figure 5.8 Crossfooting Illustration

Change Properties

Access stores the information controlling the data in the Data Properties dialog box. You can control the data's appearance by changing the data's background color or font color and size. It is generally a good idea to visually separate aggregating statistics from data points. You can do so by changing the font color or background color of the total row. This makes PivotTable output easier to understand. To change a format property, right-click the value or values to format and select Properties from the shortcut menu. Make sure the Format tab is active and select the appropriate formats. After formatting the first field, use the arrow in the Select box to define the next field you want to format. In addition to changing formats, you can also sort or delete PivotTable fields.

The Captions tab in the Properties dialog box sheet helps you customize the data presentation. Access uses default names for aggregating statistics. Sometimes the defaults are not easy to understand. They might say AverageofDaysOnMarket. This field name describes the data, but is too long to be easily understood. You can change the way it displays in the PivotTable view by establishing a caption. Click the Caption tab and select the field you wish to caption in the select box. Then type the name you want to display on the PivotTable, for example, Ave Market Days. You may only apply or modify a PivotTable caption by using the field properties if the caption was created with a caption in PivotTable view. If the field caption was created in the table's Design view, you cannot override it with a different caption.

In the following hands-on exercise, you will create a PivotTable, add and remove fields, calculate summary statistics, and display or hide detail.

Hands-On Exercises

1 | Create and Use a PivotTable

Skills covered: 1. Create a PivotTable from a Query **2.** Add Fields Using the Design Grid **3.** Remove Fields Using the Design Grid. **4.** Calculate Summary Statistics and Alter Formats and Captions **5.** Add and Rearrange PivotTable Fields **6.** Remove a Field and Modify Summary Calculations

Step 1
Create a PivotTable from a Query

Refer to Figure 5.9 as you complete Step 1.

a. Use Windows Explorer to locate the file named *chap5_ho1-3_insurance.accdb*. Copy the file and rename the copied file as **chap5_ho1-3_insurance_solution.accdb**.

b. Open *chap5_ho1-3_insurance_solution.accdb*. Click **Options** on the Security Warning toolbar, click **Enable this content** in the Microsoft Office Security Options dialog box, and click **OK**.

c. Rename the *Your_Name Raises and Bonuses* query with your name.

d. Copy the *Your_Name Raises and Bonuses* query and name the copy **Copy Of Your_Name Raises and Bonuses**.

You created a copy of the query in which to practice. If all goes well, you can delete the original and rename the copy by deleting the words *Copy Of*. If you run into problems, delete the copied query, recopy the original, and start the exercise again.

e. Open the **Copy Of Your_Name Raises and Bonuses** query. Click the **View down arrow** in the Views group on the Design tab and select **PivotTable View** from the menu.

f. Compare your screen to Figure 5.9.

The Drop Filter Fields Here, Drop Column Fields Here, Drop Row Fields Here, and Drop Totals or Detail Fields Here drop zones appear in the main part of the window. The PivotTable Field List box shows on the right side of the window.

TROUBLESHOOTING: If the drop zones do not appear, click Drop Zones in the Show/Hide group on the Design tab to display the drop zones. If the PivotTable Field List box does not appear, click Field List in the Show/Hide group to display the PivotTable Field List box.

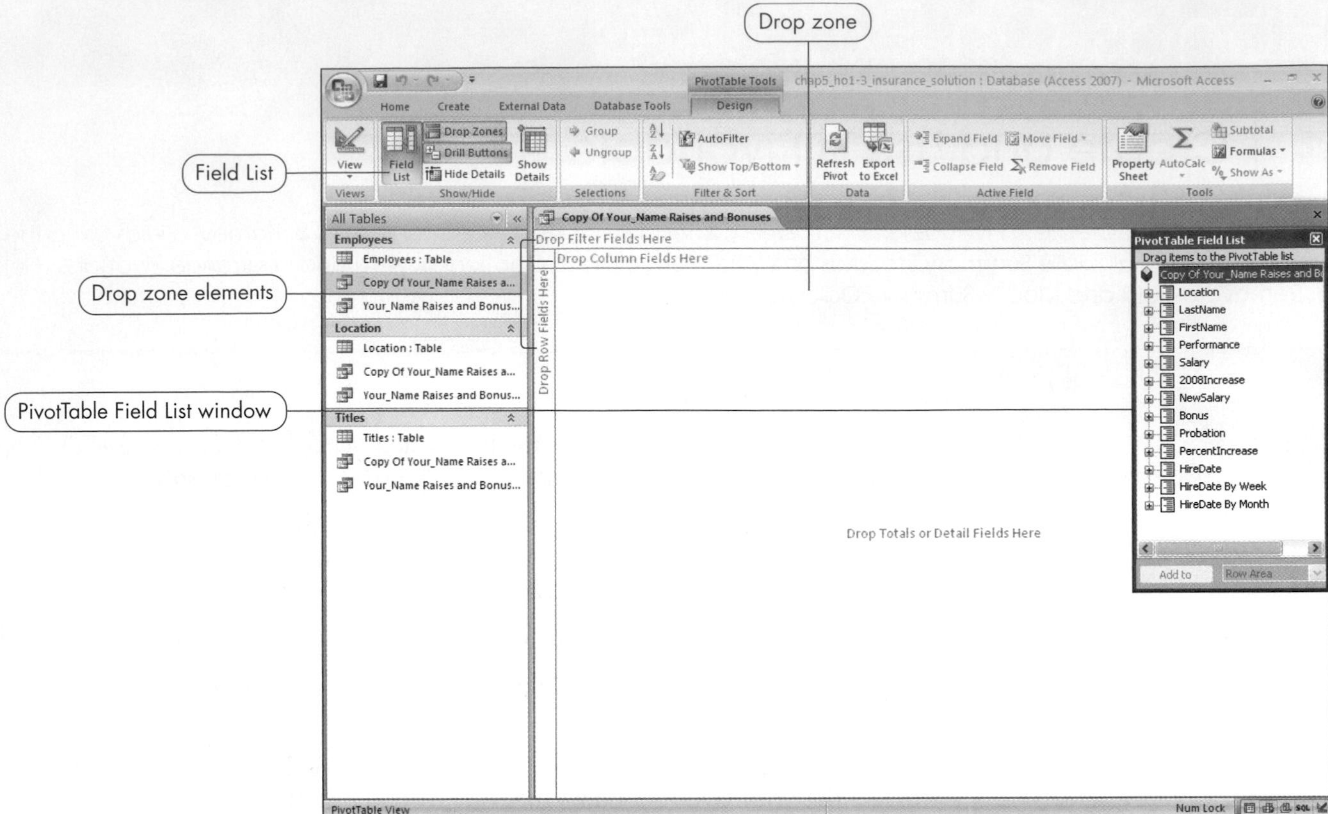

Figure 5.9 PivotTable Workspace

Step 2
Add Fields Using the Design Grid

Refer to Figure 5.10 as you complete Step 2.

a. Click the **Location** field in the PivotTable Field List box and drag it to the **Drop Row Fields Here** drop zone.

   Alternatively, click the **arrow** beside the Add to button on the bottom of the PivotTable Field List box. Select **Row Area** and click **Add to**.

   TROUBLESHOOTING: PivotTables and PivotCharts consume system resources. They require huge amounts of memory and CPU time to run. Be patient. It may take a second or two for your command to execute.

b. Click and drag the **Performance field** from the PivotTable Field List box to the **Drop Column Fields Here drop zone.**

c. Click the **PercentIncrease** field in the PivotTable Field List Pane. Click the **Drop Zone location arrow**, select **Detail Data**, and click **Add to**.

d. Activate a data point by clicking *3.00%* in the Atlanta row and the Average column. Save your query.

   Because you set the data to display details, a scroll bar turns on to let you scroll to view other data points.

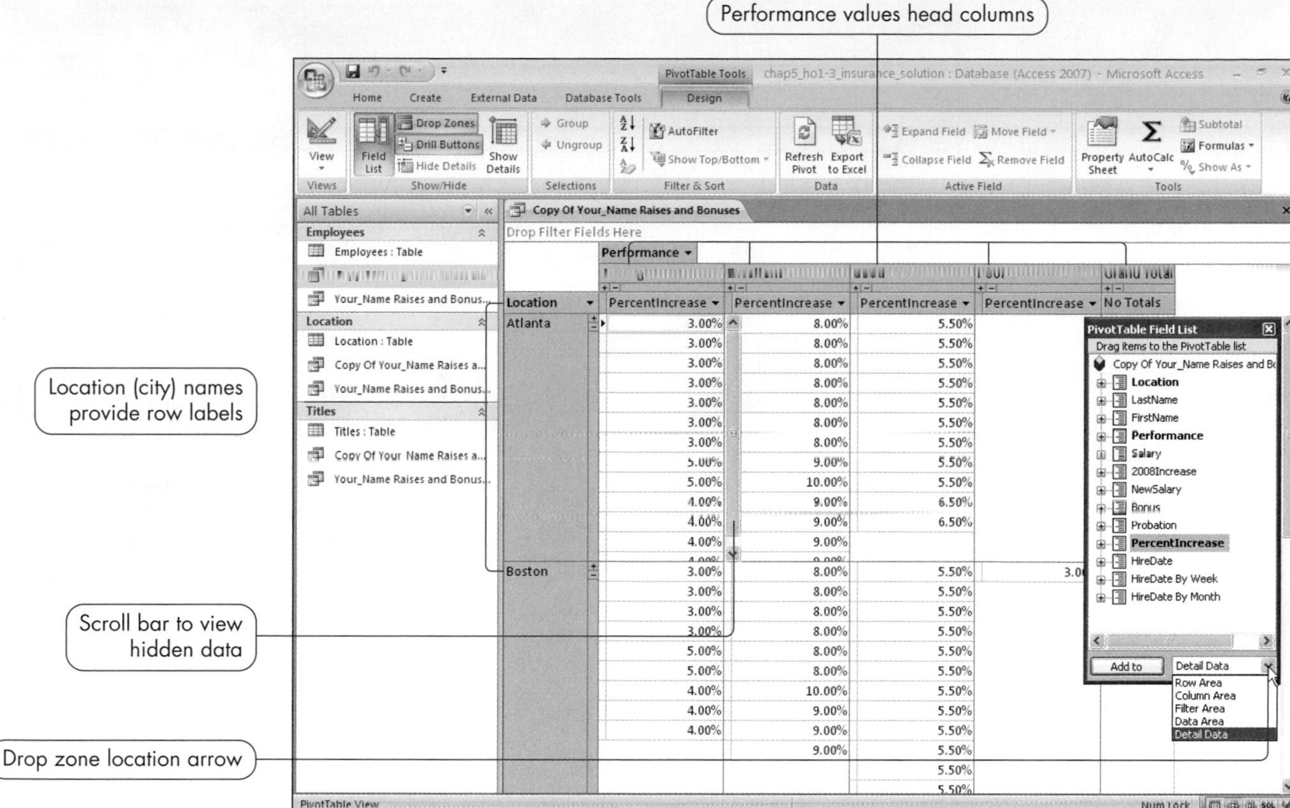

Figure 5.10 A PivotTable Showing Detail

Step 3
Remove Fields Using the Design Grid

Refer to Figure 5.11 as you complete Step 3.

a. Click any of the **PercentIncrease** labels (look for the gray background) to select the values.

   All of the detail values select and turn blue.

b. Check to make sure that **Detail Data** displays as the choice in the Drop Zone location box. Then click the **Bonus** field in the PivotTable Field List box. Click **Add to**.

c. Click any of the **Bonus** labels (look for the gray background) to select the values.

d. Click **Remove Field** in the Active Field group on the Design tab.

   The Bonus field data disappear from the PivotTable, and the space it consumed is reallocated to the remaining fields.

e. Click **Save** on the Quick Access Toolbar.

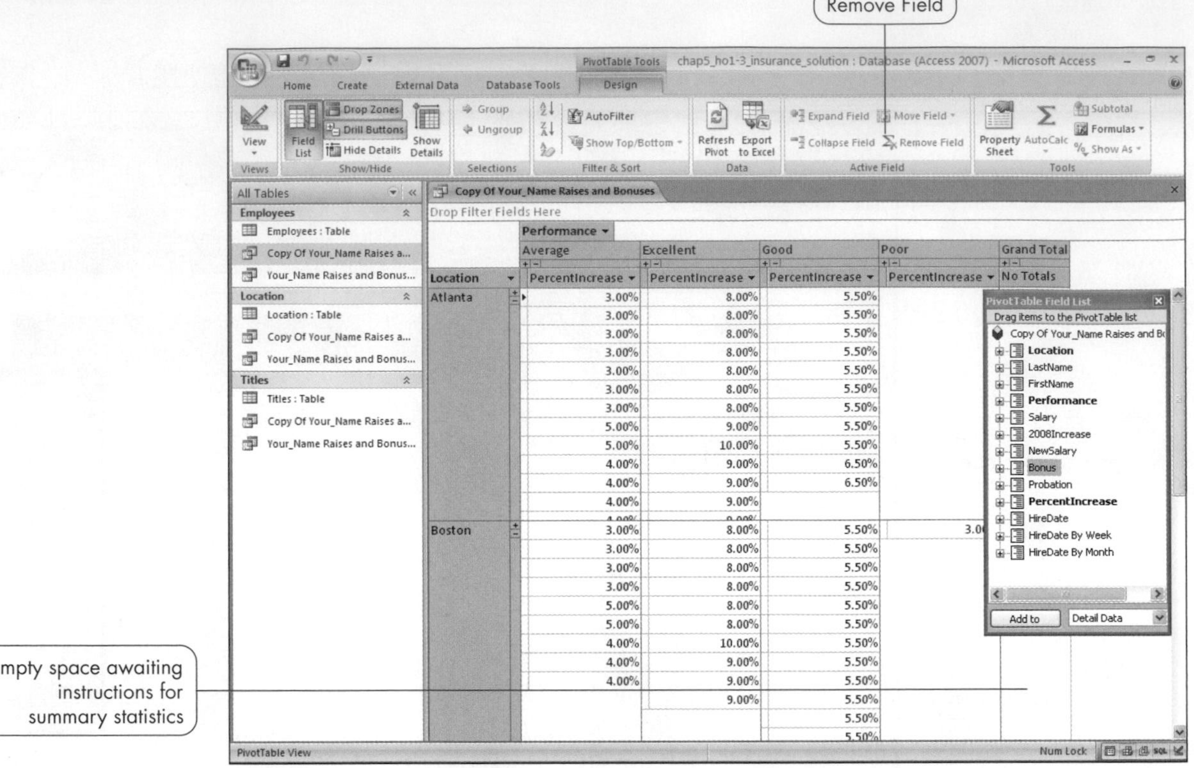

Figure 5.11 Bonus Field Added and Removed

Step 4
Calculate Summary Statistics and Alter Formats and Captions

Refer to Figure 5.12 as you complete Step 4.

a. Click the **PercentIncrease** column head to select it.

   All of the values turn blue.

b. Click **AutoCalc** in the Tools group on the Design tab. Select **Average** from the drop-down menu.

   The Grand Total column is no longer empty. It displays 5.96% for the Average of PercentIncrease summary statistic for the Atlanta location. You decide that viewing this level of detail is not helpful and decide to collapse the details.

c. Click **Hide Details** in the Show/Hide group on the Design tab.

   The details collapse, and the columns get wider because the column labels change to Average of PercentIncrease. The longer title needs a wider column to display.

d. Right-click the **Average of PercentIncrease** column label and select **Properties** from the shortcut menu.

   The Properties window for a pivoted field differs from the properties for table or query fields in that fewer options are available for PivotTable fields.

e. Click the **Captions tab** and position your insertion point in the box beside the word *Caption*. It should say *Average of PercentIncrease*. Click or type to change the caption property to **Average Increase**. Click the **red close button** in the top-right corner of the Properties window.

   Not only do the column headings change but also the columns get more narrow to fit the smaller labels.

f. Right-click the **Performance** label, select **Properties**, and click the **Format tab**. In the *Cell format* section, click the **Background Color drop-down arrow** and select **White** (first column, last row). With the Properties window still open, click the **Location** label and set its background color to **White**.

TROUBLESHOOTING: If your colors did not come out as expected, use the arrow in the *Select box* of the Properties box and reapply the color change.

g. Close the Properties window. Save the changes made to the PivotTable view.

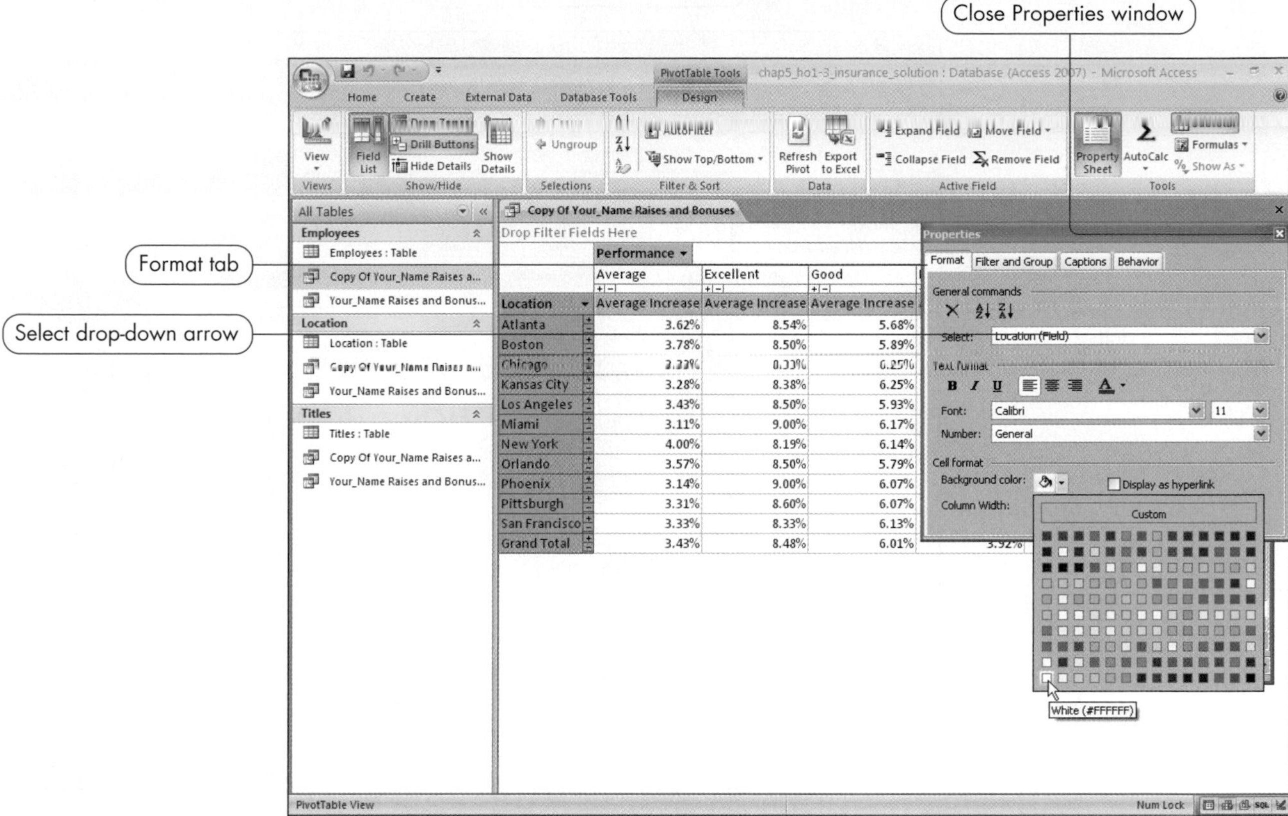

Figure 5.12 Applying Fill Property

Step 5 Add and Rearrange PivotTable Fields

Refer to Figure 5.13 as you complete Step 5.

a. Click **Field List** in the Show/Hide group on the Design tab to display the PivotTable Field List pane, if necessary. Scroll down if necessary to find the HireDate By Month field in the PivotTable Field List pane.

b. Click and drag **HireDate By Month** to the left of the city names. When the thick blue line displays to the left of the Location column, release the mouse.

You added a second row field. The dates are grouped by year and then by location within each year. When you scroll, you see that only two locations, Atlanta and Miami, have employees that have worked for the company since 1990. If you scroll through the PivotTable data, you will discover that many locations have employees that started working in the years since 2000.

c. Click the **Years** label to select the column.

You know the column is selected because it highlights.

d. Click **Years** and drag it to the right. When the thick blue line is between *Location* and *Average Increase*, release the mouse.

You have exchanged the positions of the two row fields. Now, each location name appears only once in the report, but the years display over and over. Both displays could meet a managerial decision maker's needs. If the question that is most important is "Are the percent increases equitable between locations?," then you would display the location information first. If the question is "Are the percent increases equitable among employees with similar lengths of service?," you would present the data with the years in the left position.

e. Position your mouse over the first record in the **Excellent** column (8.00%). The box that appears drills the data and explains about the underlying data. Save the changes made to the PivotTable view.

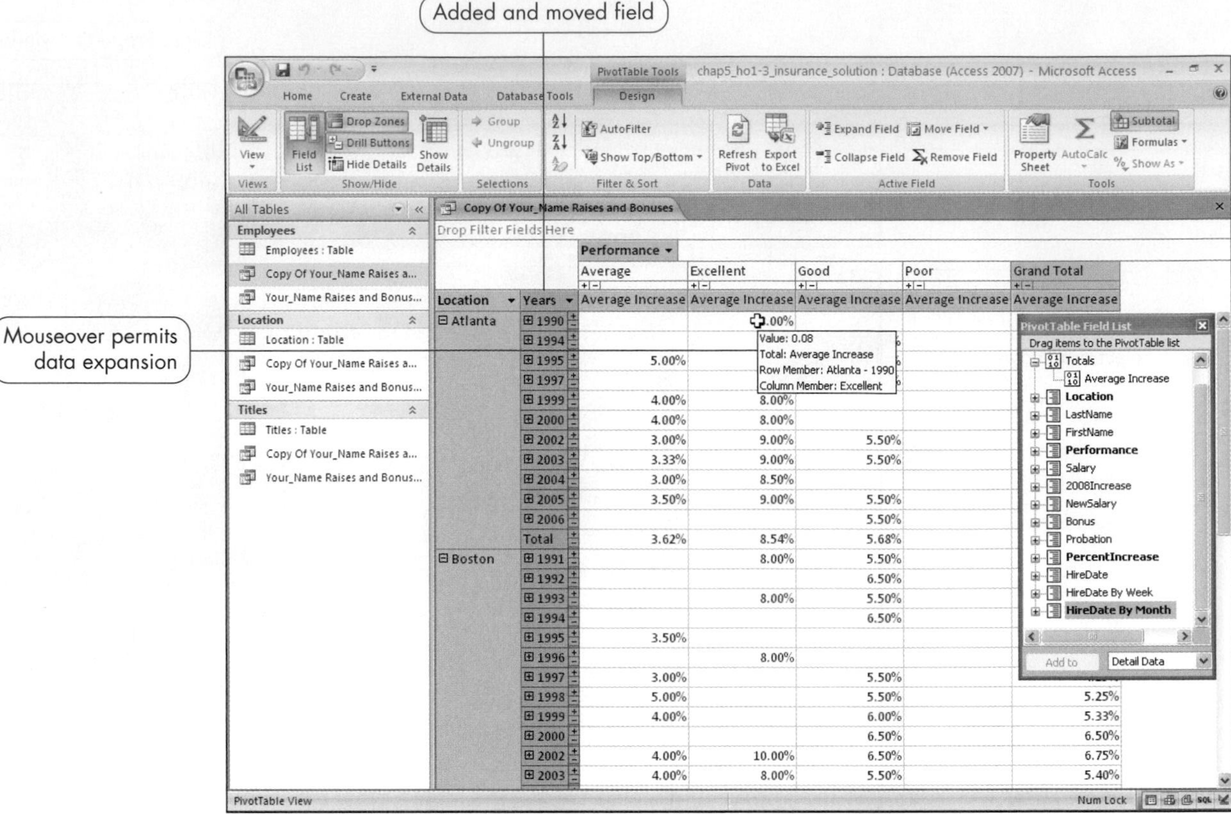

Figure 5.13 Expanded Information

Step 6
Remove a Field and Modify Summary Calculations

Refer to Figure 5.14 as you complete Step 6.

a. Click the **Performance** label. Click **Show Details** in the Show/Hide group.

   The table expands to display the hidden detail.

b. Click any **PercentIncrease** label, and then click **Remove Field** in the Active Field group.

   The PivotTable frame remains, but the detail data no longer appear.

   TROUBLESHOOTING: If your Remove Field tool is dim, it is probably because you did not have a detail active when you attempted to use the Remove Field feature. You must not only have details displayed, but you must also have one active for the Remove Field tool to be available.

c. Click the **Average Increase** label below the Grand Total label, and then click **Remove Field** in the Active Field group to remove this data.

d. Click **Field List**, if needed, in the Show/Hide group to display the PivotTable Field List window, and then click the **Bonus** field to select it and drag it to the Detail area of the PivotTable.

   Do not be concerned if no bonus values display in the Average or Poor.

e. Click any value in the detail area of the Bonus field to select it. Click **AutoCalc** in the Tools group. Select **Sum**.

TROUBLESHOOTING: If your AutoCalc tool is dim, it is probably because you did not have a detail active when you attempted to use the AutoCalc feature. You must not only have details displayed, you must also have one active for the AutoCalc tool to be available.

f. Click a **Bonus** label to select it. All of the Bonus values should highlight. Click **Hide Details** in the Show/Hide group.

g. Compare your work to Figure 5.14. If your work matches, continue following the steps. If your work does not match, close the query without saving changes, reopen the query, and rework Steps 6a through 6e.

h. Save and close your query.

i. Select and delete the original *Your_Name Raises and Bonuses* query. Rename the *Copy Of Your_Name Raises and Bonuses* query by deleting the words *Copy Of*.

j. Click the **Office Button**, select **Manage**, and select **Compact and Repair Database**.

k. Click the **Office Button**, select **Manage**, and select **Back Up Database**. Type **chap5_ho1_insurance_solution** and click **Save**.

You just created a backup of the database after completing the first hands-on exercise. The original database *chap5_ho1-3_insurance_solution* remains onscreen. If you ruin the original database as you complete the second hands-on exercise, you can use the backup file you just created.

l. Close the file and exit Access if you do not want to continue with the next exercise at this time.

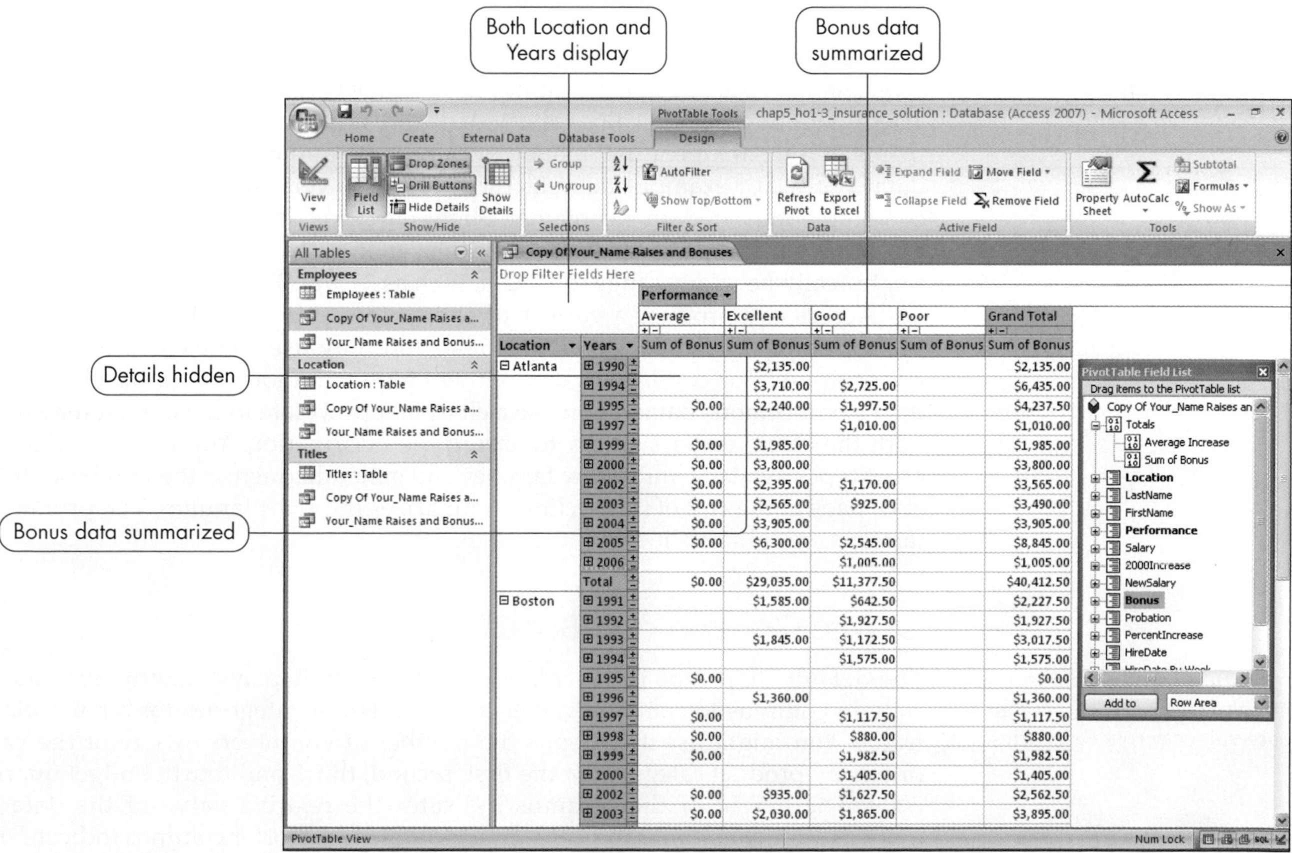

Figure 5.14 Analyzed Data Changed to Bonus

Charts Convey Information

Microsoft Office provides many tools to help you identify and extract only the records needed at the moment. After these records are identified, the decision maker needs to convert the data into information to make it useful. One of the best methods of distilling and summarizing data is to present it in a pictorial form—a chart. Well-designed charts facilitate data interpretation because charts make information clear graphically. You can present a chart differently to emphasize different data aspects. For example, if the proportion of patients receiving emergency room care differs dramatically on different days of the week, you might optimally express this difference with a pie chart. In most hospitals, the pie slices for emergency room care on Monday through Thursday will be about the same size, but the slices representing Friday, Saturday, and Sunday patient care will be much larger. An administrator in charge of scheduling can tell at a glance that more nurses need to be scheduled on the weekends. The same information could be presented in a bar or column chart, but those types of charts would not convey the same visual impact. If the old adage that a picture is worth a thousand words is true, then a well-designed chart is worth 10,000 words.

In this section, you learn about discrete and continuous data and the basics of good chart design. You will learn to create a PivotChart from PivotTable data. Finally, you will learn how to edit the chart to improve its readability.

Selecting an Appropriate Chart Type

Discrete data describe classifications and are measured and quantified in increments.

Continuous data describe a continuum of values.

Before you can create a chart, you need to understand a little about data. You will use two different types of data to create Access charts, discrete and continuous. ***Discrete data*** describe classifications or categories, such as names of the countries that a company ships orders to, or quantifiable data, such as the number of male and female volunteers for a charity drive. Discrete data typically measure in integer (whole number) values and cannot be meaningfully subdivided. For example, you might have 250 customers in Texas, but you would not have 250.7 Texan customers. ***Continuous data*** describe a continuum of smaller increments and are easily scaled. These data may be logically subdivided into smaller and smaller units. Measurements of time, temperature, money, volume, size, and distance illustrate continuous data values. For example, manufactured products very rarely are exactly the weight or volume indicated on a container. Slight variances may exist. Manufacturers may randomly sample products to measure the variance. A beverage marked as 32 ounces might really be in any range of values, such as 31.7 or 32.25 ounces.

Access can produce a variety of chart types. You must learn what chart type appropriately expresses each data type. You may use some chart types to depict either discrete or continuous data; other charts are more suited for either discrete data or continuous data. If you use a chart inappropriate to the data, it may interfere with the chart reader's ability to absorb the information. You may distill all of the chart types available into a few families and generalize across the families. The reference page at the end of this section summarizes the chart families. The primary chart families are column, line, pie, and other.

Create Column and Bar Charts

A ***column chart*** displays quantitative data vertically to compare values across categories.

The default chart type is the ***column chart***, which displays quantitative data vertically in columns to compare values across different categories for a particular time frame. You might use it to depict the number of volunteers by city or the value of orders by product category for the first, second, third, and fourth budget quarters in 2009. The height of the columns indicates the relative value of the data being depicted. Taller columns indicate larger values, and shorter columns indicate smaller values.

A ***bar chart*** displays quantitative data horizontally to compare values across categories.

A ***bar chart*** also displays quantitative data to compare values across different categories. The width of the bars indicates the relative value of the data being depicted. Wider bars indicate larger values, and smaller bars indicate smaller values. Column and bar charts differ only in orientation. A column chart displays data series vertically in columns, whereas a bar chart displays data series horizontally, left to right. You may be able to use either a column or a bar chart to depict the same data; however, one chart may optimize comprehension of the data better. A bar chart may be preferable when the categorical labels are too wide to fit easily on the horizontal axis of a column chart. By plotting the data on a bar chart, the longer categorical labels might be easier to read.

Create Line Charts

A ***line chart*** plots data points to compare trends over time.

The ***line chart*** family, including the area and scatter plot chart types, describes continuously distributed data and should only be used to plot continuous data. You may use this chart family with all time series data. The basic line chart shows trends over time. For example, a line chart is appropriate to depict the number of college graduates over the last 25 years at a particular institution or the number of cellular phones in the United States over the last 10 years.

A ***scatter plot chart*** shows relationships between two variables.

Another member of the line chart family is the scatter plot chart. The ***scatter plot chart*** shows relationships between two variables. For example, you might use a scatter plot chart to examine average monthly temperatures and ice cream sales. Presumably, that chart would show lots of data points clustered during the warmest months and fewer data points during the colder months of the year. Scatter plot charts would also be appropriate to compare ACT scores and grade point averages, to compare number of hours of exercise per week and body fat percentage, or to compare number of hours practicing the piano and ratings at a music contest.

Create Pie and Doughnut Charts

A ***pie chart*** shows proportion to the whole for a single data series.

A ***doughnut chart*** shows proportion to the whole for multiple data series.

A ***pie chart*** describes parts in relation to a whole. Instead of showing values, the values are converted to percentages of the total value. The larger the slice of the pie, the larger the percentage a category represents of the total. For example, you can use a pie chart type to depict the proportion each product category contributes to the total revenue for a year. A pie chart is also appropriate to depict the proportion of undergraduate male students by class: seniors, juniors, sophomores, and freshmen. A ***doughnut chart*** also shows proportions in relationship to a whole, but a doughnut chart can also display more than one series of data. For example, a doughnut chart could use one ring to show the proportion of male students by class and the second ring to show the proportion of female students by class.

The other chart family compares values across categories and is most often used in the social sciences. For example, a psychologist might compare the results of an individual's personality attribute test to a population's normal test results.

Identifying Chart Elements

Figure 5.15 shows a PivotChart view of an Access PivotTable. Each PivotTable created also generates a PivotChart. When you created a PivotTable in Hands-On Exercise 1, you also created a PivotChart, even if you have not looked at it yet. Because the two views are linked, any changes you make to the chart will affect the table and any changes made to the table will change the chart. You may already know some of the terminology for a PivotChart because it is the same as in the other chart applications in Microsoft Office 2007. Some of the terms differ slightly. The plot area, title, and legend remain the same.

The **legend** tells which color represents the data for each data series.

The **axes** are the vertical and horizontal scales displaying the information to be plotted.

The **gridlines** are the lines that extend across the chart.

The **chart title** displays a name describing the data depicted in a chart.

The ***legend*** tells which color represents the data for each data series, such as blue for Product A, green for Product B, and red for Product C. The legend may display anywhere in the chart area. The ***axes*** are the vertical and horizontal scales displaying the information to be plotted. The axis may be edited to more correctly display the information that you wish to describe. In a column or line chart, the vertical axis, known as the Y-axis, typically displays quantitative values, and the horizontal axis, known as the X-axis, typically displays categories or time periods. The ***gridlines*** are the lines that extend across the chart. Use them as placeholders to make data interpretation easy. The ***chart title*** displays a name describing the data depicted in the chart. The other chart elements derive their names from the data used to create them. For example, in the chart shown in Figure 5.15, the field buttons are named Performance, Location, and Title because those are the names of the fields employed for row, filter, and column drop zones. (Here the word Title refers to the field name used in the table, not the chart title.) Figure 5.16 shows the PivotTable view of the same data.

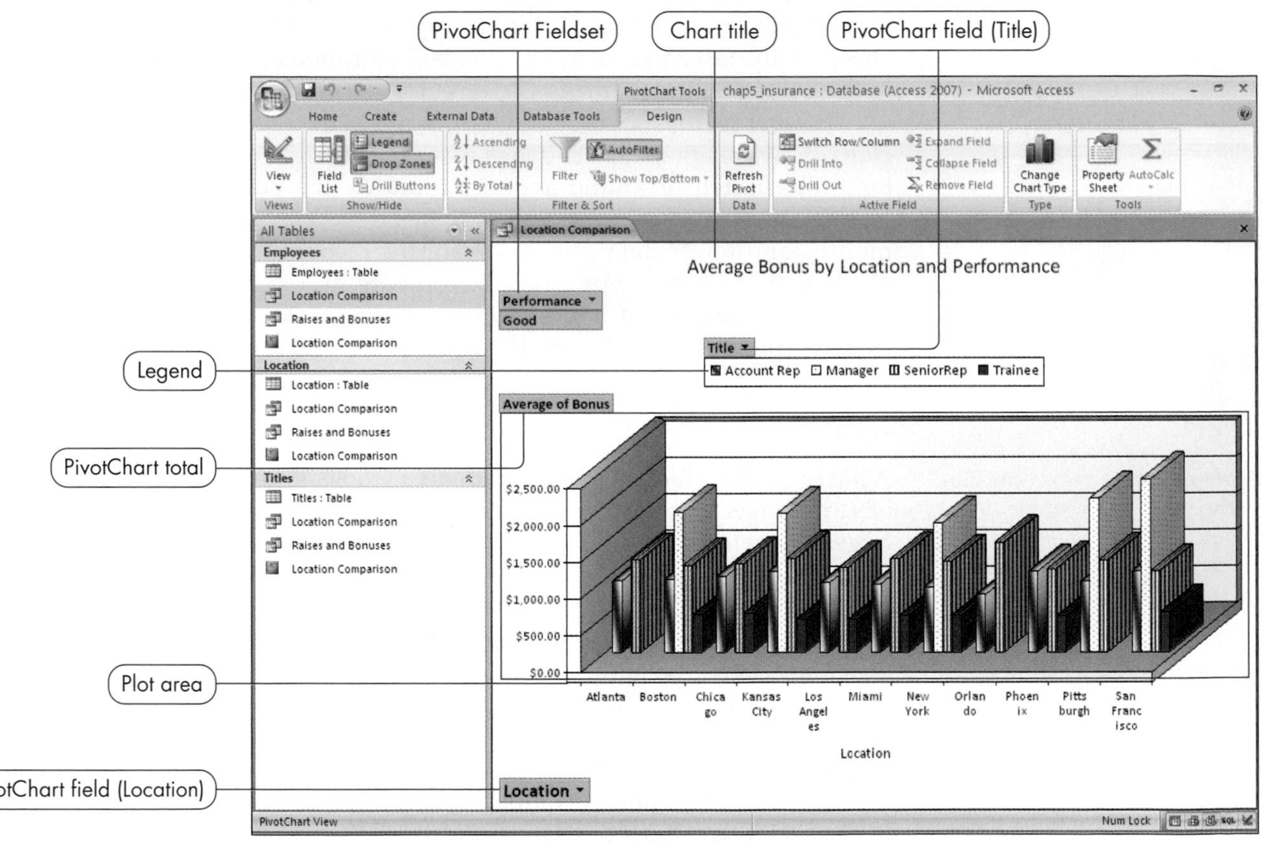

Figure 5.15 PivotChart: Average Bonus by Title and Location

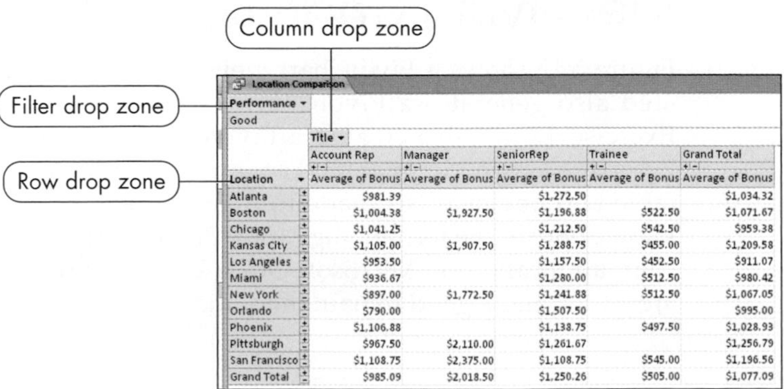

Location Comparison

Performance: Good

Location	Account Rep Average of Bonus	Manager Average of Bonus	SeniorRep Average of Bonus	Trainee Average of Bonus	Grand Total Average of Bonus
Atlanta	$981.39		$1,272.50		$1,034.32
Boston	$1,004.38	$1,927.50	$1,196.88	$522.50	$1,071.67
Chicago	$1,041.25		$1,212.50	$542.50	$959.38
Kansas City	$1,105.00	$1,907.50	$1,288.75	$455.00	$1,209.58
Los Angeles	$953.50		$1,157.50	$452.50	$911.07
Miami	$936.67		$1,280.00	$512.50	$980.42
New York	$897.00	$1,772.50	$1,241.88	$512.50	$1,067.05
Orlando	$790.00		$1,507.50		$995.00
Phoenix	$1,106.88		$1,138.75	$497.50	$1,028.93
Pittsburgh	$967.50	$2,110.00	$1,261.67		$1,256.79
San Francisco	$1,108.75	$2,375.00	$1,108.75	$545.00	$1,196.56
Grand Total	$985.09	$2,018.50	$1,250.26	$505.00	$1,077.09

Figure 5.16 PivotTable

Figure 5.17 displays a filtered view of the same chart in which you see only the Account Rep data being plotted. All of the PivotChart fields contain arrows that will produce a filterable drop setting when clicked. If you apply a filter to display only a single position title in the chart, the underlying table also changes. Figure 5.18 displays the changes to the PivotTable after its associated chart was changed. The PivotTable and PivotChart views are locked together. Although you only see one of them at a time, any changes made to one also change the other.

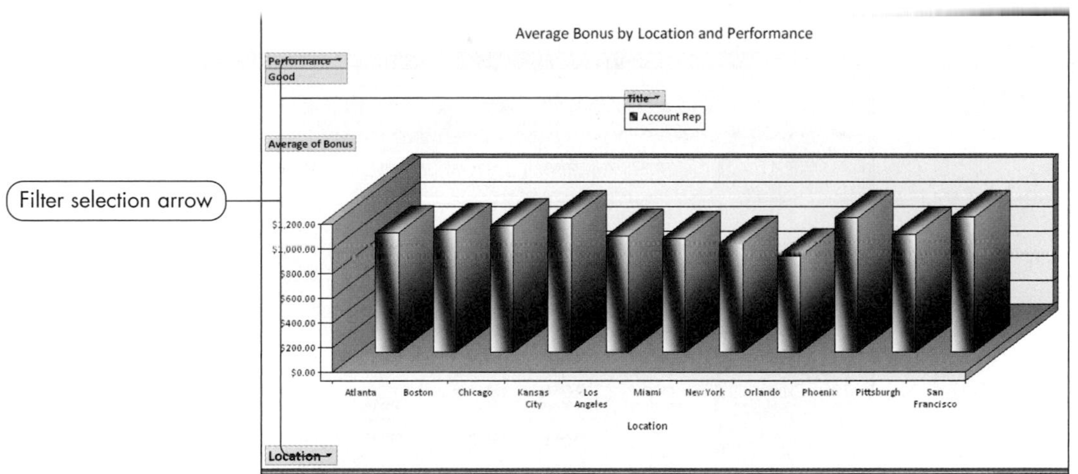

Figure 5.17 PivotChart Filtered to Account Reps by Location

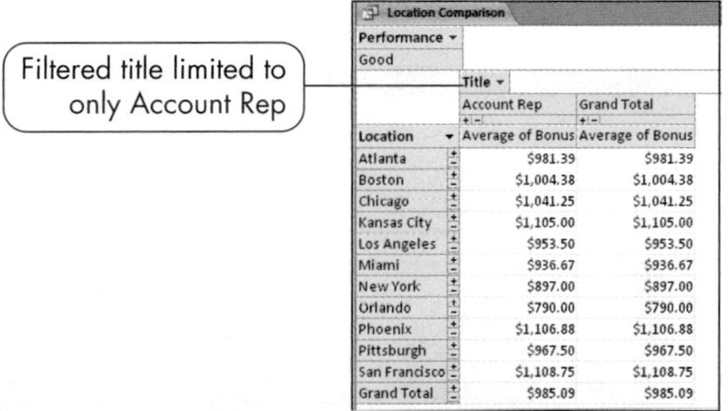

Location	Account Rep Average of Bonus	Grand Total Average of Bonus
Atlanta	$981.39	$981.39
Boston	$1,004.38	$1,004.38
Chicago	$1,041.25	$1,041.25
Kansas City	$1,105.00	$1,105.00
Los Angeles	$953.50	$953.50
Miami	$936.67	$936.67
New York	$897.00	$897.00
Orlando	$790.00	$790.00
Phoenix	$1,106.88	$1,106.88
Pittsburgh	$967.50	$967.50
San Francisco	$1,108.75	$1,108.75
Grand Total	$985.09	$985.09

Figure 5.18 Changes in a PivotChart Change the PivotTable

TIP PivotTables and PivotCharts Locked

Remember that the PivotTables and PivotCharts change together. You will spend time editing a chart to make it display perfectly, make a change in the PivotTable view, and discover that the chart has changed, too. Remember, these are *views* of the object. You may make changes to either view, but the change will automatically update the other.

Editing a PivotChart

Once you realize the power of the PivotTables and PivotCharts, you may be tempted to add more and more data to the drop zones. Figures 5.15–5.18 show only a single performance classification at a time. If you need to examine the pay equity among different locations, you will also need to know if the pay raises are equitable inside performance classifications. For example, a sales representative in Chicago with a good rating should receive about the same bonus as a good Account Rep in Miami or

Boston. It is easy to drag the Performance field from the filter area to the row area of the PivotTable design grid. The table data become slightly more complex, but remain intelligible (see Figure 5.19). However, the PivotChart gives so much information that it no longer functions. Charts have a purpose: They help readers extract complex information from complex data quickly and easily. Figure 5.20 shows a chart that is so complex that readers cannot decipher it.

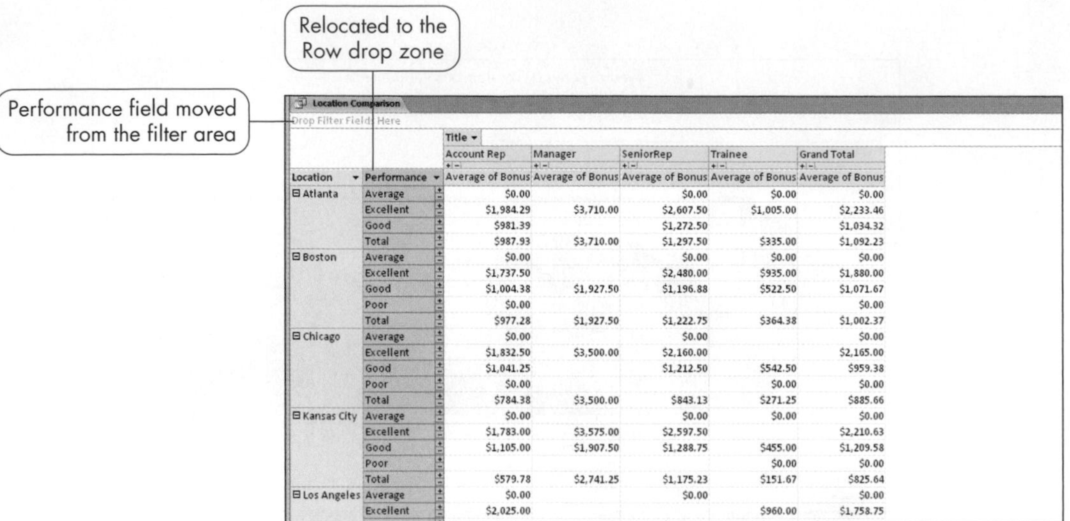

Location	Performance	Account Rep Average of Bonus	Manager Average of Bonus	SeniorRep Average of Bonus	Trainee Average of Bonus	Grand Total Average of Bonus
Atlanta	Average	$0.00		$0.00	$0.00	$0.00
	Excellent	$1,984.29	$3,710.00	$2,607.50	$1,005.00	$2,233.46
	Good	$981.39		$1,272.50		$1,034.32
	Total	$987.93	$3,710.00	$1,297.50	$335.00	$1,092.23
Boston	Average	$0.00		$0.00	$0.00	$0.00
	Excellent	$1,737.50		$2,480.00	$935.00	$1,880.00
	Good	$1,004.38	$1,927.50	$1,196.88	$522.50	$1,071.67
	Poor	$0.00				$0.00
	Total	$977.28	$1,927.50	$1,222.75	$364.38	$1,002.37
Chicago	Average	$0.00		$0.00		$0.00
	Excellent	$1,832.50	$3,500.00	$2,160.00		$2,165.00
	Good	$1,041.25		$1,212.50	$542.50	$959.38
	Poor	$0.00			$0.00	$0.00
	Total	$784.38	$3,500.00	$843.13	$271.25	$885.66
Kansas City	Average	$0.00		$0.00	$0.00	$0.00
	Excellent	$1,783.00	$3,575.00	$2,597.50		$2,210.63
	Good	$1,105.00	$1,907.50	$1,288.75	$455.00	$1,209.58
	Poor				$0.00	$0.00
	Total	$579.78	$2,741.25	$1,175.23	$151.67	$825.64
Los Angeles	Average	$0.00		$0.00		$0.00
	Excellent	$2,025.00			$960.00	$1,758.75

Figure 5.19 Moved Performance Field

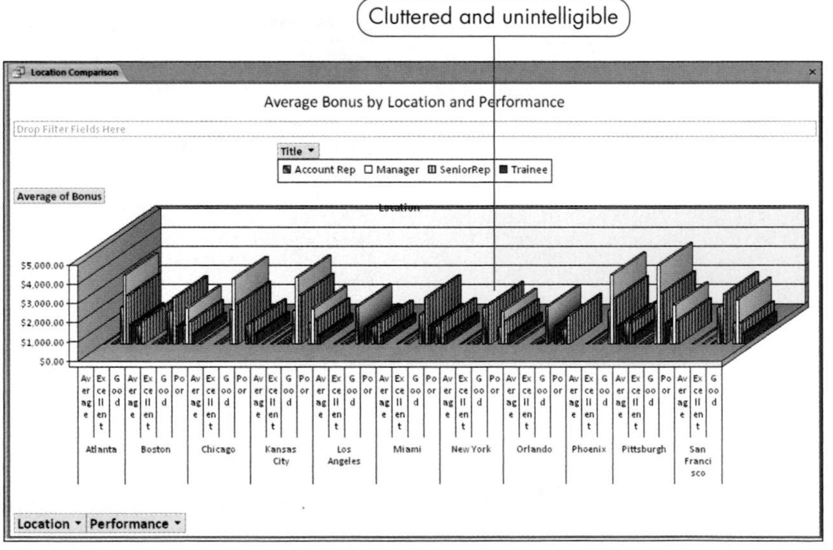

Figure 5.20 Unusable Chart

Change General Chart Properties

Editing an Access PivotChart is similar to editing a chart in Excel. First, you must select the element you wish to edit and then perform needed edits. The big difference is that you select the element through using the Properties window instead of double-clicking it. For example, let us say that you do not like the gray bars reflecting the managerial bonuses and you wish to change them. If you click an individual gray bar, you may edit it, but the edits will not automatically apply to all of the manager bars. To change all of a data series at the same time, you must first select the series. Click Property Sheet in the Tools group on the Design tab. The Properties window (shown in Figure 5.21) contains several tabs. You use the General tab to select the area of the chart for editing. In this illustration, the selected Manager field highlights all of the chart data points. These data points reflect manager bonuses. The selected objects display with a blue highlighted border.

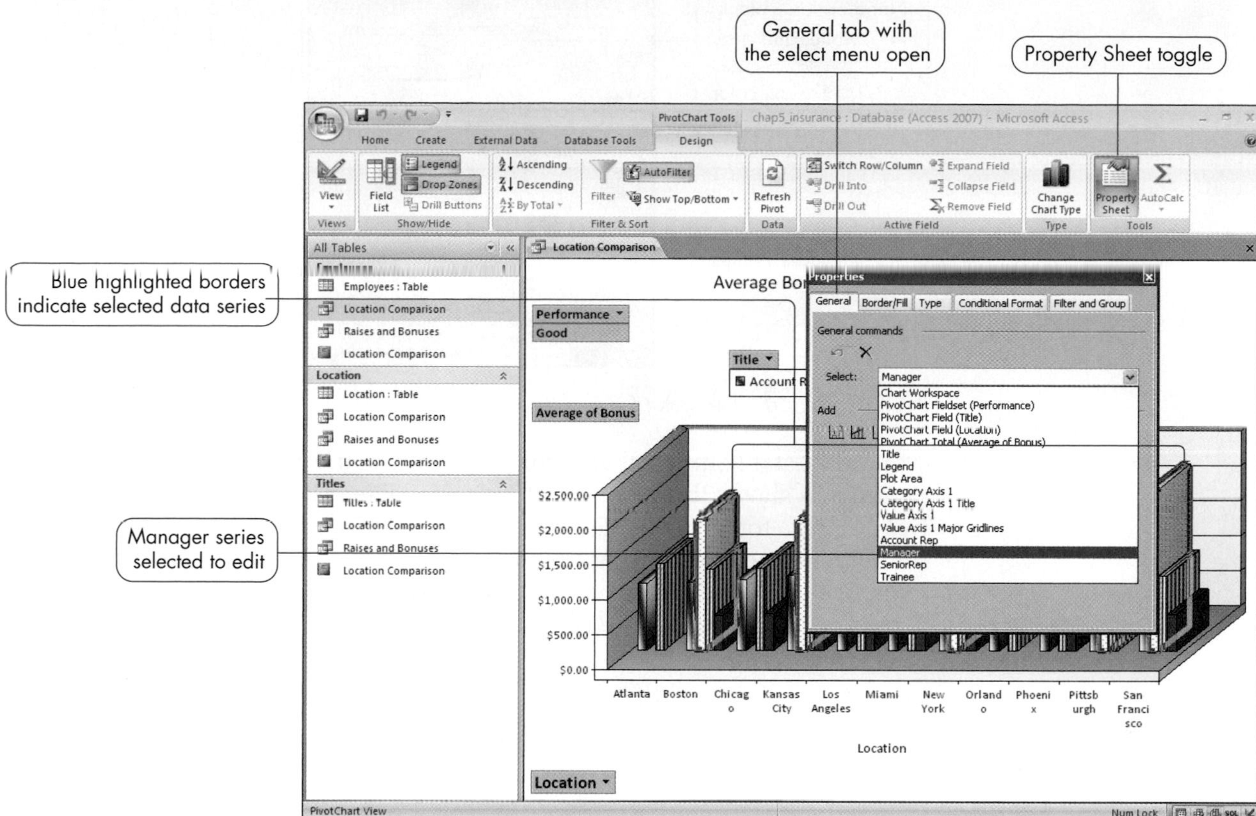

Figure 5.21 Selected Manager Data Series

Change Border and Fill Properties

The Border/Fill tab contains the editing tools you need to control the border or line surrounding the chart object's size and color. You can also define the object's internal color and pattern. You may specify fill types by clicking the Fill Type drop-down arrow in the *Fill* section and selecting from the available types (see Figure 5.22). For example, you may want to change from a solid color to a pattern or picture fill. In addition to changing the fill type, you can change the fill color by clicking the Color drop-down arrow in the *Fill* section (see Figure 5.23). Limit the number of colors you use on your charts. Too many colors may detract from your chart's aesthetics and interfere with the chart's ability to communicate. You need to remember that not everybody sees colors in the same way. Color discernment problems may make your chart unintelligible to some readers. Experiment and have fun, but produce your final chart by limiting the number of colors to only one or two.

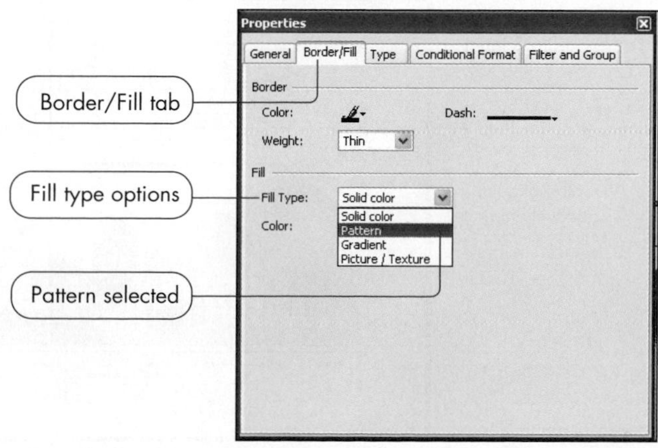

Figure 5.22 Border/Fill Tab and Fill Type Options

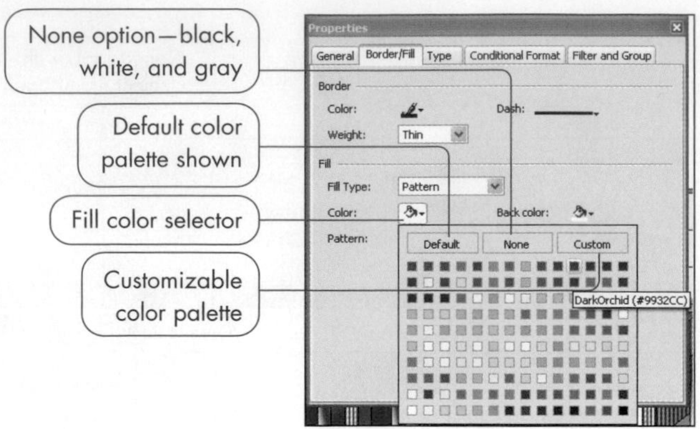

Figure 5.23 Fill Color Options

After establishing fill and color options, you will specify the pattern options. Figure 5.24 shows the range of patterns available. All patterns require you to specify two colors, a foreground color and a back color. Just as with color selection, limit the number and type of patterns you use in your charts. Readers may become confused looking at a chart with too many bold patterns.

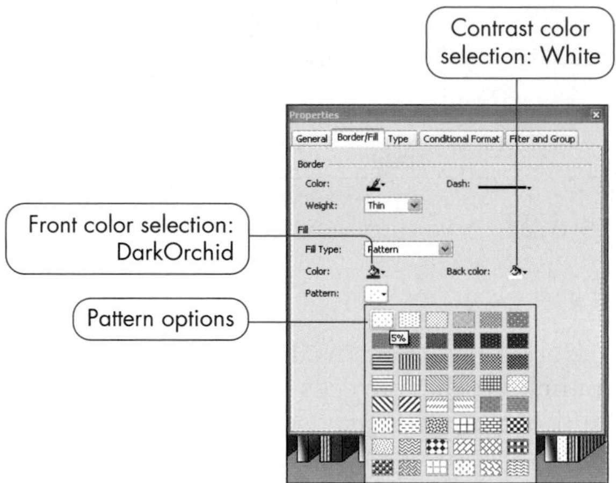

Figure 5.24 Pattern Options

Change Chart Workspace Options

Once the data series have been formatted to your liking, you may experiment with some of the other chart design features. From the General tab, select Chart Workspace to investigate options available for the chart in its entirety. The 3D View tab contains several options governing the appearance of your chart. Figure 5.25

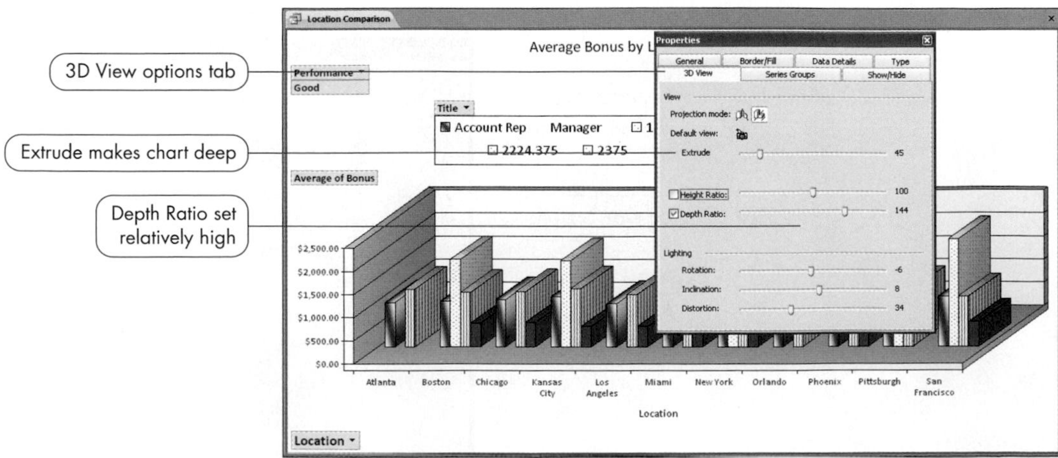

Figure 5.25 3D Adjustments

shows the option set selected to produce the chart displayed in this section. Some of the options have been modified to produce the chart shown in Figure 5.26.

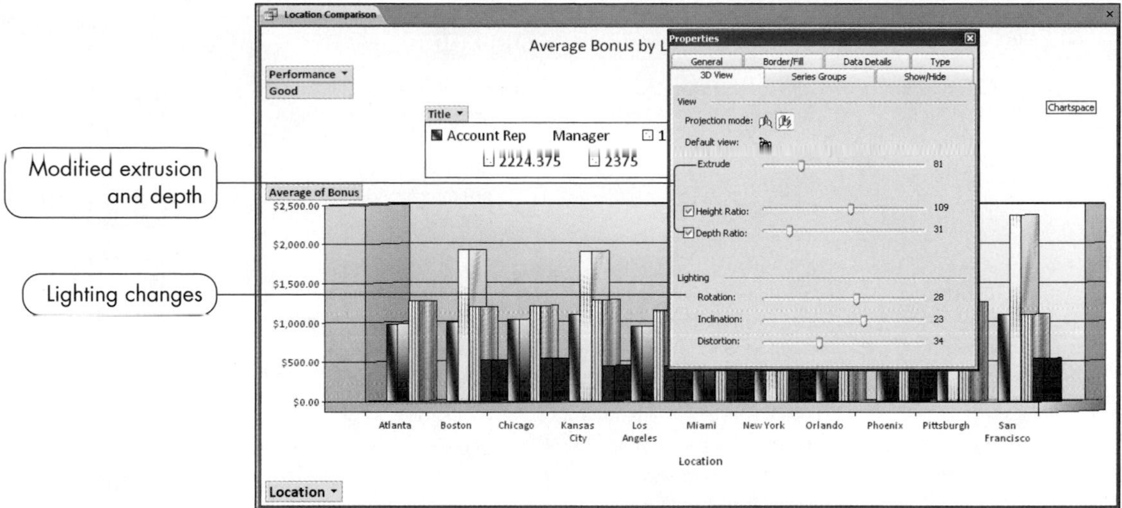

Figure 5.26 Lighting and Depth Options Varied

TIP Chart Art and Science

Learning how to control the elevation and lighting chart options is more art than science. You need to experiment with these options and learn how to control them. Just remember to save your chart prior to experimentation. If you create a chart that you dislike, you can close the object without saving changes and reopen it, reverting back to the saved version.

Adapt to Changes in Data Needs

You assembled the data necessary for PivotTable and PivotChart creation in a query to make your analysis work easier. However, data needs change. You may easily add fields to the PivotTable or PivotChart views. Activate the Field List pane by clicking the Field List in the Show/Hide group. The Field List window opens. Locate the needed field and drag it from the Field List window to the desired position on the PivotTable design grid. If you realize that you need to analyze data that you did not include in the original query design, you must switch to the design view of the query and add the field. Then when you change to the PivotTable view, the newly added field will display in the Field List window. To remove a PivotTable field, you must first display the details of the field you wish to remove. When the details display, click the field's gray title box and press Delete. If the field you wish to remove is a total field, you can delete it either by pressing Delete or with the Remove Field tool in the Active Field group on the Design tab.

In the next hands-on exercise, you will examine the PivotChart, edit it, modify it in design and structure, and save the changes.

Chart Families | Reference

Family Name	Chart Types	Use	Example	Illustration
Column	Column, Bar, Stock in two and three dimensions	Compares values across categories.	Plot number of students enrolled in pre-nursing programs, pre-med, pre-accounting, and pre-information systems courses.	
Line	Area and Line in two and three dimensions, XY Scatter	May only be used with continuously distributed data to show trends over time. Place time measurements on the X axis.	Plot volunteer hours donated by month. Display sales data by quarter.	
Pie	Pie and Doughnut	May be used only with discrete data to show proportions to the whole. Further, you must know the whole prior to using. If one observation is missing, you cannot draw a pie chart.	Show proportion of last week's revenue generated by product line.	
Other	Radar	Compare criteria. Several axes (one axis per criteria) radiate outward from a common center. Grid lines circle a uniform distance from the center. The purpose of the radar chart is to look at the "whole" of the object, rather than an individual piece. Radar charts are popular in the Eastern cultures, like Japan, because they look at a total picture.	Evaluate a car. Each criterion has a spoke from the middle. One spoke is labeled fuel economy, one handling, one acceleration, one styling, and one ride. The gridlines are at 2, 4, 6, 8, and 10. People were asked to rate the car in each of these areas and the average rating is plotted on the spoke for its criteria.	
Other	Polar	Plots data points as a function of distance from the center and angle around a circular grid.	Time series, directional, or scientific data needing a different analytical perspective.	
Other	Bubble	A variation of a scatter chart to show how sets of things compare according to various factors. The size of the bubbles show the relative size of the data being plotted.	Salaries by job title with the size of the bubble representing the percentage of the total salary budget.	

Hands-On Exercises

2 | PivotCharts and Modifications

Skills covered: 1. Remove a PivotChart Field **2.** Add a PivotChart Field **3.** Change AutoCalc Calculation and Set PivotChart Properties and Captions **4.** Edit Series Colors and Patterns

Step 1
Remove a PivotChart Field

Refer to Figure 5.27 as you complete Step 1.

a. Open the *chap5_ho1-3_insurance_solution* file if necessary and click **Options** on the Security Warning toolbar. Then click the **Enable this content option** in the Microsoft Office Security Options dialog box and click **OK**.

TROUBLESHOOTING: If you create unrecoverable errors while completing this hands-on exercise, you can delete the *chap5_ho1-3_insurance_solution* file, copy the *chap5_ho1_insurance_solution* backup database you created at the end of the first hands-on exercise, and open the copy of the backup database to start the second hands-on exercise again.

b. Select the **Your_Name Raises and Bonuses query**, copy it, and paste the copy in a blank space in the All Tables pane. Accept the default name for the copy.

You want to practice editing a PivotChart, but do not want to destroy your work from Hands-On Exercise 1. You may practice safely in the copy.

c. Open the **Copy Of Your_Name Raises and Bonuses query**. Click the **View down arrow** in the Results group on the Design tab and select **PivotChart View** from the shortcut menu.

Remember all PivotTables create PivotCharts. You have a chart, but it is not useful in its current form. You need to identify the element that clutters your chart. The Sum of Bonus displays on the Y-axis and the Locations display along the X-axis. That is what you would like. You determine the problem with the chart comes from trying to display the year each employee was hired.

d. Click the **Years** control (the gray box) in the lower-left corner and drag it off the chart into the All Tables pane. As you drag, your mouse pointer changes shape by adding a red X to the pointer. Drop the **Years field control** anywhere you see the red X.

Your chart now displays two series, red and green. However, the chart needs a legend to indicate what red means or what green represents.

e. Click **Legend** in the Show/Hide group on the Design tab.

The chart legend appears on the right side. It tells you that red bars indicate an Excellent review performance, and green bars indicate Good. You should wonder where the poor and average data series are in the chart. Why are there no blue or purple bars? The legend indicates that they exist. You need to examine the data to determine why there are missing bars.

TROUBLESHOOTING: You never want to waste your time editing a chart that contains flawed or missing data. You might end up making a pretty picture of garbage. It is attractive, but it remains useless to the decision maker.

f. Save your changes. Click **View** in the Views group on the Design tab and select **Design View** from the shortcut menu.

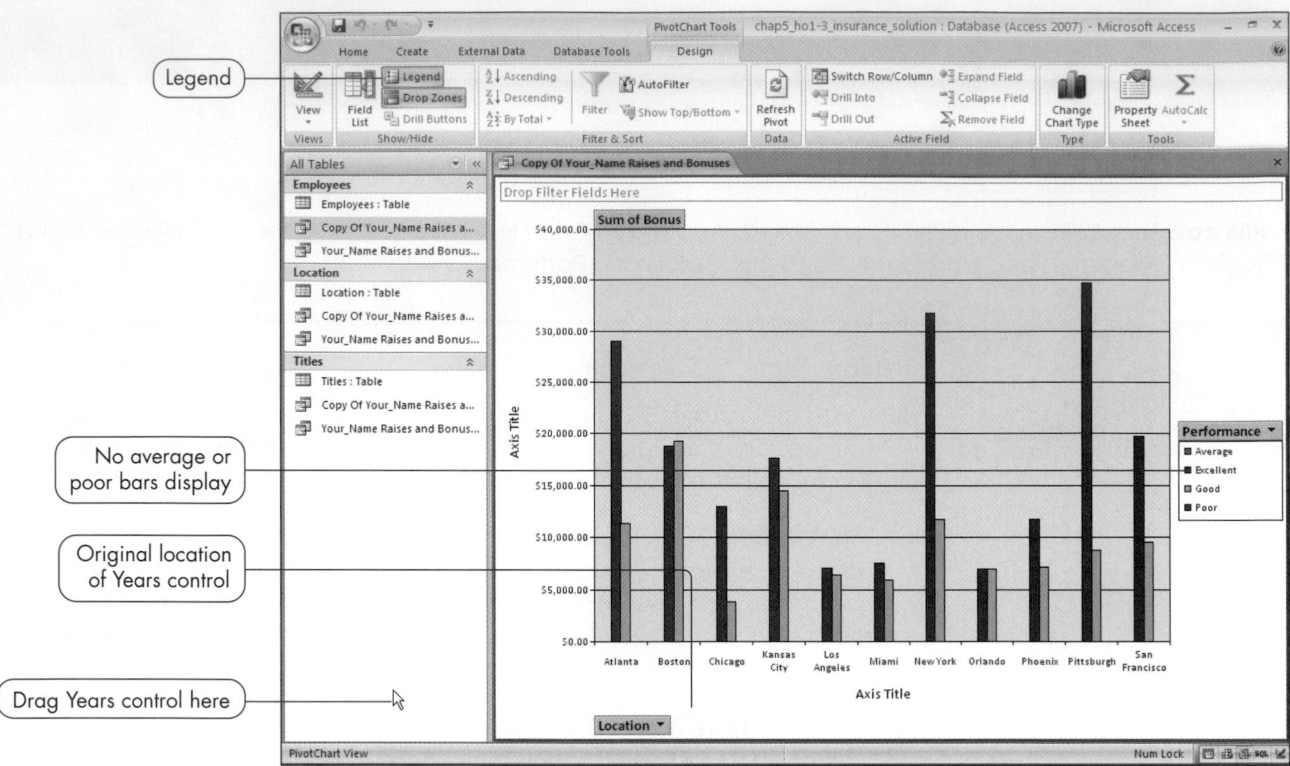

Figure 5.27 Bonus Chart After Year Field Removed

Step 2
Add a PivotChart Field

Refer to Figure 5.28 as you complete Step 2.

a. Scroll right in the Design view and click in the Bonus field. Click **Builder** in the Query Setup group on the Design tab.

   The Expression Builder dialog box opens to reveal the formula used to compute employee bonuses. Careful examination reveals that employees with an excellent rating receive bonuses of 5% of last year's salary and good-rated employees receive 2½% of last year's salary as a bonus. Employees with a performance rating of poor or average receive no bonus; therefore, no colored columns appear for these two data series in the chart.

b. Click **Cancel** in the Expression Builder dialog box to exit without changing anything.

c. Click the **View down arrow** in the Results group and select **PivotChart View** from the shortcut menu.

d. Click **Sum of Bonus** in the top-left corner of the chart. Drag it off the chart until you see that the mouse pointer has a red X. Release the mouse button.

   The bars disappear from the chart, but the chart structure—the names of the locations and the currency format on the Y-axis—remains.

e. Activate the Chart Field List pane by clicking **Field List** in the Show/Hide group if necessary.

   The Chart Field List window displays.

f. Click the **PercentIncrease** field and drag it to the top of the chart. When a blue-outlined row appears on the top of the chart, a ScreenTip by your mouse pointer displays *Drop Data Fields Here*. Release the mouse button to drop the PercentIncrease field.

   Your chart should now display the *Sum of PercentIncrease*.

g. Save your PivotChart.

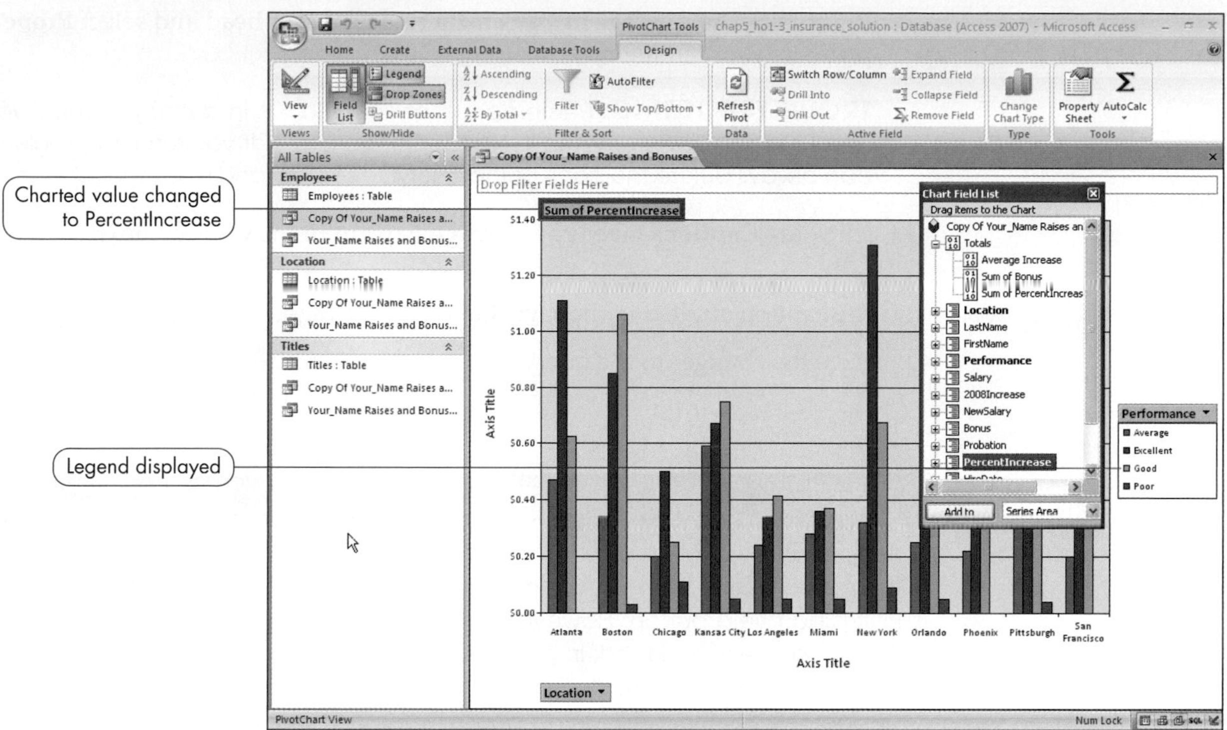

Figure 5.28 PercentIncrease Chart

TIP PivotTable Power

Once the PivotTable or PivotChart framework has been constructed, you can add and subtract fields to reassess the data. This power gives you an ability to dissect and reassemble data to obtain a complete picture of the activities they depict.

Step 3 Change AutoCalc Calculation and Set PivotChart Properties and Captions

Refer to Figure 5.29 as you complete Step 3.

a. Right-click the **Sum of PercentIncrease** field button, select **AutoCalc**, and then select **Average** from the shortcut menu.

   You know that summing a percentage field is generally a bad idea, but believe that displaying the average increase by performance category will contain useful information. You realize that the Y-axis labels have retained the currency format. You need to change them to display percentages.

b. Right-click **any number in the Y-axis** and select **Properties** from the shortcut menu.

   All of the numbers on the Y-axis highlight with a blue border.

c. Click the **Format tab** in the Properties window.

d. Click the **Number drop-down arrow**.

e. Select **Percent** on the drop-down menu.

   You notice that the field button label, Average of PercentIncrease, is awkward and want it to display *Average Increase*. Unfortunately, you cannot set a field caption in PivotChart view. However, you remember that any changes made to a PivotTable affect the chart. You decide to change the field caption in the PivotTable view.

f. Right-click the query tab and select **PivotTable View**.

   Notice that the PivotTable now displays the Average of PercentIncrease by location. It no longer has the year of hire field displayed.

g. Right-click the **Average of PercentIncrease** column head and select **Properties** from the shortcut menu.

TROUBLESHOOTING: Remember that your work is in a copy of the PivotTable and PivotChart you created in Hands-On Exercise 1. If you run into problems, you can always delete the copy of the query, recopy it, and start again.

h. Click the **Captions tab**. Type **Average Percent** in the Caption box.

i. Right-click the query tab and select **PivotChart View**. Check to make sure that the caption applied in the PivotTable view changed the PivotChart.

j. Save the changes to the query.

TIP Keep Looking

As you work in PivotTables and PivotCharts more frequently, you learn to appreciate their power and their limitations. Access does not provide a way to caption a PivotChart field button. However, you *can* caption a PivotTable field. When you cannot accomplish a task in one view, switch to the other and look for what you need to do there. Often you will find it. Because the two views represent two perspectives of the data, any changes made one place affect the other view.

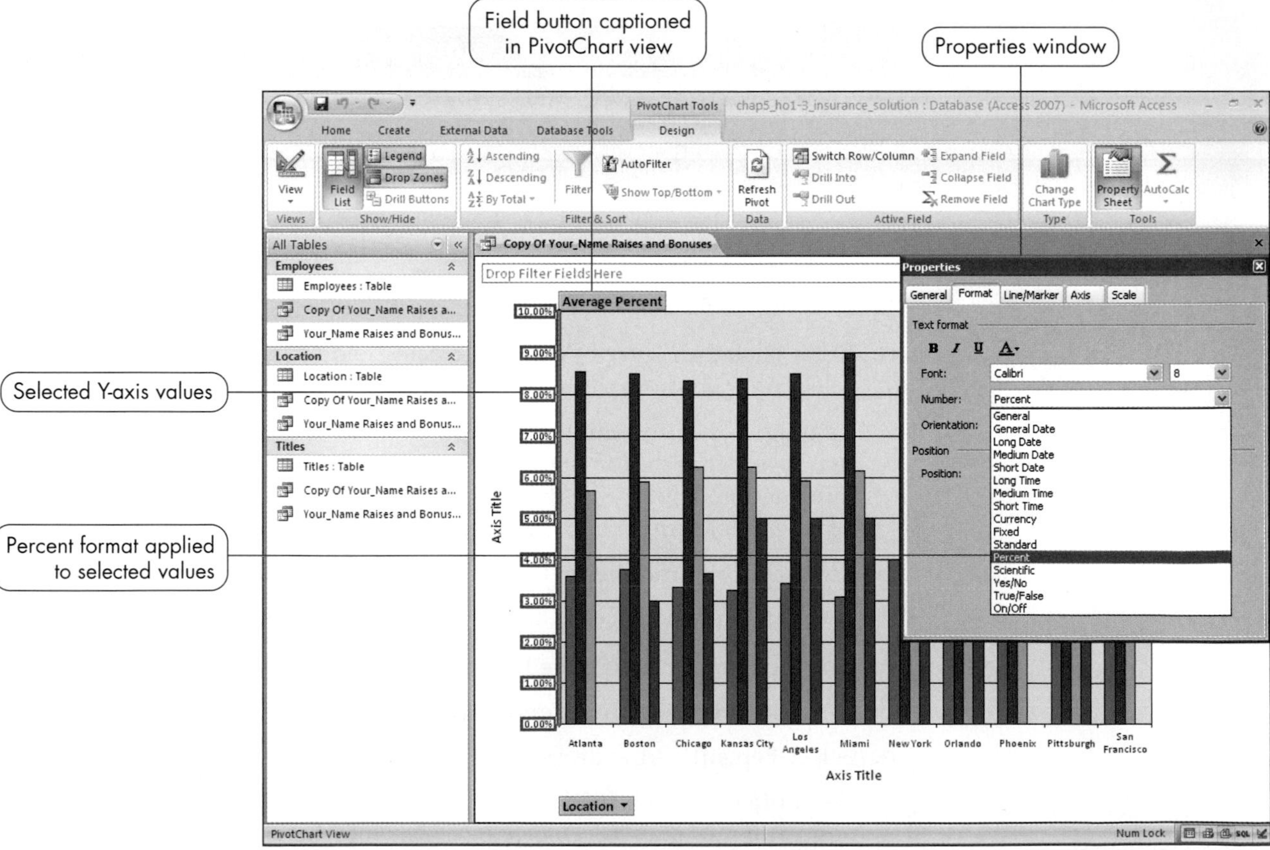

Figure 5.29 Caption and Format Changes Applied

Step 4
Edit Series Colors and Patterns

Refer to Figure 5.30 as you complete Step 4.

a. Click the **General tab** in the Properties window, and then click the **Select drop-down arrow**. Click **Average** near the bottom of the list.

   The blue bars that represent the Average data series all highlight.

b. Click the **Border/Fill tab**. Click the **Fill Color drop-down arrow** and click **BlueViolet** (fifth column, first row on the palette).

   The first series of data color changes to BlueViolet.

c. Click the **General tab** in the Properties window and then click the **Select drop-down arrow**. Click the **Excellent** series near the bottom of the list.

   The red bars that represent the Excellent data series all highlight.

d. Click the **Border/Fill tab**. Click the **Fill Color drop-down arrow** and click **Medium Turquoise** (sixth column, fourth row on the palette).

e. Click the **Fill Type drop-down arrow** and select **Pattern**.

f. Click the **Pattern drop-down arrow** and select **Dark Horizontal**.

g. Click the **Back Color drop-down arrow** and select **BlueViolet** (fifth column, first row).

h. Click the **General tab** in the Properties window, and and then click the **Select drop-down arrow**. Click the **Good** series near the bottom of the list. Click the **Border/Fill tab**. Click the **Fill Color drop-down arrow** and click **Medium Turquoise** (sixth column, fourth row).

i. Click the **General tab** in the Properties window, and then click the **Select drop-down arrow**. Click the **Poor** series near the bottom of the list. Click the **Border/Fill tab**, click the **Fill drop-down arrow**, and click **Medium Turquoise** (sixth column, fourth row). Click the **Fill Color drop-down arrow** and select **Pattern** and set the Back color to **BlueViolet** (fifth column, first row). Click the **Pattern drop-down arrow** and select **Dotted Diamond** (last column, fourth row). Close the Properties window.

j. Capture a screenshot by pressing **Prnt Scrn**. Launch Word, type your name and section number, and paste your screenshot into a Word document. Save the Word file as **chap5_h02_insurance_solution.docx**.

   TROUBLESHOOTING: Some notebook computers have Print Screen as a function. If the words Print Screen on the key are a different color, you must press **Fn+Print Screen**.

k. Return to Access. Click the **Performance field button arrow** on the legend. Click the **All check box** to deselect all the check marks. Click the **Poor check box**. Click **OK**.

   You have filtered the chart to focus attention on the pay increases awarded poor performers in the company. You see a wide variation among the locations.

l. Right-click the **Axis Title label** on the bottom of the chart and select **Properties** from the shortcut menu. Click the **Format tab** and type **Poor Performance** in the Captions box.

m. Click the axis title along the Y-axis and press **Delete** to remove it. Close the Properties window. Click **Legend** in the Show/Hide group to turn it off. Capture a screenshot and paste it in the same Word file as the earlier one. Print the Word document.

n. Close the *Copy Of Your_Name Raises and Bonuses query*. Save the changes. Rename the query **Your_Name Poor Performance**.

o. Click the **Office Button**, select **Manage**, and then select **Compact and Repair Database.**

p. Click the **Office Button** again, select **Manage**, and then select **Back Up Database**. Type **chap5_ho2_insurance_solution** as the file name and click **Save**.

You just created a backup of the database after completing the second hands-on exercise. The original database *chap5_ho1-3_insurance_solution* remains onscreen. If you ruin the original database as you complete the third hands-on exercise, you can use the backup file you just created.

q. Close the file and exit Access if you do not want to continue with the next exercise at this time.

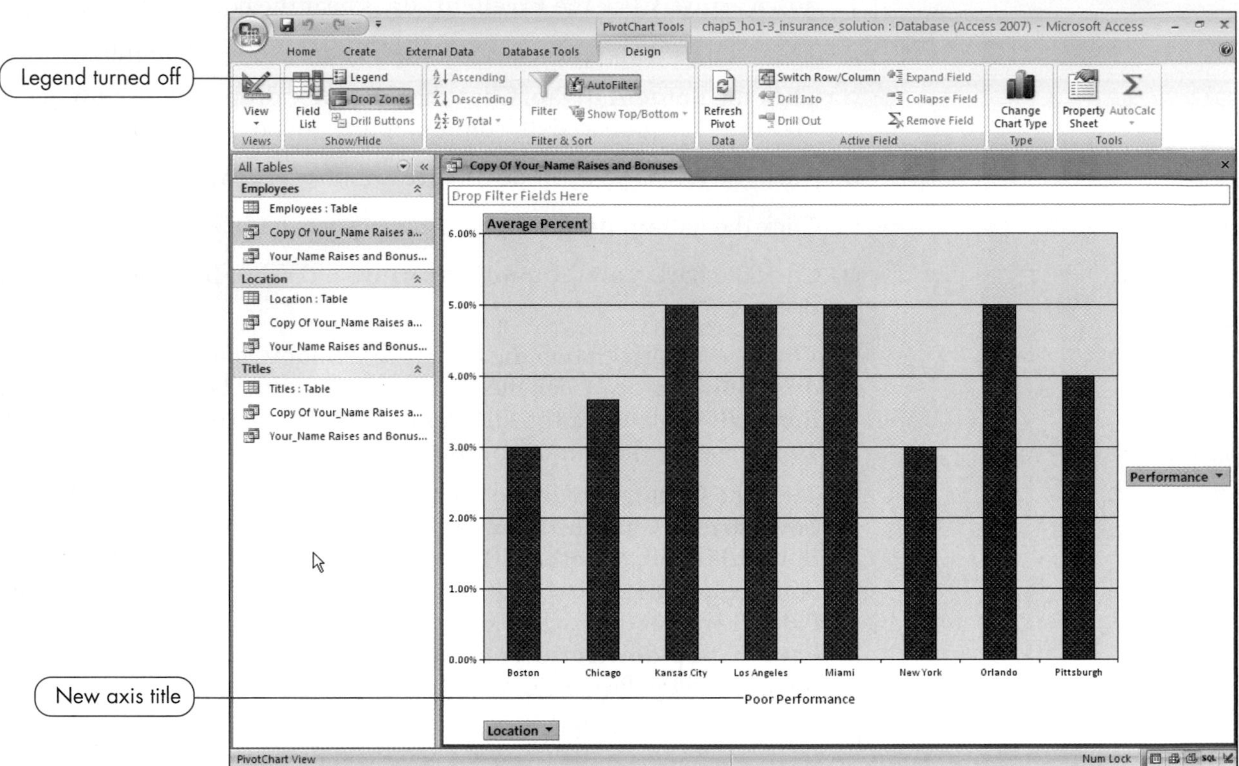

Figure 5.30 Average Increase of Employees Classified as Poor Performers

Calculations in PivotTables and PivotCharts

> The power of a relational database lies in the software's ability to organize data and combine items in different ways to obtain a complete picture of the events the data describe.

As you learn about the more advanced features available in Microsoft Access 2007, you may wonder, who uses this stuff? Most organizations have two groups of people who use these sophisticated tools. The first group is the Information Technology (IT) staff. They may be classified as the professional query writers and data guardians. The second group may be classified as the data users in the organization—those who work in Finance, Marketing, or Human Resources and who use the data to make decisions about the organizational operation. The power of a relational database lies in the software's ability to organize data and combine items in different ways to obtain a complete picture of the events the data describe. But that power will only be realized when the data are delivered to the decision maker in the appropriate form. The PivotTable and PivotChart views may appeal more to these users because these objects more closely resemble the spreadsheet software they are familiar with.

In this section, you will learn how to perform calculations in a PivotTable. You learn how to create a calculated detail field and a calculated total field.

Creating Calculations in a PivotTable

The ***calculated detail field*** generates a new field that performs the stipulated calculation on all of the detail records.

The ***calculated total field*** would be used to customize aggregating data.

Access provides several ways of calculating values. You have already created calculated fields in a query using the Expression Builder. You may also calculate values within the PivotTable structure. Performing calculations differs from aggregating, although you often use the two operations in the same query. You perform calculations at the detail level. The ***calculated detail field*** generates a new field that performs the stipulated calculation on all of the detail records. For example, suppose you had detail information in a query that communicated the number of units in stock and the unit cost for each product in your firm's inventory. Your insurance company or bank may need to know the value of the inventory. You could calculate it by multiplying the number of units by the unit cost values. A ***calculated total field*** would be used to customize aggregated data. When the sum, average, minimum, and so forth do not satisfy your data analysis needs, you may generate custom total calculations. This is most often used to calculate a percent of the total. You might use a sum aggregate to add the detail calculations for the value of inventory to determine the total value of the inventoried items. You might then create a calculated total field to calculate the percent of the total inventory value for each item.

Return to the earlier value of inventory illustration. Figure 5.31 shows a PivotTable ready to have a calculation performed. In this case, you would need to know the value of all of the inventory items, so you would select a calculated detail field. Figure 5.32 displays the Properties window where you enter the calculated formula. The syntax will be familiar to you. Do not begin the calculation with an equal sign; enclose all field names in brackets; and use standard operands, +, -, *, /, and ^. After typing your formula, click Change.

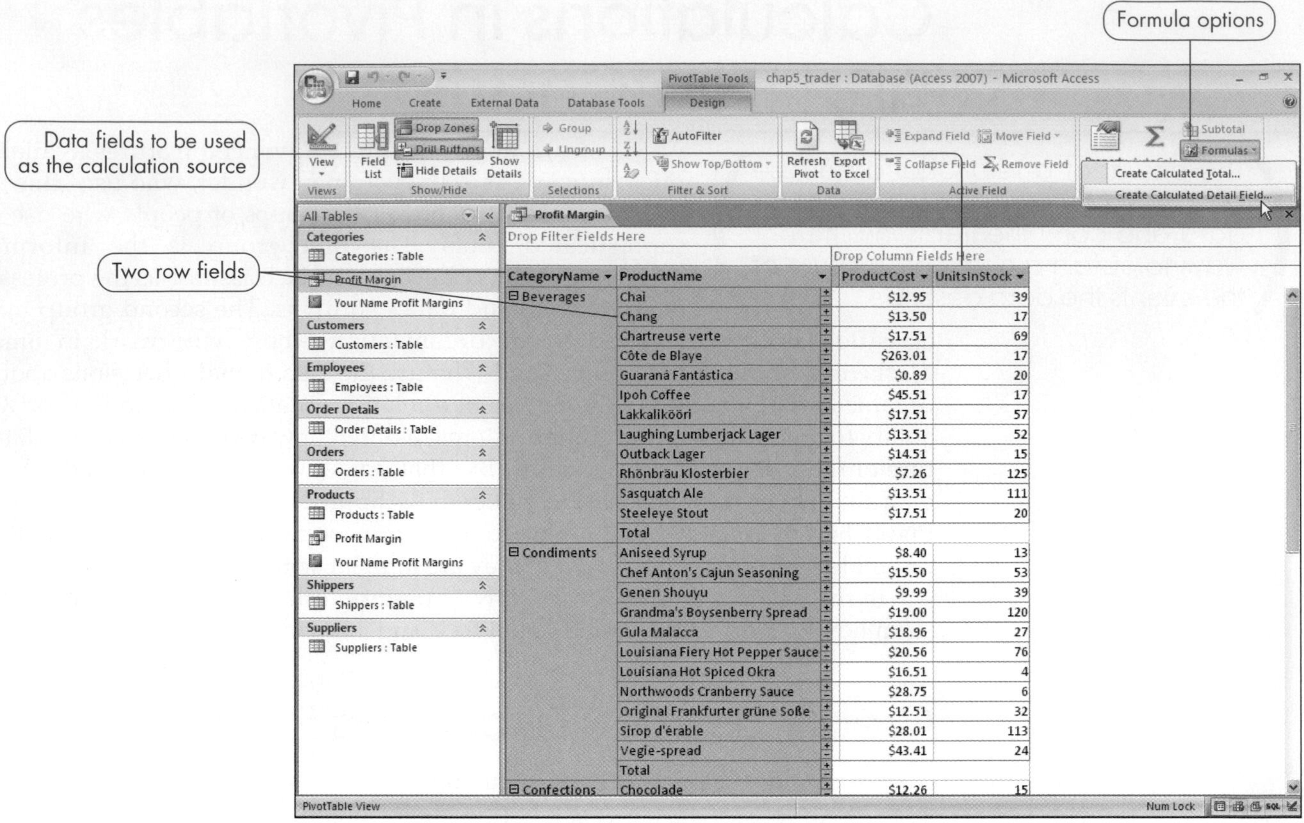

Figure 5.31 Setup for Calculated Fields

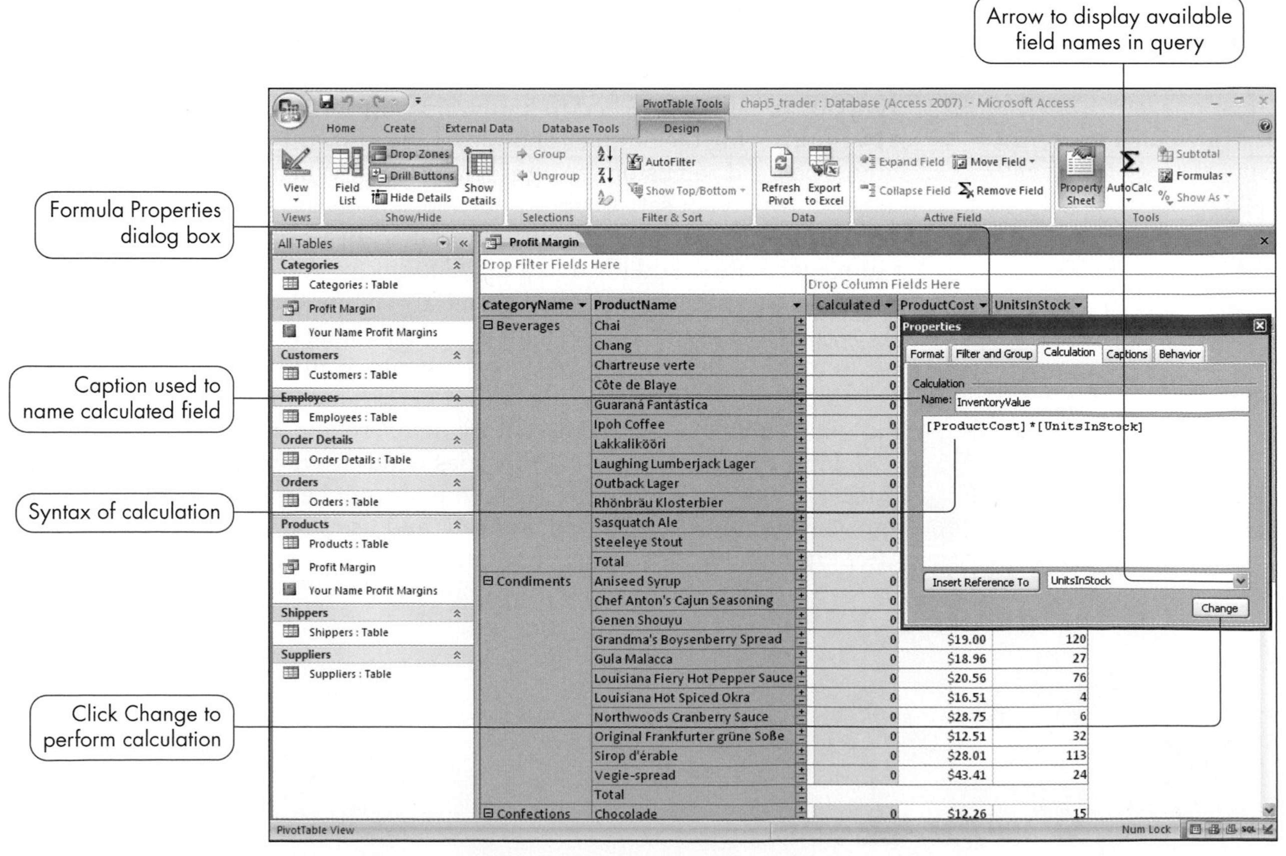

Figure 5.32 Syntax for Calculated Fields

After the calculation executes, you may treat the calculated PivotTable field like any other. You may use it as a source for summary calculations. Figure 5.33 shows the newly calculated field highlighted and ready to serve as input for a sum aggregate that will calculate total inventory values by product category. Figure 5.34 displays currency-formatted results of the Sum function, and Figure 5.35 displays only the category totals. Although the individual product names needed to be displayed to calculate the value of the inventory, after you complete the calculation, you may drag the (now extraneous) detail off the PivotTable design grid.

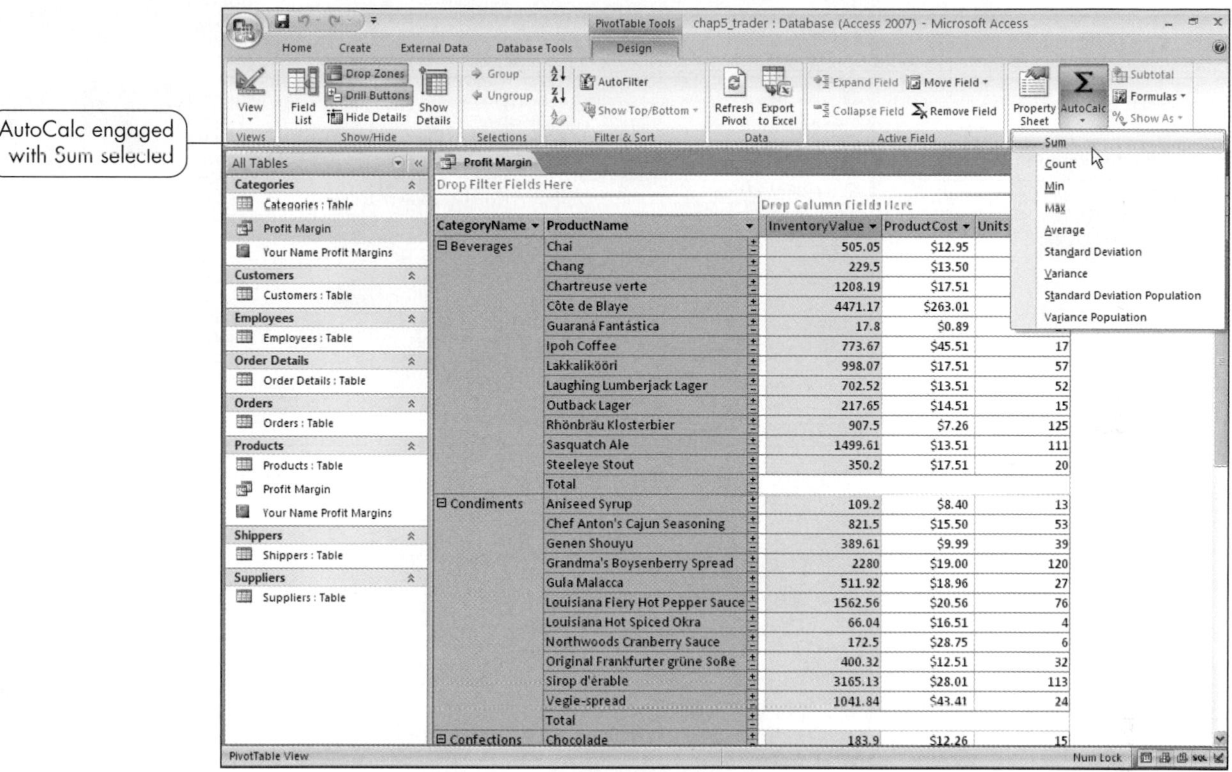

Figure 5.33 Setup for Summarizing a Calculated Field

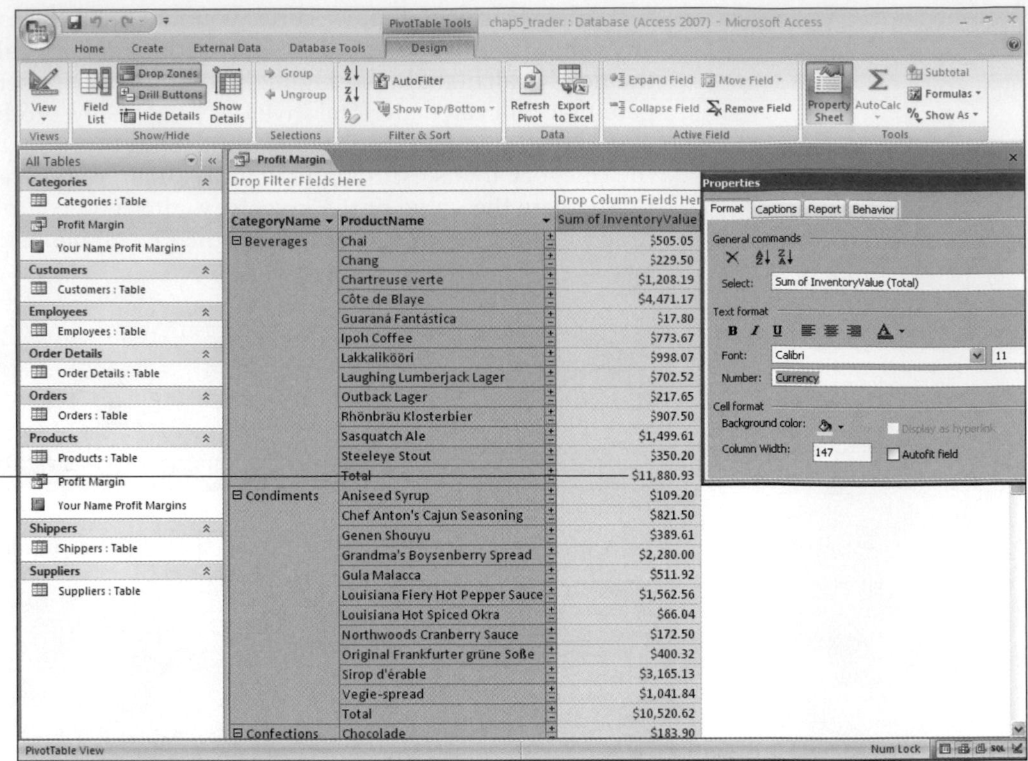

Figure 5.34 Summary Calculation Performed on a Calculated Field

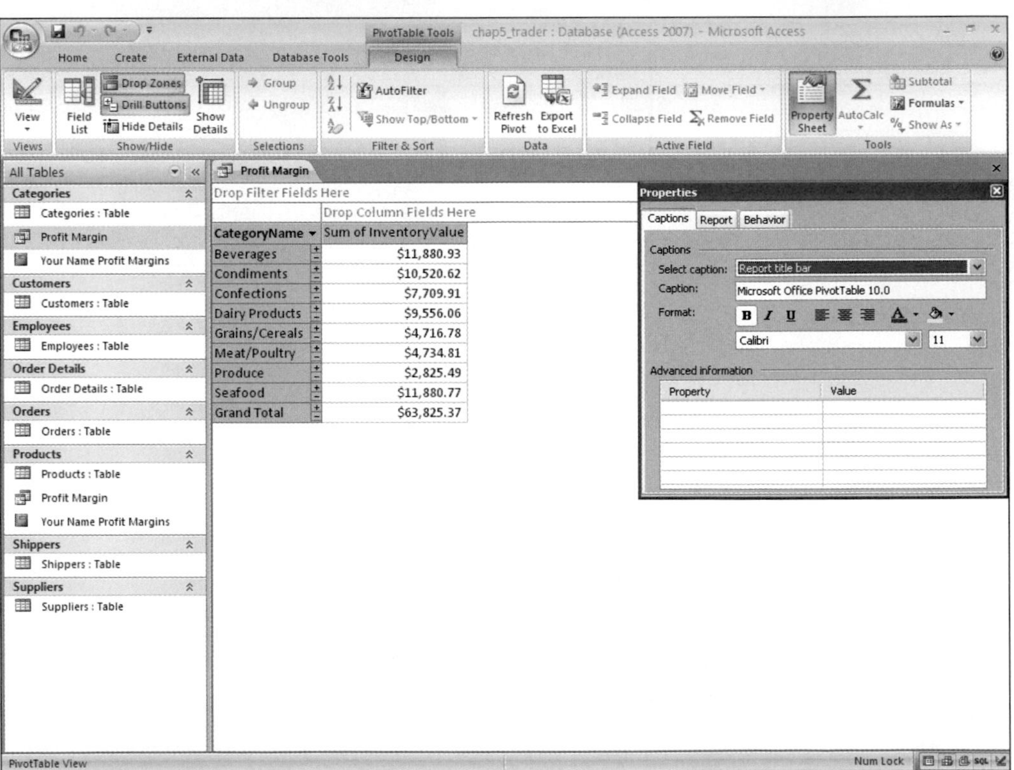

Figure 5.35 Details Removed

In the next hands-on exercise, you will calculate employee pay raises by using a Cost of Living Index. Because this organization employs workers in locations across the country, you will need to make adjustments to worker salaries to compensate them for cost of living differences. It is more expensive to live in New York City than it is in Pittsburgh or Phoenix. Your company recognizes this difference in cost of living and adjusts employee salaries to compensate them for the increased living expenses incurred in some places.

Hands-On Exercises

3 | Calculating Field Values in PivotTables

Skills covered: 1. Add a Field to a PivotTable **2.** Identify and Add Fields Needed for Calculations **3.** Create a PivotTable Calculation and Apply Formatting **4.** Total a Calculated Field and Change Formatting **5.** Set Captions

Step 1 Add a Field to a PivotTable

Refer to Figure 5.36 as you complete Step 1.

a. Open the *chap5_ho1-3_insurance_solution* file if necessary, click **Enable this Content** on the Security Alert toolbar, click the **Enable this content option** in the Microsoft Office Security Options dialog box, and click **OK**.

TROUBLESHOOTING: If you create unrecoverable errors while completing this hands-on exercise, you can delete the *chap5_ho1-3_insurance_solution* file, copy the *chap5_ho2_insurance_solution* database you created at the end of the second hands-on exercise, and open the copy of the backup database to start the third hands-on exercise again.

b. Open the **Location table**. Examine the values in the CostOfLiving field.

It reflects that a market basket of goods and services purchased in Phoenix costs about $1.00, whereas the same items purchased in San Francisco cost $1.71. You need to apply the cost of living factor to the NewSalary field. The data in the CostOfLiving field may be found in the Statistical Abstract at: http://www.census.gov/compendia/statab/prices/consumer_price_indexes_cost_of_living_index.

c. Close the **Location table**. Copy the *Your_Name Raises and Bonuses* query and paste it using the **default name**. Open the **Copy Of Your_Name Raises and Bonuses** query in Design view.

You need the CostOfLiving field added to this query.

d. Double-click the **CostOfLiving** field in the Location table to add it to the query design grid. Click **Run** in the Results group on the Design tab to run the query. Scroll right to make sure the CostOfLiving field is successfully added.

You cannot add new fields to the PivotTable view. The field must be in the query before you use a PivotTable to examine it.

e. Save the query. Right-click the query tab and select **PivotTable View** from the shortcut menu.

f. Click the **Years** column head and drag it off the grid to remove it from the PivotTable view. Click the **Performance** column head and drag it off the grid. Click the **Sum Of Bonus** column head and drag it off the grid.

g. Click **Show Details** in the Show/Hide group.

The details of the Bonus field display. You removed the summary statistic, but now you need to remove the details also.

h. Click the **Bonus** detail field and drag it off the grid. Save the changes.

You have removed the fields that you do not need from the drop zones.

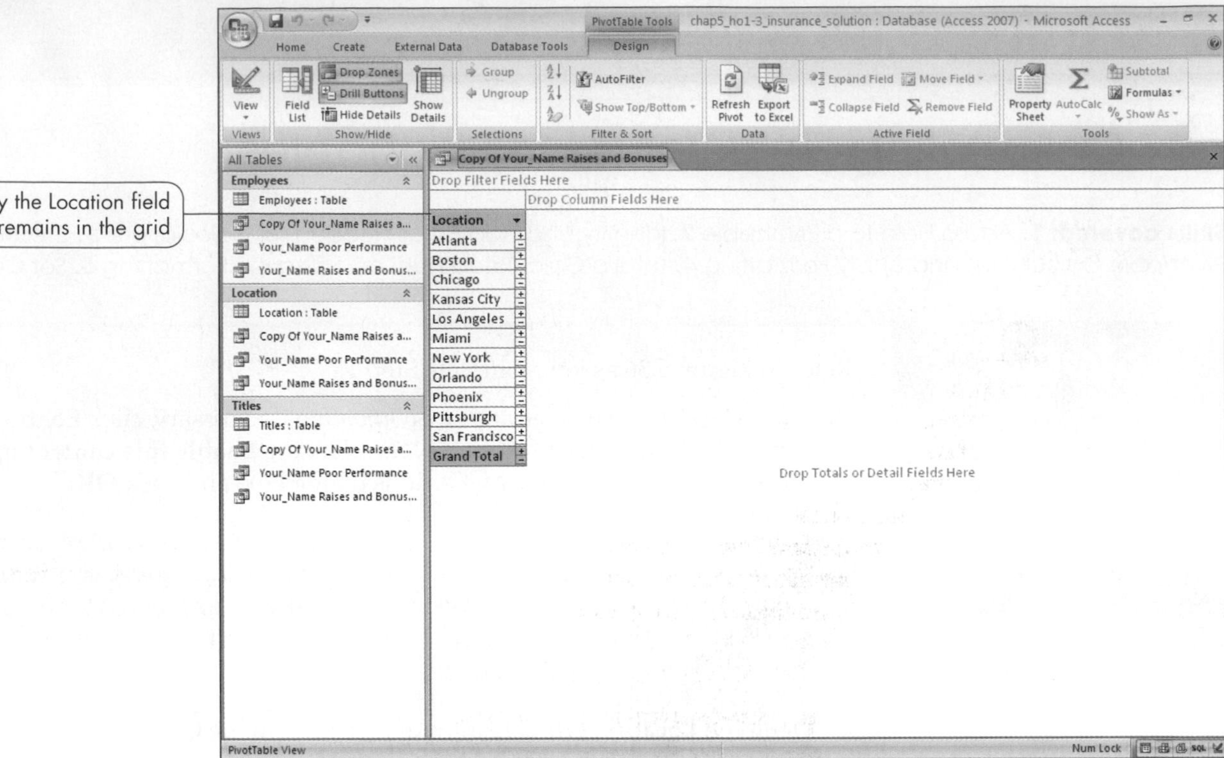

Figure 5.36 Unnecessary Fields Removed

Step 2
Identify and Add Fields Needed for Calculations

Refer to Figure 5.37 as you complete Step 2.

a. Click **Field List** in the Show/Hide group. Click the **LastName** field in the Field List pane and drag it to the right of the Location field in the **Drop Row Fields Here zone**.

   Your query should now display the names of the employees in each city. You need to add the fields necessary to calculate the cost of living increase. You will need to multiply each employee's NewSalary by the CostOfLiving field.

b. Click the **NewSalary** field in the Field List pane and drag it to the **Drop Totals or Detail Fields Here zone** in the PivotTable grid.

c. Click the **CostOfLiving** field in the Field List pane and drag it to the **Drop Totals or Detail Fields Here zone** in the PivotTable grid.

   Examine Figure 5.37. If your work matches, save the query. If not, remove fields from the drop zones and try again.

d. Save your query.

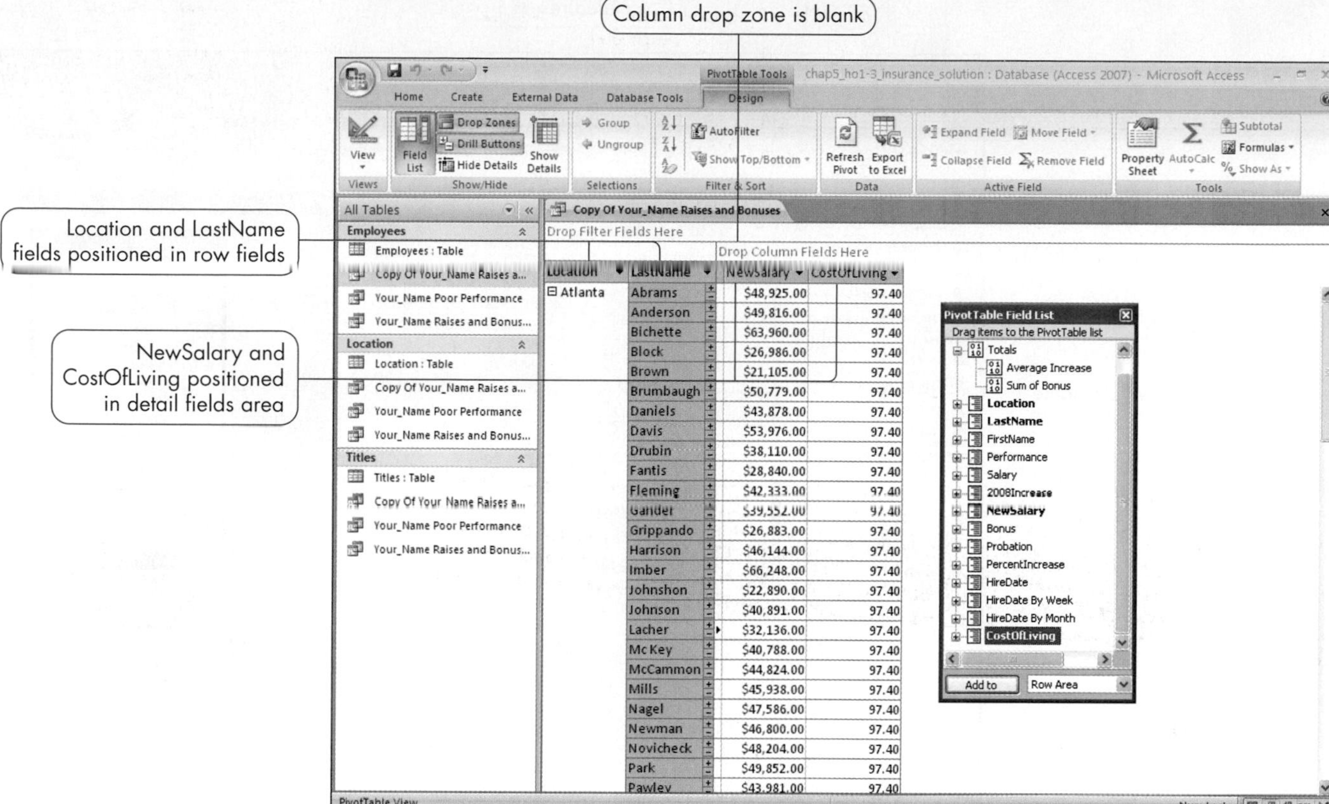

Figure 5.37 Filtered Query Results

Step 3
Create a PivotTable Calculation and Apply Formatting

Refer to Figure 5.38 as you complete Step 3.

a. Click **Formulas** in the Tools group. Select **Create Calculated Detail Field**.

The Formula Properties window opens.

b. Ensure that the Calculation tab is selected. Type **AdjustedSalary** in the Name box.

You have instructed Access to name the newly calculated field AdjustedSalary.

c. Press **Tab**.

A new column is added to the Detail area named Calculated. The value of each record is zero.

d. Type **[NewSalary]*[CostOfLiving]/100**.

You need to divide by 100 because the recorded cost of living figures actually are percentages stored as integers. You do not need to divide all calculated PivotTable fields by 100. This calculation is unique to this circumstance.

e. Click **Change** in the Properties window. Examine the results.

The first Atlanta employee's adjusted salary dropped from $48,925 to $47,652.95. The cost of living in Atlanta is lower than that in the rest of the country. Atlanta employees' salaries get lowered to adjust for the cost of living. Your calculated answer does not yet have a currency format.

f. Scroll down until you see the Boston employees.

The cost of living in Boston is higher than in the rest of the country. The first Boston employee's salary increased from $58,448 to $79,138.59 after the cost of living adjustment.

g. Compare your work to Figure 5.38. If it is correct, save the query.

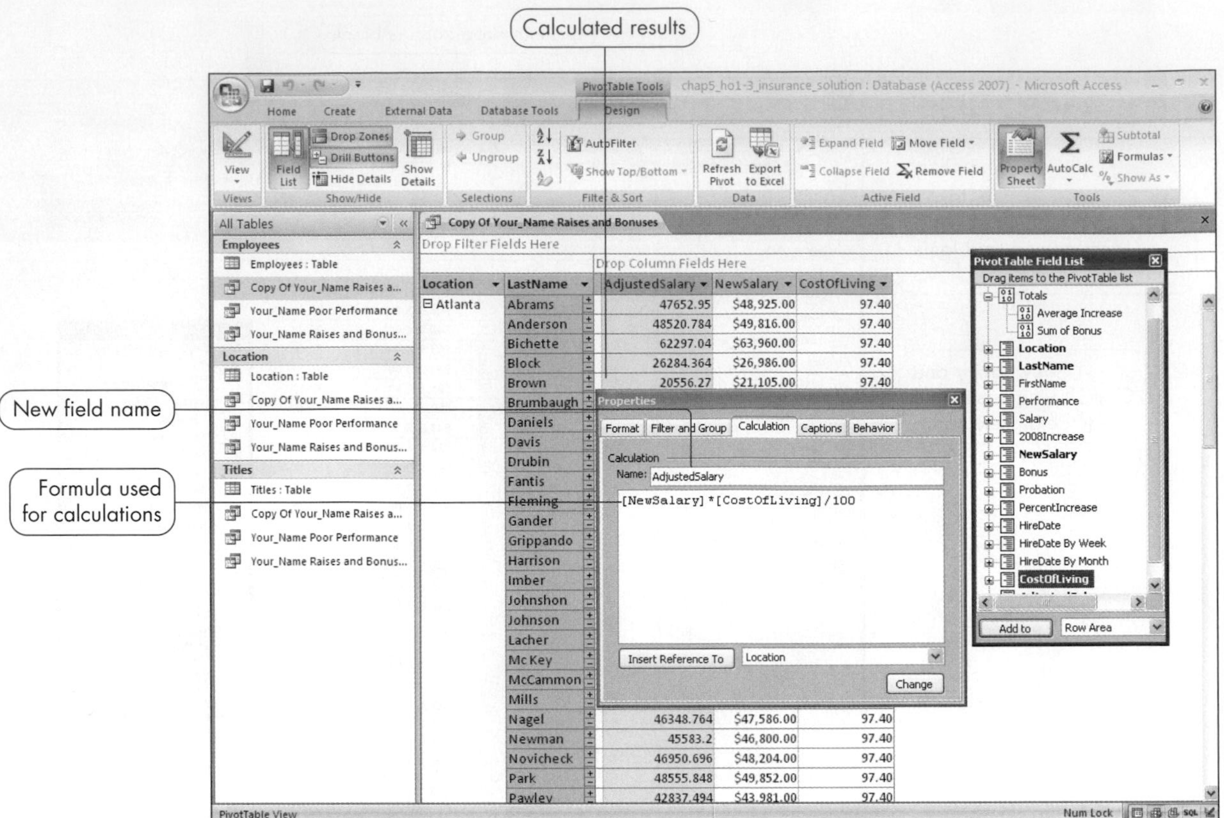

Figure 5.38 Custom Calculation

Step 4

Total a Calculated Field and Change Formatting

Refer to Figure 5.39 as you complete Step 4.

a. With the AdjustedSalary field active, click the **Format tab** in the Properties window. Click the **Number drop-down arrow** and select **Currency**.

TROUBLESHOOTING: If your AdjustedSalary field is not highlighted with a blue background, you can reactivate it by clicking its column heading.

b. Click the **Captions tab** in the Properties window. Insert a space between *Adjusted* and *Salary* in the Caption box. The column head now has a space.

If you scroll the Field List box, you will see that the actual field name is still AdjustedSalary (without the space). The caption is a method of making the database data more user-friendly.

c. Close the Properties window.

d. With the Adjusted Salary still active, click **AutoCalc** in the Tools group. Select **Sum** from the menu.

Each employee's data are summed. This looks like it is simply repeating the information. You need to know the total salaries for each city.

e. Activate the **NewSalary** field by clicking the column head. Click **AutoCalc** and **Sum**.

f. Activate the **CostOfLiving** field by clicking the column head. Click **AutoCalc** and **Average**.

g. Click **Hide Details** in the Show/Hide group.

h. Drag the **LastName** field off the grid.

With details hidden and the LastName field removed, the PivotTable collapses to display the total of all salaries in each city.

i. Save the query.

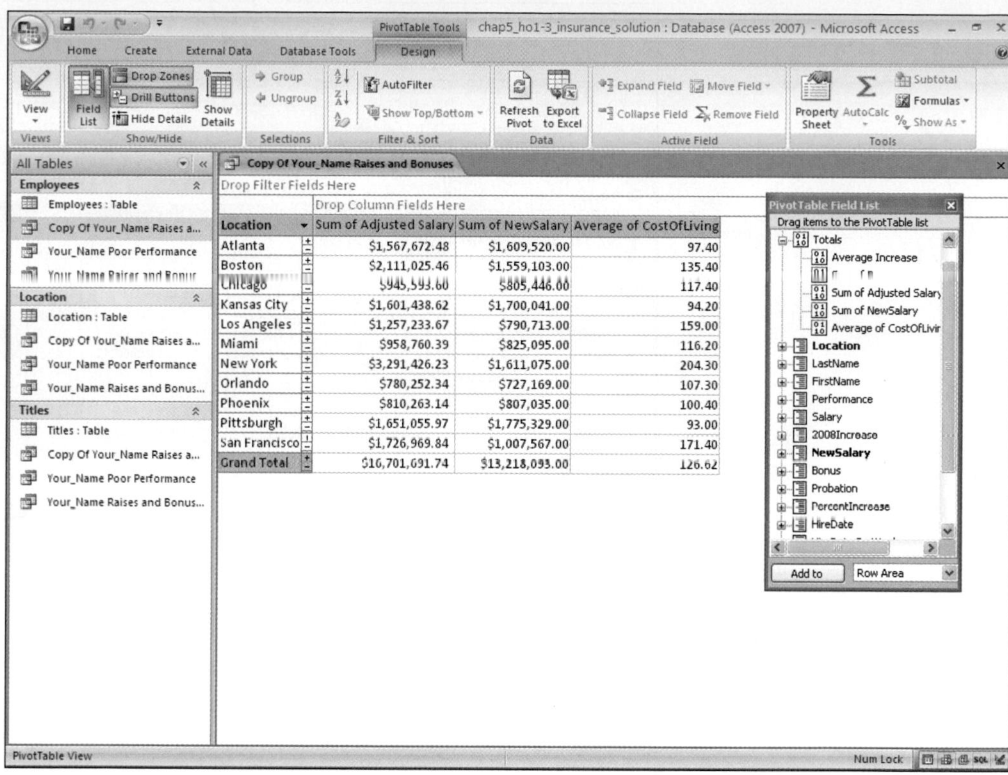

Figure 5.39 Totaled PivotTable with Details Collapsed

Step 5
Set Captions

Refer to Figure 5.40 as you complete Step 5.

a. Click the column head to select the **Sum of AdjustedSalary** field. Click **Property Sheet** in the Tools group.

b. Click the **Captions tab** (if necessary). Type **Total Adjusted Salary** in the Caption box.

c. Select the **Sum of NewSalary** field. Type **Total New Salary** in the Caption box.

When you selected a different field in the PivotTable, the Caption box updates to reflect the selected field.

d. Select the **Average of CostOfLiving** field. Type **Cost of Living** in the Caption box.

e. Examine Figure 5.40. If your results match, save the query.

f. Close the query.

g. Rename the *Copy of Your_Name Raises and Bonuses* query as **Your_Name Total Location Cost of Living**.

h. Click the **Office Button**, select **Manage**, and select **Compact and Repair**. Close the file and exit Access.

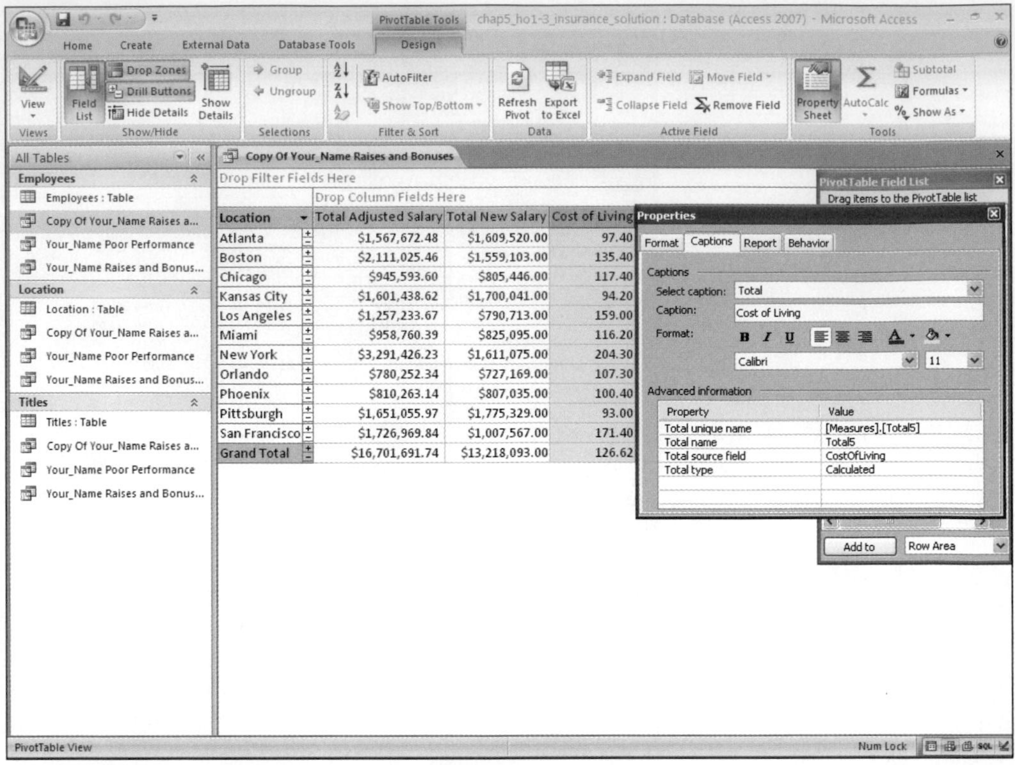

Figure 5.40 Query Results with Details Removed

Summary

1. **Create a PivotTable view.** The PivotTable view provides a method of summarizing and aggregating data. For example, an organization might need a weekly report summarizing payroll and overtime authorization by department. Because only one data source may be used for a PivotTable, you will typically use a query as the source for constructing a PivotTable, as queries may be based on multiple tables. Once the source data are assembled in a query, switch to PivotTable view. The PivotTable view is a GUI device that lets you arrange your data visually by dragging and dropping different fields into the appropriate drop zones: row, detail, column, and filter. The power of a PivotTable is its flexibility. Experienced users tend to put the field with the most possible choices in the row area and shorter ones in columns.
2. **Calculate aggregate statistics.** After you assemble data in the PivotTable view, Access provides tools to help analyze and extract the information. The PivotTable view provides the same aggregating functions as found in reports and other query views. The types of calculations available depend on the data types. The primary aggregate statistics include sum, count, min, max, average, standard deviation, standard deviation population, and variance population.
3. **Modify a PivotTable.** You add fields to a drop zone by clicking them in the PivotTable Field List window and dragging them to the appropriate drop zones. Once the PivotTable grid has been established, you can easily add and remove data fields to analyze. Should you decide that displaying certain fields makes the information too cluttered to be useful, you can remove them from the grid. Accountants use crossfooting by summing the rows, summing the columns, and making sure the totals match. It provides an important check figure. You can also modify a PivotTable by changing its properties. The Properties sheet enables you to add captions and format data in the PivotTable.
4. **Select an appropriate chart type.** One of the best methods of distilling and summarizing data is to present it in a pictorial form—a chart. Well-designed charts facilitate data interpretation. You can create PivotCharts from your PivotTable. Before you create a chart, you identify data types. Discrete data describe classifications and cannot be meaningfully subdivided. Continuous data describe a continuum of smaller increments and are easily scaled. Access can produce a variety of chart types. Column and bar charts are the most common and can be used to compare data across different categories. Line and scatter charts are used to depict data on a time line. Pie and doughnut charts depict percentages of a whole most effectively. Each PivotTable created also generates a PivotChart. Because the two views are linked, any changes you make to the chart will affect the table and any changes made to the table will change the chart.
5. **Identify chart elements.** The chart title describes the chart and its purpose. The legend provides a color-coded mapping of the data series in the chart. The axes in column, bar, line, and scatter charts typically indicate quantities and descriptions.
6. **Edit a PivotChart.** You edit an Access PivotChart similarly to editing a chart in Excel. First you must select the element you wish to edit and then perform needed edits. The big difference is that you select the element through using the Property sheet instead of double-clicking it. Be careful to add data that enhances the chart. You can overdo a PivotTable or PivotChart easily by putting too much data in it.
7. **Create calculations in a PivotTable.** Access provides several ways of calculating values. You have already created calculated fields in a query using the Expression Builder. You may also use the Expression Builder to create calculated fields in PivotTables.

Key Terms

Axes 338	*Crossfooting* 327	*Drop zone* 321
Bar chart 337	*Data aggregate* 324	*Filter field* 323
Calculated detail field 351	*Data mining* 319	*Gridlines* 338
Calculated total field 351	*Demographics* 319	*Legend* 338
Chart title 338	*Detail field* 321	*Line chart* 337
Column chart 336	*Discrete data* 336	*Pie chart* 337
Column field 322	*Doughnut chart* 337	*Row field* 321
Continuous data 336	*Drill button* 322	*Scatter plot chart* 337

Multiple Choice

1. When creating a PivotTable or PivotChart, in what order should fields be dragged to the drop zone?
   (a) Outside (Row, Column, Filter, or Page), then inside (Detail).
   (b) Inside (Detail), and then outside (Row, Column, Filter, or Page).
   (c) The order of the outside (Row, Column, Filter, or Page) is not important.
   (d) Both A and C.

2. You have a database query containing fields for donor's city and contribution type. If you want to find out which cities donors of volunteer hours live in, what order should the row fields be dropped in?
   (a) Contribution needs to be to the right of city.
   (b) Contribution needs to be to the left of city.
   (c) You may only drop one field into a row drop zone.
   (d) Drop order is unimportant.

3. You have a PivotTable that calculates an aggregate sum for each volunteer's city. How do you remove the city field from the PivotTable?
   (a) Click the Hide Detail tool if the details are hidden; activate a detail and press Delete.
   (b) Click the Hide Detail tool if the details are hidden; activate a detail and click the Remove Field tool.
   (c) Click the Hide Detail tool to hide the details; then click the gray column header and press Delete.
   (d) Both A and B.

4. You want to draw a chart that shows last month's sales by product line. The chart needs to show which product line sold the greatest proportion of total sales. Which chart type would most appropriately express these data?
   (a) Line chart
   (b) Column chart
   (c) Bubble chart
   (d) Pie chart

5. You want to draw a chart that shows donations over the past five years. Which chart type would most appropriately express these data?
   (a) Line chart
   (b) Column chart
   (c) Radar chart
   (d) Pie chart

6. You have created a 3D column chart that shows physician specialties in five different hospitals. The specialties are listed along the X-axis and the legend displays different colors for each of the hospitals. How do you change the color of one of the hospital's bars for each of the specialties?
   (a) Open the Properties window and select the series using the Select box on the General tab. Then change the series color using the Fill Color box on the Border/Fill tab of the Properties window.
   (b) Double-click any data point in the series to select the series. Then change the series color by right-clicking and selecting the Fill Color box.
   (c) Double-click any data point in the series to select the series. Then change the series color using the Fill Color box on the Border/Fill tab of the Properties window.
   (d) Open the Properties window and select the series using the Select box on the General tab. Then change the series color using the Fill Color box on the Filter and Group tab of the Properties window.

7. You have a PivotChart that summarizes employee bonuses by performance category and city. You have multiple series with different colors to indicate the different performance categories in each city. The little box that should tell the reader that the blue bars represent the excellent performance category is missing. What is the name of the box?
   (a) Property
   (b) Plot area
   (c) Legend
   (d) Series selector

8. You have a saved PivotTable that summarizes employee bonuses by performance category and city. You change to PivotChart view and decide that you need to filter for only the excellent performance category. What will happen to the PivotTable?
   (a) Nothing, it is saved.
   (b) The PivotTable will also be filtered for the excellent performance category.
   (c) You must return to the PivotTable view and filter the PivotTable to change the chart.
   (d) All of the aggregating statistics will be unchanged in the PivotTable but the details will disappear.

...continued on Next Page

Multiple Choice Continued...

9. The practice of using advanced statistical techniques to analyze patterns and relationships and to examine data in large databases is called:
   (a) Database management
   (b) Data drilling
   (c) Market analysis
   (d) Data mining

10. You have a query with fields for OrderTotal, TaxRate, and Shipping. You want to create a calculated detail field that calculates the appropriate sales tab and then adds it to the Shipping and OrderTotal fields. Which of the following expressions uses proper syntax and will correctly calculate the answer?
    (a) [OrderTotal]*[TaxRate]+[OrderTotal]+[Shipping]
    (b) [TaxRate]+[OrderTotal]+[Shipping]
    (c) [OrderTotal]*([TaxRate]+[OrderTotal]+[Shipping])
    (d) [OrderTotal]+[TaxRate]+[OrderTotal]*[Shipping]

11. You have a field in a PivotTable or PivotChart that should display with a currency format but does not. How do you change a field's format in a PivotTable or PivotChart?
    (a) Activate the field, right-click it, and select Properties. In the Properties window, select the Format tab and set the Number format to currency.
    (b) Activate the field and click the Property Sheet tool. In the Properties window, select the Format tab and set the Number format to currency.
    (c) Neither A nor B are correct.
    (d) Both A and B are correct.

12. You need to calculate an average of the PercentIncrease field in a query that shows each employee's base salaries. To do this you would:
    (a) Use the Formulas tool.
    (b) Right-click into the first blank row in the design grid and select Average from the shortcut menu.
    (c) Use the AutoCalc tool.
    (d) Use the Formulas tool and select Average.

13. You need to remove a field from a PivotTable. How do you do this?
    (a) Activate the field and press Delete.
    (b) Activate the field and drag it. When the mouse pointer shape changes to a small gray rectangle, drop it.
    (c) Activate the field and drag it. When the mouse pointer shape changes to a red X, drop it.
    (d) Both A and B are correct.

14. You have applied a filter to display only the job titles for the Sales Representatives. You enter the filter drop-down arrow and deselect the check box beside Sales Representative. What will happen to the PivotTable when you close the filter window?
    (a) Nothing.
    (b) All of the data disappear.
    (c) The PivotTable will display all of the job title's data because there is no applied filter.
    (d) You have insufficient information to answer this question.

15. You have created a PivotChart that displays hundreds of tiny, multi-colored bars. You cannot understand it. What is the most likely cause?
    (a) You selected an inappropriate chart type.
    (b) You forgot to group the bars.
    (c) You created the chart from complex, unfiltered PivotTable data.
    (d) You selected a text field for the Data Fields drop zone.

Practice Exercises

1 Miles Real Estate Sales Analysis

Nancy Miles offered you a position as the Data Manager of a small real estate firm that specializes in the sale of residential housing. Your firm sells homes in several different communities. For the last several months the employees have been recording their activities in an Access database. Nancy asked for you to mine the data and produce a summary of the sales activities by community. Refer to Figure 5.41 to verify your work.

a. Copy the partially completed file in *chap5_pe1_realestate.accdb* from the Exploring Access folder to your production folder. Rename it **chap5_pe1_realestate_solution**. Double-click the file name to open it. Click **Options** on the Security Warning toolbar, click **Enable this content** in the Microsoft Office Security Options dialog box, and then click **OK**.
b. Click the **Database Tools tab** and click **Relationships** in the Show/Hide group. Examine the table structure, relationships, and fields. Once you are familiar with the database, close the Relationships window.
c. Open the **Agents table** and replace *Your_Name* with your name in the first and last name fields. Close the Agents table. Rename the **Your_Name Sales Report** query and open it in Datasheet view.
d. Right-click the **Your_Name Sales Report query tab** and select **PivotTable View** from the shortcut menu.
e. If necessary, click **Field List** in the Show/Hide group on the Design tab to turn on the PivotTable Field List pane.
f. Drag the **LastName** field from the PivotTable Field List to the **Drop Column Fields Here** zone. Drag the **Subdivision** field from the PivotTable Field List to the **Drop Row Fields Here** zone. Drag the **SalePrice** field from the PivotTable Field List to the **Drop Totals or Detail Fields Here** zone.
g. Click any of the **SalePrice** column heads to activate all of the SalePrice data points. Click **AutoCalc** in the Tools group and select **Sum** from the list.
h. Click **Property Sheet** in the Tools group. Click the **Format tab** (if necessary) and set the *Number* format to **Currency**.
i. Click **Hide Details** in the Show/Hide group.
j. Click the **Office Button**, select **Print**, and then select **Print Preview**.
k. Click **Landscape** in the Page Layout group. Click **Margins** in the Page Layout group and select **Wide**.
l. Click the **Office Button** and select **Print**. Select **Quick Print** and click **OK**. Save and close the query.
m. Click the **Office Button**, select **Manage**, and select **Compact and Repair Database**. Close the file.

...continued on Next Page

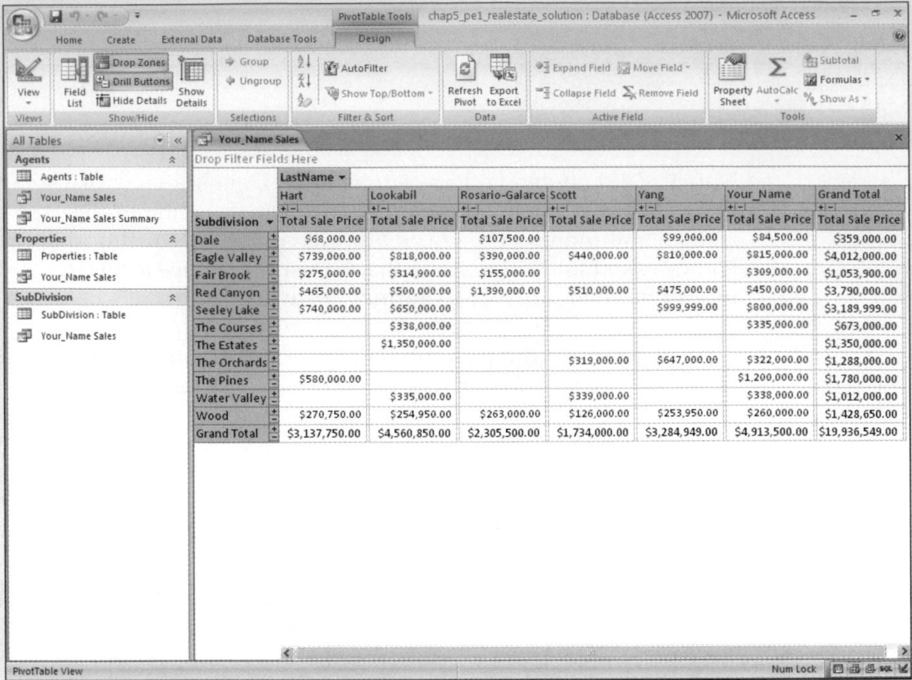

Subdivision	Hart	Lookabil	Rosario-Galarce	Scott	Yang	Your_Name	Grand Total
	Total Sale Price	Total Sale Price	Total Sale Price	Total Sale Price	Total Sale Price	Total Sale Price	Total Sale Price
Dale	$68,000.00		$107,500.00		$99,000.00	$84,500.00	$359,000.00
Eagle Valley	$739,000.00	$818,000.00	$390,000.00	$440,000.00	$810,000.00	$815,000.00	$4,012,000.00
Fair Brook	$275,000.00	$314,900.00	$155,000.00			$309,000.00	$1,053,900.00
Red Canyon	$465,000.00	$500,000.00	$1,390,000.00	$510,000.00	$475,000.00	$450,000.00	$3,790,000.00
Seeley Lake	$740,000.00	$650,000.00			$999,999.00	$800,000.00	$3,189,999.00
The Courses		$338,000.00				$335,000.00	$673,000.00
The Estates		$1,350,000.00					$1,350,000.00
The Orchards				$319,000.00	$647,000.00	$322,000.00	$1,288,000.00
The Pines	$580,000.00					$1,200,000.00	$1,780,000.00
Water Valley		$335,000.00		$339,000.00		$338,000.00	$1,012,000.00
Wood	$270,750.00	$254,950.00	$263,000.00	$126,000.00	$253,950.00	$260,000.00	$1,428,650.00
Grand Total	$3,137,750.00	$4,560,850.00	$2,305,500.00	$1,734,000.00	$3,284,949.00	$4,913,500.00	$19,936,549.00

Figure 5.41 Sorted and Filtered Query Results

2 Real Estate City Analysis

Ms. Miles asks that you examine all of the listed properties by community. Your firm offers properties for sale in several cities. Each city may be divided into one or more subdivisions. Some of the houses are located in formal subdivisions that have community pools, tennis courts, and bike trails. You need to group the listed properties by city and then by the subdivision. You also need to indicate which agent listed each property. Finally, you need to summarize the value of the listed properties. Ms. Miles asks that you present the information in both tabular and graphical form. Refer to Figures 5.42 and 5.43 to verify your work.

a. Copy the partially completed file in *chap5_pe2_realestate.accdb* from the Exploring Access folder to your production folder. Rename it **chap5_pe2_realestate_solution**. Double-click the file name to open it. Click **Options** on the Security Warning toolbar, click **Enable this content** in the Microsoft Office Security Options dialog box, and then click **OK**.
b. Copy the **City Listings** query, then paste it as **Your_Name City Listings** in the Navigation Pane.
c. Open the **Agents table** and replace *Your_Name* with your name in the first and last name fields. Close the Agents table.
d. Open the **Your_Name City Listings** query, right-click the query tab, and select **PivotTable View** from the shortcut menu.
e. If necessary, click **Field List** in the Show/Hide group to turn on the PivotTable Field List pane. Drag the **City** field from the PivotTable Field List and drop it in the **Drop Row Field** zone.
f. Drag the **Subdivision** field from the PivotTable Field List and drop it in the **Drop Row Field** zone to the right of the City field.
g. Drag the **LastName** field from the PivotTable Field List and drop it in the **Drop Column Field** zone.
h. Drag the **ListPrice** field from the PivotTable Field List and drop it in the **Drop Totals or Detail Field** zone.
i. Click any of the ListPrice column heads to select. Click **AutoCalc** in the Tool group and select **Sum** from the list.

...continued on Next Page

j. Capture a screenshot of the first page of the PivotTable by pressing **Prnt Scrn**. Launch Word and type your name and section number at the top of the page. Press **Enter**. Paste the screenshot into the Word document and save the file as **chap5_pe2_realestate_solution.docx**. Keep the Word document open.

k. Right-click the query tab and select **PivotChart**. Close the PivotTable Field List window.

l. Click the **LastName Field Button** arrow. Click the **All** check box to clear it. Click the **Your_Name** box to select it. Keep the selection list of the agent's name open.

m. Capture a screenshot of the first page of the PivotChart by pressing **Prnt Scrn**. Switch to the Word document. Press **Enter**. Paste the screenshot into the Word document and save the file as **chap5_pe2_realestate_solution.docx**. Print the Word document.

n. Save and close the query. Click the **Office Button**, select **Manage**, and then select **Compact and Repair Database**. Close the file.

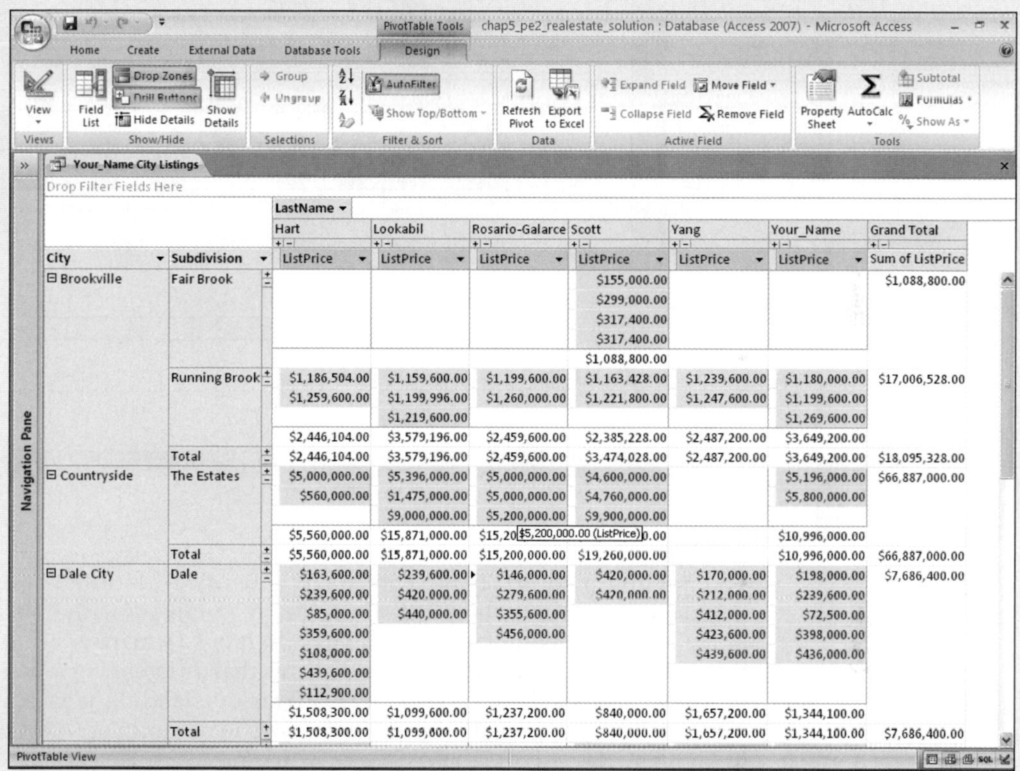

Figure 5.42 PivotTable

...continued on Next Page

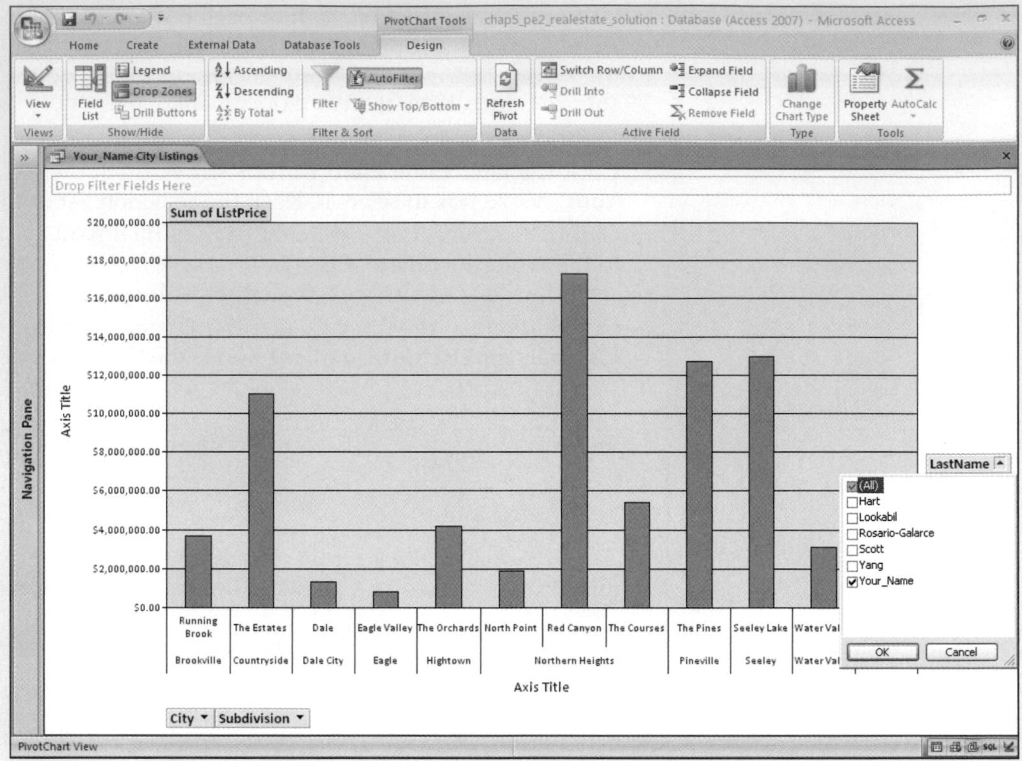

Figure 5.43 PivotChart

3 Bank Loans

You are interning in a bank. Each day you work with different employees and help them with their computer applications questions. Today, you work with Robert Wigman, one of the directors of the bank. Mr. Wigman asked you to help him summarize the sums of all the loan payments by type and interest rate. Mr. Wigman explains that different borrowers pay differing rates of interest. The bank needs to know how many loans are outstanding at each of the different interest rates. He also needs you to prepare a chart that shows total mortgage loan payments by interest rate. Refer to Figures 5.44 and 5.45 to verify your work.

a. Copy the partially completed file *chap5_pe3_nationalbank.accdb* from the Exploring Access folder to your production folder. Rename it **chap5_pe3_nationalbank_solution.accdb**. Double-click the file name to open it. Click **Options** on the Security Warning toolbar, click **Enable this content** in the Microsoft Office Security Options dialog box, and then click **OK**.

b. Rename the *Your_Name Loan Payment query* with your name. Open the query; right-click the query tab and select **PivotTable View**.

c. If necessary, click **Field List** in the Show/Hide group to turn on the PivotTable Field List window. Drag the **InterestRate** field from the PivotTable Field List and drop it in the **Drop Row Field Here Field** zone. Drag the Type field from the PivotTable Field List and drop it in the **Drop Column Field Here** zone. Drag the **Payment** field from the PivotTable Field List and drop it in the **Drop Detail Field Here** zone.

d. Click a **Payment Column head** to select the payments. Click **AutoCalc** in the Tools group and select **Sum** from the list.

e. Click **Hide Details** in the Show/Hide group.

f. Capture a screenshot of the PivotTable by pressing **Prnt Scrn**. Launch Word, then type your name and section number at the top of the page. Press **Enter**. Paste the screenshot into the Word document and save the file as **chap5_pe3_nationalbank_solution.docx**. Keep the Word document open.

...continued on Next Page

g. Return to Access. Right-click the query tab and switch to **PivotChart View**. Click the plot area to select the chart and click **Change Chart Type** in the Type group. In the Properties box, select the 3D Stacked Column Type (second row, third column).

h. Click the **General tab** in the Properties window. Click the **Select arrow** and select **C**. Click the **Border/Fill tab**. Click the **Fill Color arrow** and change the color to **MediumBlue** (second row, fourth column from the right).

i. Click the **General tab** in the Properties window. Click the **Select arrow** and select **M**. Click the **Fill Type arrow** and select Gradient. Click the **Color arrow** and select **Yellow** (sixth row, fourth column). Click the **Border/Fill tab**. Click **Two Color**. Click the **Back color arrow** and change the color to **MediumBlue** (second row, fourth column from the right). Click **Style** and select **Horizontal End** (first row, second column).

j. Click the **General tab** in the Properties window. Click the **Select arrow** and select **O**. Click the **Border/Fill tab**. Click the **Color arrow** and change the color to **Yellow** (sixth row, fourth from the right).

k. Click **Legend** in the Show/Hide group.

l. Close the Properties sheet and the PivotTable Field List window. Capture a screenshot of the PivotChart by pressing **Prnt Scrn**. Return to Word, then type **Enter** after the screenshot of the PivotTable. Paste the screenshot into the Word document and save the document as **chap5_pe3_nationalbank_solution.docx**. Print and close the Word document.

m. Save and close the query. Click the **Office Button**, select **Manage**, and select **Compact and Repair Database**.

n. Close the file.

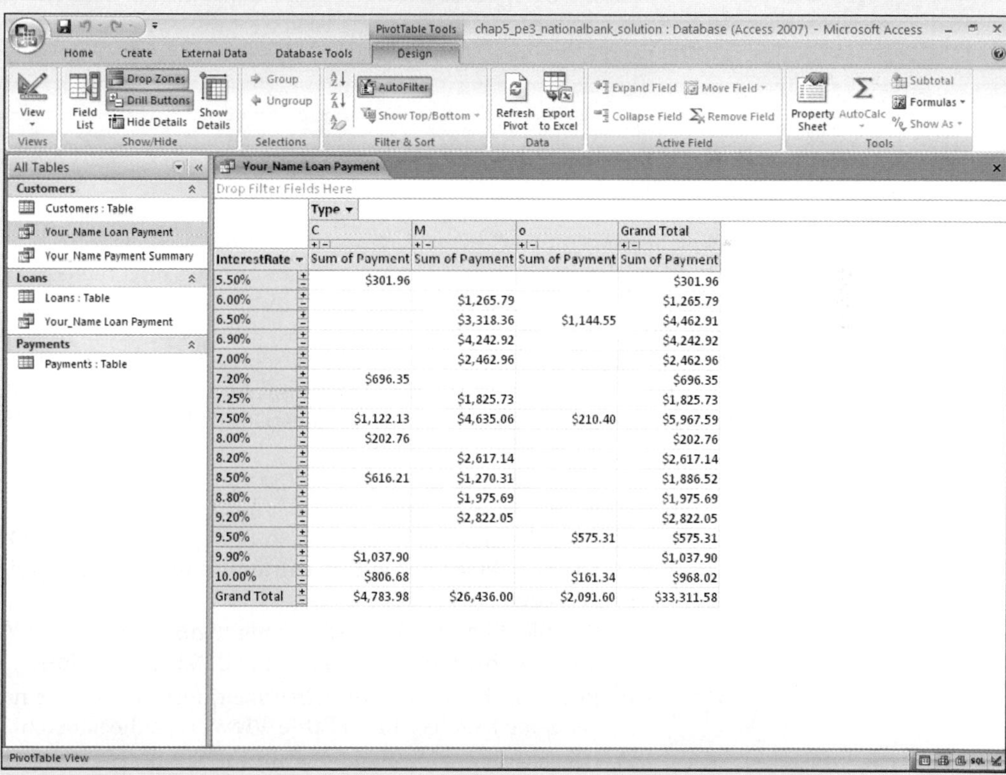

Figure 5.44 PivotTable

...continued on Next Page

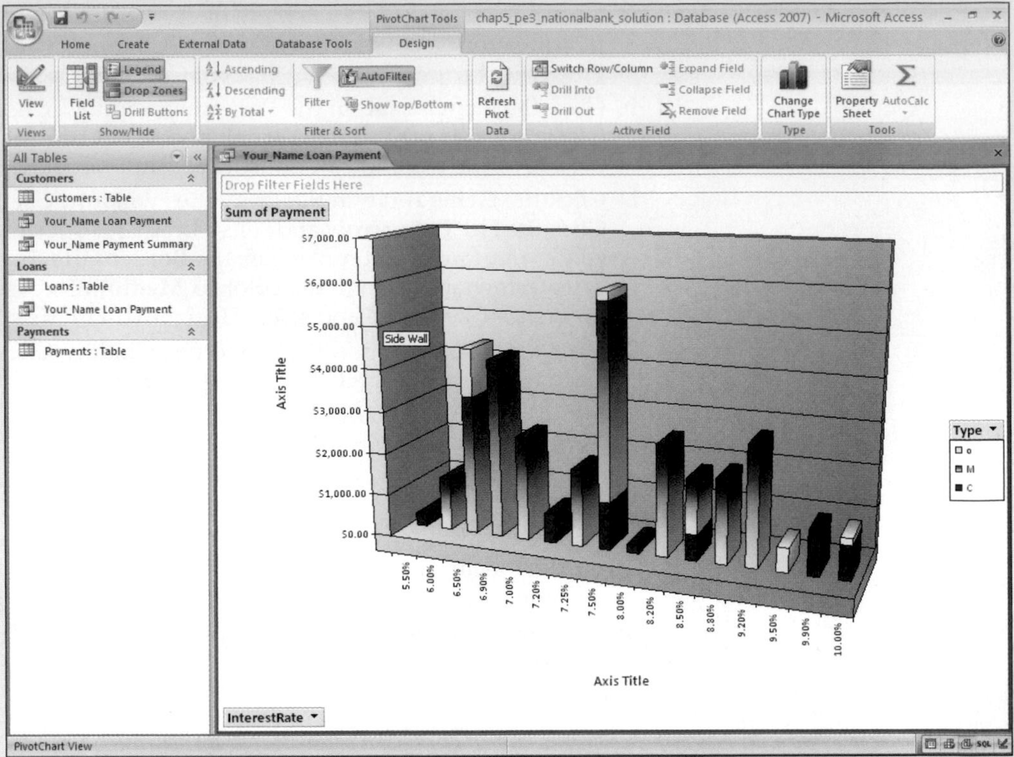

Figure 5.45 PivotChart

4 Custom Coffee

The Custom Coffee Company is a small service organization that provides coffee, tea, and snacks to offices. Custom Coffee also provides and maintains the equipment for brewing the beverages. Although the firm is small, its excellent reputation for providing outstanding customer service has helped it grow. Part of this customer service is because the firm owner set up a database to organize and keep track of customer purchases. You need to use the data mining techniques from the chapter to help convert the data into information. You need to calculate order profits and produce a chart that shows weekly profit by salesperson. Refer to Figures 5.46 and 5.47 to verify your work.

a. Copy the partially completed file *chap5_pe4_coffee.accdb* from the Exploring Access folder to your production folder. Rename it **chap5_pe4_coffee_solution.accdb**. Double-click the file name to open the file. Click **Options** on the Security Warning toolbar, click **Enable this content** in the Microsoft Office Security Options dialog box, and then click **OK**.
b. Double-click the **Sales Rep table** to open it. Replace *Your_Name* with your name. Close the table by clicking Close in the database window.
c. Rename the *Your_Name Revenue* query with your name. Open it and right-click the *query tab* to select **PivotTable View** from the shortcut menu.
d. If necessary, click **Field List** in the Show/Hide group to turn on the PivotTable Field List window. Drag the **OrderDate by Week** field from the PivotTable Field List and drop it in the **Drop Row Field Here** zone. Drag the **LastName** field from the PivotTable Field List and drop it in the **Drop Column Field Here** zone. Drag the **Revenue** and **TotalCost** fields from the PivotTable Field List and drop them in the **Drop Totals or Detail Fields Here** zone.
e. Click the **Year 2008 drill button** to expand to display the weeks.
f. Click **Formulas** in the Tools group, and then select **Create Calculated Detail Field**. In the Calculation Properties box, click in the Name box and type **Profit**. In the Calculation box, delete the zero and type **[Revenue] – [TotalCost]**. Click **Change**.

...continued on Next Page

g. Click the **Profit column head** to select the column, click **AutoCalc** in the Tools group, and select **Sum**. Use the same method to calculate totals for the Revenue and Total cost fields.

h. Click the **Profit column head** to select the column and click the **Format tab** in the Properties box. Click the **Number arrow** and select **Currency**. Click the **Sum of Profit column head** to select the column and click the **Format tab** in the Properties box. Click the **Number arrow** and select **Currency**.

i. Click **Hide Details** in the Show/Hide group. Close the Properties window and the PivotTable Field List. Capture a screenshot of the PivotTable by pressing **Prnt Scrn**. Launch Word, and then type your name and section number at the top of the page. Press **Enter**. Paste the screenshot into the Word document and save the document as **chap5_pe4_coffee_solution.docx**. Keep the Word document open.

j. Return to Access. Right-click the query tab and select **PivotChart View** from the shortcut menu.

k. Click the plot area to select the chart, then click **Change Chart Type** in the Type group. Choose a **line chart** and the first sub-chart option.

l. Click the **field button** for the **Sum of Revenue** field and drag it off the chart. Drop it when you see the red X attached to the mouse pointer. Drag the **Sum of Cost** field off the chart.

m. Click the X-axis Axis Title box and select the Format tab in the Properties sheet. Click in the Caption box, delete *Axis Title*, and type **January Weeks**. Click the Y-axis Axis Title box and press **Delete**.

n. Close the Properties window and the PivotTable Field List window. Click **Legend** to display the legend. Capture a screenshot of the PivotChart by pressing **Prnt Scrn**. Return to Word, press **Enter** after the screenshot of the PivotTable, and paste the screenshot. Save the Word document as **chap5_pe4_coffee_solution.docx**. Print and close the Word document.

o. Save the query. Click the **Office Button**, select **Manage**, and then select **Compact and Repair**. Close the file.

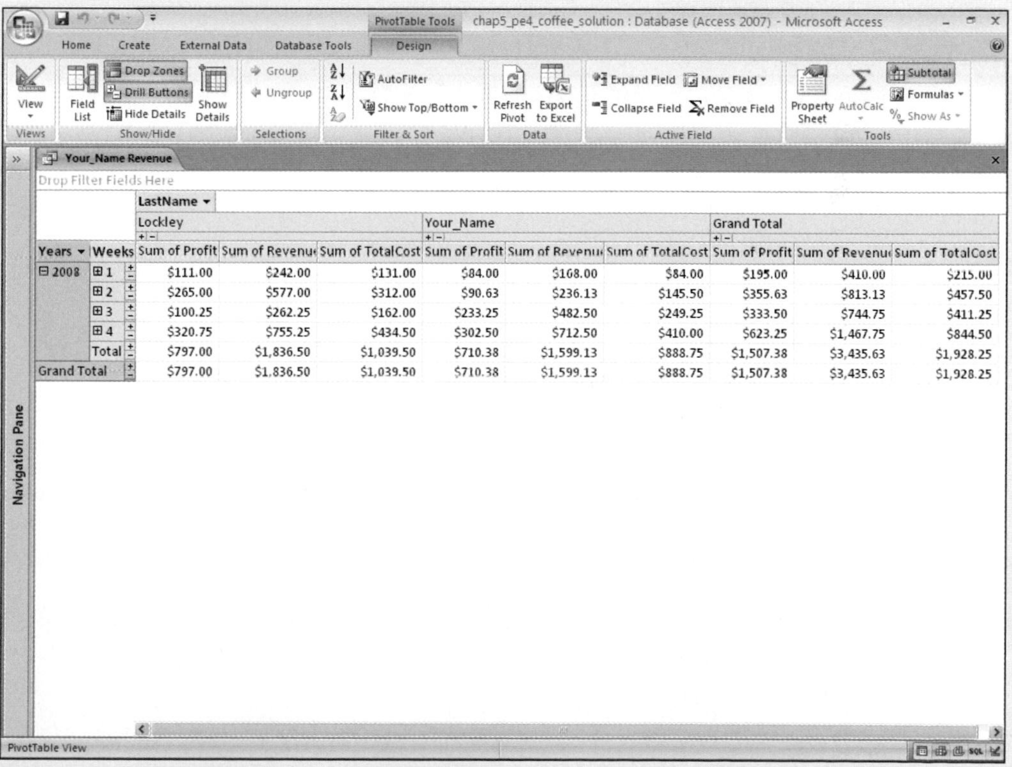

	LastName									
		Lockley			Your_Name			Grand Total		
Years	Weeks	Sum of Profit	Sum of Revenue	Sum of TotalCost	Sum of Profit	Sum of Revenue	Sum of TotalCost	Sum of Profit	Sum of Revenue	Sum of TotalCost
2008	1	$111.00	$242.00	$131.00	$84.00	$168.00	$84.00	$195.00	$410.00	$215.00
	2	$265.00	$577.00	$312.00	$90.63	$236.13	$145.50	$355.63	$813.13	$457.50
	3	$100.25	$262.25	$162.00	$233.25	$482.50	$249.25	$333.50	$744.75	$411.25
	4	$320.75	$755.25	$434.50	$302.50	$712.50	$410.00	$623.25	$1,467.75	$844.50
	Total	$797.00	$1,836.50	$1,039.50	$710.38	$1,599.13	$888.75	$1,507.38	$3,435.63	$1,928.25
Grand Total		$797.00	$1,836.50	$1,039.50	$710.38	$1,599.13	$888.75	$1,507.38	$3,435.63	$1,928.25

Figure 5.46 PivotTable

...continued on Next Page

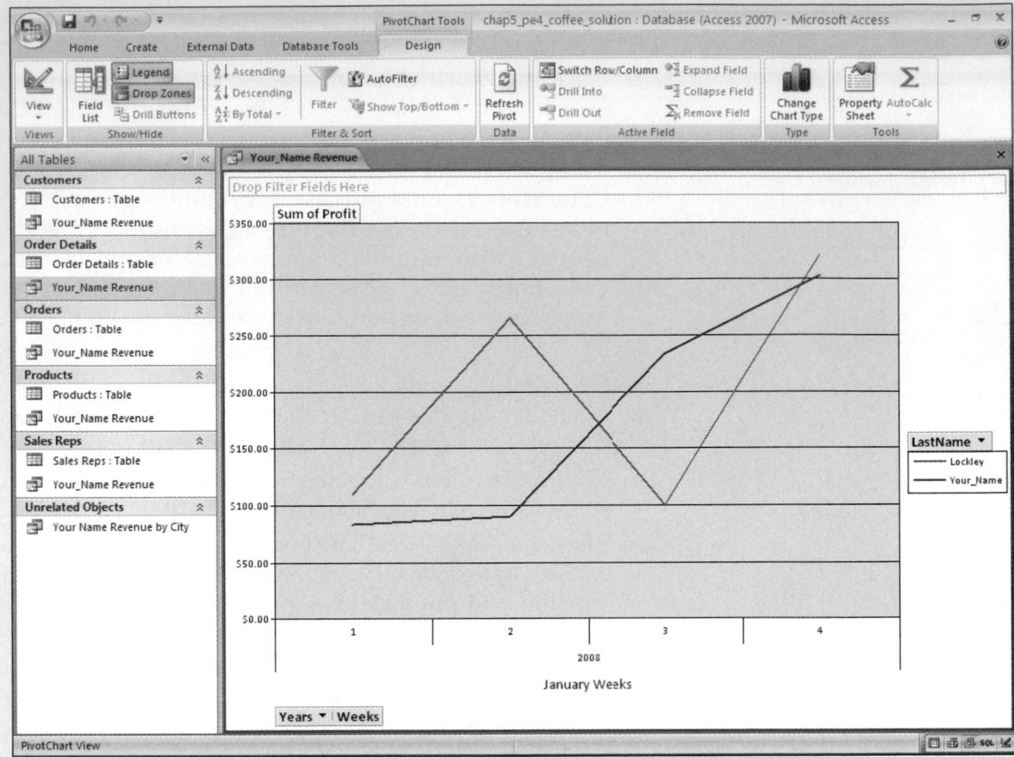

Figure 5.47 PivotChart of January Weekly Profits

Mid-Level Exercises

1 The Northwinds Traders

The Northwinds Traders is a small, international specialty foods distribution firm. It sells products in a variety of different categories, including beverages and condiments. The Sales Manager has asked you to provide her with a chart that shows beverage sales by month for 2007. She will use the chart to review each salesperson's performance in the annual review meeting. Refer to Figure 5.48 to verify your work.

a. Locate the file named *chap5_mid1_traders.accdb*, copy it to your production folder, and rename it **chap5_mid1_traders_solution.accdb**. Open the file and enable the content.

b. Rename the *Your_Name Revenue* query with **your name**. Open the Employees table and replace *Your_name* in the first and last name fields with your name.

c. Open the *Your_Name Revenue* query and switch to PivotTable view.

d. Add the **ShippedDate By Month** field to the row drop zone. Expand the 2007 values to display the months. Deselect the 2008 values.

e. Remove the **Quarters** field from the PivotTable.

f. Add the **CategoryName** field to the filter zone. Uncheck the All box and select **Beverages.** Add the **LastName** field to the column drop zone. Uncheck the All box and select the **Your_Name** box.

g. Use the Properties window to enter **Total Revenue** as the Sum of Revenue caption.

h. Switch to **PivotChart view**. Change the chart type to Line and the subtype to 3D line (first column, third row). Display the legend.

i. Change the series line color to DarkGreen (fifth row, last column). Change the plot area color to Violet (first row, fourth column). Change the Y-axis title to **Revenue** and change the X-axis title to **Beverages**.

j. Print the chart. Compact and repair the database. Close the database.

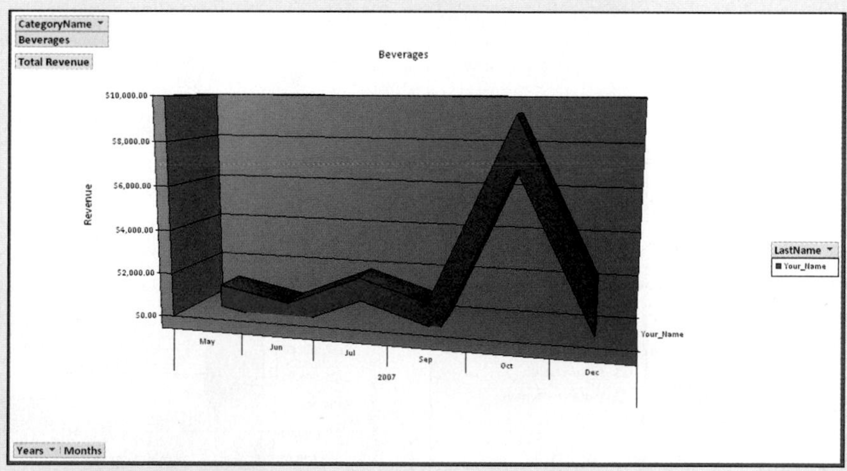

Figure 5.48 PivotChart Displaying Your Sales of Beverages

...continued on Next Page

2 Hotel Chain

You are the general manager of a large hotel chain. Your establishment provides a variety of guest services ranging from rooms and conferences to weddings. You need to calculate the total revenue generated by service type and city. You want a chart that provides quickly interpretable information. Finally, you need to sort the data by total revenue in descending order. Refer to Figure 5.49 to verify your work.

a. Locate the file named *chap5_mid2_memrewards.accdb*, copy it to your production folder, and rename it **chap5_mid2_memrewards_solution.accdb**. Open the file and enable the content. Rename the *Revenue* query as **Your_Name Revenue**. Open it in PivotTable view.

b. Use the *City* field for the **Row Field**, the *ServiceName* field for the **Column Field**, and the *NoInParty* and *PerPersonCharge* fields for the **Detail Fields**.

c. Create a *Calculated Detail Formula Field* that calculates **Revenue** by multiplying PerPersonCharge by NoInParty.

d. Use the AutoCalc tool to **Sum** the Revenue field. Format it as currency.

e. Hide the details of the PivotTable.

f. Create a PivotChart. Use a stacked 3D column chart (second row, third column). Caption the *X-axis title* with **your_name**. Caption the *Y-axis title* with the **Total Revenue.** Display a legend.

g. Modify the Rotation and Inclination options of the 3D View Properties to approximate Figure 5.49.

h. Capture a screenshot of the PivotChart. Open Word, launch a new blank document, type **your name and section number**, and press **Enter**. Press **Ctrl+V** or click Paste. Print the Word document. Save it as **chap5_mid2_memrewards_solution.docx**. Close the Word document.

i. Compact, repair, and close the database.

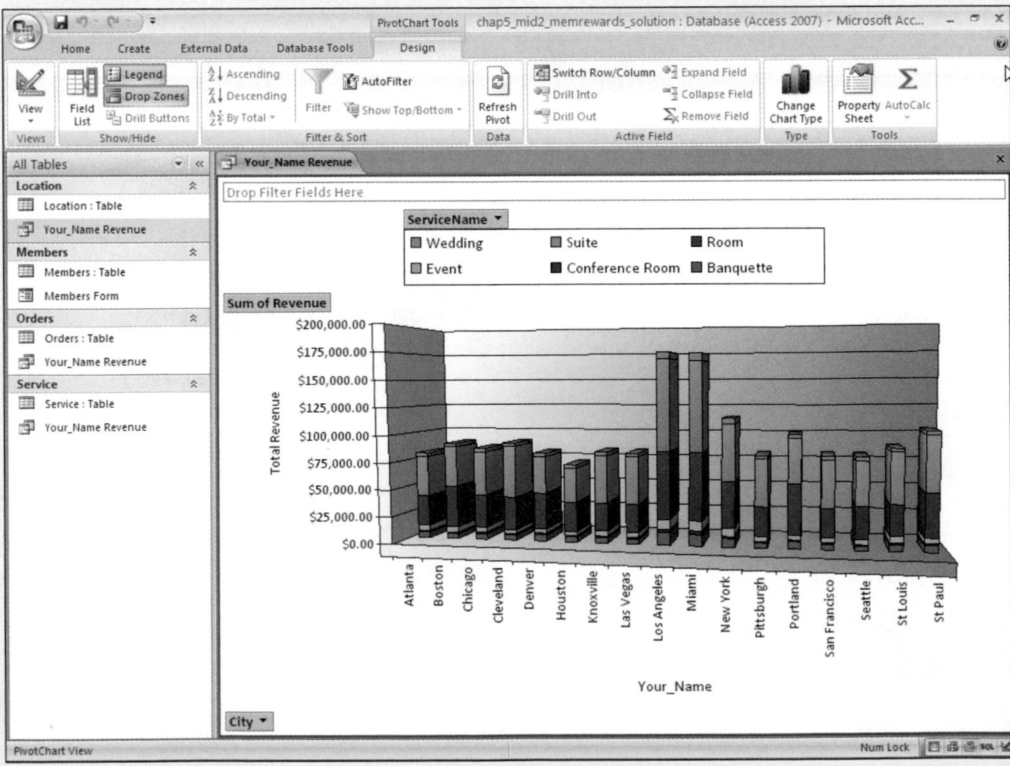

Figure 5.49 Stacked Column Chart

...continued on Next Page

3 Nesting Pivoted Data for a Hotel Chain

You are the general manager of a large hotel chain. Your establishment provides a variety of guest services ranging from rooms and conferences to weddings. You need to examine the total revenue generated by service type in each city and quarter. Refer to Figures 5.50 and 5.51 to verify your work.

a. Locate the file named *chap5_mid3_memrewards.accdb*, copy it to your production folder, and rename it **chap5_mid3_memrewards_solution.accdb**. Open the file and enable the content. Rename the *Revenue query* as **Your_Name Revenue**. Open the query and switch to the PivotTable view.

b. Drag the **City** and **ServiceName** fields to the row drop zone. Nest the service names inside each city. Drag the **ServiceDate By Month** field to the column drop zone. Limit the dates to only 2007 and display them by **quarter**. Display only the third- and fourth-quarter data.

c. Add the **Revenue** field to the detail drop zone and sum it.

d. Capture a screenshot of the PivotTable. Open Word, launch a new blank document, type your name and section number, and press **Enter**. Press **Ctrl+V** or click Paste. Save the document as **chap5_mid3_memrewards_solution.docx**. Press **Enter**. Keep the Word document open and return to Access.

e. Save the changes and close your query. Rename the query **Your_Name Revenue by City**.

f. Copy the query and name the copy as **Your_Name Revenue by Service**. Open the Revenue by Service query and modify the PivotTable so that the services are the primary group, and the city names nest within each service.

g. Capture a screenshot of the PivotTable. Return to Word and paste your second PivotTable below the first. Save the Word document as as **chap5_mid3_memrewards_solution.docx**. Close the Word document and return to Access.

h. Save your query. Compact, repair, and close the database.

...continued on Next Page

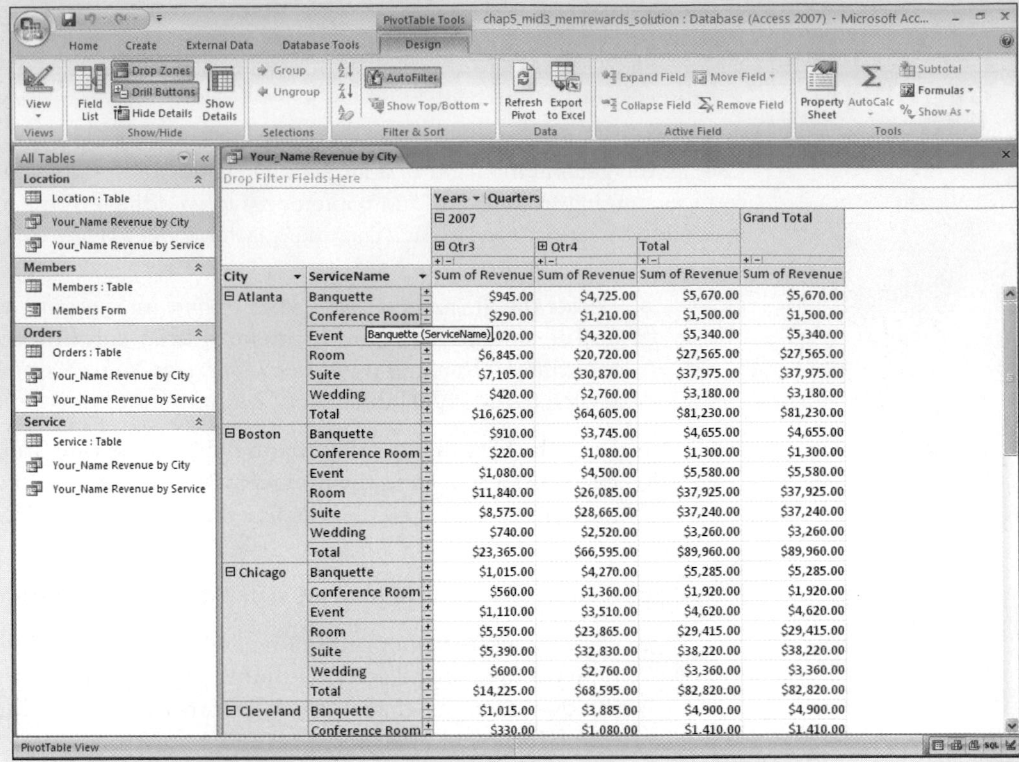

Figure 5.50 Revenue by City PivotTable

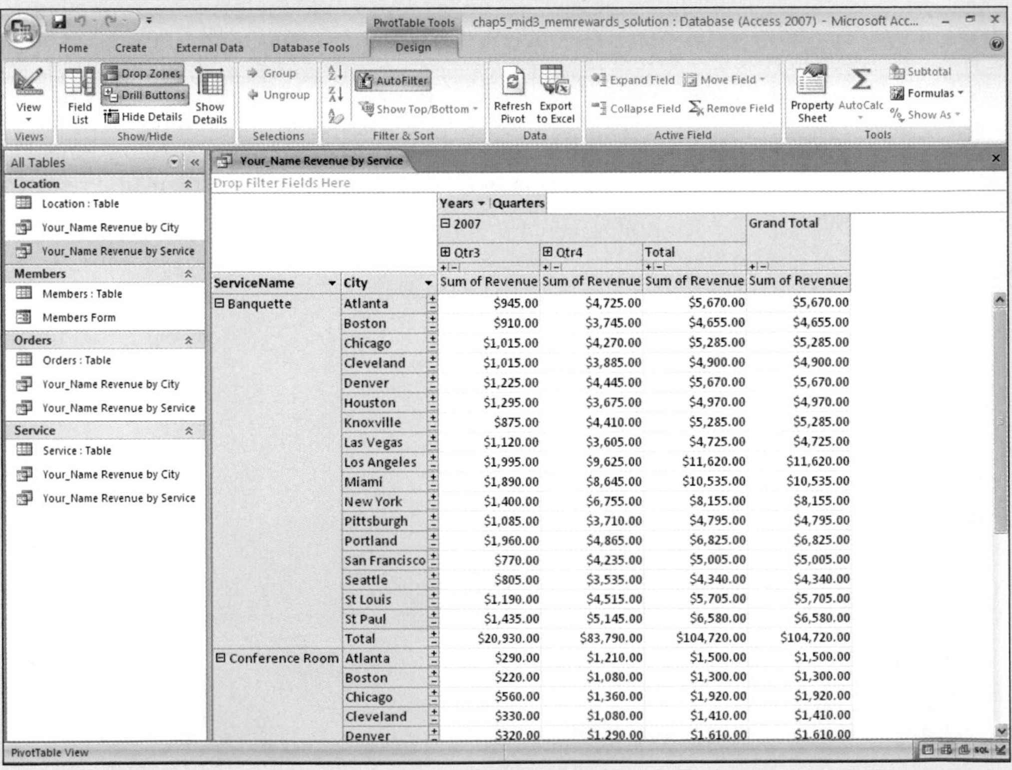

Figure 5.51 Revenue by Service PivotTable

Capstone Exercise

(Replacements, Ltd., is a real company. The data in the case file are actual data. The customer and employee information has been changed to ensure privacy. However, the inventory and sales records reflect actual transactions.)

You work as an associate marketing manager at Replacements, Ltd. Your responsibilities include browsing the Replacements Web site, www.replacements.com. There you learned that Replacements, Ltd. (located in Greensboro, NC) has the world's largest selection of old and new dinnerware, including china, stoneware, crystal, glassware, silver, stainless, and collectibles. You need to oversee the marketing of some of the patterns in the inventory. You need to discover which patterns produce the most revenue. You want to create a chart that displays the revenue generated from the sale of the patterns for which you are responsible. After you complete the work, you will compact and repair the database and make a backup of it.

Database File Setup

You need to copy an original database file, rename the copied file, and then open the copied database to complete this capstone exercise. After you open the copied database, you will replace an existing employee's name with your name.

a. Locate the file named *chap5_cap_replacements.accdb* and copy it to your working folder.

b. Rename the copied file as **chap5_cap_ replacements.accdb_solution**.

c. Open the *chap5_cap_replacements_solution.accdb* file and enable the content.

d. Open the **Employees Table** form.

e. Navigate to record 55 and replace *Carmen Thomas*'s name with your name. Press **Enter** and close the table.

f. Rename the Revenue query as **Your_Name Revenue**. Open the query.

Switch to PivotTable View and Lay Out the PivotTable Zones

You need to create a PivotTable to display sales information by pattern name. You will need to filter it to display only the sale of the patterns for which you are responsible.

a. Open the query in **PivotTable view**.

b. Place the **LongPatName** field in the row drop zone and the **LastName** field in the column drop zone.

c. Filter the **LastName** field so that only **Your_Name** displays.

d. Place the **Qty** and **Price** fields in the detail fields drop zone.

e. Save the query.

Create a Calculated Field

You need to create a field that calculates revenue as the product of price and quantity.

a. Highlight the **Price** field.

b. Click the Formula tool and use it to create a calculated detail field.

c. Name the field **Revenue**.

d. Multiply Price by Qty to perform the calculation.

Calculate Totals and Format the Results

You need to calculate totals for each pattern.

a. Make sure the Revenue field is still selected.

b. Apply the **Sum** function to the Revenue field.

c. Click the **Format tab** in the Properties window.

d. Apply the **Currency** for the **Revenue** field.

e. Apply the **Currency Format** for the **Sum of Revenue** field.

f. Hide the details.

g. Save your PivotTable changes.

Create and Format a PivotChart

Now that you are satisfied that the data summary is complete, graphically depict it.

a. Switch to PivotChart View and select a **3D Bar chart**.

b. From the General tab of the Properties sheet select **Your_Name** to select all of the chart bars.

c. Select the Border/Fill tab, then select the **Gradient** Fill Type and *Preset*: **Ocean** color scheme.

d. Print the chart. Save and close the query.

e. Compact and restore the database.

f. Close the file.

Mini Cases

Use the rubric following the case as a guide to evaluate your work, but keep in mind that your instructor may impose additional grading criteria or use a different standard to judge your work.

Determining Row and Column Data for PivotTables and PivotCharts

GENERAL CASE

The *chap5_mc1_traders.accdb* file contains data from an international specialty foods distribution firm. You have a query that assembles the necessary fields but need to mine these data to determine profits by item for each salesperson and country to which the goods were shipped. You will use this information to reward sales performance and to analyze where your customers are using the products you sell. Copy the *chap5_mc1_traders.accdb* file, rename the copied file as **chap5_mc1_traders_solution.accdb**, open the copied file, and enable the content. Use the skills from this chapter to perform several tasks. Open the Employees table and replace Your_Name with your name. Rename the Your_Name Revenue query with your name. Use the PivotTable view to calculate profits by subtracting total costs from revenue. Summarize and total the cost, revenue, and profit data by salesperson and the country of shipment. Draw a chart that displays your profits by country. Print the chart. Compact, repair, and back up your database.

Performance Elements	Exceeds Expectations	Meets Expectations	Below Expectations
Profit calculation	Calculated fields accurate.	Calculated fields accurate.	Output missing or incorrect.
Data summaries	Appropriate summaries and aggregating calculations performed.	Most of the requested summaries and aggregates present and accurate.	Output missing or inaccurate.
Detail manipulation	Appropriate levels of details displayed and formatted correctly.	Appropriate levels of details displayed with some formatting problems.	Insufficient understanding of detail manipulation.
Chart construction	Data are presented in an easy-to-interpret, aesthetically pleasing chart.	Data are presented in a chart with some aesthetic issues or minor clarity problems.	Chart is illegible or incomprehensible.

Combining Name Fields

RESEARCH CASE

This chapter introduced you to the power of using Access PivotTables and PivotCharts, but you have much more to explore. Copy the *chap5_mc2_coffee.accdb* file, rename the copied file as **chap5_mc2_coffee_solution.accdb**, open the file, and enable the content. Open the Your_Name Revenue query and set it to PivotTable view. You need to share these data with a coworker who does not have Access on her computer. She has Word, Excel, and PowerPoint. Use Help to research how to share this information with your coworker. After you successfully get the file into a usable form for your coworker, write your instructor explaining how you accomplished this step. Save and print the output that you generated for your coworker and name it **chap5_ mc2_coffee_ solution**, using the appropriate extension for the software that you used. Compact, repair, and back up your database.

Performance Elements	Exceeds Expectations	Meets Expectations	Below Expectations
Use online Help	Appropriate articles located, and instructions indicate comprehension.	Appropriate articles located, but instructions did not demonstrate comprehension.	Articles not found.
Data successfully transferred to another application	A Word or Excel file and printout submitted demonstrating file sharing.	A Word or Excel file and printout submitted with some minor problems from file sharing.	Files missing or incomprehensible.
Summarize and communicate	Instructions clearly written and could be used as directions.	Instruction text indicates some understanding but also weaknesses.	Instructions missing or incomprehensible.
File management	Database was correctly compacted, repaired, and backed up.	Database was successfully compacted but not backed up or vice versa.	Files not submitted.

Coffee Revenue Queries

DISASTER RECOVERY

A coworker called you into her office and explained that she was having difficulty with Access 2007 and asked you to look at her work. You are employed by the Human Resources Department of a large insurance company with offices and employees nationwide. Your coworker is trying to analyze the year-end salary adjustments for all of the positions and offices in the country to ensure pay equity. Copy the *chap5_mc3_insurance.accdb* file, rename the copied file as **chap5_mc3_insurance_solution.accdb**, open the file, and enable the content. Your coworker explains she cannot understand the chart. She intended that it should show the average new salary for each position title and performance rating. She needs to examine this information to determine if the excellently rated workers in all positions earn higher average salaries than do good-, average-, or poor-rated workers. Find the source of the error and correct it. Run and print the chart or charts. Compact, repair, and back up your database.

Performance Elements	Exceeds Expectations	Meets Expectations	Below Expectations
Error identification	Correct identification and correction of all errors.	Correct identification of all errors and correction of some errors.	Errors neither located nor corrected.
Reporting	Chart(s) designed and printed successfully.	Printout submitted, but with errors.	No printout submitted for evaluation.

chapter 6 | **Access**

Data Protection

Integrity, Validation, and Reliability

After you read this chapter, you will be able to:

1. Establish data validity **(page 383)**.
2. Create and modify a lookup field **(page 386)**.
3. Create and modify a multivalued lookup field **(page 389)**.
4. Work with input masks **(page 390)**.
5. Create forms by using the Form Tool **(page 400)**.
6. Create custom forms in Design view **(page 413)**.
7. Create subforms **(page 416)**.
8. Design functional formats **(page 417)**.

Hands-On Exercises

Exercises	Skills Covered
1. DATA PROTECTION (page 394) **Open:** chap6_ho1-3_nationalbank.accdb **Save as:** chap6_ho1-3_nationalbank_solution.accdb **Back up as:** chap6_ho1_nationalbank_solution.accdb	• Establish Required and Default Field Properties • Create and Test Validation Rules and Text • Create a Lookup Field • Modify a Lookup Field Value • Create a Multivalued Lookup Field • Create and Edit Input Masks
2. FORM CREATION TOOLS (page 407) **Open:** chap6_ho1-3_nationalbank_solution.accdb (from Exercise 1) **Save as:** chap6_ho1-3_nationalbank_solution.accdb (additional modifications) **Back up as:** chap6_ho2_nationalbank_solution.accdb	• Use the Form Tool and Identify Form Controls • Create a Split Form • Create a Multiple Items Form • Create a Datasheet Form • Create PivotTable and PivotChart Forms
3. CUSTOMIZING FORMS (page 421) **Open:** chap6_ho1-3_nationalbank_solution.accdb (from Exercise 2) **Save as:** chap6_ho1-3_nationalbank_solution.accdb (additional modifications)	• Use the Blank Form Tool to Create a Form • Create a Form in Design View • Add Action Buttons and Controls • Create and Edit a Form with a Subform • Customize a Form by Moving Controls and Adding a Theme

CASE STUDY

Simplify Data Entry

You work as an office manager at the Real Estate Agency. Your firm helps people buy and sell homes. The office has several agents who work with clients to help them find a match between their housing needs and what they can afford. The agents may work with home buyers, sellers, or both. The properties for sale are located in a variety of communities. Your agency maintains a database containing information about the homes, the agents, and the subdivisions in which the properties are located. The agents do not take prospective purchasers into a home unless the homeowner knows they are coming. Sometimes a prospective home purchaser needs to visit a property with very little notice. The agent needs to find the homeowner quickly and obtain permission to show the property. The agency owner asked you to add a new database table that will contain information about the clients the agents assist. You need to design a customer contact table, design a form, and make the form easy for the non-technical staff in the firm to use. You will need to think through the design of the table carefully. Some of the fields you will need are obvious, such as customers' first and last names. Other fields need to serve the unique needs of the real estate agents.

How can you help them reach a client quickly and easily? A prospective home purchaser has strong opinions about which subdivision he or she wants to live in. You need to consider how to capture the customer's preferences and enable the agents to use their time and the customer's time efficiently. For example, a customer who must have at least four bedrooms and two bathrooms would not want to spend an hour looking at a two-bedroom, one-bath house. An agent would not want to spend time showing a $750,000 house to a customer who qualifies for a $200,000 mortgage. When properly designed, your table will help your firm provide better customer service and make more efficient use of the agent's time. After you determine what fields to store in the table, you need to design a form based on the table. All of the agents need to use this table and its data. Therefore, your form must be designed in a way that will accommodate the least skilled agents in the firm. You should consider how to design the form to facilitate accurate data entry.

Your Assignment

- Read the chapter, paying special attention to the tools described that help protect data integrity and validity.
- Copy the *chap6_case_realestate.accdb* file to your production folder, rename it **chap6_case_realestate_solution.accdb**, and enable the content.
- Open the Relationships window and examine the relationships among the tables and the fields contained within each of the tables to become acquainted with this database.
- Create a new Customers table. Include fields for contact information, assuming that many of the customers are couples, so the information about names and cell phone numbers needs to be listed separately for each individual. Include fields to record the minimum number of bedrooms and bathrooms the couple wants. Finally, include information about which communities the couple wants to live in.
- Determine which fields should be required, how large each field should be, and what type of data you should define.
- Create a multivalued lookup for the subdivision.
- Create input masks for the phone numbers.
- Create a form that will facilitate data entry. Arrange the form logically and attractively. Add at least two action buttons to simplify the form's use. Test the form by populating at least one record.
- Submit your file to your instructor for evaluation. Compact and repair the database file.

Data Validity

Your friend e-mailed you a fun Web quiz that claims to measure your love of chocolate. After answering all of the questions, you submit your answers. Before you can learn your score, a pop-up window opens that asks you to log in or join as a new user of the free service. Because you have no account, you click the new-user link. A form containing many questions appears, requiring you to type answers in little boxes. You fill out your name, e-mail, password, birth date, gender, and education. As you enter your birth date, you receive an error message telling you that you need to format your birth date as MMDDYYYY. You fix the birth date and click the Submit button. The boxes return with the daytime phone box (which you missed) and an error message saying, "We're sorry, you need to provide your daytime phone number." You type your phone number, resubmit, and wonder if you will ever find out your chocolate love score. Perhaps you receive another error message about neglecting to provide your state. Eventually, you create an account, log in to it, and receive your score.

In completing the new-user information profile, you interacted with a database form over the Internet. The form refused to accept any answers until you answered all of the required questions and submitted your answers in a predetermined format. The software provided you with hints about what you did wrong and instructions about how to fix your data. Eventually, you and everyone else taking the chocolate lovers quiz provide the Web site with organized data. All of the records contain a daytime phone number; all of the birth dates are formatted identically. You found out how much you love chocolate, and the Web site owner collected demographic and psychographic information about you.

In this section, you explore establishing safeguards on table data to protect it from data-entry and user error. As you acquire these skills you shift from being the data user to becoming the individual in the organization who administers, manages, and protects the organization's data.

Establishing Data Validity

You already know about GIGO—Garbage In Garbage Out. No organization's management can make decisions unless they are able to trust the source data. Good data management practices include data validation as a critical component of the data systems. ***Data validation*** is a set of constraints or rules that help control the type and accuracy of the data entered into a field. Access provides some data validation automatically. For example, you cannot enter text into a numerically defined field or type a primary key value that duplicates another record's primary key value. Access supports the following data validation methods that help ensure the integrity of data by defending the data against user errors:

Data validation is a set of constraints or rules that help control the type and accuracy of the data entered into a field.

- **Required**—Sets the required property of a field to force data entry, such as a daytime phone number.
- **Default Values**—Specifies the default property of a field to automatically enter a specific value. For example, if most of your organization's donors live in North Carolina, you can set the default value of the state field to NC. The data entry operator can overwrite the default value with a different state abbreviation when needed.
- **Validation Rule**—Limits the type of text a user can enter into a field. For example, if all of your school's course numbers are larger than 100, then you could establish a validation rule to prohibit values under 100 on a registration form.
- **Validation Text**—Provides the error message telling users what they did wrong and gives them instructions on what they need to do to fix it. For example, the validation text for the rule violation above might be, "You have entered an invalid course number. Please recheck the number and enter a value greater than 100."
- **Lookup Lists**—Specifies the field values be limited to a predefined drop-down list of values. For example, class status in a university's database might be Freshman, Sophomore, Junior, Senior, Graduate, or Other.

- **Multiple Value Fields**—Accepts several different field values in a single record. For example, a single employee might be assigned to work on several different projects concurrently.
- **Input Masks**—Uses non-stored characters to force conformity on the data entered. For Example, a Social Security number (SSN) field might be entered and stored as 123456789. However, what the data entry operator sees on the screen is 123-45-6789. The hyphens do not need to be typed, nor are they stored with the entered data.
- **Logical**—Compares values in two fields and establishes rules governing their interaction. For example, a university database might have fields storing the enrollment and graduation dates for each student. To help prevent data entry errors, you might create a rule that the graduation date value must be larger than the enrollment date value.

Establish Required and Default Field Values

A required field is one that cannot be blank when you create a new record. You have already learned about setting the required property of a field. All primary keys must be required fields for the relational power of the database to work. The default Required setting is No for all the remaining fields, which enables you to create a record with missing data in those fields. However, to ensure the integrity of a database table, you should require that data be entered for critical fields. With the table open in Design view, click in the top half of the grid to select the field you need to require. Then switch to the Field Properties grid in the lower section of the Design view, click the Required property drop-down arrow, and select Yes (see Figure 6.1). When you create a new record or modify an existing record, you must enter data into the required field.

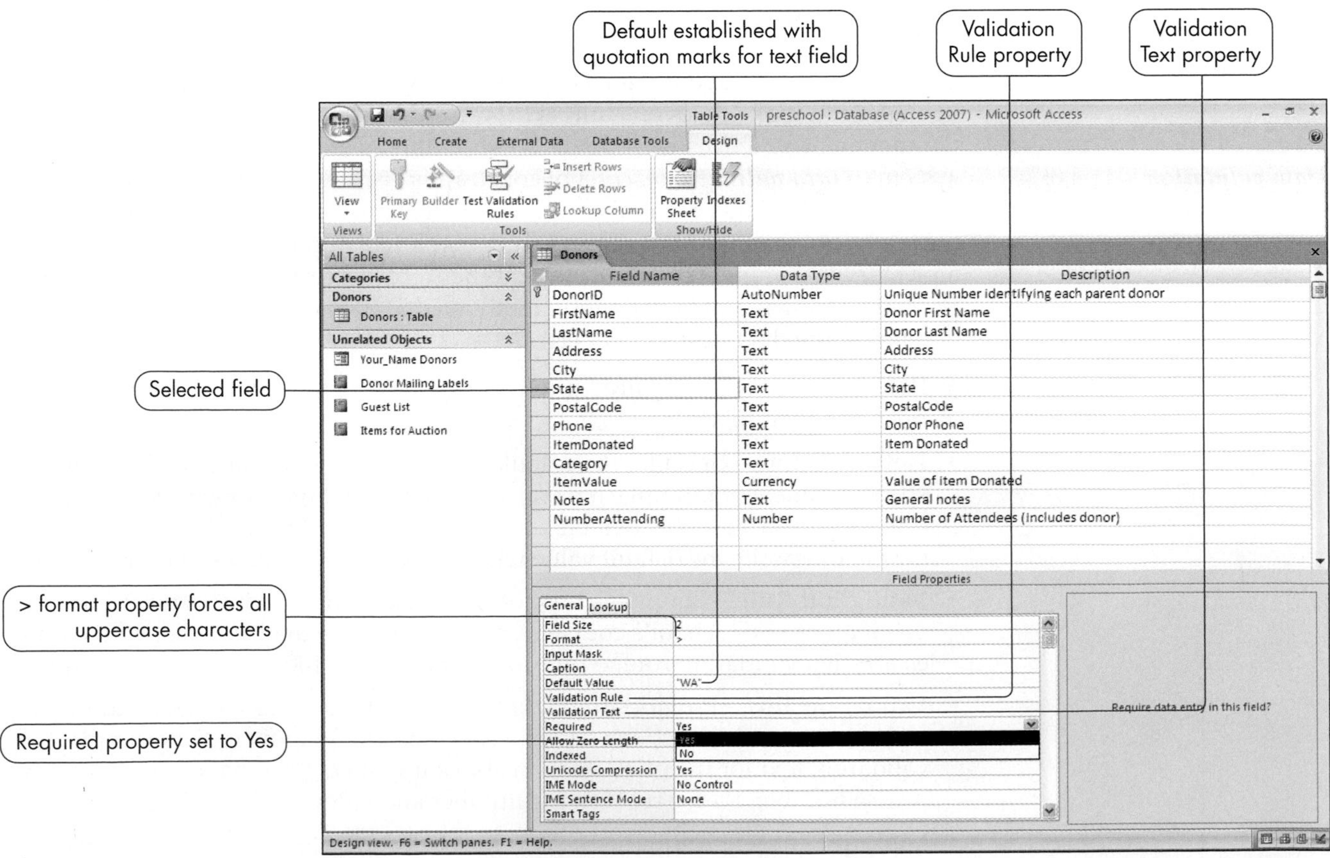

Figure 6.1 Required and Default Properties

TIP Existing Blank Fields Value

If you set the Required property to Yes after data has already been entered in a table, you see the message *Data integrity rules have been changed; existing data may not be valid for the new rules. This process may take a long time. Do you want the existing data to be tested with the new rules?* If you click Yes, you will be prompted to keep the new required setting, revert to the old optional setting, or to stop testing the existing data for the requirement. However, keeping the required setting does not indicate *which* records do not contain the required field. To find existing records that contain empty values for a particular field, you can sort the table by that field in Datasheet view. Records with empty values for the sorted field appear at the top of the sorted table.

When a majority of new records you add contain a common element, such as the same city or state, you can set a default value for that field to reduce data-entry time. You establish a field's default property by selecting the field in the table's Design view in the top part of the grid and then clicking the Default Value property in the Field Properties grid in the lower part of the window. For example, the South Vancouver Pre-school's donors primarily live in Washington. Figure 6.1 displays the default value of the State field set to *WA*. You may enter different two-character state abbreviations when necessary, but the presumption is that the majority of donors live in Washington.

TIP Current Date Default Value

You can enter Date() in the Default Value box to retrieve the current computer date and use it as the default value in a date field. When you create a new record, Access inserts the current date in the date field for the new record.

Set a Validation Rule and Generate Validation Text

A ***validation rule*** is a restriction that specifies which values are allowed in a field.

A ***validation rule*** is a restriction that specifies that data entered in a field are allowed; data that do not meet the restriction are prevented from being stored in a particular field. For most data types, you can enter one validation rule by specifying an expression in the Validation Rule property. For example, you can type >0 in the Validation Rule property to ensure that only values greater than zero are entered.

When you break a validation rule, you must provide Access with the required information in the desired format before you can move on. You have probably experienced frustration when filling out a data form on a Web site and not being able to move to the next task without knowing why. Good database design not only protects the data by using validation but also tells the user when a rule has been violated and what is needed to fix the situation. Access helps you communicate by entering error message text in the Validation Text property in the Field Properties grid. You use ***validation text*** to inform users about what they have done incorrectly and instruct them about what they need to do to correct the problem. Examples of good validation text messages might be *Please enter a daytime phone number* or *The birth date needs to be formatted using the MMDDYYYY form of data entry.* Enter the rule and text in the respective properties in the Field Properties grid, as shown in Figure 6.1.

Validation text informs users about what they have done incorrectly and instructs them about what needs to be done.

TIP Validation Rule Violations

If you add a validation rule to an already populated table, you may violate your own rule because records with inappropriate values may be stored in the table. Access warns you if existing table data violate the newly established rule. You can remove the rule, switch to Datasheet view, find and correct the rule violators, and then return to Design view and reapply the rule.

You may choose to employ different layers of validation. For example, suppose you were developing a table or form for each academic department to use to enter the courses they plan on offering during the summer. You could add a validation rule that forces the course number to fall between 100 and 599 for undergraduate classes: >=100 and <= 599. If a department head attempts to enter 650 for a class that should be 560, he or she receives an error message and a prompt suggesting a method to fix the problem. Simply having a validation rule does not prevent users from skipping the field. Unless you set the Required property to Yes, having a validation rule will not force data entry for the field. Generally, if a field is important enough to require validation, it is also important enough to insist on data entry.

Creating and Modifying a Lookup Field

A ***lookup field*** provides a predefined list of values from which to select.

Good database planning identifies the database fields containing repetitive data and designs the table and form structure to facilitate the data entry. If all of the donated items are classified as a product, service, gift certificate, or other, then it makes life easier to limit data entry options to a drop-down list. Whoever does the data entry will have their choices limited to the appropriate category. This will help ensure uniformity and consistency during data entry. A ***lookup field*** provides the user with a predefined list of values to select, which decreases the amount of time for entering data. Frequently, the values that need to be entered in one table have already been stored as a related field in a different table. For example, if all payments are limited to cash, check, credit, or other online payment methods, data entry will be faster and more accurate when clicking and selecting from a list option is available.

The ***Lookup Wizard*** helps create, populate, and relate the lookup field.

Suppose the field might contain only three values, Cash, Credit, or Check. If the data entry operators were typing, they might misspell Credit as Credir or Cerdit. Then, a query set to return all of the purchases made using Credit last month would not include some of the necessary records. The mistyped values would not be selected in the query. Perhaps that query will be used to generate the bills to send to the customer. If the query did not select the record, no request for payment will be sent. Data entry errors add costs to the organization. They add costs because the information they generate is wrong and the decisions made based on the misinformation will also be wrong. Errors add costs because the organization needs to hire someone to find and fix the errors. And finally, incorrect data may lead to poor customer service and result in the loss of a customer. If the database table or form used for data entry contains a lookup field with pre-specified (and correctly typed) values of Cash, Credit, or Check, the chance of data entry error reduces. The lookup will not prevent a data entry misclassification of a Cash sale as a Credit one, but it will prevent misspelling the word Credit. Access provides a Lookup Wizard to help you establish the lookup column and values. The ***Lookup Wizard*** helps create the lookup field, populates the appropriate values, and if needed, establishes the necessary table relationships.

TIP Three Ways to Launch the Lookup Wizard

If your table or form is open in Datasheet view, you may launch the Lookup Wizard by clicking Lookup Column in the Fields & Columns group on the Datasheet tab. Alternatively, you can open the Field List pane by clicking Add Existing Fields in the Fields & Columns group on the Datasheet tab. Click the plus sign to view all of the fields in the selected table, identify the field that will serve as the lookup source, drag it to the Datasheet view, and drop it when you see the insertion line. From this point, follow the remaining steps in the Lookup Wizard. Finally, you may open the destination table in Design view and activate the field that you want to make into a lookup in the Field Name column. If it is a newly created field, you must select the data type in the Data Type column. Type the name of the field, and then click into the Data Type column and select Lookup Wizard.

Create the Lookup Field

Suppose the South Vancouver Pre-school's auction categorizes donations as Service, Products, Gift Certificates, and Other. Because these values do not exist anywhere in the database, you would create a new table, Categories, and populate the Category field with four records containing the appropriate values. Then you would create Category as a foreign field in the Donors table. Figure 6.2 illustrates the Donor table in Design view with the Data Type column of the Category field set to launch the Lookup Wizard. Although you can simply type the values into a list using the Lookup Wizard, it is not recommended. It can create problems later when you run queries or reports that are query-based. Having a separate table to look up values also means that you can establish referential integrity between the tables. This uses the database power to protect queried results. Using a lookup list violates the rules of good database design.

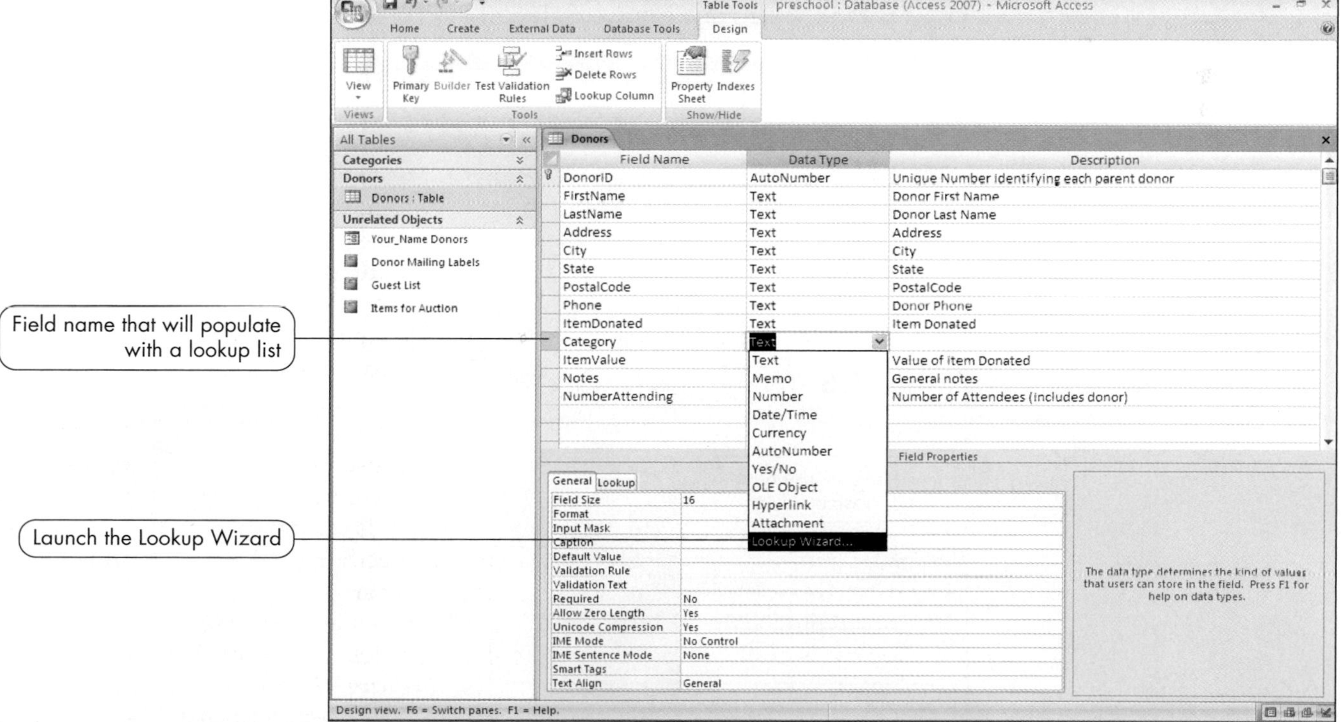

Figure 6.2 Launch the Lookup Wizard

The first screen in the Lookup Wizard asks that you identify the source data. Figure 6.3 shows the Categories table selection. The next screen asks you to select the field or fields for the lookup column (see Figure 6.4). Next, the wizard asks that you specify a sort order for the list box (see Figure 6.5). The next screen asks you to establish the column width for the lookup column. You want to make it wide enough to display the longest value, but not so wide that it obscures the rest of the form or table in which it is used (see Figure 6.6). You make width adjustments by moving your mouse over the right column boundary, and when the pointer changes to the double-headed arrow, click and drag to the appropriate width. Figure 6.7 shows the name of the lookup field and gives you a choice of single (default) or multiple values. Most lookups will not need a multiple value. Figure 6.8 shows a category being selected from the populated lookup field in Datasheet view.

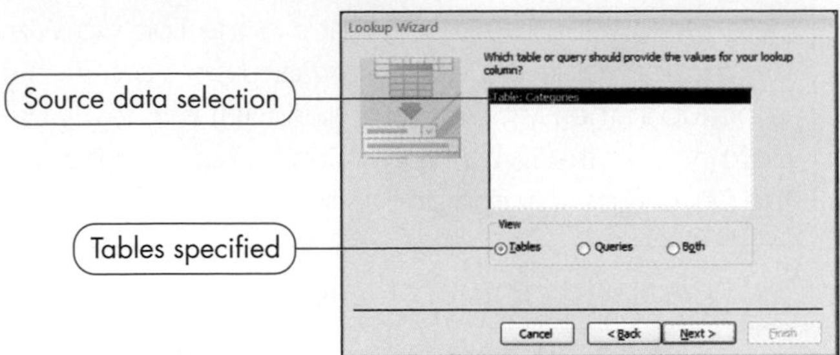

Figure 6.3 Lookup Column Data Source Specification

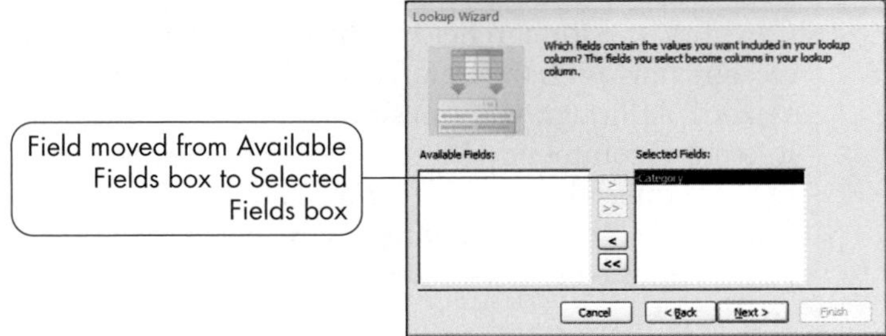

Figure 6.4 Select the Necessary Field(s)

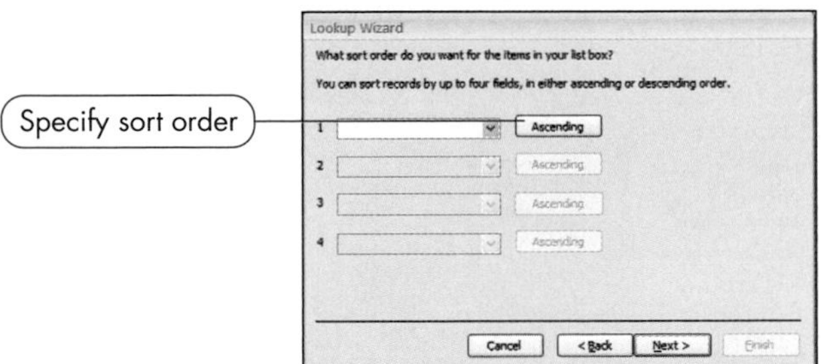

Figure 6.5 Lookup Column Sort Order

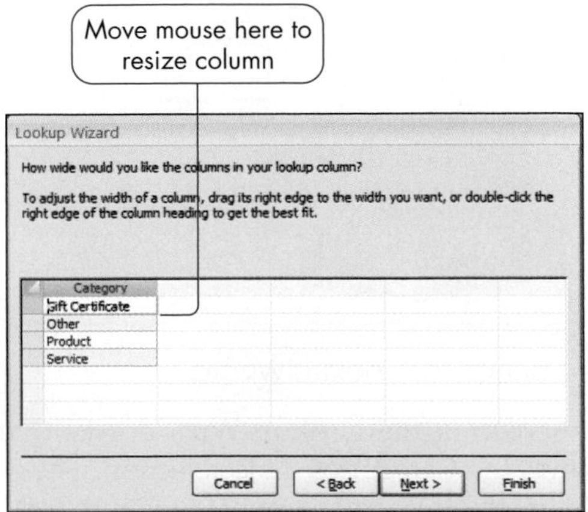

Figure 6.6 Column Width Adjustment

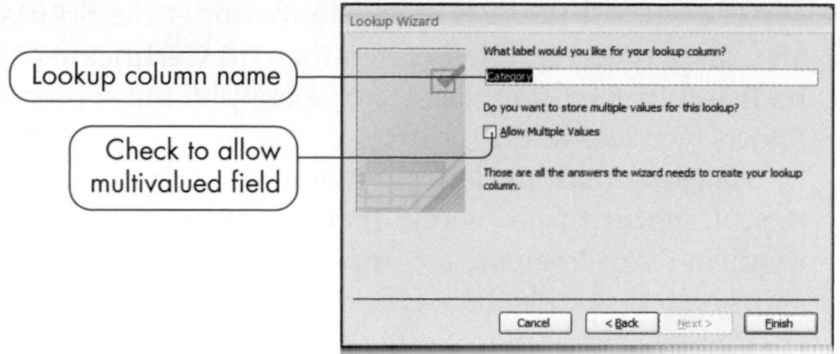

Figure 6.7 Name Specification

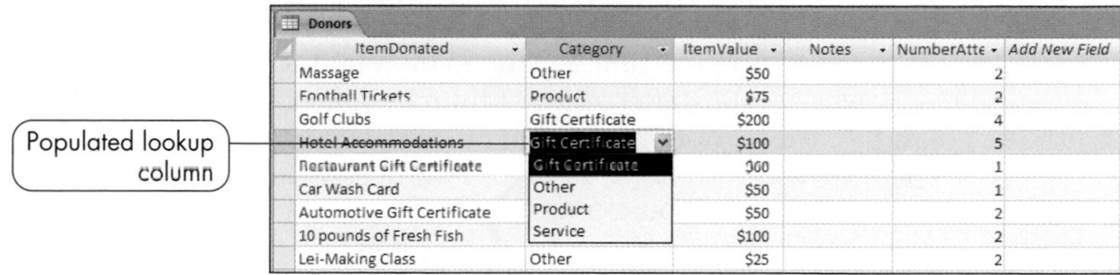

Figure 6.8 Lookup Column in Use

Modify a Lookup by Adding and Deleting Values

Data needs change. You can edit, delete, or add values to the lookup field to accommodate changed data needs. For example, the school workers cataloging the auction donations complain that the categories are too restrictive. They want the Other category removed from the lookup column list and the Service category changed to be Personal Service and Sports Services. You agree to make the necessary changes. You begin changing a lookup column by identifying the source of the lookup data. These lookup data are stored in the Category table. You need to open the Category table, delete Other, and add (or edit) Personal Service and Sports Services. Move off the record and close the Category table. As soon as the changes are made, the new lookup values are available for use in the lookup column in the Donors table (see Figure 6.9). Someone would need to go through the table data and reclassify all of the former other categories.

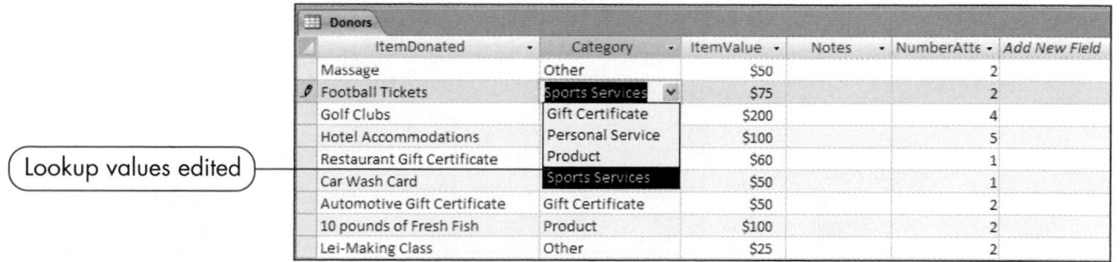

Figure 6.9 Edited Lookup Column in Use

Creating and Modifying a Multivalued Lookup Field

Often, data do not fit easily into narrowly defined classifications. For example, you have Sports Services and Gift Certificate categories. Would you classify the donation of golf lessons as Sports Services or Gift Certificate? Once the Donors table is populated with hundreds of items, it will become difficult for prospective bidders at the auction to find the items on which they wish to bid. The event chair plans on publishing auction lists by category to help bidders find items. However, the existing classification system will list the golf lessons only under the Sports Services category. You want to also display the golf lessons in the Gift Certificate category. Other items should also be listed in two categories. For example, the football tickets should be classified as Sports Services and Product.

A ***multivalued field*** is one defined to accept multiple choices for a single field.

These situations describe a need for a database that will support multiple choices. A ***multivalued field*** is one that accepts multiple choices for a single field without requiring you to create a complex design. You have worked in one-to-many relationships between table data. One customer ID can show up on multiple orders, but many customers cannot place a single order. These situations describe events that should be structurally designed in a many-to-many relationship. Access 2007 provides a way to do this. By checking the Allow Multiple Values check box in the appropriate Lookup Wizard (see Figure 6.7), you produce a field that accepts multiple values. Figure 6.10 shows the results of a field with multiple values in the first record. The values display in the table separated by commas. The second record displays the Category Field List box after Allow Multiple Values was selected. The user specifies one or more categories by checking the appropriate check boxes.

(Access works hard so that you do not need to.)

These steps are deceptively simple. Access works hard so that you do not need to. Access creates a succession of hidden system tables and the affiliated relationships for them. It appears as though you are working with a single field. Under the surface, Access creates a series of juncture tables and stores them independently.

TIP When Not to Use a Multivalued Lookup Field

Most databases (including earlier versions of Access) could not do multivalued fields—or at least not do them easily. If a possibility exists that your database will start its life in an Access environment and eventually migrate to a larger, SQL-based environment, you should not create any multivalued fields. Using them violates the basic premise of the relational model in database design. A multivalued field will not export to a SQL environment because it cannot function in a relational environment with rigidly enforced referential integrity. The database administrator cannot accurately predict the results of queries or query-based reports when the parameter field is multivalued.

Figure 6.10 Multivalued Field Specifications

Working with Input Masks

An ***input mask*** specifies the exact formatting of the input data while minimizing data storage.

Designing databases well requires that the designers anticipate how the users will interact with and populate the tables. Good designers facilitate data entry and minimize the required storage space in their databases. An ***input mask*** specifies the exact formatting of the input data while minimizing data storage requirements. For example, you are used to viewing (and thinking about) Social Security numbers with hyphens (e.g., 123-45-6789) and telephone numbers with parentheses and hyphens, such as (405) 555-1234. In a database with thousands of records, the parentheses and hyphens consume unnecessary storage space, take time for data entry operators to type, and may interfere with sorting the data. The parentheses and hyphens add value and help data users understand the information stored in the data with greater accuracy. People need them, but the computer does not. Because people in the United States are accustomed to seeing the Social Security number with the hyphens in place, you can create an input mask to display the data with the hyphens in position but store and use the data in a "hyphenless" format. In the case of the phone number, the input mask also serves as a prompt to the data entry operator to remember to enter the area code as well as the seven-digit phone number. It also helps ensure consistency in data entry. Different data entry operators might enter a phone number in a variety of ways, such as (810) 555-2222, 801-555-2222, or with the international form, 810.555.2222. Good database design anticipates and eliminates inconsistent data input. You may use the Input Mask Wizard or create a customized input mask.

Use the Input Mask Wizard

The ***Input Mask Wizard*** helps generate and test masks.

The ***Input Mask Wizard*** helps generate and test masks so you spend less time creating and correcting data masks. You launch the Input Mask Wizard by opening the table in Design view and activating the field you want to mask in the top portion of the Design grid. Click the Input Mask property in the Field Properties grid. After you click in the Input Mask property, click Builder in the Tools group on the Design tab or click Build on the right side of the Input Mask property (see Figure 6.11) to launch the Input Mask Wizard. Specify settings in the Input Mask dialog box. Figure 6.12 shows the first screen in the Input Mask Wizard dialog box. In this step, you select or edit an existing mask.

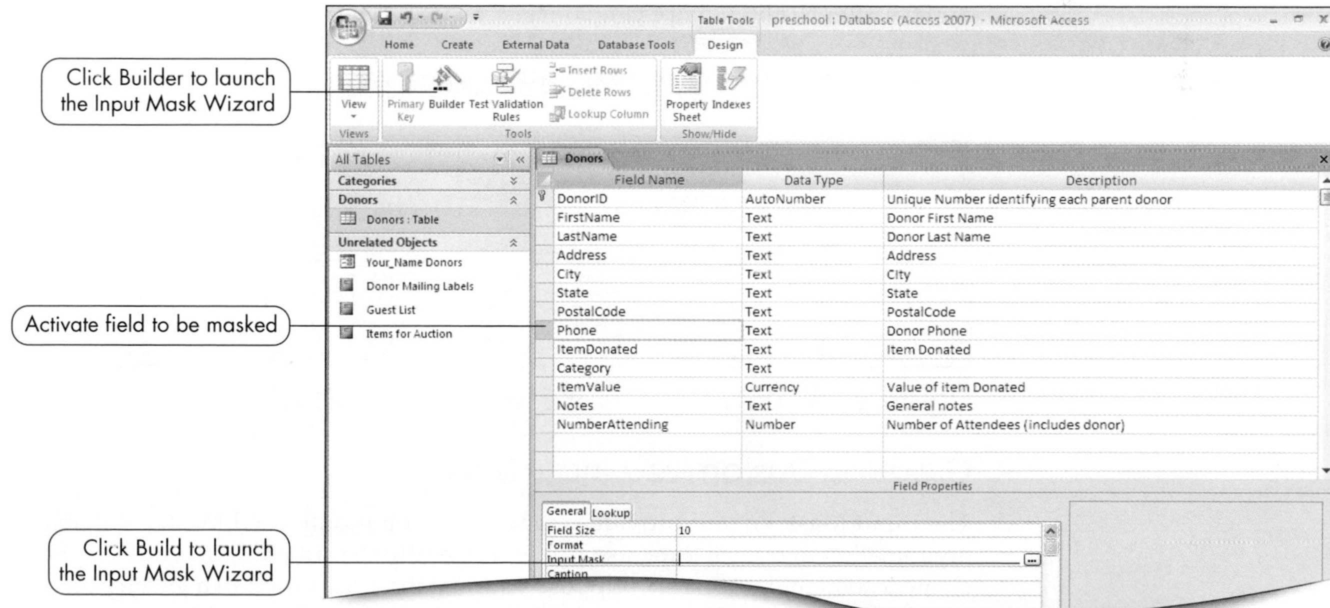

Figure 6.11 Launching the Input Mask Wizard

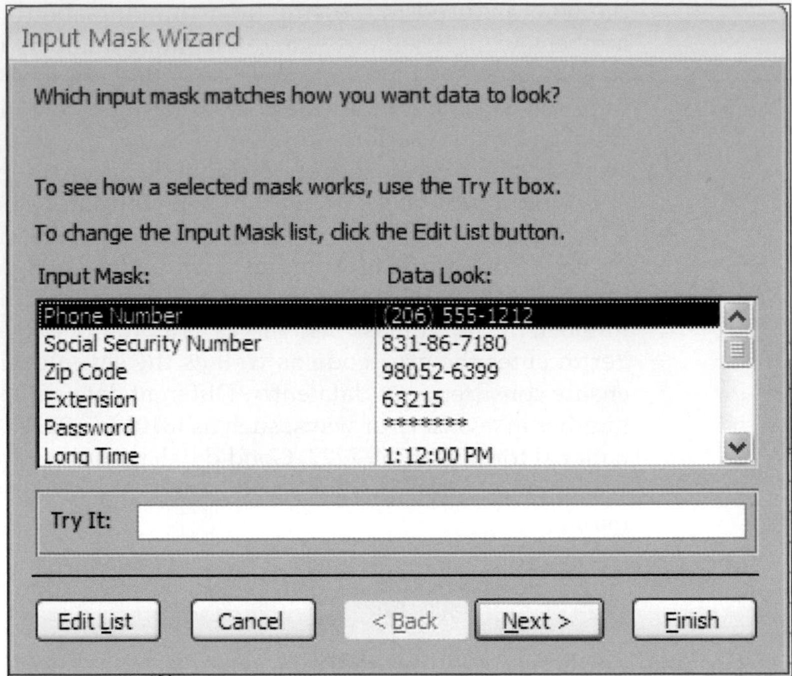

Figure 6.12 Input Mask Wizard

The second step in the Input Mask Wizard enables you to select a placeholder character, such as an underscore (_) or a pound sign (#), to display in the field in Datasheet view until you type the data. The last step enables you to specify if you want the symbols, such as the parentheses and hyphens, to be stored with the data. After you apply the mask, the correct syntax !(999) 000-0000;;_ appears in the Input Mask property. This mask prompts the data entry operator to enter an area code with each phone number entered in the database table or form (see Figure 6.13). The underscore placeholder appears for each digit as you type the phone number.

Data displayed with mask placeholder character

Phone numbers appear in same format

Donors

Donor	FirstNam	LastName	Address	City	S	PostalCo	Phone	ItemDonated	ItemValue
1	Shelly	Martin	123 North Street	Vancouver	WA	98664-	(360) 555-1000	Massage	$
2	Kelly	Kripton	456 North Street	Vancouver	WA	98664-	(9) ___-____	Football Tickets	$
3	Kim	Jansen	678 North Street	Cascade Park	WA	98684-	(360) 555-1002	Golf Clubs	$2
4	Donna	Reed	901 North Street	Woodland	WA	98674-	(360) 555-1003	Hotel Accomodations	$1
5	Huong	Pham	P.O. Box ABC	Vancouver	WA	98664-	(360) 555-1004	Restaurant Gift Certificate	$
6	George	Martin	555 Kaminini Street	Vancouver	WA	98664-	(360) 555-1005	Car Wash Card	$
7	Marion	McMahon	2216 Catharine Street	Vancouver	WA	98664-	(360) 555-1006	Automotive Gift Certificate	$
8	Catherine	McQuaide	31 Oakmont Circle	Cascade Park	WA	98684-	(360) 555-1007	10 pounds of Fresh Fish	$1
9	Christopher	Martinez	15709 Holly Grove Rd.	Cascade Park	WA	98684-	(360) 555-1008	Lei-Making Class	$
10	G	Mican	3509 Carla Drive	Woodland	WA	98674-	(360) 555-1009	Starbucks Gift Card	$
11	George	McFall	123 North Street	Woodland	WA	98674-	(360) 555-1010	Movie Tickets + Popcorn	$
12	Kristen	Kripton	456 North Street	Cascade Park	WA	98684-	(360) 555-1011	Free Photography Sitting	$

Figure 6.13 Datasheet View of a Field with an Input Mask

Create a Customized Input Mask

The Input Mask Wizard provides many of the commonly used masks. Because each organization and each database needs differently described data, you may need to create a custom input mask. Suppose your database was used in a jewelry store. The items in inventory all begin with FJ (Fall's Jewelers), followed by two characters describing the item type (WA–watch, RI–ring, BR–bracelet, etc.), followed by a five-digit inventory number. FA-RI-02345 might identify an emerald ring. The mask would be !"FJ-">AA"-"00000.

The exclamation point forces the data input to move from left to right. The "FJ-" is a character literal. All inventory numbers will begin with what is enclosed in the hyphens, in this case, FJ. The greater than symbol (>) in the mask converts whatever is typed to uppercase characters. Using it will mean that the data entry operators do not need to press Shift on the keyboard to produce uppercase letters. The next part is another character literal to produce the next hyphen. Finally, a five-digit identification number is mandatory. The data entry operator types ri02345, and Access displays FA-RI-02345. Table 6.1 describes the characters and uses of input mask codes.

Table 6.1 Some Common Input Mask Characters and Uses

Character	Description	Requires Entry
0	Digit (0 to 9) Plus + and Minus – not allowed	Yes
9	Digit or space Plus + and Minus – not allowed	No
#	Digit or Space Plus + and Minus – allowed Spaces display as blanks but are not stored	No
L	Letter (A to Z)	Yes
?	Letter (A to Z)	No
A	Letter (A to Z)	Yes
a	Letter (A to Z)	No
<	Converts all characters entered to lowercase letters	No
>	Converts all characters entered to uppercase letters	No
\	Turns the next character into a literal \(displays (\Q displays Q	No
.(period)	Decimal placeholder	No
- or /	Date separators Jun-5-2008 or 6/5/2008	No
!	Forces the value to be input from left to right	Not Applicable

In the first hands-on exercise, you will use Access features that help protect data from data entry errors, facilitate the data entry process, and ensure that the decision makers have all of the data necessary to answer their questions. You will create field properties that require information, notify data entry operators of rule violations, simplify data entry, and prompt data entry operators to enter data in the desired format.

Hands-On Exercises

1 | Data Protection

Skills covered: 1. Establish Required and Default Field Properties **2.** Create and Test Validation Rules and Text **3.** Create a Lookup Field **4.** Modify a Lookup Field Value **5.** Create a Multivalued Lookup Field **6.** Create and Edit Input Masks

Step 1
Establish Required and Default Field Properties

Refer to Figure 6.14 as you complete Step 1.

a. Use Windows Explorer to locate the file named *chap6_ho1-3_nationalbank.accdb*. Copy the file to your production folder and rename the copied file as **chap6_ho1-3_nationalbank_solution.accdb**.

b. Open *chap6_ho1-3_nationalbank_solution.accdb* and click **Options** on the Security Warning toolbar, click **Enable this content** in the Microsoft Office Security Options dialog box, and click **OK**.

c. Rename the *Your_Name Loan Payment* query with your name.

d. Open the **Customers table** in Datasheet view and replace *Your_Name* in the First Name and Last Name fields with your name.

e. Right-click the **Customers tab** and select **Design View** from the shortcut menu.

f. In the top portion of the table Design grid, click in the **PhoneNumber** field to select it. In the Field Properties grid, click in the **Required** property. Click the **drop-down arrow** on the right of the Required property, and then select **Yes** from the list.

   You changed the data entry process so that a phone number is required for each customer.

g. In the top portion of the table Design grid, click in the **AccountType** field to select it. In the Field Properties grid, click in the **Default Value** property and type **Gold**. Press **Enter**.

   As soon as you click outside the Default Value property, Access adds quotation marks around the default property because it is a text string. Because most of the bank's customers are Gold level accounts, you set the default value to display the most frequently occurring field value. You need to test the changes you made to the table design.

h. Click **Save** on the Quick Access Toolbar. If you get a warning about testing the data integrity rules, click **Yes**. Right-click the **Customers tab** and select **Datasheet View** from the shortcut menu. Because this is a small database, testing the data integrity will not take a long time.

   Look at the new record row. The AccountType field has already been entered as Gold.

i. Create a new record. Type **Aaron**, **Thomasson**, **409 Cook Road**, **Stoneboro**, **PA**, **16137**, in the appropriate fields. When you get to the Phone Number field, skip it and type **Platinum** in the **AccountType** field.

j. Click into a different record. An error message appears, reminding you that you must enter a value in the Customers.PhoneNumber field. Click **OK** and type **7245551212**. Close the Customers table.

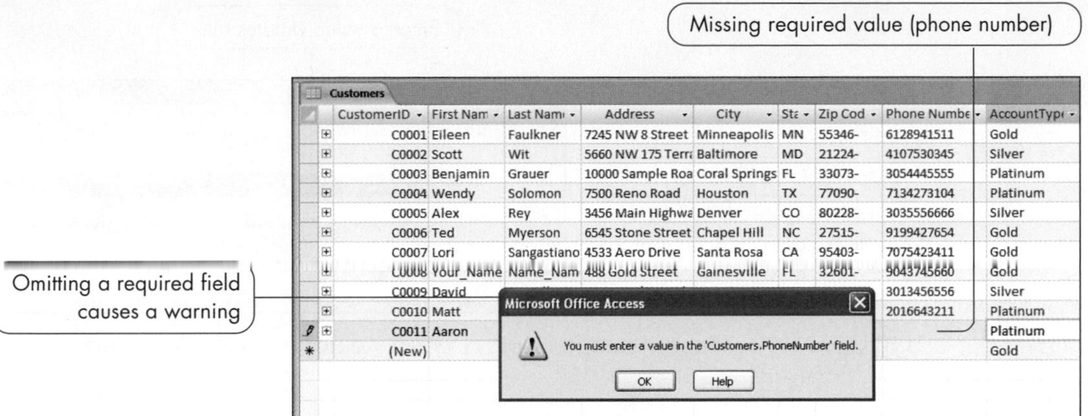
Missing required value (phone number)
Omitting a required field causes a warning
Microsoft Office Access
You must enter a value in the 'Customers.PhoneNumber' field.
OK
Help

Figure 6.14 Data Validation

Step 2
Create and Test Validation Rules and Text

Refer to Figure 6.15 as you complete Step 2.

a. Right-click the **Loans table** in the All Tables pane and select **Design View** from the shortcut menu.

b. Click the **InterestRate** field on the top of the Design grid.

c. Click in the **Validation Rule** property in the Field Properties grid.

   You will establish a rule that notifies data entry operators if they attempt to enter an interest rate that is greater than an acceptable boundary. Notice that an ellipsis button appears at the right of the property row. If the validation rule is complicated, you can launch the Expression Builder and use it to establish correct syntax. This rule is simple, and you do not need to use the Builder.

d. Type **<0.25** in the Validation Rule property box.

e. Click in the **Validation Text** property and type **The interest rate you entered is too high. Enter this value as a decimal, e.g. type .055 to enter 5.5%.**

   When a data entry operator enters an interest rate that is too high, a message will appear, giving guidance about what needs to be done differently.

f. Save the design changes. Read the message about changed data integrity rules. Click **Yes**. Right-click the **Loans tab** and select **Datasheet View** from the shortcut menu.

   Access tests the data in the table to make sure that none of the interest rates are too high.

g. Click in the **InterestRate** field of the first record. Edit the value by typing **.26**. Press **Enter**.

   You should receive an error message containing the validation text you typed in Step 2e.

h. Read the message. Click **OK** in the error message box. Edit the first record to display **.062** for the interest rate field. Press **Enter**.

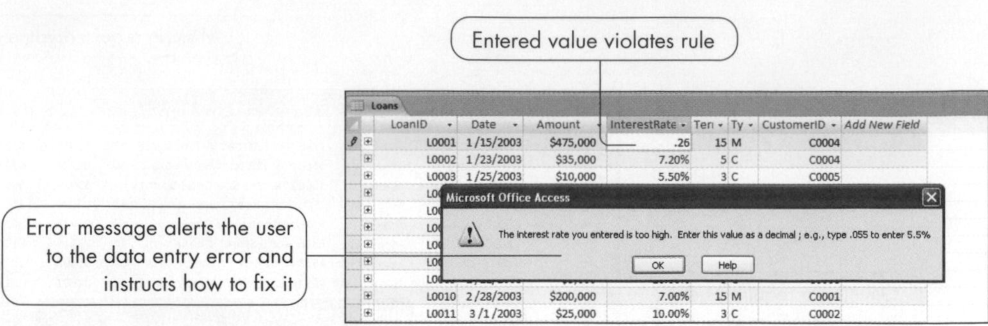

Figure 6.15 Error Message Displays when Validation Rule Is Violated

Step 3
Create a Lookup Field

Refer to Figure 6.16 as you complete Step 3.

a. Click the **Datasheet tab** and click **Lookup Column** in the Fields & Columns group.

   The Lookup Wizard launches.

b. Verify that the **I want the lookup column to look up the values in a table or query** option is selected. Click **Next**.

c. Click the **Table: LoanTypes** and click **Next**.

d. Click the **LoanName** field in the Available Fields box to select it. Click the **Move to Selected Fields button** to move the field to the Selected Fields box. Click **Next**.

   You decide that the ascending sort order meets your needs.

e. Click **Next**. Make sure that the **Hide key column (recommended) check box** is selected. Adjust the column width by moving your mouse over the LoanName column heading's right boundary. When the mouse pointer shape changes to a two-headed arrow, click and drag right about one-fourth inch. Click **Next**.

f. Name the lookup column **LoanType**. Click **Finish**. Click in the first record of the LoanType field. Click the **arrow** and select **Mortgage**. Press **Enter**. The next record is a car loan. Type **C**. Press **Enter**. Use the Type column as a reference to populate the LoanType field for the rest of the records.

   A new column, LoanType, has been added. If you had the InterestRate field active at the end of Step 2, the new column inserts to the left of the interest rate column.

   TROUBLESHOOTING: It does not matter where the Loan type column appears in your file. It only matters that it has been created. If necessary, switch to Design view and reorder the fields to match the order in Figure 6.16.

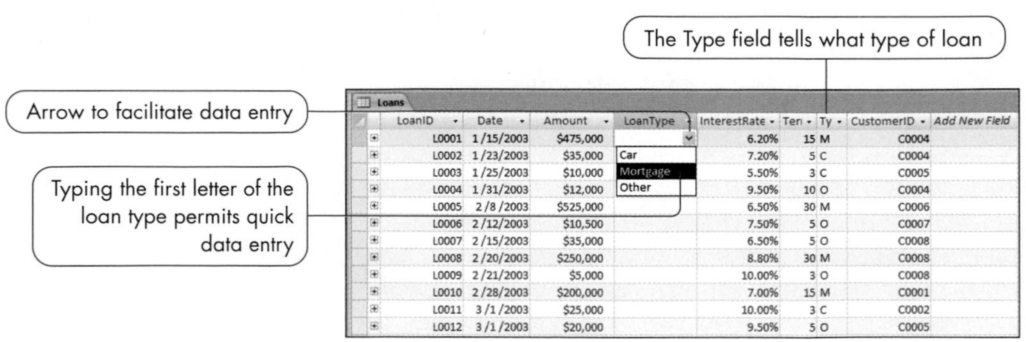

Figure 6.16 A Lookup Column

Step 4
Modify a Lookup Field Value

Refer to Figure 6.17 as you complete Step 4.

a. Open the **LoanTypes** table in Datasheet view.

b. Click in the **LoanName** field in the third record, Other, to select it. Type **Personal** and press **Enter**.

You decide that the Other loan category would be more professional if named Personal.

c. Close the LoanTypes table.

The Loans table should still be open in Datasheet view. If it is not, open it.

d. Examine the data in the LoanType field.

The word Other no longer appears. It has been replaced with Personal. You wonder why the changes in the LoanType table change the Loans table. You decide to do some research.

e. Click the **Database Tools tab** and click **Relationships** in the Show/Hide group.

The Relationships window displays a relationship between the Loans and LoanType table. Access created the relationship for you as you worked through the Lookup Wizard.

f. Close the Relationships window.

All Other loans display as Personal

Other disappears from the list

Loans

LoanID	Date	Amount	LoanType	InterestRate	Ten	Ty	CustomerID	Add New Field
L0001	1/15/2003	$475,000	Mortgage	6.20%	15	M	C0004	
L0002	1/23/2003	$35,000	Car	7.20%	5	C	C0004	
L0003	1/25/2003	$10,000	Car	5.50%	3	C	C0005	
L0004	1/31/2003	$12,000	Personal	9.50%	10	O	C0004	
L0005	2/8/2003	$525,000	Car	6.50%	30	M	C0006	
L0006	2/12/2003	$10,500	Mortgage	7.50%	5	O	C0007	
L0007	2/15/2003	$35,000	Personal	6.50%	5	O	C0008	
L0008	2/20/2003	$250,000	Mortgage	8.80%	30	M	C0008	
L0009	2/21/2003	$5,000	Personal	10.00%	3	O	C0008	
L0010	2/28/2003	$200,000	Car	7.00%	15	M	C0001	
L0011	3/1/2003	$25,000	Car	10.00%	3	C	C0002	
L0012	3/1/2003	$20,000	Personal	9.50%	5	O	C0005	
L0013	3/3/2003	$56,000	Mortgage	7.50%	5	C	C0009	
L0014	3/10/2003	$129,000	Mortgage	8.50%	15	M	C0010	
L0015	3/11/2003	$200,000	Mortgage	7.25%	15	M	C0003	
L0016	3/21/2003	$150,000	Mortgage	7.50%	15	M	C0001	
L0017	3/22/2003	$100,000	Mortgage	7.00%	30	M	C0001	
L0018	3/31/2003	$15,000	Personal	6.50%	3	O	C0003	
L0019	4/1/2003	$10,000	Car	8.00%	5	C	C0002	

Figure 6.17 Edited Lookup Column

Step 5
Create a Multivalued Lookup Field

Refer to Figure 6.18 as you complete Step 5.

a. Right-click the **Loans tab** and select **Design View** from the shortcut menu.

b. Click the **LoanType** field in the Field Name list to select it. Click the **Lookup Tab** in the Field Properties grid.

Now that a Lookup column exists, you can modify its properties to make adjustments to it.

c. Click the **Allow Multiple Values** property to select it. Click the arrow on the right of the property box and select **Yes**. Click **Yes** in the warning box.

Access warns you that you will not be able to undo this change after the table is saved. You are sure about this change.

d. Save the changes to the design of the Loans table. Right-click the **Loans tab** and select **Datasheet View** from the shortcut menu.

e. Click the arrow in the first record of the LoanType field. Add a check to the **Car check box**. Click **OK**.

   You have identified that this loan is a mortgage that was also used to purchase a car. The new loan type displays as Car, Mortgage.

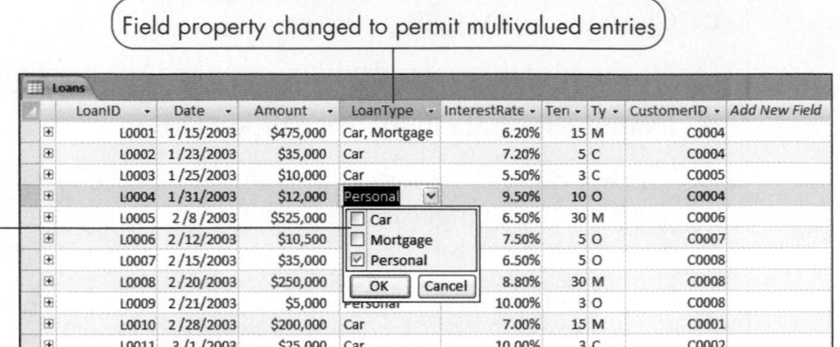

Figure 6.18 Expanded Information

Step 6
Create and Edit Input Masks

Refer to Figure 6.19 as you complete Step 6.

a. Open the **Customers table** in Design view.

b. Click the **PhoneNumber** field in the FieldName column.

c. Click the **Input Mask** property in the Field Properties grid to select it. Click **Build** on the right side of the Input Mask property box.

   This activates the Input Mask Wizard. The Phone Number input mask is already selected.

d. Click in the **Try It** box of the Input Mask Wizard dialog box. (___) ___-____ displays. Position the insertion point at the left edge and type **5556667777** to see if the mask displays the phone numbers as you want them displayed.

   TROUBLESHOOTING: You need to reposition the insertion point next to the open parentheses to make the number fit.

e. Click **Next**. You do not need to adjust the mask or the placeholder character, so click **Next** again.

f. Click the **With the symbols in the mask** option. Click **Next** and click **Finish**. Save the table, right-click the **Customers tab**, and select **Datasheet View** from the shortcut menu.

   The phone numbers display in an easier-to-read format. Parentheses enclose the area codes, and hyphens separate the prefix and suffix portions of the number. You worry that all of the extra characters will consume too much storage space and decide to edit the mask. The easiest edit method is to launch the Input Mask Wizard again.

g. Right-click the **Customers tab** and select **Design View** from the shortcut menu. Click **Build** on the right side of the Input Mask property box. Click **Next** twice.

h. Make sure that **Without the symbols in the mask** is selected and click **Finish**. Save the table, right-click the **Customers tab**, and select **Datasheet View** from the shortcut menu.

i. Click the **Office Button**, select **Manage**, and select **Compact and Repair Database**.

j. Click the **Office Button**, select **Manage**, and then select **Back Up Database**. Type **chap6_ho1_nationalbank_solution** and click **Save**.

You just created a backup of the database after completing the first hands-on exercise. The original database *chap6_ho1-3_nationalbank_solution* remains onscreen. If you ruin the original database as you complete the second hands-on exercise, you can use the backup file you just created.

k. Close the file and exit Access if you do not want to continue with the next exercise at this time.

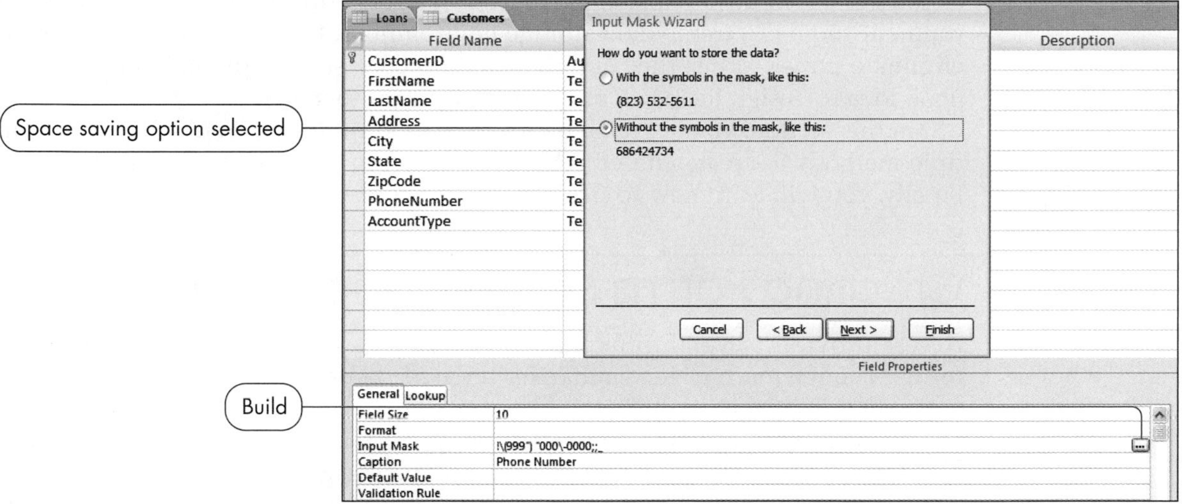

Figure 6.19 Input Mask Wizard Displaying Corrected Options

Forms

Although some data entry operators prefer entering data in the grids provided in Access tables because they find it to be quicker, most database data entry users and designers prefer forms for data entry control. Grid data entry speed may introduce errors. Especially in very long or wide tables, the data entry operators entering the data can accidentally change records in the middle of an edit. They correctly enter the data for the first five fields of the record, then jump to the previous row and overwrite existing data with values that belong in the next record. Now, two records have incorrect or incomplete data.

Typically, a form user sees only a single record at a time, so this eliminates the record-jumping problem. Using forms enables data entry to multiple tables concurrently. If a field in a record is stored as an object, like an Excel chart or a Word memo, viewing the record in a form will display the actual object. Viewing the same record in the Datasheet view of a table will display only an icon or text displaying the object's file name. Finally, forms may be designed to emulate the paper documents already in use in the organization. This facilitates the transition from the paper environment to an electronic data storage environment. Databases do not necessarily eliminate paper forms; they supplement and coexist with them. Therefore, it is a good idea to design the paper and electronic forms to match.

In this section, you learn the basics of good form design. You will discover multiple methods to create and edit Access forms. You will work with action buttons. Finally, you will learn how to create calculated controls.

Creating Forms by Using the Form Tool

Access provides several different methods of creating, editing, and embellishing forms. The reference page summarizes these methods. Once you create a form, you may edit and customize the form using either the Layout or Design views. Forms are almost never born fully functional. The designer creates a form, and the users test it and offer suggestions for its improvement. The designer adjusts the form and the users test it again. The collaborative design process between the database administrative and use staff continues throughout the life of the form. Because data needs in the organization change, forms designed long ago and used for years sometimes need to be redesigned. The form creation process provides the database administration staff a window into how the rest of the organization functions. It empowers the database users with the ability to alter the tools they use daily. Ideally, a form should simplify data entry. Form users may need access to only a few fields in a table that contains many. The form designer needs to strike a delicate balance between providing users access to everything they need to do their jobs without cluttering the form with extraneous fields. The users of the data know what they need and often offer detailed descriptions of what they want. By listening to their suggestions, your forms will function more effectively, the users' work will be easier, and your data will suffer fewer user-generated errors.

(Ideally, a form should simplify data entry.)

Form Creation Methods | Reference

Method	Location	Use
Form Tool	With a table or query open, Create Tab, Forms group	Creates a simple form displaying all of the fields in the source object.
Split Form Tool	With a table or query open, Create Tab, Forms group	Creates a two-part form that includes all of the source fields. In it, one view is a form displaying a single record and the other is a Datasheet view of the source object. The two views synchronize and edits made in either place update the other.
Multiple Items Tool	With a table or query open, Create Tab, Forms group	Creates a tabular form that includes all of the fields from the source. It closely resembles a datasheet of a table or query. This creation method moves beyond the datasheet view by permitting inclusion of action buttons, graphic elements, and other controls.
Datasheet Tool	With a table or query open, Create Tab, Forms group, More Forms Tool, Datasheet Tool	Creates a form that looks exactly like the data source. This creation method moves beyond the Datasheet view by permitting inclusion of action buttons, graphic elements, and other controls while locking the source data in a split database environment.
Form Wizard	Close source object. Create Tab, Forms Group, More Forms, Form Wizard	Creates a form that may source one or more tables or queries and may include or exclude fields. It is more selective than the three earlier methods. You may define data grouping and sorting. You may select from a number of themes to enhance your form.
Blank Form Tool	Close source object. Create Tab, Forms Group, Blank Form	Very quick form creation tool—especially suitable for forms containing only a few fields.
PivotChart Tool	With a table, form or query open, Create Tab, Forms group, PivotChart	Like the PivotChart view of a table or query, you can create and save forms in pivot views. Often, multiple different pivots of the data need to be stored. Saving a pivot as a form provides additional storage capabilities.
PivotTable Tool	With a table, form or query open, Create Tab, Forms group, More Forms, PivotTable	Like the PivotTable view of a table or query, you can create and save forms in pivot views. Often, multiple different pivots of the data need to be stored. Saving a pivot as a form provides additional storage capabilities.
Modal Dialog Tool	Close source object. Create Tab, Forms Group, More Forms, Modal Dialog	Creates a dialog box that empowers the form user to filter and select only the fields and records necessary.
Form Design	Close source object. Create Tab, Forms Group, Form Design Tool	Creates a blank form in Design view. You may completely customize all aspects of the form.

The ***Form Tool*** gives you a one-click method of form creation.

The ***Form Tool*** gives you a one-click method of form creation. Have the source object open, click the Create tab, and then click Form in the Forms group. The newly created form opens in Layout view ready for customizing edits. You may generate many forms, even complicated ones, using this method, and then use the Layout view to edit and customize your work. Figure 6.20 shows an open table with the form tool highlighted ready to generate a form. Figure 6.21 shows the form open in Layout view ready to customize.

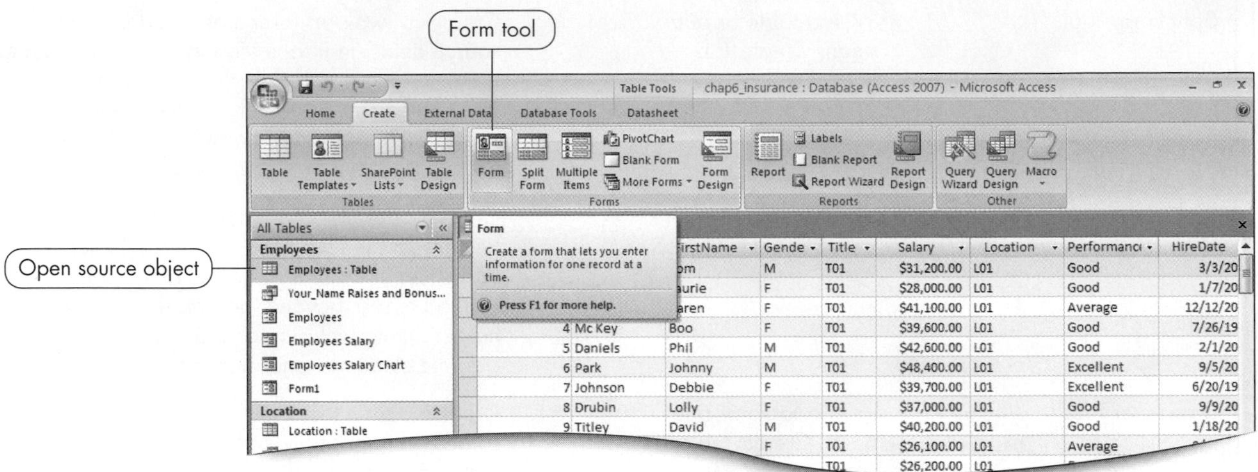

Figure 6.20 Setup for Form Creation

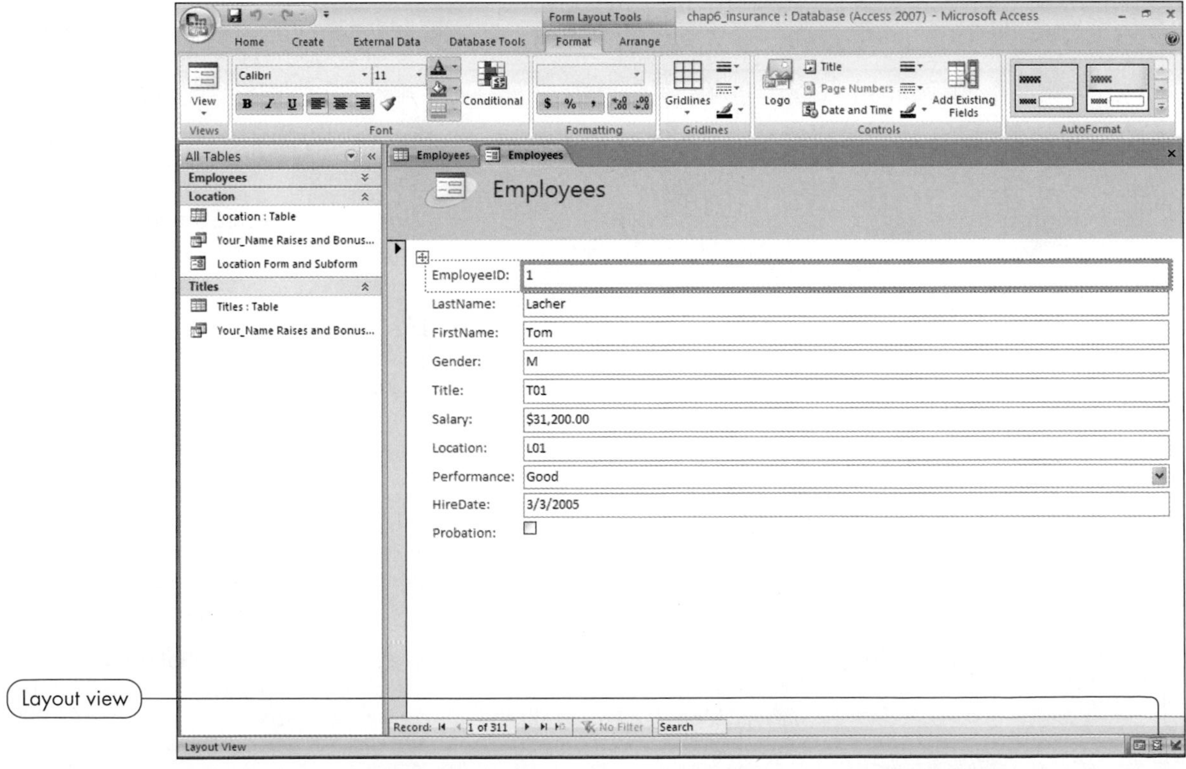

Figure 6.21 Newly Created Form Opened in Layout View

You need to understand the boxes displayed in the Layout view prior to editing the new form. Every item on the form is a control. Form controls operate like report controls. They may be bound, unbound, or calculated.

- **Bound Controls**—contain the data fields from the underlying source document. Each record is tied to the underlying data source. Every field on a form must have a unique bound control.
- **Unbound Controls**—contain labels (text boxes) providing the user with guidance on what to do with the bound control boxes. For example, the unbound control might display a label, FAX Number, and the bound control for that record would store the FAX for that employee. Unbound controls also contain aesthetic elements, lines, or borders. Use unbound controls to perform calculations in a form.
- **Calculated Controls**—contain the instructions (formulas) that generate the calculations displayed in a form.

Good form design generally dictates that you should have at least one unbound control for every bound control to identify or label the form data. As you edit the form, you will discover that each bound control generates an unbound label. If you move the label, the bound control moves along with it. If you move the bound control, the label moves, too. You may ungroup the controls and move them separately, but the default is that they are a matched set.

Use Design Elements

Attractive form design can enhance the form and make it more usable. You will generally use sans serif fonts for the form labels and a different font or color for the user-entered information. This approach helps the form user distinguish between the places where they are expected to interact with the data and the labels. Form designers frequently shade the background of the bound controls a different color from the labels. You may consider right-aligning the labels and following them with a colon while left-aligning the bound controls. You should group like objects together and separate the group visually from the rest of the form by drawing a box around it. Simply altering the white space between the group and the rest of the form will provide a sufficient visual boundary. You often see these techniques used in recurrent groups on a form like addresses. In an address group on a form, the street, suite, city, state, and postal code will be arranged as though on an envelope's address, and knitted together by having a box drawn around them. The users will guide you in effective design. They will request a larger font or a different background color if they believe making those changes will make it easier for them to see the record's data.

Create a Split Form

A ***split form*** provides a data interaction method that combines a form with a datasheet.

New to Access 2007, ***split forms*** provide a data interaction method that combines a form with a datasheet. Although forms are intended to provide a user-friendly interface for entering and updating data, they are not universally well received. Some users, especially those who do data entry exclusively, complain that form usage slows them down. You can imagine that in an organization that rewards data entry operators for efficiency and accuracy, anything that slows the data entry engenders complaints. Using a split form (see Figure 6.22) helps designers because they can apply data protection afforded by viewing a single record at a time. It helps the users because they can locate records quickly using the datasheet portion of the form. Then they can edit the record using the form. The users see the same data presented in both views. The views are synchronized at all times. If you select a field in one part of the form, the same field selects in the same record in the other part of the form. You may add, edit, or delete records in either view. The ***form splitter bar*** divides the two portions of the form. Users may reallocate space between the views by clicking and dragging the form splitter bar up or down. The form designer may disable this ability and hide the splitter bar from the users' view by setting the splitter bar property to No. The splitter bar position can be set to default to the designed position each time the form is launched by setting the save splitter position property to Yes. You can create a split form by opening the record source in Datasheet view. Click the Create tab and click the Split Form tool in the Forms group.

The ***form splitter bar*** divides the two portions of the form.

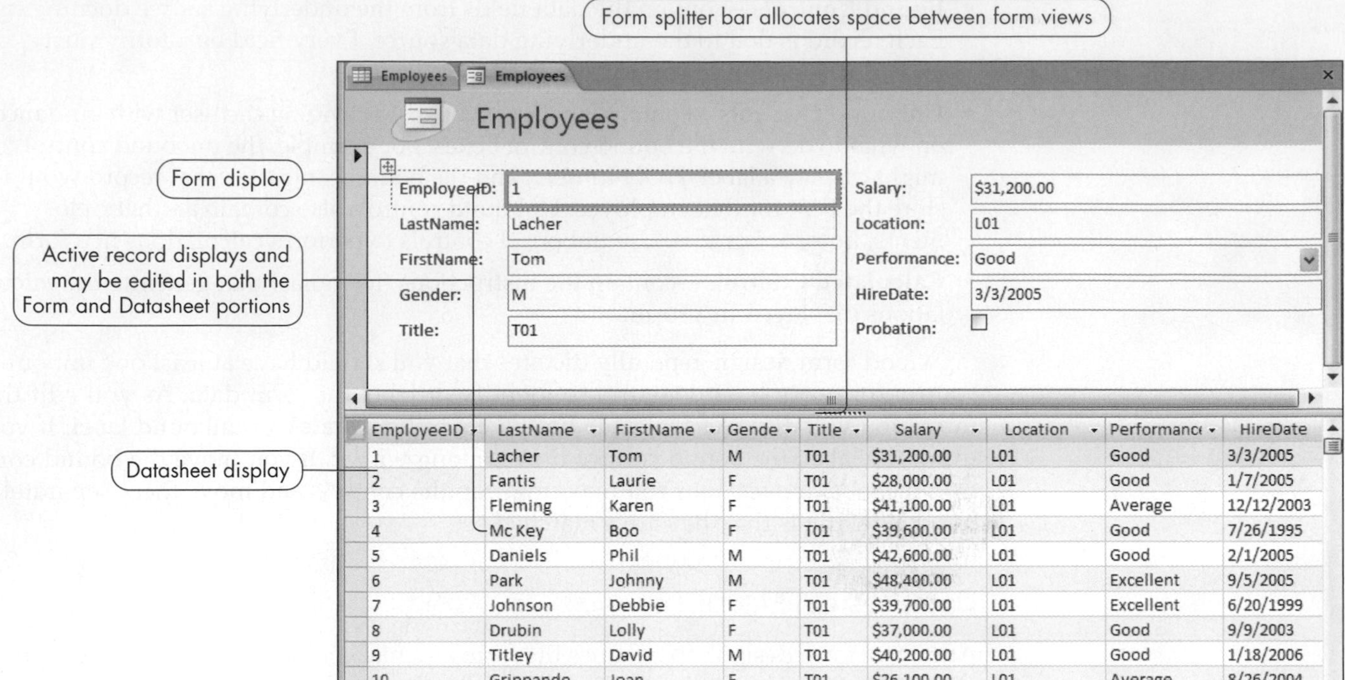

Figure 6.22 Split Form

Create a Multiple Items Form

The ***multiple items form*** creates a form that shows many records in a datasheet with one item in each row.

A form created using the Form Tool displays only a single record at a time. The *multiple items form* creates a form that shows many records in a datasheet with one item in each row. This facilitates data entry and updates because scrolling the records in a multiple items form is faster than navigating the form that shows only a single record at a time. Like the split form, the multiple items form is new to Access 2007. It provides developers another tool that will help them deliver the organization's users what they want. You create a multiple items form by first opening the data source and clicking Multiple Items in the Forms group on the Create tab. Figure 6.23 shows a multiple items form.

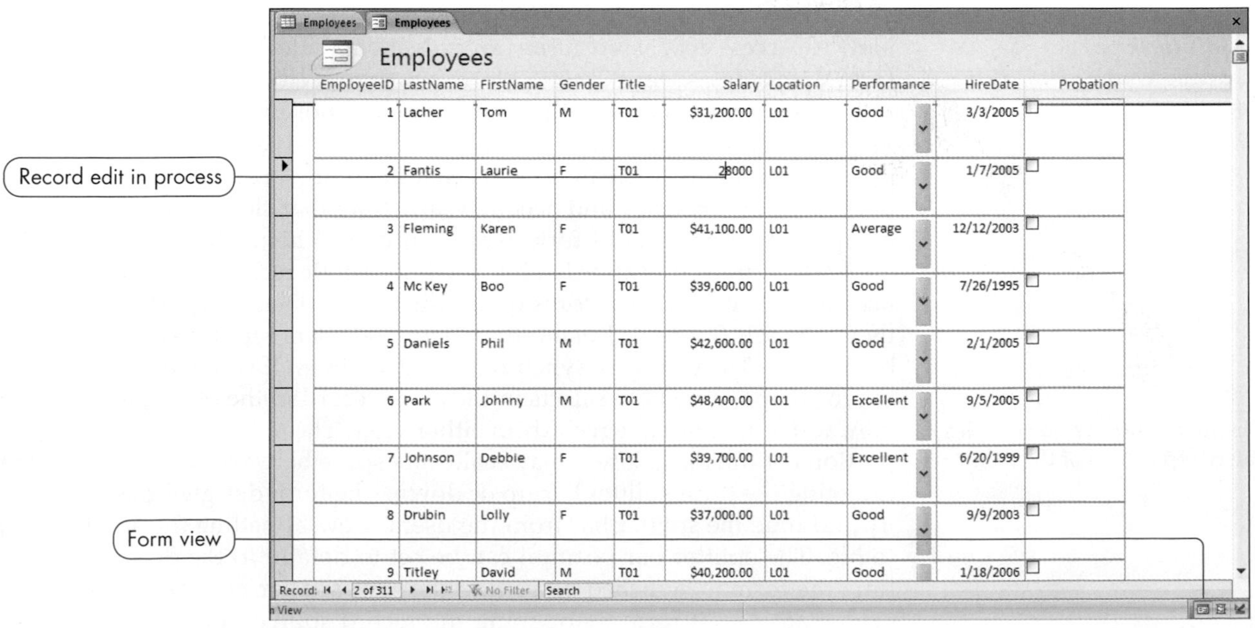

Figure 6.23 Multiple Items Form

Create a Datasheet Form

A ***datasheet form*** creates a form that looks exactly like the underlying data source.

Access provides a ***datasheet form*** that creates a form that looks exactly like the underlying data source, generally a table. This might be especially useful when a split database environment is introduced. The database managers can lock down the tables and protect the data from accidental damage while providing the users a form that looks exactly like the datasheet they were accustomed to using. One hallmark of introducing procedural change in data management is making the change transparent to the user. In other words, change the way the data are protected, but do not change the daily interaction of the users with the data. The datasheet form accomplishes this. Figure 6.24 shows a datasheet form.

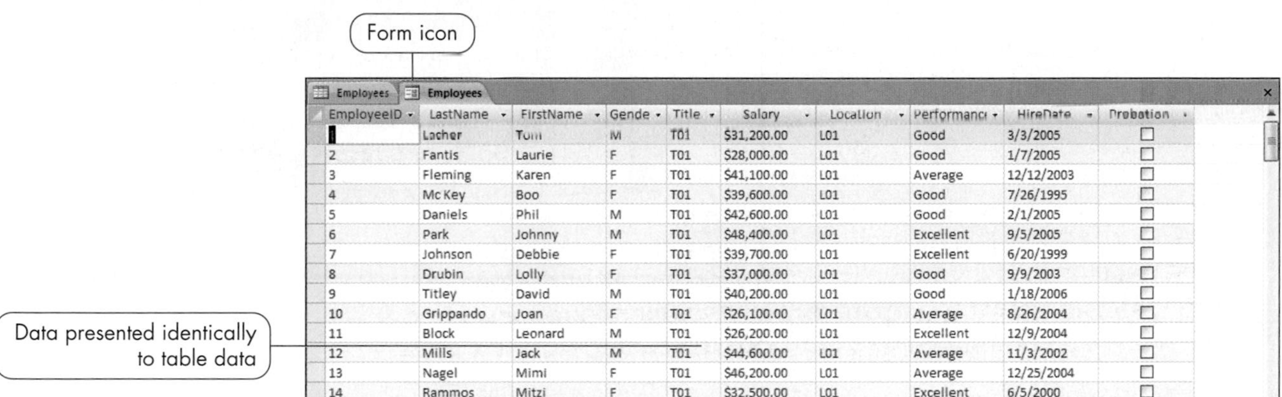

EmployeeID	LastName	FirstName	Gende	Title	Salary	Location	Performanc	HireDate	Probation
1	Lacher	Tom	M	T01	$31,200.00	L01	Good	3/3/2005	☐
2	Fantis	Laurie	F	T01	$28,000.00	L01	Good	1/7/2005	☐
3	Fleming	Karen	F	T01	$41,100.00	L01	Average	12/12/2003	☐
4	Mc Key	Boo	F	T01	$39,600.00	L01	Good	7/26/1995	☐
5	Daniels	Phil	M	T01	$42,600.00	L01	Good	2/1/2005	☐
6	Park	Johnny	M	T01	$48,400.00	L01	Excellent	9/5/2005	☐
7	Johnson	Debbie	F	T01	$39,700.00	L01	Excellent	6/20/1999	☐
8	Drubin	Lolly	F	T01	$37,000.00	L01	Good	9/9/2003	☐
9	Titley	David	M	T01	$40,200.00	L01	Good	1/18/2006	☐
10	Grippando	Joan	F	T01	$26,100.00	L01	Average	8/26/2004	☐
11	Block	Leonard	M	T01	$26,200.00	L01	Excellent	12/9/2004	☐
12	Mills	Jack	M	T01	$44,600.00	L01	Average	11/3/2002	☐
13	Nagel	Mimi	F	T01	$46,200.00	L01	Average	12/25/2004	☐
14	Rammos	Mitzi	F	T01	$32,500.00	L01	Excellent	6/5/2000	☐

Figure 6.24 Datasheet Form

Create PivotTable and PivotChart Forms

The PivotTable and PivotChart features of a form operate almost the same as they do in a query or table view. You use PivotTables and PivotCharts to summarize lengthy data using complex criteria and to represent the summary graphically. You may create a PivotChart by clicking the PivotChart in the Forms group on the Create tab. The PivotTable is found in More Forms in the Forms group on the Create tab. Once you create the Pivot grid, you drag field names from the Field List box and drop them on the appropriate position in the drop zones. Unlike the PivotTable and PivotChart views of a table or query, PivotTables and PivotCharts in forms exist independently of each other. Although you may choose to display the same data in PivotTable and PivotChart, you may also choose to display one set of criteria graphically and another in tabular form. You may change either the PivotTable or PivotChart without affecting the other. Figures 6.25 and 6.26 display Pivot Forms.

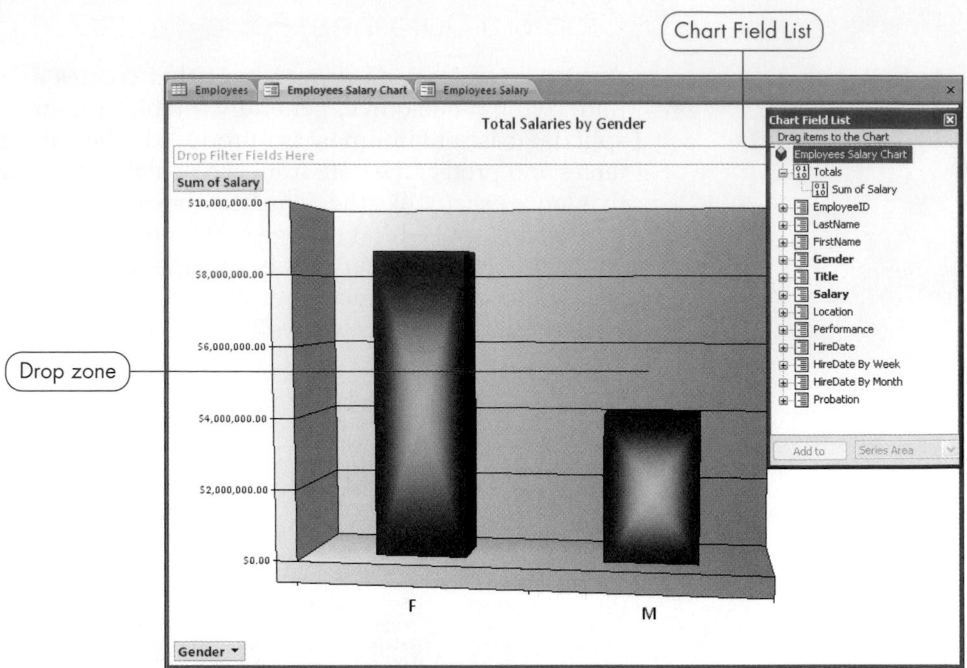

Figure 6.25 PivotChart Form

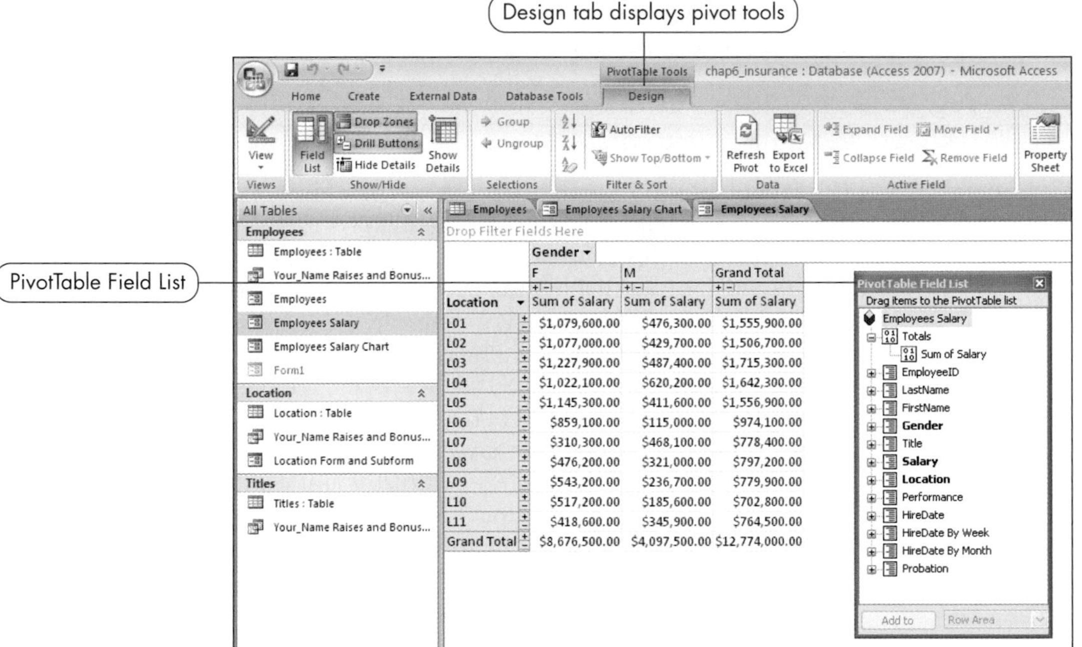

Location	F Sum of Salary	M Sum of Salary	Grand Total Sum of Salary
L01	$1,079,600.00	$476,300.00	$1,555,900.00
L02	$1,077,000.00	$429,700.00	$1,506,700.00
L03	$1,227,900.00	$487,400.00	$1,715,300.00
L04	$1,022,100.00	$620,200.00	$1,642,300.00
L05	$1,145,300.00	$411,600.00	$1,556,900.00
L06	$859,100.00	$115,000.00	$974,100.00
L07	$310,300.00	$468,100.00	$778,400.00
L08	$476,200.00	$321,000.00	$797,200.00
L09	$543,200.00	$236,700.00	$779,900.00
L10	$517,200.00	$185,600.00	$702,800.00
L11	$418,600.00	$345,900.00	$764,500.00
Grand Total	$8,676,500.00	$4,097,500.00	$12,774,000.00

Figure 6.26 PivotTable Form May Display Different Data from PivotChart

TIP Form Wizard

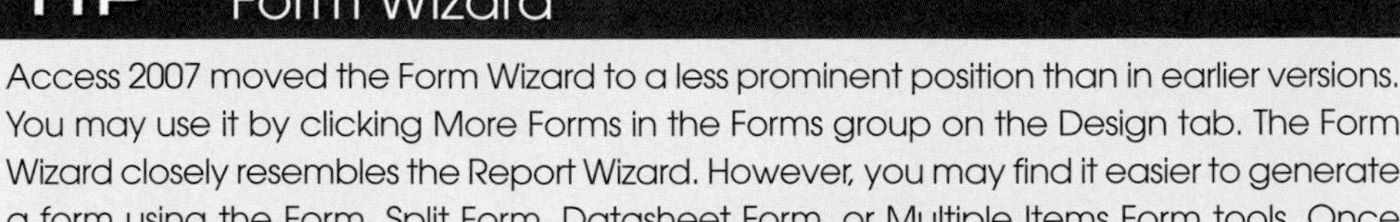

Access 2007 moved the Form Wizard to a less prominent position than in earlier versions. You may use it by clicking More Forms in the Forms group on the Design tab. The Form Wizard closely resembles the Report Wizard. However, you may find it easier to generate a form using the Form, Split Form, Datasheet Form, or Multiple Items Form tools. Once you create a form, you may edit the form in either the Layout view or Design view.

In the second hands-on exercise, you will create a series of forms using the many form creation tools available in Access 2007.

Hands-On Exercises

2 | Form Creation Tools

Skills covered: 1. Use the Form Tool and Identify Form Controls **2.** Create a Split Form **3.** Create a Multiple Items Form **4.** Create a Datasheet Form **5.** Create PivotTable and PivotChart Forms

Step 1
Use the Form Tool and Identify Form Controls

Refer to Figure 6.27 as you complete Step 1.

a. Open the *chap6_ho1-3_nationalbank solution* file, if necessary, and click **Options** on the Security Warning toolbar. Then click **Enable this content** in the Microsoft Office Security Options dialog box and click **OK**.

TROUBLESHOOTING: If you create unrecoverable errors while completing this hands-on exercise, you can delete the *chap6_ho1-3_nationalbank_solution* file, copy the *chap6_ho1_nationalbank_solution* backup database you created at the end of the first hands-on exercise, and open the copy of the backup database to start the second hands-on exercise again.

b. Open the **Payments table**. Click the **Create tab** and click **Form** in the Forms group.

You created a simple form that may be used to record customers' loan payments. The form opens in Layout view ready to edit.

c. Slowly move your mouse over the top of the **P** in *P0001*.

As you move up, the mouse pointer shape changes to a double-headed arrow. Continue moving the pointer up until the pointer shape changes to a bold down arrow.

d. When the pointer shape changes to the bold down arrow, click.

Gold selection boxes appear around the form's four bound controls. These items are bound to the values stored in the underlying table.

e. With the gold borders displayed, move your mouse over the right margin. When the pointer shape changes to a double-headed arrow, click and drag the right boundary left about five inches. Close the Properties Sheet, if necessary.

The Payments table is open.

f. Click the **Payment table tab** to switch to the table. The first record indicates a payment of $4,242.92. Click in the first record in the AmountReceived field. Select the field's current value and type **4342.92** and press **Enter**.

g. Click the **Payments form tab** to return to the form. Look at the amount received in the first record. It should show $4,342.92.

This value is a bound control. It is tied to the value stored in the underlying data source.

h. Click the **PaymentID** label to select it. Click it again to turn on Edit mode. Move the insertion point to the left of *I* and insert a space between *Payment* and *ID*.

This is an unbound control. While working in Layout view, you may edit the unbound control. This label is cosmetic. It might say anything without having any effect on any table data. Of course, you want to label the controls in your forms descriptively, so you would not want it to say just anything.

i. Type **Ctrl+S** to save the form and name it **Your_Name Payments Form**. Click **OK**. Close the form.

TROUBLESHOOTING: If you cannot easily recover from an error you make altering a form's layout, you can close the form without saving changes. This will return you to the table. Simply click the Form tool and recreate the form to start over again.

The column heading for the first column in the Payments table still says PaymentID (no space). That is because the edit you performed was on the unbound label control. It had no effect on the table data because they are not tied or bound to the table.

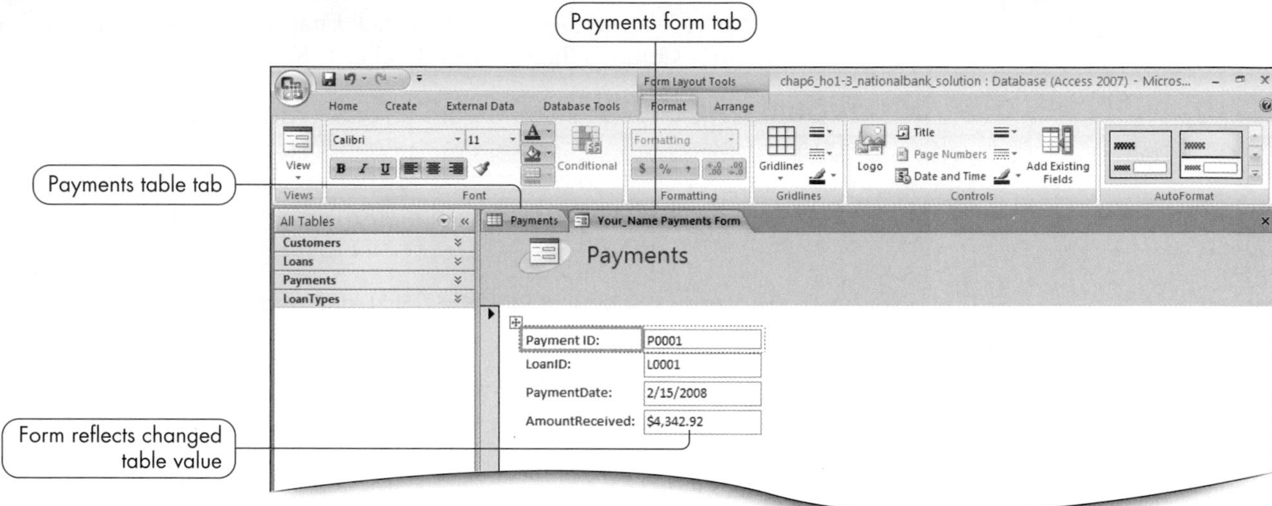

Figure 6.27 Edited Payments Form

Step 2
Create a Split Form

Refer to Figure 6.28 as you complete Step 2.

a. With the Payments table open, click the **Create tab**, and then click **Split Form** in the Forms group.

   You created a new form using the split view. The top half of the screen displays the form, and the lower portion displays the table data in a close representation of the Datasheet view.

b. Click the **AmountReceived** field in the sixth record, P0006. Edit it to be **260.40**. Press **Shift+Enter**. Press **Tab**.

   Shift+Enter saves the changes without changing to a different record.

c. Look at the form in the top portion of the window.

   It displays $260.40 for the payment in March for record 6.

d. Right-click the **Payments form tab** and switch to **Form View** from the shortcut menu.

   You will edit this record further by changing the payment date. Most forms open in the Layout view when they are first created. You cannot modify form data in the Layout view.

e. Click in the **PaymentDate** field in the form and edit it to display **3/10/2008**.

f. Click the **Next Record** navigation. Look at the date for record 6 in the Datasheet view.

The date now displays 3/10/2008. It does not matter whether changes are made to the split form by using the top or the bottom portion of the form. Any change in either place affects the other.

g. Move your mouse over the boundary between the form and datasheet portions of the window. When the pointer shape changes to a double-headed arrow, click and drag the datasheet portion of the window up about two inches.

h. Save your form as **Your_Name Payments Split**. Close the form.

Both the Payments and Split Payments forms are sourced on the same table. Any changes you make in either form will immediately reflect in the Payments table.

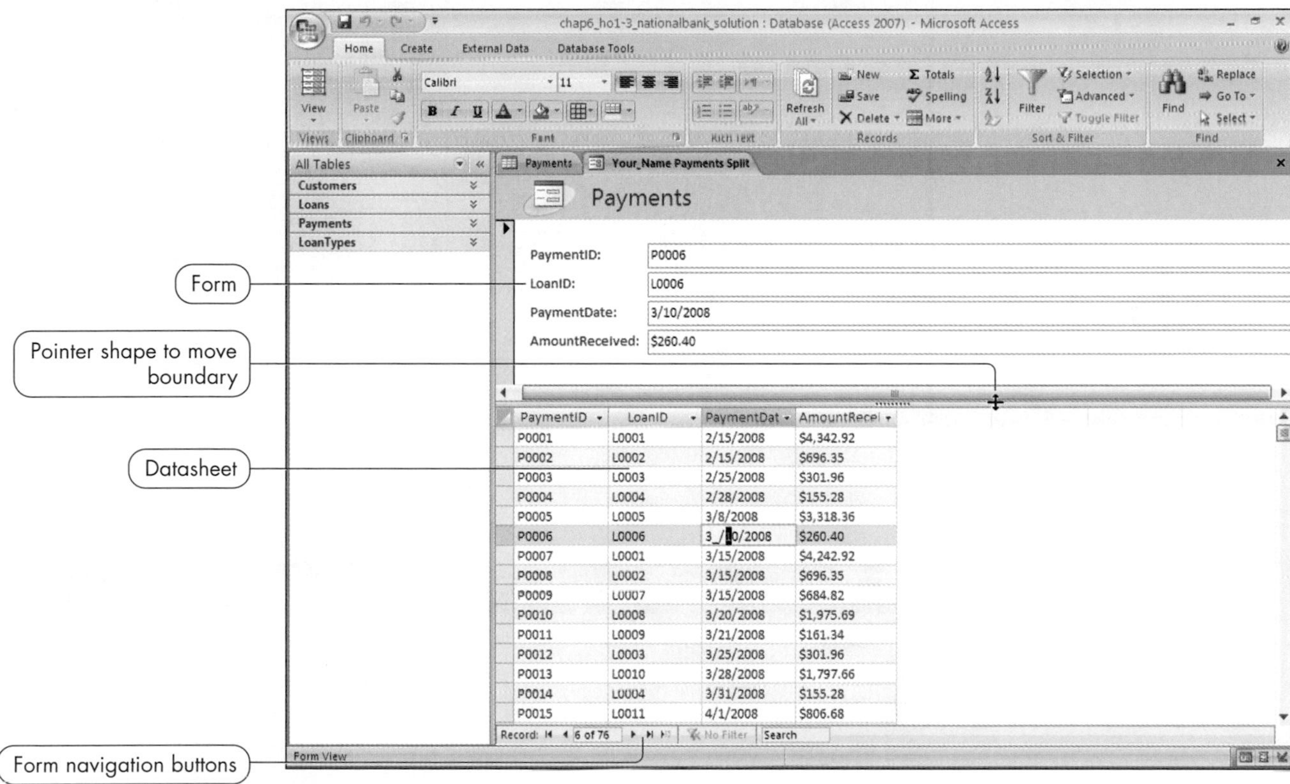

Figure 6.28 Split Form

Step 3
Create a Multiple Items Form

Refer to Figure 6.29 as you complete Step 3.

a. Open the **Payments table** (if necessary), click the **Create tab**, and click **Multiple Items** in the Forms group.

You created a multiple items form. It opens in Layout view for you to edit. You decide that if the row heights were shortened, more records would display on the screen at a time.

b. Click any value in the **PaymentID** field. Move your mouse pointer over the bottom of the cell. When the pointer shape changes to a double-headed arrow, click and drag up.

The rows move closer together.

c. Right-click the value and select **Properties** from the shortcut menu to display the Property Sheet window.

d. Click the **Height property box** on the Format tab and edit it to display **0.2"**.

e. Save the form as **Your_Name Payments Multi**. Close the form.

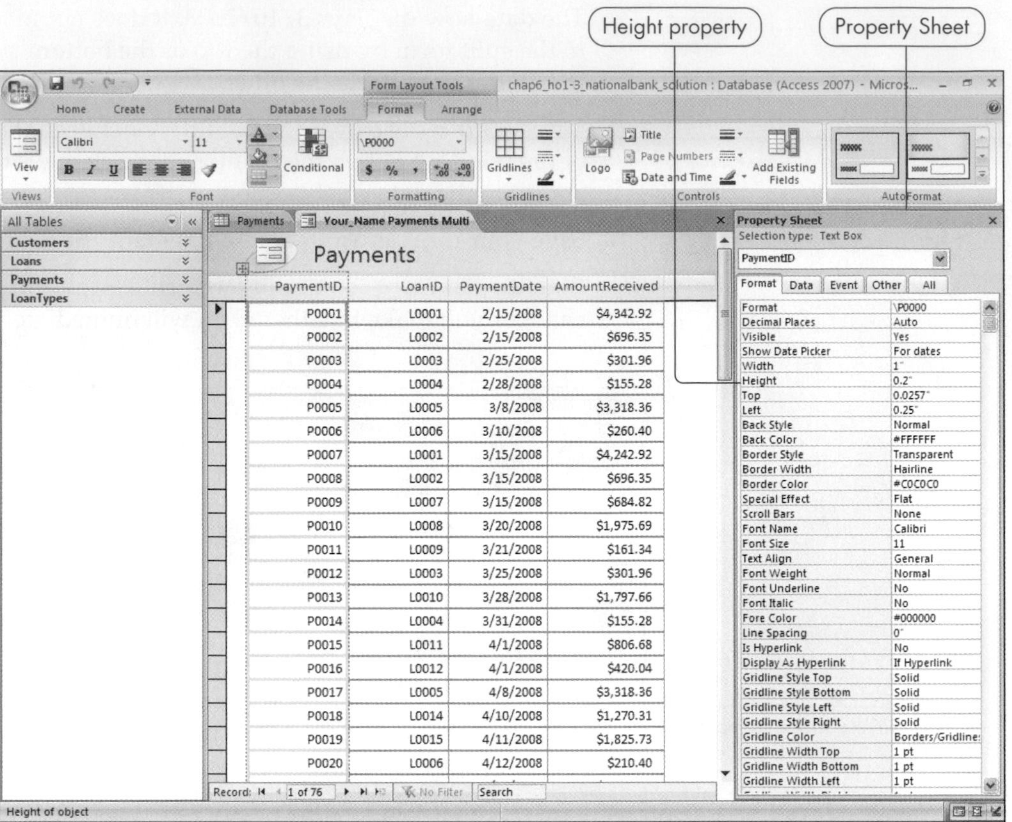

Figure 6.29 Multiple Items Form in Layout View

TIP Why so many choices?

Access provides numerous choices for form creation because most database users interact with the database through forms. Users have strong opinions about how the forms they use should look and behave.

Step 4
Create a Datasheet Form

Refer to Figure 6.30 as you complete Step 4.

a. Open the **Payments table** (if necessary), click the **Create tab**, and click **More Forms** in the Forms group. Then select **Datasheet**.

The form opens in the Datasheet view.

b. Right-click the **Payments form tab**. This form is different from the others with which you have worked. It displays only a Datasheet and Design view. Click **Design View**.

Although the form in Datasheet view looks exactly like the table, you can see the dramatic difference in structure when you switch and look at the form in Design view. This does not look anything like a table Design view. It does not act like the Design view of a table, either. Make no mistake; this is a form.

c. Right-click the **Payments Form tab** and select **Datasheet View**.

d. Click the **Payments table tab**. Return to the **Payments form**.

The only cosmetic difference between the two is the form and table icons on the tabs.

e. Save the form as **Your_Name Payments Datasheet** and keep the form open for the next step.

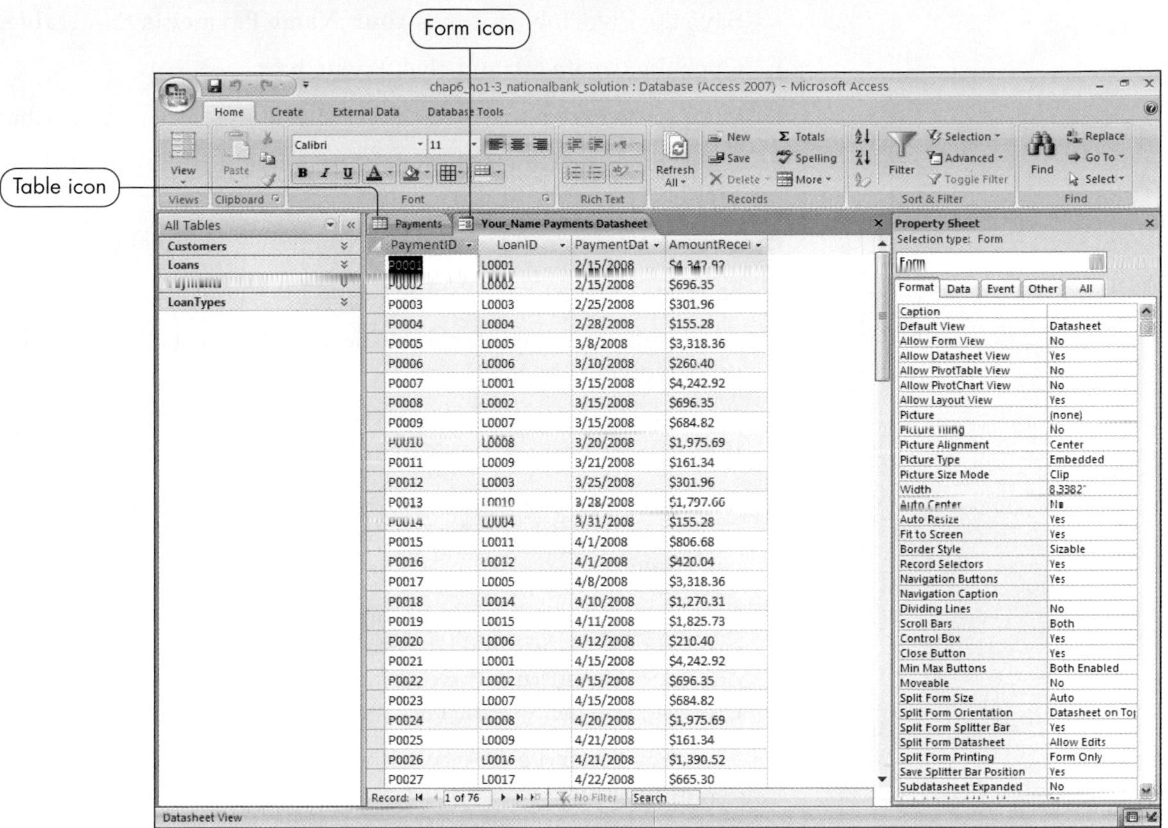

Figure 6.30 Datasheet Form in Datasheet View

Step 5
Create PivotTable and PivotChart Forms

Refer to Figure 6.31 as you complete Step 5.

a. Open the **Your_Name Payments Datasheet form** (if necessary), click the **Create tab**, and click **More Forms** in the Forms group. Then select **PivotTable**.

The form opens in the PivotTable view Design grid.

b. Click in the middle of the Design grid.

The PivotTable Field list box should turn on.

TROUBLESHOOTING: If the PivotTable Field List box fails to open, click the Field List Tool in the Show/Hide group on the Design tab.

c. Click the **AmountReceived** field in the PivotTable Field List box and drag it to the **Drop Totals or Detail Fields Here drop zone**.

d. Click the **LoanID** field in the PivotTable Field List box and drag it to the **Drop Row Fields Here drop zone**.

e. Click the **PaymentDate by Month** field in the PivotTable Field List box and drag it to the **Drop Column Fields Here drop zone**.

f. Click the **AmountReceived** column to make it the active column in the PivotTable, and then click **AutoCalc** in the Tools group and select **Sum**.

g. Click **Hide Details** in the Show/Hide group.

h. Click **Expand Details** next to 2008 (the box containing the plus sign) to display quarterly details.

The yearly data expands to display totals by quarter.

i. Save the PivotTable form as **Your_Name Payments PivotTable**.

j. Click the **Create tab** and click **PivotChart**.

k. Click anywhere in the gray part of the chart to turn on the Chart Field List box.

l. Drag the **LoanID** field from the Chart Field List box to the **Drop Category Fields Here** box.

m. Drag the **AmountReceived** field from the Chart Field List box to the **Plot area**.

n. Save the chart as **Your_Name Payments PivotChart**. Close the PivotChart.

Although you based the PivotChart on the PivotTable, the table does not change when you change the chart.

o. Close the open database objects. Click the **Office Button**, select **Manage**, and then select **Compact and Repair Database**.

p. Click the **Office Button** again, select **Manage**, and then select **Back Up Database**. Type **chap6_ho2_nationalbank_solution** as the file name and click **Save**.

You just created a backup of the database after completing the second hands-on exercise. The original database *chap6_ho1-3_nationalbank_solution* remains onscreen. If you ruin the original database as you complete the third hands-on exercise, you can use the backup file you just created.

q. Close the file and exit Access if you do not want to continue with the next exercise at this time.

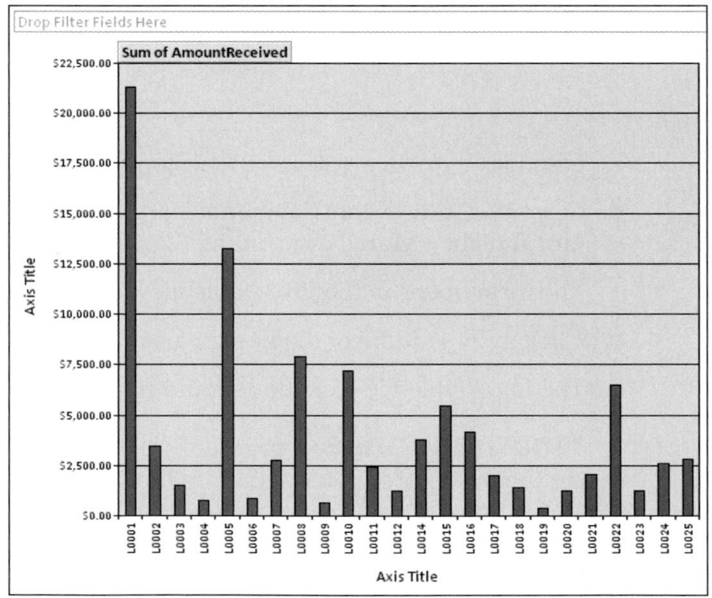

Figure 6.31 PivotChart Form

Form Customization

You can now create a variety of forms, but everything you have accomplished so far has been standard. Because much of the day-to-day work in an organization's database is accomplished using forms, you need to develop skills to make your forms fit the tasks. Your forms need to facilitate the users' work and make their lives easier. Designers spend many hours conversing with the form users, watching them work, and developing innovations that (hopefully) make the users' work lives easier.

In this section, you will learn how to create a form using Design view, add action buttons, perform calculations, create and modify subforms, and apply formatting and conditional formatting to enhance your form's usability.

Creating Custom Forms in Design View

Access provides several ways of creating forms. You have already used many of them. Design view gives you the power to completely customize the form. The Design view of a form is like a blueprint for a building. You do not see the data in a form Design view, you see only the controls, or placeholders, that will store and display your data. The form does not run while you are in Design view, and updates and changes to data do not display. There are some actions which may only be accomplished in Design view. Other actions, like applying or modifying formats or styles, may be done in either Design or Layout views. You will need to experiment to see which method suits your style. Use Design view when you need to do the following:

- Modify Form Properties, i.e., Default View or Allow Form View
- Change the form section sizes
- Add different types of controls, i.e., pictures, lines, rectangles, and calculations
- Edit control source properties directly in the text box

Use the Design Grid

You launch a new form in Design view by clicking the Create tab and then clicking Form Design. A blank workspace and the tools that you will use to create the form display. Figure 6.32 identifies many of the tools. You probably do not need to memorize each icon's purpose because the tip boxes and Microsoft Help will always remind you. Most form designers use only a select few of these tools and generally customize their Ribbons to display only the tools they employ.

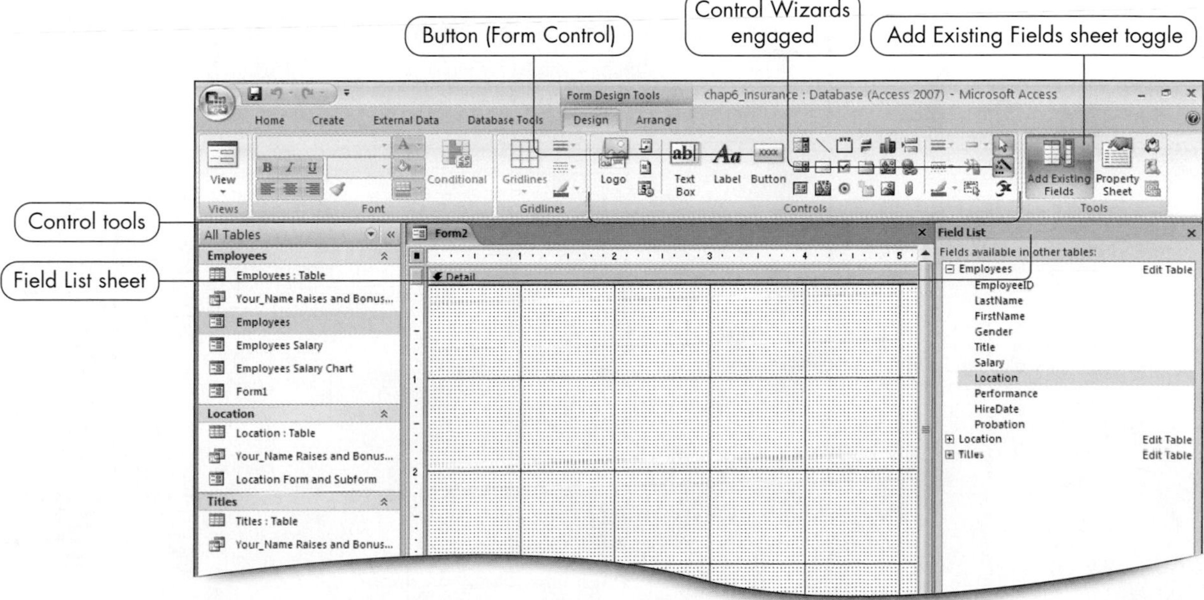

Figure 6.32 Blank Form in Design View

The Add Existing Fields tool is engaged, and the Field List displays in Figure 6.32. To add fields to the form, you need only click them in the Field List sheet and drag them onto the Design grid. Notice that the Design grid contains two grids, a fine and a wide hatch. These provide you with placement guides to help you align the form data. Do not worry about positioning a control incorrectly; after the control is on the Design grid, you can select it and move it easily. The default Design grid displays only the detail section of the form. You will use the tools to add additional sections, for example a header. You click the Title tool to create both the form header area and the label that will eventually contain the form title.

TIP Text Box or Label

You may wonder when to use a text box and when to use a label on a form. If the control is bound, use a text box because it creates two boxes on the form. The first contains the control's label and the second is a placeholder for the record value to display. The values displayed in the right box will change as the user navigates through the records displayed in the form. Use a label when you need something displayed on the form that does not change as the user navigates through records. Examples of when to use labels might include form titles, indications of form authorship or the date of last revision, or the company slogan.

Figure 6.33 displays a form in Design view with some controls and design elements added. By clicking the Title tool in the controls group, you may add a form header and the label to contain the form title. The label is selected, and it contains size handles that you may use to change its size. The Property Sheet displays that the caption is Form1. It is a good idea to change to a more descriptive form title. You can change the space allocation between the form header and detail areas by moving your mouse over the boundary bar until its shape changes to the move cross and then clicking and dragging to the desired location. This form also displays an example of a

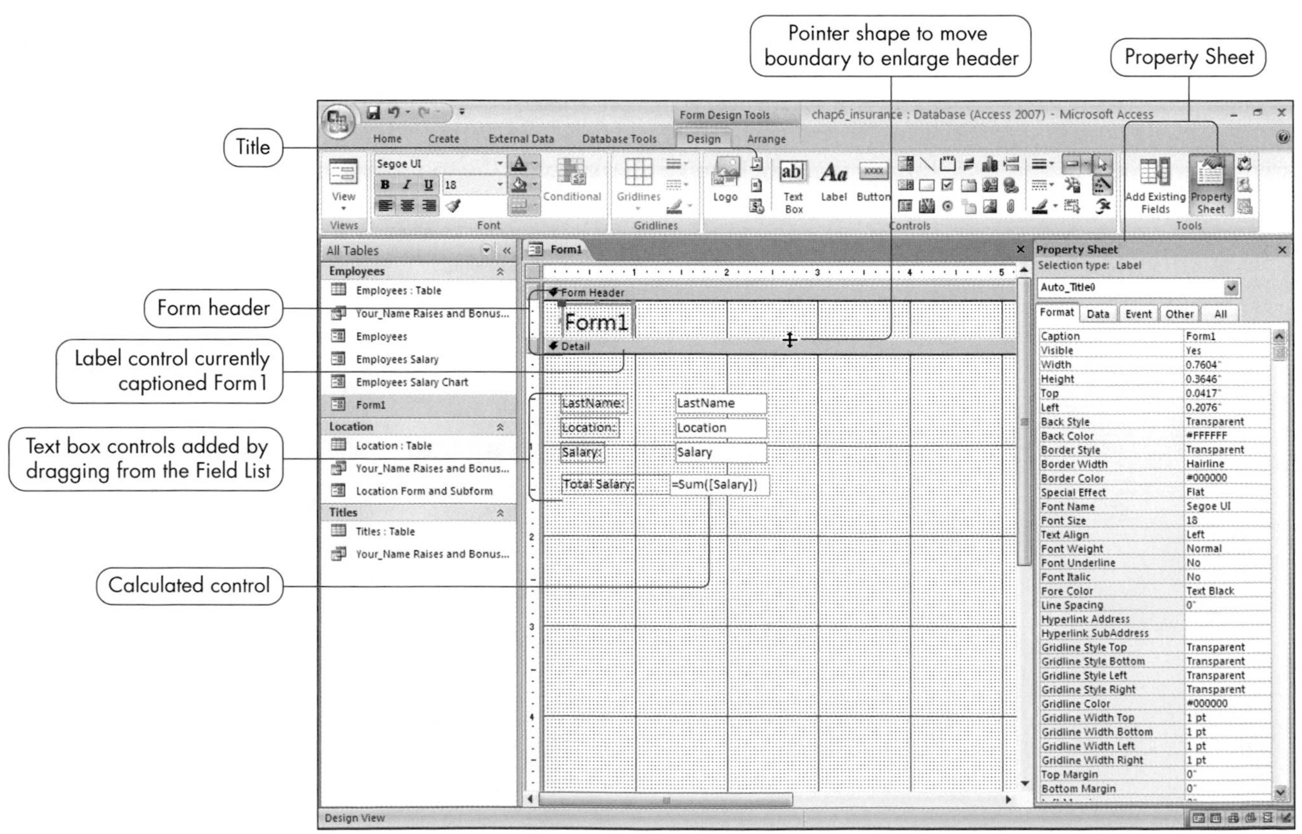

Figure 6.33 Simple Form in Design View

calculated control. The last control uses the sum function (generated with the Expression Builder) to calculate the total of all employees' salaries.

Add Action Buttons

The Button tool in the Controls group provides powerful and user-friendly form additions. When you click it, your mouse pointer shape changes to a rectangle attached to a plus sign. This means that you need to click and drag on the Design grid to position and size the button you want to create. The Command Button Wizard launches as soon as you release the mouse. Access provides many alternatives for form commands. The first wizard screen, shown in Figure 6.34, offers different categories of actions. The second screen of the wizard gives you options about the button content. In this case, the default printer picture communicates the button's action well. You could browse to a different picture or simply use text to describe the button's action (see Figure 6.35). The last wizard screen lets you name the button. Figure 6.36 shows the form as the user will engage it in Form view.

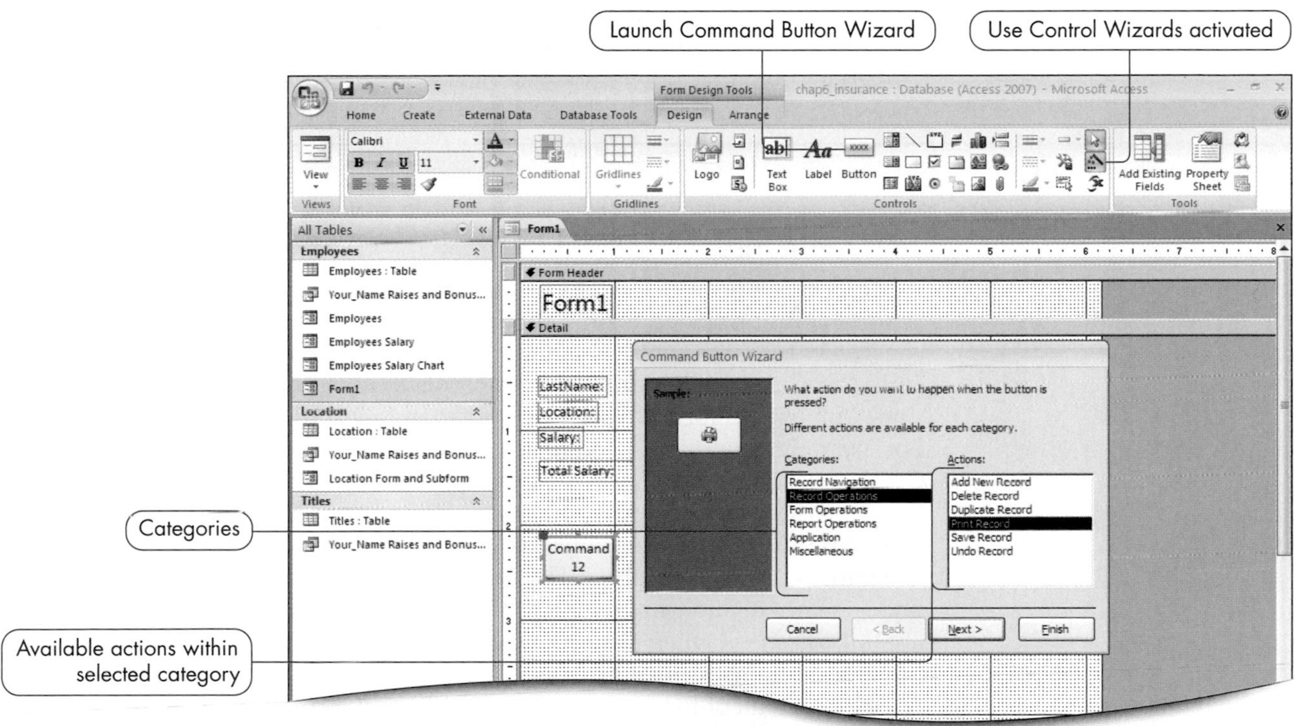

Figure 6.34 First Command Button Wizard Screen

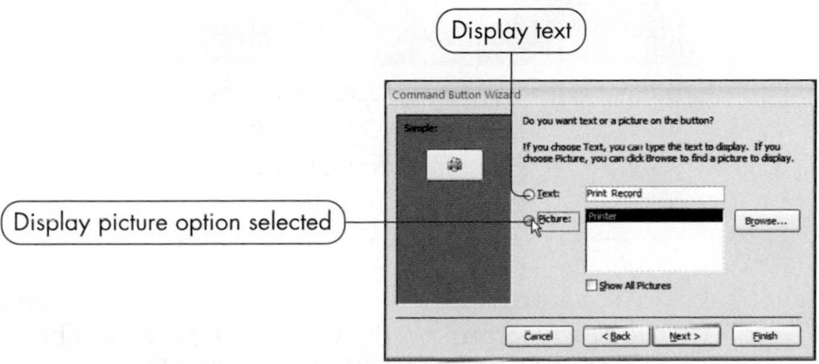

Figure 6.35 Button Information Selected

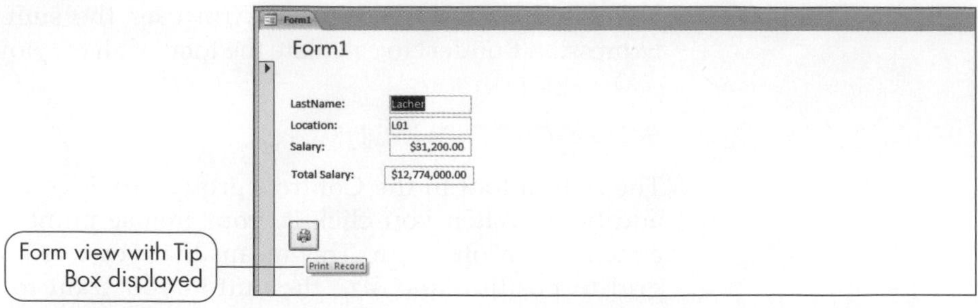

Figure 6.36 Form Displayed in Form View

TIP Adjust, View, and Save Often

Working with the Design view can be confusing because data do not display. The secret is to make a small adjustment, switch from Design view to Form view, look at the change, and if you like the results, save your form. If you do not like the results, return to Design view, click Undo on the Quick Access Toolbar, and try again. You do not want to make multiple changes without viewing them in Form view as you make each change. You will probably not be able to undo several changes at once.

Creating Subforms

A ***subform*** is a form that exists inside another form.

A ***subform*** is a form that exists inside another form. Sometimes subforms are called parent/child or nested form structures. The primary form (parent) may be edited separately from the subform (child) and the subform is stored and edited separately from the parent. Alternatively, both forms may be viewed and edited at the same time. You use subforms to show information that sources two or more related tables. For example, you might need to see the order history displayed as a subform in the Customers table. That way, a customer service representative can scroll past orders to tell the customer the name of the product that he or she purchased last month. This presupposes that a relationship, generally one-to-many, exists between the Customers and Orders tables. The primary form (customers) is the one portion of the one-to-many relationship, whereas the subform (orders) is the many part. The forms are linked so that when a specific customer's data display in the primary form, only the related items in the Orders table display in the subform. If the forms linkages were broken, all of the records in the Orders table would display in the subform.

TIP Establish the Relationships Prior to Creating Subforms

Because the subform depends on the one-to-many relationship with the parent form to display only the related records, it is much less work if the relationship exists before you create either the form or subform. When the relationship exists, open the parent table and use the Form tool. The default is a form containing the appropriate subform.

Access provides several methods of subform creation. You can use the Form tool in the Forms group on the Create tab when a table is open that displays its relationships to a related table with the Expand Detail symbols displayed. Figure 6.37 shows a location table with the Kansas City employees (the related table) with the details displayed. Figure 6.38 shows the form created from this table opened to the fourth record, Kansas City. A user in the firm could easily scroll the performance ratings of the Kansas City employees to get an overview of the supervisor's rating style.

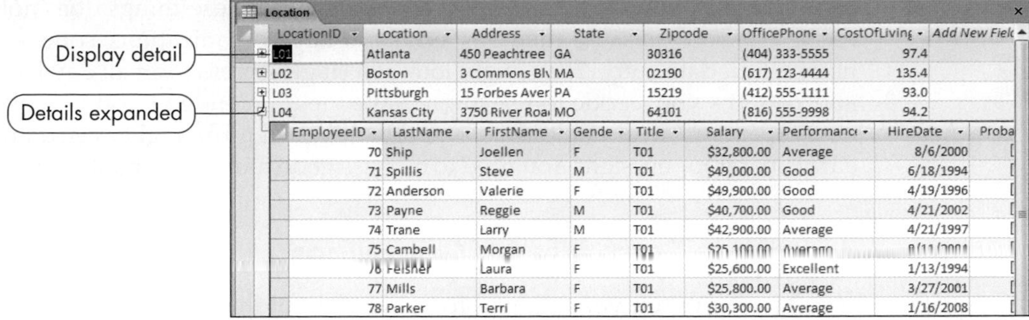

Figure 6.37 Table with Relationship Indicated

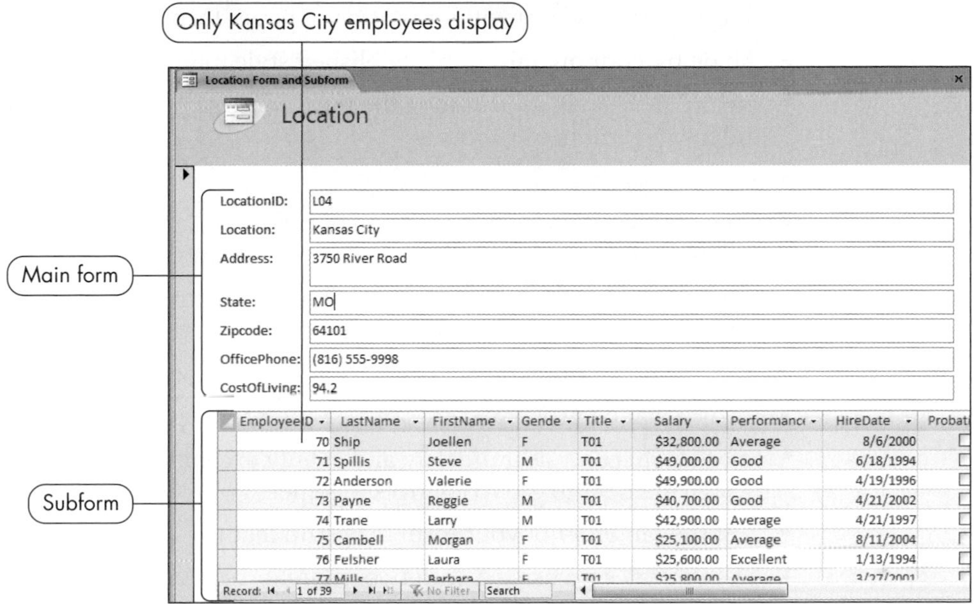

Figure 6.38 Form with Subform Displayed in Form View

Another way to generate a form with a subform is to create both forms separately. Open the main form in Design view and make sure the Control Wizard tool in the controls group is engaged. Drag the form that you wish to make the subform from the Navigation Pane and drop it on the main form's design grid. Access will create the subform and establish the linkages between the form and its subform based on the predetermined relationships in the database. If Access cannot determine how to establish the relationship, you will need to do so yourself. You would need to use the Link Child and Link Master properties in the Property Sheet. The ***Link Child Field*** property governs which field or fields in the subform link to the main form. The ***Link Master Field*** property governs which field or fields in the main form link to the subform.

The ***Link Child Field*** property governs which field or fields in the subform link to the main form.

The ***Link Master Field*** property governs which field or fields in the main form link to the subform.

You can create a form with a subform by using the Form Wizard. If you specify more than one table as the data source for the form, you will be given an option of specifying how to view the data. Make sure that you select the table that will become the main form to answer the wizard. Finally, you can create a form and its subforms completely in Design view. You may have more than one subform in a form. You may also nest multiple subforms if the appropriate relationships preexist.

Designing Functional Formats

Access provides an extremely wide range of formatting options. You can change foreground and background colors and patterns, add emphasis by shadowing or embossing controls or by changing fonts, and add boxes and lines to visually group form elements. You might add other graphic elements like pictures or designs to add clarity or excitement to the form. You can improve a form's usability by changing the form navigation tab order. Just because you *can* do these things does not necessarily mean that you *should* do them. Especially in large organizations, some employees do nothing but data entry. They might look at a single Access form all day long. The colors and patterns you decide to use might have the unintended effect of making the data entry operators' lives unpleasant. A poorly designed form might even damage the data entry operators' eyesight. You need to exercise good judgment about your form's design.

Adhere to Form Design Guidelines

(When in doubt, leave it out.)

When you create a form, you should adhere to the following design guidelines to ensure a professional, readable form.

- Design the Access form to match the paper form as closely as possible if the Access form coexists with or replaces a paper form.
- Abide by your organization's published style manual if such a style manual exists.
- Ensure that navigation among the form controls progresses from the upper left to the lower right in most forms.
- Avoid scrolling.
- Consider the Windows convention of right-aligning text boxes with labels and follow with a colon, and then left-align the bound control.
- Employ different fonts and/or fill colors for controls the form user engages and controls that provide the user information.
- Right-align all numeric fields with the possible exception of an ID field.
- Ensure that control boxes are large enough to display data completely.
- Space form controls uniformly and evenly except when you use empty space as a design element to group controls together.
- Test the tab order of your form to ensure that the navigation sequence is logical.
- Test your design using a variety of monitor resolutions. Even though you might set your monitor to display 2,084 by 786 pixels, your form's users might prefer 800 by 600.
- Select font and background colors and/or patterns with sufficient contrast to make the data easily visible.
- When there is any indication that a special effect (i.e., shadowing or embossing) detracts from the form's utility, omit it. When in doubt, leave it out.
- If the primary users of the form come from outside your organization (customers or business partners), build in contact information on every screen. This might include your logo, organization name, address, your Web site's link, and telephone number.
- Ask yourself if you would like to interact with the form you created—all day, every day. Would the themes and colors you select give you a headache after staring at them for a few hours? If so, the form users will also get headaches and complain.

Add Themes and Design Elements

Access makes forms easily. Customizing the form sometimes takes more work. Figure 6.39 shows a newly created Access form in Layout view with the controls selected. You decide that the controls for the first- and last-name fields should be on the same row. To change the form layout, you must first remove the default layout, using either Layout or Design views. Click the box with the four-headed arrow in the upper left, and the controls select. Employ the Remove tool in the Control Layout group on the Arrange tab. This "ungroups" the controls and enables you to position the controls on the form where you want them. Click the control you wish to reposition and drag it. You may reposition several controls at once by shift-clicking. You may also adjust the order in which the controls respond as the data entry operator presses Tab to navigate the form. This will open a dialog box where you can click and drag the field names to change the tab navigation order.

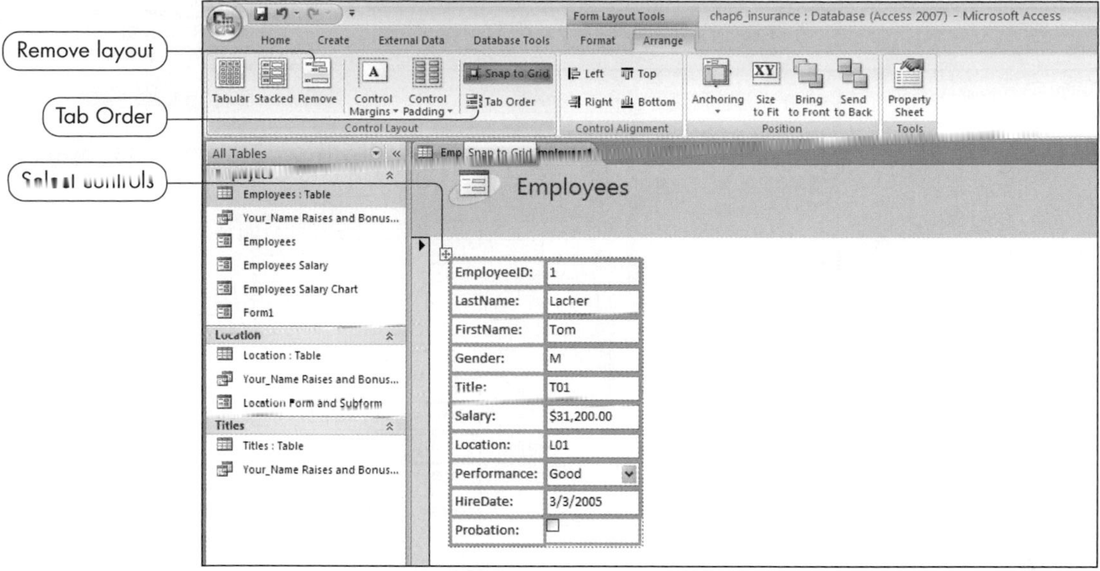

Figure 6.39 Removing the Default Layout Permits Individual Control Placement

Figure 6.40 shows the repositioned controls and adds a theme. Add themes to your forms by using AutoFormat on the Format tab. If you need more extensive design enhancement, you will need to use Design view. Figure 6.41 displays a form in Design view. Additional unbound controls add information and visual appeal. The designer added a label to the left of the FirstName field control and format-painted from the existing controls. Adding a rectangle using the rectangle control visually grouped the part of the form that serves to identify the employee. You may do this by using the rectangle tool in the Controls group on the Design tab. The mouse pointer shape changes to a rectangle attached to a crosshair. Click on the form and drag to create the appropriately sized rectangle (see Figure 6.42). With the newly added rectangle active, the designer added a shadowed special effect. Finally, the designer added

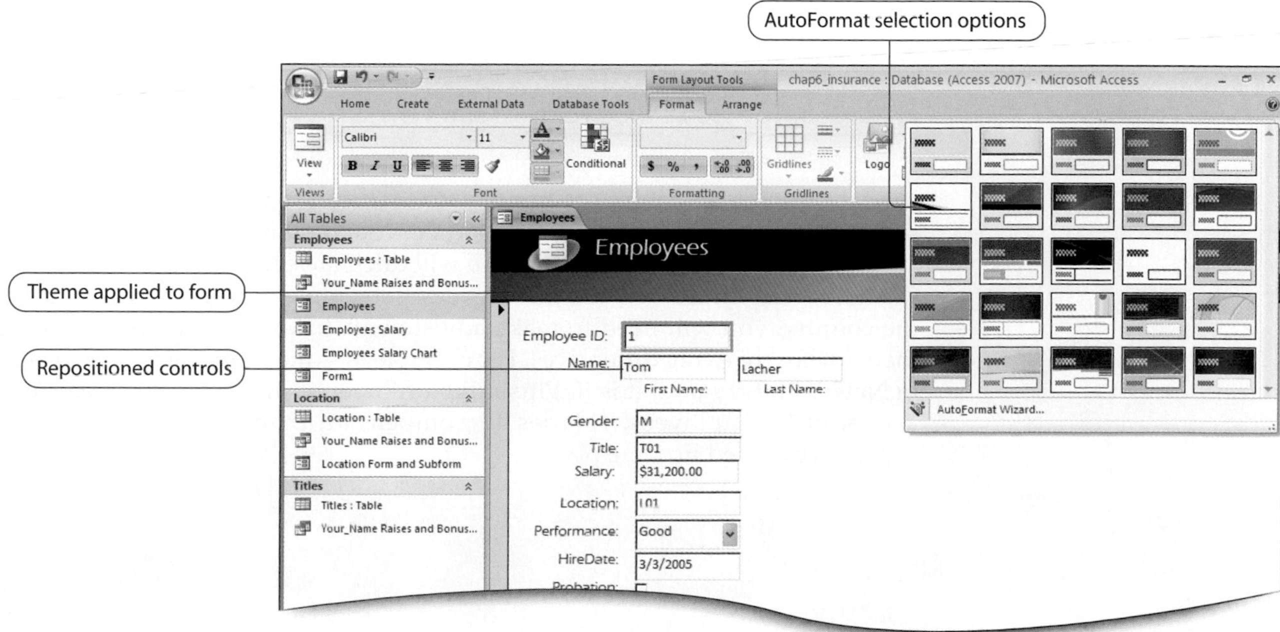

Figure 6.40 Repositioned and Formatted Form

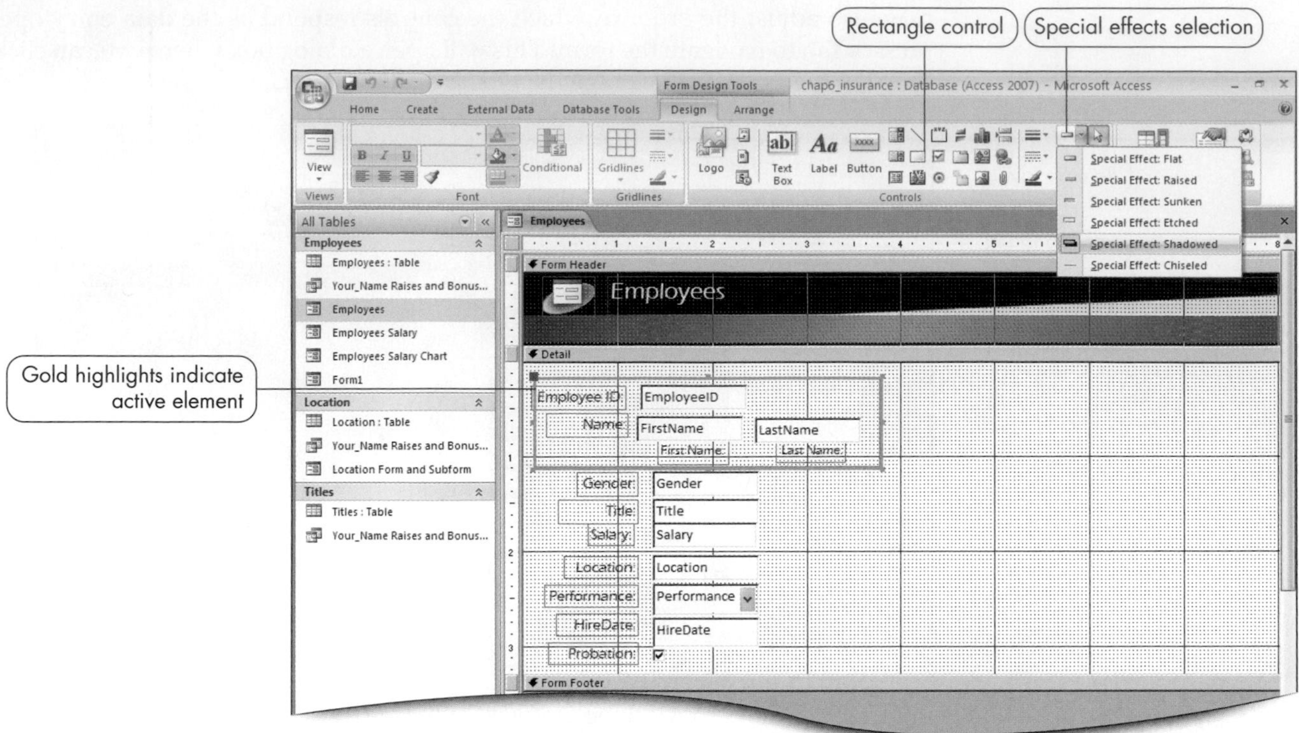

Figure 6.41 Add Controls Using Design View

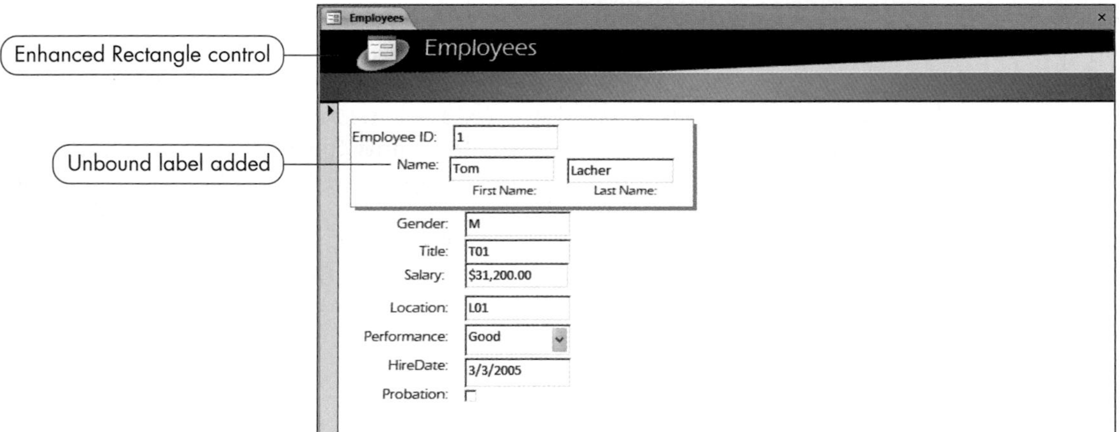

Figure 6.42 Completed Form in Form View

special effects to the controls to indicate where the user should enter data. Figure 6.42 shows the completed form as the user will encounter it in Form view.

In the third hands-on exercise, you will calculate employee pay raises by using a Cost of Living Index. Because this organization employs workers in locations across the country, you will need to make adjustments to worker salaries to compensate them for cost of living differences. For example, it is more expensive to live and work in New York City than it is in Pittsburgh or Phoenix. Your company recognizes this and adjusts employees' salaries to compensate them for the increased living expenses incurred in some places.

Hands-On Exercises

3 | Customizing Forms

Skills covered: 1. Use the Blank Form Tool to Create a Form **2.** Create a Form in Design View **3.** Add Action Buttons and Controls **4.** Create and Edit a Form with a Subform **5.** Customize a Form by Moving Controls and Adding a Theme

Step 1
Use the Blank Form Tool to Create a Form

Refer to Figure 6.43 as you complete Step 1.

a. Open the *chap6_ho1-3_nationalbank_solution* file if necessary, click the **Options** button in the Security Alert toolbar, click the **Enable this content option** in the Security Alerts dialog box, and click **OK**.

TROUBLESHOOTING: If you create unrecoverable errors while completing this hands-on exercise, you can delete the *chap6_ho1-3_nationalbank_solution* file, copy the *chap6_ho2_nationalbank_solution* database you created at the end of the second hands-on exercise, and open the copy of the backup database to start the third hands-on exercise again.

b. Close any open objects in the database and click the **Create tab**. Click **Blank Form** in the Forms group.

A blank form opens in Layout view with the Field List pane open. You should see collapsed views of the tables in the database. Click the plus boxes to view the lists of the fields in each table.

TROUBLESHOOTING: If the Field List pane fails to open, click Add Existing Fields in the Controls group on the Format tab. If the Field list displays but no table names are displayed, click the Show all tables link at the top of the Field List pane.

c. Click the **plus** sign next to the **Loans table** in the Field List pane to expand it.

The available fields in the Loans table display under the table name. The LoanType field contains another plus. That is the field you created a Multivalued lookup for earlier in the chapter.

d. Double-click the **Date** field in the Field List pane to add it to the form.

The Date field moves to the default position in the upper left of the form. A tip box with a lightning symbol displays under the control.

e. Click the **lightning box**, and then click **Show in Tabular Layout**.

The form layout changes to tabular, like a spreadsheet with the column heads above the data. You determine that you want the default Stacked layout for this form.

f. Click the **lightning box**, and then click **Show in Stacked Layout**.

g. Double-click the **Amount and LoanType** fields in the Field List pane to add them to the form.

Because the LoanType field is a lookup field, it adds to the form as a Smart Tag, and the form user may select one or more options from a drop-down list.

h. Click **Title** in the Controls group on the Format tab. Type **Your_Name Payment Receipt** in the title control at the top of the form. Save the form as **Your_Name Payment Receipt**. Close the form.

The Title's control expands to accommodate the form title.

i. Open the form in Form view. Click the **Office Button** and select **Print**. Click **Selected Record(s)** in the Print dialog box and click **OK**. Close the form.

Figure 6.43 Payment Receipt in Form View

Step 2 Create a Form in Design View

Refer to Figure 6.44 as you complete Step 2.

a. Close all database objects if necessary. Click **Form Design** in the Forms group on the Create tab.

   A blank form opens in Design view with the Field List pane open. You should see collapsed views of the tables in the database. Click the plus boxes to view the lists of the fields in each table.

   TROUBLESHOOTING: If the Field List pane fails to open, click Add Existing Fields in the Controls group on the Format tab. If the Field List displays but no table names are displayed, click the Show all tables link at the top of the Field List box.

b. Click the **CustomerID** field in the Customers table's Field List pane and drag it to the *Detail Fields* area of the Pivot grid. Drop it at the intersection of the second vertical line and the first horizontal line.

   TROUBLESHOOTING: If you position the control boxes incorrectly, you can click and drag to reposition them or, if the controls remain active, use the cursor (arrow) keys to reposition the controls. Both the text box and label boxes move together.

c. Double-click the **FirstName, LastName, and AccountType** fields to add them to the Design grid. Position them in columns under the CustomerID field.

TIP Shift-Click to Select Multiple Controls

If you click a control in Design view, release the mouse, and press and hold Shift, you can select multiple items and interact with them collectively.

d. Click **Title** in the Controls group on the Format tab. Type **Your_Name Customer** in the box that says **Form1**.

e. Right-click the **Form1 tab** and select **Form View** from the shortcut menu. Check to make sure the controls align. Right-click the **Form1 tab** and select **Design View** from the shortcut menu. If necessary, adjust the control layout.

You look at the form as the user will encounter it in Form view but make adjustments to it in Design view or Layout view.

f. Save your form and name it **Your_Name Customer**.

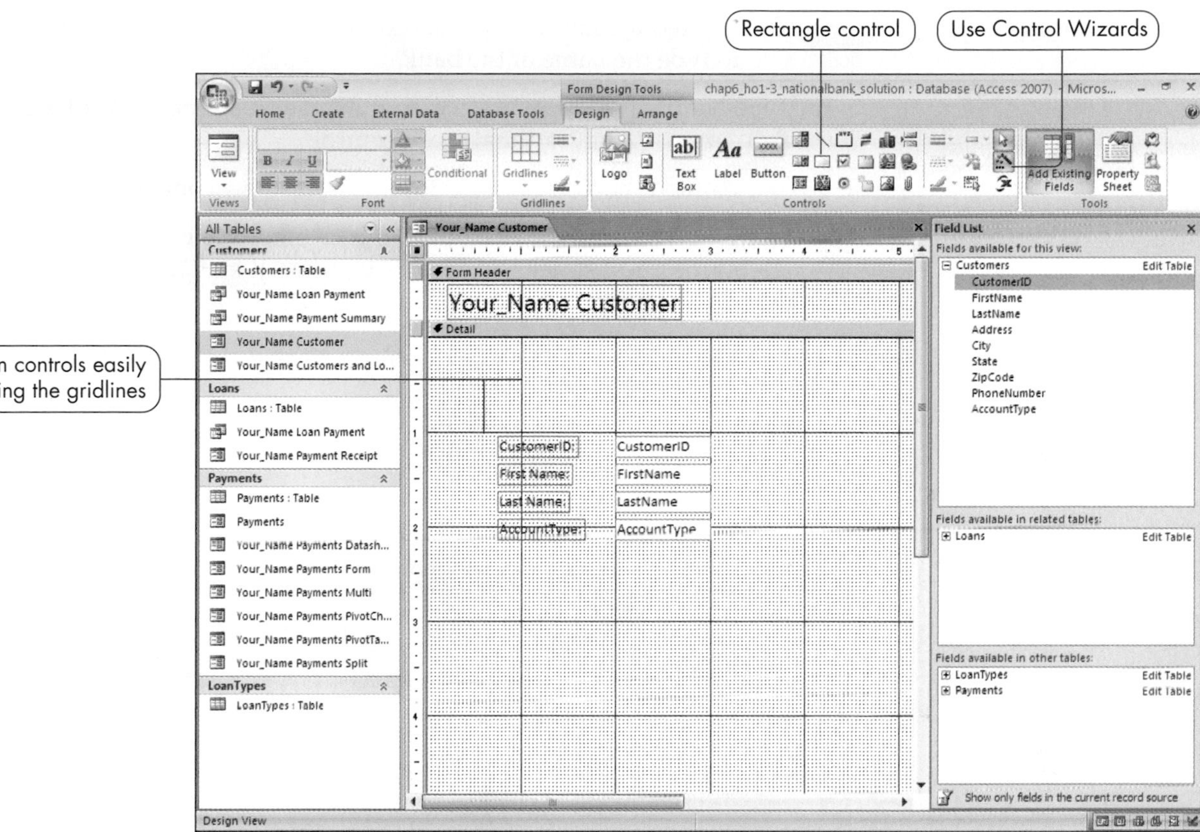

Figure 6.44 Design View of the Customer Form

Step 3
Add Action Buttons and Controls

Refer to Figure 6.45 as you complete Step 3.

a. Check to make sure the Use Control Wizards tool is engaged (see Figure 6.44). Click **Button** in the Controls group on the Design tab.

The Button tool turns gold and waits for instruction from you about where to position the button on the form.

b. Click on the first vertical grid under the AccountType control box.

Access places a button named, for the time being, Command1. (Your button may have a different number. That is OK.) The Command Button Wizard dialog box launches. This button will provide form users a navigation tool to go to the next record.

c. Select, if necessary, **Record Navigation** in the Categories box and **Go To Next Record** in the Actions box. Click **Next**.

You decide that you want a picture on this button.

d. Select the **Picture** option and **Go To Next**. Click **Next**.

e. Name the button **Next** and click **Finish**.

Your Button changes shape and shows a right triangle.

f. Switch to **Form View** by right-clicking the **Your_Name Customer tab** and use the button. Navigate through a few records to make sure it works. If it functions as expected, return to **Design View** (right-click the tab) and save your changes.

You want to add the Bank Name to the form header area. To do this, you need a control.

g. Click **Label** in the Controls group on the Design tab. Click the vertical Gridline on the **four-inch mark** in the Form Header area and drag to the **six-inch mark**.

You created a control. The insertion point is flashing inside the label, ready for you to type the name of the bank.

h. Type **National Bank**. Click the **Your_Name Customer** control. Click the **Format Painter**. Click the **National Bank** control.

You painted the title control's format on the new control.

i. Switch to Form view to examine your changes. Return to Design view. Make any needed adjustments. Compare your work to Figure 6.45. If it is correct, save and close the form.

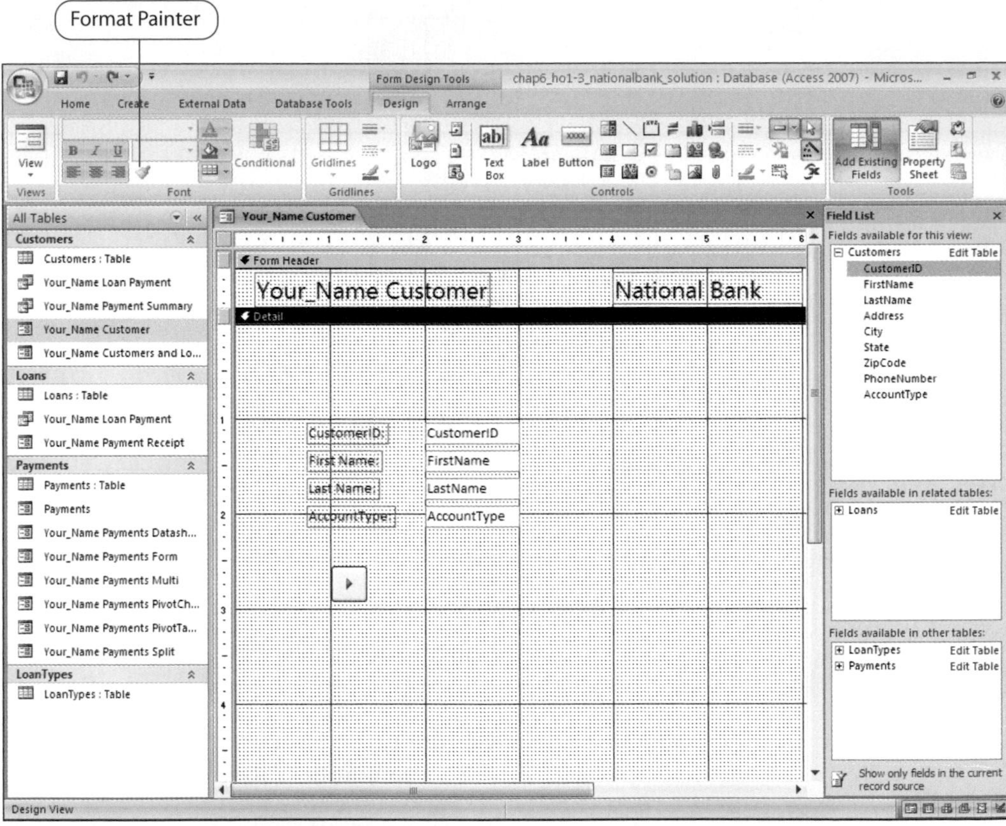

Figure 6.45 National Bank Customer Form in Design View

Step 4 Create and Edit a Form with a Subform

Refer to Figure 6.46 as you complete Step 4.

a. Open the **Customers table** in Datasheet view. Click the **Create tab** and click **Form** in the Forms group.

Access creates the form and associated subform and opens them in Layout view ready for editing. Notice that both the form and subform have separate navigation bars. The first customer has three mortgages with the bank. The subform record indicator displays record 1 of 3 and the form record indicates record 1 of 11.

b. Click the Form Navigation **Next Record** button.

You see data about Scott Wit, who has two car loans.

c. Click the Subform Navigation **Next Record** button.

The active record becomes Mr. Wit's $10,000 car loan.

d. Click the column leading **Term** in the subform. A gold border surrounds the Term column. Click and drag the **right boundary right** to make the column wider.

e. Switch to **Design View** by right-clicking the tab. Click **Yes** in the Save dialog box and save the form as **Your_Name Customers and Loans**.

The subform appears as a link to the table data and looks blank.

f. Right-click the subform and select **Properties** from the shortcut menu. Click the **Data tab** in the Property Sheet, if necessary. Examine the Link Master Fields and Link Child Fields properties.

Access used the existing relationships among the tables to generate the form and subform with all of the properties appropriately selected.

g. Save the form.

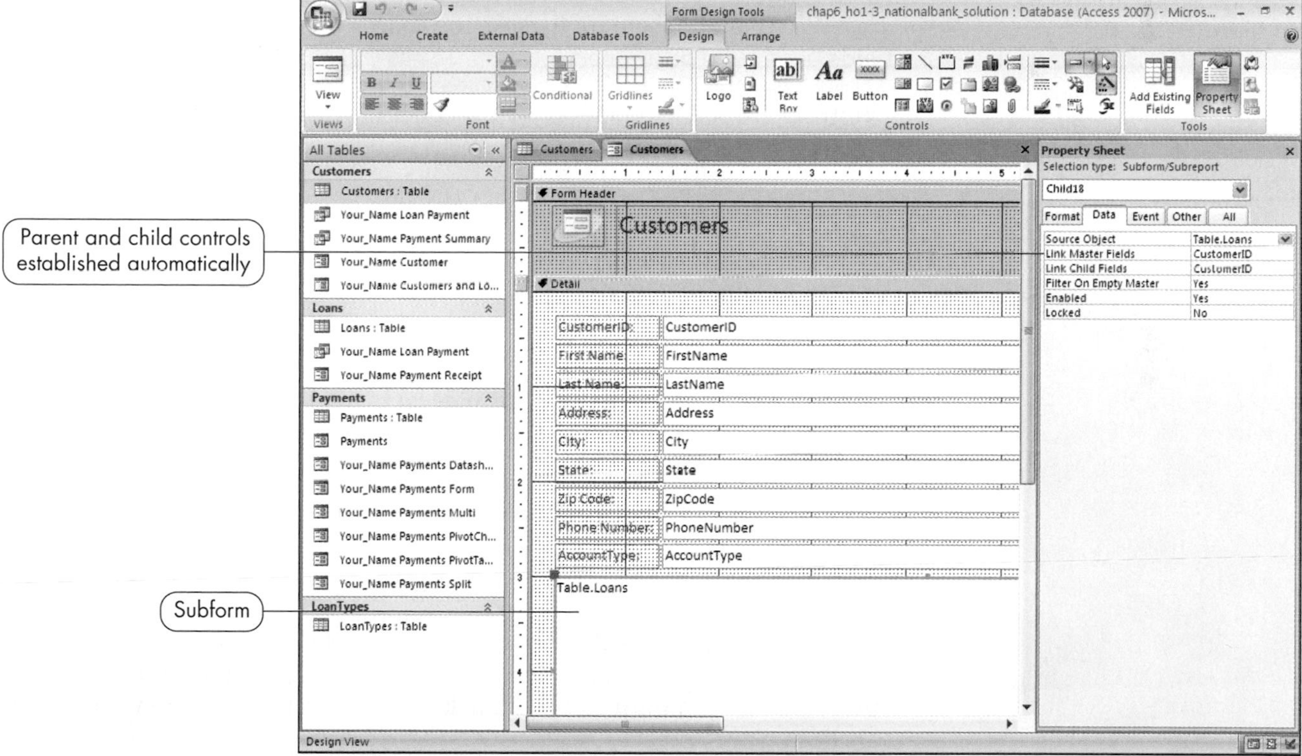

Figure 6.46 Form with Subform in Design View

Step 5
Customize a Form by Moving Controls and Adding a Theme

Refer to Figure 6.47 as you complete Step 5.

a. Click the **CustomerID field** in the main form. Locate the box in the upper left that contains the plus sign. Click the box.

All of the controls in the main form select. You want to move the city, state, and Zip fields to the same row to conserve space. You must first remove the currently applied layout.

b. Click the **Arrange tab** and click **Remove** in the Control Layout group. Close the Property Sheet.

The controls are still selected, but each control has a size handle permitting you to interact with the fields separately.

c. Click the **City Field Text** box (the right one) to select it. The gold selection boundary should be only around the right city box. Move your mouse over the right edge of the City control and when the pointer shape changes to a two-headed arrow, click and drag the boundary left to the three-inch mark. Repeat with the **State** and **Zip Code** boxes. Make the Zip Code box about one inch wide.

d. Move the mouse pointer over any boundary of the Zip Code box and when the pointer shape changes to the **four-headed move arrow**, click and drag it **up** and position it so the *right boundary* is on the **8" vertical grid** mark and it is on the same row as the City field.

e. Click the **State Field** text box to select it and move the mouse over a boundary. When the pointer shape changes to the **four-headed move arrow**, click and drag it **up** and position it between the City and Zip Code fields on the same row.

f. Click the **Phone Number label** to select it and make it **wider** so the word Number is no longer cut off, if necessary. Press **Shift** as you click to select the labels and text boxes for Phone Number and Account Type. When all four boxes are selected, move them **up** to close the space where the State and Zip Code fields used to be positioned.

TROUBLESHOOTING: If you select too many controls, simply click off onto the Design grid to deselect everything and try again.

g. Edit the labels so that spaces appear in field names and nothing is cut off.

h. Click **Tab Order** in the Control Layout group on the Arrange tab. Click the row selector beside **CustomerID**. With your mouse pointer still in the row selector area, drag the selected CustomerID field **down** and drop it below the AccountType field. Click **OK**.

You altered the order that the form accepts tab commands. After entering the AccountType, the data entry operator will move to the CustomerID field at the top of the main form.

i. Save the form and change to the **Layout view** by right-clicking the form tab.

j. Click **More** to see the list of AutoFormats in the AutoFormats group on the Format tab. Select **Concourse** (second row, first column).

k. Click anywhere in the **subform** to select it. A gold box surrounds it. Click the **Home tab** and click **Totals** in the Records group. Click in the **Total Row** of the subform in the **Amount** column. Click the **arrow** and select **Sum** from the listed functions. Save and close the form.

The Totals tool enables you to use common aggregating functions in a form exactly like you may do in a table or query. You notice that the Column headings in the subform need spaces in them. You may not alter a field property in a subform. You may add a caption to the table that the subform sources.

l. Open the **Loans table** in Design view. Create a caption that includes a space for the LoanID, LoanType, and InterestRate fields. Save the changes and close the Loans table. Reopen the Your_Name Customers and Loans form in Layout view. Look in the subform for any necessary column-width adjustments and make them.

m. Look at your form in Form view and press **Tab** on the keyboard to test the tab order change. Save and close the form.

n. Click the **Office Button**, select **Manage**, and select **Compact and Repair**. Close the file and exit Access.

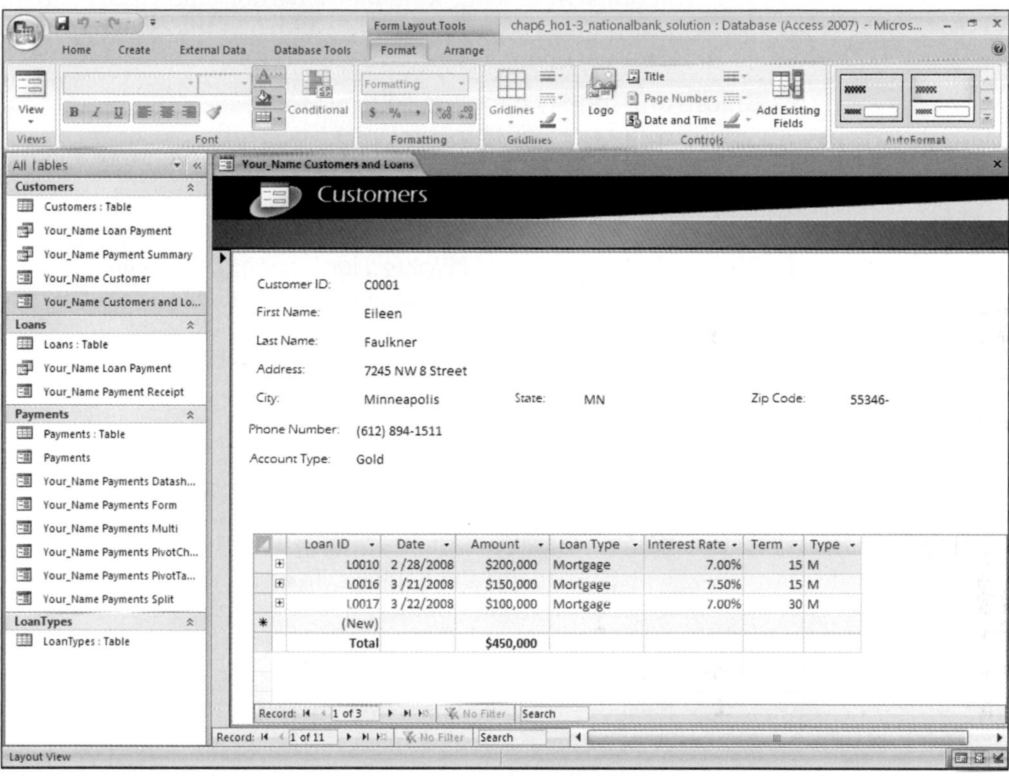

Figure 6.47 Formatted Form

Summary

1. **Establish data validity.** Database administrators establish safeguards on table data to protect them from data-entry and user error. As you learn these skills you shift from being a person in the organization who uses data to becoming the individual in the organization who administers, manages, and protects the organization's data. Data validation is a set of tools that help control the type and accuracy of the data entered into a field. Although Access provides some data validation automatically, you will need to augment the validation to help defend the data against user errors. Simply requiring that a field be filled out can help. Use a default value when the majority of your data will be the same value. Validation text informs users about what they have done incorrectly and instructs them about what needs to be done. When you break a validation rule, you must provide Access with the required information in the desired format before you can move on.
2. **Create and modify a lookup field.** Increase data entry speed and accuracy by providing the user with a predefined list of values. The Lookup Wizard helps create, populate, and relate the lookup field. Users select field values from a drop-down list. Change the values of a lookup table by opening the lookup table and changing the values in the table. The changes are immediately available.
3. **Create and modify a multivalued lookup field.** Sometimes, a database needs to support multiple choices. These choices are often represented by check boxes on a form in which you can choose multiple options. A multivalued field is one defined to accept multiple choices for a single field without requiring you to create a complex design. It is similar to a many-to-many relationship. Select the Allow Multiple Values check box in the appropriate Lookup Wizard to define this. Under the surface, Access creates a series of juncture tables and stores them independently.
4. **Work with input masks.** An input mask specifies the exact formatting of the input data while minimizing data storage requirements. You are used to viewing (and thinking about) Social Security numbers with hyphens in them, for example 123-45-6789, and telephone numbers with parentheses and hyphens. To conserve space in an Access database using an input mask for a Social Security number field, only the digits are stored in the table as 123456789, but the mask displays with the hyphens to make the data more readable for the user.
5. **Create forms by using the Form Tool.** Forms enable data entry in one or more tables with more flexibility in presentation to the user. They often resemble paper forms and facilitate the switch from paper to electronic data storage. For example, the last time you entered your name, e-mail address, and other information and clicked a submit button, you worked in a form. They also enable displaying objects such as graphics, charts, or other Office files. Access provides several different methods of creating, editing, and embellishing forms. After a form is created, you will edit it many times to satisfy the users' data entry needs. The Form tool gives you a one-click method of form creation. Split Forms provide a data interaction method that combines a form with a datasheet. The Multiple Items form creates a form that shows many records in a datasheet with one item in each row. Access provides a Datasheet Form that creates a form that looks exactly like the underlying data source. You use PivotTables and PivotCharts to summarize lengthy data using complex criteria and to represent the summary graphically.
6. **Create custom forms using Design view.** You can create a form using Design view, add action buttons, perform calculations, create and modify subforms, and apply formatting and conditional formatting to enhance your form's usability. Design view gives you the power to completely customize the form. The Design view of a form is like a blueprint for a building. You do not see the data in a Design view form; you see only the controls, or placeholders, that will store and display your data. Some actions may only be accomplished in Design view. Other actions, like applying or modifying formats or styles, may be done in either Design or Layout views. Use the Design grid. You launch a new form in Design view by clicking the Create tab and then clicking the Design View Tool. A blank workspace and the tools that you will use to create the form display. The Design grid contains two grids, a fine and a wide hatch. These provide you with placement guides to help you align the form data. The default Design grid displays only the detail section of the form. You will use the tools to add additional sections and controls, for example a header and a calculated control such as a sum. The Button tool in the Control group provides powerful and user-friendly form additions. The Command

...continued on Next Page

Button Wizard launches as soon as you create a button on a form. Access provides many alternatives for form commands, such as print, next record, and go to.

7. **Create subforms.** A subform is a form that exists inside another form. The primary form (parent) may be edited separately from the subform (child), and the subform is stored and edited separately from the parent. Alternatively, both forms may be viewed and edited at the same time. You use subforms to show information that sources two or more related tables such as customers and orders. Access provides several ways to create nested forms, including through an option in the Form Wizard.

8. **Design functional formats** The colors and patterns you decide to use might have the unintended effect of making the data entry workers' lives unpleasant. You may need to rearrange the controls on a form. To change the form layout you must first remove the default layout using either Layout or Design views. Click the box with the four-headed arrow in the upper left and the controls select. Employ the Remove tool in the Control Layout group on the Arrange tab. You can apply themes, colors, and special effects to most form elements. If you are not sure that the special effects add to the form's utility, omit them.

Key Terms

Multiple Choice

1. Database administrators establish safeguards on table data to protect it from data-entry and user error to ensure:
   (a) Referential integrity
   (b) Data validity
   (c) Hierarchical structure
   (d) Normalization

2. Which of the following is not an example of a data validation tool?
   (a) You cannot enter text into a date field.
   (b) Primary keys can contain duplicate values.
   (c) Defined default values.
   (d) Input masks, Lookup lists, Multiple Value Fields, Logical rule.

3. To make a field required, you should:
   (a) Set the required value in the Form Wizard.
   (b) Set the required button on the form design toolbox.
   (c) Set the required value in the field properties box in the table's Design view.
   (d) Click the Required/Default command in the table design group.

4. A good validation text message should:
   (a) Be generic, e.g., "You made a mistake."
   (b) Tell the users what they did incorrectly.
   (c) Offer the user guidance.
   (d) Inform the user about the error and offer guidance on correction.

5. This is the field from the source data that contains values to be summarized in a lookup table.
   (a) Lookup field
   (b) Page field
   (c) Item
   (d) Data field

6. To alter available selections in a lookup table, you should:
   (a) Add, change, or delete the records in the underlying table.
   (b) Type the desired value in the drop-down list in the form as you fill it out.
   (c) Modify the lookup property.
   (d) Click the lookup table command on the lookup table group.

7. A multivalued lookup field would most likely be represented on a form by:
   (a) An option where you put a dot in a circle to select
   (b) A drop-down list where you Ctrl + click multiple options
   (c) Check boxes beside items in a list where you put an X in the box to select
   (d) Both b and c

8. Which of the following is true about input masks?
   (a) Input masks store extra characters in records such as hyphens in Social Security numbers and parentheses and hyphens in U.S. phone numbers to speed data entry.
   (b) Input masks display the hyphens in a Social Security number field or parentheses and hyphens in a U.S. phone number field and store them in the record.
   (c) Input masks display the hyphens in a Social Security number field or parentheses and hyphens in a U.S. phone number field, but do not store them in the record.
   (d) Input masks should not be overused because they use slightly more storage space.

9. You have a Customers table open in Datasheet view. It is related to an Orders table, and you can click an expand button and examine the orders placed by the customer. If you click the Form tool, what will result?
   (a) You will create a form based on the Customers table and a subform based on the Orders table. The Customers table will be the child.
   (b) You will create a form based on the Customers table and a subform based on the Orders table. The Customers table will be the parent.
   (c) You will create a form based on the Orders table and a subform based on the Customers table. The Customers table will be the parent.
   (d) You will create a form based on the Orders table and a subform based on the Customers table. The Customers table will be the child.

10. This type of form provides a data interaction method that combines a form with a datasheet:
    (a) Multiple items form
    (b) Tabular form
    (c) Datasheet form
    (d) Split form

Multiple Choice Continued...

11. The following are examples of forms available to create in Access except:
    (a) Multiple items forms
    (b) Datasheet forms
    (c) Spreadsheet forms
    (d) PivotTable and PivotChart forms

12. The Design view for a form gives you the power to:
    (a) Customize the form.
    (b) Make formatting and style changes, but not alter the functionality of the form.
    (c) View the data as it will be presented in the form.
    (d) All of the above.

13. Where do you find the tools to add Action buttons to a form you are designing?
    (a) You can download button code from Microsoft.com to use as an add-in.
    (b) The Button Wizard in the controls toolbox
    (c) The Button tool in the Control group launches the Command Button Wizard and creates buttons per your specifications.
    (d) Buttons have to be programmed in Visual Basic and imported to Access for forms.

14. Which of the following is not true about subforms?
    (a) The primary form (parent) may be edited separately from the subform (child), and the subform is stored and edited separately from the parent.
    (b) Subforms are created automatically when you use the Subform Design Wizard.
    (c) Both forms may be viewed and edited at the same time.
    (d) You use subforms to show information that sources two or more related tables such as customers and orders.

15. Why should you design forms for your databases?
    (a) To present users with a format that is familiar and easy to use
    (b) To make the database run more quickly and efficiently
    (c) To display differing views of PivotTables and PivotCharts
    (d) a and c but not b

Practice Exercises

1 National Conference Data Entry

You are the intern assigned to the Dean of Students' Office and spend most of your time scheduling and planning the National Conference. Others in the office also work on the conference, but you find that sometimes they omit needed information or make errors that you must find and fix. For example, some people in the office enter phone numbers as (910) 555-1101, while others enter them as 910-555-1101. Some people skip the phone number field completely. You decide to add some verification and requirement properties to the database to help protect the data. Refer to Figure 6.48 to verify your work.

a. Copy the partially completed file *chap6_pe1_natconf.accdb* from the Exploring Access folder to your production folder. Rename it **chap6_pe1_natconf_solution**. Double-click the file name to open it. Click **Options** on the Security Warning toolbar, click **Enable this content** in the Microsoft Office Security Options dialog box, and click **OK**.
b. Open the **Speakers table** and replace *Your_Name* with your name in the FirstName and LastName fields.
c. Right-click the table tab and select **Design View** from the shortcut menu. Click the **PhoneNumber** field in the Field Name column to activate it. Change the Required property in the Field Properties pane to **Yes**.
d. Click the Input Mask property for the PhoneNumber field and click **Build** on the right side. Click **Yes** to the alert message on saving the changes to the table. Click **Yes** in the Data Integrity Warning dialog box. In the Input Mask Wizard dialog box, make sure that the **Phone Number** is selected in the Input Mask Column.
e. Click the **Try It box**. Click to the left edge of the phone number placeholders and type **2227775555**. Click **Next**.
f. In the next wizard screen, click the **Placeholder character drop-down arrow** and select #. Click in the **Try it** box and make sure that the mask displays **(###) ###-####**. Click **Next**.
g. Store the data **Without the symbols in the mask**. Click **Next**. Click **Finish**.
h. Make sure that the PhoneNumber field is still active. Capture a screenshot by pressing **Prnt Scrn**. Launch Word. Type your name and section number on the first line, and then press **Enter**. Paste the screenshot in the Word document, print, and save the file as **chap6_pe1_natconf_solution.docx**.
i. Toggle back to the Access database. Save the changes to the table design.
j. Click the **Office Button**, select **Manage**, and select **Compact and Repair** the file. Close the file.

...continued on Next Page

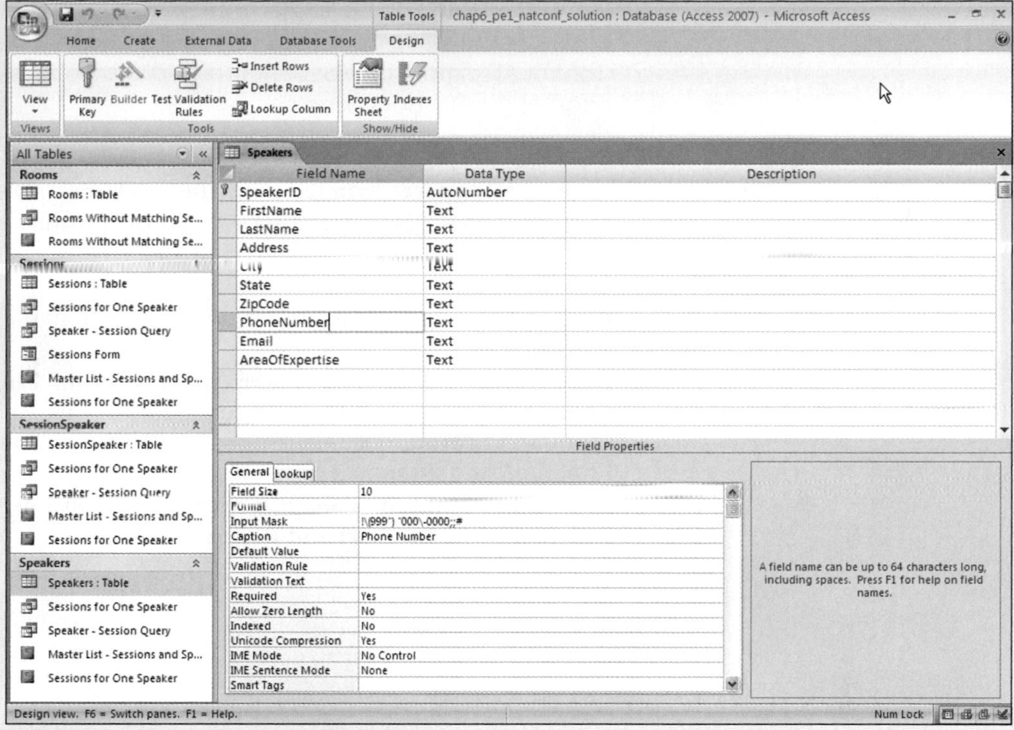

Figure 6.48 Table Property Changes

2 National Conference Form Design

You discover that a coworker entered information in the Speakers table incorrectly. He entered the first half of a new record correctly, but then jumped to a different record and overwrote the information correctly stored with incorrect data. When you discovered the error, it took you a long time to find the correct information and correct both records. You decide that a form would help your coworkers enter data more accurately and help eliminate a stray mouse click damaging data in other records. You need to create a form that will help the office workers add new speakers and sessions to the database as plans are finalized. After creating the form, you will need to customize it to be more attractive and functional. Refer to Figure 6.49 to verify your work.

a. Copy the partially completed file *chap6_pe2_natconf.accdb* from the Exploring Access folder to your production folder. Rename it **chap6_pe2_natconf_solution**. Double-click the file name to open it. Enable the security content by clicking the **Options** button in the Security Warning bar. Select **Enable this content**, and then click **OK**.

b. Open the **Speakers table** and replace *Your_Name* with your name in the FirstName and LastName fields. Close the Speakers table.

c. Open the **Speaker-Session query** in Datasheet view. Click **Form** in the Forms group on the Create tab.

d. Move the mouse to the right boundary of the selected control. When the pointer shape changes to the double-headed arrow, click and drag the right boundary left to make the column about one-half as wide.

e. Locate and click the **box with the plus sign** in it in the *upper-left corner* of the form in Layout view. All the controls select. Click the **Arrange tab**, and then click the **Remove Tool** in the Control Layout group. Click anywhere on the white space to deselect the controls.

f. Click the control for the Session ID, **S01**. Move your mouse over the right boundary. When the pointer shape changes to the double-headed arrow, click and drag the right boundary **right** to make the column about *one-half inch wide*.

g. Click the control for the Session Title, **Understanding Diversity within the University**. With the mouse pointer in the four-headed-arrow, move the control **up** and position it beside the *Session ID, S01*.

...continued on Next Page

TROUBLESHOOTING: You can click on the S01 control box, and then Shift+click on the Session Title control to select both boxes. Then on the Arrange tab, in the Control Alignment group, click Top to align the Session Title box even with the top edge of the S01 control box.

h. Click the **SessionTitle label** and press **Delete**. Edit the SessionID and StartingTime labels to add **spaces**. Edit the form title to be **Speaker – Session Form**.

i. Make the text boxes wider to match the Session Title text box width. (You might find it easier to use the Design view grid to align the boxes.) Save the form as **Your_Name Speaker-Session Form**.

j. Right-click the form tab and select **Form View** from the shortcut menu. Navigate to the third record.

k. Capture a screenshot of the third record by pressing **Prnt Scrn**. Open a Word document. Type your name and section number on the first line, then press **Enter**. Paste the screenshot into the Word document and save the file as **chap6_pe2_natconf_solution.docx**. Print the Word document. Close Word.

l. Save and close the form and any open objects. Click the **Office Button**, select **Manage**, and then select **Compact and Repair**. Close the file.

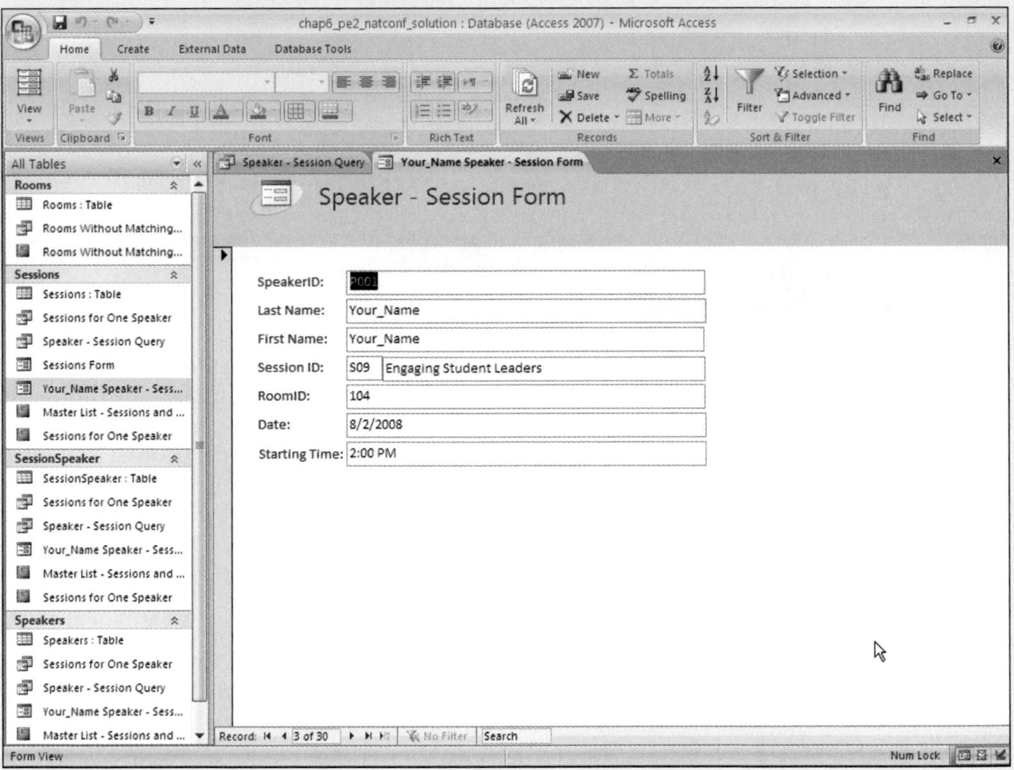

Figure 6.49 Edited Form

3 Lifelong Learning

The Lifelong Learning Physicians Association asks that you help simplify their data entry tasks. They want a form that will enroll new physicians as members. Because the data entry clerks sometimes misspell the members' specializations, you decide to create a lookup table. If all of the specialty areas are spelled uniformly, a query or a filter to examine data subsets by specialty will return predictable and accurate results. After creating the lookup and the form, you will populate the table with each physician's area of specialty. Refer to Figure 6.50 to verify your work.

a. Copy the partially completed file *chap6_pe3_physicians.accdb* from the Exploring Access folder to your production folder. Rename it **chap6_pe3_physicians_solution.accdb**.

...continued on Next Page

Double-click the file name to open it. Click **Options** in the Security Warning bar, select **Enable this content**, and click **OK**.

b. Open the **Physicians table** in Datasheet view. Click in the Add New Field column in the first row. Click the **Datasheet tab**, and then click **Lookup Column** in the Fields & Column group to launch the Lookup Wizard.

c. In the first wizard screen, select **I want the lookup column to look up the values in a table or query**. Click **Next**. In the second screen, select **Table:Specialization**. Click **Next**. In the next screen, double-click the **Specialization** field to move it to the *Selected Fields box*. Click **Next twice**. Adjust the column width to make sure that all of *Exercise Physiology* displays. Ensure that the **Hide Key column check box** is selected. Click **Next**. In the final screen, name the lookup **Specialization.** Click **Finish**. Save the table.

d. Click the **Create tab**, and then click **Form** in the Forms group. Click the **subform boundary** at the bottom of the form to select it. With the large gold rectangle surrounding the subform, press **Delete**.

e. Right-click the **Physicians form tab** and Switch to **Form View** by selecting it from the shortcut menu. Use the form to populate the Specialization Field with the following information. Add yourself as a new record. Your specialization is Gerontology.

First Name	Last Name	Specialization
Bonnie	Clinton	Obstetrics
Warren	Brasington	Hematology
James	Shindell	General Medicine
Edward	Wood	Cardiology
Michelle	Quintana	Internal Medicine
Kristine	Park	Exercise Physiology
William	Williamson	General Medicine
Holly	Davis	Cardiology
Steven	Fisher	Internal Medicine
David	Tannen	Hematology
Jeffrey	Jacobsen	Internal Medicine
Patsy	Clark	Cardiology

f. Save the form as **Your_Name Physicians**. Capture a screenshot of the form with your record displayed by pressing **Prnt Scrn**. Launch Word, and then type **Your_Name and section number** at the top of the page. Press **Enter**. Paste the screenshot into the Word document. Keep the Word document open.

g. Return to Access. Click the **Physicians table tab** to display the table data. Close and open the Physicians table again. Check to make sure that your newly added record displays.

h. Capture a screenshot of the Physicians table by pressing **Prnt Scrn**. Return to Word and press **Enter** after the screenshot of the form. Paste the screenshot into the Word document and save the file as **chap6_pe3_physicians_solution.docx**. Print and close the Word document.

i. Save and close the table and form. Click the **Office Button**, select **Manage**, and select **Compact and Repair**. Close the file.

...continued on Next Page

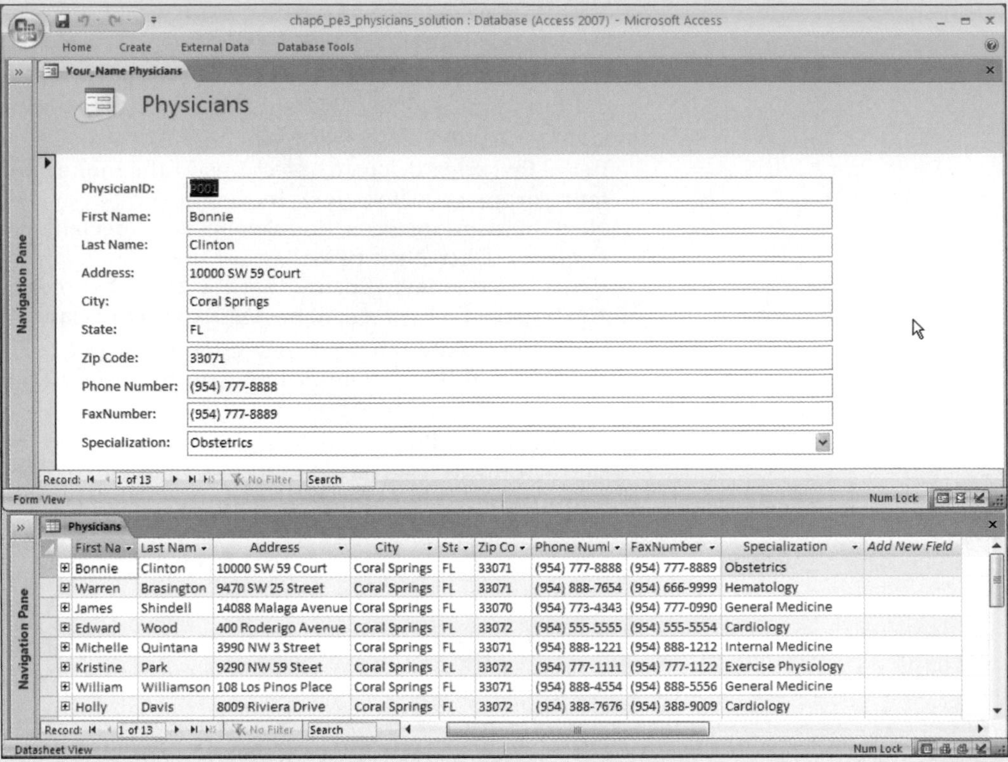

Figure 6.50 Form and Table

4 Custom Coffee

The Custom Coffee Company is a small service organization that provides coffee, tea, and snacks to offices. Custom Coffee also provides and maintains the equipment for brewing the beverages. Although the firm is small, its excellent reputation for providing outstanding customer service has helped it grow. Part of its good customer service record is because the firm owner set up a database to organize and keep track of customer purchases. You need to add a form to help track customer purchases. Because the Customers and Orders tables have a one-to-many relationship, the form created needs to be a form based on the Customers table and a subform showing the Orders each customer has placed. You will also need to add additional fields to the form. Refer to Figure 6.51 to verify your work..

a. Copy the partially completed file *chap6_pe4_coffee.accdb* from the Exploring Access folder to your production folder. Rename it **chap6_pe4_coffee_solution.accdb**. Double-click the file name to open the file. Click **Options** in the Security Warning bar, select **Enable this content**, and click **OK**.

b. Double-click the **Sales Rep table** to open it. Replace *Your_Name* with your name. Close the table by clicking Close in the database window.

c. Double-click the **Customers table** to open it. Click **Form** in the Forms group on the Create tab. The form and subform are too long to fit on a single screen, so you need to rearrange the controls.

d. Move your mouse over the *right boundary* of the first control and when the pointer shape changes to the double-headed arrow, click and drag **left** until all of the control text boxes are about two inches wide.

e. Click the **Box with the plus sign** in it in the upper-left corner of the form. Click the **Arrange tab** and click **Remove** in the Control Layout group. **Click** the *Contact label* and **Shift+click** the *text box* controls to select them both, drag them up, and position them in the same row as the Customer Name.

...continued on Next Page

f. Reposition the remaining main form controls as shown in Figure 6.51. Delete the label controls for Address2, City, State, and Zip.

g. Click the *subform border* to activate it. Find the Move box in the upper-left corner. Click and drag the Move box up. Save your form as **Your_Name Customers**.

h. Right-click the Form tab and select **Design View** from the shortcut menu. Display the **Field List pane** by clicking **Add Existing Fields** in the Tools group on the Design tab.

i. Click the **plus sign** beside the Sales Reps table to display the fields. Find and select the **LastName** field in the Sales Reps table. Drag the **LastName** field to the form and drop it *above the Sales Rep ID field*. Save the form. Close the Field List pane.

j. Right-click the form tab and select **Layout View** from the shortcut menu. Click the **Sales Rep ID** label and use Format Painter to copy the formatting to the **LastName** label. Click the **Next Record** button six times to view Record 7. Press **Tab** to test the tab order of the form controls. The LastName field is out of order. Right-click the *form tab* and select **Layout View** from the shortcut menu. Click **Tab Order** in the Control Layout group on the Arrange tab.

k. Click the **LastName field row selector** (the gray box to the left of the field name). Once selected, drag the row selector box and the associated field name **up** and drop it *under the Fax field*.

l. Move the Tab Order box to the upper-right corner of the screen and press **Prnt Scrn**. Click **OK** to close the Tab Order box.

m. Launch Word, change to **Landscape** orientation, and type **Your_name** and **section number**. Press **Enter**. Paste the screenshot into the Word document and save the file as **chap6_pe4_coffee_solution.docx**. Print and close the Word document.

n. Save the form. Click the **Office Button**, select **Manage**, and then select **Compact and Repair**. Close the file.

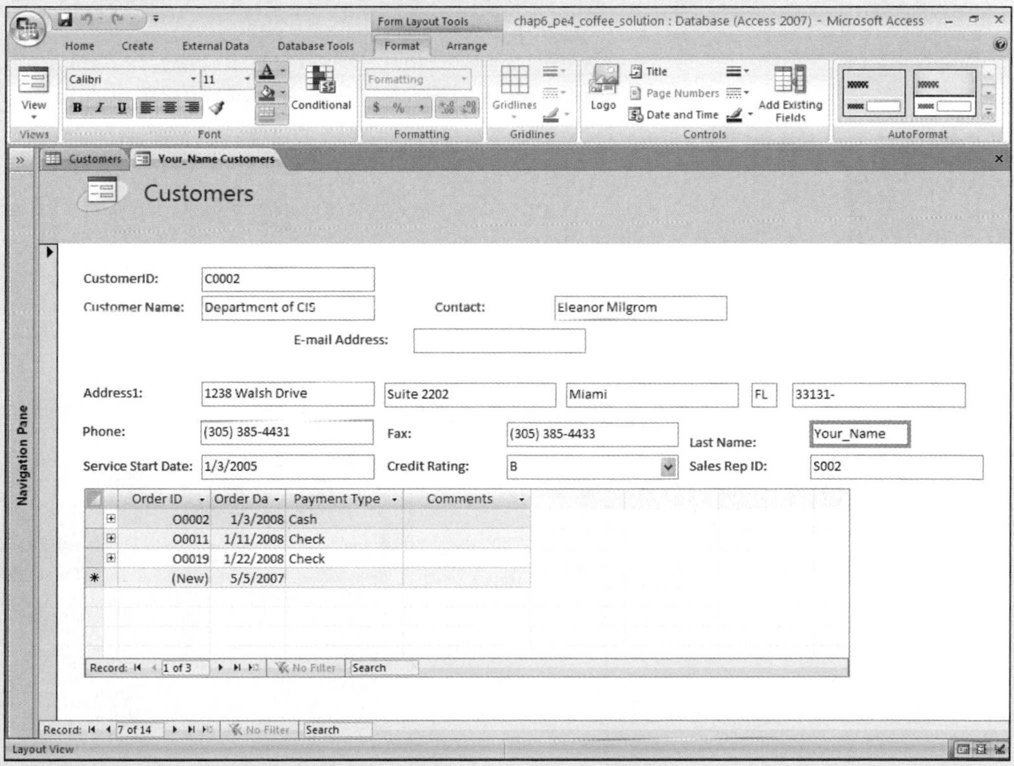

Figure 6.51 Form, Subform, and Rearranged Controls

Mid-Level Exercises

1 Create a Lookup and Edit a Form

The Parent Teachers Organization (PTO) at the South Vancouver Pre-school holds a silent auction each spring to help supply the classrooms. Parents and grandparents donate items to the auction and are invited to a dinner at which they can place bids. To help the school keep track of the donations, you prepared an Access form. You gave the form to the chairperson of the Auction Committee, who requested changes to the form design. You need to add a button that will print the form. You also need to create a lookup field to categorize donated items. The form also needs to display the items' value. Refer to Figure 6.52 to verify your work.

a. Locate the file named *chap6_mid1_preschool.accdb*, copy it to your production folder, and rename it **chap6_mid1_preschool_solution.accdb**. Open the file and enable the content.

b. Rename the *Donors* form as **Your_Name Donors**. Open the Donor table and replace Shelly Martin's name in the first and last name fields with your name.

c. Create a multivalued lookup field that uses the Category field in the Categories table as the data source. Name the field **Category**. Look at the ItemDonated field and use your best judgment to populate the new field with data.

d. Open the **Your_Name Donor** form in Layout view. Add the **ItemValue** field to the form under the Item Donated field. Add the **Category** field under the Number Attending field. Match the formatting of the other controls on the form.

e. Switch to **Design view**. Add a button between the Add New Record and Close Form buttons that prints the active record.

f. Change to **Form View** to test the Tab navigation. Fix any Tab order problems in Layout or Design views. Test the action buttons.

g. Capture a screenshot of the form that has the Tab Order dialog box open. Move the **Tab Order box** to the *top-right corner* of the screen before capturing the screenshot.

h. Launch Word, type **Your_Name and section number**, and press **Enter**. Paste the screenshot and save the file as **chap6_mid1_preschool_solution.docx**.

i. Print and close the Word document. Compact and repair the database. Close the database.

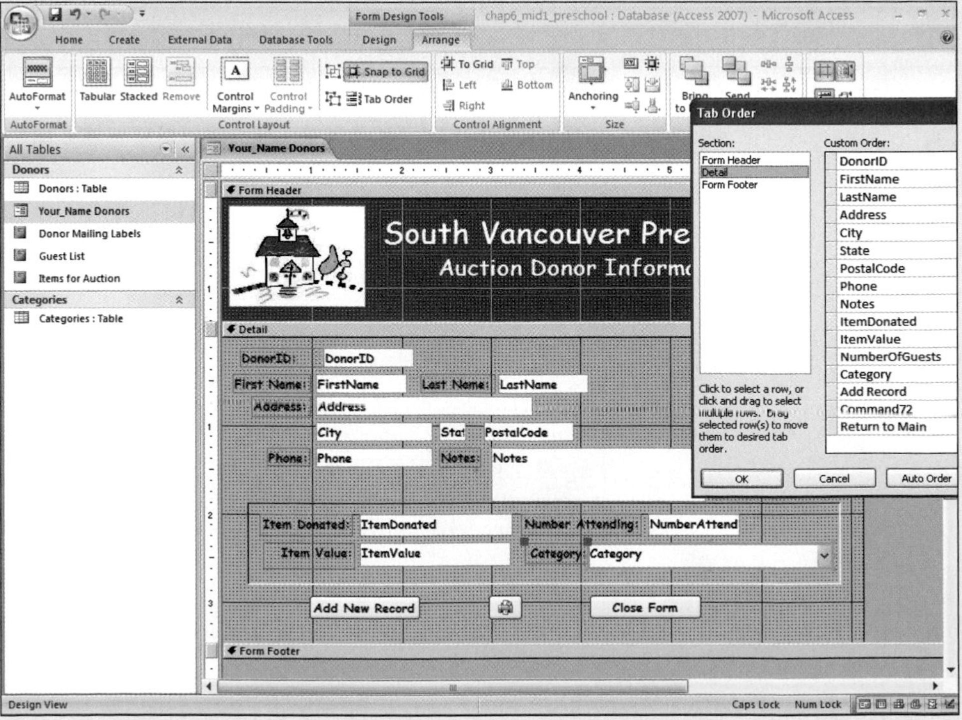

Figure 6.52 Edited Donation Form

...continued on Next Page

2 Create a Split Form, Filter a Form, and Add Summary Calculations

You are the general manager of a large hotel chain. Your establishment provides a variety of guest services ranging from rooms and conferences to weddings. You and your staff need to quickly determine how often the customer uses your services. You need a form that will show an individual record's detail as well as showing other records. Refer to Figure 6.53 to verify your work.

a. Locate the file named *chap6_mid2_memrewards.accdb*, copy it to your production folder, and rename it **chap6_mid2_memrewards_solution.accdb**. Open the file and enable the content. Rename the *Revenue* query as **Your_Name Revenue**. Open it in Datasheet view.

b. Create a split form. Select a control in the right column in the top of the form and make the second column about two inches wide. Save the form.

c. Change the Text Align property for the PerPerson Charge and Revenue fields to be right-aligned. Add spaces in the Controls in the left column where needed. Save the form.

d. Right-click the City field for the first record and select **Equals "Las Vegas"**. Sort the records by last name.

e. Click **Totals** in the Records group on the Home tab to turn on the Total row. Click into the Total row in the Revenue column, click the **arrow**, and select **Sum**.

f. Capture a screenshot of your form displaying only Las Vegas activities. Paste it into Word under a line giving your name and section number.

g. Return to Access and remove the filters. Apply a new filter that displays only records for Joe Little.

h. Capture a screenshot of your form displaying only Joe's activities. Paste it into Word under the other screenshot. Save and print the Word document.

i. Return to Access. Compact, repair, and close the database.

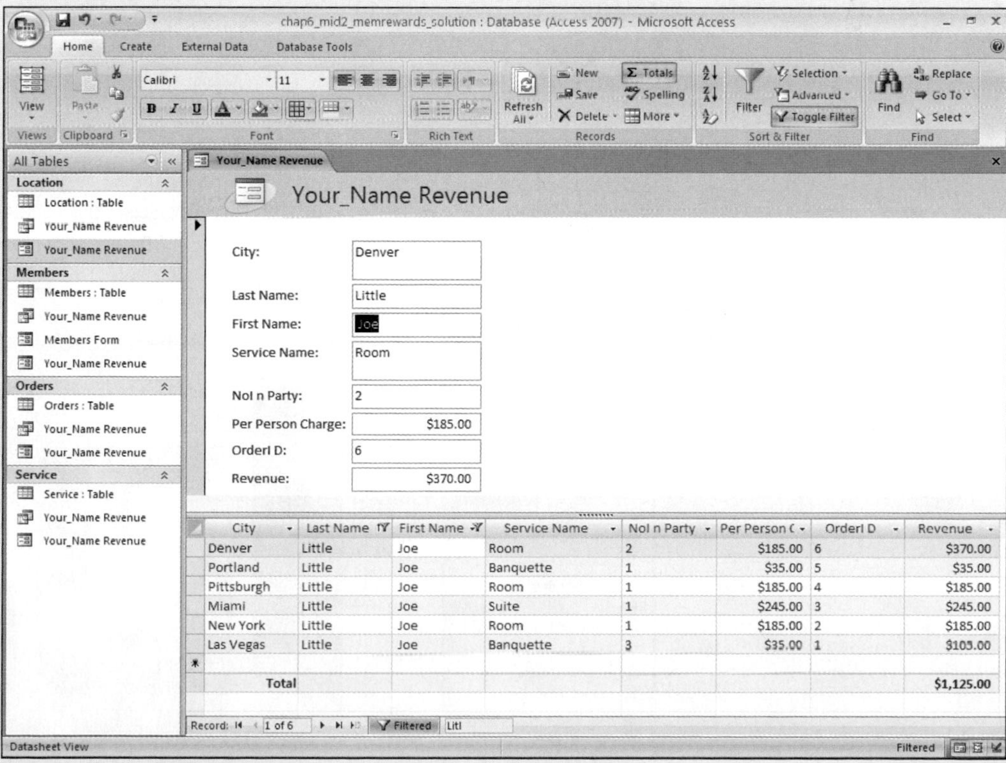

Figure 6.53 Sorted, Filtered Table

...continued on Next Page

3 Create PivotTable and PivotChart Forms with Calculations

You are the marketing manager of an international specialty food wholesaler. You need a form that will help you track sales performance and profitability by product line and employee. You will need to calculate profit by subtracting total costs from revenue. You want to have the ability to examine both aggregates and details. Refer to Figure 6.54 to verify your work.

a. Locate the file named *chap6_mid3_traders.accdb*, copy it to your production folder, and rename it **chap6_mid3_traders_solution.accdb**. Open the file and enable the content. Rename the *Revenue query* as **Your_Name Revenue**. Open the **Employees** table and replace *Your_Name* with your first and last names. Close the table and open the query.

b. Create a PivotTable (located in More Forms in the Forms group on the Create tab). Display the PivotTable Field List pane.

c. Add the **CategoryName** field to the Drop Row Fields Here zone. Add the **LastName** field to the Drop Column Fields Here zone. Add the **Revenue** and **TotalCost** fields to the Detail Drop zone.

d. Calculate **Profit** for each order by using the **Create Calculated Detail Field** tool under Formulas in the Tools group on the Design tab. Profit is the difference between Revenue and TotalCost. Name the newly created field **Profit**. Format it as **Currency**.

e. Click the *Profit* column head to select all of the records and calculate a sum by using the **AutoCalc** tool. Calculate the sum of Revenue and Total Cost.

f. Hide the details. Display only your sales figures. Save the form as **Your_Name Revenue Pivot Form**. Print the PivotTable form.

g. Create a PivotChart that uses the PivotTable as its data source. Use Figure 6.54 as a guide to format your chart. Print the chart in landscape orientation. Save it as **Your_Name Revenue Pivot Chart**.

h. Save your query. Compact, repair, and close the database.

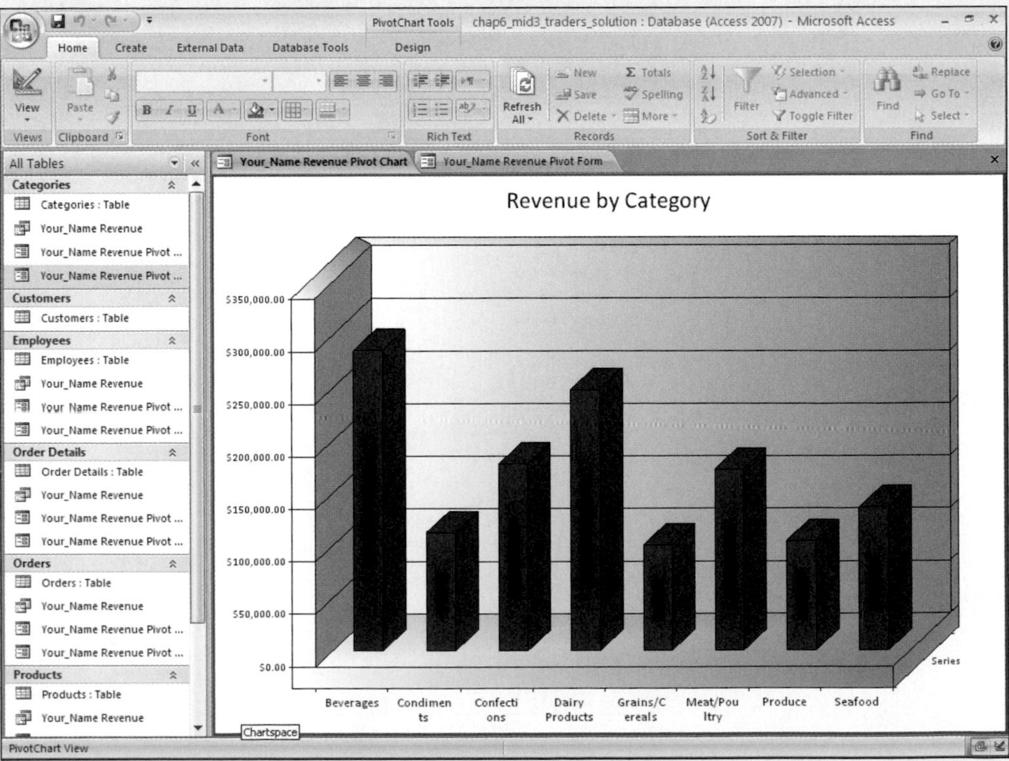

Figure 6.54 Pivot Views of Data

Capstone Exercise

(Replacements, Ltd. exists. The data in the case file are actual data. The customer and employee information has been changed to ensure privacy. However, the inventory and sales records reflect actual transactions.)

You work as an associate information technology trainee at Replacements, Ltd. In preparation for your first day on the job you have browsed the Replacements Web site, www.replacements.com. There you learned that Replacements, Ltd. (located in Greensboro, NC) has the world's largest selection of old and new dinnerware, including china, stoneware, crystal, glassware, silver, stainless, and collectibles. Your task is to create a form that data entry associates may use to add new items to the inventory. You will create a lookup table to classify merchandise as China, Crystal, or Flatware. After you test the newly created form's function, you will compact and repair the database.

Database File Setup

You need to copy an original database file, rename the copied file, and then open the copied database to complete this capstone exercise. After you open the copied database, you will replace an existing employee's name with your name. Finally, you will create a new table that will be the source for a lookup.

a. Locate the file named *chap6_cap_replacements.accdb* and copy it to your production folder.

b. Rename the copied file as **chap6_cap_replacements_solution.accdb**.

c. Open the *chap6_cap_replacements_solution.accdb* file and enable the content.

d. Open the **Employees table**.

e. Navigate to record 33 and replace *Sherol Cowan's* name with your name. Press **Enter** and close the table.

f. Create a new table.

g. Populate the new table by clicking in the first row in the *Add New Field* column. Type **China** and press **Enter**. Click in the second row in the column (now named *Field1*) and type **Flatware**. In the next row, type **Crystal**. Right-click the column head, Field1, and rename it **Category**. Save the table and name it **Product Lines**. Close the table.

Establish Validation Rules and Text

You need to edit the Inventory table design to validate data. Specifically, you need to require the SKU for each new record and set a validation rule to contain values of 0 or higher.

a. Open the **Inventory table** in Design view.

b. Set the property to require a value for the SKU field.

c. Establish a validation rule for the OnHandQty field that is at least zero. Require this field.

d. Create validation text for the OnHandQty: **Please enter the number of this product in inventory. If there are none on hand enter 0 (zero).**

e. Save the table and test the data with the new rules. Switch to Datasheet view.

Test the Validation Rule

You need to test the newly created rule to see if it works and if the error message is helpful.

a. Click any field in the OnHandQty column and write down the value it contains.

b. Delete the value and press **Enter**. You receive the required field error message. Read it and click **OK**.

c. Type a negative number, such as –3. Read the validation text.

d. Click **Undo** or type the original OnHandValue in the table.

Create and Format a Form

You need to create a form that will be used to check new purchases into inventory.

a. Create a form. Because the table is in relationship with the Orders table, the form generates a subform.

b. Delete the subform.

c. Apply the Opulent (second column, fourth row) AutoFormat.

d. Apply the **Currency Format** to the **Retail** field.

e. Right-align all of the labels. Add a sunken special effect to the text box controls.

f. Delete the form icon image in the title. Change the title to Your_Name Inventory. Add spaces where necessary in the control labels and align them.

g. Make the form controls about three inches wide. Remove the default layout and make the width of the last three controls about 1.5".

Create a Lookup

Now that you are satisfied that the form shows the necessary information, you can begin to make it easy to use.

a. Switch to Design view and deselect the controls.

b. Click the **Combo Box** tool in the Controls group on the Design tab. Click on the Design grid below the ProductCategoryId controls.

c. In the List Box Wizard, select an existing table as the source and select the **Product Lines** table. Select the Category field and instruct Access to remember this value for later use.

d. Save the form as Your_Name Inventory. Print a single record.

e. Compact and repair the database. Close the file.

Mini Cases

Use the rubric following the case as a guide to evaluate your work, but keep in mind that your instructor may impose additional grading criteria or use a different standard to judge your work.

Determining What Fields to Include on a Form

GENERAL CASE

The *chap6_mc1_traders.accdb* file contains data from an international specialty foods distribution firm. Copy the *chap6_mc1_traders.accdb* file to your production folder, name it **chap6_mc1_traders_solution.accdb**, and open the copied file. Use the skills from this chapter to perform several tasks. Open the Orders table and use it to create a form. The form will be used in the warehouse to tell the packers what items to place in each box. It will be printed on custom dye-cut labels and used in three places. One part of the form needs to group the shipping address information together. Another should generate a packing list (i.e., how many of each item have been boxed and shipped). It needs to include the name of the product (not just the identification numbers). The third grouping of information on the form needs to show the order number, the company name, the date of shipment, and the name of the shipping company (use a lookup table). Format the labels to have spaces where needed and apply an attractive format. Save and title the form as **Your_Name Packing Form**. Adjust the tab order as necessary. Compact and repair the database.

Performance Elements	Exceeds Expectations	Meets Expectations	Below Expectations
Group arrangement	Controls are grouped logically and functionally. The groups are visually separated from each other.	Most of the items that should be together are grouped; there is some visual distinction between groups.	Output missing or incorrect.
Lookup	Appropriate and functional lookups created. Unnecessary fields removed.	Lookups created and function. Unnecessary fields exist.	Output missing or inaccurate.
Detail manipulation	Appropriate levels of details displayed and formatted correctly.	Appropriate levels of details displayed with some formatting problems.	Insufficient understanding of detail manipulation.

Identifying Good and Poor Form Design

RESEARCH CASE

This chapter introduced you to the power of using Access forms, but you have much more to explore. Now that you have learned a little about form design and usage, go to the Web and find one form that you consider well designed and easy to use. Capture a screenshot of the good form and paste it into a Word file. Write a paragraph describing why you selected this form as an illustration of a well-designed, easy-to-use form. Identify which fields in your form are required. Describe the features like validation text messages that made the form useful. Identify how the form used lookups and other labor-saving features. Return to the Web and find a form that you believe has design flaws. The flaws may be aesthetic (you might dislike the background color) or they might be functional (the tab order is not logical). Capture a screenshot and paste it in the Word document. Write a paragraph describing what is wrong with this form and how you would fix it. Save the file as **chap6_mc2_goodform_solution.docx**.

Performance Elements	Exceeds Expectations	Meets Expectations	Below Expectations
Found examples of a well-designed and a poorly designed form	Both forms located and presented as directed. There were clear distinctions between the good and poor designs.	Both forms located and presented as directed. There were some distinctions between the good and poor designs.	Forms not found or there was insufficient evidence of design differences.
Form element identification	The screenshots were clearly labeled, identifying most relevant form elements.	Screenshots labeled with many relevant form design items.	Labels missing or incorrect.
Summarize and communicate	Identifications and descriptions clearly written and accurate.	Identifications and descriptions clearly written and mostly accurate, indicating some understanding but also weaknesses.	Identifications and descriptions missing, inaccurate, or incomprehensible.
Diagnosis and treatment	Most of the problems with the poorly designed form diagnosed, and the recommended actions would solve most problems.	Many problems identified, and most of the recommended actions would solve the problems.	Problems only partially identified, and no clear understanding of how to resolve presented.

Design a Form That Functions

DISASTER RECOVERY

A coworker called you into his office, explained that he was having difficulty with Access 2007, and asked you to look at his work. Copy the *chap6_mc3_physicians.accdb* file to your production folder, name it **chap6_mc3_physicians_solution.accdb**, and open the file. Your coworker explains he cannot use the form. He intended that it should provide an easy method of enrolling new volunteers into medical studies. However, he indicates several problems. The phone numbers are accurate but difficult to understand. The form controls need to be grouped more logically, with one grouping for the contact information for the volunteers, a second for their medical information, and a third for the study they are interested in joining. The study needs to be identified by name, not ID number. Rework the form with these guides in mind. Add formatting. Test the tab order. Compact, repair, and back up your database.

Performance Elements	Exceeds Expectations	Meets Expectations	Below Expectations
Error identification	Correct identification and correction of all errors.	Correct identification of all errors and correction of some errors.	Errors neither located nor corrected.
Data interaction	The phone number and study title display appropriately.	One but not both controls have been fixed.	Neither control repaired.
Grouping	Form controls visually grouped logically and attractively.	Most controls grouped logically, but there may be an item or two out of position.	No visual definition of form groupings.

Advanced Queries

Using Queries to Change Data

After you read this chapter, you will be able to:

1. Maintain databases with action queries **(page 448)**.
2. Update data with an update query **(page 448)**.
3. Add records to a table with an append query **(page 451)**.
4. Create a table with a make table query **(page 453)**.
5. Delete records with a delete query **(page 454)**.
6. Provide flexibility with a parameter query **(page 468)**.
7. Summarize data with a crosstab query **(page 472)**.
8. Find unmatched records with a query **(page 477)**.
9. Find duplicate records with a query **(page 480)**.

Hands-On Exercises

Exercises	Skills Covered
1. CREATE AND USE ACTION QUERIES (page 458) **Open:** chap7_ho1-3_replacement.accdb **Save as:** chap7_ho1-3_replacement_solution.accdb and chap7_ho1_replacement_solution.docx **Back up as:** chap7_ho1-3_replacement_solution_2007-03-15.accdb, chap7_ho1-3_replacement_solution_2007-03-15_(1).accdb, chap7_ho1-3_replacement_solution_2007-03-15_(2).accdb, and chap7_ho1_replacement_solution.accdb	• Set Up to Create an Update Query • Verify the Update Criterion • Create an Append Query • Construct a Table Using a Make Table Query • Delete Records Using a Delete Query • Construct and Run a Delete Query
2. ADDITIONAL QUERIES (page 484) **Open:** chap7_ho1-3_replacement_solution.accdb (from Exercise 1) **Save as:** chap7_1-3_ho1_replacement_solution.accdb (additional modifications) and chap7_ho2_replacement_ solution.docx	• Create a Crosstab Query • Edit a Crosstab Query • Construct a Parameter Query • Build a Find Unmatched Records Query • Create a Find Duplicates Query

CASE STUDY

Coffee Delivery

You work for a small firm that sells and delivers coffee and snack products to local offices. You have responsibility for servicing some of the customer accounts and also for administering and maintaining the firm's database. You designed and set up the database last month, in January. You designed a table for customer information, one for information about the employees, one for information about the products your firm sells, one to record order data—customer's id, date of order, and payment method—and one for the details of the order—what products were ordered and in what quantity.

At the beginning of February you created two new tables for the database. The new tables duplicate the structure of the Orders and Order Detail tables. You entered all of the new order information in the Feb Orders and Feb Order Details tables. It is now the end of the month, and you need to do some housekeeping and maintenance on the firm's database. You will append the February orders to the orders table and the order details for February to the order details table. You will (after checking to ensure the data appended properly) delete the data in the February orders and order details tables and rename the tables March. The tables will be used to record transaction data for the current month. Next you will use a crosstab query to summarize the sales data by salesperson and product. Finally you will update the prices in the products table to reflect cost changes. You will also put some of the Access queries to work for you to make data updates and summaries.

Case Study

Your Assignment

- Read the chapter, paying special attention to action queries and crosstab queries.
- Copy the *chap7_case_coffee.accdb* file to your production folder, rename it **chap7_case_coffee_solution.accdb**, and enable the content.
- Open the Relationships window and examine the relationships among the tables and the fields contained within each of the tables to become acquainted with this database.
- Append the data stored in the Feb Orders table to the Orders table and the data stored in the Feb Order Details table to the Order Details table. Rename the Orders table as **Orders Archive**. Rename the Order Details table as **Order Details Archive**. Save the append query as **Archive Last Month's Orders**.
- After you are sure the data from both tables have been safely appended, create a delete query to purge the Feb Orders and Feb Order Details tables. Rename the (now empty) tables **March Orders** and **March Order Details**.
- Create a select query that includes the following fields: CustomerName, ProductName, Quantity, OrderDate, Cost, MarkupPercent, and the sales rep's LastName. Save the query as **Profit**.
- Calculate price by multiplying cost by the markup percent and adding cost. Calculate profit by subtracting total cost (cost times quantity) from total revenue (price times quantity).
- Create a crosstab query that summarizes profit by sales rep and product name. Use the Sum aggregate. Add a Total Row that sums all of the columns. Save the query as **Profit_Crosstab**. Print the output.
- Copy the crosstab query and name the copy **Daily Profit_Crosstab**. Edit the query in Design view. In this query you need to summarize profit by the OrderDate and LastName fields. Use the Sum aggregate. Add a Total Row that sums all of the columns. Print the output.
- Update the cost of the products by using an update query that adds 20% to every product's cost for products that require refrigeration. Run the update. Print the Products table.
- Compact, repair, and close the database file.

Action Queries

You have already worked extensively with queries. All of the queries you have used so far have been select queries. You have used select queries to combine related records from various tables, established parameters to examine specific subsets of records, calculated values, created totals queries, and used PivotTables and PivotCharts to analyze your data. You recognize the power provided by select queries to search for information and massage it into a useful summary. A select query provides you with flexibility. When the underlying data change, simply rerunning the query will update them and provide you with the most up-to-date information. When you have select queries that perform similar tasks, for example, identifying last month's banquette sales in the Boston and Miami hotels, you create the query with one set of parameters. After you create the original query, you can copy it, rename the copied query, and change the parameters to extract data from a different city or service type. Alternatively, Access gives you the ability to omit one or more parameters in a query and establish a set of prompts for the query user to fill in the missing data using a parameter query. Using either method each time you run the original or copied and altered select query, it extracts the most recent records and updates the output.

An ***action query*** alters data in a database by making a table, adding records to an existing table, deleting specific records, or updating records.

Access 2007 provides many additional query types that you can use to alter data. Access provides a number of data altering queries known collectively as action queries. An ***action query*** performs an action—altering data in a database—by making a table, adding records to an existing table, deleting specific records, or updating records. Action queries, although powerful, tend to be less flexible. Most of them do not update automatically. Because action queries change data, you generally run them only once. Any time you attempt to launch an action query, Access warns you that you are about to change data in the specified number of records and gives you a chance to change your mind. In most organizations, the professional IT staff, the database administrators, and managers create and run the action queries. However, in many small and midsized companies, the owner may perform database administrative responsibilities.

TIP Database Administrator Career Possibility

Database administrators organize and protect data. Because Sarbanes-Oxley Act (SOX) and PNPI regulations govern how data is stored and retrieved, an organization's database administration has become more important. With the volume of sensitive data growing rapidly, data integrity, backup systems, and database security have become increasingly important aspects of the job of database administrators. According to the U.S. Bureau of Labor Statistics' *Occupational Outlook Handbook* (http://www.bls.gov/oco/ocos042.htm), you need a bachelor's degree in Management Information Technology, Information Systems, or Computer Science to work in this field. In 2004 database administrators earned a median income of $60,650. The outlook for this position is expected to grow much above average (exceeding 27% per year) over the next ten years.

In this section, you will learn about action queries and how they are used to maintain databases. Specifically, you will create the following types of action queries: update, append, make table, and delete. Finally, you will explore some of the more powerful tools used in database maintenance. These tools may help your queries run more quickly and will automate some routine maintenance chores like database compaction and backups. In this section, you explore several different action queries used for database maintenance.

Maintaining Databases with Action Queries

Professional database administrators spend much of their time performing database maintenance tasks. Even if you are not seeking a career as a database administrator or manager, you may need some of these skills. Many small and midsize organizations use Access databases as their primary database. You may be the entrepreneur who establishes and runs a small firm one day. You recognize that Access provides a powerful data organization and information generating tool and will wish to use it to help run your business more efficiently. You will probably not spend all of your time working with the database, but you will be responsible for the data stored there. Many Access databases are not designed or maintained by professional IT staff. They are designed and maintained by the firm's owner or family member. Because the data stored in the database contributes to the organization's operation, it may be critical to the organizational mission. Mission critical data must be intentionally and systematically maintained. You have already used a critically important maintenance procedure each time you back up an existing database file. Access provides a set of action queries to help you protect and ensure the efficacy of your organization's data.

Action queries not only search for the required information; they *alter* it. Not only can you change data stored in a database with an action query, you *permanently* change the data. You cannot undo data alteration performed with an action query. Therefore, you should move slowly and cautiously when employing these powerful tools by backing up, testing, and previewing the changes you propose. Backing up and restoring the backup provides you with some insurance to help you recover from a disaster. But it is better to avoid creating the disaster in the first place. You generally will want to create a simple select query first to examine your parameter settings and test your logic before committing to an irreversible change.

Avoid mistakes . . . examine your parameter settings and test your logic before committing to an irreversible change.

Updating Data with an Update Query

An ***update query*** changes the values in at least one record in a table.

Access provides you with four different types of action queries. An ***update query*** searches through a database table and changes or updates the values in at least one field. For example, the telephone company announces that all of your customers in specific postal codes will now have a different area code. You might construct an update query to identify records of all customers who live in the specific postal codes and change their area code to the new area code. Another example might be in a database storing information about student athletes and their academic eligibility. At the end of each semester you would create an action query to identify any academically ineligible athletes and change their playing status and/or their financial aid. You might also use an update query to increase all the product prices by 10% by combining the action query with a calculated expression.

The first step in update query creation involves record source identification. Most of the time update queries are performed on data stored in a single table. You may also update data from multiple tables. You create a new query in Design view and click Show Tables. Identify and add the table(s) storing the data to be updated. Thus far, the query is a select query. You need to change the query type by clicking Update in the Query Type group on the Query Tools Design tab. Add the field or fields you will use to establish criteria that determine which records will be updated. As with a select query, specify the conditions on the Criteria row for the respective fields. For example, assume you want to increase the price of all crystal dishes, which have a product category ID of 2. You add the ProdCategoryID field and specify 2 in the Criteria row.

Next, add the field or fields you want to change. For example, with the crystal products, you would add the Retail field, which contains the retail price that you want to change. The change may be either a constant value or a calculation you enter in the Update To row for the respective field in the design grid. For example, in the

Update To row, enter the expression that would calculate the amount of the price increase and add it back to the current retail price.

Finally, add any additional fields that you will use to verify that the update will select and change the appropriate records. For example, you might want to add a parameter to prompt for a specific piece of crystal so that you can preview which records will be updated. Figure 7.1 displays an update query that will reduce the price of the Crystal (2) inventory by 15%. The expression multiplies the current retail price by 15% and then subtracts that result from the current retail price. The final result replaces the retail price value in the table.

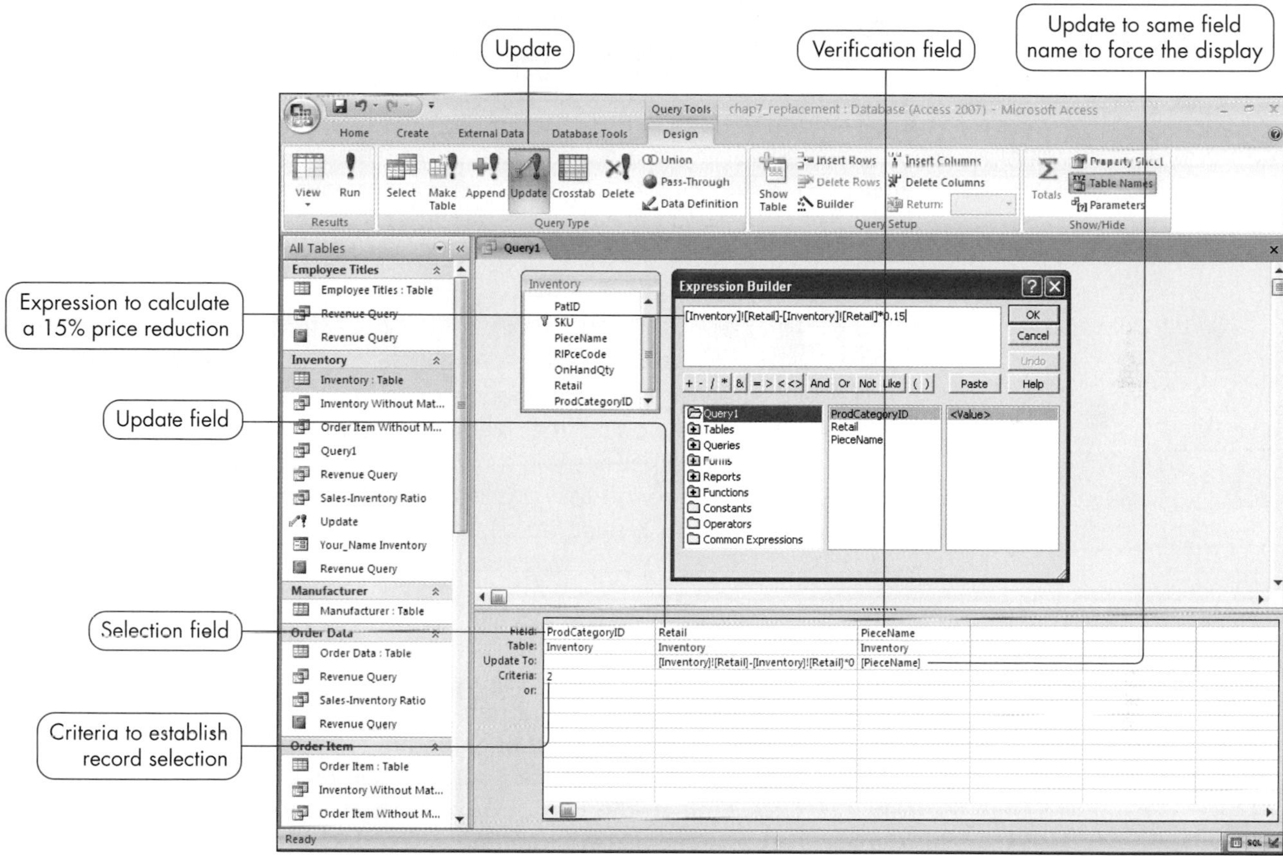

Figure 7.1 Update Query Setup

When you create select queries, you change from Design view to the Datasheet view by running the query. However, you do not want to run an action query without testing your logic. For example, the update query displayed in Figure 7.1 includes the PieceName field. This text field is updated to itself (changing nothing) so that you can verify which records will be updated when the query runs. Access displays only the fields you specify in the update query. However, adding a verification field, like PieceName, and updating it to itself will force the display and provide you with reassurance that you will change the appropriate data. You can view the query in Datasheet view by right-clicking the query tab and selecting Datasheet View. This permits you to preview the action prior to running the query. Figure 7.2 shows the preview of the query setup in the previous step. The price of the Crystal Champagne Bucket ($324.98) has not been updated. You are checking to make sure that the appropriate records have been selected.

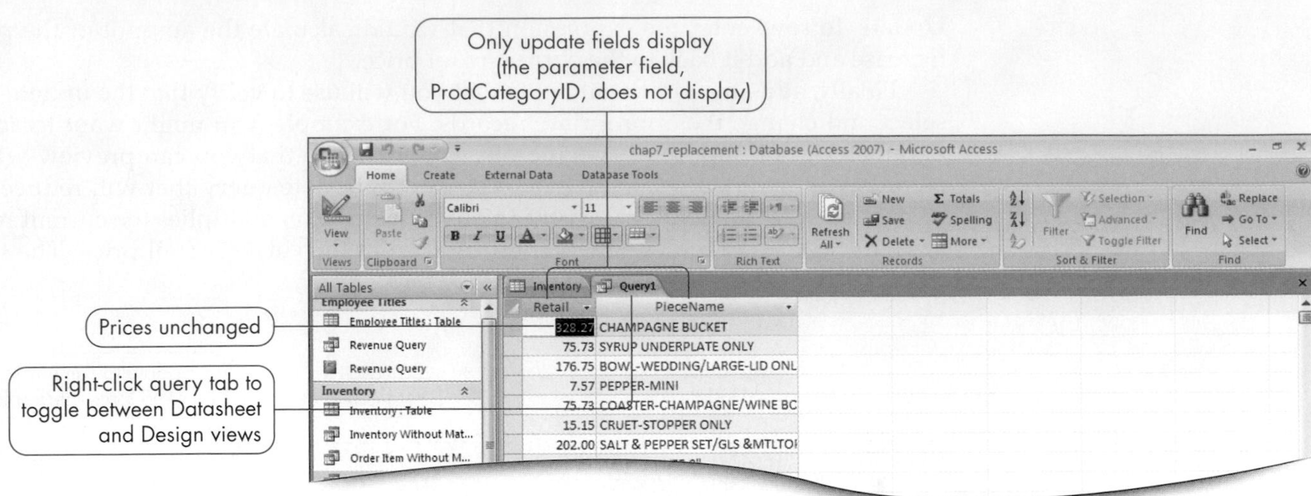
Only update fields display (the parameter field, ProdCategoryID, does not display)
Prices unchanged
Right-click query tab to toggle between Datasheet and Design views
chap7_replacement : Database (Access 2007) - Microsoft Access

Figure 7.2 Datasheet View of Update Query

TIP Viewing and Running

In a select query, you do not change data—you select only a subset of data to examine. Therefore, you run the select query and view the returned results simultaneously. In an action query, you should *preview* the selected records first by right-clicking the query design tab and selecting Datasheet View. The Datasheet view lets you see the criteria selected prior to changing data.

Now that you are confident that only the Crystal prices will change, you may return to Design view and run the update query. Access warns you that you are about to update 974 records and that you cannot reverse the change (Figure 7.3). When you click Yes, it seems as though nothing happens. Access does not display the changed records. However, the records specified by the query criteria have changed. You can click Find in the Find group on the Home tab to display the Find and Replace dialog box so that you can find a record to double-check that it was updated. Figure 7.4 shows the Inventory table and the altered price of the Crystal Champagne Bucket of $276.23. An exclamation point icon indicates an update query in the navigation bar.

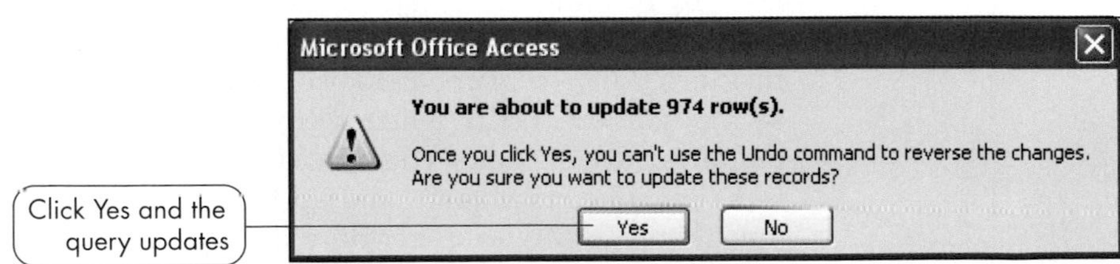
Microsoft Office Access
You are about to update 974 row(s).
Once you click Yes, you can't use the Undo command to reverse the changes.
Are you sure you want to update these records?
Yes
No
Click Yes and the query updates

Figure 7.3 Update Query Warning

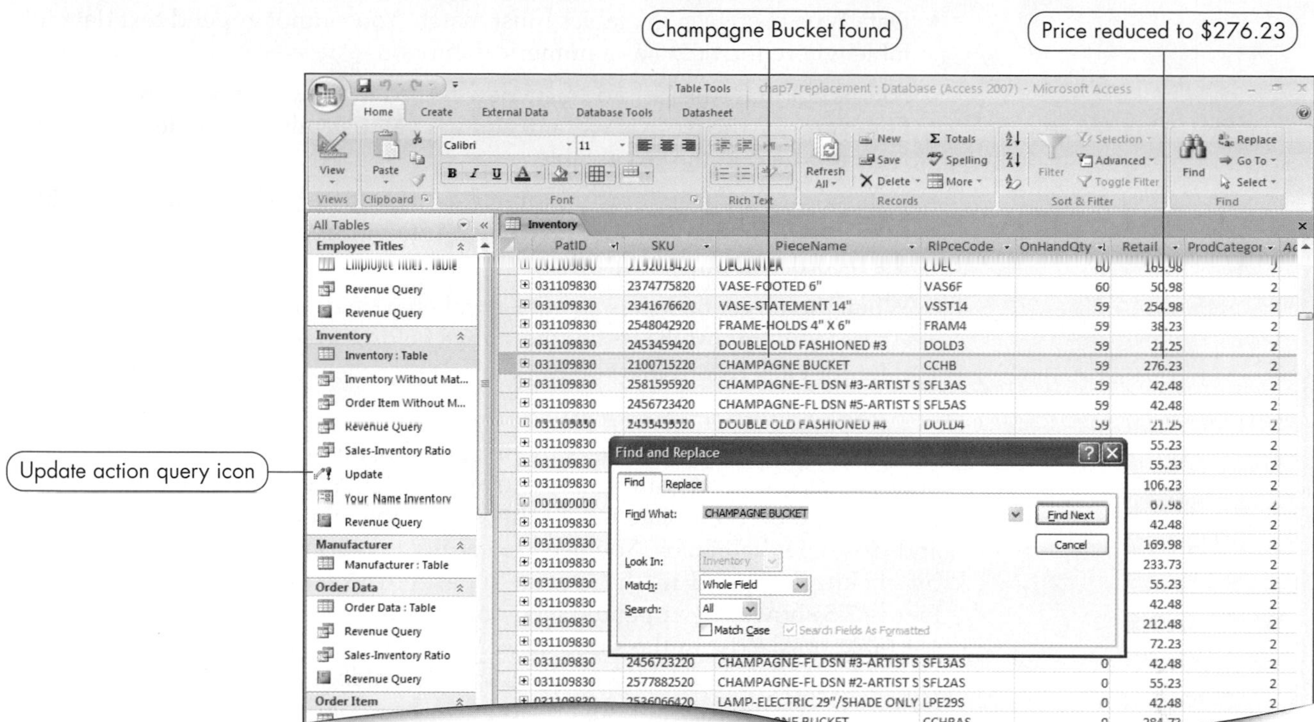

Figure 7.4 Inventory Table Reflecting Price Changes

TIP Do NOT Rerun Action Queries

After you run the action query, it looks like nothing has happened except that the warning box disappears. You might be tempted to click Run again. Do not! In this example, you would discount the crystal prices by an additional 15%. When you save an update query, you should indicate that it is an update query in the query name.

Adding Records to a Table with an Append Query

An ***append query*** selects at least one record from one table and adds the record(s) to a different, existing table.

The second type of update query is the append query. An ***append query*** selects at least one record from a table and adds those records to a different existing table. Unless a saved table sort order relocated the appended records, they will be added to the bottom of the table. You use an append query type to copy records from one table or database to a different table or database. Your school probably uses an append query at the end of each term to identify the students who graduated and moves those student records to an alumni table. You might also use an append query in conjunction with an update or delete query by using the append query to identify the records to be altered or deleted and then moving them to a new table. That way, you can have another set of eyes examine your logic and make *absolutely* certain that the action you are about to take is the correct one.

Often organizations will store the most active records (today's or this week's activities) in one table and then append them to a more permanent table for storage. The append query will work only if the records match between the two tables. The tables are the source and the target tables. The following rules for data matching are important:

- Data types between the tables must match. You cannot append text data into a table where the field has a numeric definition.
- All the normal rules for adding a new record in the target table must be honored. For example, the records will not add if a value is missing in the source table in a required field in the target table.
- If the source table has one or more fields that do not exist in the target table, you may ignore them. If the target table has nonrequired fields not in the source table, the record will import, and the missing field values will be left blank.
- When the target table has an auto-numbered field, then do not import that field. Access will import the rest of the source fields and generate an auto-numbered field for each record that follows the rules for the field specified in the field's design.

You begin the append query by first opening the source table—the table that contains the records you want to copy to another table. Then click Query Design in the Other group on the Create tab. In the Show Table dialog box, select the source table and close the dialog box. You need to specify that you are creating an append query by clicking Append in the Query Type group on the Query Tools Design tab. Figure 7.5 shows the Append dialog box where you specify the target table. The target table may exist in the same database or in a different database. If you need to append to a different database, click Another Database and use the Browse button to locate the appropriate file. An append query can only work if the target table exists somewhere. If it does not already exist, you must use a make table query, not an append query.

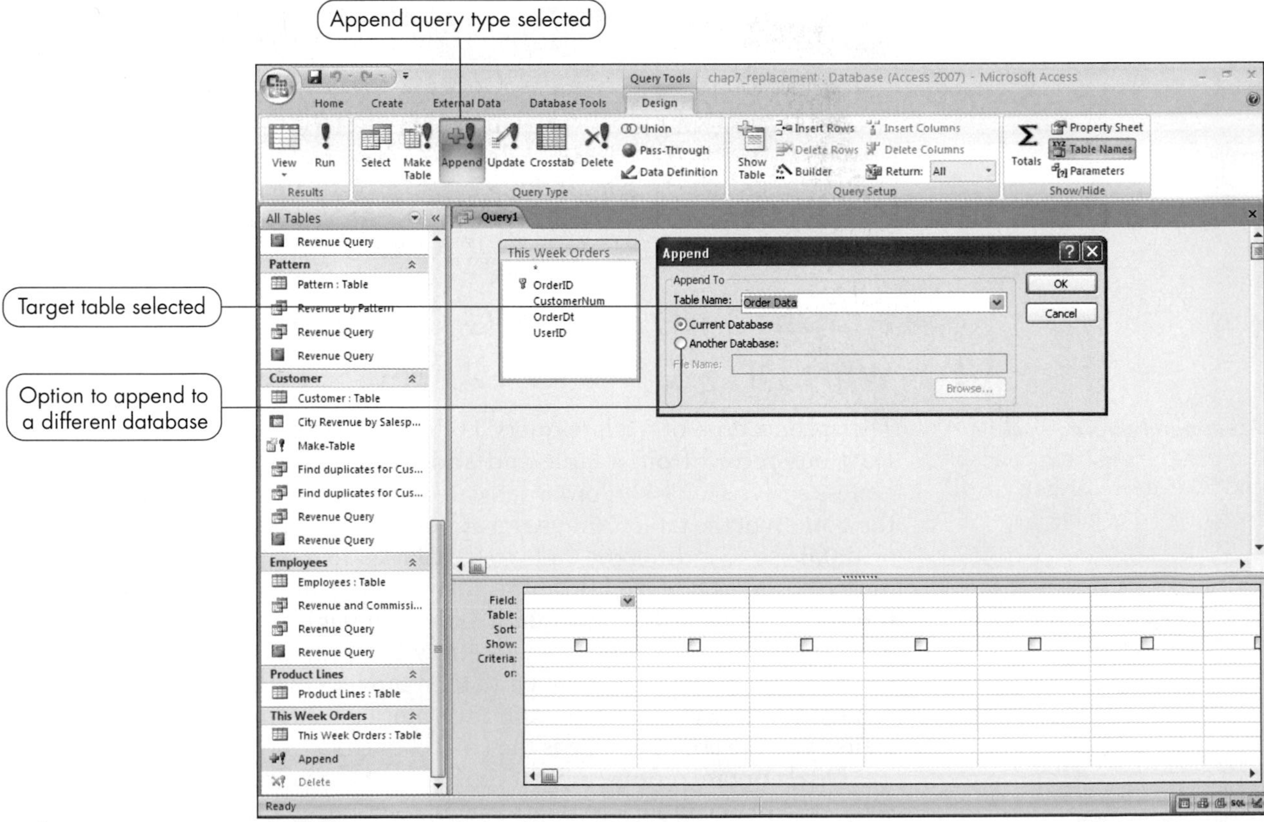

Figure 7.5 Setup for Append Query

After establishing the source and target, you need to add the records to the design grid. The OrderID field in the target table shown in Figure 7.6 is an auto-numbered field, so you should not import the corresponding OrderID field from the source table. As you add fields, Access will look for an appropriate destination field and fill it in automatically in the Append To field row. If Access cannot identify where a field needs to be placed, it will leave a blank in the Append To row and you will need to specify the destination field name. You may use the Criteria row to identify the records you wish to copy. Because no criteria were specified, Access will append all the records in the source table. Right-click the query tab and preview the records selected to be appended. After verifying the records, return to Design view and run the query. You will receive an action message telling you that you are about to append the number of records selected. If you click Yes, you cannot undo the action. Open the target table and verify that you added the new records.

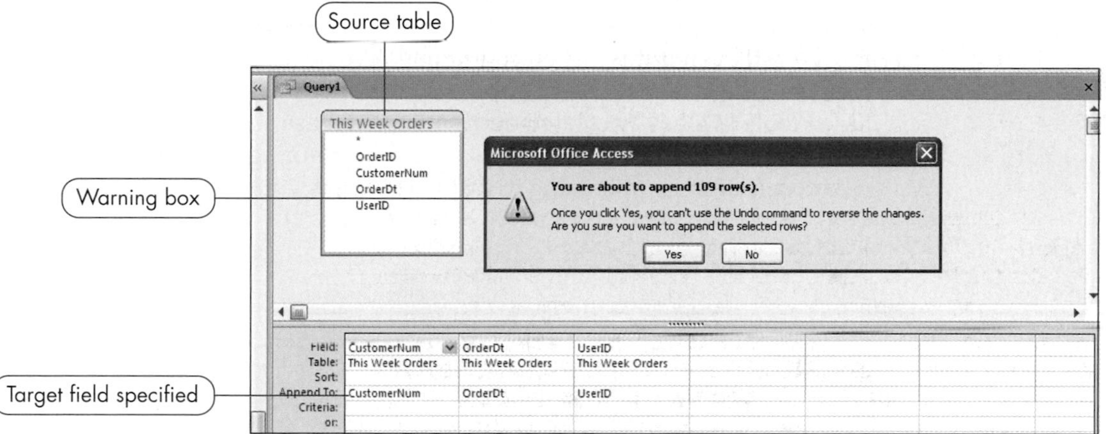

Figure 7.6 Field Specifications for an Append Query

TIP Appends Do Not Always Position at the End of a File

The technical definition of append is to add to the end of a file. However, if sort conditions are imposed on the target table, the sort command will supersede the append command. For example, if you append new employees to a table that is sorted in ascending order by the last and then first name fields, the appended records will appear in alphabetical order intermixed with the existing table data.

Creating a Table with a Make Table Query

A ***make table query*** selects at least one record and uses the record(s) to create a new table.

The third type of action query is the make table query. A ***make table query*** selects at least one record and uses it (them) to create a new table. Your school has a large database that stores information about students. Inside, it is information about the classes students have completed and are registered for this term, their majors, and emergency contact information. The advising center for the College of Arts and Sciences needs to know all of the students enrolled in their classes as well as all of their majors in various programs. Because the school database is so large, running a query to extract this information may take a long time. Additionally, these data are relatively static. Once the term has begun, class registration and student major declaration do not change much. The school IT department might create a make table query to identify the students enrolled in classes offered by the College of Arts and Sciences and all of the students with declared majors. Once selected, these data are exported to a database table located in the advising office. When a student goes to the advising office to change her major from biology to biochemistry, her records may be found and returned more quickly because the database does not need to also search through students in majors outside of the College of Arts and Sciences. At the end of the term, the changes made in the database resident in the advising office may be transferred back to the university database using an update query.

Database administrators commonly use the make table query to archive (historically store) inactive records. You might make a table of inactive customers or of products no longer sold. In fact, SOX mandates that information be stored for specified periods. Perhaps a customer has died and your firm no longer needs contact information or records of past purchases for marketing purposes. However, SOX regulations require that that information be archived and available to auditors and Securities and Exchange Commission (SEC) investigators.

The processes of creating append and make table queries are almost the same. The difference is that in an append query the table must already exist for you to append to it. You can use the make table query to copy some or all records from a source to a target table even if the target table does not exist. The target database must exist, even if it is a shell containing no objects. Figure 7.7 displays the setup for a make table query that will copy the customer table from the source database to a target table in a newly created destination database. Like the other action queries, you need to preview the record selection prior to running the query. After you verify the record selection by switching to Datasheet view, you can run and save the query.

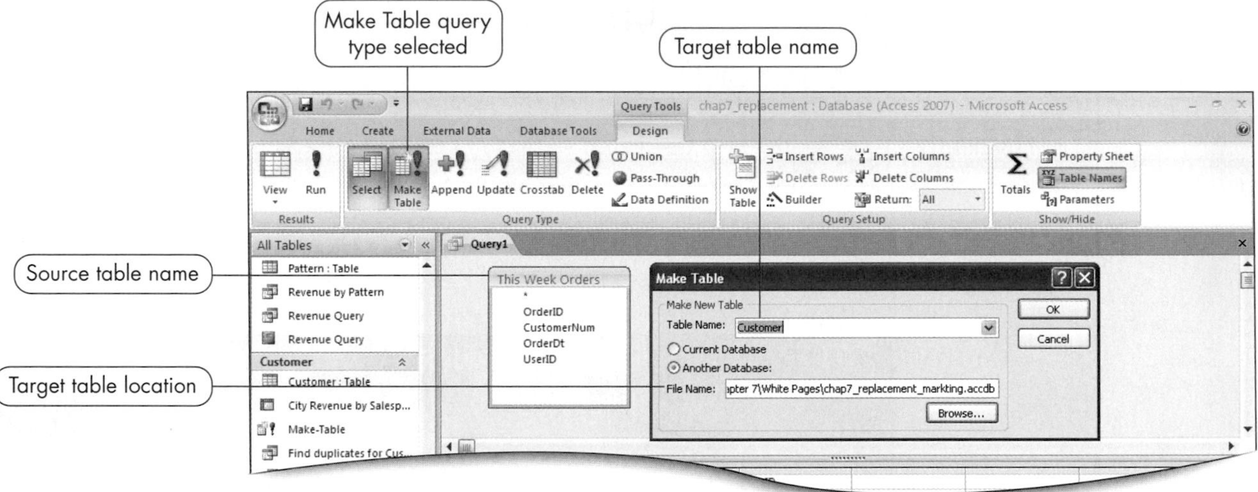

Figure 7.7 Setup for a Make Table Query

Deleting Records with a Delete Query

A ***delete query*** selects at least one record and removes it from the database.

The final action query, the ***delete query***, selects at least one record and removes it from the database. The words *remove* and *delete* cause anxiety for database administrators and managers. These IT professionals are responsible for protecting and ensuring the efficacy of an organization's precious, priceless data. Inappropriate deletions might result in job loss. Further, deletion of data that SOX regulations mandate could result in a criminal conviction and imprisonment! Nevertheless, you sometimes need to identify and delete large quantities of data. For example, after you safely copy the inactive customer and transaction data to an archival table using a make table or append query, you may want to delete those records from the original table. Of course, you will cautiously and carefully verify the records selected to be deleted. Access provides tools to help you ensure that the selected records are the appropriate ones. You might use this after successfully appending records to an archival table, verifying the results and then purging the now archived records from the source table.

TIP Cascade Deletes

Suppose you want to delete records from a table that is related with referential integrity enforced to another table. For example, you discontinue a relationship with one of your suppliers and want to remove that firm from the supplier's table. You would then also need to delete the related records in the other table so that the related records do not become orphaned. In the earlier example, you would remove all of the products listed in your products table that you purchase from the ex-supplier. Access provides a tool for you to easily accomplish this. Open the Relationships window. Find and edit the relationship between the two tables (Suppliers and Products) by right-clicking the join line and selecting edit from the shortcut menu. Select the Cascade Delete option. Save the relationship changes. Create a delete query to delete the supplier and all of the related records in the products table will also be deleted.

Perhaps the easiest and most dangerous action query of all is the delete query. A careless database administrator can do a great deal of damage to organizational data in very little time with this powerful tool. A wise database administrator always runs a backup utility prior to creating a delete action query. Earlier, you were introduced to an append query where you copied order information from the current week's order table to the order table. You probably would take this action on the same day each week. However, the other database objects that support order entry, i.e., forms, probably point to the This Week Orders table. You would want to delete the records from last week's orders after copying them to the Order table.

The delete query begins the same way as all of the other action queries. Click Query Design in the Other group on the Create tab. From the Show Table dialog box, select the table containing the records you wish to delete. Click Delete in the Query Type group on the Query Tools Design tab to specify the type of query you wish to create. The Sort and Show rows disappear from the design grid, and a Delete row appears. Add the fields that you will use to specify the criterion. In Figure 7.8, the criterion is the OrderDt field. If you fail to specify criterion, Access will delete all the records in the table. Figure 7.8 displays the criterion to delete the records for the week ending 7/27/2008.

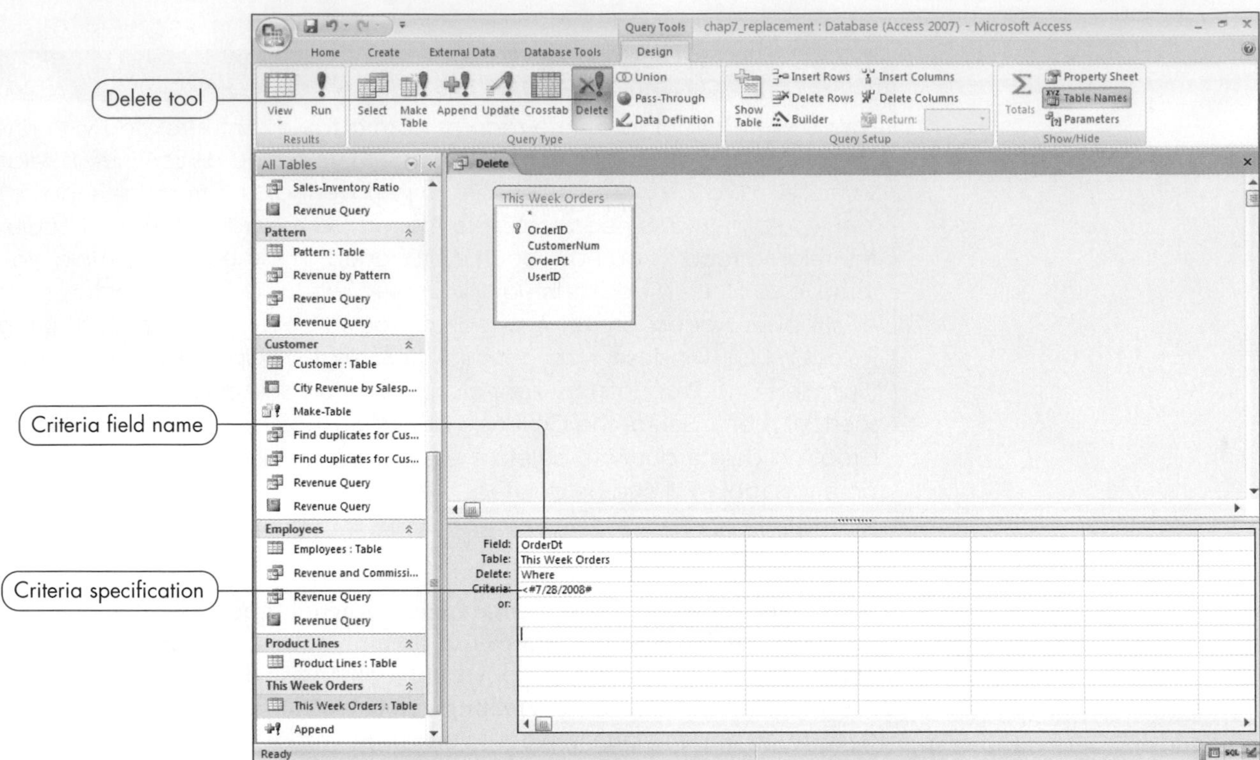

Figure 7.8 Setup for a Delete Query

TIP Hide a Query

This section introduced you to four powerful and potentially dangerous queries. Access flags the action queries differently from other queries to help protect database data by displaying specific icons to the left of each respective action query (see Figure 7.9). These icons match their command icons in the Query Type group on the Query Tools tab. Many query writers do not save action queries at all to help prevent them from being run accidentally. Because some action queries run regularly, you might wish to save them. An easy way to prevent them from being accidentally run is for you to hide them until you need to use them. You hide a query (or any other database object) by right-clicking it in the object pane and then selecting Object Properties from the shortcut menu. Set the Attributes to Hidden. To restore a hidden object to view, right-click the title bar of the object pane and select Navigation Options from the short-cut menu. Then, in the dialog box, set the Display Options to Show Hidden Objects.

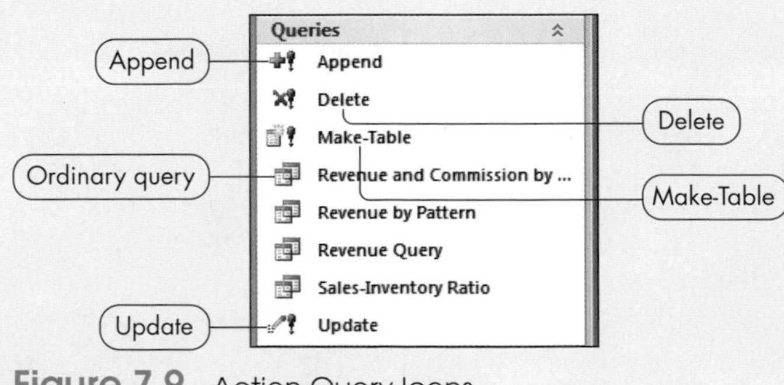

Figure 7.9 Action Query Icons

You will experiment with creating and running action queries in the first hands-on exercise using the data from Replacements, Ltd. Replacements is an international firm that inventories china, crystal, and flatware pattern pieces. Their customers replace broken or damaged items or use Replacements to extend their service. You are a database administrator and need to perform several database management operations. You will run an update query to identify all of the pieces in inventory from a specified manufacturer and increase their prices by 15%. You will use an append query to add the new employees to the Employees table. Then you will make a table of the employees who are no longer with the firm. You will use a delete query to try to remove the employees who no longer work for Replacements, Ltd., from the Employees table. This will clarify referential integrity rules. Finally, you will delete job titles that are no longer used from the Employee Titles table.

Hands-On Exercises

1 | Create and Use Action Queries

Skills covered: 1. Set Up to Create an Update Query **2.** Verify the Update Criterion **3.** Create an Append Query **4.** Construct a Table Using a Make Table Query **5.** Delete Records Using a Delete Query **6.** Construct and Run a Delete Query

Step 1
Set Up to Create an Update Query

Refer to Figure 7.10 as you complete Step 1.

a. Use Exploring to locate the file named *chap7_ho1-3_replacement.accdb*. Copy the file and rename it **chap7_ho1-3_replacement_solution.accdb**.

b. Open the *chap7_ho1-3_replacement_solution.accdb* file. Click **Options** on the Security Warning toolbar. Click **Enable this content** in the Microsoft Office Security Options dialog box and click **OK**.

c. Rename the *Inventory* table with your name, such as **Your_Name Inventory**. Open it. Also open the **Pattern** and **Manufacturer tables**.

d. Click the **Your_Name Inventory tab** to position that table on top of the other two.

e. Click the **Create tab**, and then click **Query Design** in the Other group.

   The Show Table dialog box opens.

   TROUBLESHOOTING: If the Show Table dialog box does not launch, click Show Table in the Query Setup group on the Design tab.

f. Double-click the **Your_Name Inventory**, **Pattern**, and **Manufacturer tables** to add these tables to the query design grid. Close the Show Table dialog box.

   You need to increase the price of one manufacturer's china patterns by 15% to offset rising procurement costs. The manufacturer's name is Spode China. Look in the Manufacturer table to find the MfgID for Spode China. Write it down. Now look for the pattern names in the LongPatName field of the Pattern table and identify Spode China patterns. You should find two. Write the long pattern names down so that you can verify that your query is updating the correct prices.

g. Click the **Query1 tab** to return to the query design grid. Click **Update** in the Query Type group on the Design tab.

   You changed the query type from a select to an update query.

h. Double-click the **MfgID** field in the Manufacturer table to add it to the design grid. Once it is added, type **=801190** in the Criteria row of the design grid. Double-click the **Retail** field in the Your_Name Inventory table to add it to the design grid.

   You added the criteria to select only Spode China pieces to update the prices.

i. Click the **Update To row** under the **Retail field** in the design grid. Click **Builder** in the Query Setup group on the Design tab.

   The Expression Builder launches.

j. Type **= [Your_Name Inventory]![Retail] * 1.15** in the Expression Builder dialog box.

   You used an expression identifier. An identifier in an expression is [Collection name]![Object name].[Property name].

k. Click **OK** to insert the expression and click **Builder** to open the Expression Builder dialog box again. Compare your screen to Figure 7.10. Click **OK** to close the Expression Builder dialog box.

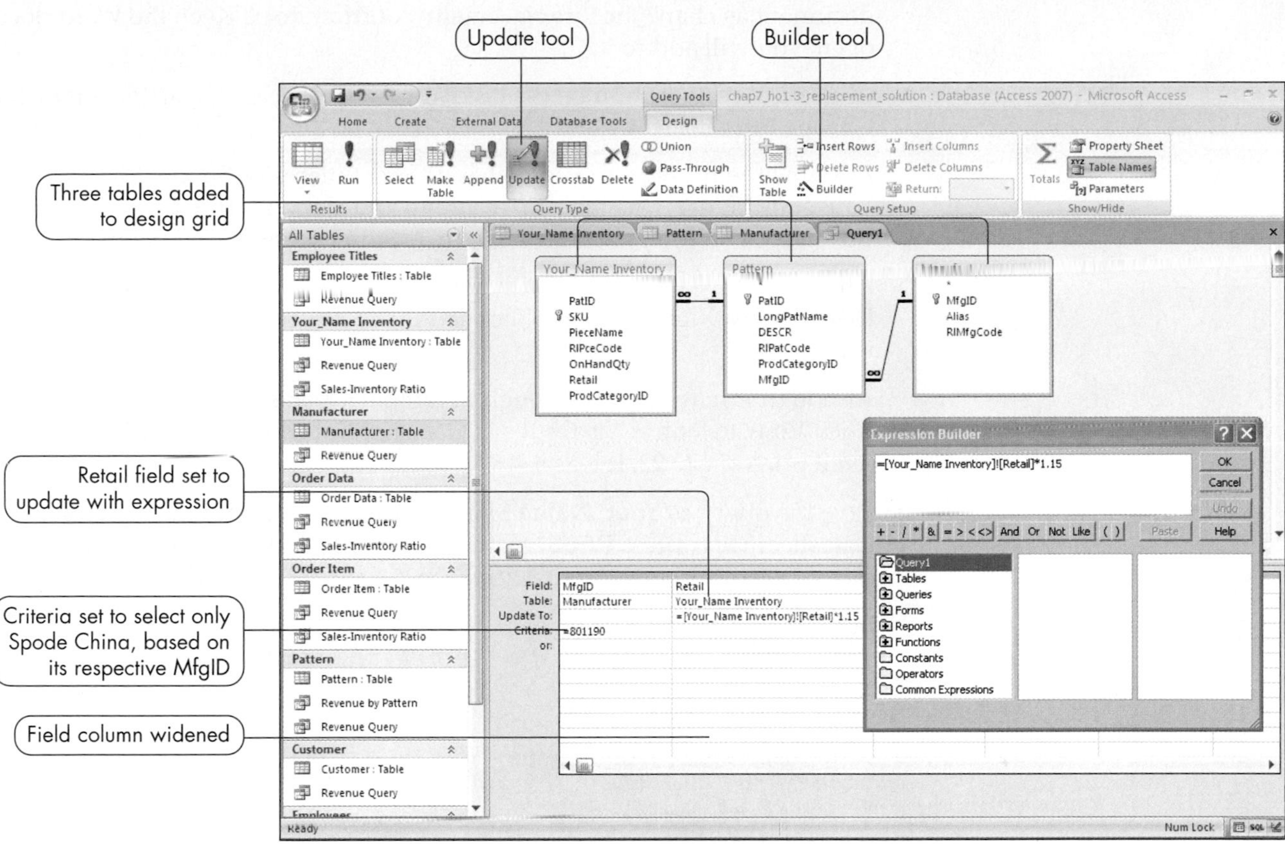

Figure 7.10 Update Query Setup

Step 2
Verify the Update Criterion

Refer to Figures 7.11 and 7.12 as you complete Step 2.

a. Double-click the **RlMfgCode** field in the Manufacturer table to add it to the design grid. Double-click the **PieceName** in the Your_Name Inventory table to add it to the design grid.

If you had run the update query at the end of Step 1, it would have changed prices. However, you need to make sure that only the Spode China pattern prices update.

b. Click **View** in the Results group on the Design tab to change to Datasheet view and examine the output without running the query.

You should see a list of prices (34.98, 10.00, 5.00, 7.00) but nothing else. Access ignores all fields in an update query that are not updated. You need to "trick" the software into providing you with the manufacturer and pattern names by updating the fields without making any changes.

c. Click **View** to return to Design view. In the Update To row of the RlMfgCode field type **[RlMfgCode]**. Be sure to include the brackets. In the Update To row of the PieceName field, type **[PieceName]**. Be sure to include the brackets here, too.

You instructed Access to update the field and overwrite the old information. However, you are updating the records on themselves. The data do not change; they simply display for you to verify your logic.

d. Capture a screenshot by pressing **PrntScrn**. Launch **Word**. Open a new document and type your name and section number on the first line. Press **Enter**. Paste the screenshot into the Word file and press **Enter** again. Save the Word document as **chap7_ho1_replacement_solution.docx**. Keep the Word document open; you will add to it.

e. Click the **Access button** on the taskbar to make Access the active window again. Change to Datasheet view.

   Examine the results and verify that different pieces of Spode (SP) prices display. You should use the tabs to examine the data in the Pattern, Your_Name Inventory, and Manufacturer tables to ensure your work is correct.

f. After you are sure that you will update the correct data, click **View** to return to Design view. Run the query. Click **Yes** in the *You are about to update 1129 row(s)* warning.

   Although it may seem as though nothing happened, your prices have changed. Click **View** to look at the results in Datasheet view. The RELISH-3 Part now has a retail price of $40.22. It was $34.98.

g. Save the query as **Your_Name Spode Price Update**. With the query showing in Datasheet view, press **PrntScrn**, return to the open Word document, and paste this screenshot below the first screenshot. Save the Word document.

   Because you set the data to display details, a scroll bar turns on to let you scroll to view other data points.

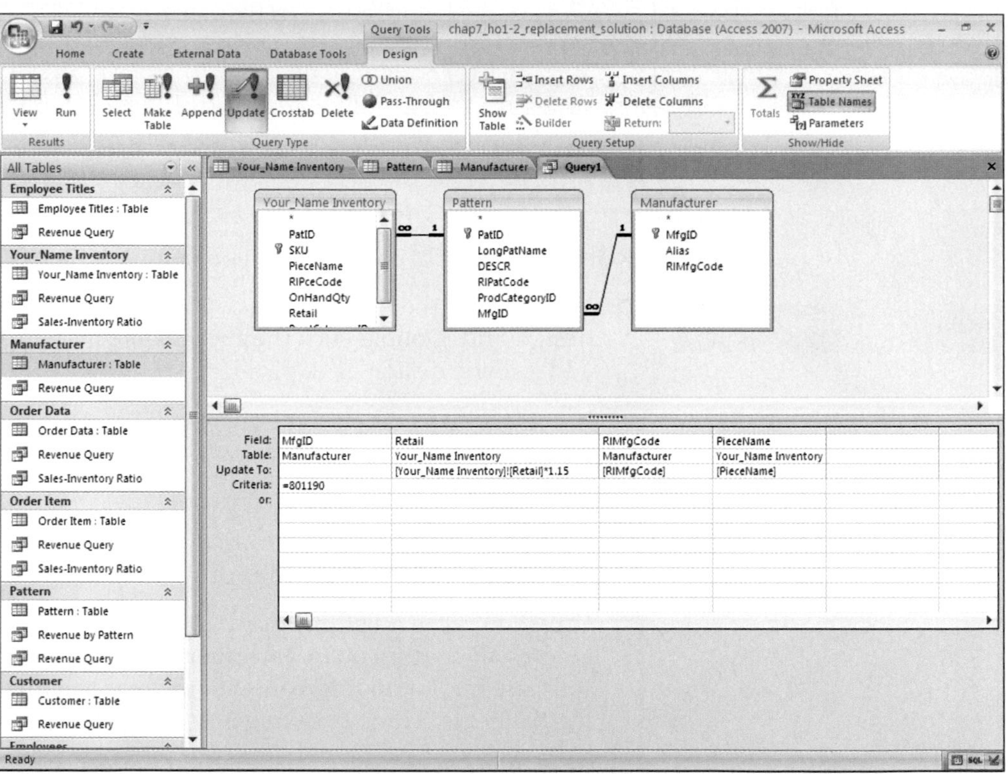

Figure 7.11 Update Query Setup

Figure 7.12 Update Query Results

Step 3 Create an Append Query

Refer to Figures 7.13 and 7.14 as you complete Step 3.

a. Close all open objects in your database. Click the **Office Button**, select **Manage**, and then select **Back Up Database**. Accept the default backup name.

   You have run two action queries and have three more to complete in this exercise. You need to have a backup to restore in the event of an error. You backed up the file before opening the database so you did not need to back up prior to running the action queries.

b. Open the **New Employees table** in Datasheet view. Add yourself as a new record. Type **8966000** in the UserID field, **0626266** in the TitleID field, your last and first names in the respective name fields, and **9/11/08** in the HireDate field. You may invent an address or use your real address, city, state, postal code, and phone. Press **Shift+Enter** to save the record.

c. Click the **Create tab** and click **Query Design** in the Other group. Double-click the **New Employees table** to add it to the design grid. Close the Show Table dialog box.

   So far, this is a simple select query. You need to tell Access that you want to append the newly hired employees to the Employees table.

d. Click **Append** in the Query Type group on the Design tab.

   The Append dialog box opens, asking you to supply the target table information.

e. Click the **Table Name drop-down arrow** and select **Employees**. Make sure that the **Current Database** option is selected and click **OK**.

   The Append To row appears on the design grid, ready for you to add fields. You need all of the fields in the New Employees table added to the Employees table.

f. Double-click the title bar of the New Employees table in the top of the design grid. All of the fields are selected. Drag the selected fields to the design grid and drop them to add all fields in the table to the design grid.

g. Click **View** in the Results group and preview the data you are about to append.

   You should see four rows and ten fields.

h. Click **View** in the Views group to return to Design view. Press **PrntScrn** to capture a screenshot. Go to your open Word document and paste the screenshot below the second screenshot. Save the Word document and return to Access.

i. Run the query. Click **Yes** in the *You are about to append 4 row(s)* warning box. Open the **Employees table**. Sort the table in descending order by the HireDate field and check to make sure the four records were added.

j. Press **PrntScrn** to capture a screenshot of the Employees table. Go to your Word document and paste the screenshot below the third screenshot. Save the Word document and return to Access.

k. Click the **Query1 tab**, click **Save** on the Quick Access Toolbar, and save the query as **Your_Name Append**.

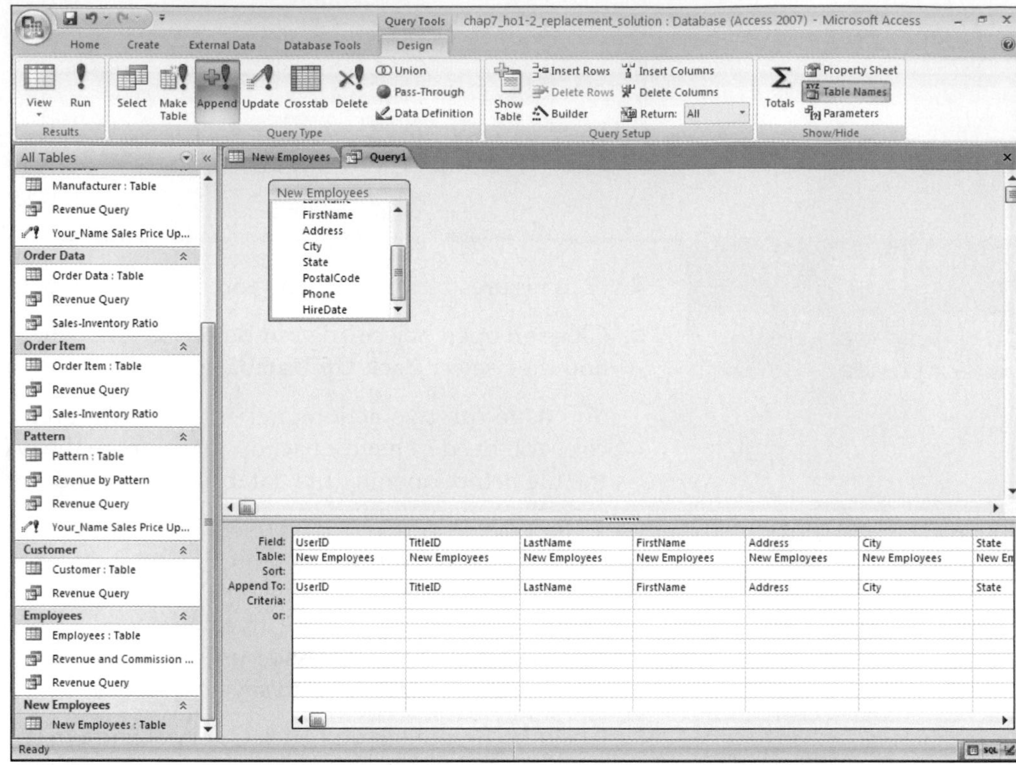

Figure 7.13 Append Query Setup

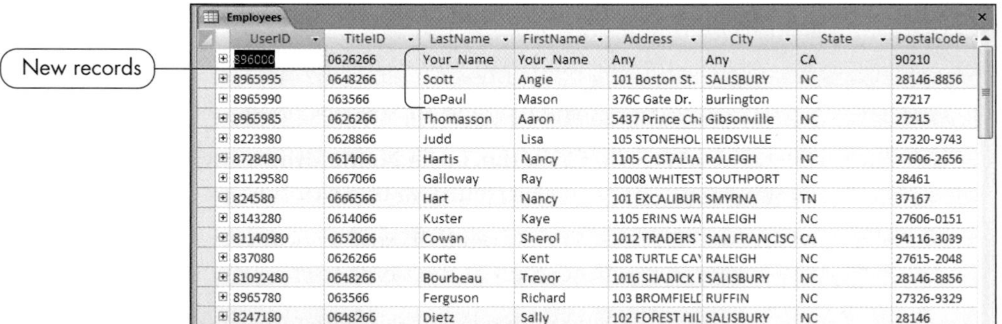

UserID	TitleID	LastName	FirstName	Address	City	State	PostalCode
896000	0626266	Your_Name	Your_Name	Any	Any	CA	90210
8965995	0648266	Scott	Angie	101 Boston St.	SALISBURY	NC	28146-8856
8965990	063566	DePaul	Mason	376C Gate Dr.	Burlington	NC	27217
8965985	0626266	Thomasson	Aaron	5437 Prince Ch	Gibsonville	NC	27215
8223980	0628866	Judd	Lisa	105 STONEHOL	REIDSVILLE	NC	27320-9743
8728480	0614066	Hartis	Nancy	1105 CASTALIA	RALEIGH	NC	27606-2656
81129580	0667066	Galloway	Ray	10008 WHITEST	SOUTHPORT	NC	28461
824580	0666566	Hart	Nancy	101 EXCALIBUR	SMYRNA	TN	37167
8143280	0614066	Kuster	Kaye	1105 ERINS WA	RALEIGH	NC	27606-0151
81140980	0652066	Cowan	Sherol	1012 TRADERS	SAN FRANCISC	CA	94116-3039
837080	0626266	Korte	Kent	108 TURTLE CA	RALEIGH	NC	27615-2048
81092480	0648266	Bourbeau	Trevor	1016 SHADICK	SALISBURY	NC	28146-8856
8965780	063566	Ferguson	Richard	103 BROMFIELD	RUFFIN	NC	27326-9329
8247180	0648266	Dietz	Sally	102 FOREST HIL	SALISBURY	NC	28146

Figure 7.14 Sorted and Appended Records in the Employees Table

Step 4
Construct a Table Using a Make Table Query

Refer to Figures 7.15 and 7.16 as you complete Step 4.

a. Click the **Office Button**, select **Manage**, and then select **Back Up Database**. Accept the default backup name.

You have run two action queries and have two more to complete in this exercise. You need to have a backup to restore in the event of an error. If you work this step on the same day as you worked the last step, Access will append *_(1)* at the end of the backup file name to distinguish it from the earlier backup.

b. Click **Query Design** in the Other group on the Create tab.

Some of the employees listed in the Employees table no longer work for Replacements, Ltd. You need to retain this information to provide references, but do not need it cluttering the working table of the database.

c. Double-click the **Employees table** to add it to the query. Close the Show Table dialog box.

You need all of the information stored in the Employees table to be stored in the archived, Former Employees table.

d. Double-click the title bar of the Employees table in the top of the design grid. All of the fields are selected. Drag the selected fields to the design grid and drop them to add all fields in the table to the design grid.

e. Add a criterion to select the terminated employees by typing **Is Not Null** in the Criteria row of the TermDate field.

You have instructed Access to select only those employees with some value entered in the termination date field.

f. Click **View** in the Results group on the Design tab to change to Datasheet view to test your criterion.

You should find nine employees that are no longer with the company. You have tested the logic of your criterion, but so far this is a select query. You need to convert it to a make table query.

g. Click **View** to change back to Design view.

h. Click **Make Table** in the Query Type group on the Design tab.

The Make Table dialog box opens and asks that you name and provide storage location information for the new table. You want to archive these data, but the new table can reside in the same database.

i. Type **Your_Name Former Employees** in the Table Name box. Make sure the **Current Database** option is selected. Click **OK**. Run the query.

j. Click **Yes** in the *You are about to paste 9 row(s) into a new table* warning box. Examine the Navigation pane to make sure that your new table exists. (You may need to scroll to find it.) Save the query as **Your_Name Make Table**.

TROUBLESHOOTING: If your table did not come out properly, delete the query and the newly created table. You can try this query again by beginning from Step 4b. Alternatively, you could close the file and open the backup.

k. With the query open in Design view, press **PrntScrn** to capture a screenshot. Switch to Word, press **Enter**, and paste the screenshot below the fourth screenshot.

l. Return to Access. Click the **arrow** in the Navigation pane title bar and switch to the **Object Type** view. Close the query. Open the **Former Employees table** in Datasheet view. Press **PrntScrn** to capture a screenshot. Switch to Word, press **Enter**, and paste the screenshot below the fifth screenshot. Save the Word document, return to Access, and close all open database objects.

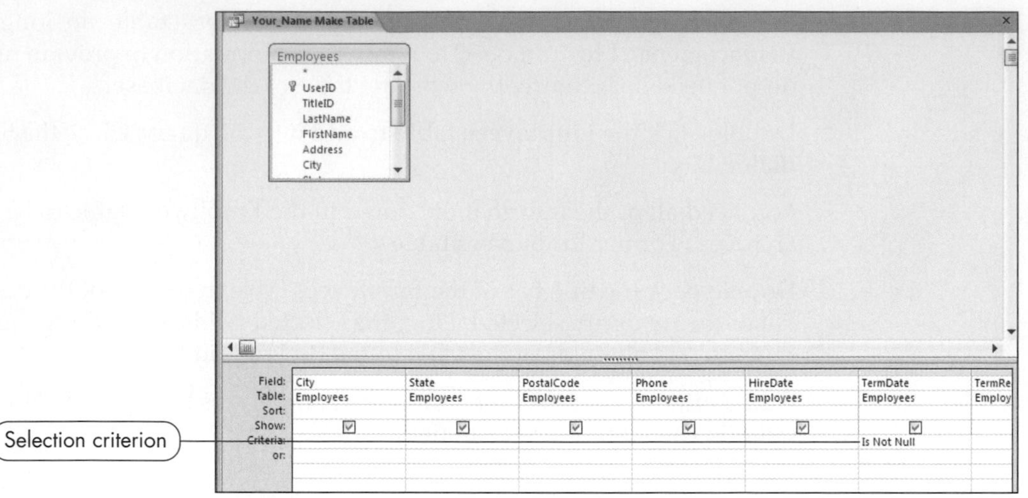

Figure 7.15 Make Table Query

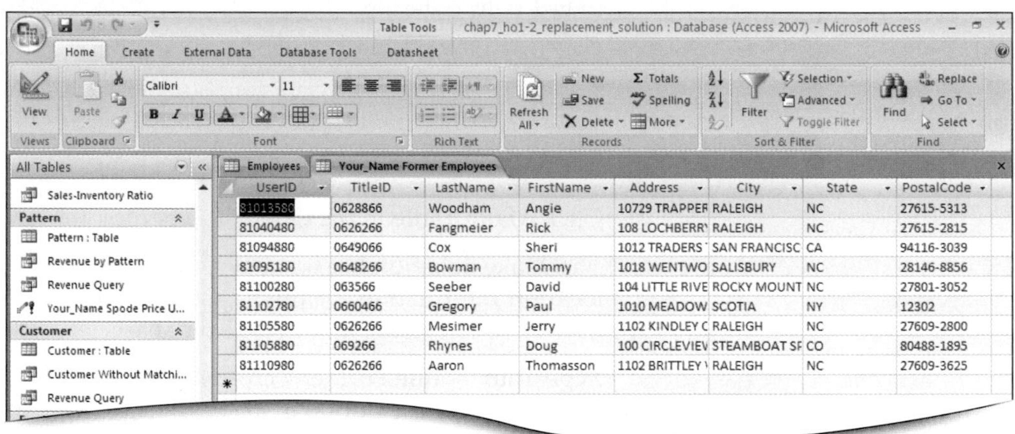

Figure 7.16 New Table

Step 5
Delete Records Using a Delete Query

Refer to Figure 7.17 as you complete Step 5.

a. Click the **Office Button**, select **Manage**, and then select **Back Up Database**. Accept the default backup name.

You have run three action queries and have one more to complete in this exercise. You need to have a backup to restore in the event of an error. If you work this step on the same day as you worked the last steps, Access will append *_(2)* at the end of the backup file name to distinguish it from the earlier backups.

b. Open the **Employees table** in Datasheet view. Click **Query Design** in the Other group on the Create tab.

You are going to create and save a select query that identifies the same terminated employees as in the previous step. You will run it as a select query to make sure you have correctly identified the nine records for deletion prior to changing it to a delete query. This table contains 119 records.

c. Double-click the **Employees table** in the Show Table dialog box to add it to the query. Close the Show Table dialog box.

d. Double-click the title bar of the Employees table in the top of the design grid. All of the fields are selected. Drag the selected fields to the design grid and drop them to add all fields in the table to the design grid. Close the Employees table.

e. Type **Is Not Null** in the Criteria row for the TermDate field. Run the query.

Check to ensure that there are nine records.

f. Click **View** in the Results group to switch to Design view. Click **Delete** in the Query Type group on the Design tab.

The design grid changes so that a Where clause displays in the Delete row for all of the fields. You have only set a criterion on the TermDate field. The other fields are no longer needed. You may remove them from the delete query without changing its performance.

g. Run the query. Click **Yes** in the *You are about to delete 9 row(s) from the specified table* warning box.

Another warning box appears. This one tells you that Access cannot delete the nine records due to key violations. Access is telling you that these former employees have related records in other tables, i.e., the Orders table. The database administrator who designed the relationships wisely did not check the cascade delete option. If that option were selected, all of the orders in the orders table that were on the many side of the one-to-many relationship with the Employees table would be deleted! This might result in SOX noncompliance because the Order table contains revenue data. You can run a delete query on the many side of the one-to-many relationship without altering the relationship.

TROUBLESHOOTING: If you need to delete records in a table that are on the one side of a one-to-many relationship, you must first edit the relationship to permit cascade deletes. Save and close the delete query. Close any open tables or queries related to the delete query. Open the Relationships window by clicking Relationships in the Show/Hide group on the Database Tools tab. Right-click the relationship connector line you wish to edit and select Edit Relationship from the short-cut menu. Select the Cascade Delete Related Records option in the Edit Relationships dialog box. Click OK. Save the design changes to the Relationships window and close it. Open the delete query. It will run on opening. You will receive a warning about deleting records in the parent table, but will receive no message about deleting all of the related records in the child table(s). You can potentially delete hundreds of records across many tables.

h. Click **No** in the Warning box. Save the query as **Your_Name Delete Employees**. Close the query.

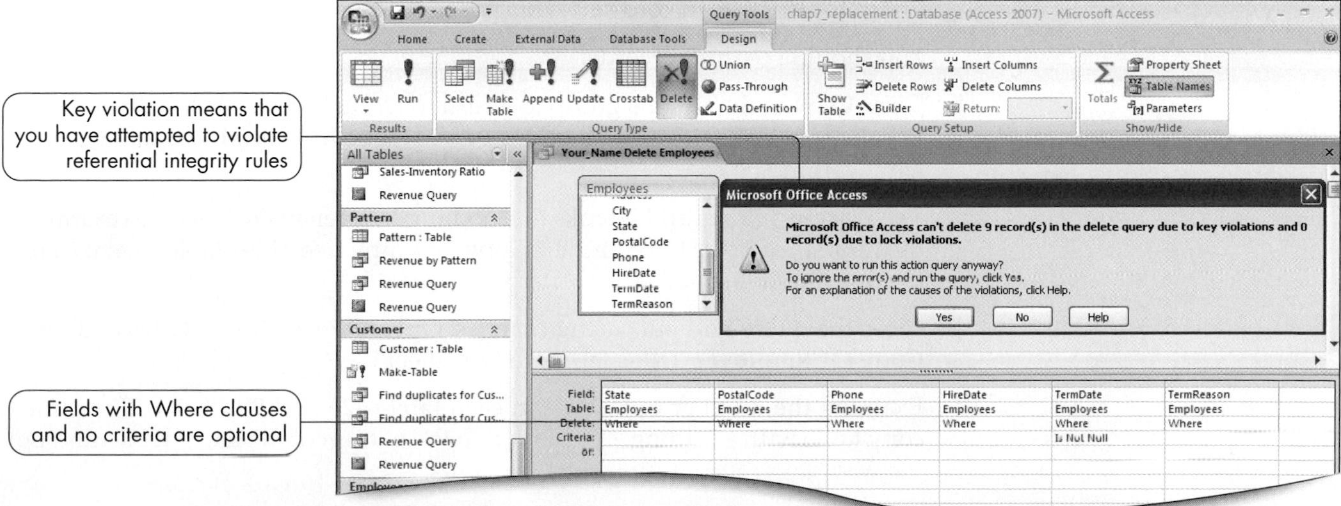

Figure 7.17 Delete Action Blocked Because Cascade Delete Option Not Selected

Step 6
Construct and Run a Delete Query

Refer to Figure 7.18 as you complete Step 6.

a. Right-click the **Employee Titles table** in the Navigation pane and select **Copy** from the shortcut menu. Right-click in the Navigation pane and select **Paste**. Check to make sure that the **Structure and Data** option is selected in the Paste Table as dialog box. Accept the default name. Click **OK**.

   You are about to delete unnecessary titles from the Employee Titles table. Because the change you will make cannot be undone, you will first make a backup of the table as a precaution. The job titles no longer in use are the ones with the word "Trainee" in them.

b. Click the **Create tab** and click **Query Design** in the Other group.

c. Double-click the **Employee Titles table**. Close the Show Table dialog box.

d. Double-click the **TitleID** and **Description** fields to add them to the design grid.

   You need to establish a criterion to select the position descriptions that contain the word Trainee.

e. In the Criteria row of the Description field, type **Like * Trainee**.

   Like * instructs Access to select all of the records ending in the word Trainee.

f. Run the query.

   The query should return three records all containing the word Trainee. Now that you have verified the record selection you can convert the query to a delete query.

   TROUBLESHOOTING: If your query returns a different number of records, check the criterion against the instructions in Steps 6d and 6e. Make sure the select query is accurate prior to converting it to a delete query.

g. Click **View** to return to Design view. Click **Delete** in the Query type group on the Design tab.

   The Sort and Show rows disappear from the design grid and a Delete row is created. Only one field has a criterion established in the Where clause, so you may remove the other field.

h. Click **above** the TitleID field when your mouse pointer shape is a bold arrow and the first column should select. Press **Delete**. Click **View** in the Results group to verify the record selection.

   You should see three records.

i. Click **View** in the Results group to return to Design view. Click **Run** in the Results group. Click **Yes** in the *You are about to delete 3 row(s) from the specified table* warning box.

   The warning closes and it looks like nothing happened. You need to examine the Employee Titles table and the Copy Of Employee Titles table to make sure the deletion happened.

j. Close the query without saving changes. Open the **Employee Titles** and the **Copy Of Employee Titles tables** in Datasheet view.

   Examine the number of records in each table—26 and 29. You will rename the copy table with a leading Z to move it to the bottom of the list of tables and out of the way.

k. Close the Copy Of Employee Titles table. Right-click it in the Navigation pane and select **Rename** from the shortcut menu. Position your insertion point left of the C in Copy. Type a **Z** and press **Enter**.

l. Compare your work to Figure 7.18. Press **PrntScrn** to capture a screenshot of the Employee Titles table in Datasheet view. Switch to Word, press **Ctrl+End** to move to the end of the document, press **Enter**, and then paste the screenshot. Save, print, and close the Word document.

m. Click the **Office Button**, select **Manage**, and select **Back Up Database**. Name the backup **chap7_ho1_replacement_solution.accdb**. Close the file and exit Access if you do not want to continue with the next exercise at this time.

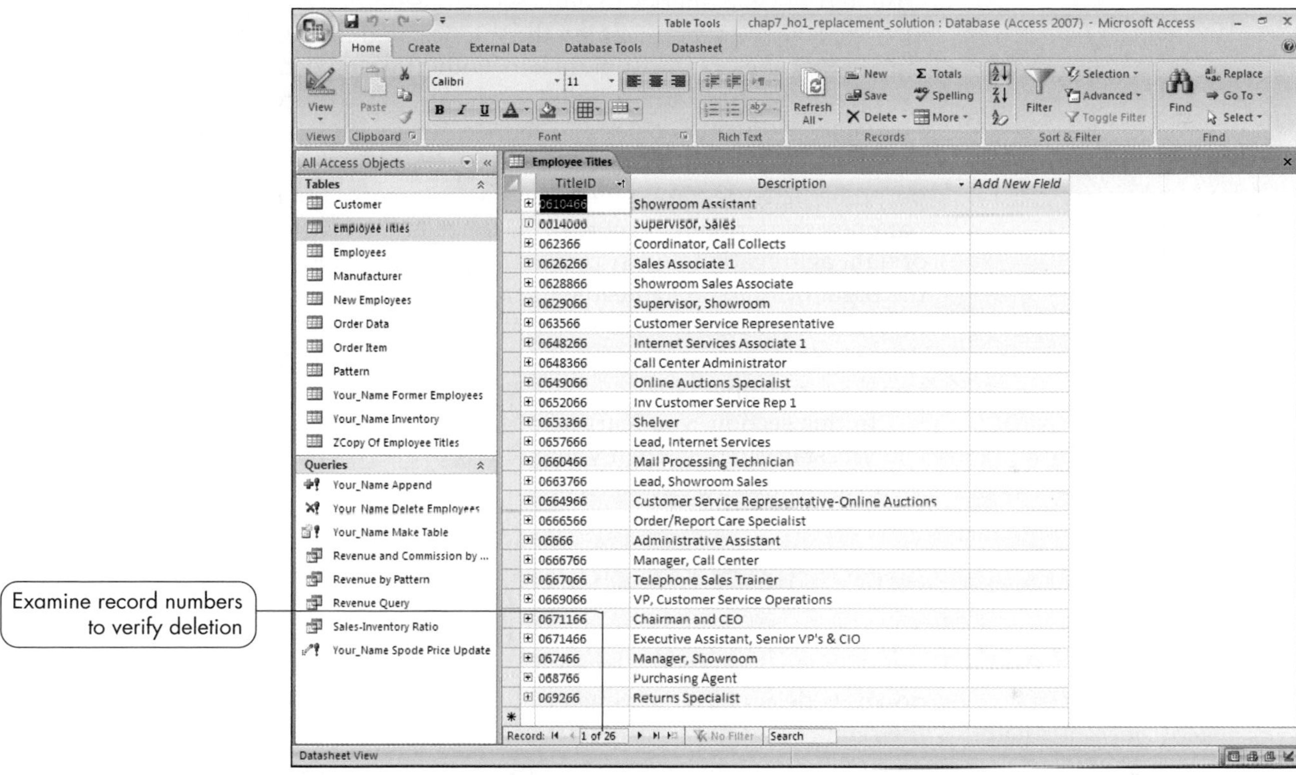

Figure 7.18 Delete Query Results

Queries for Informed Decision Making

Microsoft Access provides you with many tools that you may use to identify and extract only the records needed at the moment. There remain several query types for you to explore. Much of the power of a relational database lies in its ability to present decision makers with information needed to make decisions. Access provides powerful and flexible queries to empower decision makers. You have constructed select queries, copied them, renamed the queries, and altered criteria to construct queries that equip different decision makers with differing data. For example, you created a query identifying the revenue from banquet services in Boston and in Miami. However, many other cities and service types exist in the Member Reward database. It is likely that decision makers in other cities will request query information to support their activities. You will learn how to set up a query and let the user supply the parameter criterion to meet their data needs. You have also learned several methods of data aggregation and summarization. Depending on the database structure and the organizational data needs, the aggregating methods you already know may be insufficient to provide your organizational decision makers with the information they need. Here, too, Access's flexibility and versatility will provide you with additional aggregating tools.

In this section, you learn additional query types. You will construct parameter and crosstab queries. Then you will create queries that find unmatched records and queries that find duplicate records.

Providing Flexibility with a Parameter Query

A parameter query provides more flexibility than any other query type in Access. It simultaneously provides query designers with the ability to set up a query and lock down its design. The parameter query provides users with the ability to customize their data requests. A ***parameter query*** is a select query where one or more pieces of information are intentionally omitted by the designer and interactively selected by the user. The parameter query is not a separate type of query; it is still a select query. However, it is designed so that the query user has control of what records get selected.

A ***parameter query*** is a select query where one or more pieces of information are intentionally omitted by the designer and interactively selected by the user.

For example, the advising office in the College of Arts and Sciences advises students with many different majors. They might have a database that contains data about graduation requirements for each of the majors in the school. To graduate with a degree in Art History a student must take different classes than someone wishing to graduate with a degree in Chemistry. When an Art History major has a question for the advisor, the advisor may launch a query to find the necessary information. Before running, the query generates a parameter box (like a dialog box) that asks the advisor to supply the student's major. The advisor types the major in the box, presses enter, and the query runs. The query output will display only the necessary course requirements for an Art History major. When the next student in need of advising visits the advisor, the advisor launches the same query but supplies the next student's major, and the query will return the course requirements for the Chemistry student. The volunteer coordinator for a charity event may receive a request for a volunteer with cut flower arranging skills. The coordinator launches a query and fills in the missing parameter, flower arranging. The query will search the database of volunteer skills and return all the records listing flower arranging.

The extended flexibility of the parameter query means that users can interact with the database and run custom queries. After you properly construct one parameter query, you may apply it to many data requests. You may also construct parameters for reports. As you set up and run queries or reports, you will quickly spot when you need to use a parameter. You will find yourself copying a query (such as Miami Suite Revenue), pasting it, renaming the copy (such as Boston Suite Revenue), opening the copy in Design view, and changing a criterion. The parameter query may be based on one or more tables or queries and may be applied to select, crosstab, make table, append, and update queries. You may apply parameters to more than one field, but need to limit the number of parameters in a query to under three. Access can easily handle more. However, the query users will encounter a separate dialog box for each parameter and get irritated as box after box appears and must be addressed.

Create a Parameter Query

Open a select query in Design view and identify the field you want to turn into the parameter. Position your insertion point in the criteria row of that field. Type the text that you want to appear in the dialog box encased in brackets [ ]. The text should instruct the user what to do, such as [Enter the City Name here.]. When a user runs the query, this text will appear as a prompt in the Enter Parameter Value dialog box (see Figure 7.19). If you need additional parameters added for additional fields, move to the criteria row for the next field and type the user instructions encased in brackets in that field.

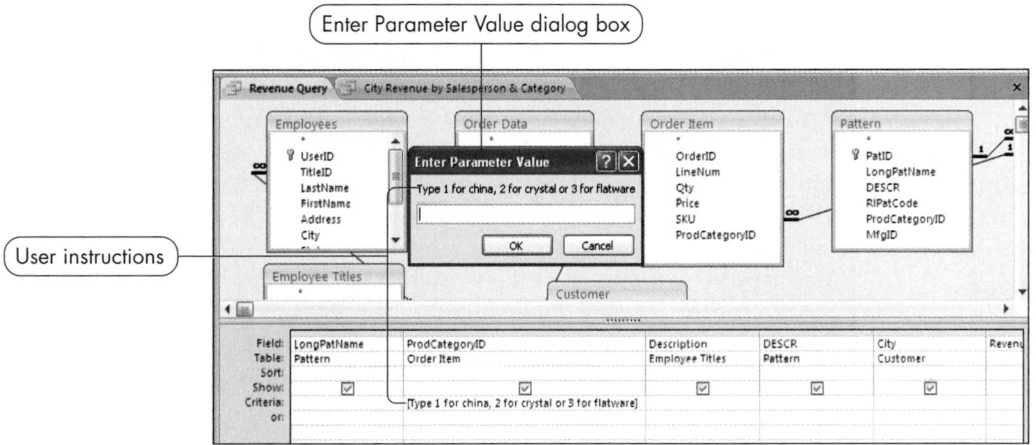

Figure 7.19 Parameter Setup

Suppose you need to establish more sophisticated criteria, for example, orders generating revenue greater than a specified amount or volunteers who donated time over a range of years. You may do this by adding an operand outside of the brackets. For example, if you want to see orders after a specific date, type **>[Enter Starting Date, example 6/1/2005]**. Figure 7.20 shows the Enter Parameter value dialog box resulting from the previous expression.

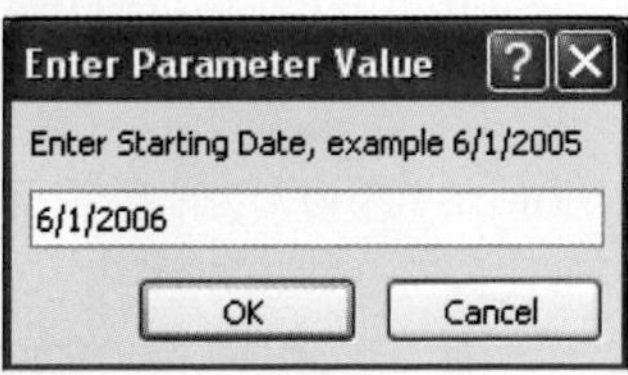

Figure 7.20 Parameter Dialog Box Requests User Input

You may combine operands and instructions to further expand the criteria selection. For example, if you want to see orders between date ranges, you would type: Between [Enter Starting Date, example 6/1/2006] and [Enter Ending Date, example 6/30/2006]

The above expression will generate two dialog boxes, one each for the starting and ending date. Figure 7.21 shows the Enter Parameter Value for the ending date. After the user supplies the missing date criteria by typing them in the Enter Parameter Value dialog box, Access will treat the criteria exactly like any other between statement. As far as Access is concerned, the criterion was established as: Between #6/1/2006# and #6/30/2006#

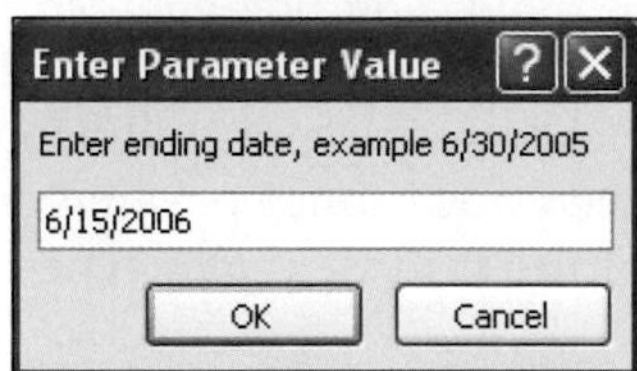

Figure 7.21 Ending Date Parameter Dialog Box

You may also expand the flexibility of how the criterion is applied to the records searched. If you combine a like operator with the bracket instructions, you could return a wider variety of results. Suppose the inventory in the jewelry department has a product ID that begins with JE for jewelry, then has a six digit ID number and ends with a two character descriptor such as WA for watch. A product ID of JE338445WA would be for a watch and JE228837RI would represent a ring. You can set up a parameter query to identify all of the products that end with a product descriptor by using the Like keyword (formula A below). Alternatively, you could search for the jewelry department's entire inventory by using expression B. The quotation marks and asterisk at the beginning and end of the criteria instructs Access to search a character string using a wildcard character.

A Like "*" & [Type the two letter product descriptor, example WA]

B Like [Type the two letter department descriptor, example JE] & "*"

TIP Select Unrelated Fields for Row and Column Fields

As you set up the parameter queries, remember you are writing the instruction sets in the dialog box for data users in the organization. Your instructions need to guide the user to successfully extract the information they need. The users will become frustrated if their queries do not return the expected results. Setting up a parameter on a field containing long numbers or difficult-to-spell words may result in data entry errors and misspellings in the dialog box. The query will run, but return no results because the criteria were not met. The users will call the help desk and claim the database is not working, and this will reflect poorly on your performance evaluation.

Create Parameter Reports

The easiest way to create a parameter report is to base the report on a parameter query. In other words, once you establish and test the parameters in the query, they will transfer to any report that sources the query and the field containing the parameter. If you want to add parameters to a report that sources a query that is not a parameter query, you have two options. The first is to open the report's source query in Design view and add the necessary parameter. After you save the query design changes, the next time you run the report the parameters will display. Alternatively, you can open the report in Design view, open the Property Sheet, and click the Record Source Property ellipsis. This opens the source query in Design view, where you can add the needed parameters.

Use the Query Parameter Dialog Box

Access provides a method for you to organize and keep track of all of the parameters used in a query. This is especially helpful when different user groups use the same query but need to extract differing layers of information from it. The marketing manager may be interested in product sales for a specific category while the sales managers need to know sales by city. The database administrator might supply the same basic query to the different user groups around the organization with a subtle difference. Access provides a Query Parameter organization system to help the database administrator keep up with the different parameters required by different users in an organization. Organization of the parameter is simple; you first display the Query Parameters dialog box by clicking Parameter in the Show/Hide group on the Design tab. Use the Parameter column of the dialog box to name the parameter descriptively. You may name the parameter anything that you wish as long as you do not use a field name that is used in the query. Use the right column to tell Access what data type is stored in the parameter's field.

Figure 7.22 shows a query open in Design view with the Query Parameters dialog box opened. This query has two different parameters stored in it—City Name and Category. You would create the parameter in the Query Parameter box and use it in the design grid. In the Criteria row, type the parameter name encased in brackets. (If you forget the brackets, your query likely will run but return no results. This query does not have a city named City Name in the records.) The same data entry prompting dialog boxes appear when you run the query using this method of parameter creation as the other method. You can alter the order in which the prompt boxes appear by changing the row order in the Query Parameters dialog box.

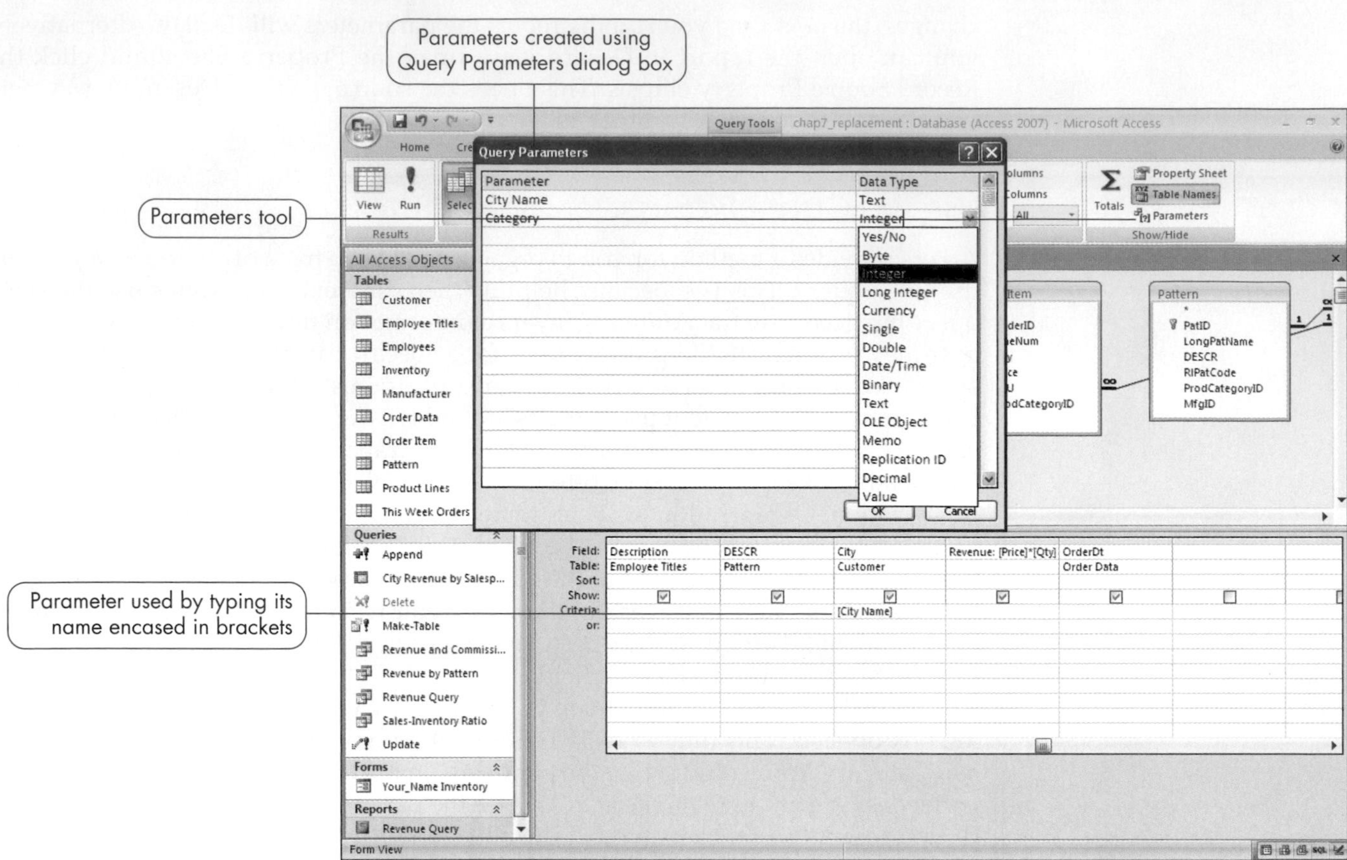

Figure 7.22 Parameter Organization

Summarizing Data with a Crosstab Query

A ***crosstab query*** summarizes values by two sets of unrelated facts.

Access does an excellent job of ordering details and retrieving them in various forms for differing data needs. Sometimes decision makers need to see every detail; sometimes they need a big picture view of the data, such as an aggregate. ***Crosstab queries*** summarize values in a grid by two unrelated sets of facts in the database. The grid design permits summarization and aggregation. For example, you might construct a crosstab query to examine total revenue generated by salesperson and by product classification. The resulting output compresses the data into a grid with the salesperson's name identifying the set of facts stored in the grid's rows. The product classification names group across the top of the columns. Each cell in the grid contains the aggregating data describing the intersection of the rows and columns.

Crosstab queries resemble PivotTables. The differences between crosstabs and PivotTables lie in who builds them and who uses the information generated by them. PivotTables give tremendous flexibility and power to the users of database information—the managerial decision maker. Once properly trained, managers can construct and use PivotTables to summarize data and convert it into useful information. PivotTables empower the end users of the data. Information Systems (IS) professionals construct most crosstab queries. The typical line manager uses the information generated from a crosstab query. In other words, the marketing manager both builds and uses the PivotTable information. But the IS professional in the organization builds the crosstab query. The information it generates is used by the marketing manager. You may have good reasons not to use PivotTables. Not all line managers have time to learn how to construct PivotTables. Not all database administrators are comfortable with granting users in the organization query construction privileges. Your organization may even have policies prohibiting it.

Group and Summarize Data

Row headings describe the set of facts listed horizontally in a crosstab query.

Column headings describe the set of facts listed vertically in a crosstab query.

The grouping in a crosstab query comes from your definitions of row and column headings. ***Row headings*** describe the set of facts listed horizontally in a crosstab query. ***Column headings*** describe the set of facts listed vertically in a crosstab query. The summarizing or aggregating in a crosstab comes from your instructions about what type of aggregating to perform. The summarizing values appear once for each grouping level. If you need to know the average grade point average (GPA) by class standing (freshman, sophomore, junior, or senior) for each different major, use the major field for the row heading, the class standing as the column heading, and the average GPA for the summarizing field. If you want to know total revenue by product for each of the past three years, place the product field as the row heading, the date field for the column heading, and the sum of revenue as the summarizing field. You may add additional row grouping fields for additional flexibility.

TIP Select Unrelated Fields for Row and Column Fields

Crosstab queries will only work when you select unrelated fields for row and column headings. You could not use Product Categories as the column field and Product Name as the row headings because a relationship is established between those fields. The result would be a grid that looks like stair steps. First, you would see all of the products in the first category listed in the second column. Then the products for the second category would list under the first, but in the third column. The fourth column would list the third category below the first two and so on. The column grouping field should not be related to any of the row grouping fields.

Use the Crosstab Query Wizard

You will probably want to use the Crosstab Query Wizard to help you build your first crosstab queries. Just as with a PivotTable, the crosstab query requires that you assemble all of the data into a single source. You may only reference one object (table or query) in a crosstab query. If you want to use fields stored in different tables, then first assemble the needed data in a single query. Once the data are assembled in a single source and you have created any calculated fields, launch the Crosstab Query Wizard by clicking Query Wizard in the Other group on the Create tab.

The New Query dialog box appears, asking that you identify the type of query to build (see Figure 7.23). After you select Crosstab Query Wizard and click OK, the Crosstab Query Wizard starts so that you can identify the source data. You may display only tables, queries, or a combination of both by selecting the appropriate object in the View section (see Figure 7.24). The next step in the Crosstab Query Wizard, shown in Figure 7.25, asks you to identify up to three row heading fields. You make your selection by double-clicking the field name or by using the move to Selected Fields buttons. Access previews the layout in the Sample area. If you selected the fields in the wrong order, use the move buttons to return the Selected Fields to the Available Fields box and try again. In the next wizard screen (see Figure 7.26), you select the fields for the column headings. Figure 7.27 displays the setup to aggregate the revenue field with a sum function. Here, you must provide information for both the summarization field (revenue) and what type of calculation to perform (sum). The final screen gives you the opportunity to name the query descriptively and provide information on how to view the query (see Figure 7.28).

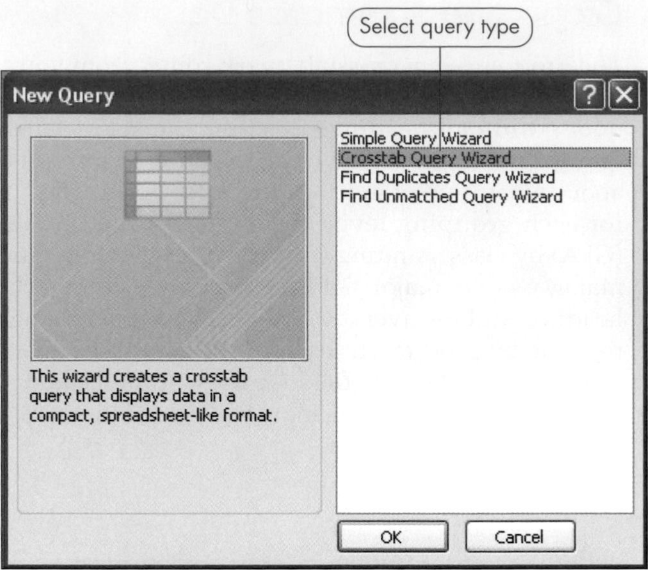

Figure 7.23 New Query Dialog Box

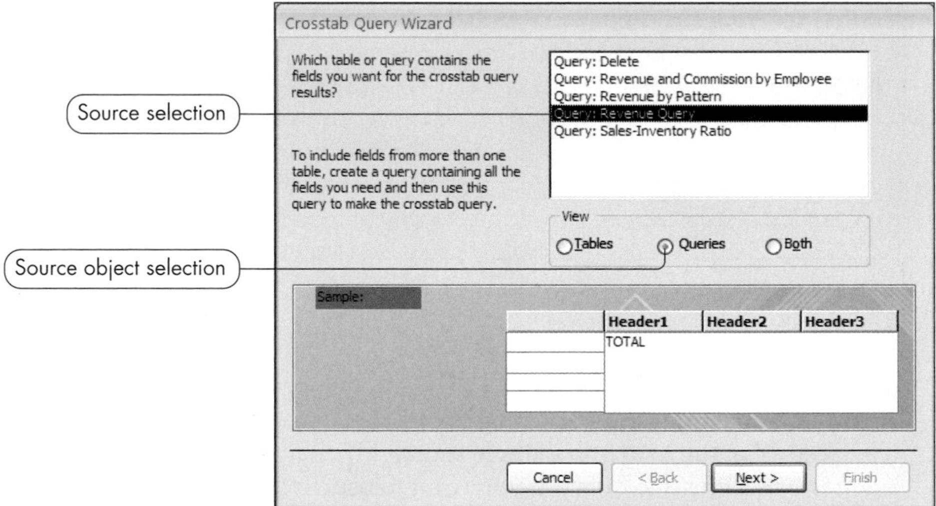

Figure 7.24 Select the Data Source

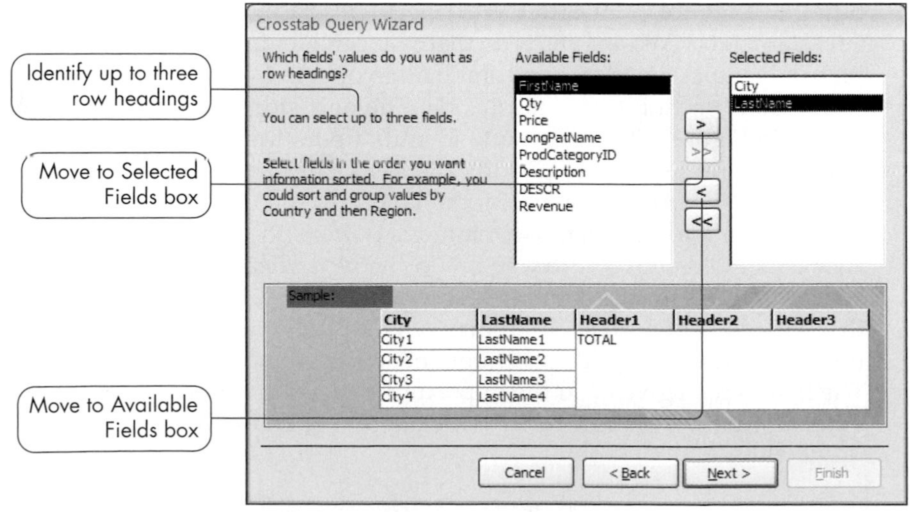

Figure 7.25 Row Head Selection

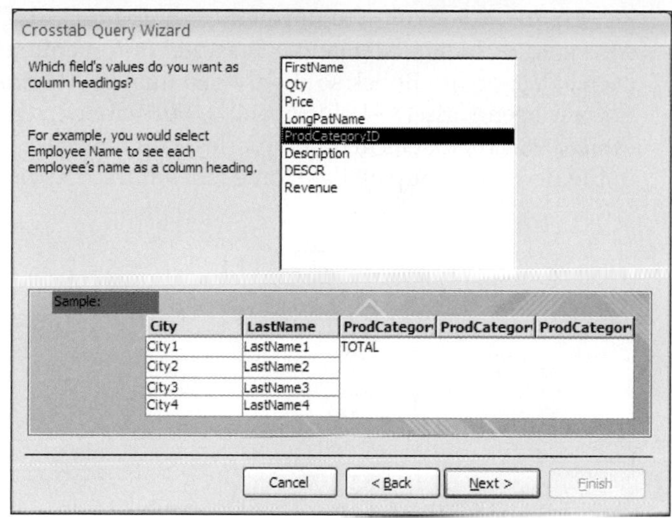

Figure 7.26 Column Heading Selection

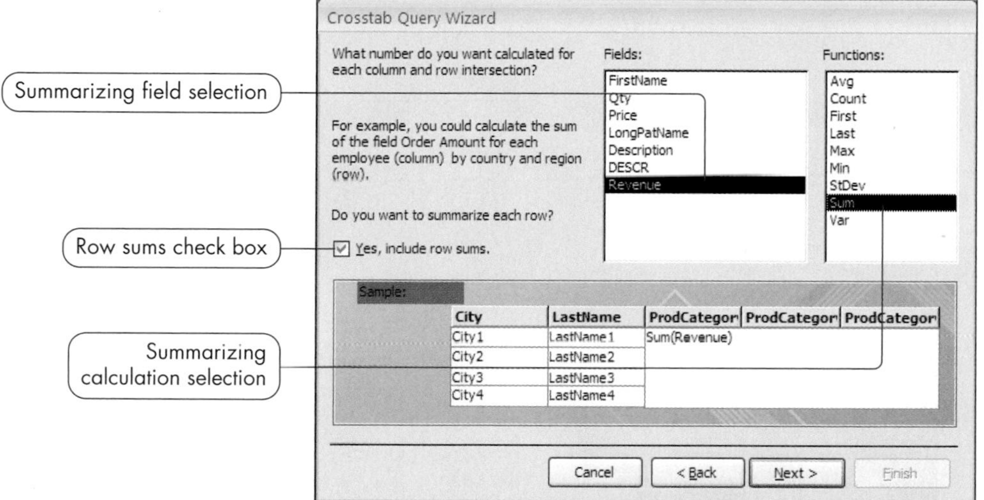

Figure 7.27 Specify Calculation Type and Data

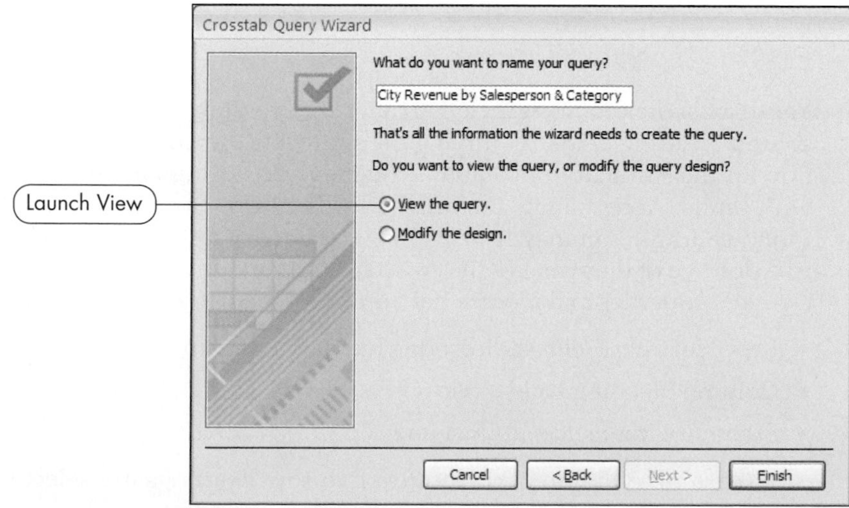

Figure 7.28 Descriptive Query Name

Figure 7.29 shows the finished crosstab query in Datasheet view. Three salespersons sold orders in Alamance. The Total of Revenue column displays aggregates for each salesperson. Bolick sold only one item in Alamance for 18.895 (the results have not yet been formatted as currency), but VanSchoich had two sales in that city that totaled 98.415. Just as in other queries, you may display a total row by clicking Totals in the Records group on the Home tab. Figure 7.30 displays the query in Design view.

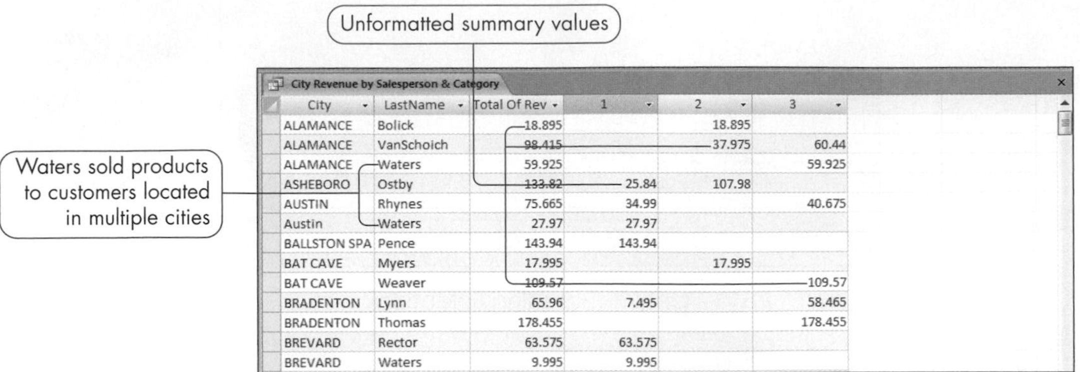

City	LastName	Total Of Rev	1	2	3
ALAMANCE	Bolick	18.895		18.895	
ALAMANCE	VanSchoich	98.415		37.975	60.44
ALAMANCE	Waters	59.925			59.925
ASHEBORO	Ostby	133.82	25.84	107.98	
AUSTIN	Rhynes	75.665	34.99		40.675
Austin	Waters	27.97	27.97		
BALLSTON SPA	Pence	143.94	143.94		
BAT CAVE	Myers	17.995		17.995	
BAT CAVE	Weaver	109.57			109.57
BRADENTON	Lynn	65.96	7.495		58.465
BRADENTON	Thomas	178.455			178.455
BREVARD	Rector	63.575	63.575		
BREVARD	Waters	9.995	9.995		

Figure 7.29 Unformatted Crosstab Output

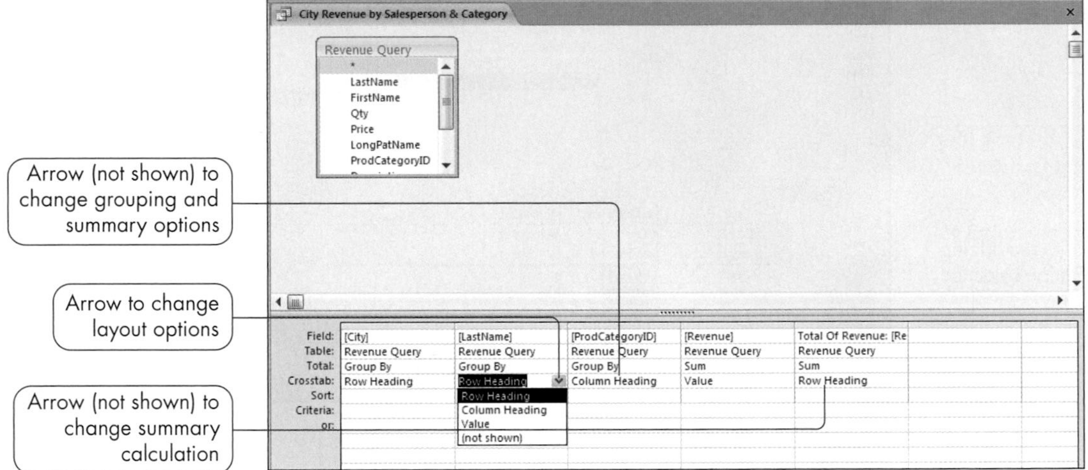

Figure 7.30 Crosstab Query in Design View

Edit a Crosstab Query

You may switch to Design view to alter the crosstab structure by changing row and column heading fields, modifying the aggregating statistic, or altering the field selection for the summary calculation. You may add additional fields to the query design with limits. Access limits the number of fields for the crosstab for the row and column headings. You may have as many summary fields as you wish, but more than two or three of them makes the crosstab structure unwieldy and difficult to read. You change properties and modify field order for a crosstab as you do in a select query.

- Row Heading Field—at least one but may have up to three
- Column Heading Field—one and only one
- Summarizing Field—at least one

Reexamine Figure 7.29. Because two row headings are selected, the summary value, sum of revenue, has been calculated on the second layer (the salesperson) only. This crosstab provides an accurate sum of each salesperson's revenue generation by product category, but does not aggregate by city. If you want to know the total revenue generated from orders shipped to each city, you would need to remove the LastName field from the design grid. Figure 7.31 shows alterations to the query's design. The LastName field was removed. The Revenue and Total of Revenue fields have currency formats applied. Figure 7.32 shows the output from the edited query.

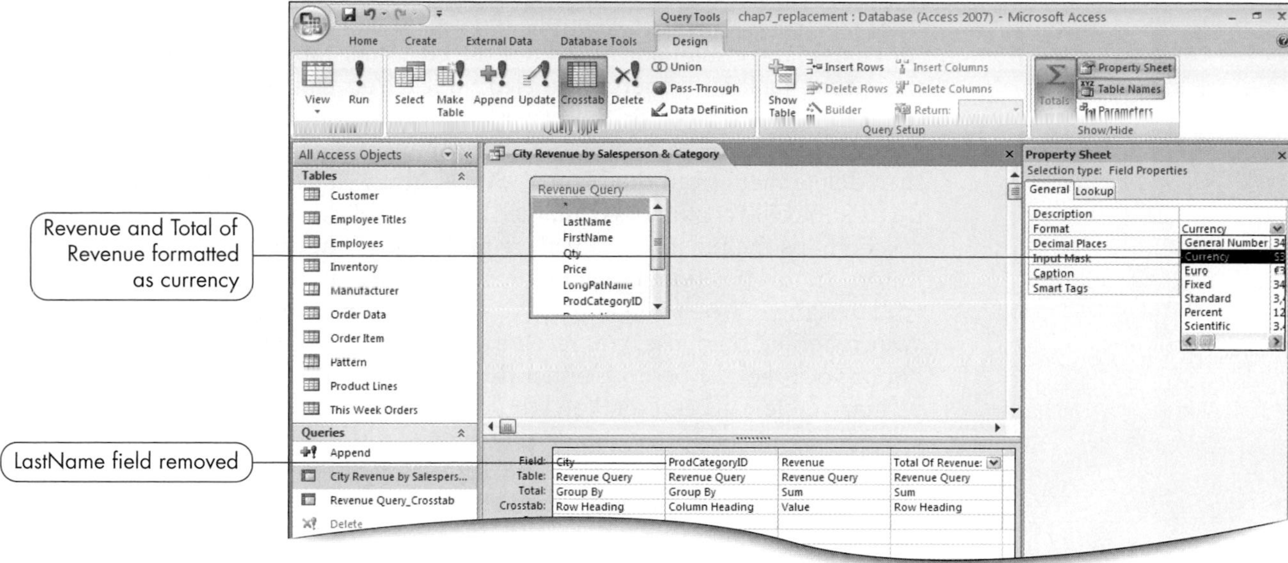

Figure 7.31 Edited Crosstab Query in Design View

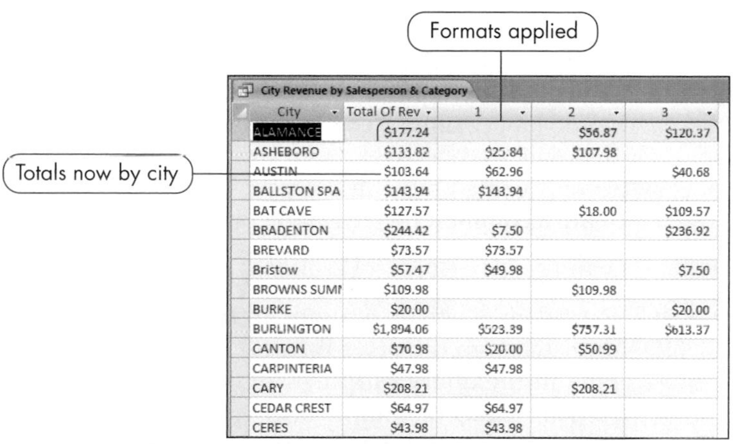

City	Total Of Rev	1	2	3
ALAMANCE	$177.24		$56.87	$120.37
ASHEBORO	$133.82	$25.84	$107.98	
AUSTIN	$103.64	$62.96		$40.68
BALLSTON SPA	$143.94	$143.94		
BAT CAVE	$127.57		$18.00	$109.57
BRADENTON	$244.42	$7.50		$236.92
BREVARD	$73.57	$73.57		
Bristow	$57.47	$49.98		$7.50
BROWNS SUMI	$109.98		$109.98	
BURKE	$20.00			$20.00
BURLINGTON	$1,894.06	$523.39	$757.31	$613.37
CANTON	$70.98	$20.00	$50.99	
CARPINTERIA	$47.98	$47.98		
CARY	$208.21		$208.21	
CEDAR CREST	$64.97	$64.97		
CERES	$43.98	$43.98		

Figure 7.32 Edited Crosstab Query in Datasheet View

Finding Unmatched Records with a Query

Most organizations can supply order information on all of the customers who placed orders last month. However, some of the firm's customers may not have purchased anything last month. These customers have records in the firm's database's customer table, but because they did not order anything, they did not produce any revenue. Maybe the marketing department should send them an e-mail offering a discount on their next purchase to reenergize them. Access offers a specialized query that will help you help the marketing manager. The ***find unmatched query*** compares records in two related tables and returns the records found in only one table, but not both of the tables.

The ***find unmatched query*** compares records in two related tables and returns the records found in one table, but not both of the tables.

Use a Find Unmatched Query

You may encounter situations where two tables in a database have similar information stored in them but also have occasions of data redundancy. For example, you might have a table named E-commerce Clients and a different table named

Customers. Both store information about the customer name and contact information. But you discover that much of the regular customer's information is duplicated in (or conflicted by) the E-commerce Clients table because those customers make purchases both in the traditional fashion and online. Some of the fields in both tables contain duplicated information (not a good idea in database design). Other fields are unique to each table. For example, the E-commerce Clients table may contain a field for customers' e-mail addresses but the customer table does not store that information. Your task is to merge the two tables. You can find those records that exist uniquely in one table or the other in an unmatched query. After you find those records, you can use a make table query or an append query to preserve the data and then delete them from their source tables. You will need a union query to merge the fields about the customers contained in both tables.

Perhaps the most useful feature of this query applies only to database administrators. In this position, you will inherit databases to manage that may not have been well designed. When you attempt to apply referential integrity between the tables in your inherited database, you receive an error message telling you that Access cannot honor your request because either duplicate records exist or no unique index for the primary table has been set. You would then run an unmatched query on the primary key field in one table that should match to its counterpart field as a foreign field. This will let you identify the problematic records, track down the correct information, and make the repairs to the table data that eventually will lead to your being able to enforce referential integrity.

Create a Find Unmatched Query Using the Wizard

Suppose you want to find a list of products that are in inventory but no one has ever purchased. You could create an unmatched records query to identify them. You begin by clicking the Query Wizard in the Other group on the Create tab. In the New Query dialog box, select the Find Unmatched Query Wizard and click OK. In the first screen of the Find Unmatched Query Wizard, you need to select the first of the two tables that will serve as sources for this query (see Figure 7.33). You will need to select the second related table in the next screen. This query will only work if the two tables share a common field (usually primary/foreign). The Order Items table contains the field SKU that is the primary key in the inventory table (see Figure 7.34). Access searches for and finds the shared SKU field in the next screen. If the two tables share more than one field in common, you would need to specify the field to use to find the unmatched records (see Figure 7.35). In the next step, you identify what fields to display in the query output. Use the arrows to move the fields you select from the *Available fields* box to the *Selected fields* box. Figure 7.36 shows that all of the fields have been selected for the query. The final screen lets you name the query and decide how to open it initially. The default name actually describes the query's purpose and content, so you keep it (see Figure 7.37).

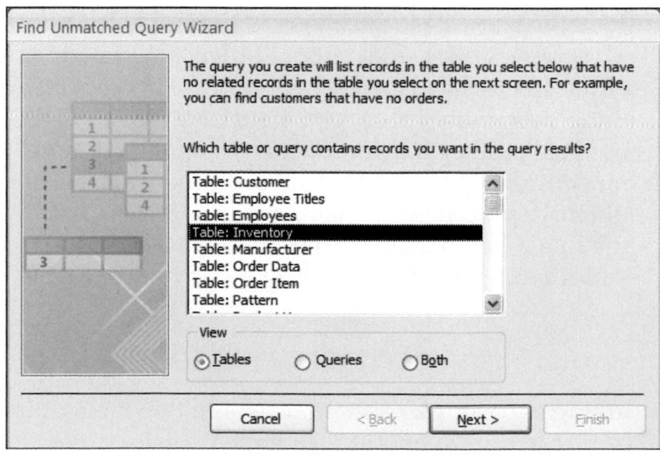

Figure 7.33 Select the First Table

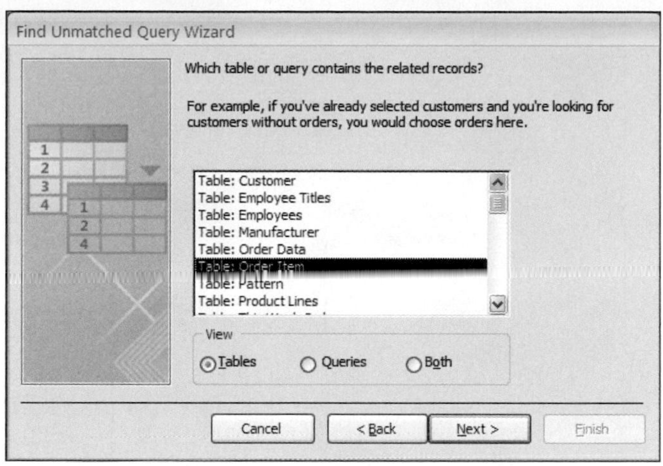

Figure 7.34 Select the Second Table

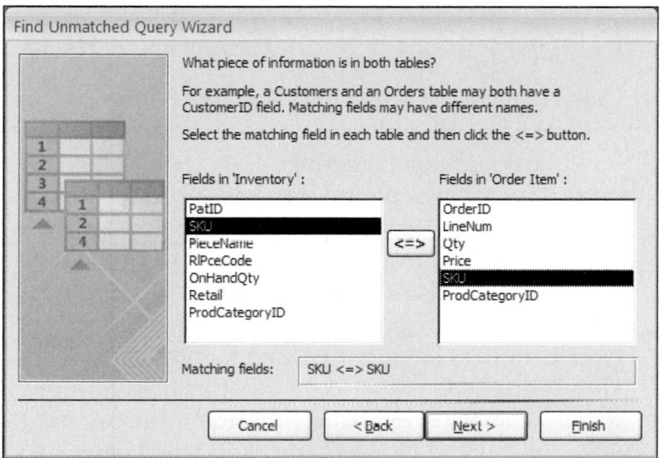

Figure 7.35 Identify the Common Field

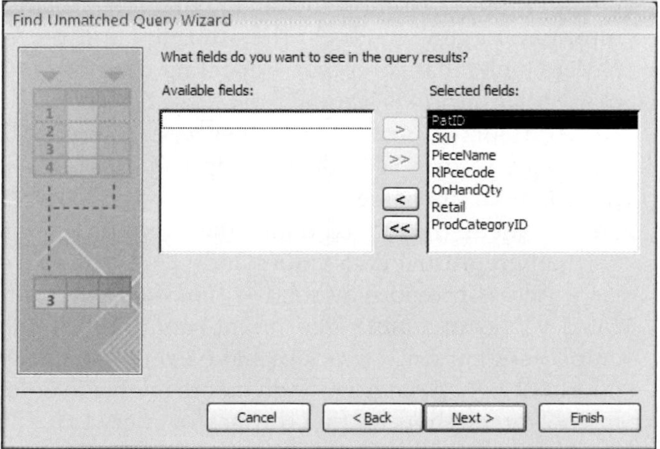

Figure 7.36 Select Fields to Display in Query Output

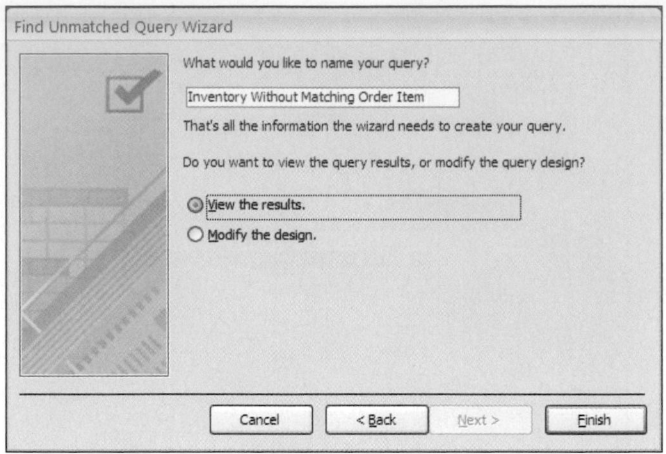

Figure 7.37 Name the Query

Finding Duplicate Records with a Query

Data are incorrectly entered. Tired data entry operators lose focus and enter the same order twice, and multiple databases addressing similar needs exist independently in multiple departmental settings. For example, both the marketing and sales departments might maintain separate databases containing customer information. Sometimes data are duplicated in a database by error. However, not all duplicated data in a database are the result of an error. Most of the data duplication is designed into the database as a result of the primary key-foreign key relationship. For example, the CustomerID field needs to be the unique identifier in the customer's table with no two customers having the same ID number and each customer having only one ID. However, the CustomerID will appear as a foreign key field in other tables in the database such as the table containing the orders. Because of the one-to-many relationship sourced on the CustomerID field between the Customers and Orders tables, a CustomerID may be repeated in the Orders table. One customer may place many different orders. If the CustomerID field value duplicates in the Customers table—where it is the primary key—that is poor database design. Referential integrity cannot be enforced. Users of the data in that system cannot fully trust the accuracy of the information generated. On the other hand, if the CustomerID field repeats in the Orders table, that is normal. Repeating data values on the many side of the one-to-many relationship is standard database design.

The ***find duplicates query*** helps you identify duplicated values in a table.

Additionally, many data values repeat naturally in a table. The city field will contain many records with duplicating values. The LastName field may contain many records with the name of Smith, Lee, or Patel. These duplicated data values are not errors. Not all duplicated data values found in a database are cause for alarm. Both naturally repeating data values and values stored in a foreign key field repeat regularly. Access provides a tool, the ***find duplicates query***, to help you identify duplicated values in a table. You might run a find duplicates query to determine which employees currently work or have ever worked with a customer. If you inherit a poorly designed database and you are unable to enforce referential integrity between tables, you might run a find duplicates query to identify the duplicating values in the primary key field. Once you identify the problem records, you can repair or eliminate them, enforce referential integrity, and trust the database information more completely. Finding duplicate fields and knowing what to do with them remains one of the greatest challenges for database administrators. This may be the part of database administration that is more art than science. The administrator must exercise judgment to determine which duplicate data are in the database by design and which are there due to errors. The administrator needs to know the data contained in the database and how the organization uses the data to make the appropriate decisions about the duplications.

TIP Ignore Duplicate Values in a Query

Suppose you are out of stock of a particular item and need to notify the customers who ordered the item that it will be delayed. You might source a select query on the customer and order tables to accumulate all of the order information and contact information in a single location. Then you would set the parameters to select the out-of-stock item. Finally, you would telephone the customer and explain the delay. But what would happen if the out-of-stock item was a frequently ordered one and the customer had placed several different orders for it on different days? You could call the same customer repeatedly or you could set the query to hide duplicate values. Open the query in Design view and display the Property Sheet by clicking it in the Show/Hide group on the Design tab. Click any empty space on the design grid and the Property Sheet title will change to Selection Type: Query Properties. Find the Unique Values property and change it from No to Yes.

Launch the Query Wizard by clicking its tool in the Other group on the Create tab. In the New Query dialog box, select Find Duplicates Query Wizard. Select the table or query that contains the data source for your query in the next screen and click Next. In the Find Duplicates Query Wizard, Access asks that you identify the field or fields that might contain duplicate information (see Figure 7.38). Figure 7.39 shows the setup to identify customers that may have duplicate city information. Here the state was also included because several states have cities with the same name. Next, you need to tell Access which fields (in addition to those already selected) you want to include in the displayed results (see Figure 7.40). The final screen gives you an opportunity to name the query and decide how to initially view it (see Figure 7.41).

In the second hands-on exercise, you will improve your querying skills as you work further with the Replacements, Ltd., data.

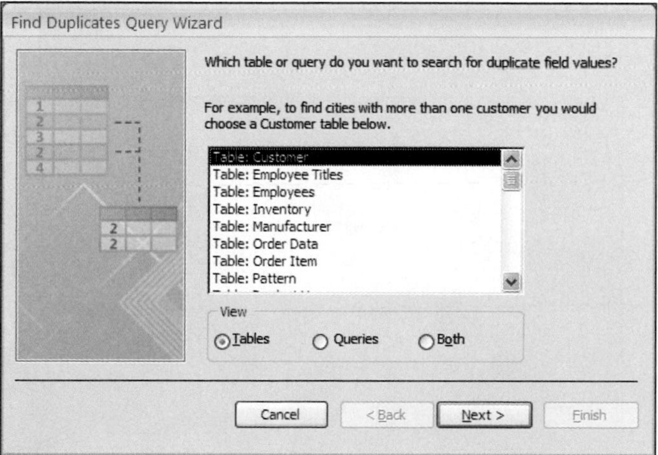

Figure 7.38 Table Selection

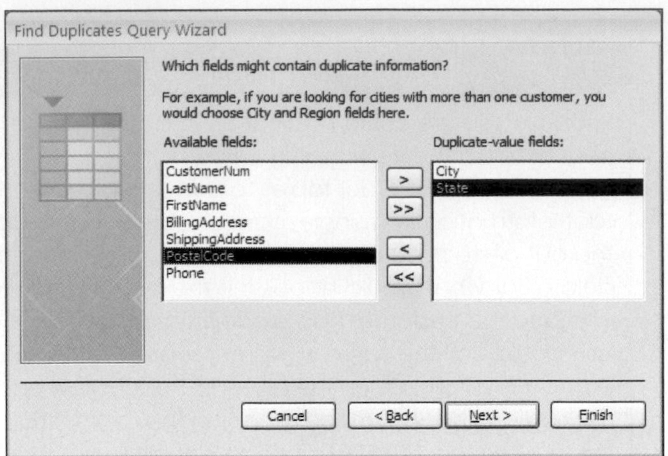

Figure 7.39 Duplicate Field Identification

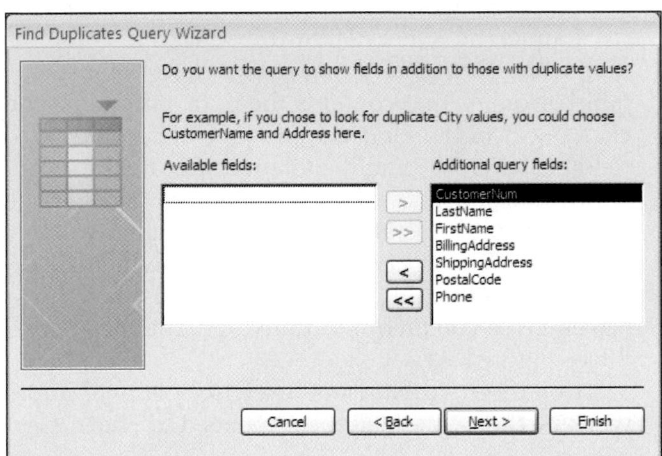

Figure 7.40 Select Fields to Display

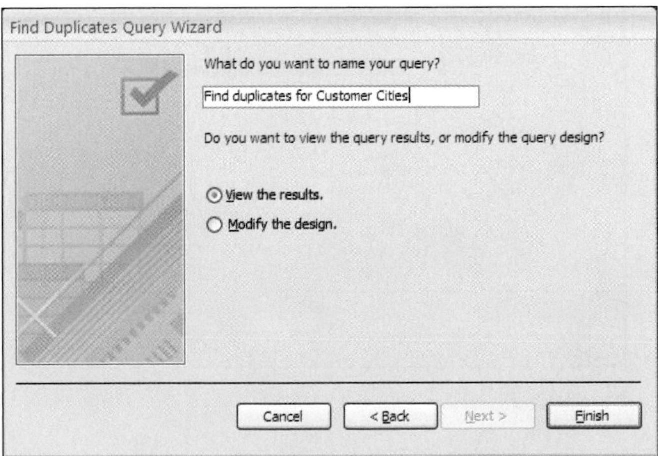

Figure 7.41 Query Naming

Data Summarization and Aggregation Methods | Reference

Means	Necessary Security Level	Who Prepares	Flexibility Level	Location	View
Total Row	Low	End User	Low	Table, Query, Report	Datasheet Report
End users with virtually no administrative privileges can toggle on or off a total row and use it to generate different aggregating summary values (a sum one place and a count or a minimum another) for different fields. Relatively unsophisticated data users can accomplish this with a small training investment required.					
Group Totaling in Reports	High	Database Professionals or Advanced End Users	High	Report	Layout or Design
Database professionals historically prepared most grouped and nested reports. They will continue to do so in Access 2007. However, with the addition of the Layout view, these operations are now in reach of advanced data end users. A select group of end users may be trained to customize the reports they need. The database administrators may need to rethink security level assignment to facilitate empowering the organization's data users.					
Totals Query	High	Database Professionals or Advanced End Users	Medium	Query	Design
These are not new to Access 2007. End users without query creation privileges in a database work around the database's security by copying data from a query in the organizational database and pasting it to a database stored locally on the user's desktop. Then they create and use the Totals queries to make decisions. This practice may lead to multiple copies of a database existing in multiple locations within an organization.					
PivotTable	Mid	End User or Database Professional	High	Query or Table	PivotTable
The PivotTable creation in Access 2007 is much easier than in earlier versions of the software. Organizational data users, if provided training, can generate customized PivotTable views of their data. The database staff will need to provide both the necessary training and technical support for end users. If the database administration locks the data security too tightly, the data users develop workarounds like copying data to a duplicate database stored locally.					
PivotChart	Mid	End User or Database Professional	High	Query or Table	PivotChart
The PivotChart creation in Access 2007 is much easier than in earlier versions of the software. Organizational data users, if provided training, can generate customized PivotChart views of their data. The database staff will need to provide both the necessary training and technical support for end users.					
Crosstab Query	High	Database Professional	Medium	Query	Design
This data aggregation tool belongs exclusively to the database professional. It is the secure, IT department controlled alternative to PivotTables and PivotCharts. Crosstabs do not have as much design flexibility as do PivotTables. However, after providing end user training on how to use the PivotTable view and answering the same end user's questions repeatedly, constructing a Crosstab for the user to look at but not alter may be the most effective resource allocation.					

Hands-On Exercises

2 | Additional Queries

Skills covered: 1. Create a Crosstab Query **2.** Edit a Crosstab Query **3.** Construct a Parameter Query **4.** Build a Find Unmatched Records Query **5.** Create a Find Duplicates Query

Step 1
Create a Crosstab Query

Refer to Figure 7.42 as you complete Step 1.

a. Open the *chap7_ho1-3_replacement_solution* file, if necessary, and click **Options** on the Security Warning toolbar. Then click the **Enable this content option** in the Microsoft Office Security Options dialog box and click **OK**.

   TROUBLESHOOTING: If you create unrecoverable errors while completing this hands-on exercise, you can delete the *chap7_ho1-3_replacement_solution* file, copy the *chap7_ho1_replacement_solution* backup database you created at the end of the first hands-on exercise, and open the copy of the backup database to start the second hands-on exercise again.

b. Click **Query Wizard** in the Other group on the Create tab.

c. Select the **Crosstab Query Wizard**. Click **OK**.

   This launches the wizard. You need to construct a query that shows revenue by state and salesperson. The data to construct this query are assembled in the Revenue Query.

d. Click **Queries** in the *View* section of the Crosstab Query Wizard dialog box. Then click **Query: Revenue Query**. Click **Next**.

   It does not matter to Access whether you use the State or the Salesperson field as the row heading. But it is a good idea to use the field with more values as the row heading. There are more salespeople than states, so use the LastName field as the row heading.

e. Double-click the **LastName** field in the *Available Fields* box to move it to the *Selected Fields* box. Click **Next**.

   TROUBLESHOOTING: You can also use the move arrows to move the selected fields from the Available to the Selected boxes or back again.

f. Click the **State** field to select it as the column heading. Click **Next**.

g. Click the **Revenue** field in the *Fields* box to select it as the summarizing field. Click **Sum** in the *Functions* box to tell Access what aggregate to perform. Click **Next**.

h. Change the query name to **Your_Name Revenue by Salesperson and State**. Make sure the option to **View the Query** is selected. Click **Finish**.

i. Examine the results.

   The query runs and returns results. You should notice many empty rows. If you open and examine the data in the Revenue query, you will see that not all of the salespeople sold items in every state. These data are accurate, but cumbersome. You will edit the crosstab in the next step.

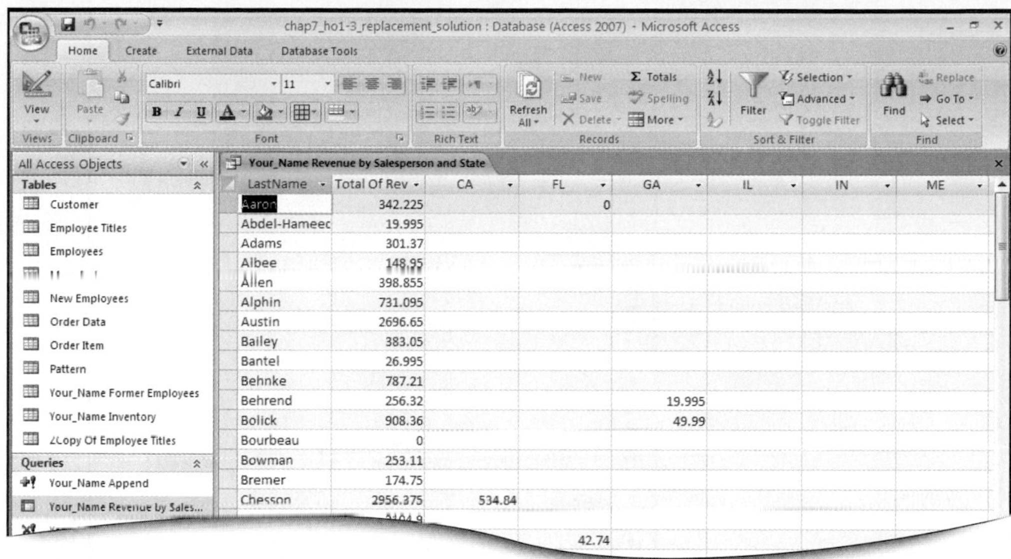

Figure 7.42 Crosstab Query Results

Step 2
Edit a Crosstab Query

Refer to Figures 7.43 and 7.44 as you complete Step 2.

a. Right-click the query tab and select **Design View** from the shortcut menu.

b. Click into the **Field row** of the second column (it says *State*) to activate the arrow. Click the **Arrow** and change from the State field to the **Alias** field.

   You changed the column field from State to Alias—the manufacturer's name.

c. Right-click the **Field row** of the third column (*Revenue*). Select **Properties** from the shortcut menu. Click the **Format** box in the Property Sheet on the General tab. Click the selection arrow and choose **Currency**. Click the **Field row** for the *Total of Revenue* field. Click the **Format** box in the Property Sheet on the General tab. Click the selection arrow and choose **Currency**. Close the Property Sheet.

   The total column formatted as currency but the totals for the individual columns did not. If you needed these values formatted as currency, use the crosstab query as a basis for a report. The formatting options in a report are more responsive than those in a query.

d. Save the changes and close the query.

   The query name no longer describes the data. You need to rename the query.

e. Right-click the *Your_Name Revenue by SalesPerson and State* in the Navigation pane. Select **Rename**, type **Your_Name Revenue by SalesPerson and Mfg**, and press **Enter**.

f. Open the query in Datasheet view. Press **PrntScrn** to capture a screenshot. Launch Word, type your name and section number, and press **Enter**. Click **Paste** to paste the screenshot in the Word document and press **Enter**.

g. Return to Access. Click **View** in the Views group on the Home tab to switch to Design view. Press **PrntScrn** to capture a screenshot. Switch to Word. Click **Paste** and press **Enter**. Save the Word document as **chap7_ho2_replacement_solution.docx**. Return to Access and close the query.

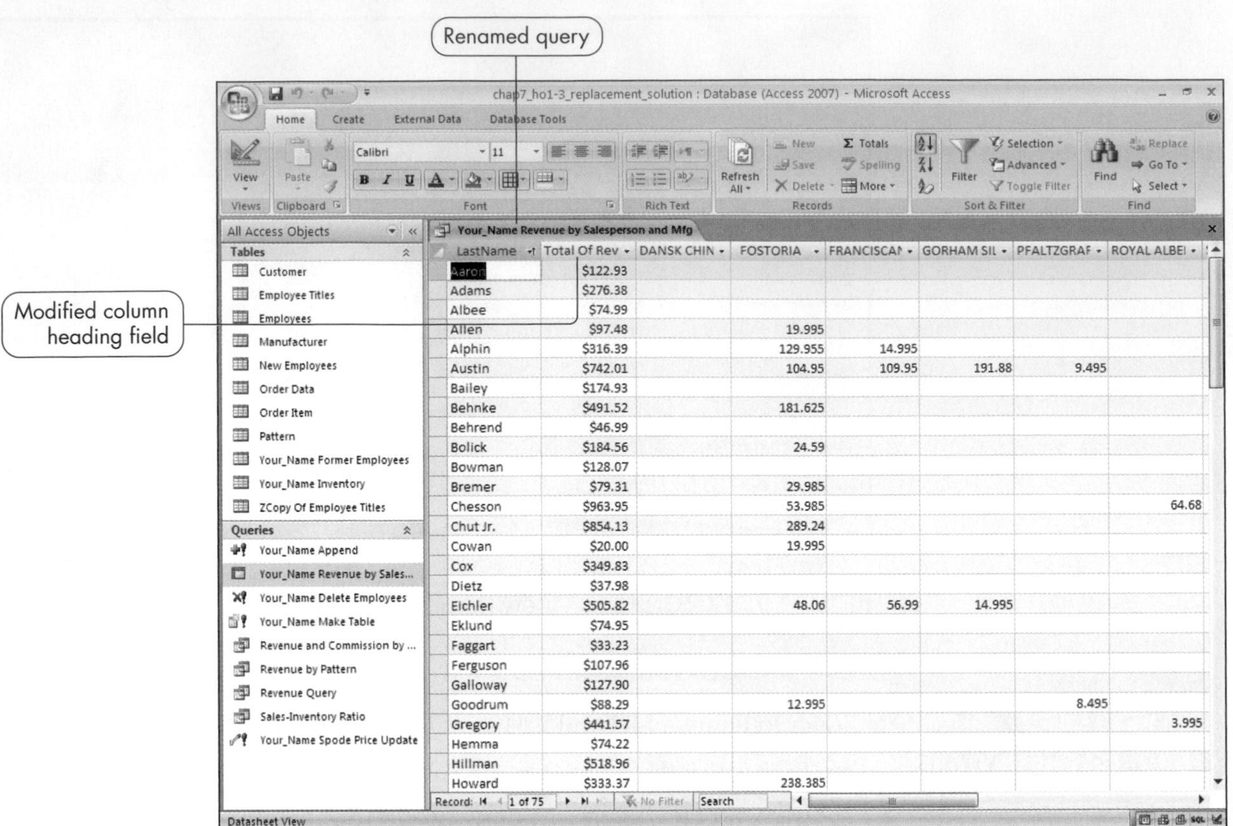

Figure 7.43 Crosstab Query Results

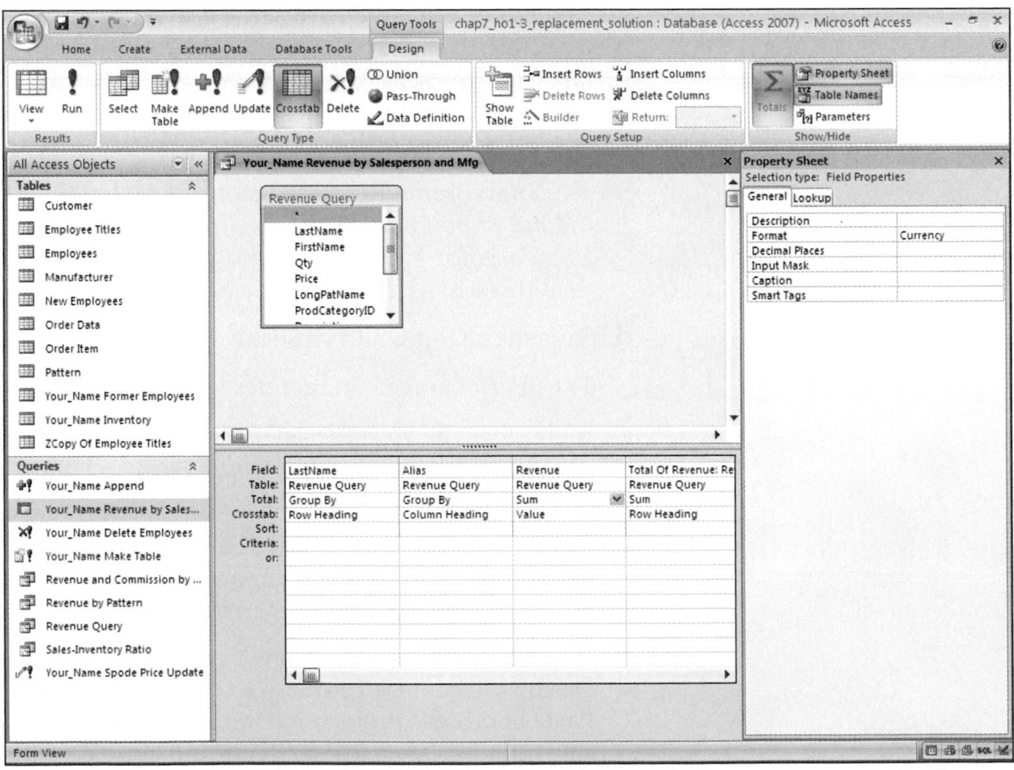

Figure 7.44 Crosstab Query Design

Step 3
Construct a Parameter Query

Refer to Figure 7.45 as you complete Step 3.

a. Click the **Create tab**, and then click **Query Design** in the Other group to create a new select query.

b. Double-click the **Employee Titles** and **Employees tables** in the Show Table dialog box to add them to the design grid. Close the Show Table dialog box.

   You are going to create a phone list query. If the query user knows the employee's title, he or she can create a phone directory showing all of the phone numbers of the employees with that position in the company.

c. Double-click the **Description** field from the Employee Titles table to add it to the design grid. Double-click the **FirstName**, **LastName**, and **Phone** fields in the Employees table to add them to the design grid.

d. Click in the **Criteria row** for the Description field. Type **[Type the Position Title Here]**. Do not forget the brackets.

e. Click the **Design tab** and click **Run** in the Results group.

   The Enter Parameter Value dialog box opens.

f. Type **Showroom Assistant** and press **Enter**.

   Only one employee, Jan Meyers, has that position.

g. Save the query as **Your_Name Employee Phone by Position**. Close the query.

   TROUBLESHOOTING: Remember that you need to encase the parameter query instructions with brackets. If your query did not return Jan Meyers, open it in Design view and make sure the brackets are there. If they are, run the query again and carefully type Showroom Assistant.

h. Open the **Your_Name Employee Phone by Position query**. The Enter Parameter Value dialog box launches asking for a position title. Type **Sales Associate 1**. (That is the number one.) Press **Enter**.

i. Click any record in the LastName field. Click **Sort Descending** in the Sort & Filter group on the Home tab.

j. Save the changes to the query. Press **PrntScrn**. Go to Word, press **Ctrl+End**, and then press **Enter**. Paste the screenshot below the other two in the document. Return to Access and change to Design view. Press **PrntScrn**. Go back to Word, press **Ctrl+End**, and then press **Enter**. Paste the screenshot below the other three in the document. Save the document. Return to Access and close the query.

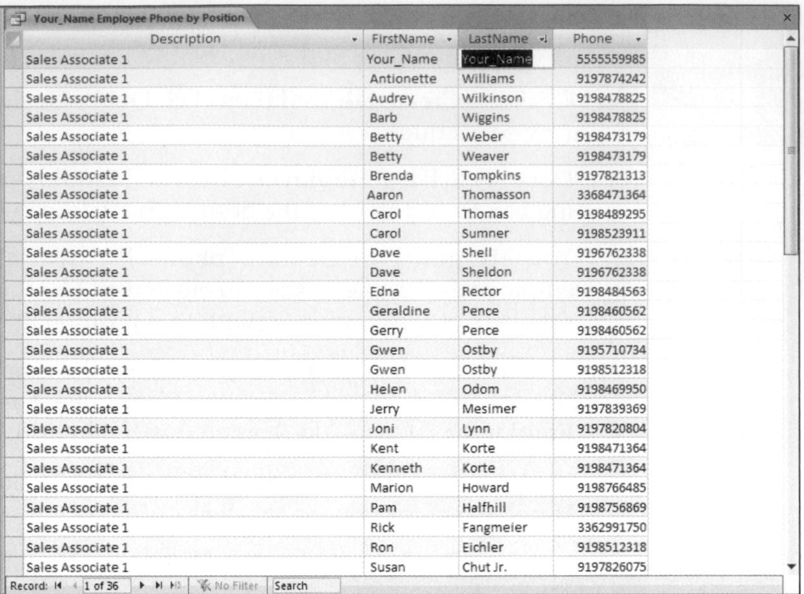
Your_Name Employee Phone by Position

Description	FirstName	LastName	Phone
Sales Associate 1	Your_Name	Your_Name	5555559985
Sales Associate 1	Antionette	Williams	9197874242
Sales Associate 1	Audrey	Wilkinson	9198478825
Sales Associate 1	Barb	Wiggins	9198478825
Sales Associate 1	Betty	Weber	9198473179
Sales Associate 1	Betty	Weaver	9198473179
Sales Associate 1	Brenda	Tompkins	9197821313
Sales Associate 1	Aaron	Thomasson	3368471364
Sales Associate 1	Carol	Thomas	9198489295
Sales Associate 1	Carol	Sumner	9198523911
Sales Associate 1	Dave	Shell	9196762338
Sales Associate 1	Dave	Sheldon	9196762338
Sales Associate 1	Edna	Rector	9198484563
Sales Associate 1	Geraldine	Pence	9198460562
Sales Associate 1	Gerry	Pence	9198460562
Sales Associate 1	Gwen	Ostby	9195710734
Sales Associate 1	Gwen	Ostby	9198512318
Sales Associate 1	Helen	Odom	9198469950
Sales Associate 1	Jerry	Mesimer	9197839369
Sales Associate 1	Joni	Lynn	9197820804
Sales Associate 1	Kent	Korte	9198471364
Sales Associate 1	Kenneth	Korte	9198471364
Sales Associate 1	Marion	Howard	9198766485
Sales Associate 1	Pam	Halfhill	9198756869
Sales Associate 1	Rick	Fangmeier	3362991750
Sales Associate 1	Ron	Eichler	9198512318
Sales Associate 1	Susan	Chut Jr.	9197826075

Record: 1 of 36 No Filter Search

Figure 7.45 Parameter Query Results

Step 4
Build a Find Unmatched Records Query

Refer to Figure 7.46 as you complete Step 4.

a. Click the **Create tab**, and then click **Query Wizard** in the Other group. Select the **Find Unmatched Query Wizard** in the New Query dialog box and click **OK**

The marketing manager has asked you to identify the customers who have not placed orders. You will create an unmatched query to find the customers in the Customer table who have no orders in the Order Data table. You can do this because the two tables are related with a primary and foreign key on the customerNum field.

b. Click the **Customer table** to select it. Click **Next**.

You have selected the first of the two tables required for an unmatched query.

c. Click the **Order Data table** to select it, and then click **Next**.

You specified the location of the second table. The next screen in the wizard asks you to identify a common field, but Access has already identified the field that exists in both tables. Because the primary and foreign keys do not need to have the same field name for relational integrity enforcement, this step is in the wizard in case the fields have different names.

d. Click **Next**.

e. Add all of the fields to the query by clicking the **Add All button**, >>. Click **Next**.

f. Accept the default name, select the option to View the results, and click **Finish**.

You see 431 customers without matching orders. Their contact information has been included in the query. Someone from the marketing department will contact these customers and try to discover why they are inactive.

g. Press **PrtScrn** to capture a screenshot. Switch to Word and paste your screenshot at the end of the Word document. Save the Word document as **chap7_ho2_replacement_solution.docx**.

h. Return to Access. Close the Customers Without Matching Order Data query. Save the changes.

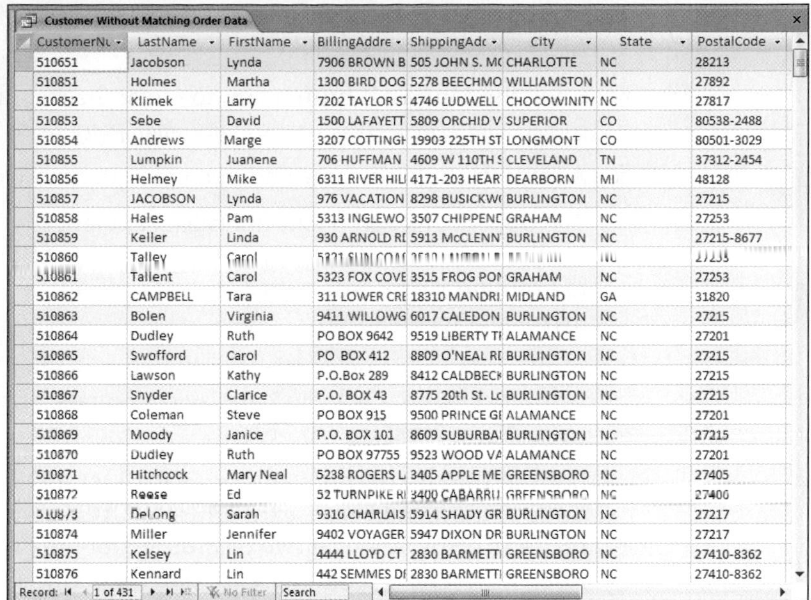

Customer Without Matching Order Data

CustomerNu	LastName	FirstName	BillingAddre	ShippingAdc	City	State	PostalCode
510651	Jacobson	Lynda	7906 BROWN B	505 JOHN S. M(	CHARLOTTE	NC	28213
510851	Holmes	Martha	1300 BIRD DOG	5278 BEECHMO	WILLIAMSTON	NC	27892
510852	Klimek	Larry	7202 TAYLOR S'	4746 LUDWELL	CHOCOWINITY	NC	27817
510853	Sebe	David	1500 LAFAYETT	5809 ORCHID V	SUPERIOR	CO	80538-2488
510854	Andrews	Marge	3207 COTTINGH	19903 225TH ST	LONGMONT	CO	80501-3029
510855	Lumpkin	Juanene	706 HUFFMAN	4609 W 110TH S	CLEVELAND	TN	37312-2454
510856	Helmey	Mike	6311 RIVER HILI	4171-203 HEAR'	DEARBORN	MI	48128
510857	JACOBSON	Lynda	976 VACATION	8298 BUSICKW(	BURLINGTON	NC	27215
510858	Hales	Pam	5313 INGLEWO	3507 CHIPPENE	GRAHAM	NC	27253
510859	Keller	Linda	930 ARNOLD RI	5913 McCLENN'	BURLINGTON	NC	27215-8677
510860	Talley	Carol	[illegible]	[illegible]	[illegible]	[illegible]	[illegible]
510861	Tallent	Carol	5323 FOX COVE	3515 FROG PON	GRAHAM	NC	27253
510862	CAMPBELL	Tara	311 LOWER CRE	18310 MANDRI	MIDLAND	GA	31820
510863	Bolen	Virginia	9411 WILLOWG	6017 CALEDON	BURLINGTON	NC	27215
510864	Dudley	Ruth	PO BOX 9642	9519 LIBERTY TI	ALAMANCE	NC	27201
510865	Swofford	Carol	PO BOX 412	8809 O'NEAL RI	BURLINGTON	NC	27215
510866	Lawson	Kathy	P.O.Box 289	8412 CALDBECK	BURLINGTON	NC	27215
510867	Snyder	Clarice	P.O. BOX 43	8775 20th St. Lc	BURLINGTON	NC	27215
510868	Coleman	Steve	PO BOX 915	9500 PRINCE GI	ALAMANCE	NC	27201
510869	Moody	Janice	P.O. BOX 101	8609 SUBURBAI	BURLINGTON	NC	27215
510870	Dudley	Ruth	PO BOX 97755	9523 WOOD VA	ALAMANCE	NC	27201
510871	Hitchcock	Mary Neal	5238 ROGERS L	3405 APPLE ME	GREENSBORO	NC	27405
510872	Reese	Ed	52 TURNPIKE RI	3400 CABARRU	GREENSBORO	NC	27406
510873	DeLong	Sarah	9316 CHARLAIS	5914 SHADY GR	BURLINGTON	NC	27217
510874	Miller	Jennifer	9402 VOYAGER	5947 DIXON DR	BURLINGTON	NC	27217
510875	Kelsey	Lin	4444 LLOYD CT	2830 BARMETTI	GREENSBORO	NC	27410-8362
510876	Kennard	Lin	442 SEMMES DI	2830 BARMETTI	GREENSBORO	NC	27410-8362

Record: 1 of 431 No Filter Search

Figure 7.46 Find Unmatched Query Results

Step 5
Create a Find Duplicates Query

Refer to Figure 7.47 as you complete Step 5.

a. Open the **Your_Name Inventory table** in Datasheet view and examine the records.

   One of the shelvers called you to explain that he had made a mistake. His job is to unpack the boxes of incoming merchandise, inspect it for damage, record its arrival in the database, and then place it in inventory in the warehouse so that it can be found again. He believes that he somehow entered most of the morning shipments incorrectly. He did the data entry using the RIPceCode instead of the SKU. He is afraid that he incorrectly duplicated values in the database. You need to examine his work and see if he made errors.

b. Click **Query Wizard** in the Other group on the Create tab to launch the Query Wizard.

   You need to run a Find Duplicates query.

c. Click **Find Duplicates Query Wizard** to select it, and then click **OK**.

d. Click **Table: Your_Name Inventory** to select it, and then click **Next**.

   You have identified the table where you believe the problem data exists.

e. Double-click the **SKU** in the *Available fields* box to move it to the *Duplicate-value fields* box. Click **Next**.

   Because the SKU is the primary key field in this table, you first want to check to ensure that it contains no duplicates.

f. Click the **Move All button**, >>, to move the rest of the fields in the table from the *Available fields* box to the *Additional query fields* box. Click **Next**.

g. Accept the default name and open the query to view the results. Click **Finish**.

   The query runs and opens in Datasheet view; however, it contains no records. The SKU is the primary key for this table. Referential integrity rules should prevent any duplicate data entry. Because the shelver believed there might be a problem, you decided to check.

h. Close and delete this query. Create another query following Steps 5b, 5c, and 5d.

i. Double-click the **RlPceCode** in the *Available fields* box to move it to the *Duplicate-value fields* box. Click **Next**.

j. Click the **Move All button**, >>, to move the rest of the fields in the table from the *Available fields* box to the *Additional query fields* box. Click **Next**.

k. Accept the default name and open the query to view the results. Click **Finish**.

   The query runs and opens in Datasheet view. It contains many duplicate records for the RlPceCode field. The shelver was unpacking crystal, so you apply a filter to examine the records with 2 as the ProdCategoryID. That way you can examine these data more closely.

l. Scroll right until you see the ProdCategoryID field. Look for a record with a value of 2. Right-click the **2** and select **Equals 2** from the shortcut menu. Examine the first two records.

   Both of the first records are for DOUBLE OLD FASHIONED (SET OF 2) in the same pattern, but because the OnHandQty is zero, you do not believe the shelver made an error. The next two records are for bread and butter plates, but the PatID (the pattern number) values are different. The next two records for beer glasses also show different pattern numbers. After examining the rest of the duplicated data, you conclude there was no error.

m. Press **PrntScrn** to capture a screenshot. Switch to Word and paste your screenshot at the end of the Word document. Save, print, and close the Word document. Save and close the query.

n. Click the **Office Button**, select **Manage**, and then select **Compact and Repair Database**. Close the file.

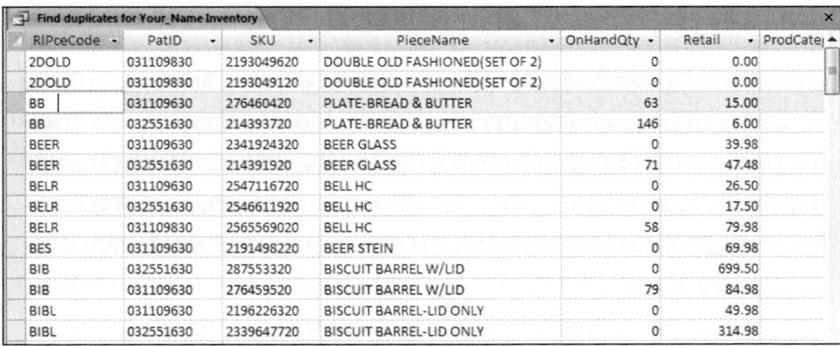

Find duplicates for Your_Name Inventory

RlPceCode	PatID	SKU	PieceName	OnHandQty	Retail	ProdCate
2DOLD	031109830	2193049620	DOUBLE OLD FASHIONED(SET OF 2)	0	0.00	
2DOLD	031109830	2193049120	DOUBLE OLD FASHIONED(SET OF 2)	0	0.00	
BB	031109630	276460420	PLATE-BREAD & BUTTER	63	15.00	
BB	032551630	214393720	PLATE-BREAD & BUTTER	146	6.00	
BEER	031109630	2341924320	BEER GLASS	0	39.98	
BEER	032551630	214391920	BEER GLASS	71	47.48	
BELR	031109630	2547116720	BELL HC	0	26.50	
BELR	032551630	2546611920	BELL HC	0	17.50	
BELR	031109830	2565569020	BELL HC	58	79.98	
BES	031109630	2191498220	BEER STEIN	0	69.98	
BIB	032551630	287553320	BISCUIT BARREL W/LID	0	699.50	
BIB	031109630	276459520	BISCUIT BARREL W/LID	79	84.98	
BIBL	031109630	2196226320	BISCUIT BARREL-LID ONLY	0	49.98	
BIBL	032551630	2339647720	BISCUIT BARREL-LID ONLY	0	314.98	

Figure 7.47 Find Duplicate Results

Summary

1. **Maintain a database with action queries.** You have already worked extensively with select queries. Access provides a number of data altering queries known collectively as action queries. An action query changes data in a database by making a table, appending records to an existing table, deleting specific records, or updating records. You cannot undo data alteration performed with an action query. Therefore, you should be careful when creating and running these types of queries.
2. **Update data with an update query.** An update query changes the values in at least one record. Most of the time update queries are performed on data stored in a single table. You create a new query in Design view and add the table(s) and fields storing the data to be updated. You tell Access to change the query type by selecting Update. Add the field or fields you will use to establish criteria that will inform Access which records to update. Next add the field or fields you want to change. The change may either be a constant created by typing a value into the Update To box in the design grid or a calculation. Finally, you add any additional fields that you will use to verify that the update will select and change the appropriate records.
3. **Add records to a table with an append query.** Often, organizations will store the most active records (today's or this week's activities) in one table and then append them to a more permanent table for storage. This query type will only work if the records match between the two tables. The tables are the source and the target (where you are heading) tables. An append query can work only if the target table exists somewhere. If it does not already exist, you must use a make table query, not an append query. After establishing the source and target, you need to select the records from the source and add them to the target table. After verifying and running an append table query, you see an action message telling you that you are about to append the number of records selected. If you click Yes, you cannot undo the action. Open the target table and verify that you added the new records.
4. **Create a table with a make table query.** The processes of creating append and make table queries are almost the same. The difference is that the table must exist for you to append to it. You can use the make table query to copy some or all records from a source to a target table even if the target table does not exist. The target database must exist, even if it is a shell containing no objects.
5. **Delete records with a delete query.** Database administrators usually run a backup utility prior to creating a delete action query. Earlier you were introduced to an append query where you copied order information from the current week's order table to the order table. You probably would take this action on the same day each week. However, the other database objects that support order entry, such as forms, probably point to the This Week Orders table. You would want to delete the records from last week's orders after copying them to the Orders table. Many query writers do not save action queries at all to help prevent them from being run accidentally. Because some action queries run regularly, you might wish to save them. An easy way to prevent them from being accidentally run is for you to hide them until you need to use them.
6. **Provide flexibility with a parameter query.** A parameter query provides more flexibility than any other query type in Access. You can set up a query and lock its design while providing others with the ability to customize their data request. A parameter query is a select query where one or more pieces of data are interactively selected by the user. However, it is designed so that the query user has control of what records get selected. The extended flexibility of the parameter query means that users can interact with the database and run custom queries without knowing much about Access. One parameter query, properly constructed, may be applied to many data requests. As you set up and run queries or reports, you will quickly spot when you need to use a parameter. As you set up the parameter queries, remember you are writing the instruction sets in the dialog box for users in the organization. Your instructions need to guide the user to successfully extract the information they need. The users will become frustrated if their queries do not return the expected results.
7. **Summarize data with a crosstab query.** Sometimes decision makers need to see every detail; sometimes they need a big picture view of the data, an aggregate. Crosstab queries summarize values in a grid by two unrelated sets of facts in the database. The grid design permits summarization and aggregation. Crosstab queries resemble PivotTables. The differences

...continued on Next Page

between crosstabs and PivotTables lie in who builds them and who uses the information generated by them. PivotTables give tremendous flexibility and power to the users of database information—the managerial decision maker. Not all line managers can be taught how to construct PivotTables. Not all database administrators are comfortable with granting users in the organization query construction privileges. You will probably want to use the wizard to help you build your first crosstab queries. Just as with a PivotTable, the crosstab query requires that you assemble all of the data into a single source.

8. **Find unmatched records with a query.** The unmatched query compares records in two related tables and returns the records found in one, but not both of the tables. You might use an unmatched query to merge similar tables or extract data such as inactive accounts. Perhaps the most useful feature of this query applies only to database administrators. When you attempt to apply referential integrity between the tables in your inherited database, you receive an error message telling you that Access cannot honor your request because either duplicate records exist or no unique index exists for the primary table. You would then run an unmatched query on the primary key field in one table that should match to its counterpart field as a foreign field. This will let you identify the problematic records, track down the correct information, and make the repairs to the table data that eventually will lead to your being able to enforce referential integrity.

9. **Find duplicate records with a query.** Sometimes, data are duplicated in a database by error. However, not all duplicated data in a database are the result of an error. Most of the data duplication is designed into the database as a result of the primary key-foreign key relationship. Additionally, many data values repeat naturally in a table. Finding duplicate fields and knowing what to do with them remains one of the greatest challenges for database administrators. This may be the part of database administration that is more art than science. The administrator must exercise judgment to determine which duplicate data are in the database by design and which are there due to errors.

Key Terms

Action query 447
Append query 451
Column heading 473
Crosstab query 472
Delete query 454
Find duplicates query 480
Find unmatched query 477
Make table query 453
Parameter query 468
Row heading 473
Update query 448

Multiple Choice

1. Which of the following is true about action queries?
   (a) An action query alters data in a database by making a table or deleting records, but cannot add records to an existing table.
   (b) An action query alters data in a database by making a table, appending records to an existing table, deleting specific records, or updating records
   (c) An action query alters data in a database, appending records only to a preexisting table, deleting specific records, or updating records.
   (d) An action query alters data in a database by making a table, appending records to an existing table, deleting specific records, or updating records and by duplicating records in a table for redundancy.

2. Which statement is true?
   (a) Users use action queries more frequently than database administrators.
   (b) You can preview your results numerous times, so it is ok to run action queries as often as you like.
   (c) Action queries should be carefully executed because you cannot undo data changes.
   (d) Action queries are easy to hack and should not be saved for data security and SOX compliance.

3. You are a database administrator for the athletic department in a large university. At the start of the season, the coaches need to have a report of players' academic eligibility status for the men's and women's basketball teams. As an excellent Access database administrator, you will do which of the following to get this information?
   (a) Go to the registrar's office and have them run a select query finding basketball players with GPAs greater than NCAA guidelines and tell the coaches who is eligible.
   (b) Go into your Access database, which pulls GPA data from the registrar's database, and run an update query to mark the eligibility field for all athletes based on NCAA GPA guidelines. Then run a report from a select query selecting basketball players who are academically eligible and a separate report of who is academically ineligible. Provide both reports as an e-mail attachment to the coaches.
   (c) Go into your Access database, which pulls GPA data from the registrar's database, and run an append query to mark the eligibility field for all athletes based on NCAA GPA guidelines. Then print records for this semester only to give to the coaches.
   (d) Go into your Access database, which pulls GPA data from the registrar's database, and construct and run a make table query to pull all ineligible athletes' records out of the table. Print this table for the coaches.

4. Your company has merged with another company. You are the lead database administrator for the newly combined company. You have the task of merging two customer databases into one database that maintains all customer data. You got lucky, each company used a five digit primary key of account number. You have appended primary keys with an extra digit so each company's customer databases do not have repeated account numbers. The merger of databases has been as seamless for your customers as possible. You discover, though, that the two companies had many of the same customers, now with duplicate entries and different account numbers. Why is this a problem and how should it be resolved?
   (a) Customers may inadvertently use the wrong account number to place orders. Each record should be reviewed and duplicates should be eliminated manually to avoid confusion.
   (b) It is poor database design to have duplicate data. You should append one table to the other and do a select query ordering all records in alphabetical order to find duplicates and run a delete query on every other record.
   (c) It shouldn't affect overall performance of the database to have duplicated records.
   (d) It is poor database design to have duplicate entries in a table. You can find those records that exist uniquely in one table or the other in a find duplicates query.

5. What is the primary difference between crosstab queries and PivotTables?
   (a) While they present data very similarly, users create crosstab queries and database administrators create PivotTables.
   (b) While they present data very similarly, database administrators create crosstab queries and users create PivotTables.
   (c) Crosstab queries can be constructed to pull from multiple tables or queries, while PivotTables can only pull from a single source of data.
   (d) PivotTables create charts by default and crosstab queries do not.

Multiple Choice Continued...

6. You realize that widespread data corruption exists in a table you maintain and decide the best way to clean up the corrupt files will be to make a new table with all the same data definitions and records. Given this scenario, which of the following would be the best way to accomplish this task?
   (a) You should make a new table, taking great care to define each field as it was defined in the corrupt table, then append the records to the table using an append query.
   (b) In database utilities, on the data tab, click the cleanup command to clean up any data corruption.
   (c) You should use a make table query and specify that you want all records to populate the new table.
   (d) You should use a copy table query and specify that you want all records to populate the new table.

7. Which is the best way to avoid damaging the integrity of your data when running an action query?
   (a) Use the test command in the Database Tools tab to test your logic before making any changes.
   (b) Use the Undo command as you need it when you make a mistake.
   (c) Run a select query with the same parameters you will use for the action query, and then run the test command from the Database Tools tab.
   (d) Backup your database, and then create a simple select query first to examine your logic before committing to an irreversible change through an action query.

8. Assuming that you have Zip codes in all tables containing telephone numbers, what steps should you take to change your tables containing the area code field when a new area code is announced?
   (a) Click the update query in the create query group. Select the affected Zip code field in the selection criteria box and the area code field in the update field box.
   (b) Create a new query in the Design view, selecting all Zip codes where an area code change has occurred. Select Update and select the area code field. In the update field, enter the new area code. Run the query when you are confident of your logic.
   (c) Create a new append query in the Design view. Select the appropriate Zip and area codes to append the new area code.
   (d) Create a new query in Design view, selecting all Zip codes where an area code change has occurred. Select Append and select the area code field. In the append field, enter the new area code. Run the query when you are confident of your logic.

9. You are the owner of a growing drop shipping business. You have kept all orders online in your orders table, but have noticed serious performance degradation because the table has gotten very large. You decide to archive all filled orders and to write a business procedure that archives filled orders weekly at the close of business on Friday. This will ensure that your active order table never grows too cumbersome, again. Once you have created the new archive table, what steps will be necessary to carry out this weekly process in Access?
   (a) Back up the database. Create a new query selecting all records with a fill date prior to the close of business on Friday. Click Append in query type group and choose your archive table. When you are confident that you have your parameters straight, view your query and run it. Make a similar delete query to delete the records after they have been archived. Save these queries and hide them so users do not accidentally archive or delete orders.
   (b) Back up the database. Create a new query selecting all records with a fill date prior to the close of business on Friday. Click Append in query type group and choose your archive table. When you are confident that you have your parameters straight, view your query and run it. Your append query will automatically delete the records from the orders table.
   (c) Run the archive utility in Database Maintenance Utilities.
   (d) Back up the database. Create a new query selecting all records. Click Append in query type group and choose your archive table. When you are confident that you have your parameters straight, view your query and run it. You will need to re-create this query every time you archive orders.

10. You hid some action queries so that users wouldn't accidentally archive and delete data that should be part of active databases. Now you need to run the queries you wrote. How do you go about finding your saved hidden queries?
   (a) Right-click in the area of the object pane where you hid the query and select show all.
   (b) Click the Office Button, click Access Options, and click show hidden objects in the Trust Center tab.
   (c) Click Show/Hide hidden objects in the database tools tab.
   (d) Right-click the title bar of the object pane and select Navigation Options. Select Show Hidden Objects.

11. Why would you use a parameter query?
    (a) Because users need to be able to query the database and select records matching shifting criteria to complete their jobs.
    (b) To determine parameters such as field length as you design a new database.
    (c) Because the DBA should perform most queries and not allow the user much access to live data.
    (d) To provide a set of disaster recovery parameters for SOX compliance.

12. How should you quickly and easily construct a crosstab query?
    (a) Click Crosstab Query on the Create tab.
    (b) Run the Query Wizard, selecting Crosstab for the query type.
    (c) Click Crosstab Query on the Database Tools tab.
    (d) It is easier to make PivotTables, and you should avoid crosstab queries.

13. Which of the following criteria would yield a parameter query that would allow for some human error on remembering exact product codes?
    (a) Like "*" & [Type the two-letter product descriptor, example WA]
    (b) [Type the two-letter product descriptor, example JE]
    (c) Neither
    (d) Both

14. What is a parameter report?
    (a) It is a report based on a parameter query.
    (b) It is a report of the data parameters for a table.
    (c) It is a report designed from the report Design view by clicking on the ellipsis for record source.
    (d) Both (a) and (c), but not (b).

15. As a tired database administrator late on a Friday evening when you want to meet your friends after work, you accidentally run the append action query two times on a mission critical table. You realize what you have done immediately and take effective corrective action by doing which of the following?
    (a) Restore the database to the backup you made right before beginning the archive and running the append and delete queries, again, only once.
    (b) Launch the Query Wizard by clicking its tool in the Other group on the Create tab. Select the Find Duplicates Query Wizard. Enter the appropriate criteria to find the duplicate records.
    (c) Neither (a) nor (b).
    (d) Either (a) or (b), but not both.

Practice Exercises

1 Miles Real Estate Sales Analysis

Nancy Miles offered you a position as the data manager of a small real estate firm that specializes in the sale of residential housing. The firm has enjoyed strong growth and expects that the growth will continue. Ms. Miles recognizes the value of a well-constructed and maintained database. She recognizes that creating a fulltime position for you will be expensive. However, the firm will not realize its growth potential without a dependable and reliable database. Your firm sells homes in several different communities. For the last several months, the employees have been recording their activities in an Access database. You have decided to add a table to the database that stores the listings of the sold properties. You will use the Make Table action query to create the new table. Refer to Figure 7.48 to verify your work.

a. Copy the partially completed file *chap7_pe1_realestate.accdb* from the Exploring Access folder to your production folder. Rename it **chap7_pe1_realestate_solution**. Double-click the file name to open it. Click **Options** on the Security Warning toolbar, click **Enable this content** in the Microsoft Office Security Options dialog box, and then click **OK**.
b. Click the **Database Tools tab** and click **Relationships** in the Show/Hide group. Examine the table structure, relationships, and fields. Once you are familiar with the database, close the Relationships window.
c. Open the **Agents table** and replace *Your_Name* with your name in the first and last name fields. Close the Agents table.
d. Click the **Create tab** and click **Query Design** in the Other group.
e. Double-click the **Properties table** in the Show Table dialog box to add it to the design grid. Click **Close**.
f. Double-click the title bar of the Properties table in the top of the design grid. All of the fields are selected. Drag the selected fields to the design grid and drop them to add all fields in the table to the design grid.
g. Set criteria to select only the sold properties by typing **True** in the Sold field's Criteria row on the design grid.
h. Click **Run** in the Results group on the Design tab to run the query as a select query. Scroll the results to make sure that the sold properties were selected.
i. Click **View** in the Views group on the Home tab to return to Design view. Change the query type by clicking **Make Table** in the Query Type group on the Design tab.
j. Type **Your_Name Sold Properties** in the Make Table dialog box to name the query. Store the new table in the current database. Click **OK**.
k. Click **Run** in the Results group on the Design tab. Click **Yes** in the *You are about to paste 54 row(s) into a new table* warning box. Save the query as **Your_Name Sold Properties Query**. Close the query.
l. Open the **Your_Name Sold Properties table** in Datasheet view. Press **PrntScrn**. Launch Word and type **Your_Name** and section number. Press **Enter** and press **Ctrl+V** to paste the screenshot in the Word document. Save the document as **chap7_pe1_realestate_solution.docx**. Print and close the Word file. Return to Access.
m. Click the **Office Button**, select **Manage**, and select **Compact and Repair Database**. Close the file.

...continued on Next Page

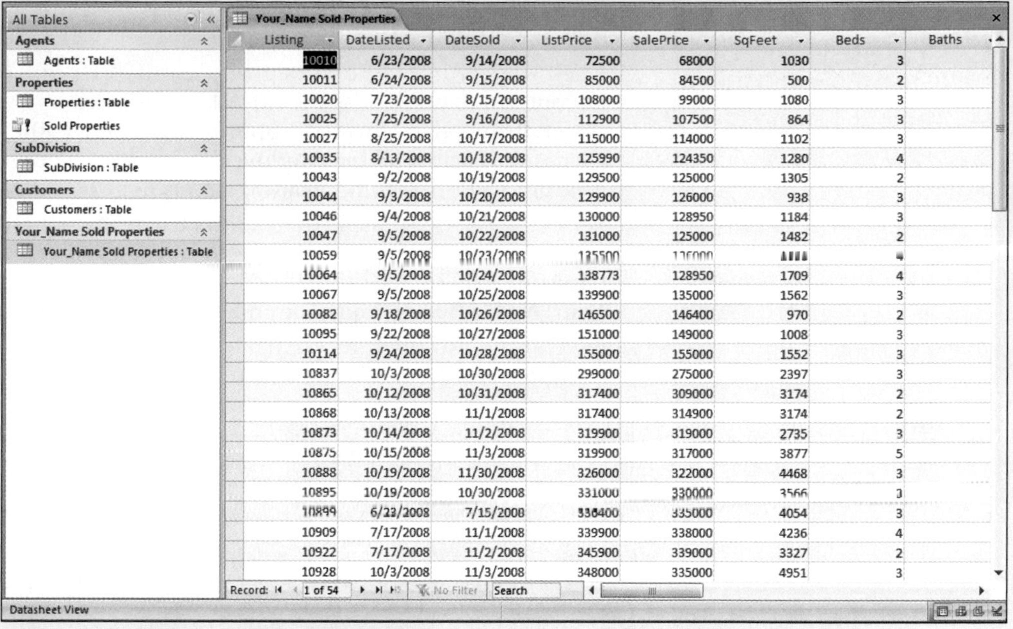

Listing	DateListed	DateSold	ListPrice	SalePrice	SqFeet	Beds	Baths
10010	6/23/2008	9/14/2008	72500	68000	1030	3	
10011	6/24/2008	9/15/2008	85000	84500	500	2	
10020	7/23/2008	8/15/2008	108000	99000	1080	3	
10025	7/25/2008	9/16/2008	112900	107500	864	3	
10027	8/25/2008	10/17/2008	115000	114000	1102	3	
10035	8/13/2008	10/18/2008	125990	124350	1280	4	
10043	9/2/2008	10/19/2008	129500	125000	1305	2	
10044	9/3/2008	10/20/2008	129900	126000	938	3	
10046	9/4/2008	10/21/2008	130000	128950	1184	3	
10047	9/5/2008	10/22/2008	131000	125000	1482	2	
10059	9/5/2008	10/23/2008	135500	[illegible]	[illegible]	[illegible]	
10064	9/5/2008	10/24/2008	138773	128950	1709	4	
10067	9/5/2008	10/25/2008	139900	135000	1562	3	
10082	9/18/2008	10/26/2008	146500	146400	970	2	
10095	9/22/2008	10/27/2008	151000	149000	1008	3	
10114	9/24/2008	10/28/2008	155000	155000	1552	3	
10837	10/3/2008	10/30/2008	299000	275000	2397	3	
10865	10/12/2008	10/31/2008	317400	309000	3174	2	
10868	10/13/2008	11/1/2008	317400	314900	3174	2	
10873	10/14/2008	11/2/2008	319900	319000	2735	3	
10875	10/15/2008	11/3/2008	319900	317000	3877	5	
10888	10/19/2008	11/30/2008	326000	322000	4468	3	
10895	10/19/2008	10/30/2008	331000	330000	3566	3	
10899	6/23/2008	7/15/2008	336400	335000	4054	3	
10909	7/17/2008	11/1/2008	339900	338000	4236	4	
10922	7/17/2008	11/2/2008	345900	339000	3327	2	
10928	10/3/2008	11/3/2008	348000	335000	4951	3	

Figure 7.48 Sold Properties Table

2 Real Estate City Analysis

Ms. Miles asks that you examine all of the listed properties by community. Your firm offers properties for sale in several cities. Each city may be divided into one or more subdivisions. Some of the houses are located in formal subdivisions that have community pools, tennis courts, and bike trails. You need to group the sold properties by the subdivision and by which agent listed each property. Finally, you need to summarize the value of the sale price by calculating the average price for each subdivision. Refer to Figure 7.49 to verify your work.

a. Copy the partially completed file *chap7_pe2_realestate.accdb* from the Exploring Access folder to your production folder. Rename it **chap7_pe2_realestate_solution**. Double-click the file name to open it. Click **Options** on the Security Warning toolbar, click **Enable this content** in the Microsoft Office Security Options dialog box, and then click **OK**.

b. Open the **Agents table** and replace *Your_Name* with your name in the first and last name fields. Close the Agents table.

c. Create a select query to assemble the necessary fields in a single source. Click the **Create tab,** and then click **Query Design** in the Other group. Add the **Properties**, **Agents**, and **SubDivision tables** to the design grid by double-clicking them in the Show Table dialog box. Click **Close**.

d. Add the necessary fields to the design grid. Double-click **Subdivision** in the SubDivision table, **Sold** and **SalePrice** in the Properties table, and **LastName** in the Agents table. Click in the Criteria row for the Sold field and type **True**. Right-click the SalePrice field and select **Properties**. In the Properties Sheet *Format box*, select **Currency**. Click **Run** in the Results group. Save the query as **Your_Name Subdivision Summary**. Close the query.

e. Click **Query Wizard** in the Other group on the Create tab. Select **Crosstab Query Wizard** and click **OK**. Select the **Queries** option in the *View* section and select the **Your_Name Subdivision Summary** query. Click **Next**.

f. Double-click the **Subdivision** field to select it and move it to the *Selected Fields* box. You want the Subdivision field to be the row heading field. Click **Next**.

g. Click the **LastName** field to select it as the column heading. Click **Next**.

h. Click the **SalePrice** field in the *Fields* box and the **Avg** function in the *Functions* box. Click **Next**.

...continued on Next Page

i. Name the query **Your_Name Subdivision Summary_Crosstab**. Select the **View** option. Click **Finish**.

j. Click **Report** in the Reports group on the Create tab. Click **Landscape** in the Page Layout group on the Page Setup tab. Right-click any value of an employee's sales and select **Properties**. In the Property Sheet, click the box beside *Format* and select **Currency**. Format all the employees' sale price averages as currency. Click the heading *Total of Sale Price* column heading and change it to **Average Sale Price**.

k. Select the Average Sale Price column. Click **Totals** in the Grouping & Totals group and select **Average** from the list. Select each Salesperson one at a time, click **Totals** in the Grouping & Totals group, and select **Average** from the list. Save the report as **Your_Name Subdivision Summary_Crosstab**. Print and close the report.

l. Save and close the query. Click the **Office Button**, select **Manage**, and then select **Compact and Repair Database**. Close the file.

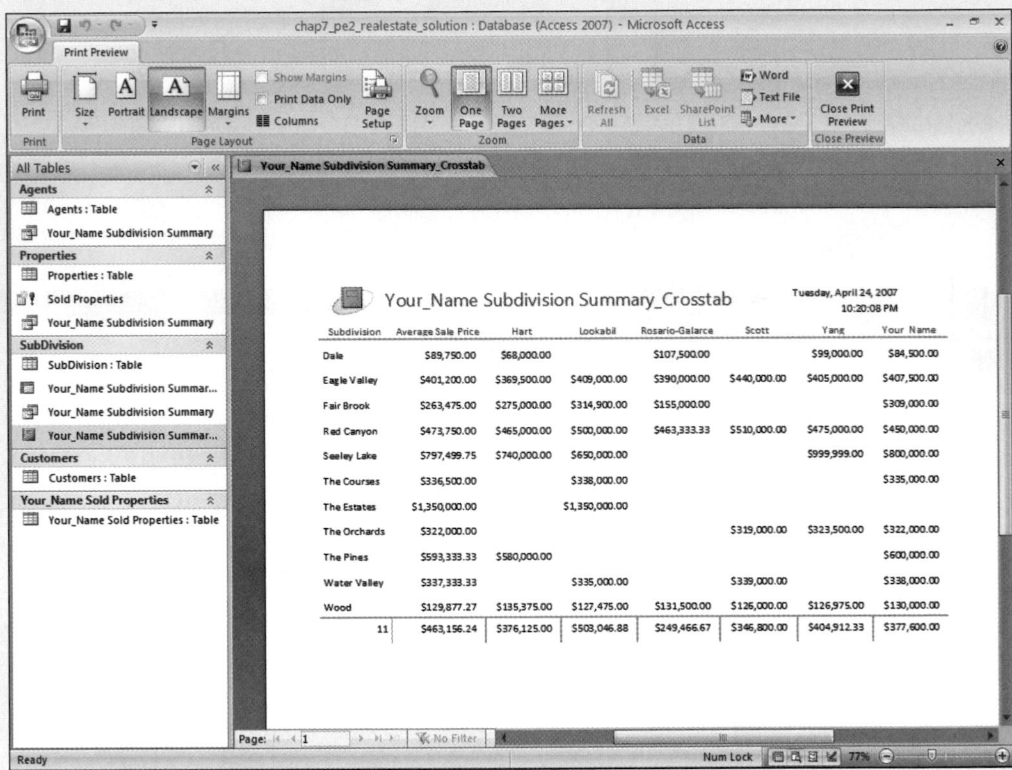

Your_Name Subdivision Summary_Crosstab — Tuesday, April 24, 2007 10:20:08 PM

Subdivision	Average Sale Price	Hart	Lookabil	Rosario-Galarce	Scott	Yang	Your Name
Dale	$89,750.00	$68,000.00		$107,500.00		$99,000.00	$84,500.00
Eagle Valley	$401,200.00	$369,500.00	$409,000.00	$390,000.00	$440,000.00	$405,000.00	$407,500.00
Fair Brook	$263,475.00	$275,000.00	$314,900.00	$155,000.00			$309,000.00
Red Canyon	$473,750.00	$465,000.00	$500,000.00	$463,333.33	$510,000.00	$475,000.00	$450,000.00
Seeley Lake	$797,499.75	$740,000.00	$650,000.00			$999,999.00	$800,000.00
The Courses	$336,500.00		$338,000.00				$335,000.00
The Estates	$1,350,000.00		$1,350,000.00				
The Orchards	$322,000.00				$319,000.00	$323,500.00	$322,000.00
The Pines	$593,333.33	$580,000.00					$600,000.00
Water Valley	$337,333.33		$335,000.00		$339,000.00		$338,000.00
Wood	$129,877.27	$135,375.00	$127,475.00	$131,500.00	$126,000.00	$126,975.00	$130,000.00
11	$463,156.24	$376,125.00	$503,046.88	$249,466.67	$346,800.00	$404,912.33	$377,600.00

Figure 7.49 Crosstab Results Converted to a Report

3 National Bank

You are the database administrator for a bank. One of the directors, Robert Wigman, asked that you help him adjust some of the loans' interest rates. Mr. Wigman explained that the interest rates of some loans are fixed for the duration of the loan, whereas other loan rates adjust when market conditions cause interest rates to increase or decrease. The Federal Funds Rate increased by a quarter of a percent this week. You need to use an action query to revise the adjustable rate loans' interest rates. You will create a select query to make sure that the calculations are correct, and then convert it to an action query. Refer to Figure 7.50 to verify your work.

a. Copy the partially completed file *chap7_pe3_nationalbank.accdb* from the Exploring Access folder to your production folder. Rename it **chap7_pe3_nationalbank_solution.accdb**. Double-click the file name to open it. Click **Options** on the Security Warning toolbar, click **Enable this content** in the Microsoft Office Security Options dialog box, and then click **OK**.

...continued on Next Page

b. Create a query by clicking **Query Design** in the Other group on the Create tab. Double-click the **Loans table** in the Show Table dialog box to add it to the design grid. Click **Close**.

c. Add the **LoanID**, **InterestRate**, and **Adjustable** fields to the design grid by double-clicking them one at a time. Run the query by clicking **Run** in the Results group on the Design tab. Save the query as **Your_Name Interest Adjustment**.

d. Click **View** in the Views group on the Home tab to return to Design view. Click in the **Field row** of the *first empty column* to position your insertion point there. Click **Builder** in the Query Setup group on the Design tab.

e. Type **= [InterestRate] + 0.0025** in the Expression Builder dialog box. Click **OK**. Click **Run** in the Results Group on the Design tab.

f. Make the calculated field column wider to view the results, if necessary. They display in scientific notation. Click **View** in the Views group to return to Design view. Right-click the *Expr1 field* and select **Properties** from the shortcut menu. Click *Format* in the Property Sheet and select **Percent**. Click *Decimal Places* and select **3**. Close the Property Sheet. Run the query. Examine the calculated results to verify your logic.

g. Click **View** in the Views group to return to Design view. Type **Yes** in the Criteria row of the Adjustable field. Run the query. Examine the output. Click **View** in the Views group to return to Design view.

h. Click **Update** in the Query Types group on the Design tab. Type **[LoanID]** in the *UpdateTo* row for the LoanID field. Type **[Loans]![InterestRate] + 0.0025** in the *Update To* row of the InterestRate field. Make sure that **Yes** remains in the *Criteria* row of the Adjustable field.

i. Click **View** in the Results group to preview the data to be updated. Verify that the same ten records will be updated when the query is run. Click **View** in the Views group to return to Design view.

j. Click **Run** in the Results group. Click **Yes** in the Warning box. Save and close the query.

k. Open the **Loans table** in Datasheet view. Click the **Office Button**, select **Print**, and select **Print Preview**. Click **Landscape** in the Page Layout section of Print Preview. Print the Loans table. Close Print Preview.

l. Click the **Office Button**, select **Manage**, and select **Compact and Repair Database**. Close the file.

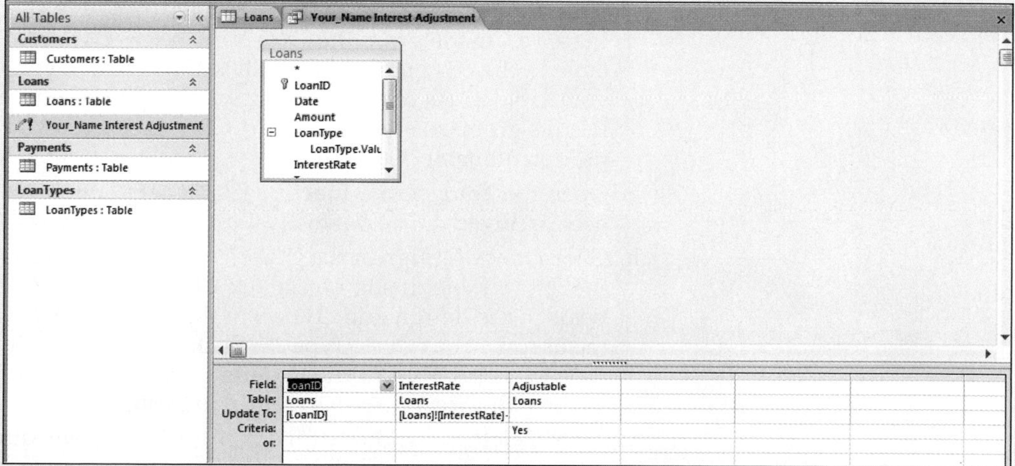

Figure 7.50 Update Query Design View

4 Custom Coffee

The Custom Coffee Company is a small service organization that provides coffee, tea, and snacks to offices. Custom Coffee also provides and maintains the equipment for brewing the beverages. Although the firm is small, its excellent reputation for providing outstanding customer service has helped it grow. Part of this is because the firm's owner set up a database to organize and keep track of customer purchases. The firm only has two employees. Both of you serve customers and

...continued on Next Page

make deliveries. You also have the responsibility for maintaining the database. Since you deliver orders to a number of cities, you decide to create a query that lists all of the customers and the profits they generate for each city. You believe that you can reduce the delivery costs by combining several orders in one trip. You also want to identify the inactive customers. While in their city, you can "drop" in on a customer who has not made an order recently if you know who they are. You need to use the advanced querying techniques from this chapter to help convert the data into information. You need to modify the existing profit query so that it will ask for a city each time it is run. You also need to identify the inactive customers and make a table of them. Finally, you will delete the inactive customers from the Customers table. Refer to Figure 7.51 to verify your work.

a. Copy the partially completed file *chap7_pe4_coffee.accdb* from the Exploring Access folder to your production folder. Rename it **chap7_pe4_coffee_solution.accdb**. Double-click the file name to open the file. Click **Options** on the Security Warning toolbar, click **Enable this content** in the Microsoft Office Security Options dialog box, and then click **OK**.

b. Double-click the **Sales Rep table** to open it. Replace *Your_Name* with your name. Close the table by clicking **Close** in the database window.

c. Rename the *Your_Name Profit* query with your name. Open it in Design view. In the criteria row for the City field, type **[What City?]**. In the Criteria row for the *LastName* field, type **Your_Name**.

d. Click **Run** in the Results group. Type **Miami** in the dialog box asking for which city you want data displayed. Click **OK**. There should be 26 records of your sales in Miami. Click the **Office Button,** select **Print,** and select **Print Preview**. Click **Landscape** in the Page Layout group on the Print Preview tab. Print the query results. Close Print Preview. Save and close the query.

e. Click **Query Wizard** in the Other group on the Create tab. Click **Find Unmatched Query Wizard**. Select the **Customer table** as the first table. Click **Next**. Select the **Order table** as the second table. Click **Next**. Access identifies the CustomerID field as the common field. Click **Next**. Use the Move All button, **>>**, to move all of the fields in the *Available fields* box to the *Selected fields* box. Click **Next**. Click **Finish**. You will find that four customers have placed no orders. Save the query. You decide to create a new table to store inactive customers.

f. Click **View** in the Views group to switch to Design view. Click **Make Table** in the Query Type group on the Design tab to change the query type. Type **Your_Name Inactive Customers** in the *Table Name* box of the Make Table dialog box. Store the new table in the current database. Click **OK**. Click **View** in the Results group to preview your table. Click **View** in the Views group to return to Design view. Click **Run** in the Results group to create the table. Click **Yes** in the Warning box. Save the query using the default name. Close the query.

g. Open the **Your_Name Inactive Customers table** to verify that the four records have been archived. Write down the CustomerID numbers. Close the table.

h. Click **Query Design** in the Other group on the Create tab. Double-click **Customers** in the Show Table dialog box. Click **Close**. Add the **CustomerID** and **CustomerName** fields to the design grid. Type **9** in the criteria row of the CustomerID field. Click into the **or** row below the 9. Type **15**. Click into the next row down; type **16**. In the next row type **17**. Click **Run** in the Results group to preview your intended deletions. Click **View** in the Views group to return to Design view.

i. Click **Delete** in the Query type group. Click **View** in the Results group to preview your intended deletions. Click **View** in the Views group to return to Design View. **Run** the query. Click **Yes** to the warning about deleting four rows. Save the query as **Delete Inactive**. Close the query.

j. Click the **Office Button**, select **Manage**, and then select **Compact and Repair**. Close the file.

...continued on Next Page

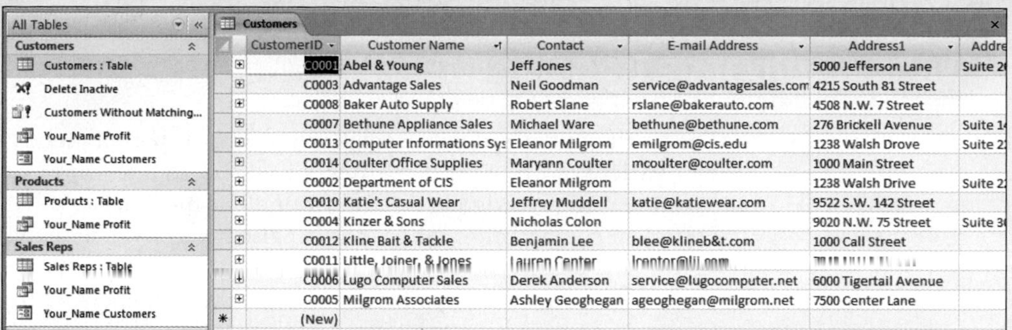

Figure 7.51 Customer Table After Inactive Customers Deleted

Mid-Level Exercises

1 The Northwinds Traders

The Northwinds Traders is a small international specialty foods distribution firm. It sells products in a variety of different categories, such as Beverages and Condiments. The sales manager has asked you to provide her with a list of all of the inactive customers (no orders since 1/1/2007) with their contact information. The list also needs to include the salesperson's name so she knows to whom to assign the contact duty. You decided that this information will be needed often, so you will use a parameter query to help identify the customers who have not ordered recently. Refer to Figure 7.52 to verify your work.

a. Locate the file named *chap7_mid1_traders.accdb*, copy it to your production folder, and rename it **chap7_mid1_traders_solution.accdb**. Open the file and enable the content.

b. Rename the *Your_Name Profit* query with your name. Open the Employees table and replace *Your_Name* in the first and last name fields with your name.

c. Create a select query based on the Orders table. Add a parameter instructing the query user to **Please Type Cutoff Date – Example 1/1/2007**. Set the parameter so that only orders greater than the user specified cutoff date get selected. Run and save the query as **Recent Orders**.

d. Create an unmatched query to identify the customers who are in the Customers table but not in the Recent Orders query. Save this query as **Customers Without Recent Orders**. Make sure that you identify the CustomerID field as the common field. Use all of the Customer fields as output. Save the query as **Customers Without Matching Recent Orders**. Run, save, and close this query.

e. Create a select query that uses the Customers Without Matching Recent Orders query, the Orders table, and the Employees table as data sources. You need to drag the **CustomerID** field from the Customers Without Matching Recent Orders query in the design grid to the **CustomerID** field in the Orders table to establish a relationship. Add the **CompanyName**, **ContactName**, and **Phone** fields from the Customers Without Matching Recent Orders query to the new query. Add the **LastName** field from the Employees table to the new query. Save the query as **Contact Information for Inactive Customers**. Run the query and examine the results. You should see the same customer name frequently duplicated. Return to Design view.

f. Run the query. Sort it by the **LastName** field. Save the query as **Contact Information for Inactive Customers**.

g. Print the results. Compact and repair the database. Close the database.

...continued on Next Page

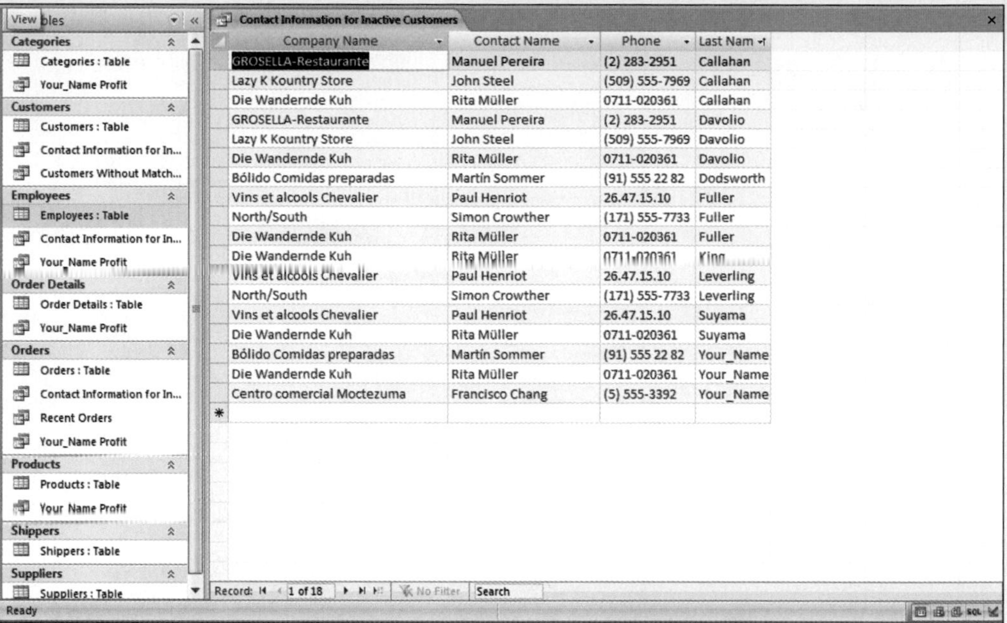

Figure 7.52 Completed Select Query Based on a Parameter and Unmatched Queries

2 Hotel Chain

You are the general manager of a large hotel chain. Your establishment provides a variety of guest services ranging from rooms and conferences to weddings. You need to calculate the total revenue generated by service type and city. Refer to Figure 7.53 to verify your work.

a. Locate the file named *chap7_mid2_memrewards.accdb*; copy it to your production folder and rename it **chap7_mid2_memrewards_solution.accdb**. Open the file and enable the content. Rename the *Revenue* query as **Your_Name Revenue**.

b. Create a crosstab query. Use the City field for the **Row Headings**, the ServiceName field for the **Column Headings**, and the Revenue field for the **calculation for each column and row intersection**. Sum the **Revenue** field.

c. Save the query as **Your_Name Revenue_Crosstab**.

d. Format the sums of service in each city and the total revenue as currency.

e. Use Print Preview to set a landscape orientation.

f. Print the query.

g. Create a new select query that displays Revenue by Service type. Save it as **Revenue by Service**. Apply a parameter that will select the service type. Use **Type the Name of the Service – Example Wedding** as the user instructions in the dialog box. Run the query to display room rentals. Sort the results in ascending order by City name. Save the query.

h. Capture a screenshot of the sorted Room Revenue query. Open Word, launch a new blank document, type your name and section number, press **Enter**, and paste the screenshot. Print the Word document. Save it as **chap7_mid2_memrewards_solution.docx**. Close the Word document.

i. Compact and repair and close the database.

...continued on Next Page

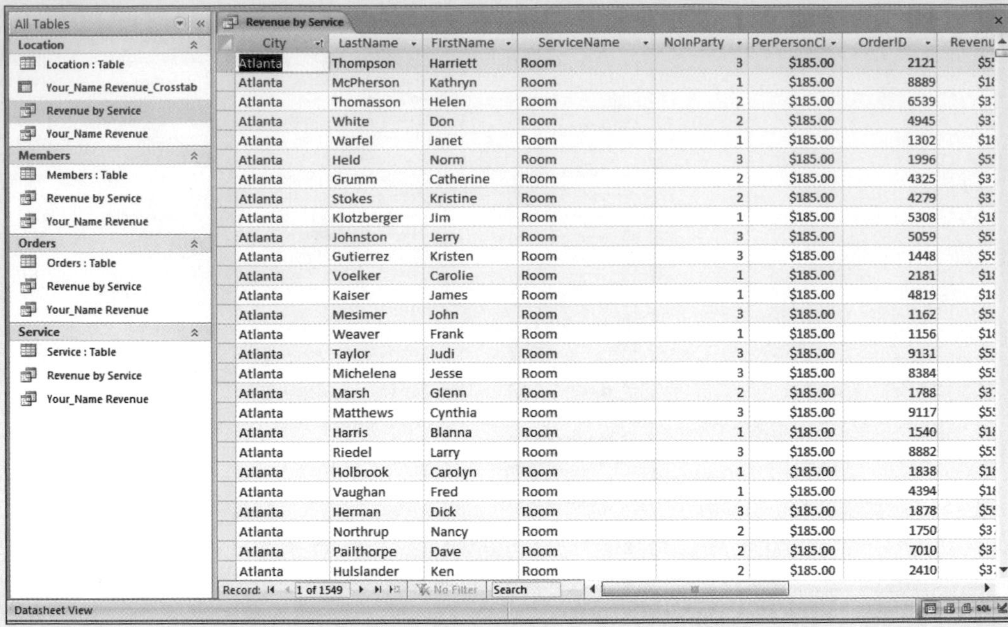

Figure 7.53 Parameter Query Displaying Room Revenue

3 Miles Real Estate

Nancy Miles offered you a position as the data manager of a small real estate firm that specializes in the sale of residential housing. Your firm sells homes in several different communities. For the last several months, the employees have been recording their activities in an Access database. This morning, Ms. Miles told you that one of the agents did not receive a commission for listing a home. She wants you to figure out what is wrong with the database and fix it to ensure accuracy. You will create a find unmatched query to help you find the data errors. Refer to Figure 7.54 to verify your work.

a. Locate the file named *chap7_mid3_realestate.accdb*; copy it to your production folder and rename it **chap7_mid3_realestate_solution.accdb**. Open the file and enable the content. Rename the *Sales Report query* **Your_Name Sales Report** query. Open the Agents table and replace *Your_Name* with your name.

b. Open the Relationships window and examine the relationships in this database. You discover no relationship exists between the Agents and Properties table. When you attempt to create the relationship between the ID field in the Agents table and the ListingAgent field in the properties table, you cannot enforce referential integrity. Read the error message. Close the Relationships window.

c. Create a find unmatched query that sources the Agents and Properties tables. Save the query as **Properties without Matching Agents**. Run the query and scroll to discover the ID of the listing agent for the properties listed.

d. Open the Agents table and examine the ID field. Report your discovery to Ms. Miles.

e. Ms. Miles tells you that the incorrectly listed agent should be agent 3 for all of the unmatched properties. Make the changes to the Properties table to correct the data entry error.

f. Open the Relationships window and establish the relationship between the **ID** field in the Agents table and the **ListingAgent** field in the Properties table. Enforce referential integrity. Capture a screenshot of the corrected relationship window.

...continued on Next Page

g. Open Word, launch a new blank document, type your name and section number, press **Enter**, and paste the screenshot. Print the Word document. Save it as **chap7_mid3_realestate_solution.docx**. Close the Word document.

h. Return to Access. Close the Relationships window and save your changes.

i. Create a new query that uses the Agents and Properties tables as the source. Include the LastName field from the Agents table and the Listing, ListPrice, ListingAgent, and Address fields from the Properties table. Add a criterion that limits the ListingAgent field to 3. Run, print, and save your query as **Your_Name Listings**.

j. Compact, repair, and close the database.

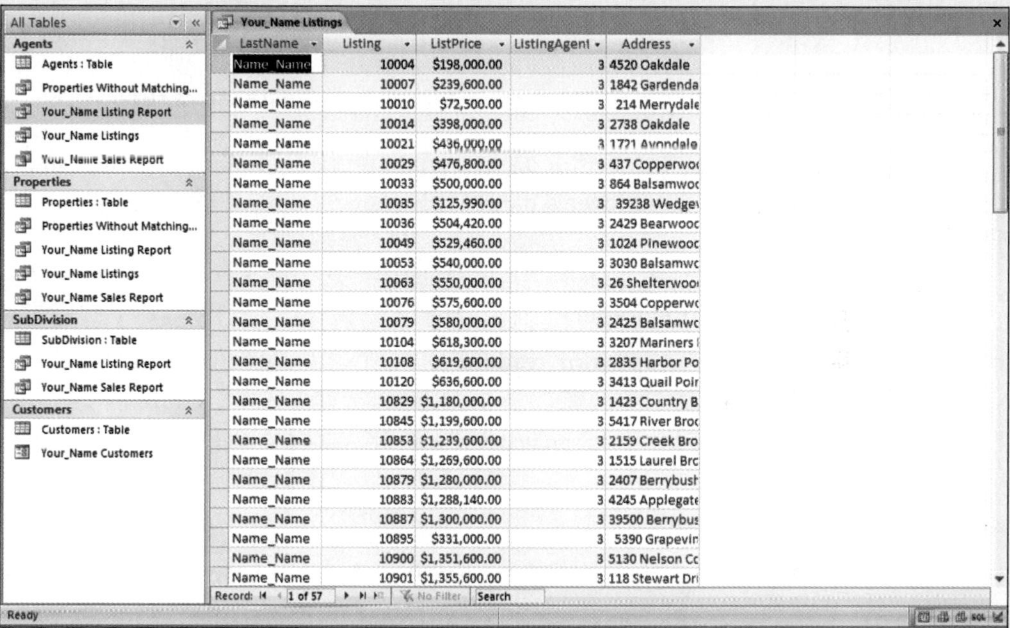

LastName	Listing	ListPrice	ListingAgent	Address
Name_Name	10004	$198,000.00	3	4520 Oakdale
Name_Name	10007	$239,600.00	3	1842 Gardenda
Name_Name	10010	$72,500.00	3	214 Merrydale
Name_Name	10014	$398,000.00	3	2738 Oakdale
Name_Name	10021	$436,000.00	3	1721 Avondale
Name_Name	10029	$476,800.00	3	437 Copperwo
Name_Name	10033	$500,000.00	3	864 Balsamwo
Name_Name	10035	$125,990.00	3	39238 Wedge
Name_Name	10036	$504,420.00	3	2429 Bearwooc
Name_Name	10049	$529,460.00	3	1024 Pinewooc
Name_Name	10053	$540,000.00	3	3030 Balsamwc
Name_Name	10063	$550,000.00	3	26 Shelterwoo
Name_Name	10076	$575,600.00	3	3504 Copperwc
Name_Name	10079	$580,000.00	3	2425 Balsamwc
Name_Name	10104	$618,300.00	3	3207 Mariners
Name_Name	10108	$619,600.00	3	2835 Harbor Po
Name_Name	10120	$636,600.00	3	3413 Quail Poir
Name_Name	10829	$1,180,000.00	3	1423 Country B
Name_Name	10845	$1,199,600.00	3	5417 River Broc
Name_Name	10853	$1,239,600.00	3	2159 Creek Bro
Name_Name	10864	$1,269,600.00	3	1515 Laurel Brc
Name_Name	10879	$1,280,000.00	3	2407 Berrybusł
Name_Name	10883	$1,288,140.00	3	4245 Applegate
Name_Name	10887	$1,300,000.00	3	39500 Berrybus
Name_Name	10895	$331,000.00	3	5390 Grapevir
Name_Name	10900	$1,351,600.00	3	5130 Nelson Cc
Name_Name	10901	$1,355,600.00	3	118 Stewart Dri

Figure 7.54 Query Results Showing Repaired Data

Capstone Exercise

You work as an associate database manager at Northwind Traders. This is a small international gourmet foods wholesaler. Your responsibilities include maintaining the firm's database and ensuring the dependability of the data. You need to update the database by increasing the price of all of the beverage and dairy products by 10%. You need to make a table of discontinued products. You will summarize profits by salesperson and category. When you have completed the work, you will compact and repair the database and make a backup of it.

Database File Setup

You need to copy an original database file, rename the copied file, and then open the copied database to complete this capstone exercise. After you open the copied database, you will replace an existing employee's name with your name.

a. Locate the file named *chap7_cap_traders.accdb* and copy it to your production folder.

b. Rename the copied file **chap7_cap_traders _ solution.accdb**.

c. Open the *chap7_cap_traders_solution.accdb* file and enable the content.

d. Open the **Employees table**.

e. Navigate to record 3 and replace *Pa Lor's* name with your name. Press **Enter** and close the table.

f. Rename the Profit query **Your_Name Profit**.

Identify and Update Selected Category Prices

You need to create a select query to identify all of the products in the beverage and dairy products categories. You will use the select query to test your logic. Once you are sure you are selecting the appropriate categories, you will create an update query to increase the prices by 10%. You will create a crosstab to summarize profit data. You will create a parameter query that will enable the user to identify a specific time period.

a. Create a new select query that includes the **CategoryID** and **CategoryName** from the Categories table and the **UnitPrice** and **ProductName** fields from the Products table. Run the query and identify the CategoryID for Beverages and for Dairy Products.

b. Add the appropriate CategoryID as a criterion to limit the query output to only Beverages and Dairy Products.

c. Convert the query to an update query. Update the **UnitPrice** field by increasing it by **10%**. (A product that used to have a price of $100 will have a $110 price following the update.) Set the criteria so that only Beverages and Dairy Products prices change. Use the CategoryName and ProductName fields as verification fields.

d. View the query in Datasheet view prior to running it to make sure you have selected the appropriate criteria.

e. Return to Design view. Run and save the query as **Update Prices**.

Create a New Table

Now that you have identified the discontinued products, you need to create a new table that will store the discontinued products. If they are archived, you can use the archive when necessary to answer customer questions.

a. Create a select query that identifies all of the discontinued products.

b. Once you are sure that the logic is sound, convert the select query to a make table query.

c. Name the table **Discontinued Products**.

d. Save the query as **Discontinued Products Query**.

Calculate Summary Statistics and Aggregate the Data

The sales manager has requested that you create summary statistics that will help him identify the most profitable categories sold by each salesperson. You need to create a crosstab query that shows Profits by Salesperson and Category.

a. Open the Your_Name Profit query in Design view and add the LastName field from the Employees table to the design grid. Run the query and save the design changes. Close it.

b. Use the Query Wizard to create a crosstab query that sums profits by Salesperson and Category. Name it **Your_Name Profit_Crosstab**.

c. Add a Total Row to sum the columns.

d. Apply the **Currency** format for the Profit field.

e. Apply the **Currency** format for the Total of Profit field.

f. Set the query to print in landscape orientation. Print it.

g. Save your changes. Close the query.

Create a Parameter Query

You want to keep track of your own sales activities. You copy the Profit query and use the copy that will prompt you for a date parameter each time it is run.

a. Copy the Your_Name Profit query and paste it as Profit by Period. Open it in Design view.

b. Establish parameters that will select, through user prompts, starting and ending dates for the query.

c. Establish criteria that limit the query results to only your sales figures.

d. Run the query and stipulate June 2007 for the date parameters. View the results in Print Preview. Change to landscape view and print the query results.

e. Compact and repair the database.

f. Close the file.

Mini Cases

Use the rubric following the case as a guide to evaluate your work, but keep in mind that your instructor may impose additional grading criteria or use a different standard to judge your work.

Determining Row and Column Data for Crosstab Queries

GENERAL CASE

A database contains data from an international china, crystal, flatware, and collectables firm. You have a query that assembles some of the necessary fields but need to mine these data to determine revenue by long pattern name for each category of goods shipped. You will use this information to analyze what your customers are buying. Copy the *chap7_mc1_replacements.accdb* file, rename the copied file **chap7_mc1_replacements_solution.accdb**, open the copied file, and enable the content. Open the Employees table and replace Bev Waters, name with your name. Rename the Revenue query **Your_Name Revenue**. Calculate total revenue. Create a crosstab query to summarize the total revenue data by category and the long pattern name (LongPatName). Format the results of the crosstab as currency. Print the results. Compact, repair, and back up your database.

Performance Elements	Exceeds Expectations	Meets Expectations	Below Expectations
Profit calculation	Calculated fields accurate.	Calculated fields accurate.	Output missing or incorrect.
Data summaries	Appropriate summaries and aggregating calculations performed.	Most of the requested summaries and aggregates present and accurate.	Output missing or inaccurate.
Row and Column Manipulation	Appropriate selections and formatted correctly.	Appropriate selections with some formatting problems.	Insufficient understanding of crosstab setup manipulation.

Consequences of Updates

RESEARCH CASE

You know how to delete hundreds of records in a database—and even cascade the delete operation to related records in other database tables. You know that you can update selected records—and potentially alter the value of stored information from past transactions. Performing these types of database procedures, has the power to do great good by automating database administration functions. It also has the potential to do great harm. Your assignment is to place yourself in an administrative position for a database in an organization with which you are familiar. What are the consequences of running a poorly planned or executed action query on the organization's data? You may wish to include consequences to SOX noncompliance or HIPAA regulations. You also need to describe a situation where appropriately using an action query will save the organization lots of time. Write a memo to your instructor; save the file as **chap7_mc2_solution.docx**.

Performance Elements	Exceeds Expectations	Meets Expectations	Below Expectations
Use online help	Appropriate articles located, and instructions indicate comprehension.	Appropriate articles located, but instructions did not demonstrate comprehension.	Articles not found.
Demonstrate an understanding of action queries' appropriate use	Clearly articulates an application of appropriate action query use.	Demonstrates some understanding of the potential but fails to the communicate clearly appropriate usage.	Definitional understanding but no application generalization demonstration.
Demonstrate an understanding of action queries' damage potential	Clearly articulates ramifications and consequences of inappropriate action query use.	Demonstrates some understanding of the damage potential but fails to communicate consequences.	Definitional understanding but no application generalization demonstration.
Summarize and communicate	Discussion clearly written and communicative.	Discussion indicates some understanding but also weaknesses.	Discussion missing or incomprehensible.

Accidentally Rerun Update Query

DISASTER RECOVERY

A coworker called you into his office, explained that he made an error using an update query in Access 2007, and asked you to look at his work. You work for Northwind Traders, an international specialty foods distributor. Your coworker was asked to update the prices on all of the categories of food requiring refrigeration: Dairy Products, Meat/Poultry, Produce, and Seafood. Because the transportation costs for refrigerated products have increased, Northwinds has decided to increase the prices of these products by 25%. Your coworker constructed an update query to increase the prices but he believes that he may have run it twice. Fortunately he backed up the table data prior to running the update query. He still has the old prices, but he cannot figure out how to replace the twice updated products table with the backup. Copy the *chap7_mc3_traders.accdb* file, rename the copied file **chap7_mc3_traders_solution.accdb**, open the file, and enable the content. Replace the Products table with the Copy of Products table. Examine the update query logic and run it if appropriate. Print the updated Products table, then compact, repair, and back up your database.

Performance Elements	Exceeds Expectations	Meets Expectations	Below Expectations
Error identification	Correct identification and correction of all errors.	Correct identification of all errors and correction of some errors.	Errors neither located nor corrected.
Problem solving	Appropriate steps taken to resolve the problem successfully.	Appropriate steps taken to resolve the problem partially but not completely.	Errors neither located nor corrected.

chapter 8 | **Access**

Get Connected

Exchanging Data Between Access and Other Applications

Objectives

After you read this chapter, you will be able to:

1. Create a hyperlinked field **(page 513)**.
2. Attach files and graphics to records **(page 516)**.
3. Add and use a table attachment field **(page 517)**.
4. Export database objects as HTML files **(page 530)**.
5. Import or link to HTML files **(page 533)**.
6. Share XML data **(page 537)**.
7. Share data with Excel **(page 542)**.
8. Collect data through e-mail messages **(page 552)**.
9. Manage e-mail replies **(page 557)**.

Hands-On Exercises

Exercises	Skills Covered
1. MAKE CONNECTIONS (page 522) **Open:** chap8_ho1-2_realestate.accdb **Use:** chap8_ho1_house_folder and chap8_ho1_agents_folder **Save as:** chap8_ho1_realestate_solution.accdb and chap8_ho1_realestate_solution.docx **Back up as:** chap8_ho1_insurance_solution.accdb	• Create a Hyperlinked Field • Edit a Hyperlinked Field • Add and Use Table Attachment Fields • Add and Use Attachment Fields in Forms and Reports • Create and Use a Multiple Attachment Field in a Form
2. SHARE DATA (page 547) **Open:** chap8_ho1-2_realestate_solution.accdb (from Exercise 1) **Save as:** chap8_ho1-2_realestate_solution.accdb (additional modifications), chap8_ho2_realestate_solution.docx, chap8_ho2_agents_solution.xlsx, chap8_ho2_agents_solution.html, and chap8_ho2_agents_solution.xml	• Export Objects as HTML Files • Import and Link to an HTML File • Share XML Data and Import from Access • Export Access Data to Excel

CASE STUDY

Data Exchange

Case Study

You work for the Office of Student Life on campus. This year, the National Student Success Conference will be held on your campus. The organization serves campus communities by conducting and sharing research about helping students succeed in college. It recommends actions that might improve graduation rates, community cohesiveness, and general measures of student happiness. The members come from university administrators, professors, counselors, and student organizations. Each year, the organization meets to present the new research and to share ideas about programs and policies that work on their campuses. The speakers and conference participants come from differently sized institutions located nationwide.

You are responsible for the database that stores the information about the conference agenda, speakers, room assignments, schedules, and participants. As the conference speakers accept their assignments, they provide you with pictures and curriculum vita that you will use to publicize the event. You have a folder containing each speaker's picture and other files that you need to integrate into the database. You also need to generate a form that will display each speaker's picture and schedule. You also need to generate an HTML file to e-mail to your supervisor, who is on vacation and is using Internet cafés to keep in touch.

Your Assignment

- Read the chapter, paying special attention to learning the vocabulary of attachments, hyperlinked fields, and data exports.
- Copy the *chap8_case_natconf.accdb* file to your production folder, rename it **chap8_case_natconf_solution.accdb**, and enable the content.
- Open the Relationships window and examine the relationships among the tables and the fields contained within each of the tables to become acquainted with this database.
- Create an attachment field in the Speakers table. Use it to attach the speakers' pictures and curriculum vita. The files are stored in a folder named *chap8_case_pixcv_folder*.
- Create a form that displays each speaker's picture and the time, place, and topic of each presentation.
- Create a report, grouped by each speaker, that displays their pictures and the time, place, and topic of their presentations.
- Export the report as an HTML file named **chap8_case_natconf_solution.htm**. Print the output.
- Compact, repair, and close the database file.

Access and the World Wide Web

The ***Uniform Resource Locator (URL)*** is a short string identifying the documents, image, or downloadable files stored on a Web server.

Access supports a variety of ways to access the Internet. You may define a table field as a hyperlinked field and use it to store a Web address. The address is a ***Uniform Resource Locator (URL)*** that stores a unique address for each file on the Web site. For example, http://www.prenhall.com/exploring is the URL for the main Web page for the Exploring series. The Web page may include documents, images, or downloadable files stored on a Web server. Web pages typically contain many text, design, and image files. The linked source may be stored as an HTML file, an e-mail address, or a file stored in any format where the link is the file name and path for a document stored locally, on an intranet or extranet.

HyperText Markup Language (HTML) and ***Extensible HyperText Markup Language (XHTML)*** are widely used languages to create Web pages.

The ***eXtensible Markup Language (XML)*** is a general-purpose language that supports a wide variety of applications by defining data in well-formed documents.

Access also gives you the option of attaching files to a record in a database through an attachment field. You can import from and export to HTML files. You may import data published on the Internet from a governmental agency such as the U.S. Department of Agriculture and store it as an object in your Access database. You could also export a database object, complete with formatting, as an HTML file and publish it on your organization's Web site. ***HyperText Markup Language (HTML)*** and ***Extensible HyperText Markup Language (XHTML)*** are widely used languages to create Web pages. HTML contains tags that mark up the text file, giving instructions on text style and position; it displays data. Even very old browser technology supports HTML documents. Unfortunately, many Web pages contain bad HTML code. The bad code displays information correctly only if the browser software is installed on a computer. If you try to view the same page using a mobile device, for example, a cell phone or a handheld device, the bad code interferes. These devices perform more dependably when the Web documents were created using XML. The ***eXtensible Markup Language (XML)*** is a general-purpose language that supports a wide variety of applications by defining data in well-formed documents. The XML solution creates another set of problems. Some older browsers do not support XML, so users of older browsers will not be able to view the data. XHTML provides a compromise solution. XHTML combines the cosmetic aspects of HTML with the data-defining aspects of XML. It can be used both by old browsers and mobile devices.

In this section, you will create a hyperlinked field to store Web addresses. In addition, you learn how to attach files and graphics to records. Finally, you learn how to attach and use a table attachment field in forms and reports.

Creating a Hyperlinked Field

If you define a field as a hyperlinked field, Access stores the address that enables you to get to the data, but not the data values. The data stored in the database are the address of the file or Web site where the data may be found. The values ascribed to the data will be stored in the original location. When you open the table and click on a record value within a hyperlinked field, Access launches the appropriate software, such as a Web browser or Excel, and you can view and interact with the file. If you make any changes to the file, you need to save those changes within the host application. Access runs in the background while you work elsewhere. Of course, the Access user must have permission to view and interact with the files stored in a hyperlinked field. That permission must come from the source document storage permissions. Most Web pages grant the public read and scan but not write or editing privileges. Hyperlinks to non-browser application files, such as Word documents or Excel workbooks, are a little more complex. For example, Joe could create a record providing the file name and path to an Excel workbook stored in a folder on his desktop. Other users of the database table would only be able to open and interact with Joe's Excel workbook if they had been granted the rights to do so by Joe or the network administration staff. Absent the privilege, they would receive an error message.

Access makes hyperlinked field creation uncomplicated. You need only define the table field as a hyperlink data type in the table's Design view. Figure 8.1 illustrates the hyperlinked field data type selection, and Figure 8.2 shows the three types of possible hyperlinks: URL, path/filename, and e-mail address.

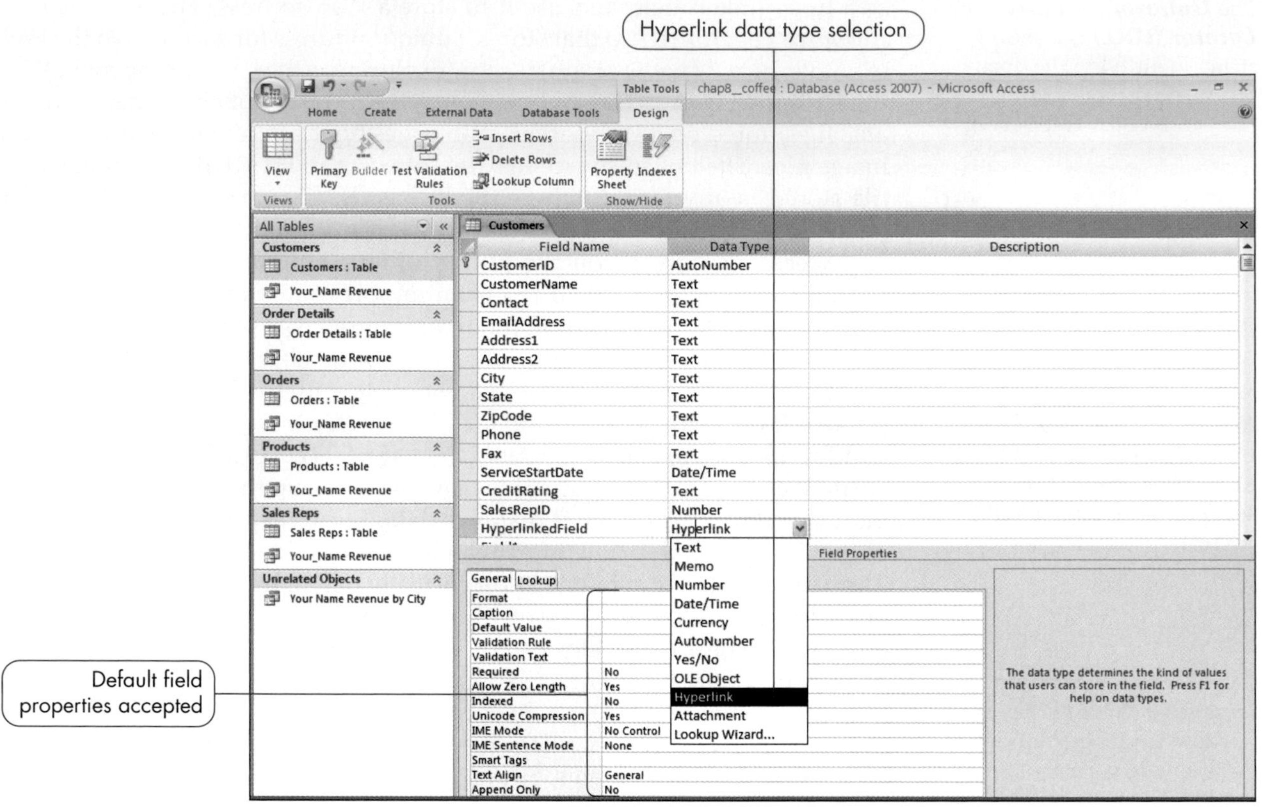

Figure 8.1 Creating a Hyperlinked Field

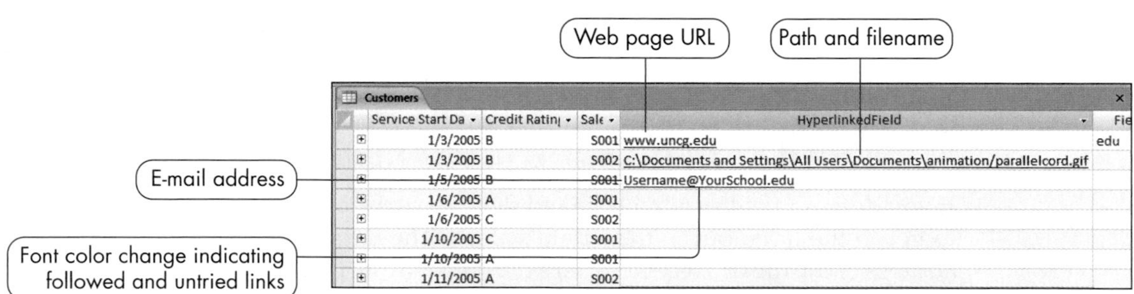

Figure 8.2 Types of Linked Field Values

TIP Editing and Removing a Hyperlinked Field

Editing a hyperlinked field requires that you select the field and then make the necessary changes. You must press Tab or an arrow key to select the record. Once you select the record, you must retype the entire value. As soon as you attempt to click to position the insertion point, Access interprets your click as a command to follow the link and launches the appropriate software. Many database designers define e-mail and hyperlinked fields as simple text fields and store the appropriate URLs or e-mail addresses. Users who need to follow the links copy and paste the information in the appropriate application. The users who do not need to follow the link can click the field value without jumping to some other application. If you need to remove a hyperlink, right-click the hyperlinked field, select Hyperlink, and select Remove Hyperlink. If you need to edit many hyperlinked field values, open the table in Design view, change the data type from Hyperlink to Text, change to Datasheet view to make the edits, return to Design view, and then change the data type back to Hyperlink. If you need to edit only a few links, right-click the hyperlink and select Edit from the shortcut menu.

You can use the Insert Hyperlink dialog box (see Figure 8.3) to specify additional settings for hyperlinked data. To do this, right-click the data in a hyperlink data field, select Hyperlink, and select Edit Hyperlink. The Insert Hyperlink dialog box enables you to specify whether you want to link to an existing file or Web page or link to an e-mail address. In addition, you can specify text that displays in the data field for a particular record instead of displaying the actual Web page, file, or e-mail address. For example, if you create a record for this textbook, you might want to include a hyperlink field that goes to http://www.prenhall.com/exploring. Instead of displaying the URL in the field, you might want to display the text, *Click to download student files for Exploring Access 2007*. You can create a ScreenTip to appear when the user positions the mouse over the hyperlinked text, similar to ScreenTips that appear when you move your mouse over commands on the Ribbon.

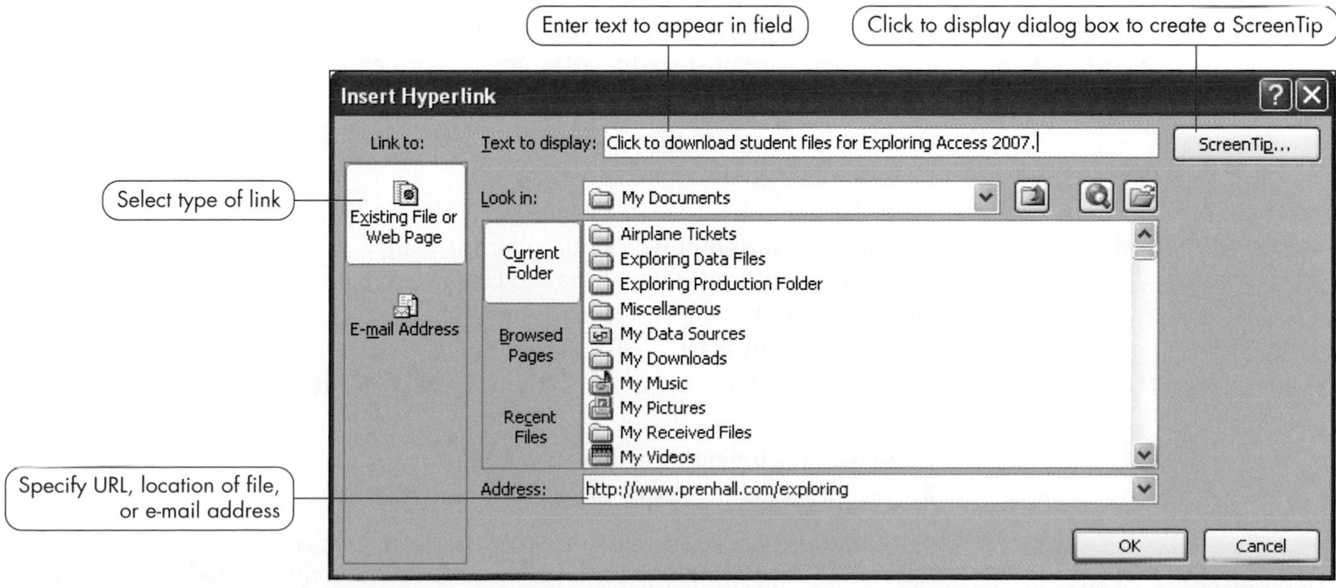

Figure 8.3 Insert Hyperlink Dialog Box

Attaching Files and Graphics to Records

Object Linking and Embedding (OLE) is a standard for linking or embedding an object from one application into another.

Versions of Access prior to Access 2007 used ***Object Linking and Embedding (OLE)*** to manage file attachments. OLE is a standard that enables you to create an object in one application and link or embed that object within another application. In previous versions of Access, the OLE process created a bitmap image of the document and stored that. In other words, you did not save a Word document, but you saved a picture of a Word document. Bitmap images are not compressed the way .jpg or .gif image files are. This created problems for database administrators because bitmap image files are very large. The large file sizes required additional storage resources and slowed the database operation. Additionally, the bitmapped images could not be viewed by Access users unless they had the appropriate OLE server software installed locally. For example, an Employee table might contain a picture of the employee stored in a JPEG format. Database users could not view the employee's picture unless they had the OLE server for JPEG installed on their computers. Access 2007 permits true file attachment and solves many of the OLE issues. Attachments use storage more efficiently, help your database files run more quickly, and avoid the OLE server installation problem.

(Access solves this . . . by creating a series of hidden systems tables that operate in the background and permit database normalization.)

Suppose you had a table of employees in your organization's database. You might wish to include a picture of the employee as well as the Word document containing each employee's most recent performance review. If an employee won a community service award, you might decide to scan the newspaper story and attach it to the employee's record, also. You can accomplish this by creating an attachment field and attaching all of the files relating to that employee in one field. A database for a real estate office might attach several pictures of listed property, both interior and exterior views. At first glance, this may appear to violate one of the basic rules of database design: store data in its smallest parts. Access solves this design issue for you by creating a series of hidden systems tables that operate in the background and permit database normalization. ***Normalization*** is a process that examines the structure of database tables to prevent inconsistent or illogical data operations. Normalization helps the database administrator identify and eliminate redundant data. Data redundancy consumes storage, slows the database operation, and may create errors.

Normalization is a process that examines the structure of database tables to prevent inconsistent or illogical data operations.

To include attachment files in a field, you should follow these guidelines and restrictions:

- Because true file attachment is new to Access 2007, you must use the .accdb format. You cannot share file attachments with earlier .mdb Access files.
- Once a table field has been set as an Attachment data type, it cannot be altered. Of course, the values stored in the field remain alterable; it is the data type definition that may not be changed.
- Many files and file types can be stored in the same attachment field. For example, you can save the employee's photo for the company ID badge, the pictures of the employee's children taken at the last company picnic, the employee's performance review as a Word document, and an Excel workbook containing the employee's requests for reimbursable expenses.
- File size for each file must be less than 256 MB, and the total of all attached files must be less than 2 GB.
- Open the attachment directly in the table, form, or report by double-clicking it.
- Add, edit, and manage file attachments with the Attachment dialog box.
- Attachments opened from forms and reports may be edited directly in the application if the application is installed locally. Attachments opened from a report are read only. If you edit them, you must save the file using a different file name.
- Access compresses all attachment files except for those stored in a pre-compressed format, i.e., .jpg or .zip.

Adding and Using a Table Attachment Field

Suppose you were the manager of a coffee service firm. You provide coffee, coffee brewing equipment, and snacks to customers in diverse locations. Although you and the firm owner make most of the deliveries, you occasionally hire part-time workers to assist you. You decide it would be good marketing to store a digital photo of your customers in the database. That way a new part-timer could enter an office and easily identify the person who places the order. Your customers will receive better service if a part-time employee knows who to look for. You might also store copies of faxed orders or e-mail messages from the customer or a map providing directions to their office in the same attachment field. You can add an attachment field to an existing table. Open your table in Datasheet view and scroll to the first empty column, indicated by *Add a New Field*. Click Data Type down arrow in the Data Type & Formatting group on the Datasheet tab. Select Attachment from the drop-down list (see Figure 8.4). Access places a paperclip icon in the field header row and records the number of attachments stored in each record (see Figure 8.5). Launch the Attachments dialog box by double-clicking the record's paperclip. Figure 8.6 shows the Attachments dialog box that opens when a record has no attachments. Add an attachment by clicking the Add button and then browsing to the selected file and attaching it by clicking the Open button. The Attachments dialog box remains open until you click OK. You may open the Attachment dialog box again by double-clicking the appropriate record's paperclip. Remove an attachment by selecting it in the Attachments dialog box and clicking Remove.

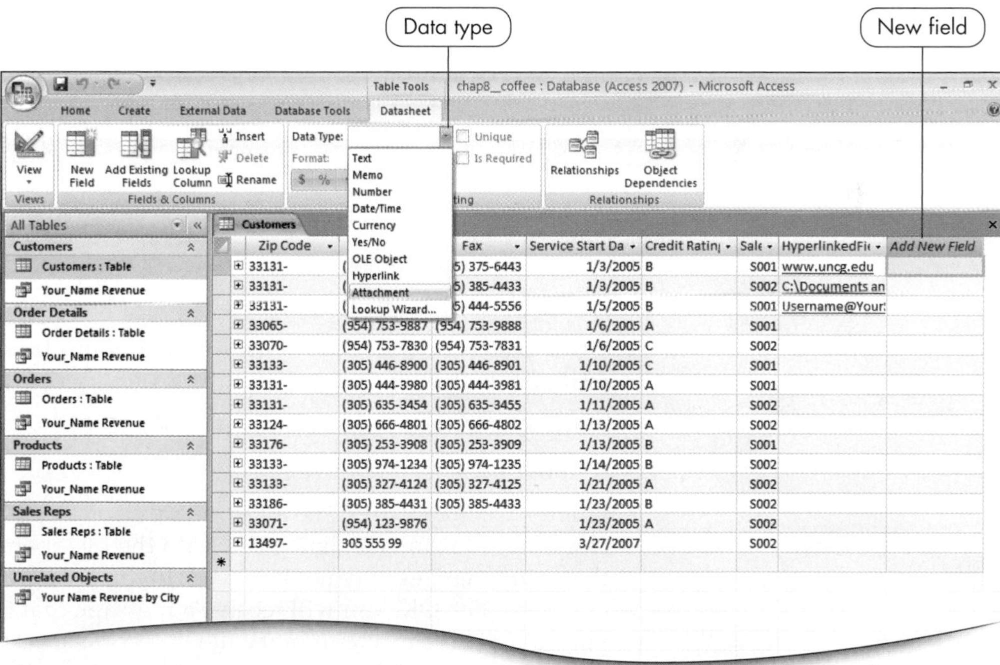

Figure 8.4 Create an Attachment Field

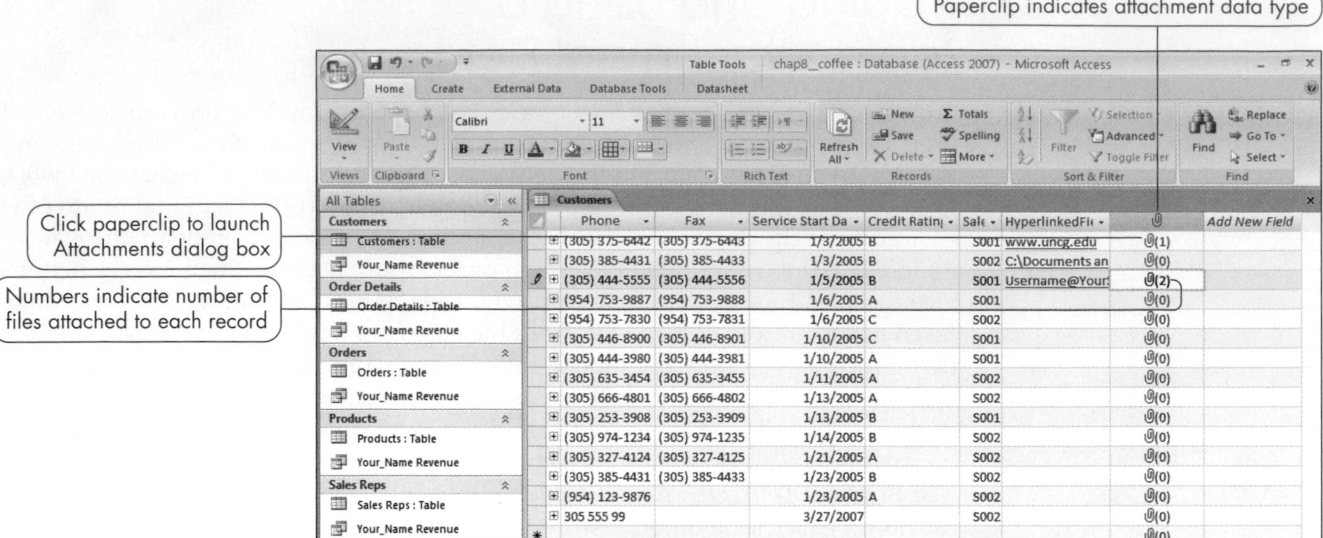

Figure 8.5 Newly Created Attachment Field with a Few Attachments Added

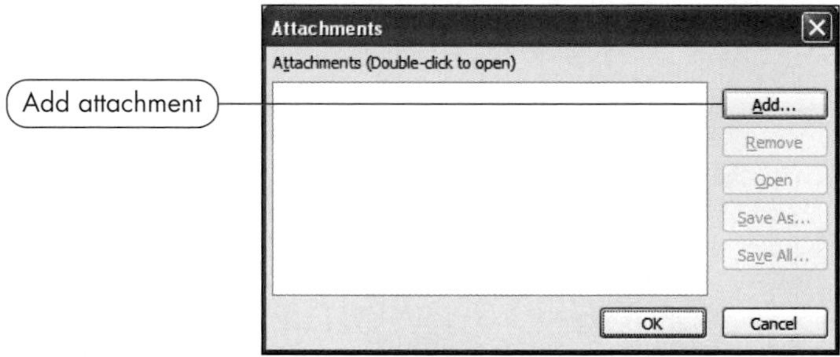

Figure 8.6 Attachments Dialog Box Options

You control most of the interactions with the attachment field's contents by using the Attachments dialog box. With it you can:

- **Add**—Click to add one or more files to a record.
- **Remove**—Click to remove previously attached files.
- **Open**—Click to launch the appropriate application and open the file. If you try to close the Attachments dialog box with the file open, you will receive a warning that your changes may not be saved. If you are sure you have saved your changes, click OK. You will receive a message that the changes were saved to your hard drive in a temporary file. Access asks if you would like to save your updates to the database (see Figure 8.7).
- **Save As**—Use to save the attached file to a local storage location. You must remember to add it back into the database if you make changes.
- **Save All**—Save all of the attachments to a record to a local, temporary folder.

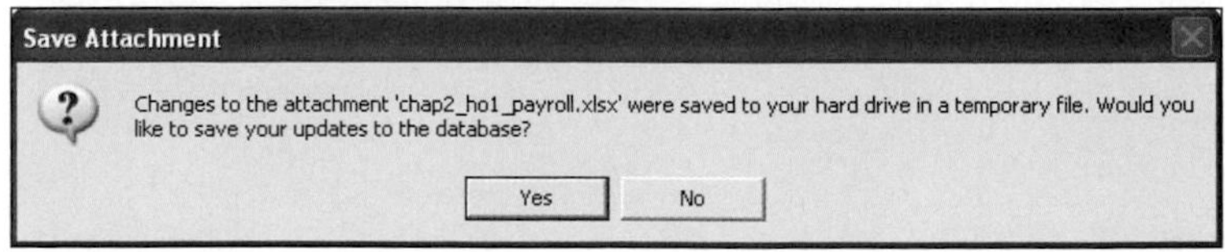

Figure 8.7 Automatic Integration of Managed Attachments

TIP Deleting Temporary Files

Each time you open an attachment from within Access, it creates a temporary file locally. Because many attachment files store pictures and picture files tend to be large, over time these temporary files will consume a great deal of space on your hard drive. You may wish to remove the temporary files, but first you must find them. To discover where Access has stored all of the temporary files, launch Windows Internet Explorer. Click Internet Options on the Tools menu. Click Settings on the General tab. The Settings dialog box appears, and the path to the folder displays in the Temporary Internet Files folder section in Current Location. Use the path to find the temporary files and delete them. If you use Internet Explorer 7, launch it. Go to Tools and select Delete Browsing History.

Add Attachment Controls in Forms and Reports

An ***attachment control*** is a control that lets you manage and use attached files.

In a form or report you interact with attachments using an attachment control. An ***attachment control*** is a control that lets you manage and use attached files while working with forms and reports. If the attachment is an image, it will display as a thumbnail in the form or report as you navigate records. When the attached file is a document, you will see the icon representing the application. In order to use an attachment control, you must previously have defined an attachment field in the source table. If you create the report or form after a field in the source has been defined as an attachment field, the attachment control will be created automatically. If you need to create an attachment control in a previously created form or report, you must first create the attachment field in the table, and then add it to the report or form.

Open the form or report in Design view. Click Add Existing Fields in the Tools group on the Design tab. Use the Field List pane to find the appropriate field. An expand symbol displays to the left of the field name, indicating that the field is expandable and collapsible. Drag the unindented reference of the field to the form or report Design view and drop it in the appropriate location. If you position the control in the wrong place, click it to select and drag it to a more appropriate spot. Access places the bound attachment control and the associated text box on the form or report. Additionally, Access will set the control's properties that bind the control to the data source for you. If necessary, use the Format Painter to paint the formats of the other controls onto the newly added attachment control. Alternatively, use the Property Sheet to format the new control. Resize the bound control, if necessary, to ensure that the thumbnail displays appropriately. Save your changes, then switch to Form or Report view. After looking at the object, return to Design or Layout view for subsequent modifications (see Figure 8.8).

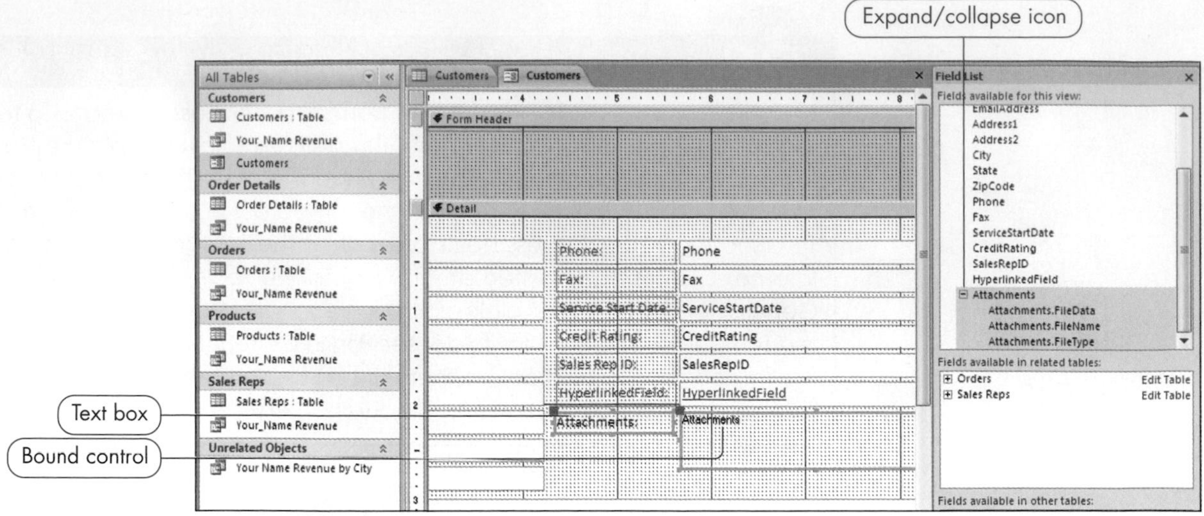

Figure 8.8 Design View of Attachment Control

Use an Attachment Field in a Form or Report

Once created, the attachment field may be used in a form by double-clicking it (alternatively, single click and use the Mini toolbar to navigate attachments or add/delete record attachments). When you work in a form with a subform (as shown in Figure 8.9), the Mini toolbar appears faded and then is fully visible. The first two buttons navigate among attachments, and the third launches the Attachments dialog box (see Figure 8.10). You use the Attachments dialog box to add, remove, or open the attachment files.

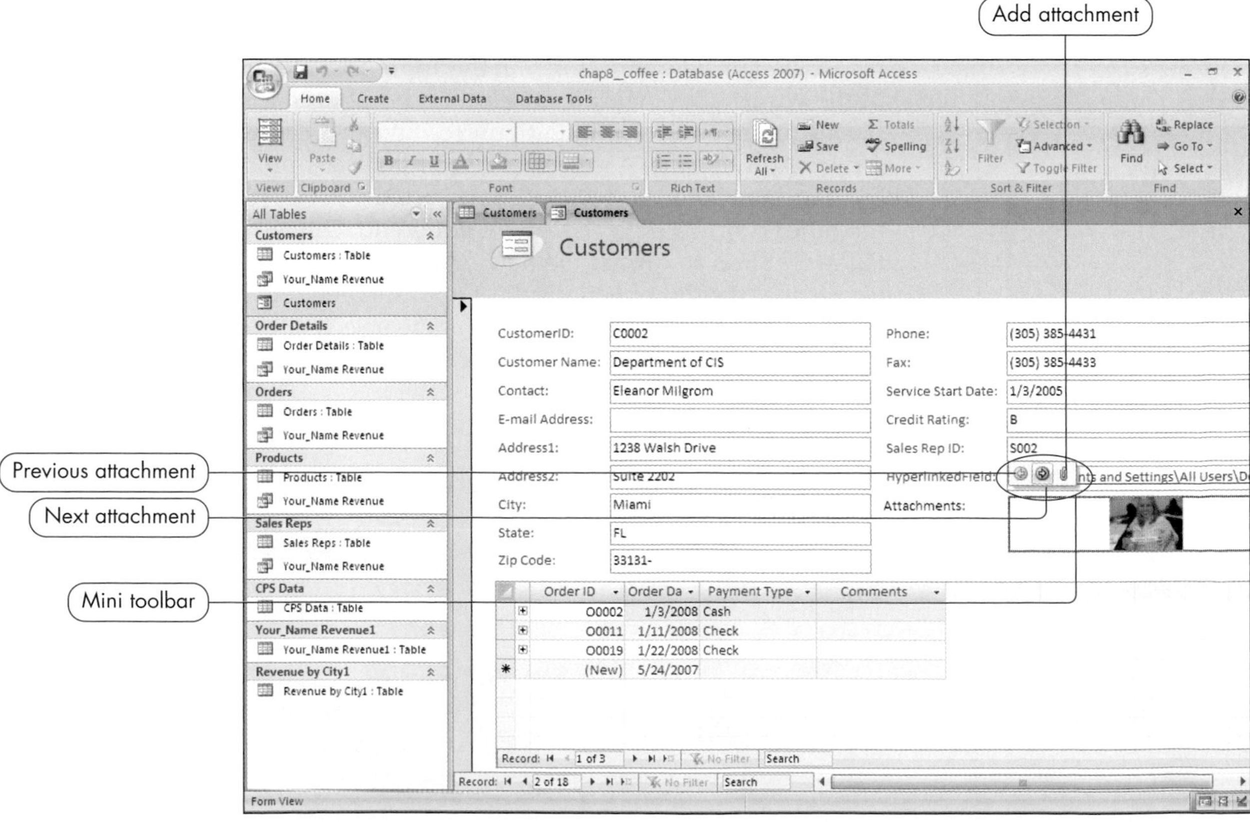

Figure 8.9 Ghosted Mini Toolbar

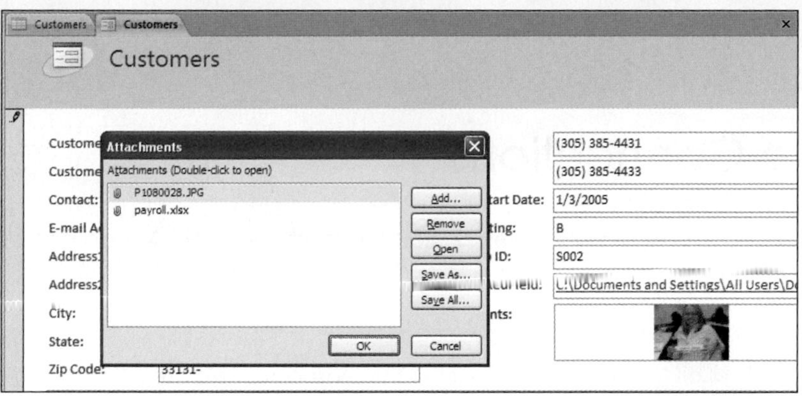

Figure 8.10 Use to Manage Attachment Files

In the first hands-on exercise, you will work with the database from a real estate company. You will add and edit a hyperlinked field that will link properties to the appropriate school district's home pages. You will create and use an attachment field (some with multiple attachments) in an Access table, and you will add attachment controls to a form and a report.

Hands-On Exercises

1 | Make Connections

Skills covered: 1. Create a Hyperlinked Field **2.** Edit a Hyperlinked Field **3.** Add and Use Table Attachment Fields **4.** Add and Use Attachment Fields in Forms and Reports **5.** Create and Use a Multiple Attachment Field in a Form

Step 1 Create a Hyperlinked Field

Refer to Figure 8.11 as you complete Step 1.

a. Use Exploring to locate the file named *chap8_ho1-2_realestate.accdb*. Copy the file and rename it **chap8_ho1-2_realestate_solution.accdb**.

b. Open the *chap8_ho1-2_realestate_solution.accdb* file. Click **Options** on the Security Warning toolbar, click **Enable this content** in the Microsoft Office Security Options dialog box, and click **OK**.

c. Rename the Your_Name Sales Report query, the Your_Name Agents form, and Your_Name Sales Report report with your name. Open the **Agents table** and replace *Your_Name* with your name. Close the Agents table.

d. Open the **SubDivision table** in Design view. In the blank row below the BikeTrail field name, type **SchoolDistrict**. Click the **Data Type drop-down arrow** and select **Hyperlink**. In the Field Properties window for the newly created field, type **School District** in the Caption property box. Right-click the **SubDivision table tab** and select **Datasheet View** from the shortcut menu. Click **Yes** when prompted to save the table changes.

You created a new text field to store the URLs of the school district's Web sites.

e. Type the URL **http://abss.k12.nc.us** in the SchoolDistrict field for records 1, 6, 7, 9, and 12.

Fair Brook, North Point, Red Canyon, The Courses, and The Pines are all located in the Alamance-Burlington School System. The URL is http://abss.k12.nc.us.

f. Type the URL **http://www.guilford.k12.ct.us** in the SchoolDistrict field for records 2, 3, 8, and 11.

King's Forest, Dale, Seeley Lake, and The Orchards are in the Guilford District.

g. Type the URL **http://www.orange.k12.nc.us** in the SchoolDistrict field for the remaining records.

The remaining subdivisions (records 4, 5, 10, 13, and 14) are in Orange County School District.

TROUBLESHOOTING: If you make a typing mistake, you cannot click in the field to correct the error because it has been defined as a hyperlinked field. Use the arrow keys to navigate to the record that you need to edit. The entire field value selects. Delete it and enter the information again.

h. Test the accuracy of the URL by clicking the links. Click **Yes** in the Microsoft Office Access Security Notice dialog box.

A browser should launch and the requested school district's Web site should open. You realized that you entered an inaccurate URL when you visited the link for the Guilford Schools. These schools are in Connecticut, not in North Carolina. The houses are in North Carolina. You will fix the links in the next step.

i. Widen the SchoolDistrict field. Move your mouse over the right column boundary in the title row. When the mouse pointer shape changes to a cross, click and drag right until the entire URL displays in Datasheet view. Compare your screen to Figure 8.11.

j. Press **PrntScrn** to capture a screenshot. Launch Word. Type your name and section number and press **Enter**. Press **Ctrl+V** to paste the screenshot and press **Enter**. Save the Word document as **chap8_ho1_realestate_solution.docx** and keep it open.

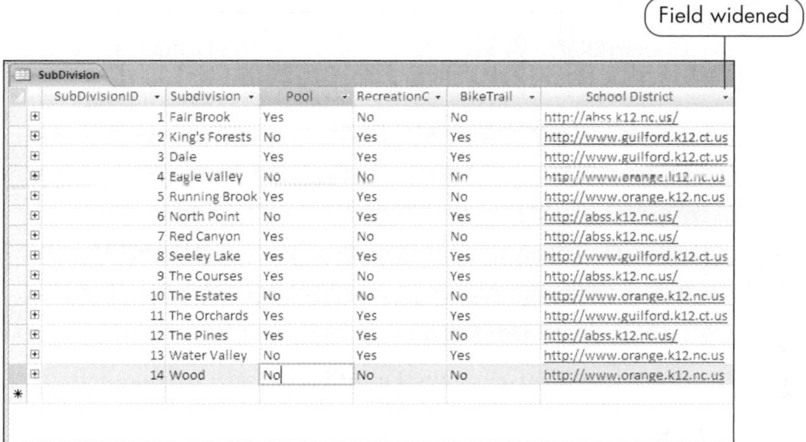

SubDivisionID	Subdivision	Pool	RecreationC	BikeTrail	School District
1	Fair Brook	Yes	No	No	http://abss.k12.nc.us/
2	King's Forests	No	Yes	Yes	http://www.guilford.k12.ct.us
3	Dale	Yes	Yes	Yes	http://www.guilford.k12.ct.us
4	Eagle Valley	No	No	No	http://www.orange.k12.nc.us
5	Running Brook	Yes	Yes	No	http://www.orange.k12.nc.us
6	North Point	No	Yes	Yes	http://abss.k12.nc.us/
7	Red Canyon	Yes	No	No	http://abss.k12.nc.us/
8	Seeley Lake	Yes	Yes	Yes	http://www.guilford.k12.ct.us
9	The Courses	Yes	No	Yes	http://abss.k12.nc.us/
10	The Estates	No	No	No	http://www.orange.k12.nc.us
11	The Orchards	Yes	Yes	Yes	http://www.guilford.k12.ct.us
12	The Pines	Yes	Yes	No	http://abss.k12.nc.us/
13	Water Valley	No	Yes	Yes	http://www.orange.k12.nc.us
14	Wood	No	No	No	http://www.orange.k12.nc.us

Figure 8.11 Hyperlinked Field in Datasheet View

Step 2 Edit a Hyperlinked Field

Refer to Figure 8.12 as you complete Step 2.

a. Return to Access. Use the arrow keys to select the first instance of the Guilford Schools link in Record 2. Press **Delete** and type the correct link **http://www.guilford.k12.nc.us**.

   This method of editing works, but it requires a lot of typing. You decide to temporarily turn the hyperlinks off to finish editing the table.

b. Click **View** in the Views group on the Design tab to change to Design view.

c. Click the **Data Type drop-down arrow** for the SchoolDistrict field and select **Text**. Save the design changes. Read the warning that some data may be lost and click **Yes**.

   You instructed Access to convert the hyperlinked field to a simple text field to simplify editing the URLs.

d. Click **View** in the Views group on the Home tab to change to Datasheet view.

   Examine the field values in the SchoolDistrict field. When Access converted the hyperlink to text, it inserted pound signs [#] at the beginning and end of the text.

e. Edit the remaining Guilford URLs to the North Carolina Guilford (**nc**), not the Connecticut one (**ct**).

f. Click **View** to return to Design view. Click the **Data Type arrow** column for the SchoolDistrict field and select **Hyperlink** from the list. Save the design changes.

g. Click **View** in the Views group on the Design tab to change to Datasheet view. The hyperlinks should again function. Test a few.

Your visited links (purple) may differ from those shown

SubDivision

SubDivisionID	Subdivision	Pool	RecreationC	BikeTrail	School District	Add New F
1	Fair Brook	Yes	No	No	http://abss.k12.nc.us/	
2	King's Forests	No	Yes	Yes	http://www.guilford.k12.nc.us	
3	Dale	Yes	Yes	Yes	http://www.guilford.k12.nc.us	
4	Eagle Valley	No	No	No	http://www.orange.k12.nc.us	
5	Running Brook	Yes	Yes	No	http://www.orange.k12.nc.us	
6	North Point	No	Yes	Yes	http://abss.k12.nc.us/	
7	Red Canyon	Yes	No	No	http://abss.k12.nc.us/	
8	Seeley Lake	Yes	Yes	Yes	http://www.guilford.k12.nc.us	
9	The Courses	Yes	No	Yes	http://abss.k12.nc.us/	
10	The Estates	No	No	No	http://www.orange.k12.nc.us	
11	The Orchards	Yes	Yes	Yes	http://www.guilford.k12.nc.us	
12	The Pines	Yes	Yes	No	http://abss.k12.nc.us/	
13	Water Valley	No	Yes	Yes	http://www.orange.k12.nc.us	
14	Wood	No	No	No	http://www.orange.k12.nc.us	

Figure 8.12 Hyperlinked Field in Datasheet View

Step 3
Add and Use Table Attachment Fields

Refer to Figure 8.13 as you complete Step 3.

a. Close all open objects in your database. Open the **Properties table** in Design view.

   You will add a new field that will permit you to attach related files. The first files you need to attach are some pictures of the properties.

b. Right-click the **DateListed field row selector** and select **Insert Rows** from the shortcut menu.

   A new row adds between the Listing and DateListed fields.

c. Type **Photo** in the Field Name column and press **Tab** to move to the Data Type column. Click the **Data Type drop-down arrow** and select **Attachment**. Look in the Field Properties to make sure that the Required property is set to **No**. Save the changes to the table design. Return to **Datasheet view**.

   The newly created field should occupy the second column position. It will display with paperclip symbols and zero in parentheses to indicate the number of attachments for each record.

d. Click in the **Listing field** in the first record of the table. Click **Find** in the Find group on the Home tab or press **Ctrl+F** and specify the following in the Find and Replacement dialog box:

   - Type **10011** in the **Find What box**.
   - Check to make sure the **Listing** field displays in the **Look In** box.
   - Check to make sure that **Whole Field** is selected in the **Match** box.
   - Click **Find Next**.

   Find will take you to the Listing field of the 11th record.

e. Without closing the Find and Replace dialog box, double-click the **paperclip** in record 11 to launch the Attachments dialog box. Click **Add**.

f. Locate and double-click the file named **10011.jpg** found in the folder named *chap8_ho1_house_folder*.

   The picture of the house attaches to the record. It displays in the Attachment dialog box.

g. Double-click the **10011.jpg** attachment in the **Attachments (Double-click to open)** window of the dialog box. When you finish looking at the house, click **Close**. Click **OK** to close the Attachment box.

h. Click **Find What** box in the Find and Replace box and find listing **10043**.

TROUBLESHOOTING: You must remember to look for the listing number in the Listing field. Make sure the *Look In* box is set to Listing.

i. Add the file **10043.jpg** to the attachment field for record listing *10043*. Click **OK**. Use the Find and Replace dialog box to find the next record, *10067*. Attach the file **10067.jpg** to it.

You will add photos for several other records.

j. Use the Find and Replace dialog box to locate records **10865**, **10888**, **10899**, **10935**, **10968**, **11028**, **11042**, **11118**, **11141**, and **11171**. Attach the appropriate photo file to each record. Click **Save** on the Quick Access Toolbar. Close the table.

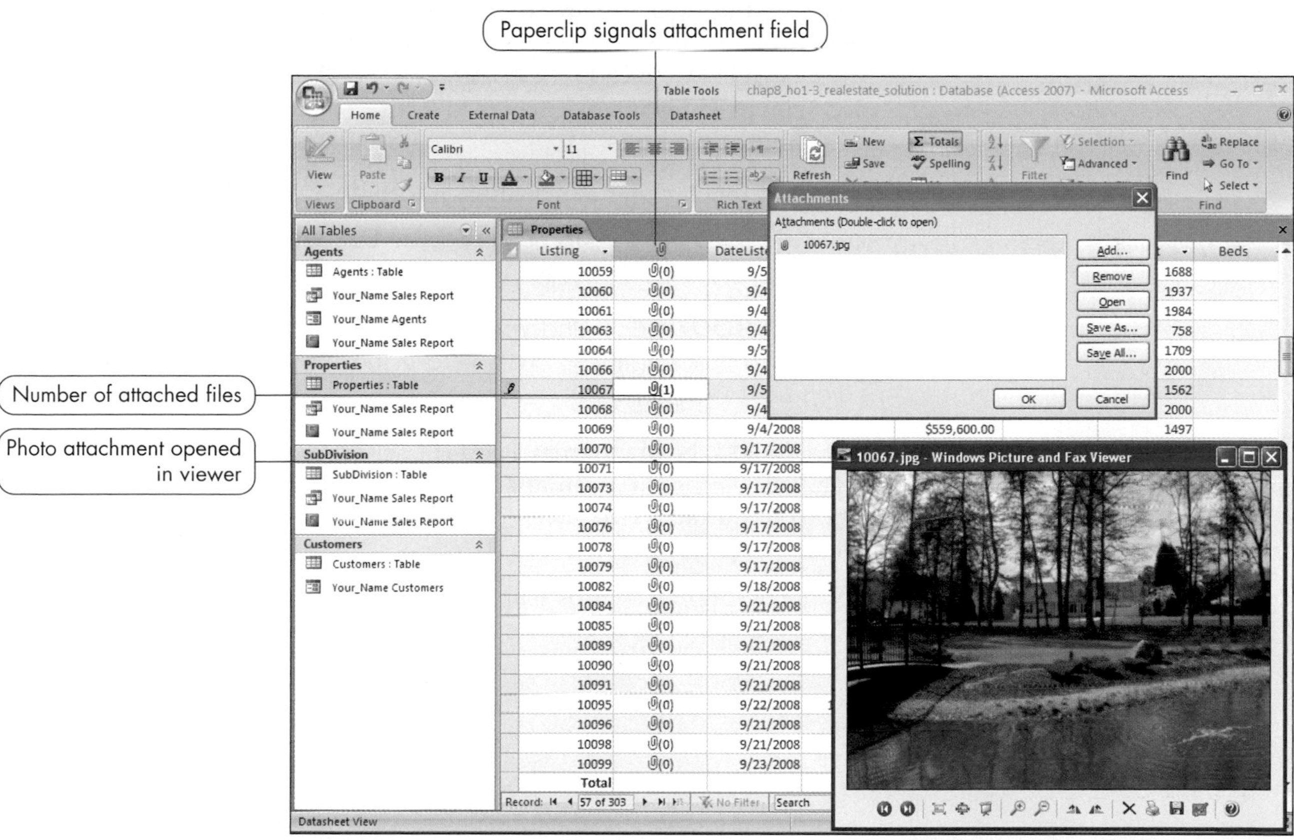

Figure 8.13 Attachment Field

Step 4
Add and Use Attachment Fields in Forms and Reports

Refer to Figure 8.14 as you complete Step 4.

a. Open the **Your_Name Sales Report query** in Design view and change the parameter from *Your_name* to your last name. Run, save, and close the query.

b. Open the report named **Your_Name Sales Report** in Layout view. Click **Add Existing Fields** in the Controls group on the Format tab. Locate the Photo field in the Field List pane below the Properties table. Click to select the **Photo** field.

The Photo field displays with subcomponents for the FileData, FileName, and FileType. All the subcomponents select along with the attachment field, Photo. This report sources a query that sources the Properties table. You made changes to the table design after the query and report that source the table were created and stored. When you attempt to add the new field to the old report, you will receive notification that Access must create a new query to include the new field.

c. Click the **Commission field** to select it. Double-click the **Photo** field in the Field List pane to add it to the report.

You selected the Commission field before adding the Photo field to control the position of the new field on the report. Read the alert box. Access tells you that it needs to make a new query in order to add this field and asks your permission. It also warns you that this report will no longer source the Your_Name Sales Report query.

d. Click **Yes** to accept the change. Close the Field List pane.

Because the Photo field is in the Properties table and the Properties table was not a record source for the underlying query, Access creates a new query and changes the report source to the new one. Then Access creates a new control that displays the photo in thumbnail view.

e. Right-click the **Sales Report tab** and select **Design View** from the shortcut menu. Right-click the photo control in the Detail section and select **Properties**. On the Format tab, click in the box controlling *Display As* (the first row) and select **Icon** from the menu. Change to **Print Preview** (right-click the report tab) and examine the results.

You decide that you like the pictures so you do not want to keep this change.

f. Right-click the **Sales Report tab** and select **Design View**. Click **Undo** on the Quick Access Toolbar to restore the thumbnails.

TROUBLESHOOTING: If Undo did not restore the thumbnails, open the Property Sheet by right-clicking the Photo control in the Detail section. Change the Display as property to Image/Icon.

You could add the photo from an attachment field to the report because you had previously defined it as an attachment field in the table. In the next step you want to use attachment fields in a form. However, you must first create the attachment field in the source table.

g. Click the report title control *Your_Name Sales Report* to select it. Click again inside the control box to edit. Replace *Your_Name* with your name. Print and close the report.

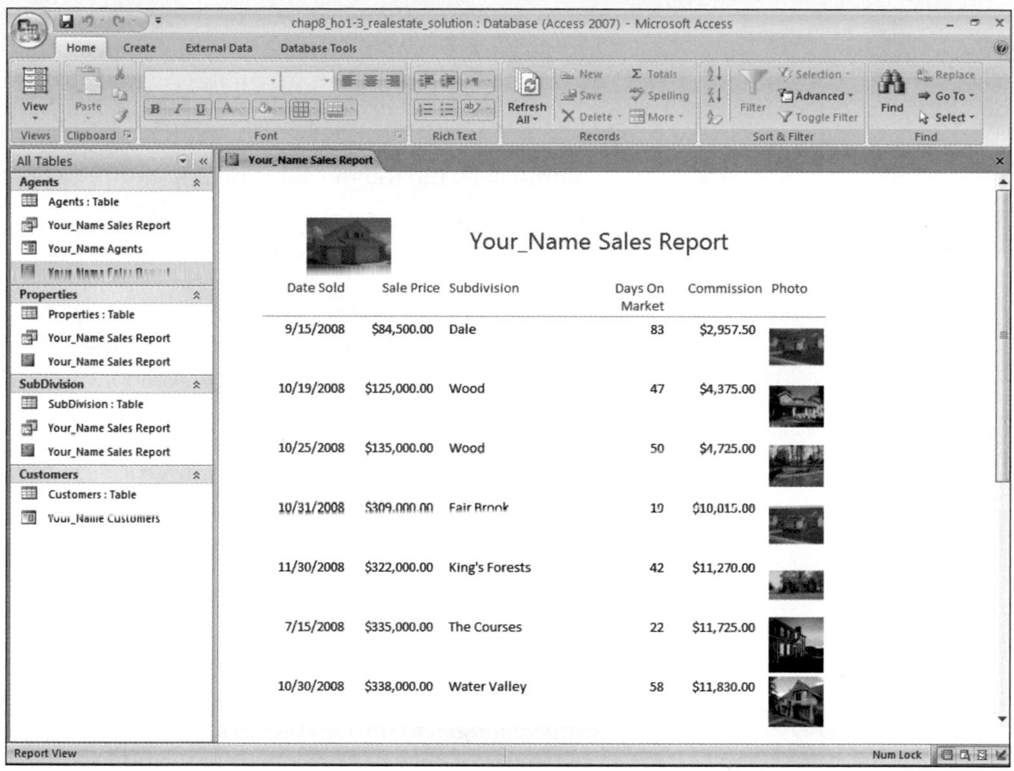

Figure 8.14 Attachment Field in a Report

Step 5
Create and Use a Multiple Attachment Field in a Form

Refer to Figure 8.15 as you complete Step 5.

a. Open the **Agents table** in Design view. Add a new field in the first blank row under Field Name. Name the new field **RelatedFiles**. Click the **Data Type drop-down arrow** for the new field and select **Attachment**. In the Field Properties box, type **Photo and Related Files** in the Caption property.

b. Save the design changes and click **View** in the Views group on the Design tab to return to Datasheet view.

   You need to attach an employee photo for all employees and Word files for the most recent performance reviews for some employees.

c. Double-click the **paperclip** in the first record *Juan*. The Attachments dialog box opens. Click the **Add** button. Locate and open the *chap8_ho1_agents* folder. Find and double-click **juan.jpg** to attach it. Click **OK** in the Attachments box to close it.

   The paperclip now shows that one file is attached to Juan's record. The next record, Kia Hart, has two attachments: a picture and a Word file containing her performance review.

d. Double-click the **paperclip** in Kia Hart's record to open the Attachment dialog box. Click **Add**. Navigate to and double-click **kia.jpg** to attach it to the record. Click **Add** again and attach the file named **Kia Hart Performance Evaluation.docx**. Click **OK** to close the Attachments dialog box.

   Kia's record should indicate two attachments.

e. Attach the other agents' pictures to their records by following the instructions in Step 5c. You may use the photo named *your_name* or use an actual photo of yourself when you get to your record. Attach the **Your_Name Performance Evaluation.docx** document to your record as well as the photo. Close the table.

f. Open the **Your_Name Agents form** in Layout view. Click any white area in the form's background to activate the detail area of the form. Click **Add Existing Fields** in the Controls group on the Format tab.

The Field List pane opens.

g. Double-click the **RelatedFiles** field to add it to the form.

The field adds to the bottom of the form and shows the attached picture as a thumbnail under the other fields. You want the picture control moved to the left of the other fields and enlarged.

TROUBLESHOOTING: If your field adds elsewhere on the form, ignore its position for now. The next steps tell you how to ungroup and move the control to the necessary position.

h. Click **Remove** in the Control Layout group on the Arrange tab to ungroup the RelatedFields control from the other fields.

i. Position the mouse pointer over the picture. It will change shape to the four-headed move arrow shape. Click and drag the control and text box up and left. Click the Photo and Related Files text box to select it. Drag it down to position it below the photo control.

j. Move your mouse over a corner of the Attachment control. When the pointer shape changes to the double-headed diagonal arrow, make the control larger (see Figure 8.15 for approximate size and layout position).

k. Click **View** in the Views group on the Home tab to change to Form view. Use the Record selector arrow to advance to record 2, Kia Hart's record.

This record has two attachments. The Word file displays as an icon.

l. Double-click the **Word icon** to launch the Attachments dialog box. Click **Open**. Read to find Kia's overall rating. Close the Word file. Click **OK** in the Attachments dialog box.

m. Change the *Performance Review* to match the memo. Click the **Attachment** control to activate the mini-toolbar. Click the **green arrow** to display the next attachment.

n. Advance to the next record by clicking the **Next Record** navigation button. Use Steps 5l and 5m to match your performance review to the memo and display the picture. With the picture displayed, capture a screenshot by pressing **PrntScrn**. Paste the screenshot in the Word document *chap8_ho1_realestate_solution.docx*. Save, print, and close the Word document.

o. Close the form. Back up the database and name the backup **chap8_ho1_realestate_solution.accdb**. Close the file and exit Access if you do not want to continue with the next exercise at this time.

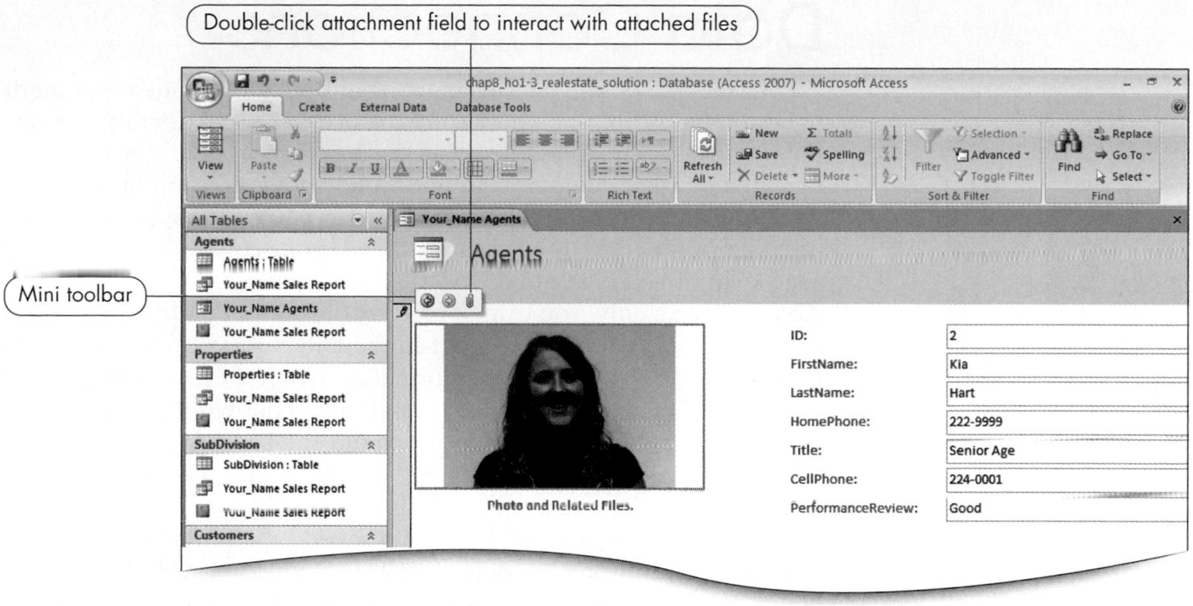

Double-click attachment field to interact with attached files

Mini toolbar

Figure 8.15 Attachment Field in a Form

Data Connections

HTML serves not only as the language of the Internet but also a method of exchanging data that is not limited by software licenses. Occasionally, you will need to share data stored in an Access database with someone who does not have the program installed on their computer. For example, a coworker might need to review the sales data while on vacation and uses an Internet café to examine the report. As long as the café computers have a browser installed, your coworker can examine the data you send them if you create an HTML file. Access permits creation of an HTML file from Access objects only. You cannot convert the entire database into HTML, but you can convert individual objects stored in the database to HTML. Once the conversion is complete, you may share the information with others by publishing it on a Web site or by attaching it to an e-mail and sending it. Following an export, the HTML version of the object is no longer connected to the database. Any changes made to the object will not update the HTML file, nor will the relationships to other database objects be affected.

In this section, you will examine several methods of data exchange, including exporting and importing objects as HTML files, as XML data, and as Excel workbooks. You will also learn about saving the export (or import) steps to facilitate regular data exchanges.

Exporting Database Objects as HTML Files

You may need to create HTML files from Access objects for different uses. If you need to provide data to a vacationing coworker, you may do so using an HTML file. If you need to publish an Access object to a Web site, you can export it as an HTML file and then upload it to a Web server. Access gives you the options of retaining the formatting in the source file or using a template (stored formatting instructions) so the exported data match the rest of the Web site's design. Depending on the type of object from the database you need to export, you will use different Access views to launch the export process. You may export a form or report by first opening the object in Form, Report, or Layout view. When you need to export a table or query, open the object in Datasheet view. After opening the source object, click More in the Export group on the External data tab, then select HTML Document from the list. Figure 8.16 shows a report open in Layout view ready to export. The Export – HTML Document dialog box opens (see Figure 8.17). You need to specify the export destination and options. Here the option to export with formatting and layout and the options to open the exported file are selected. The next dialog box asks you to select output options. If you want to publish this report to a Web site designed with a template, select the appropriate template by selecting the browse option (see Figure 8.18). Because you want to preserve the formatting in the source report, select the Default encoding option. Figure 8.19 shows the export opened in Internet Explorer 7.

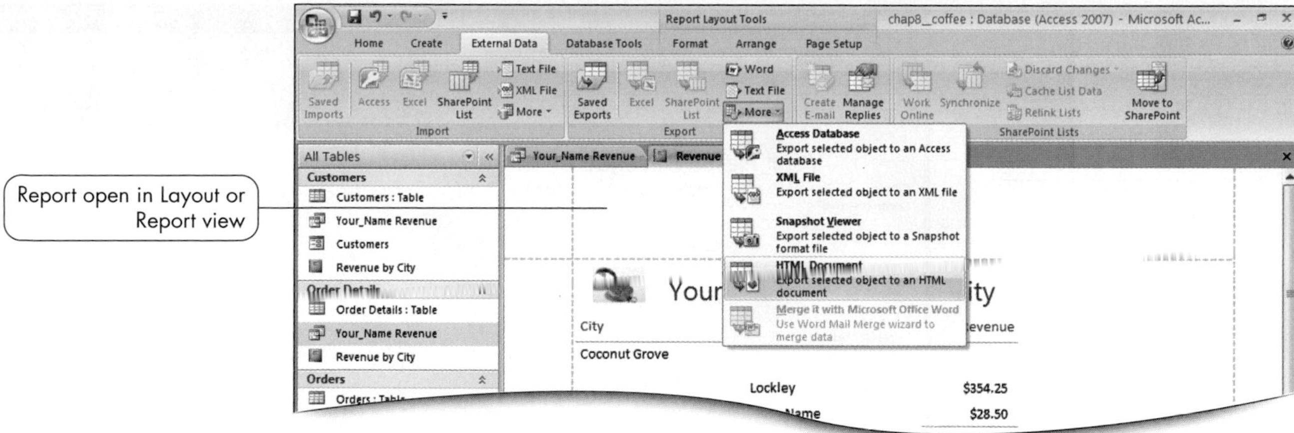

Figure 8.16 Export More Options

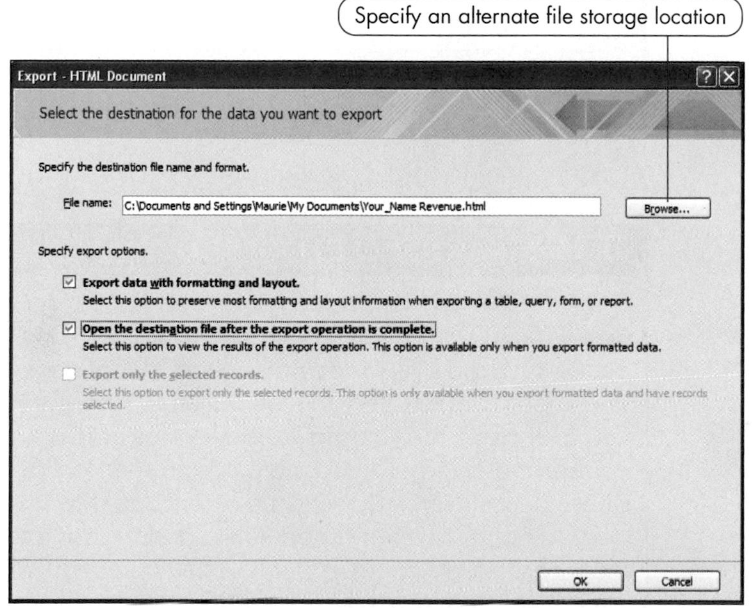

Figure 8.17 Export – HTML Document Dialog Box

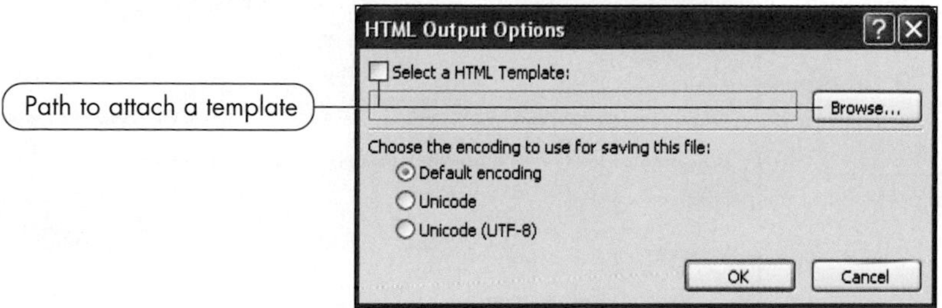

Figure 8.18 Encoding Options

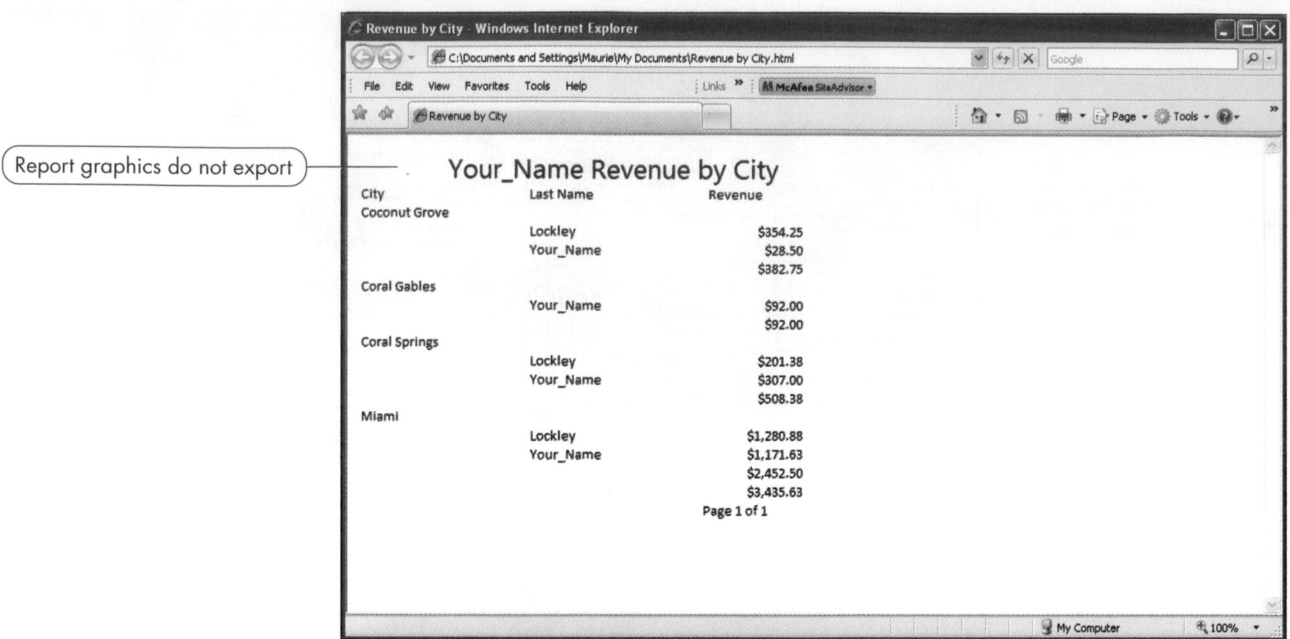

Figure 8.19 Exported Report Open in Browser

TIP Saving Export or Import Steps

Some data exports and imports between Access and other applications occur regularly. You might receive weekly sales data from an Excel user or publish a price list on the Web site every Friday afternoon. In that case, the final screen of the Export and Import Wizard offers you the option to save the Export (Import) Steps. Because you may have many data exchanges as part of the routine database maintenance and update, Access provides a method of saving your export or import steps. The last dialog box offers a check box to indicate that you need to save the steps, a name for the procedure file and a description of the event. Additionally, the wizard will (if you have Outlook 2007 installed) create a task in Outlook that will remind you that it is time to repeat the operation. Figure 8.20 shows the options selected to repeat the Sales by City report data export the next time it is needed.

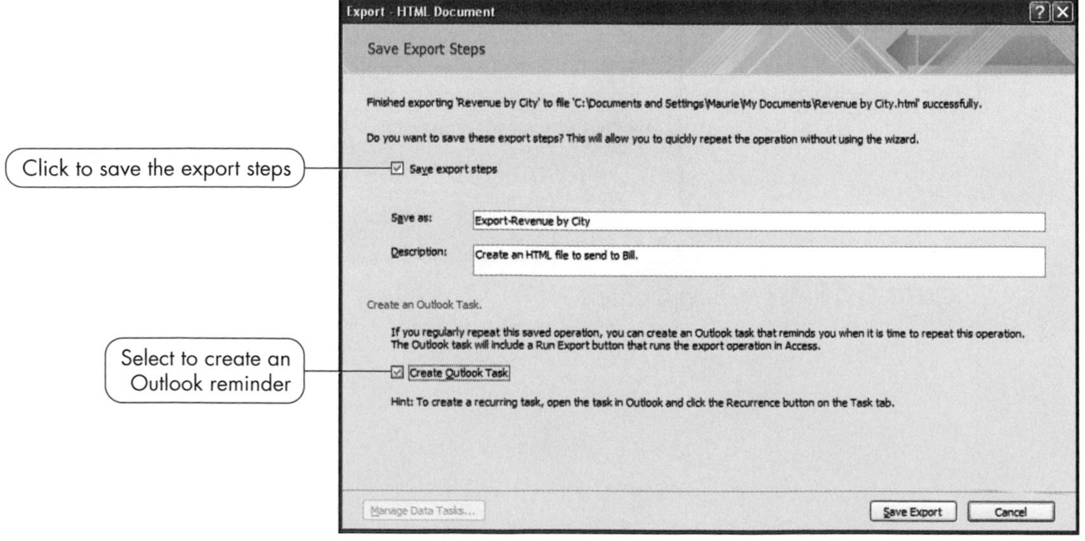

Figure 8.20 Saved Export or Import Steps

Importing or Linking to HTML Files

Data needed by your organization may be published on the Internet, extranet, or intranet in an HTML document. You need to exercise caution when using other people's data. It may be copyright protected, and unauthorized use may result in litigation. Many federal and state government agencies publish data to the Web as a service. These data may be imported or linked to an Access database either directly from the Web site or by using a slightly more circular method by using Excel as an intermediary. For example, the U.S. Department of Agriculture publishes data describing food and nutrition, invasive plants and insect populations, and the most insured crops. The Bureaus of the Census and Labor Statistics publish data about people and communities in the form of the Current Population Survey (CPS). These data are used by government policymakers and legislators and for planning and evaluating government programs. They are also used by the press, students, academics, and the general public. For example, the March Supplement of the CPS publishes data about total money income by race, Hispanic origin, sex, and work experience. Because these data are in the public domain, you may link to or import them to your Access databases.

TIP Copyright Data

Most Web sites are copyrighted, legally protected content. It is against the law for you to link to them or copy and paste the contents without obtaining the site owner's permission. Web sites from your church, your favorite restaurant, your dream car, and your favorite vacation planner are all privately owned and copyrighted Web sites. You cannot legally use or link to materials published there. If you do, the site owner may bring suit against you for damages. Some of these suit awards are substantial. If you ask the owners' permission to use the information on their sites, they will typically give you permission. You may link to or copy the material. Courtesy and copyright law requires that you ask the site owners first.

If you link to the data, you will need to instruct Access to follow the link and collect the most recent information each time the table is opened. In the Navigation pane, right-click the linked table and select the Linked Table Manager from the menu. Select the table or tables that need updating and click OK in the Linked Table Manager dialog box and in the successful update message box. Close the Linked Table Manager dialog box and open the table.

Figure 8.21 displays a USDA Web page from http://www.rma.usda.gov/news/2007/03/topten.html. To import these data to an Access file, you must first display and save the source code that generates the Web page. The following instructions work if the browser is Internet Explorer. If you use a different browser, you may need to discover how to make your browser reveal the source code. All browsers have this capability. Click the browser's View menu and select Source from the list. Notepad opens and reveals the underlying HTML code (see Figure 8.22). Save the Notepad file, but type the period and extension to force HTML coding, such as filename.htm. You have created a local file to import. Return to the database and click More in the Import Data group on the External Data tab.

TIP HTML or Excel Imports

Although Access imports HTML relatively easily, sometimes you need to know how to identify the table data by viewing the source code in order to get a "clean" data import. A good workaround is to select the data needed in the Web browser and copy it. Open a blank Excel workbook and paste the copied data into it. If you need to clean the data, it is sometimes easier to do so in Excel than it is in the HTML code. After you clean up the data, save the Excel workbook and use it as the import source for transferring the data to Access. Most governmental data-sharing Web sites include easy-to-use data export to Excel utilities that do the necessary data cleaning automatically before the exported data reach you.

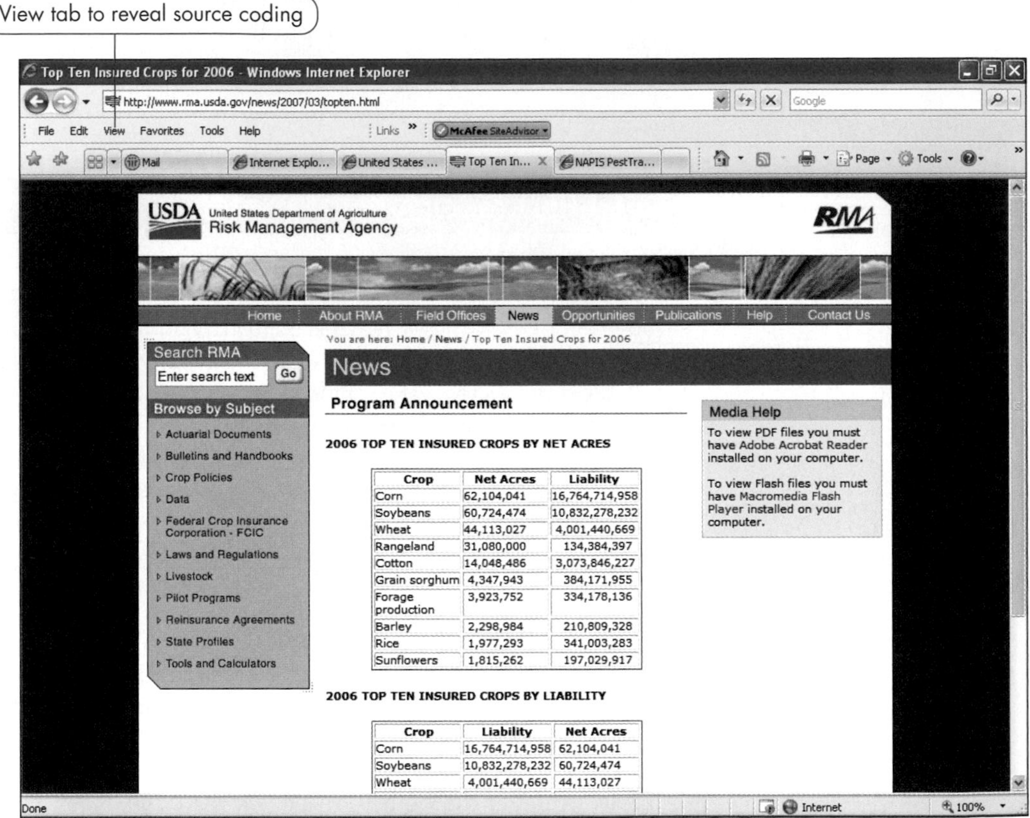

Figure 8.21 Table Data on Web Serves as an Import or Link Source

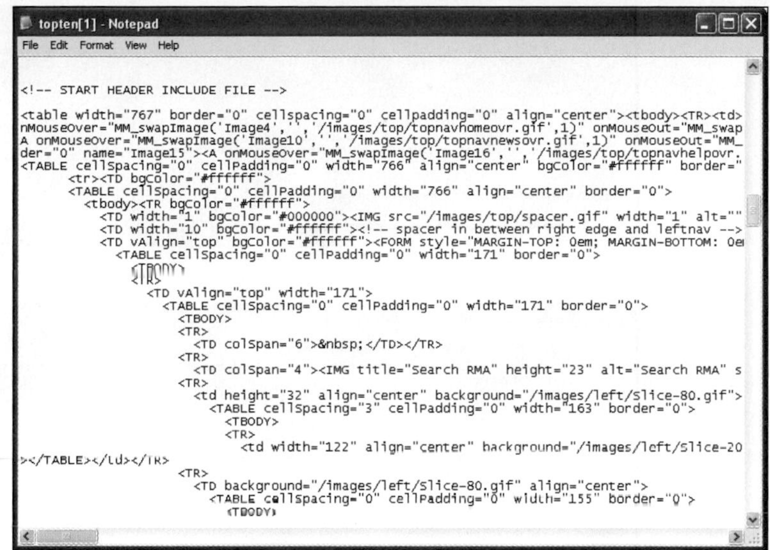

Table data start point

Figure 8.22 Inventory Table Reflecting Price Changes

Importing data from an HTML source is essentially the same as importing Excel data. You launch the Import Wizard and let it guide you through the process. Use the first screen of the Import Wizard to select the .htm file you created with Notepad (see Figure 8.23). This screen offers you the options for Import or Link. When you need to use the data only one time, select Import. If the data on the Web site change frequently and you need to ensure that your database remains current, then you should select Link. When linked, Access will return to the Web site each time the data in that table are used to import the most current information again. After making the import type selections, click OK. If you did not edit the Notepad file to contain only the table data, you will need to preview the different data options Access offers. Figure 8.24 displays the needed data, but many different options had to be viewed before the correct table is displayed. Click Next.

The next wizard screen asks you to identify if the first table row contains column headings. Most Web tables do, so be sure that you select the checkbox before clicking Next. The next screen asks you to identify the data type. The first time you attempt to import, accept the defaults and see what happens. If it does not work, delete the newly created tables and try again using different data type definitions (see Figure 8.25). Depending on the data you import, select your own primary key or let Access select one for you in the next screen of the wizard. Finally, name the table for importation and click Finish.

If the import is for table data stored on a Web site, for example, tariff data that may change relatively often, you may wish to save the import steps. Alternatively, you may link the imported Access table to the data published on the Web in the first screen of the wizard and have Access check for updates automatically. When you complete the Import Wizard, the imported data function within the database in the same fashion as table data created in other ways (see Figure 8.26). You may wish to open the table in design view and adjust the formatting.

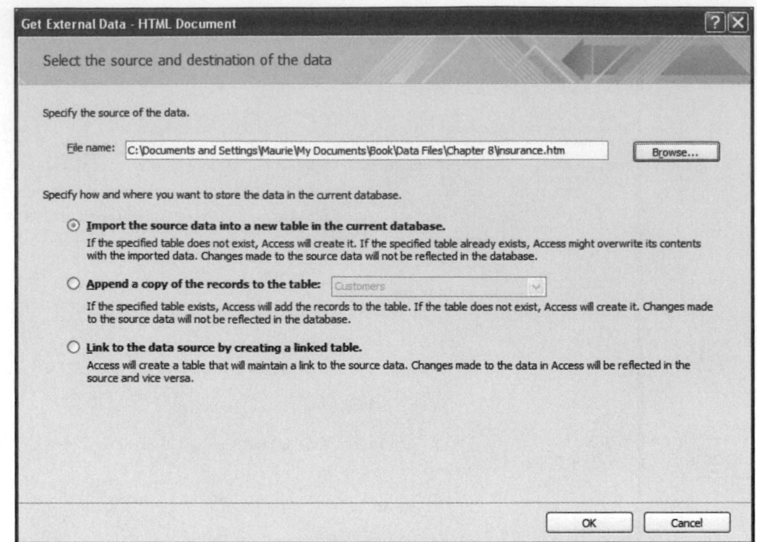

Figure 8.23 Source Identification

Try different table options until you find the needed data

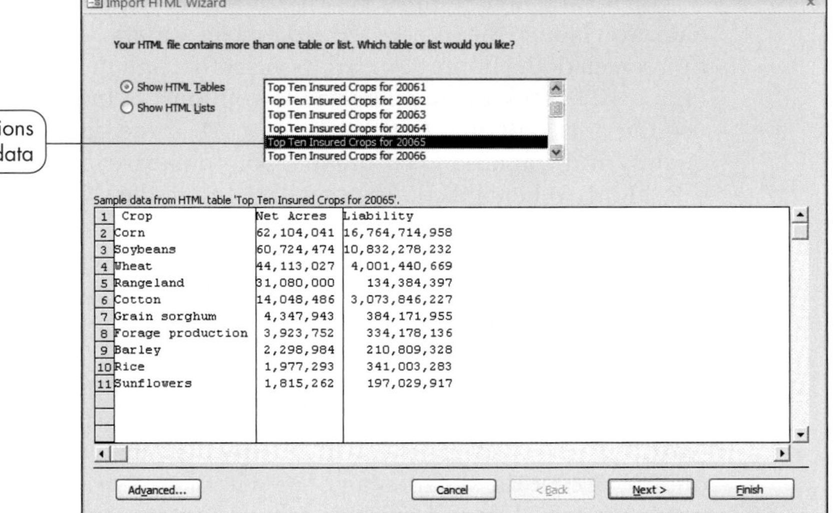

Figure 8.24 Select Appropriate Data

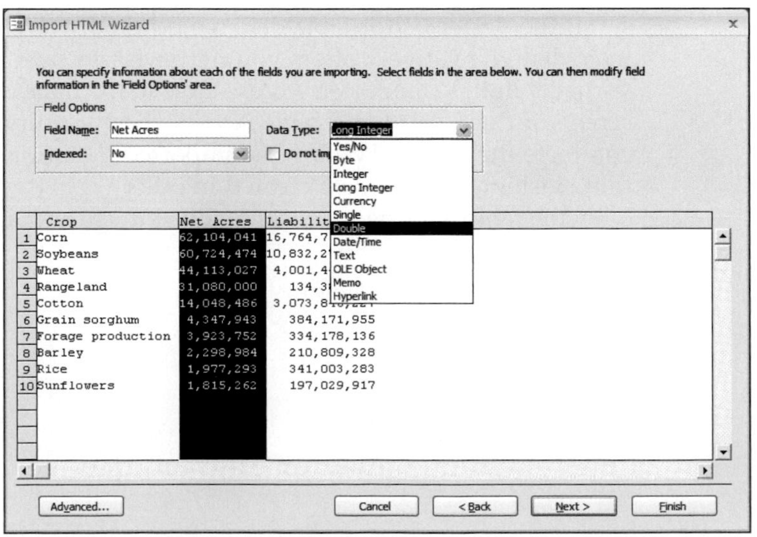

Figure 8.25 Define Data Type

Top Ten Insured Crops for 20065

ID	Crop	Net Acres	Liability	Add New Field
1	Corn	62104041	16764714958	
2	Soybeans	60724474	10832278232	
3	Wheat	44113027	4001440669	
4	Rangeland	31080000	134384397	
5	Cotton	14048486	3073846227	
6	Grain sorghum	4347943	384171955	
7	Forage product	3923752	334178136	
8	Barley	2298984	210809328	
9	Rice	1977293	341003283	
10	Sunflowers	1815262	197029917	
(New)				

Figure 8.26 Imported Table

TIP Numeric Data Type Selection

Sometimes the HTML data imports, but it contains errors. Access will generate a failed import error log table. Open the error log table and examine it. Identify the first field that failed to import correctly. Often, import failures are caused by an incorrectly defined data type. When the field is a numeric one, set the data type to Double in the wizard and the data will probably import correctly. After the import is complete, try redefining to a smaller data definition type.

Sharing XML Data

The eXtensible Markup Language (XML) is another general-purpose language that supports a wide variety of applications. XML and HTML have different purposes. HTML focuses on how things look, whereas XML sticks exclusively to the structure of content. Developers use the XML format when they need to be able to exchange complex data structures across a variety of platforms with dependability and reliability. Access can both receive imports from XML files and create XML files when exporting Access objects. You have learned that importing data from an HTML Web site is sometimes easier if you use Excel to clean up the import before taking it to Access. This also applies to XML data imports. The data used in the following example come from the U.S. Department of Census Current Population Studies and can be found at http://factfinder.census.gov.

Import XML objects into an Access database by using the Import XML File tool in the Import group on the External Data tab. The first screen of the Get External Data — XML File wizard asks you to identify the location of the data source by browsing (see Figure 8.27). After you locate the XML file, click OK. The Import XML dialog box launches. You may use the expand button(s) to view the data structure as shown in Figure 8.28. Because the XML format supports complex data structures, you want to select the Structure and Data option most of the time. Access supports not only XML but also XSD and XSL file structures as exports. An ***XML Schema Definition (XSD)*** describes how to formally describe the data structures within an XML file structure. It makes sure that each element within a file structure conforms to the data definition provided for the structure. For example, if the data were defined as numeric, the XML schema would disallow text entries. An ***Extensible Stylesheet Language (XSL)*** describes how data are presented to the user over the Web. With this you can not only provide the field values but also a descriptive label and format the label to be bold italic. Access enables exports on XML only or XML supported by either the corresponding XLS or XSD files, or both. Figure 8.29 shows the newly imported table. Access offers you the option of saving the import steps for later reuse.

An ***XML Schema Definition (XSD)*** describes how to formally describe the data structures within an XML file structure.

An ***Extensible Stylesheet Language (XSL)*** describes how data are presented to the user over the Web.

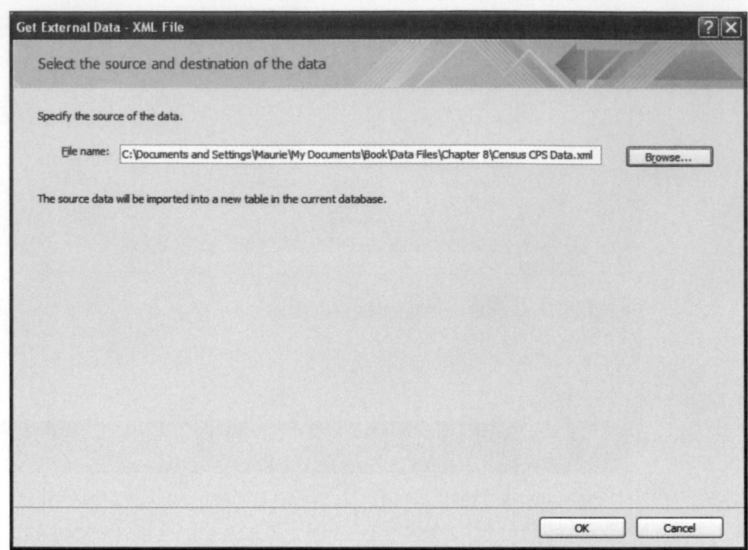

Figure 8.27 Get External Data – XML File Dialog Box

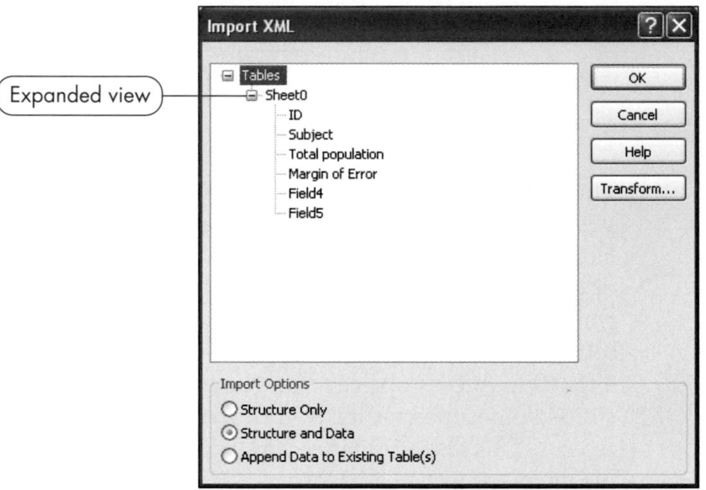

Figure 8.28 Import XML Dialog Box

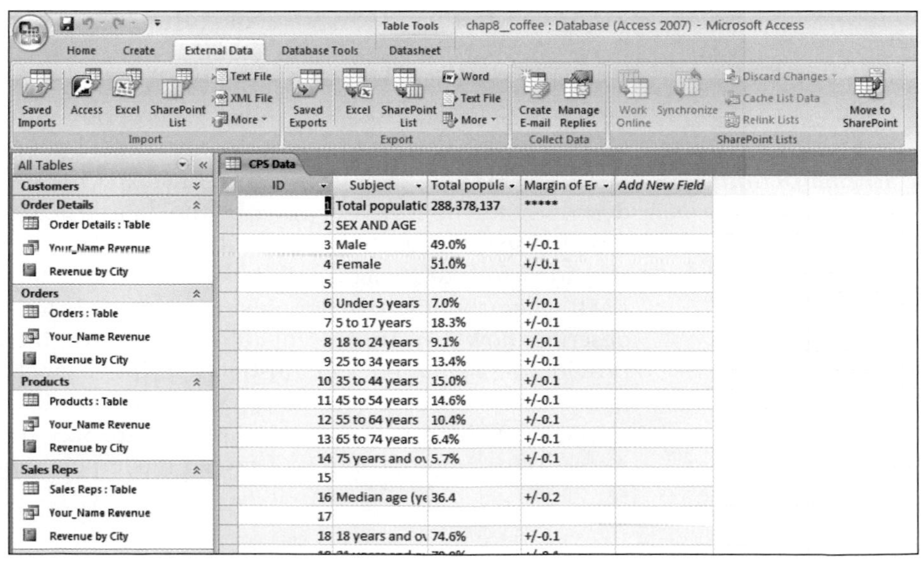

Figure 8.29 Imported Table

Exporting XML objects yields more power and a greater level of sophistication than exporting an object as an HTML file. HTML exports handle table and query data exports without issue. However, more complex object structures tend to confuse the export process. Figure 8.30 shows a grouped, nested, aggregated report that was based on a query using fields from five different tables and containing several calculated fields. In other words, it demonstrates a sophisticated and complex data structure. To export this report as an XML file, select More in the Export group on the External data tab and select XML from the list. This launches the Export Wizard (see Figure 8.31). After you identify the destination file name and location, click OK. The Export XML dialog box launches, as shown in Figure 8.32. Select the appropriate options and click OK. The wizard resumes and asks if you want to save the export steps.

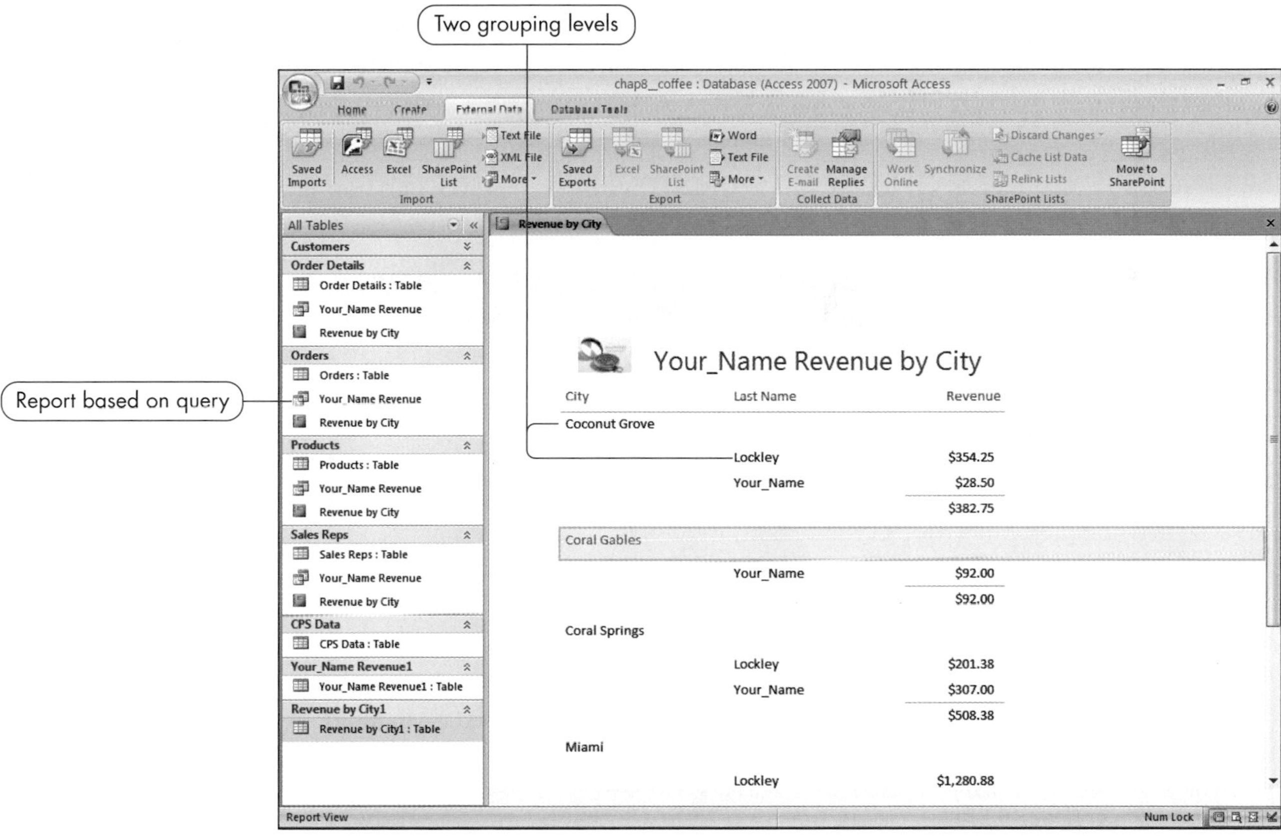

Figure 8.30 Complex Data Structure

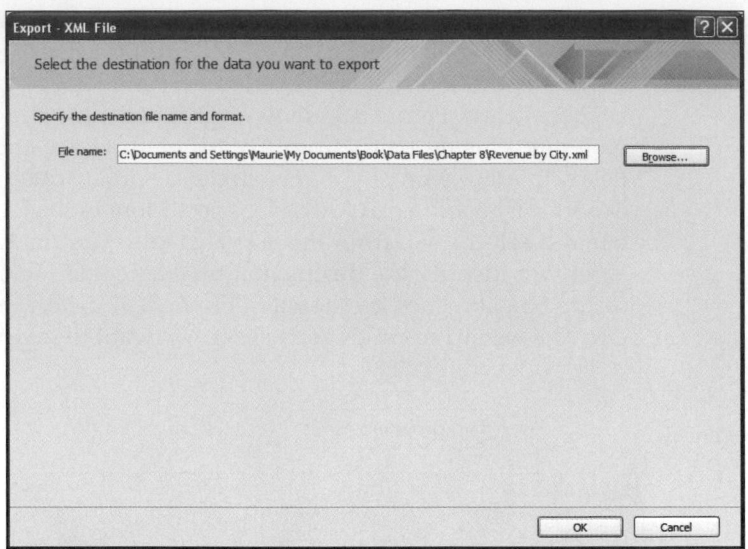

Figure 8.31 Export – XML File Wizard Launch

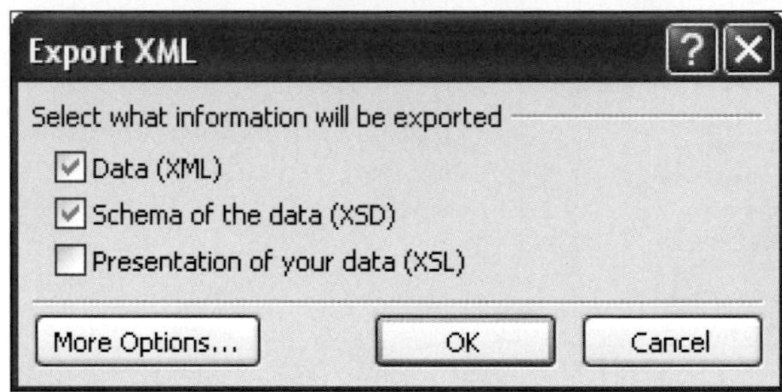

Figure 8.32 XML Export Options

To demonstrate the resulting XML file, you can import it back into Access as a table. Figure 8.33 displays the imported XML table. The XML export and import were able to find the related table records stored in the query that acted as the source for the grouped report, which served as the XML export source. The XML file structure traces through the convoluted data relationships and faithfully recreates them. The data recipients need to re-aggregate and summarize the data, but they at least have the data. If you export the same report as an HTML file and then import it to the database, the resulting table looks like Figure 8.34. HTML simply cannot perform well when the data are complex.

(The XML file structure traces through convoluted data relationships and faithfully recreates them.)

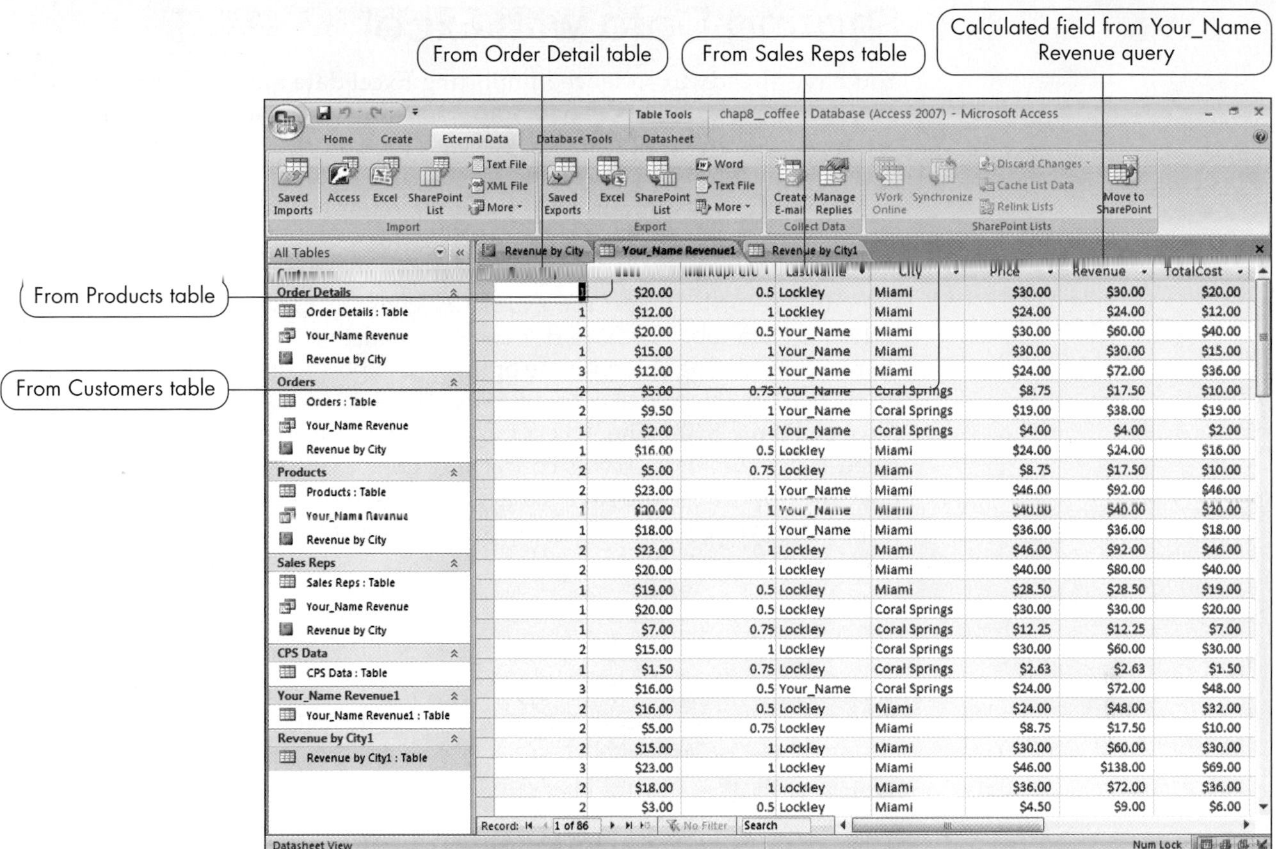

Figure 8.33 Complex Data Structure Survives XML Export

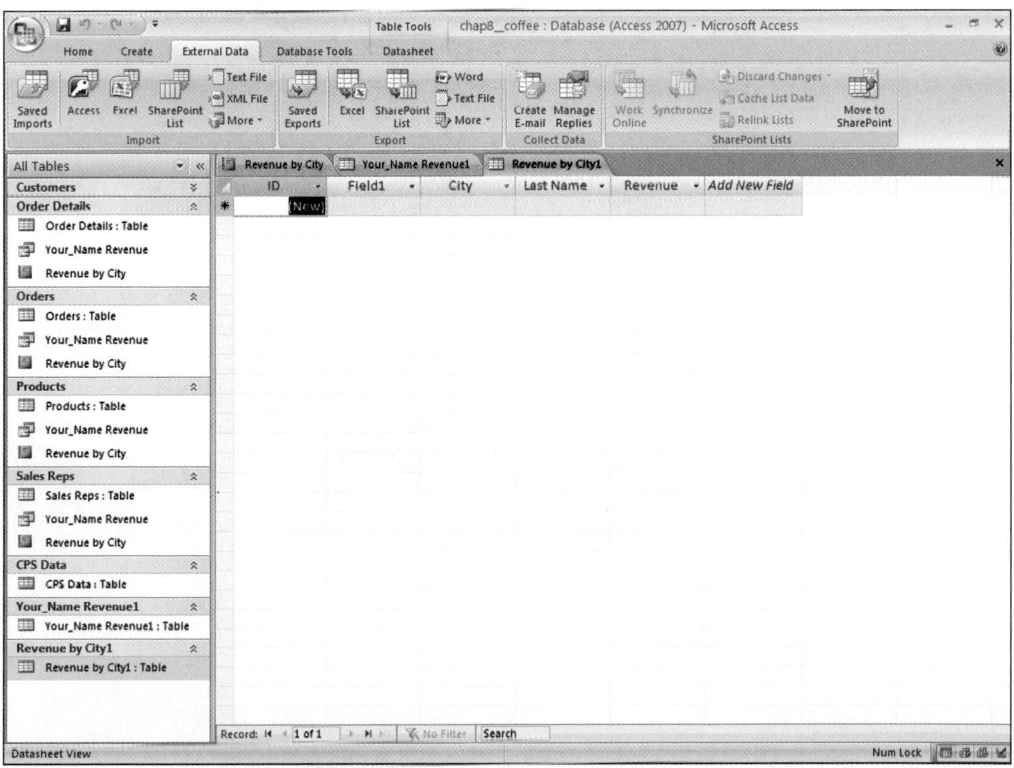

Figure 8.34 Results of HTML Export of Complex Data

Sharing Data with Excel

You have already experienced importing Excel data and converting it to Access. You may easily prepare Access data for export to Excel. The exported results depend on the type of source object within Access you export. If the source is a table that displays relationships with data stored in related tables as shown in Figure 8.35, your exported file will contain only the table data; it will contain none of the links to related data. This figure displays the Customers table with the links to the Orders and Order Detail tables expanded. You will be able to export only parent data, not the child records. Begin the export by clicking Excel in the Export group on the External Data tab. The Export – Excel Spreadsheet dialog box launches. Figure 8.36 displays the dialog box with the options to export formatting and open the file based on the export selected. Access prepares the data for export, exports it, and opens the file (see Figure 8.37). The Access tab on the task bar flashes to remind you that unfinished tasks remain in Access concerning the export. When you return to Access, you have the opportunity to save the export steps. If you want, you can create an Outlook task so that your To Do list prompts you the next time the data need to be updated to Excel (see Figure 8.38).

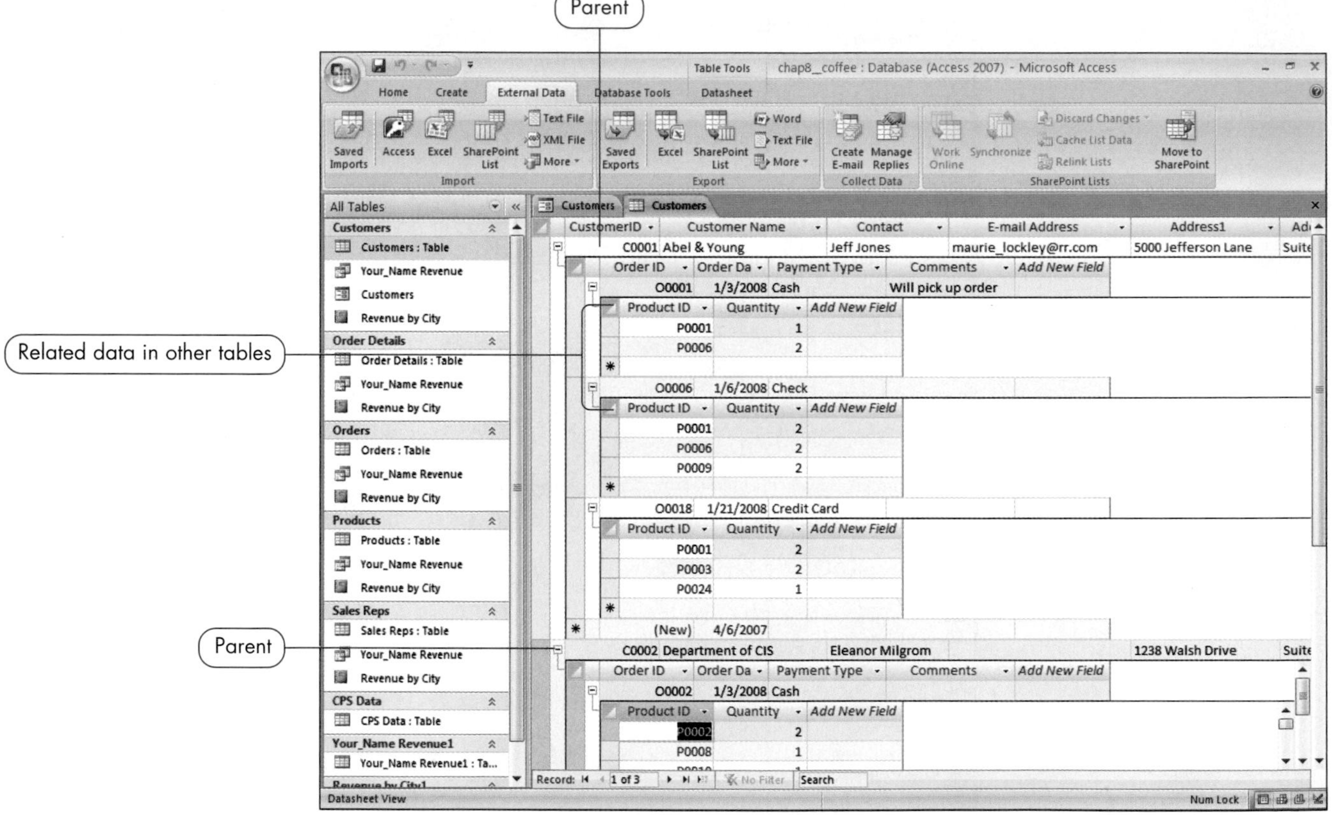

Figure 8.35 Access Table as Export Source

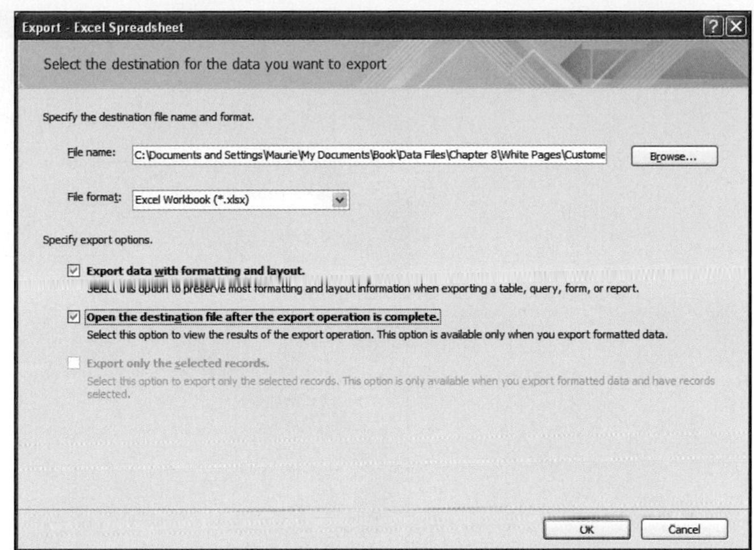

Figure 8.36 Export — Excel Spreadsheet Wizard

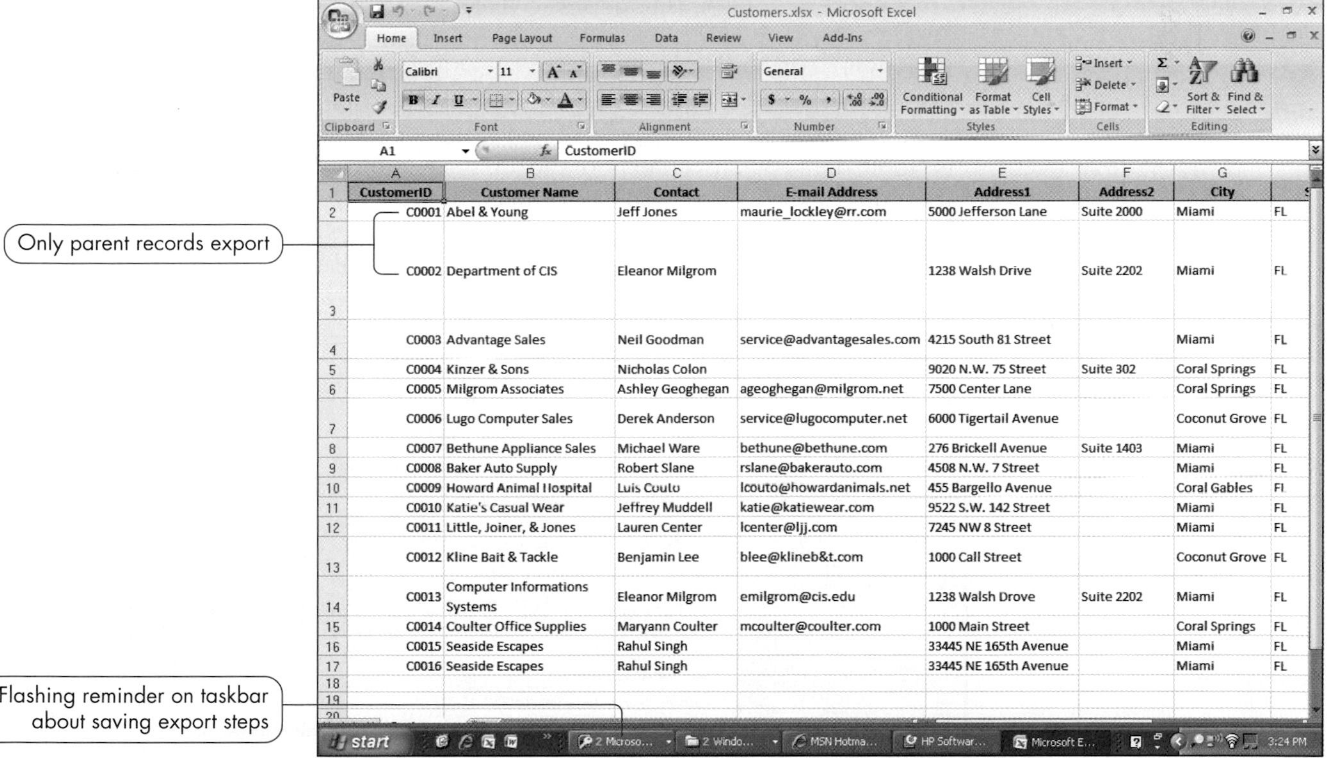

	A	B	C	D	E	F	G	
1	CustomerID	Customer Name	Contact	E-mail Address	Address1	Address2	City	
2	C0001	Abel & Young	Jeff Jones	maurie_lockley@rr.com	5000 Jefferson Lane	Suite 2000	Miami	FL
3	C0002	Department of CIS	Eleanor Milgrom		1238 Walsh Drive	Suite 2202	Miami	FL
4	C0003	Advantage Sales	Neil Goodman	service@advantagesales.com	4215 South 81 Street		Miami	FL
5	C0004	Kinzer & Sons	Nicholas Colon		9020 N.W. 75 Street	Suite 302	Coral Springs	FL
6	C0005	Milgrom Associates	Ashley Geoghegan	ageoghegan@milgrom.net	7500 Center Lane		Coral Springs	FL
7	C0006	Lugo Computer Sales	Derek Anderson	service@lugocomputer.net	6000 Tigertail Avenue		Coconut Grove	FL
8	C0007	Bethune Appliance Sales	Michael Ware	bethune@bethune.com	276 Brickell Avenue	Suite 1403	Miami	FL
9	C0008	Baker Auto Supply	Robert Slane	rslane@bakerauto.com	4508 N.W. 7 Street		Miami	FL
10	C0009	Howard Animal Hospital	Luis Couto	lcouto@howardanimals.net	455 Bargello Avenue		Coral Gables	FL
11	C0010	Katie's Casual Wear	Jeffrey Muddell	katie@katiewear.com	9522 S.W. 142 Street		Miami	FL
12	C0011	Little, Joiner, & Jones	Lauren Center	lcenter@ljj.com	7245 NW 8 Street		Miami	FL
13	C0012	Kline Bait & Tackle	Benjamin Lee	blee@klineb&t.com	1000 Call Street		Coconut Grove	FL
14	C0013	Computer Informations Systems	Eleanor Milgrom	emilgrom@cis.edu	1238 Walsh Drove	Suite 2202	Miami	FL
15	C0014	Coulter Office Supplies	Maryann Coulter	mcoulter@coulter.com	1000 Main Street		Coral Springs	FL
16	C0015	Seaside Escapes	Rahul Singh		33445 NE 165th Avenue		Miami	FL
17	C0016	Seaside Escapes	Rahul Singh		33445 NE 165th Avenue		Miami	FL

Figure 8.37 Exported Data in Excel

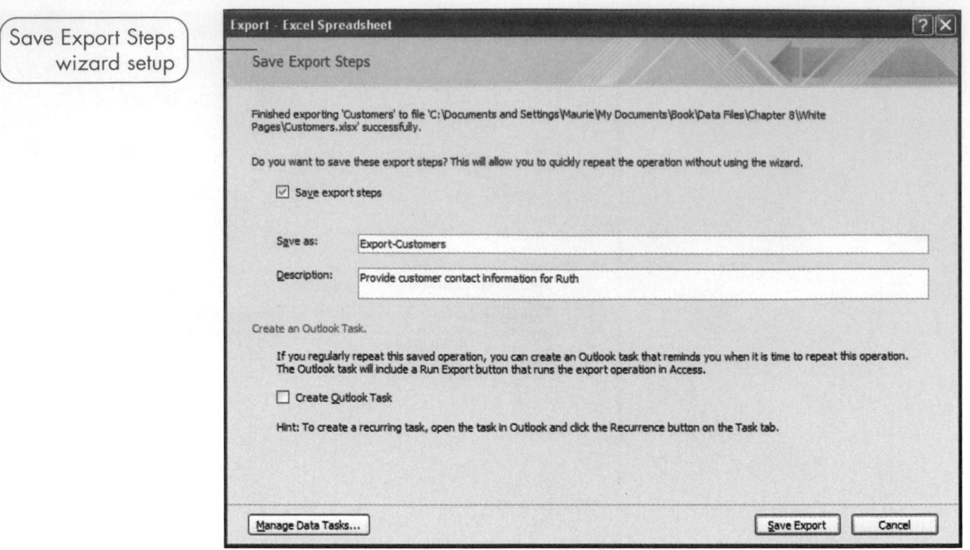

Figure 8.38 Save and Name the Export to Excel

Exporting tables and queries to Excel results in a spreadsheet containing only parent records. When you export forms and reports from Access to Excel, most of the time the results of the export revert to the underlying source data within Access. For example, if you have a grouped report in Access that uses a query as its source, the resulting data export to Excel will match the query formatting. Most forms are based on table data. When you export a form, the resulting Excel worksheet resembles the table data source more than the form. Figure 8.39 displays an Access form that has a hyperlinked field and an attachment field. It also contains a subform displaying related records from the Order ID and Product ID tables.

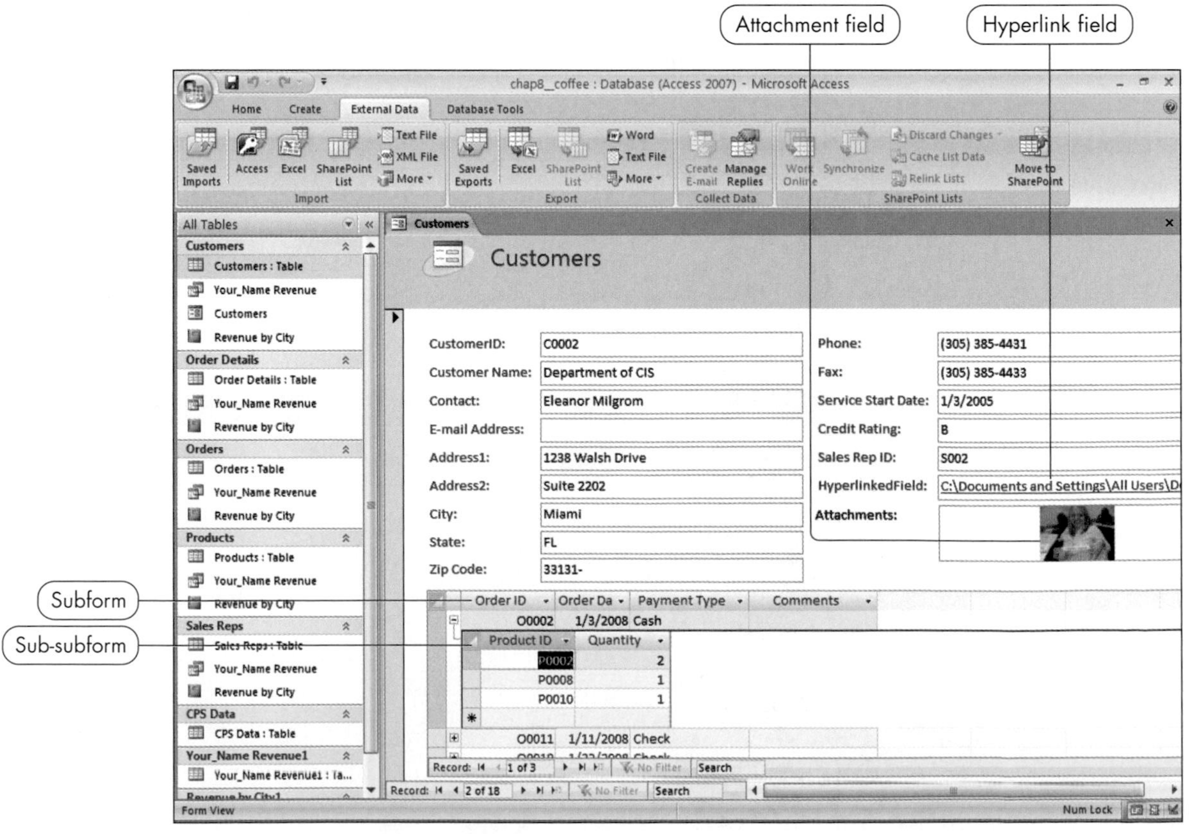

Figure 8.39 Access Form and Subform with Complex Data Types

TIP Exporting to Excel Reasons

The reason most people export data to Excel is to enable users to use Excel's analysis, charting, and other capabilities. Consequently, it is appropriate that exported spreadsheets contain only the raw records.

Examine the resulting export shown in Figure 8.40 (some columns were hidden to highlight the appropriate fields). The form data revert to a table format. The e-mail and hyperlinked fields export without issue because they are data types supported by Excel. However, the attachment field displays only the number of attachments and the green triangle indicates an error. When you click the error indicator in Excel, the message cryptically indicates that a number has been stored as text. The underlying issue is that Excel has no facility to support an attachment field. Excel guessed at what was needed in this column, but it guessed incorrectly. The hidden columns containing more ordinary data exported without problem. Although not illustrated, exporting a complex report containing grouping levels and hidden details yields a similar result. Excel reverts to the underlying query data and eliminates grouping and aggregating statistics.

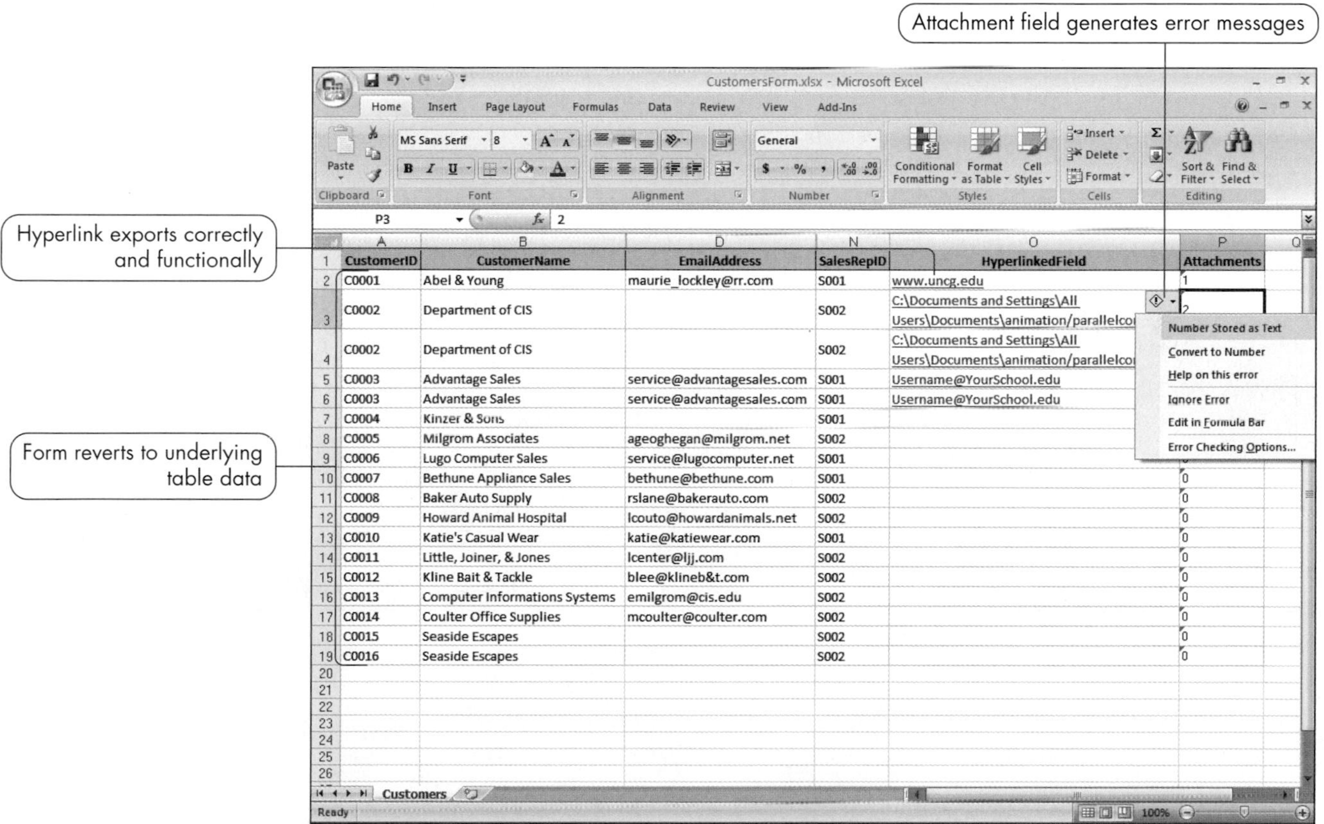

Figure 8.40 Exported Form Data in Excel

In the next hands-on exercise, you will work with importing and exporting data in many forms: HTML, XML, and Excel.

File Sharing Summary | Reference

File Type	Extension	Connections with Access
Word	.docx .doc	• Copy and paste contents into a Memo field • Copy a Word table and paste into a new Access table • Use Access table or query data as a source for a Word mail merge • Copy an Access report from Design view and paste into a new Word file. • Export an Access object as a Word file. This creates an .rtf file. You may open the .rtf in Word and use Save As to convert the file to a .doc or .docx format. • Attach this file type to an attachment field in a table and use it in Access forms and reports.
Text	.txt .rtf	• You may view the source code of a Web page, copy the code, and paste it into a text file. Then you may use the import HTML tool to convert the txt file into an Access table. • Export an Access object as a Word file. This creates an .rtf file. You may open the .rtf in Word and use Save As to convert the file to a .doc or .docx format. • Text files also contain comma or tab delimited data which may be imported to an Access table using the Import Other tool. • Copy and paste contents into a Memo field. • Attach this file type to an attachment field in a table and use it in Access forms and reports.
Excel	.xlsx .xls	• Import Excel files using the Import from Excel tool. • Export Excel files using the Export to Excel tool. • Copy and paste Access table, query, or report (in Report view) data from Access to Excel. • Save the import or export steps for frequently occurring procedures. • Attach this file type to an attachment field in a table and use it in Access forms and reports.
HyperText Markup Language	.html .xhtml	• If you need to publish an Access object to a Web site, you can export it as an HTML file and then upload it to a Web server. • You may also export Access objects as HTML files to facilitate data sharing with someone who does not have a license to Microsoft Office. • Access can use HTML files in two ways—importing and linking. Using the Import HTML tool converts the data found on the web to an Access table. Linking the data to the Web site permits the Access user to revisit the Web site and download the most current data. Often it is easier to create a text file containing only the table data from the Web site. You may clean the text data using a text editor or Excel to facilitate data conversion.
eXtensible Markup Language	.xml .xsd .xsl	• Access may use .xml files as data sources through the Import XML tool. • Access supports not only XML but also XSD and XSL file structures as exports. • An .xsd (XML Schema Definition) describes how to formally describe the data structures within an XML file structure. It makes sure that each element within a file structure conforms to the data definition provided for the structure. • An XSL (Extensible Stylesheet Language) describes how data are presented to the user over the Web.

Hands-On Exercises

2 | Share Data

Skills covered: 1. Export Objects as HTML Files **2.** Import and Link to an HTML File **3.** Share XML Data and Import from Access **4.** Export Access Data to Excel

Step 1 Export Objects as HTML Files

Refer to Figure 8.41 as you complete Step 1.

a. Open the *chap8_ho1-2_realestate_solution* file, if necessary, and click **Options** on the Security Warning toolbar. Then click the **Enable this content option** in the Microsoft Office Security Options dialog box and click **OK**.

   TROUBLESHOOTING: If you create unrecoverable errors while completing this hands-on exercise, you can delete the *chap8_ho1-2_realestate_solution* file, copy the *chap8_ho1_realestate_solution* backup database you created at the end of the first hands-on exercise, and open the copy of the backup database to start the second hands-on exercise again.

b. Open the **SubDivision table** in Datasheet view. Click **More** in the Export group on the External data tab and select **HTML Document**.

   The Export — HTML Document Wizard launches.

c. Click **Browse** and select your solutions folder. Click in the **File name** box and type **chap8_ho2_realestate_solution.html**. Click **Save**.

   Now that you have told Access where to save the export, the export options become available for your use.

d. Check the **Export data with formatting and layout** and **Open the destination file after the export operation is complete** options. Click **OK**.

   You do not need to use a Web template because these data will be e-mailed as an attachment to a customer without MS Office installed on their computer.

e. Check to make sure that the Default encoding option is selected and click **OK**.

   A browser launches and the file displays in the browser window as an HTML table.

   TROUBLESHOOTING: You may not be permitted full access to the browser window until you return to Access and complete the export operation.

f. Click the flashing **Access button** on the taskbar to return to Access. You do not need to save these export steps. Click **Close**.

g. Use the taskbar to return to the browser window. Click some of the hyperlinks to ensure that they still function after the export. You may need to use the browser's back button to return to the SubDivision table.

h. Save and close the HTML file. Close the SubDivision table.

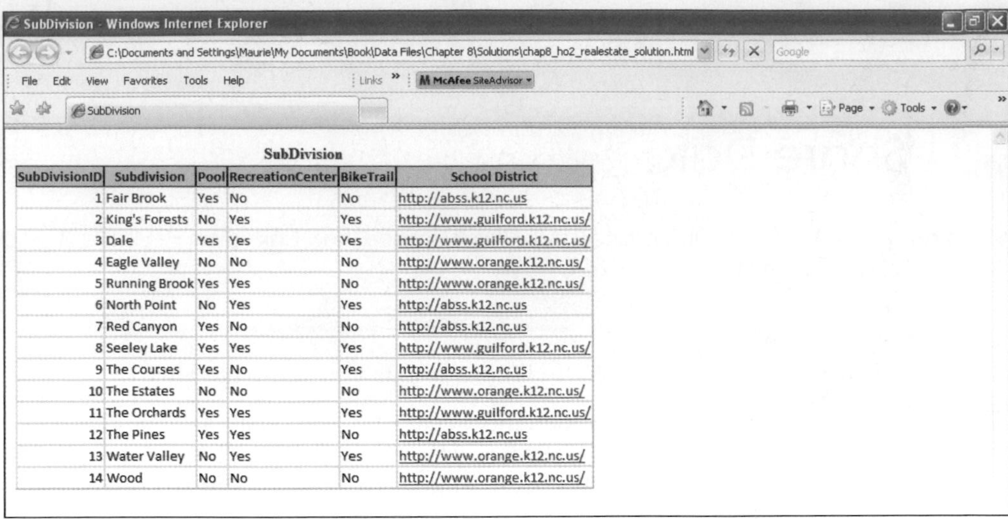

SubDivision

SubDivisionID	Subdivision	Pool	RecreationCenter	BikeTrail	School District
1	Fair Brook	Yes	No	No	http://abss.k12.nc.us
2	King's Forests	No	Yes	Yes	http://www.guilford.k12.nc.us/
3	Dale	Yes	Yes	Yes	http://www.guilford.k12.nc.us/
4	Eagle Valley	No	No	No	http://www.orange.k12.nc.us/
5	Running Brook	Yes	Yes	No	http://www.orange.k12.nc.us/
6	North Point	No	Yes	Yes	http://abss.k12.nc.us
7	Red Canyon	Yes	No	No	http://abss.k12.nc.us
8	Seeley Lake	Yes	Yes	Yes	http://www.guilford.k12.nc.us/
9	The Courses	Yes	No	Yes	http://abss.k12.nc.us
10	The Estates	No	No	No	http://www.orange.k12.nc.us/
11	The Orchards	Yes	Yes	Yes	http://www.guilford.k12.nc.us/
12	The Pines	Yes	Yes	No	http://abss.k12.nc.us
13	Water Valley	No	Yes	Yes	http://www.orange.k12.nc.us/
14	Wood	No	No	No	http://www.orange.k12.nc.us/

Figure 8.41 HTML Export Results

Step 2
Import and Link to an HTML File

Refer to Figure 8.42 as you complete Step 2.

a. Click **More** in the Import group on the External Data tab. Select **HTML Document**.

The Get External Data – HTML Document wizard launches. You need to create a link to these data that will update as the Web site updates. These data come from the U.S. Department of Census, Health and Human Services Current Population Survey: www.census.gov.hhes/www/income05/statemhi3.html.

b. Click the **Link to the data source by creating a linked table** option. Browse to and select the file named **chap8_ho2_income.htm**. Click **Open**. Click **OK**.

The Link HTML Wizard opens to the first screen. These data contain a header row.

c. Click the **First Row Contains Column Headings check box** in the wizard.

The title row contains parentheses. Access tells you that they will be removed in a warning box.

d. Read the warning and click **OK**. Click **Next**.

The data display and you may identify the data types. The State column imported as a text field. You do not need to change it.

e. Click the **Median Income** column heading. Click the **Data Type drop-down arrow** and select **Double**. Click the **Standard error** column heading and change it to a **Double** data type. Change all of the remaining data fields to **Double**. You must scroll to see them all.

The final field that you need to import is headed *Lower than state of interest*. A number of fields are so narrow that they look like stripes. You do not need to import them.

f. Click the unnecessary fields to the right of the *Lower than State of interest* field one at a time and click the **Do not import field check box**. Click **Next**. Name the Linked Table *Income*. Click **Finish**. Read the message and click **OK**.

Access gives you a message indicating that it has completed the linked import.

g. Open the Income table in Datasheet view. Press **PrntScrn** to capture a screenshot. Switch to Word. In a new document, type your name and section number. Click **Paste** and press **Enter**. Save the Word document as **chap8_ho2_realestate_solution.docx**. Close the table.

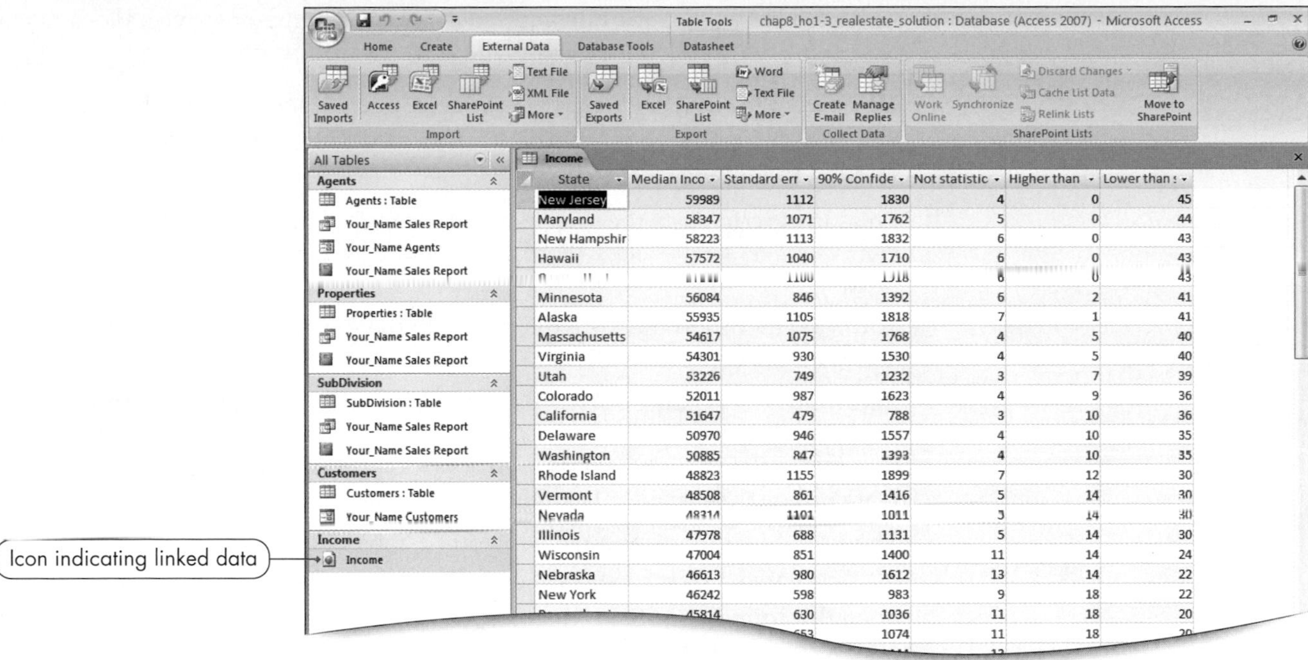

Figure 8.42 Linked HTML Data

Step 3
Share XML Data and Import from Access

Refer to Figure 8.43 as you complete Step 3.

a. Click **Access** in the Import group on the External Data tab. Make sure the **Import tables, queries, forms, reports, macros, and modules into the current database** option is selected. Click **Browse**. Select **chap8_ho2_realestate.accdb**, click **Open** in the File Open dialog box, and click **OK** in the Get External Data – Access Database dialog box.

A coworker created a complex nested report in a backup copy of the database to test it. After testing, you decide that it is a good report and wish to import it to the production copy of the database.

b. Click the **Reports tab** in the Import Objects dialog box and select **Your_Name Sales Report Qtr 3 and 4**. Click the **Options** button. Make sure that **Relationships** is selected in the *Imports* section. Click **OK**. You do not need to save the import steps. Click **Close**.

The new report imports into the database and is ready to use.

c. Rename the *Your_Name Sales Report Qtr 3 and 4* report with your name. Open it in Layout view. Open the Property Sheet Pane. Click the **Data tab**. Change the Data Source Property from *Your_name* to your actual name. Click the report title control and edit it to display your name**.** Save and close the report.

d. Click **More** in the Export group on the External Data tab. Select **XML File** from the list.

e. Click **Browse** to your solutions folder. Name the file **chap8_ho2_realestate_solution.xml**. Click **Save** and click **OK**.

The Export XML dialog box opens.

f. Check **Data (XML)** and click **OK**. Click **Close** without saving the export steps.

You wonder what the exported report data look like, so you open them in a browser to examine the results.

g. Launch a browser. Click **File** and select **Open**. You may receive a blocked content security message. If you do, **Allow Blocked Content**.

TROUBLESHOOTING: If you have trouble locating the file from within the browser, you can navigate to the folder in a file management program like Windows Explorer and double-click it to open.

h. Press **PrntScrn**. Paste the screenshot at the end of the previously created *chap8_ho2_realestate_solution.docx* Word document. Save the Word document. Close the browser.

You want to import the XML file back into the Access file to see how Access interacts with the complex XML data structures.

i. Return to Access. Click **XML File** in the Import group on the External Data tab. Click **Browse**. Navigate to the *chap8_ho2_realestate_solution.xml* file in your production folder. Select it and click **Open**. Click **OK**. Make sure that the **Structure and Data** option is selected. Click **OK**. Click **Close** without saving the import steps.

The XML file imports as a table to your database.

j. Open the **Your_Name Sales Report1 table** and examine it. You may want to open the Your_Name Sales Report Qtr 3 and 4 report and compare the source and output documents. Return to the Your_Name Sales Report1 table. Press **PrntScrn**. Paste the screenshot at the end of the previously created *chap8_ho2_realestate_solution.docx* Word document. Save the Word document. Return to Access and close the table.

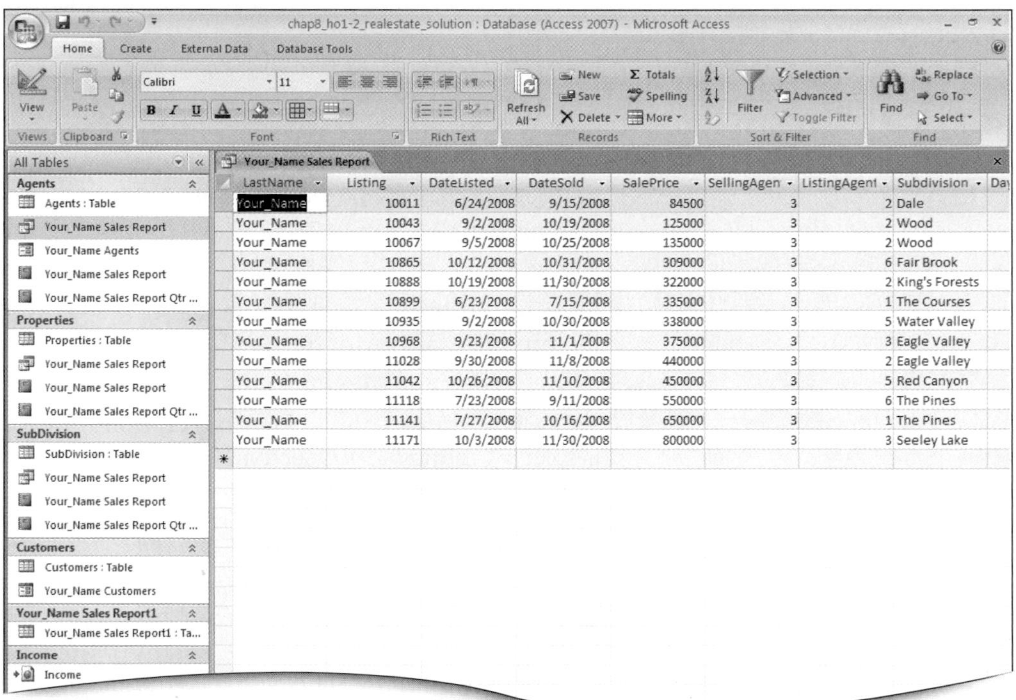

Figure 8.43 Results of Importing XML Data

Step 4
Export Access Data to Excel

Refer to Figure 8.44 as you complete Step 4.

a. Open the **Agents table** in Datasheet view. Click **Excel** in the Export group on the External Data tab.

You need to create an Excel file containing the contact information for all of the agents to share with an Excel user in the office.

b. Select the **Export data with formatting and layout** option. Select the **Open the destination file after the export operation is complete** option. Click **Browse** and navigate to the folder containing your solution files.

c. Name the file **chap8_ho2_agents_solution.xlsx**. Click **Save**. Click **OK**.

You specified the location and name for the exported file. After a pause for Excel to launch and the file to open, the newly exported file opens in Excel. The Access tab on the taskbar flashes to remind you that you have unfinished tasks in Access.

d. Click the **Access button** on the taskbar to return to Access. Click the **Save Export Steps check box**. The file name should display in the Save as box. Type **Agent contact information for Juan to use at home** in the Description box. Click **Save Export**.

You notice that the Agents table incorrectly stores your old cell phone number. You need to update the data.

e. Click the **CellPhone** field in the third record and edit the number to be **224-0022**. Click into a different record to save the data edit. Close the table.

Your number is stored correctly in Access, but you exported the data before making the edit.

f. Use the taskbar to examine the data in Excel. Your cell phone number there is still the old one. Close the Excel workbook. Return to Access. Click **Saved Exports** in the Export group on the External Data tab. Click **Run** in the Manage Data Tasks Wizard. Click **Yes** in the warning box asking if you want to update the existing file. Click **Yes** in the second warning box.

The Manage Data Tasks wizard exports the data to the same Excel file and opens the workbook. Your cell phone should now display the 224-0022 number. Notice that the attachment field failed to export correctly because Excel does not support that file type.

g. Click the flashing **Access button** on the taskbar. Click **OK** in the information box telling you that the export is finished. Return to Access. Capture a screenshot by pressing **PrntScrn**. Paste your screenshot at the end of the Word document created in the previous exercises, *chap8_ho2_realestate_solution.docx*. Save and close the Word document.

TROUBLESHOOTING: You cannot update an existing Excel workbook if the file is open. If you cannot run the export utility, make sure the Excel workbook is closed and try again.

h. Return to Access. Click on the message window that tells you the table was exported. Close the Manage Data Tasks wizard query. Click the **Office Button**, select **Manage**, and select **Compact and Repair Database**. Close Access.

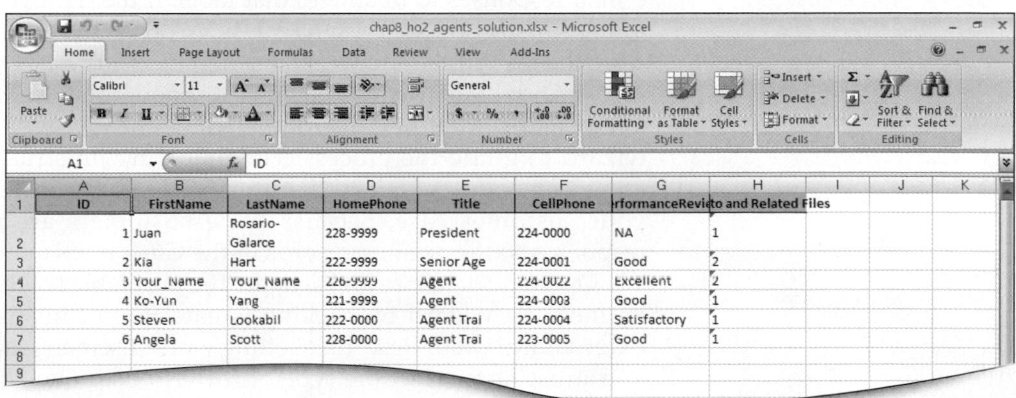

ID	FirstName	LastName	HomePhone	Title	CellPhone	rformanceRevi	to and Related Files
1	Juan	Rosario-Galarce	228-9999	President	224-0000	NA	1
2	Kia	Hart	222-9999	Senior Age	224-0001	Good	2
3	Your_Name	Your_Name	226-9999	Agent	224-0022	Excellent	2
4	Ko-Yun	Yang	221-9999	Agent	224-0003	Good	1
5	Steven	Lookabil	222-0000	Agent Trai	224-0004	Satisfactory	1
6	Angela	Scott	228-0000	Agent Trai	223-0005	Good	1

Figure 8.44 Exported Access Table Displayed in Excel

E-Mail Management with Access and Outlook

Access 2007 contains a powerful and astonishingly easy-to-use tool that facilitates e-mail delivery and response management. In order to utilize this feature in Access, you must also have Microsoft Outlook installed. Organizations might use this tool to empower interactive marketing, to facilitate customer relationship management, or to coordinate communications with the organizational suppliers or business partners. You must have an e-mail distribution list stored either in Outlook or in an Access table to use this feature. You can then use the Create E-mail tool in Access to generate an e-mail message that is an Access form. When the recipient completes the form and replies to your message, Outlook can connect to the appropriate Access table (after your review of the response) and automatically append the e-mailed responses as new records in the table.

(Access 2007 . . . facilitates e-mail delivery and response management.)

You have probably encountered similar systems on e-commerce sites or possibly at your school. Many universities send an e-mail message to students at the end of the term asking for their feedback on their courses and instructors. The student opens the e-mail and sees a mixture of multiple-choice questions and fill-in-the-blank questions to record their responses. The questions might be "Compared to your other classes, how would you rate the level of work expected in this course? Is it much above average, above average, average, below average, or much below average?" At most schools, student responses will be collected and summarized, and the results distributed to the faculty and administration. Access provides a natural environment to collect, analyze, and summarize the responses to this type of instrument. Even if Outlook is not installed, handwritten form data can be entered into an Access table for analysis and summarization. New to Access and Outlook 2007 is the ability to automate this critically important customer feedback interaction tool.

In this section, you learn how to create e-mail with Access and Outlook and manage the replies.

Collecting Data Through E-Mail Messages

Many schools do not support Outlook. Because this section requires the use of both Outlook and Access, a hands-on exercise is not provided at the end of this section. The topic supports customer relationship management in many small and midsized organizations; it must be addressed.

Suppose you want to contact all of your firm's customers and ask them to verify the information stored about them in your firm's database. You need to make sure that the address and phone numbers are correct and that the contact person remains the same. Those data are likely stored in your Customers table, so you want the e-mail responses to update to that table. If the data you want to collect are in a customer satisfaction survey, you might create a new table or query in your database to store the responses. You would need to carefully design the table that will receive the response data using the principles of good database design that you have encountered earlier. After you determine where the data will be stored, Access provides a wizard to guide the process. The following illustration is an example of sending e-mail messages to a group of prospective customers in expectation of increasing your customer base. Because these customers are new, you will append their responses to the existing records in the Customers table.

Open the database and activate the host table by clicking it in the Navigation bar. Launch the wizard by clicking Create E-mail in the Collect Data group on the External Data tab. Read the Getting started screen (see Figure 8.45) and click Next. You must next select the type of form to use. The choices are HTML or InfoPath forms. Because you are not sure if all of your customers have InfoPath installed, you elect to use an HTML form (see Figure 8.46). Because this e-mail will be sent to prospective customers, you will select the Collect new information option and click Next. If you are sending an e-mail to your current customers asking that they review and correct the information stored about them in your database, select the *Update existing information* option. You **must** have the recipient's e-mail address stored in a field of the table to which you wish to append the returns (see Figure 8.47). The next screen asks you to identify which fields should be designed into the e-mail form. Use the arrow buttons to move one or more fields from the *Fields in table* box to the *Fields to include in E-mail message box*. The third box, *Field Properties*, lets you set a caption that describes what to enter in each of the form's boxes (see Figure 8.48). Click Next.

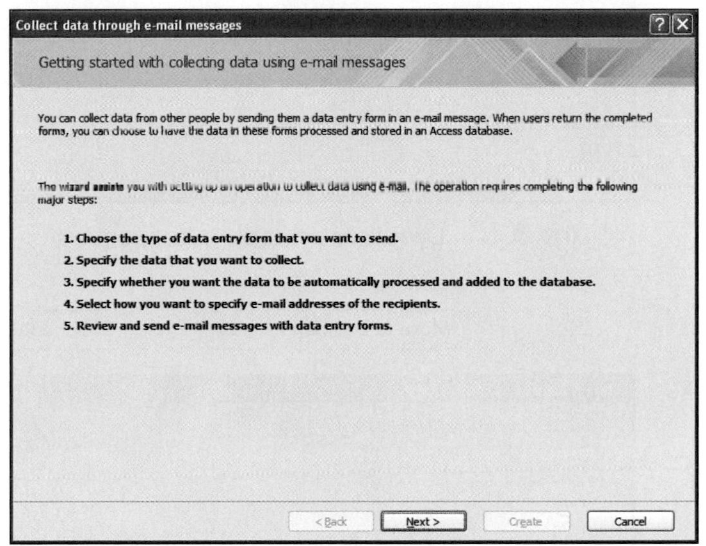

Figure 8.45 Collect Data Through E-Mail Wizard Welcome

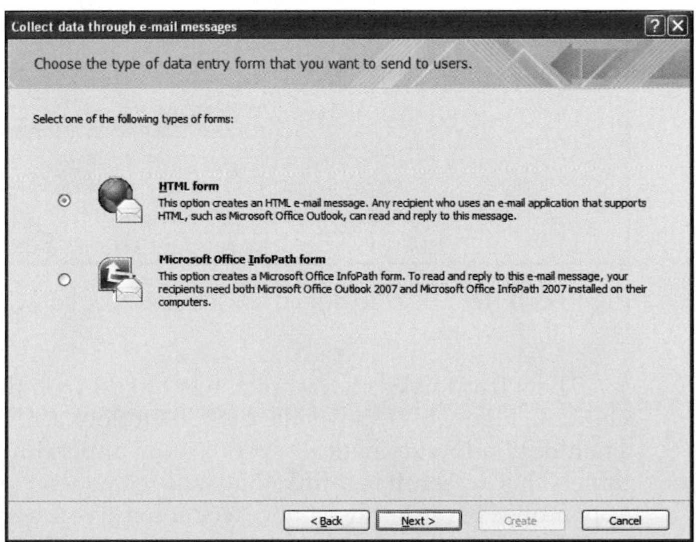

Figure 8.46 Specify Form Type

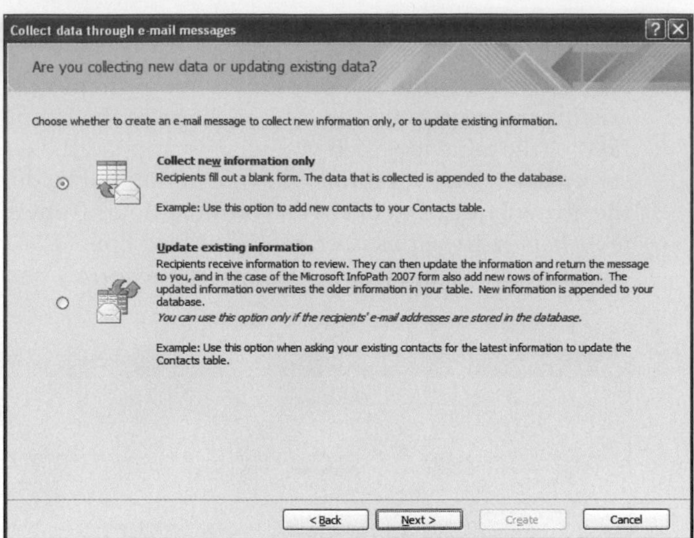

Figure 8.47 Directions on Reply Management

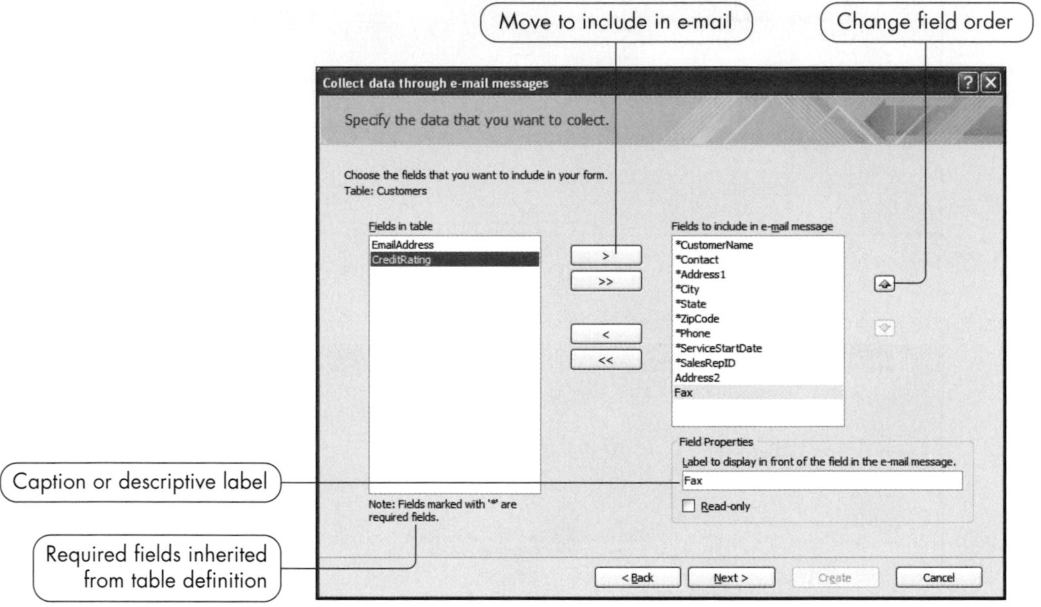

Figure 8.48 Field Selection, Order, and Caption Options

The wizard now lets you pick what to do with the replies both in Access and in Outlook. Figure 8.49 shows the default Outlook folder that stores the replies as well as an option to automatically process (by appending) the replies to the Customers table. This screen has a link that will let you set properties to control the auto-appending. Because this is new technology, you decide against selecting the automatically processed responses. Next, the wizard needs to know where the e-mail addresses of the intended recipients are stored. You may select from the current table, a field in a different table, or your Outlook contacts list (see Figure 8.50).

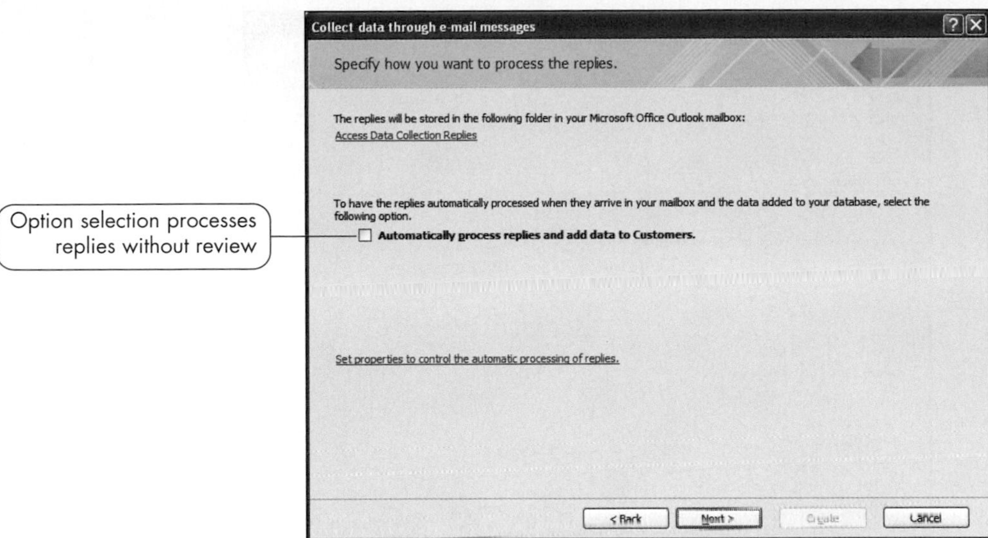

Figure 8.49 Directions on Reply Processing

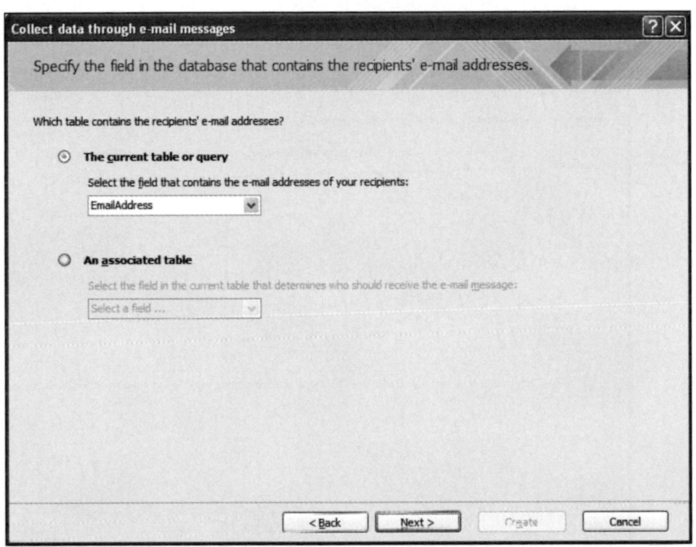

Figure 8.50 E-Mail Address Location

The next screen (see Figure 8.51) lets you customize the e-mail's subject and instructions. It also lets you specify where in the address the e-mail address will display. To protect your customers' privacy, you should consider sending the original e-mail to yourself and entering all of the remaining addresses in a Bcc (Blind Carbon Copy) field. As you move to the next step of the wizard, Access examines your e-mail addresses and reports the results to you. The table that served as a source for the e-mail address field in this example did not have e-mail addresses for all records. Access warns about this in the wizard prior to sending the messages. Access also reminds you how to examine the responses to the message as they arrive by clicking the Manage Replies tool (see Figure 8.52). The next step shows the valid e-mail addresses found in the table and gives you a chance to review the recipients prior to e-mailing. You may deselect any of the individual addresses to abort the send to that person. Click Next.

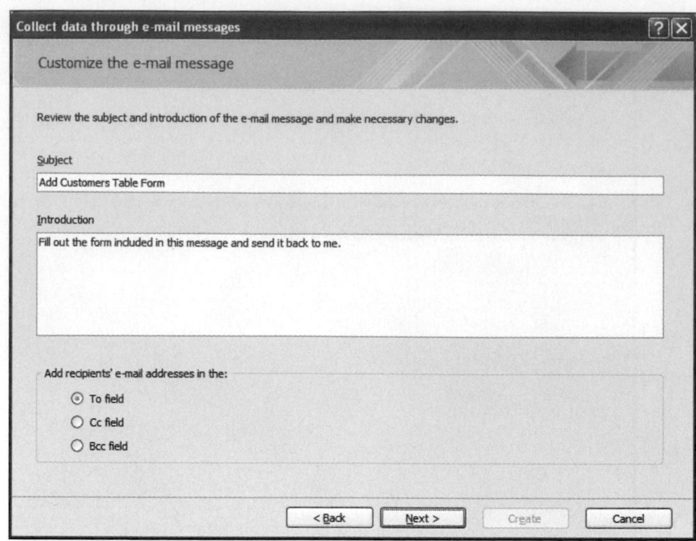

Figure 8.51 E-Mail Address Location and Customizing Options

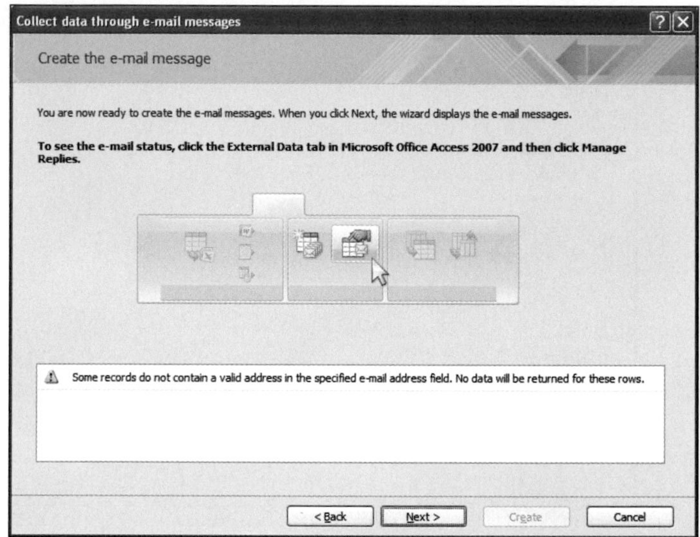

Figure 8.52 Access Pre-Tests Addresses

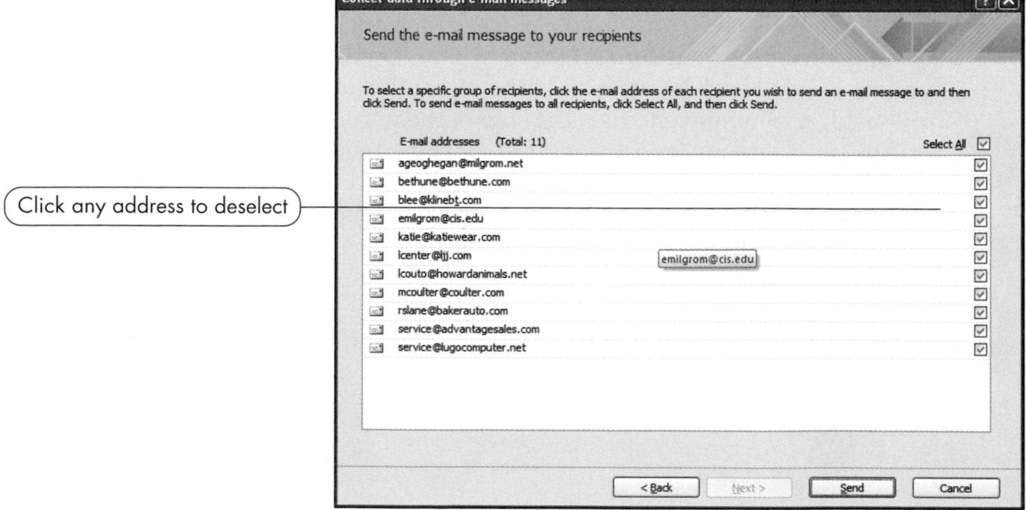

Figure 8.53 Preview Recipient Addresses

The wizard offers you a chance to review all of your instructions about generating the e-mail and about what to do with the replies when they arrive. Figure 8.54 displays the summary wizard screen. You need to review this screen very carefully. You would not want to send multiple e-mails to your customers because you had incorrectly specified an Access option and needed to correct it.

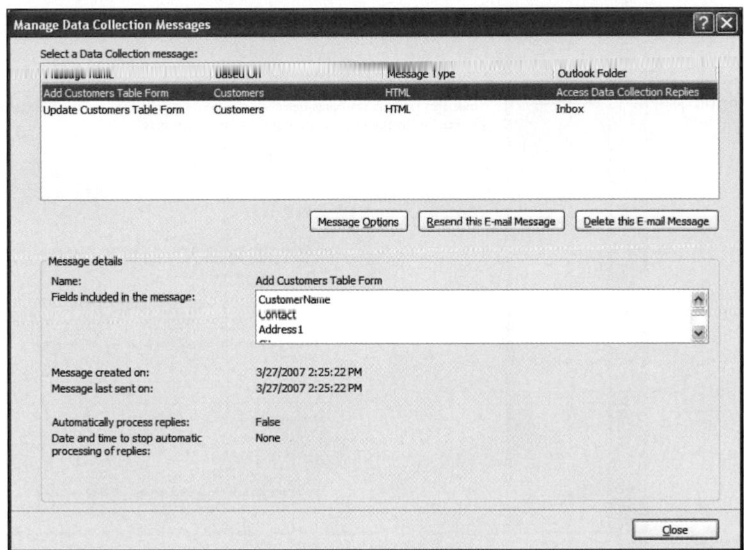

Figure 8.54 Review Message Options

Managing E-Mail Replies

Although this is a long wizard, it is easy to use and the guidance offered is clear. Access creates a form and loads it into an e-mail message (see Figure 8.55). Figure 8.56 examines some of the response options available. One important option is the ability to limit the number of replies to process and the duration of the process period. Your organization's Internet Service Provider (ISP) needs to know this information to allocate sufficient resources to process your mass e-mailing efficiently. The messages are addressed and sent through Outlook. Figure 8.57 displays an Outlook screen with the e-mail message received from a customer displayed. After you preview the response, you may right-click the message in the inbox and select Export data to Access from the shortcut menu. Alternatively, you can open the e-mail and use the Export to Access tool in the Microsoft Office group. The Export data to Microsoft Access dialog box launches. After you click OK, you receive the message box shown in Figure 8.58. You may click OK and continue reading and processing your e-mail within Access. Figure 8.59 shows the new record appended to the Customers table in Access.

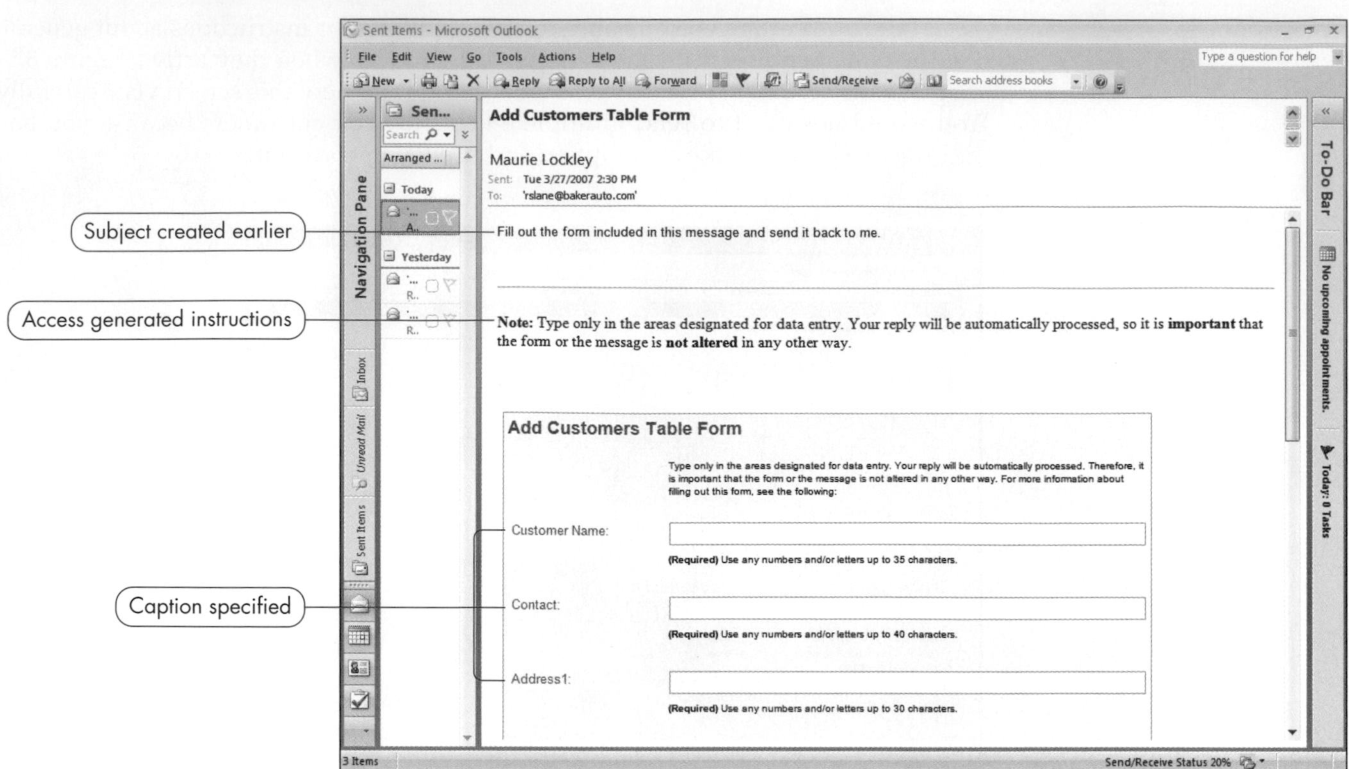

Figure 8.55 Preview E-Mail Message and Form

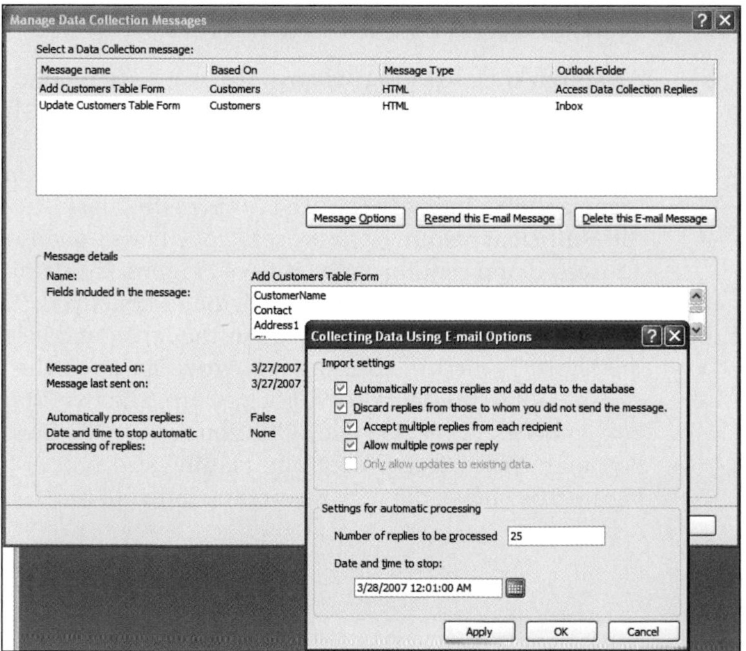

Figure 8.56 Data Collection Options

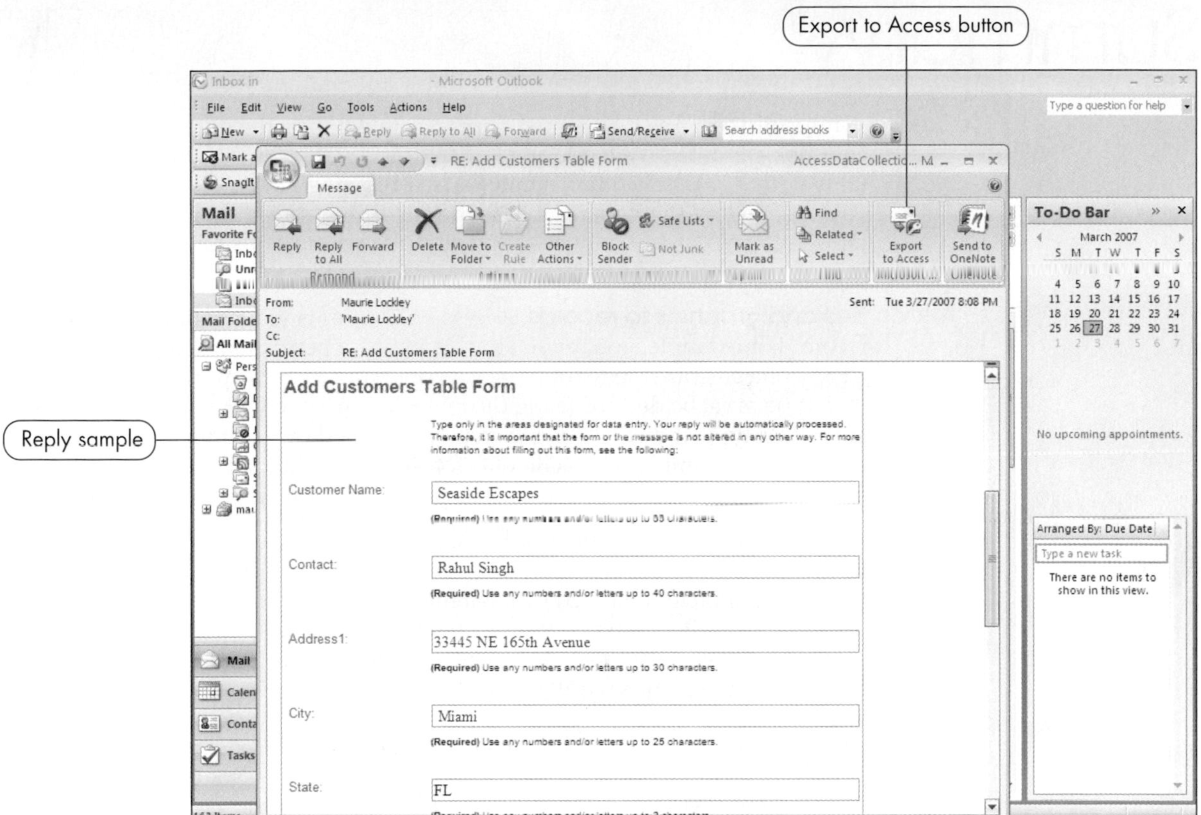

Figure 8.57 Reply Management

Figure 8.58 Export Notification

Customers

CustomerID	Customer Name	Contact	E-mail Address	Address1	Addre
C0001	Abel & Young	Jeff Jones	maurie_lockley@rr.com	5000 Jefferson Lane	Suite 2
C0002	Department of CIS	Eleanor Milgrom		1238 Walsh Drive	Suite 2
C0003	Advantage Sales	Neil Goodman	service@advantagesales.com	4215 South 81 Street	
C0004	Kinzer & Sons	Nicholas Colon		9020 N.W. 75 Street	Suite 3
C0005	Milgrom Associates	Ashley Geoghegan	ageoghegan@milgrom.net	7500 Center Lane	
C0006	Lugo Computer Sales	Derek Anderson	service@lugocomputer.net	6000 Tigertail Avenue	
C0007	Bethune Appliance Sales	Michael Ware	bethune@bethune.com	276 Brickell Avenue	Suite 1
C0008	Baker Auto Supply	Robert Slane	rslane@bakerauto.com	4508 N.W. 7 Street	
C0009	Howard Animal Hospital	Luis Couto	lcouto@howardanimals.net	455 Bargello Avenue	
C0010	Katie's Casual Wear	Jeffrey Muddell	katie@katiewear.com	9522 S.W. 142 Street	
C0011	Little, Joiner, & Jones	Lauren Center	lcenter@ljj.com	7245 NW 8 Street	
C0012	Kline Bait & Tackle	Benjamin Lee	blee@klineb&t.com	1000 Call Street	
C0013	Computer Informations Sys	Eleanor Milgrom	emilgrom@cis.edu	1238 Walsh Drove	Suite 2
C0014	Coulter Office Supplies	Maryann Coulter	mcoulter@coulter.com	1000 Main Street	
C0015	Seaside Escapes	Rahul Singh		33445 NE 165th Avenue	
(New)					

Figure 8.59 Processed Reply Appended to Access Table

Like any powerful tool, the ability to generate e-mail and automatically process responses in Access should be judiciously and carefully used. Most e-mail systems limit the number of messages that may be sent in a single event. Most ISPs also impose limits on the number of e-mail messages that you may send. Still, a small- or mid-sized business that uses both Access and Outlook has a powerful customer relationship management and direct marketing tool added to its option set.

Summary

1. **Create a hyperlinked field.** You must appropriately define the data type to store in a field when it contains a link to a Web address (URL) or to a data file, like an Excel workbook. Editing a table with hyperlinked fields may cause problems. If you click a cell to edit it, you will activate and follow the hyperlink. Use the cursor and press Tab to position the cursor for editing. Links to files can only be followed if the permissions on the file and folder have been set to permit sharing.
2. **Attach files and graphics to records.** Access 2007 permits you to attach multiple files to a field in a record. For example, you might attach a photo, a performance review, a payment schedule, or a copy of a customer letter of praise or complaint to an employee record. The attachment field data type must be defined using the table design view. Once the field is defined as an attachment data type, it displays as a paperclip followed by a number in parentheses. The number indicates the number of attachments for the record. You interact with attachments through the Attachment dialog box, which lets you add, delete, edit, and open attachments.
3. **Add and use a table attachment field.** Once a field has been defined as an attachment field, the Datasheet view of the table displays a paperclip icon as the field heading. Each record displays the paperclip followed by a parenthetically expressed number. The number indicates the number of files attached to a given record. You may populate the attachment field by using the Attachment dialog box. With it, you may add or remove files and images. You may also open, save as, or save all of the attachments to a given record. Although you may use an attachment in a form or report, the field delimitation must come from the underlying table. After the attachment field is defined in the table, the form or report treats different types of attachments differently. Pictures display as thumbnails. Other document types display as the software logo. Multiple attachments in a form or a report may be navigated among by using the Mini toolbar. After you select the appropriate attached file, you can open it by double-clicking it.
4. **Export database objects as HTML files.** HTML not only serves as the language in which many Web sites are published, it is also useful as a communication facilitator. Even if customers or coworkers does not have Microsoft Office installed, they can open and read a file transmitted to them in HTML code. Access provides an export wizard that makes it easy for you to save objects from a database as HTML files.
5. **Import or link to HTML files.** Access can use HTML files in two ways: importing and linking. An import is a one and done procedure. It visits the source, for example, a Web site, and captures the published information and returns it to your database. Once there, you can link the information to the rest of the database tables and use it like you would use any other data within the database. Alternatively you can link to the external data source. If linked to a Web site, each time the linked Access table is opened or used, Access revisits the source and checks for updated information. You right-click the table in the Navigation pane and select the Linked Table Manager to force the update. A linked table in Access displays with an icon different from other table icons so you know it is a dynamic data source.
6. **Share XML data.** Like HTML, XML is widely used to publish Web pages. XML can handle far more complex data types than HTML can. Using the import and export external data wizards you exported complex data to XML and then imported it back into Access as a table. Like HTML data, XML data can be shared with anyone with access to newer browser software.
7. **Share data with Excel.** Many organizations purchase licenses for all users for Microsoft Excel, but only purchase Access licenses for those users who need the power generated from database software. Access facilitates data exchange with Excel in three ways. You can import Excel data into an Access table, you can export Access data as an Excel workbook, or you can add an Excel file as an attachment to an appropriately defined field in an Access table, form, or report. Access provides import and export wizards to facilitate data exchange with Excel.
8. **Collect data through e-mail messages.** If you have both Access and Outlook installed on your computer, Office 2007 provides a powerful means of using the tools to facilitate communication. You can create and send e-mails to e-mail addresses stored in Access or Outlook by using Outlook.

...continued on Next Page

9. **Manage e-mail replies.** You may also manage the replies by appending them to an existing Access table or by creating a new table in Access to receive the e-mailed replies. The wizard creates a form that the e-mail recipient fills out. Upon receipt of the response, the wizard helps the organization manage the replies through the manage response wizard. This software interaction will help small businesses improve customer relationship and interactive marketing management.

Key Terms

Attachment control 519
Extensible HyperText Markup Language (XHTML) 513
eXtensible Markup Language (XML) 513
Extensible Stylesheet Language (XSL) 537
HyperText Markup Language (HTML) 513
Normalization 516
Object Linking and Embedding (OLE) 516
Uniform Resource Locator (URL) 513
XML Schema Definition (XSD) 537

Multiple Choice

1. Which of the following is true about importing data from the Internet to your database?
   - (a) Anything published on the Internet is fair game for copying and downloading.
   - (b) Access stores the data found on a Web site in a field defined as a hyperlink data type. You do not need a live Internet connection to view data.
   - (c) Editing a hyperlinked data field is no different from editing any other type of data.
   - (d) Many items published on governmental Web sites are available to use without risking copyright violations.

2. Which statement is true?
   - (a) You may attach only one file per record in a table.
   - (b) You may use attachment files in forms and reports, but you must first define them in the table.
   - (c) Attached files that are picture files display as thumbnails in queries.
   - (d) Attachment files tend to be larger than OLE files.

3. You need to attach an employee's most recent performance review to his/her record in the employee's table. The field has already been defined as an attachment type and has last year's performance rating attached. Which describes the correct action?
   - (a) You open the employee's record in a form, find and delete the old attachment, and then add the new file.
   - (b) You open the employee's record in the table, find and delete the old attachment, and then add the new file.
   - (c) You may add the new file in either a form or a table and do not need to delete anything.
   - (d) Create a hyperlink to the file and specify the file name and path to the file storage location on your hard drive.

4. Which statement about attachment files in a form or a report is true?
   - (a) If the attachment control is sufficiently large, the attached application files such as Word or PowerPoint will display in thumbnails.
   - (b) If an attachment field contains several attachments including one picture file, only the picture file will display in a form or report. You will never see the Word icon.
   - (c) Only graphic files display as thumbnails; all other file types display as the logo.
   - (d) If you open an attached Excel file and make changes to it, the changes will not be stored in the database.

5. You might save an Access object as an HTML file structure to accomplish all of the following except to:
   - (a) Perform complex calculations.
   - (b) Share data with someone with limited access to application software.
   - (c) Share data with someone with limited computer use skills.
   - (d) Publish it on the Internet.

6. What type of software is needed to view an HTML file and its formatting?
   - (a) Web page creation software like FrontPage or Dreamweaver
   - (b) A browser
   - (c) WordPad or any simple text editor
   - (d) Antivirus software

7. The primary difference between an import and a link is the way edits are handled. Which statement is correct?
   - (a) Changes made to an imported source file after the import are ignored.
   - (b) Changes made to a linked source file after the import are ignored.
   - (c) Changes made in the linked destination file will update the source file.
   - (d) Changes made in the imported destination file will update the source file.

8. XML data import more completely and generates fewer errors than HTML data. Why?
   - (a) HTML is best edited and viewed in a text program, like WordPad. It is too complex for Access to use well.
   - (b) XML data is generally too complex for Access to understand.
   - (c) Because HTML and XML are open source, they do not work well with proprietary software like Access.
   - (d) XML is capable of dealing with more complex data types than HTML. Because Access also uses complex data types, the XML imports go more smoothly.

9. You need to create Access data for an Excel user to use, interact with, and save locally. The user needs updates weekly. How should you accomplish this most efficiently?
   (a) Display the needed data in Access, select it, copy it, and paste it into Excel. Save and send the file.
   (b) Use the Excel tool in the Export Data group on the External Data tab.
   (c) Use the Excel tool in the Import Data group on the External Data tab.
   (d) Use the Excel tool in the Export Data group on the External Data tab and save the export steps.

10. You decide to use Access and Outlook to send e-mail to your customers and manage their replies. Where should you store the e-mail addresses?
    (a) In an Access table
    (b) In an Outlook distribution list
    (c) In either Access or Outlook
    (d) Within the e-mail wizard

11. You decide to use Access and Outlook to send e-mail to your customers and manage their replies. You want to send a form for the recipient to fill out and then have the replies processed and appended to a table in your database. How do you build the form?
    (a) You do not need to build a form; the wizard creates the form based on the fields specified.
    (b) You do not need to build a form; simply attach an existing Access form to the e-mail and send it.
    (c) You must create the form in Access and base it on the appropriate table prior to launching Outlook.
    (d) You use Outlook to generate the form.

12. Data exports sometimes yield surprising results. Formats change, aggregating statistics disappear, and spacing sometimes gets odd. Access data exports that yield the fewest surprises tend to source on:
    (a) Tables
    (b) Queries
    (c) Simple data structures found in tables and queries
    (d) Reports

13. You have sent an e-mail form using Access and Outlook requesting feedback on the customer service in your organization. You should set the manage replies to:
    (a) Automatically append to your Access table
    (b) Append following review
    (c) Be stored in a special Outlook folder and appended when you open the folder
    (d) Be stored in a special Outlook folder and appended following your review

14. You have used the export wizard to export the Inventory form data to Excel: The Inventory form sources the Inventory table. The resulting exported data, viewed in Excel, will look like:
    (a) The Inventory table
    (b) The Inventory form
    (c) Neither the Inventory table nor the Inventory form
    (d) None of the above because you cannot export data from a form

15. You exported data from the Properties table to Excel. The table contained an attachment field and a hyperlink field. What will the results in Excel look like?
    (a) The hyperlinked field will generate an error message but the attachment field will export and function.
    (b) The attachment field will generate an error message but the hyperlinks will export and function.
    (c) Neither data type is supported by Excel so neither will function.
    (d) Both data types are supported by Excel and will export and function without problems.

Practice Exercises

1 Northwind Traders Inactive Customers

The Northwinds Traders is a small international specialty foods distribution firm. As part of a concerted customer relationship management effort, the Sales Manager has asked you to provide her with a list in Excel of all of the inactive customers (no orders since 11/1/2007) with their contact information. The list also needs to include the salesperson's name so she knows to whom to assign the contact duty. You decided that this information will be needed often, so you will create an Excel workbook and save the export steps to help identify the customers who have not ordered recently. Refer to Figure 8.60 to verify your work.

a. Copy the partially completed file *chap8_pe1_traders.accdb* from the Exploring Access folder to your production folder. Rename the copied file **chap8_pe1_traders_solution**. Double-click the file name to open it. Click **Options** on the Security Warning toolbar, click **Enable this content** in the Microsoft Office Security Options dialog box, and then click **OK**.

b. Click the **Database Tools tab** and click **Relationships** in the Show/Hide group. Examine the table structure, relationships, and fields. Once you are familiar with the database, close the Relationships window.

c. Open the **Employees table** and replace *Your_Name* with your name in the first and last name fields. Close the Employees table.

d. Open the **Contact Information for Inactive Customers query** in Datasheet view. Type **11/1/2007** in the parameter box and click **OK**. Type **11/1/2007** in the Enter Parameter Value box. Click **OK.** (You must enter the date twice.)

e. Click **Excel** in the Export group on the External data tab. Click **Browse** and navigate to your production folder. Type **chap8_pe1_traders_solution.xlsx** in the *File name* box of the File Save dialog box. Click **Save**.

f. Select the options to **Export data with formatting and layout** and **Open the destination file after the export operation is complete**. Click **OK**.

g. Examine the exported data in Excel. If it is correct, click the flashing **Microsoft Access** button on the taskbar.

h. Click the **Save export steps check box**. Type **Contact Information for Inactive Customers** in the *Description box* in the Save Export Steps Wizard. Click **Save Export**.

i. Click **Excel** on the taskbar. Print and close the Excel workbook.

j. Click **Access** on the taskbar, if necessary, to return to Access. Close the query. Click **Saved Exports** in the Export Group on the External Data tab. Click **Run**.

k. Click **Yes** to update the existing file. Click **Yes** again. Type **10/1/2007** in the Enter Parameter Value box. Click **OK**. Type **10/1/2007** in the Enter Parameter Value box. Click **OK**. (You must enter the date twice.)

l. Print and close the Excel workbook. Return to Access. Click **OK** in the Successful Export message box. Close the Manage Data Task Wizard.

m. Click the **Office Button**, select **Manage**, and select **Compact and Repair Database**. Close the file.

...continued on Next Page

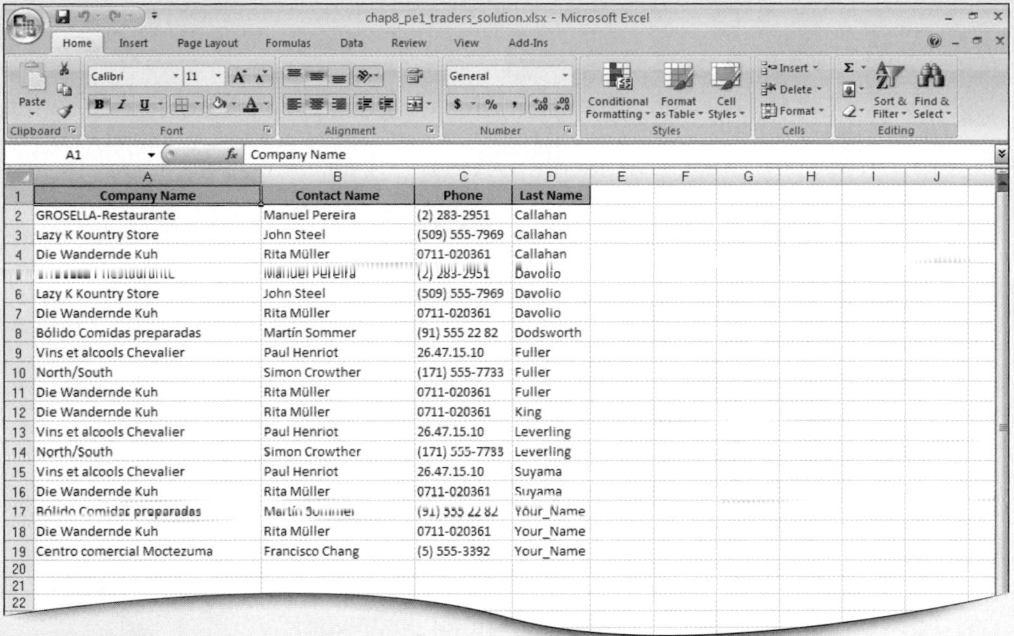

	Company Name	Contact Name	Phone	Last Name
2	GROSELLA-Restaurante	Manuel Pereira	(2) 283-2951	Callahan
3	Lazy K Kountry Store	John Steel	(509) 555-7969	Callahan
4	Die Wandernde Kuh	Rita Müller	0711-020361	Callahan
5	[illegible]	Manuel Pereira	(2) 283-2951	Davolio
6	Lazy K Kountry Store	John Steel	(509) 555-7969	Davolio
7	Die Wandernde Kuh	Rita Müller	0711-020361	Davolio
8	Bólido Comidas preparadas	Martín Sommer	(91) 555 22 82	Dodsworth
9	Vins et alcools Chevalier	Paul Henriot	26.47.15.10	Fuller
10	North/South	Simon Crowther	(171) 555-7733	Fuller
11	Die Wandernde Kuh	Rita Müller	0711-020361	Fuller
12	Die Wandernde Kuh	Rita Müller	0711-020361	King
13	Vins et alcools Chevalier	Paul Henriot	26.47.15.10	Leverling
14	North/South	Simon Crowther	(171) 555-7733	Leverling
15	Vins et alcools Chevalier	Paul Henriot	26.47.15.10	Suyama
16	Die Wandernde Kuh	Rita Müller	0711-020361	Suyama
17	Bólido Comidas preparadas	Martín Sommer	(91) 555 22 82	Your_Name
18	Die Wandernde Kuh	Rita Müller	0711-020361	Your_Name
19	Centro comercial Moctezuma	Francisco Chang	(5) 555-3392	Your_Name

Figure 8.60 November Inactive Customers

2 Northwind Traders Product Price Updates

You manage the database for Northwind Traders, an international specialty foods company. One of the purchasing managers in the company, Ms. Chu, asked you to make her work easier. She visits the Web site for a firm from which Northwinds purchases some of the products they sell each day. She examines the product prices published on the Web site for the Plutzer Company and then updates the Products table in the database with the new prices when they change. Ms. Chu wonders if you could set the database up to automate the price updating process. You decide that you will link the Products table to the Plutzer Company Web site and import the product prices automatically. Refer to Figure 8.61 to verify your work.

a. Copy the partially completed file *chap8_pe2_traders.accdb* from the Exploring Access folder to your production folder. Rename the copied file **chap8_pe2_traders_solution**. Double-click the file name to open it. Click **Options** on the Security Warning toolbar, click **Enable this content** in the Microsoft Office Security Options dialog box, and then click **OK**.

b. Locate the file named *chap8_pe2_plutzer.html*. Copy it to your production folder. Rename the copied file **chap8_pe2_plutzer_solution.html.**

c. Click **More** in the Import group on the External Data tab. Select **HTML Document** from the list. Click **Browse** in the Get External Data — HTML Document Wizard. Locate and select the file named *chap8_pe2_plutzer_solution.html* in the File Open dialog box. Click **Open**.

d. Click the **Link to the data source by creating a linked table** option. Click **OK**.

e. Click the **First Row Contains Column Headings check box**. Click **Next**.

f. Accept the default data types and indexing options. Click **Next**.

g. Type **Price List Plutzer** as the Linked Table Name. Click **Finish**. Click **OK** in the resulting message box.

h. Click **Start**, point to **All Programs**, select **Accessories**, and click **WordPad** to launch WordPad. Click the **Open button** to launch the Open dialog box. Locate and select your data folder. Click in the *Files of Type* box and select **All Documents (*.*)** to make the file name display. Select the file named *chap8_pe2_plutzer_solution.html*. Save it as **chap8_pe2_plutzer_solution.html**.

...continued on Next Page

i. Press **Ctrl+F** to launch the Find dialog box. Type **Your_Name** in the *Find What* box. Close the Find dialog box. Type your first and last names to replace the highlighted *Your_Name* in the HTML code.

j. Below and to the right of your name is the price of the cheese, *$11.60*. You may need to scroll right to locate it. Change the price to **$12.60**. Save and close the WordPad file.

k. Return to Access. Right-click the **Price List Plutzer table** in the Navigation pane and select **Linked Table Manager**. Click the **Price List Plutzer check box**. Click **OK**, and then click **OK**. Close the Linked Table Manager dialog box.

l. Open the linked **Price List Plutzer table**. Press **PrntScrn**. Launch Word. Type your name and section number and press **Enter**. Press **Ctrl+V** to paste the screenshot. Save the Word document as **chap8_pe2_traders_solution.docx**. Print and close the Word document.

m. Return to Access. Click the **Office Button**, select **Manage**, and then select **Compact and Repair Database**. Close the file.

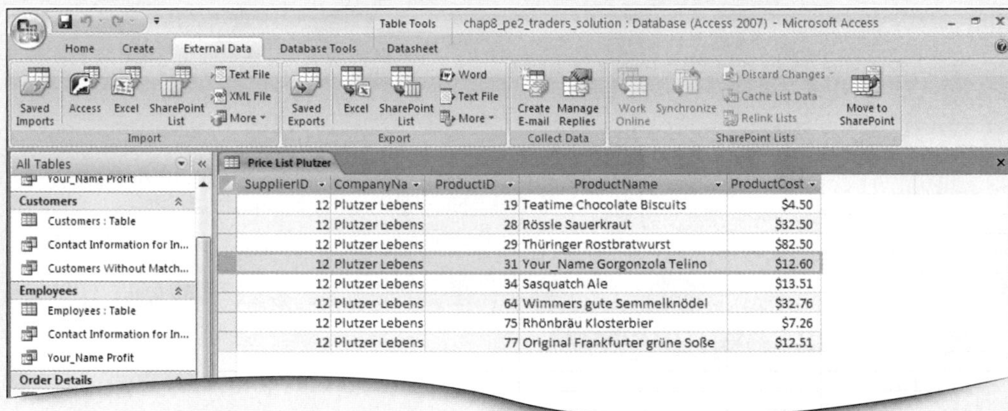

Figure 8.61 Linked HTML Import

3 National Bank

You are the database administrator for a bank. One of the directors, Susan Mohney, asked that you help her with a customer relationship management problem. She wants to attach pictures of the customers to the records in the Customers table so that she can do a better job of remembering names. You will need to create an attachment field in the Customers table and attach the picture files to the records. Refer to Figure 8.62 to verify your work.

a. Copy the partially completed file *chap8_pe3_nationalbank.accdb* from the Exploring Access folder to your production folder. Rename the copied file **chap8_pe3_nationalbank_solution.accdb**. Double-click the file name to open it. Click **Options** on the Security Warning toolbar, click **Enable this content** in the Microsoft Office Security Options dialog box, and then click **OK**.

b. Open the **Customers table** in Datasheet view and replace *Your_Name* with your name.

c. Scroll right until you find the Add New Field column, then click in the first record. Click **Data Type** in the Data Type & Formatting group on the Datasheet tab and select **Attachment**.

d. Double-click the **paperclip** in the first record. Click **Add** in the Attachments dialog box. Locate and open the *chap8_pe3_customers* folder. Double-click the file named *C0001.jpg* to attach it to the record, and then click **OK**.

e. Double-click the **paperclip** in the second record. Click **Add**. Double-click the file named *C0002.jpg* to attach it to the record, and then click **OK**. Repeat until all of the records have picture files attached. You may use either the provided picture for record 8 or attach a picture of yourself.

...continued on Next Page

f. Click **Report** in the Reports group on the Create tab to create a report.

g. Edit the report in Layout view. Display only columns for the CustomerID, FirstName, LastName, PhoneNumber, AccountType, and Field1 (the picture field) fields. Delete the columns you do not need by clicking the column heading and pressing **Delete**.

h. Rename *Field1* on the report as **Picture**. Add spaces to the column headings for Customer ID and Account Type.

i. Save the report as **Your_Name Customers and Pictures**. Print and close the report.

j. Capture a screenshot of the Customers table in Datasheet view by pressing **PrntScrn**. Launch Word. Type your name and section number. Press **Enter** and press **Ctrl+V** to paste the screenshot. Save the Word document as **chap8_pe3_nationalbank_solution.docx**. Print and close the Word document.

k. Return to Access. Click the **Office Button**, select **Manage**, and select **Compact and Repair Database**. Close the file.

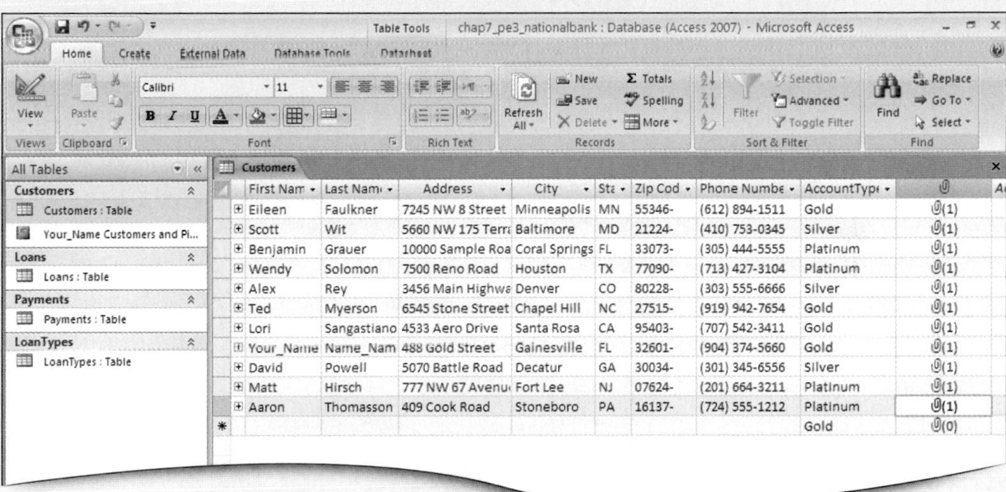

Figure 8.62 Attachment Field

4 Custom Coffee

The Custom Coffee Company is a small service organization that provides coffee, tea, and snacks to offices. Custom Coffee also provides and maintains the equipment for brewing the beverages. Although the firm is small, its excellent reputation for providing outstanding customer service has helped it grow. Part of this is because the firm owner set up a database to organize and keep track of customer purchases. You need to create an XML file to share data with the firm's employees when they are out of the office. Eventually the file you create will be published on a password-protected Web site. Refer to Figure 8.63 to verify your work.

a. Copy the partially completed file *chap8_pe4_coffee.accdb* from the Exploring Access folder to your production folder. Rename the copied file **chap8_pe4_coffee_solution.accdb**. Double-click the file name to open the file. Click **Options** on the Security Warning toolbar, click **Enable this content** in the Microsoft Office Security Options dialog box, and then click **OK**.

b. Double-click the **Sales Rep table** to open it. Replace *Your_Name* with your name. Close the table.

c. Rename the *Your_Name SalesOutside Miami* report with your name. Open it in Report view.

d. Click **More** in the Export group on the External Data Tab. Select **XML File** from the list. Click **Browse**. Navigate to and select your solutions folder. In the File Save dialog box, click in the *File name* box and type **chap8_pe4_coffee_solution.xml**. Click **Save**. Click **OK**.

...continued on Next Page

e. Click the options for **Data (XML), Schema of the data (XSD),** and **Presentation of your data (XSL)** in the Export XML dialog box. Click **OK**.

f. Do not save the export steps. Click **Close**.

g. Close the report. Click **XML File** in the Import Group on the External Data tab. Click **Browse**. Double-click **chap8_pe4_coffee_ solution.xml**. Click **OK**. Make sure the option for Structure and Data is selected. Click **OK**. Close the wizard without saving the import steps.

h. Double-click the newly imported **Your_Name sales outside of Miami table**.

i. Capture a screenshot of the table in datasheet view by pressing **PrntScrn**. Launch Word. Type your name and section number. Press **Enter** and press **Ctrl+V** to paste the screenshot. Save the Word document as **chap8_pe4_coffee_solution.docx**. Print and close the Word document.

j. Click the **Office Button**, select **Manage**, and then select **Compact and Repair Database**. Close the file.

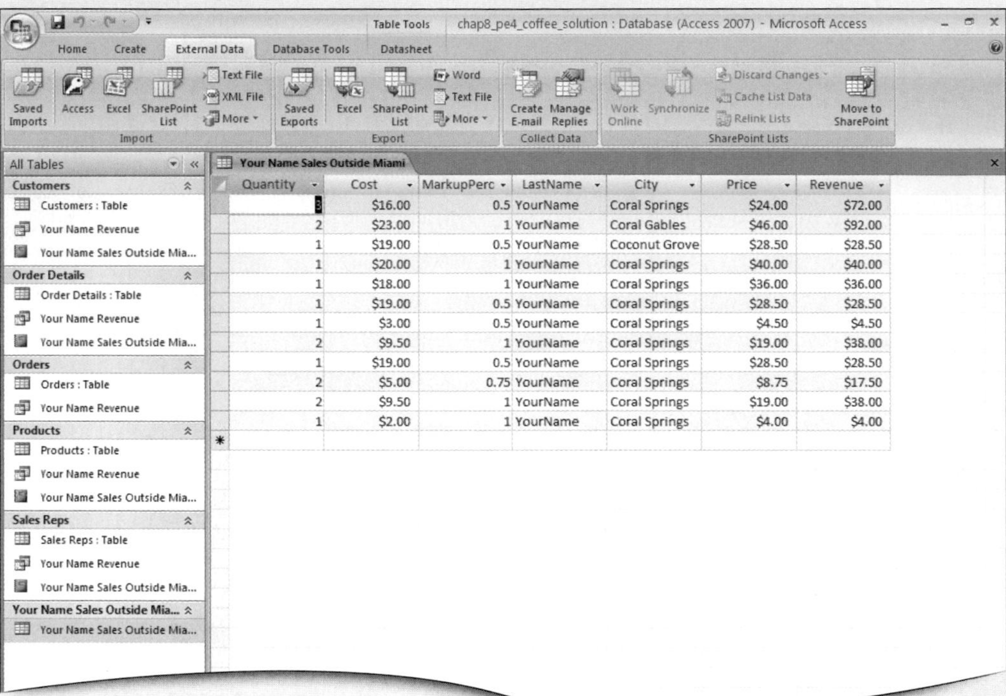

Figure 8.63 Exported and Then Imported XML File

Mid-Level Exercises

1 The Northwinds Traders

The Northwinds Traders is a small international specialty foods distribution firm. It sells products in a variety of different categories: Beverages, Condiments, etc. The sales manager has asked you to provide her with a list of Revenue, Total Cost, and Profit figures by category. She needs the file in an Excel format. There is a query that has the necessary data. You will need to summarize it by category and export the summary to Excel. You decide that this information will be needed often, so you will create an Excel file and save the export steps to make it easier to re-export the query data the next time it is needed. Refer to Figure 8.64 to verify your work.

a. Locate the file named *chap8_mid1_traders.accdb*, copy it to your production folder, and rename it **chap8_mid1_traders_solution.accdb**. Open the file and enable the content.

b. Rename the Your_Name Profit query with your name.

c. Create a new select query based on the Your_Name Profit query. Add the CategoryName, Revenue, TotalCost, and Profit fields to the new query. Turn this into a summary query grouped by CategoryName by employing the Totals tool. Sum the Revenue, TotalCost, and Profit fields. Format the numeric fields as currency. Name the new query **Your_Name Profit by Category**. Save and close it.

d. Export this query to Excel. Save the Excel workbook as **chap8_mid1_traders_solution.xlsx**. Close the workbook.

e. Return to Access. Save the export steps. Type **Profit by Category** as the export description.

f. Open the **Your_Name Profit by Category query** in Design view.

g. Use the Property Sheet to caption the CategoryName column as **Category Name**, the SumofRevenue column as **Total Revenue,** the SumofTotalCost column as **Total Cost**, and the SumofProfit column as **Profit**.

h. Run and save the query. Use the Manage Data Tasks tool to re-export it to Excel. Capture a screenshot of the Excel workbook. Launch Word and type your name and section number. Press **Enter**. Paste the screenshot. Save the Word document as **chap8_mid1_traders_solution.docx**. Print the Word document.

i. Compact and repair the database. Close the database and all other files.

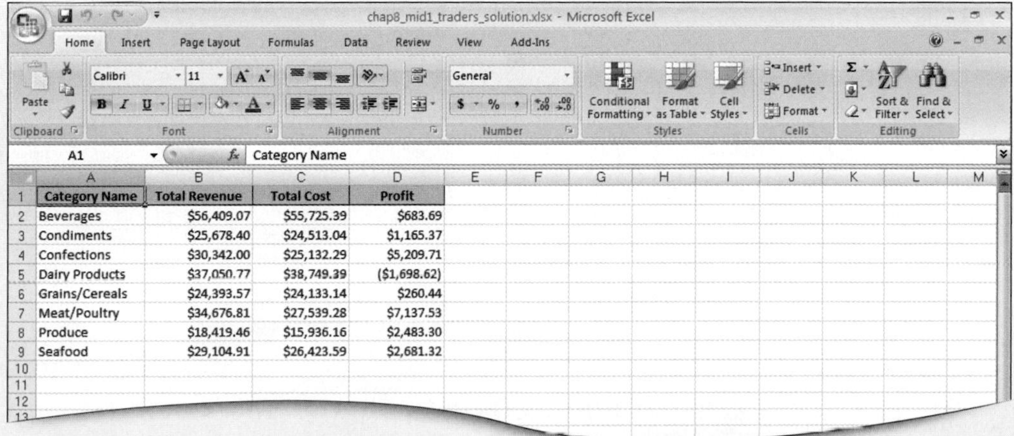

Category Name	Total Revenue	Total Cost	Profit
Beverages	$56,409.07	$55,725.39	$683.69
Condiments	$25,678.40	$24,513.04	$1,165.37
Confections	$30,342.00	$25,132.29	$5,209.71
Dairy Products	$37,050.77	$38,749.39	($1,698.62)
Grains/Cereals	$24,393.57	$24,133.14	$260.44
Meat/Poultry	$34,676.81	$27,539.28	$7,137.53
Produce	$18,419.46	$15,936.16	$2,483.30
Seafood	$29,104.91	$26,423.59	$2,681.32

Figure 8.64 Exported Access Query

...continued on Next Page

2 Hotel Chain

You are the general manager of a large hotel chain. Your establishment provides a variety of guest services ranging from rooms and conferences to weddings. You need to add a new field to an existing table and enter each hotel's Web site as a hyperlinked field. Refer to Figure 8.65 to verify your work.

a. Locate the file named *chap8_mid2_memrewards.accdb*, copy it to your production folder, and rename it **chap8_mid2_memrewards_solution.accdb**. Open the file and enable the content.

b. Open the **Locations table**. Create a new field. Enter the URL of each hotel in the newly created field. For each hotel, the URL will be http://www.BigHotel.CityName.com (replace CityName with the city where the hotel is located). When a city has more than one location, name the second one http://www.BigHotel.CityName2.com. Do not use spaces in the city names; for example, http://www.BigHotel.LosAngeles2.com is correct.

c. Define the data type as Hyperlink. Name the field **Web site**.

d. Make the column wide enough to completely display the URL.

e. Capture a screenshot. Launch Word. Type your name and section number on the first line. Press **Enter**. Paste your screenshot into the Word document. Save the Word document as **chap8_mid2_memrewards_solution.docx**.

f. Print the Word document.

g. Compact, repair, and close the database.

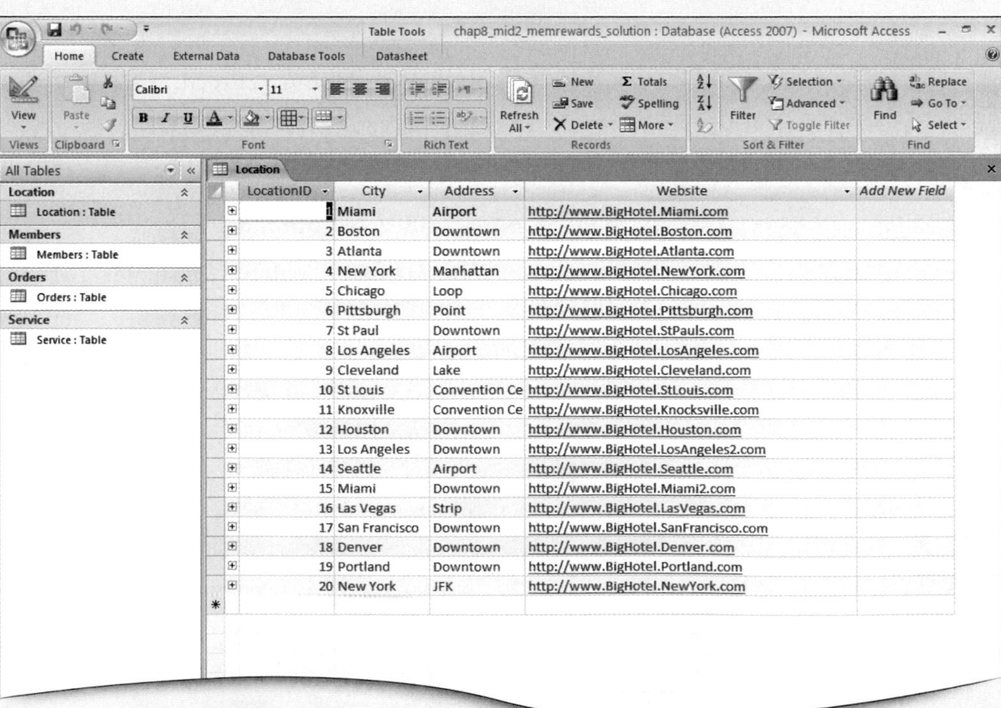

Figure 8.65 Hyperlinked Data Field

...continued on Next Page

3 JC Raulston Arboretum

The JC Raulston Arboretum at NC State University has added a new feature to its Web site. There is a search engine that helps gardeners locate specific plants in the Arboretum, look at pictures of the plant, and discover a little about it. The volunteers have been photographing plants in the garden and need your help matching the digital prints with the scientific plant names stored in the database. You have been asked to add an attachment field to a newly created table in the database and attach the pictures of the plants to the appropriate records. You also need to create a report showing the plant names and the pictures so that the horticultural experts can verify that you have attached the appropriate pictures to the records. Refer to Figure 8.66 to verify your work.

a. Locate the file named *chap8_mid3_arboretum.accdb*, copy it to your production folder, and rename it **chap8_mid3_arboretum_solution.accdb**. Open the file and enable the content. Open the **Plant Pictures table**.

b. Create a new attachment field named **Picture** in the Plant Pictures table.

c. Use the new field and the Attachment dialog box to add the picture files for each plant to the record. Some plants have several pictures. You will find the picture files on the student data disk in a folder named *chap8_mid3_plantpix_folder*.

d. Create a report based on the Plant Pictures table. Title the report **Your_Name Plant Pictures**.

e. Add the picture of the Magnolia "Elizabeth" to the report's logo area. Enlarge it to be about twice the original size. Move the report title control right and down to approximate the layout shown in Figure 8.66.

f. Make the attachment controls about twice the original size. Activate each attachment and use the Mini toolbar to locate the last attachment for each record. If a plant has three attachments, the highest numbered attachment for that plant should display in the report control.

g. Save the report as **Your_Name Plant Pictures**.

h. Print and close the report. Print and close the table. Compact, repair, and close the database.

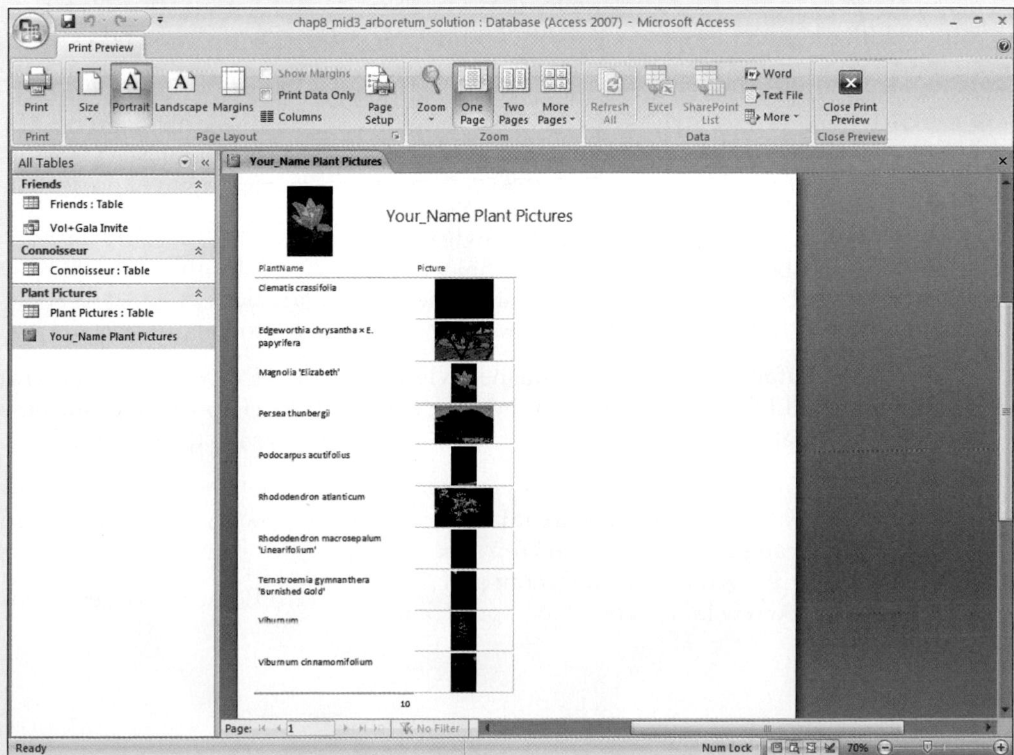

Figure 8.66 Report Displaying Resized Attachment Controls

Capstone Exercise

You work as an associate database manager at Replacements Ltd. This firm specializes in finding difficult to replace, no longer manufactured china, crystal, silver, and collectables. Today you need to create and test a hyperlink field to a manufacturer's Web site. The human resource manager has asked that you design a form that stores the information about each employees including their pictures and performance review files. You also need to export a query for a remotely located employee to view using a browser. Finally you will export a revenue query to Excel. When you have completed the work, you will compact and repair the database and make a backup of it.

Database File Setup

You need to copy an original database file, rename the copied file, and then open the copied database to complete this capstone exercise. After you open the copied database, you will replace an existing employee's name with your name.

a. Locate the file named *chap8_cap_replacement.accdb* and copy it to your production folder.

b. Rename the copied file **chap8_cap_replacement_solution.accdb**.

c. Open the *chap8_cap_replacement_solution.accdb* file and enable the content.

d. Open the **Employees table**.

e. Navigate to record 15 and replace *Your_Name* with your name. Press **Enter** and close the table.

f. Rename the Your_Name Revenue query with your name. Rename the Your_Name Revenue_crosstab query with your name.

Create Attachment and Hyperlinked Fields

You need to modify two tables in the database, the Manufacturers table and the Employees table. Some of the manufacturers with whom you do business continue to manufacture new china, crystal, and flatware. You have been asked to create a hyperlink field that links to their Web sites. You have also been asked to add an attachment field to the employees' records that will permit the attachment of their most recent performance reviews and photos.

a. Open the **Manufacturers table** in Datasheet view, create a new field named **Web site**, and define it as a hyperlink data type.

b. Add the appropriate URLs to the following two fields and test each link to make sure it launches a browser and locates the appropriate Web site. Waterford is http://www.waterford.com and Lenox is http://www.Lenox.com. Save, print, and close the table.

c. Open the **Employees table** and create a new field that is the Attachment data type. Only one department has completed the performance reviews so far. The files you need are on the student data disk in a folder named *chap8_cap_review_folder*. The files have been named with the UserID number for each employee.

d. Use Find in the EmployeeID field to locate the appropriate employee, then attach his/her picture and performance review file to the attachment field.

e. Save the design changes to the table and leave the table open.

Create a New Form

You need to create a form that will display the Employees table data, including the newly attached photos and performance reviews.

a. Create a form based on the Employees table and open it in layout view. Enlarge the attachment control.

b. Find your name. Use the Mini toolbar to display your picture. Print only the form containing your information.

c. Find the form containing Michelle Bowden's information. Use the Mini toolbar to display the Word icon indicating a Word file has been attached. Print only the form containing Ms. Bowden's information.

d. Save the form as **Your_Name Employees**. Close the form and table.

Export a Query to an HTML File

You need to create an HTML file to send to a remotely located employee who is using a borrowed computer without Microsoft Office installed on it.

a. Open the **Your_Name Revenue query**. Add a total row and sum the Revenue field. Make sure the field property is set to Currency. Save the changes to the query.

b. Export this query to an HTML file. Save the file as **chap8_cap_replacement_solution.html**. Do not save the export steps.

c. Open the exported file in a browser to verify the work. Print the file from the browser. Close the browser.

d. Return to Access. Close the query.

Export Data for an Excel User and Save the Export

You need to export a crosstab query with formatting and layout to Excel and save the export steps for reuse.

a. Open the **Your_Name Revenue_Crosstab query** in Datasheet view.

b. Export the query to an Excel workbook named **chap8_cap_replacement_solution.xlsx**.

c. After the export finishes, save the export steps with a description of Create an Excel file for Mary Hughes.

d. Print and close the Excel workbook.

e. Compact and repair the database.

f. Close the file.

Mini Cases

Use the rubric following the case as a guide to evaluate your work, but keep in mind that your instructor may impose additional grading criteria or use a different standard to judge your work.

Creating Attachment Fields

GENERAL CASE

The *chap8_mc1_preschool.accdb* file contains data from a small preschool. Each year they raise money through a silent auction and a dinner. You are maintaining the database tracking the donated items. The auction chairperson believes the auction will raise more money if the literature about what has been donated contains pictures of the items. Copy the *chap8_mc1_preschool.accdb* file, rename the copied file **chap8_mc1_preschool_solution.accdb**, open the copied file, and enable the content. Use the skills from this chapter to perform several tasks. Open the Donors table and replace Your_Name with your name. Create a new field that is an attachment field. Populate it with at least five pictures of donated items. You may use clip art or the Internet or your camera to create the pictures. Add the pictures to the items for auction report. Print the results. Compact, repair, and back up your database.

Performance Elements	Exceeds Expectations	Meets Expectations	Below Expectations
Field creation and population	Field created and populated.	Field created, but pictures were not descriptive or insufficient.	Data missing or incorrect.
Using an attachment field in a report	The new field successfully integrated into the report.	The new field was added to the report, but mispositioned.	Field missing or inaccurate.

Exporting to Excel

RESEARCH CASE

The *chap8_mc2_replacement.accdb* file contains data from an international china, crystal, flatware, and collectables firm. This chapter introduced you to the power of data sharing. You now know how to import and export data from and to many different types of file formats. The provided file gives you two queries displaying the same information. The Your_Name Revenue query summarizes revenue by salesperson and pattern name using a PivotTable. When in datasheet view, the Your_Name Revenue query contains the data needed to construct the PivotTable. The Your_Name Revenue_Crosstab query provides the same information but uses a crosstab query to aggregate and summarize the data. Rename the queries with your name. Export the queries to Excel, naming the exported files **chap8_mc2_replacement_crosstab.xlsx**, **chap8_mc2_replacement_datasheet.xlsx**, and **chap8_mc2_replacement_pivot.xlsx**. Compare the resulting data. If you need to share data with an Excel user, which type of query yields better exported results? Would you select a different source for the data export for different users of data? Why? Write a memo to your instructor that explains the results of the exports and when you might use the different sources; save the file as **chap8_mc2_replacement_solution.docx**.

Performance Elements	Exceeds Expectations	Meets Expectations	Below Expectations
Query exports	All three exports successfully created and named.	Two of the three export files successfully created.	Export files missing, incomplete, or corrupted.
Demonstrates an understanding of the export results	Clearly articulates the differences in output that result from the different inputs.	Demonstrates some understanding of the differences, but failed to identify causal comprehension.	Inability to identify any differences beyond cosmetic issues.
Demonstrates an understanding of how different users of data in an organization have differing data needs	Clearly articulates differing data needs and user skills. Correctly identified what type of data to supply to different user types.	Clearly articulates differing data needs and user skills but was not able to connect data types to different user types.	Failed to communicate comprehension of either different users or different data needs.
Summarize and communicate	Discussion clearly written and communicative.	Discussion indicates some understanding but also weaknesses.	Discussion missing or incomprehensible.

Exporting to Word

DISASTER RECOVERY

A coworker called you into his office and asked for your help. You work for a real estate firm and manage the databases. You are often called upon to help the other employees of the firm locate the data they need in order to do their work. Your task today is to generate an Access report that can be used by an MS Word user. The file must have the docx extension because the user cannot find any files using the Word open dialog box if the file has any other extension. Copy the *chap8_mc3_realestate.accdb* file, rename the copied file **chap8_mc3_realestate_solution.accdb**, open the file, and enable the content. Open the Your_Name Sales report. Change the title by replacing Your_Name with your name. Export it to Word. Save the Word document as **chap8_mc3_realestate_solution.docx.** Print the Word document. Compact, repair, and back up your database.

Performance Elements	Exceeds Expectations	Meets Expectations	Below Expectations
Problem identification	Correct identification and correction of all problems.	Correct identification of all errors and correction of some problems.	Errors neither located nor corrected.
Problem solving	Appropriate steps taken to resolve the problem successfully.	Appropriate steps taken to resolve the problem partially but not completely.	Errors neither located nor corrected.

chapter 9 | **Access**

Bulletproofing the Database

Protecting Data and Analyzing Database Performance

After you read this chapter, you will be able to:

1. Encrypt and password-protect a database **(page 579)**.
2. Digitally sign and publish the database **(page 581)**.
3. Save the database as an ACCDE file **(page 582)**.
4. Analyze database documentation **(page 590)**.
5. Analyze database performance **(page 592)**.
6. Analyze database table structure and relationships **(page 593)**.
7. Move data to new database files **(page 596)**.
8. Analyze and optimize object relationships in an Access database **(page 606)**
9. Create usable switchboards **(page 611)**.

Hands-On Exercises

Exercises	Skills Covered
1. MANAGING AND SECURING THE DATA (page 584) **Open:** chap9_ho1_students.accdb **Save as:** chap9_ho1_students_solution.accdb, chap9_ho1_students_solution.accdc, and chap9_ho1_students_solution.accde	• Open a Database with Exclusive Access • Encrypt a Database with a Password • Create a Digital Signature • Apply a Digital Signature and Create a New Package for Distribution • Convert the Database to the ACCDE File Format
2. USING DATABASE TOOLS (page 601) **Open:** chap9_ho2_coffee.accdb **Save as:** chap9_ho2_coffee_solution.accdb and chap9_ho2_coffee_solution_be.accdb	• Analyze Relationships in the Database • Use Performance Analyzer and Optimize the Database • Manually Complete the Optimization Process After Optimization • Split the Database into a Back-end and Front-end
3. BUILD A BASIC SWITCHBOARD (page 613) **Open:** chap9_ho3_students.accdb **Save as:** chap9_ho3_students_solution.accdb	• Start the Switchboard Manager • Complete the Switchboard • Test the Switchboard • Insert the Clip Art • Set Startup Options • Examine Object Dependencies

CASE STUDY

Projects Plus

You recently were asked to secure the Access database that Rupee Patel, vice president of Sales at your company, uses to keep track of customers and their purchases. Ms. Patel is concerned that as the database grows, it might not function properly, as she quickly built it without an understanding as to what tables are and how they should be related. She would like some type of documentation as backup to database design when you finish your work on this project, but she isn't sure what she wants. You mention that Access can produce documentation to suit her needs and that you will provide this as part of your solution.

Ms. Patel also mentions that she wants to give her junior manager, Micah Fecarotta, access to the database so that he can add customer and sales information. However, other employees should not be able to open the database because it contains vital company information. She asks you how she can catch unauthorized modifications to the database. You mention that you will need to do some research to come up with the best solution to that request. Finally, Ms. Patel asks you to add a switchboard to the database so that Micah can add his information in a familiar Windows environment. She also mentions that she is worried that Micah might inadvertently delete something important, such as a table or report, since he is unfamiliar with how to directly enter data into a database. You ask Ms. Patel if other people might later be given the ability to add customer and purchase information to the database. She says that she doesn't think so, but looks away and adds, "Maybe Greta. Next year, she will probably be promoted."

Case Study

Your task is to analyze the performance of the database, implement all suggestions, and create a switchboard. You also decide to split the database, keeping the database tables in a network folder, providing Micah with a front-end copy of the database that he can use to enter data when he is connected to the local area network. You also need to digitally sign and encrypt the database with a password.

Your Assignment

- Read the chapter, paying special attention to analyzer and documenter tools, data dictionary, splitting a database, and making an ACCDE database.
- Copy the *chap9_case_marketing.accdb* file to your production folder and rename it **chap9_case_marketing_solution.accdb**.
- Open each table and familiarize yourself with the data.
- Open the Relationships window and acquaint yourself with the tables, fields, and relationships among the tables in the database.
- Analyze database performance by selecting all database objects and implement any suggested recommendations.
- Create a data dictionary for the database. Format the report in landscape orientation. Print the last page of the report.
- Create a switchboard for the Employee Details form, Open Projects list form, All Open Projects report, and Deliverables by Assigned To report. Also add a switchboard item to exit the database.
- Password-protect the database. Use **P@ssw0rd** as the password.
- Save the file as **chap9_case_marketing_password_solution.accdb**.
- Split the database into a front- and back-end. Save the databases as **chap9_case_marketing_fe_solution.accdb** and **chap9_case_marketing_be_solution.accdb**.

Data Protection

The growing problem of identify theft, the outright destruction of corporate records, and new data retention rules passed by the U.S. Congress emphasize how urgent it is that electronic data be strongly protected. The Sarbanes-Oxley Act (SOX) of 2002 mandates that all electronic documents, which include databases, be securely maintained for five years.

Security is broadly defined as the protection of assets from unauthorized access, change, or destruction and can be broken down into two general categories: physical security and logical security. Physical security involves protecting assets you can touch, such as computers, routers, tapes, and vaults. Security of nonphysical, or logical, assets protects databases and the rules that allow and restrict access to the data. Anything that endangers an asset is a threat. The measures that you take to protect your assets are known as ***countermeasures***.

Countermeasures are steps taken to protect a company's assets.

The depth and number of your countermeasures depend upon the potential threats to your physical and logical data and their value to your organization. If your database catalogs your music collection, you might deem that data as having low value and perhaps password-protect the database, placing the database in a folder on your computer that restricts who can open objects in the folder. However, if your database contains contact information about your customer base and the products they purchase, you would probably consider that data a strategic company asset and implement a number of countermeasures in order to physically and logically safeguard it so that only people who have a "need to know" have access to its contents.

(You can do three basic things to secure your database.)

Carrying this example one step further, if your database contains payroll data, SOX requires that this data be stored intact, with no changes to its data, for the entire five-year retention period. Failure to follow these rules can result in loss of your job, imprisonment, and large fines.

Database security always begins with identifying the risk you face, determining a course of action you will take to protect the data, and estimating the cost of the security measures planned. After you protect data, you can use the Table Analyzing Wizard and the Performance Analyzer to improve database performance. You can do three basic things to secure your database. Each of these denies (or impedes) access to the database in some way. These are:

1. Require a password to open the database.
2. Digitally sign databases you create and open them in trusted locations.
3. Save the database with the .accde file extension.

In this section, you learn how to manage data. Specifically, you will learn about security precautions available from within Microsoft Access that can be utilized to protect your database from threats to its logical security.

Encrypting and Password-Protecting a Database

Encryption encodes a file so that unintelligible text appears if another program is used to gain unauthorized access to the file.

Access 2007 incorporates stronger encryption techniques to help keep your databases secure. ***Encryption*** is the process of encoding the contents of a file, making the contents unreadable if the file is opened through tampering tools. Encrypting a database makes its contents unintelligible to other programs and is especially useful when you intend to distribute, e-mail, or store your database on removable media such as a USB jump drive, tape, or disk. Encryption is accomplished through the use of a math formula, or algorithm, that converts the plain, unencrypted data (a password or an entire database) into meaningless data, or secret code, that makes no sense without the exact math formula used to encrypt the data. Because trillions of secret codes can be generated, encrypted data are virtually impossible to break.

A ***password*** prevents unauthorized access or modification of a secured file.

One of the first methods to encrypt a database is to assign a password to the database. A ***password*** is a security mechanism in the form of characters that prevents unauthorized access or modification of a secured file. Passwords typically include a combination of letters and numbers. A good password should be impossible for unauthorized users to guess. In particular, use at least six or eight characters that combine uppercase and lowercase letters, numbers, and symbols to make the password more difficult for others to guess. A weak password is File07. A stronger password is Exp7msA8. Be sure to remember the passwords you assign to your files. If you forget a password, you will not be able to recover the contents of the file.

TIP Additional Password Tips

You can find additional password tips by searching for the key term *password* in Access Help. Click the *Help protect your personal information with strong passwords* to display information on Microsoft's Web site.

Exclusive access enables one person to have sole access to a database.

The imposition of a password and encryption is easily done, but it requires that the database be opened with ***exclusive access***. This means that you have sole access to the database while you are establishing the password, and that others are prevented from opening or using the database during that time. To open a database with exclusive access, display the Open dialog box, select the database you want to open, click the Open drop-down arrow, and select Open Exclusive.

After opening a database in exclusive mode, you are ready to assign a password. To do this, click Encrypt with Password in the Database Tools group on the Database Tools tab (see Figure 9.1). The Set Database Password dialog box opens so that you can enter and verify a password. The database is encrypted when you click OK in the Set Database Password dialog box. Once the password is set, close the database and then open it again as usual. When you open the database, the Password Required dialog box appears. You must enter the correct password and click OK to open the database now.

Password-protect and encrypt the database

Convert an existing database to ACCDE file format

Figure 9.1 The Database Tools Tab Illustrating Password Protection and Encryption

TIP Remove a Password

If you want to remove a password, you must open the database using the Open Exclusive option. Then click Decrypt Database in the Database Tools group on the Database Tools tab. In the Unset Database Password dialog box, enter the password and click OK.

Digitally Signing and Publishing the Database

A ***digital signature*** is an electronic, encryption-based stamp that confirms the validity of the file.

Digital signatures are electronic, encryption-based, secure stamps of authentication that confirm who authorized the file, that the file is valid, and that no changes have been made to the file after its authentication. You can apply digital signatures to databases, documents, spreadsheets, or macros that you create. By digitally signing and distributing your database, you ensure other users that the database has not been tampered with. In other words, if users trust the entity that created the digital signature, they can trust your database by allowing any macros or Visual Basic (VB) code to run when they use the database.

A ***certification authority (CA)*** is a commercial company that validates digital signatures.

To obtain a digital signature, you must purchase one from a qualified ***certification authority (CA)*** or you can create one yourself. CAs are commercial companies, such as VeriSign, that issue and validate identities using digital signatures for a fee. Choose a CA if you need a high-level of security. Most countries have stringent laws that regulate CAs so that purchasers can be sure that their digital signatures are valid.

A ***timestamp*** encrypts the date and time as part of a digital signature.

You can create a self-signed personal digital signature using Microsoft Office Tools and attach it immediately before you distribute the database file to other users. Keep in mind that a digital signature does not prove that you own the database. By use of a timestamp, it can prove that you were the last person to modify it. You provide the ***timestamp*** information to others when you distribute, or publish, your database. By examining the timestamp on your database, you can prove that it has or has not been modified since you applied your signature. A timestamp is a combination of the date and time that is encrypted as part of the digital signature. For a timestamp to be truly valid to others, it must be passed through some timestamping service provider. Again, this can be a commercial entity or a server located on your network. Further discussion of this process is outside the scope of this textbook.

You can digitally sign and publish your database simultaneously from within Access 2007. To digitally sign and publish your database, click the Office Button, click Publish, and select Package and Sign. When the Select Certificate dialog box opens (see Figure 9.2), select an existing certificate. When you click OK, the database is packaged, or converted to the new .accdc file format, and digitally signed with your certificate.

Figure 9.2 Package a Database by Applying a Digital Signature

Saving the Database as an ACCDE File

Access Database Executable (ACCDE) files remove VBA code, deny certain permissions, and prohibit use of database objects.

Access 2007 introduces the new file extension *.accde*. ***Access Database Executable (ACCDE)*** files remove all VBA source code, deny users permission to make design and name changes to forms or reports within the database, and prohibit users from creating new forms and reports. In other words, users can execute the VBA code, but they cannot modify it. The ACCDE file type replaces the MDE (Microsoft Database Executable) file type from earlier versions of Access.

You create a database with the .accde file extension within Access 2007. This is a simple process that saves your existing database with the new file extension, making a copy of the last saved edition of your database. When you click Make ACCDE in the Database Tools group on the Database Tools tab (see Figure 9.1), the Save As dialog box opens. The *File name* box displays the same main name as the original database with the *.accde* extension. The *Save as type* box displays ACCDE File (*.accde). Click Save to save the database with the .accde file format.

Before you can convert a database to the .accde file format, you must first open the database with Exclusive Access. When you open a file in this way, anyone else who attempts to open the database will receive a "file already in use" message. This means that only you will be able to make changes to the database when you have it open and that other users can open a read-only copy of the database.

Once a database is converted to .accde, it cannot be converted back to its source format (.accdb). Therefore, keep your original database—the database as it existed before being converted to the .accde file format—in a safe place. This will really come in handy in cases where you convert your database to .accde and later find out that one or more of its underlying objects (in this case, a form, report, VBA code, or VBA module) needs to be changed. Without your original database, you would not be able to make these changes. You would be forced to create the database again.

As you have observed in the exercises throughout this textbook, Access supports many different file types. A typical Access 2007 database will have the .accdb file extension. Microsoft includes database templates in Access 2007. When you first open Access, the left pane lists Template Categories. Click Local Templates to view templates stored on your computer. Table 9.1 lists common Access 2007 file types.

Table 9.1 Access 2007 File Types

.accdb	Microsoft Office Access 2007 Database
.accdc	Microsoft Office Access Digitally Signed Database Package
.accde	Microsoft Office Access Database Executable
.accdt	Microsoft Office Access 2007 Database Template

In the first hands-on exercise, you will practice all of the security measures discussed in this section. Table 9.2 recaps the highlights from this section.

Table 9.2 Security Measures and Their Intended Results

Countermeasure	Result
Password-protect and encrypt	Makes the database unintelligible to other programs. Forces users to enter a password to open the database.
Digital signature	Provides proof to others that you last modified the database. Not very secure without some type of CA.
Make ACCDE	Removes VB code from database and stops users from making changes to database forms and reports.

Database Tools | Reference

Command	Name	Description
	Object Dependencies	Shows database objects that use the selected object. For example, shows queries that are dependent on the selected table.
	Database Documenter	Launches the Documenter so that you can obtain a report that documents objects—tables, queries, forms, reports, macros, and modules—in a database. For example, Documenter lists all field names in a table and their attributes, such as data type and size. The generated documented reports helps database designers analyze database design.
	Analyze Performance	Launches the Performance Analyzer to analyze objects—tables, queries, forms, reports, macros, and modules—and provide recommendations, suggestions, and ideas for optimizing the database to improve efficiency. The user can then select which changes to implement.
	Analyze Table	Launches the Table Analyzer Wizard that analyzes tables to identify duplicate information and recommends design changes to eliminate redundancy by splitting tables into two or more related tables, specify primary keys, rename tables, etc.
	Access Database	Splits a database into two files: (1) the back-end database that contains the original tables; (2) the front-end database in which the tables are removed and replaced with links to the tables that are moved to the back-end database; the front-end database contains queries, forms, and reports.
	Switchboard Manager	Builds switchboards with up to eight buttons to open a form in Add Mode or edit Mode, open a report, design application, exit the application, and run a macro or code. The designer selects the specific objects, such as a form, to open. Also enables the designer to edit, delete, and move up or down the items on the switchboard.
	Encrypt with Password	Displays the Set Database Password dialog box so that you can enter a password to protect the database against unauthorized opening and changes. Requires that you first open the database in Exclusive Access mode prior to setting the password.
	Make ACCDE	Creates an execute-only copy of the database by removing Visual Basic code and stops users from making changes to database forms and reports.

Hands-On Exercises

1 | Managing and Securing the Data

Skills covered: 1. Open a Database with Exclusive Access **2.** Encrypt a Database with a Password **3.** Create a Digital Signature **4.** Apply a Digital Signature and Create a New Package for Distribution **5.** Convert the Database to the ACCDE File Format

Step 1
Open a Database with Exclusive Access

Refer to Figure 9.3 as you complete Step 1.

a. Use Windows Explorer to locate the file named *chap9_ho1_students.accdb*. Copy the file to your production folder and rename it **chap9_ho1_students_solution.accdb**.

b. Start Microsoft Access. Click the **Office Button** and select **Open**.

TROUBLESHOOTING: Carefully follow the steps that follow so that you open the database properly. If you do not open the database with exclusive access, you will not be able to encrypt and password-protect the database.

c. Select the *chap9_ho1_students_solution.accdb* database file. Do not double-click the file or click Open.

d. Click the **Open drop-down arrow** and select **Open Exclusive**.

The database is now open and you have exclusive rights to its contents. No other user can modify the database when you have it open in exclusive mode.

e. Click **Options** on the Security Warning toolbar, click **Enable this content** in the Microsoft Office Security Options dialog box, and click **OK**.

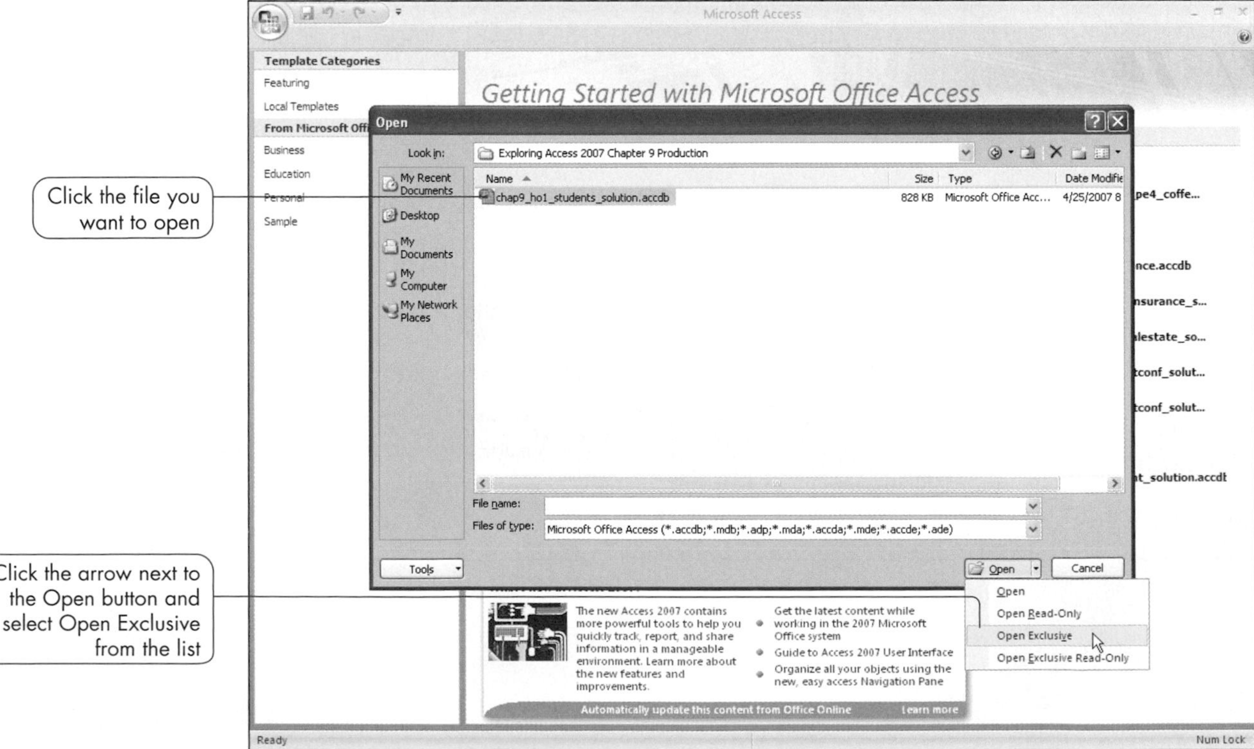

Figure 9.3 Open Exclusive Option

Step 2
Encrypt a Database with a Password

Refer to Figures 9.4 and 9.5 as you complete Step 2.

a. Click the **Database Tools tab** and click **Encrypt with Password** in the Database Tools group.

TROUBLESHOOTING: If the dialog box shown in Figure 9.4 appears, close the database and start again at Step 1. The database was not opened with exclusive access and cannot be encrypted.

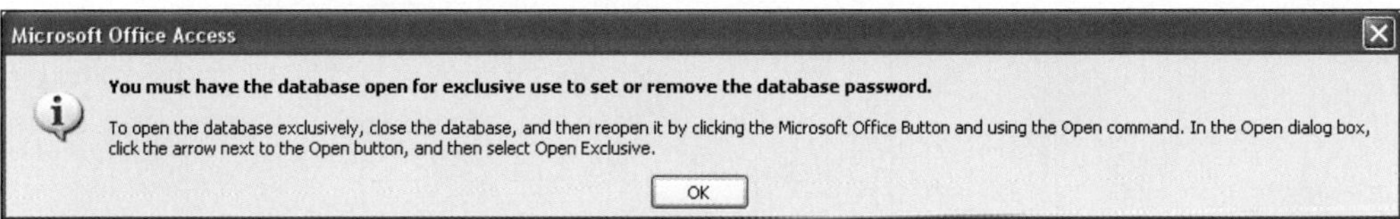

Microsoft Office Access
You must have the database open for exclusive use to set or remove the database password.
To open the database exclusively, close the database, and then reopen it by clicking the Microsoft Office Button and using the Open command. In the Open dialog box, click the arrow next to the Open button, and then select Open Exclusive.
OK

Figure 9.4 Password Cannot Be Applied

The Set Database Password dialog box opens (see Figure 9.5).

b. Enter the password **P@ssw0rd** in the **Password** box and enter the same password in the **Verify** box. Click **OK** to set the password and encrypt the database.

You need to test the password to be sure that it works.

c. Close the *chap9_ho1_students_solution* database, and then open it again as you would normally.

The Password Required dialog box opens, prompting you to enter the password to open the database.

d. Type **P@ssw0rd** in the **Enter database password** box and click **OK**.

e. Repeat Step 1e to enable the content.

Figure 9.5 Enter your Password Twice to Encrypt the Database

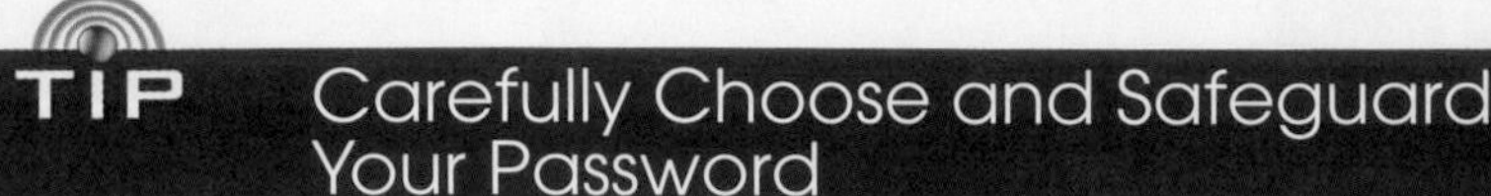

TIP Carefully Choose and Safeguard Your Password

A good password should be easy to remember, but difficult to break. One way to create such a password is to think of a sentence and use the first letter in each word to create the password. For example, "My grandmother's birthday is March 26" yields Mgbi@M23M26 as the password. It looks like a series of random characters, but it's easy to remember because you created the sentence in the first place. Note the combination of upper- and lowercase letters, numbers, and special characters. This complexity makes it difficult to break a password of eight characters or more. Be sure that you remember the password, or you will not be able to open the database in the future.

Step 3 Create a Digital Signature

Refer to Figure 9.6 as you complete Step 3.

a. Click **Start**, point to **All Programs**, point to **Microsoft Office**, point to **Microsoft Office Tools**, and select **Digital Certificate for VBA Projects**.

b. Type **TestCert** in the **Your certificate's name** box and click **OK**.

   The SelfCert Success dialog box appears, confirming that you successfully created a new certificate.

c. Click **OK**.

Figure 9.6 Create Digital Certificate Dialog Box

Step 4
Apply a Digital Signature and Create a New Package for Distribution

Refer to Figures 9.7 and 9.8 as you complete Step 4.

a. With the *chap9_ho1_students_solution* file open in Access, click the **Office Button**, point to the **Publish**, and select **Package and Sign**.

   The Select Certificate dialog box appears so that you can select the certificate you want to use for the database.

b. Select **TestCert**, the name of the certificate that you want to use to digitally sign this database, and then click **OK**.

   The Create Microsoft Office Access Signed Package dialog box opens so that you can change the name of the digitally signed database if you want. Notice that the file extension is changed to *.accdc*. The digitally signed file name is *chap9_ho1_students_solution.accdc*, and the regular database is *chap9_ho1_students_solution.accdb*.

c. Click **Create** to make a new signed package.

   Your database is now packaged with your digital signature so that you can deliver the database to other people who trust your certificate. The signed database closes, and then the original database opens again.

Figure 9.7 Select Certificate Dialog Box

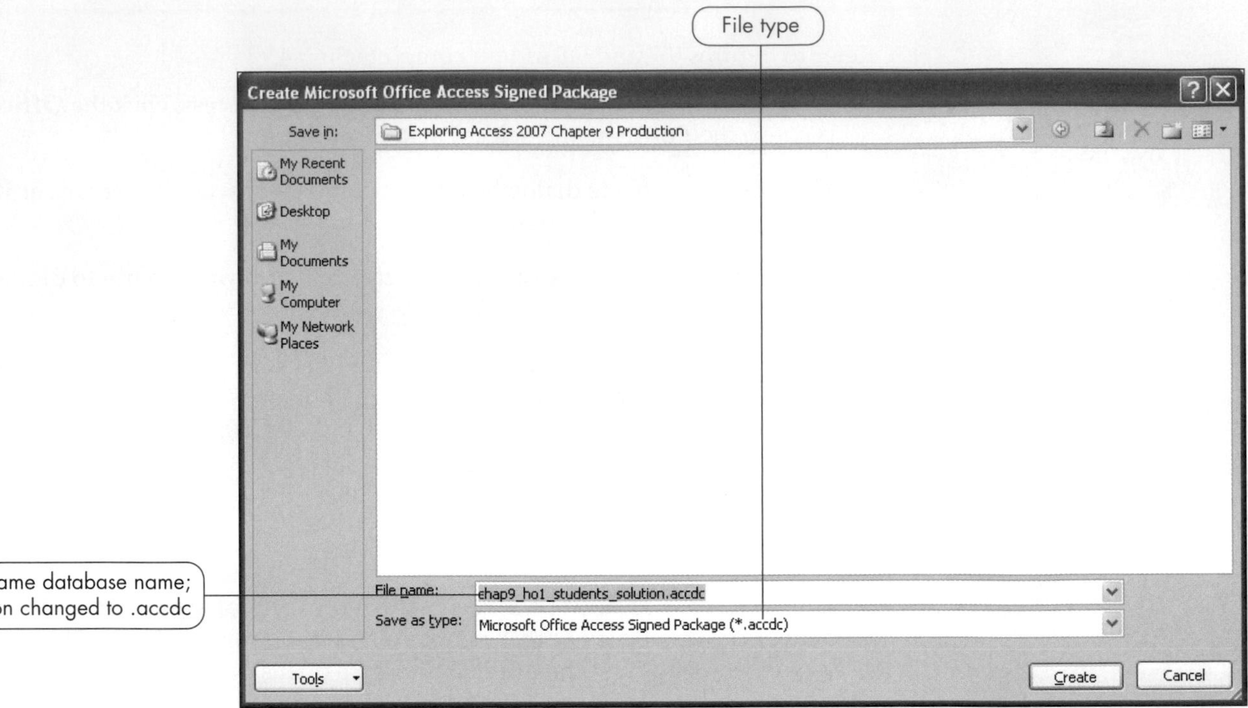

Figure 9.8 Creating a New Signed Package

TIP View the Certificates Currently Installed on Your Computer

Follow these steps to view, export, or remove certificates on your computer through Internet Explorer: Open Internet Explorer, display the Tools menu, select Internet Options, and click the Content tab. Click Certificates for the listing of all of the certificates currently installed on your computer.

Step 5 Convert the Database to the ACCDE File Format

Refer to Figure 9.9 as you complete Step 5.

a. Click the **Database Tools tab** and click **Make ACCDE** in the Database Tools group on the Database Tools tab.

   The Save As dialog box opens. The default *Save as type* is ACCDE File (*.accde), and the suggested file name is *chap9_ho1_students_solution.accde*.

b. Click **Save** to create an .accde copy of your database.

c. Close the file. Exit Access if you do not want to continue with the next exercise at this time.

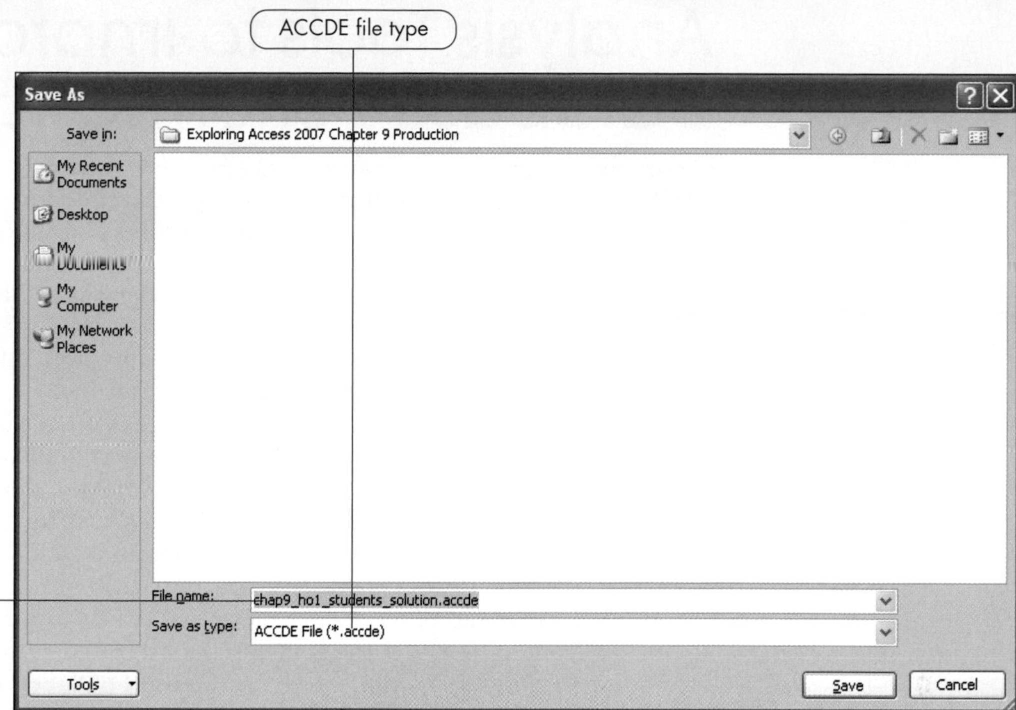

Figure 9.9 The Make ACCDE Save As Dialog Box

TIP How do I know which database is open?

When you select Make ACCDE in the Database Tools group, you make a copy (refer to Figure 9.9) of the database that is currently open within Access 2007. After you create an .accde file, Access does not open it; a copy is created in the location you selected in Step 5a. The original .accdb database file opens again. If you want to open the .accde file, close the open database and open the .accde copy as you would open any other Access database.

Analysis Tools to Improve Database Performance

Compared to competing database management systems (DBMS), Access is easy to use and provides solid performance in a production environment. Often, Access databases are created to solve an immediate business problem. A supervisor asks you to create a database to store inventory data for a small shop in the plant. Then, other departments learn of the database and ask for their data to be added to the database. As new tables, forms, and data are added to the database, its performance may decline because reports and queries take a long time to run. This slower performance is often due to the fact that Access databases are often created and modified by accountants, biologists, and managers who lack formal training in how to construct a database that performs well, even as the database undergoes dramatic change in its structure and size. For example, a field biologist creating 10 new tables might not understand how to relate the tables so that queries against these tables run quickly.

(Access provides three useful tools database administrators can use to create documentation, analyze database performance, and rework table structure.)

Many database administrators believe that if a database runs slowly, things will speed up tremendously if the database is migrated out of Access and into an enterprise-level or large DBMS, such as Microsoft SQL Server 2005. This is far from true since performance has more to do with database design than it does with the platform or computer under which the database runs. However, many good reasons exist to use Access rather than move to a large DBMS. Some of these reasons include wizards to create tables, forms, and reports and a graphical user interface (GUI) that is intuitive to Access users. Relating database tables is much easier to accomplish through a GUI than a command line interface. Access can also run on a desktop computer and does not require its own dedicated server as might a SQL Server DBMS. Access provides three useful tools that database administrators can use to create documentation, analyze database performance, and rework table structure.

In this section, you use data analysis tools. These tools are the Database Documenter, Performance Analyzer, and Table Analyzer and are available in the Analyze group on the Database Tools tab (see Figure 9.10).

These tools assist you in analyzing the database

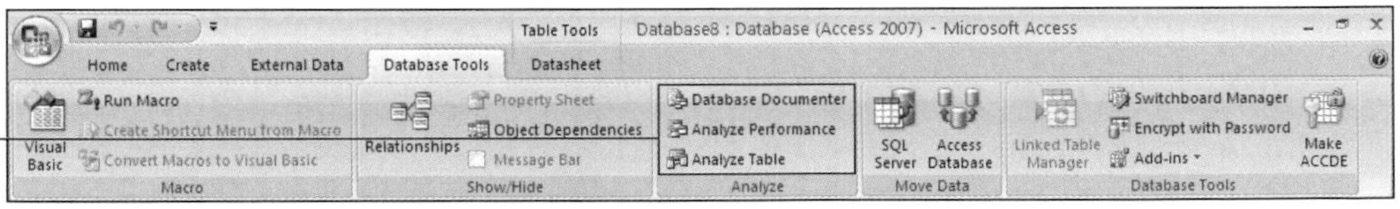

Figure 9.10 Database Analysis Tools

Analyzing Database Documentation

The ***Database Documenter*** creates documentation about all database objects.

The ***Database Documenter*** creates a data dictionary that itemizes and lists the attributes for any object in the database. For example, the Documenter lists the background color, caption, font size, and much more for every text box found in the database. This report can easily run hundreds of pages long for even a small database. Why would you want to generate so much information about your database? Suppose a database needs to be enhanced by adding more tables and forms to its existing structure. The Documenter can provide us with all of the existing table field names and their attributes. It also provides the names of every button and field on all of your forms, saving designers from being forced to open a form and examine each of its elements. Of course, these are just a few of the many reasons database designers find the Documenter such a great tool!

To use Database Documenter, click Database Documenter in the Analyze group on the Database Tools tab. The Documenter dialog box opens so that you can select objects to include in the report (see Figure 9.11). Each tab on the dialog box represents a database object that can be documented. After you select one or more objects, click OK to generate the report.

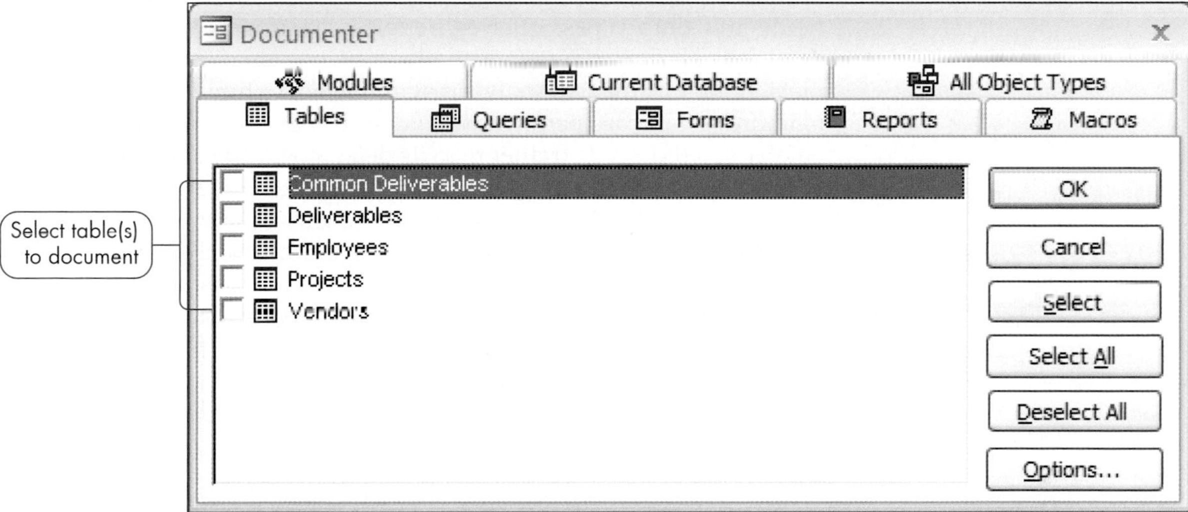

Figure 9.11 Documenter Dialog Box

The Documenter then creates a data dictionary that contains detailed information about the objects in your database. You should notice that the Print Preview tab is visible after the Documenter completes, which enables you to format and print the data dictionary (see Figure 9.12).

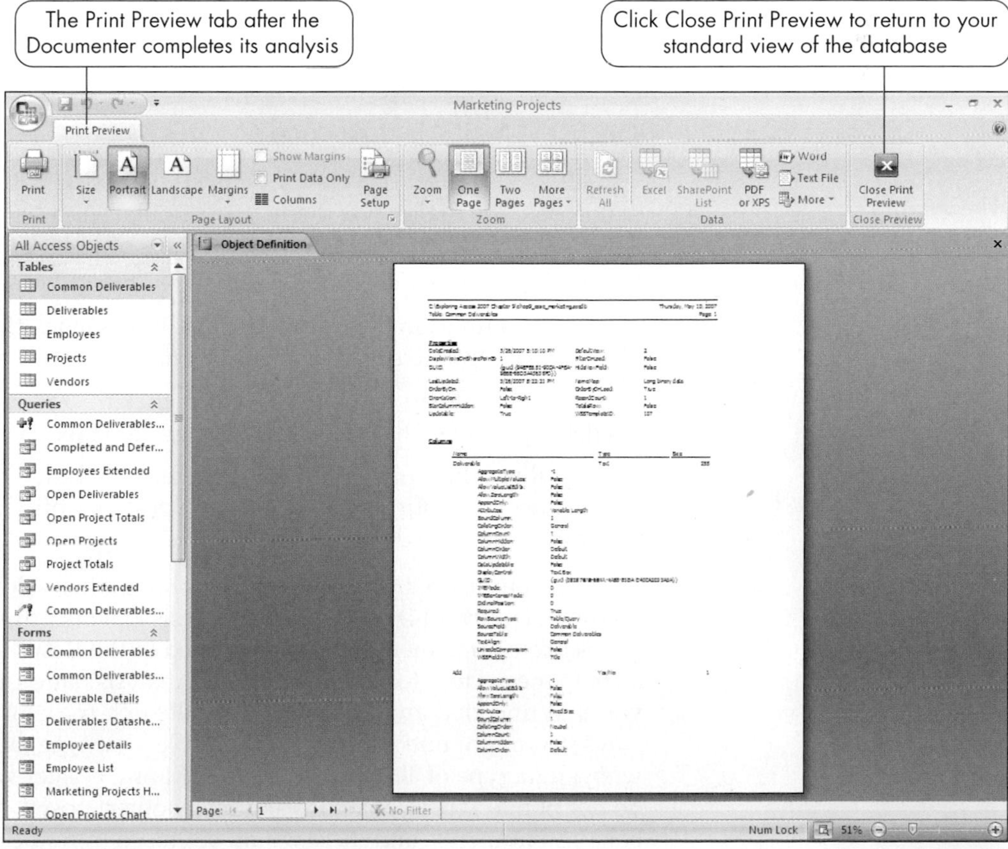

Figure 9.12 The Documenter in Print Preview

Analyzing Database Performance

The ***Performance Analyzer*** improves performance by recommending design changes to database objects.

The Performance Analyzer dialog box looks similar to that of the Documenter. However, the ***Performance Analyzer*** functionality is quite different, as it works to improve database performance by identifying choices made during database design that will slow performance when the database is put into a production or work environment. This is accomplished by analyzing any (or all) objects in the database such as fields and data types, queries, reports, and forms. Each tab in the Performance Analyzer window represents an object we can analyze. After object analysis is complete, the Performance Analyzer recommends optimizations that you can implement to improve database performance. For example, one optimization might be to save the database in the .accde (rather than its default .accdb) file format. This improves performance because an .accde file stores less design information about many of its objects.

To launch the Performance Analyzer, click Analyze Performance in the Analyze group on the Database Tools tab (refer to Figure 9.10) to display the Performance Analyzer dialog box shown in Figure 9.13. The Tables tab is selected. However, if users inform you that the database generally runs slow (e.g., reports take a long time to complete), you might choose to analyze All Object Types in an attempt to improve performance.

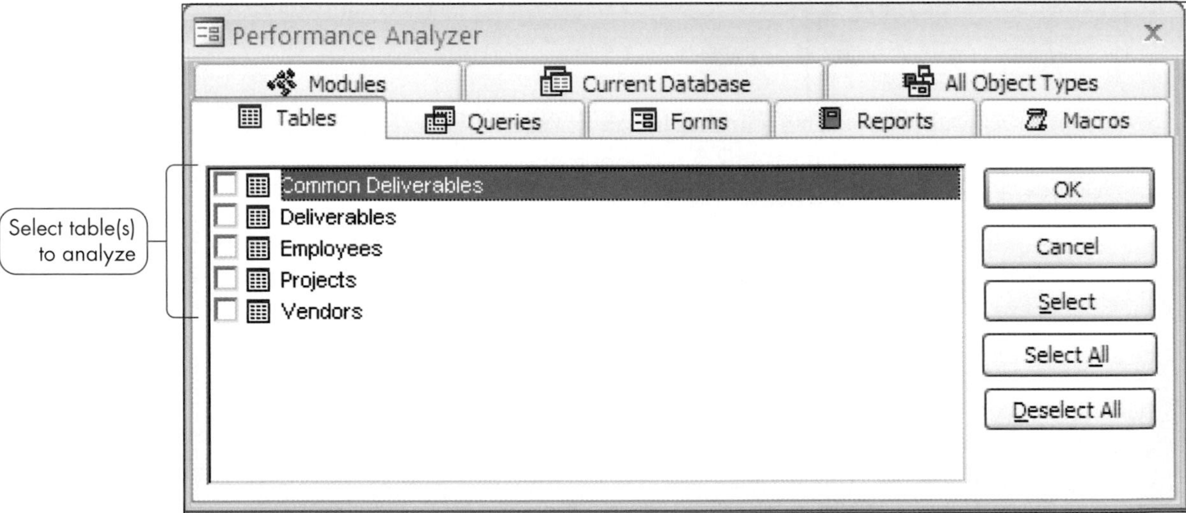

Figure 9.13 The Performance Analyzer Window

After you select objects for analysis and click OK in the Performance Analyzer dialog box, the dialog box displays a Results Analysis pane, as shown in Figure 9.14. An analysis results in three different types of potential solutions. An Analysis Note provides a brief description of a potential problem and its possible solution.

- **Recommendation**. Read the Analysis Notes, click the specific Recommendation, and click Optimize. The item's icon changes to Fixed after optimization.
- **Suggestion**. Read the Analysis Note, click the specific Recommendation, and click Optimize. The item's icon changes to Fixed after optimization.
- **Idea**. Read the Analysis Note and determine how you will manually implement this idea into your database. Access does not optimize Ideas, as these materially change database design.

You optimize a database by implementing (this is done when you click Optimize as shown in Figure 9.14) one or more Analysis Results. Always carefully read the Analysis Notes *before* implementing any item listed in the Results Analysis pane. Implementing an item means to select it in the Results Analysis pane and click Optimize. On occasion, you will find that an optimization results in a trade-off that affects your database in ways you might not consider. For example, changing an existing field named ZipCode with a data type of Text to a data type of Long Integer will erase any existing data that do not fit that type. Canadian (and many other) postal codes are alphanumeric (alphabetic and numeric), and these would be erased from the database. Often, changing data types as recommended will slightly improve performance.

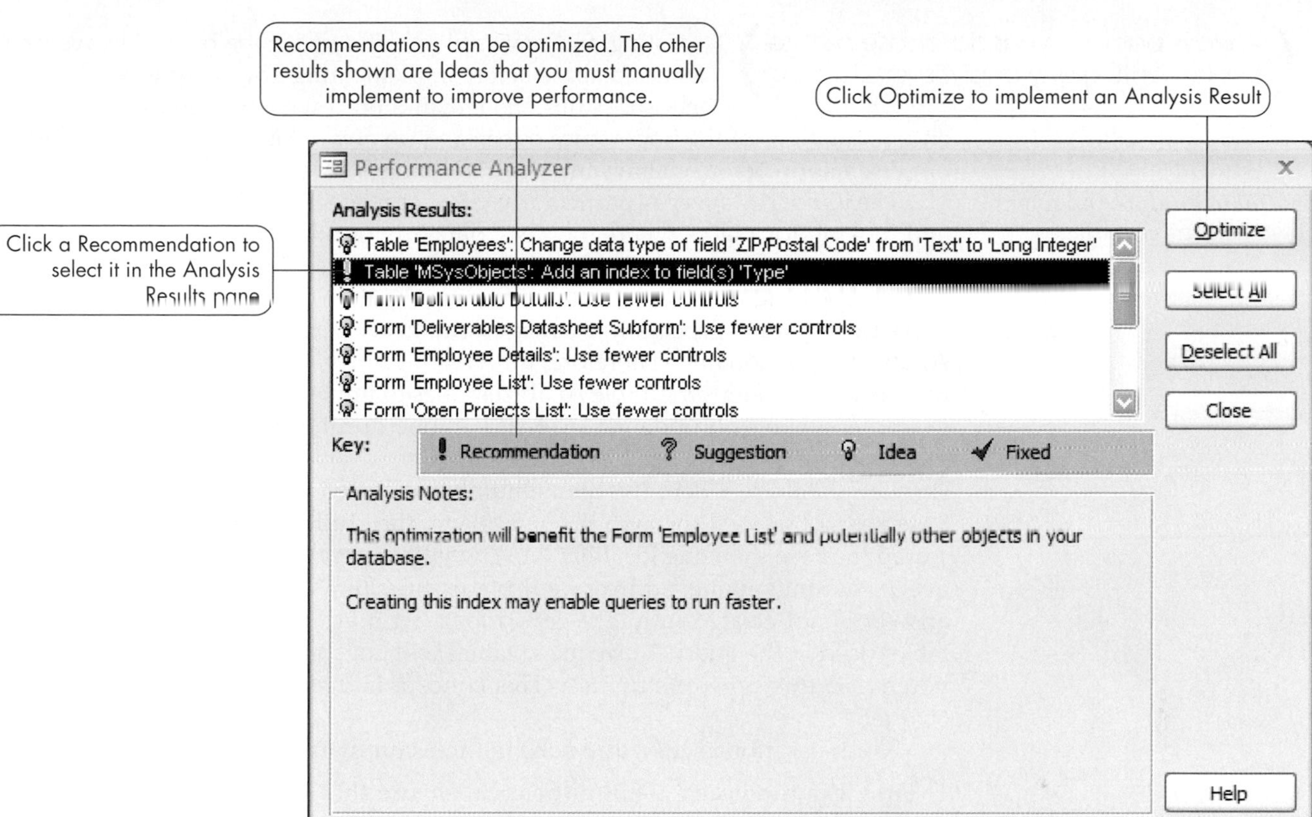

Figure 9.14 The Analysis Results Pane Window

An item that appears frequently in the Results Analysis pane is *Add an index*. This is a harmless fix that will slightly improve performance when implemented. Adding an index is similar to having a phone book that lists people by last name and again by phone number. Each one of these is an index. When you add an index to a table, you reduce the number of times that the database needs to ask the hard drive for information when a report or query is run. For large reports or queries, the time savings can be substantial. On the other hand, adding more than one or two indices to a table can decrease database performance because every time we add a new record to a database, the index needs to be recalculated. In a large database, this means that every time you add a new record to the database, the index is re-created, resulting in a longer period of time for each record saved. This would be similar to processing and printing a new phone book each time a family moved in or out of your city.

TIP Back Up Database Before Optimizing It

When analysis reveals many Recommendations and Suggestions, it is tempting to select them all and click Optimize. Do not do this without first considering the Analysis Note for each one. Then, only optimize after you have made a backup copy of your database. This way, you can revert back to the copy if the optimization yields results you did not anticipate.

Analyzing Database Table Structure and Relationships

Even when you apply all of the design principles discussed earlier, you often are unable to fully evaluate a database until it is put into a work environment. Inevitably, this leads to requests for new queries or reports. People will also decide that more data should be captured in the database, which means that more tables (and relationships between

(Always back up your database before implementing any analysis results.)

existing and new tables) will need to be built. Always back up your database before implementing any analysis results. We cannot stress this enough, and our own (sometimes painful) experience reminds us of the importance of backing up any database, document, workbook, or presentation before making any material changes.

The ***Table Analyzer*** examines how tables are constructed.

The ***Table Analyzer*** is particularly good at inspecting data stored in your tables and looking for places where the same data are found in more than one row. This is known as repeating data, which reflects poor database design. The process of eliminating repeating rows of data and designing the database with logical dependencies is part of a larger process known as normalization, and this process drives Table Analyzer functionality. Therefore, a review of normalization will help us to better understand the steps the Table Analyzer takes to improve database performance. For example, when you update a student's phone number in the database, you might often assume that you need to do this only once. This is true only in a properly constructed database where the phone number is stored in one location. When a database has not passed through normalization, the student's phone number might be stored in more than one location. Now, what happens when you run a report listing every student's name, address, and phone number? As you probably guessed, the answer is not clear. You might get a report with either number, depending on the tables used in the query. Normalized tables will not contain this design flaw and help you avoid this type of situation. This concept is discussed more fully later in the chapter.

Normalization is generally done in three cumulative stages, or levels, where:

First Normal Form (1NF) is the first normalization process, which requires that repeating groups be eliminated from a table.

Second Normal Form (2NF) is the second normalization process, which removes partial dependencies.

Third Normal Form (3NF) is the third normalization process, which removes transitive dependencies.

1. First, examine each column (field) to ensure that it does not duplicate another field in that table and that each field allows only a single value for each record. For example, if a field is named MovieCategories, you would not want another field in the same table to contain movie categories. In addition, group related fields together and create separate tables for each group. Within each table, create a unique field known as a primary key to identify each distinct record. The process of ensuring that each field contains different data, thus, eliminating repeating groups, grouping related fields into separate tables, and identifying a primary key for each table is called ***First Normal Form (1NF)***.
2. Next, examine entire columns, searching for the same column value in different table rows. For example, if a table named MovieActorNames contains a field named ActorLastName, listing the name Green for the same actor in more than one row would reflect poor design. Consider the work involved in updating our records should the actor's last name change. As before, creating a new table and establishing proper relationships between primary and foreign keys resolves this problem. This process of removing partial dependencies and further removing duplicate data is known as second normal form or 2NF ***Second Normal Form (2NF)***.
3. The third step of database normalization is where every column in a table depends upon that table's primary key to obtain its value. The process of removing transitive dependencies, fields that do not depend on the primary key, is known as ***Third Normal Form (3NF)***. As you will recall, the primary key uniquely identifies one row of data from every other row of data in the database. As an example, consider a table that stores an individual's first name, last name, address, city, state, and zip code. The primary key for this table is an AutoNumber (Access generates the number and guarantees that it will not be repeated within the database). As you probably guessed, no field value in the table depends on the primary key for its value, so this table would not be 3NF. However, if you replace the AutoNumber field with a CustomerID field in which you assign a value, the other columns are related or dependent upon the primary key value.

Taking normalization to this extreme (where every field depends on the primary key for its value) is usually not necessary and depends on factors such as your desired level of database stability and how many tables you can effectively manage. Normalization is a skill that is attained through designing many databases. A database with a large number of tables requires the skill of an experienced database administrator. With these normalization concepts in mind, the Table Analyzer will examine table relationships (or their lack thereof), suggesting improvements in how tables might be better related to each other.

To analyze a table, click Analyze Table in the Analyze group on the Database Tools tab to launch the Table Analyzer Wizard (see Figure 9.15). The output from this process should be tables that pass through normalization, resulting in the creation of additional tables in your database. The Table Analyzer Wizard explains problems for which it will search, how it will attempt to fix problems it identifies, and asks you to identify a table for analysis. You can take some control of the process by deciding which fields should be included in new tables created by the Table Analyzer Wizard or you can choose to let the wizard decide on your behalf.

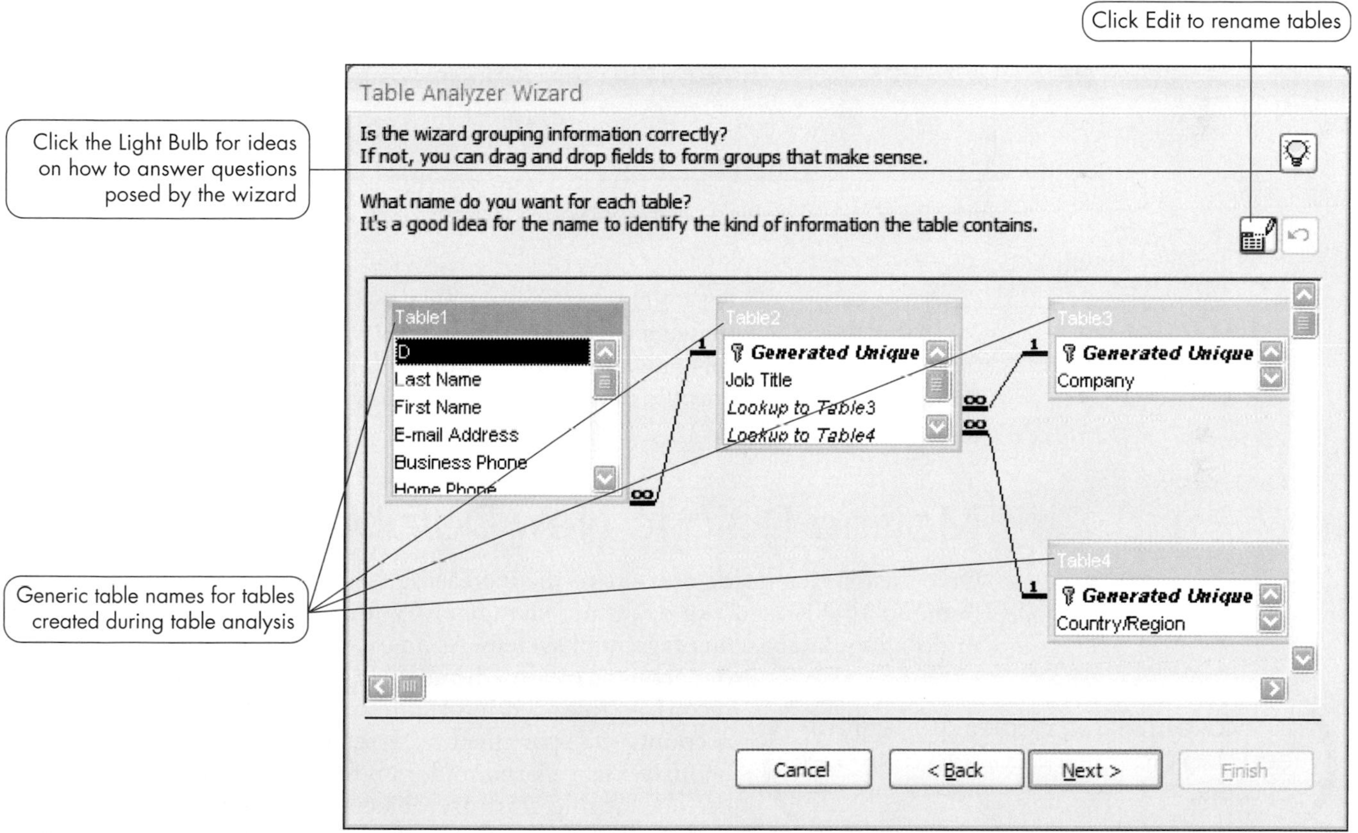

Figure 9.15 Inside the Table Analyzer Wizard

You might decide to click through the entire Table Analyzer Wizard, but we do not recommend doing so. Closely examine each question the wizard asks of you and decide whether to allow the action suggested. When the Table Analyzer Wizard creates new tables, you are also asked to name them and fix any data stored in fields that appear to be incorrect (typos or outright errors). The last step of this process is to click Finish so that the wizard can create and relate the new tables. At this last window, you can also choose to create a query that references the original tables in the database. This query will not pull data from new tables created by the Table Analyzer Wizard and serves as another form of backup for your existing database (see Figure 9.16).

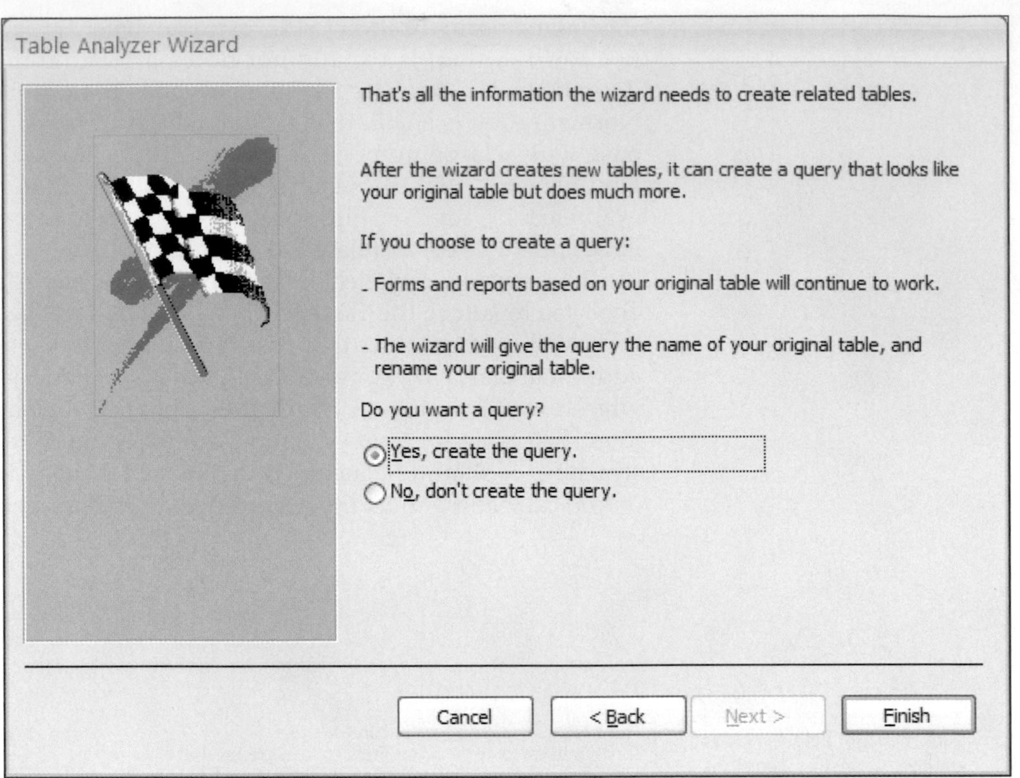

Figure 9.16 Finishing up the Table Analyzer Wizard

After the Table Analyzer Wizard completes, examine your new table structure. Click the Database Tools tab, and within the Show/Hide group, click Relationships. From there, you can add the new tables to your view and visually analyze and edit the table relationships.

Moving Data to New Database Files

On occasion, the needs of users or the increasing size and use of the database may demand that you make dramatic changes to your database structure or to its underlying database management system. As an example, consider the accounting department of a medium-sized company that uses Access to record its financial information. Each of the 10 people in the accounting department accesses the same database, simultaneously, via a shared folder on the local area network. Most of the accounting staff use objects such as forms, queries, and reports that are customized to fit their needs. Staff members complain that they often are confused by the quantity of objects from which they must choose. They mention that they would prefer to not see the objects that they do not use and that this would save them considerable time each day since they often run reports or queries and subsequently find out that they chose the wrong item from the list.

(. . . Make multiple copies of the front-end and provide this copy to a number of users.)

Management may decide that the best solution would be to split the database into two files: one that contains the tables and one that contains everything else (such as reports, forms, queries, and VB code).

Split a Database

Suppose the accounting staff also is frustrated because forms, reports, and queries used by payroll accountants are continuously changed by general ledger accountants, resulting in lost time as the payroll accountants are forced to invest additional time to re-create the original objects. Further, the general ledger accountants may be frustrated because they cannot find the queries they regularly use because the database contains over 100 queries. Again, splitting the database into a back-end and a front-end can solve this problem.

The ***back-end*** of a database contains its tables, but not its forms, reports, or queries.

The ***front-end*** of a database contains its forms, reports, and queries, but not its tables.

When you split a database, you are creating two copies of the same database. One copy, the ***back-end***, is a database that contains only the database tables. The other copy, the ***front-end***, contains everything else. You place the back-end on the network, and you give a copy of the front-end to those who need to use the back-end tables. For example, you would give the front-end to each accountant who needs to use the back-end tables. Therefore, you have one back-end with as many front-end copies of the database as you need.

One advantage of splitting the database into two files (a back-end and a front-end) is that you can now make multiple copies of the front-end and provide these copies to a number of users. These users can, in turn, customize the objects on their (front-end) copy of the database and link their front-end to the back-end tables. All of this is invisible to other users, who also have a copy of the front-end and who also connect to the back-end database tables.

Returning to the accounting department example, each accountant has a copy of the front-end on his or her computer and each accountant links her front-end to the back-end file that resides on a local area network server. None of the accountants can see the objects in the front-end that are on someone else's computer. This means that the payroll accountant will not be able to modify or delete objects found on the general ledger accountant's front-end copy of the database. Of course, any changes made by any of the accountants, through their individual front-end connection, to the data in the tables on the back-end is available to any of these databases.

Click the Database Tools tab and click Access Database in the Move Data group to launch the Database Splitter (see Figure 9.17).

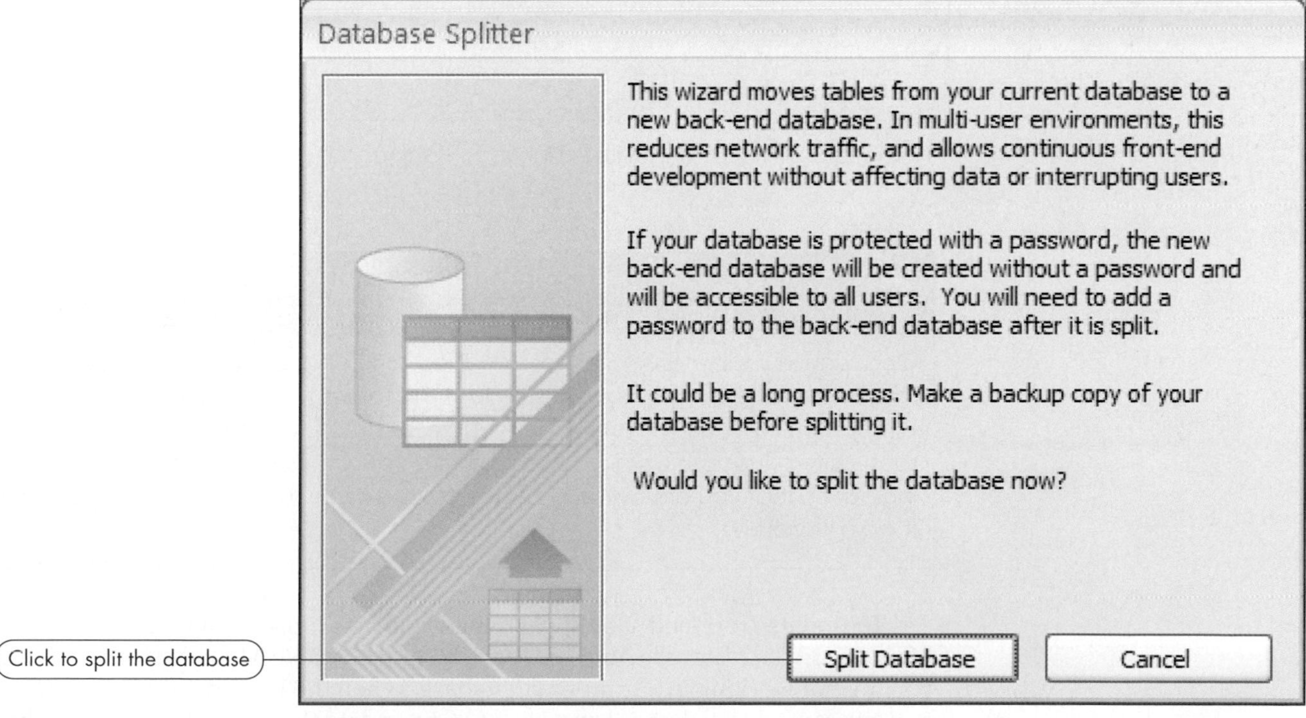
Database Splitter
This wizard moves tables from your current database to a new back-end database. In multi-user environments, this reduces network traffic, and allows continuous front-end development without affecting data or interrupting users.
If your database is protected with a password, the new back-end database will be created without a password and will be accessible to all users. You will need to add a password to the back-end database after it is split.
It could be a long process. Make a backup copy of your database before splitting it.
Would you like to split the database now?
Click to split the database
Split Database
Cancel

Figure 9.17 Click Split Database to Create a Back-End Copy of the Database

The **Database Splitter** creates the front-end and back-end simultaneously.

The ***Database Splitter*** creates the front-end and back-end simultaneously. During the split process, you are asked to name and save the back-end. Access adds the acronym "be" to the file name. After you save the back-end, the database that remains open is the front-end. You are also prompted to backup the database as part of the database split process.

You can verify that you are working in the front-end copy of the database by close examination of how its tables appear in the Navigation pane. Tables in the front-end copy of the database appear with small, right-pointing arrows just to the left of the table name (see Figure 9.18). Additionally, when you point at (but do not click) a table name, a pop-up appears that provides the path to the physical table to which your front-end database is linked. As users add data to a (back-end) table to which a (front-end) database is linked, it becomes available to other front-end users linked to the same back-end database.

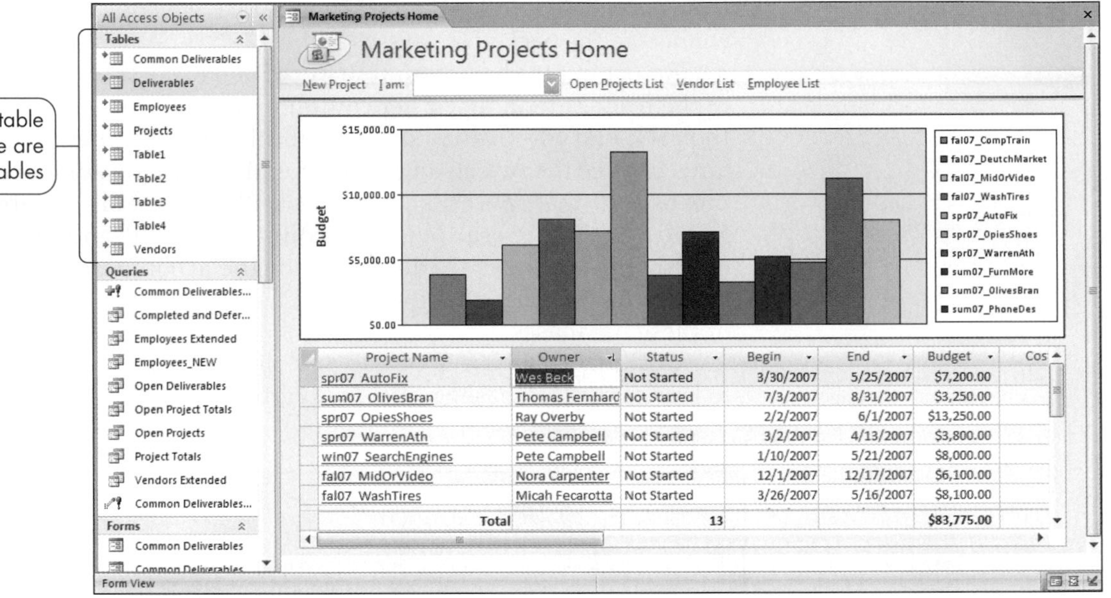

Figure 9.18 Front-end Tables Linked to Back-end Database

TIP How do I determine that my front-end reflects current table structure?

Occasionally, table structures are modified to fit changing business needs. If table structure changes, you must be sure that the tables to which the front-end is linked are current. How do you know that your table structure is not valid? If you add new records to or update existing records and an error message appears, this is a good indication that you are trying to add data to a table that is no longer structured as it was previously.

To update front-end tables, click the Database Tools tab and click Linked Table Manager in the Database Tools group. The Linked Table Manager icon is dimmed if you are not working in a front-end database. When the Linked Table Manager dialog box appears, click Select All and click OK to update the front-end to reflect the most recent back-end table structure.

Link to Other Databases

A large copy shop you do business with keeps an Access database about office supply products it sells. However, the manager of the store does not want to have more than one copy of the password-protected database on the network. Further, he wants his purchasing agents to have access to the tables, but not to queries, forms, or reports in the database. He also believes that splitting the database, which you suggested as a possible solution, is too difficult for him to perform. You recognize that another solution to this problem is to let users link their new, blank databases to the existing Access database. This, in effect, imports the existing data into the new database.

If the manager provides the database password to his purchasing agents, they can each create new, empty databases and then link these directly to the database on the network. After you create a new blank database, click the External Data tab and click Access in the Import group (see Figure 9.19). These steps launch the Get External Data – Access Database Window (see Figure 9.20).

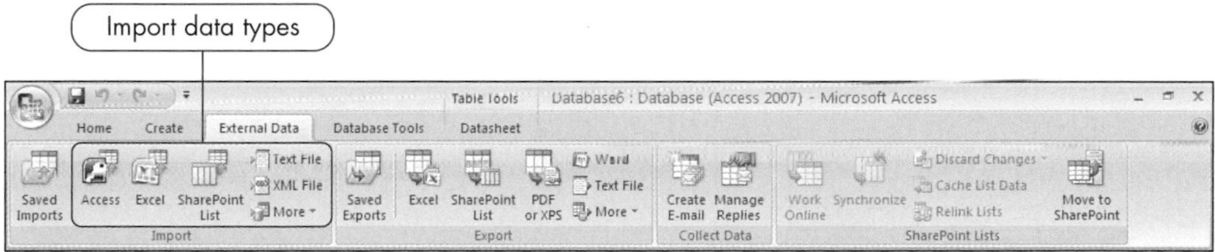

Figure 9.19 Link Your Database to Other Data Providers

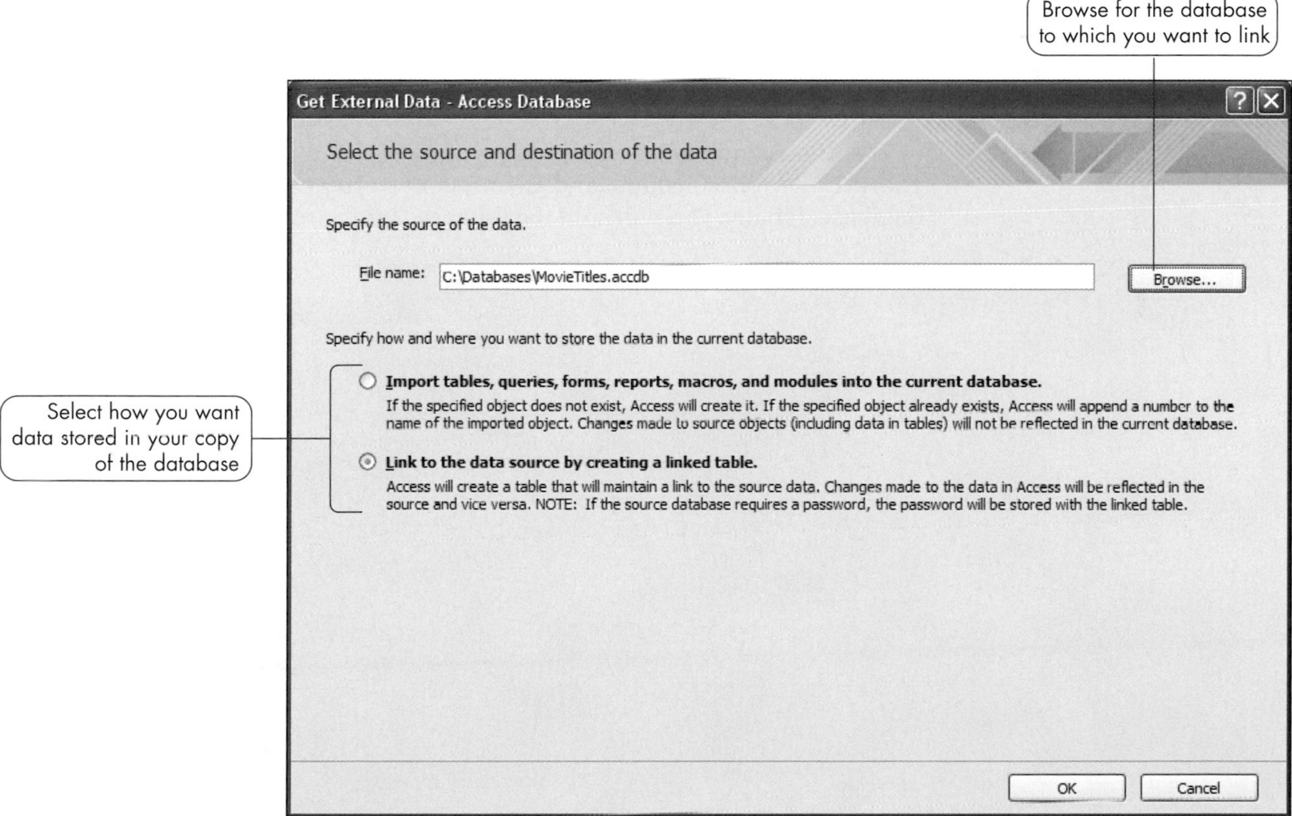

Figure 9.20 Select the Source and Destination of the Data to Create the Link

Complete the three tasks shown and click OK to create the link. And, with functionality similar to the Database Splitter, as you add data to the linked table, it (the new data) becomes available to other users linked to the same database. And, just as with front-end databases, the purchasing agents will see arrows on the left of the table name, and when they point at the table name in their database, a pop-up will appear, revealing the path to the physical table to which they are linked (see Figure 9.21).

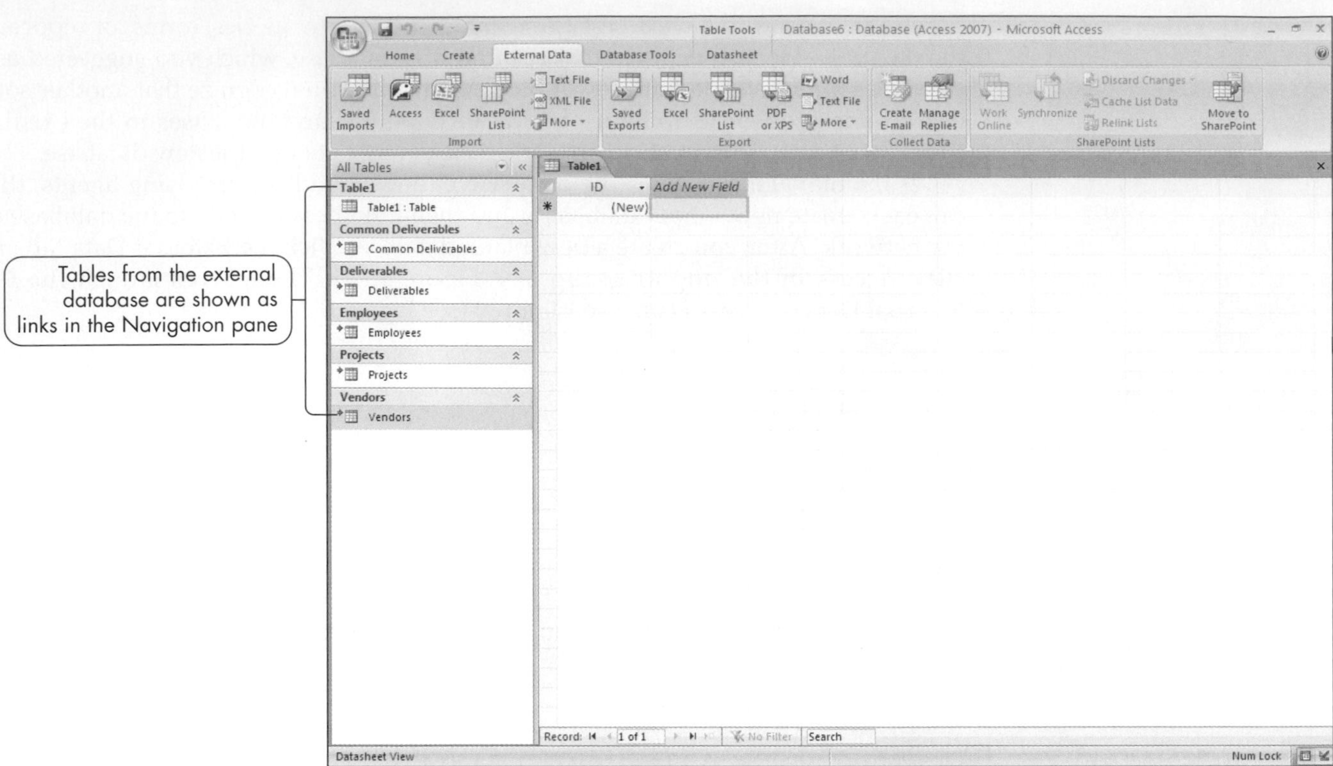

Figure 9.21 Navigation Pane After Linking to an External Database

In the second hands-on exercise, you use tools to analyze the database. You will analyze the relationships, and then use Performance Analyzer and optimize the database. Finally, you will split the database into a front-end and a back-end.

Hands-On Exercises

2 | Using Database Tools

Skills covered: 1. Analyze Relationships in the Database **2.** Use Performance Analyzer and Optimize the Database **3.** Manually Complete the Optimization Process After Optimization **4.** Split the Database Into a Back-end and Front-end

Step 1
Analyze Relationships in the Database

Refer to Figure 9.22 as you complete Step 1.

a. Use Windows Explorer to locate the file named *chap9_ho2_coffee.accdb*. Copy the file to your production folder and rename it **chap9_ho2_coffee_solution.accdb**.

b. Open the *chap9_ho2_coffee_solution.accdb* database.

c. Click **Options** on the Security Warning toolbar, click **Enable this content** in the Microsoft Office Security Options dialog box, and click **OK**.

d. Click the **Database Tools tab** and click **Relationships** in the Show/Hide group.

Take note of the relationships between the tables and verify that no relationship exists between the Customers and Sales Reps tables. Do you see the primary key in the table listed as a foreign key in the table (see Figure 9.22)? There should be a relationship here. Do not fix this error. You will run the Performance Analyzer to see if it catches this design error.

e. Click **Close** to exit the Relationships window.

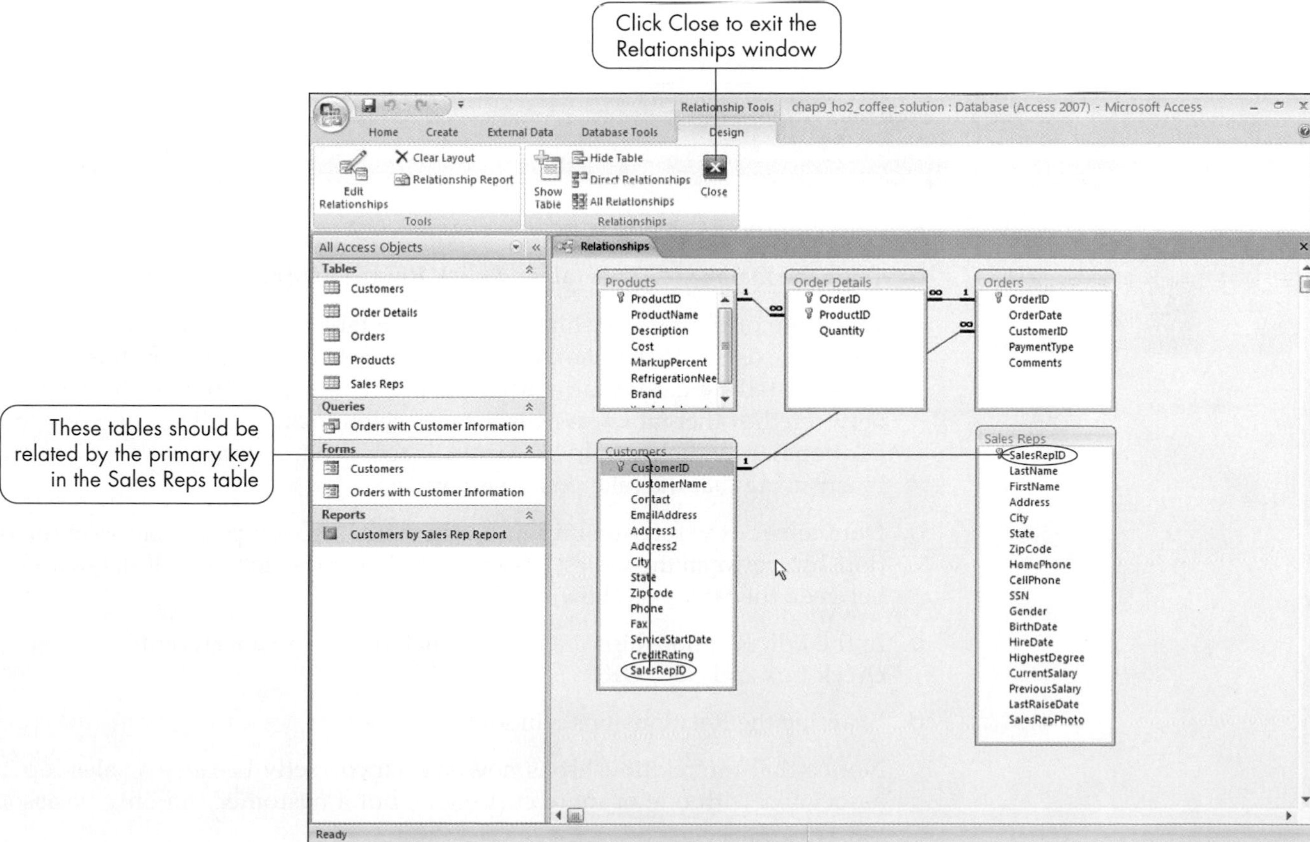

Figure 9.22 Examining the Relationships in the Database

Step 2
Use Performance Analyzer and Optimize the Database

Refer to Figure 9.23 as you complete Step 2.

a. Click the **Database Tools tab** and click **Analyze Performance** in the Analyze group.

b. Click the **All Object Types tab**, click **Select All**, and click **OK** to start the Performance Analyzer.

c. Click the highlighted result, as shown in Figure 9.23, and click **Optimize** to implement this fix. Click **Close** to exit the Performance Analyzer.

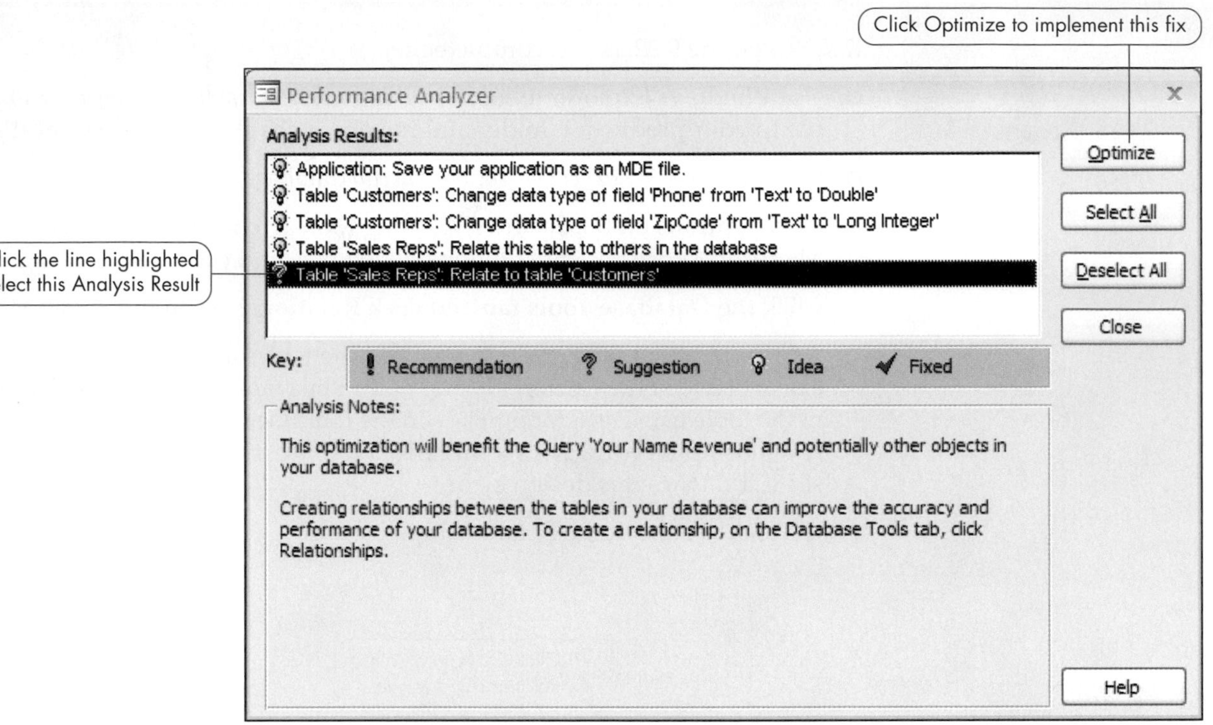

Figure 9.23 Implement a Suggestion Using Performance Analyzer

Step 3
Manually Complete the Optimization Process After Optimization

Refer to Figure 9.24 as you complete Step 3.

a. Click the **Database Tools tab** and click **Relationships** in the Show/Hide group.

Take note of the relationships between the tables and verify that a proper relationship exists between the Customers and Sales Reps tables. But, is the relationship created by the Performance Analyzer complete? Look at the relationships between the other tables. Why is the new relationship not listed as a one-to-many relationship (which would be correct)? You need to complete the Optimization by ensuring that the relationship is correct.

b. Double-click the **relationship line**, which is a visual representation of the relationship between the tables, based on the key indicated, to edit the relationship between the tables, as shown in Figure 9.24.

c. In the Edit Relationships dialog box, click the **Enforce Referential Integrity check box** and click **OK**.

d. Examine the Relationships window.

Notice that the relationship is now shown correctly because a sales rep can be associated with one or more customers, but a customer can only be associated with one sales rep.

e. Click **Close** to exit Relationship Tools. Make a mental note to always verify fixes you implement made by any analysis tool.

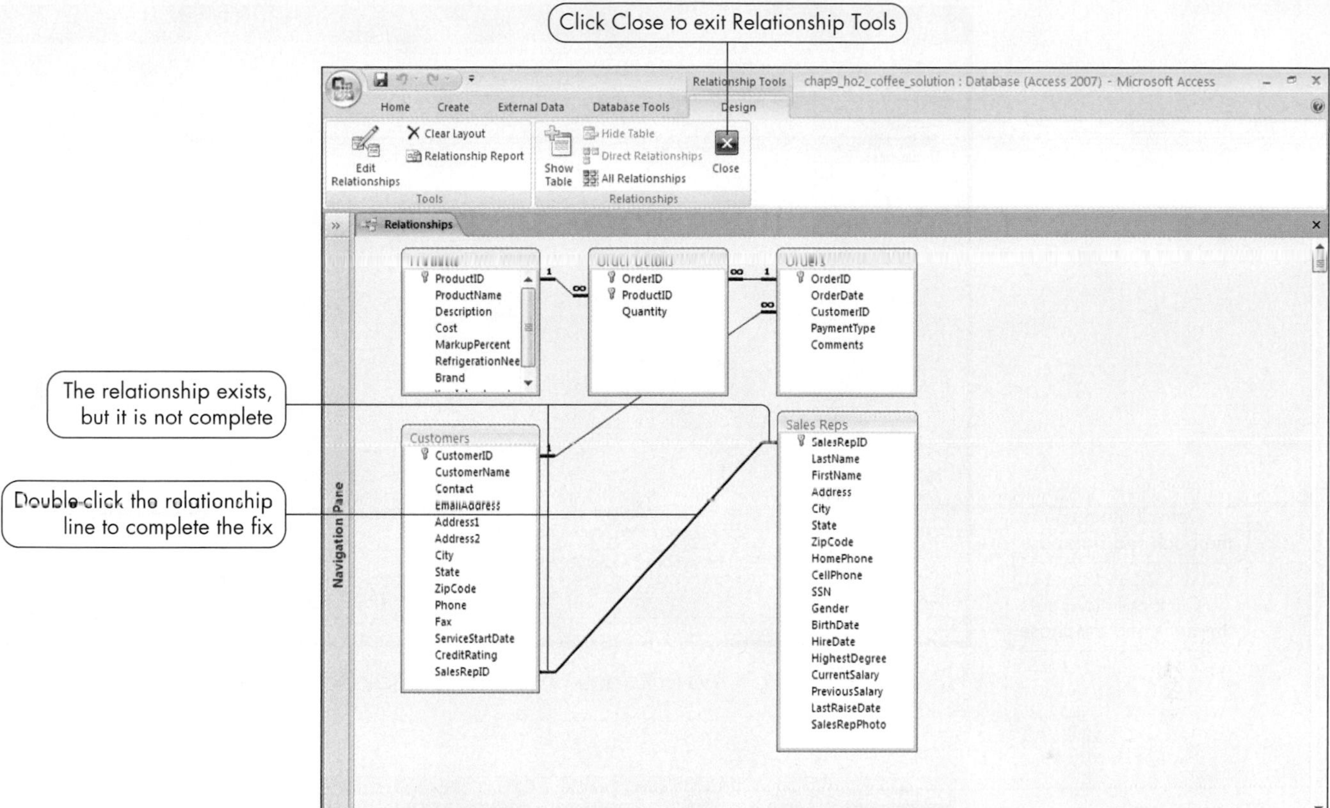

Figure 9.24 Edit the Relationship Between Tables to Complete Optimization

Step 4
Split the Database into a Back-end and Front-end

Refer to Figures 9.25 through 9.27 as you complete Step 4.

a. Click the **Database Tools tab** and click **Access Database** in the Move Data group.

   The Database Splitter dialog box opens.

b. Click **Split Database** to create a back-end copy of the existing database.

   The Create Back-end Database dialog box opens. Access maintains the original file name but adds *be* before the extension to indicate a back-end database.

c. Select your production folder. Accept the default database name shown in the *File name* box (see Figure 9.25) and click **Split**.

   The Database Splitter message box informs you that the database successfully split.

d. Click **OK**.

   The front-end copy of the database is open. The back-end database is saved but is not open.

e. Double-click the **Customers form** to open it and click **Add Record** to add a new customer to the database. Enter data on the form, as shown in Figure 9.26.

f. Click **Add Record** so that Access adds the Customer ID. Close the form.

   You added the record to the back-end. Let us verify that the record is in the back-end copy of the database.

g. Point at the **Customers table**.

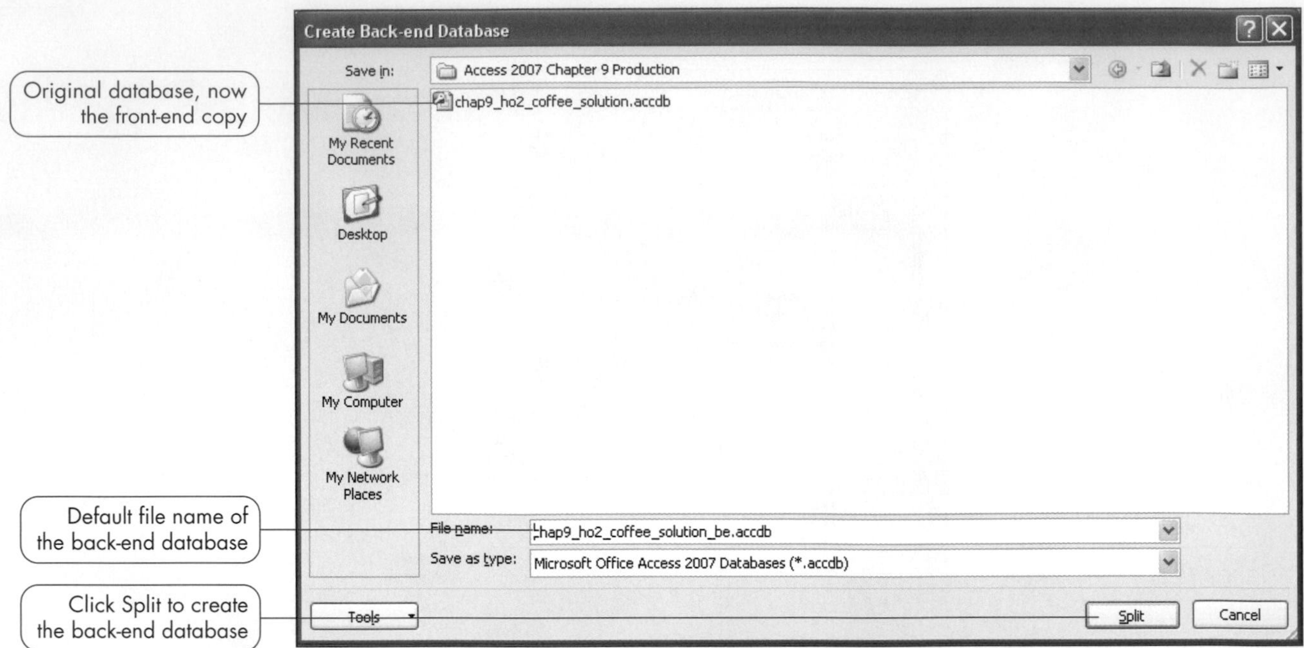

Figure 9.25 Split the Database into a Front-end and Back-end

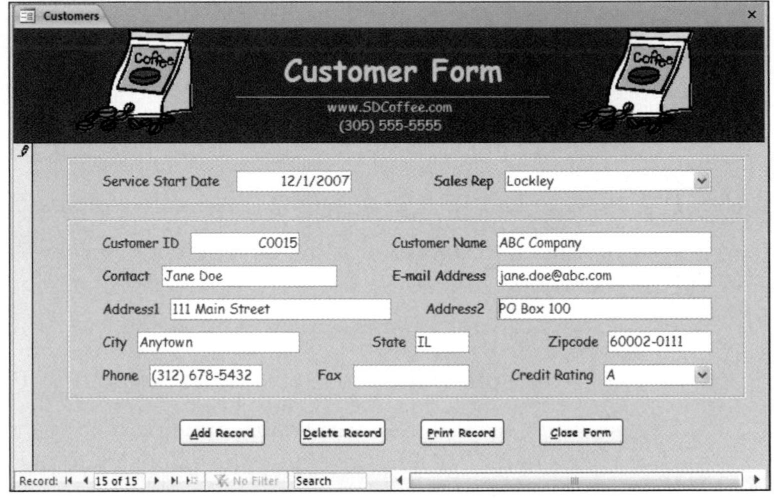

Figure 9.26 Enter the Data as Shown to Add a New Record

A ScreenTip appears that provides the path to the physical table to which we are linked (see Figure 9.27). Note *be* in the file name shown in the ScreenTip. Do not close the front-end database.

h. Click the **Office Button** and select **Open**. Locate the *chap9_ho2_coffee_solution_be.accdb* back-end database you created and open it.

When you open the back-end database, the front-end database closes automatically.

i. Double-click the **Customers table** in the *chap9_ho2_coffee_solution_be.accdb* database to open it.

Notice that the last record in the back-end database table is the record you entered through the front-end copy of the database.

j. Close the back-end database. Exit Access if you do not want to continue with the next exercise at this time.

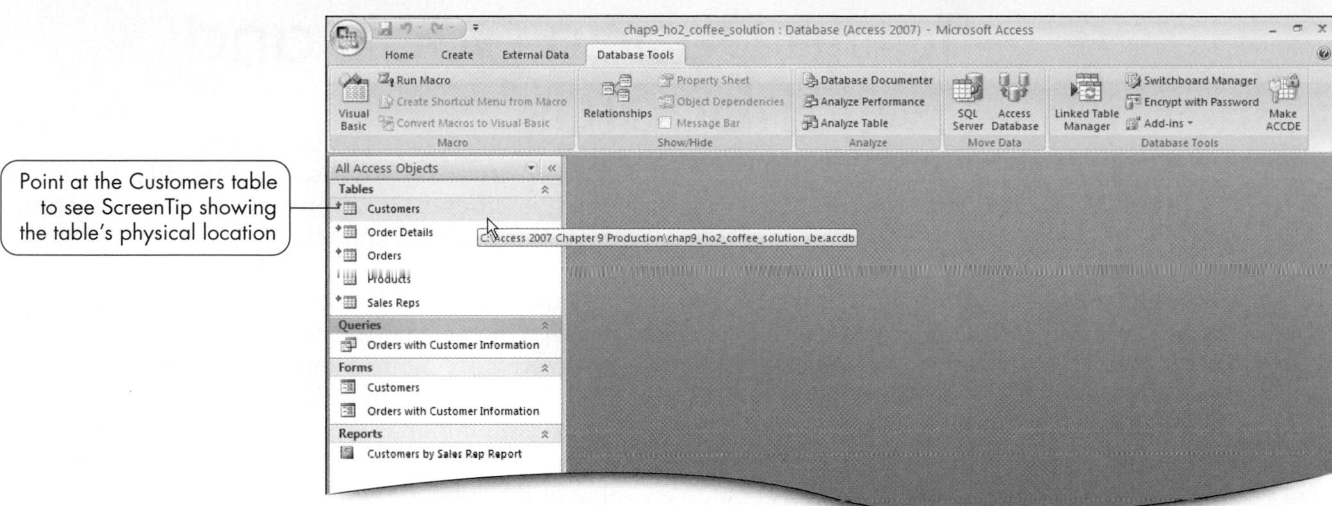

Figure 9.27 Determine the Table's Physical Location

Table Design Goals and Switchboards

We "know" that the designs for the databases you used in this chapter are "good designs," but knowing something is different from proving it. Normalization is a way of organizing a database so that the storage and retrieval of its data is more efficient. It is a multistep process that continually refines the design of a database until all redundant data have been eliminated. This is accomplished by examining the ***dependencies*** (relationships) between the fields in a table and eliminating the partial and transitive dependencies (both terms are defined shortly) that may exist.

A ***dependency*** is the extent to which fields in a table are related to each other through the table's primary key.

The end result is a design in which every field within a table is functionally dependent on the primary key. This is an important concept and, indeed, it is the ultimate goal of the normalization process. A field is said to be functionally dependent on the primary key if a given value of the primary key (e.g., a student number) yields only one value of the dependent field (e.g., the student's name). This sounds complicated, but the normalization process can be summed up by a single phrase: "The key, the whole key, and nothing but the key, so help me Codd." This simple sentence not only gives credit to Edgar Codd, who first postulated the relational model, but it also states the essence of good database design: Namely, the value of every field in a table is dependent on the primary key, on the entire primary key, and on nothing but the primary key.

(. . . The key, the whole key, and nothing but the key, so help me Codd.)

In this section, you learn how to analyze and optimize object relationships. Specifically, you learn more about normalization. In addition, you learn how to create a switchboard to facilitate a user-friendly database.

Analyzing and Optimizing Object Relationships in an Access Database

Consider the database for an order entry system for a retail establishment that focuses on customers, products, and orders. The system maintains the usual customer data (name, address, phone, and so on). It also keeps track of the available products, storing for each product the product number, name, and price. And finally, it maintains data about every order, storing the date of the order, the customer who placed the order, the products that were ordered, and the quantity of each product in that order.

(. . . Our goal is a database that is accurate, dependable, and scalable.)

The database should be able to supply information about a specific customer (i.e., phone number and address). It should also be able to supply the name of the customer who placed a particular order and/or retrieve all orders that were placed by a specific customer. The database must be able to list all of the products that are carried by the store and/or compute the cost of a particular order. The potential queries are endless.

You may already see the two distinct relationships that exist within this system. A one-to-many relationship exists between customers and orders; that is, one customer can place many orders, but a given order is associated with only one customer. A many-to-many relationship exists between orders and products; that is, one order can contain many products, and the same product can appear in many orders. This insight enables you to create the required tables and to bypass some or all of the steps in the normalization process. It is important, however, to go through normalization at least once so that you will better understand the theoretical foundation of database design.

We are also quite aware that comfort in this process comes only with experience. So, focus on the principles and how these relate to the goal, which is a database that is accurate, dependable, and scalable. When clerks enter data, they need to know that the data are being recorded properly. Additionally, when managers run reports, they must have confidence that the reports accurately reflect the data stored in the database. Management uses database reports to make business decisions based on where they think they are now and where they think they will be at some future date.

Understand Normalization

An ***atomic field*** is one that contains only one value.

Normalization is a multistep process in which you progress from one normal form to the next until the design is acceptable. Part (a) of Figure 9.28 shows the raw data with no normalization; that is, all of the data exist in a single Orders table. This design contains many potential anomalies and is further complicated because each record is of variable length, depending on the number of products that appear in a specific order. Hence, the first step in the normalization process is to eliminate the repeating groups (the product information and quantity) that occur in each order record. Fields that contain only one value (no repeating groups of data) are known as ***atomic fields***. The result is the first normal form (1NF) that is illustrated in Part (b) of Figure 9.28, where the original Orders table has been converted to an Order Details table.

The Order Details table contains a record for each product in each order (as opposed to a single record for each order in the original Orders table). Every record in the new table is the same length as every other record. The primary key of the new table is a composite key consisting of the OrderID and the ProductID. (The remaining fields contain the product information for the selected product, the quantity ordered, the date of the order, the CustomerID, and the associated customer information.) This design is significantly better than the unstructured data, but a significant problem still exists because the product information depends on only part of the composite primary key (the ProductID, as opposed to the combination of OrderID and ProductID). This is known as a partial dependency, and it has to be eliminated.

The second step in the normalization process removes the partial dependencies to create the second normal form (2NF) in Part (c) of Figure 9.28. Two additional tables, a Products table and an Orders table, are created. The Products table contains three fields: ProductID, Product Name, and Price; the Product Name and Price depend on the ProductID (the primary key), which is the proper design. The partial dependency is eliminated, but another type of dependency is present in the Orders table. The date of the order and the CustomerID depend on the OrderID, which is as it should be, because the OrderID is the primary key. The problem is that the customer information depends on the CustomerID, as opposed to the OrderID. This is known as a transitive dependency, and it has to be eliminated.

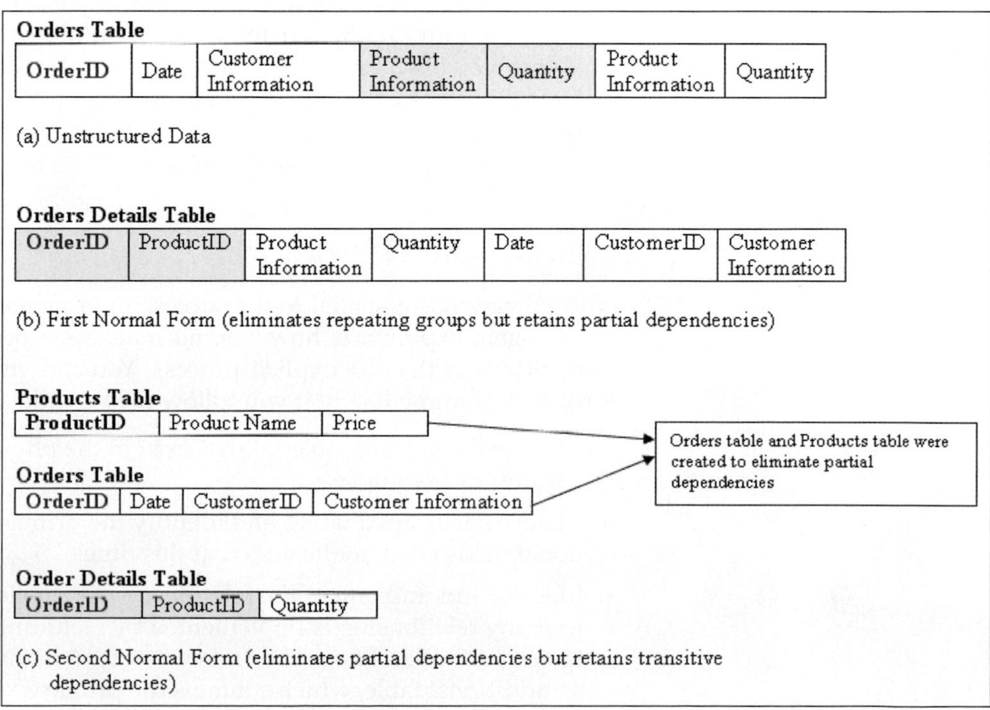

Figure 9.28 Unstructured, First Normal Form, and Second Normal Form

The third step in the normalization process removes the transitive dependencies to create the third normal form (3NF) in Figure 9.29. The database now contains four tables: Customers, Products, Orders, and Order Details. Every field in every table is functionally dependent on the primary key of that table; that is, a given value of the primary key always yields the same value of the dependent field. Think again of our summary phrase, "the key, the whole key, and nothing but the key"; that is, every field in every table depends on the value of the primary key, the entire primary key, and nothing but the primary key.

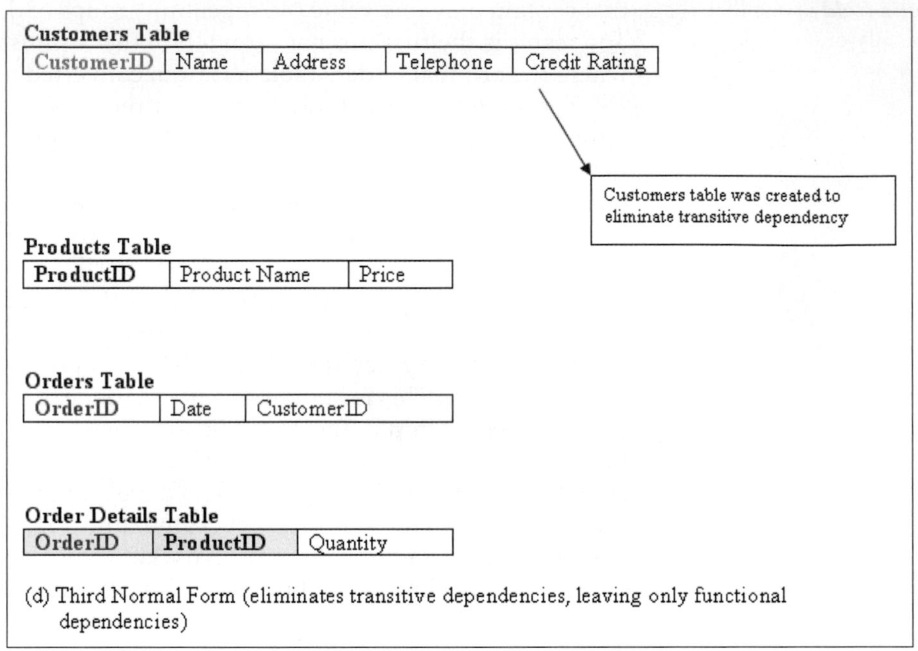

Figure 9.29 Third Normal Form

You might wonder why arriving at third normal form is important. A table that has not passed the normalization process might experience strange occurrences as data is added to, updated, and deleted from the database. Consider a simple update operation for an existing customer listed in the database. If a customer who rents DVD movies has her address and other contact information stored in the DVD Rentals table, we cannot update her record in the database without updating the record, or row of data, of every rental in this customer's purchasing history. Similar design errors can cause anomalies when we add or delete records.

Create Third Normal Form

Normalization is essential to the successful implementation of a relational database. As you gain experience, however, normalization becomes intuitive and more of an implicit rather than an explicit process. You can, in fact, arrive at the third normal form almost immediately if you follow these guidelines:

- Identify the entities (objects) that exist in the physical system, each of which requires its own table.
- Create the required tables and identify the primary key in each table. The additional fields need not be added at this time.
- Identify and implement the relationships that exist in the physical system. A one-to-many relationship is implemented by including the primary key of the "one" table as a foreign key in the "many" table. A many-to-many relationship requires an additional table, which contains the primary keys of the individual entities.
- Complete each table in the database by including any other fields that are necessary to produce the information that is required of the database.

- Study the completed design to ensure that the value of every field in every table is dependent on the primary key of that table, the entire primary key, and nothing but the primary key.
- Ask "questions" of the finished database to determine the completeness of the design; if you cannot answer a specific question, you will have to add fields to one or more tables and repeat some (or all) of the previous steps.

Let us return to the original description of the order entry database and apply these guidelines to arrive immediately at the third normal form. Three distinct entities exist in the physical system: customers, orders, and products, each of which requires its own table. A one-to-many relationship exists between customers and orders; that is, one customer can have many orders, but a given order is associated with only one customer. Thus, you take the primary key of the "one" table (the Customers table) and place it as a foreign key in the "many" table (the Orders table).

A many-to-many relationship between products and orders, which requires a new Order Details table. The primary key for this table is the combination of ProductID and OrderID. The only additional field in this table is the quantity (of that particular product in that particular order) that was ordered. At this point you are very close to the third normal form shown in Figure 9.29. All you have to do to complete the design is to add the remaining fields in each table to satisfy the information requirements of the system.

TIP Query the Database

You have completed the design of the order entry system. It is a good design without data duplication that enables us to add, edit, or modify the records for a customer, product, or order. Equally important, the design enables us to retrieve detailed information about any customer, product, or order. Consider, for example, the following queries in conjunction with Figure 9.30.

Query:	Which customers ordered a gazebo?
Answer:	Bob Barker and Jennie Jones are the only two customers who ordered a gazebo.
Method:	Search the products table for "gazebo" to determine the ProductID (P0007), then take this value to the Order Details table to identify the orders that contained this product, orders O0006 and O0009. Now look in the Orders table to determine the associated CustomerID for each order (C0004 and C0007),then look in the Customers table to find the associated customer names, which are Bob Barker and Jennie Jones.
Query:	What is the total cost of order O0010? Which products are in the order, and how many units of each product?
Answer:	The total cost of order O0010 is $262.00. The order is composed of four orchids that cost $16 each and two three-foot fountains that sell for $99 each.
Method:	Search the Order Details table for the first record for order O0010 to determine the associated ProductID (P0017) and quantity, search the Products table to find the name of this product and its price, and then multiply the price ($16) by the quantity (4 units) to get the cost of this item ($64). Repeat this process for every record in the Order Details table for order O0010 (there is only one additional record for two units of product P0018), then add the subtotals to arrive at the total cost of the order.

Remember too, that once the database has been implemented in Access, the answers to these and other queries are available with the click of a mouse. You will be pleased at what you can do with Access, but your success depends on the validity of your design.

CustomerID	Last Name	First Name	Address	City	State	Zip Code	Phone Number
C001	Fecarotta	Micah	1234 Main	Ft. Lauderdale	FL	33120	305-555-5678
C002	Patel	Rupee	578 Burn St	Miami	FL	33123	305-356-5601
C003	Willie	Mark	992 Fern Dr	Coral Gables	FL	33146	305-358-1902
C004	Barker	Bob	143 Home St	Miami	FL	33124	305-281-0186
C005	Smith	Gregg	181 Post	Miami	FL	33214	305-857-2684
C006	Madden	Ken	468 Ridge	Miami	FL	33120	305-891-5522
C007	Jones	Jennie	181 Edge	Coral Gables	FL	32147	305-543-4121
C008	Trapani	Josie	928 128th	Coral Gables	FL	33145	305-440-4613

(a) Customers Table (partial list)

OrderID	CustomerID	Order Date
O0001	C0005	03-02-2007
O0002	C0006	03-03-2007
O0003	C0001	03-06-2007
O0004	C0002	03-07-2007
O0005	C0001	03-08-2007
O0006	C0004	03-08-2007
O0007	C0003	03-09-2007
O0008	C0006	03-10-2007
O0009	C0007	03-10-2007
O0010	C0001	03-10-2007

(b) Orders Table (partial list)

ProductID	Product Name	Price
P0001	6" potted plant	$10.99
P0007	Gazebo	$499.00
P0017	Orchid of the week	$16.00
P0018	3' fountain	$99.00

(c) Product Table (partial list)

OrderID	ProductID	Quantity
O0001	P0002	2
O0001	P0003	1
O0001	P0005	3
O0001	P0006	2
O0004	P0003	2
O0004	P0010	2
O0006	P0007	1
O0009	P0007	1
O0009	P0001	1
O0009	P0016	3
O0010	P0017	4
O0010	P0018	2

(d) Order Details Table (partial list)

Figure 9.30 Tables to Address Queries

Creating Usable Switchboards

Many people who use databases are not technically inclined and prefer that the tables, queries, and other technical objects be managed by others. Part of the job of database administrators is to hide the complexity of the technology from users so that they can focus on their work rather than the tool or tools they use every day to get things done. Compounding this is solid evidence that users prefer to work in simple windows that make sense to them and flow with the logic of what they are trying to perform. Users prefer easy to navigate windows in which clicking buttons and selecting options are intuitive over a design that is difficult to figure out.

Database forms and switchboards, therefore, are excellent tools you can employ to satisfy users and at the same time ensure that quality data is entered into the tables. In earlier versions of Access a common way to make your database easy to use as well as control access to its underlying structure was through the implementation of switchboards. Even though Access 2007 reduced support for switchboards, the functionality is still available through the ***Switchboard Manager***. Plus, switchboards created in earlier versions of Access will, for the most part, function correctly. The ***switchboard*** is a menu or a series of menus that ties the objects in the database together so that the database is easy to use. The interface displays a menu (or series of menus) enabling a nontechnical person to open the various objects within the database, and to move easily from one object to another. The switchboard is quite powerful, but it is also very easy to create. All of the work is done by the Switchboard Manager, an Access utility that prompts you for information about each menu. You supply the text of the item, as it is to appear on the switchboard, together with the underlying command (e.g., Open Form in Add Mode).

The ***Switchboard Manager*** enables you to create switchboards.

A ***switchboard*** is a form that acts as a menu, making the database easier to use.

(. . . Hide the underlying database objects from users.)

You can hide the underlying database objects from users by setting Access Options to open the database so that only the switchboard is visible. However, a savvy user can display all hidden database objects by simply pressing F11, as you will see in the next exercise. If your database requires the security that comes from setting user permissions and rights, you may need to consider a more robust platform such as Microsoft SQL Server 2005.

For example, an accounts receivable clerk is just getting acquainted with Access and can't determine how to get started entering customer contact data after opening the database. You might create a switchboard to simplify that user's experience until he becomes more familiar with how Access functions. To hide database objects, click the Office Button and click Access Options. In the left pane, click Current Database (see Figure 9.31). Then, clear the Display Navigation Pane check box. When users open the database, the switchboard will open and all of the other database objects, such as forms, queries, and reports, will be hidden.

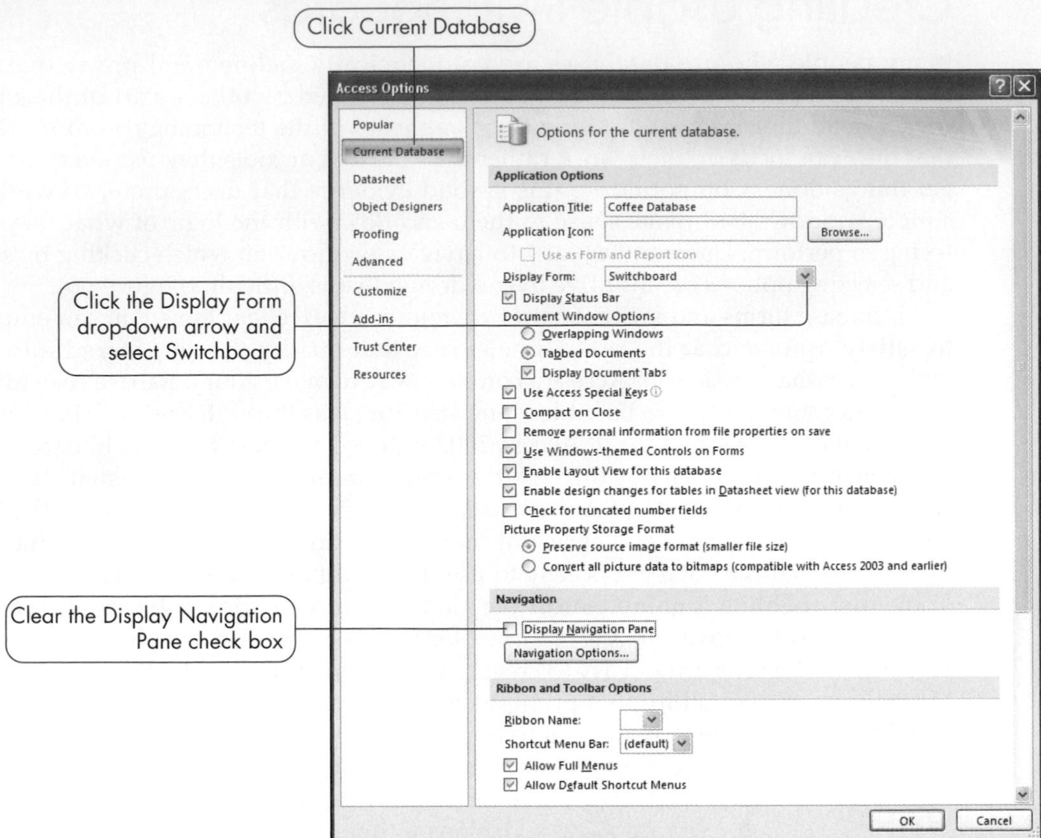

Figure 9.31 Hide Database Objects Using Access Options

In the third hands-on exercise, you use the Switchboard Manager to create a switchboard. The switchboard will open a form, two reports, and exit the application. In addition, you will change startup options and examine object dependencies.

3 | Build a Basic Switchboard

Skills covered: 1. Start the Switchboard Manager **2.** Complete the Switchboard **3.** Test the Switchboard **4.** Insert the Clip Art **5.** Set Startup Options **6.** Examine Object Dependencies

Step 1
Start the Switchboard Manager

Refer to Figures 9.32 and 9.33 as you complete Step 1.

a. Use Windows Explorer to locate the file named *chap9_ho3_students.accdb*. Copy the file to your production folder and rename it **chap9_ ho3_students_ solution.accdb**.

b. Open the *chap9_ho3_students_solution.accdb* database.

c. If necessary, click **Options** on the Security Warning toolbar, click **Enable this content** in the Microsoft Office Security Options dialog box, and click **OK**.

   Notice that the Student List form is opened automatically when you open the database. After you create the Switchboard, you will set it to open instead of the Student List form when the database first opens.

d. Click the **Database Tools tab** and click **Switchboard Manager** in the Database Tools group.

   The Switchboard Manager message box appears, stating that it was not able to find a valid switchboard in your database. You are asked if you want to create a switchboard.

e. Click **Yes** to confirm that you want to create a new switchboard.

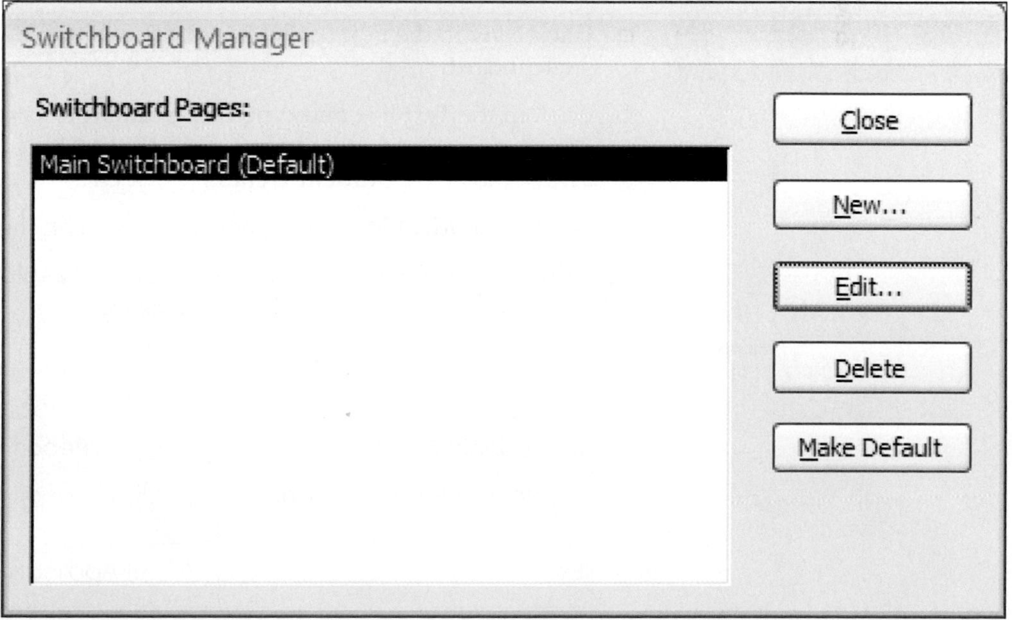

Figure 9.32 Start the Switchboard Manager

Because this database does not currently have any switchboards, Access creates a default page to get you started (see Figure 9.32).

f. Click **Edit** to display the Edit Switchboard Page dialog box. Click **New** to add an item to this page, which in turn displays the Edit Switchboard Item dialog box (see Figure 9.33). Add the first switchboard item as follows.

   If the text *New Switchboard Command* is not selected, select it and type **Add New Student**.

   Click the **Command drop-down arrow** and select **Open Form in Add Mode**.

   Click the **Form drop-down arrow** and select **Student Details**.

g. Click **OK** to create the switchboard item.

   The Edit Switchboard Item dialog box closes and the item appears in the Edit Switchboard Page dialog box.

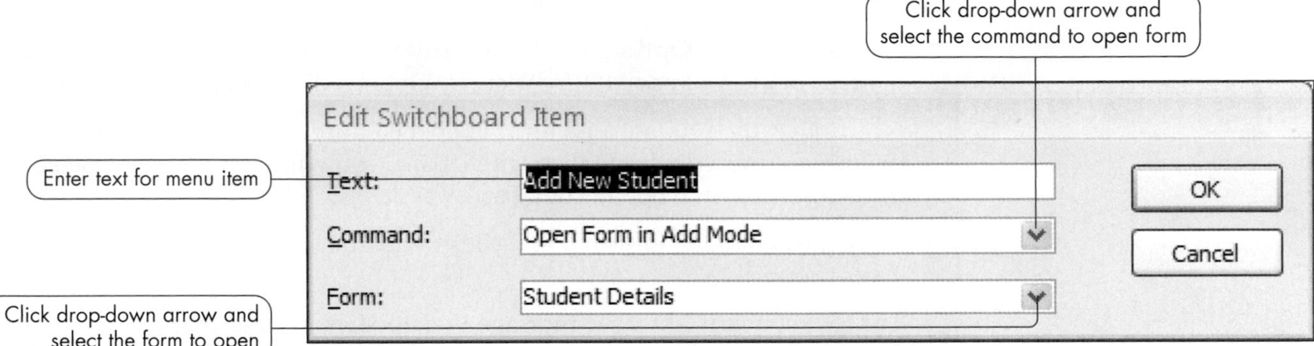

Figure 9.33 Edit the Switchboard Manager

Step 2 Complete the Switchboard

Refer to Figure 9.34 as you complete Step 2.

a. Click **New** in the Edit Switchboard Page dialog box to add a second item to the switchboard.

b. Click in the **Text** box and type **Edit Student Record**. Click the **Command drop-down arrow** and select **Open Form in Edit Mode**. Click the **Form drop-down arrow** and select **Student Details**. Click **OK**.

   The Edit Student Record appears as an item on the switchboard.

c. Add the remaining items to the switchboard as shown in Figure 9.34. The menu items function and should be added as follows:

Text	Command	Form or Report
All Students Report	Open Report	All Students
Guardian Information Report	Open Report	Guardian Information
Exit	Exit Application	

d. Click **Close** to close the Edit Switchboard Page dialog box. Then click **Close** to exit the Switchboard Manager.

   In Form view or Layout view of the switchboard form, the header displays *Main Switchboard*. In Design view, the header displays the name of the file, *chap9_ho3_students_solution*.

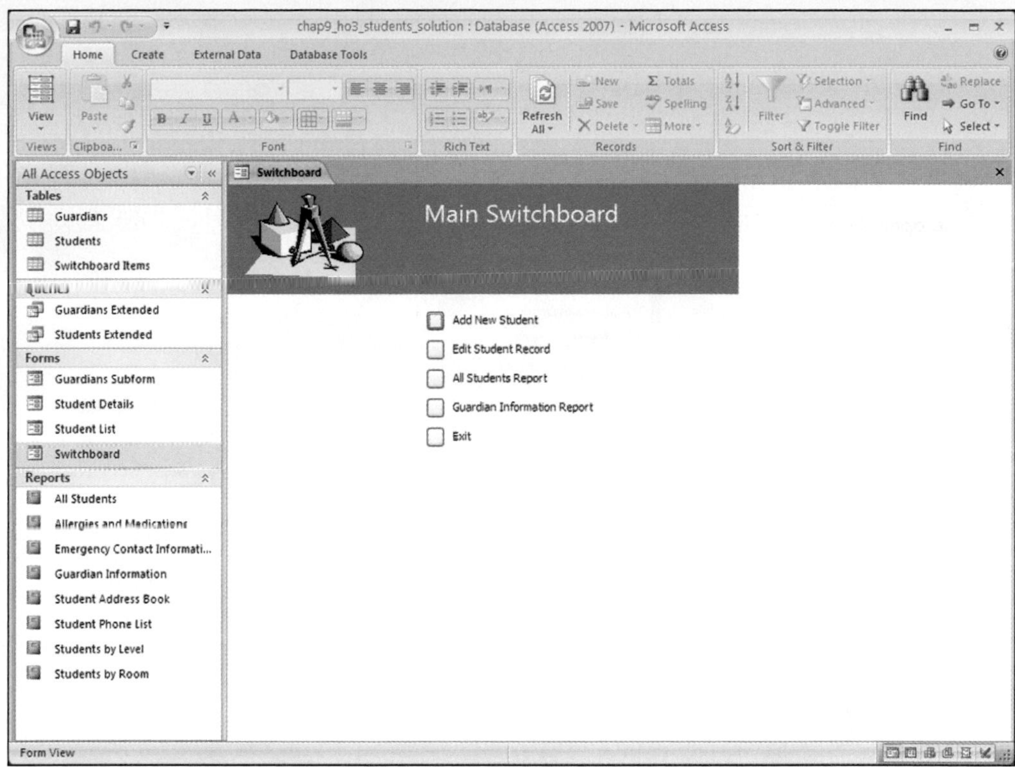

Figure 9.34 Complete the Switchboard

Step 3
Test the Switchboard

Refer to Figure 9.35 as you complete Step 3.

a. Double-click the **Switchboard form** to open the Main Switchboard as shown in Figure 9.35.

   Do not be concerned about the design of the switchboard at this time, as your immediate objective is to make sure that the buttons work.

b. Click the **Add New Student button**.

   The Student Details form opens, ready for you to enter a new record.

c. Click **Close** to close the Student Details form.

d. Test the remaining items on the switchboard. If you test the Exit button, reopen the database.

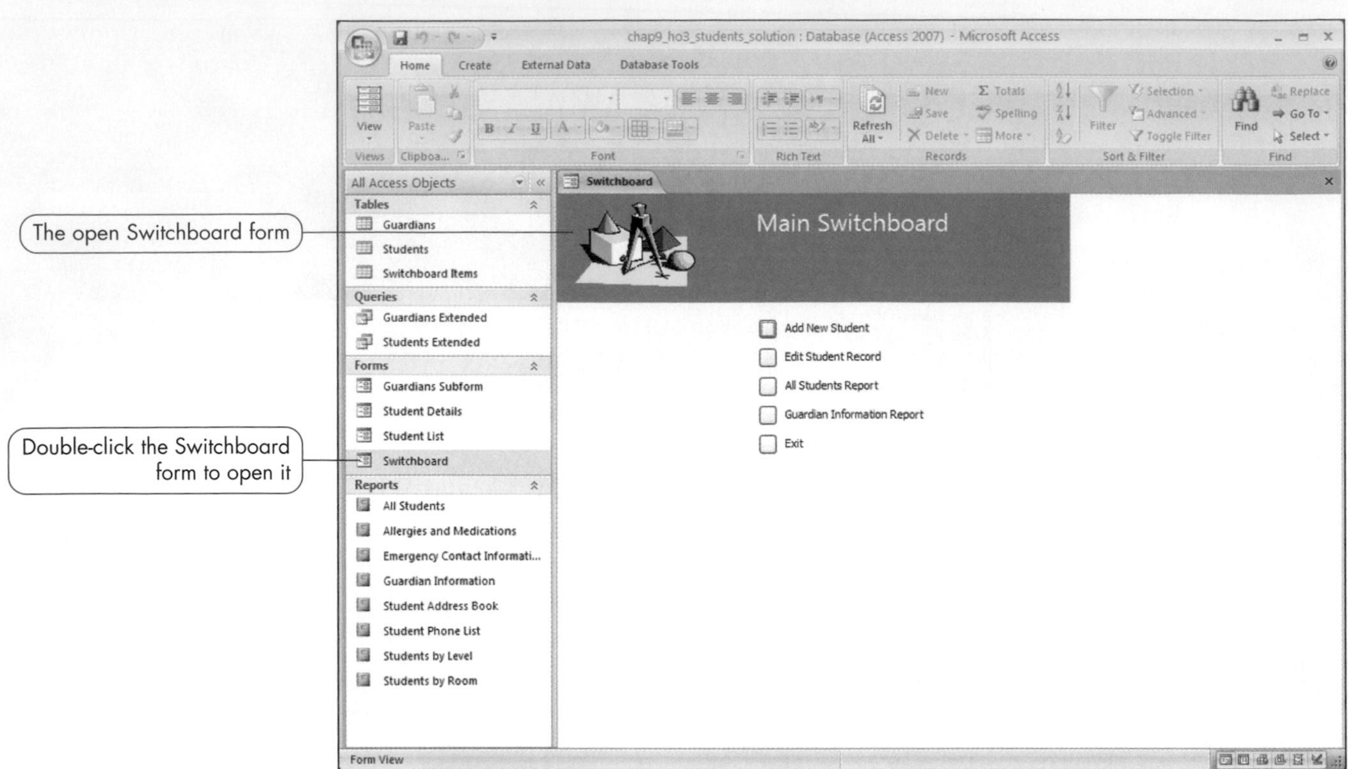

Figure 9.35 Open and Test the Switchboard

TIP Modify the Switchboard Table

You can modify an existing switchboard in one of two ways—by using the Switchboard Manager or by making changes directly in the underlying table of switchboard items. In the Navigation Pane, under Tables, double-click Switchboard Items to open it. You can manually add entries to the switchboard in the table that opens. We encourage you to experiment, but start by changing one entry at a time. The ItemText field is a good place to start.

However, be careful about changing any of the items on a switchboard that you created using the Switchboard Wizard. In a large application with a good number of forms and subordinate switchboards, such changes could cause items on some or all switchboards to become inoperable.

Step 4 Insert the Clip Art

Refer to Figure 9.36 as you complete Step 4.

a. Right-click the **Switchboard tab** and select **Design View**.

b. Drag the **Form Header** lower detail line down so that it is at approximately 1.25 inches. If necessary, close the Field List window. Next, select the **green rectangle background element** and drag its lower edge down as shown in Figure 9.36.

c. Click **Image** in the Controls group on the Design tab. Draw a 1-inch square to the left of the label you see in the header. When you release the mouse button, navigate to the **Exploring Access folder**. Select the **academic_symbols.wmf** image and click **OK**.

   An image of academic symbols is inserted in the Image control.

d. Right-click the image and select **Properties**. Click the **Size Mode drop-down arrow** in the Property Sheet window and select **Stretch**. Close the Property Sheet window.

e. Click the green rectangle background that is to the left of the Item Text control in the Detail section. Press **Delete** to remove the green background. Click the remaining dark gray square in the Detail section and press **Delete** to remove it. Click **Save**.

TROUBLESHOOTING: Sometimes it is difficult to click the appropriate handle of an object so that you can move or resize it. Single-clicking an object will reveal where its sizing handles and exact outer edges are located. To resize an object, click it to determine where its sizing handles are located. Then, click and hold your mouse button down as you expand or lessen its size. To move an object, click it to determine where its outer edges are located. Then, point at any edge of the object until your cursor turns into an icon with four arrows pointing in four different directions. Next, click and hold your mouse button down and move the object to its desired location.

f. Double-click **Switchboard** below Forms in the Navigation pane.

Your image is in the header, and the buttons no longer have image holders in the Detail section.

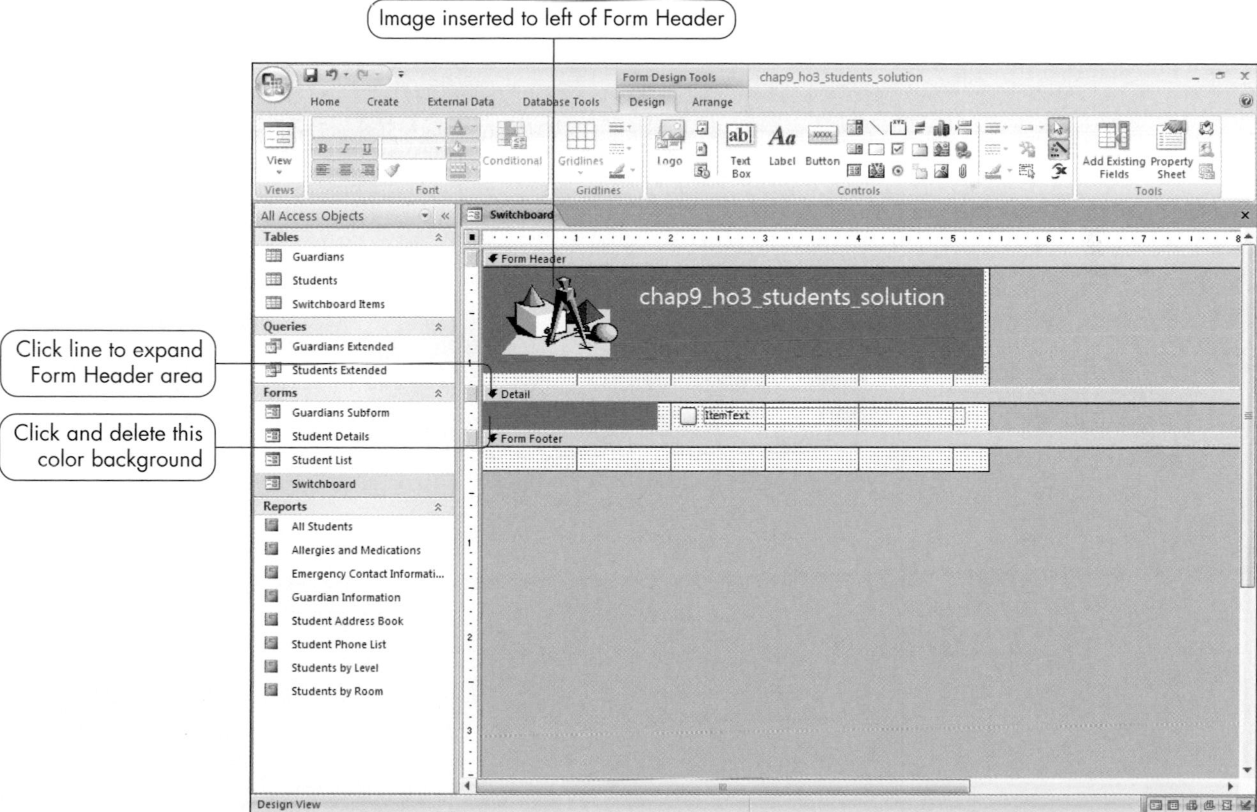

Figure 9.36 Insert the Clip Art

Step 5
Set Startup Options

Refer to Figure 9.37 as you complete Step 5.

a. Click the **Office Button** and click **Access Options**.

b. In the left pane of Access Options, click **Current Database**.

   The *Options for the current database* is displayed.

c. In the *Application Options* section, click the **Display Form drop-down arrow** and select **Switchboard**. Type **Student Database** in the **Application Title** text box at the top of the window to add a personal touch.

   This step will cause the Switchboard form to display when the database is opened. The title bar will display Student Database instead of the file name.

d. Further down on the screen, in the *Navigation* section, clear the **Display Navigation Pane check box**. Click **OK** to close the Access Options dialog box.

   A Microsoft Office Access message box appears, indicating that you must close and then reopen the current database for the specified option to take effect.

e. Click **OK** to close the message box. Then close and reopen the database. Enable the content.

   When you reopen the database, the title bar displays *Student Database* instead of the file name. The Switchboard form is displayed, and the Navigation pane is hidden.

f. Press **F11** to display the Navigation pane.

   All database objects are now visible.

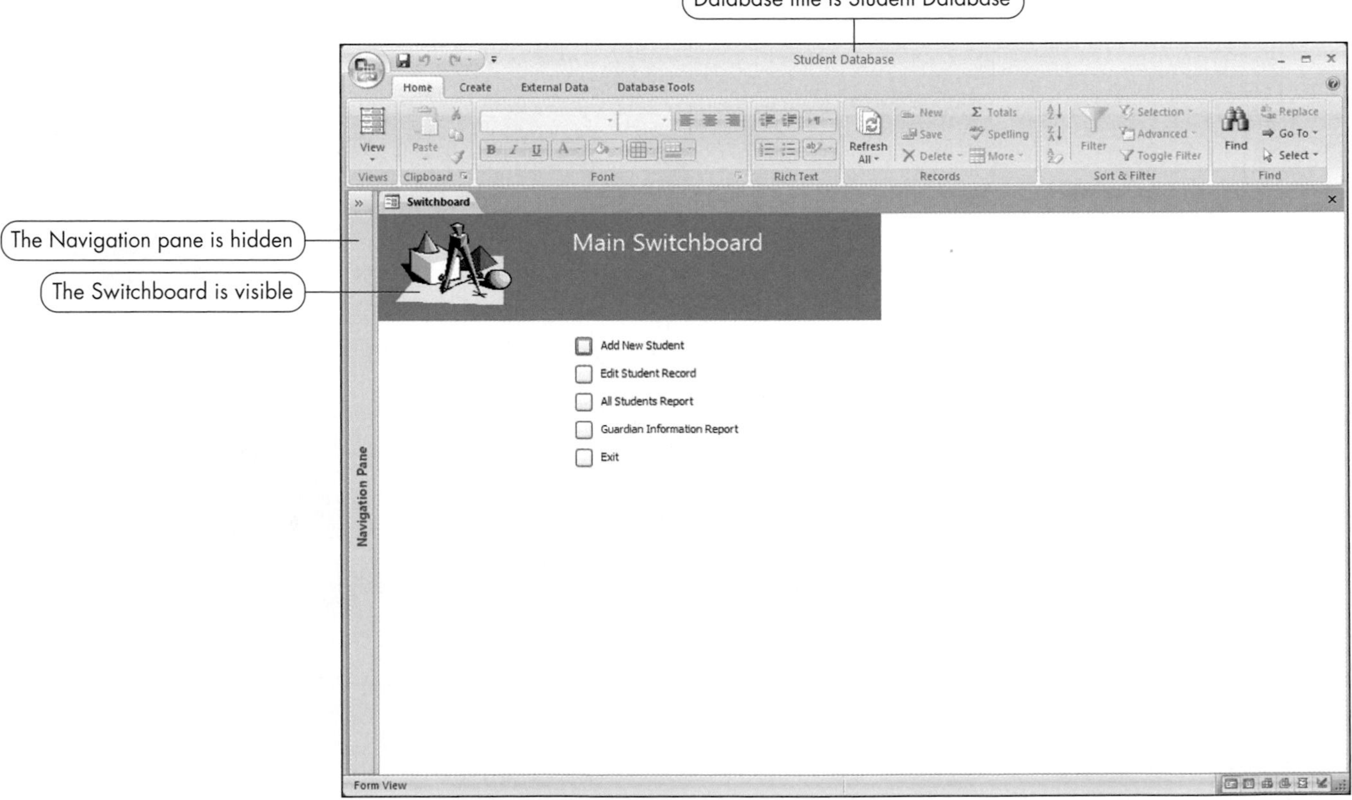

Figure 9.37 Open the Database with Startup Options Enabled

TIP Using Access Special Keys

If Use Special Access Keys is enabled in Access Options, the following keyboard shortcuts are available: (a) F11 displays and hides the Navigation pane; (b) Ctrl+Break stops Access from downloading records from a database server, such as Microsoft SQL Server; (c) Ctrl+G displays the VBA Immediate window; (d) Alt+F11 opens the VBA Editor.

Step 6 Examine Object Dependencies

Refer to Figure 9.38 as you complete Step 6.

a. Click the **Database Tools tab** and click **Object Dependencies** in the Show/Hide group. Click **OK** to update database object dependencies. Click **Yes** if you are prompted to continue.

b. Open the **Switchboard** in Design view if it is not already open. In the Object Dependencies window, click the **Objects that I depend on** option.

   In the Object Dependencies window, you should see the Switchboard Items table, indicating that the switchboard is dependent on this underlying table.

c. Close the Switchboard form. Close the database.

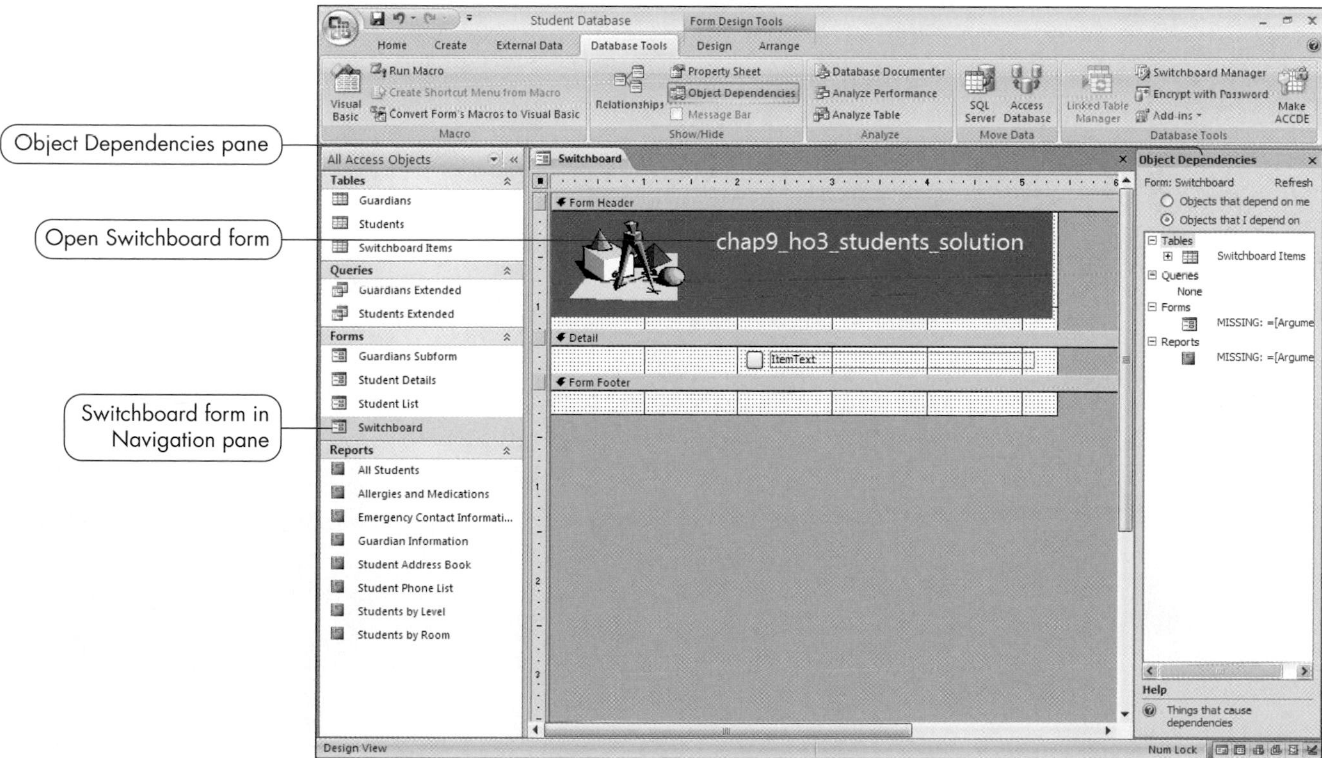

Figure 9.38 The Completed Switchboard and Object Dependencies

TIP Searching for Clip Art

The Image control functions differently in Access than in other Office applications since it does not display the Clip Art task pane. You can search for clip art by starting the Clip Organizer as a separate application. Click Start, point at All Programs, click Microsoft Office, click Microsoft Office Tools, then click Microsoft Clip Organizer. Select a clip art from within the Clip Organizer and click Copy. Return to Access, open the form in Design view, and click Paste.

Summary

1. **Encrypt and password-protect a database.** The amount of security you implement for a database depends upon the value of the data in the database. Database security revolves around requiring users to provide a username and password to open a database. Passwords typically contain a combination of letters and numbers. A good password should be impossible for unauthorized users to guess. A general rule for assigning a password is to use at least six or eight characters that combine uppercase and lowercase letters, numbers, and symbols to make the password more difficult for others to guess.
2. **Digitally sign and publish the database.** A digital signature is an electronic, encryption-based stamp that confirms the validity of the file. You can create a digital signature and apply it to a database to create a signed package. Digital signatures can be purchased from a qualified certification authority (CA).Your digital signature can prove who signed the package and when the database was last modified. When you attach a digital certificate and package the database, the database is saved with the .accdc file format.
3. **Save the database as an ACCDE file.** Converting an existing database to the .accde file format protects its forms, reports, and VB code from modification by users of the database. The .accde file format removes design features from the database so that these objects cannot be changed. Before converting a database to the .accde file format, you must open the original database with Exclusive Access.
4. **Analyze database documentation.** The Database Documenter produces a full report about every object in the database. This report can prove useful when you need to reference existing database objects or completely reconstruct the database. For example, the Documenter can provide information about existing table field names and their attributes.
5. **Analyze database performance.** The Performance Analyzer quickly examines database objects to suggest actions you can take to optimize performance. Actions include ideas, recommendations, and suggestions. Some actions can be automatically implemented, whereas others must be completed manually.
6. **Analyze database table structure and relationships.** Database performance is directly tied to its design. The Table Analyzer inspects table design and suggests normalization procedures that might improve performance.
7. **Move data to new database files.** When a database is used by a number of people, it may be wise to split the database into a front-end and a back-end. The back-end contains database tables, whereas the front-end contains everything else such as forms, queries, reports, and VB code. Each front-end copy of the database is independent of the other front-end databases. Database splitting enables users to create and manage their own front-end objects, knowing that these will not be deleted or modified by any other user.
8. **Analyze and optimize object relationships in an Access database.** Relationships between tables are based on dependencies. The goal of database design is creating tables in which every field is functionally dependent on that table's primary key. You reach this level of dependency through normalization, a process that reviews each row and field in a table to eliminate duplicate data and design databases with logical dependencies. First Normal Form (1NF) ensures that each field in a row only contains one value. We can look at this as horizontal analysis. Second Normal Form (2NF) searches columns for the same value in different columns to remove partial dependencies. This can be called vertical analysis. Third Normal Form (3NF) occurs when every field in a row of data depends on the primary key for its value.
9. **Create usable switchboards.** A switchboard is a user interface that enables a nontechnical person to open the objects in an Access database by selecting buttons from a menu. The switchboard is created through the Switchboard Manager, a tool that prompts you for the information about each menu item. The switchboard itself is stored as a form within the database that reads data from an underlying table of switchboard forms.

Key Terms

Access Database Executable (ACCDE) 582
Atomic field 607
Back-end 597
Certification Authority (CA) 581
Countermeasure 579
Database Documenter 590
Database Splitter 598
Dependency 606
Digital signature 581
Encryption 579
Exclusive access 580
First Normal Form (1NF) 594
Front-end 597
Password 580
Performance Analyzer 592
Second Normal Form (2NF) 594
Switchboard 611
Switchboard Manager 611
Table Analyzer 594
Third Normal Form (3NF) 594
Timestamp 581

Multiple Choice

1. Which of the following is created by the Switchboard Manager?
   (a) A Switchboard Items table
   (b) A Switchboard form
   (c) Both A and B
   (d) Neither A nor B

2. How do you insert art into a switchboard?
   (a) Start the Switchboard Manager, and then use the Insert Clip Art command.
   (b) Open the Switchboard form in Design view, and then add the clip art using the same techniques as for any other form.
   (c) Right-click the Switchboard form and select Insert Clip Art from the menu.
   (d) None of the above.

3. Switchboards can be used to:
   (a) Stop unauthorized persons from opening an Access database
   (b) Insert clip art into a database table
   (c) Jump between different databases
   (d) Hide database objects from nontechnical users

4. The Performance Analyzer:
   (a) Creates documentation relating to every object in the database
   (b) Displays recommendations in a results analysis window
   (c) Searches for rows of repeating data and suggests design changes to improve performance
   (d) Is a wizard that provides step-by-step instructions on the creation of tables and forms

5. The Database Documenter:
   (a) Creates a data dictionary relating to every object in the database
   (b) Displays recommendations in a Results Analysis window
   (c) Searches for rows of repeating data and suggests design changes to improve performance
   (d) Is a wizard that provides step-by-step instructions on the creation of tables and forms

6. The Table Analyzer:
   (a) Creates documentation relating to every object in the database
   (b) Displays recommendations in a Results Analysis window
   (c) Searches for rows of repeating data and suggests design changes to improve performance
   (d) Is a wizard that provides step-by-step instructions on the creation of tables and forms

7. How often should backups of the database be made?
   (a) Weekly, at the very end of the work week.
   (b) Daily at midnight.
   (c) Whenever a material change is made to the database structure.
   (d) Backups should be made as needed by users and stored on a network server.

8. How is a digital signature best defined?
   (a) A scanned copy of the database owner's signature.
   (b) Digital signatures are not supported in Office 2007.
   (c) Provides a timestamp that can help prove who last modified the database.
   (d) An e-mail that details who last made changes to the attached database.

9. Which of the following is true about encrypted databases?
   (a) Database encryption scrambles the contents of the database such that it can't be opened by other programs.
   (b) Once a database is encrypted, it can only be opened with its password.
   (c) Both A and B.
   (d) Neither A nor B.

10. What should you do if you lost or misplaced the password for your payroll database?
    (a) Run SelfCert to decrypt the database from the owner's computer.
    (b) Use Digital Certificate for VBA Projects Decrypt to remove the password.
    (c) Microsoft Support can decrypt the database upon license validation.
    (d) The database cannot be opened without the password.

Multiple Choice Continued...

11. What does password complexity mean?
    (a) The password is at least 8 characters long with uppercase, lowercase, and special characters.
    (b) The password is not easy to break.
    (c) The password is so complex that users must write it down to remember it.
    (d) Password complexity only applies to computer logins.

12. You open a database with exclusive access. What can other users do?
    (a) Open the database and make changes to it. Any changes made will be kept.
    (b) Other users cannot open the database when it is already open with exclusive access.
    (c) No rules apply. Exclusive access is a database setting that can be turned on or off.
    (d) Other users can open but cannot modify the database. Any changes made will be lost.

13. Your company needs to safeguard its databases from falling into the wrong hands. What can it do?
    (a) Password-protect every company database
    (b) Keep its databases on USB jump drives and hide them in the office manager's unlocked desk
    (c) Both A and B
    (d) Neither A nor B

14. You want to personalize a database you created for a customer. How is this accomplished?
    (a) Open the VBA Editor, select Load, and type in the database name.
    (b) Open Access Options and enter the title in the Database Title text box.
    (c) Right-click the Access title bar, select Database Title, and type in the title.
    (d) You cannot specify an Access database title.

15. When is a database in third normal form?
    (a) Every field in a row is atomic.
    (b) Columns do not contain repeating rows of data.
    (c) Every field gets its value based on the value of the primary key.
    (d) All of the above.

16. When is a database in first normal form?
    (a) Every field in a row is atomic.
    (b) Columns do not contain repeating rows of data.
    (c) Every column has a primary key.
    (d) Every field gets its value based on the value of the primary key.

17. How is normalization best defined?
    (a) User analysis of data entry that steps through three normal forms.
    (b) Atomicity at the third normal form.
    (c) A three-step process where rows, columns, and then fields (by column) are examined.
    (d) A difficult concept to implement where Codd's law of growth is examined.

Practice Exercises

1 Look Ahead

The Look Ahead Company employs sales reps who represent a number of major manufacturers by providing complete schematic pricing for customers. The company maintains basic employee contact and salary information in an Access database and hired a new payroll assistant, Ella, who, among other tasks, maintains this database. Ella is unfamiliar with Access and you are tasked with creating the switchboard. The switchboard contains five commands, three of which reference reports and an employee form. Your task is to create the switchboard and to test each switchboard item to ensure that each functions properly. You also need to set Access Options so that the switchboard displays when the database opens and hides the Navigation pane. Refer to Figure 9.39 to verify your work.

a. Copy the partially completed *chap9_pe1_lookahead.accdb* file from the Exploring Access folder to your production folder. Rename it **chap9_pe1_lookahead_solution**. Double-click the file name to open it. Enable the security content by clicking **Options** in the Security Warning bar. Select **Enable this content**, and then click **OK**.
b. Click **Switchboard Manager** in the Database Tools group on the Database Tools tab. Click **Yes** to create a new switchboard.
c. Click **Edit** in the Switchboard Manager dialog box and click **New** to create a new switchboard item.
d. Type **Add New Employee**, select **Open Form in Add Mode**, and select **Employees** in the Text, Command, and Form fields, respectively. Click **OK** to add the new item.
e. Click **New** to create a new switchboard item. Type **Employee Master List**, select **Open Report**, and select **Employee Master List** in the Text, Command, and Form fields, respectively. Click **OK** to add the new item.
f. Click **New** to create a new switchboard item. Type **Employees by Location**, select **Open Report**, and select **Employees by Location** in the Text, Command, and Form fields, respectively. Click **OK** to add the new item.
g. Click **New** to create a new switchboard item. Type **Employees by Title**, select **Open Report**, and select **Employ by Title** in the Text, Command, and Form fields, respectively. Click **OK** to add the new item.
h. Close the Edit Switchboard Page and the Switchboard Manager.
i. Double-click **Switchboard** under Forms in the Navigation pane and test each button on the switchboard to be sure that the commands work properly.
j. Click **Add New Employee** to add a new employee in the database. Type **8888**, **Blackwood**, and **Robert** in the Employee ID, Last Name, and First Name fields, respectively. Click **Location** and select **Chicago**, then click **Title** and select **Trainee**. Type **50000**, **M**, and select **Excellent** in the Salary, Gender, and Performance fields, respectively. Click **Close Form**.
k. Click **Employee Master List** to display the report that lists all employees. Note the new employee is listed in the report. Close the report.
l. Click the **Office Button**, click **Access Options**, and click **Current Databases**. In the Application Options section, click the **Display Form drop-down arrow** and select **Switchboard** as the form to display when the database is opened.
m. Clear the **Display Navigation Pane check box** in the Navigation section to hide the pane when the database is opened. Click **OK** to close Access Options.
n. Close the database file in Access.

...continued on Next Page

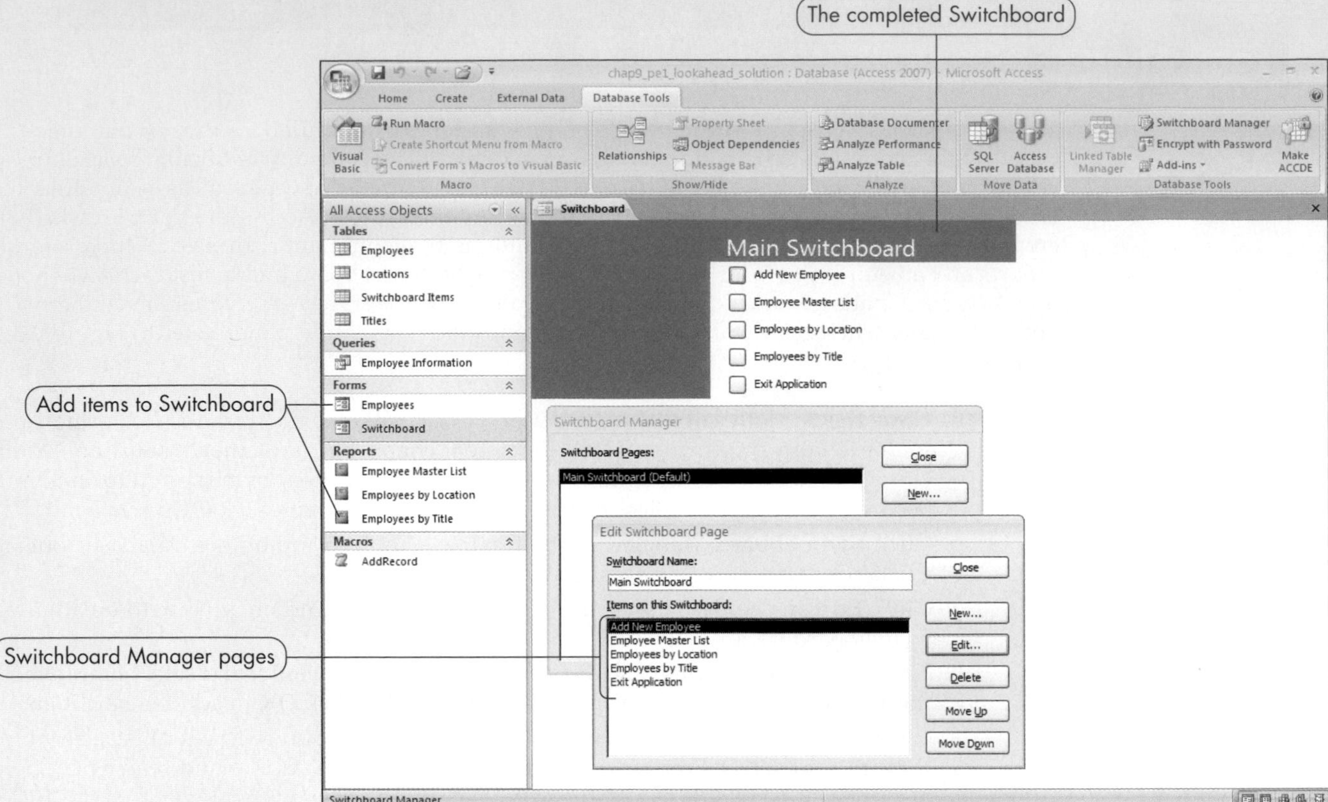

Figure 9.39 The Completed Switchboard

2 Metro Zoo

The Metro Zoo serves a small rural community. The zoo employs four trainers who manage three different exhibits and care for approximately 200 animals. A database has been created with three tables: exhibits, trainers, and animals. A one-to-many relationship exists between exhibits and animals. One exhibit can have many different animals, but a specific animal is assigned to only one exhibit. A one-to-many relationship also exists between trainers and animals. One trainer can have many animals, but a specific animal has only one trainer. The zoo hired you to optimize this database, which was created by one of the zoo managers. Your assignment is to make sure that tables are related correctly and implement any optimization ideas you deem worthwhile. You also decide to protect the database and its objects by adding password-protection, a digital signature, and protection of database objects by creating an ACCDE copy.

a. Copy the partially completed file *chap9_pe2_metrozoo.accdb* from the Exploring Access folder to your production folder. Rename it **chap9_pe2_metrozoo_password _solution**. *Do not double-click the file or click open.*
b. Click the **Open drop-down arrow** on the right side of the Open button and select **Open Exclusive**. The database is now open and you have exclusive rights to its contents. No other user can modify the contents of this database when you have it open in exclusive mode.

   If necessary, click **Options** on the Security Warning toolbar, click **Enable this content** in the Microsoft Office Security Options dialog box, and click **OK**.
c. Click **Relationships** in the Show/Hide group on the Database Tools tab. Right-click the page that opens and select **Show Table**. Select the **Animals**, **Exhibits**, and **Trainers tables** and click **Add**. Click **Close**.

   The tables are not currently related to each other. Relate the tables as displayed in Figure 9.40.

...continued on Next Page

Click **ExhibitID** in the Exhibits table and drag to **ExhibitID** in the Animals table. Click **TrainerID** in the Trainers table and drag to **TrainerID** in the Animals table. Remember to enable and **Enforce Referential Integrity** on each relationship. Click **Save** and click **Close**.

d. Click **Analyze Performance** in the Analyze group on the Database Tools tab. In the Performance Analyzer window, click the **All Object Types** pane and click **Select All**. Click **OK** to analyze the database.

   The Analysis Results pane indicates that the database is not saved in a compiled state. You decide not to implement this idea since very little VBA code resides in this database.

e. Click **Close** to exit Performance Analyzer.

f. Click **Database Documenter** in the Analyze group on the Database Tools tab. In the Documenter window, click the **All Object Types tab** and click **Select All**. Click **OK** to create complete documentation for the database. Click **Close Print Preview** to close the report.

g. Click the **Office Button** and click **Access Options**. In the left pane, click **Current Database**. In the Application Title text field, type **Metro Zoo**. Click **OK** to close Access Options.

h. Click the **Database Tools tab** and click **Encrypt with Password** in the Database Tools group.

i. Enter the password **P@ssw0rd** in the Password box and enter the same password in the Verify box. Click **OK** to set the password and encrypt the database.

   You need to test the password to be sure that it works.

j. Close the *chap9_pe2_metrozoo_password_solution* database, and then open it again as you normally would open it.

   The Password Required dialog box opens, prompting you to enter the password to open the database.

k. Type **P@ssw0rd** in the Enter database password box and click **OK**. If necessary, click **Options** on the Security Warning toolbar, click **Enable this content** in the Microsoft Office Security Options dialog box, and click **OK**.

l. Click **Start**, point to **All Programs**, point to **Microsoft Office**, point to **Microsoft Tools**, and select **Digital Certificate for VBA Projects**.

m. Type **TestCert_pe2** in the Your certificate's name box and click **OK**.

   The SelfCert success dialog box appears, confirming that you successfully created a new certificate. Click **OK**.

n. Click the **Office Button**, point to **Publish**, and select **Package and Sign**.

   The Select Certificate dialog box appears so that you can select the certificate you want to use for the database.

o. Select **TestCert_pe2**, the name of the certificate that you want to use to digitally sign this database, and then click **OK**.

   The Create Microsoft Office Access Signed Package dialog box opens so that you can change the name of the digitally signed database if you want. Change the file name to **chap9_pe2_metrozoo_signed_solution.accdc**.

p. Click **Create** to make a new signed package.

   Your database is now packaged with your digital signature so that you can deliver the database to other people who trust your certificate. The signed database closes, and then the original database opens again.

q. Click the **Database Tools tab** and click **Make ACCDE** in the Database Tools group.

   The Save As dialog box opens. The default *Save as* type is ACCDE File (*.accde), and the default name is *chap9_pe2_metrozoo_solution.accde*.

r. Click **Save** to create an .accde copy of your database.

s. Close the database.

...continued on Next Page

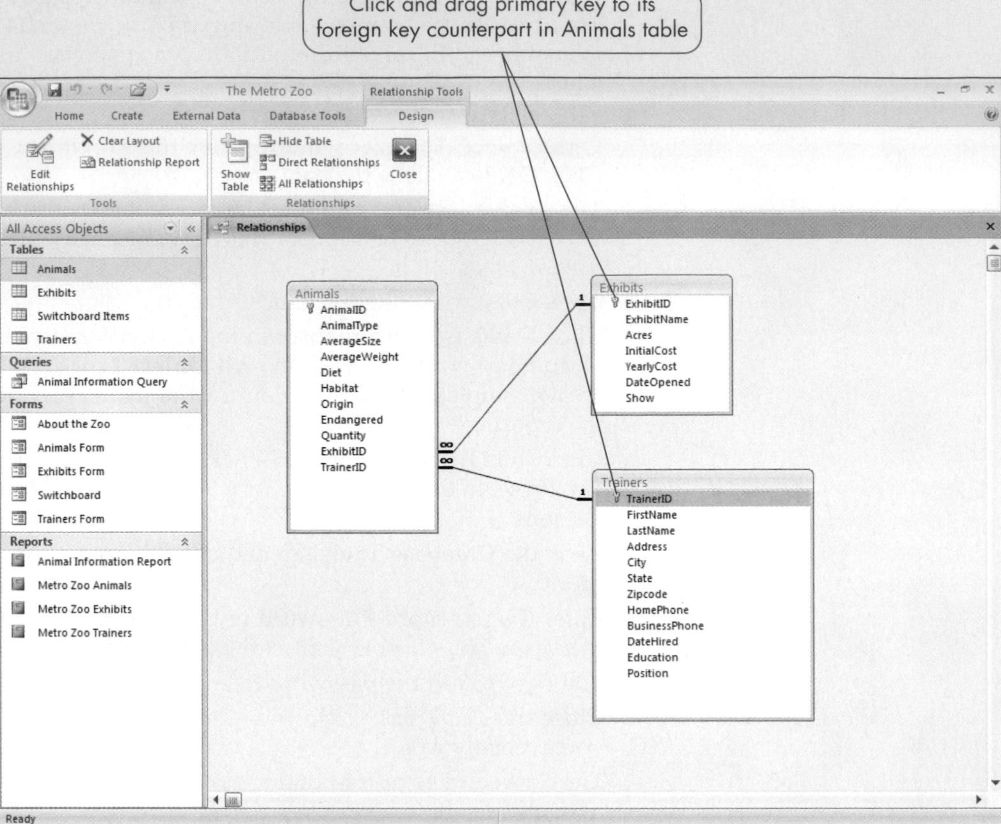

Figure 9.40 Edit Relationships

3 The SD Coffee Company

The SD Coffee Company delivers ground coffee and coffee supplies to employers who provide this perk to their employees. Sales reps service accounts throughout the state and place orders for products through the corporate Web site using handheld devices. The company stores its sales rep, customer, product, and order information in an Access database. The database was almost completed when the accountant who created the database, Nicoli, left the company. The database works but management is worried that the VBA code might be mistakenly altered or deleted by Nicoli's replacement, Faith. You are tasked with hiding the VBA code. You decide to use Analysis tools to accomplish this task. Refer to Figure 9.41 to verify your work.

a. Copy the partially completed file *chap9_pe3_sdcoffee.accdb* from the Exploring Access folder to your production folder. Rename it **chap9_pe3_sdcoffee_solution**. Double-click the file name to open it. Click **Options** on the Security Warning toolbar, click **Enable this content** in the Microsoft Office Security Options dialog box, and click **OK**.

b. Click **Analyze Performance** in the Analyze group on the Database Tools tab to display the Performance Analyzer dialog box. Click the **All Object types tab**, click **Select All** to select every object in the database, and then click **OK** to display the results, as shown in Figure 9.41.

   The Performance Analyzer displays three types of results: ***Recommendations***, ***Suggestions***, and ***Ideas***. (Your analysis returns only the last category.) Recommendations are typically unequivocal and should (almost always) be implemented. Suggestions involve a trade-off, and they should be analyzed individually prior to implementation. Access can perform recommendations and suggestions for you; that is, select the item, and then click the Optimize button. The user must implement ideas manually.

...continued on Next Page

c. Select the first idea, **The application is not saved in a fully compiled state,** then read the analysis note at the bottom of the dialog box. Close the Performance Analyzer dialog box. Click **Visual Basic** in the Macro group on the Database Tools tab. Click the **Debug** menu and select **Compile Coffee** as suggested. Click **Save**.

d. Close the VBA Editor to return to the Database window. Repeat Step b to rerun the Performance Analyzer.

Look briefly at several of the other ideas. Some have no merit, such as changing the data type of the ZipCode field, whereas other ideas are more worthwhile but are best evaluated by the developer. We do not intend to make you a VBA expert, but we did want to acquaint you with the concept of performance analysis.

e. Close the database.

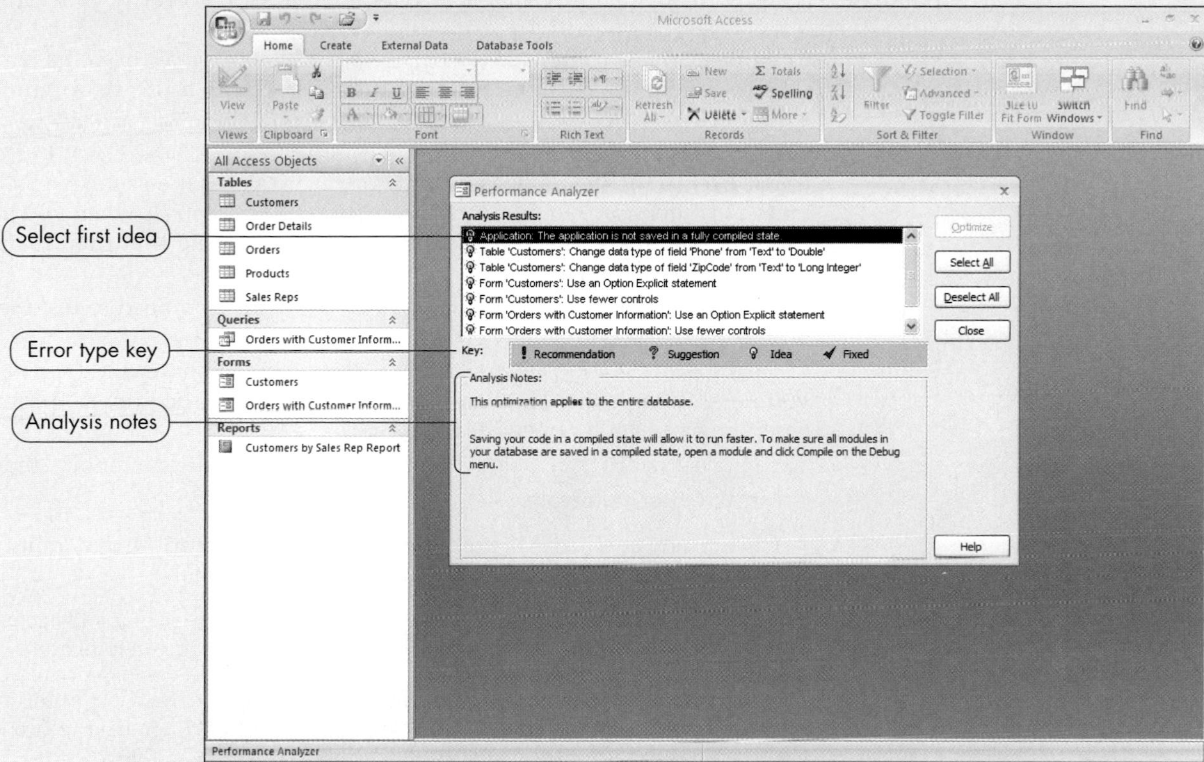

Figure 9.41 The Performance Analyzer

Mid-Level Exercises

1 The Fishing Pole

The Fishing Pole sells boats and yachts to upscale customers in the Miami, Florida area. You work in the accounting department and created a database to store customer information. The database is not yet complete, as you have a large amount of purchase history to import. You know that you also need to add more tables as you revamp your work. The accounting manager tells you that he wants the ability to open the database and run reports based on customer information you enter in the database. The accounting manager is not a technical person and you want to restrict any damage that he might do to your underlying tables. You need to create a switchboard to display reports and the About Fishing Pole form, hide the Navigation pane. You also decide to protect the database and its objects by adding password-protection, a digital signature, and protection of database objects by creating an ACCDE copy. Refer to Figure 9.42 to verify your work.

a. Copy the partially completed file *chap9_mid1_fishingpole.accdb* from the Exploring Access folder to your production folder. Rename it **chap9_mid1_fishingpole_password_solution**. Do not double-click the file or click open.

b. Click the **Open drop-down arrow** on the right side of the Open button and select **Open Exclusive**. The database is now open and you have exclusive rights to its contents. No other user can modify the contents of this database when you have it open in exclusive mode. If necessary, enable the content. Note that this database contains tables, forms, and reports.

c. Encrypt the database with the password **P@ssw0rd**. You need to test the password to be sure that it works.

d. Close the *chap9_mid1_fishingpole_password_solution* database, and then open it again as you normally open it. The Password Required dialog box opens, prompting you to enter the password to open the database.

e. Type the password you assigned in Step c and enable the content if needed.

f. Create a digital certificate:

   - Click **Start**, point to **All Programs**, point to **Microsoft Office**, point to **Microsoft Tools**, and select **Digital Certificate for VBA Projects**.
   - Type **TestCert_mid1** as the certificate name. The SelfCert success dialog box appears, confirming that you successfully created a new certificate. Click **OK**.

g. Package and sign the database within Access, using the TestCert_mid1 certificate you created. The Create Microsoft Office Access Signed Package dialog box opens so that you can change the name of the digitally signed database if you want.

h. Change the file name to **chap2_mid_fishingpole_signed_solution.accdc**. Create the new signed package. Your database is now packaged with your digital signature so that you can deliver the database to other people who trust your certificate. The signed database closes, and then the original database opens again.

i. Make an ACCDE version of the database. Change the file name to **chap9_mid_fishingpole_solution.accde**. Save the ACCDE database.

j. Create a switchboard that looks similar to Figure 9.42:

   - Make sure the Customers Report and Customers by State Report open when the user clicks the respective button on the switchboard. The About The Fishing Pole Switchboard (form) should be set to Open Form in Edit Mode.
   - Test each switchboard item to be sure that they all work properly.

k. Set Access options:

   - Display the Access Options window.
   - Click **Current Database** and select Switchboard as the Display Form setting.
   - Type **The Fishing Pole** as the application title.
   - Clear the **Display Navigation Pane check box**.
   - Close and reopen the database. Notice that when you reopen the database that the switchboard is displayed and the Navigation pane is hidden.

...continued on Next Page

l. Press **F11** to display the Navigation pane.
m. Close the database.

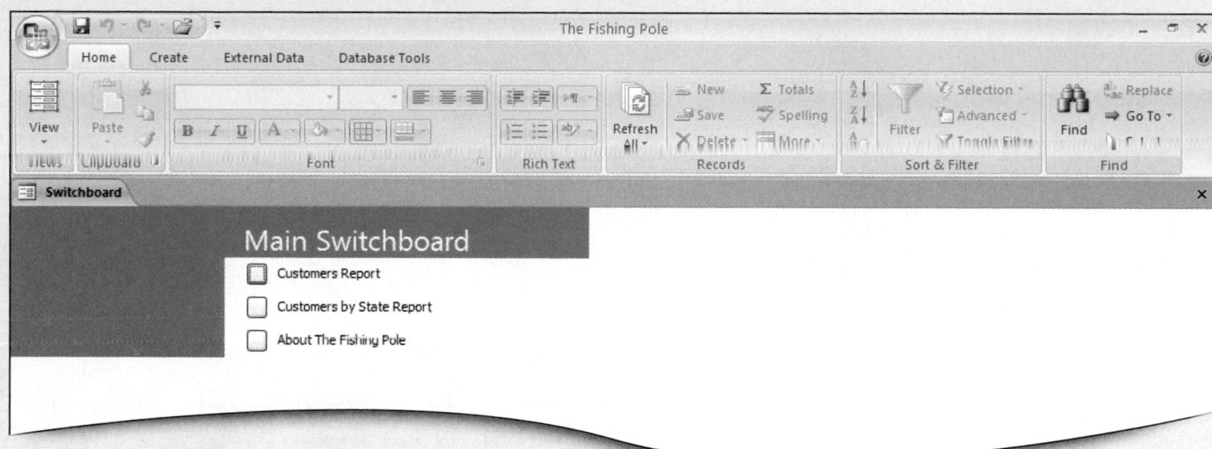

Figure 9.42 Database Opened in Switchboard View

2 The Computer Store

You are the database administrator for The Computer Store, a home-grown business handling PC repair and server administration in your geographic area. Accounting staff are complaining that the queries and reports they create are subsequently modified by other accountants and bookkeepers. Your assignment is to analyze database performance, create a front-end for the users, and keep the tables on a back-end database. Before splitting the database, also create backup documentation. Refer to Figure 9.43 as you complete your work.

a. Copy the partially completed file *chap9_mid2_computerstore.accdb* from the Exploring Access folder to your production folder. Rename it **chap9_mid2 computerstore_solution**. Double-click the file name to open it. Enable the security content.
b. Use the Database Documenter to document all object types in the database. Close the generated report after viewing it.
c. Use the Performance Analyzer to analyze all object types in the database. The Analysis Results pane indicates that the database is not saved in a compiled state. You decide not to implement this idea since very little VBA code resides in this database. The other ideas are not useful and you decide not to implement them as well.
d. Split the database as shown in Figure 9.43. Take note of the back-end database name and its location. Notice how Access appended the acronym "be" to the current database name. Save the back-end database with its default name.
e. Close the *chap9_mid2_computerstore_solution* database and open the *chap9_mid2_computerstore_solution_be* back-end database from Step d. Notice that only tables are contained in the back-end database.
f. Close the back-end database and open the front-end database. The front-end will have its original file name (*chap9_mid2_computerstore_solution.accdb*). The front-end database contains the forms, queries, and reports that are no longer sited within the back-end. Tables are links to the back-end indicated by blue arrows to the left of the table name in the Navigation Pane.
g. Close the *chap9_mid2_computerstore_solution* front-end database.

...continued on Next Page

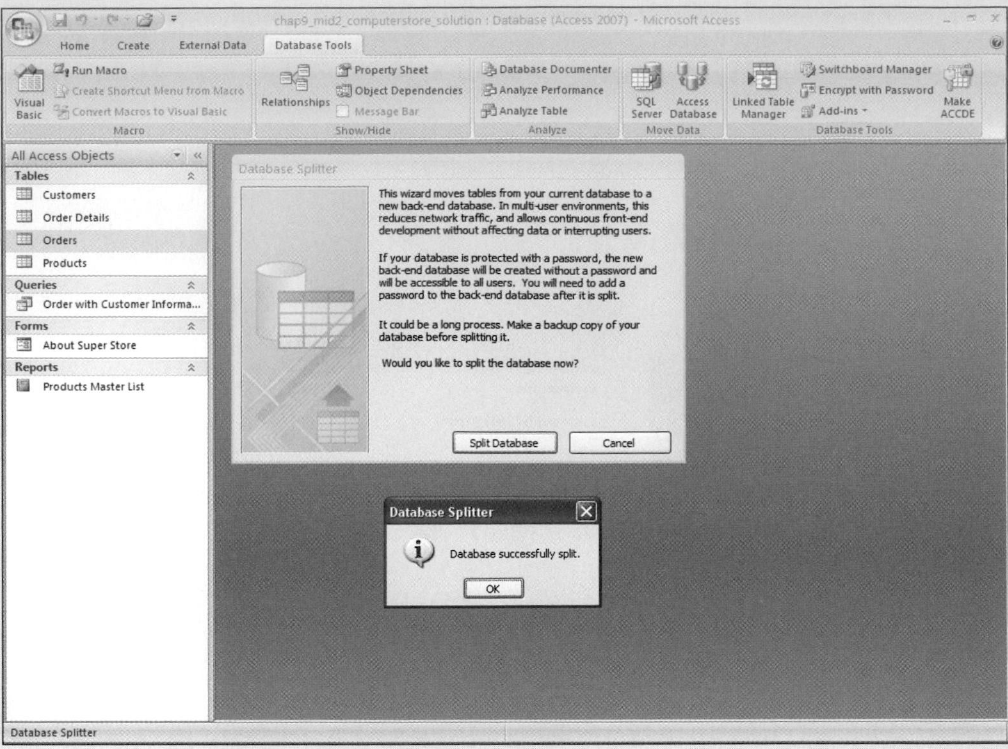

Figure 9.43 The Database Splitter Dialog Box

3 Create a Database in Third Normal Form

You create databases to generate extra cash, and a couple of friends, Dave and Jon, ask you to create a database to hold movie information for them. Dave wants to store the movie title, major actor, the character played by that actor, movie category, and the date the film was created in a database. Dave further tells you that this database will be placed on his Web site and that his Web administrator will optimize it so that users can add, modify, or view the movies stored in the database. Your assignment is to create the database tables and relate them together with referential integrity. Dave gives you a printout that is displayed below. Your goal is to create a prototype database for Dave and Jon to preview, in the third normal form. Refer to Figure 9.44 as you complete your work.

a. Create a new, blank database named **chap9_mid3_movietitles_solution.accdb**. Display **Table 1** in Design view.
b. Rename the table **Movies**. Rename the ID primary key field name **pk_MovieID**. Add the following fields: **MovieTitle**, **fk_ActorID**, **CharacterPlayed**, and **DateMade**. Set the data types to AutoNumber, Text, Number, Text, and DateTime, respectively. In the DateMade Field Properties, change the Format attribute to **MediumDate**. Save and close the table.
c. Create a new table named **Categories**. Change the primary key field name from ID to **pk_CategoryID**. Add a field named **Category** and accept its default data type. Open this table and type in the following values: **Action**, **Animation**, **Comedy**, **Crime**, **Drama**, **Family**, **Fantasy**, **Film-noir**, **Horror**, **Musical**, **Mystery**, **Romance**, **Sci-fi**, **Thriller**, **War**, **Western**. Save and close the table.
d. Add a field named **fk_CategoryID** to the Movies table. Set its data type to **Lookup**. Create a relationship to the **Categories** table. (Add both fields to the Lookup when asked to do so by the Wizard.) Close the Movies table.
e. Create a new table named **Actors**. Change the ID primary key field name to **pk_ActorID**. Add two new fields to the database: **ActorFirstName** and **ActorLastName**. Accept the default **Text** data types. Save and close the table. You have achieved third normal form in the design process.
f. Relate the tables and enforce referential integrity. (Remember to always drag the primary key to its foreign key counterpart in another table). Save and close the Relationships window.

...continued on Next Page

g. Use the **Forms Wizard** to create a form similar to that shown in Figure 9.44. Save the form and open it in Form view.

h. Add the following movies to your database:

Nbr	Movie Titles	Major Actor	Character Played	Category	Date Made
1	Pinnochio	Dickie Jones	Pinocchio	Animation	1940
2	Old Yeller	Fess Parker	Jim Coates	Family	1957
3	Red River	John Wayne	Thomas Dunson	Western	1948
4	Les Miserables	Richard Jordan	Jean Valjean	Drama	1978
5	Citizen Kane	Orson Welles	Charles Foster Kane	Mystery	1941

i. Close the *chap9_mid3_movietitles_solution* database.

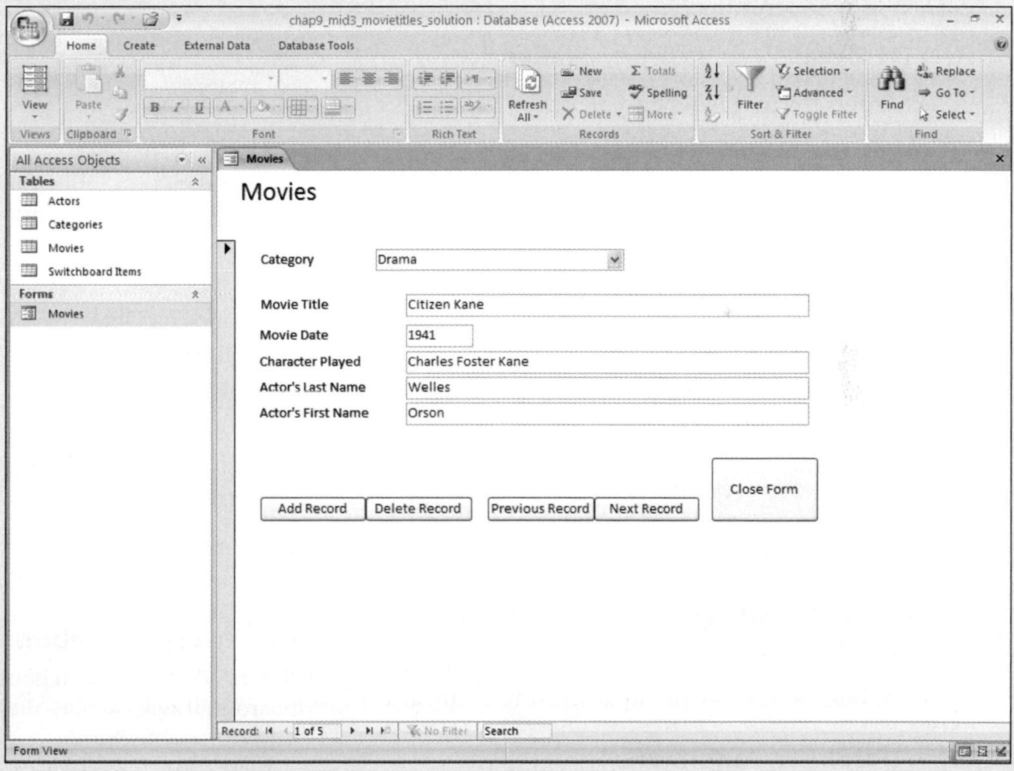

Figure 9.44 Movie Form

Capstone Exercise

Your company handles room registration, speaker coordination, and other functions for national conferences that are held at your campus throughout the year. The sales department mails schedules to speakers and building coordinators. The database has undergone a amount of change lately and it appears that unauthorized personnel have opened the database and made changes to dates that do not fit the schedule. These changes have been fixed, but someone also deleted database relationships. This was not fixed. You have been asked to secure the database, make it difficult for users to locate tables and queries, restore database relationships, and optimize its performance. You are also to produce a data dictionary.

Restore Database Relationships

You need to open the original database *chap9_cap_natconf.accdb* and restore its database relationships.

a. Locate the file named *chap9_cap_natconf.accdb* and copy it to your production folder.

b. Rename it **chap9_cap_natconf_solution.accdb**.

c. Select **Open Exclusive** when you open *chap9_cap_natconf_solution.accdb*.

d. Open the Relationships window to examine table relationships.

e. Add the **Speakers**, **SessionsSpeaker**, and **Sessions** tables to the Relationships window. Restore relationships by dragging **primary keys** to **their foreign key location**.

f. Enable referential integrity for all relationships you create.

g. Capture a screenshot of the Relationships screen. Press **PrintScrn**, open Word, type your name and section number, and press **Enter**. Paste the screenshot in the Word document. Save the document as **chap9_cap_natconf_relationships_solution.docx**. Close the Word document.

h. Save changes and close the Relationships window.

Analyze Database Performance

You want to verify that the database will perform properly when it is used in a production environment. Run Performance Analyzer to examine database performance and take note of the recommendation to create an MDE file.

a. Open the Performance Analyzer dialog box, click the **All Objects Type tab**, click **Select All**, and click **OK**.

b. Examine the Analysis Results, noting that most of the ideas are not worth implementing.

c. The first recommendation suggests creating an MDE file. You will do that later.

d. Close the Performance Analyzer.

Create the Data Dictionary

Since the database is complete, create backup documentation. This can be used in case the database needs to be re-created or if you later decide to add other objects to the database. Run the Database Documenter to create the data dictionary.

a. Open the Documenter dialog box, click the **All Object Types tab**, click **Select All**, and click **OK**.

b. Navigate to the report's Relationships page. This should be the last page of the report.

c. Look over the relationships and make sure they are reported correctly. The **Attributes: Enforced** entry refers to referential integrity being applicable to that relationship.

d. Close the Object Definition window.

e. If necessary, click Close Print Preview.

Split the Database

Protect database table design by creating a back-end and creating front-end database copies for users. This will let users customize forms, queries, and reports without fear of losing their work.

a. Open the Database Splitter and select the option to split the database. At the Create Back-end Database window, do not click Split until Step b.

b. Click **Split** to create the back-end database containing the tables. The front-end copy of the database remains open.

c. Continue using the open front-end copy of the database.

Create the Switchboard

You need to run Switchboard Manager to create a switchboard that will display the three reports in the database. In addition, you want to set Access options so that the Navigation pane is hidden and the Switchboard form loads when the database is opened.

a. Open the Switchboard Manager and edit the existing switchboard.

b. Add all three reports to the switchboard.

c. Close the Switchboard Manager and open **Access Options**.

d. Set the database to open the switchboard when the database is opened. Also disable **Access Special Keys** and clear the **Display Navigation Pane check box**.

e. Test the switchboard. Close and reopen the database to test that the other functionality is correct.

f. Capture a screenshot of the switchboard. Press **PrintScrn**, open Word, and launch a new blank document. Type your name and section number, and press **Enter**. Paste the screenshot in the Word document. Save it as **chap9_cap_natconf_switchboard_solution.docx**. Close the Word document.

Encrypt the Database with a Password and Create the ACCDE File

Make sure you have the database open with Exclusive access before completing these steps. You need to encrypt the database with a password. In addition, you want to convert the database to the ACCDE file format.

a. Display the Set Database Password dialog box.

b. Set the database password to **P@ssw0rd**. Type the same password in both text boxes.

c. Close and reopen the database to test the password.

d. Convert the database to ACCDE file format. Notice the file extension changes from .accdb to .accde during the conversion.

e. Close the database.

Mini Cases

Use the rubric following the case as a guide to evaluate your work, but keep in mind that your instructor may impose additional grading criteria or use a different standard to judge your work.

Split a Database

GENERAL CASE

The owner of a small bookstore called and asked for your assistance. Accountants are accidentally modifying and deleting reports and queries that belong to bookkeepers. Open *chap9_mc1_bookstore.accdb* file. Create a front-end and back-end. Append **fe_solution** and **be_solution** to each file name, respectively. You are to encrypt the back-end database with the password **B@ckEnd1** and encrypt the front-end with the password **Fr0nt@end**.

Performance Elements	Exceeds Expectations	Meets Expectations	Below Expectations
Create split database	Front-end and back-end created and named correctly.	Front-end and back-end created but not named correctly.	Either front-end or back-end created with correct or incorrect file naming.
Database encrypted	Each database encrypted with assigned password. Passwords not saved to a file in the same folder as database files.	Each database encrypted with assigned password.	Either front-end or back-end encrypted with incorrect password.

Data Dictionaries

RESEARCH CASE

Your company uses a large Access 2007 database to store its customer information. The Accounting Department uses and maintains this database. Marketing, Sales, and Production now want to create new databases that link their (newly added) data to the existing accounting database to improve customer relations and revenue forecasting. Currently, no documentation exists that supports the existing database, and you recall that a data dictionary can be generated from within Access. Your assignment is to do online research to determine exactly what a data dictionary is, what its Access output will include, and your professional opinion as to whether or not you believe you should create a data dictionary before the other databases begin the requirements stage. Use a memo template in Word and a business casual writing style in your (minimum) two-page write-up. Save the document as **chap9_mc2_ datadictionary_solution.docx**.

Performance Elements	Exceeds Expectations	Meets Expectations	Below Expectations
Use Online help	Appropriate articles located and memo indicates comprehension. comprehension.	Appropriate articles located, but memo did not demonstrate Articles not located.	Research items used on occasion in written.
Prepare written report	Research items heavily used in written communication.	Research items used on occasion in written.	Research items not used.
Summarize and communicate	Memo clearly written and could be used to make a decision.	Memo text indicates some understanding of concepts but contains weaknesses.	Memo is not completed or is in comprehensible.
Aesthetics	Memo template correctly employed.	Template employed, but format is missing one or two required items.	Template not used or output cannot be understood.

Troubleshoot Using Performance Analyzer

DISASTER RECOVERY

A loan officer, Greta, at the credit union you work at frantically calls you to ask for your help in fixing her database. Greta tells you that her database was working fine until a loud thunderbolt hit the building late this morning. Greta's computer lost power during the storm and since she rebooted, she is unable to enter loan payment information. Greta needs to get deposits entered so that she can provide the branch vice president, Rip, a report in 30 minutes. The report was due two hours ago. Rip wants a small write-up explaining what happened and what you did to fix the problem. Your task is to analyze the database to determine what needs to be fixed and then implement the fix in the database. You also need to write the document Rip requested. Use a memo template in Word and a business casual writing style in your write-up. The loan officer's database is *chap9_mc3_nationalbank.accdb*. Save your final database as **chap9_mc3_nationalbank_solution.accdb**.

Performance Elements	Exceeds Expectations	Meets Expectations	Below Expectations
Error identification	Memo indicates use of Performance and Table Analyzer.	Memo indicates use of either Performance or Table Analyzer.	Memo does not indicate that Performance and Table Analyzer were used.
Error fixed	Memo indicates that all ideas were implemented (optimized).	Memo indicates that the table relationship was restored. No other ideas were implemented.	Memo does not indicate that any ideas were implemented.
Summarize and communicate	Memo clearly written and could be used to make a decision.	Memo text indicates some understanding of concepts but contains weaknesses.	Memo is not completed or is incomprehensible.
Aesthetics	Memo template correctly employed.	Template employed, but format is missing one or two required items.	Template not used or output cannot be understood.

Macros and Visual Basic for Applications

Customizing a Database

After you read this chapter, you will be able to:

1. Understand the purpose of macros in Access databases **(page 641)**.
2. Create embedded macros using wizards **(page 643)**.
3. Create macros using the Macro Builder **(page 644)**.
4. Assign macros to events **(page 646)**.
5. Use SQL conditions to control macro actions **(page 648)**.
6. Understand Visual Basic for Applications (VBA) **(page 658)**.
7. Use the Visual Basic Editor **(page 658)**.
8. Create procedures **(page 660)**.
9. Declare and use variables **(page 662)**.
10. Manage data using SQL **(page 666)**.

Hands-On Exercises

Exercises	Skills Covered
1. CUSTOMIZING A DATABASE USING MACROS (page 652) **Open:** chap10_ho1-2_acme.accdb **Save as:** chap10_ho1_acme_solution.accdb	• Create an Embedded Macro on a Form • Create an Embedded Macro on a Report • Create a Standalone Macro • Assign a Macro to an Event • Create a Macro with an SQL Expression on a Form
2. CUSTOMIZING A DATABASE USING VBA (page 668) **Open:** chap10_ho1-2_acme.accdb (from Exercise 1) **Save as:** chap10_ho2_acme_solution.accdb	• Create Global Procedures • Create Sub Procedures That Call Global Procedures • Write Procedures That Handle Events • Set Database Properties and Test Procedures

CASE STUDY

ACME Consulting

ACME Consulting is a small consulting firm that provides consulting services to information technology companies. ACME has a team of almost 20 consultants in four regional offices throughout the United States. Recently the company implemented a 401(k) retirement plan for all employees. The plan is open to all employees, and a participant may elect to contribute up to 9% of monthly gross pay into a personal retirement account. For employees who have been with the company for more than 30 days, the company will match the employee's contribution by a percentage that varies according to the length of employment. The programming for performing these calculations has been completed.

The database has a menu form with buttons, but the buttons have not been programmed to do anything. The menu form contains six buttons that require customization. When the programming is complete, these buttons will open the History form that shows the year-to-date retirement contribution for each employee; open the Employee form to enter and edit employee data; open the Retirement Summary report for all employees; open the Retirement Summary report for employees by region, with the region (East, Midwest, Rocky Mountain, West) entered by the user at the time the report is run; open the Office Locations report; and close the database. In addition, the Employee and History forms each contain a button to close the form, but these buttons also have not been programmed. The Retirement Summary and Office Locations reports each also have a button to close the report, but the buttons have not been programmed.

Your task is to program the database using macros and VBA procedures. You will use macros for the procedures that open the Employee and History forms and the Office Locations report. You will use VBA procedures to close the forms and reports, and to close and exit the database. For each procedure that closes a form, report, or the database, you will need to verify the user's intent to complete the close action. Finally, you will use VBA procedures to display the Retirement Summary report, because the source data for the report will be defined using Structured Query Language (SQL). The VBA procedure to display the Retirement Summary report by region will include an SQL WHERE clause that will store the region name as a variable so the report will display only records for employees in a specific region.

Your Assignment

- Copy the file named *chap10_case_acme.accdb* to your production folder. Rename it **chap10_case_acme_solution.accdb**. Open the copied file and enable the content.
- Create macros to display the Employee form, the History form, and the Office Locations report.
- Define global variables and a public procedure that will close any form or any report.
- Create local procedures to close the Employee form, the History form, and the Retirement Summary report when the button to close the form or report is clicked. These procedures use a decision structure to verify the user's intent to close the form or report.
- Create a local procedure to exit the database when the Exit button is clicked. Use a decision structure to verify the user's intent to close the database.
- Create two local procedures to display the Retirement Summary report—one report listing all employees and one listing the employees in a specific region. Use SQL statements to define the source data for each report, and for the report listing employees in a specific region, use an SQL WHERE clause to select the records.
- Set the database startup properties so that a database title is displayed, the Menu form opens, and the Navigation pane is hidden.
- Test the database functionality for each macro and procedure you created.

Programming with Macros

Access developers have a variety of tools available to create database tables, queries, forms, and reports, but at times a database requires additional functionality that can only be accomplished through programming. Two ways exist to customize an Access 2007 database with programming—using macros or writing procedures using Visual Basic for Applications (VBA). In general, it is easier to create a macro than a VBA procedure, because Access includes tools for automating macro design. In this chapter you will learn how to program a database using macros and VBA.

In this section, you will learn to create macros first because you can create Access macros using tools such as the Command Button Wizard and the Macro Builder. In addition, you learn about SQL and how to incorporate SQL statements into macros.

Understanding the Purpose for Macros in Access Databases

A ***macro*** automates tasks by adding functionality to database objects.

A *macro* in Access is a tool that enables you to automate database tasks and add functionality to objects such as forms, reports, and the controls your forms and reports contain. Think of a macro as a simplified programming language for automating a repetitive task or performing a specific action. You can use macros to group a series of commands and instructions as a single command to accomplish repetitive or routine tasks automatically. After you create a macro, you can perform all its tasks by running the macro. For example, you might create a macro to import weekly sales data from an Excel workbook into an Access table, run a query to update prices to reflect a storewide sale, or run a report to ensure that the same sequence of steps are performed each time you run the macro. You actually were exposed to macros when you created switchboards with buttons that display forms or reports or run queries.

You can create macros in most Microsoft Office 2007 applications. Word and Excel include the Macro Recorder to record steps into a macro. PowerPoint requires you to use VBA to create macros. When you create a macro in Word, Excel, and PowerPoint, Office stores the macro as a VBA procedure. Access handles macros differently. In addition, Access has expanded capabilities for creating, managing, and using macros. In Access, macros are most often used with forms and reports. This is because forms are typically used to enter and edit records, and reports display and summarize data. Forms and reports contain controls. A *control* is an object like a text box, list box, or command button. Controls display data or respond to events. A form or report might include a text box control that performs a calculation and displays and formats the result. A command button usually responds to a user clicking the button, similar to when you click a dialog box button in Access, the program responds by performing a task.

A ***control*** is an object that displays data or responds to an event.

Access 2007 supports two categories of macros: standalone macros and embedded macros. A ***standalone macro*** is a database object that you create and use with more than one control. Standalone macros appear in the Navigation pane. Figure 10.1 shows the names of three standalone macros.

A ***standalone macro*** is a database object that you create and use with more than one control.

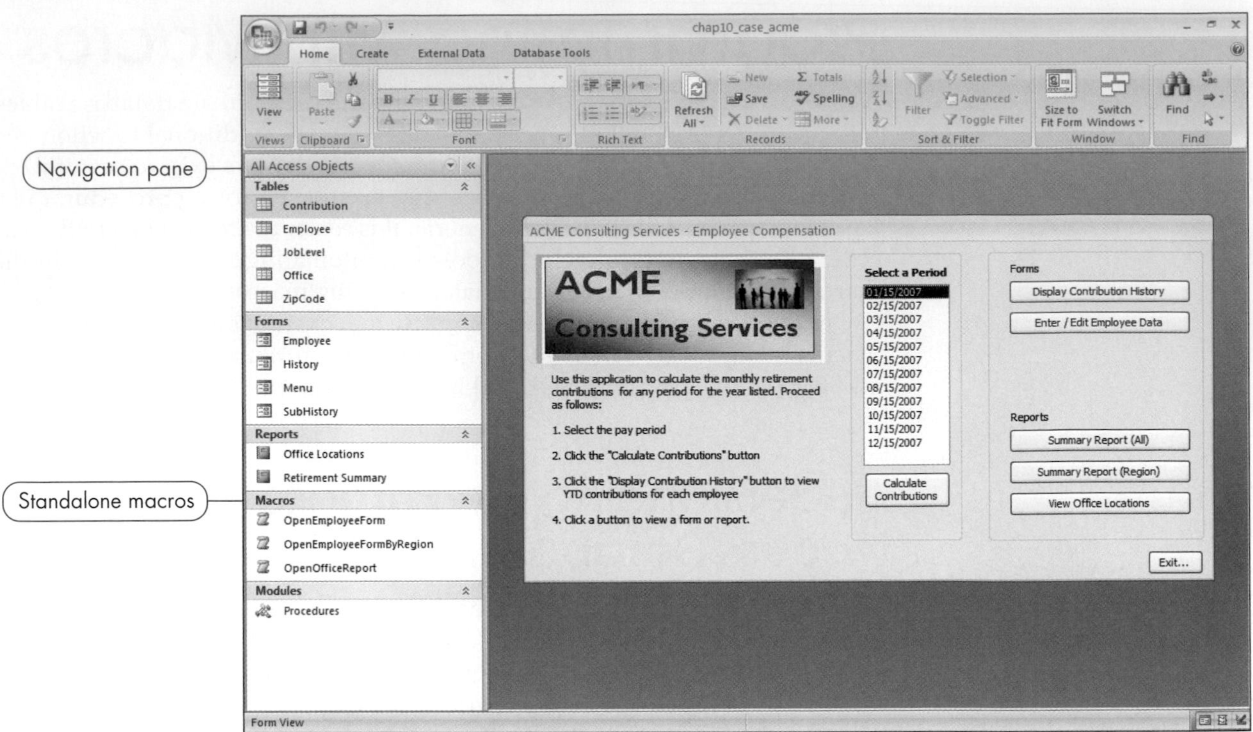

Figure 10.1 Standalone Macros in the Navigation Pane

An ***embedded macro*** is a macro that belongs to a single database object or control.

An ***embedded macro*** is a macro that belongs to a single object or control. Access provides two ways to create an embedded macro: by creating an object such as a command button with a wizard or by modifying the event property of the object or control. When you assign actions to an event (such as clicking a button), Access embeds a macro in the object or control. You can also add a control to a form or report and then use the Macro Builder to create and embed the macro. Regardless of which method you use, the Event tab in the object's Property Sheet enables you to open and edit the embedded macro. Figure 10.2 shows how an embedded macro appears in the Property Sheet for a control.

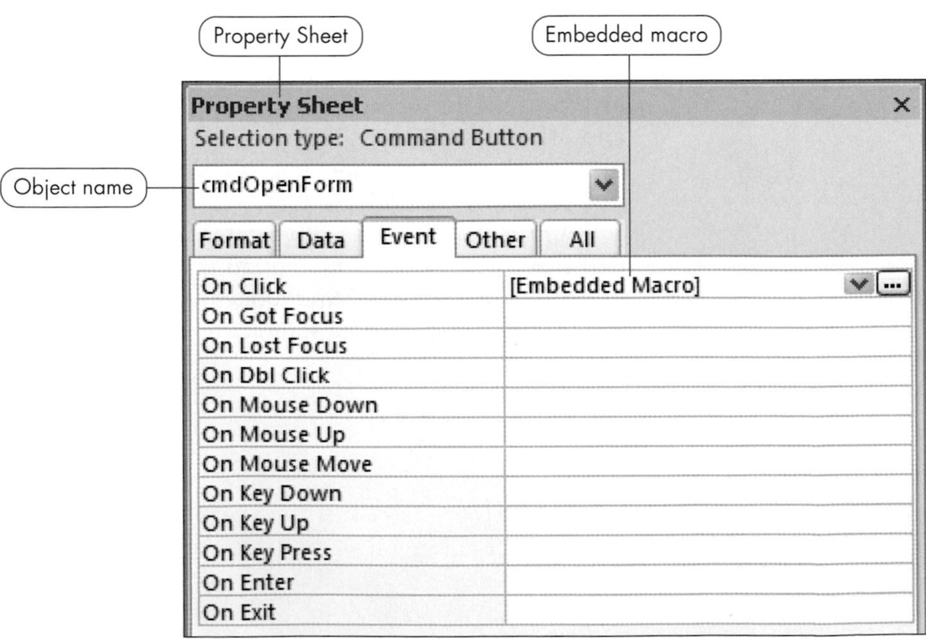

Figure 10.2 Embedded Macro Shown in an Object's Property Sheet

A ***macro group*** is a group of macros stored in a single macro object.

In Access, you can also create a *macro group*, which is a group of macros stored in a single macro object. A macro group requires that each macro in the group has a unique name. The group also has a name, and the macro group appears in the Navigation pane. You can run the individual macros in the group by running the macro group. A macro group is helpful when you have a large number of macros, and some of the macros have related functionality. Table 10.1 summarizes the macros supported by Access 2007.

Table 10.1 Access 2007 Macro Types

Macro Type	Description
Embedded Macro	A macro that belongs to (is embedded in) a specific object or control. An embedded macro does not appear in the Navigation pane. Use an embedded macro when a single object needs to run the macro.
Standalone Macro	A macro that belongs to the Access database. A standalone macro appears in the Navigation pane and is available to any control or object in the database. Use a standalone macro when the macro needs to be available for multiple objects.
Macro Group	A group of macros stored as a single macro object. A macro group is useful for organizing a related group of macros. Each macro in the group must have a unique name. The named macro group will appear in the Navigation pane and is available to any object or control in the database.

Creating Embedded Macros Using Wizards

Embedded macros are new in Access 2007. An embedded macro will not appear in the Navigation pane because it belongs to a specific object. The simplest method for creating an embedded macro is to create a control, such as a command button, and use the control's wizard to define the actions the macro will perform. For example, you might add a button on a Customers form to close the form when a user clicks the button.

To add a command button to a form, create a new form or open a form in Design view. Click the Design tab to view the available controls. Click Button in the Controls group on the Design tab and drag a button onto the form. When you release the mouse button, the Command Button Wizard begins. Figure 10.3 shows the first step in the Command Button Wizard.

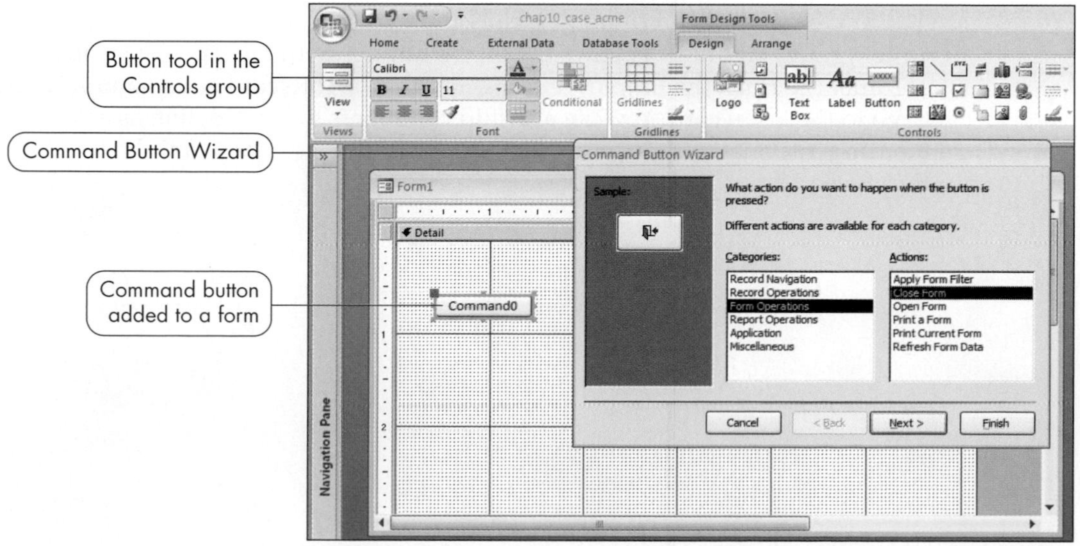

Figure 10.3 Using the Command Button Wizard to Create an Embedded Macro

The Command Button Wizard guides you through the steps for defining the actions performed by the button, selecting the format for the button, and saving the control. When you complete the wizard, Access automatically saves and embeds the macro. You can modify the macro by viewing the button's properties and selecting the embedded macro in the button's On Click event. The On Click event detects when a button is clicked and then executes a series of commands, such as commands in a macro.

TIP Editing an Embedded Macro

When you edit an embedded macro by opening the event for the control, Access opens the embedded macro in the Macro Builder. You can then use any of the commands or properties available in the Macro Builder to modify the embedded macro. However, the macro remains embedded in the object.

Creating Macros Using the Macro Builder

The ***Macro Builder*** is a tool for creating and editing Access macros.

Although the Command Button Wizard provides a simple interface for creating an embedded macro, an embedded macro is not available to objects other than the control where the macro is embedded. Access has a tool called the ***Macro Builder*** for creating and editing standalone macros. This tool provides an interface for selecting the actions and the arguments for a macro. Actions are the basic building blocks for macros. The Macro Builder contains a list of actions you can select. Common actions open a report, find a record, display a message box, or apply a filter to a form or report, just to name a few. For example, a database administrator for a pharmacist might create a macro that uses the OpenForm action to open the Supplier form, or a college professor creates a macro that uses the OpenTable action to open the Section001 table to see grades and use the ApplyFilter action to filter the table to show students earning an A grade.

You assign actions to the macro by selecting an action from the Action drop-down list. A macro can contain a single action or many actions. For example, you might need to use both the OpenTable and ApplyFilter actions in one macro. Certain actions require an argument, which is a value that provides information to the action. A macro argument is similar to a function argument in Excel. For example, the Excel SUM function's argument requires a range of cells that contain values that need to be summed. In an Access macro action, the argument indicates the specifics. For example, the OpenForm action requires an argument to specify *which* form to open.

To launch the Macro Builder, click the Create tab, and then click Macro in the Other group. Figure 10.4 shows the Macro Builder with the OpenForm action and its argument to open the Employee form, and the GoToRecord action and its argument to go to the last record. You can also add comments for each action as a way of documenting the macro's purpose. An example of a comment might be "Open the Employee Mailing List Report."

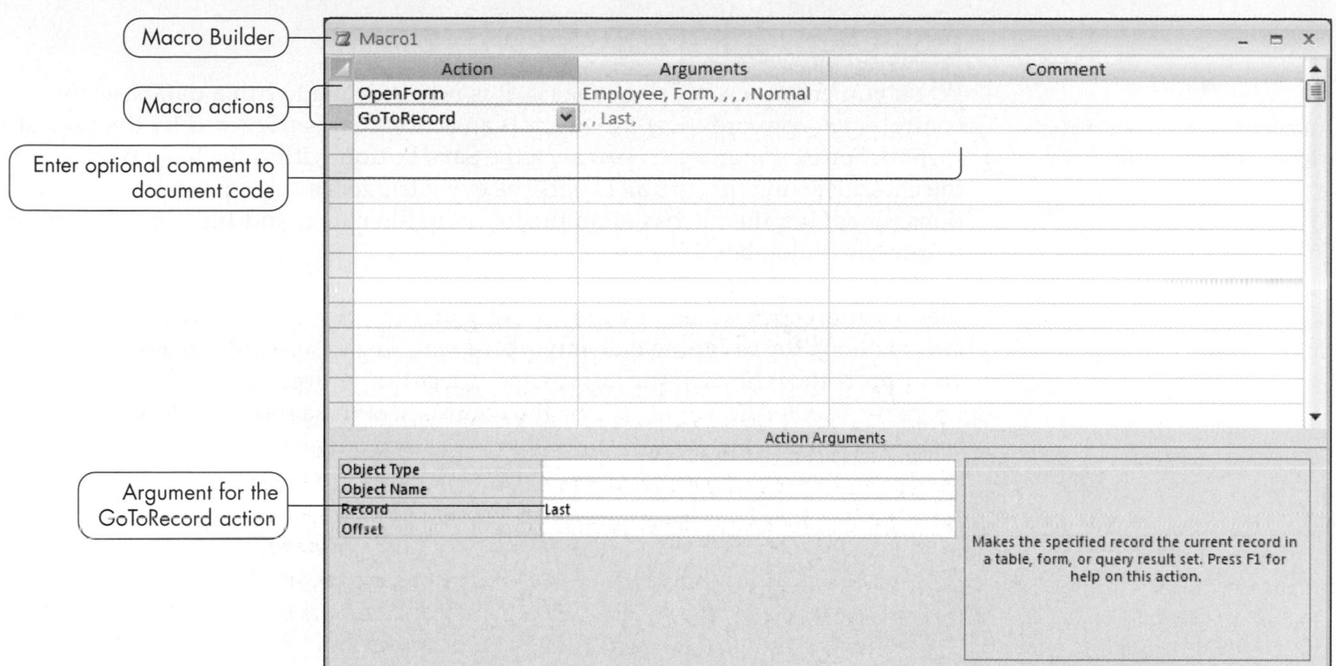

Figure 10.4 The Macro Builder

When you create a macro using the Macro Builder, you give the macro a unique name. Some database programmers prefer Pascal Case, in which the first word in the macro name is an action verb describing the macro's purpose, no spaces within the name, and an uppercase letter for each major word—for example, OpenEmployeeForm starts with the verb *Open* that describes the macro's purpose and uses uppercase letters for the O, E, and F. After you name a macro, the macro name appears in the Navigation pane. You can run the macro from the Navigation pane, from within a macro group, from another macro, from a VBA module, or in response to an event that occurs on a form, report, or control. Notice the icon that represents a macro object in Figure 10.1.

After creating a macro, you can test its functionality by running the macro. To run a macro, click the Database Tools tab, click Run macro in the Macro group, select the macro from the Macro Name drop-down list, and click OK. Alternatively, double-click or right-click the macro name in the Navigation pane and select Run, as shown in Figure 10.5.

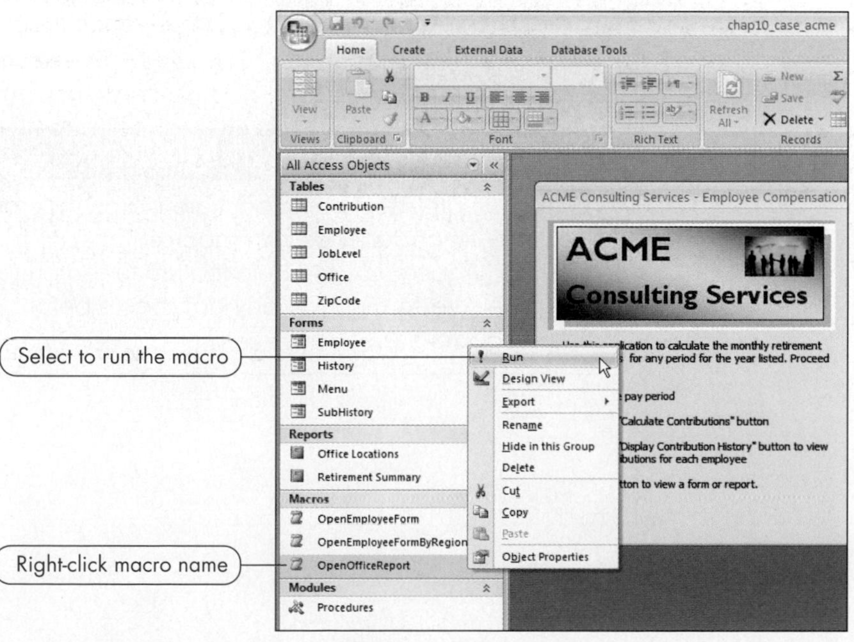

Figure 10.5 Running a Macro from the Navigation Pane

Assigning Macros to Events

An ***event*** is an action that is triggered by the user or the system.

When you create a standalone macro, it is not associated with a database object or a control on a form or report. An *event* is an action that is triggered by the user or the system. For example, when you click the Save button within the Save As dialog box, the clicking action triggers an event. The event triggers a set of programming instructions for saving the file based on the location, file name, and file type you specified within the dialog box.

You assign a macro to an event—such as the On Click event property that handles a button click event—by modifying a property for the control. Access provides two methods for assigning a macro to an event. The easiest way to assign a macro to an event is to right-click the button and select Properties. This method displays the Property Sheet. The Event tab for the control lists the properties to which you can assign the macro. Figure 10.6 shows how to assign a macro to the On Click event.

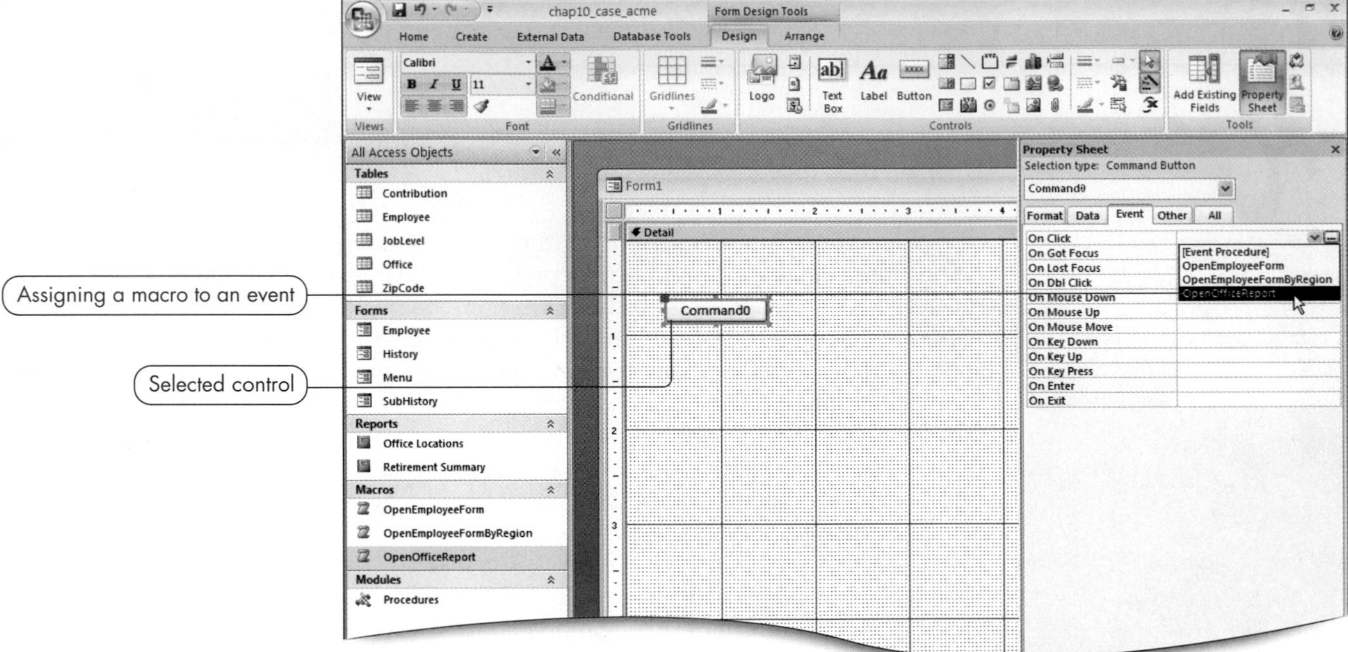

Figure 10.6 Assigning the OpenOfficeReport Macro to the On Click Event

TIP More About Macros

This section provides a brief background on macros. Access 2007 offers an extensive array of capabilities with macros. To learn more about creating and using macros in Access, use the Help feature to search for information and online tutorials. Make sure to back up any databases before experimenting with additional macro capabilities.

Design Controls | Reference

Command	Name	Description
ab|	Text Box	A text box is the standard control for users to enter and display data on a form or report. When you display a form, you see text boxes for the fields so that you can enter, edit, or delete data for a record.
Aa	Label	A label contains descriptive information that does not change, such as the heading for a text box or a column of data. For example, in a form, you see labels that represent the field names or their captions to the left of the text boxes that display data for a record.
XXXX	Button	A command button adds functionality by launching an event and processing procedures. For example, a Close command button closes a dialog box or window, or a Display button can be used to display a report from a switchboard.
	Combo Box	A combo box lists data in a field and also enables the user to add a value to the list.
	List Box	A list box displays a list of choices from which the user selects one.
	Sub form/Sub report	A sub form or sub report lists data from a related table or query.
	Line	A line enhances the appearance of a form or report. It helps to divide sections within the form or report.
	Rectangle	A rectangle enhances the appearance of a form or report, and can be used as a border for other controls.
	Bound Object Frame	The bound object frame control is used to display OLE objects, such as a picture, where each record in the database displays a different picture in the control.
	Option Group	The option group control will group other controls, such as radio buttons, to enable users to select one option in the group.
	Check Box	The check box control enables users to select one or more options within a group.
	Option Button	An option button enables users to make a single choice within a group on a form or report.
	Toggle Button	The toggle button control is usually bound to a yes/no field.
	Tab Control	The tab control enables multiple tabs for a form, where each tab contains unique information.
	Insert Page	The insert page control displays a page from another application.
	Insert Chart	The insert chart control displays a chart that is bound to rows and columns of data.
	Unbound Object Frame	The unbound object frame control group objects.
	Image	The image control, which is bound to an image, displays on the form or report.
	Insert or Remove Page Breaks	The page break control determines where data breaks on a report.
	Insert Hyperlink	The hyperlink control displays a link to an external data source, such as a Web page or a document.
	Attachment	The attachment control is used to attach an external document.

Using SQL Conditions to Control Macro Actions

A ***condition*** specifies certain criteria that must be met before an action will be performed.

When you begin programming a database using macros, you will find times when you need a macro action to perform a task that meets a specific condition. For example, a macro might open a form and display employee records, but rather than showing all records, the macro lists employees from a specific region only. A ***condition*** specifies certain criteria that must be met before an action will be performed. In this example, the condition specifies which region will filter the employee records.

You specify a condition for a macro action using the Macro Builder. The Where Condition is an argument for the action. You define a Where Condition by typing a valid expression for the argument or by clicking the Build button in the Where Condition row to open the Expression Builder. Figure 10.7 shows the Expression Builder for defining the Where Condition for a macro action.

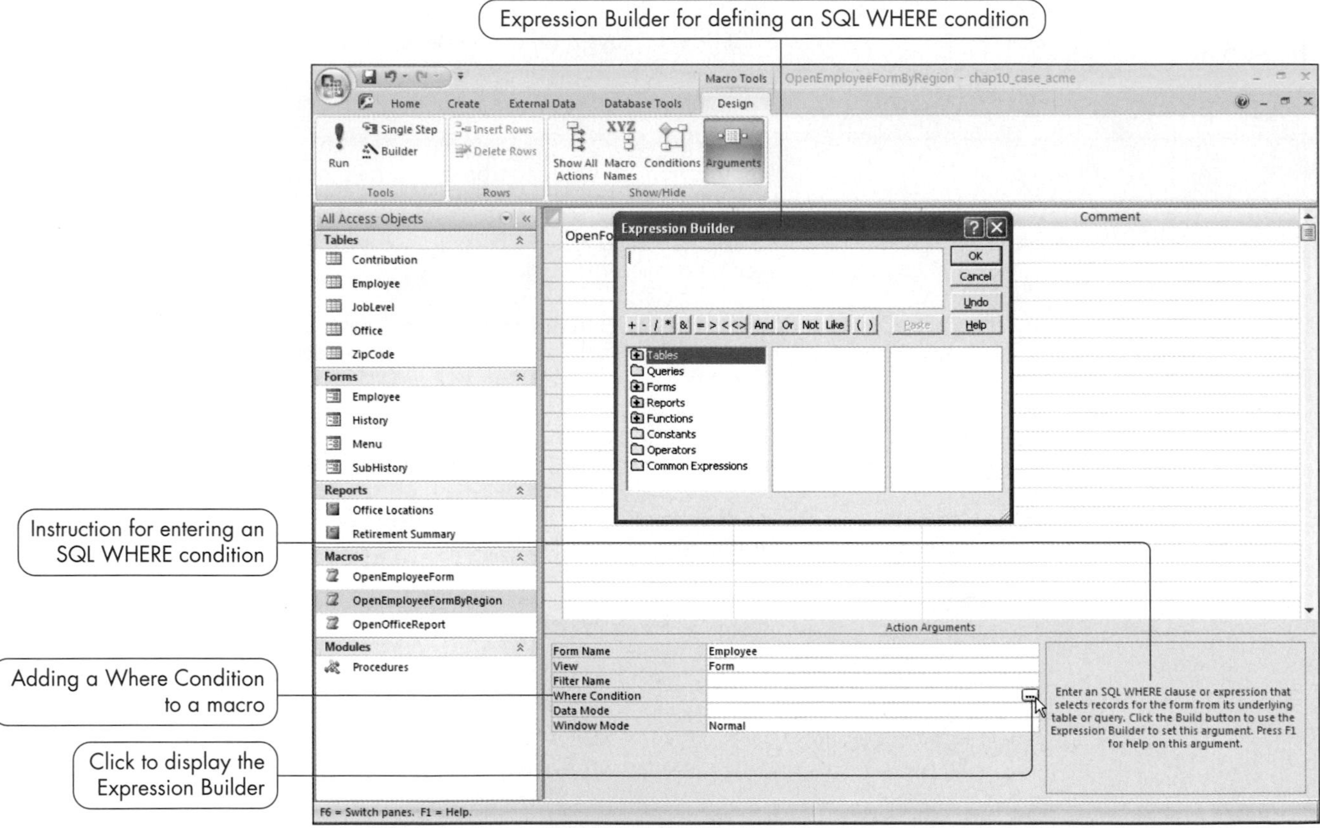

Figure 10.7 Defining a Macro Condition

Understand the Basics of Structured Query Language

Structured Query Language (SQL) is a language for defining and processing database queries.

By now, you know that Microsoft Access is a relational database. Edger Codd is the father of the relational model. In 1970, Codd wrote a theoretical paper entitled "A Relational Model of Data for Large Shared Data Banks" that transformed the world of database management. Codd proposed a method for breaking data into two-dimensional tables consisting of rows and columns, called relations. After Codd conceptualized and developed the relational database concept, IBM created a technology in the late 1970s for combining fields stored in multiple tables into a single relation, or view. This technology—called ***Structured Query Language (SQL)*** and pronounced Sequel—is now the industry-standard method for defining and processing database queries. Microsoft has developed its own version of SQL, called Microsoft Access SQL, which complies with the ANSI SQL standard.

Figure 10.7 shows the Where Condition in the Action Arguments grid. This indicates that an SQL WHERE clause or expression is required. To better understand macro conditions, you need to know the basics of SQL. All Access queries use Microsoft Access SQL. You can view the SQL statements underlying a query by listing the query in SQL View. Figure 10.8 shows both the Design view and the SQL view of an Access query. In Design view, the Field row displays the fields used in the query. In SQL view, the SELECT statement lists the fields that are selected.

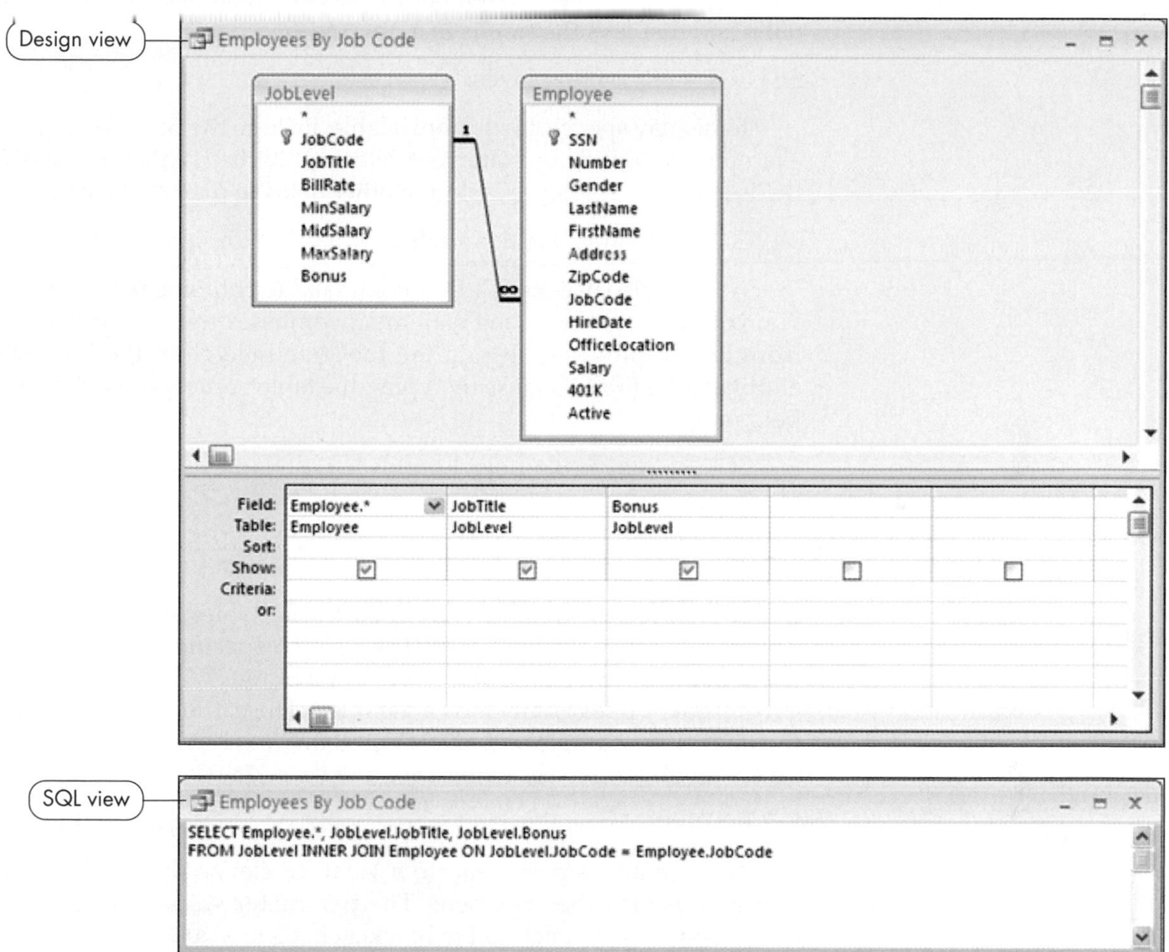

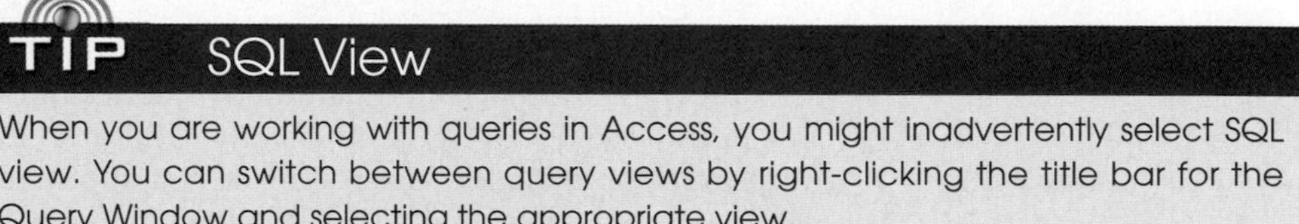

Figure 10.8 Query in Design View and SQL View

TIP SQL View

When you are working with queries in Access, you might inadvertently select SQL view. You can switch between query views by right-clicking the title bar for the Query Window and selecting the appropriate view.

An ***SQL statement*** is a statement that uses keywords that belong to the SQL definition language.

SQL expressions consist of text that includes SQL statements and clauses. An ***SQL statement*** is a statement that uses keywords that belong to the SQL definition language. SQL statements are written as text. An SQL statement ends with a semicolon character.

Select Records with the SELECT Statement and FROM Clause

A ***SELECT statement*** instructs Access to return fields from one or more database tables.

The ***FROM clause*** specifies the table containing the data returned by the query.

The ***SELECT statement*** instructs Access to return fields from one or more database tables. When a query or expression containing a SELECT statement runs, Access searches the specified table (or tables), extracts the chosen fields, and displays the results. The ***FROM clause*** specifies the table containing the data returned by the query. You can use the asterisk character (*) to select all fields in a table. For example, the following SELECT statement displays *all* fields and records from the Employee table and displays the results in a datasheet:

```
SELECT * FROM Employee;
```

To display specific fields from a table, include the field names in the statement. For example, the following statement selects only the LastName, FirstName, and Salary fields from the Employee table; the other fields in the Employee table are not selected:

```
SELECT LastName, FirstName, Salary FROM Employee;
```

You can also use the SELECT command to combine records from different tables. For example, the following statement combines the Number and LastName fields from the Employee table and the JobCode field from the JobLevel table. You can eliminate the FROM clause by typing the table name followed by a period (.) and the field name:

```
SELECT Employee.Number, Employee.LastName, JobLevel.JobCode;
```

Specify Source Tables with the WHERE Clause

The ***WHERE clause*** specifies which records from the tables listed in the FROM clause are affected by a SELECT, UPDATE, or DELETE statement.

In addition to selecting fields from particular tables, a query typically specifies conditions that must be met. The ***WHERE clause*** specifies which records from the tables listed in the FROM clause are affected by a SELECT, UPDATE, or DELETE statement. If your query does not include a WHERE clause, the query will return all rows from the table. For example, the following example returns the last name, first name, and salary for all employees who earn more than $75,000:

```
SELECT LastName, FirstName, Salary FROM Employee WHERE Salary>75000;
```

You can add a parameter to a WHERE clause that enables the user to enter a value to use for the statement. The parameter value defines the criterion for the query and must be enclosed in bracket characters, just as when you create a parameter query in Design view. For example, in the following SELECT statement, the WHERE clause specifies a salary greater than the value entered by the user, who defines the minimum salary for the query:

```
SELECT LastName, FirstName, Salary FROM Employee WHERE Salary>[Enter the minimum salary];
```

Previously, you created parameter queries in Design view. Creating the parameter in the SQL view creates the same result: the Enter Parameter Value dialog box appears, displaying the message. The text appearing between the bracket characters defines the message that will display when the query runs, as shown in Figure 10.9.

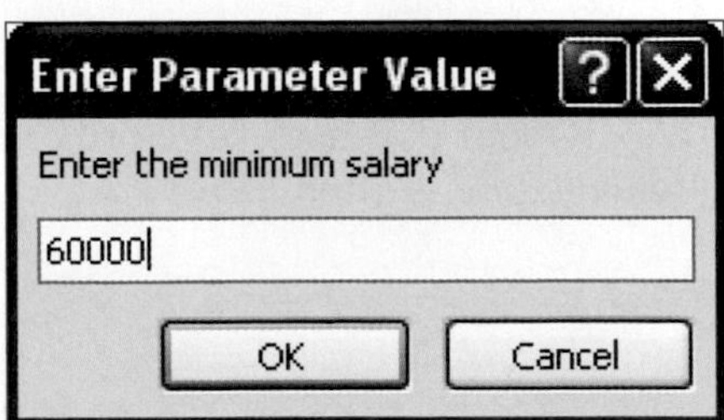

Figure 10.9 Query with a Parameter Value Supplied by the User

Sort Records with the ORDER BY Clause

The ***ORDER BY clause*** is used in queries to indicate which field is used to sort the records in a recordset in either ascending or descending order.

Typically, you want the query results to be arranged in a particular order. For example, you might want to arrange the records in alphabetical order by last name or descending order by salary. The ***ORDER BY clause*** is used in queries to indicate which field is used to sort the records in a recordset in either ascending or descending order. If you add sort order information in a query using the design grid, Access adds the appropriate ORDER BY clause into the underlying SQL statement. The following example selects the LastName, FirstName, and Salary fields from the Employee table, and then sorts the records in alphabetical order based on the LastName field:

SELECT LastName, FirstName, Salary FROM Employee ORDER BY LastName;

By default, the ORDER BY clause sorts records in ascending order. To sort in descending order, add the DESC clause to the statement. The following SELECT statement returns the LastName, FirstName, and Salary fields from the Employee table with the recordset sorted in descending order by the LastName field.

SELECT LastName, FirstName, Salary FROM Employee ORDER BY LastName DESC;

Learn SQL

SQL commands typically appear in uppercase letters, and SQL statements always end with a semicolon. You can add hard returns in SQL statements to make them more readable, or you can combine all of the statements together into a single line of text.

The easiest way to learn more about SQL is to create Access queries in Design view and then view these queries in SQL view. Although some statements might seem complex at first, the more you work with SQL, the easier it will be to understand the SQL statements. Table 10.2 summarizes common SQL statements and clauses.

Table 10.2 Common SQL Statements and Clauses

Statement	Purpose
SELECT	Selects specified fields from one or more tables to return in a query
FROM	Specifies the table or tables from which to return fields in a query
WHERE	Sets a condition for the data returned in a query
ORDER BY	Determines how the rows in a query are ordered: ascending or descending

In the first hands-on exercise, you will create embedded and standalone macros. After creating macros, you will assign a macro to an event and use an SQL expression.

Hands-On Exercises

1 | Customizing a Database Using Macros

Skills covered: 1. Create an Embedded Macro on a Form **2.** Create an Embedded Macro on a Report **3.** Create a Standalone Macro **4.** Assign a Macro to an Event **5.** Create a Macro with an SQL Expression on a Form

Step 1
Create an Embedded Macro on a Form

Refer to Figure 10.10 as you complete Step 1.

a. Use Windows Explorer to locate the file named *chap10_ho1-2_acme.accdb*. Copy the file to your production folder and rename it **chap10_ho1_acme_solution .accdb**.

b. Open the *chap10_ho1_acme_solution.accdb* file.

   You now have to enable the content in order to create macros.

c. Click **Options** on the Security Warning toolbar, click **Enable this content** in the Microsoft Office Security Options dialog box, and then click **OK**.

d. Open the **History form** in Design view.

   An embedded macro belongs to a specific Access object. You will embed the macro in this form.

e. Right-click the **Close button** in the Form Footer and select **Build Event**. Click **Macro Builder** in the Choose Builder dialog box and click **OK**.

   The Macro Builder is the tool you will use to create the macro. When you choose to build a macro as the source for the event, Access opens the Macro Builder.

f. Click the **Action drop-down arrow** in the first row of the Macro Builder and select **Close**.

   A macro consists of one or more actions you define using the Macro Builder. This defines the first action for the macro: closing an object.

g. Click the **Object Type** row in the Action Arguments grid. Click the **Object Type drop-down arrow** and select **Form**.

   Some macro commands require arguments; the argument you need here is the kind of object to close (a form).

h. Click the **Object Name** row in the Action Arguments grid. Click the **Object Name drop-down arrow** and select **History**.

   The Object Name argument specifies the name of the form the macro will close.

i. Click **Save** in the Quick Access Toolbar. Click **Close** in the Close group on the Macro Tools Design tab.

   Save your changes to the form before closing the Macro Builder.

j. Save changes to the form and display the form in Form view.

   When you switch to Form view, you will again save the form. The macro is now ready for testing.

k. Click the **Close button** on the form to verify that the macro closes the History form.

   Always test the macro before closing the form. The macro should perform the action of closing the form when you click the Close button.

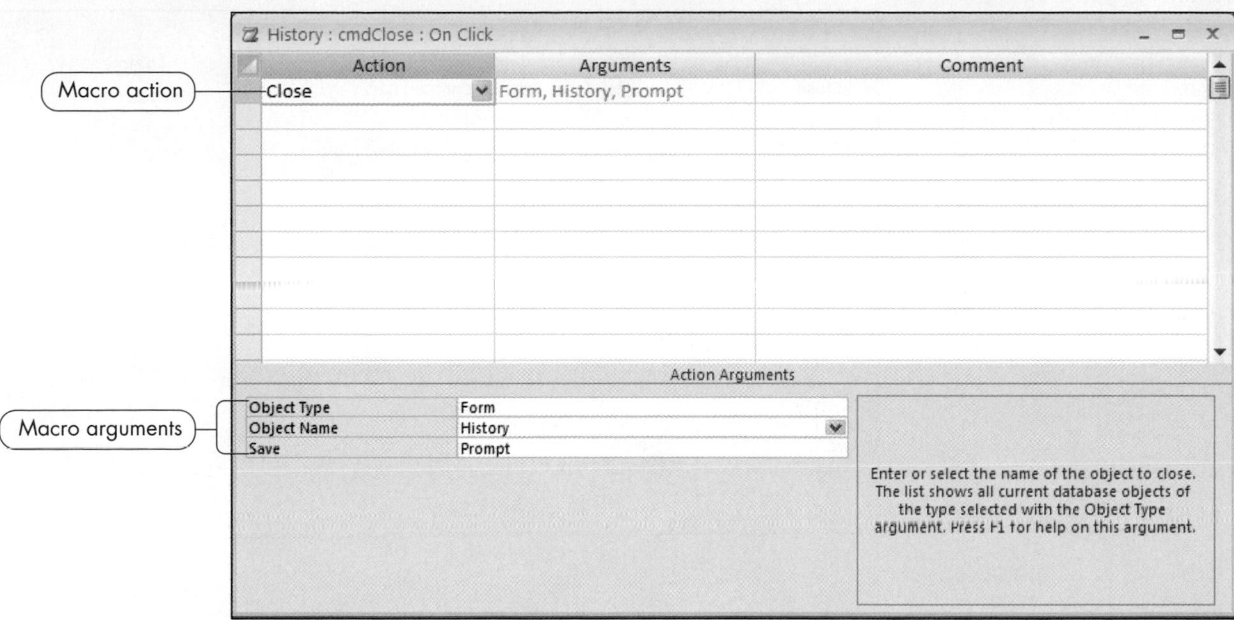

Figure 10.10 Embedded Macro to Close the History Form

Step 2
Create an Embedded Macro on a Report

Refer to Figure 10.11 as you complete Step 2.

a. Open the **Retirement Summary report** in Design view.

b. Right-click the **Close button** in the Report Header and select **Build Event**. Click **Macro Builder** in the Choose Builder dialog box and click **OK**.

   The process for creating an embedded macro to close a report is similar to the macro you created in the previous step. Begin by opening the Macro Builder.

c. Click the **Action drop-down arrow** in the first row of the Macro Builder. Scroll the list and select **Close**.

   This action for the first step of this macro is to close a report object.

d. Click the **Object Type drop-down arrow** in the Action Arguments grid and select **Report**.

   This action requires an argument specifying the object type—a report.

e. Click the **Object Name drop-down arrow** in the Action Arguments grid, and then select **Retirement Summary**.

   Select the object name parameter from the list of report objects. Make sure you select the correct report name.

f. Click **Save** on the Quick Access Toolbar. Click **Close** in the Close group on the Macro Tools Design tab.

   You have saved the report with the embedded macro and closed the Macro Builder.

g. Save changes to the report and display the report in Report view.

   Save the report to save the embedded macro.

h. Click the **Close button** on the report to verify that the macro closes the Retirement Summary report.

   Test the macro before closing the report.

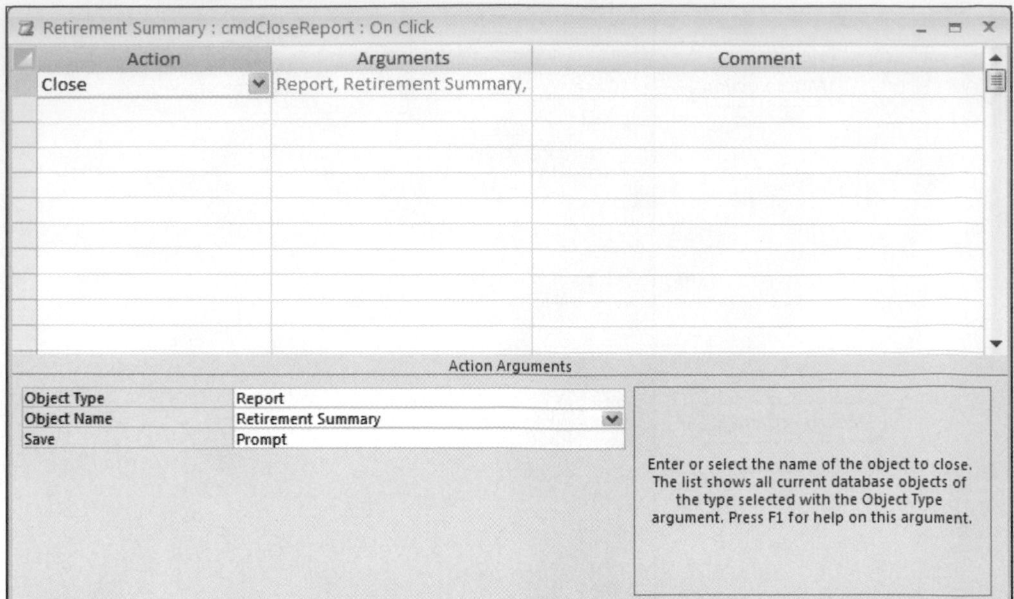

Figure 10.11 Embedded Macro to Close the Retirement Summary Report

Step 3
Create a Standalone Macro

Refer to Figure 10.12 as you complete Step 3.

a. Click the **Create tab** and click **Macro** in the Other group to launch the Macro Builder.

   This is also an embedded macro, but the actions will differ from the macros you created in the previous steps.

b. Click the **Action drop-down arrow** in the first row, scroll through the list, and select **MsgBox**.

   This macro will display a message box on the screen. Access uses the MsgBox action to display a message.

c. Click in the **Message** row in the Action Arguments grid and type **The database will now close.**

   The action requires an argument that defines the message that will display.

d. Click the **Type drop-down arrow** in the Action Arguments grid and select **Information**.

   This argument specifies the icon that will appear in the message box: the Information icon.

e. Click in the **Title** row in the Action Arguments grid and type **Close Database**.

   This argument specifies the title that will display in the title box of the message box.

f. Click the **Action drop-down arrow** in the second row and select **CloseDatabase**.

   When the user clicks the OK button in the message box, the second action will close the database.

g. Compare your macro actions and arguments to Figure 10.12. When your actions and arguments match those in the figure, click **Save**. Name the macro **Close Database**.

   It is important that you check the macro actions before you save the macro and close the Macro Builder.

h. Click **Close** in the Macro Builder title bar.

The Macro Builder closes.

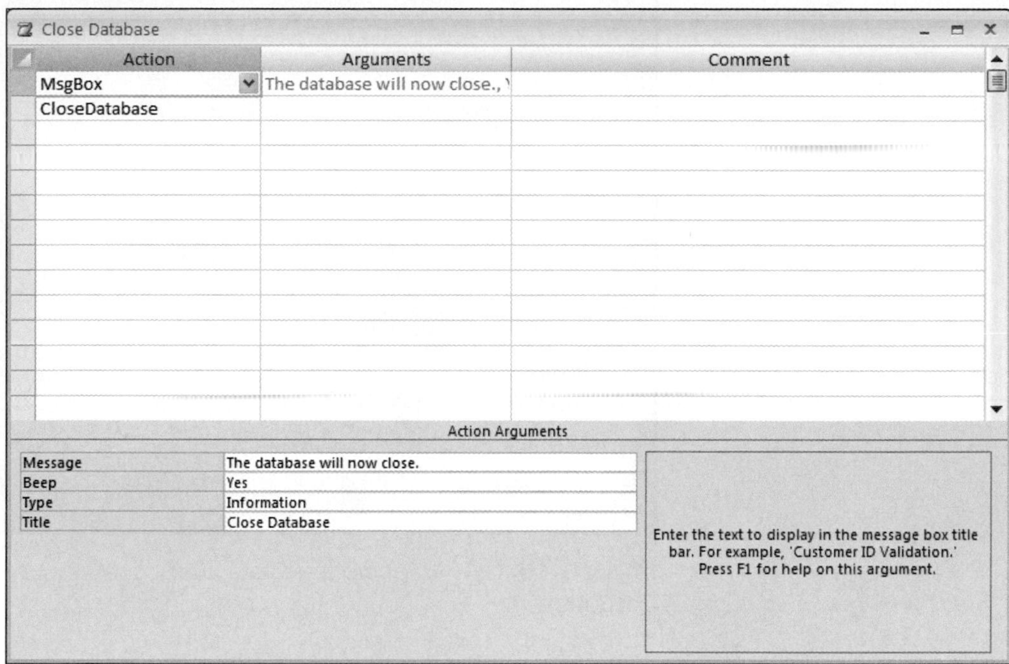

Figure 10.12 Actions and Arguments for the Close Database Macro

Step 4
Assign a Macro to an Event

Refer to Figure 10.13 as you complete Step 4.

a. Open the **Menu form** in Design view.

b. Right-click the **Exit button** on the form and select **Build Event**. Select **Macro Builder** in the Choose Builder dialog box and click **OK**.

This macro will be embedded in the Menu form.

c. Click the **Action drop-down arrow** in the first row, scroll through the list, and select **RunMacro**.

The first action for this macro is to run another macro.

d. Click the **Macro Name drop-down arrow** in the Action Arguments grid and select **Close Database**.

This action requires an argument specifying which macro to run.

e. Click **Save**. Click **Close** in the Close group on the Macro Tools Design tab.

You have saved the macro and closed the Macro Builder.

f. Save changes to the Menu form and switch to Form view to test the macro.

g. Click the **Exit button** on the form.

The Close Database message box appears with the message, *The database will now close.*

h. Click the **OK button** in the message box.

The *chap10_ho1_acme_solution* database closes.

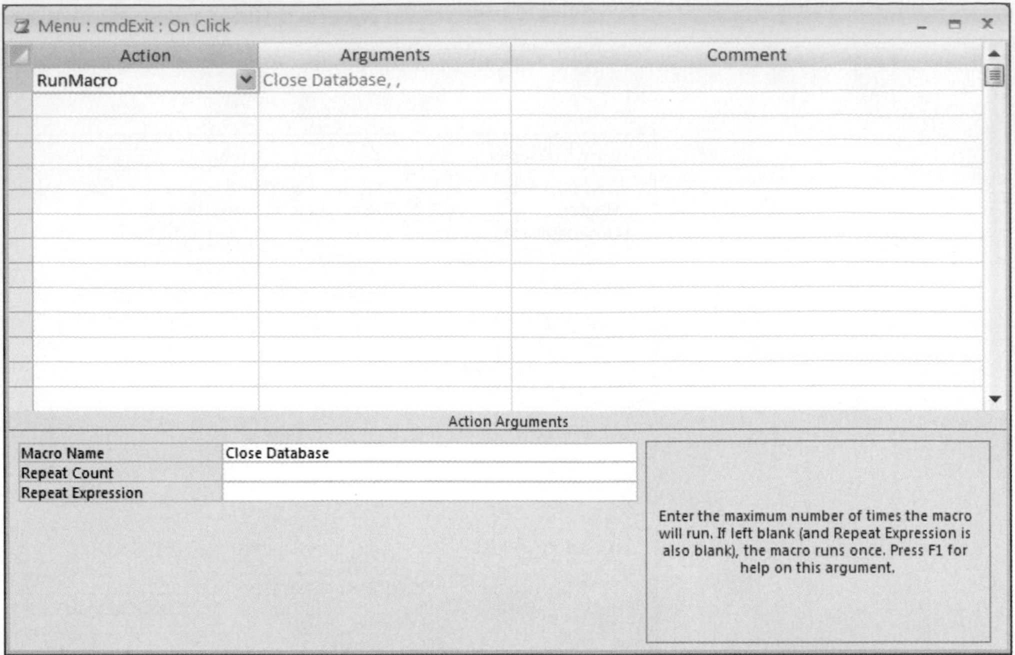

Figure 10.13 Assigning the Close Database Macro to the On Click Event for the Exit Button

Step 5
Create a Macro with an SQL Expression on a Form

Refer to Figure 10.14 as you complete Step 5.

a. Open the *chap10_ho1_acme_solution.accdb* file.

b. Click **Options** on the Security Warning toolbar, click **Enable this content** in the Microsoft Office Security Options dialog box, and then click **OK**.

c. Open the **Menu form** in Design view.

d. Right-click the **Summary Report (Region) button** on the form and select **Build Event**. Click **Macro Builder** in the Choose Builder dialog box and click **OK**.

   This macro is similar to the macro that closes a report; this macro will open a report for viewing.

e. Click the **Action drop-down arrow** in the first row, scroll through the list, and select **OpenReport**.

   This specifies the first macro action: opening a report.

   The action requires an argument that specifies the database object to open—a report.

f. Click the **Report Name drop-down arrow** in the Action Arguments grid and select **Retirement Summary**.

   The action also requires an argument for the report to open; make sure you select the correct report from the list.

g. Click in the **Where Condition** row in the Action Arguments grid and type **[Office].[Region]=[Enter Region Name]** as the condition.

   The action to open a report will accept an argument defining which records to display in the report. You entered an SQL statement to specify the Region field from the Office table and prompt the user to enter the region.

h. Click **Save**. Click **Close** in the Close group on the Macro Tools Design tab.

i. Save changes to the Menu form and display the form in Form view.

j. Click the **Summary Report (Region) button**. When you are prompted for a region, type **West** and click **OK**.

   The Enter Parameter Value dialog box appears, prompting you to enter the region name. When you type a region, such as West, and click OK, Access displays records in which West is listed as the region.

   TROUBLESHOOTING: If you type an invalid region name, the report will not display any records.

k. Click **Close** on the report to close the report and return to the menu.

   The macro opens the report; when you are finished viewing the report, you close it manually.

l. Close the database.

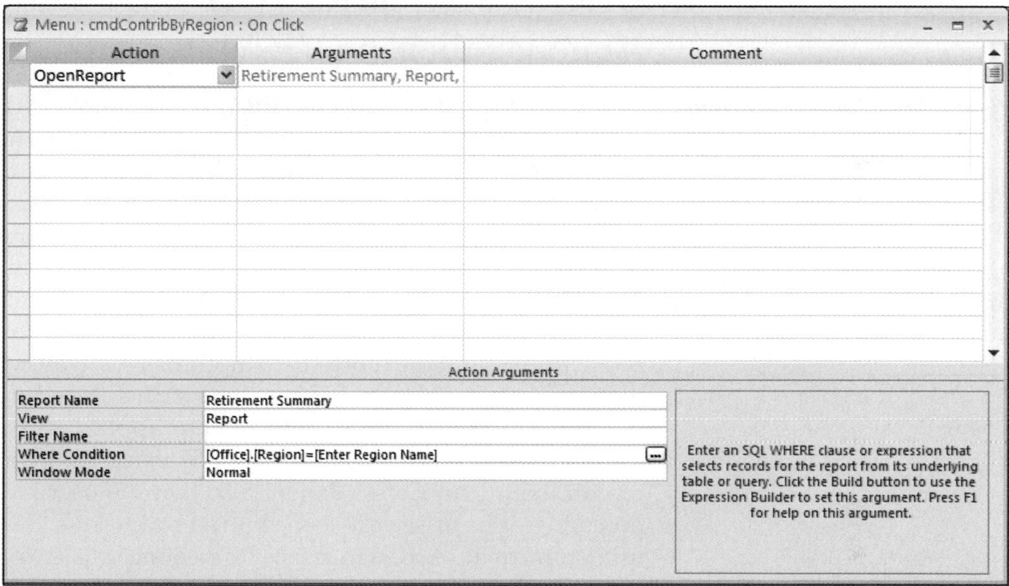

Figure 10.14 Macro with a Condition

Programming with VBA

Now that you have used macros to customize a database, you are probably aware that macros have limited functionality, in that you are limited to a list of options and arguments. Although the Macro Builder gives you a more structured interface than the Visual Basic Editor, programming with VBA provides greater functionality, because macros only include a limited set of actions you can include. In contrast, VBA has hundreds of actions you can run in response to events. VBA code is contained in class modules for forms and reports, or in modules that are not tied to specific objects.

In this section, you learn the basics of database programming with VBA. Next, you learn how to use the Visual Basic Editor. You also learn how to modify a form by adding controls that run macros and VBA procedures.

Understanding Visual Basic for Applications (VBA)

Visual Basic for Applications (VBA) is a programming language that you can use to create and customize Office applications.

A ***host application*** is the specific Office application that supports VBA.

Visual Basic for Applications (VBA) is a programming language that you can use to create and customize Office applications to enhance their functionality. VBA—which is included with Microsoft Office 2007—is a subset of a more powerful language, Visual Basic, which is a general-purpose programming language for creating Windows-based applications. VBA requires a ***host application*** (such as Word, Excel, Access, or PowerPoint) that contains the VBA procedures that add functionality to your Office applications. Because VBA has a consistent user interface and utilizes the same technology in all Office applications, some of the procedures you write in one application can be exported to another. This way, your programming efforts are reduced, because you can re-use some of the procedures you create.

You can use VBA to customize your applications or to enhance objects you created with Access wizards. For example, you might want to modify a command button for exiting an Access database so that the user has an opportunity to cancel the procedure if he or she clicks the button by mistake. Seasoned programmers use VBA to customize the Access interface by creating data entry forms, adding custom menus to the host application, and hiding and displaying interface elements depending upon user access. Office developers also use VBA to create custom functions, perform calculations using variables and constants, and process database records.

Using the Visual Basic Editor

The ***Visual Basic Editor*** is a workspace text editor for writing and editing VBA procedures.

You create and edit VBA statements in ***Design time***.

An application runs VBA statements in ***Run time***.

Before you can customize Access databases with VBA, you need to understand how VBA works within the host application. To customize a database, you will write a set of VBA program statements that perform a series of actions in response to an action on the part of a user, such as clicking a button, selecting a menu option, or opening a form. All Microsoft Office applications use the same tool for working with VBA, the ***Visual Basic Editor***. The Visual Basic Editor is a workspace text editor for writing and editing VBA procedures and includes other tools for working with program code. You can use the Visual Basic Editor to create procedures, declare variables and constants, perform calculations, and obtain input and display messages. When you create a VBA procedure using the Visual Basic Editor, you enter your code statements in ***Design time***, the mode for designing or creating programming code. When you run your procedure to test the code, VBA runs the procedure in ***Run time***, the mode during which a program is being executed. The Visual Basic Editor is *smart*, meaning that it will add color to specific code elements and highlight code errors in red. The Visual Basic Editor also supports automatic completion of certain statements you enter. After creating a procedure, you can test the procedure by running it from within the Visual Basic Editor.

You can launch the Visual Basic Editor in a number of ways: from the Macro group in the Database Tools tab, from the Event property of an object or control, or by pressing Alt+F11. Figure 10.15 shows the Visual Basic Editor. The Visual Basic

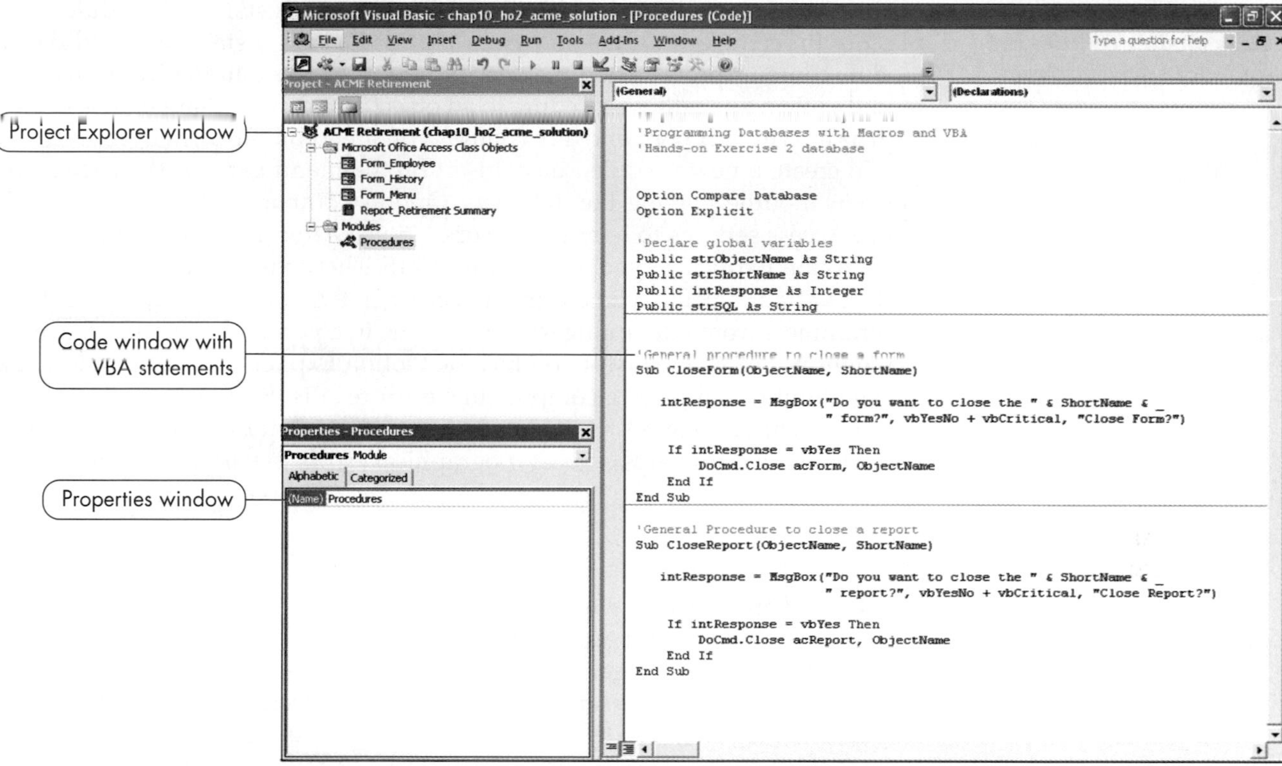

Figure 10.15 The Visual Basic Editor

Editor contains three primary windows: the Project Explorer window, the Properties window, and the Code window.

The Project Explorer shows the name of the current database and lists class objects and modules, which serve as containers for code. Figure 10.15 shows *ACME Retirement (chap10_ho2_acme_solution)*, which is the name of the database—indicated in the title bar. The Modules section shows the selected module named Procedures. The Properties window displays the properties or attributes you can set for the currently selected item in the Project Explorer window. The Properties window is similar to the Property Sheet you use to set properties for other database objects.

The Code window displays the code statements for the currently selected Procedures module. Figure 10.15 shows code statements that handle a click event to close a form and a report. As you review the lines of code, you will notice that some of the words appear in different colors. Lines appearing in green and that begin with an apostrophe character are ***comments***. Programmers often include comments in code for documenting procedures; comments do not execute at run time. Comments should be brief, yet descriptive. Furthermore, programmers typically place comments at the beginning of the blocks of code to state the purpose for the procedure. Comments are very helpful if you are reviewing code that you previously wrote or code that someone else wrote. Think of comments as internal documentation explaining what the code will do.

A ***comment*** is a line in a VBA statement that explains the code's purpose.

Figure 10.15 also has words appearing in blue; these are ***keywords***. A keyword is a word or symbol recognized as part of the Visual Basic programming language; for example, a statement, function name, or operator. The program statements follow a specific ***syntax***, which refers to the rules for entering the statements. If you enter code incorrectly, the Visual Basic Editor displays the syntax error in red. Statements that appear as black are free of syntax errors.

A ***keyword*** is a word or symbol recognized as part of a particular programming language.

Code ***syntax*** refers to the rules for entering VBA statements.

Creating Procedures

A ***standard module*** stores procedures that can be called by any event in the application.

A ***class module*** contains procedures for a specific object.

The code procedures are contained within modules. VBA has two types of modules: standard modules and class modules. A ***standard module*** stores procedures that can be called by any event in the application, such as a general procedure that will open or close any form or report. You must explicitly create a standard module. For example, the Procedures module shown in Figure 10.15 is a standard module. A ***class module*** contains procedures for a specific object. Access automatically creates a class module when you add a procedure to an object or a control that belongs to an object, such as a form or report, and any controls contained on the form or report.

To create a new module, select Insert on the menu bar and then select Module. The new module contains the statement, Option Compare Database, which tells VBA to use Access settings to handle code operations. After that line of code, you should type Option Explicit, as shown in Figure 10.15. This code requires that you explicitly declare variables before you use them in other statements. This requirement prevents programmers from attempting to store a value in a variable or manipulate a variable that does not exist already. If you include Option Explicit and attempt to use a variable without declaring it, a compile-time error results. Furthermore, Option Explicit detects when you have a variable name in a statement does not match a declared variable name. This helps detect typographical errors in variable names.

Create Events

You learned about events when you associated a standalone macro with a user event. VBA procedures perform actions in response to events. An event is an action occurring at run time that triggers a program instruction, such as when the user clicks a button. For example, you can write VBA code to specify what the object will do in response to the event. The system triggers some events, such as when Access opens a form. Users trigger other events by performing specific actions, such as selecting an item in a list, selecting a menu option, clicking a button, or opening a form or report.

A ***sub procedure*** is a procedure that performs an action.

A ***function procedure*** is a procedure that performs an action and returns a value.

A ***property procedure*** is a procedure that creates or manipulates a custom property.

VBA supports three different kinds of procedures. A ***sub procedure*** is a procedure that performs an action. A ***function procedure*** is a procedure that performs an action and returns a value. Function procedures always begin with the **Function** keyword and end with the **End Function** keyword. For example, a function procedure might calculate the payment in a loan and display the returned value (the payment) in a message box. A ***property procedure*** is a procedure that creates or manipulates a custom property. Property procedures are useful when you want to assign a custom property to an object. For example, you might create a property procedure that displays a previously hidden label on a form when an event occurs. Most of the procedures you create with VBA will be either sub procedures or function procedures.

A ***public procedure*** is a procedure that is available to any object in an application.

A ***private procedure*** is a procedure that is available only to a specific object or module.

All procedures are either public or private. A ***public procedure*** is available to any object in an application, which means that the code for an object anywhere in the application can use the code statements in a public procedure. A ***private procedure*** is available only to a specific object or module. Procedures are public by default, unless the procedure is associated with a specific event, such as clicking a button. Why does it matter if a procedure is public or private? If only one object or control needs to run a procedure, a private procedure is sufficient. However, if multiple objects in a database need to run a procedure, such as a general procedure to close any form, you will need to use a public procedure.

Create and Modify Sub Procedures

You create all procedures using the Visual Basic Editor. To create a procedure, you enter a **Sub** statement, the name of the procedure, and a pair of parentheses. The code statements appear after the declaration of the procedure. A sub procedure concludes with the **End Sub** statement. Figure 10.16 shows a code procedure in the Visual Basic Editor. The procedure is based on the Click event for the Exit button, indicated by Private Sub cmdExit_Click(). It displays a message box that asks *Do you want to exit the Compensation application?* The message box contains the critical icon as a visual cue to the user, along with Yes and No buttons, and *Exit Application* in the title bar.

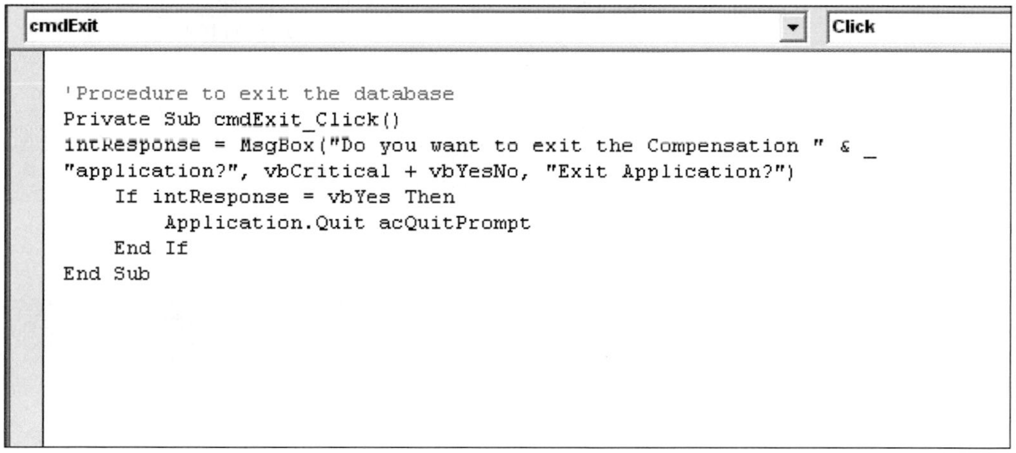

```
cmdExit                                   Click

'Procedure to exit the database
Private Sub cmdExit_Click()
intResponse = MsgBox("Do you want to exit the Compensation " & _
"application?", vbCritical + vbYesNo, "Exit Application?")
    If intResponse = vbYes Then
        Application.Quit acQuitPrompt
    End If
End Sub
```

Figure 10.16 Code Displayed in the Visual Basic Editor

A ***decision structure*** is a programming structure that performs a logical test to compare statements and branch to appropriate statements based on the comparison.

This procedure will exit a database. The procedure uses a ***decision structure*** to validate the user's intent to exit the application. The If-Then statement makes a comparison between program statements. Based on the result of that comparison, the program executes statements in a certain order. If the result of the comparison is true, one statement executes (exits the application), but if the result of the comparison is false, an alternative statement executes (the procedure ends). In this example, the decision structure tests to see if the user clicked the Yes button in the message box. If that is true, the application exits. If the comparison is false (i.e., the user clicked No), the application does not exit.

This comparison uses a relational operator to compare two statements and determine if the comparison is true or false. An expression is a combination of variables and operators that performs a calculation or returns a value. Such a comparison is a logical test, which is always contained within a decision structure. In programming, you can use a logical test within your program statements to respond to conditions that vary. VBA uses the relational operators listed in Table 10.3.

Table 10.3 VBA Relational Operators

Relational Operator	Tests whether the	Example
=	two operands are equal	txtLastName.Text = "Smith"
<>	two operands are not equal	Val(txtLoanAmount.Text)<>0
<	first operand is less than the second operand	Val(txtLoanAmount.Text) <250000
>	first operand is greater than the second operand	Val(txt401K.Text)>100000
<=	first operand is less than or equal to the second operand	sngConversionResult<=300
>=	first operand is greater than or equal to the second operand	decGrossPay>=500

TIP Making Code Readable with the Continuation Character

Some of the statements in a procedure may be long and extend to the right of the Code window. To make the code in procedures easier to read in the Code window, use the ***continuation character***. You can continue a code statement to additional lines by using a space and the underscore character (_). If the code statement includes a text string enclosed in quotes, you will need to end the line with a quote character.

The ***continuation character*** enables you to break code statements into multiple lines.

Declaring and Using Variables

A ***variable*** stores a value that can change while the application is running.

Variables are basic elements in every programming language. A ***variable*** stores a value that can change while the application is running. Variables store values in computer memory, and your code statement can change the value at any time. Because variables are stored in computer memory, a value for a variable exists only while a program is running. You can set the initial value for a variable (called initializing the variable) in program code and then change the value as necessary. For example, a string variable named strLastName could store the names of employees. Smith and Jones are examples of valid entries for the string data type. A currency variable named curSalary will store an employee's annual salary; 45000 is a valid entry for this data type.

Select a Data Type

The ***data type*** for a variable determines the kind of data the variable can store.

All variables require a ***data type***, which determines the kind of data the variable can hold and how the data is stored in the computer's memory. Because variables are stored in memory, it is a good programming practice to create variables that use the minimal amount of memory necessary to store various kinds of information like text and numbers. Because each data type has different memory requirements, you can conserve computer memory, increase the speed of your application, and minimize programming errors by carefully selecting the most appropriate data type for the kind of data your application needs to store. Table 10.4 lists the data types for variables in VBA.

Table 10.4 VBA Data Types

Data Type	Data Stored in the Variable	Memory Used
Boolean	True or False.	2 bytes
Byte	A single ASCII character (ASCII code 0–255).	1 byte
Currency	Stores values for calculations involving money and for fixed-point calculations in which accuracy is particularly important. The ranges of values for this data type are –922,337,203,685,477.5808 to 922,337,203,685,477.5807.	8 bytes
Date	Date in an eight-character format: 01/01/2007. Stores dates as a number ranging from January 1, 1900 to December 31, 9999.	8 bytes
Decimal	Decimal values +/– 79,228,162,514,264,337,593,543,950,335 with no decimal point to +/– 7.9228162514264337593543950335 with 28 places to the right of the decimal. The smallest non-zero number is +/–0.0000000000000000000000000001.	14 bytes
Double (double-precision floating-point)	Double-precision floating-point numbers with 14 digits of accuracy. Values range from –1.79769313486231E308 to 4.94065645841247E-324 for negative values and 4.94065645841247E-324 to 1.79769313486232E308 for positive values.	8 bytes
Integer	Whole numbers ranging from –32,768 to 32,767.	2 bytes
Long (long integer)	Whole numbers ranging from –2,147,483,648 to 2,147,483,647.	4 bytes
Object	Stores a reference to any application object.	4 bytes
Single (single-precision floating-point)	Single-precision floating-point numbers with six digits of accuracy. Values range from –3.402823E38 to –1.401298E-45 for negative values and 1.401298E-45 to 3.402823E38 for positive values.	4 bytes
String (fixed length)	Alphanumeric data including letters, digits, and other characters. "Adam Smith" is an example of a text string.	1 to approximately 64 K characters
String (variable length)	Alphanumeric data including letters, digits, and other characters.	0 to 2 billion characters
Variant	This is the default type if no type is assigned.	Up to 22 bytes plus the length of a text string
Type (user defined)	Structured data that contain data appropriate to the required elements in a range.	Size depends upon the data definition

Specify the Variable Scope

The variable ***scope (accessibility)*** limits which procedures can access the value stored in a variable.

A ***local variable*** is available to the procedure associated with a specific database object or control.

A ***module-level variable*** is available to any procedure within a module.

A ***global variable*** is available to any procedure in a database.

The ***Dim statement*** declares a variable.

When you declare a variable, you must also specify its accessibility. The ***accessibility***—or ***scope***—specifies which program statements will have access to the value stored in the variable. If you declare a variable within a procedure so that the value is only accessible to the procedure, it is a ***local variable*** and has procedure scope. This means the value stored in the variable is only available to the procedure. The variable declaration shown in Figure 10.16 is a local variable. If the value in the variable must be accessible to any procedure within an Access form, it is a ***module-level variable*** and has module scope. This means that any procedure contained in the module can get or change the variable. A ***global variable*** has accessibility to any procedure within a database, which means that any procedure can get or change what is stored in the variable.

You declare a local or module-level variable using the ***Dim statement***. For example, *Dim strLastName as String* declares a string variable for storing a person's last name. The scope you intend for the variable determines where you declare it. You can add the declaration statement within a procedure to create a procedure-level variable, or you can declare the variable at the top of a module, in the Declarations section, to create a module-level variable. To use the value stored in a variable or constant in all procedures in a project, use the Public statement instead of the Dim statement. Remember that if Option Explicit is turned on, you must explicitly declare a variable before assigning a value to it. If Option Explicit is not set, you can declare a variable implicitly, or by simply naming the variable in a procedure. If a procedure contained the statement *strLastName = "Smith"* and Option Explicit was not set, the statement declares the variable the first time it is used. This can lead to problems, because a code statement might need to reference a variable, but misnames it, thereby declaring a new variable. Most programmers require explicit variable declaration.

Name the Variable

When you declare a variable, you must give the variable a unique name. Most programmers prefer descriptive names that tell the purpose of a variable or constant and the kind of data it contains. A commonly used standard for naming variables in VBA is to begin the name with the first three characters indicating the data type (in lowercase) and the remainder specifying the variable's purpose (beginning with an uppercase letter). For example, a variable for storing the number of units might be named *intQuantity*, where *int* indicates the data type (Integer) and *Quantity* is a descriptive name for the values the variable holds (number of units). The first three characters appear in lowercase, with the remaining part of the variable name appearing as descriptive words that begin with uppercase letters. If the descriptive name includes more than one word, the first character of each word is capitalized. This standard of using lowercase to start the identifying name and then using an uppercase character for each succeeding word is called Camel Casing. Table 10.5 lists the three-character designation for each data type and an example of how to apply the Camel Casing convention.

Table 10.5 Three-Character Identifiers for Data Types in Variable Names

Data Type	Prefix	Example of a Named Variable
Boolean	bln	blnEmploymentStatus
Currency	cur	curNetPay
Decimal	dec	decTotalInventory
Date (Time)	dtm	dtmNet30
Double	dbl	dblSpeedOfLight
Integer	int	intQuantity
Long	lng	lngPopulation
Object	obj	objCurrent
Single	sng	sngSalesTax
String	str	strAddress

TIP Naming Variables

Variable names should be descriptive of the data stored in the variable. Here are a few examples of variable declarations.

```
Public strObjectName As String
Public strShortName As String
Public intResponse As Integer
Public strSQL As String
Dim intCount As Integer
Dim strCriteria As String
```

Assign Values to Variables

After you declare a variable, you can assign a value to the variable using the equals sign (=) relational operator. To assign a value, specify the variable name, enter the equals sign, and assign a value. The value must be the appropriate data type, or you will receive a run time error. For example, you cannot assign a string value (alpha character) to an integer variable; *intCount = "A"* is invalid. If the assigned value is text, you will need to enclose the string in quotes. Here are three examples of variable assignments:

```
strLastName = "Smith"
intCounter = 1
curSalary = 75000
```

Call a Procedure

At times, a sub procedure will need to invoke, or call, another procedure. When calling a procedure, you can use the optional Call keyword, or simply include the name of the procedure in the code statements. Figure 10.17 shows a procedure that calls a procedure to close a form.

```
(General)

Option Compare Database

Private Sub cmdClose_Click()
    strObjectName = "Customers"
    Call CloseForm(strObjectName)
End Sub
```

Figure 10.17 A Procedure That Stores a Value and Calls Another Procedure

Pass Arguments to a Called Procedure

A called procedure can accept information from the procedure that is calling it. For example, the procedure shown in Figure 10.17 requires the name of the form to close. You can store the form name in a string variable, such as *strObjectName = "Customers"*. Then you can pass the contents of this variable to the called procedure; the strObjectName variable is for storing the form name. Figure 10.18 shows the code statements that accept the argument that is passed and closes the appropriate form. Notice that the argument name is enclosed in parentheses.

```
(General)                                                    CloseForm

'General procedure to close a form
Sub CloseForm(ObjectName)

intResponse = MsgBox("Do you want to close the " & ObjectName & _
" form?", vbYesNo + vbCritical, "Close Form?")

    If intResponse = vbYes Then
        DoCmd.Close acForm, ObjectName
    End If
End Sub
```

Figure 10.18 A Called Procedure that Accepts an Argument

Managing Data Using SQL

Earlier in this chapter you learned how to use SQL statements to define a WHERE condition in a macro. You can also use SQL statements in VBA procedures to specify the data source for objects such as queries, forms, and reports.

To use SQL in a VBA procedure you will need to declare a string variable to store the SQL statement, and then assign the string to the variable. Figure 10.19 shows a procedure that uses an SQL string to define the records for a report. Study the statements carefully. Notice the SELECT statement selects fields from tables, an INNER JOIN connects the tables, and the WHERE clause provides the condition for selecting records.

```
cmdContribByRegion                                   Click

Private Sub cmdContribByRegion_Click()

'Assign the report name to the strObjectName variable
strObjectName = "Retirement Summary"

strSQL = "SELECT Employee.LastName, Employee.FirstName, Office.Region, " & _
"Contribution.PayDate, Contribution.[401KEmployee], " & _
"Contribution.[401KMatch], Contribution.[401KTotal] " & _
"FROM (Office INNER JOIN Employee " & _
"ON Office.[OfficeNumber] = Employee.[OfficeLocation]) " & _
"INNER JOIN Contribution ON Employee.[SSN] = Contribution.[SSN]" & _
"WHERE (((Office.Region)=[Enter Region Name]));"

'Open the Address List Report
DoCmd.OpenReport strObjectName, acViewReport

'Assign the SQL query as the recordsource for the report
Reports(strObjectName).RecordSource = strSQL

'clean up the public strSQL variable
strSQL = ""

End Sub
```

Figure 10.19 Using an SQL String in a Variable to Specify Records for a Report

The procedure assigns the SQL statement to a variable. The SQL statements for this assignment are more complex than the SQL examples earlier in this chapter, because the INNER JOIN statement is required to extract data from related tables. When you create a query from multiple tables, Access uses a JOIN statement to combine data from the tables into the query results.

TIP Creating SQL Statements

Although SQL statements are difficult to construct from scratch, you can easily create SQL strings by creating an Access query and then viewing the query in SQL view. You can copy the test directly from the SQL view window into a VBA procedure. The SQL string must be enclosed in quotes. If the SQL statement is long, you may want to use the continuation character to make the statement easier to read in the Code window.

In the next hands-on exercise, you will create procedures and modify the menu form to open and close forms and reports and to exit the database.

2 | Customizing a Database Using VBA

Skills covered: 1. Create Global Procedures **2.** Create Sub Procedures That Call Global Procedures **3.** Write Procedures That Handle Events **4.** Set Database Properties and Test Procedures

Step 1 Create Global Procedures

Refer to Figure 10.20 as you complete Step 1.

a. Use Windows Explorer to locate the file named *chap10_ho1-2_acme.accdb*. Copy the file and rename it **chap10_ho2_acme_solution.accdb**.

b. Open the *chap10_ho2_acme_solution.accdb* file.

c. Click **Options** on the Security Warning toolbar, click **Enable this content** in the Microsoft Office Security Options dialog box, and then click **OK**.

d. Press **Alt+F11** to open the Visual Basic Editor.

   You will begin this exercise by adding a module to the project, and then creating defining global variables and procedures. These actions require the Visual Basic Editor.

e. Click **Insert** on the menu bar and select **Module**.

   The global variables and global procedures require a module, which you have now added to the database.

f. Place the insertion point in the Code window below the *Option Compare Database* statement. Type the following code statements:

```
Option Explicit

'Declare global variables
Public strObjectName As String
Public strShortName As String
Public intResponse As Integer
Public strSQL As String

'General procedure to close a form
Sub CloseForm(ObjectName, ShortName)

  intResponse = MsgBox("Do you want to close the " & ShortName & _
                "form?", vbYesNo + vbCritical, "Close Form?")

  If intResponse = vbYes Then
    DoCmd.Close acForm, ObjectName
  End If
End Sub

'General Procedure to close a report
Sub CloseReport(ObjectName, ShortName)

  intResponse = MsgBox("Do you want to close the " & ShortName & _
    " report?", vbYesNo + vbCritical, "Close Report?")

  If intResponse = vbYes Then
    DoCmd.Close acReport, ObjectName
  End If
End Sub
```

Refer to Figure 10.20 as necessary. The statements you entered declare four public variables and two general procedures. The comments, indicated by green, in the code explain the purpose of the statements.

TROUBLESHOOTING: Type the code statements exactly as shown. Use the continuation character to continue the code on a subsequent line. Also make sure you do not have an extra End Sub after the last End Sub. Compare your statements to Figure 10.20.

g. Click **Save**. Type **Procedures** in the Save As dialog box for the module. Click **OK**.

This saves the module you added to the database. The code statements are contained in the module.

```
(General)                                        (Declarations)

Option Compare Database

Option Explicit

'Declare global variables
Public strObjectName As String
Public strShortName As String
Public intResponse As Integer
Public strSQL As String

'General procedure to close a form
Sub CloseForm(ObjectName, ShortName)

    intResponse = MsgBox("Do you want to close the " & ShortName & _
                    " form?", vbYesNo + vbCritical, "Close Form?")

    If intResponse = vbYes Then
        DoCmd.Close acForm, ObjectName
    End If
End Sub

'General Procedure to close a report
Sub CloseReport(ObjectName, ShortName)

   intResponse = MsgBox("Do you want to close the " & ShortName & _
                    " report?", vbYesNo + vbCritical, "Close Report?")

    If intResponse = vbYes Then
        DoCmd.Close acReport, ObjectName
    End If
End Sub
```

Figure 10.20 Code Statements for a Global Procedure

Step 2
Create Sub Procedures That Call Global Procedures

Refer to Figures 10.21 through 10.23 as you complete Step 2.

a. Double-click the **Form_Employee form** in the Visual Basic Editor Project Explorer.

This opens the class module for the form.

b. Place the insertion point in the Code window. Type the following code statements:

```
Sub cmdClose_Click()
  strObjectName = "Employee"
  strShortName = "Employee Records"
  CloseForm strObjectName, strShortName
End Sub
```

This procedure assigns a string to two variables and passes the form name and short name to the global procedure that closes a form.

c. Click **Save**.

You have saved the changes to the class module.

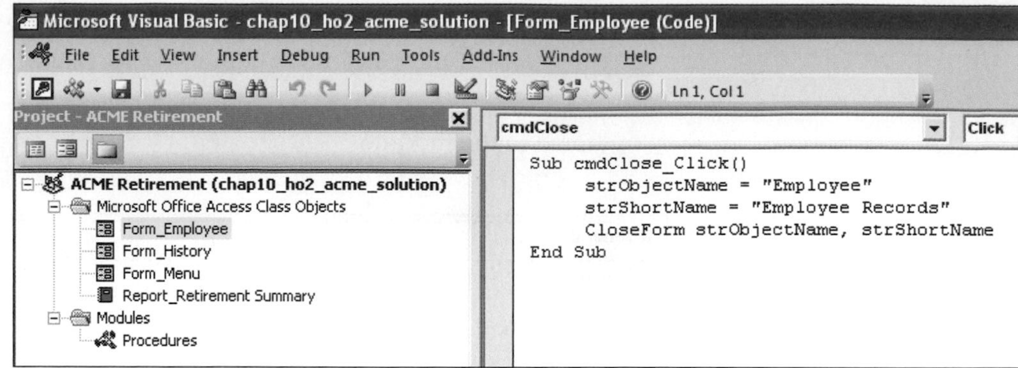

Figure 10.21 Code Statements for a Local Procedure

d. Double-click the **Form_History form** in the Visual Basic Editor Project Explorer.

This opens the class module for the form.

e. Place the insertion point in the Code window. Type the following code statements:

```
Private Sub cmdClose_Click()
strObjectName = "History"
strShortName = "Contribution History"
CloseForm strObjectName, strShortName
End Sub
```

This procedure assigns a string to two variables and passes the form name and short name to the global procedure that closes a form.

f. Click **Save**.

You have saved the changes to the class module.

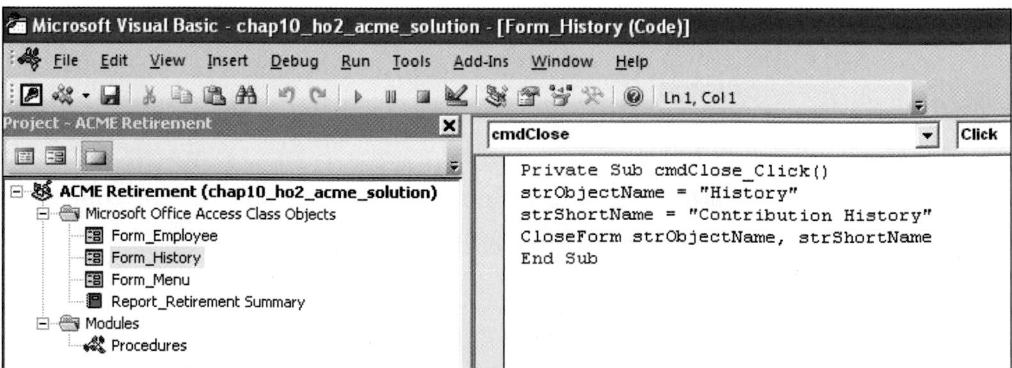

Figure 10.22 Code Statements for a Local Procedure

g. Double-click the **Report_Retirement Summary report** in the Visual Basic Editor Project Explorer.

This opens the class module for the report.

h. Place the insertion point in the Code window. Type the following code statements:

```
Private Sub cmdCloseReport_Click()
strObjectName = "Retirement Summary"
strShortName = "Retirement"
CloseReport strObjectName, strShortName
End Sub
```

This procedure assigns a string to two variables and passes the form name and short name to the global procedure that closes a report

i. Click **Save**.

You have saved the changes to the class module.

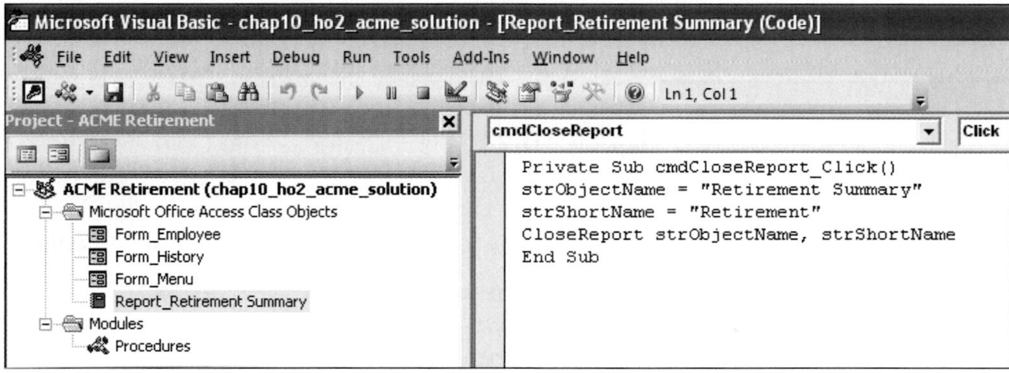

Figure 10.23 Code Statements for a cmdCloseReport Local Procedure

Step 3
Write Procedures That Handle Events

Refer to Figures 10.24 through 10.26 as you complete Step 3.

a. Double-click the **Form_Menu form** in the Visual Basic Editor Project Explorer.

This opens the class module for the form.

b. Place the insertion point in the Code window. Type the following code statements:

```
Private Sub cmdEmployeeForm_Click()
  'Display the form
  DoCmd.OpenForm ("Employee"), , , , acFormEdit
End Sub

Private Sub cmdHistoryForm_Click()
  'Display the form
  DoCmd.OpenForm ("History"), , , , acReadOnly
End Sub

Private Sub cmdExit_Click()
  'Exit the application
  intResponse = MsgBox("Do you want to exit the Compensation " & _
  "application?", vbCritical + vbYesNo, "Exit Application?")
      If intResponse = vbYes Then
          Application.Quit acQuitPrompt
      End If
End Sub
```

The first two procedures open the Employee and History forms, respectively. The third procedure closes the Menu form.

c. Click **Save**.

You have saved the changes to the class module.

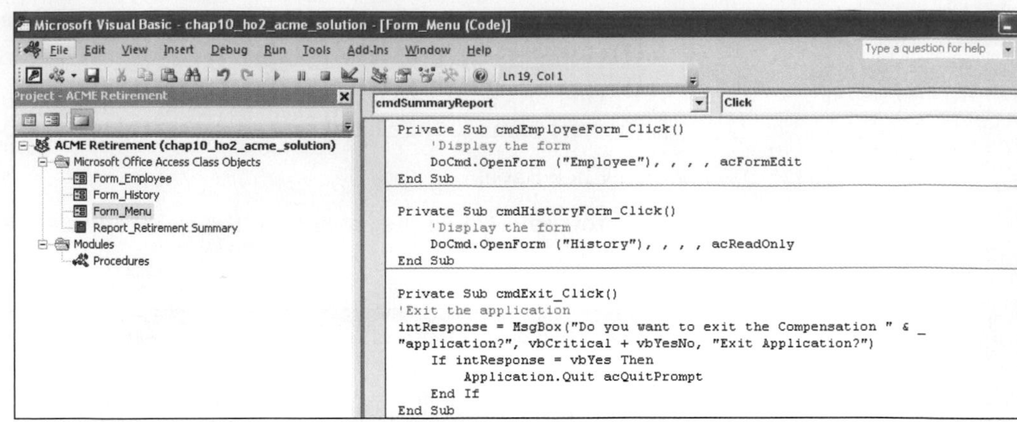

Figure 10.24 Code Statements to Open and Close Objects

d. Press **Enter**. Type the following code statements:

```
'This procedure defines an SQL query as the record source
'for the "Retirement Summary" report; the SQL statement
'returns all records

'Assign the report name to the strObjectName variable
strObjectName = "Retirement Summary"

'Declare a variable to store the SQL statement, define the
'SQL string

strSQL = "SELECT Employee.LastName, Employee.FirstName, " & _
"Office.Region, Contribution.PayDate, " & _
    "Contribution.[401KEmployee], " & _
"Contribution.[401KMatch], Contribution.[401KTotal]" & _
"FROM (Office INNER JOIN Employee ON Office.[OfficeNumber] = " & _
"Employee.[OfficeLocation])" & _
"INNER JOIN Contribution ON Employee.[SSN]=Contribution.[SSN];"

'Open the Address List Report
DoCmd.OpenReport strObjectName, acViewReport

'Assign the SQL query as the record source for the report
Reports(strObjectName).RecordSource = strSQL

'clean up the public strSQL variable
strSQL = ""

End Sub
```

This procedure defines the SQL string and stores this as a variable that is set as the source for the report.

e. Check your code against the code in Figure 10.25 to ensure correct line breaks, spacing, etc. Click **Save** to save the changes to the class module.

```
Private Sub cmdSummaryReport_Click()
'This procedure defines an SQL query as the record source
'for the "Retirement Summary" report; the SQL statement returns all records

'Assign the report name to the strObjectName variable
strObjectName = "Retirement Summary"

'Declare a variable to store the SQL statement, define the SQL string

strSQL = "SELECT Employee.LastName, Employee.FirstName, " & _
"Office.Region, Contribution.PayDate, Contribution.[401KEmployee], " & _
"Contribution.[401KMatch], Contribution.[401KTotal]" & _
"FROM (Office INNER JOIN Employee ON Office.[OfficeNumber] = " & _
"Employee.[OfficeLocation])" & _
"INNER JOIN Contribution ON Employee.[SSN] = Contribution.[SSN];"

'Open the Address List Report
DoCmd.OpenReport strObjectName, acViewReport

'Assign the SQL query as the record source for the report
Reports(strObjectName).RecordSource = strSQL

'clean up the public strSQL variable
strSQL = ""

End Sub
```

Figure 10.25 Code Statements to Assign an SQL Record Source and Display a Report

f. Press **Enter**. Type the following code statements:

```
Private Sub cmdContribByRegion_Click()

'Assign the report name to the strObjectName variable
strObjectName = "Retirement Summary"

strSQL = "SELECT Employee.LastName, Employee.FirstName, " & _
      "Office.Region, " & _
"Contribution.PayDate, Contribution.[401KEmployee], " & _
"Contribution.[401KMatch], Contribution.[401KTotal] " & _
"FROM (Office INNER JOIN Employee " & _
"ON Office.[OfficeNumber] = Employee.[OfficeLocation]) " & _
"INNER JOIN Contribution ON Employee.[SSN] = " & _
      "Contribution.[SSN]" & _
"WHERE (((Office.Region)=[Enter Region Name]));"

'Open the Address List Report
DoCmd.OpenReport strObjectName, acViewReport

'Assign the SQL query as the record source for the report
Reports(strObjectName).RecordSource = strSQL

'clean up the public strSQL variable
strSQL = ""

End Sub
```

This procedure defines the SQL string and stores it as a variable that is set as the source for the report. The SQL string includes a WHERE clause to filter the results by region.

g. Check your code against the code in Figure 10.26 to ensure correct line breaks, spacing, etc. Click **Save** to save the changes to the class module.

h. Close the Visual Basic Editor.

You are finished with the code for the application, so you have closed the Visual Basic Editor.

```
Private Sub cmdContribByRegion_Click()

'Assign the report name to the strObjectName variable
strObjectName = "Retirement Summary"

strSQL = "SELECT Employee.LastName, Employee.FirstName, Office.Region, " & _
"Contribution.PayDate, Contribution.[401KEmployee], " & _
"Contribution.[401KMatch], Contribution.[401KTotal] " & _
"FROM (Office INNER JOIN Employee " & _
"ON Office.[OfficeNumber] = Employee.[OfficeLocation]) " & _
"INNER JOIN Contribution ON Employee.[SSN] = Contribution.[SSN]" & _
"WHERE (((Office.Region)=[Enter Region Name]));"

'Open the Address List Report
DoCmd.OpenReport strObjectName, acViewReport

'Assign the SQL query as the record source for the report
Reports(strObjectName).RecordSource = strSQL

'clean up the public strSQL variable
strSQL = ""

End Sub
```

Figure 10.26 Code Statements to Assign an SQL Record Source and Display a Report

Step 4
Set Database Properties and Test Procedures

Refer to Figure 10.27 as you complete Step 4.

a. Click the **Office Button** and click **Access Options**.

   You will set the options for the current database.

b. Click **Current Database**.

   This displays the page for setting the options for the current database.

c. Type **chap10_h02_acme–solution** in the **Application Title** box.

   This defines the title that will appear in the title bar for the database.

d. Click **Display Form drop-down arrow** and select **Menu**, if necessary.

   This sets the Menu form as the default form that displays when the database is first opened.

e. Uncheck **Display Navigation Pane**.

   This hides the Navigation pane. Because the menu form and the buttons on each object include code for opening and closing the forms and reports, users do not need to use the Navigation pane.

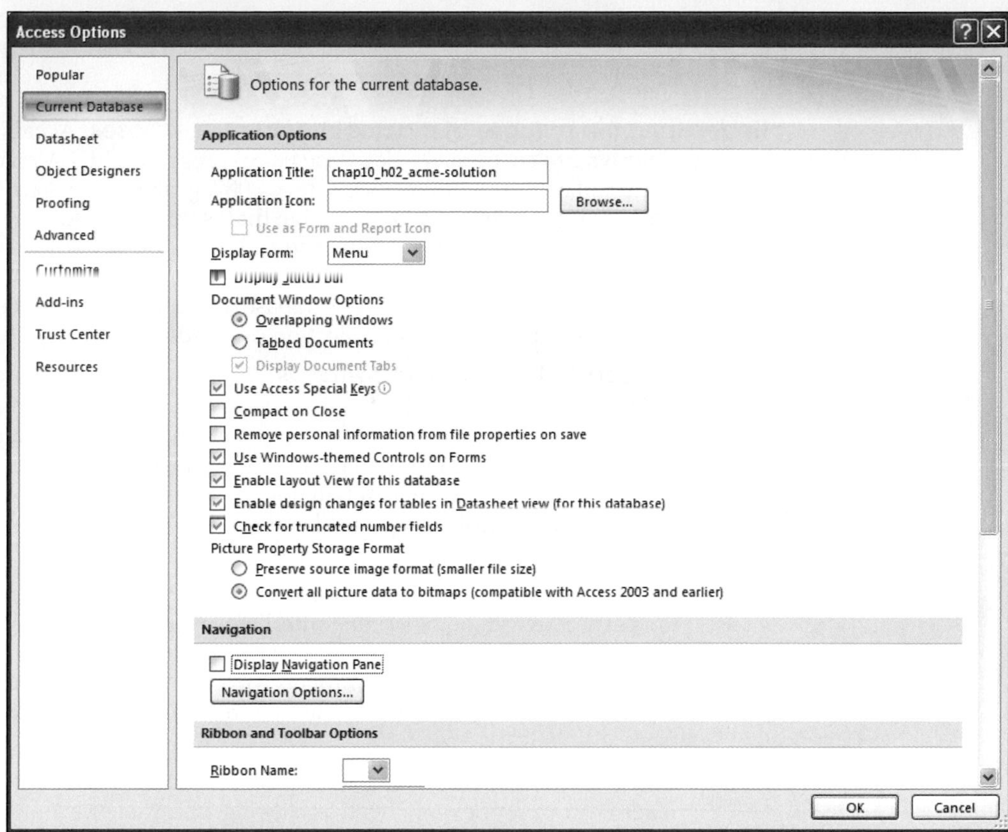

Figure 10.27 Setting the Database Properties

f. Click **OK**.

This closes the Access Options dialog box.

g. Click **OK** when the message appears explaining that the database will need to be closed for the changes to take effect.

This message informs you that you must close and reopen the database before the changes you have made are applied.

h. Close the database.

You must close and reopen the database before you can test the menu form.

i. Open the *chap10_ho2_acme_solution* database file again and enable the database content.

The changes you made to the database options are now in effect. Notice that the Menu form displays and the Navigation pane is hidden.

j. Click each button on every database form and report. Each button should open a form or report, and the Close button on the Employee form, History form, and Retirement Summary report should close the form or report. A message will appear for each action, verifying your intent to perform the action. The Exit button on the Menu form will verify your decision to exit the database, and then close the file.

Test the functionality. If you need to make any changes, refer to the appropriate steps for entering the code statements. If you made an error in the SQL statement for the report, the report may open in Design view. If so, review the SQL code in the figures, and correct and save your SQL code.

k. If you did not use the Exit button to close the database, click **Exit** to close.

If you test the Exit button, the database will close. If you did not test this button, you will need to close the database manually.

Summary

1. **Understand the purpose of macros in Access databases.** Access macros are an easy and efficient way to customize a database using programming. A macro is an object that stores a collection of actions. Unlike other Office 2007 applications, Access macros are not stored in VBA procedures, but in a macro language that is unique to Access. A standalone macro is available to any object within a database and will appear in the Navigation pane. An embedded macro belongs to a specific database object or control, and although it is not available to other objects or controls in the database, it is retained with the control or object when it is copied. A macro group is a collection of standalone macros that are stored in a single macro.
2. **Create embedded macros using wizards.** The easiest way to create an embedded macro on a control such as a command button is to use a wizard, such as the Command Button Wizard. Not all controls open a wizard automatically, but when you add a button control to a form or report, the wizard guides you through selecting the action that will occur when the button is clicked. An embedded macro will not appear in the Navigation pane, but you can edit a macro in the control's Property Sheet.
3. **Create macros using the Macro Builder.** The Macro Builder in Access is a tool for creating macros. You can launch the Macro Builder from the Other group on the Create tab or from the Property Sheet for an object or control. The Macro Builder consists of three columns—a column for specifying the action to perform, a column for specifying any required arguments, and a column for entering comments to document the macro's purpose. You can also specify conditions for the macro using the Action Arguments section in the Macro Builder.
4. **Assign macros to events.** After you create a standalone macro or a macro group, you can assign this macro to the event for a database object or control. The events that are associated with a macro can be user events, such as clicking a button, or events associated with an object, such as loading a form. The purpose of a macro is to automate repetitive tasks or set the database in a predictable state, so a macro is typically associated with one or more events.
5. **Use SQL conditions to control macro actions.** You can specify a condition that will determine how a macro will run. A condition specifies certain criteria that must be met before an action will be performed. You can use any expression that evaluates to true or false. You can use the SQL WHERE clause to define conditions for a macro. You can also use a valid expression created with the Expression Builder.
6. **Understand Visual Basic for Applications (VBA).** VBA is a programming language you can use to add functionality to a database. VBA works within a host application, such as Access, Word, or Excel. As a subset of a more powerful programming language (Visual Basic), VBA provides a consistent interface for customizing Office applications.
7. **Use the Visual Basic Editor.** The Visual Basic Editor is a tool you can use to create code statements for programming a database. You can open the Visual Basic Editor by pressing Alt+F11, and from within the editor, create or modify code statements for any database object or globally for the entire database. The Visual Basic Editor is smart, in that it will automatically highlight errors you make when entering or modifying code statements. You can also test a procedure from within the Visual Basic Editor by running the procedure.
8. **Create procedures.** VBA code statements are typically stored in procedures. VBA supports three kinds of procedures: sub procedures, function procedures, and property procedures. Beginning programmers use sub procedures, which perform a task, and function procedures, which return a value. You create procedures by typing code statements in the Visual Basic Editor. The code procedures must follow a specific syntax, and the editor contains logic to assist you with entering the statements correctly. The accessibility or scope of a procedure will vary, depending upon where you create the procedure. All procedures are stored in modules. Class modules belong to specific objects, like a form or report, and the procedures are available to the object itself, or any control that also belongs to the object. Code modules store procedures that are available to any object within the database.
9. **Declare and use variables.** Variables are storage locations in memory that store a value while a program is running. A variable must be declared using the Dim, Private, or Public statement, and require a name and a data type as well. The data type for a variable determines what kind of data the variable can store and how it is represented in memory.
10. **Manage data using SQL.** Structured Query Language (SQL) is a language for returning data from one or more tables. You can use SQL statements in VBA procedures to define the data source for a form or report.

Key Terms

Accessibility (scope) 664
Class module 660
Comment 659
Condition 648
Continuation character 662
Control 641
Data type 662
Decision structure 661
Design time 658
Dim statement 664
Embedded macro 642
Event 646
FROM clause 650
Function procedure 660
Global variable 664
Host application 658
Keyword 659
Local variable 664
Macro 641
Macro Builder 644
Macro group 643
Module-level variable 664
ORDER BY clause 651
Private procedure 660
Property procedure 660
Public procedure 660
Run time 658
Scope (accessibility) 664
SELECT statement 650
SQL statement 649
Standalone macro 641
Standard module 660
Structured Query Language (SQL) 648
Sub procedure 660
Syntax 659
Variable 662
Visual Basic Editor 658
Visual Basic for Applications (VBA) 658
WHERE clause 650

Multiple Choice

1. Which statement about macros in Access 2007 is false?
   (a) Access 2007 supports embedded macros.
   (b) A macro group is a collection of macros stored as a single object.
   (c) You can view a macro's actions in the Visual Basic Editor.
   (d) A standalone macro will appear in the Navigation pane.

2. Which tool automatically creates an embedded macro?
   (a) Macro Builder
   (b) Command Button Wizard
   (c) Command button tool
   (d) Form Wizard

3. A database requires an event associated with the On Click event for a button that will open a form. No other objects or controls need to use this event. What should you create to most efficiently accomplish this?
   (a) A standalone macro
   (b) A VBA sub procedure
   (c) An SQL statement
   (d) An embedded macro

4. A recommended three-character identifier for a string variable is:
   (a) str
   (b) txt
   (c) chr
   (d) val

5. Which statement about the Macro Builder is true?
   (a) The Macro Builder is available in Word, Excel, PowerPoint, and Access.
   (b) The Macro Builder enables you to choose actions from a list.
   (c) The Macro Builder supports user-defined actions.
   (d) The Macro Builder stores macro events in a VBA procedure.

6. The recommended naming convention for variables is to precede the variable name with a ___ character prefix.
   (a) 1
   (b) 2
   (c) 3
   (d) 4

7. Which SQL statement will return records from a table?
   (a) SELECT
   (b) DESC
   (c) WHERE
   (d) ORDER BY

8. Which keyword makes a variable available to all objects in a database?
   (a) Global
   (b) Dim
   (c) Private
   (d) Public

9. Which data type is best suited for storing an employee's street address?
   (a) Boolean
   (b) Decimal
   (c) Currency
   (d) String

10. A VBA procedure invokes another procedure. Which keyword is optional in the procedure that is invoking the other procedure?
    (a) Get
    (b) Run
    (c) Call
    (d) Locate

11. Which character assigns a value to a variable?
    (a) >
    (b) %
    (c) =
    (d) ;

12. Which character is required at the end of an SQL statement?
    (a) >
    (b) :
    (c) ;
    (d) *

Multiple Choice Continued...

13. Which combination of characters will allow a VBA code statement to continue on the next line in the Code Window?

(a) $ —
(b) * ;
(c) ' '
(d) & _

14. Which key combination will launch the Visual Basic Editor?

(a) Alt+F11
(b) Ctrl+F8
(c) F1
(d) Shift+F9

15. You are creating an SQL string in a VBA procedure that uses the WHERE clause, but with a value supplied by the user. Which characters are required to define the criteria?

(a) Brackets — [ ]
(b) Parentheses — ( )
(c) Ampersands — & &
(d) Asterisks — * *

Practice Exercises

1 Relational, Inc. (Macros)

Relational, Inc., is a small company that provides data integration services. The company has a simple database for managing employee records and listing employees in reports: a master list of all employees, employees by title, and employees by location. The menu has five buttons, one that opens the Employees form, three that open each of the employee reports, and one that closes the database. Your task is to create the menu as shown, and use embedded macros to open and display the Employee form, open each report, and close the database. Refer to Figure 10.28 to verify your work.

a. Use Windows Explorer to locate the file named *chap10_pe1_relational.accdb*. Copy the file and rename it **chap10_pe1_relational_solution.accdb**.
b. Open the *chap10_pe1_relational_solution.accdb* file.
c. Click **Options** on the Security Warning toolbar, click **Enable this content** in the Microsoft Office Security Options dialog box, and then click **OK**.
d. Click the **Create tab** and click **Blank Form** in the Forms group. Switch to Design view.
e. Add the title label to the form:
    - Click **Label** in the Controls group on the Design tab.
    - Click and drag below the 0.5″ mark on the horizontal ruler to the 5.25″ mark. Adjust the height, as shown in Figure 10.28.
    - Type **Relational, Inc., Employee Database** in the label control.
    - Select the outside border of the label control, click **Bold**, and then click **Center** in the Font group on the Design tab.
    - Change the font size to **12 pt**.
f. Add the Forms label to the form:
    - Click **Label** in the Controls group on the Design tab.
    - Click and drag below the 0.5″ mark on the horizontal ruler to the 2″ mark, with this label control below the title label control. Adjust the height as shown in Figure 10.28.
    - Type **Forms** in the label control.
    - Select the outside border of the label control, click **Bold**, and then click **Center** in the Font group on the Design tab.
    - Change the font size to **11 pt**.
g. Add the Reports label to the form by adapting Step f to place the control on the form, as shown in Figure 10.28. Type **Reports** in the label control.
h. Add the View/Edit Employees button:
    - Click **Button** in the Controls group on the Design tab.
    - Click and drag the button to align with the left and right edges of the Forms label. Adjust the height as shown in Figure 10.28.
    - Select **Form Operations** in the **Categories** list of the Command Button Wizard, then select **Open Form** in the **Actions** list and click **Next**.
    - Select **Employees** when prompted to select the form to open and click Next.
    - Make sure the **Open the form and show all the records** option is selected and click **Next**.
    - Click the **Text option**, type **View/Edit Employees**, and click **Next**.
    - Type **cmdOpenEmployeeForm** as the name of the button and click **Finish**.
i. Add the Master Employee List button:
    - Click **Button** in the Controls group on the Design tab.

...continued on Next Page

- Click and drag the button to align with the left and right edges of the Reports label. Adjust the height as shown in Figure 10.28.
- Select **Report Operations** in the **Categories** list of the Command Button Wizard, then select **Preview Report** in the **Actions** list and click **Next**.
- Select **Employee Master List** when prompted to select the report to open and click **Next**.
- Click the **Text option**, type **Master Employee List**, and click **Next**.
- Type **cmdPreviewMasterList** as the name of the button and click **Finish**.

j. Add the Employees (By Location) button by adapting Step i. Select the **Employees by Location** report, type **Employees (By Location)** for the button text, and type **cmdPreviewByLocation** as the name.

k. Add the Employees (By Title) button by adapting Step i. Select the **Employees by Title** report, type **Employees (By Title)** for the button text, and type **cmdPreviewByTitle** as the name.

l. Add a button that quits the database. Position the button control as shown in Figure 10.28:

- Select **Application** in the **Categories list** of the Command Button Wizard, then select **Quit Application** in the **Actions** list and click **Next**.
- Click the **Text option**, type **Exit**, and click **Next**.
- Type **cmdExit** as the name of the button and click **Finish**.

m. Click the form to select it and click **Property Sheet** in the Tools group on the Design tab, if needed, to display the Property Sheet for the form.

n. Click the **Format tab** and set the following properties:

- Caption: Employees
- BorderStyle: Dialog
- Scroll Bars: Neither

o. Click **Save**. Type **Menu** as the form name.

p. Open the **Menu form** in Form view. Check the functionality of each button. Check the Exit button as the last function to test, so the database closes when your testing is complete.

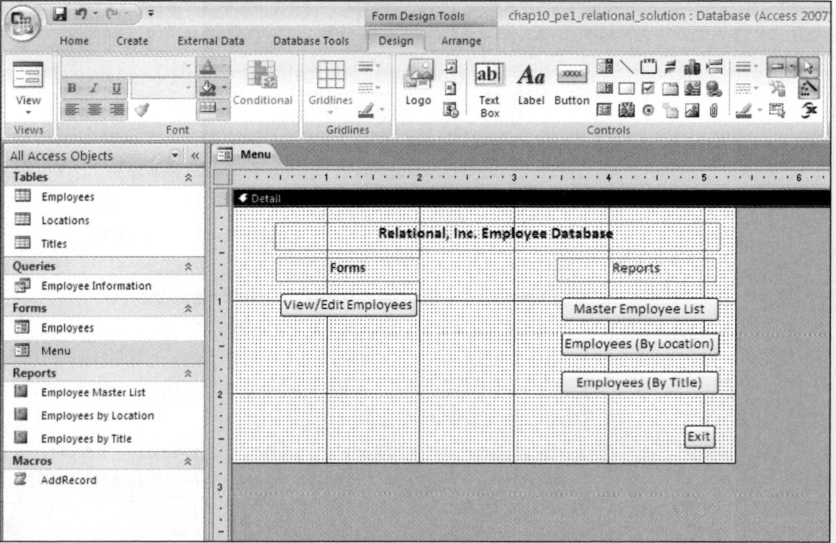

Figure 10.28 Relational, Inc., Database Menu

2 Relational, Inc. (VBA)

In this chapter, you learned how to program databases using both macros and VBA procedures. In this exercise, you will create a copy of the Relational, Inc., database from the previous exercise and use the Database Tools tab to convert the embedded macros to VBA procedures. You will then modify the VBA procedures in the Menu class module so that a single called procedure will display any of the reports, and the operation to close the database includes an IF-Then statement verifying the user's intent to close the database. Refer to Figure 10.29 to verify your work.

a. Use Windows Explorer to copy the *chap10_pe1_relational_solution.accdb* file you created in Practice Exercise 1. Copy the file and rename the copy **chap10_pe2_relational_solution.accdb**.
b. Open the *chap10_pe2_relational_solution.accdb* file.
c. Click **Options** on the Security Warning toolbar, click **Enable this content** in the Microsoft Office Security Options dialog box, and then click **OK**.
d. Open the **Menu form** in Design view.
e. Click the **Database Tools tab** and click **Convert Form's Macros to Visual Basic** in the Visual Basic group.
f. Uncheck the options to add error handling and include macro comments. Click **Convert**. When the message appears indicating that the conversion is complete, click **OK**.
g. Press **Alt+F11** to open the Visual Basic Editor. Display the Project Explorer if it is not currently visible. Expand the database object and open the class module for the Menu form.
h. Delete any comments in the Code window.
i. Place the insertion point in the Code window just below the *Option Compare Database* statement. Type the following code statements:

```
Dim strReportName As String

Sub DisplayReport(ReportName)
  DoCmd.OpenReport strReportName, acViewPreview, , , acWindowNormal
End Sub
```

j. Locate the sub procedure that handles the click event for the **cmdPreviewMasterList** button. Highlight the code statement beginning with *DoCmd* and press **Delete**. Type the following statements:

```
strReportName = "Master Employee List"
Call DisplayReport (strReportName)
```

k. Locate the sub procedure that handles the click event for the **cmdPreviewByLocation** button. Highlight the code statement beginning with *DoCmd* and press **Delete**. Type the following statements:

```
strReportName = "Employees by Location"
Call DisplayReport (strReportName)
```

l. Locate the sub procedure that handles the click event for the **cmdPreviewByTitle** button. Highlight the code statement beginning with *DoCmd* and press **Delete**. Type the following statements:

```
strReportName = "Employees by Title"
Call DisplayReport (strReportName)
```

m. Locate the sub procedure that handles the click event for the **cmdExit** button. Highlight the code statement beginning with *DoCmd* and press **Delete**. Type the following statements:

```
intResponse = MsgBox("Do you want to exit the Compensation " & _
"application?", vbCritical + vbYesNo, "Exit Application?")

      If intResponse = vbYes Then
            Application.Quit acQuitPrompt
      End If
```

...continued on Next Page

n. Compare your code statements to Figure 10.29. When your statements match those shown in the figure, click **Save**.
o. Close the Visual Basic Editor.
p. Click **Save**.
q. Check the functionality of each button. Check the Exit button as the last function to test, so the database closes when your testing is complete.

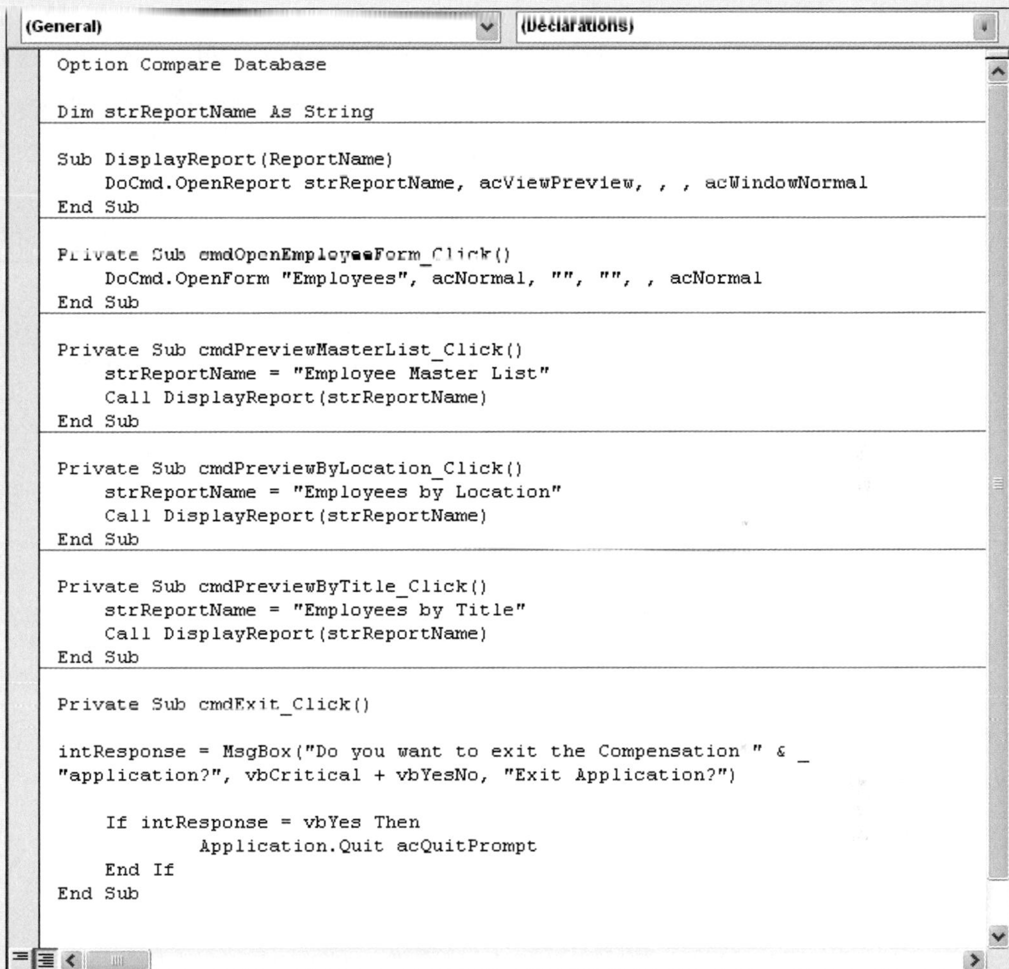

```
Option Compare Database

Dim strReportName As String

Sub DisplayReport(ReportName)
    DoCmd.OpenReport strReportName, acViewPreview, , , acWindowNormal
End Sub

Private Sub cmdOpenEmployeeForm_Click()
    DoCmd.OpenForm "Employees", acNormal, "", "", , acNormal
End Sub

Private Sub cmdPreviewMasterList_Click()
    strReportName = "Employee Master List"
    Call DisplayReport(strReportName)
End Sub

Private Sub cmdPreviewByLocation_Click()
    strReportName = "Employees by Location"
    Call DisplayReport(strReportName)
End Sub

Private Sub cmdPreviewByTitle_Click()
    strReportName = "Employees by Title"
    Call DisplayReport(strReportName)
End Sub

Private Sub cmdExit_Click()

intResponse = MsgBox("Do you want to exit the Compensation " & _
"application?", vbCritical + vbYesNo, "Exit Application?")

    If intResponse = vbYes Then
            Application.Quit acQuitPrompt
    End If
End Sub
```

Figure 10.29 Relational, Inc., VBA Procedures

Mid-Level Exercises

1 Northwind Traders—Reporting

At times a report lists data in a table, but the table does not contain any records. In this case Access typically displays a blank page. In this exercise, you will create an embedded macro to the On No Data event of a report that displays a message rather than a blank page. Refer to Figure 10.30 to verify your work.

a. Locate the file named *chap10_mid1_traders.accdb*, copy it to your production folder, and rename it **chap10_mid1_traders_solution.accdb**. Open the file and enable the content.

b. Open the **Customer report** in Design view. Display the Property Sheet.

c. Click the **Event tab**. Create a new macro for the *On No Data* event.

d. In the first row, select the **Beep** action. In the second row, select the **MsgBox** action and type **No Records found** as the message to display. In the third row, select the **CancelEvent** action.

e. Save and close the report.

f. Open the **Customers table** and delete all records.

g. Run the report. Verify that a message is displayed.

h. Close the database.

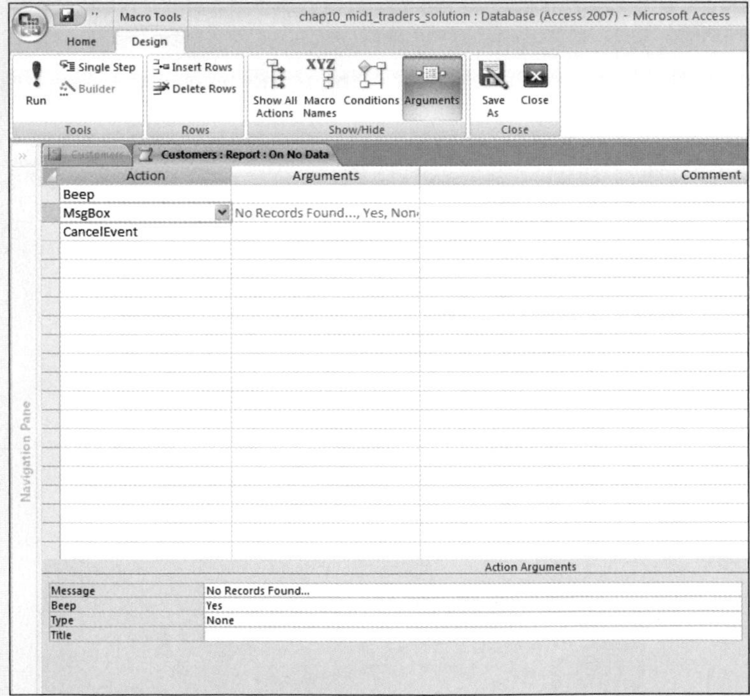

Figure 10.30 Macro Displaying a Message When No Records Are Found on a Report

...continued on Next Page

2 Northwind Traders—Employee Salaries

In the hands-on exercises, you have worked with employee data from ACME, Inc., as you have learned to program databases using macros and VBA. In this exercise, you will modify an existing query by adding a criterion to the Criteria row, view the SQL for the query, and construct an SQL string from the query that sets the record source for a report. You will make these changes in the Northwind Traders database. Refer to Figure 10.31 to verify your work.

a. Locate the file named *chap10_mid2_salaries.accdb*, copy it to your production folder, and rename it **chap10_mid2_salaries_solution.accdb**. Open the file and enable the content.

b. Open the **Salaries query** in Design view. Modify the query so that it returns records for employees whose salary exceeds $65,000.

c. View the query in SQL view. Select and copy the text for the query.

d. Close the query. Save the query when prompted.

e. Open the **Salaries report** in Design view.

f. Display the Property Sheet for the report.

g. Click the **Data tab**.

h. Right-click the *Record Source* row and paste the text you copied in Step c.

i. Save the changes.

j. View the Zoom window for the Record Source in the Property Sheet. Compare your SQL statements to those shown in Figure 10.31.

k. Close the report.

l. Open the report. Verify that all salaries displayed are greater than $65,000.

m. Close the database.

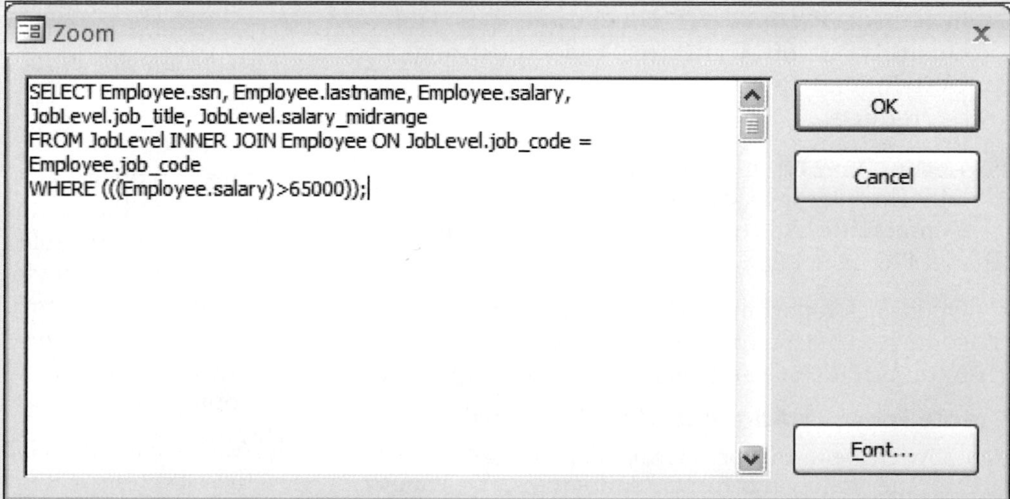

Figure 10.31 SQL Statements Defining a Report's Record Source

Capstone Exercise

You work for Northwind Traders, a small international gourmet foods wholesaler. The company has a database for managing the business. This database contains tables and queries. You have been appointed as the database developer responsible for creating forms, additional reports, and a menu for opening and closing the forms and reports. After you create the additional forms and reports, you will use macros and VBA procedures to add functionality to the menu.

Database File Setup

You need to copy an original database file, rename the copied file, and then open the copied database to complete this capstone exercise. After you open the copied database, you will replace an existing employee's name with your name.

a. Locate the file named *chap10_cap_traders.accdb* and copy it to your production folder.

b. Save the copied file as **chap10_cap_traders_solution.accdb**.

c. Open the *chap10_cap_traders_solution.accdb* file and enable the content.

Create Reports

You will need to create two additional reports: one listing the products and another listing the suppliers. The fields and report name are listed below. Modify the report design so that all data are displayed and the report headings are descriptive.

a. Create a new report based upon the Products table. Include the **ProductID**, **ProductName**, **QuantityPerUnit**, **UnitPrice**, **ProductCost**, and **UnitsInStock** fields in the report. Save the report as **Products**.

b. Create a new report based upon the Suppliers table. Include the **CompanyName**, **ContactName**, **ContactTitle**, **Address**, **City**, **PostalCode**, **Country**, and **Phone** fields. Save the report as **Suppliers**.

c. Open each report included in the database. Add a command button in the report header. Name the button **cmdClose** and change the caption to **Close**.

Create Forms to Add and Edit Table Data

You now create forms for entering and editing table data. Create the following forms: Employees, Customers, Suppliers, and Products.

a. Create a new form based upon the Employees table. Include all fields on the form. Save the form as **Employees**. Add a command button to the form footer. Name the button **cmdClose**. Change the caption to **Close**.

b. Create a new form based upon the Customers table. Include all fields on the form. Save the form as **Customers**. Add a command button to the form footer. Name the button **cmdClose**. Change the caption to **Close**.

c. Create a new form based upon the Suppliers table. Include all fields on the form. Save the form as **Suppliers**. Add a command button to the form footer. Name the button **cmdClose**. Change the caption to **Close**.

d. Create a new form based upon the Products table. Include all fields on the form. Save the form as **Products**. Add a command button to the form footer. Name the button **cmdClose**. Change the caption to **Close**.

Create a Menu Form

The database does not include a menu. The menu form will contain labels and buttons. The labels provide descriptive information about the form. The form will include seven buttons: four to display each of the forms, two to preview the reports, and one to exit the database.

a. Create a new blank form. Open the Property Sheet for the form. Type **Northwind Traders** as the caption for the form. Remove the record selectors, control box, and close button. Disable the min and max buttons.

b. Add three labels to the form. Type **Northwind Traders** as the caption for the first label. Center the label near the top of the form. Format the label so the title stands out on the form. Type **Forms** as the caption for the second label and **Reports** as the caption for the third label. Position the Forms label to the left side of the form and the Reports label to the right side.

c. Add four buttons to the form. Each of these buttons will open a form for entering and editing records in the **Customers**, **Employees**, **Products**, and **Suppliers** tables (these are the forms you created in the previous section). Position each button under the **Forms** label. As you create each button, add an embedded macro to open one of the forms. Set the button text and button name as appropriate.

d. Add two additional buttons to the form. Each of these buttons will open a report: the **Products** and **Suppliers** reports (also created in the previous section). Position each button under the **Reports** label. As you create each button, add an embedded macro to open each report. Set the button text and button name as appropriate.

e. Add one more button to the form, but do not embed a macro. Set the caption property to **Exit** and the name to **cmdExit**.

f. Save the form.

Capstone Exercise Continued...

Create VBA Procedures

Now that you have created the Menu form, you are ready to use VBA procedures to add functionality to the database.

a. Open the Visual Basic Editor. Add a module named Procedures to the database.

b. Create two global procedures: one that will close any form and another that will close any report. These procedures will accept a parameter specifying which form or report to close. The procedure will also verify the user's intent to close a specific form or report. Declare a global variable to store the name of the object passed to each procedure.

c. Add a procedure to the Close buttons on each form and report in the database. The procedure for each object will store the name of the object in a global variable.

d. Add a procedure to the cmdExit button on the Menu form. This procedure will verify the user's intent to exit and will then exit the database.

Set Database Startup Options

Change the Access Options for the database.

a. Type Northwind Traders as the database title. Display the Menu form when the database is opened.

b. Set the Navigation pane option so that the pane is not displayed.

c. Save and close the database.

Test the Database

You are now ready to test the database. Open the database and enable the content. Test each button on the menu and on the forms and reports. Test the Exit button last. Make any required modifications. Close the database when your testing is complete.

Mini Cases

Use the rubric following the case as a guide to evaluate your work, but keep in mind that your instructor may impose additional grading criteria or use a different standard to judge your work.

Using an Embedded Macro with SQL WHERE Condition to Open a Form

GENERAL CASE

Macros are useful because they add functionality to database objects and controls. For example, you can create a macro attached to a Form Open event that filters the form to only display specific records. Locate the *chap10_mc1_coffee.accdb* file. Create a copy named **chap10_mc1_coffee_solution.accdb**. Open the file. Create an embedded macro for the On Open event that uses an SQL WHERE clause that displays customers from Miami, who have a credit rating of "A." Use AND to connect the two WHERE conditions, enclosing each condition in parenthesis.

Performance Elements	Exceeds Expectations	Meets Expectations	Below Expectations
Macro creation	Embedded in the Form Open event.	Calculated fields are accurate.	Macro was not created.
WHERE clause	Contains a WHERE clause that is accurate.	Contains an inaccurate WHERE clause.	No WHERE clause.
Macro functionality	Macro runs without error and returns four records.	Macro runs but does not return four records.	Macro does not run.

Using a VBA Procedure to Perform a Calculation

RESEARCH CASE

You can perform many kinds of calculations using VBA procedures and variables. Explore the Help system within the Visual Basic Editor to find out how to extract a value from a text box on a form, assign the text string to a numeric variable, perform a calculation, and return the result in a message box. Locate the *chap10_mc2_401k.accdb* file and make a copy named **chap10_mc2_401k_solution.accdb**. Open the database. Create a procedure that handles the Click event for the cmd401k button. The procedure will declare variables to store captured information and the calculated value, and will calculate the monthly 401K contribution based upon the annual salary and contribution percentage. Use a message box to display the result. Use the Format function to format the result as currency.

Performance Elements	Exceeds Expectations	Meets Expectations	Below Expectations
Variables	Uses variables of an appropriate data type.	Uses variables, sub-optimum data type.	No variables.
Procedure	Runs without error and calculates correctly.	Runs but does not return the correct values.	Does not run.
Message box	Displays correct result formatted as currency.	Displays correct result but not formatted as currency.	Does not display a result.

Correcting Code Errors

DISASTER RECOVERY

The Visual Basic Editor will highlight code errors if you make a mistake entering statements. This is beneficial for anyone writing code, because it is impossible to program without inadvertently making an error. Locate the *chap10_mc3_bonus.accdb* file. Make a copy and save it as **chap10_mc3_bonus_solution.accdb**. Open the database, and then launch the Visual Basic Editor. Find three code errors and correct them. Add remark statements (preceded with an apostrophe character) to document the errors. Print the code from your modified procedure.

Performance Elements	Exceeds Expectations	Meets Expectations	Below Expectations
Errors	Three errors found, documented, and corrected.	Three errors found but not documented.	Errors not found.
Procedure	Procedure runs and returns correct values.	Procedure runs.	Procedure does not run.

Glossary

All key terms appearing in this book (in bold italic) are listed alphabetically in this Glossary for easy reference. If you want to learn more about a feature or concept, use the Index to find the term's other significant occurrences.

Access Database Executable Files that remove all VBA source code, deny users permission to make design and name changes to forms or reports within the database, and prohibit users from creating new forms and reports.

Access function Predefined formula that performs an operation using input supplied as arguments and returns a value.

Access speed Measures the time it takes for the storage device to make the file content available for use.

Accessibility (scope) Specifies which program statements will have access to the value stored in a variable.

Action query Type of query that alters data in a database by making a table, adding records to an existing table, deleting specific records, or updating records.

Aggregate A collection of many parts that come together from different sources and are considered a whole.

And operator Returns only records that meet all criteria.

Append Process of adding new records to the end of the table.

Append query An action query that searches a table based on a condition, selects at least one record from one table, and adds the selected record(s) to a different, existing table.

Argument A necessary input component required to produce the output for a function.

Atomic field A field that contains only one value (no repeating groups of data).

Attachment control A control that lets you manage and use attached files within a form or report.

AutoNumber field A field that assigns a unique identifying number to each record.

Axes The vertical and horizontal scales displaying plotted data in a line, column, bar, or scatter chart.

Back end A database that contains database tables, but not database forms, reports, or queries. Protects and stores data so that users cannot inadvertently destroy or corrupt the organization's vital data.

Bar chart A chart that displays quantitative data horizontally in rows to compare values across different categories; useful when categorical labels are wide and fit better on the Y axis instead of the X axis.

Bound control A control that enables you to pull information from the underlying table or query data.

Calculated control Uses an expression as opposed to a record value as its data source.

Calculated detail field The portion of a PivotTable or PivotChart that generates a new field and performs the stipulated calculation on all of the detail records.

Calculated field A field that derives its value from a formula that references one or more existing fields.

Calculated total field A data field used to customize aggregated data.

CamelCase notation Field-naming style that uses no spaces in multi-word field names, but uses uppercase letters to distinguish the first letter of each new word.

Caption property Specifies a label other than the field name that appears at the top of a column in Datasheet view, forms, and reports.

Cascade delete Searches the database and deletes all of the related records.

Cascade update Connects any primary key changes to the tables in which it is a foreign key.

Cascades Permit data changes to travel from one table to another.

Certification Authority (CA) Commercial companies that issue and validate identities using digital signatures for a fee.

Chart title The area of a chart that displays a name describing the data depicted in a chart.

Class module Contains procedures for a specific object.

Clipboard A memory location that holds up to 24 items for you to paste into the current document, another file, or another application.

Column chart A chart that displays quantitative data vertically in columns to compare values across different categories.

Column field The data field that you assign to group data vertically into columns.

Column headings Labels that describe the set of facts listed vertically in a crosstab query.

Command An icon on the Quick Access Toolbar or in a group on the Ribbon that you click to perform a task. A command can also appear as text on a menu or within a dialog box.

Comment A brief, yet descriptive line in a VBA statement that explains the code's purpose; typically placed before a block of code; a statement that documents the code but is not executed by the program.

Condition Specifies certain criteria that must be met before an action will be performed; specified on the Criteria line in the Design view of a query or part of an SQL statement.

Constant An unchanging value, like a birthdate.

Contextual tab A specialty tab that appears on the Ribbon only when certain types of objects are being edited.

Continuation character The underscore symbol that enables you to break code statements into multiple lines for readability.

Continuous data Classification of data in which values fall on a continuum, such as continuum of ounces in a container.

Control A form or report object like a text box, list box, or command button that displays, positions, and formats data or responds to an event.

Copy The process of making a duplicate copy of the text or object leaving the original intact.

Countermeasure Measures or steps that a company takes to protect its assets.

Criteria row Position in a query design grid where criteria may be entered.

Criterion (criteria, pl) A rule or norm that is the basis for making judgments.

Crossfooting The sum of a total row compared to the sum of a column total to verify that the two totals match.

Crosstab query A query that summarizes calculated values by two sets of unrelated facts.

Currency The medium of exchange, in the United States, currency formatted values display with a dollar sign.

Cut Process of removing the original text or an object from its current location.

Data aggregate A collection of many parts that come together from different sources to form a whole, such as a sum or average derived from many values.

Data mining The process of analyzing large volumes of data to identify patterns and relationships.

Data redundancy Occurs when unnecessary duplicate information exists in a database.

Data type Determines the type of data that a table field or programming variable can hold, such as a Decimal or Integer data type, and how the data is stored in the computer's memory.

Data validation A set of constraints or rules that help control the type and accuracy of the data entered into a field.

Database A file that consists of one or more tables and the supporting objects used to get data into and out of the tables.

Database Documenter Tool that creates a data dictionary that itemizes and lists the attributes for any object in the database.

Database Splitter Tool that creates the front-end and back-end databases simultaneously.

Dataset A container for records that satisfy the criteria specified in the query, provides the answers to the user's questions.

Datasheet form A form that has the same appearance as the Datasheet view of a table.

Datasheet view A grid containing columns (fields) and rows (records) where you add, edit, and delete records in a database table.

Date arithmetic A mathematical expression that calculates lapsed time.

Date formatting Affects the date's display without changing the serial value.

Date/time field A field that facilitates calculations for dates and times.

DatePart function Enables users to identify a specific part of a date, such as only the year.

Decision structure A programming structure that performs a logical test to compare statements; based on the comparison, the structure branches to respective statements to execute.

Delete query An action query that searches a table based on a condition, and then deletes the records that match the condition.

Demographics Data describing population segments by age, gender, race, education, and other variables.

Dependency The extent to which fields in a table are related to each other through the table's primary key.

Design time Mode in which you create and edit VBA statements.

Design view Displays the infrastructure of a table, form, or report without displaying the data.

Detail field The data field that contains individual values to be summarized.

Detail section Repeats once for each record in the underlying record source.

Dialog box A window that provides an interface for a user to select commands.

Dialog Box Launcher A small icon that, when clicked, opens a related dialog box.

Digital signature Electronic, encryption-based, secure stamp of authentication that confirms who authorized the file, that the file is valid, and that no changes have been made to the file after its authentication.

Dim statement A programming statement that declares a local or module-level variable.

Discrete data Classification of data that is measured and quantified in discrete, unique increments, such as the number of males and females in a class.

Doughnut chart A chart that shows values as percentages to the whole for multiple data series.

Drill button The plus (+) or minus (–) sign that enables you to show or collapse details, respectively, in a PivotTable.

Drop zone An area in the PivotTable or PivotChart design grid where you drop fields to organize the data. Primary drop zones include row field, column field, data field, and filter field.

Duplex printer A printing device that prints on both sides of the page.

Embedded macro A macro object that belongs to a single object or control and is used to automate tasks based on an event.

Encryption The process of encoding the contents of a file, making the contents unreadable if another program is used to gain unauthorized access to the file.

Enhanced ScreenTip Displays when you rest the mouse pointer on a command on the Quick Access Toolbar or Ribbon.

Event An action occurring at run time that triggers a program instruction, such as when the user clicks a button.

Exclusive access Enables one person to have sole access to a database while establishing a password.

Expression A formula used to calculate new fields from the values in existing fields.

Expression Builder A tool to help you create a formula that performs calculations easily.

Extensible HyperText Markup Language (XHTML) A hybrid popular authoring language to create Web pages; combines features of HTML and XML.

eXtensible Markup Language (XML) A general-purpose language that supports a wide variety of applications by defining data in well-formed documents; enables designers to create customized tags specific to their needs.

Extensible Stylesheet Language (XSL) Describes how data are presented to the user over the Web; specifies how content and style are separated for HTML or XML files.

Field A basic entity, data element, or category, such as a book title or telephone number.

Field List pane Displays a list of all of the tables and fields in the database.

Field row The area in the query design grid that specifies fields to be used in a query.

Field size property Defines how much space to reserve for each field.

Filter Condition that helps you find a subset of data meeting your specifications.

Filter by Form Permits selecting the criteria from a drop-down list, or applying multiple criterion.

Filter by Selection Selects only the records that match the pre-selected criteria.

Filter field The data field that you use to create criteria to filter data in a PivotTable.

Find Locates a word or group of words in a file.

Find duplicates query A query that identifies duplicated values in a specific field within a table.

Find unmatched query A query that compares records in two related tables and returns the records found in only one table, but not both of the tables.

First Normal Form (1NF) The first normalization process that requires that repeating groups be eliminated from a table.

Flat or non-relational Data contained in a single page or sheet (not multiple).

Font A complete set of characters—upper- and lowercase letters, numbers, punctuation marks, and special symbols with the same design.

Foreign key A field in one table that also is stored in a different table as a primary key.

Form An interface that enables you to enter or modify record data.

Form splitter bar Divider between the form and datasheet areas of a split form; enables you to click and drag it up or down to change the height of the two areas.

Form Tool A tool that creates an automatic form for the open table; uses all fields from the table in the form.

Format Painter Feature that enables you to copy existing text formats to other text to ensure consistency.

Formatting text Changes an individual letter, a word, or a body of selected text.

FROM clause A portion of a SQL statement that specifies the table containing the data returned by the query.

Front end A database that contains the objects, like queries, reports and forms, needed to interact with data, but not the tables where the record values reside. Database GUI used by end users to prevent users from having direct access to the database.

Function procedure A group of programming statements that perform an action and return a value to the statement that called the function.

Gallery Displays a set of predefined options that can be clicked to apply to an object or to text.

Global variable A variable that is available to any procedure in a database.

Go To Moves the insertion point to a specific location in the file.

Gridlines The lines that extend across the plot area of a chart; help guide the reader's eyes from the axis values to the data points.

Group Categories that organize similar commands together within each tab on the Ribbon.

Group footer section(s) Appear at the end of each grouping level.

Group header section(s) Appear once at the start of each new grouping level in the report.

Host application Contains the VBA procedures that add functionality to Office applications.

HyperText Markup Language (HTML) Widely used authoring language to create Web pages; defines structure and formatting through with HTML tags.

IIF function The function that evaluates a condition and executes one action when the condition is true and an alternate action when the condition is false.

Indexed property A list that relates the field values to the records that contain the field value.

Inequity Examines a mathematical relationship such as equals, not equals, greater than, less than, greater than or equal to, or less than or equal to.

Input mask Specifies the exact formatting of the input data while minimizing data storage; useful to ensure consistent data entry of phone numbers, zip codes, etc. Displays placeholder for required characters until data entry is complete for the field for a particular record.

Input Mask Wizard The tool that helps you generate and test an input mask for a field.

Insert The process of adding text in a document, spreadsheet cell, database object, or presentation slide.

Insertion point The blinking vertical line in the document, cell, slide show, or database table designating the current location where text you type displays.

Key Tip The letter or number that displays over each feature on the Ribbon and Quick Access Toolbar and is the keyboard equivalent that you press. Press Alt by itself to display Key Tips.

Keyword A word or symbol recognized as part of a specific programming language, such as VBA, that has special meaning within that language.

Label Wizard Asks you questions and then, depending on how you answer, generates the report formatted to print on mailing labels.

Landscape orientation Page orientation is wider than it is long, resembling a landscape scene.

Layout view Alter the report design while viewing the data.

Legend The area of a chart that identifies which color represents the data for each data series.

Line chart A chart that plots data points to compare trends over time. Lines connect the data points for a particular data series.

Link Child Field Property that specifies which field or fields in the subform link to the main form.

Link Master Field Property that specifies which field or fields in the main form link to the subform.

Live Preview A feature that provides a preview of how a gallery option will affect the current text or object when the mouse pointer hovers over the gallery option.

Local variable A variable that is available to the procedure associated with a specific database object or control.

Lookup field A field that provides a predefined list of values from which to select.

Lookup Wizard A tool that helps create, populate, and relate the lookup field in a table.

Macro An Access tool that enables you to automate database tasks and add functionality to objects, such as forms, reports, and the controls contained in forms and reports.

Macro Builder A tool for creating and editing standalone macros; the interface enables you to select action and arguments to build the macro.

Macro group A collection of macros stored in a single macro object; each macro within the macro group must have a unique name.

Mailing labels Self-stick, die-cut labels that you print with names, addresses, and postal barcodes.

Make table query An action query that searches a table based on a condition, selects at least one record that matches the condition, and uses the selected record(s) to create a new table.

Manual duplex Operation that enables you to print on both sides of the paper by printing first on one side and then on the other.

Mini toolbar A semitransparent toolbar of often-used font, indent, and bullet commands that displays when you position the mouse over selected text and disappears when you move the mouse away from the selected text.

Module-level variable A variable that is available to *any* procedure within a module.

Multiple items form A continuous form that shows many records in a datasheet with one item in each row.

Multivalued field A field that accepts more than one value for a single field.

Nested groups Provide a power-layering tool to organize information.

Normalization A process that examines the structure of database tables to prevent inconsistent or illogical data operations.

Not operator Returns the opposite of the specified criteria.

Null The formal, computer term for a missing value.

Object An entity that contains the basic elements of the database. Access uses six types of objects—tables, queries, forms, reports, macros, and modules.

Object Linking and Embedding (OLE) A standard that enables you to create an object in one application and then link or embed that object within another application, such as creating an image and using that image within a table field in Access.

Office Button Icon that, when clicked, displays the Office menu.

Office menu List of commands (such as New, Open, Save, Save As, Print, and Options) that work with an entire file or with the specific Microsoft Office program.

One-to-many relationship Exists when each record in the first table may match one, more than one, or no records in the second table. Each record in the second table matches one and only one record in the first table.

Operand Field or value being operated or manipulated in an expression.

Or operator Returns records meeting any of the specified criteria.

ORDER BY clause Portion of an SQL statement used in queries to indicate which field is used to sort the records in a record set in either ascending or descending order.

Order of precedence Rules that establish the sequence by which values are calculated.

Overtype mode Replaces the existing text with text you type character by character.

Page footers Appear once for each page in the report at the bottom of the pages.

Page headers Appear once for each page in the report at the top of the pages.

Parameter query A select query where one or more specific conditional values are intentionally omitted by the designer and interactively selected by the user, thus providing flexibility for running the query. The parameter is enclosed in brackets []. When you run a parameter query, the Enter Parameter Value dialog box appears so that you can enter the specific value to query the database.

Password A security mechanism in the form of characters that prevents unauthorized access or modification of a secured file.

Paste Places the cut or copied text or object in the new location.

Performance Analyzer Tool that improves database performance by identifying choices made during database design that will slow performance when the database is put into a production or work environment.

Pie chart A chart that shows proportion of each category to the whole for a single data series.

PivotChart view Displays a chart of the associated PivotTable view.

PivotTable view Provides a convenient way to summarize and organize data about groups of records.

PMT function Calculates a periodic loan payment given a constant interest rate, term, and original value.

PNPI Federal laws governing the safeguarding of personal, non-public information such as Social Security numbers (SSNs), credit card or bank account numbers, medical or educational records, or other sensitive data.

Portrait orientation Page orientation is longer than it is wide—like the portrait of a person.

Presentation graphics software A computer application, such as Microsoft PowerPoint, that is used primarily to create electronic slide shows.

Primary key The field that makes each record in a table unique.

Print Preview view Displays the report as it will be printed.

Private procedure A programming procedure—group of programming statements—that is available only to a specific object or module.

Property A characteristic or attribute of an object that determines how the object looks and behaves.

Property procedure A programming procedure that creates or manipulates a custom property.

Public procedure A programming procedure—group of programming statements—that is available to any object in an application.

Query A database object that enables you to ask questions about the data stored in a database and returns the answers in the order from the records that match your instructions.

Query design grid Displays when you select a query's Design view; it divides the window into two parts.

Query sort order Determines the order of items in the query datasheet view.

Query Wizard A tool that facilitates new query development.

Quick Access Toolbar A customizable row of buttons for frequently used commands, such as Save and Undo.

Record A complete set of all of the data (fields) about one person, place, event, or idea.

Redo Command that reinstates or reserves an action performed by the Undo command.

Referential Integrity The set of rules that ensure that data stored in related tables remain consistent as the data are updated.

Relational Database Management System Data are grouped into similar collections, called tables, and the relationships between tables are formed by using a common field.

Relational database software A computer application, such as Microsoft Access, that is used to store data and convert it into information.

Repeat Provides limited use because it repeats only the last action you performed. The Repeat icon is replaced with the Redo icon after you use the Undo command.

Replace The process of finding and replacing a word or group of words with other text.

Report A printed document that displays information professionally from a database.

Report footer section Prints once at the conclusion of each report.

Report header section Prints once at the beginning of each report.

Report view Provides you the ability to see what the printed report will look like and to make temporary changes to how the data are viewed.

Report Wizard Asks you questions and then, depending on how you answer, generates the report.

Ribbon The Microsoft Office 2007 GUI command center that organizes commands into related tabs and groups.

Row field The source field that you assign to group data horizontally into rows.

Row headings Labels that describe the set of facts listed horizontally in a crosstab query.

Run a query Processes the query instructions and displays records that meet the conditions.

Run time Time during which an application runs or executes VBA statements.

Sarbanes Oxley Act (SOX) Protects the general public and companies' shareholders against fraudulent practices and accounting errors.

Scatter plot chart A chart that shows relationships between two variables, such as attendance record and final course grade.

Scope (accessibility) Specifies which program statements will have access to the value stored in a variable.

Second Normal Form (2NF) The second normalization process that removes partial dependencies.

Select query Searches the underlying tables to retrieve the data that satisfy the query parameters.

SELECT statement SQL statement that returns fields from one or more database tables.

Shortcut menu A list of commands that appears when you right-click an item or screen element.

Show row The area in a query design grid that controls whether the field will display in the query results.

Sort Lists those records in a specific sequence, such as alphabetically by last name or rearranges data based on a certain criteria.

Sort Ascending Provides an alphabetical list of text data or a small-to-large list of numeric data.

Sort Descending Arranges the records with the highest value listed first.

Split form A data interaction method that combines a form with a datasheet so that you can see data for a single record in the form area and view a list of table records in the datasheet at the same time.

Spreadsheet program A computer application, such as Microsoft Excel, that is used to build and manipulate electronic spreadsheets.

SQL statement A statement containing keywords that belong to the SQL definition language, field names, and table names that create an instruction for processing database commands; ends with a semicolon.

Standalone macro A database macro object that automates tasks and may be used by more than one control; it is not restricted to a single control.

Standard module Stores procedures that can be called by any event in the application, such as a general procedure that will open or close any form or report.

Status bar The horizontal bar at the bottom of a Microsoft Office application that displays summary information about the selected window or object and contains View buttons and the Zoom slider. The Word status bar displays the page number and total words, while the Excel status bar displays the average, count, and sum of values in a selected range. The PowerPoint status bar displays the slide number and the Design Theme name.

Structured Query Language (SQL) The industry-standard method for defining and processing database queries.

Sub procedure A block of programming statements that performs an action.

Subform A form that exists within another form; used to show the one-to-many relationship between two tables. When a record is selected in the main form, the subform shows the related records from the related table.

Switchboard A menu or series of menus that ties the objects in the database together so that the database is easy to use.

Switchboard Manager An Access utility that prompts you for information about each menu and enables you to create switchboards.

Syntax The rules by which the words and symbols of an expression are correctly combined or the rules for designing programming statements for a particular language, such as VBA.

Tab Looks like a folder tab and divides the Ribbon into task-oriented categories.

Table A collection of records. Every record in a table contains the same fields in the same order.

Table Analyzer Tool that examines how tables are constructed and looks for places where the same data is found in more than one row.

Table row The second row of the query design grid that specifies the tables from which the fields are selected to create a query.

Template A file that incorporates a theme, a layout, and content that can be modified.

Third Normal Form (1NF) The third normalization process that removes transitive dependencies.

Timestamp Encrypts the date and time as part of a digital signature and proves who was the last person to modify the database.

Title bar The shaded bar at the top of every window; often displays the program name and filename.

Total row Displays as the last row in the Datasheet view of a table or query and provides a variety of summary statistics.

Totals query Organizes query results into groups by including a grouping field and a numeric field for aggregate calculations.

Unbound controls Do not have any record source for their contents.

Undo Command cancels your last one or more operations.

Uniform Resource Locator (URL) A short string identifying the documents, image, or downloadable files stored on a

Web server, such as http://www.prenhall.com/exploring is a URL that stores the main Web page for the Exploring series information.

Update query An action query that searches a table based on a condition and then changes a specific value to another value in at least one record in a table.

User interface The meeting point between computer software and the person using it.

Validation rule A restriction that specifies which values are allowed in a field.

Validation text Message that informs users about what they have done incorrectly and instructs them about what needs to be done.

Variable Reserved memory location with a user-defined descriptive name that stores a value that can change while the application is running.

Virus checker Software that scans files for a hidden program that can damage your computer.

Visual Basic Editor A workspace text editor for writing and editing VBA procedures; includes other tools for working with program code.

Visual Basic for Applications (VBA) A programming language used within Office 2007 to create and customize Office applications to enhance their functionality.

WHERE clause Portion of an SQL statement that specifies which records from the tables listed in the FROM clause are affected by a SELECT, UPDATE, or DELETE statement.

Word processing software A computer application, such as Microsoft Word, that is used primarily with text to create, edit, and format documents.

Work-around Acknowledges that a problem exists, and develops a sufficing solution.

XML Schema Definition (XSD) Describes how to formally describe the data structures within an XML file structure.

Zoom slider Enables you to increase or decrease the magnification of the file onscreen.

Multiple Choice Answer Keys

Office Fundamentals, Chapter 1

1. b
2. c
3. d
4. a
5. d
6. c
7. b
8. c
9. d
10. a
11. c
12. d
13. c
14. a
15. d

Access 2007, Chapter 1

1. b
2. b
3. d
4. d
5. b
6. b
7. b
8. c
9. c
10. c
11. c
12. a
13. c
14. d
15. a

Access 2007, Chapter 2

1. b
2. c
3. b
4. a
5. d
6. b
7. d
8. c
9. b
10. b
11. d
12. d
13. b
14. c
15. c
16. b
17. c
18. b
19. d
20. b

Access 2007, Chapter 3

1. a
2. c
3. e
4. d
5. b
6. c
7. a
8. a
9. a
10. c
11. a
12. b
13. b
14. c
15. d

Access 2007, Chapter 4

1. b
2. d
3. d
4. c
5. c
6. b
7. d
8. c
9. b
10. d
11. a
12. c
13. a
14. c
15. d
16. a
17. b
18. b

Access 2007, Chapter 5

1. a
2. b
3. d
4. d
5. a
6. a
7. c
8. b
9. d
10. a
11. d
12. c
13. b
14. a
15. c

Access 2007, Chapter 6

1. b
2. a
3. c
4. d
5. a
6. a
7. d
8. c
9. b
10. d
11. c
12. a
13. c
14. b
15. d

Access 2007, Chapter 7

1. b
2. c
3. b
4. d
5. b
6. c
7. d
8. b
9. a
10. d
11. a
12. b
13. a
14. d
15. d

Access 2007, Chapter 8

1. d
2. b
3. c
4. c
5. a
6. b
7. c
8. d
9. d
10. c
11. c
12. c
13. d
14. a
15. b

Access 2007, Chapter 9

1. c
2. b
3. d
4. b
5. a
6. c
7. c
8. c
9. c
10. d
11. a
12. b
13. a
14. b
15. d
16. a
17. c

Access 2007, Chapter 10

1. c
2. b
3. d
4. a
5. b
6. c
7. a
8. d
9. d
10. c
11. c
12. c
13. d
14. a
15. a

Index

E

F

G

H

I

J

K

L

M

N

P

Q

R

S

T

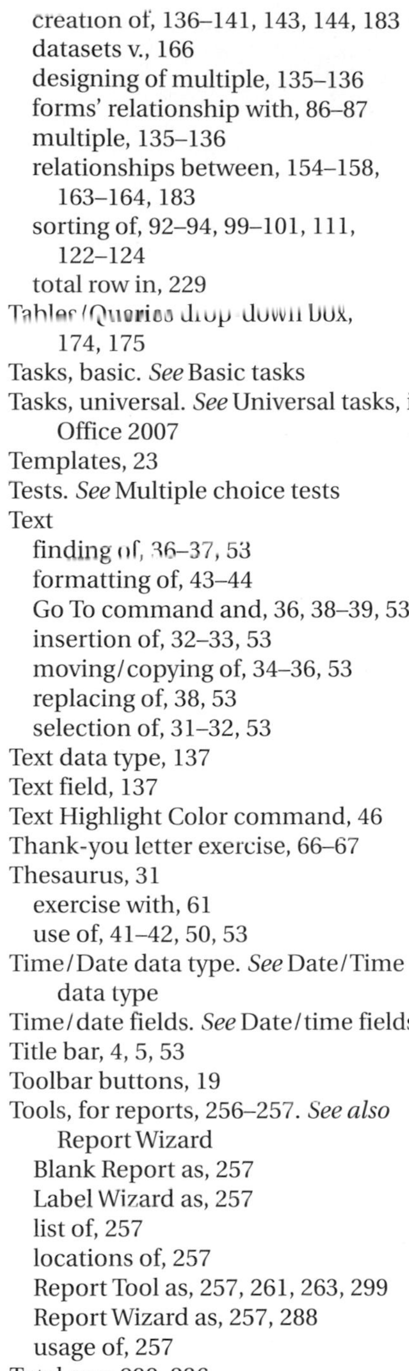